Lives of Jesus Series

LEANDER E. KECK, *General Editor*

THE LIFE OF JESUS

CRITICALLY EXAMINED

by

DAVID FRIEDRICH STRAUSS

Edited and with an Introduction by

PETER C. HODGSON

Translated from the Fourth German Edition by

George Eliot

SIGLER PRESS
Ramsey, NJ

SIGLER PRESS EDITION 1994

Library of Congress Catalog Card Number 94-65347

ISBN 0-9623642-6-6

FOREWORD TO THE SERIES

In a time when a premium is placed on experimentation for the future and when theological work itself values "new theology," the reasons for reissuing theological works from the past are not self-evident. Above all, there is broad consensus that the "Lives of Jesus" produced by our forebears failed both as sound history and as viable theology. Why, then, make these works available once more?

First of all, this series does not represent an effort to turn the clock back, to declare these books to be the norm to which we should conform, either in method or in content. Neither critical research nor constructive theology can be repristinated. Nevertheless, root problems in the historical-critical study of Jesus and of theological reflection are perennial. Moreover, advances are generally made by a critical dialogue with the inherited tradition, whether in the historical reconstruction of the life of Jesus or in theology as a whole. Such a dialogue cannot occur, however, if the tradition is allowed to fade into the mists or is available to students only in handbooks which perpetuate the judgments and clichés of the intervening generation. But a major obstacle is the fact that certain pivotal works have never been available to the present generation, for they were either long out of print or not translated at all. A central aim, then, in republishing certain "Lives of Jesus" is to encourage a fresh discovery of and a lively debate with this tradition so that our own work may be richer and more precise.

Titles were selected which have proven to be significant for ongoing issues in Gospel study and in the theological enterprise as a whole. H. S. Reimarus inaugurated the truly critical investigation of Jesus and so was an obvious choice. His *On the Intention of Jesus* was reissued by the American Theological Library Association in 1962, but has not really entered the discussion despite the fact that questions he raised have been opened again, especially by S. G. F. Brandon's *Jesus and the Zealots*. Our edition, moreover, includes also his previously untranslated discussion of the resurrection and part of D. F. Strauss's evaluation of Reimarus. That Strauss's *Life of Jesus* must be included was clear from the start. Our edition, using George Eliot's translation, will take account of Strauss's shifting views as well. Schleiermacher's *Life of Jesus* will be translated, partly because it is significant for the study of Schleiermacher himself and partly because he is the wellspring of repeated concern for the inner life of Jesus. One of the most influential expressions of this motif came from Wilhelm Herrmann's *The Communion of the Christian with God*, which, while technically not a life of Jesus, emphasizes more than any other work the religious significance of Jesus' inner life. In fresh form, this emphasis has been rejuvenated in the current work of Ernst Fuchs and Gerhard Ebeling who concentrate on Jesus' own faith. Herrmann, then, is a bridge between Schleiermacher and the present. In such a series, it was also deemed important to translate Strauss's critique of Schleier-macher, *The Christ of Faith and the Jesus of History,* for here important critical issues were exposed. Probably no book was more significant for twentieth-century study of Jesus than Johannes Weiss's *Jesus' Proclamation of the Kingdom of God,* for together with Albert Schweitzer, Weiss turned the entire course of Jesus-research and undermined the foundations of the prevailing Protestant the-ology. From the American scene, Shailer Mathews's *Jesus on Social Institutions* was included. There can be no substantive dialogue with our own theological tra-dition which ignores his work, together with that of Shirley Jackson Case. Case's *Jesus: A New Biography* was originally planned for inclusion, but its availability in two other editions has made that unnecessary. Doubtless other works could have been included with justification; however, these will suffice to enliven the theological scene if read perceptively.

In each case, an editor was invited to provide an introductory essay and anno-tations to the text in order to assist the reader in seeing the book in perspective. The bibliography will aid further research, though in no case was there an attempt to be comprehensive. The aim is not to produce critical editions in the technical sense (which would require a massive apparatus), but a useable series of texts with guidance at essential points. Within these aims the several editors enjoyed considerable latitude in developing their contributions. The series will achieve its aim if it facilitates a rediscovery of an exciting and controversial his-tory and so makes our own work more fruitful.

The present volume is edited by Peter C. Hodgson, Associate Professor of Theology at Vanderbilt Divinity School. After winning honors in history at Princeton, he continued his education at Yale (B.D., M.A., Ph.D., 1959–63) where his work in systematic and historical theology again earned him distinction. Professor Hodgson is unusually well equipped to edit Strauss's *Life of Jesus.* His dissertation on Strauss's teacher, F. C. Baur, was published as *The Formation of Historical Theology: A Study of Ferdinand Christian Baur* (Harper, 1966); two years later, he edited and translated Baur's *On the Writing of Church History* (Oxford, 1968). Both books manifest his capacity for careful historical scholar-ship. In numerous articles he has shown also his ability to grasp and interpret contemporary theological issues. He is concerned with constructive theological thinking as well, and has published his own Christology as *Jesus—Word and Pres-ence* (Fortress, 1971). Not least important for the task at hand is Professor Hodgson's concern as a theologian to take biblical study seriously; his first pub-lished article, in fact, was a study of the title, Son of Man, in the Synoptic Gos-pels. These multiple competencies have made possible this definitive English edi-tion of Strauss's *Life of Jesus.* That Strauss changed his mind several times as the book was repeatedly revised is well known; but not until now could the stu-dent trace some of the significant shifts between the various editions. Moreover, by relying on letters and other recently available material, Professor Hodgson has been able to relate these shifts to Strauss's life in detail. In short, the pres-ent edition will doubtless prove to be indispensable for future study of one of the most fascinating and important figures in nineteenth century Protestantism—David Friedrich Strauss.

LEANDER E. KECK

ACKNOWLEDGMENTS

Without the help of several graduate assistants this work could not have been completed. I am especially grateful to Voris G. Brookshire, who undertook the arduous task of comparing the German editions and checking the accuracy of the English translation. His work provided the basis for a critical study of the text and for an analysis of the variations between the German editions. Mr. Brookshire also prepared the bibliographies. James O. Duke helped to translate the Author's Prefaces included in this edition, while John C. Shelley translated the concluding section of the third edition of *The Life of Jesus*.

I am also indebted to my colleague, Professor Leander E. Keck, who persuaded me to undertake the editorial assignment for this volume in the Lives of Jesus Series, and who has provided many of the resources with which the task has been completed. In the fall semester 1970 Professor Keck and I taught jointly a seminar on Strauss and the historical Jesus. The participants in that seminar made a distinct contribution to this work, and I am grateful to all of them. The University Research Council provided funds to support the project, and the Divinity and University Libraries lent important assistance as well. Dr. Walter Sachs of Stuttgart furnished some manuscript materials used in preparing the Introduction, and offered the editor valuable bibliographical and interpretive counsel during a conversation in the spring of 1969.

In the Editor's Introduction, citations of *The Life of Jesus* are placed in parentheses and abbreviated *LJ*. Page references are to the 1892 edition of the Eliot translation, reprinted in this volume. Editorial notes are abbreviated "ed.n." and are found in the Annotations at the back of the work. They are keyed to the page numbers of the text and are located on the pages by asterisks and daggers, while author's footnotes are designated by arabic numerals.

Peter C. Hodgson

Vanderbilt University
December 1971

CONTENTS

INTRODUCTION.

DEVELOPMENT OF THE MYTHICAL POINT OF VIEW IN RELATION TO THE GOSPEL HISTORIES.

FIRST PART.

HISTORY OF THE BIRTH AND CHILDHOOD OF JESUS.

CHAPTER I.

ANNUNCIATION AND BIRTH OF JOHN THE BAPTIST.

CHAPTER II.

CHAPTER III.

CHAPTER IV.

CHAPTER V.

SECOND PART.

HISTORY OF THE PUBLIC LIFE OF JESUS.

CHAPTER I.

RELATIONS BETWEEN JESUS AND JOHN THE BAPTIST.

CHAPTER II.

BAPTISM AND TEMPTATION OF JESUS.

CHAPTER III.

LOCALITY AND CHRONOLOGY OF THE PUBLIC LIFE OF JESUS.

CHAPTER IV.

JESUS AS THE MESSIAH.

CHAPTER V.

THE DISCIPLES OF JESUS.

CHAPTER VI.

THE DISCOURSES OF JESUS IN THE THREE FIRST GOSPELS.

CHAPTER VII.

DISCOURSES OF JESUS IN THE FOURTH GOSPEL.

CHAPTER VIII.

EVENTS IN THE PUBLIC LIFE OF JESUS, EXCLUSIVE OF THE MIRACLES.

CHAPTER IX.

MIRACLES OF JESUS.

CHAPTER X.

THE TRANSFIGURATION OF JESUS, AND HIS LAST JOURNEY TO JERUSALEM.

THIRD PART.

HISTORY OF THE PASSION, DEATH, AND RESURRECTION OF JESUS.

CHAPTER I.

RELATION OF JESUS TO THE IDEA OF A SUFFERING AND DYING MESSIAH ; HIS DIS-
COURSES ON HIS DEATH, RESURRECTION, AND SECOND ADVENT.

CHAPTER II.

MACHINATIONS OF THE ENEMIES OF JESUS ; TREACHERY OF JUDAS ; LAST SUPPER WITH
THE DISCIPLES.

CHAPTER III.

RETIREMENT TO THE MOUNT OF OLIVES, ARREST, TRIAL, CONDEMNATION, AND
CRUCIFIXION OF JESUS.

CHAPTER IV.

DEATH AND RESURRECTION OF JESUS.

CHAPTER V.

THE ASCENSION.

CONCLUDING DISSERTATION.

THE DOGMATIC IMPORT OF THE LIFE OF JESUS.

EDITOR'S INTRODUCTION:

Strauss's Theological Development from 1825 to 1840

PETER C. HODGSON

THE ALIENATED THEOLOGIAN

A PROMINENT religious thinker of our time has characterized his own attitude and that of many of his contemporaries by describing the emergence of the "alienated theologian," who continues in his professional role and is "concerned with the articulation of the faith of the Christian community but who is himself as much a doubter as a believer." Antecedents of an alienated theology may be traced to the rationalists of the eighteenth century and the Protestant liberals of the nineteenth century, whose alienation was "milder or more serious" depending upon whether the doctrines they doubted were peripheral or more central to the Christian faith. In the past decade, however, a more radical form of doubt has emerged among the death-of-God theologians.

> In them, the dubiety is not so much about marginal doctrine as about the essence of faith itself: the existence of God. What makes this new phenomenon especially interesting is that these professional theologians do not leave the Christian community or give up theology. They are still preoccupied with the significance of Jesus Christ for human life, and they read and comment on the work of other more orthodox theologians. Nevertheless, they are deeply estranged from the faith and their work reflects this estrangement. They are "unhappy lovers" of Christian theology.[1]

Although unintended, these sentences precisely describe the posture and dilemma of David Friedrich Strauss, who was perhaps the first of the modern "unhappy lovers" of Christian theology. His dubiety went to the heart of the matter: the question of the relation between God and the world. Strauss was not an atheist, but he was unable to believe in a transcendent, personal God who intervenes supernaturally in the course of nature and history (*LJ*, 79) and who reserves eternal blessedness to the end of history, at which time the righteous will be rewarded and sinners condemned. In place of what he took to be orthodox theism, Strauss posited a pantheism that asserted the ultimate identity of God and the world and the immanence of time and eternity.[2]

The crisis of belief in God precipitated a crisis in Christology and first became perceptible there, at least for Strauss. Neither the supernatural God-man of orthodox doctrine, nor a historical Jesus whose teaching was molded by eschato-logical-apocalyptic imagery, accorded well with Strauss's view of the God-world

---

[1] Van A. Harvey, "The Alienated Theologian," *McCormick Quarterly* 23 (May 1970): 234–65. Quotation from p. 235.
[2] Gotthold Müller, *Identität und Immanenz: Zur Genese der Theologie von David Friedrich Strauss* (Zürich: EVZ-Verlag, 1968), pp. 252–59. I return to this matter in greater detail below (see especially n. 98).

relation. So Strauss set out to write a destructive critique of the biblical and doctrinal views of Christ, which would enable him to abstract the true essence of Christian faith from the religious imagery with which it had been entangled, an imagery that could be traced to Jesus himself. Yet rather like the radical theologians of our time (as well as the great radical at the turn of our century, Albert Schweitzer), he found himself strangely drawn to Jesus, the apocalyptic enthusiast he discovered behind the Gospel accounts, and was unable to let him go, regardless of the ambivalence of his attitude toward him. The great offense of the faith of Christianity was for Strauss its futuristic eschatology, yet his fascination with eschatology and his struggle against it continued to the end of his career. It is this fascination and struggle that make him so distinctly contemporary and render a renewed study of *The Life of Jesus* worthwhile.

Strauss was, to use Van Harvey's image, a straggler at the edge of the camp of Israel.[3] He no longer could enter the camp of faith and affirm its rites and practices, but neither could he leave it, for he continued to draw spiritual sustenance from it. Strauss was, in fact, during the period with which we are concerned (1825–1840), a very religious man engaged in an intensely religious quest and struggle. The quest was for a consciousness of the underlying identity of the divine and human, the infinite and finite. At the conclusion of his doctoral dissertation, he says: "We believe in a restoration of all things because everything, each in its own place, is an object of the divine beneficence and is a melodious voice in the great harmony that praises the creator."[4] This statement expresses Strauss's romantic pathos for the presence of and participation in the divine, a pathos born in part of the experience of God's absence. He therefore considered himself a defender of religion against its real enemies, the naturalists and atheists who cut the nerve center of divine-human unity by an exclusive veneration of man and the espousal of abstract ideals.[5] Thus, in enumerating at the end of *The Life of Jesus* the alternatives left open to the critical and speculative theologian, he decisively rejects that of forsaking the ministerial office, for the faith could then no longer "resist the attacks of the critical and speculative laity" (*LJ*, 783; see also 757–58). Moreover, he points out, it would be unreasonable to expect one who believes "he has penetrated into the deepest mysteries of theology . . . just at this point in his career to abandon theology."

But this abandonment was forced upon Strauss by the violent reaction to *The Life of Jesus*, which forever destroyed the prospects of a university professorship, to say nothing of a pulpit. Had Strauss received the teaching position he coveted and had his scholarship been honestly recognized by theology and the church, his career might well have taken a different and more productive course. But as things stood, he became a free-lance theologian who dabbled in biography, in poetry, in philosophy—knowing that he was neither a historian, nor an artist, nor a philosopher. The theologian who cannot abandon theology, yet cannot practice it, is truly the alienated theologian. It was the lack of a viable vocation that turned Strauss into a bitter antagonist of the Christian faith and caused him finally to embrace the flat bourgeois materialism he earlier recognized as the deadly enemy of true religion.

Yet the lack of vocation was the consequence not merely of outer circumstance but also of inner personal failure and weakness. The inner weakness pre-

---

[3] Harvey, "The Alienated Theologian," pp. 235–38.

[4] Strauss, *Die Lehre von der Wiederbringung aller Dinge in ihrer religionsgeschichtlichen Entwicklung* (1831), in Müller, *Identität und Immanenz*, p. 82. For discussion of this work, see below, pp. xxi–xxii.

[5] See Strauss, "Vergängliches und Bleibendes im Christenthum," *Freihafen* 1:3 (1848): 31–32.

vented him from becoming a tragic figure, as Karl Barth rightly recognizes.[6] Strauss himself was aware of the weakness and perceived it in the form of a vacillation of interests and an inability to hold to a coherent life-course. To his friend Ernst Rapp he wrote in 1837: "Many theological points, which at one time lay very close to my heart, no longer interest me, and I often wish I could escape the entire business. It is similar to the experience I had when I concluded my philosophical lectures in Tübingen: my interest in philosophy as such began to die out and since then has never reawakened. Perhaps I am again shedding a skin, but what is to replace the theological skin I do not yet see."[7] He mentions the possibility of art and literature but acknowledges a lack of literary imagination. He is certain that he will never make a true scholar, for he is too dependent upon mood and is too preoccupied with himself. Yet he is unable to abandon theology, to which it was his fate to have been "called."[8] As an "inbetween creature"[9] who lacked a vocation and sensed inner warring drives, Strauss was unable to become a constructive thinker and to create an independent theological position, which had been his original intent. His "sole talent," he later acknowledged, was that of "logical-rhetorical representation,"[10] which is perhaps the destined role of the alienated theologian.

In this role Strauss was devastatingly effective. He destroyed all previous attempts, by both rationalists and supernaturalists, to construct a historical portrayal of the founding events of the Christian faith, and he reflected to his age the confusion and ambiguity with which this task had been approached.[11] The negative results of his criticism were doubly effective because Neo-Protestant theology had sought to replace supernatural revelation and the infallible magisterium of the church, which were the bases of authority in orthodox Protestantism and Catholicism, by an appeal to history and to religious consciousness. Yet here was a critical method that "made the historical correlate of faith uncertain in the same way as Feuerbach's psychology of religion made its metaphysical correlate uncertain."[12] One might welcome these results as demonstrating the necessary independence of Christian faith from any form of historical corroboration or denial, as Karl Barth does. Or one could attempt to show the inadequacies of Strauss's critical method and the inaccuracies of his historical findings. The latter course is the only defensible one if a critical theology is to survive; but Strauss did his work so thoroughly that for many years no one could offer an adequate response. For this reason he was feared and reviled, and even today his work retains its undoubted impact.

The lasting theological significance of Strauss can be summarized under at least the following points:

(1) *The Life of Jesus* represented a watershed in the development of a critical method for the study of the Gospels, in virtue of both its destruction of all previous methods of interpretation and its positive elaboration of the mythical criterion. However much Strauss's own method has been surpassed, the fundamen-

---

[6] Karl Barth, *Protestant Thought: From Rousseau to Ritschl*, trans. Brian Cozens (New York: Harper & Row, 1959), p. 363, against the judgment of Albert Schweitzer, *The Quest of the Historical Jesus*, 3rd ed. (London: Adam & Charles Black, 1954), p. 68.

[7] Strauss to Ernst Rapp, 7 May 1837 (*Ausgewählte Briefe von David Friedrich Strauss*, ed. Eduard Zeller [Bonn: Verlag von Emil Strauss, 1895], p. 35).

[8] *Ausgewählte Briefe*, pp. 36, 263.

[9] Heinrich Maier, *Briefe von David Friedrich Strauss an L. Georgii* (Tübingen: J. C. B. Mohr, 1912), p. 14.

[10] Strauss to Ernst Rapp, 10 April 1841 (*Ausgewählte Briefe*, p. 101).

[11] F. C. Baur recognized this destructive role as Strauss's true significance. See *Kritische Untersuchungen über die kanonischen Evangelien* (Tübingen: L. F. Fues, 1847), pp. 48–50.

[12] Barth, *Protestant Thought*, p. 31. Van Harvey offers a similar judgment in "D. F. Strauss' *Life of Jesus* Revisited," *Church History* 30 (1961): 194.

tal developments in form criticism and redaction criticism of our century may be traced back to him; and in his discussion of individual pericopes he anticipated many of the critical questions that are still debated.

(2) Strauss called radically into question the appeal to history as a basis of faith, and he seriously undermined the historical character of the Christian faith, not so much by frontal attack as by the cumulative weight of his minutely detailed analysis. He set the context for the debates over "faith and history," "authority," "absoluteness," and "relativism" that have preoccupied religious thinkers for over a century. He forced much deeper reflection on the precise manner in which the certainty of faith has its ground in the relative events of history, and he demanded an assessment of Jesus free of the dogmatic presuppositions and religious interests of the interpreter.

(3) Strauss perceived the futuristic eschatology of primitive Christianity to be a fundamental stumbling block for the modern secular mind, and he attributed this eschatology to Jesus as well, depicting him as an apocalyptic enthusiast with whom we can have little sympathy today. Eschatology is the secret motif of *The Life of Jesus,* lending the work a distinctly contemporary caste. Strauss prepared the way for Johannes Weiss and Albert Schweitzer, to whom the apocalyptic Jesus remained ultimately an enigma; for Rudolf Bultmann's program of demythologizing, which sought to translate eschatological images into existential ones; and for the current theologies of hope, in their efforts to reassess the significance of eschatology and its role in the birth of Christianity.

(4) The radically immanent theology Strauss proposed as an alternative to biblical eschatology, and his passionate critique of transcendence in any form, caught the essence of the idealist-romantic polemic against the transcendent, separated deity of orthodoxy, although it was probably based on a misreading of Hegel's dialectic; and it anticipated the mystical vision of divine immanence propounded by Thomas Altizer and others in our time. (Strangely enough, Altizer holds to an eschatological vision, whereas Strauss regarded eschatology as the most dangerous mode of transcendence.) The recognition of the potentially demonic character of transcendence, and the corresponding emphasis upon the autonomy of man, which have played such an important though fateful role in recent attempts to move beyond neoorthodoxy, owe something to Strauss. The question he poses for us is whether any form of belief in transcendence is credible, and whether a recognizably Christian theology can survive without it.

(5) As an "alienated theologian," Strauss is representative of the Protestant theological movement from the beginnings of the nineteenth century to the present, and increasingly of Catholic and Jewish religious thought as well. We have all experienced alienation—from the symbols and myths of biblical religion, from the doctrines and creeds of our traditions, from contemporary ecclesiastical practices, from the secularization and dehumanization of our culture. Moreover, we have all sensed the loss of vocation. In Strauss the alienation manifested itself with unusual clarity because of his disjunctive logic, critical acumen, personal honesty, autobiographical proclivities, and literary genius.

The latter remark deserves further comment. *The Life of Jesus* is a work of art—in the world of theology, a literary event of the first magnitude. Its logic is not displayed on the surface like the steps of a pyramid. Rather it could be likened to a great tapestry: threads woven through each other, making each incomplete without the other.[13] A good example is provided by the chapter on the

---

[13] I am indebted to Ray Gingerich, a student in the Strauss seminar at Vanderbilt, for this observation.

miracles of Jesus: the logic of this chapter and its cumulative impact are revealed only gradually, giving it a novellike quality. What makes for literary excellence, however, also lends the work a certain theological opacity. Ideas and motifs are not presented systematically but are woven in and out of each other in an increasingly complex fabric—precisely the fabric of the Gospel story itself. To help readers find their way through seven hundred fifty pages of difficult text, I have provided a synthesis of Strauss's portrayal of the life of Jesus at a later point in this Introduction (pp. xxxi–xxxvi). From this summary it will be possible to locate critical passages where the logic of the book and its author's convictions become apparent.

In the spring of 1838, upon completion of the third edition of *The Life of Jesus,* Strauss wrote to a friend: "I now know from experience thrice repeated that every six years or so an old scholar dies off in me. Thus it is that the whole foundation of my thought is no longer the same as when I first wrote the book."[14] If the "every six years or so" is construed literally down to 1838, the critical periods in Strauss's theological development between 1825 and 1840 may be distinguished as follows: (a) 1825–1831. Philosophical and theological studies at the University of Tübingen, cu¹minating with a year in the parish ministry and a doctoral dissertation on "The Doctrine of the Restoration of All Things." (b) 1831–1837. A half-year of study in Berlin, the direct impact of Hegel, the sketching of a theological program combining critical analysis and speculative reconstruction, philosophical lectures in Tübingen, preparation for and publication of the first two editions of *The Life of Jesus.* (c) 1837–1839. The desire for a less polemical mode of existence, the abortive call to Zürich, the general weakening of theological interests, and the quest for a more positive Christology, culminating in the third edition of *The Life of Jesus.* (d) 1839–1840. Return to the original negative conclusions of *The Life of Jesus* in a fourth edition of the work, and open attack upon Christendom in the *Christliche Glaubenslehre.* In the next four sections of this Introduction, I shall examine these four periods in detail. Following publication of the *Glaubenslehre,* Strauss did no further work in theology for over twenty years, until his essay on Reimarus of 1862, and his new life of Jesus, *Das Leben Jesu für das deutsche Volk bearbeitet,* 1864. During the intervening period he wrote biography, essays, and poetry, ventured into politics, and experienced a disastrous marriage which ended in legal separation (but not divorce) after five years. This period of Strauss's life, and especially his return to a theological authorship in the 1860s, are matters that lie beyond the province of this Introduction.

ROMANTICISM, MYSTICISM, IDEALISM:
THE STUDENT YEARS IN TÜBINGEN (1825–1831)[15]

David Friedrich Strauss was born January 27, 1808, in Ludwigsburg, near Stuttgart, the son of a merchant. From 1821 to 1825 he studied at the seminary

---

[14] Strauss to Ernst Rapp, 17 March 1838 (*Ausgewählte Briefe,* p. 58).

[15] Crucial for the study of this period in Strauss's development is Gotthold Müller's recent book, *Identität und Immanenz: Zur Genese der Theologie von David Friedrich Strauss.* Müller publishes for the first time Strauss's doctoral dissertation of 1831, "The Doctrine of the Restoration of All Things in Its Religious-Historical Development," and the book concentrates on an analysis of Strauss's education and interests prior to the writing of this manuscript. Thus important background materials are made available for understanding the philosophical and theological milieu out of which *The Life of Jesus* emerged.

in Blaubeuren, one of four preparatory seminaries provided by the state of Württemberg for the training of candidates for the ministry prior to their university education at Tübingen. In Blaubeuren Strauss was a student of Ferdinand Christian Baur, who became and remained his most influential teacher.

In 1825 both Strauss and Baur went to Tübingen. Strauss's first two years there were taken up with philosophical study, as was the custom. But he learned more outside the classroom than within it. The chief influences on him at the time were romanticism, mysticism, and natural philosophy. He became associated with a romantic circle that included Eduard Mörike and Ludwig Bauer, and wrote a "romantic national tragedy," *Zauberei und Spengler*, which was produced at Blaubeuren. On his own he studied intensively J. G. Fichte and especially the philosophy of nature of Friedrich Schelling. Through the latter he became acquainted with the medieval mystics, Jacob Boehme, and the Swabian mystic Friedrich Christian Oetinger.[16] In the spring of 1827, he made the first of several pilgrimages to Weinsberg, where the poet-physician Justinus Kerner had under treatment a remarkable woman. Strauss was deeply affected by this and similar experiences, which were the source of his fascination with the cures of certain types of physical ailments by magnetic or hypnotic means—a fascination that was to play a fateful role in the third edition of *The Life of Jesus*.[17]

During the period 1827–1830 Strauss studied theology, but with the exception of Baur the theological faculty did not interest him, and he engaged in further philosophical reading of his own, above all in Schelling. In 1828 he wrote a prize essay for the Catholic theological faculty, titled "De resurrectione carnis," of which he later remarked: "I proved exegetically and by the philosophy of nature the resurrection of the dead, with complete conviction, and as I dotted the last *i* it was clear to me that there is nothing to the entire story."[18] Shortly thereafter he read for the first time Schleiermacher's *Glaubenslehre*, which served to facilitate a transition from his romantic and mystical affinities to the rigor of Hegelian dialectic. Hegel himself was virtually unknown in Tübingen prior to the winter of 1828–29, when a tutor in the evangelical seminary, who had recently returned from a period of study in Berlin, lectured on his thought. That same winter Strauss and a small circle of friends began a thorough study of Hegel's *Phenomenology of Spirit*, which they interpreted in the "liberal sense," i.e., as superseding religion and theology in a purely philosophical vision.[19] According to Müller, Strauss thought he had discovered in Hegel an answer to the question that came to preoccupy him during his entire course of study, namely, how to overcome the tension between a religion based on supernatural revelation and an immanent philosophy of consciousness. He persistently interpreted Hegel monistically where the latter insisted upon dialectical distinctions.[20]

Following the completion of his studies at Tübingen Strauss took a parish in Kleiningersheim from the fall of 1830 through the summer of 1831. There he continued his study of Hegel and engaged in a struggle with his conscience. A friend, Christian Märklin, had also taken a parish, and the two engaged in correspondence on mutual problems. Hegel had drawn a crucial distinction between *Vorstellung* (religious imagery) and *Begriff* (philosophical concept), according to which the same content or truth (the unity of God and world, the reconciliation

[16] Müller, *Identität und Immanenz*, pp. 39–43, 196, 202–3.

[17] Ibid., pp. 41–42, 205–6; William Nast, "Recollections of David Friedrich Strauss," *The New Princeton Review* 4 (1887): 345–46.

[18] Strauss to Friedrich Vischer, 8 Feb. 1838 (*Ausgewählte Briefe*, p. 52).

[19] Ibid. See also Müller, *Identität und Immanenz*, pp. 44–46, 222–24.

[20] Müller, *Identität und Immanenz*, pp. 225–27.

of finite and infinite spirit) could be expressed in different forms. This permitted one to criticize the religious forms without losing their essential content. But Märklin pointed out that as a preacher he was finding it necessary to give explicitly as the essence or content of Christianity what according to Hegel merely has the form of religious imagination (e.g., the devil, the virgin birth, the empty tomb, the miracles of Jesus). For ordinary Christians the imaginative forms were themselves the content of faith. Consequently he was unable to preach with an easy conscience. In attempting to answer his friend, Strauss revealed his uncertainty. The only alternative, he says, is to hold to the unity of content that exists between imagery and conception, and whenever possible substitute concepts for the less edifying religious images (or myths). At those points where the congregation is not ready for concepts, we must either speak to them in images or terminate religious fellowship with them—and such scruples are not called for. Yet at one point Strauss confesses: "But you say, this whole game with images instead of concepts, etc., is dishonest, self-contradictory, and must collapse—yes, you may be right about this."[21]

In the spring of 1831, while still in Kleiningersheim, Strauss wrote a brief doctoral dissertation on "The Doctrine of the Restoration of All Things in Its Religious-Historical Significance." The only extant piece of theological writing by Strauss prior to the *Life of Jesus*, it is of fundamental significance for an interpretation of the latter work. Its central argument is that the *apokatastasis ton pantōn*, the restoration of all finite things to the creator, and the concomitant overcoming of the awareness of contradiction between finite and infinite spirit, must be *de-eschatologized*. All religions have postponed this restoration to the distant future, including Christianity despite its own inner principle. The reason is "the practical standpoint of Jesus and the apostles"; i.e., they were too motivated by a concern to secure salvation for the righteous and damnation for the sinners, and they thought of the kingdom of God in "practical" rather than in "speculative" terms. Although Origen espoused the idea of an *apokatastasis*, even he postponed it to the "expected world of pure spirit and pure goodness." The first real advance in understanding came with Schleiermacher, although it is concealed by ambiguity. The doctrine of individual immortality required him to postpone the *apokatastasis* to the hidden future, when errant souls will at last enter into vital community with Christ. Yet according to Schleiermacher, evil for God is essentially nothingness, nonexistent, rather than a quasi-personal agency (the devil) which could be vanquished only at the end of time in a cosmic struggle. "Therefore," continues Strauss, "the *apokatastasis pantōn* for Schleiermacher is not something future but eternally present, and his restoration of all things means that the world in every moment is the best possible." The ambiguities in Schleiermacher were overcome by Hegel. "Hegel rightly denies that religion already provides the spiritual man with a present resolution of all the contradictions of his pious consciousness. For many religions, as we have said, have postponed that resolution to the distant future; and he ascribes this [resolution] to the true philosophy, which, subjectively considered, is the restoration of all things."[22]

---

[21] Strauss to Christian Märklin, 26 Dec. 1830 (*Ausgewählte Briefe*, pp. 3–7); Müller, *Identität und Immanenz*, pp. 228–31. The same solution is proposed at the end of the *Life of Jesus*, pp. 783–84.

[22] Strauss, *Die Lehre von der Wiederbringung aller Dinge*, in Müller, *Identität und Immanenz*, pp. 50, 58–62, 80–81; Strauss to Gustaf Binder, 14 June 1831 (Müller, *Identität und Immanenz*, pp. 85–87).

Thus in his earliest writing we find Strauss already preoccupied with the problem of eschatology, a preoccupation that is the hidden motif of *The Life of Jesus* and that led finally to his denial of the Christian faith, first in the *Glaubenslehre* and then irrevocably in *Der alte und der neue Glaube*. The dissertation in its historical sections evidences an uncritical use of sources and a rationalistic exegesis of texts, which give few hints of the critical and dialectical talents so impressively displayed just four years later. Philosophically Strauss identifies himself as a "radical" Hegelian: religion and philosophy are viewed as irreconcilable alternatives (the one calling for a future, the other for an eternally present, dissolution of the antithesis between finite and infinite spirit); and a nondialectical, timeless reconciliation of spirit is advocated, in which no consciousness of opposition is tolerated. In fact, the dissertation appears to be based on a monistic-immanent philosophy of identity, having its roots not so much in Hegel as in Spinoza, Schelling, and the German mystics (Boehme, Oetinger, and von Baader).[23] The monistic identity of God and the world, and the immanence of time and eternity, cut the nerve of true Hegelian dialectic, as well as of the religious perception of the future as an image of transcendence. The presence of God is conceived as timeless immediacy rather than as the coming of future, liberating power—which is the genius of both the Bible and Hegel.

CRITICAL ANALYSIS AND PROPOSALS FOR A SPECULATIVE RECONSTRUCTION: THE FIRST TWO EDITIONS OF *THE LIFE OF JESUS* (1831–1837)

STUDY IN BERLIN AND THE ORIGINAL PLAN FOR A LIFE OF JESUS

Strauss apparently decided that the only way to resolve the tension between his interpretation of Hegel and his desire to be a theologian and pastor was to talk with the great philosopher directly. Accordingly he made plans for a period of study in Berlin and arrived there in October 1831. Scarcely had he begun to attend lectures when Hegel died of cholera on November 14. Strauss learned this news from Schleiermacher during his first visit with the latter, to whom he is reputed to have blurted out, "But it was for his sake that I came here!" He first thought to leave Berlin at once, but then consoled himself with the thought, "Here Hegel has died, to be sure, but not died out." Hegel continued to live in his disciples—Marheinecke, Henning, Michelet—all of whom Strauss heard.[24] He also read a full transcription by students of Schleiermacher's lectures on the life of Jesus from the summer semester of 1831. Although Strauss was severely critical of these lectures at the time, the third edition of his own *Life of Jesus* (1838) approximates Schleiermacher's views on certain critical matters, e.g., the unsurpassable religious consciousness of Jesus, his unusual curative powers, and the validity of the Gospel of John as a source of knowledge about Jesus' self-understanding. On each of his major concessions Strauss moves in the direction of Schleiermacher! Yet when the latter's lectures on the life of Jesus were pub-

---

[23] Müller, *Identität und Immanenz*, pp. 100–101, 113–18, 252–59. See below, n. 98.
[24] *Ausgewählte Briefe*, pp. 8–11; Eduard Zeller, *David Friedrich Strauss in seinem Leben und seinen Schriften*, 2nd ed. (Bonn: Verlag von Emil Strauss, 1874), pp. 25–26.

lished in 1864, Strauss was quick to deliver the coup de grace with his critique of 1865, *Der Christus des Glaubens und der Jesus der Geschichte.*

Prior to reading Schleiermacher's lectures, Strauss already had in mind a plan for a life of Jesus of his own. He described it in a letter to Christian Märklin from Berlin in February 1832, and with greater clarity five years later at the beginning of his third series of *Streitschriften.*[25] He notes that Hegel and his students were ambiguous about the relation between *Vorstellung* and *Begriff.* "The most important question . . . concerns the nature of the relation of the historical data of the Bible, especially the Gospels, to the concept. Does the historical character adhere to the content [of Christian faith], thus demanding recognition from the concept [*Begriff*] as well as the imagination [*Vorstellung*], since the content is the same for both, or is it reduced to the mere form [of imagination], to which conceptual thinking is not bound?" Marheinecke, Göschel, and the right-wing Hegelians had emphasized the affirmative side of the relation of the concept to history at the expense of the negative. This is not satisfying because it leads back to the orthodox systems. Therefore the idea has occurred to Strauss of a dogmatics that would present the biblical imagery, show how the latter is defined by church dogma through heretical distortions, then demonstrate that dogma itself is annulled in the polemics of deism and rationalism in order to be reestablished and purified by means of conceptual thinking. Then he continues:

> Because of the seemingly special importance of the relation of the concept to the Gospel history, it occurred to me first of all to work through the life of Jesus in this fashion. My first plan, sketched during a period of study in Berlin, . . . was to have three parts. The first, positive or traditional part, would contain an objective presentation of the life of Jesus according to the Gospels, a description of the way Jesus lives subjectively in the faithful, and the mediation of these two aspects in the second article of the Apostles' Creed. The second, negative or critical part, would for the most part annul the life history of Jesus as history; the third part would re-establish dogmatically what had been destroyed. Together with this original plan the designation of the project as "life of Jesus" developed, and one could not say that it was inappropriate. When in its execution the projected first part fell away, the third became a mere appendix, and the second grew into the real body of the book, I did not want . . . to surrender the original designation, and thought to make it appropriate to the altered plan by the addition, "critically examined."[26]

Ironically, Strauss originally expected the second part to be the most difficult, although it would have the most assistance from Celsus through the English and French deists; whereas the third, constructive part would be for him the easiest.[27] When it came to the actual writing of the book, he decided to give only a brief sketch of the dogmatic reestablishment of christological doctrine,

---

[25] *Ausgewählte Briefe,* pp. 12–15; *Streitschriften zur Vertheidigung meiner Schrift über das Leben Jesu und zur Charakteristik der gegenwärtigen Theologie,* No. 3 (Tübingen: C. F. Osiander, 1837), pp. 57–60. While still in Kleiningersheim, Strauss outlined a plan for an entire Christian dogmatics, based on Hegelian dialectics, similar to the one proposed here for a life of Jesus. This plan formed the basis for the *Christliche Glaubenslehre* of 1840. (Maier, *Briefe von Strauss an Georgii,* p. 4.)

[26] *Streitschriften,* No. 3, pp. 57–60; quotations from pp. 57, 59–60. Strauss had been criticized by Carl Ullmann and August Tholuck for giving the book a misleading title in order to gain a larger reading public. Ullmann said the book should have been titled, "Critique of the Evangelical History." See *Streitschriften,* p. 134.

[27] Strauss to Christian Märklin, 6 Feb. 1832 (*Ausgewählte Briefe,* p. 15).

which was to be made the subject of a separate work, because the ultimate goal of historical criticism can "only lie beyond dogmatic criticism" (*LJ*, § 144; ed.nn. 757*, 758*). Yet the promised constructive part was missing from the *Glaubenslehre* as well.

THE FIRST AND SECOND EDITIONS OF *THE LIFE OF JESUS*, 1835–1836

Strauss returned to Tübingen as a tutor in the evangelical seminary in the summer of 1832. He lectured with brilliant success on logic and metaphysics (summer semester 1832), history of philosophy since Kant (winter semester 1832–33), and history of ethics (summer semester 1833). But after only three semesters he gave up his lectures to begin work on a life of Jesus in the fall of 1833. He took extensive notes on everything in the ancient and modern literature related to the interpretation and criticism of the Gospels. As a consequence of these extensive preparatory studies, the second, critical part grew ever more extensive and eventually absorbed the entire project. The sketch of the individual Gospel accounts, which originally was to constitute a separate first part, was divided up and used to preface each of the critical sections, while the second article of the Apostles' Creed was reserved to the Concluding Dissertation (§ 145). The manuscript itself, which covered 1500 printed pages, was written in little over a year. The first volume appeared in the early summer, the second in the late fall, of 1835. It was a work of youthful genius, whose author was just twenty-seven years old.[28]

Strauss expected that the book would be welcomed by serious and enlightened men of all persuasions as a liberation from the fetters of dogmatism and as a basis for the revitalization of the true essence of the Christian faith. He also was confident that it would bring him a teaching appointment.[29] Instead, the negative reaction was perfectly extraordinary. On all sides complaints were heard of Strauss's negativity, sarcastic sense of humor, and heartless coldness—a charge to which he opened himself by the infamous reference in the Preface to the *Kaltblütigkeit* of the investigation. On July 23, 1835, he was relieved of his position as tutor and exiled to the Lyceum in Ludwigsburg, where he was to teach philology. He could have transferred to the philosophical faculty in Tübingen, but declined doing so because he had lost interest in purely philosophical questions and was intent on pursuing an academic career in theology. For the moment he was satisfied to have the free time for completion of the second volume of his work. But he soon grew restless at the Lyceum and while in Ludwigsburg had to live with his parents, where he came into continual conflict with his father. So in the fall of 1836 he departed for Stuttgart and began a free-lance career of writing and research.[30]

Already by the spring of 1836 a second edition was necessary. Strauss asked his friends for suggested improvements, "since I can learn nothing from the reviews of opponents."[31] Baur responded with the most concrete suggestions, urging Strauss to add a section on the relation of myth to Christianity, and another on external evidences for the age and authenticity of the Gospels.[32] Strauss agreed

[28] Strauss, *Streitschriften*, No. 3, pp. 60–61; Zeller, *David Friedrich Strauss*, pp. 29–32.
[29] Maier, *Briefe von Strauss an Georgii*, pp. 8–10.
[30] Ibid., pp. 8–10, 12–13; Zeller, *David Friedrich Strauss*, pp. 43–44.
[31] Maier, *Briefe von Strauss an Georgii*, p. 14.
[32] Ibid., p. 15; and Strauss to F. C. Baur, 1 May 1836 (Ernst Barnikol, "Der Briefwechsel zwischen Strauss und Baur," *Zeitschrift für Kirchengeschichte* 73 [1962]: 82–83).

to do so but indicated that in Ludwigsburg he lacked the necessary literary and critical tools for an adequate study of these questions, and that in particular he "felt insecure" on the matter of external evidences for the Gospels. Consequently, he restricted himself for the most part to a reworking and expansion of materials already found in the last part of § 12 of the first edition, with only limited reference to additional literature. The discussion of external evidences for the Gospels was included in the new § 13, and the analysis of Christian mythology in the new § 14. Strauss also added a discussion of "Criteria by which to Distinguish the Mythical in the Gospel Narrative" (now § 16); it was the only addition that contained wholly new material. Apart from these three sections, the revisions to the second edition are not extensive. They were prepared hastily during the spring and summer of 1836, while Strauss was still teaching at the Lyceum in Ludwigsburg. The first two editions will be considered together in the analysis of the method and contents of the work which follows.

THE "NEGATIVE-CRITICAL OR DIALECTICAL" METHOD

THE DIALECTICAL CRITIQUE OF SUPERNATURALISM AND RATIONALISM

In the Preface to the first edition Strauss points out that both the supernaturalists and the rationalists accepted the Gospel stories as true accounts of the history of Jesus. The difference between them was that, whereas the supernaturalists interpreted the miracles as instances of immediate divine intervention, the rationalists attributed these stories to misapprehensions on the part of the original witnesses, or explained them on a naturalistic basis. They considered "the miraculous in the sacred history as a drapery which needs only to be drawn aside, in order to disclose the pure historic form" (*LJ*, 50). In neither case was the historical authenticity of the reports questioned. Strauss's method throughout the book is to establish the necessity of the mythical interpretation by moving through the supernaturalistic and rationalistic interpretations of each incident in the Gospels. These interpretations are made to refute each other, the arguments of rationalists being used against supernaturalists, and vice versa. First the supernaturalists are demolished. Then "the natural explanation, by its own unnaturalness, ever brings us back to the mythical," upon the application of which "the innumerable, and never otherwise to be harmonized, discrepancies and chronological contradictions in the gospel histories disappear, as it were, at one stroke" (*LJ*, 55, 56–57). This dialectical procedure is *the* characteristic method of the book, rather than the *direct* application of the criteria for distinguishing the mythical enumerated in § 16—criteria that were specified for the first time in the second edition only after the main body of the analysis had been completed. Strauss systematizes his method in a way not entirely congruous with the application of it. The dialectical procedure he in fact follows is undoubtedly dramatic, and its cumulative effect upon the orthodoxy and rationalism of his day must have been devastating indeed.

Nevertheless, Strauss's attitude toward supernaturalism and rationalism is an ambivalent one. On the one hand, he gives the impression of greater sympathy for the supernaturalists because of the often deceptive and paralogistic character of the rationalistic explanation (see *LJ*, 130, n. 8). At least the supernaturalists were closer to the actual intent of Scripture and openly acknowledged miraculous assumptions, secretly shared by the rationalists as well, e.g., that the New Testament writers always spoke and wrote what was just and true. The effort to penetrate to the rational core of the narrative often required extravagant, illogical, indeed revolting constructions (*LJ*, 140). Yet Strauss has no hesitation about demolishing the supernaturalist views, often with a biting sense of humor. On the other hand, when the mythical interpretation does not apply, Strauss's own inclination is invariably toward a rationalist rather than a supernaturalist explanation. Good examples are his treatment of the intellectual development of Jesus (*LJ*, 202–4), and especially his psychological interpretation of the cures (*LJ*, §§ 92–96), and of the visions the disciples experienced of the risen Lord (*LJ*, § 140, ed.n. 735*). Psychology permitted Strauss a more refined rationalism and he did not hesitate to employ it when it suited his purposes; in this respect he was distinctly modern. As we shall discover shortly, Strauss's interpretation of history was basically rationalistic.

THE POSITIVE CRITERION: THE MYTHICAL INTERPRETATION

In the third and fourth editions, Strauss added a typology (§ 15) of myths and other forms of unhistorical material found in the Gospels, which helps to clarify his rather obscure survey of the Mythical School (§§ 8–12),[33] and is especially important for an understanding of his own mythical interpretation.

(1) *Evangelical myths* are products of an *idea*—specifically, messianic ideas and expectations, which are found either in "pure" form (i.e., unrelated to Jesus), or as modified by the general impression left by Jesus, or as applied to specific individual facts, which may or may not be recoverable. By "idea" in this context Strauss means the *religious imagery* (*religiöse Vorstellung*) characteristic of a particular people or religious community (*LJ*, 65). Ideas in this sense are to be distinguished from the ideal, essential content of Christianity—the idea of divine-human unity—as defined by speculative-conceptual thought. To be sure, Strauss was of the conviction, together with Hegel, "that the primitive Christian *Zeitideen* represented in the mythologoumena are to be viewed on their part as realizations of the true and eternal idea of God-manhood in the mode and at the level of *Vorstellung*."[34] But the distinction between *Vorstellung* and *Begriff* is preserved. Religion is by definition *imaginative* (perception in the mode of *Vorstellung*) and therefore *mythical* (*LJ*, 80), for myths are expressions in storylike form of temporally conditioned religious ideas. This definition has the effect of greatly enlarging the role of myth, for where true religion is found so also is myth, as its proper mode of expression. For Strauss, the terms *Religion, Vorstellung*, and *Mythos* become largely synonymous. "Pure" myths are direct expressions of religious imagination, without an admixture of the historical; "historical" myths are also expressions of religious imagination, but influenced to a greater or lesser extent by particular historical events and personages.

(2) *Legends* are products of the formation of *oral tradition*,[35] in the course of

---

[33] On the Mythical School, see Christian Hartlich and Walter Sachs, *Der Ursprung des Mythosbegriffes in der modernen Bibelwissenschaft* (Tübingen: J. C. B. Mohr, 1952), chap. 3. Hartlich and Sachs include in the Mythical School J. G. Eichhorn, J. P. Gabler, J. G. Herder, G. L. Bauer, and the early Schelling.

[34] Ibid., pp. 137–39; quotation from p. 139.

[35] One of Strauss's most important insights concerned the existence of a period of the oral transmission of traditions, prior to the first written documents, during which legends and myths began to form shortly after Jesus' death (*LJ*, 73–74). Because he lacked the tools of form criticism by which to analyze the formative process of oral tradition, he had no way of tracing these traditions back to their more primitive and historically authentic forms, and thus of bridging the gulf between the events themselves and the earliest written documents. His historical skepticism was enlarged by the honest recognition of a methodological impasse. For further analysis, see ed.n. 74*.

which the original facts are distorted and exaggerated, and the original mythical "ideas" (if any) have disappeared.

(3) *Additions of the author* are traceable neither to ideas nor to tradition, but to the literary designs of the author.

(4) *Historical materials* are comprised of the residue left over after subtracting the "forms of the unhistorical" enumerated above, as well as the kernel of fact that is undoubtedly hidden in many myths and legends. Strauss clearly does not deny that such historical materials are found in the Gospels, indeed in considerab'e abundance, but he believes it is often very difficult to identify them (*LJ*, 91). His intent is to examine the entire story of Jesus (not just the infancy and ascension narratives) for the presence of myth, but this is not to imply that all the details of the life of Jesus are mythical (*LJ*, 63, 65; see ed.n. 65*).

Strauss intends the mythical interpretation as a *positive criterion of the unhistorical* in the Gospel stories (*LJ*, 87, 89–90). In this respect his method differs subtly but crucially from the so-called negative criterion of contemporary form criticism. The latter is intended as a limiting criterion of dissimilarity for purposes of locating the contexts where authentic sayings of Jesus are most likely to be found. Norman Perrin formulates it as follows: "The earliest form of a saying we can reach may be regarded as authentic if it can be shown to be dissimilar to characteristic emphases both of ancient Judaism and of the early Church."[36] The contrast between a *negative criterion of the historical* (Perrin) and a *positive criterion of the unhistorical* (Strauss) may be shown by the following comparison:

Perrin: If the earliest form of a saying can be shown to be *dissimilar to* emphases both of ancient Judaism and of the early Church . . .	Strauss: If the contents of a narrative *accords with* ideas existing within the circle from which the narrative proceeded . . .
it may be regarded as *authentic*.	it is probable that such a narrative is of *mythical origin*.[37]

With the concept of myth, Strauss uses a *positive* criterion to achieve *negative* results. Whereas the historian is ordinarily interested in defining critically what is historical, *Strauss has no criterion for isolating authentic historical materials*. It is by no means necessarily the case that, where the mythical criterion fails to apply, historical traditions are present. Where myth is absent, legends or additions of the author may abound rather than history. The mythical criterion can define with reasonable precision what is myth, but beyond that we are left foundering in a sea of uncertainty. A good example is Strauss's treatment of the miracles. Outside the province of the "miracles proper," which are purely mythical (§§ 100–104), the results are in many cases uncertain. Jesus may or may not have performed natural cures (§§ 92–99), and Strauss argues both ways from the same evidence in the first and third editions (see ed.n. 415*).

---

[36] Norman Perrin, *Rediscovering the Teaching of Jesus* (New York: Harper & Row, 1967), p. 39. It is not thereby implied that the sayings of Jesus at one with Judaism or early Christianity are necessarily inauthentic, merely that they cannot be shown to be authentic or inauthentic without the application of a second criterion, the "criterion of coherence" (p. 43).

[37] Adapted from *LJ*, 89. To be sure, Strauss also has a *negative* criterion of the *un*historical, which will be discussed in the next subsection.

With such a procedure, it is inevitable that the negative effects of Strauss's mythical interpretation should be greatly extended beyond the actual presence of myth in the New Testament. For good reason, therefore, Baur characterized Strauss's method as "negative-critical or dialectical." *Negative* results are obtained, according to Baur, by combining the mythical criterion, as the basic critical canon, with an analysis of individual stories abstracted from their literary context. The method is *dialectical* because Strauss brings together opposing interpretations (supernaturalist and rationalist) and opposing accounts (by different Evangelists), showing them to be mutually contradictory and destructive.[38]

Despite the careful methodological elaboration of §§ 15–16 (added in the second and third editions), the criteria of the mythical are applied unsystematically in the main body of the analysis. The following incidents in the story of Jesus contain the most extensive mythical elements: the birth and childhood narratives (§§ 17–43), relations between Jesus and John the Baptist (§§ 44–56). the miracles of Jesus (§§ 91–104), the transfiguration (§§ 105–7), the entrance into Jerusalem (§ 110), precise predictions of the passion (§ 111), many details of the passion story (§§ 121, 126, 129–32, 135–36), the resurrection and ascension (§§ 137–43). Although the presence of myth may be detected in every portion of the story of Jesus (not just the beginning and the end, *LJ*, 64–65), the Gospel accounts are by no means exclusively mythical in Strauss's view, and he allows a greater residue of history to stand than has generally been credited him. He has no doubts that Jesus actually lived, that he was a disciple of John the Baptist, that he conducted a ministry in Galilee, that he came to regard himself as the Messiah, that he called disciples, that his discourses as contained in the Synoptic Gospels are by and large authentic (although not especially important), that he went to Jerusalem with a messianic plan, that he predicted his second advent as the glorified Son of Man, that he had premonitions of his death and bade farewell to his disciples, and that he was arrested, tried, condemned, and crucified. These data provide a rather considerable base for a critically reconstructed portrayal of Jesus, although Strauss never attempts to assemble the scattered pieces into a coherent representation. In the first *Life of Jesus* he is simply not interested in such positive sketches. Nevertheless, some surprising data are excluded from the mythical interpretation: above all, Jesus' alleged messianic claims and apocalyptic predictions. Why these sayings are attributed by Strauss to Jesus himself rather than to the mythology of the primitive Jewish-Christian community will be considered in due course.

THE NEGATIVE CRITERION: RATIONAL LAWS OF HISTORY

In addition to myth as a positive criterion, Strauss also provides a *negative* criterion of the *unhistorical* in § 16. An account is not historical (a) when it is "irreconcilable with the known and universal laws which govern the course of events" (laws of causality, succession, and psychology); and (b) when it is inconsistent with itself or contradicts another account (*LJ*, 88). Hartlich and Sachs conjecture that Strauss added this discussion of "criteria" in the second edition in an effort to distinguish his critical method from Hegel and to show that it was free of specific speculative presuppositions. "What 'presuppositions' do lie at the basis of his criticism he himself precisely delineates: they have a purely *empirical-rational* character. These are not presuppositions of a specific

[38] Baur, *Kritische Untersuchungen über die kanonischen Evangelien*, pp. 41–46.

philosophical standpoint, but those of *scientific scholarship generally, in the specific field of historical scholarship.*"[39]

Although Hartlich and Sachs are correct in describing Strauss's historical method as "empirical-rational," their latter contention is open to debate. An empirical-rational hermeneutics has a philosophical basis just as clearly as does a speculative one, and it is misleading to suggest that rationalism offers the *only* valid presupposition for scientific historical scholarship. Already in Strauss's time, under the influence of Schleiermacher and Hegel, hermeneutics was moving beyond the limited perspective of rationalism;[40] and one can argue that it was to the impoverishment rather than the advantage of Strauss's historical method that he turned back from speculative philosophy to rationalism. That he did make such a turn, however, is indisputable. Strauss's rationalism is most clearly evident in his formulation of and adherence to "known and universal [historical] laws," and in the dialectical procedure by which he contrasts conflicting interpretations and accounts to the discredit of the underlying event; but in addition it may be suggested that the mythical interpretation and the insights provided by psychology, of which he was especially fond, merely permit a more refined rationalism. Moreover, he drew a clear distinction between the negative-critical task of historiography and the positive-constructive task of philosophy; the former was intended to clear the ground for the latter.[41] He was not interested in a *critical* philosophy (e.g., Kant) and a *constructive* historiography (e.g., Schleiermacher, Baur). Rather he moved from a rationalist historiography to a speculative transfiguration of historical data into philosophical truths. It is difficult to escape the suspicion that a marriage of convenience existed between these two operations.

CRITICISM OF STORIES, NOT WRITINGS

Baur's fundamental objection to Strauss's exegetical method was that his analysis concentrated upon the individual *stories* that comprise the Gospel accounts, not upon the *writings* (the Gospels themselves) that contain these stories.[42] Therefore he was unable to determine critically how the Evangelists intended to *use* the stories. If their intentions could be determined with some degree of certainty, then it would be possible to establish more original and authentic forms of the stories by projecting backwards through the process of tradition (for Baur, a literary rather than an oral tradition) which had brought them to their present form. The "firm ground of concrete historical truth" is first attained by establishing a critical perspective on the writings, from the basis of which the historicity of individual pericopes can be evaluated. Such a perspective, according to Baur, represents a genuinely "historical understanding" of the Gospels; any other procedure is abstract, negative, or dialectical.[43]

[39] Hartlich and Sachs, *Der Ursprung des Mythosbegriffes*, p. 147 (italics are the authors'). This is the central theme of their chapter on Strauss; cf. pp. 121–22, 124, 134, 139–41. Van Harvey concurs in this judgment: Strauss's criteria are "a common operational assumption of almost all modern critical historiography." "D. F. Strauss' *Life of Jesus* Revisited," pp. 198–200, 204.

[40] Hans-Georg Gadamer, *Wahrheit und Methode: Grundzüge einer philosophischen Hermeneutik*, 2nd ed. (Tübingen: J. C. B. Mohr, 1965), pp. 162–204, 324–44.

[41] Cf. *LJ*, 757: the task is "to re-establish dogmatically [i.e., speculatively] that which has been destroyed critically."

[42] Cf. *LJ*, 461: ". . . the credibility of the narratives should not be concluded from the assumed origin of the book which contains them, but on the contrary, our judgment of the book must be founded on the nature of its particular narratives."

[43] Baur, *Kritische Untersuchungen über die kanonischen Evangelien*, pp. 41–46, 71–74.

When Baur called for a new section in *The Life of Jesus* concerned with *external* evidence for the age and authenticity of the Gospels, he apparently had in mind a critical attempt at establishing the historical and theological context of the writings, which would be the first step in gaining a perspective on the intentions of the authors and their use of materials from the tradition. But in the section added at Baur's urging (§ 13), Strauss delimits "external evidence" to the date and authority of the opinions of antiquity regarding the origin of the Gospels (*LJ*, 70), and offers only the briefest summary of this evidence as it bears on each of the four Gospels (*LJ*, 71–73). In the course of the analysis itself, he supplements this discussion by drawing together some judgments on the historical credibility, theological intentions, and literary characteristics of the Gospels, based on *internal* and *comparative* evidence.[44] He concludes that, while none of the Gospels can be eyewitness reports, Matthew is relatively the most historically reliable because it reflects an earlier stage in the formation of oral tradition, while Luke, Mark, and John represent progressively more remote stages. Indeed, because of the imaginative embellishments found in Mark's narrative sections, this Gospel has "almost an apocryphal appearance"; while the literary constructions of the author of the Fourth Gospel are quite apparent and render his account useless as a historical source.[45] Characteristically Strauss buries these conclusions in the body of the text and makes little of them, because he is basically uninterested in the historical credibility of the *writings*. His true delight and skill is in a dialectical critique of the isolated units of synoptic tradition.

Because the external testimony is inconclusive, Strauss argues, the credibility of the Gospel writings stands or falls with the credibility of the stories they contain, and the determination of the latter demands an investigation of the internal evidence. "To investigate the internal grounds of credibility *in relation to each detail given in the Gospels*, (for it is with them alone we are here concerned) and to test the probability or improbability of their being the production of eyewitnesses, or of competently informed writers, is the sole object of the present work" (*LJ*, 70; italics mine). Thus the Gospels are broken down into their smallest literary units (the "stories"), and each unit is examined independently, in comparison with parallel units in the other Gospels, to test its general credibility. Do the parallel accounts contradict each other? Do they violate the known and universal laws of history? Do they give evidence of the presence of myth? Are they products of eyewitnesses, or of subsequent tradition, or of the Evangelists? Because the stories are abstracted from their literary, historical, and theological context, the negative results are inevitably accentuated and the credibility of the Gospel writings as a whole called into question. Even if individual pericopes are established as authentic, their present location in the evangelical writings is not original, but the work of the Evangelists. ". . . the discourses of Jesus, like fragments of granite, could not be dissolved by the flood of oral tradi-

---

[44] See esp. *LJ*, § 84, "General Comparison of the Manner of Narration that Distinguishes the Several Evangelists."

[45] On Mark, *LJ*, 389–90, ed.n. 501*; on John, §§ 80–83. For a recent defense of Matthean priority and the literary dependence of Mark on Matthew and Luke—a theory which originated with J. J. Griesbach in the eighteenth century and is rejected by the prevailing consensus of New Testament critics today—see William R. Farmer, *The Synoptic Problem* (New York: Cambridge University Press, 1965). Karl Lachmann in 1835 was the first to suggest that Mark may have been the earliest, not the latest, of the Synoptic Gospels. (Farmer, *The Synoptic Problem*, pp. 16–17.) Although within twenty-five years this view had been widely accepted by New Testament critics, culminating in the Holtzmannian two-document hypothesis of 1863, at the time Strauss wrote *The Life of Jesus* the Griesbach hypothesis remained largely unquestioned.

tion; but they were not seldom torn from their natural connexion, floated away from their original situation, and deposited in places to which they did not properly belong.... Matthew, like an able compiler, though far from being sufficiently informed to give each relic in its original connexion, has yet for the most part succeeded in judiciously associating analogous materials; while the two other Evangelists have left many small fragments just where chance threw them, in the intervals between longer discourses" (*LJ*, 342).

In much of this Strauss anticipates form criticism, which is greatly to his credit. Like Strauss, form criticism endeavors to isolate the literary units of synoptic tradition and to examine them in regard to their kerygmatic (for Strauss, mythical) function. But it differs in its intent to define and classify these units according to literary form, and to trace them back through the formative process of oral tradition to the earliest and most authentic stage attainable. The latter operation presupposes a critical perspective on the writings that contain these forms and the tradition that mediates them (i.e., redaction criticism). Strauss allows for historical development of the stories through tradition, but lacks both the form-critical tools and the perspective on the writings necessary to trace it. The stories are simply analyzed as presented in the Gospels, without an accompanying history of the synoptic tradition. Baur's overemphasis of "tendency criticism" (or redaction criticism) should be viewed as a reaction to Strauss's one-sided criticism of stories apart from their literary context and traditio-historical development. The best results can be obtained from a combination of the two methods, and indeed Strauss and Baur *together* lay the foundations of modern form criticism and redaction criticism.

THE CRITICAL RESULTS AND THEIR CHRISTOLOGICAL SIGNIFICANCE

As already noted, Strauss was uninterested in providing a synthetic portrayal of the life of Jesus, based on materials that had withstood the critical fires and had proven to be historically sound. Such a disinterest made his work appear more historically skeptical than it really was. For Strauss did arrive at positive historical results in his investigation, and it is not impossible to determine what they are, as Schweitzer has contended.[46] But the positive results had a purely negative significance as far as Christology is concerned.

The birth, infancy, and childhood narratives are largely mythical (§§ 17–43). But there is no question that Jesus came under the tutelage of John the Baptist, whose proclamation of a coming messianic kingdom he continued once John had been imprisoned. It was from the influence of John that Jesus first began to formulate his own messianic project, but at first he did not identify himself with the messianic figure anticipated by John. Jesus remained the disciple of the Baptist and continued to pay him homage, even when he had far surpassed his predecessor. (*LJ*, 233, 239, 246, 286–87.) Although there was a period early in his ministry when Jesus referred to the messianic Son of Man as a future figure, different from himself, he came eventually to identify himself with that figure. "Jesus held and expressed the conviction that he was the Messiah; this is an indisputable fact" (*LJ*, 284; cf. 281–83, 288–90, 656). Here Strauss is curiously uncritical and brief in assessing the evidence, and he has no hesitation in attributing to Jesus messianic claims and titles (Son of Man, Son of God, *Christos*) that more likely are products of the early Christian community. The mythical interpretation would seem to apply in an obvious way to the messianic claims of

---

[46] Schweitzer, *The Quest of the Historical Jesus*, p. 90.

Jesus, which accord so well with the popular imagination of late Judaism and the religious needs of primitive Christian faith. Possibly for two reasons, one historical, the other theological, Strauss draws back from the mythical interpretation at this point. The historical reason is hinted at briefly: "... the fact that his disciples after his death believed and proclaimed that he was the Messiah, is not to be comprehended, unless, when living, he had implanted the conviction in their minds" (*LJ*, 284). The Bultmannian school attributes the rise of faith in Jesus as the Messiah solely to the impact of the resurrection experience on the disciples, whereas for Strauss the resurrection is of little significance either historically or theologically. In proportion as the resurrection diminishes in significance as the focal point of Christian faith, the necessity of proving Jesus' messiahship from his own claim increases.[47] The theological reason resides in the fact that Jesus' messianic consciousness as interpreted by Strauss could be of only limited significance for Christian faith: his vision was restricted by Jewish theocratic expectations, which he attempted to spiritualize or depoliticize,[48] but only by means of an apocalyptic fanaticism. Such a Jesus cannot have been the God-man of orthodox faith, and we are driven to the speculative conclusion that the idea of God-manhood is properly realized only in the human race as a whole.

Only one of the work's twenty chapters is devoted specifically to the sayings and teachings of Jesus in the synoptic tradition. (A second chapter treats the Johannine discourses, which Strauss regards as compositions of the Evangelist.) This apportionment of space already signals a de-emphasis on the importance of the teaching of Jesus for a christological interpretation of his person. Strauss's chief interest is in a comparative analysis of the arrangement of the discourses in the three Gospels, and in the process of oral tradition by which various forms, contexts, and combinations were given to the original fragments of sayings (*LJ*, 342, 355, 361, 363). Insofar as he interests himself in the content and meaning of these sayings at all, the suggestion is that they contain little that is essentially original or profound, and that in this as in other respects Jesus shared the limitations and prejudices of his age (*LJ*, 359). Although supposing himself to be the Messiah, Jesus did not intend to break with Judaism but merely presented himself as a teacher in the Mosaic tradition (*LJ*, 338–39); his pronouncement of eschatological blessings and woes (regarded by Strauss as unquestionably authentic) had much in common with Ebionitism (*LJ*, 337, 351); the parables were analogous to rabbinic literature in form and content (*LJ*, 348, ed.n. 345*); his high estimation of external poverty can probably be traced to the Essenes (*LJ*, 351, 358); his controversies with the scribes and Pharisees were thoroughly rabbinic in argumentation (*LJ*, 358). There is considerable irony in the fact that Strauss's relentless criticism of the synoptic *narratives* forced subsequent theology to shift almost exclusively to Jesus' *teaching* as the only firm basis for a christo-

---

[47] It could be argued that both positions are extreme: the Christian kerygma cannot be intelligibly reduced to a resurrection-experience alone (Bultmann); but neither is it necessary to attribute overt messianic claims to Jesus to account for the expectations and fears of his contemporaries that he was the Messiah (Strauss). These expectations and fears could have been aroused by the unique authority of his teaching, his announcement that the kingdom of God had come near, his defiance of religious and political authority, his possible association with Zealots.

[48] Strauss consistently refuses, in contrast with Reimarus, to attribute a political or revolutionary role to Jesus, and he overlooks any possible relation of Jesus to the Zealots (*LJ*, 293–96, 331, 402, 558, 584). This refusal may reflect Strauss's own political conservatism, or his belief that such an interpretation is a characteristic ploy of the enemies of Christianity, or his recognition that a political Messiah would not comfortably fit his interpretive categories, by which he proposed to convert *religious* images and myths into philosophical concepts.

logical construction—a move Strauss himself refused to make. This is true first of Baur, then of the liberal Lives of Jesus in the latter part of the nineteenth century, and later of the Bultmannian and post-Bultmannian concentration on the words of Jesus.

As his brief career drew toward its denouement, Jesus predicted (according to Strauss) that shortly after the destruction of Jerusalem and its temple, and within the term of the contemporary generation, he would visibly make his second advent in the clouds of heaven as the messianic Son of Man and terminate the existing dispensation (*LJ*, 296, 584, 589–90, 596). Although he may at first have thought that he would attain his messianic glorification without the intervention of death (*LJ*, 656; see ed.nn. 596*, 656*), he later came to recognize that suffering and death were part of the office and destination of the Messiah, the means by which the messianic age would be ushered in through the supernatural power of God rather than by political revolution; and he sought to prepare his disciples for this eventuality (*LJ*, 572–73, 633–34, 656). Here Strauss confronts and openly acknowledges the fundamental difficulty with the Christian faith which he had first sensed in his doctoral dissertation: the futuristic eschatology and apocalyptic enthusiasm of Jesus. "They who shrink from this view, merely because they conceive that it makes Jesus an enthusiast [*Schwärmer*], will do well to reflect how closely such hopes corresponded with the long cherished messianic idea of the Jews, and how easily, in that day of supernaturalism, . . . an idea, in itself extravagant, . . . might allure even a reasonable man beneath its influence" (*LJ*, 296). Later he remarks that inferences from the discourse on the second advent, such as those drawn by Reimarus, to the effect that Jesus was in error or that the apostles engaged in premeditated deception, "would inflict a fatal wound on Christianity." But Strauss himself clearly draws the first inference (*LJ*, 584–85). The "fatal wound" cannot be ameliorated by appeal to a philosophical interpretation of the second coming—"instead of a merely future, to make it a perpetual coming"—more congenial to the modern mind, for such immanental views simply do not accord with the meaning of the New Testament apocalypses (*LJ*, 589–90). The only remaining possibility is that these texts represent a *vaticinium post eventum* and hence cannot be attributed to Jesus but to primitive Christian apocalyptic. But in § 116 Strauss rejects this possibility as well, for reasons that are not entirely clear, except that such apocalypses may well have been "part of the popular conception in the time of Jesus" and simply adapted by him to his own circumstances (*LJ*, 594–96). Moreover, holding to the authenticity of Jesus' apocalyptic predictions underscores the necessity not merely of an *interpretation* but of an *annulment* of these "religious" views in Christianity, which is the task to be carried forward by the speculative reconstruction of Christology.[49]

Strauss's treatment of the passion story need not be summarized in detail. He considers large segments of it to have been reworked from the mythical point of

---

[49] In the *New Life of Jesus*, Strauss does attribute these apocalyptic predictions to the primitive church rather than to Jesus himself. Although it served his constructive purposes, the possibility that the real historical Jesus was an apocalyptic fanatic profoundly disturbed Strauss, for in his view it implied Jesus' insanity, and he twice attempted to draw back from this position, but without lasting success. See below, p. xlv, and Albert Schweitzer, *The Psychiatric Study of Jesus* (Boston: Beacon Press, 1958), pp. 34–35.

On the existence of a primitive Christian apocalyptic and the attendant interpretive issues, see Ernst Käsemann, "The Beginnings of Christian Theology," and "On the Topic of Primitive Christian Apocalyptic," in *Journal for Theology and the Church* 6 (New York: Herder and Herder, 1969): 17–46, 99–133.

view of the early church (e.g., the accounts of the Last Supper, the events in Gethsemane, the denial by Peter, the death of Judas, the trials before Pilate and Herod, and many details of the crucifixion scene). Nevertheless he holds it likely that "Jesus on that evening in the garden experienced a violent access of fear, and prayed that his sufferings might be averted" (*LJ*, 640); that when queried by the Sanhedrin and by Pilate he openly acknowledged his messianic claim (*LJ*, 656, 670–71); and that if the cry of God-forsakenness is authentic (which Strauss doubts), Jesus would have died bitterly disappointed at the failure of his messianic plan (*LJ*, 687–89). That Jesus really did die, and was not physically resuscitated after a merely apparent death (as the rationalists claim), cannot be doubted (§ 139). Because the idea of "resurrection" includes the blatantly supernatural notion of the return to life of a dead man (*LJ*, 735), a rational person must conclude that "either Jesus was not really dead, or he did not really rise again" (*LJ*, 736). Since the former is excluded by the historical evidence, we have no alternative than to doubt the reality of the resurrection itself (*LJ*, 737–39). The empty tomb reports are shown to be the product of legend (§ 137), while the appearances of the crucified Jesus to the disciples are subjective visions or hallucinations, which may be interpreted psychologically as instances of primitive Christian enthusiasm (*LJ*, 739–44), and which also engendered the myth of his visible ascension into heaven (§ 143).[50]

The dogmatic reconstruction of Christology by means of speculative philosophy, of which the Concluding Dissertation is intended merely as a foretaste,[51] fortunately is not contingent upon the particular founding events of Christianity, and indeed benefits when the mind is driven from the forms of popular religious imagination to a purely philosophical conceptuality. Strauss notes the ambiguity in Hegel's understanding of the relation between *Vorstellung* and *Begriff*, which had given rise to his own project of a life of Jesus in the first place. Do the historical data concerning Jesus adhere to the *content* of Christian faith (the idea of God-manhood), thus demanding recognition from the *concept* as well as the *imagination*, or are they reducible to the mere form of imagination, to which conceptual thinking is not bound?[52] The leading theologians of the Hegelian school (Philipp Marheinecke, Karl Rosenkranz, Kasim Conradi, and at this point in his career, Bruno Bauer), appealing to passages in Hegel's *Lectures on the Philosophy of Religion*, all asserted the former on the grounds that the idea of divine-human unity must once have fully appeared in a sentient historical individual as the basis of the popular religious consciousness of this ideal. The necessity and truth of the Gospel history of Jesus is thus deduced from the ideal content of Christian faith. Precisely this deduction is questioned by Strauss. Neither the necessity nor the truth of any particular historical individual as the God-man can be deduced from "general propositions on the unity of the divine and human natures." This is by no means to deprive the idea of God-manhood of all reality, but merely to assert that its full manifestation need not (and indeed could not) have been restricted to a single individual. "Is not the idea of the unity of the divine and human natures a real one in a far higher sense, when I regard the whole race of mankind as its realization, than when I single out one man as such a realization?" (*LJ*, 779–80).

Thus Jesus was not the God-man in an exclusive and perfect sense; but he might still have played a peculiar and decisive role, in virtue of the intensity of

---

[50] For a detailed analysis of Strauss's interpretation of the resurrection, see ed.n. 735*.

[51] For an analysis of the structure and argument of the Concluding Dissertation, see ed.n. 757*.

[52] *Streitschriften*, No. 3, p. 57 (paraphrased); see *LJ*, 777–79.

his God-consciousness, in the realization of the unity of God and man for the human race as a whole. But now Strauss's argument takes its final, most radical and fateful turn (*LJ*, 780–81). He contends that Jesus was at best a fortuitous occasion for the development of the idea of humanity. *Some such* occasion was necessary, given the subjective religious needs of the ancient world, which could perceive this idea only in the concrete figure of an individual. Jesus served the purpose because of the pathos of his suffering and death, which helped humanity to bear its afflictions. "But the science of our time can no longer suppress the awareness that the relation to an individual belongs only to the temporally conditioned and popular form of this doctrine"—not to its essential content and truth.[53] When the mind has learned to grasp the latter philosophically, the former (meaning the story of Jesus) ceases to be essential and indeed may be cast wholly aside. This freedom from history is granted philosophically, in Strauss's view, but it is also corroborated critically. Not only is Jesus not the God-man of orthodox faith; but also, in view of the futuristic eschatology, apocalyptic fanaticism, and messianic delusions disclosed by the foregoing investigation, Jesus can scarcely continue to play the decisive role in mediating to the whole of mankind the consciousness of divine and human unity—a consciousness that is eternally present rather than restricted to the near or distant future. The facts of the case as well as the dialectics of consciousness require that "the object of faith [be] completely changed; instead of a sensible, empirical fact, it [must] become a spiritual and divine idea, which has its confirmation no longer in history but in philosophy" (*LJ*, 780–81). From the historical point of view, Jesus could have been a highly distinguished person, who by means of his exalted character exercised a decisive influence on subsequent humanity (*LJ*, 773). But in point of fact Strauss cannot believe even that about him, and his "speculative reconstruction" ends with a trivial bourgeois secularism in place of Christology (*LJ*, 781).

Strauss's difficulty stemmed in part from the way he conceived the distinction between religious image (*Vorstellung*) and philosophical concept (*Begriff*). While contending for the ultimate identity of their content, he believed that the forms of imaginative and conceptual thinking must be kept strictly separate, and moreover that the latter could *replace* the former, *fulfilling the same religious need in a more adequate way*. This is clear from his proposed solution to the problem of the conflict between the consciousness of the theologian and that of the church at the end of *The Life of Jesus* (*LJ*, 783), and especially from his Tübingen lectures on "Logic and Metaphysics" of 1832. In the latter he contended that it is "equally comforting," personally speaking, whether I represent the unity of divine and human spirit in the form of images as the ascension of Jesus, or abstractly in the form of concepts. My faith in a reward or a retribution is no less firm, whether I represent it imaginatively as a future judgment of the world, or grasp it conceptually as already accomplished in the context of everyday life.[54] Since conceptual thinking is as existentially satisfying as the symbolic and mythical forms of religious imagination, and since it entails a more precise grasp

---

[53] This argument is advanced in a paragraph contained in the first and second editions, but omitted from the third and fourth editions. See ed.n. 780*. What follows is based on material found in all the editions.

[54] "Vorlesungen über Logik und Metaphysik," University of Tübingen, Summer Semester 1832 (Schiller National-Museum, Marbach, No. 6828), 15th folio, pp. 15–16; 16th folio, pp. 1–2. A typescript of the section of these lectures on the relation of *Vorstellung* and *Begriff* was furnished me by Walter Sachs, who has pointed out that with this argument Strauss moved beyond Hegel's own position.

of the essential content of faith, Strauss proposed to annul the religious forms entirely and replace them by a purely speculative vision—a proposal not shared by Hegel himself, who never advocated a break with religion on philosophical grounds, and who believed that philosophy must continue to be funded by religious experience.[55] But Strauss cut speculative theology off from the rich tradition of religious imagination and historical experience, thereby not permitting theology and philosophy to be fructified by the fundamental symbols of religious consciousness.[56] Instead of a *hermeneutics* of symbols and religious myths, he proposed to *destroy* them, together with the historical tradition in which they were imbedded. It is no wonder that his constructive program remained barren and unfruitful, falling back upon the "anonymous, flatly bourgeois morality"[57] of his time.

THE QUEST FOR A MORE POSITIVE CHRISTOLOGY:
THE THIRD EDITION OF *THE LIFE OF JESUS* (1837–1839)

CONCESSIONS IN THE MAKING, 1837–1838

In the fall of 1836 Strauss moved to Stuttgart where he eked out an existence as a free-lance author. Apparently almost from the start he had doubts about the severity of his conclusions: an old scholar was beginning to die off. Several factors conspired to bring this about. For one thing, he was beginning to despair of ever being offered a teaching appointment. His name was anathema in the German universities. No less than three times he was proposed for a position at Zürich (in Switzerland) by liberals on the theological faculty there—in June 1836, February 1837, and January 1839. Twice they were defeated, but on the third try they won, by a single vote of the Educational Council. The call was approved by the Large Senate of Canton Zürich, and on February 3, Strauss was appointed Professor of Dogmatics and Church History. But the public outcry, inflamed by a Faith Committee of conservative churchmen, was so great that the government was forced to hold a referendum in which the citizens of Zürich supported a petition revoking the call by a vote of 39,225 to 1,048. Because Strauss had already accepted the appointment, the government was required to pension him at a salary of 1000 francs, paid annually for the rest of his life.[58] The concessions in the third edition were initially unrelated to the Zürich affair, for Strauss began to prepare the revisions in the summer of 1837, at a time when he was not being actively considered for an appointment at Zürich and had very little hope of being called.[59] Later, however, he took advantage of the changes in the third edition to bolster his cause when it became apparent once again that he was under consideration.[60]

---

[55] See Emil Fackenheim, *The Religious Dimension in Hegel's Thought* (Bloomington, Ind.: Indiana University Press, 1967), chaps. 5, 6.

[56] Cf. Paul Ricoeur, *The Symbolism of Evil*, trans. Emerson Buchanan (Boston: Beacon Press, 1969), pp. 350–51, on the relation between symbolism and philosophical reflection.

[57] Barth, *Protestant Thought*, p. 366.

[58] Adolf Hausrath, *David Friedrich Strauss und die Theologie seiner Zeit*, 2 vols. (Heidelberg: Fr. Bassermann, 1876, 1878), I:342–411.

[59] See Strauss to Ernst Rapp, 17 Aug. 1837; and Strauss to Eduard Zeller, 8 Dec. 1837 (*Ausgewählte Briefe*, pp. 38, 46). The third possibility of an appointment at Zürich did not develop until the summer of 1838, after the third edition had been published, and Strauss expressed at the time little confidence that he would be seriously considered. See Strauss to Ludwig Georgii, 19 June 1838 (Maier, *Briefe von Strauss an Georgii*, p. 23).

[60] See Strauss to Ferdinand Hitzig, 14 June 1838 (Hausrath, *David Friedrich Strauss*, I:18 [Appendix]).

Strauss was a sensitive, temperamental man, and his condition as a theological outcast began to weigh on him heavily. From letters written during this period it is evident that he genuinely desired to assume a less polemical posture and to achieve an accommodation with his serious critics.[61] In 1837 he began publishing a series of *Streitschriften*, polemical writings against his critics. The first pieces were vigorous, sarcastic attacks on his orthodox opponents—J. C. L. Steudel, C. A. Eschenmayer, W. Menzel—written in late 1836 and early 1837. But a shift in mood had occurred by the summer and fall of 1837, while he was writing the third number. Now he was attempting to come to terms with the objections raised by critics comprising the so-called Hegelian Center (Carl Rosenkranz) and the Mediating Theology (Carl Ullmann, Julius Müller), and he was prepared to shift ground.[62]

Moreover, Strauss had been stung by the criticisms of his former teacher, Baur. In an article published in May 1836, the latter defended the right of free criticism and its value for faith, but distinguished his own "positive" method from Strauss's "negative" criticism and dialectical argumentation.[63] Strauss reacted bitterly to this criticism, but within a few months was prepared to take Baur's suggestions to heart. The latter visited Strauss several times late in 1836 and in 1837, undoubtedly clarifying his criticisms at length. The tone of Strauss's letters indicates that during this period Baur had become once again a trusted counselor, to whom he turned frequently for advice and support.

In 1838 Strauss published a monologue, "Transient and Permanent Elements in Christianity,"[64] which bore some marked affinities to Baur's religio-historical comparison of Socrates and Christ.[65] Strauss's work was intended as an appeal to the "cultured despisers" of religion, in defense of the enduring truths of Christianity and against the mounting paganism of the time. He perceived the point of contact with the educated public to be that of the "cult of genius," and undertook to demonstrate that true genius has a religious basis, above all in Christ. "As little as humanity can be without religion, so little can it be without Christ. . . . And this Christ . . . is an historical, not a mythical, figure, an individual, not merely a symbol. To this historical, personal Christ belongs everything from his life in which his religious perfection is portrayed: his discourses, his moral actions and suffering." Once we have surrendered outmoded dogmas, "Christ remains for us the highest that we can know and conceive in the domain of religion, without whose presence in the soul no true piety is possible; indeed, there remains for us in him the essence of Christianity."[66] Zeller notes the influence not only of Baur but also of Schleiermacher in this essay, and suggests that it represents the closest approximation to positive (i.e., historical) Christianity of any of Strauss's writings.[67] It also provides the clearest and most concise

[61] See *Ausgewählte Briefe*, pp. 35, 46, 47–48; Adolf Rapp, ed., *Briefwechsel zwischen Strauss und Vischer*, 2 vols. (Stuttgart: Ernst Klett Verlag, 1952), I:39; Hausrath, *David Friedrich Strauss*, I:331–32.

[62] *Streitschriften*, No. 3, pp. 120–26, 127–79.

[63] Baur, "Abgenöthigte Erklärung gegen einen Artikel der *Evangelischen Kirchenzeitung*," *Tübinger Zeitschrift für Theologie* 9:3 (1836): 200–208, et passim.

[64] "Vergängliches und Bleibendes im Christenthum," *Freihafen* 1:3 (1838): 1–48. Strauss reissued it in booklet form, with an essay on Justinus Kerner, under the title, *Zwei friedliche Blätter*, during the conflict over his call to Zürich early in 1839.

[65] Baur, "Das christliche des Platonismus oder Sokrates und Christus," *Tübinger Zeitschrift für Theologie* 10:3 (1837): 1–154. Strauss spoke appreciatively of this essay in a letter dated 31 March 1837 (Barnikol, "Der Briefwechsel zwischen Strauss und Baur," pp. 98–99).

[66] Strauss, "Vergängliches und Bleibendes im Christenthum." pp. 31–32, 33–48: quotations from pp. 47–48.

[67] Zeller. *David Friedrich Strauss*. p. 51.

expression of the revised Christology articulated in the third edition of *The Life of Jesus,* and it indicates the significant extent to which Strauss sought to modify the conclusions of the first two editions.[68]

THE THIRD EDITION OF *THE LIFE OF JESUS,* 1838

Preparations for the third edition were made in the summer and fall of 1837 while Strauss was writing the third issue of *Streitschriften.* It was ready for the press by mid-winter and appeared the following spring, with a Preface dated April 8, 1838. The contrast between the brilliant, biting polemic of the Preface to the second volume of the first edition, and the accommodating, defenseless mood of the Preface to the third edition, written just two-and-a-half years later, is startling. The work, moreover, had been thoroughly revised. By far the largest number of substantive changes (ninety-nine in all) were not retained in the fourth edition, which restored the readings of the second. These comprise the famous "concessions" and concern three major points: the possible authenticity of the Fourth Gospel, the unity of the divine and the human in the religious consciousness of Jesus, and the allowance of an intermediary category of miracles (cures based on unusual powers of nature, analogous to animal magnetism).

In the Preface Strauss contends that these changes "are all more or less related to the fact that a renewed study of the Fourth Gospel, on the basis of de Wette's commentary and Neander's *Leben Jesu Christi,* has made me again doubtful of my earlier doubt concerning the authenticity and credibility of this Gospel. It is not that I have become convinced of its authenticity, merely that I am no longer certain of its inauthenticity. . . . As a consequence my work as it now appears, by comparison with its earlier form, . . . has lost in unity but hopefully has gained in truth." This remark is partially misleading. It is true that the new assessment of Jesus' religious consciousness gains support from the Johannine discourses, the core of which are now considered to be authentic, but the more positive Christology of the third edition clearly is based on other factors besides a renewed study of the Fourth Gospel. Moreover, the interest in Jesus' cures based on unusual powers of nature is not related to the latter study, since most of the Johannine miracles fall into the category of "absolute" miracles that violate the laws of nature. Thus Strauss only partly admits to the extent of substantive changes in the new edition. On the other hand, his acknowledgment of vacillating judgments and his remark that the work has lost its unity are ingenuous; for despite the great skill with which these changes are made, the fact cannot be concealed that they have the effect of blunting the underlying philosophical thesis of the work and of destroying its analytical clarity on many points.

THE POSSIBLE AUTHENTICITY OF THE FOURTH GOSPEL

Prior to the first editions of Strauss's *Life of Jesus,* only Carl Gottlieb Bretschneider in his *Probabilia de Evangelii et Epistolarum Joannis* (Leipzig, 1820).

---

[68] Precisely what Strauss's motives were in undertaking these revisions remains unclear. On the one hand he expressed to friends a slackening of interest in scholarly theological issues, a sense that many historical questions regarding the origin of Christianity could never be settled, and a desire to abandon theology entirely. On the other hand he envisioned for himself a more constructive and positive theological position, for personal as well as polemical reasons, which would require not merely a revision but a totally new work, which he anticipated for a fourth edition, should it become necessary. Perhaps the experiment with the third edition served both these purposes and permitted its author to languish for a while in his irresolve. See *Ausgewählte Briefe,* pp. 35–36, 46–48, 49–50, 58, 61–62.

had questioned the apostolic authorship and historical credibility of the Gospel of John—the favorite of the Gospels for the post-Enlightenment German theologians (e.g., Schleiermacher). But in an article published in July of 1837,[69] Bretschneider revised his position, now contending that the core of many of the discourses of Jesus in the Fourth Gospel is authentic, while the form has been reshaped by the Evangelist. Strauss now found himself standing alone on a matter of critical importance, against the combined judgment of the biblical and theological scholarship of his day. Even those critics who dealt with him impartially had reaffirmed at least the possibility of apostolic authorship: Ferdinand Hitzig at Zürich, F. C. Baur in an article published in 1836,[70] and Wilhelm de Wette in the first volume of his new biblical commentary.[71]

Strauss himself contended in the Preface, as we have seen, that the combined impact of de Wette and August Neander caused him once again to be "doubtful of my earlier doubt concerning the authenticity and credibility of [the Fourth] Gospel." It is true that in the other editions as well his position remained conjectural and to some degree equivocal. He presented negative evidence but often without drawing specific conclusions. The brief discussion of *authorship* in the Introduction left the matter unsettled (*LJ*, 73). At the end of the chapter on the Johannine discourses he merely says, "These and a few other ideas, variously combined by an ingenious author, compose the bulk of the discourses attributed to Jesus by John" (*LJ*, 386). His most precise statement on the matter of apostolic authorship is buried in the conclusion to the section on the twelve disciples of Jesus. The allusion to "the disciple whom Jesus loved" in John 21:20 could scarcely have been written by the apostle and intended as a self-reference; "but a venerator of John, issuing perhaps from a Johannine school [translation corrected], might very naturally be induced to designate the revered apostle, under whose name he wished to write, in this half honourable, half mysterious manner" (*LJ*, 330). In the third edition, Strauss merely removes these and other negative judgments, substituting for them more positive suggestions. His clearest statement occurs in the revised conclusion to § 83, at the end of the chapter on Johannine discourses: "I do not venture to assert that the Johannine discourses contain anything that represents a formidable obstacle to their being interpreted in part from the individual character of John and in part from the composition of the Gospel in his old age" (ed.n. 386*; 3rd ed., I:741).

On the matter of the Johannine *discourses,* Strauss forthrightly denied their authenticity in the other editions. "We . . . hold it to be established, that the discourses of Jesus in John's gospel are mainly free compositions of the Evangelist." By contrast with the fragmentary character of the sayings of Jesus in the Synoptic Gospels, the discourses in the Fourth are unified and fluid in transition —"indicative of a pliable, unresisting mass, such as is never presented to a writer by the traditional sayings of another, but such as proceeds from the stores of his

---

[69] C. G. Bretschneider, "Erklärung über die mythische Auffassung des historischen Christus," *Allgemeine Kirchenzeitung,* July 1837, Nos. 104–6. Cited by Strauss in the third edition, I:740 (ed.n. 386*).

[70] Baur, "Abgenöthigte Erklärung gegen einen Artikel der *Evangelischen Kirchenzeitung," Tübinger Zeitschrift für Theologie* 9:3 (1836): 288–90. In this article Baur defended himself against E. W. Hengstenberg's charge that he had questioned the authenticity of John by contending that he had not yet expressed a critical judgment on this Gospel in any of his writings, and that he had no desire to deny the historical authority of John without good cause. But shortly after the appearance of Strauss's third edition, Baur did in fact reach a negative judgment on the Fourth Gospel.

[71] Wilhelm de Wette, *Kurzgefasstes exegetisches Handbuch zum Neuen Testament,* 3 vols. (Leipzig. 1836–1848). See Hausrath, *David Friedrich Strauss,* I:317–18.

own thought, which he moulds according to his will. For this reason the contributions of tradition to these stores of thought . . . were not so likely to have been particular, independent dicta of Jesus, as rather certain ideas which formed the basis of many of his discourses, and which were modified and developed according to the bent of mind of Alexandrian or Greek culture" (*LJ*, 386; cf. 368, 371, 380–81, 384, 385). In the third edition, Strauss does not deny that the discourses in their present form are compositions of the Evangelist, but he suggests that these compositions are based on authentic fragments of sayings of Jesus (not merely on certain general ideas that may have formed the basis of his sayings), which have been constructed into unified speeches by the author, who could well have been the Apostle John (ed.n. 386*). Although this modification appears to be slight, it opens the door to the possibility that the *substance* if not the form of Jesus' self-referential speeches in the Fourth Gospel, where his intensity of God-consciousness and awareness of identity with the Father are quite explicit, may be historically authentic.[72]

THE RELIGIOUS CONSCIOUSNESS OF JESUS

The critical heart of the third edition was not its position on the Fourth Gospel but its revised portrayal of the person of Jesus. Gone were the futuristic eschatology, the apocalyptic fanaticism, and the messianic delusions, which in the other editions had rendered Jesus so religiously and philosophically inaccessible to the modern mind. They were replaced by an intensity of God-consciousness and an equilibrium of inner life that made him the central figure in the mediation of the idea of divine-human unity to the whole of mankind. According to the third edition, the origin of Jesus' religious consciousness can be traced back to the inner spark of genius already evident upon his first visit to the temple at the age of twelve (ed.n. 194*). He remained independent of John the Baptist in regard to his messianic project, which at first he concealed from public exposure, and he did not share the latter's apocalyptic enthusiasm (ed.nn. 234*, 237*, 246*, 284*). He understood himself as Messiah in a strictly religious, nonpolitical, nonapocalyptic sense (ed.nn. 283*, 284*, 288†, 295*, 402*, 573*). He elevated the title, Son of God, "from its Jewish-theocratic sense to a religious-metaphysical significance," as is already evident from his sense of being about his Father's business as a twelve-year-old in the temple.

The same interiority of spiritual communion [with God] is later expressed by Jesus in the words, "All things have been delivered to me by my Father; and no one knows the Son except the Father, and no one knows the Father except the Son and any one to whom the Son chooses to reveal him" (Matt. 11:27). But this understanding of the concept "Son of God" predominates in the Fourth Gospel in a special way: e.g., when Jesus says of himself that he speaks and does nothing of his own accord but only what he has learned as the Son from the Father (5:19; 12:49, etc.), who moreover is in him (17:21), and in regard to his sublimity over him (14:28; cf. Lk. 18:18–19 par.), yet is also one with him (Jn. 10:30).[73]

[72] The third edition tends to equivocate on the historicity of *narrative* material in the Gospel of John, whereas the other editions usually decide in favor of the Synoptics when it is a question of conflicting accounts. The equivocation is especially evident in the third edition's treatment of the Johannine account of relations between Jesus and John the Baptist, and the conversation with Nicodemus. On the other hand, Strauss now decides in favor of the Fourth Evangelist's representation that Jesus made several trips to Jerusalem during his public ministry; and he questions the authenticity of the narrative of the woman taken in adultery (John 8:1 ff.), defended in the other editions. See ed.nn. 230*, 271*, 409*.

[73] 3rd ed., I:535, ed.n. 288†. The same theme is repeated many times in the third edition.

These historical findings provide the basis for the "mediating" Christology propounded in the new section at the end of the Concluding Dissertation in the third edition (replacing § 152 of the other editions):[74] while not the God-man in the orthodox sense, nevertheless in view of his intensity of God-consciousness and personality as religious genius, Jesus is the essential figure by whom the idea of God-manhood was and continues to be mediated to humanity as a whole. The new conclusion required modifications to § 151 as well. Strauss omitted a paragraph from the first and second editions in which he argued that Jesus was merely an accidental occasion for the emergence of the idea of humanity, whereas "the science of our time can no longer suppress the awareness that the relation to an individual belongs only to the temporally conditioned and popular form of this doctrine."[75] But now he rediscovers the Hegelian dictum: "All actions, including world-historical actions, culminate with individuals as subjects giving actuality to the substantial."[76] Strauss continues: "Especially in the field of religion, . . . all new epochs and characteristic formations are attached to a prominent personality. . . . As a result of this sort of reflection, Jesus belongs to the category of highly gifted individuals who in the various spheres of life are called to raise the development of spirit in humanity to higher levels. These are individuals whom in fields outside of religion, namely those of art and science, we are accustomed to call geniuses." Moreover, it can be demonstrated that the religious genius is superior to all other geniuses, mediating a special revelation of the divine.[77]

But whether Jesus himself was in fact such a genius cannot be demonstrated from these philosophical considerations. This is the fundamental mistake of those theologians to the right and the center of the Hegelian school (e.g., Göschel, Gabler, Rosenkranz). Such an argument confuses the notion of *the* individual with *an* individual. "It belongs to the essence of the idea that it should appear in *the* individual, that it should make the human individual the bearer of its absolute content, insofar as individuality, subjectivity, is according to Hegel the final pinnacle of spirit. But that *any particular* individual must be the full realization of the idea exclusively, by no means belongs to the essence of the idea. . . ." To be sure, some individuals are more fully penetrated by the idea than others, and in the field of religion an individual is conceivable who has fully attained the goal of the mediation of the human and the divine. "But only the *conceivability*, not the *necessity*, of such an individual is philosophically deducible. That precisely Jesus was really this individual, and that only he and none other either before or after him has attained this *non plus ultra* of religious development, can only be demonstrated historically, not philosophically."[78] Strauss was convinced that the new edition of his book had in fact demonstrated historically that Jesus was this individual. The argument is based on evidence from synoptic and Johannine discourses, which purport to show that Jesus expressed an awareness of per-

---

[74] See ed.n. 781†. This section is translated in full on pp. 798–802.

[75] See ed.n. 780*. In the third edition, the concluding paragraph of § 151 (beginning in the Eliot translation at p. 780/12b), was intended to represent a left-Hegelian position that would be refuted or qualified in the concluding section, whereas in the other editions it represented Strauss's own position.

[76] G. W. F. Hegel, *Grundlinien der Philosophie des Rechts* (Berlin, 1821), § 348. Quoted by Strauss in the 3rd ed., II:770; and in the *Streitschriften*, No. 3, p. 70, cf. p. 125.

[77] 3rd ed., II:771–72. *Streitschriften*. No. 3, pp. 70–72: "Vergängliches und Bleibendes im Christenthum," pp. 30–32.

[78] *Streitschriften*, No. 3, pp. 125–26; cf. pp. 73–74. Italics in the first quotation are Strauss's: in the second, mine. See also *LJ*, 3rd ed., II:778.

fect unity with God, thus overcoming the basic religious dilemma of mankind, the antithesis between finite and infinite spirit.[79] Strauss is now prepared to argue that the dissolution of this antithesis and the "restoration of all things" did in fact take place in the self-consciousness of Jesus rather than being postponed to the distant future. Rather than exhibiting apocalyptic disharmonies, the Jesus of the third edition embodies the romantic ideal of a harmonious inner equilibrium of life.

The only remaining question is whether Jesus could be equaled or surpassed by another, future figure in whom the unity of divine and human life will be even more intensively realized. Strauss contends that in principle Jesus' religious consciousness was the highest that can be conceived. But because sinlessness and absolute perfection are incompatible with finite human existence, and because the highest incarnation of God in the sphere of religion still requires completion through the revelation of the divine life in the other spheres of human existence as well, it cannot be denied that the religious consciousness first fully achieved and expressed by Jesus is capable "of purification and further development in details through the progressive formation of the human spirit." Therefore Strauss was led to formulate his "disappearing minimum" theory, which was also utilized by Baur and had been anticipated in the work of Wilhelm de Wette: "We conceive Christ as the one in whose self-consciousness the unity of the divine and the human first appeared with sufficient energy to reduce to a disappearing minimum all hindrances of this unity in the whole range of his soul and life."[80]

THE QUESTION OF MIRACLE

Such a view of Jesus tempted Strauss to reexamine some of the miracle traditions he had earlier rejected as mythical. In the third edition he writes: "It is natural to expect that, corresponding to new points of development in spiritual life, new phenomena of a bodily character should also occur, brought about by the new spiritual power. Accordingly it may be presupposed of Christ that he, who exercised such a remarkable influence on the rest of human nature, should also . . . have given evidence of a remarkable power to affect the bodily side of human nature."[81] Strauss adds that such "bodily endowments" cannot of themselves serve as proof of Jesus' exalted religious consciousness and moral dignity, for persons in whom such bodily powers are displayed—e.g., somnambulists gifted with hypnotic clairvoyance and telepathy—often suffer from mental depression and illness. Despite this warning, an endeavor is made in the third edition to discover hypnoticlike powers in the cures of Jesus, with at least the implication that these cures may serve as further evidence of his messianic dignity.

In all the editions Strauss distinguishes between two basic types of miracle: miacle in the strict or proper sense (*Mirakel*), which involves a supernatural exercise of power over inanimate nature or animals and requires a direct divine intervention in the causal nexus; and miracle in the loose or common sense

---

[79] 3rd ed., II:775, 777. See also *Streitschriften*, No. 3, pp. 74, 152–53. Strauss's preoccupation with this dilemma can be traced back to the doctoral dissertation of 1831.

[80] 3rd ed., II:777–79; *Streitschriften*, No. 3, p. 74: "Vergängliches und Bleibendes im Christenthum," pp. 45–47.

[81] 3rd ed., II:9 (see ed.n. 415*). Strauss cites Schleiermacher's *Glaubenslehre*, § 14, in defense of this point, which is indicative of the fact that his views in the third edition often approximate those of Schleiermacher.

(*Wunder*), such as cures of human beings based on ordinary powers of nature, medicinal and psychical. The chapter on miracles is organized according to this typology: §§ 92–99 analyze the cures of Jesus, categorized by type and treated in an order of descending historical probability: §§ 101–4 examine Jesus' exercise of power over nature (the sea, loaves and fishes, water turned into wine, the fig-tree); while § 100 is a transitional type, for it involves a revivifying power exercised on the human organism. All the miracles in the strict sense are clearly products of mythical tradition, and the same applies to many of the cures, for the miraculous power of healing was considered an attribute of the Messiah. Yet in instances of cures of persons with mental derangement or nervous disorders, such as the demoniac of Capernaum, a historical substratum can be uncovered that yields to a natural or psychological explanation.[82]

In the third edition Strauss introduces a third category of miracle, intended to stand between the first two: cures based on *unusual* powers of nature, analogous to "animal magnetism" or hypnotism. These cures can still be explained on the basis of nature, as with the second type, but they display uncommon or extraordinary powers, similar to the absolute miracles of the first type. Strauss has in mind cures involving touch, cures based on the hypnotic power of will or on clairvoyance, and cures at a distance (mental telepathy).[83] This third category of miracles enables him to upgrade the authenticity of many of the cures earlier dismissed as legendary, enlarging upon his long-standing interest in the occult and abnormal. It is not without significance that the possibility of an explanation of the cures on the basis of magnetism or hypnotism is already envisioned in the first and second editions, but is rejected because the circumstances recounted in the Gospels do not fit the known instances when patients have been cured magnetically.[84] Thus it is only a relatively short step, involving no change in principle, to argue (on the alleged basis of an improved familiarity with the phenomenon) that some of the magnetic/hypnotic analogies do in fact apply. In this respect, the third edition moves in the direction not of supernaturalism but of rationalism. It is not surprising, therefore, that the modified treatment of miracle did not improve the author's standing with his orthodox opponents at all. And the argument from these data could easily be shifted to imply that Jesus, like modern-day somnambulistic cure artists, was suffering from "a disordered state of nerves" (cf. *LJ*, 470).

ANTICIPATIONS OF THE *NEW LIFE OF JESUS*, 1864

It is not the intention of this Introduction to trace Strauss's theological and personal development beyond 1840. But some brief comments are called for on the relation between the third edition of the first *Life of Jesus* and the so-called *New Life of Jesus* of 1864 (*Das Leben Jesu für das deutsche Volk bearbeitet*). Nowhere in the Preface to the latter work is there any mention of its approximation to the third edition of the "critical" *Life of Jesus*, nor indeed is there an acknowledgment of significant variations between the several editions of the earlier work. The *New Life* differs from the third edition of the first *Life* in that it does not contend for the authenticity of the Fourth Gospel,[85] nor does it allow

---

[82] See *LJ*, 413–15, 435–36, 496.

[83] 3rd ed., II:4–10 (ed.n. 415*). See also "Vergängliches und Bleibendes im Christenthum," pp. 20–25.

[84] See *LJ*, 445, 496, and esp. 470.

[85] *A New Life Of Jesus*, 2 vols. (London: Williams and Norgate, 1865), I:115–49, 270–73.

for cures analogous to animal magnetism,[86] but it does retain the third edition's more positive estimate of Jesus' religious consciousness, although in subdued form. Thus Strauss has excised the most critically dubious features of the third edition (its position on the Gospel of John and on miracles), and has attempted once again to lay the historical foundations for a constructive Christology. And once again he has come within the orbit of Baur's influence. In a letter to Baur shortly before the latter's death, in September 1860, he hints at his intention to return to a theological authorship, to write a work for the people since the theologians are not able to understand, and to be guided primarily by the historical scholarship of Baur and his students.[87] The new *Life of Jesus* is in fact a rather feeble popularization of the analysis of the origins of Christianity contained in the first volume of Baur's church history.

Strauss pointedly contrasts the "analytical" method of the first *Life of Jesus* with the "synthetic" method of the *New Life.* "We shall therefore on this occasion start from the presumable historical kernel of the history of Jesus, which in the earlier work was never represented as a unity."[88] The positive data are synthesized in the First Book, "Historical Outline of the Life of Jesus," whereas the "Mythical History" is reserved to the Second Book. The synthetic portrayal of Jesus partially returns to the "religious genius" theory of the third edition, although based now on the Sermon on the Mount, as the nucleus of the synoptic speeches, rather than on the Gospel of John.[89] Jesus conceived of God as the personification of "indiscriminating benevolence" or "comprehensive love," which was the original principle of his own nature, and in this respect he was "conscious of his own harmony with God."[90] He spiritualized the law, purged the messianic idea of political elements, and used the title "Son of Man" in a moral-religious sense.[91] Although he spoke of the *future* as a time of perfection—antiquity could perceive the supersensual only in terms of temporal distance—he did not refer to his *own* second coming as the Son of Man glorified on the clouds of heaven. Had he done so he would have to be considered a fanatic enthusiast; but these apocalyptic predictions are more likely the product of Jewish Christianity after the fall of Jerusalem.[92] In a letter to Wilhelm Lang, Strauss explained his reversal on this matter from the first *Life of Jesus*: "I too have constantly repeated the fact that we are not permitted to transport our Western mode of conception into the Eastern world, to which the personalities of the New Testament still belong. But the hard nut of the second coming was too difficult for me; I have not been able to swallow it. ... I find in the earlier sayings of Jesus, above all the Sermon on the Mount, so rational a tendency that I cannot properly credit him with an idea that in my view lies so close to insanity."[93] Strauss must have found it equally difficult to swallow this "hard

[86] Ibid., pp. 360–70.

[87] Strauss to Baur, 5 Sept. 1860 (Barnikol, "Der Briefwechsel zwischen Strauss und Baur," p. 124). See also *A New Life of Jesus,* I:viii, xiii. Precisely what Strauss's motives were in returning to theological scholarship are not easy to determine. According to Zeller, his biography of Ulrich von Hutten (1857) and the twenty-fifth anniversary of the first *Life of Jesus* (1860) served to reawaken his interests, but surely other factors must have been involved. Zeller, *David Friedrich Strauss,* pp. 86–91.

[88] *A New Life of Jesus,* I:217.

[89] Ibid., pp. 282–83.

[90] Ibid., pp. 279–80.

[91] Ibid., pp. 277–78, 303–13.

[92] Ibid., pp. 322–32.

[93] Strauss to Wilhelm Lang, 16 Oct. 1864, quoted in Theobald Ziegler, *David Friedrich Strauss* (Strassburg: Karl J. Trübner, 1908), II:608–9.

nut" in the third edition of the first *Life*, although he did not deny Jesus' predictions of his own second advent in that volume (see ed.n. 596*), and his uncertainty on such a fundamental interpretive question reflects the fact that biblical eschatology remained the critical theological stumbling block throughout his career.

An ominous note is struck at the very end of the *New Life*. The happiness of mankind is not, after all, dependent upon belief in Jesus. Although the latter stands in the first class among the "improvers of the ideal of humanity," the "exemplar has been, after him, still further developed, more perfectly finished, its different features brought into better proportion with each other." In particular, his Jewish one-sidedness required supplementation from Greek and Roman culture and from "the further development of mankind and its history."[94] Jesus is no longer viewed as the *"non plus ultra* of religious development," as in the third edition; and the way is open for the final reversal which ensued in *The Old Faith and the New* of 1872: Jesus was at best a "noble enthusiast," whom "we shall not be desirous to choose . . . as the guide of our life." Therefore, concludes Strauss, "we must acknowledge we are no longer Christians," although we may still have a religion—the religion of cosmic evolution.[95]

ATTACK UPON CHRISTENDOM: THE *GLAUBENSLEHRE* AND THE FOURTH EDITION OF *THE LIFE OF JESUS* (1839–1840)

The anti-Christian pantheism of *The Old Faith and the New* was first enunciated in *The Christian Faith, Its Doctrinal Development and Conflict with Modern Science*,[96] the first volume of which appeared simultaneously with the fourth edition of *The Life of Jesus* in 1840. It is difficult to summarize briefly the argument of Strauss's second great work, more ambitious in scope than the first, and considered by some to be an even more significant scholarly product. It is intended to transfer the critical operation from history to dogma, i.e., from the story of Jesus to the whole of Christian doctrine—in order, by destroying all traditional forms of belief, to prepare for the final reconstruction of Christian faith at the purely speculative level. The method of the book is summed up by the famous statement, "The true criticism of dogma is its history." The history of dogmas is presented individually from the origin of Christianity to the present, with the intent of showing that each dogma contains the seeds of its own destruction, seeds that began to bear fruit with the critical spirit of Renaissance humanism and the Reformation, and have fully ripened in rationalism and idealism.[97]

The philosophical perspective of the book is that of a monistic pantheism. Upon near completion of the first volume in February 1840, Strauss wrote Ernst Rapp that the sections on the doctrines of God, creation, and the original state of man "seem to me especially important because all the principles of our criticism of Christianity lie here; hitherto they have not been adequately expressed. I have surrounded and assaulted theism from all sides, and have come forth openly with the language of pantheism. The only consideration that causes me to

---

[94] *A New Life of Jesus*, II:434–38.

[95] *The Old Faith and the New*, trans. Mathilde Blind (American ed.: New York: Henry Holt and Co., 1874), pp. 92, 107.

[96] *Die christliche Glaubenslehre in ihrer geschichtlichen Entwicklung und im Kampfe mit der modernen Wissenschaft dargestellt*, 2 vols. (Tübingen: C. F. Osiander, 1840–1841).

[97] *Glaubenslehre*, I, § 6 (esp. p. 71); cf. also *LJ*, ed.n. 757*.

express myself here and there more mildly than I would like is that my book not be censored."[98] The monistic, anti-eschatological character of the pantheism becomes especially apparent in the final sections of the second volume on "The Doctrine of Immortality in Modern Reflection." Strauss contends that immortality must be understood as immanent and pancosmic (absorption in the World-All) rather than as futuristic and personal-individual. Schleiermacher's dictum in the *Reden*—"to become one with the infinite in the midst of finitude, and to be eternal in every moment"—represents everything that modern science is able to say about immortality. Strauss quotes the words of Angelus Silesius:

> Mensch, wo du deinen Geist schwingst über Ort und Zeit,
> So kannst du jeden Blick sein in der Ewigkeit.
> Ich selbst bin Ewigkeit, wenn ich die Zeit verlasse,
> Und mich in Gott und Gott in mich zusammenfasse.

To which is added his theological swan song: "Herewith our work for the time being is ended. For transcendence is indeed the one enemy—in its eschatological form, the final enemy—with which speculative criticism has to contend in all forms, and wherever possible to overcome."[99]

What caused this sudden reversal from the more positive direction of the third edition of *The Life of Jesus*? Almost at once Strauss realized that he had made a mistake. In May of 1838 Baur had questioned his judgment in defending the authenticity of the Johannine discourses, and without this resource he apparently was unable to sustain his mediating Christology. The concessions of the third edition had no effect on Strauss's orthodox opponents. Letters from this period indicate that Strauss was depressed and discouraged following publication of the third edition, and that the final resolution of the Zürich affair in the spring of 1839 terminated his desire for a teaching position, setting him free to pursue his own interests without regard to the opinions of the ecclesiastical and academic establishment.[100] Already by the fall of 1838 he had resolved to begin work on the dogmatics he had projected ever since 1831, of which *The Life of Jesus* was intended merely as the first stage.[101] He worked intensively throughout 1839, and by March of 1840 the first volume was completed.

[98] Strauss to Ernst Rapp, 27 Feb. 1840 (*Ausgewählte Briefe*, p. 90). The precise sense in which Strauss can be considered a pantheist is not clear from this statement. Pantheism in the strict sense is the doctrine that God's absolute being is identical with the world: God is All, and the All is God. Depending upon how this identity is nuanced, pantheism can assume either acosmic or atheistic forms. *Acosmic pantheism* holds that there is properly speaking no world apart from God, or at least that the world has no positive differentiation or finitude; whereas *atheistic pantheism* holds that finite things in their finitude and interrelatedness are to be taken as God. Both acosmism and atheism are monistic doctrines, by contrast with *panentheism* (viewed by some as a form of pantheism), according to which all things are "in" God, or have their being in God, without God being absorbed into the world, or the world into God. Strauss's position appears to be monistic rather than panentheistic. In the earlier writings, his pantheism takes an acosmic form, while at the end of his career he shifts to an atheistic position. The *Glaubenslehre* stands between these two positions and could be interpreted either way. By contrast, Hegel's position is clearly panentheistic (see *The Logic of Hegel*, trans. William Wallace, 2nd ed. [Oxford: Oxford University Press, 1892], §§ 50, 151; and *Hegel's Philosophy of Mind*, trans. William Wallace and A. V. Miller [Oxford: Oxford University Press, 1971], § 573).

[99] *Glaubenslehre*, II, §§ 106–10, esp. pp. 737–39. See also Müller, *Identität und Immanenz*, pp. 255, 259.

[100] *Ausgewählte Briefe*, pp. 77, 85–86, 89; Maier, *Briefe von Strauss an Georgii*, p. 28.

[101] Barnikol, "Der Briefwechsel zwischen Strauss und Baur," pp. 107–8. Cf. Maier, *Briefe von Strauss an Georgii*, p. 4; and *Ausgewählte Briefe*, p. 12.

He set aside the second volume in order to prepare a fourth edition of *The Life of Jesus*, which was ready by June of 1840. He wrote Georgii: ". . . after the disfigurement the book experienced in the third edition, I am firmly resolved to let it be reprinted without any alterations according to the second edition, and in part the first."[102] This impression, however, is partly misleading. The fourth edition is in fact a composite of the second and third editions. In form and detail (e.g., citations of literature) it is closer to the third edition than to the second, retaining most of the minor changes and formal improvements adopted in the third edition. But in substance it approximates the second edition, since all but sixteen of the substantive revisions (or concessions) of the third edition have been abandoned and the readings of the second edition, indeed in some instances of the first, restored. Of the four editions, the first is the most consistent in its uncompromising radicalism. The second edition already contains some moderating revisions, most of which are retained in the third and fourth editions. In a few places the fourth edition restores the more radical readings of the first (at places where the second edition anticipates more sweeping revisions in the third), but its substantive position is nearly identical to the second. It also retains the additional sections of the Introduction (§§ 13–16), the separate concluding section (§ 152), and the many refinements in style, form of argument, precision of analysis, and citations of critical literature provided by the second and third editions. Moreover, it is easier to reconstruct the earlier editions from the fourth than vice versa. For these reasons, despite the fact that the original version of Strauss's work had the profoundest historical impact and is undeniably appealing in its rigorous purity,[103] it is not unfortunate that the fourth edition was destined to appear in the splendid English of George Eliot.

THE ELIOT TRANSLATION

ELIOT, BRABANT, HENNELL, AND STRAUSS

In May of 1839 Strauss was visited by an eccentric English physician, R. H. Brabant, who had given up his practice several years before to pursue the study of theology. Brabant knew all about the famous liberal theologians of Germany. He had read Strauss's *Leben Jesu* with enthusiasm, and was struck by the similarities between it and a book published in England in 1838 by a Unitarian businessman, Charles Christian Hennell, *An Inquiry Concerning the Origin of Christianity*. Brabant and Strauss spent a week discussing Hennell, upon which Strauss agreed to arrange for a German translation of the *Inquiry*. He asked Georgii to do the work and it appeared the following year.[104]

In 1841 the British politician and attorney Joseph Parkes, with a group of friends, decided to request an English translation of Strauss's book and agreed to put up the funds, believing that the work would further social and political reform in England by weakening the hold of Anglican orthodoxy. They approached Hennell, whose *Inquiry* they greatly admired; he asked his sister, Sara Sophia Hennell, to undertake the work, but she declined. In 1839 Charles Hennell had been invited to visit Dr. Brabant. Within a week he proposed to

---

[102] Strauss to Georgii, 31 May 1840 (Maier, *Briefe von Strauss an Georgii*, p. 34). See also *Ausgewählte Briefe*, p. 91, and the Preface to the fourth edition, dated 17 October 1840.

[103] The first edition was selected for reprinting by the Wissenschaftliche Buchgesellschaft, 1969. Strauss himself provided by his will that any further editions of the work should be made according to the original version (*A New Life of Jesus*, I:ix).

[104] Strauss to Christian Märklin, 31 May 1839 (*Ausgewählte Briefe*, pp. 87–88); Strauss to Ludwig Georgii, 4 June 1839 (Maier, *Briefe von Strauss an Georgii*, pp. 29–30).

Brabant's daughter, Rufa, but because his lungs were unsound her father opposed the match. Rufa now agreed at Charles's request to undertake the translation to be sponsored by Parkes, but she completed only 257 pages of the German text (see ed.n. 166*) before she and Charles were finally married, on November 1, 1843. This brought the translation project to a halt, for Rufa discovered that she could not handle both Strauss and a marriage, and a new translator was sought.[105]

George Eliot[106] was born November 22, 1819. She was reared in a strict evangelical context but freed herself of its influence after moving to Foleshill, near Coventry, in 1841, where she became acquainted with the Rev. John Sibree (the translator of Hegel) and Mr. and Mrs. Charles Bray. She read works in science, deism, and rationalism, began to teach herself German, engaged in an intensive study of the New Testament in 1841, and was "liberated" by Hennell's *Inquiry*. Mrs. Bray was Caroline Hennell, another sister of Charles; through her Eliot became acquainted with all the members of the Hennell family. They recognized her brilliance, so it was only natural that they turned to her after Rufa Brabant Hennell had to give up the translation. George Eliot took it on early in 1844, at the age of twenty-three, and finished the work in a year and a half. Charles and Sara Hennell were to serve as consultants, but they rarely were needed. The translation, like the original, was a work of youthful genius.[107]

From letters written during the period, glimpses of her progress can be obtained.[108] The decision was made not to revise the material already translated by Rufa Brabant (through § 33), but Eliot found a rendering of the Concluding Dissertation by Dr. Brabant to be unusable. She finished the actual work on the translation by the summer of 1845, and spent the next nine months reading proofs, checking and rechecking the accuracy of her work. Strauss was asked to supply a Latin preface, which he agreed to do. The book was published in three volumes on June 15, 1846, by Chapman Brothers, London. Mary Ann Evans's name did not appear; for her labors she was paid £ 20. The translation was of the highest quality, combining to a remarkable degree both accuracy and fluency. Not only did it give Strauss an impact on English and American religious thought he never otherwise could have attained, but also it helped to set the intellectual course for George Eliot's own literary career. She grew impatient with Strauss's belaboring of the miracle stories and his minute dissection of the passion narratives (it was said of her by a friend that she was "Strauss-sick" at his treatment of the crucifixion scene). But at the end she wrote: "I do really like reading our Strauss—he is so klar und ideenvoll but I do not know *one* person who is likely to read the book through, do you?"[109]

In 1851 Eliot went to work for John Chapman, the publisher of her translation, as assistant editor of the *Westminster Review*. The Chapman house was a gathering place for liberals of all stripes: Unitarians, Spencerian evolutionists, Comtean positivists, left-Hegelians, Marxists. In 1854 her translation of Feuer-

---

[105] Gordon S. Haight, *George Eliot: A Biography* (New York: Oxford University Press, 1968), pp. 47, 49, 52–53; Haight, ed., *The George Eliot Letters* (New Haven: Yale University Press, 1954), I:lvi–lvii, 171n., 171–72.

[106] She was baptized Mary Anne Evans. In 1837 she began to write *Mary Ann*, in 1850 it became *Marian*, and in 1880 she reverted to *Mary Ann*. In 1857 she adopted the pseudonym *George Eliot* upon publication of her first novel, *Amos Barton*. (Haight, *Eliot*, pp. 3n., 219–20.)

[107] Haight, *Eliot*, pp. 52–54, 59; *Letters*, I:xliii–xliv.

[108] Haight, *Letters*, I:169–219.

[109] Haight, *Letters*, I:187, 206–7, 218.

bach's *Essence of Christianity* was published. The same year she began living with George Henry Lewes as his wife. Lewes was separated from his wife, Agnes Jervis, but could not obtain a legal divorce. Lewes and Eliot went to Germany where he wrote his biography of Goethe and she completed her translation of Spinoza's *Ethics*. She met Strauss briefly on that visit, in Cologne, July 30, 1854; and a second time in Munich, July 6, 1858. Upon the occasion of their second meeting, Strauss wrote Ernst Rapp: "She is in her thirties, not bad looking, an almost transparent face, expressive more of feeling than of spirit. Between a man and a woman as translator there always exists a mystical marriage."[110]

TEXT, TRANSLATION, AND NOTES

George Eliot translated the fourth German edition, although the other editions were in the possession of the Brabants and Hennells, and they were apparently at least partially aware of the variations between them.[111] The translation has been carefully checked for accuracy; it does contain a few omissions and errors, the more serious of which are noted in the Annotations. The text of the present volume is reproduced from the second English edition, published in 1892 by Swan Sonnenschein in London and Macmillan in New York, with an Introduction by Otto Pfleiderer (omitted from the present edition). Although no alterations were made in the text of the 1846 edition, the type was reset in 1892 and the book was published in one volume rather than three. The text of the 1892 edition begins on arabic page 39, which was numbered consecutively with page xxxviii, the last of thirty-eight pages of prefatory matter bearing roman numerals.

Footnotes are handled cavalierly through the first thirty-three sections, that portion of the text which was translated by Rufa Brabant. For example, many footnoted references to recent critical works in German are omitted from the English text. Sometimes the note is given without being translated at all, nor are Greek passages translated. When George Eliot took over the translation at § 34, these policies improved but were not entirely rectified. Often footnotes are reduced in length or citations of passages are eliminated. Beginning with § 39, a translation of Greek passages cited in the footnotes is given if the sense of the Greek does not appear in the text to which it refers. Translations of the Greek New Testament are given in the English Authorized Version.

I have rejected as too cumbersome any attempt to provide missing footnotes, to take note of them in the Annotations, or to supplement the bibliographical data for each note. Rather I have provided a bibliography of modern authors cited by Strauss, which includes full data on most of the books (not journal articles) cited. Interested readers can thus readily verify particular citations. For missing footnotes in the first thirty-three sections, it will be necessary to consult the German original. In the latter part of the work a number of footnoted cross-references contain the words "Vol. I" or "Vol. II" before the section numbers. This is an erroneous carry-over from the three-volume English edition of 1846 and should be disregarded.

---

[110] Strauss to Rapp, 16 July 1858 (*Ausgewählte Briefe*, p. 394); Haight, *Eliot*, pp. 145–48, 150–51, 261; *Letters*, I:xliv–xlvi; II:171, 472.

[111] See the letter from Sara Hennell to Rufa Brabant Hennell, January 1844 (Haight, *Letters*, I:171).

The translation of the terms "myth," "mythical," "mythology," and "mythological" is complicated by Eliot's use of the now archaic "mythus" and "mythi," as well as by a double meaning found in the German term *Mythos* and the English "mythology." *Mythos* in Strauss's German can refer either to a myth or to the literary genre comprised of myths ("mythology" in the loose English sense). Eliot translates this term by "mythus" or "mythi" (plural). When she uses the definite article, "the mythus," the sense is usually that of a literary genre or body of myths ("mythology," as we would more naturally say). "Mythology" in English can refer either to the literary genre comprised of myths (the loose sense), or to the science which treats of myth (the strict sense). In this work *Mythologie* is restricted in usage to the strict sense and in consistently translated "mythology."

The systematic distinction between *Vorstellung* and *Begriff* is somewhat blurred by the translation. Eliot translates *Vorstellung* variously as "conception," "idea," "representation," "imagery." "Conception" and "idea" blur the contrast with *Begriff*, which is also rendered by these terms. "Representation" is possible for *Vorstellung*, but it is awkward in English and does not convey the meaning naturally. The difficulty with "imagery" is that *Vorstellung* is not quite the same as *Bild* ("image") and *Phantasie* ("imagination"), although Strauss sometimes uses these terms in the same context. Nevertheless, "imagery" and "image" represent the best choices for *Vorstellung*, while "conception" and "concept" should be reserved for *Begriff*. The translations of a few other terms are noted in the Annotations.

The fourth German edition contains only the Prefaces to the first volume of the first edition and to the fourth edition. The marvelously polemical Prefaces to the second volume of the first edition and to the second edition were deleted in the third; and the accommodating Preface to the third edition was for good reason excluded from the fourth. Because they help to chronicle the evolution of the work, I have included translations of all the German Prefaces, while the Latin Preface to the English edition has been omitted. A translation is also provided of the concluding section of the third edition, which contains a sketch of Strauss's mediating Christology. The editor's notes in the Annotations are restricted to substantive variations between the German editions. major interpretive issues, and questions of text and translation.

AUTHOR'S PREFACES

PREFACE TO THE FIRST GERMAN EDITION, VOLUME I*

IT APPEARED to the author of the work, the first half of which is herewith submitted to the public, that it was time to substitute a new mode of considering the life of Jesus, in the place of the antiquated systems of supranaturalism and naturalism. This application of the term "antiquated" will in the present day be more readily admitted in relation to the latter system than to the former. For while the interest excited by the explanations of the miracles and the conjectural facts of the rationalists has long ago cooled, the commentaries now most read are those which aim to adapt the supernatural interpretation of the sacred history to modern taste. Nevertheless, in point of fact, the orthodox view of this history became superannuated earlier than the rationalistic, since it was only because the former had ceased to satisfy an advanced state of culture, that the latter was developed, while the recent attempts to recover, by the aid of a mystical philosophy, the supernatural point of view held by our forefathers, betray themselves, by the exaggerating spirit in which they are conceived, to be final, desperate efforts to render the past present, the inconceivable conceivable.

The new point of view, which must take the place of the above, is the mythical. This theory is not brought to bear on the evangelical history for the first time in the present work: it has long been applied to particular parts of that history, and is here only extended to its entire tenor. It is not by any means meant that the whole history of Jesus is to be represented as mythical, but only that every part of it is to be subjected to a critical examination, to ascertain whether it have not some admixture of the mythical. The exegesis of the ancient church set out from the double presupposition: first, that the Gospels contained a history, and secondly, that this history was a supernatural one. Rationalism rejected the latter of these presuppositions, but only to cling the more tenaciously to the former, maintaining that these books present unadulterated, though only natural, history. Science cannot rest satisfied with this half-measure: the other presupposition also must be relinquished, and the inquiry must first be made whether in fact, and to what extent, the ground on which we stand in the Gospels is historical. This is the natural course of things, and thus far the appearance of a work like the present is not only justifiable, but even necessary.

It is certainly not therefore evident that the author is precisely the individual whose vocation it is to appear in this position. He has a very vivid consciousness that many others would have been able to execute such a work with incomparably superior erudition. Yet on the other hand he believes himself to be at least possessed of one qualification which especially fitted him to undertake this task.

* Translated by George Eliot.

The majority of the most learned and acute theologians of the present day fail in the main requirement for such a work, a requirement without which no amount of learning will suffice to achieve anything in the domain of criticism— namely, the internal liberation of the feelings and intellect from certain religious and dogmatical presuppositions; and this the author early attained by means of philosophical studies. If theologians regard this absence of presupposition from his work as unchristian, he regards the believing presuppositions of theirs as unscientific. Widely as in this respect the tone of the present work may be contrasted with the edifying devoutness and enthusiastic mysticism of recent books on similar subjects; still it will nowhere depart from the seriousness of science, or sink into frivolity; and it seems a just demand in return, that the judgments which are passed upon it should also confine themselves to the domain of science, and keep aloof from bigotry and fanaticism.

The author is aware that the essence of the Christian faith is perfectly independent of his criticism. The supernatural birth of Christ, his miracles, his resurrection and ascension, remain eternal truths, whatever doubts may be cast on their reality as historical facts. The certainty of this can alone give calmness and dignity to our criticism, and distinguish it from the naturalistic criticism of the last century, the design of which was, with the historical fact, to subvert also the religious truth, and which thus necessarily became frivolous. A dissertation at the close of the work will show that the dogmatic significance of the life of Jesus remains inviolate: in the meantime let the calmness and sang-froid* with which, in the course of it, criticism undertakes apparently dangerous operations, be explained solely by the security of the author's conviction that no injury is threatened to the Christian faith. Investigations of this kind may, however, inflict a wound on the faith of individuals. Should this be the case with theologians, they have in their science the means of healing such wounds, from which, if they would not remain behind the development of their age, they cannot possibly be exempt. For the laity the subject is certainly not adequately prepared; and for this reason the present work is so framed, that at least the unlearned among them will quickly and often perceive that the book is not destined for them. If from curiosity or excessive zeal against heresy they persist in their perusal, they will then have, as Schleiermacher says on a similar occasion, to bear the punishment in their conscience, since their feelings directly urge on them the conviction that they understand not that of which they are ambitious to speak.

A new opinion, which aims to fill the place of an older one, ought fully to adjust its position with respect to the latter. Hence the way to the mythical view is here taken in each particular point through the supranaturalistic and rationalistic opinions and their respective refutations; but, as becomes a valid refutation, with an acknowledgment of what is true in the opinions combated, and an adoption of this truth into the new theory. This method also brings with it the extrinsic advantage, that the work may now serve as a repertory of the principal opinions and treatises concerning all parts of the evangelical history.

* *Kaltblütigkeit* is rendered in the Eliot translation as "insensibility," though Eliot herself preferred "sang-froid." She was willing to defer to "coldbloodedness" at the suggestion of the Hennells. Later she wrote "dispassionate calmness," which was finally changed to "insensibility." (Gordon S. Haight, ed., *The George Eliot Letters* [New Haven: Yale University Press, 1954], I:217.) Her original choice of "sang-froid" was the best, for it conveys both the negative and positive overtones of the German term, which can mean both callousness, ruthlessness, insensitivity, *and* equanimity, composure, coolness in trying circumstances. That Strauss had the latter, positive connotation in mind is evident from the parallel expression "calmness and dignity" in the preceding sentence. But the negative meaning was also intended, and was taken by Strauss's critics as the dominant characteristic of the work.

The author has not, however, aimed to give a complete bibliographical view of this department of theological literature, but, where it was possible, has adhered to the chief works in each separate class of opinions. For the rationalistic system the works of Paulus remain classical, and are therefore preeminently referred to; for the orthodox opinions, the commentary of Olshausen is especially important, as the most recent and approved attempt to render the supranatural interpretation philosophical and modern; while as a preliminary to a critical investigation of the life of Jesus, the commentaries of Fritzsche are excellently adapted, since they exhibit, together with uncommon philological learning, that freedom from prejudice and scientific indifference to results and consequences, which form the first condition of progress in this region of inquiry.

The second volume, which will open with a detailed examination of the miracles of Jesus, and which will conclude the whole work, is already prepared and will be in the press immediately on the completion of the first.

Tübingen, 24 May 1835

PREFACE TO THE FIRST GERMAN EDITION, VOLUME II*

I ought to rejoice that the second and final volume of this work is able to appear so shortly after the first. Now that a survey of the whole is possible, it might be hoped that many misunderstandings could be corrected and many harsh judgments softened. Yet just as those who protested most loudly about the first volume orally were those who had read not a page of it, so also up to now only those have judged it in writing from whom I can expect no understanding, even if they should read this second part. Thus I do not intend to indulge myself in false delights, but neither do I intend to allow myself to be disturbed henceforth by the cries of owls, which to be sure I awakened much too inconsiderately by a harsh light.

From the criticisms of the first volume that have appeared up to now, I have been able to draw nothing of benefit for the second, partly because it was already largely printed by the time they came to my attention, and partly because of the character of these criticisms themselves.

The first that I had occasion to read was a review by Dr. Paulus in the literary supplement to the *Allgemeine Kirchenzeitung*. To the author himself I am indebted for the liberal and appreciative manner with which he, despite his completely different view, still treated my work. His most important objection to my method is that even if something is mythical in a narrative, it does not follow that everything in it must be mythical. That would doubtless have been a very false conclusion, had I in fact drawn it, but I merely claimed that everything *might* be mythical. Whether it is really so must be determined from the character of the individual narratives, and on this basis I have decided in every case, if I recall properly. I was especially touched to read of the joy my honored old compatriot had over the progress of scholarly freedom in Württemberg, by virtue of which one is now able to write such things without fear—this at a time when I had already been removed from my tutorial post in the Tübingen seminary because of my writings.

As could not otherwise be expected from his vigilance, Dr. Steudel at once considered himself obliged to point out the pernicious effects of my book in his

* Translated by Peter C. Hodgson.

Vorläufig zu Beherzigendes [*Preliminary Considerations*].* This man has often enough been told that it is unseemly to make a moral issue out of scientific discussions, to raise his views about opponents to the level of conscience, and to brand those who are not orthodox as irreligious. Nevertheless, again this time he has struck his customary note. To be sure, it is much more expedient to speak about petty things instead of engaging the issue, and occasionally to wound the opponent by malicious insinuations, especially when such practices are already quite common. But that nothing is accomplished thereby is as clear as day. Or rather, something is accomplished by it, namely, the discrediting of one's opponent in the eyes of the public at large, which does not understand the affair. But for that purpose no doctor of theology is needed; it could be safely left to the gossip of religious societies and the hullabaloo of the tractarians.

My work has also been criticized, supposedly from the standpoint of philosophy, by Professor Eschenmayer in a brochure entitled, *Der Ischariotismus unserer Tage.*† This monstrous product of the legitimate marriage of theological ignorance and religious intolerance, consecrated by a somnambulent philosophy, is so evidently absurd as to render any word of defense superfluous. Its title, moreover, has become for me the occasion of perhaps too presumptive a reminder—of Lessing, to be specific, who also was once slandered by a Viennese paper as a second Judas Iscariot because he was said to have been paid 1000 Ducats for the publication of the *Fragments* of his unknown author‡ by the Amsterdam Jewish Society, which is surely a much more serious charge than that brought against me by Herr E. Incidentally, Dr. Steudel's *Vorläufig zu Beherzigendes* could have reminded me of Lessing—if I may make light of prototypes and predictions—for against Lessing as well there appeared an *Etwas Vorläufiges* [*Something Preliminary*] by Hauptpastor Goeze (may his memory be praised!), which that cheerful man preferred to call the *Vorläufige Etwas* [*Preliminary Something or Other*] on account of its elusiveness. And so I want to close the Preface to this second volume of my allegedly shocking work with the words Lessing used to explain why he had not stopped with the publication of the first sample of those bothersome *Fragments*, as I have not with the first part of this book. I am not stopping, he said, "because I am convinced that this scandal is merely a bogey with which certain people would like to frighten away any and every spirit of investigation, because it does no good at all to want to cut out only half a cancer, and because air must be given to the fire if it is to be extinguished."

Ludwigsburg, October 1835

---

* Steudel was the last remaining representative of the old Tübingen theology on the faculty at the time and was instrumental in having Strauss dismissed from his tutorial post. Concerning his writing Strauss at this point appended the following note:

"The full title runs: *Preliminary Considerations for an Evaluation of the Question Concerning the Historical or Mythical Basis of the Life of Jesus, How the Canonical Gospels Represent the Same, Held Before the Consciousness of a Believer Who Is Counted Among the Supernaturalists, to the Comfort of the Soul,* by Dr. Johann Christian Friedrich Steudel. Specially reprinted from the *Tübinger Zeitschrift für Theologie,* Tübingen, 1835; 88 pp."

† C. A. Eschenmayer was professor of philosophy in Tübingen for many years, and in earlier days had been a critical admirer and student of Schelling. He also had an interest in the hypnotic cures of somnambulists, which perhaps accounts for Strauss's reference here to "a somnambulent philosophy"; and in 1827, when Strauss was a student in Tübingen, Eschenmayer helped to establish the latter's contact with Justinus Kerner.

‡ Reimarus.

PREFACE TO THE SECOND GERMAN EDITION*

In the short time between the appearance of the first edition and the completion of the second, this work has already experienced all the major stages of
reception and opinion on the part of the public that a work of its kind can
experience.

Differing as it does from the views of most theologians and the remainder of
the public, precisely on a matter for which a different opinion is accustomed to
pass as godlessness, it could, upon first acquaintance, only evoke in unprepared
minds a vague astonishment, passing over into horror—an impression which,
having been occasioned by a writing, could not fail for many to be resolved once
again into written expressions. Hence those slanderous articles in the pietistic
journals, e.g., the New Year's capuchin in the so-called *Evangelische Kirchenzeitung*; hence the numerous brochures the tone of which I indicated in the Preface
to the second volume of the first edition—whose entire contents (aside from a
few general comments on my way of interpreting the Gospel history, and, as
with Harless, a specification of its most disturbing results) amount to only the
more or less violent loathing of the author because of his views and probably
also because of his character and person. This sort of reply is on no higher a
plane than those screams often heard from women upon the sudden report of a
nearby shot; such a scream does not take into account the fact that the shot
perhaps missed or hit the wrong target, but only that a shot actually was fired.
If upon such a hue and cry even a cautious government should find itself
carried away for a moment to want to take action against the danger of those
shots, then perchance a reasonable and clearheaded man may intervene with the
advice that here a false alarm exists and no real danger is present. The latter
service is provided, for the time being from the standpoint of a merely general
evaluation, by the academic opinion concerning my work written by Neander,
to whom I cannot avoid expressing my thanks and my high esteem for his
willingness to have his much respected voice heard in so worthy a manner in
my affair.

Gradually, however, as the immediacy of the first impact gradually receded,
some critics began to give an account of the details of the work, whose individual
results they examined together with the evidence. Now for the first time, it
appears, can the public be guaranteed a correct appraisal and the author a true
instruction. In fact, during the transition from the first class of essays on my
book to the second, there were a few that pleased me, such as the review to
which Professor Weisse in Leipzig later confessed, and another in the *Blätter für
katholische Theologie*. I happily admit to much useful instruction from the latter
writings, which decidedly belong to the second class. However, these authors
apply themselves for the time being only to scrutinizing the book, not in the
same fashion to its subject matter, which is the real issue. They ask only how I
treat the Gospel history on the whole and in detail, and whether much does not
have to be said against my view and for the church's. But they totally fail to
undertake an independent investigation of the whole of the Gospel history from
the point of view they defend against me, or to ask whether such an investigation, consistently executed, could be placed in harmony with the scholarly
demands of our time. Now it is to be expected, if one does not enter into the
individual cases of application, or takes no regard for the relation of those specific points to the whole, that nearly always the validity of the ecclesiastical view
is established against the mythical—sometimes in truth, sometimes only in

* Translated by Peter C. Hodgson.

appearance. Consequently, the illusion of a boundless superiority and a thoroughgoing dogmatism develops in the criticisms that take this point of view. From this is readily formed the vain habit of granting nothing at all to the opponent on any point. This habit utilizes a dishonest, chicanerous method, and allies itself, moreover, to an arrogant and even sarcastic tone, insofar as one is conscious of confronting—on the broad basis of tradition and under the firm protection of ecclesiastical and state power—an apparently isolated phenomenon. All this has been expressed angrily against me in the writings especially of Diaconus Hoffmann and Professor Kern, and doubtless of others as well. Much as I have been attracted by the possibility of dealing with these opponents at each and every point in the second edition, I must nevertheless resist it, in order not to enlarge my work unduly or to tear it asunder by polemical encounters. I hope, however, to be able to find time soon to answer them in a series of special writings.

Not until men turn away from the tendency of my work to the issue itself, not until they determine the extent to which the life of Jesus can be investigated at the present level of scholarship and general consciousness, or even a single Gospel treated, without making use of my research—not until then (but then indeed with certainty) can I hope that by no means everything I achieved will be thrown wantonly away, but that the hitherto much reviled stone which I brought to light or cleaned off will have been incorporated into the new edifice of theological scholarship. Also not until I am able to see how others, without this or that assumption borrowed from me or from others they substitute for me, are capable of forming a comprehensive view of the Gospel history, will I find myself enlightened in this objective way that I have gone too far here and there, or have grasped at straws. Among this latter class of writings, one has appeared recently to my special delight: de Wette's *Erklärung des Evangeliums Matthäi*, a work in which I find my efforts on many points appreciated by an old master of biblical criticism in such a way as to compensate for the derogatory judgments of so many others, who appear to have learned something of criticism for the first time either from my book or only shortly before, which is clear as day from my reviewer in the *Berliner Jahrbücher*. From the pages of a work such as de Wette's I have taken note of some rather blatant errors and contradictions on my part, and insofar as it was still possible and I could agree, I have already corrected my work in a few places according to his pointers.

A thorough revision of the work could scarcely be expected in this second edition in view of the short intervening time and my current circumstances, which are unfavorable to sustained scholarly studies. Nevertheless, I have subjected the entire work to another thorough review, and on all points have endeavored to utilize, for the sake of its improvement, the objections of opponents, the advice of friends, and what I have learned from my own further research: notably, to complete existing gaps, to retract untenable positions, and to support the proven findings all the more strongly; and I hope that my good intentions will not be completely misjudged.

Ludwigsburg, 23 September 1836

PREFACE TO THE THIRD GERMAN EDITION*

DUE to the necessity of a third edition of *The Life of Jesus* I was interrupted in the preparation of my *Streitschriften*, the second volume of which was intended

* Translated by Peter C. Hodgson.

to deal with the objections of the more detailed opposing writings, topically arranged, on individual aspects of my critical view of the Gospel history. But in the main work itself I have now worked through the issues with my principal opponents, and thus any further continuation of the *Streitschriften* has been rendered superfluous.*

One will discover that I have not taken the objections of my opponents lightly but have allowed myself to be penetrated by their full strength and significance, in order to revise at once without hesitation whenever they seemed to me to be right; but whenever I found my earlier views unshaken I stood firm. I have sought to learn as much as possible from everyone. How much I owe to de Wette in this matter I have already indicated elsewhere. Neander's profound insight was often no less helpful in discovering the unity which had hidden itself from me amidst the conflicts, although in his case I must judge that frequently the conflicts prior to the unity are not given their due. By his caution in clinging to the ancients, his sincerity in admitting his doubts, and his self-effacing love of truth, he puts to shame the dishonest zeal of those who, like Hoffmann, appear less concerned that the truth be made known than that their boastfully uttered words yield not an inch to their opponents for the sake of truth. Nevertheless, I owe a great deal to this latter knowledgeable and discerning opponent, especially on the infancy narrative. Likewise, I have drawn out of Kern's inflated professorial tone a number of appropriate comments, and from the high horse of Tholuck's versatility, in spite of its occasionally unsteady gait, I have gained a more adequate point of view for this and that passage. Even Theile's formless and at times passionate writing is of some value. Only in Osiander's book could I discover no light for all its fumes and smoke, at least none that he kindled without his superior predecessors. Weisse's work on the evangelical history, which I hail as a welcome addition in many respects, could no longer be used for this first volume.

The changes offered by this new edition are all more or less related to the fact that a renewed study of the Fourth Gospel, on the basis of de Wette's commentary and Neander's *Leben Jesu Christi*, has made me again doubtful of my earlier doubt concerning the authenticity and credibility of this Gospel. It is not that I have become convinced of its authenticity, merely that I am no longer certain of its inauthenticity. From among the peculiarly striking and frustrating features of credibility and incredibility, of proximity to and distance from the truth, which exist in this most remarkable Gospel, I had emphasized in the first composition of my work, with one-sided polemical zeal, only what seemed to me the adverse and unfavorable side. In the meanwhile the other side has gradually come into its own for me; but I am still not in the position to sacrifice without further ado the opposing observations, as nearly all present-day theologians up to de Wette do. As a consequence my work as it now appears, by comparison with its earlier form as well as with works by others proceeding from the opposing point of view, has lost in unity but hopefully has gained in truth over both.

Regarding the style of my writing, I had luxuriated in great sensual confidence

---

* The second volume of *Streitschriften* was never published. The first volume was comprised of three numbers or series, each with separate pagination. Strauss wrote the third of these numbers during the fall and winter of 1837, at the same time as he began preparations for the third edition of *The Life of Jesus*. In it he discussed the relation of his work to Hegelian philosophy, and the criticisms leveled against him by the Hegelian theologians and the Mediating school, anticipating many of the changes to come in the third edition of the main work. The reason given here for not continuing the *Streitschriften* is partly misleading, because it is clear that Strauss had lost his appetite for further polemical debate.

because it had been praised by otherwise hostile critics, until recently Ewald raised the charge, among others, of a confusion of tongues against my work. In this revision, then, I paid attention to this matter also, and in fact discovered that I had let myself go too far. For this reason I have weeded out hundreds of such patches and have allowed them to remain only where it seemed beneficial for brevity and definiteness of expression, or suitable as a change. I am speaking of foreign words which have crept into German in unseemly fashion; for I could not accept the reproach that I frequently interlaced my writing with New Testament words and sentences in the original, since this sort of mixture of tongues must be permitted anyone who writes a book about something in a foreign language.

Finally, I feel obliged to thank the anonymous author of the *apologia* on behalf of my person and work, on account of the goodwill with which he attempted to sympathize with my views and intentions, despite the fact they are not his own, and for the impartiality and generosity with which he was able to resolve many misunderstandings of them and to dismiss many misinterpretations.

Stuttgart, 8 April 1838

PREFACE TO THE FOURTH GERMAN EDITION*

As THIS new edition of my critical examination of the life of Jesus appears simultaneously with the first volume of my *Dogmatik*, it will not be expected to contain any essential alterations. Indeed, even in the absence of other labours, I should scarcely have been inclined to undertake such on the present occasion. The critical researches prompted by the appearance of my work have, after the stormy reaction of the first few years, at length entered on that quiet course, which promises the most valuable assistance towards the confirmation and more precise determination of the negative results at which I have arrived. But these fruits still require some years for their maturing; and it must therefore be deferred to a future opportunity to enrich this work by the use of them. I could not persuade myself to do so, at least in the present instance, by prosecuting a polemic against opposite opinions. Already in the last edition there was more of a polemical character than accorded with the unity and calmness proper to such a work; hence I was in this respect admonished rather to abridge than to amplify. But that edition also contained too much of compliance. The intermingling voices of opponents, critics, and fellow labourers, to which I held it a duty attentively to listen, had confused the idea of the work in my mind; in the diligent comparison of divergent opinions I had lost sight of the subject itself. Hence on coming with a more collected mind to this last revision, I found alterations at which I could not but wonder, and by which I had evidently done myself injustice. In all these passages the earlier readings are now restored, and thus my labour in this new edition has chiefly consisted in whetting, as it were, my good sword, to free it from the notches made in it rather by my own grinding, than by the blows of my enemies.

Stuttgart, 17 October 1840

* Translated by George Eliot.

TEXT OF THE ELIOT TRANSLATION

THE LIFE OF JESUS.

⁓୧ଛଛ৩ⵜ

INTRODUCTION.

DEVELOPMENT OF THE MYTHICAL POINT OF VIEW IN RELATION TO THE GOSPEL HISTORIES.

----

§ I.

NEVITABLE RISE OF DIFFERENT MODES OF EXPLAINING SACRED HISTORIES.

WHEREVER a religion, resting upon written records, prolongs and extends the sphere of its dominion, accompanying its votaries through the varied and progressive stages of mental cultivation, a discrepancy between the representations of those ancient records, referred to as sacred, and the notions of more advanced periods of mental development, will inevitably sooner or later arise. In the first instance this disagreement is felt in reference only to the unessential—the external form : the expressions and delineations are seen to be inappropriate ; but by degrees it manifests itself also in regard to that which is essential : the fundamental ideas and opinions in these early writings fail to be commensurate with a more advanced civilisation. As long as this discrepancy is either not in itself so considerable, or else is not so universally discerned and acknowledged, as to lead to a complete renunciation of these Scriptures as of sacred authority, so long will a system of reconciliation by means of interpretation be adopted and pursued by those who have a more or less distinct consciousness of the existing incongruity.

A main element in all religious records is sacred history ; a history of events in which the divine enters, without intermediation, into the human ; the ideal thus assuming an immediate embodiment. But as the progress of mental cultivation mainly consists in the gradual recognition of a chain of causes and effects connecting natural phenomena with each other; so the mind in its development becomes ever increasingly conscious of those mediate links which are indispensable to the realization of the ideal ;[1] and hence the discrepancy between the modern culture and the ancient records, with regard to their historical portion, becomes so apparent, that the immediate intervention of the divine in human affairs loses its probability. Besides, as the humanity of these records is the humanity of an early period, consequently of an age

----

[1] [This passage varies slightly from the original, a subsequent amplification by Dr. Strauss being incorporated with it.—TR.] *

comparatively undeveloped and necessarily rude, a sense of repulsion is like-wise excited. The incongruity may be thus expressed. *The divine cannot so have happened* ; (not immediately, not in forms so rude ;) or, *that which has so happened cannot have been divine* :—and if a reconciliation be sought by means of interpretation, it will be attempted to prove, either that the divine did not manifest itself in the manner related,—which is to deny the historical validity of the ancient Scriptures ; or, that the actual occurrences were not divine—which is to explain away the absolute contents of these books. In both cases the interpretation may be partial or impartial : partial, if under-taken with a determination to close the eyes to the secretly recognised fact of the disagreement between the modern culture and the ancient records, and to see only in such interpretation the original signification of these records ; im-partial, if it unequivocally acknowledges and openly avows that the matters narrated in these books must be viewed in a light altogether different from that in which they were regarded by the authors themselves. This latter method, however, by no means involves the entire rejection of the religious documents ; on the contrary, the essential may be firmly retained, whilst the unessential is unreservedly abandoned.

§ 2.

DIFFERENT EXPLANATIONS OF SACRED LEGENDS AMONG THE GREEKS.

Though the Hellenistic religion cannot be said to have rested upon written records, it became enshrined in the Greek poems, for example, in those of Homer and Hesiod ; and these, no less than its orally transmitted legends, did not fail to receive continually varying interpretations, successively adapted to the progressive intellectual culture of the Greeks. At an early period the rigid philosophy of the Greeks, and under its influence even some of the Greek poets, recognized the impossibility of ascribing to Deity manifestations so grossly human, so immediate, and so barbarous, as those exhibited and represented as divine in the wild conflicts of Hesiod's Theogony, and in the domestic occupations and trivial pursuits of the Homeric deities. Hence arose the quarrel of Plato, and prior to him of Pindar, with Homer ; [1] hence the cause which induced Anaxagoras, to whom the invention of the allegorical mode of interpretation is ascribed, to apply the Homeric delineations to vir-tue and to justice ; [2] hence it was that the Stoics understood the Theogony of Hesiod as relating to the action of the elements, which, according to their notions, constituted, in their highest union, the divine nature.[3] Thus did these several thinkers, each according to his own peculiar mode of thought, succeed in discovering an absolute meaning in these representations : the one finding in them a physical, the other an ethical signification, whilst, at the same time, they gave up their external form, ceasing to regard them as strictly historical.

On the other hand, the more popular and sophistical culture of another class of thinkers led them to opposite conclusions. Though, in their estima-tion, every semblance of the divine had evaporated from these histories ; though they were convinced that the proceedings ascribed to the gods were not godlike, still they did not abandon the historical sense of these narratives.

---

[1] Plato, de Republ. ii. p. 377. Steph. ; Pindar, Nem. vii. 31.
[2] Diog. Laërt. L. ii. c. iii. No. 7.
[3] Cic. de Nat. Deor. i. 10. 15. Comp. Athenag. Legat. 22. Tatian, c. Græc. Orat. 21. Clement. homil. 6, 1 f.

With Evemerus [4] they transformed the subjects of these histories from gods to men, to heroes and sages of antiquity, kings and tyrants, who, through deeds of might and valour, had acquired divine honours.   Some indeed went still further, and, with Polybius,[5] considered the whole system of heathen theology as a fable, invented by the founders of states to awe the people into subjection.

§ 3.

ALLEGORICAL INTERPRETATIONS AMONG THE HEBREWS.—PHILO.

Whilst, on the one hand, the isolation and stability of the Hebrews served to retard the development of similar manifestations amongst this people, on the other hand, when once actually developed, they were the more marked ; because, in proportion to the high degree of authority ascribed to the sacred records, was the skill and caution required in their interpretation.   Thus, even in Palestine, subsequent to the exile, and particularly after the time of the Maccabees, many ingenious attempts were made to interpret the Old Testament so as to remove offensive literalities, supply deficiencies, and introduce the notions of a later age.   Examples of this system of interpretation occur in the writings of the Rabbins, and even in the New Testament ; [1] but it was at that place where the Jewish mind came into contact with Greek civilization, and under its influence was carried beyond the limits of its own national culture—namely at Alexandria—that the allegorical mode of interpretation was first consistently applied to the whole body of historical narrative in the Old Testament.   Many had prepared the way, but it was Philo who first fully developed the doctrine of both a common and a deeper sense of the Holy Scriptures.   He was by no means inclined to cast away the former, but generally placed the two together, side by side, and even declared himself opposed to those who, everywhere and without necessity, sacrificed the literal to the higher signification.   In many cases, however, he absolutely discarded the verbal meaning and historical conception, and considered the narrative merely as the figurative representation of an idea.   He did so, for example, whenever the sacred story appeared to him to present delineations unworthy of Deity, tending either to materialism or anthropomorphism, or otherwise to contain contradictions.[2]

The fact that the Jews, whilst they adopted this mode of explaining the Old Testament, (which, in order to save the purity of the intrinsic signification, often sacrificed the historical form), were never led into the opposite system of Evemerus (which preserved the historical form by divesting the history of the divine, and reducing it to a record of mere human events), is to be ascribed to the tenacity with which that people ever adhered to the supernatural point of view.   The latter mode of interpretation was first brought to bear upon the Old Testament by the Christians.

§ 4.

ALLEGORICAL INTERPRETATIONS AMONG THE CHRISTIANS.—ORIGEN.

To the early Christians who, antecedent to the fixing of the christian canon, made especial use of the Old Testament as their principal sacred record, an

[4] Diodor. Sic.   Bibl. Fragm. L. vi.   Cic. de Nat. Deor. i. 42.
[5] Hist. vi. 56.
[1] Döpke, die Hermeneutik der neutestamentlichen Schriftsteller, s. 123. ff.
[2] Gfrörer. Dähne.

allegorical interpretation was the more indispensable, inasmuch as they had made greater advances beyond the views of the Old Testament writers than even the most enlightened of the Jews.   It was no wonder therefore that this mode of explanation, already in vogue among the Jews, was almost universally adopted by the primitive christian churches.   It was however again in Alexandria that it found the fullest application amongst the Christians, and that in connexion with the name of Origen.   Origen attributes a threefold meaning to the Scriptures, corresponding with his distribution of the human being into three parts : the literal sense answering to the body ; the moral, to the soul ; and the mystical, to the spirit.[1]   The rule with him was to retain all three meanings, though differing in worth ; in some particular cases, however, he was of opinion that the literal interpretation either gave no sense at all, or else a perverted sense, in order the more directly to impel the reader to the discovery of its mystical signification.   Origen's repeated observation that it is not the purpose of the biblical narratives to transmit old tales, but to instruct in the rules of life ;[2] his assertion that the merely literal acceptation of many of the narratives would prove destructive of the christian religion ;[3] and his application of the passage " The letter killeth, but the spirit giveth life,"[4] to the relative worth of the allegorical and the literal modes of biblical interpretation, may be understood as indicating only the inferiority of the literal to the deeper signification.   But the literal sense is decidedly given up when it is said, " Every passage of Scripture has a spiritual element, but not every one has a corporeal element ; "[5]   " A spiritual truth often exists embodied in a corporeal falsehood " ;[6]   " The Scriptures contain many things which never came to pass, interwoven with the history, and he must be dull indeed who does not of his own accord observe that much which the Scriptures represent as having happened never actually occurred."[7]   Among the passages which Origen regarded as admitting no other than an allegorical interpretation, besides those which too sensibly humanised the Deity,[8] he included those which attributed unworthy action to individuals who had held intimate communion with God.[9]

It was not however from the Old Testament views alone that Origen had, in consequence of his christian training, departed so widely that he felt himself compelled, if he would retain his reverence for the sacred records, to allegorize their contents, as a means of reconciling the contradiction which had arisen between them and his own mind.   There was much likewise in the New Testament writings which so little accorded with his philosophical

---

[1] Homil. 5. in Levit. § 5.
[2] Homil. 2. in Exod. iii. : *Nolite putare, ut sæpe jam diximus, veterum vobis fabulas recitari, sed doceri vos per hæc, ut agnoscatis ordinem vitæ.*
[3] Homil. 5. in Levit. i. : *Hæc omnia, nisi alio sensu accipiamus quam literæ textus ostendit, obstaculum magis et subversionem Christianæ religioni, quam hortationem ædificationemque præstabunt.*
[4] Contra Cels. vi. 70.
[5] De principp. L. iv. § 20 : πᾶσα μὲν (γραφὴ) ἔχει τὸ πνευματικὸν, οὐ πᾶσα δὲ τὸ σωματικόν.
[6] Comm. in Joann., Tom. x. § 4 :—σωζομένου πολλάκις τοῦ ἀληθοῦς πνευματικοῦ ἐν τῷ σωματικῷ, ὡς ἂν εἴποι τις, ψεύδει.
[7] De principp. iv. 15 : συνύφηνεν ἡ γραφὴ τῇ ἱστορίᾳ τὸ μὴ γενόμενον, πῆ μὲν μὴ δυνατὸν γενέσθαι, πῆ δὲ δυνατὸν μὲν γενέσθαι, οὐ μὴν γεγενημένον.   De principp. iv. 16 : καὶ τί δεῖ πλείω λέγειν ; τῶν μὴ πάνυ ἀμβλέων μυρία ὅσα τοιαῦτα δυναμένων συναγαγεῖν, γεγραμμένα μὲν ὡς γεγονότα, οὐ γεγενημένα δὲ κατὰ τὴν λέξιν.
[8] De principp. iv. 16.
[9] Homil. 6, in Gen. iii. : *Quæ nobis ædificatio erit, legentibus, Abraham, tantam patriarcham, non solum mentitum esse Abimelech regi, sed et pudicitiam conjugis prodidisse?   Quid nos ædificat tanti patriarchæ uxor, si putetur contaminationibus exposita per conniventiam maritalem?   Hæc Judæi putent et si qui cum eis sunt literæ amici, non spiritus.*

notions, that he found himself constrained to adopt a similar proceeding in reference to them. He reasoned thus :—the New Testament and the Old are the work of the same spirit, and this spirit would proceed in the same manner in the production of the one and of the other, interweaving fiction with reality, in order thereby to direct the mind to the spiritual signification.[10] In a remarkable passage of his work against Celsus, Origen classes together, and in no ambiguous language, the partially fabulous stories of profane history, and of heathen mythology, with the gospel narratives.[11] He expresses himself as follows : " In almost every history it is a difficult task, and not unfrequently an impossible one, to demonstrate the reality of the events recorded, however true they may in fact be. Let us suppose some individual to deny the reality of a Trojan war on account of the incredibilities mixed up with the history ; as, for example, the birth of Achilles from a goddess of the sea. How could we substantiate the fact, encumbered as it is with the numerous and undeniable poetical fictions which have, in some unascertainable manner, become interwoven with the generally admitted account of the war between the Greeks and the Trojans ? There is no alternative : he who would study history with understanding, and not suffer himself to be deluded, must weigh each separate detail, and consider what is worthy of credit and may be believed without further evidence ; what, on the contrary, must be regarded as merely figurative ; (τίνα δὲ τροπολογήσει) always bearing in mind the aim of the narrator— and what must be wholly mistrusted as being written with intent to please certain individuals." In conclusion Origen says, " I was desirous of making these preliminary observations in relation to the entire history of Jesus given in the Gospels, not with the view of exacting from the enlightened a blind and baseless belief, but with design to show how indispensable to the study of this history are not only judgment and diligent examination, but, so to speak, the very penetrating into the mind of the author, in order to discover the particular aim with which each narrative may have been written."

We here see Origen almost transcending the limits of his own customary point of view, and verging towards the more modern mythical view. But if his own prepossessions in favour of the supernatural, and his fear of giving offence to the orthodox church, combined to hinder him from making a wider application of the allegorical mode of interpretation to the Old Testament, the same causes operated still more powerfully in relation to the New Testament ; so that when we further inquire of which of the gospel histories in particular did Origen reject the historical meaning, in order to hold fast a truth worthy of God ? the instances will prove to be meagre in the extreme. For when he says, in illustration of the above-mentioned passage, that amongst other things, it is not to be understood literally that Satan showed to Jesus all the kingdoms of the earth from a mountain, because this is impossible to the bodily eye ; he here gives not a strictly allegorical interpretation, but merely a different turn to the literal sense, which, according to him, relates not to an external fact, but to the internal fact of a vision. Again, even where the text offers a tempting opportunity of sacrificing the literal to the spiritual meaning, as, for example, the cursing of the fig-tree,[12] Origen does not speak out freely. He is most explicit when speaking of the expulsion of the buyers and sellers from the temple ; he characterizes the conduct of Jesus,

---

[10] De princip. iv. 16 : οὐ μόνον δὲ περὶ τῶν πρὸ τῆς παρουσίας ταῦτα τὸ πνεῦμα ᾠκονόμησεν, ἀλλ', ἅτε τὸ αὐτὸ τυγχάνον καὶ ἀπὸ τοῦ ἑνὸς θεοῦ, τὸ ὅμοιον καὶ ἐπὶ τῶν εὐαγγελίων πεποίηκε καὶ ἐπὶ τῶν ἀποστόλων, οὐδὲ τούτων πάντη ἄκρατον τὴν ἱστορίαν τῶν προσυφασμένων κατὰ τὸ σωματικὸν ἐχόντων μὴ γεγενημένων.
[11] Contra Celsum, i. 40.
[12] Comm. in Matth., Tom. xvi. 26.

according to the literal interpretation, as assuming and seditious.[13]   He
moreover expressly remarks that the Scriptures contain many more historical
than merely scriptural truths.[14]

§ 5.

TRANSITION TO MORE MODERN TIMES.—DEISTS AND NATURALISTS OF THE
17TH AND 18TH CENTURIES.—THE WOLFENBÜTTEL FRAGMENTIST.

Thus was developed one of those forms of interpretation to which the
Hebrew and Christian Scriptures, in common with all other religious records,
in relation to their historical contents, became necessarily subjected; that,
namely, which recognizes in them the divine, but denies it to have actually
manifested itself in so immediate a manner.   The other principal mode of
interpretation, which, to a certain extent, acknowledges the course of events
to have been historically true, but assigns it to a human and not a divine
origin, was developed amongst the enemies of Christianity by a Celsus, a
Porphyry, and a Julian.   They indeed rejected much of the history as altogether fabulous ; but they admitted many of the incidents related of Moses,
Jesus, and others, to be historical facts : these facts were however considered
by them as originating from common motives ; and they attributed their
apparently supernatural character either to gross fraud or impious sorcery.

It is worthy of observation that the circumstances attending the introduction of these several modes of interpretation into the heathen and Jewish
religions, on the one hand, and into the christian religion, on the other, were
different.   The religion and sacred literature of the Greeks and Hebrews had
been gradually developed with the development of the nation, and it was not
until the intellectual culture of the people had outgrown the religion of their
fathers, and the latter was in consequence verging towards decay, that the
discrepancy which is the source of these varying interpretations became
apparent.   Christianity, on the contrary, came into a world of already advanced civilization ; which was, with the exception of that of Palestine, the
Judaico-Hellenistic and the Greek.   Consequently a disagreement manifested
itself at the very beginning ; it was not now, however, as in former times, between modern culture and an ancient religion, but between a new religion and
ancient culture.   The production of allegorical interpretations among the
Pagans and the Hebrews, was a sign that their religion had lost its vitality ;
the allegories of Origen and the attacks of Celsus, in reference to Christianity,
were evidences rather that the world had not as yet duly accommodated itself
to the new religion.   As however with the christianizing of the Roman empire,
and the overthrow of the chief heresies, the christian principle gained an ever-
increasing supremacy ; as the schools of heathen wisdom closed ; and the un-
civilized Germanic tribes lent themselves to the teaching of the church ;—the
world, during the tedious centuries of the middle ages, was satisfied with
Christianity, both in form and in substance.   Almost all traces of these modes
of interpretation which presuppose a discrepancy between the culture of a
nation, or of the world, and religion, in consequence disappeared.   The reformation effected the first breach in the solid structure of the faith of the
church.   It was the first vital expression of a culture, which had now in the
heart of Christendom itself, as formerly in relation to Paganism and Judaism,
acquired strength and independence sufficient to create a reaction against the

---

[13] Comm. in Joann., Tom. x. 17.
[14] De principp. iv. 19.   After Origen, that kind of allegory only which left the historical
sense unimpaired was retained in the church ; and where, subsequently, a giving up of the
verbal meaning is spoken of, this refers merely to a trope or a simile.

soil of its birth, the prevailing religion.   This reaction, so long as it was directed against the dominant hierarchy, constituted the sublime, but quickly terminated, drama of the reformation.   In its later direction against the Bible, it appeared again upon the stage in the barren revolutionary efforts of deism ; and many and various have been the forms it has assumed in its progress down to the present time.

The deists and naturalists of the seventeenth and eighteenth centuries re-newed the polemic attacks of the pagan adversaries of Christianity in the bosom of the christian church ; and gave to the public an irregular and con-fused mass of criticisms, impugning the authenticity and credibility of the Scrip-tures, and exposing to contempt the events recorded in the sacred volume. Toland,[1] Bolingbroke,[2] and others, pronounced the Bible to be a collection of unauthentic and fabulous books ; whilst some spared no pains to despoil the biblical histories, and the heroes whose actions they celebrate, of every ray of divine light.   Thus, according to Morgan,[3] the law of Moses is a miserable system of superstition, blindness, and slavery ; the Jewish priests are de-ceivers ; and the Jewish prophets the originators of the distractions and civil wars of the two kingdoms of Judah and Israel.   According to Chubb,[4] the Jewish religion cannot be a revelation from God, because it debases the moral character of the Deity by attributing to him arbitrary conduct, partiality for a particular people, and above all, the cruel command to exterminate the Canaanitish nations.   Assaults were likewise made by these and other deists upon the New Testament : the Apostles were sus-pected of being actuated by selfish and mercenary motives ;[5] the character of Jesus himself was not spared,[6] and the fact of his resurrection was denied.[7] The miracles of Jesus, wrought by an immediate exercise of divine power in human acts and concerns, were made the particular objects of attack by Woolston.[8]   This writer is also worthy of notice on account of the peculiar position taken by him between the ancient allegorists and the modern natural-ists.   His whole reasoning turns upon the alternative ; either to retain the historical reality of the miracles narrated in the Bible, and thus to sacrifice the divine character of the narratives, and reduce the miracles to mere artifices, miserable juggleries, or commonplace deceptions ; or, in order to hold fast the divine character of these narratives, to reject them entirely as details of actual occurrences, and regard them as historical representations of certain spiritual truths.   Woolston cites the authority of the most distinguished al-legorists among the fathers in support of this view.   He is wrong however in representing them as supplanting the literal by the figurative meaning.   These ancient fathers, on the contrary, were disposed to retain both the literal and the allegorical meaning.   (A few examples in Origen, it is true, are an exception to this rule.)   It may be doubted, from the language of Woolston, which alternative was adopted by himself.   If we reason from the fact, that before he appeared as the opponent of the commonly entertained views of Christianity, he occupied himself with allegorical interpretations of the Scrip-tures,[9] we may be led to consider the latter alternative as expressing his real conviction.   On the other hand, he enlarges with so evident a predi-

[1] In his Amyntor, 1698.   See Leland's View of the Deistical Writers.
[2] See Leland.
[3] In his work entitled The Moral Philosopher.
[4] Posthumous Works, 1748.
[5] Chubb, Posthumous Works, i. 102.
[6] Ibid., ii. 269.
[7] The Resurrection of Jesus Considered, by a Moral Philosopher, 1744.
[8] Six Discourses on the Miracles of our Saviour.   Published singly, from 1727-1729.
[9] Schröckh, Kirchengesch, seit der Reform. 6 Th. s. 191.

lection on the absurdities of the miracles, when literally understood, and the manner in which he treats the whole subject is so tinged with levity, that we may suspect the Deist to put forward the allegorical interpretations merely as a screen, from behind which he might inveigh the more unreservedly against the literal signification.

Similar deistical objections against the Bible, and the divine character of its history, were propagated in Germany chiefly by an anonymous author (Reimarus) whose manuscripts were discovered by Lessing in the Wolfenbüttel library. Some portions of these manuscripts, called the "Wolfenbüttel Fragments," were published by Lessing in 1774. They consist of Essays, one of which treats of the many arguments which may be urged against revealed religion in general; the others relate partly to the Old and partly to the New Testament. It is the opinion of the Fragmentist, in relation to the Old Testament, first, that the men, of whom the Scriptures narrate that they had immediate communications with God, were so unworthy, that such intercourse, admitting its reality, compromised the character of Deity; secondly, that the result of this intercourse,—the instructions and laws alleged to have been thus divinely communicated,—were so barbarous and destructive, that to ascribe them to God is impossible; and thirdly, that the accompanying miracles were at once absurd and incredible. From the whole, it appears to him clear, that the divine communications were only pretended; and that the miracles were delusions, practised with the design of giving stability and efficiency to certain laws and institutions highly advantageous to the rulers and priests. The author finds much to condemn in the conduct of the patriarchs, and their simulations of divine communications; such as the command to Abraham to sacrifice his son. But it is chiefly Moses upon whom he seeks, in a long section, to cast all the obloquy of an impostor, who did not scruple to employ the most disgraceful means in order to make himself the despotic ruler of a free people: who, to effect his purpose, feigned divine apparitions, and pretended to have received the command of God to perpetrate acts which, but for this divine sanction, would have been stigmatized as fraudulent, as highway robbery, as inhuman barbarity. For instance, the spoiling of the Egyptians, and the extirpation of the inhabitants of Canaan; atrocities which, when introduced by the words "*Jehovah hath said it*," became instantly transformed into deeds worthy of God. The Fragmentist is as little disposed to admit the divinity of the New Testament histories. He considers the aim of Jesus to have been political; and his connexion with John the Baptist a preconcerted arrangement, by which the one party should recommend the other to the people. He views the death of Jesus as an event by no means foreseen by himself, but which frustrated all his plans; a catastrophe which his disciples knew not how else to repair than by the fraudulent pretence that Jesus was risen from the dead, and by an artful alteration of his doctrines [10].

§ 6.

NATURAL MODE OF EXPLANATION ADOPTED BY THE RATIONALISTS.—EICHHORN.—PAULUS.

Whilst the reality of the biblical revelation, together with the divine origin and supernatural character of the Jewish and Christian histories, were tenaciously maintained in opposition to the English deists by numerous English apologists, and in opposition to the Wolfenbüttel Fragmentist by the great majority of German theologians, there arose a distinct class of theologians in

[10] Fragmente des Wolfenbüttelschen Ungenannten von G. E. Lessing herausgegeben.

Germany, who struck into a new path. The ancient pagan mythology, as understood by Evemerus, admitted of two modes of explanation, each of which was in fact adopted. The deities of the popular worship might, on the one hand, be regarded as good and benevolent men ; as wise lawgivers, and just rulers, of early times, whom the gratitude of their contemporaries and posterity had encircled with divine glory ; or they might, on the other hand, be viewed as artful impostors and cruel tyrants, who had veiled themselves in a nimbus of divinity, for the pupose of subjugating the people to their domin-ion. So, likewise, in the purely human explanation of the bible histories, besides the method of the deists to regard the subjects of these narratives as wicked and deceitful men, there was yet another course open ; to divest these individuals of their immediate divinity, but to accord to them an undegraded humanity ; not indeed to look upon their deeds as miraculous ;—as little on the other hand to decry them as impositions ;—but to explain their proceed-ings as altogether natural, yet morally irreprehensible. If the Naturalist was led by his special enmity to the Christianity of the church to the former ex-planation, the Rationalist, anxious, on the contrary, to remain within the pale of the church, was attracted towards the latter.

Eichhorn, in his critical examination of the Wolfenbüttel Fragments,[1] directly opposes this rationalistic view to that maintained by the Naturalist. He agrees with the Fragmentist in refusing to recognize an immediate divine agency, at all events in the narratives of early date. The mythological re-searches of a Heyne had so far enlarged his circle of vision as to lead Eich-horn to perceive that divine interpositions must be alike admitted, or alike denied, in the primitive histories of all people. It was the practice of all nations, of the Grecians as well as the Orientals, to refer every unexpected or inexplicable occurrence immediately to the Deity. The sages of antiquity lived in continual communion with superior intelligences. Whilst these re-presentations (such is Eichhorn's statement of the matter) are always, in reference to the Hebrew records, understood verbally and literally, it has hitherto been customary to explain similar representations in the pagan histories, by presupposing either deception and gross falsehood, or the mis-interpretation and corruption of tradition. But Eichhorn thinks justice evidently requires that Hebrew and pagan history should be treated in the same way ; so that intercourse with celestial beings during a state of infancy, must either be accorded to all nations, pagan and Hebrew, or equally denied to all. The mind hesitates to make so universal an admission : first, on account of the not unfrequent errors contained in religions claiming to have been divinely communicated ; secondly, from a sense of the difficulty of ex-plaining the transition of the human race from a state of divine tutelage to one of self-dependence : and lastly, because in proportion as intelligence in-creases, and the authenticity of the records may be more and more confidently relied upon, in the same proportion do these immediate divine influences invariably disappear. If, accordingly, the notion of supernatural interposition is to be rejected with regard to the Hebrews, as well as to all other people, the view generally taken of pagan antiquity presents itself, at first sight, as that most obviously applicable to the early Hebrews ; namely, that their pre-tended revelations were based upon deceit and falsehood, or that their miracu-lous histories should be referred to the misrepresentations and corruptions of tradition. This is the view of the subject actually applied by the Fragmentist to the Old Testament ; a representation, says Eichhorn, from which the mind on a nearer contemplation recoils. Is it conceivable that the greatest men of

---

[1] Recension der übrigen, noch ungedruckten Werke des Wolfenbüttler Fragmentisten, in Eichhorns allgemeiner Bibliothek, erster Band 1tes u. 2tes Stück.

antiquity, whose influence operated so powerfully and so beneficially upon their age, should one and all have been impostors, and yet have escaped the detection of their contemporaries ?

According to Eichhorn, so perverted a view could arise only in a mind that refused to interpret the ancient records in the spirit of their age.   Truly, had they been composed with all the philosophical accuracy of the writers of the present day, we should have been compelled to find in them either actual divine interpositions, or a fraudulent pretence.   But they are the production of an infant and unscientific age ; and treat, without reserve of divine interventions, in accordance with the conceptions and phraseology of that early period.   So that, in point of fact, we have neither miracles to wonder at, on the one hand, nor deceptions to unmask on the other ; but simply the language of a former age to translate into that of our own day.   Eichhorn observes that before the human race had gained a knowledge of the true causes of things, all occurrences were referred to supernatural agencies, or to the interposition of superhuman beings.   Lofty conceptions, noble resolves, useful inventions and regulations, but more especially vivid dreams, were the operations of that Deity under whose immediate influence they believed themselves placed.   Manifestations of distinguished intelligence and skill, by which some i..dividual excited the wonder of the people, were regarded as miraculous ; as signs of supernatural endowments, and of a particular intercourse with higher beings.   And this was the belief, not of the people only, but also of these eminent individuals, who entertained no doubt of the fact, and who exulted in the full conviction of being in mysterious connexion with the Deity.   Eichhorn is of opinion that no objection can be urged against the attempt to resolve all the Mosaic narratives into natural occurrences, and thus far he concedes to the Fragmentist his primary position ; but he rejects his inference that Moses was an impostor, pronouncing the conclusion to be over-hasty and unjust.   Thus Eichhorn agreed with the Naturalists in divesting the biblical narratives of all their immediately divine contents, but he differed from them in this, that he explained the supernatural lustre which adorns these histories, not as a fictitious colouring imparted with design to deceive, but as a natural and as it were spontaneous illumination reflected from antiquity itself.

In conformity with these principles Eichhorn sought to explain naturally the histories of Noah, Abraham, Moses, etc.   Viewed in the light of that age, the appointment of Moses to be the leader of the Israelites was nothing more than the long cherished project of the patriot to emancipate his people, which when presented before his mind with more than usual vividness in his dreams, was believed by him to be a divine inspiration.   The flame and smoke which ascended from Mount Sinai, at the giving of the law, was merely a fire which Moses kindled in order to make a deeper impression upon the imagination of the people, together with an accidental thunderstorm which arose at that particular moment.   The shining of his countenance was the natural effect of being over-heated : but it was supposed to be a divine manifestation, not only by the people, but by Moses himself, he being ignorant of the true cause.

Eichhorn was more reserved in his application of this mode of interpretation to the New Testament.   Indeed, it was only to a few of the narratives in the Acts of the Apostles, such as the miracle of the day of Pentecost, the conversion of the Apostle Paul, and the many apparitions of angels, that he allowed himself to apply it.   Here too, he refers the supernatural to the figurative language of the Bible ; in which, for example, a happy accident is called—a protecting angel ; a joyous thought—the salutation of an angel ; and a peaceful state of mind—a comforting angel.   It is however remarkable that

Eichhorn was conscious of the inapplicability of the natural explanation to some parts of the gospel history, and with respect to many of the narratives took a more elevated view.

Many writings in a similar spirit, which partially included the New Testament within the circle of their explanations, appeared ; but it was Dr. Paulus who by his commentary on the Gospels [2] in 1800, first acquired the full reputation of a *christian Evemerus*. In the introduction to this work he states it to be the primary requisite of the biblical critic to be able to distinguish between what is *fact*, and what is *opinion*. That which has been actually experienced, internally or externally, by the participants in an event, he calls *fact*. The interpretation of an event, the supposed causes to which it is referred either by the participants or by the narrators, he calls *opinion*. But, according to Dr. Paulus, these two elements become so easily blended and confounded in the minds both of the original sharers in an event, and of the subsequent relators and historians, that fact and opinion lose their distinction ; so that the one and the other are believed and recorded with equal confidence in their historical truth. This intermixture is particularly apparent in the historical books of the New Testament ; since at the time when Jesus lived, it was still the prevailing disposition to derive every striking occurrence from an invisible and superhuman cause. It is consequently the chief task of the historian who desires to deal with matters of fact, that is to say, in reference to the New Testament, to separate these two constituent elements so closely amalgamated, and yet in themselves so distinct ; and to extricate the pure kernel of fact from the shell of opinion. In order to this, in the absence of any more genuine account which would serve as a correcting parallel, he must transplant himself in imagination upon the theatre of action, and strive to the utmost to contemplate the events by the light of the age in which they occurred. And from this point of view he must seek to supply the deficiencies of the narration, by filling in those explanatory collateral circumstances, which the relator himself is so often led by his predilection for the supernatural to leave unnoticed. It is well known in what manner Dr. Paulus applies these principles to the New Testament in his Commentary, and still more fully in his later production, " The Life of Jesus." He firmly maintains the historical truth of the gospel narratives, and he aims to weave them into one consecutive chronologically-arranged detail of facts ; but he explains away every trace of immediate divine agency, and denies all supernatural intervention. Jesus is not to him the *Son of God* in the sense of the Church, but a wise and virtuous human being ; and the effects he produced are not miracles, but acts sometimes of benevolence and friendship, sometimes of medical skill, sometimes also the results of accident and good fortune.

This view proposed by Eichhorn, and more completely developed by Paulus, necessarily presupposes the Old and New Testament writings to contain a minute and faithful narration, composed shortly after the occurrence of the events recorded, and derived, wherever this was possible, from the testimony of eye-witnesses. For it is only from an accurate and original report that the ungarbled fact can be disentangled from interwoven opinion. If the report be later and less original, what security is there that what is taken for the matter-of-fact kernel does not belong to opinion or tradition? To avoid this objection, Eichhorn sought to assign a date to the Old Testament histories approximating as nearly as possible to the events they record : and here he, and other theologians of the same school, found no difficulty in admitting suppositions the most unnatural: for example, that the Pentateuch was written during the passage through the wilderness. However this critic admits that

---

[2] Paulus's Commentar über das neue Testament.

some portions of the Old Testament, the Book of Judges, for instance, could not have been written contemporaneously with the events ; that the historian must have contemplated his heroes through the dim mist of intervening ages, which might easily have magnified them into giant forms.   No historian who had either witnessed the circumstances, or had been closely connected with them in point of time, could embellish after such fashion, except with the express aim to amuse at the expense of truth.   But with regard to remote occurrences it is quite different.   The imagination is no longer restricted by the fixed limits of historical reality, but is aided in its flight by the notion that in earlier times all things were better and nobler ; and the historian is tempted to speak in loftier phrase, and to use hyperbolical expressions. Least of all is it possible to avoid embellishment, when the compiler of a subsequent age derives his materials from the orally transmitted traditions of antiquity.   The adventures and wondrous exploits of ancestors, handed down by father to son, and by son to grandson, in glowing and enthusiastic representations, and sung by the poet in lofty strains, are registered in the written records of the historian in similar terms of high flowing diction.   Though Eichhorn took this view of a portion of the Old Testament Books, he believed he was not giving up their historical basis, but was still able, after clearing away the more or less evident legendary additions, to trace out the natural course of the history.

But in one instance at least, this master of the natural mode of interpretation in reference to the Old Testament, took a more elevated view :—namely, of the history of the creation and the fall.   In his influential work on primitive history,[3] although he had from the first declared the account of the creation to be poetry, he nevertheless maintained that of the fall to be neither mythology nor allegory, but true history.   The historical basis that remained after the removal of the supernatural, he stated to be this : that the human constitution had at the very beginning become impaired by the eating of a poisonous fruit.   He thought it indeed very possible in itself, and confirmed by numerous examples in profane history, that purely historical narratives might be overlaid by a mythical account ; but owing to a supranaturalistic notion, he refused to allow the same possibility to the Bible, because he thought it unworthy of the Deity to admit a mythological fragment into a book, which bore such incontestable traces of its divine origin.   Later, however, Eichhorn himself declared that he had changed his opinion with regard to the second and third chapters of Genesis.[4]   He no longer saw in them an historical account of the effects of poison, but rather the mythical embodying of a philosophical thought ; namely, that the desire for a better condition than that in which man actually is, is the source of all the evil in the world.   Thus, in this point at least, Eichhorn preferred to give up the history in order to hold fast the idea, rather than to cling to the history with the sacrifice of every more elevated conception.   For the rest, he agreed with Paulus and others in considering the miraculous in the sacred history as a drapery which needs only to be drawn aside, in order to disclose the pure historic form.

§ 7.

MORAL INTERPRETATION OF KANT.

Amidst these natural explanations which the end of the eighteenth century brought forth in rich abundance, it was a remarkable interlude to see the old

---

[3] Eichhorn's Urgeschichte, herausgegeben von Gabler, 3 Thl. s. 98. ff.
[4] Allgem. Biblioth. 1 Bd. s. 989, and Einleitung in das A. T. 3 Thl. s. 82.

allegorical system of the christian fathers all at once called up from its grave, and revived in the form of the moral interpretation of Kant. He, as a philosopher, did not concern himself with the history, as did the rationalist theologians, but like the fathers of the church, he sought the idea involved in the history : not however considering it as they did an absolute idea, at once theoretical as well as practical, but regarding it only on its practical side, as what he called *the moral imperative* and consequently belonging to the finite. He moreover attributed these ideas wrought into the biblical text, not to the Divine Spirit, but to its philosophical interpreters, or in a deeper sense, to the moral condition of the authors of the book themselves. This opinion Kant [1] bases upon the fact, that in all religions old and new which are partly comprised in sacred books, intelligent and well-meaning teachers of the people have continued to explain them, until they have brought their actual contents into agreement with the universal principles of morality. Thus did the moral philosophers amongst the Greeks and Romans with their fabulous legends ; till at last they explained the grossest polytheism as mere symbolical representations of the attributes of the one divine Being, and gave a mystical sense to the many vicious actions of their gods, and to the wildest dreams of their poets, in order to bring the popular faith, which it was not expedient to destroy, into agreement with the doctrines of morality. The later Judaism and Christianity itself he thinks have been formed upon similar explanations, occasionally much forced, but always directed to objects undoubtedly good and necessary for all men. Thus the Mahometans gave a spiritual meaning to the sensual descriptions of their paradise, and thus the Hindoos, or at least the more enlightened part of them, interpreted their Vedas. In like manner, according to Kant, the Christian Scriptures of the Old and New Testament, must be interpreted throughout in a sense which agrees with the universal practical laws of a religion of pure reason : and such an explanation, even though it should, apparently or actually, do violence to the text, which is the case with many of the biblical narratives, is to be preferred to a literal one, which either contains no morality at all or is in opposition to the moral principle. For example, the expressions breathing vengeance against enemies in many of the Psalms are made to refer to the desires and passions which we must strive by all means to bring into subjection ; and the miraculous account in the New Testament of the descent of Jesus from heaven, of his relationship to God, etc., is taken as an imaginative description of the ideal of humanity well-pleasing to God. That such an interpretation is possible, without even always too offensive an opposition to the literal sense of these records of the popular faith, arises according to the profound observations of Kant from this : that long before the existence of these records, the disposition to a moral religion was latent in the human mind ; that its first manifestations were directed to the worship of the Deity, and on this very account gave occasion to those pretended revelations ; still, though unintentionally, imparting even to these fictions somewhat of the spiritual character of their origin. In reply to the charge of dishonesty brought against his system of interpretation, he thinks it a sufficient defence to observe, that it does not pretend that the sense now given to the sacred books, always existed in the intention of the authors ; this question it sets aside, and only claims for itself the right to interpret them after its own fashion.

Whilst Kant in this manner sought to educe moral thoughts from the biblical writings, even in their historical part, and was even inclined to consider these

---

[1] Religion innerhalb der Grenzen der blossen Vernunft, drittes Stück. No. **VI.** : Der Kirchenglaube hat zu seinem höchsten Ausleger den reinen Religionsglauben.

thoughts as the fundamental object of the history : on the one hand, he derived these thoughts only from himself and the cultivation of his age, and
therefore could seldom assume that they had actually been laid down by the
authors of those writings ; and on the other hand, and for the same reason,
he omitted to show what was the relation between these thoughts and those
symbolic representations, and how it happened that the one came to be expressed by the other.

§ 8.

RISE OF THE MYTHICAL MODE OF INTERPRETING THE SACRED HISTORY, IN REFERENCE FIRST TO THE OLD TESTAMENT.

It was impossible to rest satisfied with modes of proceeding so unhistorical
on the one hand, and so unphilosophical on the other.   Added to which, the
study of mythology, now become far more general and more prolific in its
results, exerted an increasing influence on the views taken of biblical history.
Eichhorn had indeed insisted that all primitive histories, whether Hebrew or
Pagan, should be treated alike, but this equality gradually disappeared ; for
though the mythical view became more and more developed in relation to
profane history, the natural mode of explanation was still rigidly adhered to
for the Hebrew records.   All could not imitate Paulus, who sought to establish consistency of treatment by extending the same natural explanation
which he gave to the Bible, to such also of the Greek legends as presented any
points of resemblance ; on the contrary, opinion in general took the opposite
course, and began to regard many of the biblical narratives as mythi. Semler had already spoken of a kind of Jewish mythology, and had even called
the histories of Samson and Esther mythi ; Eichhorn too had done much to
prepare the way, now further pursued by Gabler, Schelling, and others, who
established the notion of the mythus as one of universal application to ancient
history, sacred as well as profane, according to the principle of Heyne : *A
mythis omnis priscorum hominum cum historia tum philosophia procedit.*[1]   And
Bauer in 1820 ventured so far as to publish a Hebrew mythology of the Old
and New Testament.[2]   The earliest records of all nations are, in the opinion
of Bauer, mythical : why should the writings of the Hebrews form a solitary
exception ?—whereas in point of fact a cursory glance at their sacred books
proves that they also contain mythical elements.   A narrative he explains,
after Gabler and Schelling, to be recognizable as mythus, first, when it proceeds from an age in which no written records existed, but in which facts were
transmitted through the medium of oral tradition alone ; secondly, when it
presents an historical account of events which are either absolutely or relatively beyond the reach of experience, such as occurrences connected with the
spiritual world, and incidents to which, from the nature of the circumstances,
no one could have been witness ; or thirdly, when it deals in the marvellous
and is couched in symbolical language.   Not a few narratives of this description occur in the Bible ; and an unwillingness to regard them as mythi can arise
only from a false conception of the nature of a mythus, or of the character of
the biblical writings.   In the one case mythi are confounded with fables, premeditated fictions, and wilful falsehoods, instead of being recognised as the
necessary vehicle of expression for the first efforts of the human mind ; in the
other case it certainly does appear improbable, (the notion of inspiration

---

[1] Ad. Apollod. Athen. Biblioth. notæ, p. 3 f.
[2] Hebraische Mythologie des alten und neuen Testaments. G. L. Bauer, 1802.

presupposed,) that God should have admitted the substitution of mythical for actual representations of facts and ideas, but a nearer examination of the scriptures shows that this very notion of inspiration, far from being any hindrance to the mythical interpretation, is itself of mythical origin.

Wegscheider ascribed this greater unwillingness to recognise mythi in the early records of the Hebrew and Christian religion than in the heathen religions, partly to the prevailing ignorance respecting the progress of historical and philosophical science; partly to a certain timidity which dares not call things manifestly identical by the same name.   At the same time he declared it impossible to rescue the Bible from the reproaches and scoffs of its enemies except by the acknowledgment of mythi in the sacred writings, and the separation of their inherent meaning from their unhistorical form.[3]

These biblical critics gave the following general definition of the mythus. It is the representation of an event or of an idea in a form which is historical, but, at the same time characterized by the rich pictorial and imaginative mode of thought and expression of the primitive ages.   They also distinguished several kinds of mythi.[4]

1st. *Historical mythi:* narratives of real events coloured by the light of antiquity, which confounded the divine and the human, the natural and the supernatural.

2nd. *Philosophical mythi:* such as clothe in the garb of historical narrative a simple thought, a precept, or an idea of the time.

3rd. *Poetical mythi:* historical and philosophical mythi partly blended together, and partly embellished by the creations of the imagination, in which the original fact or idea is almost obscured by the veil which the fancy of the poet has woven around it.

To classify the biblical mythi according to these several distinctions is a difficult task, since the mythus which is purely symbolical wears the semblance of history equally with the mythus which represents an actual occurrence.   These critics however laid down rules by which the different mythi might be distinguished.   The first essential is, they say, to determine whether the narrative have a distinct object, and what that object is.   Where no object, for the sake of which the legend might have been invented, is discoverable, every one would pronounce the mythus to be *historical*.   But if all the principal circumstances of the narrative concur to symbolize a particular truth, this undoubtedly was the object of the narrative, and the mythus is *philosophical*.   The blending of the historical and philosophical mythus is particularly to be recognised when we can detect in the narrative an attempt to derive events from their causes.   In many instances the existence of an historical foundation is proved also by independent testimony; sometimes certain particulars in the mythus are intimately connected with known genuine history, or bear in themselves undeniable and inherent characteristics of probability : so that the critic, while he rejects the external form, may yet retain the groundwork as historical.   The *poetical* mythus is the most difficult to distinguish, and Bauer gives only a negative criterion.   When the narrative is so wonderful on the one hand as to exclude the possibility of its being a detail of facts, and when on the other it discovers no attempt to symbolize a particular thought, it may be suspected that the entire narrative owes its birth to the imagination of the poet.   Schelling particularly remarks on the unartificial and spontaneous origin of mythi in general.   The unhistorical

[3] Institutiones Theol. Chr. Dogm. § 42.
[4] Ammon, Progr. quo inquiritur in narrationum de vitæ Jesu Christi primordiis fontes, etc., in Pott's and Ruperti's Sylloge Comm. theol. No. 5, und Gabler's n. theol. Journal, 5 Bd. s. 83 und 397.

which is interwoven with the matters of fact in the historical mythus is not, he observes, the artistical product of design and invention. It has on the contrary glided in of itself, as it were, in the lapse of time and in the course of transmission. And, speaking of philosophical mythi, he says: the sages of antiquity clothed their ideas in an historical garb, not only in order to accommodate those ideas to the apprehension of a people who must be awakened by sensible impressions, but also on their own account: deficient themselves in clear abstract ideas, and in ability to give expression to their dim conceptions, they sought to illumine what was obscure in their representations by means of sensible imagery.[5]

We have already remarked, that the natural mode of interpreting the Old Testament could be maintained only so long as the records were held to be contemporaneous, or nearly so, with the events recorded. Consequently it was precisely those theologians, Vater, De Wette and others who controverted this opinion, who contributed to establish the mythical view of the sacred histories. Vater[6] expressed the opinion that the peculiar character of the narrations in the Pentateuch could not be rightly understood, unless it were conceded that they are not the production of an eye witness, but are a series of transmitted traditions. Their traditional origin being admitted, we cease to feel surprised at the traces which they discover of a subsequent age; at numerical exaggerations, together with other inaccuracies and contradictions; at the twilight which hangs over many of the occurrences; and at representations such as, that the clothes of the Israelites waxed not old during their passage through the wilderness. Vater even contends, that unless we ascribe a great share of the marvellous contained in the Pentateuch to tradition, we do violence to the original sense of the compilers of these narratives.

The natural mode of explanation was still more decidedly opposed by De Wette than by Vater. He advocated the mythical interpretation of a large proportion of the Old Testament histories. In order to test the historical credibility of a narrative, he says,[7] we must ascertain the intention of the narrator. If that intention be not to satisfy the natural thirst for historical truth by a simple narration of facts, but rather to delight or touch the feelings, or to illustrate some philosophical or religious truth, then his narrative has no pretension to historical validity. Even when the narrator is conscious of strictly historical intentions, nevertheless his point of view may not be the historical: he may be a poetical narrator, not indeed subjectively, as a poet drawing inspiration from himself, but objectively, as enveloped by and depending on poetry external to himself. This is evidently the case when the narrator details as bonâ fide matter of fact things which are impossible and incredible, which are contrary not only to experience, but to the established laws of nature. Narrations of this description spring out of tradition. Tradition, says De Wette, is uncritical and partial; its tendency is not historical, but rather patriotic and poetical. And since the patriotic sentiment is gratified by all that flatters national pride, the more splendid, the more honourable, the more wonderful the narrative, the more acceptable it is; and where tradition has left any blanks, imagination at once steps in and fills them up. And since, he continues, a great part of the historical books of the Old Testament bear this stamp, it has hitherto been believed possible (on the part of the natural interpreters) to separate the embellishments and trans-

---

[5] Ueber Mythen, historische Sagen und Philospheme der ältesten Welt. In Paulus Memorabilien, 5 stuck. 1793.

[6] Vid. die Abhandlung über Moses und die Verfasser des Pentateuchs, im 3ten. Band des Comm. über den Pent. s. 660.

[7] Kritik der Mosaischen Geschichte. Einl. s. 10. ff.

formations from the historical substance, and still to consider them available as records of facts. This might indeed be done, had we, besides the marvellous biblical narratives, some other purely historical account of the events. But this is not the case with regard to the Old Testament history; we are solely dependent on those accounts which we cannot recognize as purely historical. They contain no criterion by which to distinguish between the true and the false; both are promiscuously blended, and set forth as of equal dignity. According to De Wette, the whole natural mode of explanation is set aside by the principle that the only means of acquaintance with a history is the narrative which we possess concerning it, and that beyond this narrative the historian cannot go. In the present case, this reports to us only a supernatural course of events, which we must either receive or reject: if we reject it, we determine to know nothing at all about it, and are not justified in allowing ourselves to invent a natural course of events, of which the narrative is totally silent. It is moreover inconsistent and arbitrary to refer the dress in which the events of the Old Testament are clothed to poetry, and to preserve the events themselves as historical; much rather do the particular details and the dress in which they appear, constitute a whole belonging to the province of poetry and mythus. For example, if God's covenant with Abraham be denied in the form of fact, whilst at the same time it is maintained that the narrative had an historical basis,—that is to say, that though no objective divine communication took place, the occurrence had a subjective reality in Abraham's mind in a dream or in a waking vision; in other words, that a natural thought was awakened in Abraham which he, in the spirit of the age, referred to God:—of the naturalist who thus reasons, De Wette asks, how he knows that such thoughts arose in Abraham's mind? The narration refers them to God; and if we reject the narration, we know nothing about these thoughts of Abraham, and consequently cannot know that they had arisen naturally in him. According to general experience, such hopes as are described in this covenant, that he should become the father of a mighty nation which should possess the land of Canaan, could not have sprung up naturally in Abraham's mind; but it is quite natural that the Israelites when they had become a numerous people in possession of that land, should have invented the covenant in order to render their ancestor illustrious. Thus the natural explanation, by its own unnaturalness, ever brings us back to the mythical.

Even Eichhorn, who so extensively employed the natural explanation in reference to the Old Testament, perceived its inadmissibility in relation to the gospel histories. Whatever in these narratives has a tendency to the supernatural, he remarks,[8] we ought not to attempt to transform into a natural occurrence, because this is impossible without violence. If once an event has acquired a miraculous colouring, owing to the blending together of some popular notion with the occurrence, the natural fact can be disentangled only when we possess a second account which has not undergone the like transformation; as, concerning the death of Herod Agrippa, we have not only the narrative in the Acts, but also that of Josephus.[9] But since we have no such controlling account concerning the history of Jesus, the critic who pretends to discover the natural course of things from descriptions of supernatural occurrences, will only weave a tissue of indemonstrable hypotheses:—a consideration which, as Eichhorn observes, at once annihilates many of the so-called psychological interpretations of the Gospel histories.

---

[8] Einleit. in das N. T. 1, s. 408. ff.
[9] Antiquit. xix. viii. 2.

It is this same difference between the natural and mythical modes of interpretation which Krug intends to point out, referring particularly to the histories of miracles, when he distinguishes the physical or material, from the genetic or formal, mode of explaining them. Following the former mode, according to him, the inquiry is : how can the wonderful event here related have possibly taken place with all its details by natural means and according to natural laws ? Whereas, following the latter, the question is : whence arose the narrative of the marvellous event ? The former explains the natural possibility of the thing related (the substance of the narrative) ; the latter traces the origin of the existing record (the form of the narrative). Krug considers attempts of the former kind to be fruitless, because they produce interpretations yet more wonderful than the fact itself ; far preferable is the other mode, since it leads to results which throw light upon miraculous histories collectively. He gives the preference to the exegetist, because in his explanation of the text he is not obliged to do violence to it, but may accept it altogether literally as the author intended, even though the thing related be impossible ; whereas the interpreter, who follows the material or physical explanation, is driven to ingenious subtleties which make him lose sight of the original meaning of the authors, and substitute something quite different which they neither could nor would have said.

In like manner Gabler recommended the mythical view, as the best means of escaping from the so called natural, but forced explanation, which had become the fashion. The natural interpreter, he remarks, commonly aims to make the whole narrative natural ; and as this can but seldom succeed, he allows himself the most violent measures, owing to which modern exegesis has been brought into disrepute even amongst laymen. The mythical view, on the contrary, needs no such subtleties ; since the greater part of a narrative frequently belongs to the mythical representation merely, while the nucleus of fact, when divested of the subsequently added miraculous envelopments, is often very small.

Neither could Horst reconcile himself to the atomistic mode of proceeding, which selected from the marvellous narratives of the Bible, as unhistorical, isolated incidents merely, and inserted natural ones in their place, instead of recognizing in the whole of each narrative a religious moral mythus in which a certain idea is embodied.

An anonymous writer in Bertholdt's Journal has expressed himself very decidedly against the natural mode of explaining the sacred history, and in favour of the mythical. The essential defect of the natural interpretation, as exhibited in its fullest development by Paulus's Commentary, is, according to that writer, its unhistorical mode of procedure. He objects : that it allows conjecture to supply the deficiencies of the record ; adopts individual speculations as a substitute for real history ; seeks by vain endeavours to represent that as natural which the narrative describes as supernatural ; and lastly, evaporates all sacredness and divinity from the Scriptures, reducing them to collections of amusing tales no longer meriting the name of history. According to our author, this insufficiency of the natural mode of interpretation, whilst the supernatural also is felt to be unsatisfactory, leads the mind to the mythical view, which leaves the substance of the narrative unassailed ; and instead of venturing to explain the details, accepts the whole, not indeed as true history, but as a sacred legend. This view is supported by the analogy of all antiquity, political and religious, since the closest resemblance exists between many of the narratives of the Old and New Testament, and the mythi of profane antiquity. But the most convincing argument is this : if the mythical view be once admitted, the innumerable, and never otherwise to be harmonized, discrepancies and chronological contradictions in the gospel histories disappear, as it were, at one stroke.[10]

§ 9.

THE MYTHICAL MODE OF INTERPRETATION IN REFERENCE TO THE NEW TESTAMENT.

Thus the mythical mode of interpretation was adopted not only in relation to the Old Testament, but also to the New; not, however, without its being felt necessary to justify such a step. Gabler has objected to the Commentary of Paulus, that it concedes too little to the mythical point of view, which must be adopted for certain New Testament narratives. For many of these narratives present not only those mistaken views of things which might have been taken by eye-witnesses, and by the rectification of which a natural course of events may be made out; but frequently, also, false facts and impossible consequences which no eye-witness could have related, and which could only have been the product of tradition, and must therefore be mythically understood.[1]

The chief difficulty which opposed the transference of the mythical point of view from the Old Testament to the New, was this :—it was customary to look for mythi in the fabulous primitive ages only, in which no written records of events as yet existed; whereas, in the time of Jesus, the mythical age had long since passed away, and writing had become common among the Jews. Schelling had however conceded (at least in a note) that the term mythi, in a more extended sense, was appropriate to those narratives which, though originating in an age when it was usual to preserve documentary records, were nevertheless transmitted by the mouth of the people. Bauer[2] in like manner asserted, that though a connected series of mythi,—a history which should be altogether mythical,—was not to be sought in the New Testament, yet there might occur in it single myths, either transferred from the Old Testament to the New, or having originally sprung up in the latter. Thus he found, in the details of the infancy of Jesus, much which requires to be regarded from a mythical point of view. As after the decease of celebrated personages, numerous anecdotes are circulated concerning them, which fail not to receive many and wondrous amplifications in the legends of a wonder-loving people; so, after Jesus had become distinguished by his life, and yet more glorified by his death, his early years, which had been passed in obscurity, became adorned with miraculous embellishments. And, according to Bauer, whenever in this history of the infancy we find celestial beings, called by name and bearing the human shape, predicting future occurrences, etc., we have a right to suppose a mythus; and to conjecture as its origin, that the great actions of Jesus being referred to superhuman causes, this explanation came to be blended with the history. On the same subject, Gabler[3] remarked that the notion of ancient is relative; compared with the Mosaic religion Christianity is certainly young; but in itself it is old enough to allow us to refer the original history of its founder to ancient times. That at that time written documents on other subjects existed, proves nothing,

---

[10] Die verschiedenen Rücksichten, in welchen und für welche der Biograph Jesu arbeiten kann. In Bertholdt's krit. Journal, 5 Bd. s. 235. ff.

[1] Recens-von Paulus Commentar, im neuesten theol. Journal 7, 4, s. 395 ff. (1801).

[2] Hebräische Mythologie. 1 Thl. Einl. § 5.

[3] Ist es erlaubt, in der Bibel, und sogar im N.T., Mythen anzunehmen? Im Journal für auserlesene theol. Literatur, 2, 1, s. 49 ff.

whilst it can be shown that for a long period there was no written account of the life of Jesus, and particularly of his infancy. Oral narratives were alone transmitted, and they would easily become tinged with the marvellous, mixed with Jewish ideas, and thus grow into historical mythi. 'On many other points there was no tradition, and here the mind was left to its own surmises. The more scanty the historical data, the greater was the scope for conjecture ; and historical guesses and inferences of this description, formed in harmony with the Jewish-Christian tastes, may be called the philosophical, or rather, the dogmatical mythi of the early christian Gospel. The notion of the mythus, concludes Gabler, being thus shown to be applicable to many of the narratives of the New Testament, why should we not dare to call them by their right name ; why—that is to say in learned discussion—avoid an expression which can give offence only to the prejudiced or the misinformed?

As in the Old Testament Eichhorn had been brought over by the force of internal evidence from his earlier natural explanation, to the mythical view of the history of the fall ; so in the New Testament, the same thing happened to Usteri in relation to the history of the temptation.   In an earlier work he had, following Schleiermacher, considered it as a parable spoken by Jesus but misunderstood by his disciples.[4] Soon however he perceived the difficulties of this interpretation ; and since both the natural and the supernatural views of the narrative appeared to him yet more objectionable, he had no alternative but to adopt the mythical. Once admit, he remarks, a state of excitement, particularly of religious excitement, among a not unpoetical people, and a short time is sufficient to give an appearance of the marvellous not only to obscure and concealed, but even to public and well-known facts. It is therefore by no means conceivable that the early Jewish Christians, gifted with the spirit, that is, animated with religious enthusiasm, as they were, and familiar with the Old Testament, should not have been in a condition to invent symbolical scenes such as the temptation and other New Testament mythi. It is not however to be imagined that any one individual seated himself at his table to invent them out of his own head, and write them down, as he would a poem : on the contrary, these narratives like all other legends were fashioned by degrees, by steps which can no longer be traced ; gradually acquired consistency, and at length received a fixed form in our written Gospels.

We have seen that in reference to the early histories of the Old Testament, the mythical view could be embraced by those only who doubted the composition of these Scriptures by eye-witnesses or contemporaneous writers. This was equally the case in reference to the New. It was not till Eichhorn [5] became convinced that only a slender thread of that primitive Gospel believed by the Apostles ran through the three first Gospels, and that even in Matthew this thread was entangled in a mass of unapostolic additions, that he discarded as unhistorical legends, the many narratives which he found perplexing, from all share in the history of Jesus ; for example, besides the Gospel of Infancy, the details of the temptation ; several of the miracles of Jesus ; the rising of the saints from their graves at his crucifixion ; the guard at the sepulchre, etc.[6] Particularly since the opinion, that the three first Gospels originated from oral traditions, became firmly established,[7] they have been found to

[4] Ueber den Täufer Johannes, die Taufe und Versuchung Christi, in Ullmann's u. Umbreit's theol. Studien u. Kritiken, 2, 3, s. 456 ff.
[5] Beitrag zur Erklärung der Versuchungsgeschichte, in ders. Zeitschrift, 1832, 4. Heft.
[6] Einleitung in das N. T. I, s. 422 ff. 453 ff.
[7] Besonders durch Gieseler, über die Entstehung und die frühsten Schicksale der schriftlichen Evangelien.

contain a continually increasing number of mythi and mythical embellishments.[8] On this account the authenticity of the Gospel of John, and consequently its historical credibility, is confidently maintained by most of the theologians of the present day : he only who, with Bretschneider,[9] questions its apostolic composition, may cede in this Gospel also a considerable place to the mythical element.

§ 10.

THE NOTION OF THE MYTHUS IN ITS APPLICATION TO SACRED HISTORIES
NOT CLEARLY APPREHENDED BY THEOLOGIANS.

Thus, indeed, did the mythical view gain application to the biblical history : still the notion of the mythus was for a long time neither clearly apprehended nor applied to a due extent.

Not clearly apprehended. The characteristic which had been recognised as constituting the distinction between historical and philosophical mythi, however just that distinction might in itself be, was of a kind which easily betrayed the critic back again into the scarcely abandoned natural explanation. His task, with regard to historical mythi, was still to separate the natural fact—the nucleus of historical reality—from its unhistorical and miraculous embellishments. An essential difference indeed existed : the natural explanation attributed the embellishments to the opinion of the actors concerned, or of the narrator; the mythical interpretation derived them from tradition; but the mode of proceeding was left too little determined. If the Rationalist could point out historical mythi in the Bible, without materially changing his mode of explanation ; so the Supernaturalist on his part felt himself less offended by the admission of historical mythi, which still preserved to the sacred narratives a basis of fact, than by the supposition of philosophical mythi, which seemed completely to annihilate every trace of historical foundation. It is not surprising, therefore, that the interpreters who advocated the mythical theory spoke almost exclusively of historical mythi ; that Bauer, amongst a considerable number of mythi which he cites from the New Testament, finds but one philosophical mythus ; and that a mixed mode of interpretation, partly mythical and partly natural, (a medley far more contradictory than the pure natural explanation, from the difficulties of which these critics sought to escape,) should have been adopted. Thus Bauer[1] thought that he was explaining Jehovah's promise to Abraham as an historical mythus, when he admitted as the fundamental fact of the narrative, that Abraham's hopes of a numerous posterity were re-awakened by the contemplation of the star-sown heavens. Another theologian[2] imagined he had seized the mythical point of view, when, having divested the announcement of the birth of the Baptist of the supernatural, he still retained the dumbness of Zachariah as the historical groundwork. In like manner Krug,[3] immediately after assuring us that his intention is not to explain the substance of the history, (according to the natural mode,) but to explain the origin of the narrative, (according to the mythical view,) constitutes an accidental

---

[8] Vid. den Anhang der Schulz'schen Schrift über das Abendmahl, und die Schriften von Sieffert und Schneckenburger über den Ursprung des ersten kanonischen Evangeliums.
[9] In den Probabilien.
[1] Geschichte der hebräischen Nation, Theil. i. s. 123.
[2] In Henke's Magazin, 5ten Bdes. 1tes Stuck. s. 163.
[3] Versuch über die genetische oder formelle Erklärungsart de Wunder. In Henke's Museum, i. 3. 1803.

journey of oriental merchants the basis of the narrative of the visit of the wise men from the east.   But the contradiction is most glaring when we meet with palpable misconceptions of the true nature of a mythus in a work on the mythology of the New Testament, such as Bauer's ; in which for instance he admits, in the case of the parents of John the Baptist, a marriage which had actually been childless during many years ;—in which he explains the angelic appearance at the birth of Jesus as a meteoric phenomenon ; supposes the occurrence of thunder and lightning and the accidental descent of a dove at his baptism ; constitutes a storm the groundwork of the transfiguration; and converts the angels at the tomb of the risen Jesus into white grave-clothes.   Kaiser also, though he complains of the unnaturalness of many of the natural explanations, accords to a very considerable proportion of natural explanations a place by the side of the mythical ; remarking—and the remark is in itself just—that to attempt to explain all the miracles of the New Testament in one and the same manner betrays a limited and partial comprehension of the subject.   Let it be primarily admitted that the ancient author intended to narrate a miracle, and the natural explanation is in many instances admissible.   This may be either a physical-historical explanation, as in the narrative of the leper whose approaching recovery Jesus doubtless perceived ; or it may be a psychological explanation ; since, in the case of many sick persons, the fame of Jesus and faith in him were mainly instrumental in effecting the cure; sometimes indeed good fortune must be taken into the account, as where one apparently dead revived in the presence of Jesus, and he became regarded as the author of the sudden re-animation. With respect to other miracles Kaiser is of opinion that the mythical interpretation is to be preferred ; he, however, grants a much larger space to historical, than to philosophical mythi.   He considers most of the miracles in the Old and New Testament real occurrences mythically embellished : such as the narrative of the piece of money in the fish's mouth ; and of the changing of water into wine : which latter history he supposes to have originated from a friendly jest on the part of Jesus.   Few only of the miracles are recognised by this critic as pure poetry embodying Jewish ideas ; as the miraculous birth of Jesus, and the murder of the innocents.[4]

Gabler in particular calls attention to the error of treating philosophical mythi as if they were historical, and of thus converting into facts things that never happened.[5]   He is however as little disposed to admit the exclusive existence of philosophical, as of historical mythi in the New Testament, but adopting a middle course, he decides in each case that the mythus is of this kind or of that according to its intrinsic character.   He maintains that it is as necessary to guard against the arbitrary proceeding of handling as philosophical a mythus through which a fact unquestionably glimmers, as it is to avoid the opposite tendency to explain naturally or historically that which belongs properly to the mythical clothing.   In other words : when the derivation of a mythus from a thought is easy and natural, and when the attempt to educe from it a matter of fact and to give the wonderful history a natural explanation, does violence to the sense or appears ridiculous, we have, according to Gabler, certain evidence that the mythus is philosophical and not historical.   He remarks in conclusion that the philosophical-mythical interpretation is in many cases far less offensive than the historical-mythical explanation.[6]

Yet, notwithstanding this predilection in favour of the philosophical mythus

[4] Kaiser's biblische Theologie, 1 Thl.
[5] Gabler's Journal für auserlesene theol. Literatur. ii. 1. s. 46.
[6] Gabler's neuestes theolog. Journal, 7 Bd.

in relation to biblical history, one is surprised to find that Gabler himself was ignorant of the true nature both of the historical and of the philosophical mythus. Speaking of the mythological interpreters of the New Testament who had preceded him, he says that some of them, such as Dr. Paulus, discover in the history of Jesus historical mythi only; whilst others, the anonymous E. F. in Henke's Magazine for instance, find only philosophical mythi. From this we see that he confounded not only the natural explanation with the historical-mythical view, (for in Paulus's "Commentar" the former only is adopted,) but also historical with philosophical mythi ; for the author E. F. is so exclusively attached to the historical-mythical view that his explanations might almost be considered as naturalistic.

De Wette has some very cogent observations directed equally against the arbitrary adoption either of the historical-mythical or of the natural explanation in relation to the Mosaic history. In reference to the New Testament an anonymous writer in Bertholdt's Critical Journal[7] is the most decided in his condemnation of every attempt to discover an historical groundwork even in the Gospel mythi. To him likewise the midway path struck out by Gabler, between the exclusive adoption of historical mythi on the one hand and of philosophical mythi on the other, appears inapplicable ; for though a real occurrence may in fact constitute the basis of most of the New Testament narratives, it may still be impossible at the present time to separate the element of fact from the mythical adjuncts which have been blended with it, and to determine how much may belong to the one and how much to the other. Usteri likewise expressed the opinion that it is no longer possible to discriminate between the historical and the symbolical in the gospel mythi ; no critical knife however sharp is now able to separate the one element from the other. A certain measure of *probability* respecting the preponderance of the historical in one legend, and of the symbolical in another, is the ultimate point to which criticism can now attain. *

Opposed however to the onesidedness of those critics who found it so easy to disengage the historical contents from the mythical narratives of the Scriptures, is the onesidedness of other critics, who, on account of the difficulty of the proposed separation, despaired of the possibility of success, and were consequently led to handle the whole mass of gospel mythi as philosophical, at least in so far as to relinquish the endeavour to extract from them a residuum of historical fact. Now it is precisely this latter onesidedness which has been attributed to my criticism of the life of Jesus ; consequently, several of the reviewers of this work have taken occasion repeatedly to call attention to the varying proportions in which the historical and the ideal in the pagan religion and primitive history, (the legitimate province of the mythus,) alternate ; an interchange with the historical which in the christian primitive history, presupposing the notion of the mythus to be admitted here, must unquestionably take place in a far greater degree. Thus Ullmann distinguishes not only firstly the *philosophical*, and secondly the *historical mythus*, but makes a further distinction between the latter (that is the *historical mythus*, in which there is always a preponderance of the fictitious,) and thirdly the *mythical history*, in which the historical element, though wrought into the ideal, forms the predominating constituent ; whilst fourthly in *histories of which the legend is a component element* we tread properly speaking upon historical ground, since in these histories we meet only with a few faint echoes of mythical fiction. Ullmann is moreover of opinion, and Bretschneider and others agree with him, that independently of the re-

pulsion and confusion which must inevitably be caused by the application of
the term *mythus* to that which is Christian—a term originally conceived in
relation to a religion of a totally different character—it were more suitable,
in connexion with the primitive Christian records, to speak only of Gospel
legend, (Sage) and the legendary element.[8]

George on the contrary has recently attempted not only more accurately to
define the notions of the mythus and of the legend, but likewise to demonstrate that the gospel narratives are mythical rather than legendary. Speaking
generally, we should say, that he restricts the term *mythus* to what had
previously been distinguished as philosophical mythi; and that he applies
the name *legend* to what had hitherto been denominated historical mythi.
He handles the two notions as the antipodes of each other ; and grasps them
with a precision by which the notion of the mythus has unquestionably
gained. According to George, *mythus* is the creation of a fact out of an
idea : *legend* the seeing of an idea in a fact, or arising out of it. A people, a
religious community, finds itself in a certain condition or round of institutions
of which the spirit, the idea, lives and acts within it. But the mind, following
a natural impulse, desires to gain a complete representation of that existing
condition, and to know its origin. This origin however is buried in oblivion,
or is too indistinctly discernible to satisfy present feelings and ideas. Consequently an image of that origin, coloured by the light of existing ideas, is
cast upon the dark wall of the past, which image is however but a magnified
reflex of existing influences.

If such be the rise of the *mythus*, the *legend*, on the contrary, proceeds
from given facts : represented, indeed, sometimes in an incomplete and
abridged, sometimes in an amplified form, in order to magnify the heroes of
the history—but disjoined from their true connexion ; the points of view
from which they should be contemplated, and the ideas they originally
contained, having in the course of transmission wholly disappeared. The
consequence is, that new ideas, conceived in the spirit of the different ages
through which the legend has passed down, become substituted in the stead
of the original ideas. For example, the period of Jewish history subsequent
to the time of Moses, which was in point of fact pervaded by a gradual
elevation of ideas to monotheism and to a theocracy, is, in a later legend,
represented in the exactly opposite light, as a state of falling away from the
religious constitution of Moses. An idea so unhistorical will infallibly here
and there distort facts transmitted by tradition, fill up blanks in the history,
and subjoin new and significant features—and then the mythus reappears in
the legend. It is the same with the mythus : propagated by tradition, it, in
the process of transmission, loses its distinctive character and completeness,
or becomes exaggerated in its details—as for example in the matter of
numbers—and then the mythus comes under the influence of the legend.
In such wise do these two formations, so essentially distinct in their origin,
cross each other and mingle together. Now, if the history of the life of Jesus
be of mythical formation, inasmuch as it embodies the vivid impression of
the original idea which the first christian community had of their founder,
this history, though unhistorical in its form, is nevertheless a faithful representation of the idea of the Christ. If instead of this, the history be legendary—
if the actual external facts are given in a distorted and often magnified form
—are represented in a false light and embody a false idea,—then, on the contrary, the real tenour of the life of Jesus is lost to us. So that, according to
George, the recognition of the mythical element in the Gospels is far less

---

[8] Ullmann, Recens. meines L. J., in den Theol. Studien u. Kritiken 1836. 3.

prejudicial to the true interests of the Christian faith than the recognition of the legendary element.[9]

With respect to our own opinion, without troubling ourselves here with the dogmatic signification, we need only remark in this introduction, that we are prepared to meet with both legend and mythus in the gospel history; and when we undertake to extract the historial contents which may possibly exist in narratives recognized as mythical, we shall be equally careful neither on the one part by a rude and mechanical separation, to place ourselves on the same ground with the natural interpreter; nor on the other by a hyper-critical refusal to recognize such contents where they actually exist, to lose sight of the history.

§ 11.

THE APPLICATION OF THE NOTION OF THE MYTHUS TOO CIRCUMSCRIBED.

The notion of the mythus, when first admitted by theologians, was not only imperfectly apprehended, but also too much limited in its application to biblical history.

As Eichhorn recognized a genuine mythus only on the very threshold of the Old Testament history, and thought himself obliged to explain all that followed in a natural manner; as, some time later, other portions of the Old Testament were allowed to be mythical, whilst nothing of the kind might be suspected in the New; so, when the mythus was once admitted into the New Testament, it was here again long detained at the threshold, namely, the history of the infancy of Jesus, every farther advance being contested. Ammon,[1] the anonymous E. F. in Henke's Magazine, Usteri, and others maintained a marked distinction between the historical worth of the narratives of the public life and those of the infancy of Jesus. The records of the latter could not, they contend, have been contemporaneous; for particular attention was not at that time directed towards him; and it is equally manifest that they could not have been written during the last three years of his life, since they embody the idea of Jesus glorified, and not of Jesus in conflict and suffering. Consequently their composition must be referred to a period subsequent to his resurrection. But at this period accurate data concerning his childhood were no longer to be obtained. The apostles knew him first in manhood. Joseph was probably dead; and Mary, supposing her to be living when the first and third gospels were composed, had naturally imparted an imaginative lustre to every incident treasured in her memory, whilst her embellishments were doubtless still further magnified in accordance with the Messianic ideas of those to whom her communications were made. Much also that is narrated had no historical foundation, but originated entirely from the notions of the age, and from the Old Testament predictions—that a virgin should conceive—for example. But, say these critics, all this does not in any degree impair the credibility of what follows. The object and task of the Evangelists was merely to give an accurate account of the three last years of the life of Jesus; and here they merit implicit confidence, since they were either themselves spectators of the details they record, or else had learned them from the mouth of trustworthy eye-witnesses. This boundary line between

---

[9] George, Mythus und Sage; Versuch einer wissenschaftlichen Entwicklung dieser Begriffe und ihres Verhältnisses zum christlichen Glauben, s. 11.ff. 108. ff.
[1] Work cited, § 8, note 4. Hase, Leben Jesu, § 32. Tholuck, s. 208. ff. Kern, die Hauptsachen der evangelischen Geschichte, 1st Article, Tübinger Zeitschrift für Theologie, 1836, ii. s. 39.

the credibility of the history of the public life, and the fabulousness of the history of the infancy of Jesus, became yet more definitely marked, from the circumstance that many theologians were disposed to reject the two first chapters of Matthew and Luke as spurious and subsequent additions.[2]

Soon, however, some of the theologians who had conceded the commencement of the history to the province of mythi, perceived that the conclusion, the history of the ascension, must likewise be regarded as mythical.[3] Thus the two extremities were cut off by the pruning knife of criticism, whilst the essential body of the history, the period from the baptism to the resurrection, remained, as yet, unassailed : or in the words of the reviewer of Greiling's Life of Jesus :[4] the entrance to the gospel history was through the decorated portal of mythus, and the exit was similar to it, whilst the intermediate space was still traversed by the crooked and toilsome paths of natural interpretations.

In Gabler's [5] writings we meet with a somewhat more extended application of the mythical view. He distinguishes (and recently Rosenkranz [6] has agreed with him) between the miracles wrought *by* Jesus and those operated *on him* or *in relation to him*, interpreting the latter mythically, but the former naturally. Subsequently however, we find Gabler expressing himself as if with the above mentioned theologians he restricted the mythical interpretation to the miraculous narratives of the childhood of Jesus, but this restriction is in fact a limitation merely of the admitted distinction : since though all the miracles connected with the early history of Jesus were operated in relation to him and not wrought by him, many miracles of the same character occur in the history of his public life. Bauer appears to have been guided by the same rule in his Hebrew mythology. He classes as mythical the narratives of the conception and birth of Jesus, of the Baptism, the transfiguration, the angelic apparitions in Gethsemane and at the sepulchre : miracles selected from all periods of the life of Jesus, but all operated in relation to him and not by him. This enumeration, however, does not include all the miracles of this kind.

The often referred to author of the treatise " Upon the different views with which and for which a Biographer of Jesus may work," has endeavoured to show that so limited an application of the notion of the mythus to the history of the life of Jesus is insufficient and inconsequent. This confused point of view from which the gospel narrative is regarded as partly historical and partly mythical owes its origin, according to him, to those theologians who neither give up the history, nor are able to satisfy themselves with its clear results, but who think to unite both parties by this middle course—a vain endeavour which the rigid supranaturalist pronounces heretical, and the rationalist derides. The attempt of these reconcilers, remarks our author, to explain as intelligible everything which is not impossible, lays them open to all the charges so justly brought against the natural interpretation ; whilst the admission of the existence of mythi in the New Testament subjects them to the direct reproach of being inconsequent : the severest censure which can be passed upon a scholar. Besides, the proceeding of these Eclectics is most arbitrary, since they decide respecting what belongs to the history and what to the mythus almost entirely upon subjective grounds. Such distinctions

[2] Comp. Kuinöl, Prolegom. in Matthæum, § 3 ; in Lucam, § 6.

[3] e. g. Ammon, in der Diss. : Ascensus J. C. in cœlum historia biblica, in seinen Opusc. nov.

[4] In Bertholdt's Krit. Journ. v. Bd. s. 248.

[5] Gabler's neuestes theol. Journal, Bd. vii. s. 395.

[6] Encyclopädie der theol. Wissenschaften, s. 161.

are equally foreign to the evangelists, to logical reasoning, and to historical criticism. In consistency with these opinions, this writer applies the notion of the mythus to the entire history of the life of Jesus; recognizes mythi or mythical embellishments in every portion, and ranges under the category of mythus not merely the miraculous occurrences during the infancy of Jesus, but those also of his public life; not merely miracles operated on Jesus, but those wrought by him. *

The most extended application of the notion of the philosophical or dogmatical mythus to the Gospel histories which has yet been made, was published in 1799 in an anonymous work concerning Revelation and Mythology. The writer contends that the whole life of Jesus, all that he should and would do, had an ideal existence in the Jewish mind long prior to his birth. Jesus as an individual was not actually such as according to Jewish anticipations he should have been. Not even that, in which all the records which recount his actions agree, is absolutely matter of fact. A popular idea of the life of Jesus grew out of various popular contributions, and from this source our written Gospels were first derived. A reviewer objects that this author appears to suppose a still smaller portion of the historical element in the gospels than actually exists. It would, he remarks, have been wiser to have been guided by a sober criticism of details, than by a sweeping scepticism.[7]

§ 12.

OPPOSITION TO THE MYTHICAL VIEW OF THE GOSPEL HISTORY.

In adopting the mythical point of view as hitherto applied to Biblical history, our theologians had again approximated to the ancient allegorical interpretation. For as both the natural explanations of the Rationalists, and the jesting expositions of the Deists, belong to that form of opinion which, whilst it sacrifices all divine meaning in the sacred record, still upholds its historical character; the mythical mode of interpretation agrees with the allegorical, in relinquishing the historical reality of the sacred narratives in order to preserve to them an absolute inherent truth. The mythical and the allegorical view (as also the moral) equally allow that the historian apparently relates that which is historical, but they suppose him, under the influence of a higher inspiration known or unknown to himself, to have made use of this historical semblance merely as the shell of an *idea*—of a religious conception. The only essential distinction therefore between these two modes of explanation is, that according to the allegorical this higher intelligence is the immediate divine agency; according to the mythical, it is the spirit of a people or a community. (According to the moral view it is generally the mind of the interpreter which suggests the interpretation.) Thus the allegorical view attributes the narrative to a supernatural source, whilst the mythical view ascribes it to that *natural* process by which legends are originated and developed. To which it should be added, that the allegorical interpreter (as well as the moral) may with the most unrestrained arbitrariness separate from the history every thought he deems to be worthy of God, as constituting its inherent meaning; whilst the mythical interpreter, on the contrary, in searching out the ideas which are embodied in the narrative, is controlled by regard to conformity with the spirit and modes of thought of the people and of the age.

This new view of the sacred Scriptures was opposed alike by the orthodox

[7] In Gabler's neuestem theolog. Journal, Bd. vi. 4tes Stück. s. 350.

and by the rationalistic party. From the first, whilst the mythical interpretation was still restricted to the primitive history of the Old Testament, Hess [1]
on the orthodox side, protested against it. The three following conclusions
may be given as comprising, however incredible this may appear, the substance of his book, a work of some compass ; upon which however it is unnecessary to remark further than that Hess was by no means the last orthodox
theologian who pretended to combat the mythical view with such weapons.
He contends, 1st, that mythi are to be understood figuratively ; now the
sacred historians intended their writings to be understood literally : consequently they do not relate mythi. 2ndly, Mythology is something heathen-
ish ; the Bible is a christian book ; consequently it contains no mythology.
The third conclusion is more complex, and, as will appear below, has more
meaning. If, says Hess, the marvellous were confined to those earliest
biblical records of which the historical validity is less certain, and did not
appear in any subsequent writings, the miraculous might be considered as a
proof of the mythical character of the narrative ; but the marvellous is no less
redundant in the latest and undeniably historical records, than in the more
ancient ; consequently it cannot be regarded as a criterion of the mythical. In
short the most hollow natural explanation, did it but retain the slightest vestige
of the historical—however completely it annihilated every higher meaning,—
was preferable, in the eyes of the orthodox, to the mythical interpretation.
Certainly nothing could be worse than Eichhorn's natural explanation of the
fall. In considering the tree of knowledge as a poisonous plant, he at once
destroyed the intrinsic value and inherent meaning of the history ; of this he
afterwards became fully sensible, and in his subsequent mythical interpretation, he recognized in. the narrative the incorporation of a worthy and
elevated conception. Hess however declared himself more content with
Eichhorn's original explanation, and defended it against his later mythical
interpretation. So true is it that supranaturalism clings with childlike fondness to the empty husk of historical semblance, though void of divine significance, and estimates it higher than the most valuable kernel divested of its
variegated covering.

Somewhat later De Wette's bold and thorough application of the mythical
view to the Mosaic writings ; his decided renunciation of the so-called *historical-mythical*, or more properly speaking of the natural mode of interpretation ;
and his strict opposition to the notion of the possibility of arriving at any
certainty respecting the residue of fact preserved in these writings, gave rise
to much controversy. Some agreed with Steudel in totally rejecting the
mythical view in relation to the Bible, and in upholding the strictly historical
and indeed supranatural sense of the Scriptures : whilst Meyer and others
were willing to follow the guidance of De Wette, at least as far as the principles
of Vater, which permitted the attempt to extract some, if only probable,
historical data from the mythical investment. If, says Meyer[2], the marvellousness and irrationality of many of the narratives contained in the Pentateuch,
(narratives which no one would have thought of inventing,) together with the
want of symmetry and connexion in the narration, and other considerations,
permit us not to mistake the historical groundwork of the record ; surely,
allowing the existence of an historical basis, a modest and cautious attempt
to seek out or at any rate to approximate towards a discovery of that historical

---

[1] Gränzbestimmung dessen, was in der Bibel Mythus, u. s. f., und was wirkliche
Geschichte ist. In seiner Bibliothek der heiligen Geschichte, ii. Bd. s. 155. ff.
[2] Meyer, Apologie der geschichtlichen Auffassung der historischen Bücher des A. T.,
besonders des Pentateuchs, im Gegensatz gegen die blos mythische Deutung des letztern.
Fritzsche. Kelle.

foundation is admissible. In the hope of preserving those who adopted the historical-mythical view from relapsing into the inconsistencies of the natural interpreters, Meyer laid down the following rules, which however serve rather to exhibit afresh the difficulty of escaping this danger. 1. To abstract every thing which is at once recognizable as mythical representation as opposed to historical fact ; that is the extraordinary, the miraculous, accounts of immediate divine operation, also the religious notions of the narrators in relation to final causes. 2. To proceed from that which is simple to that which is more complicated. Let a case be supposed where we have two accounts of the same event, the one natural, the other supernatural, as, for instance. the gathering of the elders by Moses, attributed, Numbers, xi. 16., to the suggestion of Jehovah, and Exodus, xviii. 14., to the counsel of Jethro. According to this rule all divine inspiration must be subtracted from the known decisions of Noah, Abraham, Moses, and others. (Precisely the proceeding which met with the censure of De Wette quoted above.) 3. As far as possible to contemplate the fact which forms the basis of a narrative, in its ·simple and common character, apart from all collateral incidents. (This however, is going too far where no basis of fact exists.) For example. The story of the deluge may be reduced thus ; a great inundation in Asia Minor, according to the legend, destroyed many wicked. (Here the supposed final cause is not abstracted.) Noah the father of Shem, a devout man, (*the teleological* notion again !) saved himself by swimming. The exact circumstances of this preservation, the character of the vessel, if such there were, which saved him, are left undetermined in order to avoid arbitrary explanations. Thus, in reference to the birth of Isaac, Meyer is satisfied with saying, that the wish and hope of the wealthy and pious Emir Abraham to possess an heir by his wife Sara was fulfilled unusually late, and in the eyes of others very unexpectedly. (Here again De Wette's censure is quite applicable.)

In like manner Eichhorn, in his Introduction to the New Testament, declared in yet stronger terms his opposition to the view advocated by De Wette. If the orthodox were displeased at having their historical faith disturbed by the progressive inroads of the mythical mode of interpretation, the rationalists were no less disconcerted to find the web of facts they had so ingeniously woven together torn asunder, and all the art and labour expended on the natural explanation at once declared useless. Unwillingly does Dr. Paulus admit to himself the presentiment that the reader of his Commentary may possibly exclain : " Wherefore all this labour to give an historical explanation to such legends? how singular thus to handle mythi as history, and to attempt to render marvellous fictions intelligible according to the rules of causality ! " Contrasted with the toilsomeness of his natural explanation, the mythical interpretation appears to this theologian merely as the refuge of mental indolence, which, seeking the easiest method of treating the gospel history, disposes of all that is marvellous, and all that is difficult to comprehend, under the vague term—mythus, and which, in order to escape the labour of disengaging the natural from the supernatural, fact from opinion, carries back the whole narration into the *camera-obscura* of ancient sacred legends.[3]

Still more decided was Greiling's [4] expression of disapprobation, elicited by Krug's commendation of the *genetic*—that is to say, mythical theory ; but each stroke levelled by him at the mythical interpretation may be turned with far greater force against his own natural explanation. He is of opinion that among all the attempts to explain obscure passages in the New Testament,

[3] Exegetisches Handbuch, i. a. s. 1, 71.
[4] Greiling in Henke's Museum. i. 4. s. 621. ff.

scarcely any can be more injurious to the genuine historical interpretation, to the ascertaining of actual facts and their legitimate objects (that is, more prejudicial to the pretensions of the natural expounder) than the endeavour to supply, by aid of an inventive imagination, the deficiencies of the historical narrative. (The inventive imagination is that of the natural interpreter, which suggests to him collateral incidents of which there is no trace in the text. The imagination of the mythical interpreter is not inventive ; his part is merely the recognizing and detecting of the fictitious.) According to Greiling the *genetic*, or mythical mode of explaining miracles, is a needless and arbitrary invention of the imagination. (Let a groping spirit of inquiry be added, and the natural explanation is accurately depicted.) Many facts, he continues, which might be retained as such are thus consigned to the province of fable, or replaced by fictions the production of the interpreter. (But it is the *historical* mythical mode of interpretation alone which substitutes such inventions, and this only in so far as it is mixed up with the natural explanation.) Greiling thinks that the explanation of a miracle ought not to change the fact, and by means of interpretation, as by sleight of hand, substitute one thing for another ; (which is done by the natural explanation only,) for this is not to explain that which shocks the reason, but merely to deny the fact, and leave the difficulty unsolved. (It is false to say we have a fact to explain ; what immediately lies before us is a statement, respecting which we have to discover whether it embody a fact or not.) According to this learned critic the miracles wrought by Jesus should be naturally, or rather psychologically, explained ; by which means all occasion to change, clip, and amplify by invention the recorded facts, till at length they become metamorphosed into fiction, is obviated—(with how much justice this censure may be applied to the natural mode of explanation has been sufficiently demonstrated.)

Heydenreich has lately written a work expressly on the inadmissibility of the mythical interpretation of the historical portions of the New Testament. He reviews the external evidences concerning the origin of the Gospels, and finds the recognition of a mythical element in these writings quite incompatible with their substantiated derivation from the Apostles, and the disciples of the Apostles. He also examines the character of the gospel representations, and decides, in reference to their form, that narratives at once so natural and simple, so complete and exact, could be expected only from eyewitnesses, or those connected with them ; and, with respect to their contents, that those representations which are in their nature miraculous are so worthy of God, that nothing short of an abhorrence of miracles could occasion a doubt as to their historical truth. The divine operations are indeed generally mediate, but according to Heydenreich this by no means precludes the possibility of occasional intermediate exertions of the divine energy, when requisite to the accomplishment of some particular object ; and, referring to each of the divine attributes in succession, he shows that such intervention in nowise contradicts any of them ; and that each individual miracle is a peculiarly appropriate exercise of divine power.

These, and similar objections against the mythical interpretation of the gospel histories, which occur in recent commentaries and in the numerous writings in opposition to my work on the life of Jesus, will find their place and refutation in the following pages. *

§ 13.

THE POSSIBILITY OF THE EXISTENCE OF MYTHI IN THE NEW TESTAMENT
CONSIDERED IN REFERENCE TO THE EXTERNAL EVIDENCES.

The assertion that the Bible contains mythi is, it is true, directly opposed
to the convictions of the believing christian. For if his religious view be
circumscribed within the limits of his own community, he knows no reason
why the things recorded in the sacred books should not literally have taken
place ; no doubt occurs to him, no reflection disturbs him. But, let his
horizon be so far widened as to allow him to contemplate his own religion in
relation to other religions, and to draw a comparison between them, the conclusion to which he then comes is that the histories related by the heathens
of their deities, and by the Mussulman of his prophet, are so many fictions,
whilst the accounts of God's actions, of Christ and other Godlike men contained in the Bible are, on the contrary, true. Such is the general notion
expressed in the theological position : that which distinguishes Christianity
from the heathen religions is this, they are mythical, it is historical.

But this position, thus stated without further definition and proof, is merely
the product of the limitation of the individual to that form of belief in which
he has been educated, which renders the mind incapable of embracing any
but the affirmative view in relation to its own creed, any but the negative in
reference to every other—a prejudice devoid of real worth, and which cannot
exist in conjunction with an extensive knowledge of history. For let us
transplant ourselves among other religious communities ; the believing
Mohammedan is of opinion that truth is contained in the Koran alone,
and that the greater portion of our Bible is fabulous ; the Jew of the present
day, whilst admitting the truth and divine origin of the Old Testament, rejects
the New ; and, the same exclusive belief in the truth of their own creed and
the falsity of every other was entertained by the professors of most of the
heathen religions before the period of the Syncretism. But which community
is right ? Not all, for this is impossible, since the assertion of each excludes
the others. But which particular one ? Each claims for itself the true faith.
The pretensions are equal; what shall decide? The origin of the several
religions ? Each lays claim to a divine origin. Not only does the Christian
religion profess to be derived from the Son of God, and the Jewish from God
himself, through Moses; the Mohammedan religion asserts itself to be
founded by a prophet immediately inspired by God ; in like manner the
Greeks attributed the institution of their worship to the gods.

" But in no other religion " it is urged " are the vouchers of a divine origin
so unequivocal as in the Jewish and the Christian. The Greek and Roman
mythologies are the product of a collection of unauthenticated legends,
whilst the Bible history was written by eye-witnesses ; or by those whose connexion with eye-witnesses afforded them opportunities of ascertaining the
truth ; and whose integrity is too apparent to admit of a doubt as to the
sincerity of their intentions." It would most unquestionably be an argument
of decisive weight in favour of the credibility of the biblical history, could it
indeed be shown that it was written by eye-witnesses, or even by persons nearly
contemporaneous with the events narrated. For though errors and false
representations may glide into the narrations even of an eye-witness, there is far
less probability of unintentional mistake (intentional deception may easily be
detected) than where the narrator is separated by a long interval from the

facts he records, and is obliged to derive his materials through the medium of transmitted communications.

But this alleged ocular testimony, or proximity in point of time of the sacred historians to the events recorded, is mere assumption, an assumption originating from the titles which the biblical books bear in our Canon. Those books which describe the departure of the Israelites from Egypt, and their wanderings through the wilderness, bear the name of Moses, who being their leader would undoubtedly give a faithful history of these occurrences, unless he designed to deceive; and who, if his intimate connexion with Deity described in these books be historically true, was likewise eminently qualified, by virtue of such connexion, to produce a credible history of the earlier periods. In like manner, of the several accounts of the life and fate of Jesus, the superscriptions assign one to Matthew and one to John : two men who having been eye-witnesses of the public ministry of Jesus from its commencement to its close were particularly capable of giving a report of it; and who, from their confidential intercourse with Jesus and his mother, together with that supernatural aid which, according to John, Jesus promised to his disciples to teach them and bring all things to their remembrance, were enabled to give information of the circumstances of his earlier years; of which some details are recorded by Matthew.

But that little reliance can be placed on the headings of ancient manuscripts, and of sacred records more especially, is evident, and in reference to biblical books has long since been proved. In the so-called books of Moses mention is made of his death and burial : but who now supposes that this was written beforehand by Moses in the form of prophecy? Many of the Psalms bear the name of David which presuppose an acquaintance with the miseries of the exile; and predictions are put into the mouth of Daniel, a Jew living at the time of the Babylonish captivity, which could not have been written before the reign of Antiochus Epiphanes. It is an incontrovertible position of modern criticism that the titles of the Biblical books represent nothing more than the design of their author, or the opinion of Jewish or Christian antiquity respecting their origin; points the first of which proves nothing; and as to the second every thing depends upon the following considerations : 1. the date of the opinion and the authority on which it rests; 2. the degree of harmony existing between this opinion and the internal character of the writings in question. The first consideration includes an examination of the external, the second of the internal grounds of evidence respecting the authenticity of the biblical books. To investigate the internal grounds of credibility in relation to each detail given in the Gospels, (for it is with them alone we are here concerned) and to test the probability or improbability of their being the production of eye-witnesses, or of competently informed writers, is the sole object of the present work. The *external grounds* of evidence may be examined in this introduction, only so far however as is necessary in order to judge whether they yield a definite result, which may perhaps be in opposition to the internal grounds of evidence; or whether the external evidence, insufficient of itself, leaves to the internal evidence the decision of the question.

We learn from the works of Irenæus, of Clemens Alexandrinus, and of Tertullian, that at the end of the second century after Christ our four Gospels were recognized by the orthodox church as the writings of the Apostles and the disciples of the Apostles; and were separated from many other similar productions as authentic records of the life of Jesus. The first Gospel according to our Canon is attributed to Matthew, who is enumerated among the twelve Apostles; the fourth to John the beloved disciple of our Lord;

the second to Mark the interpreter of Peter; and the third to Luke the companion of Paul.[1] We have, besides, the authority of earlier authors, both in their own works and in quotations cited by others.

It is usual, in reference to the first Gospel, to adduce the testimony of Papias, Bishop of Hierapolis, said to have been an auditor ἀκουστὴς of John, (probably the presbyter) and to have suffered martyrdom under Marcus Aurelius. (161–180.) Papias asserts that Matthew the Apostle wrote τὰ λόγια (τὰ κυριακὰ[2]). Schleiermacher, straining the meaning of λόγια, has latterly understood it to signify merely a collection of the sayings of Jesus. But when Papias speaks of Mark, he seems to use σύνταξιν τῶν κυριακῶν λογίων ποιεῖσθαι, and τὰ ὑπὸ τοῦ Χριστοῦ ἢ λεχθέντα ἢ πραχθέντα γράφειν as equivalent expressions. Whence it appears that the word λόγια designates a writing comprehending the acts and fate of Jesus; and the fathers of the church were justified in understanding the testimony of Papias as relating to an entire Gospel.[3] They did indeed apply this testimony decidedly to our first Gospel; but the words of the Apostolic father contain no such indication, and the manuscript, of which he speaks, cannot be absolutely identical with our Gospel; for, according to the statement given by Papias, Matthew wrote in the Hebrew language; and it is a mere assumption of the christian fathers that our Greek Matthew is a translation of the original Hebrew Gospel[4]. Precepts of Jesus, and narratives concerning him, corresponding more or less exactly with passages in our Matthew, do indeed occur in the works of other of the apostolic fathers; but then these works are not wholly genuine, and the quotations themselves are either in a form which indicates that they might have been derived from oral traditions; or where these authors refer to written sources, they do not mention them as being directly apostolic. Many citations in the writings of Justin Martyr (who died 166) agree with passages in our Matthew; but there are also, mixed up with these, other elements which are not to be found in our Gospels; and he refers to the writings from which he derives them generally as ἀπομνημονεύματα τῶν ἀποστόλων, or εὐαγγέλια, without naming any author in particular. Celsus,[5] the opponent of Christianity, (subsequent to 150) mentions that the disciples of Jesus had written his history, and he alludes to our present Gospels when he speaks of the divergence of the accounts respecting the number of angels seen at the resurrection; but we find no more precise reference to any one Evangelist in his writings, so far as we know them through Origen.

We have the testimony of the same Papias who has the notice concerning Matthew, a testimony from the mouth of John (πρεσβύτερος), that Mark, who according to him was the interpreter of Peter (ἑρμηνευτὴς Πέτρου), wrote down the discourses and actions of Jesus from his recollections of the instructions of that Apostle.[6] Ecclesiastical writers have likewise assumed that this passage from Papias refers to our second Gospel, though it does not say any thing of the kind, and is besides inapplicable to it. For our second Gospel cannot have originated from recollections of Peter's instructions, i.e., from a source peculiar to itself, since it is evidently a compilation, whether made from memory or otherwise, from the first and third Gospels.[7] As little will the remark of Papias that Mark wrote without order (οὐ τάξει) apply to our

[1] See the quotations given by De Wette in his "Einleitung in d. N. T." § 76.
[2] Euseb. H. E., iii. 39.
[3] Ullman, Credner, Lücke, De Wette.
[4] Hieron. de vir. illustr. 3.
[5] Contra Celsum, ii. 16. v. 56.
[6] Euseb. H. E. iii. 39.
[7] This is clearly demonstrated by Griesbach in his "Commentatio, quâ Marci Evangelium totum e Matthæi et Lucæ commentariis decerptum esse demonstratur."

Gospel. For he cannot by this expression intend a false chronological arrangement, since he ascribes to Mark the strictest love of truth, which, united with the consciousness that he had not the means of fixing dates, must have withheld him from making the attempt. But a total renunciation of chronological connexion, which Papias can alone have meant to attribute to him, is not to be found in the second Gospel. This being the case, what do those echoes which our second Gospel, in like manner as our first, seems to find in the most ancient ecclesiastical writers, prove?

That Luke, the companion of Paul, wrote a Gospel, is not attested by any authority of corresponding weight or antiquity with that of Papias in relation to Matthew and to Mark. The third Gospel however possesses a testimony of a particular kind in the "Acts of the Apostles;" not indeed authenticating it as the composition of Luke, but attributing it to an occasional companion of the Apostle Paul. According to the proëm to the Acts and that to the Gospel of Luke, these two books proceeded from the same author or compiler: an origin which these writings do not, in other respects, contradict. In several chapters in the second half of the Book of the Acts the author, speaking of himself together with Paul, makes use of the first person plural,[8] and thus identifies himself with the companion of that apostle. The fact is, however, that many of the details concerning Paul, contained in other parts of the book of the Acts, are so indefinite and marvellous, and are moreover so completely at variance with Paul's genuine epistles, that it is extremely difficult to reconcile them with the notion that they were written by a companion of that apostle. It is also not a little remarkable that the author, neither in the introduction to the Acts, nor in that to the Gospel, alludes to his connexion with one of the most distinguished of the Apostles, so that it is impossible not to suspect that the passages in which the writer speaks of himself as an actor in the scenes described, belong to a distinct memorial by another hand, which the author of the Acts has merely incorporated into his history. But leaving this conjecture out of the question, it is indeed possible that the companion of Paul may have composed his two works at a time, and under circumstances, when he was no longer protected by Apostolic influence against the tide of tradition; and that he saw no reason why, because he had not heard them previously from this Apostle, he should therefore reject the instructive, and (according to his notions, which certainly would not lead him to shun the marvellous,) credible narratives derived from that source. Now, it is asserted that because the Book of the Acts terminates with the two years' imprisonment of Paul at Rome, therefore this second work of the disciple of that apostle, must have been written during that time, (63–65, A.D.) before the decision of Paul's trial, and that consequently, the Gospel of Luke, the earlier work of the same author, could not have been of later date. But, the breaking off of the Acts at that particular point might have been the result of many other causes; at all events such testimony, standing alone, is wholly insufficient to decide the historical worth of the Gospel.

It were to be wished that Polycarp, (he died 167) who both heard and saw the Apostle John,[9] had left us a testimony respecting him similar to that of Papias concerning Matthew. Still his silence on this subject, in the one short epistle which has come down to us, is no evidence against the authenticity of that Gospel, any more than the more or less ambiguous allusions in several of the Apostolic fathers to the *Epistles* of John are proofs in its favour. But it is matter of surprise that Irenæus the disciple of Polycarp, who was

---

[8] Chap. xvi. 10–17 ; xx. 5–15 ; xxi. 1–17 ; xxvii. 1–28 ; xxviii. 10–16.
[9] Euseb. H. E. v. 20, 24.

called upon to defend this Gospel from the attacks of those who denied its composition by John, should neither on this occasion, nor once in his diffuse work, have brought forward the weighty authority of his Apostolic master, as to this fact.   Whether or not the fourth Gospel originally bore the name of John remains uncertain.   We meet with it first among the Valentinians and the Montanists, about the middle of the second century.   Its Apostolic origin was however (immediately after) denied by the so-called Alogi, who ascribed it to Cerinthus ; partly because the Montanists derived from it their idea of the Paraclete ; partly also because it did not harmonize with the other Gospels.[10]   The earliest quotation expressly stated to be from the Gospel of John is found in Theophilus of Antioch, about the year 172.[11]   How little reason the numerous theologians of the present day have to boast of the evidences in favour of the fourth Gospel, whilst they deny the not less well attested Apocalypse, has been well remarked by Tholuck.   Lastly, that there were two Johns, the Apostle and the Presbyter, living contemporaneously at Ephesus, is a circumstance which has not received sufficient attention in connexion with the most ancient testimonies in favour of the derivation from John, of the Apocalypse on the one hand, and of the Gospels and Epistles on the other.*

Thus these most ancient testimonies tell us, firstly, that an apostle, or some other person who had been acquainted with an apostle, wrote a Gospel history ; but not whether it was identical with that which afterwards came to be circulated in the church under his name ; secondly, that writings similar to our Gospels were in existence ; but not that they were ascribed with certainty to any one individual apostle or companion of an apostle.   Such is the uncertainty of these accounts, which after all do not reach further back than the third or fourth decade of the second century.   According to all the rules of probability, the Apostles were all dead before the close of the first century ; not excepting John, who is said to have lived till A.D. 100 ; concerning whose age and death, however, many fables were early invented.   What an ample scope for attributing to the Apostles manuscripts they never wrote !   The Apostles, dispersed abroad, had died in the latter half of the first century ; the Gospel became more widely preached throughout the Roman empire, and by degrees acquired a fixed form in accordance with a particular type.   It was doubtless from this orally circulated Gospel that the many passages agreeing accurately with passages in our Gospels, which occur without any indication of their source in the earliest ecclesiastical writers, were actually derived.   Before long this oral traditionary Gospel became deposited in different manuscripts : this person or that, possibly an apostle, furnishing the principal features of the history.   But these manuscripts were not at first compiled according to a particular form and order, and consequently had to undergo many revisions and re-arrangements, of which we have an example in the Gospel of the Hebrews and the citations of Justin.   It appears that these manuscripts did not originally bear the names of their compilers, but either that of the community by whom they were first read, as the Gospel of Hebrews ; or that of the Apostle or disciple after whose oral discourses or notes some other person had composed a connected history.   The latter seems to have been the original meaning attached to the word κατὰ ; as in the title to our first Gospel.[12]   Nothing however was more natural than the supposition which arose among the early christians, that the histories concerning Jesus which were circulated and used by the churches had been

[10] De Wette, Gieseler.
[11] Ad. Autol. ii., 22.
[12] See Schleiermacher.

written by his immediate disciples. Hence the ascription of the gospel writings generally to the apostles by Justin and by Celsus ; and also of particular gospels to those particular apostles and disciples, whose oral discourses or written notes might possibly have formed the groundwork of a gospel manuscript, or who had perhaps been particularly connected with some certain district, or had been held in especial esteem by some particular community. The Gospel of the Hebrews successively received all three kinds of appellations; being first called εὐαγγέλιον καθ' Ἑβραίους, after the community by which it was read ; somewhat later, *Evangelium juxta duodecim apostolos ;* and finally, *secundum Matthæum.**

Admitting however that we do not possess the immediate record of an eye-witness in any one of the four Gospels, it is still very incomprehensible, replies the objector, how in Palestine itself, and at a time when so many eye-witnesses yet lived, unhistorical legends and even collections of them should have been formed. But, in the first place, the fact that many such compilations of narratives concerning the life of Jesus were already in general circulation during the lifetime of the Apostles, and more especially that any one of our gospels was known to an Apostle and acknowledged by him, can never be proved. With respect to isolated anecdotes, it is only necessary to form an accurate conception of Palestine and of the real position of the eye-witnesses referred to, in order to understand that the origination of legends, even at so early a period, is by no means incomprehensible. Who informs us that they must necessarily have taken root in that particular district of Palestine where Jesus tarried longest, and where his actual history was well known? And with respect to eye-witnesses, if by these we are to understand the Apostles, it is to ascribe to them absolute ubiquity, to represent them as present here and there, weeding out all the unhistorical legends concerning Jesus in whatever places they had chanced to spring up and flourish. Eye-witnesses in the more extended sense, who had only seen Jesus occasionally and not been his constant companions, must, on the contrary, have been strongly tempted to fill up their imperfect knowledge of his history with mythical representations.

But it is inconceivable, they say, that such a mass of mythi should have originated in an age so historical as that of the first Roman emperors. We must not however be misled by too comprehensive a notion of an historical age. The sun is not visible at the same instant to every place on the same meridian at the same time of year ; it gleams upon the mountain summits and the high plains before it penetrates the lower valleys and the deep ravines. No less true is it that the historic age dawns not upon all people at the same period. The people of highly civilized Greece, and of Rome the capital of the world, stood on an eminence which had not been reached in Galilee and Judæa. Much rather may we apply to this age an expression become trite among historians, but which seems in the present instance willingly forgotten : namely, that incredulity and superstition, scepticism and fanaticism go hand in hand.

But the Jews, it is said, had long been accustomed to keep written records ; nay, the most flourishing period of their literature was already past, they were no longer a progressing and consequently a productive people, they were a nation verging to decay. But the fact is, the pure historic idea was never developed among the Hebrews during the whole of their political existence ; their latest historical works, such as the Books of the Maccabees, and even the writings of Josephus, are not free from marvellous and extravagant tales. Indeed no just notion of the true nature of history is possible, without a perception of the inviolability of the chain of finite causes, and of the impossibility of miracles. This perception which is wanting to so many minds of our own day was still more deficient in Palestine, and indeed throughout the Roman empire. And to a mind still open to the reception of the marvellous, if it be once carried away by the tide of religious enthusiasm, all things will appear credible, and should this enthusiasm lay hold of a yet wider circle, it will awaken a new creative vigour, even in a decayed people. To account for such an enthusiasm it is by no means necessary to presuppose the gospel miracles as the existing cause. This may be found in the known religious dearth of that period, a dearth so great that the cravings of the mind after some religious belief excited a relish for the most extravagant forms of worship; secondly in the deep religious satisfaction which was afforded by the belief in the resurrection of the deceased Messiah, and by the essential principles of the doctrine of Jesus.

§ 14.

THE POSSIBILITY OF MYTHI IN THE NEW TESTAMENT CONSIDERED ON INTERNAL GROUNDS.

Seeing from what has already been said that the external testimony respecting the composition of our Gospels, far from forcing upon us the conclusion that they proceeded from eye-witnesses or well-informed contemporaries, leaves the decision to be determined wholly by internal grounds of evidence, that is, by the nature of the Gospel narratives themselves : we might immediately proceed from this introduction to the peculiar object of the present work, which is an examination of those narratives in detail. It may however appear useful, before entering upon this special inquiry, to consider the general question, how far it is consistent with the character of the Christian religion that mythi should be found in it, and how far the general construction of the Gospel narratives authorizes us to treat them as mythi. Although, indeed, if the following critical examination of the details be successful in proving the actual existence of mythi in the New Testament, this preliminary demonstration of their possibility becomes superfluous.

If with this view we compare the acknowledged mythical religions of antiquity with the Hebrew and Christian, it is true that we are struck by many differences between the sacred histories existing in these religious forms and those in the former. Above all, it is commonly alleged that the sacred histories of the Bible are distinguished from the legends of the Indians, Greeks, Romans, etc., by their moral character and excellence. "In the latter, the stories of the battles of the gods, the loves of Krishna, Jupiter, etc., contain much which was offensive to the moral feeling even of enlightened heathens, and which is revolting to ours : whilst in the former, the whole course of the narration, offers only what is worthy of God, instructive, and ennobling." To this it may be answered with regard to the heathens, that the appearance of immorality in many of their narratives is merely the consequence of a subsequent misconception of their original meaning : and with regard to the Old Testament, that the perfect moral purity of its history has been contested. Often indeed, it has been contested without good grounds, because a due distinction is not made between that which is ascribed to individual men, (who, as they are represented, are by no means spotless examples of purity,) and that which is ascribed to God :[1] nevertheless it is

---

[1] This same want of distinction has led the Alexandrians to allegorize, the Deists to scoff,

true that we have commands called divine, which, like that to the Israelites on their departure out of Egypt to purloin vessels of gold, are scarcely less revolting to an enlightened moral feeling, than the thefts of the Grecian Hermes. But even admitting this difference in the morality of the religions to its full extent (and it must be admitted at least with regard to the New Testament), still it furnishes no proof of the historical character of the Bible ; for though every story relating to God which is immoral is necessarily fictitious, even the most moral is not necessarily true.

"But that which is incredible and inconceivable forms the staple of the heathen fables ; whilst in the biblical history, if we only presuppose the immediate intervention of the Deity, there is nothing of the kind." Exactly, if this be presupposed. Otherwise, we might very likely find the miracles in the life of Moses, Elias, or Jesus, the Theophany and Angelophany of the Old and New Testament, just as incredible as the fables of Jupiter, Hercules, or Bacchus : presuppose the divinity or divine descent of these individuals, and their actions and fate become as credible as those of the biblical person-ages with the like presupposition. Yet not quite so, it may be returned. Vishnu appearing in his three first avatars as a fish, a tortoise, and a boar ; Saturn devouring his children ; Jupiter turning himself into a bull, a swan, etc.—these are incredibilities of quite another kind from Jehovah appearing to Abraham in a human form under the terebinth tree, or to Moses in the burning bush. This extravagant love of the marvellous is the character of the heathen mythology. A similar accusation might indeed be brought against many parts of the Bible, such as the tales of Balaam, Joshua, and Samson ; but still it is here less glaring, and does not form as in the Indian religion and in certain parts of the Grecian, the prevailing character. What however does this prove? Only that the biblical history *might* be true, sooner than the Indian or Grecian fables ; not in the least that on this account it *must* be true, and can contain nothing fictitious.

" But the subjects of the heathen mythology are for the most part such, as to convince us beforehand that they are mere inventions : those of the Bible such as at once to establish their own reality. A Brahma, an Ormusd, a Jupiter, without doubt never existed; but there still is a God, a Christ, and there have been an Adam, a Noah, an Abraham, a Moses." Whether an Adam or a Noah, however, were such as they are represented, has already been doubted, and may still be doubted. Just so, on the other side, there may have been something historical about Hercules, Theseus, Achilles, and other heroes of Grecian story. Here, again, we come to the decision that the biblical history might be true sooner than the heathen mythology, but is not necessarily so. This decision however, together with the two distinctions already made, brings us to an important observation. How do the Grecian divinities approve themselves immediately to us as non-existing beings, if not because things are ascribed to them which we cannot reconcile with our idea of the divine ? whilst the God of the Bible is a reality to us just in so far as he corresponds with the idea we have formed of him in our own minds. Besides the contradiction to our notion of the divine involved in the plurality of heathen gods, and the intimate description of their motives and actions, we are at once revolted to find that the gods themselves have a history ; that they are born, grow up, marry, have children, work out their purposes, suffer difficulties and weariness, conquer and are conquered. It is irreconcileable with our idea of the Absolute to suppose it subjected to time and change, to

and the Supernaturalists to strain the meaning of words ; as was done lately by Hoffmann in describing David's behaviour to the conquered Ammonites. (Christoterpe auf 1838, s. 184.)

opposition and suffering ; and therefore where we meet with a narrative in which these are attributed to a divine being, by this test we recognize it as unhistorical or mythical.

It is in this sense that the Bible, and even the Old Testament, is said to contain no mythi. The story of the creation with its succession of each day's labour ending in a rest after the completion of the task ; the expression often recurring in the farther course of the narrative, God repented of having done so and so ;—these and similar representations cannot indeed be entirely vindicated from the charge of making finite the nature of the Deity, and this is the ground which has been taken by mythical interpreters of the history of the creation.   And in every other instance where God is said to reveal himself exclusively at any definite place or time, by celestial apparition, or by miracle wrought immediately by himself, it is to be presumed that the Deity has become finite and descended to human modes of operation.   It may however be said in general, that in the Old Testament the divine nature does not appear to be essentially affected by the temporal character of its operation, but that the temporal shows itself rather as a mere form, an unavoidable appearance, arising out of the necessary limitation of human, and especially of uncultivated powers of representation.   It is obvious to every one, that there is something quite different in the Old Testament declarations, that God made an alliance with Noah, and Abraham, led his people out of Egypt, gave them laws, brought them into the promised land, raised up for them judges, kings, and prophets, and punished them at last for their disobedience by exile ;—from the tales concerning Jupiter, that he was born of Rhea in Crete, and hidden from his father Saturn in a cave ; that afterwards he made war upon his father, freed the Uranides, and with their help and that of the lightning with which they furnished him, overcame the rebellious Titans, and at last divided the world amongst his brothers and children.   The essential difference between the two representations is, that in the latter, the Deity himself is the subject of progression, becomes another being at the end of the process from what he was at the beginning, something being effected in himself and for his own sake : whilst in the former, change takes place only on the side of the world ; God remains fixed in his own identity as the I AM, and the temporal is only a superficial reflection cast back upon his acting energy by that course of mundane events which he both originated and guides.   In the heathen mythology the gods have a history : in the Old Testament, God himself has none, but only his people : and if the proper meaning of mythology be the history of gods, then the Hebrew religion has no mythology.

From the Hebrew religion, this recognition of the divine unity and immutability was transmitted to the Christian.   The birth, growth, miracles, sufferings, death, and resurrection of Christ, are circumstances belonging to the destiny of the Messiah, above which God remains unaffected in his own changeless identity.   The New Testament therefore knows nothing of mythology in the above sense.   The state of the question is however somewhat changed from that which it assumed in the Old Testament : for Jesus is called the Son of God, not merely in the same sense as kings under the theocracy were so called, but as actually begotten by the divine spirit, or from the incarnation in his person of the divine λόγος.   Inasmuch as he is one with the Father, and in him the whole fullness of the godhead dwells bodily, he is more than Moses.   The actions and sufferings of such a being are not external to the Deity : though we are not allowed to suppose a *theopaschitic* union with the divine nature, yet still, even in the New Testament, and more in the later doctrine of the Church, it is a divine being that here lives and suffers, and what befals him has an absolute worth and significance.

Thus according to the above accepted notion of the mythus, the New Testament has more of a mythical character than the Old. But to call the history of Jesus mythical in this sense, is as unimportant with regard to the historical question as it is unexceptionable ; for the idea of God is in no way opposed to such an intervention in human affairs as does not affect his own immutability ; so that as far as regards this point, the gospel history, notwithstanding its mythical designation, might be at the same time throughout historically true.

Admitting that the biblical history does not equally with the heathen mythology offend our idea of Deity, and that consequently it is not in like manner characterized by this mark of the unhistorical, however far it be from bearing any guarantee of being historical,—we are met by the further question whether it be not less accordant with our idea of the world, and whether such discordancy may not furnish a test of its unhistorical nature.

In the ancient world, that is, in the east, the religious tendency was so preponderating, and the knowledge of nature so limited, that the law of connexion between earthly finite beings was very loosely regarded. At every link there was a disposition to spring into the Infinite, and to see God as the immediate cause of every change in nature or the human mind. In this mental condition the biblical history was written. Not that God is here represented as doing all and every thing himself :—a notion which, from the manifold direct evidence of the fundamental connexion between finite things, would be impossible to any reasonable mind :—but there prevails in the biblical writers a ready disposition to derive all things down to the minutest details, as soon as they appear particularly important, immediately from God. He it is who gives the rain and sunshine ; he sends the east wind and the storm ; he dispenses war, famine, pestilence ; he hardens hearts and softens them, suggests thoughts and resolutions. And this is particularly the case with regard to his chosen instruments and beloved people. In the history of the Israelites we find traces of his immediate agency at every step : through Moses, Elias, Jesus, he performs things which never would have happened in the ordinary course of nature.

Our modern world, on the contrary, after many centuries of tedious research, has attained a conviction, that all things are linked together by a chain of causes and effects, which suffers no interruption. It is true that single facts and groups of facts, with their conditions and processes of change, are not so circumscribed as to be unsusceptible of external influence ; for the action of one existence or kingdom in nature intrenches on that of another : human freedom controls natural development, and material laws react on human freedom. Nevertheless the totality of finite things forms a vast circle, which, except that it owes its existence and laws to a superior power, suffers no intrusion from without. This conviction is so much a habit of thought with the modern world, that in actual life, the belief in a supernatural manifestation, an immediate divine agency, is at once attributed to ignorance or imposture. It has been carried to the extreme in that modern explanation, which, in a spirit exactly opposed to that of the Bible, has either totally removed the divine causation, or has so far restricted it that it is immediate in the act of creation alone, but mediate from that point onwards ;—i.e., God operates on the world only in so far as he gave to it this fixed direction at the creation. From this point of view, at which nature and history appear as a compact tissue of finite causes and effects, it was impossible to regard the narratives of the Bible, in which this tissue is broken by innumerable instances of divine interference, as historical.

It must be confessed on nearer investigation, that this modern explanation, although it does not exactly deny the existence of God, yet puts aside the idea of him, as the ancient view did the idea of the world. For this is, as it has been often and well remarked, no longer a God and Creator, but a mere finite Artist, who acts immediately upon his work only during its first production, and then leaves it to itself; who becomes excluded with his full energy from one particular sphere of existence. It has therefore been attempted to unite the two views so as to maintain for the world its law of sequence, and for God his unlimited action, and by this means to preserve the truth of the biblical history. According to this view, the world is supposed to move in obedience to the law of consecutive causes and effects bound up with its constitution, and God to act upon it only mediately : but in single instances, where he finds it necessary for particular objects, he is not held to be restricted from entering into the course of human changes immediately. This is the view of modern Supranaturalism [2]; evidently a vain attempt to reconcile two opposite views, since it contains the faults of both, and adds a new one in the contradiction between the two ill-assorted principles. For here the consecutiveness of nature and history is broken through as in the ancient biblical view ; and the action of God limited as in the contrary system. The proposition that God works sometimes mediately, sometimes immediately, upon the world, introduces a changeableness, and therefore a temporal element, into the nature of his action, which brings it under the same condemnation as both the other systems ; that, namely, of distinguishing the maintaining power, in the one case from individual instances of the divine agency, and in the other from the act of creation.[3]

Since then our idea of God requires an immediate, and our idea of the world a mediate divine operation ; and since the idea of combination of the two species of action is inadmissible :—nothing remains for us but to regard them both as so permanently and immoveably united, that the operation of God on the world continues for ever and every where twofold, both immediate and mediate ; which comes just to this, that it is neither of the two, or this distinction loses its value. To explain more closely : if we proceed from the idea of God, from which arose the demand for his immediate operation, then the world is to be regarded in relation to him as a Whole : on the contrary, if we proceed from the idea of the finite, the world is a congeries of separate parts, and hence has arisen the demand for a merely mediate agency of God :—so that we must say—God acts upon the world as a Whole immediately, but on each part only by means of his action on every other part, that is to say, by the laws of nature.[4]

This view brings us to the same conclusion with regard to the historical value of the Bible as the one above considered. The miracles which God wrought for and by Moses and Jesus, do not proceed from his immediate

---

[2] Heydenreich, über die Unzulässigkeit, u. s. f. 1 stück. Compare Storr, doctr. christ. § 35, ff.

[3] If the Supranatural view contains a theological contradiction, so the new evangelical theology, which esteems itself raised so far above the old supranatural view, contains a logical contradiction. To say that God acts only mediately upon the world as the general rule, but sometimes, by way of exception, immediately,—has some meaning, though perhaps not a wise one. But to say that God acts always immediately on the world, but in some cases more particularly immediately,—is a flat contradiction in itself. On the principle of the immanence or immediate agency of God in the world, to which the new evangelical theology lays claim, the idea of the miraculous is impossible. Comp. my Streitschriften, i. 3, s. 46 f.

[4] In this view essentially coincide Wegscheider, instit. theol. dogm. § 12 ; De Wette, bibl. Dogm., Vorbereitung ; Schleiermacher, Glaubensl. § 46 f. ; Marheineke, Dogm. § 269 ff. Comp. George, s. 78 f.

operation on the Whole, but presuppose an immediate action in particular cases, which is a contradiction to the type of the divine agency we have just given.   The supranaturalists indeed claim an exception from this type on behalf of the biblical history ; a presupposition which is inadmissible from our point of view [5], according to which the same laws, although varied by various circumstances, are supreme in every sphere of being and action, and therefore every narrative which offends against these laws, is to be recognized as so far unhistorical.

The result, then, however surprising, of a general examination of the biblical history, is that the Hebrew and Christian religions, like all others, have their mythi.   And this result is confirmed, if we consider the inherent nature of religion, what essentially belongs to it and therefore must be common to all religions, and what on the other hand is peculiar and may differ in each.   If religion be defined as the perception of truth, not in the form of an idea, which is the philosophic perception, but invested with imagery ; it is easy to see that the mythical element can be wanting only when religion either falls short of, or goes beyond, its peculiar province, and that in the proper religious sphere it must necessarily exist.

It is only amongst the lowest and most barbarous people, such as the Esquimaux, that we find religion not yet fashioned into an objective form, but still confined to a subjective feeling.   They know nothing of gods, of superior spirits and powers, and their whole piety consists in an undefined sentiment excited by the hurricane, the eclipse, or the magician.   As it progresses however, the religious principle loses more and more of this indefiniteness, and ceasing to be subjective, becomes objective.   In the sun, moon, mountains, animals, and other objects of the sensible world, higher powers are discovered and revered ; and in proportion as the significance given to these objects is remote from their actual nature, a new world of mere imagination is created a sphere of divine existences whose relations to one another, actions, and influences, can be represented only after human analogy, and therefore as temporal and historical.   Even when the mind has raised itself to the conception of the Divine unity, still the energy and activity of God are considered only under the form of a series of acts : and on the other hand, natural events and human actions can be raised to a religious significance only by the admission of divine interpositions and miracles.   It is only from the philosophic point of view that the world of imagination is seen again to coincide with the actual, because the thought of God is comprehended to be his essence, and in the regular course itself of nature and of history, the revelation of the divine idea is acknowledged.

It is certainly difficult to conceive, how narratives which thus speak of imagination as reality can have been formed without intentional deceit, and believed without unexampled credulity ; and this difficulty has been held an invincible objection to the mythical interpretation of many of the narratives of the Old and New Testament.   If this were the case, it would apply equally to the Heathen legends; and on the other hand, if profane Mythology have

---

[5] To a freedom from this presupposition we lay claim in the following work ; in the same sense as a state might be called free from presupposition where the privileges of station, etc., were of no account.   Such a state indeed has one presupposition, that of the natural equality of its citizens ; and similarly do we take for granted the equal amenability to law of all events ; but this is merely an affirmative form of expression for our former negation.   But to claim for the biblical history especial laws of its own, is an affirmative proposition, which, according to the established rule, is that which requires proof, and not our denial of it, which is merely negative.   And if the proof cannot be given, or be found insufficient, it is the former and not the latter, which is to be considered a presupposition.   See my Streitschriften i. 3. s. 36 ff. *

steered clear of the difficulty, neither will that of the Bible founder upon it. I shall here quote at length the words of an experienced inquirer into Grecian mythology and primitive history, Otfried Müller, since it is evident that this preliminary knowledge of the subject which must be derived from general mythology, and which is necessary for the understanding of the following examination of the evangelic mythus, is not yet familiar to all theologians. " How," says Müller [6], " shall we reconcile this combination of the true and the false, the real and ideal, in mythi, with the fact of their being believed and received as truth? The ideal, it may be said, is nothing else than poetry and fiction clothed in the form of a narration. But a fiction of this kind cannot be invented at the same time by many different persons without a miracle, requiring, as it does, a peculiar coincidence of intention, imagination, and expression. It is therefore the work of one person :—but how did he convince all the others that his fiction had an actual truth? Shall we suppose him to have been one who contrived to delude by all kinds of trickery and deception, and perhaps allied himself with similar deceivers, whose part it was to afford attestation to the people of his inventions as having been witnessed by themselves? Or shall we think of him as a man of higher endowments than others, who believed him upon his word ; and received the mythical tales under whose veil he sought to impart wholesome truths, as a sacred revelation? But it is impossible to prove that such a caste of deceivers existed in ancient Greece (or Palestine) ; on the contrary, this skilful system of deception, be it gross or refined, selfish or philanthropic, if we are not misled by the impression we have received from the earliest productions of the Grecian (or Christian) mind, is little suited to the noble simplicity of those times. Hence an inventer of the mythus in the proper sense of the word is inconceivable. This reasoning brings us to the conclusion, that the idea of a deliberate and intentional fabrication, in which the author clothes that which he knows to be false in the appearance of truth, must be entirely set aside as insufficient to account for the origin of the mythus. Or in other words, that there is a certain necessity in this connexion between the ideal and the real, which constitutes the mythus ; that the mythical images were formed by the influence of sentiments common to all mankind ; and that the different elements grew together without the author's being himself conscious of their incongruity. It is this notion of a certain necessity and unconsciousness in the formation of the ancient mythi, on which we insist. If this be once understood, it will also be perceived that the contention whether the mythus proceed from one person or many, from the poet or the people, though it may be started on other grounds, does not go to the root of the matter. For if the one who invents the mythus is only obeying the impulse which acts also upon the minds of his hearers, he is but the mouth through which all speak, the skilful interpreter who has the address first to give form and expression to the thoughts of all. It is however very possible that this notion of necessity and unconsciousness, might appear itself obscure and mystical to our antiquarians (and theologians), from no other reason than that this mythicising tendency has no analogy in the present mode of thinking. But is not history to acknowledge even what is strange, when led to it by unprejudiced research? "

As an example to show that even very complicated mythi, in the formation of which many apparently remote circumstances must have combined, may

---

[6] Prolegomena zu einer wissenschaftlichen Mythologie, s. 110 ff. With this Ullmann, and J. Müller in their reviews of this work, Hoffmann, s. 113 f., and others are agreed as far as relates to the heathen mythi. Especially compare George, Mythus and Sage, s. 15 ff.
1 03.

yet have arisen in this unconscious manner, Müller then refers to the Grecian mythus of Apollo and Marsyas. " It was customary to celebrate the festivals of Apollo with playing on the lyre, and it was necessary to piety, that the god himself should be regarded as its author. In Phrygia, on the contrary, the national music was the flute, which was similarly derived from a demon of their own, named Marsyas. The ancient Grecians perceived that the tones of these two instruments were essentially opposed : the harsh shrill piping of the flute must be hateful to Apollo, and therefore Marsyas his enemy. This was not enough : in order that the lyre-playing Grecian might flatter himself that the invention of his god was the more excellent instrument, Apollo must triumph over Marsyas. But why was it necessary in particular that the un-lucky Phrygian should be flayed ? Here is the simple origin of the mythus. Near the castle of Celœne in Phrygia, in a cavern whence flowed a stream or torrent named Marsyas, was suspended a skin flask, called by the Phrygians, the bottle of Marsyas ; for Marsyas was, like the Grecian Silenus, a demi-god symbolizing the exuberance of the juices of nature. Now where a Grecian, or a Phrygian with Grecian prepossessions, looked on the bottle, he plainly saw the catastrophe of Marsyas ; here was still suspended his skin, which had been torn off and made into a bottle :—Apollo had flayed him. In all this there is no arbitrary invention : the same ideas might have occurred to many, and if one first gave expression to them, he knew well that his auditors, imbued with the same prepossessions, would not for an instant doubt his accuracy."

" The chief reason of the complicated character of mythi in general, is their having been formed for the most part, not at once, but successively and by degrees, under the influence of very different circumstances and events both external and internal. The popular traditions, being orally transmitted and not restricted by any written document, were open to receive every new addition, and thus grew in the course of long centuries to the form in which we now find them. (How far this applies to a great part of the New Testa-ment mythi, will be shown hereafter.) This is an important and luminous fact, which however is very frequently overlooked in the explanation of mythi ; for they are regarded as allegories invented by one person, at one stroke, with the definite purpose of investing a thought in the form of a narration."

The view thus expressed by Müller, that the mythus is founded not upon any individual conception, but upon the more elevated and general conception of a whole people (or religious community), is said by a competent judge of Müller's work to be the necessary condition for a right understanding of the ancient mythus, the admission or rejection of which henceforth ranges the opinions on mythology into two opposite divisions.[7]

It is not however easy to draw a line of distinction between intentional and unintentional fiction. In the case where a fact lay at the foundation, which, being the subject of popular conversation and admiration, in the course of time formed itself into a mythus, we readily dismiss all notion of wilful fraud, at least in its origin. For a mythus of this kind is not the work of one man, but of a whole body of men, and of succeeding generations ; the narrative passing from mouth to mouth, and like a snowball growing by the involuntary addition of one exaggerating feature from this, and another from that narrator. In time however these legends are sure to fall into the way of some gifted minds, which will be stimulated by them to the exercise of their own poetical, religious, or didactic powers. Most of the mythical narratives which have come down to us from antiquity, such as the Trojan, and the Mosaic series of legends, are presented to us in this elaborated form. Here then it would appear there must have been intentional deception : this however is only the result of an erroneous assumption. It is almost impossible, in a critical and enlightened age like our own, to carry ourselves back to a period of civilization in which the imagination worked so powerfully, that its illusions were believed as realities by the very minds that created them. Yet the very same miracles which are wrought in less civilized circles by the imagination, are produced in the more cultivated by the understanding. Let us take one of the best didactic historians of ancient or modern times, Livy, as an example. "Numa," he says, "gave to the Romans a number of religious ceremonies, *ne luxuriarentur otio animi,* and because he regarded religion as the best means of bridling *multitudinem imperitam et illis seculis rudem. Idem,"* he continues, *"nefastos dies fastosque fecit, quia aliquando nihil cum populo agi utile futurum erat."* [8] How did Livy know that these were the motives of Numa ? In point of fact they certainly were not. But Livy believed them to be so. The inference of his own understanding appeared to him so necessary, that he treated it with full conviction as an actual fact. The popular legend, or some ancient poet, had explained this fertility of religious invention in Numa otherwise ; namely, that it arose from his communication with the nymph Egeria, who revealed to him the forms of worship that would be most acceptable to the gods. It is obvious, that the case is pretty nearly the same with regard to both representations. If the latter had an individual author, it was his opinion that the historical statement could be accounted for only upon the supposition of a communication with a superior being ; as it was that of Livy, that its explanation must lie in political views. The one mistook the production of his imagination, the other the inference of his understanding, for reality.

Perhaps it may be admitted that there is a possibility of unconscious fiction, even when an individual author is assigned to it, provided that the mythical consists only in the filling up and adorning some historical event with imaginary circumstances : but that where the whole story is invented, and not any historical nucleus is to be found, this unconscious fiction is impossible. Whatever view may be taken of the heathen mythology, it is easy to show with regard to the New Testament, that there was the greatest antecedent probability of this very kind of fiction having arisen respecting Jesus without any fraudulent intention. The expectation of a Messiah had grown up amongst the Israelitish people long before the time of Jesus, and just then had ripened to full maturity. And from its beginning this expectation was not indefinite, but determined, and characterized by many important particulars. Moses was said to have promised his people a prophet like unto himself (Deut. xviii. 15), and this passage was in the time of Jesus applied to the Messiah (Acts iii. 22 ; vii. 37). Hence the rabbinical principle : as the first redeemer (*Goël*), so shall be the second ; which principle was carried out into many particulars to be expected in the Messiah after his prototype Moses.[9] Again, the Messiah was to come of the race of David, and as a second David take possession of his throne (Matt. xxii. 42 ;

---

[8] I. 19.
[9] Midrasch Koheleth f. 73, 3 (in Schöttgen, *horæ hebraicæ et talmudicæ,* 2, S. 251 f.). *R. Berechias nomine R. Isaaci dixit: Quemadmodum Goël primus* (Moses), *sic etiam postremus* (Messias) *comparatus est. De Goële primo quidnam scriptura dicit?* Exod. iv. 20 : *et sumsit Moses uxorem et filios, eosque asino imposuit. Sic Goël postremus,* Zachar. ix. 9 : *pauper et insidens asino. Quidnam de Goële primo nosti? Is descendere fecit Man, q. d.* Exod. xvi. 14 : *ecce ego pluere faciam vobis panem de cœlo. Sic etiam Goël postremus Manna descendere faciet, q. d.* Ps. lxxii. 16 : *erit multitudo frumenti in terra. Quomodo Goël primus comparatus fuit? Is ascendere fecit puteum : sic quoque Goël postremus ascendere faciet aquas, q. d.* Joel iv. 18 : *et fons e domo Domini egredietur, et torrentem Sittim irrigabit.*

Luke i. 32 ; Acts ii. 30) : and therefore in the time of Jesus it was expected that he, like David, should be born in the little village of Bethlehem (John vii. 42 ; Matt. ii. 5 f.). In the above passage Moses describes the supposed Messiah as a prophet ; so in his own idea, Jesus was the greatest and last of the prophetic race. But in the old national legends the prophets were made illustrious by the most wonderful actions and destiny. How could less be expected of the Messiah ? Was it not necessary beforehand, that his life should be adorned with that which was most glorious and important in the lives of the prophets ? Must not the popular expectation give him a share in the bright portion of their history, as subsequently the sufferings of himself and his disciples were attributed by Jesus, when he appeared as the Messiah, to a participation in the dark side of the fate of the prophets (Matt. xxiii. 29 ff. ; Luke xiii. 33 ff. ; comp. Matt. v. 12)? Believing that Moses and all the prophets had prophesied of the Messiah (John v. 46 ; Luke iv. 21 ; xxiv. 27), it was as natural for the Jews, with their allegorizing tendency, to consider their actions and destiny as types of the Messiah, as to take their sayings for predictions. In general the whole Messianic era was expected to be full of signs and wonders. The eyes of the blind should be opened, the ears of the deaf should be unclosed, the lame should leap, and the tongue of the dumb praise God (Isa. xxxv. 5 f. ; xlii. 7 ; comp. xxxii. 3, 4). These merely figurative expressions soon came to be understood literally (Matt. xi. 5 ; Luke vii. 21 f.), and thus the idea of the Messiah was continually filled up with new details, even before the appearance of Jesus.[10] Thus many of the legends respecting him had not to be newly invented ; they already existed in the popular hope of the Messiah, having been mostly derived with various modifications [11] from the Old Testament, and had merely to be transferred to Jesus,[12] and accommodated to his character and doctrines. In no case could it be easier for the person who first added any new feature to the description of Jesus, to believe himself its genuineness, since his argument would be : Such and such things must have happened to the Messiah ; Jesus was the Messiah ; therefore such and such things happened to him.[13]

Truly it may be said that the middle term of this argument, namely, that Jesus was the Messiah, would have failed in proof to his contemporaries all the more on account of the common expectation of miraculous events, if that expectation had not been fulfilled by him. But the following critique

---

[10] Tanchuma f. 54, 4. (in Schöttgen, p. 74) : R. Acha nomine R. Samuelis bar Nachmani dixit : Quæcumque Deus S. B. facturus est לבא לעתיך (tempore Messiano) ea jam ante fecit per manus justorum בעולם הזה (seculo ante Messiam elapso). Deus S. B. suscitabit mortuos, id quod jam ante fecit per Eliam, Elisam et Ezechielem. Mare exsiccabit, prout per Mosen factum est. Oculos cæcorum aperiet, id quod per Elisam fecit. Deus S. B. futuro tempore visitabit steriles, quemadmodum in Abrahamo et Sarâ fecit.

[11] The Old Testament legends have undergone many changes and amplifications, even without any reference to the Messiah, so that the partial discrepancy between the narratives concerning Jesus with those relating to Moses and the prophets, is not a decisive proof that the former were not derived from the latter. Compare Acts vii. 22, 53, and the corresponding part of Josephus Antiq. ii. & iii. with the account of Moses given in Exodus. Also the biblical account of Abraham with Antiq. i. 8, 2 ; of Jacob with i. 19, 6 ; of Joseph with ii. 5, 4.

[12] George, s. 125 : If we consider the firm conviction of the disciples, that all which had been prophesied in the Old Testament of the Messiah must necessarily have been fulfilled in the person of their master ; and moreover that there were many blank spaces in the history of Christ ; we shall see that it was impossible to have happened otherwise than that these ideas should have embodied themselves, and thus the mythi have arisen which we find. Even if a more correct representation of the life of Jesus had been possible by means of tradition, this conviction of the disciples must have been strong enough to triumph over it.

[13] Compare O. Müller, Prolegomena, s. 7, on a similar conclusion of Grecian poets.

on the Life of Jesus does not divest it of all those features to which the character of miraculous has been appropriated : and besides we must take into account the overwhelming impression which was made upon those around him by the personal character and discourse of Jesus, as long as he was living amongst them, which did not permit them deliberately to scrutinize and compare him with their previous standard. The belief in him as the Messiah extended to wider circles only by slow degrees ; and even during his lifetime the people may have reported many wonderful stories of him (comp. Matt. xiv. 2). After his death, however, the belief in his resurrection, however that belief may have arisen, afforded a more than sufficient proof of his Messiahship ; so that all the other miracles in his history need not be considered as the foundation of the faith in this, but may rather be adduced as the consequence of it.

It is however by no means necessary to attribute this same freedom from all conscious intention of fiction, to the authors of all those narratives in the Old and New Testament which must be considered as unhistorical. In every series of legends, especially if any patriotic or religious party interest is associated with them, as soon as they become the subject of free poetry or any other literary composition, some kind of fiction will be intentionally mixed up with them. The authors of the Homeric songs could not have believed that every particular which they related of their gods and heroes had really happened ; and just as little could the writer of the Chronicles have been ignorant that in his deviation from the books of Samuel and of the Kings, he was introducing many events of later occurrence into an earlier period ; or the author of the book of Daniel [14] that he was modelling his history upon that of Joseph, and accommodating prophecies to events already past ; and exactly as little may this be said of all the unhistorical narratives of the Gospels, as for example, of the first chapter of the third, and many parts of the fourth Gospel. But a fiction, although not undesigned, may still be without evil design. It is true, the case is not the same with the supposed authors of many fictions in the Bible, as with poets properly so called, since the latter write without any expectation that their poems will be received as history : but still it is to be considered that in ancient times, and especially amongst the Hebrews, and yet more when this people was stirred up by religious excitement, the line of distinction between history and fiction, prose and poetry, was not drawn so clearly as with us. It is a fact also deserving attention that amongst the Jews and early Christians, the most reputable authors published their works with the substitution of venerated names, without an idea that they were guilty of any falsehood or deception by so doing.

[14] The comparison of the first chapter of this book with the history of Joseph in Genesis, gives an instructive view of the tendency of the later Hebrew legend and poetry to form new relations upon the pattern of the old. As Joseph was carried captive to Egypt, so was Daniel to Babylon (i. 2) ; like Joseph he must change his name (7). God makes the שַׂר הַסָּרִיסִים favourable to him, as the סָרִים שַׂר הַטַּבָּחִים to Joseph (9) ; he abstains from polluting himself with partaking of the king's meats and drinks, which are pressed upon him (8) ; a self-denial held as meritorious in the time of Antiochus Epiphanes, as that of Joseph with regard to Potiphar's wife ; like Joseph he gains eminence by the interpretation of a dream of the king, which his חַרְטֻמִּים were unable to explain to him (ii.) ; whilst the additional circumstance that Daniel is enabled to give not only the interpretation, but the dream itself, which had escaped the memory of the king, appears to be a romantic exaggeration of that which was attributed to Joseph. In the account of Josephus, the history of Daniel has reacted in a singular manner upon that of Joseph ; for as Nebuchadnezzar forgets his dream, and the interpretation according to Josephus revealed to him at the same time, so does he make Pharaoh forget the interpretation shown to him with the dream. Antiq. ii. 5, 4.

The only question that can arise here is whether to such fictions, the work of an individual, we can give the name of mythi? If we regard only their own intrinsic nature, the name is not appropriate ; but it is so when these fictions, having met with faith, come to be received amongst the legends of a people or religious party, for this is always a proof that they were the fruit, not of any individual conception, but of an accordance with the sentiments of a multitude.[15]

A frequently raised objection remains, for the refutation of which the remarks above made, upon the date of the origin of many of the gospel mythi, are mainly important : the objection, namely, that the space of about thirty years, from the death of Jesus to the destruction of Jerusalem, during which the greater part of the narratives must have been formed ; or even the interval extending to the beginning of the second century, the most distant period which can be allowed for the origin of even the latest of these gospel narratives, and for the written composition of our gospels ;—is much too short to admit of the rise of so rich a collection of mythi.   But, as we have shown, the greater part of these mythi did not arise during that period, for their first foundation was laid in the legends of the Old Testament, before and after the Babylonish exile ; and the transference of these legends with suitable modifications to the expected Messiah, was made in the course of the centuries which elapsed between that exile and the time of Jesus.   So that for the period between the formation of the first Christian community and the writing of the Gospels, there remains to be effected only the transference of Messianic legends, almost all ready formed, to Jesus, with some alterations to adapt them to christian opinions, and to the individual character and circumstances of Jesus : only a very small proportion of mythi having to be formed entirely new.

§ 15.

DEFINITION OF THE EVANGELICAL MYTHUS AND ITS DISTINCTIVE CHARACTERISTICS. *

The precise sense in which we use the expression *mythus*, applied to certain parts of the gospel history, is evident from all that has already been said ; at the same time the different kinds and gradations of the mythi which we shall meet with in this history may here by way of anticipation be pointed out.

We distinguish by the name *evangelical mythus* a narrative relating directly or indirectly to Jesus, which may be considered not as the expression of a fact, but as the product of an idea of his earliest followers : such a narrative being mythical in proportion as it exhibits this character.   The mythus in this sense of the term meets us, in the Gospel as elsewhere, sometimes in its pure form, constituting the substance of the narrative, and sometimes as an accidental adjunct to the actual history.

The pure mythus in the Gospel will be found to have two sources, which in most cases contributed simultaneously, though in different proportions, to form the mythus.   The one source is, as already stated, the Messianic ideas and expectations existing according to their several forms in the Jewish mind before Jesus, and independently of him ; the other is that particular impression which was left by the personal character, actions, and fate of Jesus, and which served to modify the Messianic idea in the minds of his people.   The account of the Transfiguration, for example, is derived almost

---

[15] Thus J. Müller, theol. Studien u. Kritiken, 1836, iii. s. 839 ff.

exclusively from the former source ; the only amplification taken from the latter source being—that they who appeared with Jesus on the Mount spake of his decease.   On the other hand, the narrative of the rending of the veil of the temple at the death of Jesus seems to have had its origin in the hostile position which Jesus, and his church after him, sustained in relation to the Jewish temple worship.   Here already we have something historical, though consisting merely of certain general features of character, position, etc. ; we are thus at once brought upon the ground of the historical mythus.

The historical mythus has for its groundwork a definite individual fact which has been seized upon by religious enthusiasm, and twined around with mythical conceptions culled from the idea of the Christ.   This fact is perhaps a saying of Jesus such as that concerning " fishers of men " or the barren fig-tree, which now appear in the Gospels transmuted into marvellous histories : or, it is perhaps a real transaction or event taken from his life ; for instance, the mythical traits in the account of the baptism were built upon such a reality.   Certain of the miraculous histories may likewise have had some foundation in natural occurrences, which the narrative has either exhibited in a supernatural light, or enriched with miraculous incidents.

All the species of imagery here enumerated may justly be designated as mythi, even according to the modern and precise definition of George, inasmuch as the unhistorical which they embody—whether formed gradually by tradition, or created by an individual author—is in each case the product of an *idea*.   But for those parts of the history which are characterized by indefiniteness and want of connexion, by misconstruction and transformation, by strange combinations and confusion,—the natural results of a long course of oral transmission ; or which, on the contrary, are distinguished by highly coloured and pictorial representations, which also seem to point to a traditionary origin ;—for these parts the term *legendary* is certainly the more appropriate.

Lastly.   It is requisite to distinguish equally from the mythus and the legend, that which, as it serves not to clothe an idea on the one hand, and admits not of being referred to tradition on the other, must be regarded as *the addition of the author*, as purely individual, and designed merely to give clearness, connexion, and climax, to the representation.

It is to the various forms of the unhistorical in the Gospels that this enumeration exclusively refers : it does not involve the renunciation of the *historical* which they may likewise contain.

§ 16.

CRITERIA BY WHICH TO DISTINGUISH THE UNHISTORICAL IN THE GOSPEL NARRATIVE. *

Having shown the possible existence of the mythical and the legendary in the Gospels, both on extrinsic and intrinsic grounds, and defined their distinctive characteristics, it remains in conclusion to inquire how their actual presence may be recognised in individual cases?

The mythus presents two phases : in the first place it is not history ; in the second it is fiction, the product of the particular mental tendency of a certain community.   These two phases afford the one a negative, the other a positive criterion, by which the mythus is to be recognised.

I. *Negative.*   That an account is not historical—that the matter related could not have taken place in the manner described is evident,

First. When the narration is irreconcilable with the known and universal laws which govern the course of events. Now according to these laws, agreeing with all just philosophical conceptions and all credible experience, the absolute cause never disturbs the chain of secondary causes by single arbitrary acts of interposition, but rather manifests itself in the production of the aggregate of finite casualities, and of their reciprocal action. When therefore we meet with an account of certain phenomena or events of which it is either expressly stated or implied that they were produced immediately by God himself (divine apparitions—voices from heaven and the like), or by human beings possessed of supernatural powers (miracles, prophecies), such an account is *in so far* to be considered as not historical. And inasmuch as, in general, the intermingling of the spiritual world with the human is found only in unauthentic records, and is irreconcilable with all just conceptions; so narratives of angels and of devils, of their appearing in human shape and interfering with human concerns, cannot possibly be received as historical.

Another law which controls the course of events is the law of succession, in accordance with which all occurrences, not excepting the most violent convulsions and the most rapid changes, follow in a certain order of sequence of increase and decrease. If therefore we are told of a celebrated individual that he attracted already at his birth and during his childhood that attention which he excited in his manhood ; that his followers at a single glance recognized him as being all that he actually was ; if the transition from the deepest despondency to the most ardent enthusiasm after his death is represented as the work of a single hour; we must feel more than doubtful whether it is a real history which lies before us. Lastly, all those psychological laws, which render it improbable that a human being should feel, think, and act in a manner directly opposed to his own habitual mode and that of men in general, must be taken into consideration. As for example, when the Jewish Sanhedrim are represented as believing the declaration of the watch at the grave that Jesus was risen, and instead of accusing them of having suffered the body to be stolen away whilst they were asleep, bribing them to give currency to such a report. By the same rule it is contrary to all the laws belonging to the human faculty of memory, that long discourses, such as those of Jesus given in the fourth Gospel, could have been faithfully recollected and reproduced.

It is however true that effects are often far more rapidly produced, particularly in men of genius and by their agency, than might be expected ; and that human beings frequently act inconsequently, and in opposition to their general modes and habits ; the two last mentioned tests of the mythical character must therefore be cautiously applied, and in conjunction only with other tests.

Secondly. An account which shall be regarded as historically valid, must neither be inconsistent with itself, nor in contradiction with other accounts.

The most decided case falling under this rule, amounting to a positive contradiction, is when one account affirms what another denies. Thus, one gospel represents the first appearance of Jesus in Galilee as subsequent to the imprisonment of John the Baptist, whilst another Gospel remarks, long after Jesus had preached both in Galilee and in Judea, that " John was not yet cast into prison."

When on the contrary, the second account, without absolutely contradicting the first, differs from it, the disagreement may be merely between the incidental particulars of the narrative ; such as *time,* (the clearing of the Temple,) *place,* (the original residence of the parents of Jesus ;) *number,* (the Gadarenes, the angels at the sepulchre ;) *names,* (Matthew and Levi ;) or it may concern the essential substance of the history.   In the latter case, sometimes the character and circumstances in one account differ altogether from those in another.   Thus, according to one narrator, the Baptist recognizes Jesus as the Messiah destined to suffer ; according to the other, John takes offence at his suffering condition.   Sometimes an occurrence is represented in two or more ways, of which one only can be consistent with the reality ; as when in one account Jesus calls his first disciples from their nets whilst fishing on the sea of Galilee, and in the other meets them in Judea on his way to Galilee.   We may class under the same head instances where events or discourses are represented as having occurred on two distinct occasions, whilst they are so similar that it is impossible to resist the conclusion that both the narratives refer to the same event or discourse.

It may here be asked : is it to be regarded as a contradiction if one account is wholly silent respecting a circumstance mentioned by another?   In itself, apart from all other considerations, the argumentum ex silentio is of no weight ; but it is certainly to be accounted of moment when, at the same time, it may be shown that had the author known the circumstance he could not have failed to mention it, and also that he must have known it had it actually occurred.

II. *Positive.*   The positive characters of legend and fiction are to be recognized sometimes in the form, sometimes in the substance of a narrative.

If the form be poetical, if the actors converse in hymns, and in a more diffuse and elevated strain than might be expected from their training and situations, such discourses, at all events, are not to be regarded as historical. The absence of these marks of the unhistorical do not however prove the historical validity of the narration, since the mythus often wears the most simple and apparently historical form : in which case the proof lies in the substance.

If the contents of a narrative strikingly accords with certain ideas existing and prevailing within the circle from which the narrative proceeded, which ideas themselves seem to be the product of preconceived opinions rather than of practical experience, it is more or less probable, according to circumstances, that such a narrative is of mythical origin.   The knowledge of the fact, that the Jews were fond of representing their great men as the children of parents who had long been childless, cannot but make us doubtful of the historical truth of the statement that this was the case with John the Baptist ; knowing also that the Jews saw predictions everywhere in the writings of their prophets and poets, and discovered types of the Messiah in all the lives of holy men recorded in their Scriptures ; when we find details in the life of Jesus evidently sketched after the pattern of these prophecies and prototypes, we cannot but suspect that they are rather mythical than historical.

The more simple characteristics of the legend, and of additions by the author, after the observations of the former section, need no further elucidation.

Yet each of these tests, on the one hand, and each narrative on the other, considered apart, will rarely prove more than the possible or probable unhistorical character of the record.   The concurrence of several such indications, is necessary to bring about a more definite result.   The accounts of the visit of the Magi, and of the murder of the innocents at Bethlehem, harmonize remarkably with the Jewish Messianic notion, built upon the prophecy of Balaam, respecting the star which should come out of Jacob ; and with the history of the sanguinary command of Pharaoh.   Still this would not alone suffice to stamp the narratives as mythical.   But we have also the corroborative facts that the described appearance of the star is contrary to the physical, the alleged conduct of Herod to the psychological laws ; that Josephus, who gives in other respects so circumstantial an account of Herod, agrees with all other historical authorities in being silent concerning the Bethlehem massacre ; and that the visit of the Magi together with the flight into Egypt related in the one Gospel, and the presentation in the temple related in another Gospel, mutually exclude one another.   Wherever, as in this instance, the several criteria of the mythical character concur, the result is certain, and certain in proportion to the accumulation of such grounds of evidence.

It may be that a narrative, standing alone, would discover but slight indications, or perhaps, might present no one distinct feature of the mythus ; but it is connected with others, or proceeds from the author of other narratives which exhibit unquestionable marks of a mythical or legendary character ; and consequently suspicion is reflected back from the latter, on the former. Every narrative, however miraculous, contains some details which might in themselves be historical, but which, in consequence of their connexion with the other supernatural incidents, necessarily become equally doubtful.

In these last remarks we are, to a certain extent, anticipating the question which is, in conclusion, to be considered : viz., whether the mythical character is restricted to those features of the narrative, upon which such character is actually stamped ; and whether a contradiction between two accounts invalidate one account only, or both ?   That is to say, what is the precise boundary line between the historical and the unhistorical ?—the most difficult question in the whole province of criticism.

In the first place, when two narratives mutually exclude one another, one only is thereby proved to be unhistorical.   If one be true the other must be false, but though the one be false the other may be true.   Thus, in reference to the original residence of the parents of Jesus, we are justified in adopting the account of Luke which places it at Nazareth, to the exclusion of that of Matthew, which plainly supposes it to have been at Bethlehem ; and, generally speaking, when we have to choose between two irreconcilable accounts, in selecting as historical that which is the least opposed to the laws of nature, and has the least correspondence with certain national or party opinions.   But upon a more particular consideration it will appear that, since one account is false, it is possible that the other may be so likewise : the existence of a mythus respecting some certain point, shows that the imagination has been active in reference to that particular subject; (we need only refer to the genealogies ;) and the historical accuracy of either of two such accounts cannot be relied upon, unless substantiated by its agreement with some other well authenticated testimony.

Concerning the different parts of one and the same narrative : it might be thought for example, that though the appearance of an angel, and his announcement to Mary that she should be the Mother of the Messiah, must certainly be regarded as unhistorical, still, that Mary should have indulged this hope before the birth of the child, is not in itself incredible.   But what should have excited this hope in Mary's mind ?   It is at once apparent that that which is credible in itself is nevertheless unhistorical when it is so intimately connected with what is incredible that, if you discard the latter, you at the same time remove the basis on which the former rests.   Again, any action of Jesus represented as a miracle, when divested of the marvellous, might be thought to exhibit a perfectly natural occurrence ; with respect to some of the miraculous histories, the expulsion of devils for instance, this might with some limitation, be possible.   But for this reason alone : in these instances, a cure, so instantaneous, and effected by a few words merely, as it is described in the Gospels, is not psychologically incredible ; so that, the essential in these narratives remains untouched. It is different in the case of the healing of a man born blind. A natural cure could not have been effected otherwise than by a gradual process ; the narrative states the cure to have been immediate ; if therefore the history be understood to record a natural occurrence, the most essential particular is incorrectly represented, and consequently all security for the truth of the otherwise natural remainder is gone, and the real fact cannot be discovered without the aid of arbitrary conjecture.

The following examples will serve to illustrate the mode of deciding in such cases. According to the narrative, as Mary entered the house and saluted her cousin Elizabeth, who was then pregnant, the babe leaped in her womb, she was filled with the Holy Ghost, and she immediately addressed Mary as the mother of the Messiah. This account bears indubitable marks of an unhistorical character. Yet, it is not, in itself, impossible that Mary should have paid a visit to her cousin, during which everything went on quite naturally. The fact is however that there are psychological difficulties connected with this journey of the betrothed ; and that the visit, and even the relationship of the two women, seem to have originated entirely in the wish to exhibit a connexion between the mother of John the Baptist, and the mother of the Messiah. Or when in the history of the transfiguration it is stated, that the men who appeared with Jesus on the Mount were Moses and Elias : and that the brilliancy which illuminated Jesus was supernatural ; it might seem here also that, after deducting the marvellous, the presence of two men and a bright morning beam might be retained as the historical facts. But the legend was predisposed, by virtue of the current idea concerning the relation of the Messiah to these two prophets, not merely to make any two men (whose persons, object and conduct, if they were not what the narrative represents them, remain in the highest degree mysterious) into Moses and Elias, but to create the whole occurrence ; and in like manner not merely to conceive of some certain illumination as a supernatural effulgence (which, if a natural one, is much exaggerated and misrepresented), but to create it at once after the pattern of the brightness which illumined the face of Moses on Mount Sinai.

Hence is derived the following rule. Where not merely the particular nature and manner of an occurrence is critically suspicious, its external circumstances represented as miraculous and the like ; but where likewise the essential substance and groundwork is either inconceivable in itself, or is in striking harmony with some Messianic idea of the Jews of that age, then not the particular alleged course and mode of the transaction only, but the entire occurrence must be regarded as unhistorical. Where on the contrary, the form only, and not the general contents of the narration, exhibits the characteristics of the unhistorical, it is at least possible to suppose a kernel of historical fact ; although we can never confidently decide whether this kernel of fact actually exists, or in what it consists ; unless, indeed, it be discoverable from other sources. In legendary narratives, or narratives embellished by the writer, it is less difficult,—by divesting them of all that betrays itself as fictitious imagery, exaggeration, etc.—by endeavouring to abstract from them every extraneous adjunct and to fill up every hiatus—to succeed, proximately at least, in separating the historical groundwork.

The boundary line, however, between the historical and the unhistorical, in records, in which as in our Gospels this latter element is incorporated, will ever remain fluctuating and unsusceptible of precise attainment. Least of all can it be expected that the first comprehensive attempt to treat these records from a critical point of view should be successful in drawing a sharply defined line of demarcation. In the obscurity which criticism has produced, by the extinction of all lights hitherto held historical, the eye must accustom itself by degrees to discriminate objects with precision ; and at all events the author of this work, wishes especially to guard himself in those places where he declares he knows not what happened, from the imputation of asserting that he knows that nothing happened.

FIRST PART.

———

HISTORY OF THE BIRTH AND CHILDHOOD OF JESUS.

CHAPTER I.

ANNUNCIATION AND BIRTH OF JOHN THE BAPTIST.

§ 17.

ACCOUNT GIVEN BY LUKE.* IMMEDIATE, SUPERNATURAL CHARACTER OF
THE REPRESENTATION.

EACH of the four Evangelists represents the public ministry of Jesus as preceded by that of John the Baptist; but it is peculiar to Luke to make the
Baptist the precursor of the Messiah in reference also to the event of his
birth. This account finds a legitimate place in a work devoted exclusively to
the consideration of the life of Jesus: firstly, on account of the intimate
connexion which it exhibits as subsisting from the very commencement between the life of John and the life of Jesus; and secondly, because it constitutes a valuable contribution, aiding essentially towards the formation of a
correct estimate of the general character of the gospel narratives. The
opinion that the two first chapters of Luke, of which this particular history
forms a portion, are a subsequent and unauthentic addition, is the uncritical
assumption of a class of theologians who felt that the history of the childhood
of Jesus seemed to require a mythical interpretation, but yet demurred to
apply the comparatively modern mythical view to the remainder of the
Gospel.[1]

A pious sacerdotal pair had lived and grown old in the cherished, but
unrealized hope, of becoming parents, when, on a certain day, as the priest is
offering incense in the sanctuary, the angel Gabriel appears to him, and
promises him a son, who shall live consecrated to God, and who shall be the
harbinger of the Messiah, to prepare his way when he shall visit and redeem
his people. Zacharias, however, is incredulous, and doubts the prediction on
account of his own advanced age and that of his wife; whereupon the angel,
both as a sign and as a punishment, strikes him dumb until the time of its
accomplishment; an infliction which endures until the day of the circumcision
of the actually born son, when the father, being called upon to assign to the
child the name predetermined by the angel, suddenly recovers his speech,
and with the regained powers of utterance, breaks forth in a hymn of praise.
(Luke i. 5–25, 57–80.)

It is evidently the object of this gospel account to represent a series of
external and miraculous occurrences. The announcement of the birth of the

---

* It may here be observed, once for all, that whenever in the following inquiry the names
"Matthew," "Luke," etc., are used, it is the author of the several Gospels who is thus
briefly indicated, quite irrespective of the question whether either of the Gospels was written
by an apostle or disciple of that name, or by a later unknown author.

[1] See Kuinöl Comm. in Luc., Proleg., p. 247

forerunner of the Messiah is divinely communicated by the apparition of a celestial spirit; the conception takes place under the particular and preternatural blessing of God; and the infliction and removal of dumbness are effected by extraordinary means.   But it is quite another question, whether we can accede to the view of the author, or can feel convinced that the birth of the Baptist was in fact preceded by such a series of miraculous events.

The first offence against our modern notions in this narrative is the appearance of the angel : the event contemplated in itself, as well as the peculiar circumstances of the apparition.   With respect to the latter, the angel announces himself to be *Gabriel that stands in the presence of God*.   Now it is inconceivable that the constitution of the celestial hierarchy should actually correspond with the notions entertained by the Jews subsequent to the exile ; and that the names given to the angels should be in the language of this people.[2]   Here the supranaturalist finds himself in a dilemma, even upon his own ground.   Had the belief in celestial beings, occupying a particular station in the court of heaven, and distinguished by particular names, originated from the revealed religion of the Hebrews,—had such a belief been established by Moses, or some later prophet,—then, according to the views of the supranaturalist, they might, nay they must, be admitted to be correct.   But it is in the Maccabæan Daniel[3] and in the apocryphal Tobit,[4] that this doctrine of angels, in its more precise form, first appears ; and it is evidently a product of the influence of the Zend religion of the Persians on the Jewish mind.   We have the testimony of the Jews themselves, that they brought the names of the angels with them from Babylon.[5]   Hence arises a series of questions extremely perplexing to the supranaturalist.   Was the doctrine false so long as it continued to be the exclusive possession of the heathens, but true as soon as it became adopted by the Jews ? or was it at all times equally true, and was an important truth discovered by an idolatrous nation sooner than by the people of God ?   If nations shut out from a particular and divine revelation, arrived at truth by the light of reason alone, sooner than the Jews who were guided by that revelation, then either the revelation was superfluous, or its influence was merely negative : that is, it operated as a check to the premature acquisition of knowledge.   If, in order to escape this consequence, it be contended that truths were revealed by the divine influence to other people besides the Israelites, the supranaturalistic point of view is annihilated; and, since all things contained in religions which contradict each other cannot have been revealed, we are compelled to exercise a critical discrimination. Thus, we find it to be by no means in harmony with an elevated conception of God to represent him as an earthly monarch, surrounded by his court : and when an appeal is made, in behalf of the reality of angels standing round the throne, to the reasonable belief in a graduated scale of created intelligences,[6] the Jewish representation is not thereby justified, but merely a modern conception substituted for it.   We should, thus, be driven to the

---

[2] Paulus, exeget. Handbuch, 1 a. s. 78 f. 96.   Bauer, hebr. Mythol., 2 Bd. s. 218 f.

[3] Here Michael is called *one of the chief princes.*

[4] Here Raphael is represented as *one of the seven angels which go in and out before the glory of the holy One ;* (Tobit, xii. 15), almost the same as Gabriel in Luke i. 19, excepting the mention of the number.   This number is in imitation of the Persian Amschaspands.   Vid. De Wette, bibl. Dogmatik, § 171 b.

[5] Hieros. rosch haschanah f. lvi. 4.   (Lightfoot, horæ hebr. et talmud. in IV. Evangg., p. 723) : *R. Simeon ben Lachisch dicit : nomina angelorum ascenderunt in manu Israëlis ex Babylone.   Nam antea dictum est : advolavit ad me unus τῶν Seraphim, Seraphim steterunt ante eum,* Jes. vi. ; *at post : vir Gabriel,* Dan. ix. 21, *Michaël princeps vester,* Dan. x. 21.

[6] Olshausen, biblischer Commentar zum N.T., 1 Thl. s. 29 (2te Auflage).   Comp. Hoffmann, s. 124 f.

expedient of supposing an accommodation on the part of God : that he sent a celestial spirit with the command to simulate a rank and title which did not belong to him, in order that, by this conformity to Jewish notions, he might insure the belief of the father of the Baptist. Since however it appears that Zacharias did not believe the angel, but was first convinced by the result, the accommodation proved fruitless, and consequently could not have been a divine arrangement. With regard to the name of the angel, and the improbability that a celestial being should bear a Hebrew name, it has been remarked that the word Gabriel, taken appellatively in the sense of *Man of God*, very appropriately designates the nature of the heavenly visitant ; and since it may be rendered with this signification into every different language, the name cannot be said to be restricted to the Hebrew.[7] This explanation however leaves the difficulty quite unsolved, since it converts into a simple appellative a name evidently employed as a proper name. In this case likewise an accommodation must be supposed, namely, that the angel, in order to indicate his real nature, appropriated a name which he did not actually bear : an accommodation already judged in the foregoing remarks.

But it is not only the name and the alleged station of the angel which shock our modern ideas, we also feel his discourse and his conduct to be unworthy. Paulus indeed suggests that none but a levitical priest, and not an angel of Jehovah, could have conceived it necessary that the boy should live in nazarite abstemiousness,[8] but to this it may be answered that the angel also might have known that under this form John would obtain greater influence with the people. But there is a more important difficulty. When Zacharias, overcome by surprise, doubts the promise and asks for a sign, this natural incredulity is regarded by the angel as a crime, and immediately punished with dumbness. Though some may not coincide with Paulus that a real angel would have lauded the spirit of inquiry evinced by the priest, yet all will agree in the remark, that conduct so imperious is less in character with a truly celestial being than with the notions the Jews of that time entertained of such. Moreover we do not find in the whole province of supranaturalism a parallel severity.

The instance, cited by Paulus, of Jehovah's far milder treatment of Abraham, who asks precisely the same question unreproved, Gen xv. 8, is refuted by Olshausen, because he considers the words of Abraham, chap. v. 6, an evidence of his faith ; but this observation does not apply to chap. xviii. 12, where the greater incredulity of Sarah, in a similar case, remains unpunished ; nor to chap. xvii. 17, where Abraham himself is not even blamed, though the divine promise appears to him so incredible as to excite laughter. The example of Mary is yet closer, who (Luke i. 34) in regard to a still greater improbability, but one which was similarly declared by a special divine messenger to be no impossibility, puts exactly the same question as Zacharias ; so that we must agree with Paulus that such inconsistency certainly cannot belong to the conduct of God or of a celestial being, but merely to the Jewish representation of them. Feeling the objectionableness of the representation in its existing form, orthodox theologians have invented various motives to justify this infliction of dumbness. Hess has attempted to screen it from the reproach of an arbitrary procedure by regarding it as the only means of keeping secret, even against the will of the priest, an event, the premature proclamation of which might have been followed by disastrous consequences, similar to those which attended the announcement by the wise men of the birth of

---

[7] Olshausen, ut sup. Hoffmann, s. 135.
[8] Ut sup. s. 77.

the child Jesus.[9]   But, in the first place, the angel says nothing of such an object, he inflicts the dumbness but as a sign and punishment ; secondly, the loss of speech did not hinder Zacharias from communicating, at any rate to his wife, the main features of the apparition, since we see that she was acquainted with the destined name of the child before appeal was made to the father.   Thirdly, what end did it serve thus to render difficult the communication of the miraculous annunciation of the unborn babe, since no sooner was it born than it was at once exposed to all the dreaded dangers ?—for the father's sudden recovery of speech, and the extraordinary scene at the circumcision excited attention and became noised abroad in all the country. Olshausen's view of the thing is more admissible.   He regards the whole proceeding, and especially the dumbness, as a moral training destined to teach Zacharias to know and conquer his want of faith.[10]   But of this too we have no mention in the text ; besides, the unexpected accomplishment of the prediction would have made Zacharias sufficiently ashamed of his unbelief, if instead of inflicting dumbness the angel had merely remonstrated with him.

But however worthy of God we might grant the conduct of his messenger to have been, still many of the present day will find an angelic apparition, as such, incredible.   Bauer insists that wherever angels appear, both in the New Testament and in the Old, the narrative is mythical.[11]   Even admitting the existence of angels, we cannot suppose them capable of manifesting themselves to human beings, since they belong to the invisible world, and spiritual existences are not cognizable by the organs of sense ; so that it is always advisable to refer their pretended apparitions to the imagination.[12]   It is not probable, it is added, that God should make use of them according to the popular notion, for these apparitions have no apparent adequate object, they serve generally only to gratify curiosity, or to encourage man's disposition passively to leave his affairs in higher hands.[13]   It is also remarkable that in the old world these celestial beings show themselves active upon the smallest occasions, whilst in modern times they remain idle even during the most important occurrences.[14]   But to deny their appearance and agency among men is to call in question their very being, because it is precisely this occupation which is a main object of their existence (Heb. i. 14).   According to Schleiermacher[15] we cannot indeed actually disprove the existence of angels, yet the conception is one which could not have originated in our time, but belongs wholly to the ancient ideas of the world.   The belief in angels has a twofold root or source : the one the natural desire of the mind to presuppose a larger amount of intelligence in the universe than is realized in the human race.   We who live in these days find this desire satisfied in the conviction that other worlds exist besides our own, and are peopled by intelligent beings ; and thus the first source of the belief in angels is destroyed.   The other source, namely, the representation of God as an earthly monarch surrounded by his court, contradicts all enlightened conceptions of Deity ; and further, the phenomena in the natural world and the transitions in human life, which were formerly thought to be wrought by God himself through ministering angels, we are now able to explain by natural causes ; so that the belief in

---

[9] Geschichte der drei letzten Lebensjahre Jesu, sammt dessen Jugendgeschichte.   Tübingen 1779.   I Bd. s. 12.
[10] Bibl. Comm. I, s. 115.
[11] Hebr. Mythol. ii. s. 218.
[12] Bauer, ut sup. i. s. 129.   Paulus, exeget. Handbuch, i. a. 74.
[13] Paulus, Commentar, i. s. 12.
[14] Bauer, ut sup.
[15] Glaubenslehre, 1 Thl. § 42 und 43 (2te Ausgabe).

angels is without a link by which it can attach itself to rightly apprehended modern ideas; and it exists only as a lifeless tradition. The result is the same if, with one of the latest writers on the doctrine of angels,[16] we consider as the origin of this representation, man's desire to separate the two sides of his moral nature, and to contemplate, as beings existing external to himself, angels and devils. For, the origin of both representations remains merely subjective, the angel being simply the ideal of created perfection : which, as it was formed from the subordinate point of view of a fanciful imagination, disappears from the higher and more comprehensive observation of the intellect.[17]

Olshausen, on the other hand, seeks to deduce a positive argument in favour of the reality of the apparition in question, from those very reasonings of the present day which, in fact, negative the existence of angels; and he does so by viewing the subject on its speculative side. He is of opinion that the gospel narrative does not contradict just views of the world, since God is immanent in the universe and moves it by his breath.[18] But if it be true that God is immanent in the world, precisely on that account is the intervention of angels superfluous. It is only a Deity who dwells apart, throned in heaven, who requires to send down his angels to fulfil his purposes on earth. It would excite surprise to find Olshausen arguing thus, did we not perceive from the manner in which this interpreter constantly treats of angelology and demonology, that he does not consider angels to be independent personal entities; but regards them rather as divine powers, transitory emanations and fulgurations of the Divine Being. Thus Olshausen's conception of angels, in their relation to God, seems to correspond with the Sabellian doctrine of the Trinity; but as his is not the representation of the Bible, as also the arguments in favour of the former prove nothing in relation to the latter, it is useless to enter into further explanation. The reasoning of this same theologian, that we must not require the ordinariness of every-day life for the most pregnant epochs in the life of the human race ; that the incarnation of the eternal word was accompanied by extraordinary manifestations from the world of spirits, uncalled for in times less rich in momentous results,[19] rests upon a misapprehension. For the ordinary course of every-day life is interrupted in such moments, by the very fact that exalted beings like the Baptist are born into the world, and it would be puerile to designate as ordinary those times and circumstances which gave birth and maturity to a John, because they were unembellished by angelic apparitions. That which the spiritual world does for ours at such periods is to send extraordinary human intelligences, not to cause angels to ascend and descend,

Finally, if, in vindication of this narrative, it be stated that such an exhibition by the angel, of the plan of education for the unborn child, was necessary in order to make him the man he should become [20], the assumption includes too much ; namely, that all great men, in order by their education to become such, must have been introduced into the world in like manner, or cause must be shown why that which was unnecessary in the case of great men of other ages and countries was indispensable for the Baptist. Again, the assumption attaches too much importance to external training, too little to the internal development of the mind. But in conclusion, many of the circumstances in the life of the Baptist, instead of serving to confirm a belief

---

[16] Binder, Studien der evang. Geistlichkeit Würtembergs, ix. 2, 5. 11 ff.
[17] Compare my Dogmatik, i. § 49.
[18] Bibl. Comm., I. Thl. s. 119.
[19] Ut sup. s. 92.
[20] Hess, Geschichte der drei letzten Lebensjahre Jesu u. s. w., I. Thl. s. 13, 33.

in the truth of the miraculous history, are on the contrary, as has been justly maintained, altogether irreconcilable with the supposition, that his birth was attended by these wonderful occurrences.   If it were indeed true, that John was from the first distinctly and miraculously announced as the forerunner of the Messiah, it is inconceivable that he should have had no acquaintance with Jesus prior to his baptism ; and that, even subsequent to that event, he should have felt perplexed concerning his Messiahship (John i. 30 ; Matt. xi. 2).[21]

Consequently the *negative* conclusion of the rationalistic criticism and controversy must, we think, be admitted, namely, that the birth of the Baptist could not have been preceded and attended by these supernatural occurrences.   The question now arises, what *positive* view of the matter is to replace the rejected literal orthodox explanation ?

§ 18.

NATURAL EXPLANATION OF THE NARRATIVE.

In treating the narrative before us according to the rationalistic method, which requires the separation of the pure fact from the opinion of interested persons, the simplest alteration is this : to retain the two leading facts, the apparition and the dumbness, as actual external occurrences ; but to account for them in a natural manner.   This were possible with respect to the apparition, by supposing that a man, mistaken by Zacharias for a divine messenger, really appeared to him, and addressed to him the words he believed he heard.   But this explanation, viewed in connexion with the attendant circumstances, being too improbable, it became necessary to go a step further, and to transform the event from an external to an internal one ; to remove the occurrence out of the physical into the psychological world.   To this view the opinion of Bahrdt, that a flash of lightning was perhaps mistaken by Zacharias for an angel,[1] forms a transition ; since he attributes the greater part of the scene to Zacharias's imagination.   But that any man, in an ordinary state of mind, could have created so long and consecutive a dialogue out of a flash of lightning is incredible.   A peculiar mental state must be supposed ; whether it be a swoon, the effect of fright occasioned by the lightning,[2] but of this there is no trace in the text (no falling down as in Acts ix. 4) ; or, abandoning the notion of the lightning, a dream, which, however, could scarcely occur whilst burning incense in the temple.   Hence, it has been found necessary, with Paulus, to call to mind that there are waking visions or ecstasies, in which the imagination confounds internal images with external occurrences.[3]   Such ecstasies, it is true, are not common ; but, says Paulus, in Zacharias's case many circumstances combined to produce so unusual a state of mind.   The exciting causes were, firstly, the long-cherished desire to have a posterity ; secondly, the exalted vocation of administering in the Holy of Holies, offering up with the incense the prayers of the people to the throne of Jehovah, which seemed to Zacharias to foretoken the acceptance of his own prayer ; and thirdly, perhaps an exhortation from his wife as he left his house, similar to that of Rachel to Jacob.   Gen. xxx. 1 (!)   In

---

[21] Horst in Henke's Museum, i. 4. s. 733 f.   Gabler in seinem neuest. theol. Journal, vii. I. s. 403.

[1] Briefe über die Bibel im Volkstone (Ausg. Frankfurt und Leipzig, 1800), 1tes Bändchen, 6ter Brief, s. 51 f.

[2] Bahrdt, ut sup. s. 52.

[3] Exeget. Handb. 1, a. s. 74 ff.

this highly excited state of mind, as he prays in the dimly-lighted sanctuary, he thinks of his most ardent wish, and expecting that now or never his prayer shall be heard, he is prepared to discern a sign of its acceptance in the slightest occurrence.   As the glimmer of the lamps falls upon the ascending cloud of incense, and shapes it into varying forms, the priest imagines he perceives the figure of an angel.   The apparition at first alarms him; but he soon regards it as an assurance from God that his prayer is heard.   No sooner does a transient doubt cross his mind, than the sensitively pious priest looks upon himself as sinful, believes himself reproved by the angel, and—here two explanations are possible—either an apoplectic seizure actually deprives him of speech, which he receives as the just punishment of his incredulity, till the excessive joy he experiences at the circumcision of his son restores the power of utterance: so that the dumbness is retained as an external, physical, though not miraculous, occurrence;[4] or the proceeding is psychologically understood, namely, that Zacharias, in accordance with a Jewish superstition, for a time denied himself the use of the offending member.[5]   Re-animated in other respects by the extraordinary event, the priest returns home to his wife, and she becomes a second Sarah.

With regard to this account of the angelic apparition given by Paulus,— and the other explanations are either of essentially similar character, or are so manifestly untenable, as not to need refutation—it may be observed that the object so laboriously striven after is not attained.   Paulus fails to free the narrative of the marvellous; for by his own admission, the majority of men have no experience of the kind of vision here supposed.[5]   If such a state of ecstasy occur in particular cases, it must result either from a predisposition in the individual, of which we find no sign in Zacharias, and which his advanced age must have rendered highly improbable; or it must have been induced by some peculiar circumstances, which totally fail in the present instance.[7]   A hope which has been long indulged is inadequate to the production of ecstatic vehemence, and the act of burning incense is insufficient to cause so extraordinary an excitement, in a priest who has grown old in the service of the temple.   Thus Paulus has in fact substituted a miracle of chance for a miracle of God.   Should it be said that to God nothing is impossible, or to chance nothing is impossible, both explanations are equally precarious and unscientific.

Indeed, the dumbness of Zacharias as explained from this point of view is very unsatisfactory.   For had it been, as according to one explanation, the result of apoplexy; admitting Paulus's reference to Lev. xxi. 16, to be set aside by the contrary remark of Lightfoot,[8] still, we must join with Schleiermacher in wondering how Zacharias, nothwithstanding this apoplectic seizure, returned home in other respects healthy and vigorous;[9] and that in spite of partial paralysis his general strength was unimpaired, and his long-cherished hope fulfilled.   It must also be regarded as a strange coincidence, that the father's tongue should have been loosed exactly at the time of the circumcision; for if the recovery of speech is to be considered as the effect of joy,[10] surely the father must have been far more elated at the birth of the

---

[4] Bahrdt, ut sup. 7ter Brief, s. 60.—E. F. über die beiden ersten Kapitel des Matthäus und Lukas, in Henke's Magazin, v. 1. s. 163.   Bauer, hebr. Mythol. 2, s. 220.

[5] Exeget. Handb. 1, a. s. 77-80.

[6] Ut sup. s. 73.

[7] Comp. Schleiermacher über die Schriften des Lukas, s. 25.

[8] Horæ hebr. et talmud., ed. Carpzov. p. 722.

[9] Ut sup. s. 26.

[10] Examples borrowed from Aulus Gellius, v. 9, and from Valerius Maximus, i. 8, are cited.

earnestly-desired son, than at the circumcision ; for by that time he would
have become accustomed to the possession of his child.

The other explanation : that Zacharias's silence was not from any physical
impediment, but from a notion, to be psychologically explained, that he ought
not to speak, is in direct contradiction to the words of Luke. What do
all the passages, collected by Paulus to show that οὐ δύναμαι may signify not
only a positive *non posse*, but likewise a mere *non sustinere*,[11] prove against
the clear meaning of the passage and its context? If perhaps the narrative
phrase (v. 22), οὐκ ἠδύνατο λαλῆσαι αὐτοῖς might be forced to bear this sense,
yet certainly in the supposed vision of Zacharias, had the angel only forbidden
him to speak, instead of depriving him of the power of speech, he would
not have said : καὶ ἔσῃ σιωπῶν, μὴ δυνάμενος λαλῆσαι, but ἴσθι σιωπῶν, μηδ᾽
ἐπιχειρήσῃς λαλῆσαι.   The words διέμενε κωφὸς (v. 21) also most naturally
mean actual dumbness.   This view assumes, and indeed necessarily so, that
the gospel history is a correct report of the account given by Zacharias himself; if then it be denied that the dumbness was actual, as Zacharias affirms
that actual dumbness was announced to him by the angel, it must be admitted that, though perfectly able to speak, he believed himself to be dumb ;
which leads to the conclusion that he was mad : an imputation not to be
laid upon the father of the Baptist without compulsory evidence in the text.

Again, the natural explanation makes too light of the incredibly accurate
fulfilment of a prediction originating, as it supposes, in an unnatural, over-
excited state of mind.   In no other province of inquiry would the realization
of a prediction which owed its birth to a vision be found credible, even by
the Rationalist.   If Dr. Paulus were to read that a somnambulist, in a state
of ecstasy, had foretold the birth of a child, under circumstances in the
highest degree improbable ; and not only of a child, but of a boy ; and had
moreover, with accurate minuteness, predicted his future mode of life,
character, and position in history ; and that each particular had been exactly
verified by the result : would he find such a coincidence credible?   Most
assuredly to no human being, under any conditions whatsoever, would he
concede the power thus to penetrate the most mysterious workings of nature ;
on the contrary he would complain of the outrage on human free-will, which
is annihilated by the admission that a man's entire intellectual and moral
development may be predetermined like the movements of a clock.   And he
would on this very ground complain of the inaccuracy of observation, and
untrustworthiness of the report which represented, as matters of fact, things
in their very nature impossible.   Why does he not follow the same rule with
respect to the New Testament narrative?   Why admit in the one case what
he rejects in the other ?   Is biblical history to be judged by one set of laws,
and profane history by another ?—An assumption which the Rationalist is
compelled to make, if he admits as credible in the Gospels that which he
rejects as unworthy of credit in every other history—which is in fact to fall
back on the supranaturalistic point of view, since the assumption, that the
natural laws which govern in every other province are not applicable to sacred
history, is the very essential of supranaturalism.

No other rescue from this self-annihilation remains to the anti-supernatural
mode of explanation, than to question the verbal accuracy of the history.
This is the simplest expedient, felt to be such by Paulus himself, who remarks,
that his efforts may be deemed superfluous to give a natural explanation of a
narrative, which is nothing more than one of those stories invented either
after the death or even during the lifetime of every distinguished man to em-

---

[11] Ut sup. s. 26.

bellish his early history.   Paulus, however, after an impartial examination, is
of opinion that the analogy, in the present instance, is not applicable.   The
principal ground for this opinion is the too short interval between the birth
of the Baptist, and the composition of the Gospel of Luke.[12] We, on the
contrary, in harmony with the observations in the introduction, would reverse
the question and inquire of this interpreter, how he would render it credible,
that the history of the birth of a man so famed as the Baptist should have
been transmitted, in an age of great excitement, through a period of more
than sixty years, in all its primitive accuracy of detail?   Paulus's answer
is ready : an answer approved by others (Heidenreich, Olshausen) :—the
passage inserted by Luke (i. 5 ; ii. 39) was possibly a family record, which
circulated among the relatives of the Baptist and of Jesus ; and of which
Zacharias was probably the author.[13]

K. Ch. L. Schmidt controverts this hypothesis with the remark, that it is
impossible that a narrative so disfigured (we should rather say, so embellished)
could have been a family record ; and that, if it does not belong altogether
to the class of legends, its historical basis, if such there be, is no longer to be
distinguished.[14]   It is further maintained, that the narrative presents certain
features which no poet would have conceived, and which prove it to be a
direct impression of facts ; for instance, the Messianic expectations expressed
by the different personages introduced by Luke (chap. i. and ii.) correspond
exactly with the situation and relation of each individual.[15]   But these distinctions are by no means so striking as Paulus represents ; they are only the
characteristics of a history which goes into details, making a transition from
generalities to particulars, which is natural alike to the poet and to the popular legend ; besides, the peculiar Judaical phraseology in which the Messianic
expectations are expressed, and which it is contended confirm the opinion
that this narrative was written, or received its fixed form, before the death of
Jesus, continued to be used after that event (Acts i. 6 [16]).   Moreover we
must agree with Schleiermacher when he says : [17] least of all is it possible to
regard these utterances as strictly historical ; or to maintain that Zacharias,
in the moment that he recovered his speech, employed it in a song of praise,
uninterrupted by the exultation and wonder of the company, sentiments
which the narrator interrupts himself to indulge.   It must, at all events, be
admitted, that the author has made additions of his own, and has enriched
the history by the lyric effusions of his muse.   Kuinöl supposes that Zacharias
composed and wrote down the canticle subsequent to the occasion ; but this
strange surmise contradicts the text.   There are some other features which,
it is contended, belong not to the creations of the poet ; such as, the signs
made to the father, the debate in the family, the position of the angel on the
right hand of the altar.[18]   But this criticism is merely a proof that these
interpreters have, or determine to have, no just conception of poetry or
popular legend ; for the genuine characteristic of poetry and mythus is
natural and pictorial representation of details.[19]

[12] Ut sup. s. 72 f.
[13] Ut sup. s. 69.
[14] In Schmidt's Bibliothek für Kritik und Exegese, iii. 1, s. 119.
[15] Paulus, ut sup.
[16] Comp. De Wette, exeg. Handb., i. 2, s. 9.
[17] Über die Schriften des Lukas, s. 23.
[18] Paulus und Olshausen z. d. St., Heydenreich a. a. O. 1, s. 87.
[19] Comp. Horst, in Henke's Museum, i. 4, s. 705 ; Vater, Commentar zum Pentateuch,
3, s. 597 ff. ; Hase L. J., § 35 ; auch George, s. 33 f. 91.

§ 19.

MYTHICAL VIEW OF THE NARRATIVE IN ITS DIFFERENT STAGES.

The above exposition of the necessity, and lastly, of the possibility of doubting the historical fidelity of the gospel narrative, has led many theologians to
explain the account of the birth of the Baptist as a poetical composition ;
suggested by the importance attributed by the Christians to the forerunner of
Jesus, and by the recollection of some of the Old Testament histories, in
which the births of Ishmael, Isaac, Samuel, and especially of Samson, are
related to have been similarly announced.   Still the matter was not allowed
to be altogether invented.   It may have been historically true that Zacharias
and Elizabeth lived long without offspring ; that, on one occasion whilst in
the temple, the old man's tongue was suddenly paralyzed ; but that soon afterwards his aged wife bore him a son, and he, in his joy at the event, recovered
the power of speech.   At that time, but still more when John became a remarkable man, the history excited attention, and out of it the existing legend
grew.[1]

It is surprising to find an explanation almost identical with the natural one
we have criticised above, again brought forward under a new title ; so that the
admission of the possibility of an admixture of subsequent legends in the narrative has little influence on the view of the matter itself.   As the mode of
explanation we are now advocating denies all confidence in the historical
authenticity of the record, all the details must be in themselves equally prob-
lematic ; and whether historical validity can be retained for this or that particular incident, can be determined only by its being either less improbable
than the rest, or else less in harmony with the spirit, interest, and design of
the poetic legend, so as to make it probable that it had a distinct origin.   The
barrenness of Elizabeth and the sudden dumbness of Zacharias are here retained as incidents of this character : so that only the appearing and prediction of the angel are given up.   But by taking away the angelic apparition,
the sudden infliction and as sudden removal of the dumbness loses its only
adequate supernatural cause, so that all difficulties which beset the natural interpretation remain in full force : a dilemma into which these theologians are,
most unnecessarily, brought by their own inconsequence ; for the moment we
enter upon mythical ground, all obligation to hold fast the assumed historical
fidelity of the account ceases to exist.   Besides, that which they propose to
retain as historical fact, namely, the long barrenness of the parents of the
Baptist, is so strictly in harmony with the spirit and character of Hebrew
legendary poetry, that of this incident the mythical origin is least to be mistaken.   How confused has this misapprehension made, for example, the
reasoning of Bauer !   It was a prevailing opinion, says he, consonant with
Jewish ideas, that all children born of aged parents, who had previously been
childless, became distinguished personages.   John was the child of aged
parents, and became a notable preacher of repentance ; consequently it was
thought justifiable to infer that his birth was predicted by an angel.   What an
illogical conclusion ! for which he has no other ground than the assumption
that John was the son of aged parents.   Let this be made a settled point,
and the conclusion follows without difficulty.   It was readily believed, he proceeds, of remarkable men that they were born of aged parents, and that their
birth, no longer in the ordinary course of nature to be expected, was an-

---

[1] E. F. über die zwei ersten Kapitel u. s. w. in Henke's Magazin, v. 1, s. 162 ff., und
Bauer hebr. Mythol., ii. 220 f.

nounced by a heavenly messenger[2]; John was a great man and a prophet; consequently, the legend represented him to have been born of an aged couple, and his birth to have been proclaimed by an angel.

Seeing that this explanation of the narrative before us, as a half (so called historical) mythus, is encumbered with all the difficulties of a half measure, Gabler has treated it as a pure philosophical, or dogmatical mythus.[3] Horst likewise considers it, and indeed the entire two first chapters of Luke, of which it forms a part, as an ingenious fiction, in which the birth of the Messiah, together with that of his precursor, and the predictions concerning the character and ministry of the latter, framed after the event, are set forth ; it being precisely the loquacious circumstantiality of the narration which betrays the poet.[4] Schleiermacher likewise explains the first chapter as a little poem, similar in character to many of the Jewish poems which we meet with in their apocrypha. He does not however consider it altogether a fabrication. It might have had a foundation in fact, and in a widespread tradition ; but the poet has allowed himself so full a license in arranging, and combining, in moulding and embodying the vague and fluctuating representations of tradition, that the attempt to detect the purely historical in such narratives, must prove a fruitless and useless effort.[5] Horst goes so far as to suppose the author of the piece to have been a Judaising Christian ; whilst Schleiermacher imagines it to have been composed by a Christian of the famed Jewish school, at a period when it comprised some who still continued strict disciples of John ; and whom it was the object of the narrative to bring over to Christianity, by exhibiting the relationship of John to the Christ as his peculiar and highest destiny ; and also by holding out the expectation of a state of temporal greatness for the Jewish people at the reappearance of Christ.

An attentive consideration of the Old Testament histories, to which, as most interpreters admit, the narrative of the annunciation and birth of the Baptist bears a striking affinity, will render it abundantly evident that this is the only just view of the passage in question. But it must not here be imagined, as is now so readily affirmed in the confutation of the mythical view of this passage, that the author of our narrative first made a collection from the Old Testament of its individual traits; much rather had the scattered traits respecting the late birth of different distinguished men, as recorded in the Old Testament, blended themselves into a compound image in the mind of their reader, whence he selected the features most appropriate to his present subject. Of the children born of aged parents, Isaac is the most ancient prototype. As it is said of Zacharias and Elizabeth, "they both were advanced in their days " (v. 7) προβεβηκότες ἐν ταῖς ἡμέραις αὐτῶν, so Abraham and Sarah "were advanced in their days " בָּאִים בַּיָּמִים (Gen. xviii. 11 ; LXX : προβεβηκότες ἡμερῶν), when they were promised a son. It is likewise from this history that the incredulity of the father, on account of the advanced age of both

[2] The adoption of this opinion is best explained by a passage—with respect to this matter classical—in the Evangelium de nativitate Mariæ, in Fabricius codex apocryphus N. Ti. 1, p. 22 f., and in Thilo 1, p. 322, " Deus "—it is here said,—cum alicujus uterum claudit, ad hoc facit, ut mirabilius denuo aperiat, et non libidinis esse, quod nascitur, sed divini muneris cognoscatur. Prima enim gentis vestræ Sara mater nonne usque ad octogesimum annum infecunda fuit ? et tamen in ultimâ senectutis ætate genuit Isaac, cui repromissa erat benedictio omnium gentium. Rachel quoque, tantum Domino grata tantumque a sancto Jacob amata diu sterilis fuit, et tamen Joseph genuit, non solum dominum Ægypti, sed plurimarum gentium fame periturarum liberatorem. Quis in ducibus vel fortior Sampsone, vel sanctior Samuele ? et tamen hi ambo steriles matres habuere.—ergo—crede—dilatos diu conceptus et steriles partus mirabiliores esse solere.

[3] Neuestes theol. Journal, vii. 1, s. 402 f.
[4] In Henke's Museum, i. 4, s. 702 ff.
[5] Hase in his Leben Jesu makes the same admission ; compare § 52 with § 32.

parents, and the demand of a sign, are borrowed in our narrative. As Abraham, when Jehovah promises him he shall have a son and a numerous posterity who shall inherit the land of Canaan, doubtingly inquires, "Whereby shall I know that I shall inherit it?" κατὰ τί γνώσομαι, ὅτι κληρονομήσω αὐτήν; (sc. τὴν γῆν. Gen. xv. 8. LXX): so Zacharias—"Whereby shall I know this?" κατὰ τί γνώσομαι τοῦτο; (v. 18.) The incredulity of Sarah is not made use of for Elizabeth; but she is said to be of the daughters of Aaron, and the name Elizabeth may perhaps have been suggested by that of Aaron's wife (Exod. vi. 23. LXX). The incident of the angel announcing the birth of the Baptist is taken from the history of another late-born child, Samson. In our narrative indeed, the angel appears first to the father in the temple, whereas in the history of Samson he shows himself first to the mother, and afterwards to the father in the field. This, however, is an alteration arising naturally out of the different situations of the respective parents (Judges xiii.). According to popular Jewish notions, it was no unusual occurrence for the priest to be visited by angels and divine apparitions whilst offering incense in the temple.[6] The command which before his birth predestined the Baptist —whose later ascetic mode of life was known—to be a Nazarite, is taken from the same source. As, to Samson's mother during her pregnancy, wine, strong drink, and unclean food, were forbidden, so a similar diet is prescribed for her son,[7] adding, as in the case of John, that the child shall be consecrated to God from the womb.[8] The blessings which it is predicted that these two men shall realize for the people of Israel are similar (comp. Luke i. 16, 17, with Judges xiii. 5), and each narrative concludes with the same expression respecting the hopeful growth of the child.[9] It may be too bold to derive the Levitical descent of the Baptist from a third Old Testament history of a late-born son—from the history of Samuel (compare 1 Sam. i. 1; Chron. vii. 27); but the lyric effusions in the first chapter of Luke are imitations of this history. As Samuel's mother, when consigning him to the care of the high priest, breaks forth into a hymn (1 Sam. ii. 1), so the father of John does the same at the circumcision; though the particular expressions in the Canticle uttered by Mary—of which we shall have to speak hereafter—have a closer resemblance to Hannah's song of praise than that of Zacharias. The significant appellation *John* (יְהוֹחָנָן = Θεόχαρις), predetermined by the angel, had its precedent in the announcements of the names of Ishmael and Isaac[10]; but the ground of its selection was the apparently providential coincidence between the signification of the name and the historical destination of the man. The

---

[6] Wetstein zu Luke i. 11, s. 647 f. adduces passages from Josephus and from the Rabbins recording apparitions seen by the high priests. How readily it was presumed that the same thing happened to ordinary priests is apparent from the narrative before us.

[7] Judges xiii. 14 (LXX.):
καὶ οἶνον καὶ σίκερα (al. μέθυσμα, hebr. שֵׁכָר)
μὴ πιέτω.

Luc. i. 15.
καὶ οἶνον καὶ σίκερα οὐ μὴ πίῃ.

[8] Judg. xiii. 5:
ὅτι ἡγιασμένον ἔσται τῷ θεῷ (al. Ναζὶρ θεοῦ ἔσται) τὸ παιδάριον οὐκ τῆς γαστρός (al. ἀπὸ τῆς κοιλίας).

Luc. i. 15:
καὶ πνεύματος ἁγίου πλησθήσεται ἔτι ἐκ κοιλίας μητρὸς αὐτοῦ.

[9] Judg. xiii. 24 f. :
καὶ ηὐλόγησεν αὐτὸν Κύριος, καὶ η᾿ξήθη (al. ηὐρύνθη) τὸ παιδάριον· καὶ ἤρξατο πνεῦμα Κυρίου συμπορεύεσθαι αὐτῷ ἐν παρεμβολῇ Δὰν, ἀναμέσον Σαρὰ καὶ ἀναμέσον Ἐσθαόλ.
Comp. Gen. xxi. 20.

Luc. i. 80 :
τὸ δὲ παιδίον ηὔξανε καὶ ἐκραταιοῦτο πνεύματι, καὶ ἦν ἐν ταῖς ἐρήμοις, ἕως ἡμέρας ἀναδείξεως αὐτοῦ πρὸς τὸν Ἰσραήλ.

[10] Gen. xvi. 11. (LXX.) :
καὶ καλέσεις τὸ ὄνομα αὐτοῦ Ἰσμαήλ.
xvii. 19 : — — Ἰσαάκ.

Luc. i. 13 :
καὶ καλέσεις τὸ ὄνομα αὐτοῦ Ἰωάννην.

remark, that the name of John was not in the family (v. 61), only brought its celestial origin more fully into view.   The tablet (πινακίδιον) upon which the father wrote the name (v. 63), was necessary on account of his incapacity to speak ; but it also had its type in the Old Testament.   Isaiah was commanded to write the significant names of the child Maher-shalal-hash-baz upon a tablet (Isaiah viii. 1 ff.).   The only supernatural incident of the narrative, of which the Old Testament may seem to offer no precise analogy, is the dumbness ; and this is the point fixed upon by those who contest the mythical view.[11]   But if it be borne in mind that the asking and receiving a sign from heaven in confirmation of a promise or prophecy was usual among the Hebrews (comp. Isaiah vii. 11 ff.) ; that the temporary loss of one of the senses was the peculiar punishment inflicted after a heavenly vision (Acts ix. 8, 17 ff.) ; that Daniel became dumb whilst the angel was talking with him, and did not recover his speech till the angel had touched his lips and opened his mouth (Dan. x. 15 f.) : the origin of this incident also will be found in the legend, and not in historical fact.   Of two ordinary and subordinate features of the narrative, the one, the righteousness of the parents of the Baptist (v. 6), is merely a conclusion founded upon the belief that to a pious couple alone would the blessing of such a son be vouchsafed, and consequently is void of all historical worth ; the other, the statement that John was born in the reign of Herod (the Great) (v. 5), is without doubt a correct calculation.

So that we stand here upon purely mythical-poetical ground ; the only historical reality which we can hold fast as positive matter of fact being this : —the impression made by John the Baptist, by virtue of his ministry and his relation to Jesus, was so powerful as to lead to the subsequent glorification of his birth in connection with the birth of the Messiah in the Christian legend.[12]

[11] Olshausen, bibl. Commentar, I. s. 116.   Hoffmann, s. 146.
[12] With this view of the passage compare De Wette, Exeg. Handbuch zum N. T., i. 2, s. 12.

CHAPTER II.

DAVIDICAL DESCENT OF JESUS, ACCORDING TO THE GENEALOGICAL TABLES OF MATTHEW AND LUKE.

———

§ 20.

THE TWO GENEALOGIES OF JESUS CONSIDERED SEPARATELY AND IRRESPECTIVELY OF ONE ANOTHER.

In the history of the birth of the Baptist, we had the single account of Luke ; but regarding the genealogical descent of Jesus we have also that of Matthew ; so that in this case the mutual control of two narrators in some respects multiplies, whilst in others it lightens, our critical labour. It is indeed true that the authenticity of the two first chapters of Matthew, which contain the history of the birth and childhood of Jesus, as well as that of the parallel section of Luke, has been questioned : but as in both cases the question has originated merely in a prejudiced view of the subject, the doubt has been silenced by a decisive refutation.[1]

Each of these two Gospels contains a genealogical table designed to exhibit the Davidical descent of Jesus, the Messiah. That of Matthew (i. 1–17) precedes, that of Luke (iii. 23–38) follows, the history of the announcement and birth of Jesus. These two tables, considered each in itself, or both compared together, afford so important a key to the character of the evangelic records in this section, as to render a close examination of them imperative. We shall first consider each separately, and then each, but particularly that of Matthew, in comparison with the passages in the Old Testament to which it is parallel.

In the Genealogy given by the author of the first Gospel, there is a comparison of the account with itself which is important, as it gives a result, a sum at its conclusion, whose correctness may be proved by comparing it with the previous statements. In the summing up it is said, that from Abraham to Christ there are three divisions of fourteen generations each, the first from Abraham to David, the second from David to the Babylonish exile, the third from the exile to Christ. Now if we compute the number of names for ourselves, we find the first fourteen from Abraham to David, both included, complete (2–5) ; also that from Solomon to Jechonias, after whom the Babylonish exile is mentioned (6–11) ; but from Jechonias to Jesus, even reckoning the latter as one, we can discover only thirteen (12–16). How shall we explain this discrepancy ? The supposition that one of the names has escaped from the third division by an error of a transcriber,[2] is in the highest degree improb-

[1] Kuinöl, Comm. in Matth. Proleg., p. xxvii. f.
[2] Paulus, p. 292.

able, since the deficiency is mentioned so early as by Porphyry.[3] The insertion, in some manuscripts and versions, of the name *Jehoiakim* [4] between
Josias and Jechonias, does not supply the deficiency of the third division ; it
only adds a superfluous generation to the second division, which was already
complete. As also there is no doubt that this deficiency originated with the
author of the genealogy, the question arises : in what manner did he reckon
so as to count fourteen generations for his third series ? Truly it is possible
to count in various ways, if an arbitrary inclusion and exclusion of the first and
last members of the several series be permitted. It might indeed have been
presupposed, that a generation already included in one division was necessarily
excluded from another : but the compiler of the genealogy may perhaps have
thought otherwise ; and since David is twice mentioned in the table, it is
possible that the author counted him twice : namely, at the end of the first
series, and again at the beginning of the second. This would not indeed, any
more than the insertion of Jehoiakim, fill up the deficiency in the third
division, but give too many to the second ; so that we must, with some commentators,[5] conclude the second series not with Jechonias, as is usually done,
but with his predecessor Josias : and now, by means of the double enumeration of David, Jechonias, who was superfluous in the second division, being
available for the third, the last series, including Jesus, has its fourteen members complete. But it seems very arbitrary to reckon the concluding member
of the first series twice, and not also that of the second : to avoid which inconsistency some interpreters have proposed to count Josias twice, as well as
David, and thus complete the fourteen members of the third series without
Jesus. But whilst this computation escapes one blunder, it falls into another ;
namely, that whereas the expression ἀπὸ ᾿Αβραὰμ ἕως Δαβὶδ κ. τ. λ. (v. 17) is
supposed to include the latter, in ἀπὸ μετοικεσίας Βαβυλῶνος ἕως τοῦ Χριστοῦ,
the latter is excluded. This difficulty may be avoided by counting Jechonias
twice instead of Josias, which gives us fourteen names for the third division,
including Jesus ; but then, in order not to have too many in the second, we
must drop the double enumeration of David, and thus be liable to the same
charge of inconsistency as in the former case, since the double enumeration
is made between the second and third divisions, and not between the first and
second. Perhaps De Wette has found the right clue when he remarks, that
in v. 17, in both transitions some member of the series is mentioned twice,
but in the first case only that member is a *person* (David), and therefore to
be twice reckoned. In the second case it is the *Babylonish captivity* occurring between Josias and Jechonias, which latter, since he had reigned only
three months in Jerusalem (the greater part of his life having passed after
the carrying away to Babylon), was mentioned indeed at the conclusion of
the second series for the sake of connexion, but was to be reckoned only at
the beginning of the third.[6]

If we now compare the genealogy of Matthew (still without reference to
that of Luke) with the corresponding passages of the Old Testament, we
shall also find discrepancy, and in this case of a nature exactly the reverse of
the preceding : for as the table considered in itself required the duplication
of one member in order to complete its scheme, so when compared with the
Old Testament, we find that many of the names there recorded have been
omitted, in order that the number fourteen might not be exceeded. That is
to say, the Old Testament affords data for comparison with this genealogical

[3] Hieron. in Daniel. init.
[4] See Wetstein.
[5] *e.g.* Frische, Comm. in Matth., p. 13.
[6] Exegt. Handbuch, i. 1, s. 12 f.

table as the famed pedigree of the royal race of David, from Abraham to Zorobabel and his sons ; after whom the Davidical line begins to retire into obscurity, and from the silence of the Old Testament the genealogy of Matthew ceases to be under any control. The series of generations from Abraham to Judah, Pharez, and Hezron, is sufficiently well known from Genesis; from Pharez to David we find it in the conclusion of the book of Ruth, and in the 2nd chapter of the 1st Chronicles ; that from David to Zerubbabel in the 3rd chapter of the same book ; besides passages that are parallel with separate portions of the series.

To complete the comparison : we find the line from Abraham to David, that is, the whole first division of fourteen in our genealogy, in exact accordance with the names of men given in the Old Testament : leaving out however the names of some women, one of which makes a difficulty. It is said v. 5 that Rahab was the mother of Boaz. Not only is this without confirmation in the Old Testament, but even if she be made the great-grandmother of Jesse, the father of David, there are too few generations between her time and that of David (from about 1450 to 1050 B.C.), that is, counting either Rahab or David as one, four for 400 years. Yet this error falls back upon the Old Testament genealogy itself, in so far as Jesse's great-grandfather Salmon, whom Matthew calls the husband of Rahab, is said Ruth iv. 20, as well as by Matthew, to be the son of a Nahshon, who, according to Numbers i. 7, lived in the time of the march through the wilderness[7] : from which circumstance the idea was naturally suggested, to marry his son with that Rahab who saved the Israelitish spies, and thus to introduce a woman for whom the Israelites had an especial regard (compare James ii. 25, Heb. xi. 31) into the lineage of David and the Messiah.

Many discrepancies are found in the second division from David to Zorobabel and his son, as well as in the beginning of the third. Firstly, it is said v. 8 *Joram begat Ozias;* whereas we know from 1 Chron. iii. 11, 12, that Uzziah was not the son, but the grandson of the son of Joram, and that three kings occur between them, namely, Ahaziah, Joash, and Amaziah, after whom comes Uzziah (2 Chron. xxvi. 1, or as he is called 1 Chron. iii. 12, and 2 Kings xiv. 21, Azariah). Secondly : our genealogy says v. 11, *Josias begat Jechonias and his brethren.* But we find from 1 Chron. iii. 16, that the son and successor of Josiah was called Jehoiakim, after whom came his son and successor Jechoniah or Jehoiachin. Moreover *brethren* are ascribed to Jechoniah, whereas the Old Testament mentions none. Jehoiakim, however, had brothers : so that the mention of the *brethren of Jechonias* in Matthew appears to have originated in an exchange of these two persons.—A third discrepancy relates to Zorobabel. He is here called, v. 12, a son of Salathiel ; whilst in 1 Chron. iii. 19, he is descended from Jechoniah, not through Shealtiel, but through his brother Pedaiah. In Ezra v. 2, and Haggai i. 1, however, Zerubbabel is designated, as here, the son of Shealtiel.—In the last place, Abiud, who is here called the son of Zorobabel, is not to be found amongst the children of Zerubbabel mentioned 1 Chron. iii. 19 f. : perhaps because Abiud was only a surname derived from a son of one of those there mentioned.[8]

The second and third of these discrepancies may have crept in without evil intention, and without any great degree of carelessness, for the omission of Jehoiakim may have arisen from the similar sound of the names (יְהוֹיָקִים and

---

[7] The expedient of Kuinöl, Comm. in Matth. p. 3, to distinguish the Rahab here mentioned from the celebrated one, becomes hence superfluous, besides that it is perfectly arbitrary.

[8] Hoffmann, s. 154, according to Hug, Einl., ii. s. 271.

יְהוֹיָכִין), which accounts also for the transposition of the brothers of Jechoniah; whilst respecting Zorobabel the reference to the Old Testament is partly adverse, partly favourable. But the first discrepancy we have adduced, namely, the omission of three known kings, is not so easily to be set aside. It has indeed been held that the similarity of names may here also have led the author to pass unintentionally from Joram to Ozias, instead of to the similar sounding Ahaziah (in the LXX. Ochozias). But this omission falls in so happily with the author's design of the threefold fourteen (admitting the double enumeration of David), that we cannot avoid believing, with Jerome, that the oversight was made on purpose with a view to it.[9] From Abraham to David, where the first division presented itself, having found fourteen members, he seems to have wished that those of the following divisions should correspond in number. In the whole remaining series the Babylonish exile offered itself as the natural point of separation. But as the second division from David to the exile gave him four supernumerary members, therefore he omitted four of the names. For what reason these particular four were chosen would be difficult to determine, at least for the three last mentioned.

The cause of the compiler's laying so much stress on the threefold equal numbers, may have been simply, that by this adoption of the Oriental custom of division into equal sections, the genealogy might be more easily committed to memory[10]: but with this motive a mystical idea was probably combined. The question arises whether this is to be sought in the number which is thrice repeated, or whether it consists in the threefold repetition ? Fourteen is the double of the sacred number seven ; but it is improbable that it was selected for this reason,[11] because otherwise the seven would scarcely have been so completely lost sight of in the fourteen. Still more improbable is the conjecture of Olshausen, that the number fourteen was specially chosen as being the numeric value of the name of David[12] ; for puerilities of this kind, appropriate to the rabbinical gematria, are to be found in no other part of the Gospels. It is more likely that the object of the genealogists consisted merely in the repetition of an equal number by retaining the fourteen which had first accidentally presented itself: since it was a notion of the Jews that signal divine visitations, whether of prosperity or adversity, recurred at regular periodical intervals. Thus, as fourteen generations had intervened between Abraham, the founder of the holy people, and David the king after God's own heart, so fourteen generations must intervene between the re-establishment of the kingdom and the coming of the son of David, the Messiah. [13] The most ancient genealogies in Genesis exhibit the very same uniformity. As according to the βίβλος γενέσεως ἀνθρώπων, cap. v., from Adam the first, to Noah the second, father of men, were ten generations : so from Noah, or rather from his son, the tenth is Abraham the father of the faithful. [14]

<hr>

[9] Compare Fritsche, Comm. in Matth., p. 19 ; Paulus, exeget. Handbuch, i. s. 289 ; De Wette, exeg. Handb. in loco.
[10] Fritsche in Matth., p. 11.
[11] Paulus, s. 292.
[12] Bibl. Comm., p. 46, note.
[13] See Schneckenburger, Beiträge zur Einleitung in das N. T., s. 41 f., and the passage cited from Josephus, B. j. vi. 8. Also may be compared the passage cited by Schöttgen, horæ hebr. et talm. zu Matth. i. from Synopsis Sohar, p. 132, n. 18. *Ab Abrahamo usque ad Salomonem XV. sunt generationes ; atque tunc luna fuit in plenilunio. A Salomone usque ad Zedekiam iterum sunt XV. generationes, et tunc luna defecit, et Zedekiæ effossi sunt oculi.*
[14] De Wette has already called attention to the analogy between these Old Testament genealogies and those of the Gospels, with regard to the intentional equality of numbers. Kritik der mos. Geschichte, s 69. Comp. s. 48.

This *à priori* treatment of his subject, this Procrustes-bed upon which the author of our genealogy now stretches, now curtails it, almost like a philosopher constructing a system,—can excite no predisposition in his favour. It is in vain to appeal to the custom of Oriental genealogists to indulge themselves in similar licence ; for when an author presents us with a pedigree expressly declaring that *all the generations* during a space of time were fourteen, whereas, through accident or intention, many members are wanting,—he betrays an arbitrariness and want of critical accuracy, which must shake our confidence in the certainty of his whole genealogy.

The genealogy of Luke, considered separately, does not present so many defects as that of Matthew. It has no concluding statement of the number of generations comprised in the genealogy, to act as a check upon itself, neither can it be tested, to much extent, by a comparison with the Old Testament. For, from David to Nathan, the line traced by Luke has no correspondence with any Old Testament genealogy, excepting in two of its members, Salathiel and Zorobabel ; and even with respect to these two, there is a contradiction between the statement of Luke and that of 1 Chron. iii. 17. 19 f. : for the former calls Salathiel a son of Neri, whilst, according to the latter, he was the son of Jechoniah. Luke also mentions one Resa as the son of Zorobabel, a name which does not appear amongst the children of Zerubbabel in 1 Chron. iii. 17, 19. Also, in the series before Abraham, Luke inserts a Cainan, who is not to be found in the Hebrew text, Gen. x. 24 ; xi. 12 ff., but who was however already inserted by the LXX. In fact, the original text has this name in its first series as the third from Adam, and thence the translation appears to have transplanted him to the corresponding place in the second series as the third from Noah.

§ 21.

COMPARISON OF THE TWO GENEALOGIES—ATTEMPT TO RECONCILE THEIR CONTRADICTIONS.

If we compare the genealogies of Matthew and Luke together, we become aware of still more striking discrepancies. Some of these differences indeed are unimportant, as the opposite direction of the two tables, the line of Matthew descending from Abraham to Jesus, that of Luke ascending from Jesus to his ancestors. Also the greater extent of the line of Luke ; Matthew deriving it no farther than from Abraham, while Luke (perhaps lengthening some existing document in order to make it more consonant with the universalism of the doctrines of Paul [1] :) carries it back to Adam and to God himself. More important is the considerable difference in the number of generations for equal periods, Luke having 41 between David and Jesus, whilst Matthew has only 26. The main difficulty, however, lies in this : that in some parts of the genealogy, in Luke totally different individuals are made the ancestors of Jesus from those in Matthew. It is true, both writers agree in deriving the lineage of Jesus through Joseph from David and Abraham, and that the names of the individual members of the series correspond from Abraham to David, as well as two of the names in the subsequent portion : those of Salathiel and Zorobabel. But the difficulty becomes desperate when we find that, with these two exceptions about midway, the whole of the names from David to the foster-father of Jesus are totally different in Matthew and

---

[1] See Chrysostom and Luther, in Credner, Einleitung in d. N. T., 1, s. 143 f. Winer, bibl. Realwörterbuch, 1. s. 659.

in Luke. In Matthew, the father of Joseph is called Jacob; in Luke, Heli. In Matthew, the son of David through whom Joseph descended from that king is Solomon; in Luke, Nathan: and so on, the line descends, in Matthew, through the race of known kings; in Luke, through an unknown collateral branch, coinciding only with respect to Salathiel and Zorobabel, whilst they still differ in the names of the father of Salathiel and the son of Zorobabel. Since this difference appears to offer a complete contradiction, the most industrious efforts have been made at all times to reconcile the two. Passing in silence explanations evidently unsatisfactory, such as a mystical signification, [2] or an arbitrary change of names,[3] we shall consider two pairs of hypotheses which have been most conspicuous, and are mutually supported, or at least bear affinity to one another.

The first pair is formed upon the presupposition of Augustine, that Joseph was an adopted son, and that one evangelist gave the name of his real, the other that of his adopted, father[4]; and the opinion of the old chronologist Julius Africanus, that a Levirate marriage had taken place between the parents of Joseph, and that the one genealogy belonged to the natural, the other to the legal, father of Joseph, by the one of whom he was descended from David through Solomon, by the other through Nathan.[5] The farther question: to which father do the respective genealogies belong? is open to two species of criticism, the one founded upon literal expressions, the other upon the spirit and character of each gospel: and which lead to opposite conclusions. Augustine as well as Africanus, has observed, that Matthew makes use of an expression in describing the relationship between Joseph and his so-called father, which more definitely points out the natural filial relationship than that of Luke: for the former says Ἰακὼβ ἐγέννησε τὸν Ἰωσήφ: whilst the expression of the latter, Ἰωσὴφ τοῦ Ἡλὶ, appears equally applicable to a son by adoption, or by virtue of a Levirate marriage. But since the very object of a Levirate marriage was to maintain the name and race of a deceased childless brother, it was the Jewish custom to inscribe the first-born son of such a marriage, not on the family register of his natural father, as Matthew has done here, but on that of his legal father, as Luke has done on the above supposition. Now that a person so entirely imbued with Jewish opinions as the author of the first Gospel, should have made a mistake of this kind, cannot be held probable. Accordingly, Schleiermacher and others conceive themselves bound by the spirit of the two Gospels to admit that Matthew, in spite of his ἐγέννησε, must have given the lineage of the legal father, according to Jewish custom: whilst Luke, who perhaps was not born a Jew, and was less familiar with Jewish habits, might have fallen upon the genealogy of the younger brothers of Joseph, who were not, like the firstborn, inscribed amongst the family of the deceased legal father, but with that of their natural father, and might have taken this for the genealogical table of the first-born Joseph, whilst it really belonged to him only by natural descent, to which Jewish genealogists paid no regard.[6] But, besides the fact, which we shall show hereafter, that the genealogy of Luke can with difficulty be proved to be the work of the author of that Gospel:—in which case the little acquaintance of Luke with

---

[2] Orig. homil. in Lucam 28.
[3] Luther, Werke, Bd. 14. Walch. Ausg. s. 8 ff.
[4] De consensu Evangelistarum, ii. 3, u. c. Faust., iii. 3; amongst the moderns, for example, E. F. in Henke's Magazin 5, 1, 180 f. After Augustine had subsequently become acquainted with the writing of Africanus, he gave up his own opinion for that of the latter. Retract. ii. 7.
[5] Eusebius, H. E. i. 7, and lately e.g. Schleiermacher on Luke, p. 53.
[6] S. 53. Comp. Winer, bibl. Realwörterbuch, 1 Bd. s. 660.

Jewish customs ceases to afford any clue to the meaning of this genealogy;—
it is also to be objected, that the genealogist of the first Gospel could not
have written his ἐγέννησε thus without any addition, if he was thinking of
a mere legal paternity.   Wherefore these two views of the genealogical
relationship are equally difficult.

However, this hypothesis, which we have hitherto considered only in
general, requires a more detailed examination in order to judge of its admissi-
bility.   In considering the proposition of a Levirate marriage, the argument
is essentially the same if, with Augustine and Africanus, we ascribe the
naming of the natural father to Matthew, or with Schleiermacher, to Luke.
As an example we shall adopt the former statement : the rather because
Eusebius, according to Africanus, has left us a minute account of it.   According to this representation, then, the mother of Joseph was first married to
that person whom Luke calls the father of Joseph, namely Heli.   But since
Heli died without children, by virtue of the Levirate law, his brother, called
by Matthew Jacob the father of Joseph, married the widow, and by her
begot Joseph, who was legally regarded as the son of the deceased Heli, and
so described by Luke, whilst naturally he was the son of his brother Jacob,
and thus described by Matthew.

But, merely thus far, the hypothesis is by no means adequate.   For if the
two fathers of Joseph were real brothers, sons of the same father, they had
one and the same lineage, and the two genealogies would have differed only
in the father of Joseph, all the preceding portion being in agreement.   In
order to explain how the discordancy extends so far back as to David, we
must have recourse to the second proposition of Africanus, that the fathers of
Joseph were only half-brothers, having the same mother, but not the same
father.   We must also suppose that this mother of the two fathers of Joseph,
had twice married ; once with the Matthan of Matthew, who was descended
from David through Solomon and the line of kings, and to whom she bore
Jacob ; and also, either before or after, with the Matthat of Luke, the offspring of which marriage was Heli : which Heli, having married and died
childless, his half-brother Jacob married his widow, and begot for the deceased
his legal child Joseph.

This hypothesis of so complicated a marriage in two successive generations,
to which we are forced by the discrepancy of the two genealogies, must be
acknowledged to be in no way impossible, but still highly improbable : and
the difficulty is doubled by the untoward agreement already noticed, which
occurs midway in the discordant series, in the two members Salathiel and
Zorobabel.   For to explain how Neri in Luke, and Jechonias in Matthew,
are both called the father of Salathiel, who was the father of Zorobabel ;—not
only must the supposition of the Levirate marriage be repeated, but also that
the two brothers who successively married the same wife, were brothers only
on the mother's side.   The difficulty is not diminished by the remark, that
any nearest blood-relation, not only a brother, might succeed in a Levirate
marriage,—that is to say, though not obligatory, it was at least open to his
choice (Ruth iii. 12. f. iv. 4 f.[7]).   For since even in the case of two cousins,
the concurrence of the two branches must take place much earlier than here
for Jacob and Eli, and for Jechonias and Neri, we are still obliged to have
recourse to the hypothesis of half-brothers ; the only amelioration in this
hypothesis over the other being, that these two very peculiar marriages do not
take place in immediately consecutive generations.   Now that this extraordinary double incident should not only have been twice repeated, but that

---

[7] Comp. Michaelis, Mos. Recht. ii. s. 200.   Winer, bibl. Realwörterb. ii. s. 22 f.

the genealogists should twice have made the same selection in their statements respecting the natural and the legal father, and without any explanation,—is so improbable, that even the hypothesis of an adoption, which is burdened with only one-half of these difficulties, has still more than it can bear. For in the case of adoption, since no fraternal or other relationship is required, between the natural and adopting fathers, the recurrence to a twice-repeated half-brotherhood is dispensed with ; leaving only the necessity for twice supposing a relationship by adoption, and twice the peculiar circumstance, that the one genealogist from want of acquaintance with Jewish customs was ignorant of the fact, and the other, although he took account of it, was silent respecting it.

It has been thought by later critics that the knot may be loosed in a much easier way, by supposing that in one Gospel we have the genealogy of Joseph, in the other that of Mary, in which case there would be no contradiction in the disagreement : [8] to which they are pleased to add the assumption that Mary was an heiress.[9]   The opinion that Mary was of the race of David as well as Joseph has been long held.   Following indeed the idea, that the Messiah, as a second Melchizedec, ought to unite in his person the priestly with the kingly dignity,[10] and guided by the relationship of Mary with Elizabeth, who was a daughter of Aaron (Luke i. 36) ; already in early times it was not only held by many that the races of Judah and Levi were blended in the family of Joseph ; [11] but also the opinion was not rare that Jesus, deriving his royal lineage from Joseph, descended also from the priestly race through Mary.[12]   The opinion of Mary's descent from David, soon however became the more prevailing.   Many apocryphal writers clearly state this opinion,[13] as well as Justin Martyr, whose expression, that the virgin was of the race of David, Jacob, Isaac, and Abraham, may be considered an indication that he applied to Mary one of our genealogies, which are both traced back to Abraham through David.[14]

On inquiring which of these two genealogies is to be held that of Mary ? we are stopped by an apparently insurmountable obstacle, since each is distinctly announced as the genealogy of Joseph ; the one in the words Ἰακὼβ ἐγέννησε τὸν Ἰωσήφ, the other by the phrase υἱὸς Ἰωσὴφ τοῦ Ἠλί.   Here also, however, the ἐγέννησε of Matthew is more definite than the τοῦ of Luke, which according to those interpreters may mean just as well a son-in-law or grandson ; so that the genitive of Luke in iii. 23 was either intended to express that Jesus was in common estimation a son of Joseph, who was the son-in-law of Heli, the father of Mary [15] :—or else, that Jesus was, as was believed, a son of Joseph, and through Mary a grandson of Heli.[16]   As it may here be objected, that the Jews in their genealogies were accustomed to take no account of the

---

[8] Thus e.g. Spanheim, dubia evang. p. 1. s. 13 ff.   Lightfoot, Michaelis, Paulus, Kuinöl, Olshausen, lately Hoffmann and others.
[9] Epiphanius, Grotius.   Olshausen, s. 43.
[10] Testament XII. Patriarch., Test. Simeon c. 71.   In Fabric. Codex pseudepigr. V. T. p. 542 : ἐξ αὐτῶν (the races of Levi and Juda) ἀνατελεῖ ὑμῖν τὸ σωτήριον τοῦ θεοῦ.   Ἀνασήσει γὰρ Κύριος ἐκ τοῦ Λευῒ ὡς ἀρχιερέα, καὶ ἐκ τοῦ Ἰουδα ὡς βασιλέα κ. τ. λ.
[11] Comp. Thilo, cod. apocr. N.T. 1, s. 374 ff.
[12] Thus e.g. the Manichæan Faustus in Augustin. contra Faust. L. xxiii. 4.
[13] Protevangel. Jacobi c. 1 f. u. 10. and evangel. de nativitate Mariæ c. 1.   Joachim and Anna, of the race of David, are here mentioned as the parents of Mary.   Faustus on the contrary, in the above cited passage, gives Joachim the title of Sacerdos.
[14] Dial. c. Tryph. 43. 100. (Paris, 1742.)
[15] Paulus.   The Jews also in their representation of a Mary, the daughter of Heli, tormented in the lower world (see Lightfoot), appear to have taken the genealogy of Luke, which sets out from Heli, for that of Mary.
[16] e.g. Lightfoot, horæ, p. 750 ; Osiander, s. 86.

female line,[17] a farther hypothesis is had recourse to, namely, that Mary was an heiress, *i.e.* the daughter of a father without sons : and that in this case, according to Numbers xxxvi. 6, and Nehemiah vii. 63, Jewish custom required that the person who married her should not only be of the same race with herself, but that he should henceforth sink his own family in hers, and take her ancestors as his own.   But the first point only is proved by the reference to Numbers; and the passage in Nehemiah, compared with several similar ones (Ezra ii. 61 ; Numbers xxxii. 41; comp. with 1 Chron. ii. 21 f.), shows only that sometimes, by way of exception, a man took the name of his maternal ancestors.   This difficulty with regard to Jewish customs, however, is cast into shade by one much more important.   Although undeniably the genitive case used by Luke, expressing simply derivation in a general sense, may signify any degree of relationship, and consequently that of son-in-law or grandson ; yet this interpretation destroys the consistency of the whole passage.   In the thirty-four preceding members, which are well known to us from the Old Testament, this genitive demonstrably indicates throughout the precise relationship of a son ; likewise when it occurs between Salathiel and Zorobabel: how could it be intended in the one instance of Joseph to indicate that of son-in-law ? or, according to the other interpretation, supposing the nominative υἱὸς to govern the whole series, how can we suppose it to change its signification from son to grandson, great-grandson, and so on to the end ? If it be said the phrase Ἀδὰμ τοῦ θεοῦ is a proof that the genitive does not necessarily indicate a son in the proper sense of the word, we may reply that it bears a signification with regard to the immediate Author of existence equally inapplicable to either father-in-law or grandfather.

A further difficulty is encountered by this explanation of the two genealogies in common with the former one, in the concurrence of the two names of Salathiel and Zorobabel.   The supposition of a Levirate marriage is as applicable to this explanation as the other, but the interpreters we are now examining prefer for the most part to suppose, that these similar names in the different genealogies belong to different persons.   When Luke however, in the twenty-first and twenty-second generations from David, gives the very same names that Matthew (including the four omitted generations), gives in the nineteenth and twentieth, one of these names being of great notoriety, it is certainly impossible to doubt that they refer to the same persons.

Moreover, in no other part of the New Testament is there any trace to be found of the Davidical descent of Mary : on the contrary, some passages are directly opposed to it.   In Luke i. 27, the expression ἐξ οἴκου Δαβίδ refers only to the immediately preceding ἀνδρὶ ᾧ ὄνομα Ἰωσὴφ, not to the more remote παρθένον μεμνηστευμένην.   And more pointed still is the turn of the sentence Luke ii. 4, ἀνέβη δὲ καὶ Ἰωσὴφ—διὰ τὸ εἶναι αὐτὸν ἐξ οἴκου καὶ πατριᾶς Δαβὶδ, ἀπο-γράψασθαι σὺν Μαρίᾳ κ. τ. λ., where αὐτοὺς might so easily have been written instead of αὐτὸν, if the author had any thought of including Mary in the descent from David.   These expressions fill to overflowing the measure of proof already adduced, that it is impossible to apply the genealogy of the third Evangelist to Mary.

---

[17] Juchasin f. 55, 2. in Lightfoot s. 183, and Bava bathra, f. 110, 2. in Wetstein s. 230 f. Comp. Joseph. Vita, 1.

§ 22.

THE GENEALOGIES UNHISTORICAL.

A consideration of the insurmountable difficulties, which unavoidably embarrass every attempt to bring these two genealogies into harmony with one another, will lead us to despair of reconciling them, and will incline us to acknowledge, with the more free-thinking class of critics, that they are mutually contradictory.[1] Consequently they cannot both be true : if, therefore, one is to be preferred before the other, several circumstances would seem to decide in favour of the genealogy of Luke, rather than that of Matthew. It does not exhibit an arbitrary adherence to a fixed form and to equal periods : and whilst the ascribing of twenty generations to the space of time from David to Jechonias or Neri, in Luke, is at least not more offensive to probability, than the omission of four generations in Matthew to historical truth ; Luke's allotment of twenty-two generations for the period from Jechonias (born 617 B.C.) to Jesus, *i.e.* about 600 years, forming an average of twenty-seven years and a half to each generation, is more consonant with natural events, particularly amongst eastern nations, than the thirteen generations of Matthew, which make an average of forty-two years for each. Besides the genealogy of Luke is less liable than that of Matthew to the suspicion of having been written with a design to glorify Jesus, since it contents itself with ascribing to Jesus a descent from David, without tracing that descent through the royal line. On the other hand, however, it is more improbable that the genealogy of the comparatively insignificant family of Nathan should have been preserved, than that of the royal branch. Added to which, the frequent recurrence of the same names is, as justly remarked by Hoffmann, an indication that the genealogy of Luke is fictitious.

In fact then neither table has any advantage over the other. If the one is unhistorical, so also is the other, since it is very improbable that the genealogy of an obscure family like that of Joseph, extending through so long a series of generations, should have been preserved during all the confusion of the exile, and the disturbed period that followed. Yet, it may be said, although we recognise in both, so far as they are not copied from the Old Testament, an unrestrained play of the imagination, or arbitrary applications of other genealogies to Jesus,—we may still retain as an historical basis that Jesus was descended from David, and that only the intermediate members of the line of descent were variously filled up by different writers. But the one event on which this historical basis is mainly supported, namely, the journey of the parents of Jesus to Bethlehem in order to be taxed, so far from sufficing to prove them to be of the house and lineage of David, is itself, as we shall presently show, by no means established as matter of history. Of more weight is the other ground, namely, that Jesus is universally represented in the New Testament, without any contradiction from his adversaries, as the descendant of David. Yet even the phrase υἱὸς Δαβὶδ is a predicate that may naturally have been applied to Jesus, not on historical, but on dogmatical grounds. According to the prophecies, the Messiah could only spring from David. When therefore a Galilean, whose lineage was utterly unknown, and of whom consequently no one could prove that he was not descended from David, had acquired the

---

[1] Thus Eichhorn, Einl. in das N. T. 1 Bd. s. 425. Kaiser, bibl. Theol. 1, s. 232. Wegscheider, Institut. § 123, not. d. de Wette, bibl. Dogm. § 279, and exeget. Handbuch 1, 2, s. 32. Winer, bibl. Realwörterb. 1, s. 660 f. Hase, Leben Jesu, § 33. Fritzsche, Comm. in Matt. p. 35. Ammon, Fortbildung des Christenthums zur Weltreligion, 1, s. 196 ff.

reputation of being the Messiah ; what more natural than that tradition should under different forms have early ascribed to him a Davidical descent, and that genealogical tables, corresponding with this tradition, should have been formed? which, however, as they were constructed upon no certain data, would necessarily exhibit such differences and contradictions as we find actually existing between the genealogies in Matthew and in Luke.[2]

If, in conclusion, it be asked, what historical result is to be deduced from these genealogies? we reply: a conviction (arrived at also from other sources), that Jesus, either in his own person or through his disciples, acting upon minds strongly imbued with Jewish notions and expectations, left among his followers so firm a conviction of his Messiahship, that they did not hesitate to attribute to him the prophetical characteristic of Davidical descent, and more than one pen was put in action, in order, by means of a genealogy which should authenticate that descent, to justify his recognition as the Messiah.[3]

---

[2] See De Wette, bibl. Dogm. and exeg. Handb. 1, 1, s. 14 ; Hase, L. J.   Eusebius gives a not improbable explanation of this disagreement (ad. Steph. quæst. iii., pointed out by Credner, 1, p. 68 f.) that besides the notion amongst the Jews, that the Messiah must spring from the royal line of David, another had arisen, that this line having become polluted and declared unworthy of continuing on the throne of David (Jerem. xxii. 30), by the wickedness of its later reigning members, a line more pure though less famed was to be preferred to it.

[3] The farther considerations on the origin and import of these genealogies, which arise from their connexion with the account of the miraculous birth of Jesus, must be reserved till after the examination of the latter point.

CHAPTER III.

ANNOUNCEMENT OF THE CONCEPTION OF JESUS.—ITS SUPERNATURAL CHARACTER.—VISIT OF MARY TO ELIZABETH.

§ 23.

SKETCH OF THE DIFFERENT CANONICAL AND APOCRYPHAL ACCOUNTS.

THERE is a striking gradation in the different representations of the conception and birth of Jesus given in the canonical and in the apocryphal Gospels. They exhibit the various steps, from a simple statement of a natural occurrence, to a minute and miraculously embellished history, in which the event is traced back to its very earliest date. Mark and John presuppose the fact of the birth of Jesus, and content themselves with the incidental mention of Mary as the mother (Mark vi. 3), and of Joseph as the father of Jesus (John i. 46). Matthew and Luke go further back, since they state the particular circumstances attending the conception as well as the birth of the Messiah. But of these two evangelists Luke mounts a step higher than Matthew. According to the latter Mary, the betrothed of Joseph, being *found with child,* Joseph is offended, and determines to put her away ; but the angel of the Lord visits him in a dream, and assures him of the divine origin and exalted destiny of Mary's offspring ; the result of which is that Joseph takes unto him his wife : but knows her not till she has brought forth her first-born son. (Matt. i. 18–25.) Here the pregnancy is discovered in the first place, and then afterwards justified by the angel ; but in Luke the pregnancy is prefaced and announced by a celestial apparition. The same Gabriel, who had predicted the birth of John to Zacharias, appears to Mary, the betrothed of Joseph, and tells her that she shall conceive by the power of the Holy Ghost ; whereupon the destined mother of the Messiah pays a visit full of holy import to the already pregnant mother of his forerunner ; upon which occasion both Mary and Elizabeth pour forth their emotions to one another in the form of a hymn (Luke i. 26–56). Matthew and Luke are content to presuppose the connexion between Mary and Joseph ; but the apocryphal Gospels, the *Protevangelium Jacobi,* and the *Evangelium de Nativitate Mariae,*[1] (books with the contents of which the Fathers partially agree,) seek to represent the origin of this connexion ; indeed they go back to the birth of Mary, and describe it to have been preceded, equally with that of the Messiah and the Baptist, by a divine annunciation. As the description of the birth of John in Luke is principally borrowed from the Old Testament accounts of Samuel and of Samson, so this history of the birth of Mary is an imitation of the history in Luke, and of the Old Testament histories.

Joachim, so says the apocryphal narrative, and Anna (the name of Samuel's

---

[1] Fabricius, Codex apocryphus N. T. 1, p. 19 ff. 66 ff. ; Thilo, 1, p. 161 ff. 319 ff.

mother [2]) are unhappy on account of their long childless marriage (as were the parents of the Baptist) ; when an angel appears to them both (so in the history of Samson) at different places, and promises them a child, who shall be the mother of God, and commands that this child shall live the life of a Nazarite (like the Baptist). In early childhood Mary is brought by her parents to the temple (like Samuel) ; where she continues till her twelfth year, visited and fed by angels and honoured by divine visions. Arrived at womanhood she is to quit the temple, her future provision and destiny being revealed by the oracle to the high priest. In conformity with the prophecy of Isaiah xi. 1 f.: *egredietur virga de radice Jesse, et flos de radice ejus ascendet, et requiescet super eum spiritus Domini* ; this oracle commanded, according to one Gospel,[3] that all the unmarried men of the house of David,—according to the other,[4] that all the widowers among the people,—should bring their rods, and that he on whose rod a sign should appear (like the rod of Aaron, Numb. xvii.), namely the sign predicted in the prophecy, should take Mary unto himself. This sign was manifested upon Joseph's rod ; for, in exact accordance with the oracle, it put forth a blossom and a dove lighted upon it.[5] The apocryphal Gospels and the Fathers agree in representing Joseph as an old man ;[6] but the narrative is somewhat differently told in the two apocryphal Gospels. According to the *Evang. de nativ. Mariae*, notwithstanding Mary's alleged vow of chastity, and the refusal of Joseph on account of his great age, betrothment took place at the command of the priest, and subsequently a marriage—(which marriage, however, the author evidently means to represents also as chaste). According to the *Protevang. Jacobi*, on the contrary, neither betrothment nor marriage are mentioned, but Joseph is regarded merely as the chosen protector of the young virgin,[7] and Joseph on the journey to Bethlehem doubts whether he shall describe his charge as his wife or as his daughter ; fearing to bring ridicule upon himself, on account of his age, if he called her his wife. Again, where in Matthew Mary is called ἡ γυνή of Joseph, the apocryphal Gospel carefully designates her merely as ἡ παῖς, and even avoids using the term παραλαβεῖν or substitutes διαφυλάξαι, with which many of the Fathers concur.[8] In the *Protevangelium* it is further related that Mary, having been received into Joseph's house, was charged, together with other young women, with the fabrication of the veil for the temple, and that it fell to her lot to spin the true purple.—But whilst Joseph was absent on business Mary was visited by an angel, and Joseph on his return found her with child and called her to account, not as a husband, but as the guardian of her honour. Mary, however, had forgotten the words of the angel and protested her ignorance of the cause of her pregnancy. Joseph was perplexed and determined to remove her secretly from under his protection ; but an angel appeared to him in a dream and reassured him by his explanation. The matter was then brought before the priest, and both

---

[2] Gregory of Nyssa or his interpolator is reminded of this mother of Samuel by the apocryphal Anna when he says of her : Μιμεῖται τοίνυν καὶ αὕτη τὰ περὶ τῆς μητρὸς τοῦ Σαμουὴλ διηγήματα κ.τ.λ. Fabricius, 1, p. 6.

[3] Evang. de nativ. Mar. c. 7 : *cunctos de domo et familia David nuptui habiles, non conjugatos.*

[4] Protev. Jac. c. 8 : τοὺς χηρεύοντας τοῦ λαοῦ.

[5] It is thus in the Evang. de nativ. Mariae vii. and viii. ; but rather different in the Protev. Jac. c. ix.

[6] Protev. c. 9 : πρεσβύτης. Evang. de nativ. Mar. 8. : grandaevus. Epiphan. adv. haeres. 78, 8 : λαμβάνει τὴν Μαρίαν χῆρος, κατάγων ἡλικίαν περί που ὀγδοήκοντα ἐτῶν καὶ πρόσω ὁ ἀνήρ.

[7] Παράλαβε αὐτὴν εἰς τήρησιν σεαυτῷ. c. ix. Compare with Evang. de nativ. Mar. viii. and x.

[8] See the variations in *Thilo*, p. 227, and the quotations from the Fathers at p. 365 not.

Joseph and Mary being charged with incontinence were condemned to drink the "bitter water," [9] ὕδωρ τῆς ἐλέγξεως, but as they remained uninjured by it, they were declared innocent.   Then follows the account of the taxing and of the birth of Jesus.[10]

Since these apocryphal narratives were for a long period held as historical by the church, and were explained, equally with those of the canonical accounts, from the supranaturalistic point of view as miraculous, they were entitled in modern times to share with the New Testament histories the benefit of the natural explanation.   If, on the one hand, the belief in the marvellous was so superabundantly strong in the ancient church, that it reached beyond the limits of the New Testament even to the embracing of the apocryphal narratives, blinding the eye to the perception of their manifestly unhistorical character; so, on the other hand, the positive rationalism of some of the heralds of the modern modes of explanation was so overstrong that they believed it adequate to explain even the apocryphal miracles.   Of this we have an example in the author of the natural history of the great prophet of Nazareth;[11] who does not hesitate to include the stories of the lineage and early years of Mary within the circle of his representations, and to give them a natural explanation.   If we in our day, with a perception of the fabulous character of such narratives, look down alike upon the Fathers of the church and upon these naturalistic interpreters, we are certainly so far in the right, as it is only by gross ignorance that this character of the apocryphal accounts is here to be mistaken ; more closely considered, however, the difference between the apocryphal and the canonical narratives concerning the early history of the Baptist and of Jesus, is seen to be merely a difference of form : they have sprung, as we shall hereafter find, from the same root, though the one is a fresh and healthy sprout, and the other an artificially nurtured and weak aftergrowth.   Still, the Fathers of the church and these naturalistic interpreters had this superiority over most of the theologians of our own time ; that they did not allow themselves to be deceived respecting the inherent similarity by the difference of form, but interpreted the kindred narratives by the same method ; treating both as miraculous or both as natural ; and not, as is now usual, the one as fiction and the other as history.

§ 24.

DISAGREEMENTS OF THE CANONICAL GOSPELS IN RELATION TO THE FORM OF THE ANNUNCIATION.

After the foregoing general sketch, we now proceed to examine the external circumstances which, according to our Gospels, attended the first communication of the future birth of Jesus to Mary and Joseph.   Leaving out of sight, for the present, the special import of the annunciation, namely, that Jesus should be supernaturally begotten of the Holy Ghost, we shall, in the first place, consider merely the form of the announcement; by whom, when, and in what manner it was made.

As the birth of the Baptist was previously announced by an angel, so the conception of Jesus was, according to the gospel histories, proclaimed after the same fashion.   But whilst, in the one case, we have but one history of the apparition, that of Luke ; in the other we have two accounts, accounts however which do not correspond, and which we must now compare.   Apart from

---

[9] Numb. v. 18.
[10] Protev. Jac. x.–xvi.   The account in the Evang. de nativ. Mar. is less characteristic.
[11] "Die natürliche Geschichte des grossen Propheten von Nazaret," 1ter Band, s. 119 ff.

the essential signification the two accounts exhibit the following differences. 1. The individual who appears is called in Matthew by the indefinite appellation, *angel of the Lord*, ἄγγελος Κυρίου : in Luke by name, *the angel Gabriel*, ὁ ἄγγελος Γαβριήλ. 2. The person to whom the angel appears is, according to Matthew, Joseph, according to Luke, Mary. 3. In Matthew the apparition is seen in a dream, in Luke whilst awake. 4. There is a disagreement in relation to the time at which the apparition took place : according to Matthew, Joseph receives the heavenly communication after Mary was already pregnant : according to Luke it is made to Mary prior to her pregnancy. 5. Lastly, both the purpose of the apparition and the effect produced are different; it was designed, according to Matthew, to comfort Joseph, who was troubled on account of the pregnancy of his betrothed : according to Luke to prevent, by a previous announcement, all possibility of offence.

Where the discrepancies are so great and so essential, it may, at first sight, appear altogether superfluous to inquire whether the two Evangelists record one and the same occurrence, though with considerable disagreement; or whether they record distinct occurrences, so that the two accounts can be blended together, and the one be made to amplify the other? The first supposition cannot be admitted without impeaching the historical validity of the narrative; for which reason most of our theologians, indeed all who see in the narrative a true history, whether miraculous or natural, have decided in favour of the second supposition. Maintaining, and justly, that the silence of one Evangelist concerning an event which is narrated by the other, is not a negation of the event,[1] they blend the two accounts together in the following manner: 1, First, the angel makes known to Mary her approaching pregnancy (Luke); 2, she then journeys to Elizabeth (the same Gospel); 3, after her return her situation being discovered, Joseph takes offence (Matthew); whereupon, 4, he likewise is visited by an angelic apparition (the same Gospel [2]).

But this arrangement of the incidents is, as Schleiermacher has already remarked, full of difficulty[3]; and it seems that what is related by one Evangelist is not only not presupposed, but excluded, by the other. For, in the first place, the conduct of the angel who appears to Joseph is not easily explained, if the same or another angel had previously appeared to Mary. The angel (in Matthew) speaks altogether as if his communication were the first in this affair : he neither refers to the message previously received by Mary, nor reproaches Joseph because he had not believed it ; but more than all, the informing Joseph of the name of the expected child, and the giving him a full detail of the reasons why he should be so called, (Matt. i. 21,) would have been wholly superfluous had the angel (according to Luke i. 34) already indicated this name to Mary.

Still more incomprehensible is the conduct of the betrothed parties according to this arrangement of events. Had Mary been visited by an angel, who had made known to her an approaching supernatural pregnancy, would not the first impulse of a delicate woman have been, to hasten to impart to her betrothed the import of the divine message, and by this means to anticipate the humiliating discovery of her situation, and an injurious suspicion on the part of her affianced husband. But exactly this discovery Mary allows Joseph to make from others, and thus excites suspicions ; for it is evident that the expression εὑρέθη ἐν γαστρὶ ἔχουσα (Matt. i. 18) signifies a discovery

[1] Augustin, *de consens. evangelist.* ii. 5.
[2] Paulus, Olshausen, Fritzsche, Comm. in Matth. p. 56.
[3] Comp. de Wette's exeg. Handbuch, i. 1, s. 18. Schleiermacher, Ueber die Schriften des Lukas, s. 42 ff.

made independent of any communication on Mary's part, and it is equally clear that in this manner only does Joseph obtain the knowledge of her situation, since his conduct is represented as the result of that discovery (εὑρίσκεσθαι). The apocryphal *Protevangelium Jacobi* felt how enigmatical Mary's conduct must appear, and sought to solve the difficulty in a manner which, contemplated from the supranaturalistic point of view, is perhaps the most consistent. Had Mary retained a recollection of the import of the heavenly message—upon this point the whole ingenious representation of the apocryphal Gospel rests—she ought to have imparted it to Joseph ; but since it is obvious from Joseph's demeanour that she did not acquaint him with it, the only remaining alternative is, to admit that the mysterious communication made to Mary had, owing to her excited state of mind, escaped her memory, and that she was herself ignorant of the true cause of her pregnancy.[4] In fact, nothing is left to supranaturalism in the present case but to seek refuge in the miraculous and the incomprehensible. The attempts which the modern theologians of this class have made to explain Mary's silence, and even to find in it an admirable trait in her character, are so many rash and abortive efforts to make a virtue of necessity. According to Hess [5] it must have cost Mary much self-denial to have concealed the communication of the angel from Joseph ; and this reserve, in a matter known only to herself and to God, must be regarded as a proof of her firm trust in God. Without doubt Mary communed thus with herself : It is not without a purpose that this apparition has been made to me alone ; had it been intended that Joseph should have participated in the communication, the angel would have appeared to him also (if each individual favoured with a divine revelation were of this opinion, how many special revelations would it not require ?) ; besides it is an affair of God alone, consequently it becomes me to leave it with him to convince Joseph (the argument of indolence). Olshausen concurs, and adds his favourite general remark, that in relation to events so extraordinary the measure of the ordinary occurrences of the world is not applicable : a category under which, in this instance, the highly essential considerations of delicacy and propriety are included.

More in accordance with the views of the natural interpreters, the *Evangelium de nativitate Mariae*,[6] and subsequently some later writers, for example, the author of the Natural History of the Great Prophet of Nazareth, have sought to explain Mary's silence, by supposing Joseph to have been at a distance from the abode of his affianced bride at the time of the heavenly communication. According to them Mary was of Nazareth, Joseph of Bethlehem ; to which latter place Joseph departed after the betrothing, and did not return to Mary until the expiration of three months, when he discovered the pregnancy which had taken place in the interim. But since the assumption that Mary and Joseph resided in different localities has no foundation, as will presently be seen, in the canonical Gospels, the whole explanation falls to the ground. Without such an assumption, Mary's silence towards Joseph might, perhaps, have been accounted for from the point of view of the naturalistic interpreters, by imagining her to have been held back through modesty from confessing a situation so liable to excite suspicion. But one who, like Mary, was so fully convinced of the divine agency in the matter, and had shown so ready a

---

[4] Protev. Jac. c. 12 : Μαριὰμ δέ ἐπελάθετο τῶν μυστηρίων ὧν εἶπε πρὸς αὐτὴν Γαβριήλ. When questioned by Joseph she assures him with tears : οὐ γινώσκω, πόθεν ἐστὶ τοῦτο τὸ ἐν τῇ γαστρί μου. c. 13.

[5] Geschichte der drei letzten Lebensjahre Jesu u. s. w. 1. Thl. s. 36. Comp. Hoffmann, s. 176 f.

[6] Ch. viii.–x.

comprehension of her mysterious destination (Luke i. 38), could not possibly have been tongue-tied by petty considerations of false shame.

Consequently, in order to rescue Mary's character, without bringing reproach upon Joseph's, and at the same time to render his unbelief intelligible, interpreters have been compelled to assume that a communication, though a tardy one, was actually made by Mary to Joseph. Like the last-named apocryphal Gospel, they introduce a journey, not of Joseph, but of Mary—the visit to Elizabeth mentioned in Luke—to account for the postponement of the communication. It is probable, says Paulus, that Mary did not open her heart to Joseph before this journey, because she wished first to consult with her older friend as to the mode of making the disclosure to him, and whether she, as the mother of the Messiah, ought to marry. It was not till after her return, and then most likely through the medium of others, that she made Joseph acquainted with her situation, and with the promises she had received. But Joseph's mind was not properly attuned and prepared for such a disclosure; he became haunted by all kinds of thoughts; and vacillated between suspicion and hope till at length a dream decided him.[7] But in the first place a motive is here given to Mary's journey which is foreign to the account in Luke. Mary sets off to Elizabeth, not to take counsel of her, but to assure herself regarding the sign appointed by the angel. No uneasiness which the friend is to dissipate, but a proud joy, unalloyed by the smallest anxiety, is expressed in her salutation to the future mother of the Baptist. But besides, a confession so tardily made can in nowise justify Mary. What behaviour on the part of an affianced bride—after having received a divine communication, so nearly concerning her future husband, and in a matter so delicate—to travel miles away, to absent herself for three months, and then to permit her betrothed to learn through third persons that which could no longer be concealed!

Those, therefore, who do not impute to Mary a line of conduct which certainly our Evangelists do not impute to her, must allow that she imparted the message of the angel to her future husband as soon as it had been revealed to her; but that he did not believe her.[8] But now let us see how Joseph's character is to be dealt with! Even Hess is of opinion that, since Joseph was acquainted with Mary, he had no cause to doubt her word, when she told him of the apparition she had had. This scepticism presupposes a mistrust of his betrothed which is incompatible with his character as a *just man* (Matt. i. 19), and an incredulity respecting the marvellous which is difficult to reconcile with a readiness on other occasions to believe in angelic apparitions; nor, in any case, would this want of faith have escaped the censure of the angel who subsequently appeared to himself.

Since then, to suppose that the two accounts are parallel, and complete one another, leads unavoidably to results inconsistent with the sense of the Gospels, in so far as they evidently meant to represent the characters of Joseph and Mary as free from blemish; the supposition cannot be admitted, but the accounts mutually exclude each other. An angel did not appear, first to Mary, and also afterwards to Joseph; he can only have appeared either to the one or to the other. Consequently, it is only the one or the other relation which can be regarded as historical. And here different considerations would conduct to opposite decisions. The history in Matthew might appear the more probable from the rationalistic point of view, because it is more easy to interpret naturally an apparition in a dream; whilst that in

---

[7] Paulus, exeg. Handb. 1 a, s. 121. 145.
[8] To this opinion Neander inclines, L. J. Ch. s. 18.

Luke might be preferred by the supranaturalist, because the manner in which the suspicion cast upon the holy virgin is refuted is more worthy of God. But in fact, a nearer examination proves, that neither has any essential claim to be advanced before the other. Both contain an angelic apparition, and both are therefore encumbered with all the difficulties which, as was stated above in relation to the annunciation of the birth of the Baptist, oppose the belief in angels and apparitions. Again, in both narrations the import of the angelic message is, as we shall presently see, an impossibility. Thus every criterion which might determine the adoption of the one, and the rejection of the other, disappears; and we find ourselves, in reference to both accounts, driven back by necessity to the mythical view.

From this point of view, all the various explanations, which the Rationalists have attempted to give of the two apparitions, vanish of themselves. Paulus explains the apparition in Matthew as a natural dream, occasioned by Mary's previous communication of the announcement which had been made to her; and with which Joseph must have been acquainted, because this alone can account for his having heard the same words in his dream, which the angel had beforehand addressed to Mary : but much rather, is it precisely this similarity in the language of the presumed second angel to that of the first, with the absence of all reference by the latter to the former, which proves that the words of the first angel were not presupposed by the second. Besides, the natural explanation is annihilated the moment the narratives are shown to be mythical. The same remark applies to the explanation, expressed guardedly indeed by Paulus, but openly by the author of the Natural History of the Great Prophet of Nazareth, namely, that the angel who visited Mary (in Luke) was a human being; of which we must speak hereafter.

According to all that has been said, the following is the only judgment we can form of the origin of the two narratives of the angelic apparitions. The conception of Jesus through the power of the Holy Ghost ought not to be grounded upon a mere uncertain suspicion; it must have been clearly and positively asserted; and to this end a messenger from heaven was required, since theocratic decorum seemed to demand it far more in relation to the birth of the Messiah, than of a Samson or a John. Also the words which the angels use, correspond in part with the Old Testament annunciations of extraordinary children.[9] The appearing of the angel in the one narrative beforehand to Mary, but in the other at a later period to Joseph, is to be regarded as a variation in the legend or in the composition, which finds an explanatory counterpart in the history of the annunciation of Isaac. Jehovah (Gen. xvii. 15) promises Abraham a son by Sarah, upon which the Patriarch cannot refrain from laughing; but he receives a repetition of the assurance; Jehovah (Gen. xviii. 1 ff.) makes this promise under the Terebinth tree at Mamre, and Sarah laughs as if it were something altogether novel and unheard of by her; lastly, according to Genesis xxi. 5 ff. it is first after Isaac's birth that

---

[9] Gen. xvii. 19; LXX. (Annunciation of Isaac):

ἰδοὺ Σάρρα ἡ γυνή σου τέξεταί σοι υἱόν, καὶ καλέσεις τὸ ὄνομα αὐτοῦ Ἰσαάκ.

Judg. xiii. 5. (Annunciation of Samson) :

καὶ αὐτὸς ἄρξεται σῶσαι τὸν Ἰσραὴλ ἐκ χειρὸς Φυλιστιίμ.

Gen. xvi. 11 ff. (Annunciation of Ishmael) :

καὶ εἶπεν αὐτῇ ὁ ἄγγελος Κυρίου· ἰδοὺ σὺ ἐν γαστρὶ ἔχεις, καὶ τέξῃ υἱὸν καὶ καλέσεις τὸ ὄνομα αὐτοῦ Ἰσμαήλ. Οὗτος ἔσται——.

Matt. i. 21.

(μὴ φοβηθῇς παραλαβεῖν Μαριὰμ τὴν γυναῖκα σου—) τέξεται δὲ υἱόν, καὶ καλέσεις τὸ ὄνομα αὐτοῦ Ἰησοῦν· αὐτὸς γὰρ σώσει τὸν λαὸν αὐτοῦ ἀπὸ·τῶν ἁμαρτιῶν αὐτῶν.

Luke i. 30 ff.

καὶ εἶπεν ὁ ἄγγελος αὐτῇ—ἰδοὺ συλλήψῃ ἐν γαστρί, καὶ τέξῃ υἱόν, καὶ καλέσεις τὸ ὄνομα αὐτοῦ Ἰησοῦν. Οὗτος ἔσται——.

Sarah mentions the laughing of the people, which is said to have been the occasion of his name ; whereby it appears that this last history does not presuppose the existence of the two other accounts of the annunciation of the birth of Isaac.[10]   As in relation to the birth of Isaac, different legends or poems were formed without reference to one another, some simpler, some more embellished : so we have two discordant narratives concerning the birth of Jesus.   Of these the narrative in Matthew [11] is the simpler and ruder style of composition, since it does not avoid, though it be but by a transient suspicion on the part of Joseph, the throwing a shade over the character of Mary which is only subsequently removed ; that in Luke, on the contrary, is a more refined and artistical representation, exhibiting Mary from the first in the pure light of a bride of heaven.[12]

§ 25.

IMPORT OF THE ANGEL'S MESSAGE.—FULFILMENT OF THE PROPHECY OF ISAIAH.

According to Luke, the angel who appears to Mary, in the first place informs her only that she shall become pregnant, without specifying after what manner : that she shall bring forth a son and call his name Jesus ; He shall be great, and shall be called the Son of the Highest ($\upsilon\iota\grave{o}s$ $\upsilon\psi\acute{\iota}\sigma\tau\sigma\upsilon$) ; and God shall give unto him the throne of his father David, and he shall reign over the house of Jacob for ever.   The subject, the Messiah is here treated precisely in the language common to the Jews, and even the term *Son of the Highest*, if nothing further followed, must be taken in the same sense ; as according to 2 Sam. vii. 14, Ps. ii. 7 an ordinary king of Israel might be so named ; still more, therefore, the greatest of these kings, the Messiah, even considered merely as a man.   This Jewish language reflects in addition a new light upon the question of the historic validity of the angelic apparition ; for we must agree with Schleiermacher that the real angel Gabriel would hardly have proclaimed the advent of the Messiah in a phraseology so strictly Jewish : [1] for which reason we are inclined to coincide with this theologian, and to ascribe this particular portion of the history, as also that which precedes and relates to the Baptist, to one and the same Jewish-christian author.   It is not till Mary opposes the fact of her virginity to the promises of a son, that the angel defines the nature of the conception : that it shall be by the Holy Ghost, by the power of the Highest ; after which the appellation $\upsilon\iota\grave{o}s$ $\theta\epsilon\sigma\hat{\upsilon}$ receives a more precise metaphysical sense.   As a confirmatory sign that a matter of this kind is nowise impossible to God, Mary is

[10] Comp. de Wette, Kritik der mos. Geschichte, s. 86 ff.

[11] The vision which, according to Matthew, Joseph had in his sleep, had besides a kind of type in the vision by which, according to the Jewish tradition related by Josephus, the father of Moses was comforted under similar circumstances, when suffering anxiety concerning the pregnancy of his wife, although for a different reason.   Joseph. Antiq. II. ix. 3. "A man whose name was Amram, one of the nobler sort of Hebrews, was afraid for his whole nation, lest it should fail, by the want of young men to be brought up hereafter, and was very uneasy at it, his wife being then with child, and he knew not what to do.   Hereupon he betook himself to prayer to God.   . . .   Accordingly God had mercy on him, and was moved by his supplication.   He stood by him in his sleep, and exhorted him not to despair of his future favours.   . . .   For this child of thine shall deliver the Hebrew nation from the distress they are under from the Egyptians.   His memory shall be famous while the world lasts."

[12] Comp. Ammon, Fortbildung des Christenthums, i. s. 208 f.

[1] Ueber die Schriften des Lukas, s. 23.

referred to that which had occurred to her relative Elizabeth ; whereupon she resigns herself in faith to the divine determination respecting her.

In Matthew, where the main point is to dissipate Joseph's anxiety, the angel begins at once with the communication, that the child conceived by Mary is (as the Evangelist had already stated of his own accord, chap. i. 18), of the *Holy Ghost* (πνεῦμα ἅγιον) ; and hereupon the Messianic destination of Jesus is first pointed out by the expression, *He shall save his people from their sins.* This language may seem to sound less Jewish than that by which the Messianic station of the child who should be born, is set forth in Luke ; it is however to be observed, that under the term *sins* (ἁμαρτίαις) is comprehended *the punishment* of those sins, namely, the subjection of the people to a foreign yoke ; so that here also the Jewish element is not wanting ; as neither in Luke, on the other hand, is the higher destination of the Messiah left wholly out of sight, since under the term *to reign*, βασιλεύειν, the rule over an obedient and regenerated people is included. Next is subjoined by the angel, or more probably by the narrator, an oracle from the Old Testament, introduced by the often recurring phrase, *all this was done, that it might be fulfilled which was spoken of the Lord by the prophet* [v. 22]. It is the prophecy from Isaiah (chap. vii. 14) which the conception of Jesus after this manner should accomplish : namely, *a virgin shall be with child, and shall bring forth a son, and they shall call His name Emmanuel*—God-with-us.

The original sense of this passage in Isaiah is, according to modern research,[2] this. The prophet is desirous of giving Ahaz, who, through fear of the kings of Syria and Israel, was disposed to make a treaty with Assyria, a lively assurance of the speedy destruction of his much dreaded enemies ; and he therefore says to him : suppose that an unmarried woman now on the point of becoming a wife[3] shall conceive ; or categorically : a certain young woman is, or is about to be with child (perhaps the prophet's own wife) ; now, before this child is born, the political aspect of affairs shall be so much improved, that a name of good omen shall be given to the child ; and before he shall be old enough to use his reason, the power of these enemies shall be completely annihilated. That is to say, prosaically expressed : before nine months shall have passed away, the condition of the kingdom shall be amended, and within about three years the danger shall have disappeared. Thus, what, at all events, is demonstrated by modern criticism, that, under the circumstances stated by Isaiah in the introduction to the oracle, it is only a sign having reference to the actual moment and the near future, which could have any meaning. How ill chosen, according to Hengstenberg's[4] interpretation, is the prophet's language : As certainly as the day shall arrive when, in fulfilment of the covenant, the Messiah shall be born, so impossible is it that the people among whom he shall arise, or the family whence he shall spring, shall pass away. How ill-judged, on the part of the prophet, to endeavour to make the improbability of a speedy deliverance appear less improbable, by an appeal to a yet greater improbability in the far distant future !—And then the given limit of a few years ! The overthrow of the two kingdoms, such is Hengstenberg's explanation, shall take place—not in the immediately succeeding years, before the child specified shall have acquired the use of

---

[2] Compare Gesenius and Hitzig. Commentaren zum Jesaia ; Umbreit, Ueber die Geburt des Immanuel durch eine Jungfrau, in den theol. Studien u. Krit., 1830, 3. Heft, s. 541 ff.

[3] This explanation does away with the importance of the controversy respecting the word עַלְמָה. Moreover it ought to be decided by the fact that the word does not signify an immaculate, but a marriageable young woman (see *Gesenius*). So early as the time of Justin the Jews maintained that the word עַלְמָה ought not to be rendered by παρθένος, but by νεᾶνις. *Dial c. Tryph.* no. 43. p. 130 *E.* Comp. *Iren. adv. haer.* iii. 21.

[4] Christologie des A. T. s. I, b, s. 47.

his reason, but—within such a space of time, as in the far future will elapse between the birth of the Messiah and the first development of his mental powers; therefore in about three years. What a monstrous confounding of times ! A child is to be born in the distant future, and that which shall happen before this child shall know how to use his reason, is to take place in the nearest present time.

Thus Paulus and his party are decidedly right in opposing to Hengstenberg and his party, that the prophecy of Isaiah has relation, in its original local signification, to the then existing circumstances, and not to the future Messiah, still less to Jesus. Hengstenberg, on the other hand, is equally in the right, when in opposition to Paulus he maintains, that the passage from Isaiah is adopted by Matthew as a prophecy of the birth of Jesus of a virgin. Whilst the orthodox commentators explain the often recurring *that it might be fulfilled* (ἵνα πληρωθῇ), and similar expressions as signifying : this happened by divine arrangement, in order that the Old Testament prophecy, which in its very origin had reference to the New Testament occurrence, might be fulfilled;—the rationalistic interpreters, on the contrary, understand merely : this took place after such a manner, that it was so constituted, that the Old Testament words, which, originally indeed, had relation to something different, should admit of being so applied ; and in such application alone do they receive their full verification. In the first explanation, the relation between the Old Testament passage and the New Testament occurrence is objective, arranged by God himself : in the last it is only subjective, a relation perceived by the later author; according to the former it is a relationship at once precise and essential : according to the latter both inexact and adventitious. But opposed to this latter interpretation of New Testament passages, which point out an Old Testament prophecy as fulfilled, is the language, and equally so the spirit of the New Testament writers. The language : for neither can πληροῦσθαι signify in such connexion anything than *ratum fieri, eventu comprobari*, nor ἵνα ὅπως anything than *eo consilio ut*, whilst the extensive adoption of ἵνα ἐκβατικὸν has arisen only from dogmatic perplexity.[5] But such an interpretation is altogether at variance with the Judaical spirit of the authors of the Gospels. Paulus maintains that the Orientalist does not seriously believe that the ancient prophecy was designedly spoken, or was accomplished by God, precisely in order that it should prefigure a modern event, and vice versâ ; but this is to carry over our sober European modes of thought into the imaginative life of the Orientals. When however Paulus adds : much rather did the coincidence of a later event with an earlier prophecy assume only the *form* of a designed coincidence in the mind of the Oriental : he thus, at once, annuls his previous assertion; for this is to admit, that, what in our view is mere coincidence, appeared to the oriental mind the result of design ; and we must acknowledge this to be the meaning of an oriental representation, if we would interpret it according to its original signification. It is well known that the later Jews found prophecies, of the time being and of the future, everywhere in the Old Testament ; and that they constructed a complete image of the future Messiah, out of various, and in part falsely interpreted Old Testament passages.[6] And the Jew believed he saw in the application he gave to the Scripture, however perverted it might be, an actual fulfilment of the prophecy. In the words of Olshausen : it is a mere dogmatic prejudice to attribute to this formula, when used by the New Testament writers, an altogether different sense from that

---

[5] See Winer, Grammatik des neutest. Sprachidioms, 3te Aufl. s. 382 ff. Fritzsche, Comm. in Matth. p 49. 317 und Excurs. 1, p. 836 ff.

[6] See the Introduction, § 14.

which it habitually bears among their countrymen ; and this solely with the view to acquit them of the sin of falsely interpreting the Scripture.

Many theologians of the present day are sufficiently impartial to admit, with regard to the Old Testament, in opposition to the ancient orthodox interpretation, that many of the prophecies originally referred to near events ; but they are not sufficiently rash, with regard to the New Testament, to side with the rationalistic commentators, and to deny the decidedly Messianic application which the New Testament writers make of these prophecies ; they are still too prejudiced to allow, that here and there the New Testament has falsely interpreted the Old. Consequently, they have recourse to the expedient of distinguishing a double sense in the prophecy; the one relating to a near and minor occurrence, the other to a future and more important event ; and thus they neither offend against the plain grammatical and historical sense of the Old Testament passage on the one hand, nor distort or deny the signification of the New Testament passage on the other.[7] Thus, in the prophecy of Isaiah under consideration, the spirit of prophecy, they contend, had a double intention : to announce a near occurrence, the delivery of the affianced bride of the prophet, and also a distinct event in the far distant future, namely the birth of the Messiah of a virgin. But a double sense so monstrous owes its origin to dogmatic perplexity alone. It has been adopted, as Olshausen himself remarks, in order to avoid the offensive admission that the New Testament writers, and Jesus himself, did not interpret the Old Testament rightly, or, more properly speaking, according to modern principles of exegesis, but explained it after the manner of their own age, which was not the most correct. But so little does this offence exist for the unprejudiced, that the reverse would be the greater difficulty, that is, if, contrary to all the laws of historical and national development, the New Testament writers had elevated themselves completely above the modes of interpretation common to their age and nation. Consequently, with regard to the prophecies brought forward in the New Testament, we may admit, according to circumstances, without further argument, that they are frequently interpreted and applied by the evangelists, in a sense which is totally different from that they originally bore.

We have here in fact a complete table of all the four possible views on this point : two extreme and two conciliatory ; one false and one, it is to be hoped, correct.

1. *Orthodox view* (Hengstenberg and others) : Such Old Testament passages had in their very origin an exclusive prophetic reference to Christ, for the New Testament writers so understand them ; and they must be in the right even should human reason be confounded.

2. *Rationalistic view* (Paulus and others) : The New Testament writers do not assign a strictly Messianic sense to the Old Testament prophecies, for this reference to Christ is foreign to the original signification of these prophecies viewed by the light of reason ; and the New Testament writings must accord with reason, whatever ancient beliefs may say to the contrary.

3. *Mystical conciliatory view* (Olshausen and others) : The Old Testament passages originally embody both the deeper signification ascribed to them by the New Testament writers, and that more proximate meaning which common sense obliges us to recognize : thus sound reason and the ancient faith are reconcilable.

4. *Decision of criticism :* Very many of the Old Testament prophecies had, originally, only an immediate reference to events belonging to the time : but they came to be regarded by the men of the New Testament as actual

[7] See Bleek in den theol. Studien u. Kritiken, 1835, 2, s. 441 ff.

predictions of Jesus as the Messiah, because the intelligence of these men was limited by the manner of thinking of their nation, a fact recognized neither by Rationalism nor the ancient faith.[8]

Accordingly we shall not hesitate for a moment to allow, in relation to the prophecy in question, that the reference to Jesus is obtruded upon it by the Evangelists. Whether the actual birth of Jesus of a virgin gave rise to this application of the prophecy, or whether this prophecy, interpreted beforehand as referring to the Messiah, originated the belief that Jesus was born of a virgin, remains to be determined.

§ 26.

JESUS BEGOTTEN OF THE HOLY GHOST.   CRITICISM OF THE ORTHODOX

OPINION.

. The statement of Matthew and of Luke concerning the mode of Jesus's conception has, in every age, received the following interpretation by the church; that Jesus was conceived in Mary not by a human father, but by the Holy Ghost. And truly the gospel expressions seem, at first sight, to justify this interpretation; since the words πρὶν ἢ συνελθεῖν αὐτοὺς (Matt. i. 18) and ἐπεὶ ἄνδρα οὐ γινώσκω (Luke i. 34) preclude the participation of Joseph or any other man in the conception of the child in question. Nevertheless the terms πνεῦμα ἅγιον and δύναμις ὑψίστου do not represent the Holy Ghost in the sense of the church, as the third person in the Godhead, but rather the רוּחַ אֱלֹהִים, Spiritus Dei as used in the Old Testament : God in his agency upon the world, and especially upon man. In short the words ἐν γαστρὶ ἔχουσα ἐκ πνεύματος ἁγίου in Matthew, and πνεῦμα ἅγιον ἐπελεύσεται ἐπὶ σὲ κ. τ. λ. in Luke, express with sufficient clearness that the absence of human agency was supplied—not physically after the manner of heathen representations—but by the divine creative energy.

Though this seems to be the representation intended by the evangelists in the passages referred to concerning the origin of the life of Jesus, still it cannot be completed without considerable difficulties. We may separate what we may term the *physico-theological* from the *historical-exegetical* difficulties.

The physiological difficulties amount to this, that such a conception would be a most remarkable deviation from all natural laws. However obscure the physiology of the fact, it is proved by an exceptionless experience that only by the concurrence of the two sexes is a new human being generated ; on which account Plutarch's remark, " παιδίον οὐδεμία ποτὲ γυνὴ λέγεται ποιῆσαι δίχα κοινωνίας ἀνδρὸς,"[1] and Cerinthus's " *impossible* " become applicable.[2] It is

---

[8] The whole rationalistic interpretation of Scripture rests upon a sufficiently palpable paralogism, by which it stands or falls :

The New Testament authors are not to be interpreted as if they said something irrational (certainly not something contrary to *their own* modes of thinking).

Now according to a particular interpretation their assertions are irrational (that is contrary to *our* modes of thinking).

Consequently the interpretation cannot give the original sense, and a different interpretation must be given.

Who does not here perceive the *quaternio terminorum* and the fatal inconsequence, when Rationalism takes its stand upon the same ground with supernaturalism ; that, namely, whilst with regard to all other men the first point to be examined is whether they speak or write what is just and true, to the New Testament writers the prerogative is granted of this being, in their case, already presupposed ?

[1] Conjugial. præcept. Opp. ed. Hutton, Vol. 7. s. 428.

[2] Irenäus, adv. haer. 1, 26 : Cerinthus, Jesum subjecit non ex virgine natum, impossibile enim hoc ei visum est.

only among the lowest species of the animal kingdom that generation takes place without the union of sexes;[3] so that, regarding the matter purely physiologically, what Origen says, in the supranaturalistic sense, would indeed be true of a man of the like origin; namely, that the words in Psalm xxii. 7, *I am a worm and no man* is a prophecy of Jesus in the above respect.[4] But to the merely physical consideration a theological one is subjoined by the angel (Luke i. 37), when he appeals to the divine omnipotence to which nothing is impossible. But since the divine omnipotence, by virtue of its unity with divine wisdom, is never exerted in the absence of an adequate motive, the existence of such, in the present instance, must be demonstrated. But nothing less than an object worthy of the Deity, and at the same time necessarily unattainable except by a deviation from the ordinary course of nature, could constitute a sufficient cause for the suspension by God of a natural law which he had established. Only here, it is said, the end, the redemption of mankind, required impeccability on the part of Jesus; and in order to render him exempt from sin, a divinely wrought conception, which excluded the participation of a sinful father, and severed Jesus from all connexion with original sin, was necessary.[5] To which it has been answered by others,[6] (and Schleiermacher has recently most decisively argued this side of the question,[7]) that the exclusion of the paternal participation is insufficient, unless, indeed, the inheritance of original sin, on the maternal side, be obviated by the adoption of the Valentinian assertion, that Jesus only passed through the body of Mary. But that the gospel histories represent an actual maternal participation is undeniable; consequently a divine intervention which should sanctify the participation of the sinful human mother in the conception of Jesus must be supposed in order to maintain his assumed necessary impeccability. But if God determined on such a purification of the maternal participation, it had been easier to do the same with respect to that of the father, than by his total exclusion, to violate the natural law in so unprecedented a manner; and consequently, a fatherless conception cannot be insisted upon as the necessary means of compassing the impeccability of Jesus.

Even he who thinks to escape the difficulties already specified, by enveloping himself in a supranaturalism, inaccessible to arguments based on reason or the laws of nature, must nevertheless admit the force of the *exegetical-historical* difficulties meeting him upon his own ground, which likewise beset the view of the supernatural conception of Jesus. Nowhere in the New Testament is such an origin ascribed to Jesus, or even distinctly alluded to, except in these two accounts of his infancy in Matthew and in Luke.[8] The history of the conception is omitted not only by Mark, but also by John, the supposed author of the fourth Gospel and an alleged inmate with the mother of Jesus subsequent to his death, who therefore would have been the most accurately informed concerning these occurrences. It is said that John sought rather to record the heavenly than the earthly origin of Jesus; but the question arises, whether the doctrine which he sets forth in his prologue, of a divine

---

[3] In Henke's neuem Magazin, iii. 3, s. 369.
[4] Homil. in Lucam xiv. Comp. my Streitschriften, i. 2, s. 72 f.
[5] Olshausen, Bibl. Comm. s. 49. Neander, L. J. Ch. s. 16 f.
[6] *e. g.* by Eichhorn, Einleitung in das N. T. 1. Bd. s. 407.
[7] Glaubenslehre, 2 Thl. § 97. s. 73 f. der zweiten Auflage.
[8] This side is particularly considered in der Skiagraphie des Dogma's von Jesu übernatürlicher Geburt, in Schmidt's Bibliothek, i. 3, s. 400 ff.; in den Bemerkungen über den Glaubenspunkt: Christus ist empfangen vom heil. Geist, in Henke's neuem Magazin, iii. 3, 365 ff.; in Kaiser's bibl. Theol. 1, s. 231 f.; De Wette's bibl. Dogmatik, § 281; Schleiermacher's Glaubenslehre, 2 Thl. § 97.

hypostasis actually becoming flesh and remaining immanent in Jesus, is reconcilable with the view given in the passages before us, of a simple divine operation determining the conception of Jesus ; whether therefore John could have presupposed the history of the conception contained in Matthew and Luke ? This objection, however, loses its conclusive force if in the progress of our investigation the apostolic origin of the fourth Gospel is not established. The most important consideration therefore is, that no retrospective allusion to this mode of conception occurs throughout the four Gospels ; not only neither in John nor in Mark, but also neither in Matthew nor in Luke. Not only does Mary herself designate Joseph simply as the father of Jesus (Luke ii. 48), and the Evangelist speak of both as his parents, γονεῖς (Luke ii. 41),—an appellation which could only have been used in an ulterior sense by one who had just related the miraculous conception,—but all his contemporaries in general, according to our Evangelists, regarded him as a son of Joseph, a fact which was not unfrequently alluded to contemptuously and by way of reproach in his presence (Matt. xiii. 55 ; Luke iv. 22 ; John vi. 42), thus affording him an opportunity of making a decisive appeal to his miraculous conception, of which, however, he says not a single word. Should it be answered, that he did not desire to convince respecting the divinity of his person by this external evidence, and that he could have no hope of making an impression by such means on those who were in heart his opponents,—it must also be remembered, that, according to the testimony of the fourth Gospel, his own disciples, though they admitted him to be the son of God, still regarded him as the actual son of Joseph. Philip introduces Jesus to Nathanael *as the son of Joseph*, Ἰησοῦν τὸν υἱὸν Ἰωσὴφ (John i. 46), manifestly in the same sense of real paternity which the Jews attached to the designation ; and nowhere is this represented as an erroneous or imperfect notion which these Apostles had subsequently to relinquish ; much rather does the whole sense of the narrative, which is not to be mistaken, exhibit the Apostles as having a right belief on this point. The enigmatical presupposition, with which, at the marriage in Cana, Mary addressed herself to Jesus,[9] is far too vague to prove a recollection of his miraculous conception on the part of the mother ; at all events this feature is counterbalanced by the opposing one that the family of Jesus, and, as appears from Matt. xii. 46 ff. compared with Mark iii. 21 ff., his mother also were, at a later time, in error respecting his aims ; which is scarcely explicable, even of his brothers, supposing them to have had such recollections.

Just as little as in the Gospels, is anything in confirmation of the view of the supernatural conception of Jesus, to be found in the remaining New Testament writings. For when the Apostle Paul speaks of Jesus as *made of a woman*, γενόμενον ἐκ γυναικὸς (Gal. iv. 4), this expression is not to be understood as an exclusion of paternal participation ; since the addition *made under the law*, γενόμενον ὑπὸ νόμον, clearly shows that he would here indicate (in the form which is frequent in the Old and New Testament, for example Job xiv. 1 ; Matt. xi. 11) human nature with all its conditions. When Paul (Rom. i. 3, 4 compared with ix. 5) makes Christ *according to the flesh*, κατὰ σάρκα, descend from David, but declares him to be the son of God *according to the Spirit of Holiness*, κατὰ πνεῦμα ἁγιωσύνης ; no one will here identify the antithesis *flesh* and *spirit* with the maternal human participation, and the divine energy superseding the paternal participation in the conception of Jesus. Finally when in the Epistle to the Hebrews (vii. 3) Melchisedec is compared with *the son of God*, υἱὸς τοῦ θεοῦ, because *without father*, ἀπάτωρ, the application of the literally interpreted ἀπάτωρ to Jesus, as he

[9] Brought to bear upon this point by Neander, L. J. Ch. s. 12.

appeared upon earth, is forbidden by the addition *without mother*, ἀμήτωρ, which agrees as little with him as the immediately following *without descent*, ἀγενεαλόγητος.

§ 27.

RETROSPECT OF THE GENEALOGIES.

The most conclusive exegetical ground of decision against the supernatural conception of Jesus, which bears more closely on the point than all the hitherto adduced passages, is found in the two genealogies previously considered. Even the Manichæan Faustus asserted that it is impossible without contradiction to trace the descent of Jesus from David through Joseph, as is done by our two genealogists, and yet assume that Joseph was not the father of Jesus; and Augustine had nothing convincing to answer when he remarked that it was necessary, on account of the superior dignity of the masculine gender, to carry the genealogy of Jesus through Joseph, who was Mary's husband if not by a natural by a spiritual alliance.[1] In modern times also the construction of the genealogical tables in Matthew and in Luke has led many theologians to observe, that these authors considered Jesus as the actual son of Joseph.[2] The very design of these tables is to prove Jesus to be of the lineage of David through Joseph; but what do they prove, if indeed Joseph was not the father of Jesus? The assertion that Jesus was the son of David, υἱὸς Δαβίδ, which in Matthew (i. 1) prefaces the genealogy and announces its object, is altogether annulled by the subsequent denial of his conception by means of the Davidical Joseph. It is impossible, therefore, to think it probable that the genealogy and the history of the birth of Jesus emanate from the same author[3]; and we must concur with the theologians previously cited, that the genealogies are taken from a different source. Scarcely could it satisfy to oppose the remark, that as Joseph doubtlessly adopted Jesus, the genealogical table of the former became fully valid for the latter. For adoption might indeed suffice to secure to the adopted son the reversion of certain external family rights and inheritances; but such a relationship could in no wise lend a claim to the Messianic dignity, which was attached to the true blood and lineage of David. He, therefore, who had regarded Joseph as nothing more than the adopted father of Jesus, would hardly have given himself the trouble to seek out the Davidical descent of Joseph; but if indeed, besides the established belief that Jesus was the son of God, it still remained important to represent him as the son of David, the pedigree of Mary would have been preferred for this purpose; for, however contrary to custom, the maternal genealogy must have been admitted in a case where a human father did not exist. Least of all is it to be believed, that several authors would have engaged in the compilation of a genealogical table for Jesus which traced his descent through Joseph, so that two different genealogies of this kind are still preserved to us, if a closer relationship between Jesus and Joseph had not been admitted at the time of their composition.

Consequently, the decision of the learned theologians who agree that these genealogies were composed in the belief that Jesus was the actual son of Joseph and Mary, can hardly be disputed; but the authors or compilers of our Gospels, notwithstanding their own conviction of the divine origin of

---

[1] Augustinus contra Faustum Manichaeum, L. 23. 3. 4. 8.
[2] See Schmidt, Schleiermacher, and Wegscheider, Instit. § 123 (not. d).
[3] Eichhorn thinks this probable, Einl. in das N. T. i. s. 425, De Wette possible, exeg. Handb. i. 1, s. 7.

Jesus, received them among their materials; only that Matthew (i. 16) changed the original *Joseph begat Jesus of Mary*—Ἰωσὴφ δὲ ἐγέννησε τὸν Ἰησοῦν ἐκ τῆς Μαρίας (comp. verses 3. 5. 6) according to his own view ; and so likewise Luke (iii. 23) instead of commencing his genealogy simply with, *Jesus— the son of Joseph*—Ἰησοῦς υἱὸς Ἰωσήφ, inserts *being as was supposed*, ὤν, ὡς ἐνομίζετο κ. τ. λ.

Let it not be objected that the view for which we contend, namely, that the genealogies could not have been composed under the notion that Joseph was not the father of Jesus, leaves no conceivable motive for incorporating them into our present Gospels. The original construction of a genealogy of Jesus, even though in the case before us it consisted simply in the adapting of foreign already existing genealogical tables to Jesus, required a powerful and direct inducement ; this was the hope thereby to gain—the corporeal descent of Jesus from Joseph being presupposed—a main support to the belief in his Messiahship ; whilst, on the other hand, a less powerful inducement was sufficient to incite to the admission of the previously constructed genealogies : the expectation that, notwithstanding the non-existence of any real relationship between Joseph and Jesus, they might nevertheless serve to link Jesus to David. Thus we find, that in the histories of the birth both in Matthew and in Luke, though they each decidedly exclude Joseph from the conception, great stress is laid upon the Davidical descent of Joseph (Matt. i. 20, Luke i. 27, ii. 4) ; that which in fact had no real significance, except in connexion with the earlier opinion, is retained even after the point of view is changed.

Since, in this way, we discover both the genealogies to be memorials belonging to the time and circle of the primitive church, in which Jesus was still regarded as a naturally begotten man, the sect of the Ebionites cannot fail to occur to us ; as we are told concerning them, that they held this view of the person of Christ at this early period.[4] We should therefore have expected, more especially, to have found these genealogies in the old Ebionitish Gospels, of which we have still knowledge, and are not a little surprised to learn that precisely in these Gospels the genealogies were wanting. It is true Epiphanius states that the Gospel of the Ebionites commenced with the public appearance of the Baptist[5] ; accordingly, by the genealogies, γενεαλογίαις, which they are said to have cut away, might have been meant, those histories of the birth and infancy comprised in the two first chapters of Matthew ; which they could not have adopted in their present form, since they contained the fatherless conception of Jesus, which was denied by the Ebionites : and it might also have been conjectured that this section which was in opposition to their system had alone perhaps been wanting in their Gospel ; and that the genealogy which was in harmony with their view might nevertheless have been somewhere inserted. But this supposition vanishes as soon as we find that Epiphanius, in reference to the Nazarenes, defines the genealogies, (of which he is ignorant whether they possessed them or not,) as *reaching from Abraham to Christ*, τὰς ἀπὸ τοῦ Ἀβραὰμ ἕως Χριστοῦ[6] ; consequently, by the genealogies which were wanting to some heretics, he evidently understood the genealogical tables, though, in relation to the Ebionites, he might likewise have included under this expression the history of the birth.

How is the strange phenomenon, that these genealogies are not found among that very sect of Christians who retained the particular opinion upon which they were constructed, to be explained ? A modern investigator has

---

[4] Justin Mart. Dial. cum Tryphone, 48 ; Origines contra Celsum, L. 5, 61. Euseb. H. E. 3. 27.
[5] Epiphan. haeres. 30, 14.
[6] Haeres. 29, 9.

advanced the supposition, that the Jewish-christians omitted the genealogical tables from prudential motives, in order not to facilitate or augment the persecution which, under Domitian, and perhaps even earlier, threatened the family of David.[7] But explanations, having no inherent connexion with the subject, derived from circumstances in themselves of doubtful historical validity, are admissible only as a last refuge, when no possible solution of the questionable phenomenon is to be found in the thing itself, as here in the principles of the Ebionitish system.

But in this case the matter is by no means so difficult. It is known that the Fathers speak of two classes of Ebionites, of which the one, besides strenuously maintaining the obligation of the Mosaic law, held Jesus to be the naturally begotten Son of Joseph and Mary ; the other, from that time called also Nazarenes, admitted with the orthodox church the conception by the Holy Ghost.[8] But besides this distinction there existed yet another. The most ancient ecclesiastic writers, Justin Martyr and Irenæus for example, are acquainted with those Ebionites only, who regarded Jesus as a naturally born man first endowed with divine powers at his baptism.[9] In Epiphanius and the Clementine Homilies, on the other hand, we meet with Ebionites who had imbibed an element of speculative Gnosticism. This tendency, which according to Epiphanius is to be dated from one Elxai, has been ascribed to Essenic influence,[10] and traces of the same have been discovered in the heresies referred to in the Epistle to the Colossians ; whereas the first class of Ebionites evidently proceeded from common Judaism. Which form of opinion was the earlier and which the later developed is not so easily determined ; with reference to the last detailed difference, it might seem, since the speculative Ebionites are mentioned first by the Clementines and Epiphanius, whilst Ebionites holding a simpler view are spoken of by Justin and by Irenæus, that the latter were the earlier ; nevertheless as Tertullian already notices in his time the Gnosticising tendency of the opinions of the Ebionites respecting Christ[11], and as the germ of such views existed among the Essenes in the time of Jesus, the more probable assumption is, that both opinions arose side by side about the same period.[12] As little can it be proved with regard to the other difference, that the views concerning Christ held by the Nazarenes became first, at a later period, lowered to those of the Ebionites[13] ; since the notices, partly confused and partly of late date, of the ecclesiastical writers, may be naturally explained as arising out of what may be called an optical delusion of the church, which,—whilst she in fact made continual advances in the glorification of Christ, but a part of the Jewish Christians remained stationary,—made it appear to her as if she herself remained stationary, whilst the others fell back into heresy.

By thus distinguishing the simple and the speculative Ebionites, so much is gained, that the failure of the genealogies among the latter class, mentioned by Epiphanius, does not prove them to have been also wanting among the

---

[7] Credner, in den Beiträgen zur Einleitung in das N. T. 1, s. 443. Anm.

[8] Orig. ut sup.

[9] See Neander, K. G. 1, 2, s. 615 f.

[10] Credner, über Essener, und einen theilweisen Zusammenhang beider, in Winer's Zeitschrift f. wissenschaftliche Theologie, 1. Bd. 2tes and 3tes Heft ; see Baur, *Progr. de Ebionitarum origine et doctrinâ ab Essenis repetendâ*, und christl. Gnosis, s. 403.

[11] De carne Christi, c. 14 : *Poterit haec opinio Hebioni convenire, qui nudum hominem, et tantum ex semine David, i.e. non et Dei filium, constituit Jesum, ut in illo angelum fuisse edicat.*

[12] Neander and Schneckenburger are of the latter, Gieseler and Credner of the former opinion.

[13] I here refer to the account of Hegesippus in Eusebius, H. E. iv. 22.

former. And the less if we should be able to make it appear probable, that the grounds of their aversion to the genealogical table, and the grounds of distinction between them and the other class of Ebionites, were identical. One of these grounds was evidently the unfavourable opinion, which the Ebionites of Epiphanius and of the Clementine Homilies had of David, from whom the genealogy traces the descent of Jesus.   It is well known that they distinguished in the Old Testament a twofold prophecy, male and female, pure and impure, of which the former only promised things heavenly and true, the latter things earthly and delusive ; that proceeding from Adam and Abel, this from Eve and Cain ; and both constituted an under current through the whole history of the revelation.[14] It was only the pious men from Adam to Joshua whom they acknowledged as true prophets : the later prophets and men of God, among whom David and Solomon are named, were not only not recognized, but abhorred.[15]   We even find positive indications that David was an object of their particular aversion.   There were many things which created in them a detestation of David (and Solomon).   David was a bloody warrior ; but to shed blood was, according to the doctrines of these Ebionites, one of the greatest of sins; David was known to have committed adultery, (Solomon to have been a voluptuary); and adultery was even more detested by this sect than murder.   David was a performer on stringed instruments ; this art, the invention of the Canaanites (Gen. iv. 21), was held by these Ebionites to be a sign of false prophecy ; finally, the prophecies announced by David and those connected with him, (and Solomon,) had reference to the kingdoms of this world, of which the Gnosticising Ebionites desired to know nothing.[16] Now the Ebionites who had sprung from common Judaism could not have shared this ground of aversion to the genealogies ; since to the orthodox Jew David was an object of the highest veneration.

Concerning a second point the notices are not so lucid and accordant as they should be ; namely, whether it was a further development of the general Ebionitish doctrine concerning the person of the Christ, which led these Ebionites to reject the genealogies.   According to Epiphanius, they fully recognized the Gnostic distinction between Jesus the son of Joseph and Mary, and the Christ who descended upon him [17] ; and consequently might have been withheld from referring the genealogy to Jesus only perhaps by their abhorrence of David.   On the other hand, from the whole tenor of the Clementines, and from one passage in particular,[18] it has recently been inferred, and not without apparent reason, that the author of these writings had himself abandoned the view of a natural conception, and even birth of Jesus [19] ; whereby it is yet more manifest that the ground of the rejection of the genealogies by this sect was peculiar to it, and not common to the other Ebionites.

Moreover positive indications, that the Ebionites who proceeded from Judaism possessed the genealogies, do not entirely fail.   Whilst the Ebionites

---

[14] Homil. 3, 23–27.
[15] Epiphan. haeres. 30, 18. comp. 15.
[16] That these were the traits in David's character which displeased the Christian sect in question, is sufficiently evident from a passage in the Clementine Homilies, though the name is not given : Homil. 3, 25 ; ἔτι μὴν καὶ οἱ ἀπὸ τῆς τούτου (τοῦ Καῒν) διαδοχῆς προελ ηλυθότες πρῶτοι μοιχοὶ ἐγένοντο, καὶ ψαλτήρια, καὶ κιθάραι, καὶ χαλκεῖς ὅπλων πολεμικῶν ἐγένοντο. Δι᾽ ὃ καὶ ἡ τῶν ἐγγόνων προφητεία, μοιχῶν καὶ ψαλτηρίων γέμουσα, λανθανόντως διὰ τῶν ἡδυ- παθειῶν ὡς τοὺς πολέμους ἐγείρει.
[17] Epiphan. haer. 30, 14. 16. 34.
[18] Homil. 3, 17.
[19] Schneckenburger, über das Evang. der Aegypter, s. 7 ; Baur, christl. Gnosis, s. 760 ff. See on the other side Credner and Hoffmann.

of Epiphanius and of the Clementines called Jesus only Son of God, but rejected the appellation Son of David, as belonging to the common opinion of the Jews [20]; other Ebionites were censured by the Fathers for recognizing Jesus only as the Son of David, to whom he is traced in the genealogies, and not likewise as the Son of God.[21]   Further, Epiphanius relates of the earliest Judaising Gnostics, Cerinthus and Carpocrates, that they used a Gospel the same in other respects indeed as the Ebionites, but that they adduced the genealogies, which they therefore read in the same, in attestation of the human conception of Jesus by Joseph.[22]   Also the ἀπομνημονεύματα cited by Justin, and which originated upon Judæo-christian ground, appear to have contained a genealogy similar to that in our Matthew ; since Justin as well as Matthew speaks, in relation to Jesus, of a γένος τοῦ Δαβὶδ καὶ Ἀβραὰμ, of a σπέρμα ἐξ Ἰακὼβ, διὰ Ἰούδα, καὶ Φαρὲς καὶ Ἰεσσαὶ καὶ Δαβὶδ κατερχόμενον [23] ; only that at the time, and in the circle of Justin, the opinion of a supernatural conception of Jesus had already suggested the reference of the genealogy to Mary, instead of to Joseph.

Hence it appears that we have in the genealogies a memorial, agreeing with indications from other sources, of the fact that in the very earliest Christian age, in Palestine, a body of Christians, numerous enough to establish upon distinct fundamental opinions two different Messianic tables of descent, considered Jesus to have been a naturally conceived human being.   And no proof is furnished to us in the apostolic writings, that the Apostles would have declared this doctrine to be unchristian ; it appeared so first from the point of view adopted by the authors of the histories of the birth in the first and third Gospels : notwithstanding which, however, it is treated with surprising lenity by the Fathers of the church.

§ 28.

NATURAL EXPLANATION OF THE HISTORY OF THE CONCEPTION.

If, as appears from the foregoing statements, so many weighty difficulties, philosophical as well as exegetical, beset the supranaturalistic explanation, it is well worth while to examine whether it be not possible to give an interpretation of the gospel history which shall obviate these objections.   Recourse has been had to the natural explanation, and the two narratives singly and conjointly have been successively subjected to the rationalistic mode of interpretation.

In the first place, the account in Matthew seemed susceptible of such an interpretation.   Numerous rabbinical passages were cited to demonstrate, that it was consonant with Jewish notions to consider a son of pious parents to be conceived by the divine co-operation, and that he should be called the son of the Holy Spirit, without its being ever imagined that paternal participation was thereby excluded.   It was consequently contended, that the section in

[20] Orig. Comm. in Matth. T. 16, 12.   Tertullian, De carne Christi, 14, s. Anm. 13 (a passage in which indeed the speculative and ordinary Ebionites are mingled together).
[21] Clement. homil. 18, 13.   They referred the words of Matth. xi. 27 : οὐδεὶς ἔγνω τὸν πατέρα, εἰ μὴ ὁ υἱὸς κ. τ. λ. to τοὺς πατέρα νομίζοντας χριστοῦ τὸν Δαβὶδ, καὶ αὐτὸν δὲ τὸν χριστὸν υἱὸν ὄντα, καὶ υἱὸν θεοῦ μὴ ἐγνωκότας, and complained that ἀντὶ τοῦ θεοῦ τὸν Δαβὶδ πάντες ἔλεγον.
[22] Haeres. 30, 14 : ὁ μὲν γὰρ Κήρινθος καὶ Κάρποκρας τῷ αὐτῷ χρώμενοι παρ᾽ αὐτοῖς (τοῖς Ἐβιωναίοις) εὐαγγελίῳ, ἀπὸ τῆς ἀρχῆς τοῦ κατὰ Ματθαῖον εὐαγγελίου διὰ τῆς γενεαλογίας βούλονται παριστᾷν ἐκ σπέρματος Ἰωσὴφ καὶ Μαρίας εἶναι τὸν χριστόν.
[23] Dial. c. Tryph. 100. 120.

Matthew represented merely the intention of the angel to inform Joseph, not indeed that Mary had become pregnant in the absence of all human intercourse, but that notwithstanding her pregnancy she was to be regarded as pure, not as one fallen from virtue. It was maintained that the exclusion of paternal participation—which is an embellishment of the original representation—occurs first in Luke in the words ἄνδρα οὐ γινώσκω (i. 34).[1]   When however this view was justly opposed by the remark, that the expression πρὶν ἢ συνελθεῖν αὐτοὺς in Matthew (i. 18) decidedly excludes the participation of the only individual in question, namely Joseph ; it was then thought possible to prove that even in Luke the paternal exclusion was not so positive : but truly this could be done only by an unexegetical subversion of the clear sense of the words, or else by uncritically throwing suspicion on a part of a well-connected narrative.   The first expedient is to interpret Mary's inquiry of the angel i. 34, thus : Can I who am already betrothed and married give birth to the Messiah, for as the mother of the Messiah I must have no husband? whereupon the angel replies, that God, through his power, could make something distinguished even of the child conceived of her and Joseph.[2]   The other proceeding is no less arbitrary.   Mary's inquiry of the angel is explained as an unnatural interruption of his communication, which being abstracted, the passage is found to contain no decided intimation of the supernatural conception.[3]

If consequently, the difficulty of the natural explanation of the two accounts be equally great, still, with respect to both it must be alike attempted or rejected ; and for the consistent Rationalist, a Paulus for example, the latter is the only course.   This commentator considers the participation of Joseph indeed excluded by Matt. i. 18, but by no means that of every other man ; neither can he find a supernatural divine intervention in the expression of Luke i. 35.   The *Holy Ghost*—πνεῦμα ἅγιον—is not with him objective, an external influence operating upon Mary, but her own pious imagination. The *power of the Highest*—δύναμις ὑψίστου—is not the immediate divine omnipotence, but every natural power employed in a manner pleasing to God may be so called.   Consequently, according to Paulus, the meaning of the angelic announcement is simply this : prior to her union with Joseph, Mary, under the influence of a pure enthusiasm in sacred things on the one hand, and by an human co-operation pleasing to God on the other, became the mother of a child who on account of this holy origin was to be called a son of God.

Let us examine rather more accurately the view which this representative of rationalistic interpretation takes of the particulars of the conception of Jesus.   He begins with Elizabeth, the patriotic and wise daughter of Aaron, as he styles her.   She, having conceived the hope that she might give birth to one of God's prophets, naturally desired moreover that he might be the first of prophets, the forerunner of the Messiah; and that the latter also might speedily be born.   Now there was among her own kinsfolk a person suited in every respect for the mother of the Messiah, Mary, a young virgin, a descendant of David; nothing more was needful than to inspire her likewise with such a special hope.   Whilst these intimations prepare us to anticipate a cleverly concerted plan on the part of Elizabeth in reference to her young relative, in the which we hope to become initiated ; Paulus here suddenly lets

---

[1] Br . . . , die Nachricht, dass Jesus durch den heil. Geist und von einer Jungfrau geboren sei, aus Zeitbegriffen erläutert.   In Schmidt's Bibl. 1, 1. s. 101 ff.—Horst, in Henke's Museum 1, 4, 497 ff., über die beiden ersten Kapitel in Evang. Lukas.

[2] Bemerkungen über den Glaubenspunkt :   Christus ist empfangen vom heil. Geist.   In Henke's neuem Magazin, 3, 3. 399.

[3] Schleiermacher, über den Lukas, s. 26 f.

fall the curtain, and remarks, that the exact manner in which Mary was convinced that she should become the mother of the Messiah must be left historically undetermined; thus much only is certain, that Mary remained pure, for she could not with a clear conscience have stationed herself, as she afterwards did, under the Cross of her Son, had she felt that a reproach rested on her concerning the origin of the hopes she had entertained of him. The following is the only hint subsequently given of the particular view held by Paulus. It is probable, he thinks, that the angelic messenger visited Mary in the evening or even at night; indeed according to the correct reading of Luke i. 28, which has not the word angel, καὶ εἰσελθὼν πρὸς αὐτὴν εἶπε, without ὁ ἄγγελος, the evangelist here speaks only of some one who had come in. (As if in this case, the participle εἰσελθὼν must not necessarily be accompanied by τὶς ; or, in the absence of the pronoun be referred to the subject, the angel Gabriel— ὁ ἄγγελος Γαβριὴλ, v. 26 !) Paulus adds : that this visitant was the angel Gabriel was the subsequent suggestion of Mary's own mind, after she had heard of the vision of Zacharias.

Gabler, in a review of Paulus's Commentary [4] has fully exposed, with commensurate plainness of speech, the transaction which lies concealed under this explanation. It is impossible, says he, to imagine any other interpretation of Paulus's view than that some one passed himself off for the angel Gabriel, and as the pretended Messenger of God remained with Mary in order that she might become the mother of the Messiah. What ! asks Gabler, is Mary, at the very time she is betrothed, to become pregnant by another, and is this to be called an innocent holy action, pleasing to God and irreproachable? Mary is here pourtrayed as a pious visionary, and the pretended messenger of heaven as a deceiver, or he too is a gross fanatic. The reviewer most justly considers such an assertion as revolting, if contemplated from the christian point of view ; if from the scientific, as at variance both with the principles of interpretation and of criticism.

The author of the Natural History of the Great Prophet of Nazareth is, in this instance, to be considered as the most worthy interpreter of Paulus ; for though the former could not, in this part of his work, have made use of Paulus's Commentary, yet, in exactly the same spirit, he unreservedly avows what the latter carefully veils. He brings into comparison a story in Josephus,[5] according to which, in the very time of Jesus, a Roman knight won the chaste wife of a Roman noble to his wishes, by causing her to be invited by a priest of Isis into the temple of the goddess, under the pretext that the god Anubis desired to embrace her. In innocence and faith, the woman resigned herself, and would perhaps afterwards have believed she had given birth to the child of a god, had not the intriguer, with bitter scorn, soon after discovered to her the true state of the case. It is the opinion of the author that Mary, the betrothed bride of the aged Joseph, was in like manner deceived by some amorous and fanatic young man (in the sequel to the history he represents him to be Joseph of Arimathea), and that she on her part, in perfect innocence, continued to deceive others.[6] It is evident that this interpretation does not differ from the ancient Jewish blasphemy, which we find in Celsus and in the Talmud ; that Jesus falsely represented himself as born of a pure virgin, whereas, in fact, he was the offspring of the adultery of Mary with a certain Panthera.[7]

---

[4] Im neuesten theol. Journal, 7. Bd. 4. Stück, s. 407 f.
[5] Antiq. xviii. 3, 4.
[6] 1ter Theil, s. 140 ff.
[7] The legend has undergone various modifications, but the name of *Panthera* or *Pandira* has been uniformly retained. Vid. Origenes c. Cels. 1, 28. 32. Schöttgen, Horæ 2, 693 ff.

This whole view, of which the culminating point is in the calumny of the Jews, cannot be better judged than in the words of Origen.   If, says this author, they wished to substitute something else in the place of the history of the supernatural conception of Jesus, they should at any rate have made it happen in a more probable manner ; they ought not, as it were against their will, to admit that Mary knew not Joseph, but they might have denied this feature, and yet have allowed Jesus to have been born of an ordinary human marriage ; whereas the forced and extravagant character of their hypothesis betrays its falsehood.[8] Is not this as much as to say, that if once some particular features of a marvellous narrative are doubted, it is inconsequent to allow others to remain unquestioned ? each part of such an account ought to be subjected to critical examination.   The correct view of the narrative before us is to be found, that is indirectly, in Origen.   For when at one time he places together, as of the same kind, the miraculous conception of Jesus and the story of Plato's conception by Apollo (though here, indeed, the meaning is that only ill-disposed persons could doubt such things [9]), and when at another time he says of the story concerning Plato, that it belongs to those mythi by which it was sought to exhibit the distinguished wisdom and power of great men (but here he does not include the narrative of Jesus's conception), he in fact states the two premises, namely, the similarity of the two narratives and the mythical character of the one [10] ; from which the inference of the merely mythical worth of the narrative of the conception of Jesus follows ; a conclusion which can never indeed have occurred to his own mind.

§ 29.

HISTORY OF THE CONCEPTION OF JESUS VIEWED AS A MYTHUS.

If, says Gabler in his review of the Commentary of Paulus, we must relinquish the supernatural origin of Jesus, in order to escape the ridicule of our contemporaries, and if, on the other hand, the natural explanation leads to conclusions not only extravagant, but revolting ; the adoption of the mythus, by which all these difficulties are obviated, is to be preferred.   In the world of mythology many great men had extraordinary births, and were sons of the gods.   Jesus himself spoke of his heavenly origin, and called God his father ; besides, his title as Messiah was—Son of God.   From Matthew i. 22, it is further evident that the passage of Isaiah, vii. 14, was referred to Jesus by the early Christian Church.   In conformity with this passage the belief prevailed that Jesus, as the Messiah, should be born of a virgin by means of divine agency ; it was therefore taken for granted that what was to be actually did occur ; and thus originated a philosophical (dogmatical) mythus concerning the birth of Jesus.   But according to historical truth, Jesus was the offspring of an ordinary marriage, between Joseph and Mary ; an explanation which, it has been justly remarked, maintains at once the dignity of Jesus and the respect due to his mother.[1]

aus Tract. Sanhedrin u. A. ; Eisenmenger, entdecktes Judenthum, 1, s. 105 ff. aus der Schmähschrift : Toledoth Jeschu ; Thilo, cod. apocr. s. 528. Comp. my Abhandlung über die Namen Panther, Pantheras, Pandera, in jüdischen und patristischen Erzählungen von der Abstammung Jesu. Athenäum, Febr. 1839, s. 15 ff.

    [8] Orig. c. Celsus i. 32.
    [9] Ibid. vi. 8.
    [10] Ibid. i. 37.
    [1] Gabler, in seinem neuesten theol. Journal, 7, 4. s. 408 f ; Eichhorn, Einleitung in das N. T. 1, s. 428 f. ; Bauer, hebr. Mythol. 1, 192 e ff. ; Kaiser, bibl. Theologie, 1, s. 231 f. ;

The proneness of the ancient world to represent the great men and bene-factors of their race as the sons of the gods, has therefore been referred to, in order to explain the origin of such a mythus. Our theologians have accumulated examples from the Greco-Roman mythology and history. They have cited Hercules, and the Dioscuri ; Romulus, and Alexander ; but above all Pythagoras,[2] and Plato. Of the latter philosopher Jerome speaks in a manner quite applicable to Jesus : sapientiæ principem non aliter arbitrantur, nisi de partu virginis editum.[3]

From these examples it might have been inferred that the narratives of the supernatural conception had possibly originated in a similar tendency, and had no foundation in history. Here however the orthodox and the rationalists are unanimous in denying, though indeed upon different grounds, the validity of the analogy. Origen, from a perception of the identical character of the two classes of narratives, is not far from regarding the heathen legends of the sons of the gods as true supernatural histories. Paulus on his side is more decided, and is so logical as to explain both classes of narratives in the same manner, as natural, but still as true histories. At least he says of the narrative concerning Plato : it cannot be affirmed that the groundwork of the history was a subsequent creation ; it is far more probable that Perictione believed herself to be pregnant by one of her gods. The fact that her son became a Plato might indeed have served to confirm that belief, but not to have originated it. Tholuck invites attention to the important distinction that the mythi concerning Romulus and others were formed many centuries after the lifetime of these men : the mythi concerning Jesus, on the contrary, must have existed shortly after his death.[4] He cleverly fails to remember the narrative of Plato's birth, since he is well aware that precisely in that particular, it is a dangerous point. Osiander however approaches the subject with much pathos, and affirms that Plato's apotheosis as son of Apollo did not exist till several centuries after him[5] ; whereas in fact Plato's sister's son speaks of it as a prevailing legend in Athens.[6] Olshausen, with whom Neander coincides, refuses to draw any detrimental inference from this analogy of the mythical sons of the gods ; remarking that though these narratives are un-historical, they evince a general anticipation and desire of such a fact, and therefore guarantee its reality, at least in one historical manifestation. Certainly, a general anticipation and representation must have truth for its basis ; but the truth does not consist in any one individual fact, presenting an accurate correspondence with that notion, but in *an idea* which realizes itself in a series of facts, which often bear no resemblance to the general notion. The widely spread notion of a golden age does not prove the existence of a golden age : so the notion of divine conceptions does not prove that some one individual was thus produced. The truth which is the basis of this notion is something quite different.

A more essential objection[7] to the analogy is, that the representations of

Wegscheider, Instit. § 123 ; De Wette, bibl. Dogmat. § 281, und exeg. Handb. 1, 1, s. 18 f., Ammon, Fortbildung des Christenth. s. 201 ff. ; Hase, L. J. § 33 ; Fritzsche, Comment. in Matth. s. 56. The latter justly remarks in the title to the first chapter : *non minus ille (Jesus) ut ferunt doctorum Judaicorum de Messiâ sententiæ, patrem habet spiritum divinum, matrem virginem.*
[2] Jamblich. vita Pythagoræ, cap. 2, ed. Kiessling.
[3] Adv. Jovin. 1, 26. Diog. Laërt., 3, 1, 2.
[4] Glaubwürdigkeit, s. 64.
[5] Apologie des L. J. s. 92.
[6] Diog. Laërt. a. a. O.: Σπεύσιππος (Sororis Platonis filius, Hieron.) δ᾽ ἐν τῷ ἐπιγραφομένῳ Πλάτωνος περδείπνῳ καὶ Κλέαρχος ἐν τῷ Πλάτωνος ἐγκωμίῳ καὶ Ἀναξιλίδης ἐν τῷ δευτέρῳ περὶ φιλοσόφων, φασὶν, Ἀθήνῃσιν ἦν λόγος, κ. τ. λ.
[7] Neander, L. J. Ch. s. 10.

the heathen world prove nothing with respect to the isolated Jews; and that the idea of sons of the gods, belonging to polytheism, could not have exerted an influence on the rigidly monotheistic notion of the Messiah. At all events such an inference must not be too hastily drawn from the expression "sons of God," found likewise among the Jews, which as applied in the Old Testament to magistrates, (Ps. lxxxii. 6, or to theocratic kings, 2 Sam. vii. 14, Ps. ii. 7,) indicates only a theocratic, and not a physical or metaphysical relation. Still less is importance to be attached to the language of flattery used by a Roman, in Josephus, who calls beautiful children of the Jewish princes children of God.[8] It was, however, a notion among the Jews, as was remarked in a former section, that the Holy Spirit co-operated in the conception of pious individuals; moreover, that God's choicest instruments were conceived by divine assistance of parents, who could not have had a child according to the natural course of things. And if, according to the believed representation, the extinct capability on both sides was renewed by divine intervention (Rom. iv. 19), it was only one step further to the belief that in the case of the conception of the most distinguished of all God's agents, the Messiah, the total absence of participation on the one side was compensated by a more complete superadded capability on the other. The latter is scarcely a degree more marvellous than the former. And thus must it have appeared to the author of Luke i., since he dissipates Mary's doubts by the same reply with which Jehovah repelled Sara's incredulity.[9] Neither the Jewish reverence for marriage, nor the prevalent representation of the Messiah as a human being, could prevent the advance to this climax; to which, on the other hand, the ascetic estimation of celibacy, and the idea, derived from Daniel, of the Christ as a superhuman being, contributed. But decided impulse to the development of the representations embodied in our histories of the birth, consisted partly in the title, *Son of God*, at one time usually given to the Messiah. For it is the nature of such originally figurative expressions, after a while to come to be interpreted according to their more precise and literal signification; and it was a daily occurrence, especially among the later Jews, to attach a sensible signification to that which originally had merely a spiritual or figurative meaning. This natural disposition to understand the Messianic title *Son of God* more and more literally, was fostered by the expression in the Psalms (ii. 7), interpreted of the Messiah: *Thou art my Son; this day have I begotten thee*: words which can scarcely fail to suggest a physical relation; it was also nurtured by the prophecy of Isaiah respecting the virgin who should be with child, which it appears was applied to the Messiah; as were so many other prophecies of which the immediate signification had become obscure. This application may be seen in the Greek word chosen by the Septuagint, παρθένος, a pure unspotted virgin, whereas by Aquila and other Greek translators the word νεᾶνις is used.[10] Thus did the notions of a *son of God* and a *son of a virgin* complete one another, till at last the divine agency was substituted for human paternal participation. Wetstein indeed affirms that no Jew ever applied the prophecy of Isaiah to the Messiah; and it was with extreme labour that Schoettgen collected traces of the notion that the Messiah should be the son of a virgin from the Rabbinical writings. This however, considering the paucity of records of the Messianic ideas of that age,[11] proves nothing in opposition to the presumption that a

---

[8] Antiq. 15. 2. 6.

[9] Gen. xviii., 14 Sept.   Luke i. 37.
μὴ ἀδυνατήσει παρὰ τῷ θεῷ ῥῆμα ;   ὅτι οὐκ ἀδυνατήσει παρὰ τῷ θεῷ πᾶν ῥῆμα.

[10] De Wette, Exeg. Handb. 1, 1, s. 17.

[11] They are to be found however in the more modern Rabbins, s. Matthæi, Religionsgl. der Apostel 2, a. s. 555 ff.

notion then prevailed, of which we have the groundwork in the Old Testament, and an inference hardly to be mistaken in the New.

One objection yet remains, which I can no longer designate as peculiar to Olshausen, since other theologians have shown themselves solicitous of sharing the fame. The objection is, that the mythical interpretation of the gospel narrative is especially dangerous, it being only too well fitted to engender, obscurely indeed, profane and blasphemous notions concerning the origin of Jesus ; since it cannot fail to favour an opinion destructive of the belief in a Redeemer, namely, that Jesus came into being through unholy means ; since, in fact, at the time of her pregnancy Mary was not married.[12] In Olshausen's first edition of his work, he adds that he willingly allows that these interpreters know not what they do : it is therefore but just to give him the advantage of the same concession, since he certainly appears not to know what mythical interpretation means. How otherwise would he say, that the mythical interpretation is fitted only to favour a blasphemous opinion ; therefore that all who understand the narrative mythically, are disposed to commit the absurdity with which Origen reproaches the Jewish calumniators ; the retaining one solitary incident, namely, that Mary was not married, whilst the remainder of the narrative is held to be unhistorical ; a particular incident which evidently serves only as a support to the other, that Jesus was conceived without human paternal participation, and with it, therefore, stands or falls. No one among the interpreters who, in this narrative, recognise a mythus, in the full signification of that term, has been thus blind and inconsequent ; all have supposed a legitimate marriage between Joseph and Mary ; and Olshausen merely paints the mythical mode of interpretation in caricature, in order the more easily to set it aside ; for he confesses that in relation to this portion of the Gospel in particular, it has much that is dazzling.

§ 30.

RELATION OF JOSEPH TO MARY—BROTHERS OF JESUS.

Our Gospels, in the true spirit of the ancient legend, find it unbecoming to allow the mother of Jesus, so long as she bore the heavenly germ, to be approached or profaned by an earthly husband. Consequently Luke (ii. 5) represents the connexion between Joseph and Mary, prior to the birth of Jesus, as a betrothment merely. And, as it is stated respecting the father of Plato, after his wife had become pregnant by Apollo : ὅθεν καθαρὰν γάμου φυλάξαι ἕως τῆς ἀποκυήσεως,[1] so likewise it is remarked of Joseph in Matthew (i. 25) : καὶ οὐκ ἐγίνωσκεν αὐτὴν (τὴν γυναῖκα αὐτοῦ) ἕως οὗ ἔτεκε τὸν υἱὸν αὐτῆς τὸν πρωτότοκον. In each of these kindred passages the Greek word ἕως (till) must evidently receive the same interpretation. Now in the first quotation the meaning is incontestably this :—that till the time of Plato's birth his father abstained from intercourse with his wife, but subsequently assumed his conjugal rights, since we hear of Plato's brothers. In reference, therefore, to the parents of Jesus, the ἕως cannot have a different signification ; in each case it indicates precisely the same limitation. So again the expression πρωτότοκος (firstborn) used in reference to Jesus in both the Gospels (Matt. i. 25, Luke ii. 7) supposes that Mary had other children, for as Lucian says : εἰ μὲν πρῶτος, οὐ μόνος· εἰ δὲ μόνος, οὐ πρῶτος.[2] Even in the same Gospels (Matt. xiii. 55,

---

[12] Bibl. Comm. 1, s. 47. Also Daub. 2 a. s. 311 f ; Theile, § 14. Neander, s. 9.
[1] Diog. Laërt. a. a. O. See Origenes c. Cels. 1, 37.
[2] Demonax, 29.

Luke viii. 19) mention is made of ἀδελφοῖς Ἰησοῦ (*the brothers of Jesus*). In the words of Fritzsche : *Lubentissime post Jesu natales Mariam concessit Matthæus* (Luke does the same) *uxorem Josepho, in hoc uno occupatus, ne quis ante Jesu primordia mutuâ venere usos suspicaretur.* But this did not continue to satisfy the orthodox ; as the veneration for Mary rose even higher, she who had once become fruitful by divine agency was not subsequently to be profaned by the common relations of life.[3] The opinion that Mary after the birth of Jesus became the .wife of Joseph, was early ranked among the heresies,[4] and the orthodox Fathers sought every means to escape from it and to combat it. They contended that according to the exegetical interpretation of ἕως οὗ, it sometimes affirmed or denied a thing, not merely up to a certain limit, but beyond that limitation and for ever ; and that the words of Matthew οὐκ ἐγίνωσκεν αὐτὴν ἕως οὗ ἔτεκε κ. τ. λ. excluded a matrimonial connexion between Joseph and Mary for all time.[5] In like manner it was asserted of the term πρωτότοκος, that it did not necessarily include the subsequent birth of other children, but that it merely excluded any previous birth.[6] But in order to banish the thought of a matrimonial connexion between Mary and Joseph, not only grammatically but physiologically, they represented Joseph as a very old man, under whom Mary was placed for control and protection only ; and the brothers of Jesus mentioned in the New Testament they regarded as the children of Joseph by a former marriage.[7] But this was not all ; soon it was insisted not only that Mary never became the wife of Joseph, but that in giving birth to Jesus she did not lose her virginity.[8] But even the conservation of Mary's virginity did not long continue to satisfy : perpetual virginity was likewise required on the part of Joseph. It was not enough that he had no connexion with Mary ; it was also necessary that his entire life should be one of celibacy. Accordingly, though Epiphanius allows that Joseph had sons by a former marriage, Jerome rejects the supposition as an impious and audacious invention ; and from that time the brothers of Jesus were degraded to the rank of cousins.[9]

Some modern theologians agree with the Fathers of the Church in maintaining that no matrimonial connexion subsisted at any time between Joseph and Mary, and believe themselves able to explain the gospel expressions which appear to assert the contrary. In reference to the term *firstborn*, Olshausen contends that it signifies an only son : no less than the eldest of several. Paulus allows that here he is right, and Clemen[10] and Fritzsche seek in vain to demonstrate the impossibility of this signification. For when it is said in Ex. xiii. 2, קַדֶּשׁ־לִי כָל־בְּכוֹר פֶּטֶר כָּל־רֶחֶם (πρωτότοκον πρωτογενὲς LXX.) it was not merely a firstborn followed by others subsequently born, who was sanctified to Jehovah, but the fruit of the body of that mother of whom no

---

[3] S. Origenes in Matthæum, Opp. ed. de la Rue, Vol. 3. s. 463.
[4] The Arian Eunomius according to Photius taught τὸν Ἰωσὴφ μετὰ τὴν ἄφραστον κυοφορίαν συνάπτεσθαι τῇ παρθένῳ. This was also, according to Epiphanius, the doctrine of those called by him Dimaerites and Antidicomarianites, and in the time of Jerome, of Helvidius and his followers. Compare on this point the Sammlung von Suicer, im Thesaurus ii., s. v. Μαρία, fol. 305 f.
[5] Comp. Hieron. adv. Helv. 6, 7, Theophylact and Suidas in Suicer, 1, s. v. ἕως, fol. 1294 f.
[6] Hieron. z. d. St.
[7] See Orig. in Matth. Tom. 10, 17 ; Epiphan. haeres. 78, 7 ; Historia Josephi, c. 2 ; Protev. Jac. 9. 18.
[8] Chrysostomus, hom. 142, in Suicer, s. v. Μαρία, most repulsively described in the Protev. Jac. xix. and xx.
[9] Hieron. ad Matth. 12, und advers. Helvid. 19.
[10] Die Brüder Jesu. In Winer's Zeitschrift für wissenschaftliche Theologie, 1, 3. s. 364 f.

other child had previously been born. Therefore the term πρωτοτοκος must of necessity bear also this signification. Truly however we must confess with Winer [11] and others, on the other side, that if a narrator who was acquainted with the whole sequel of the history used that expression, we should be tempted to understand it in its primitive sense ; since had the author intended to exclude other children, he would rather have employed the word μονογενὴς, or would have connected it with πρωτότοκος. If this be not quite decisive, the reasoning of Fritzsche in reference to the ἕως οὗ, κ. τ. λ., is more convincing. He rejects the citations adduced in support of the interpretation of the Fathers of the Church, proving that this expression according to its primitive signification affirms only to a given limit, and beyond that limit supposes the logical opposite of the affirmation to take place ; a signification which it loses only when the context shows clearly that the opposite is impossible in the nature of things.[12] For example, when it is said οὐκ ἐγίνωσκεν αὐτὴν, ἕως οὗ ἀπέθανεν, it is self-evident that the negation, during the time elapsed till death—cannot be transformed after death into an affirmation ; but when it is said, as in Matthew, οὐκ ἐ. ἀ. ἕως οὗ ἔτεκεν, the giving birth to the divine fruit opposes no impossibility to the establishment of the conjugal relations ; on the contrary it renders it possible, i.e. suitable [13] for them now to take place.

Olshausen, impelled by the same doctrinal motives which influenced the Fathers, is led in this instance to contradict both the evidence of grammar and of logic. He thinks that Joseph, without wishing to impair the sanctity of marriage, must have concluded after the experiences he had had (?) that his marriage with Mary had another object than the production of children ; besides it was but natural (?) in the last descendant of the house of David, and of that particular branch from which the Messiah should come forth, to terminate her race in this last and eternal offshoot.

A curious ladder may be formed of these different beliefs and superstitions in relation to the connexion between Mary and Joseph.

1. Contemporaries of Jesus and composers of the genealogies : Joseph and Mary man and wife—Jesus the offspring of their marriage.

2. The age and authors of our histories of the birth of Jesus : Mary and Joseph betrothed only ; Joseph having no participation in the conception of the child, and previous to his birth no conjugal connexion with Mary.

3. Olshausen and others : subsequent to the birth of Jesus, Joseph, though then the husband of Mary, relinquishes his matrimonial rights.

4. Epiphanius, Protevangelium Jacobi and others : Joseph a decrepit old man, no longer to be thought of as a husband : the children attributed to him are of a former marriage. More especially it is not as a bride and wife that he receives Mary ; he takes her merely under his guardianship.

5. Protevang., Chrysostom and others : Mary's virginity was not only not destroyed by any subsequent births of children by Joseph, it was not in the slightest degree impaired by the birth of Jesus.

6. Jerome : not Mary only but Joseph also observed an absolute virginity, and the pretended brothers of Jesus were not his sons but merely cousins to Jesus.

---

[11] Biblisches Realwörterbuch, 1 Bd. s. 664, Anm. De Wette, z. d. St. Neander L. J. Ch., s. 34.

[12] Comment. in Matth. s. 53 ff., vgl. auch s. 835.

[13] Olshausen is exceedingly unhappy in the example chosen by him in support of his interpretation of ἕως οὗ. For when it is said, *we waited till midnight but no one came*, certainly this by no means implies that after midnight some one did come, but it does imply that after midnight we waited no longer ; so that here the expression *till* retains its signification of exclusion.

The opinion that the ἀδελφοὶ (brothers) and ἀδελφαὶ Ἰησοῦ (sisters of Jesus) mentioned in the New Testament, were merely half brothers or indeed cousins, appears in its origin, as shown above, together with the notion that no matrimonial connexion ever subsisted between Joseph and Mary, as the mere invention of superstition, a circumstance highly prejudicial to such an opinion. It is however no less true that purely exegetical grounds exist, in virtue of which theologians who were free from prejudice have decided, that the opinion that Jesus actually had brothers is untenable.[14]   Had we merely the following passages—Matt. xiii. 55, Mark vi. 3, where the people of Nazareth, astonished at the wisdom of their countryman, in order to mark his well known origin, immediately after having spoken of τέκτων (the carpenter) his father, and his mother Mary, mention by name his ἀδελφοὺς (brothers) James, Joses, Simon, and Judas, together with his sisters whose names are not given [15]; again Matt. xii. 46, Luke viii. 19, when his mother and his brethren come to Jesus ; John ii. 12, where Jesus journeys with his mother and his brethren to Capernaum ; Acts i. 14, where they are mentioned in immediate connexion with his mother —if we had these passages only, we could not for a moment hesitate to recognize here real brothers of Jesus at least on the mother's side, children of Joseph and Mary ; not only on account of the proper signification of the word ἀδελφὸς, but also in consequence of its continual conjunction with Mary and Joseph. Even the passages—John vii. 5, in which it is remarked that his brethren did not believe on Jesus, and Mark iii. 21, compared with 31, where, according to the most probable explanation, the brothers of Jesus with his mother went out to lay hold of him as one beside himself—furnish no adequate grounds for relinquishing the proper signification of ἀδελφὸς.   Many theologians have interpreted ἀδελφοὺς Ἰησοῦ in the last cited passage *half brothers, sons of Joseph by a former marriage*, alleging that the real brothers of Jesus must have believed on him, but this is a mere assumption.   The difficulty seems greater when we read in John xix. 26 f. that Jesus, on the cross, enjoined John to be a son to his mother ; an injunction it is not easy to regard as suitable under the supposition that Mary had other children, except indeed these were half-brothers and unfriendly to Jesus.   Nevertheless we can imagine the existence both of external circumstances and of individual feelings which might have influenced Jesus to confide his mother to John rather than to his brothers. That these brothers appeared in company with his apostles after the ascension (Acts i. 14) is no proof that they must have believed on Jesus at the time of his death.

The real perplexity in the matter, however, originates in this : that besides the James and Joses spoken of as the brothers of Jesus, two men of the same name are mentioned as the sons of another Mary (Mark xv. 40, 47, xvi. 1, Matt. xxvii. 56), without doubt that Mary who is designated, John xix. 25, as the sister of the mother of Jesus, and the wife of Cleophas ; so that we have a James and a Joses not only among the children of Mary the mother of Jesus, but again among her sister's children.   We meet with several others among those immediately connected with Jesus, whose names are identical.   In the lists of the apostles (Matt. x. 2 ff., Luke vi. 14 ff.) we have two more of the name of James : that is four, the brother and cousin of Jesus included ; two more of the name of Judas : that is three, the brother of Jesus included ; two of the name of Simon, also making three with the brother of Jesus of the

---

[14] On this subject compare in particular Clemen, die Brüder Jesu, in Winer's Zeitschrift für wiss. Theol. 1, 3, s. 329 ff. ; Paulus, Exeg. Handbuch, 1 Bd. s. 557 ff. ; Fritzsche, a. a. O. s. 480 ff. ; Winer, bibl. Realwörterbuch, in den A. A. ; Jesus, Jacobus, Apostel.

[15] See the different names assigned them in the legend in Thilo, Codex apocryphus N.T., I, s. 360 note.

same name. The question naturally arises, whether the same individual is not here taken as distinct persons? The suspicion is almost unavoidable in reference to James. As James the son of Alpheus is, in the list of the apostles, introduced after the son of Zebedee, as the second, perhaps the younger ; and as James the cousin of Jesus is called ὁ μικρὸς (" the less ") Mark xv. 40 ; and since by comparing John xix. 25, we find that the latter is called the son of Cleophas, it is possible that the name Κλωπᾶς (Cleophas) given to the husband of Mary's sister, and the name Ἀλφαῖος (Alpheus) given to the father of the apostle, may be only different forms of the Hebrew חלפי. Thus would the second James enumerated among the apostles and the cousin of Jesus of that name be identical, and there would remain besides him only the son of Zebedee and the brother of Jesus. Now in the Acts (xv. 13) a James appears who takes a prominent part in the so-called apostolic council, and as, according to Acts xii. 2, the son of Zebedee had previously been put to death, and as in the foregoing portion of the book of the Acts no mention is made of any other James besides the son of Alpheus (i. 13), so this James, of whom (Acts xv. 13) no more precise description is given, can be no other than the son of Alpheus. But Paul speaks of a James (Gal. i. 19) *the Lord's brother*, whom he saw at Jerusalem, and it is doubtless he of whom he speaks in connexion with Cephas and John as the στύλοι (pillars) of the church—for this is precisely in character with the (Apostle) James as he appeared at the apostolic council—so that this James may be considered as identical with the Lord's brother, and the rather as the expression ἕτερον δὲ τῶν ἀποστόλων οὐκ εἶδον, εἰ μὴ Ἰάκωβον τὸν ἀδελφὸν τοῦ Κυρίου (*but other of the apostles saw I none, save James the Lord's brother.* Gal. i. 19), makes it appear as if the Lord's brother were reckoned among the apostles ; with which also the ancient tradition which represents James the Just, a brother of Jesus, as the first head of the church at Jerusalem, agrees.[16] But admitting the James of the Acts to be identical with the distinguished apostle of that name, then is he the son of Alpheus, and not the son of Joseph ; consequently if he be at the same time ἀδελφὸς τοῦ Κυρίου, then ἀδελφὸς cannot signify a brother. Now if Alpheus and Cleophas are admitted to be the same individual, the husband of the sister of Mary the mother of Jesus, it is obvious that ἀδελφὸς, used to denote the relationship of his son to Jesus, must be taken in the signification, cousin. If, after this manner, James the Apostle the son of Alpheus be identified with the cousin, and the cousin be identified with the brother of Jesus of the same name, it is obvious that Ἰούδας Ἰακώβου in the catalogue of the Apostles in Luke (Luke vi. 16, Acts i. 13), must be translated *brother of James* (son of Alpheus) ; and this Apostle Jude must be held as identical with the Jude ἀδελφὸς Ἰησοῦ, that is, with the cousin of the Lord and son of Mary Cleophas (though the name of Jude is never mentioned in connexion with this Mary). If the Epistle of Jude in our canon be authentic, it is confirmatory of the above deduction, that the author (verse 1) designates himself as the ἀδελφὸς Ἰακώβου (*brother of James*). Some moreover have identified the Apostle Simon ὁ ζηλωτὴς or Κανανίτης (*Zelotes, or the Canaanite*) with the Simon enumerated among the brothers of Jesus (Mark vi. 3), and who according to a tradition of the church succeeded James as head of the church at Jerusalem [17]; so that Joses alone appears without further designation or appellative.

If, accordingly, those spoken of as ἀδελφοὶ Ἰησοῦ were merely cousins, and three of these were apostles, it must excite surprise that not only in the Acts (i. 14), after an enumeration of the apostles, the brothers of Jesus are separ-

---

16 Euseb. H. E. 2, 1.
17 Euseb. H. E. 3, 11.

ately particularized, but that also (1 Cor. ix. 5) they appear to be a class distinct from the apostles.   Perhaps, also, the passage Gal. i. 19 ought to be understood as indicating that James, the Lord's brother, was not an apostle.[18] If, therefore, the ἀδελφοὶ Ἰησοῦ seem thus to be extruded from the number of the apostles, it is yet more difficult to regard them merely as the cousins of Jesus, since they appear in so many places immediately associated with the mother of Jesus, and in two or three passages only are two men bearing the same names mentioned in connexion with the other Mary, who accordingly would be their real mother.   The Greek word ἀδελφὸς may indeed signify, in language which pretends not to precision, as well as the Hebrew אח, a more distant relative ; but as it is repeatedly used to express the relationship of these persons to Jesus, and is in no instance replaced by ἀνεψιὸς—a word which is not foreign to the New Testament language when the relationship of cousin is to be denoted (Col. iv. 10), it cannot well be taken in any other than its proper signification.   Further, it need only be pointed out that the highest degree of uncertainty exists respecting not only the identity of the names Alpheus and Cleophas, upon which the identity of James the cousin of Jesus and of the Apostle James the Less rests, but also regarding the translation of Ἰούδας Ἰακώβου by the *brother of James* ; and likewise respecting the assumed identity of the author of the last Catholic Epistle with the Apostle Jude.

Thus the web of this identification gives way at all points, and we are forced back to the position whence we set out ; so that we have again real brothers of Jesus, also two cousins distinct from these brothers, though bearing the same names with two of them, besides some apostles of the same names with both brothers and cousins.   To find two pairs of sons of the same names in a family is, indeed, not so uncommon as to become a source of objection.   It is, however, remarkable that the same James who in the Epistle to the Galatians is designated ἀδελφὸς Κυρίου (*the Lord's brother*), must unquestionably, according to the Acts of the Apostles, be regarded as the son of Alpheus ; which he could not be if this expression signified a brother.   So that there is perplexity on every side, which can be solved only (and then, indeed, but negatively and without historical result) by admitting the existence of obscurity and error on this point in the New Testament writers, and even in the very earliest Christian traditions ; error which, in matters of involved relationships and family names, is far more easily fallen into than avoided.[19]

We have consequently no ground for denying that the mother of Jesus bore her husband several other children besides Jesus, younger, and perhaps also older ; the latter, because the representation in the New Testament that Jesus was the first-born may belong no less to the mythus than the representation of the Fathers that he was an only son.

§ 31.

VISIT OF MARY TO ELIZABETH.

The angel who announced to Mary her own approaching pregnancy, at the same time informed her (Luke i. 36) of that of her relative Elizabeth, with whom it was already the sixth month.   Hereupon Mary immediately set out on a journey to her cousin, a visit which was attended by extraordinary occurrences ; for when Elizabeth heard the salutation of Mary, the babe leaped in her womb for joy ; she also became inspired, and in her exultation poured

---

[18] Fritzsche, Comm. in Matth. p. 482.
[19] Theile, Biographie Jesu, § 18.

forth an address to Mary as the future mother of the Messiah, to which Mary
responded by a hymn of praise (Luke i. 39–56).

The rationalistic interpreter believes it to be an casy matter to give a
natural explanation of this narrative of the Gospel of Luke. He is of
opinion [1] that the unknown individual who excited such peculiar anticipations
in Mary, had at the same time acquainted her with the similar situation of her
cousin Elizabeth. This it was which impelled Mary the more strongly to confer on the subject with her older relative. Arrived at her cousin's dwelling,
she first of all made known what had happened to herself; but upon this the
narrator is silent, not wishing to repeat what he had just before described.
And here the Rationalist not only supposes the address of Elizabeth to have
been preceded by some communication from Mary, but imagines Mary to
have related her history piecemeal, so as to allow Elizabeth to throw in sentences during the intervals. The excitement of Elizabeth—such is the continuation of the rationalistic explanation—communicated itself, according to
natural laws, to the child, who, as is usual with an embryo of six months,
made a movement, which was first regarded by the mother as significant, and
as the consequence of the salutation, after Mary's farther communications.
Just as natural does it appear to the Rationalist that Mary should have given
utterance to her Messianic expectations, confirmed as they were by Elizabeth,
in a kind of psalmodic recitative, composed of reminiscences borrowed from
various parts of the Old Testament.

But there is much in this explanation which positively contradicts the text.
In the first place, that Elizabeth should have learned the heavenly message
imparted to Mary from Mary herself. There is no trace in the narrative
either of any communication preceding Elizabeth's address, or of interruptions
occasioned by farther explanations on the part of Mary. On the contrary, as
it is a supernatural revelation which acquaints Mary with the pregnancy of
Elizabeth, so also it is to a revelation that Elizabeth's immediate recognition
of Mary, as the chosen mother of the Messiah, is attributed.[2] As little will
the other feature of this narrative—that the entrance of the mother of the
Messiah occasioned a responsive movement in his mother's womb on the part
of his forerunner—bear a natural explanation. In modern times, indeed, even
orthodox interpreters have inclined to this explanation, but with the modification, that Elizabeth in the first place received a revelation, in which however the child, owing to the mother's excitement, a matter to be physiologically explained, likewise took part.[3] But the record does not represent the
thing as if the excitement of the mother were the determining cause of the
movement of the child; on the contrary (v. 41), the emotion of the mother
follows the movement of the child, and Elizabeth's own account states, that
it was the salutation of Mary (v. 44), not indeed from its particular signification, but merely as the voice of the mother of the Messiah, which produced
the movement of the unborn babe : undeniably assuming something supernatural. And indeed the supranaturalistic view of this miracle is not free
from objection, even on its own ground ; and hence the anxiety of the above-
mentioned modern orthodox interpreters to evade it. It may be possible to
conceive the human mind immediately acted upon by the divine mind, to
which it is related, but how solve the difficulty of an immediate communication of the divine mind to an unintelligent embryo? And if we inquire the
object of so strange a miracle, none which is worthy presents itself. Should

---

[1] Paulus, exeg. Handb. 1. a, s. 120 ff.
[2] S. Olshausen und de Wette, z. d. St.
[3] Hess, Geschichte Jesu, 1, s. 26 ; Olshausen, bibl. Comm. z. d. St. ; Hoffmann, s. 226;
Lange, s. 76 ff.

it be referred to the necessity that the Baptist should receive the earliest possible intimation of the work to which he was destined ; still we know not how
such an impression could have been made upon an embryo.   Should the purpose be supposed to centre in the other individuals, in Mary or Elizabeth ;
they had been the recipients of far higher revelations, and were consequently
already possessed of an adequate measure of insight and faith.

No fewer difficulties oppose the rationalistic than the supranaturalistic explanation of the hymn pronounced by Mary.   For though it is not, like the
Canticle of Zacharias (v. 67) and the address of Elizabeth (v. 41), introduced
by the formula ἐπλήσθη πνεύματος ἁγίου, *she was filled with the Holy Ghost*,
still the similarity of these utterances is so great, that the omission cannot be
adduced as a proof that the narrator did not intend to represent this, equally
with the other two, as the operation of the πνεῦμα (spirit).   But apart from
the intention of the narrator, can it be thought natural that two friends visiting
one another should, even in the midst of the most extraordinary occurrences,
break forth into long hymns, and that their conversation should entirely lose
the character of dialogue, the natural form on such occasions ?   By a supernatural influence alone could the minds of the two friends be attuned to a
state of elevation, so foreign to their every-day life.   But if, indeed, Mary's
hymn is to be understood as the work of the Holy Spirit, it is surprising that
a speech emanating immediately from the divine source of inspiration should
not be more striking for its originality, but should be so interlarded with reminiscences from the Old Testament, borrowed from the song of praise spoken
by the mother of Samuel (1 Sam. ii.) under analogous circumstances.[4]   Accordingly we must admit that the compilation of this hymn, consisting of
recollections from the Old Testament, was put together in a natural way ; but
allowing its composition to have been perfectly natural, it cannot be ascribed
to the artless Mary, but to him who poetically wrought out the tradition in
circulation respecting the scene in question.

Since then we find all the principal incidents of this visit inconceivable
according to the supernatural interpretation ; also that they will not bear a
natural explanation ; we are led to seek a mythical exposition of this as well
as the preceding portions of the gospel history.   This path has already been
entered upon by others.   The view of this narrative given by the anonymous
E. F. in Henke's Magazine [5] is, that it does not pourtray events as they actually did occur, but as they might have occurred ; that much which the sequel
taught of the destiny of their sons was carried back into the speeches of these
women, which were also enriched by other features gleaned from tradition ;
that a true fact however lies at the bottom, namely an actual visit of Mary to
Elizabeth, a joyous conversation, and the expression of gratitude to God ; all
which might have happened solely in virtue of the high importance attached
by Orientals to the joys of maternity, even though the two mothers had been
at that time ignorant of the destination of their children.   This author is of
opinion that Mary, when pondering over at a later period the remarkable life
of her son, may often have related the happy meeting with her cousin and

---

[4] Compare   Luke i. 47 with 1 Sam. ii. 1.
                           i. 49   ii. 2.
                           i. 51   ii. 3, 4.
                           i. 52   ii. 8.
                           i. 53   ii. 5.
     Particularly Luke i. 48 with 1 Sam. i. 11.
     Compare   Luke i. 50   Deut. vii. 9.
                           i. 52   Ecclesiasticus x. 14.
                           i. 54   Ps. xcviii. 3.
[5] 5 Band, 1. Stück, s. 161. f.

their mutual expressions of thankfulness to God, and that thus the history gained currency. Horst also, who has a just conception of the fictitious nature of this section in Luke, and ably refutes the natural mode of explanation, yet himself slides unawares half-way back into it. He thinks it not improbable that Mary during her pregnancy, which was in many respects a painful one, should have visited her older and more experienced cousin, and that Elizabeth should during this visit have felt the first movement of her child : an occurrence which as it was afterwards regarded as ominous, was preserved by the oral tradition.[6]

These are farther examples of the uncritical proceeding which pretends to disengage the mythical and poetical from the narrative, by plucking away a few twigs and blossoms of that growth, whilst it leaves the very root of the mythus undisturbed as purely historical. In our narrative the principal mythical feature (the remainder forms only its adjuncts) is precisely that which the above-mentioned authors, in their pretended mythical explanations, retain as historical : namely, the visit of Mary to the pregnant Elizabeth. For, as we have already seen, the main tendency of the first chapter of Luke is to magnify Jesus by connecting the Baptist with him from the earliest possible point in a relation of inferiority. Now this object could not be better attained than by bringing about a meeting, not in the first instance of the sons, but of the mothers in reference to their sons, during their pregnancy, at which meeting some occurrence which should prefigure the future relative positions of these two men should take place. Now the more apparent the existence of a dogmatical motive as the origin of this visit, the less probability is there that it had an historical foundation. With this principal feature the other details are connected in the following order :—The visit of the two women must be represented as possible and probable by the feature of family relationship between Mary and Elizabeth (v. 36), which would also give a greater suitability to the subsequent connexion of the sons. Further, a visit, so full of import, made precisely at that time, must have taken place by special divine appointment ; therefore it is an angel who refers Mary to her cousin. At the visit the subservient position of the Baptist to Jesus is to be particularly exhibited ;—this could have been effected by the mother, as indeed it is, in her address to Mary, but it were better if possible that the future Baptist himself should give a sign. The mutual relation of Esau and Jacob had been prefigured by their struggles and position in their mother's womb (Gen. xxv. 22 ff.). But, without too violent an offence against the laws of probability, an ominous movement would not be attributed to the child prior to that period of her pregnancy at which the motion of the fœtus is felt ; hence the necessity that Elizabeth should be in the sixth month of her pregnancy when Mary, in consequence of the communication of the angel, set out to visit her cousin (v. 36). Thus, as Schleiermacher remarks,[7] the whole arrangement of times had reference to the particular circumstance the author desired to contrive—the joyous responsive movement of the child in his mother's womb at the moment of Mary's entrance. To this end only must Mary's visit be delayed till after the fifth month ; and the angel not appear to her before that period.

Thus not only does the visit of Mary to Elizabeth with all the attendant circumstances disappear from the page of history, but the historical validity of the further details—that John was only half a year older than Jesus ; that the two mothers were related ; that an intimacy subsisted between the families ;—cannot be affirmed on the testimony of Luke, unsupported by other authorities : indeed, the contrary rather will be found substantiated in the course of our critical investigations.

[6] In Henke's Museum, 1, 4, s. 725. [7] Ueber den Lukas, s. 23 f.

CHAPTER IV.

BIRTH AND EARLIEST EVENTS OF THE LIFE OF JESUS.

§ 32.

THE CENSUS.

WITH respect to the birth of Jesus, Matthew and Luke agree in representing it as taking place at Bethlehem; but whilst the latter enters into a minute detail of all the attendant circumstances, the former merely mentions the event as it were incidentally, referring to it once in an appended sentence as the sequel to what had gone before (i. 25), and again as a presupposed occurrence (ii. 1). The one Evangelist seems to assume that Bethlehem was the habitual residence of the parents; but according to the other they are led thither by very particular circumstances. This point of difference between the Evangelists however can only be discussed after we shall have collected more data; we will therefore leave it for the present, and turn our attention to an error into which Luke, when compared with himself and with dates otherwise ascertained, seems to have fallen. This is the statement, that the census, decreed by Augustus at the time when Cyrenius (Quirinus) was governor of Syria, was the occasion of the journey of the parents of Jesus, who usually resided at Nazareth, to Bethlehem where Jesus was born (Luke ii. 1 ff.).

The first difficulty is that the ἀπογραφὴ (namely, the inscription of the name and amount of property in order to facilitate the taxation) commanded by Augustus, is extended to *all the world*, πᾶσαν τὴν οἰκουμένην. This expression, in its common acceptation at that time, would denote the *orbis Romanus*. But ancient authors mention no such general census decreed by Augustus; they speak only of the assessment of single provinces decreed at different times. Consequently, it was said Luke meant to indicate by οἰκουμένη merely the land of Judea, and not the Roman world according to its ordinary signification. Examples were forthwith collected in proof of the possibility of such an interpretation,[1] but they in fact prove nothing. For supposing it could not be shown that in all these citations from the Septuagint, Josephus, and the New Testament, the expression really does signify, in the extravagant sense of these writers, the whole known world; still in the instance in question, where the subject is a decree of the Roman emperor, πᾶσα ἡ οἰκουμένη must necessarily be understood of the regions which he governed, and therefore of the *orbis Romanus*. This is the reason that latterly the opposite side has been taken up, and it has been maintained, upon the authority of Savigny, that in the time of Augustus a census of the

---

[1] Olshausen, Paulus, Kuinöl.

whole empire was actually undertaken.[2]   This is positively affirmed by late Christian writers [3] : but the statement is rendered suspicious by the absence of all more ancient testimony [4]; and it is even contradicted by the fact, that for a considerable lapse of time an equal assessment throughout the empire was not effected.   Finally, the very expressions of these writers show that their testimony rests upon that of Luke.[5]   But, it is said, Augustus at all events attempted an equal assessment of the empire by means of an universal census ; and he began the carrying out his project by an assessment of individual provinces, but he left the further execution and completion to his successors.[6]   Admit that the gospel term δόγμα (decree) may be interpreted as a mere design, or, as Hoffmann thinks, an undetermined project expressed in an imperial decree ; still the fulfilment of this project in Judea at the time of the birth of Jesus was impossible.

Matthew places the birth of Jesus shortly before the death of Herod the Great, whom he represents (ii. 19) as dying during the abode of Jesus in Egypt.   Luke says the same indirectly, for when speaking of the announcement of the birth of the Baptist, he refers it to the days of Herod the Great, and he places the birth of Jesus precisely six months later ; so that according to Luke, also, Jesus was born, if not, like John, previous to the death of Herod I., shortly after that event.   Now, after the death of Herod the country of Judea fell to his son Archelaus (Matt. ii. 22), who, after a reign of something less than ten years, was deposed and banished by Augustus,[7] at which time Judea was first constituted a Roman province, and began to be ruled by Roman functionaries.[8]   Thus the Roman census in question must have been made either under Herod the Great, or at the commencement of the reign of Archelaus.   This is in the highest degree improbable, for in those countries which were not reduced in formam provinciæ, but were governed by regibus sociis, the taxes were levied by these princes, who paid a tribute to the Romans [9]; and this was the state of things in Judea prior to the deposition of Archelaus.   It has been the object of much research to make it appear probable that Augustus decreed a census, as an extraordinary measure, in Palestine under Herod.   Attention has been directed to the circumstance that the breviarium imperii, which Augustus left behind him, contained the financial state of the whole empire, and it has been suggested that, in order to ascertain the financial condition of Palestine, he caused a statement to be prepared by Herod.[10]   Reference has been made first to the record of Josephus, that on account of some disturbance of the relations between Herod

---

[2] Tholuck, s. 194 ff. Neander, s. 19.

[3] Cassiodor. Variarum, 3, 52. Isidor. Orig. 5, 36.

[4] To refer here to the *Monumentum Ancyranum*, which is said to record a census of the whole empire in the year of Rome 746 (Osiander, p. 95), is proof of the greatest carelessness. For he who examines this inscription will find mention only of three assessments *census civium Romanorum*, which Suetonius designates *census populi*, and of which Dio Cassius speaks, at least of one of them, as ἀπογραφὴ τῶν ἐν τῇ Ἰταλίᾳ κατοικούντων. See Ideler, Chronol. 2, s. 339.

[5] In the authoritative citations in Suidas are the words taken from Luke, αὕτη ἡ ἀπογραφὴ πρώτη ἐγένετο.

[6] Hoffmann, s. 231.

[7] Joseph. Antiq. 17, 13, 2. B. j. 2, 7, 3.

[8] Antiq. 17, 13, 5. 18, 1, 1. B. j. 2, 8, 1.

[9] Paulus, exeg. Handb. 1, a, s. 171. Winer, bibl. Realwörterbuch.

[10] Tacit. Annal. 1, 11. Sueton. Octav. 191. But if in this document *opes publicæ continebantur : quantum civium sociorumque in armis ; quot classes, regna, provinciæ, tributa aut vectigalia, et necessitates ac largitiones* : the number of troops and the sum which the Jewish prince had to furnish, might have been given without a Roman tax being levied in their land.   For Judea in particular Augustus had before him the subsequent census made by Quirinus.

and Augustus, the latter threatened for the future to make him feel his subjection [11] ; secondly, also to the oath of allegiance to Augustus which, according to Josephus, the Jews were forced to take even during the lifetime of Herod.[12] From which it is inferred that Augustus, since he had it in contemplation after the death of Herod to restrict the power of his sons, was very likely to have commanded a census in the last years of that prince.[13] But it seems more probable that it took place shortly after the death of Herod, from the circumstance that Archelaus went to Rome concerning the matter of succession, and that during his absence the Roman procurator Sabinus occupied Jerusalem, and oppressed the Jews by every possible means.[14]

The Evangelist relieves us from a farther inquiry into this more or less historical or arbitrary combination by adding, that this taxing was first made when Cyrenius (Quirinus) *was governor of Syria,* ἡγεμονεύοντος τῆς Συρίας Κυρηνίου; for it is an authenticated point that the assessment of Quirinus did not take place either under Herod or early in the reign of Archelaus, the period at which, according to Luke, Jesus was born. Quirinus was not at that time governor of Syria, a situation held during the last years of Herod by Sentius Saturninus, and after him by Quintilius Varus ; and it was not till long after the death of Herod that Quirinus was appointed governor of Syria. That Quirinus undertook a census of Judea we know certainly from Josephus,[15] who, however, remarks that he was sent to execute this measure, τῆς Ἀρχελάου χώρας εἰς ἐπαρχίαν περιγραφείσης, or, ὑποτελοῦς προσνεμηθείσης τῇ Σύρων [16] ; thus about ten years after the time at which, according to Matthew and Luke, Jesus must have been born.

Yet commentators have supposed it possible to reconcile this apparently undeniable contradiction between Luke and history. The most dauntless explain the whole of the second verse as a gloss, which was early incorporated into the text.[17] Some change the reading of the verse ; either of the *nomen proprium,* by substituting the name of Saturninus or Quintilius,[18] according to the example of Tertullian, who ascribed the census to the former [19] ; or of the other words, by various additions and modifications. Paulus's alteration is the most simple. He reads, instead of αὕτη, αὐτή, and concludes, from the reasons stated above, that Augustus actually gave orders for a census during the reign of Herod I., and that the order was so far carried out as to occasion the journey of Joseph and Mary to Bethlehem ; but that Augustus being afterwards conciliated, the measure was abandoned, and αὐτὴ ἡ ἀπογραφὴ was only carried into effect a considerable time later, by Quirinus. Trifling as this alteration, which leaves the letters unchanged, may appear, in order to render it admissible it must be supported by the context. The reverse, however, is the fact. For if one sentence narrates a command issued by a prince, and

---

[11] Ὅτι, πάλαι χρώμενος αὐτῷ φίλῳ, νῦν ὑπηκόῳ χρήσεται. Joseph. Antiq. 16, 9, 3. But the difference was adjusted long before the death of Herod. Antiq. 16, 10, 9.
[12] Joseph. Ant. 17, 2, 4. παντὸς τοῦ Ἰουδαϊκοῦ βεβαιώσαντος δι' ὅρκων ἦ μὴν εὐνοῆσαι Καίσαρι καὶ τοῖς βασιλέως πράγμασι. That this oath, far from being a humiliating measure for Herod, coincided with his interest, is proved by the zeal with which he punished the Pharisees who refused to take it.
[13] Tholuck, s. 192 f. But the insurrection which the ἀπογραφὴ after the depositions of Archelaus actually occasioned—a fact which outweighs all Tholuck's surmises—proves it to have been the first Roman measure of the kind in Judea.
[14] Antiq. 17, 9, 10, 1 ff. B. j. 2. 2. 2. His oppressions however had reference only to the fortresses and the treasures of Herod.
[15] Antiq. 18, 1, 1.
[16] Bell. jud. 2, 8, 1. 9, 1. Antiq. 17, 13, 5.
[17] Kuinöl, Comm. in Luc. p. 320.
[18] Winer.
[19] Adv. Marcion. 4, 19.

the very next sentence its execution, it is not probable that a space of ten years intervened.   But chiefly, according to this view the Evangelist speaks, verse 1, of the decree of the emperor ; verse 2, of the census made ten years later ; but verse 3, without any remark, again of a journey performed at the time the command was issued ; which, in a rational narrative, is impossible. Opposed to such arbitrary conjectures, and always to be ranked above them, are the attempts to solve a difficulty by legitimate methods of interpretation. Truly, however, to take πρώτη in this connexion for προτέρα, and ἡγεμονεύοντος K. not for a genitive absolute, but for a genitive governed by a comparative, and thus to understand an enrolment *before* that of Quirinus,[20] is to do violence to grammatical construction ; and to insert πρὸ τῆς after πρώτη [21] is is no less uncritical.   As little is it to be admitted that some preliminary measure, in which Quirinus was not employed, perhaps the already mentioned oath of allegiance, took place during the lifetime of Herod, in reference to the census subsequently made by Quirinus ; and that this preliminary step and the census were afterwards comprised under the same name.   In order in some degree to account for this appellation, Quirinus is said to have been sent into Judea, in Herod's time, as an extraordinary tax-commissioner [22] ; but this interpretation of the word ἡγεμονεύοντος is rendered impossible by the addition of the word Συρίας, in combination with which the expression can denote only the *Præses Syriæ.*

Thus at the time at which Jesus, according to Matt. ii. 1, and Luke i. 5, 26, was born, the census of which Luke ii. 1 f. speaks could not have taken place ; so that if the former statements are correct, the latter must be false.   But may not the reverse be the fact, and Jesus have been born after the banishment of Archelaus, and at the time of the census of Quirinus ?   Apart from the difficulties in which this hypothesis would involve us in relation to the chrono-logy of the future life of Jesus, a Roman census, subsequent to the banishment of Archelaus, would not have taken the parents of Jesus from Nazareth in Galilee to Bethlehem in Judea.   For Judea only, and what otherwise belonged to the portion of Archelaus, became a Roman province and subjected to the census.   In Galilee Herod Antipas continued to reign as an allied prince, and none of his subjects dwelling at Nazareth could have been called to Bethlehem by the census.   The Evangelist therefore, in order to get a census, must have conceived the condition of things such as they were after the deposition of Archelaus ; but in order to get a census extending to Galilee, he must have imagined the kingdom to have continued undivided, as in the time of Herod the Great.   Thus he deals in manifest contradictions ; or rather he has an exceedingly sorry acquaintance with the political relations of that period ; for he extends the census not only to the whole of Palestine, but also (which we must not forget) to the whole Roman world.

Still these chronological incongruities do not exhaust the difficulties which beset this statement of Luke.   His representation of the manner in which the census was made is subject to objection.   In the first place, it is said, the taxing took Joseph to Bethlehem, *because he was of the house and lineage of David,* διὰ τὸ εἶναι αὐτὸν ἐξ οἴκου καὶ πατριᾶς Δαβίδ, and likewise every one into his own city, εἰς τὴν ἰδίαν πόλιν, *i.e.* according to the context, to the place whence his family had originally sprung.   Now, that every individual should be registered in his own city was required in all Jewish inscriptions, because among the Jews the organization of families and tribes constituted the very basis of the state.   The Romans, on the contrary, were in the habit of taking

[20] Storr, opusc. acad. 3, s. 126 f.   Süskind, vermischte Aufsätze, s. 63.   Tholuck, s. 182 f.
[21] Michaelis, Anm. z. d. St. und Einl. in d. N.T. 1, 71.
[22] Münter, Stern der Weisen. s. 88.

the census at the residences, and at the principal cities in the district. [23] They conformed to the usages of the conquered countries only in so far as they did not interfere with their own objects.   In the present instance it would have been directly contrary to their design, had they removed individuals—Joseph for example—to a great distance, where the amount of their property was not known, and their statement concerning it could not be checked. [24] The view of Schleiermacher is the more admissible, that the real occasion which took the parents to Bethlehem was a sacerdotal inscription, which the Evangelist confounded with the better known census of Quirinus.   But this concession does not obviate the contradiction in this dubious statement of Luke.   He allows Mary to be inscribed with Joseph, but according to Jewish customs inscriptions had relation to men only.   Thus, at all events, it is an inaccuracy to represent Mary as undertaking the journey, in order to be inscribed with her betrothed in his own city.   Or, if with Paulus we remove this inaccuracy by a forced construction of the sentence, we can no longer perceive what inducement could have instigated Mary, in her particular situation, to make so long a journey, since, unless we adopt the airy hypothesis of Olshausen and others, that Mary was the heiress of property in Bethlehem, she had nothing to do there.

The Evangelist, however, knew perfectly well what she had to do there ; namely, to fulfil the prophecy of Micah (v. 1), by giving birth, in the city of David, to the Messiah.   Now as he set out with the supposition that the habitual abode of the parents of Jesus was Nazareth, so he sought after a lever which should set them in motion towards Bethlehem, at the time of the birth of Jesus.   Far and wide nothing presented itself but the celebrated census ; he seized it the more unhesitatingly because the obscurity of his own view of the historical relations of that time, veiled from him the many difficulties connected with such a combination.   If this be the true history of the statement in Luke, we must agree with K. Ch. L. Schmidt when he says, that to attempt to reconcile the statement of Luke concerning the ἀπογραφὴ with chronology, would be to do the narrator too much honour ; he wished to place Mary in Bethlehem, and therefore times and circumstances were to accommodate themselves to his pleasure. [25]

Thus we have here neither a fixed point for the date of the birth of Jesus, nor an explanation of the occasion which led to his being born precisely at Bethlehem.   If then—it may justly be said—no other reason why Jesus should have been born at Bethlehem can be adduced than that given by Luke, we have absolutely no guarantee that Bethlehem was his birth-place.

§ 33.

PARTICULAR CIRCUMSTANCES OF THE BIRTH OF JESUS.   THE CIRCUMCISION.

The basis of the narrative, the arrival of Joseph and Mary as strangers in Bethlehem on account of the census, being once chosen by Luke, the farther details are consistently built upon it.   In consequence of the influx of strangers brought to Bethlehem by the census, there is no room for the travellers in the inn, and they are compelled to put up with the accommodation of a stable where Mary is forthwith delivered of her first-born.   But the child, who upon

---

[23] Paulus.   Wetstein.
[24] Credner.
[25] In Schmidt's Bibliothek für Kritik und Exegese, 3, 1. s. 124.   See Kaiser, bibl. Theol. 1, s. 230 ; Ammon, Fortbildung, 1, s. 196 ; Credner, Einleitung, in d. N.T. 1, s. 155 ; De Wette, exeget. Handbuch.

earth comes into being in so humble an abode, is highly regarded in heaven. A celestial messenger announces the birth of the Messiah to shepherds who are guarding their flocks in the fields by night, and directs them to the child in the manger. A choir of the heavenly host singing hymns of praise next appears to them, after which they seek and find the child. (Luke ii. 6–20.) The apocryphal gospels and the traditions of the Fathers still further embellished the birth of Jesus. According to the *Protevangelium Jacobi*,[1] Joseph conducts Mary on an ass to Bethlehem to be taxed. As they approach the city she begins to make now mournful, now joyous gestures, and upon inquiry explains that—(as once in Rebecca's womb the two hostile nations struggled, Gen. xxv. 23)—she sees two people before her, the one weeping, the other laughing : *i.e.* according to one explanation, the two portions of Israel, to one of whom the advent of Jesus *was set* (Luke ii. 34) εἰς πτῶσιν, *for the fall*, to the other εἰς ἀνάστασιν, *for the rising again*. According to another interpretation, the two people were the Jews who should reject Jesus, and the heathens who should accept him.[2] Soon, however, whilst still without the city—as appears from the context and the reading of several MSS.—Mary is seized with the pains of child-bearing, and Joseph brings her into a cave situated by the road side, where, veiled by a cloud of light, all nature pausing in celebration of the event, she brings her child into the world, and after her delivery is found, by women called to her assistance, still a virgin.[3] The legend of the birth of Jesus in a cave was known to Justin [4] and to Origen,[5] who, in order to reconcile it with the account in Luke that he was laid in a manger, suppose a manger situated within the cave. Many modern commentators agree with them [6]; whilst others prefer to consider the cave itself as φάτνη, in the sense of foddering-stall.[7] For the birth of Jesus in a cave, Justin appeals to the prophecy in Isaiah xxviii. 16 : οὗτος (the righteous) οἰκήσει ἐν ὑψηλῷ σπηλαίῳ πέτρας ἰσχυρᾶς. In like manner, for the statement that on the third day the child Jesus, when brought from the cave into the stable, was worshipped by the oxen and the asses, the *Historia de Nativitate Mariae*,[8] etc. refers to Isaiah i. 3 : *cognovit bos possessorem suum, et asinus praesepe domini sui*. In several apocryphas, between the Magi and the women who assist at the birth, the shepherds are forgotten ; but they are mentioned in the *Evangelium infantiae arabicum*,[9] where it says, that when they arrived at the cave, and had kindled a fire of rejoicing, the heavenly host appeared to them.

If we take the circumstances attending the birth of Jesus, narrated by Luke, in a supranaturalistic sense, many difficulties occur. First, it may reasonably be asked, to what end the angelic apparition ? The most obvious answer is, to make known the birth of Jesus ; but so little did it make it known that, in the neighbouring city of Jerusalem, it is the Magi who give the first information of the new-born king of the Jews ; and in the future history of Jesus, no trace of any such occurrence at his birth is to be found. Consequently, the object of that extraordinary phenomenon was not to give a wide-spreading intimation of the fact ; for if so, God failed in his object. Must we then agree with Schleiermacher, that the aim was limited to an immediate opera-

---

[1] Chap. 17. Compare Historia de nativ. Mariae et de infantiâ Servatoris, c. 13.
[2] Fabricius, im Codex Apocryph. N.T. 1, s. 105, not. y.
[3] Ambrosius and Jerome. See Gieseler, K. G. 1, s. 516.
[4] Dial. c. Tryph. 78.
[5] C. Cels. 1, 51.
[6] Hess, Olshausen, Paulus.
[7] Paulus.
[8] Chap. 14.
[9] Chap. 4 in Thilo, s. 69.

tion upon the shepherds? Then we must also suppose with him, that the shepherds, equally with Simeon, were filled with Messianic expectations, and that God designed by this apparition to reward and confirm their pious belief. The narrative however says nothing of this heavenly frame of mind, neither does it mention any abiding effects produced upon these men. According to the whole tenor of the representation, the apparition seems to have had reference, not to the shepherds, but exclusively to the glorification and the proclaiming of the birth of Jesus, as the Messiah. But as before observed, the latter aim was not accomplished, and the former, by itself, like every mere empty display, is an object unworthy of God. So that this circumstance in itself presents no inconsiderable obstacle to the supranaturalistic conception of the history. If, to the above considerations, we add those already stated which oppose the belief in apparitions and the existence of angels in general, it is easy to understand that with respect to this narrative also refuge has been sought in a natural explanation.

The results of the first attempts at a natural explanation were certainly sufficiently rude. Thus Eck regarded the angel as a messenger from Bethlehem, who carried a light which caught the eye of the shepherds, and the song of the heavenly host as the merry tones of a party accompanying the messenger.[10] Paulus has woven together a more refined and matter of fact explanation. Mary, who had met with a hospitable reception in a herdsman's family, and who was naturally elated with the hope of giving birth to the Messiah, told her expectations to the members of this family; to whom as inhabitants of a city of David the communication could not have been indifferent. These shepherds therefore on perceiving, whilst in the fields by night, a luminous appearance in the air—a phenomenon which travellers say is not uncommon in those regions—they interpret it as a divine intimation that the stranger in their foddering-stall is delivered of the Messiah; and as the meteoric light extends and moves to and fro, they take it for a choir of angels chaunting hymns of praise. Returning home they find their anticipations confirmed by the event, and that which at first they merely conjectured to be the sense and interpretation of the phenomenon, they now, after the manner of the East, represent as words actually spoken.[11]

This explanation rests altogether on the assumption, that the shepherds were previously acquainted with Mary's expectation that she should give birth to the Messiah. How otherwise should they have been led to consider the sign as referring particularly to the birth of the Messiah in their manger? Yet this very assumption is the most direct contradiction of the gospel account. For, in the first place, the Evangelist evidently does not suppose the manger to belong to the shepherds: since after he has narrated the delivery of Mary in the manger, he then goes on to speak of the shepherds as a new and distinct subject, not at all connected with the manger. His words are: *and there were in the same country shepherds,* καὶ ποιμένες ἦσαν ἐν τῇ χώρᾳ τῇ αὐτῇ. If this explanation were correct he would, at all events, have said, *the shepherds etc.* οἱ δὲ ποιμένες κ. τ. λ.; besides he would not have been wholly silent respecting the comings and goings of these shepherds during the day, and their departure to guard the flock at the approach of night. But, grant these presupposed circumstances, is it consistent in Paulus to represent Mary, at first so reserved concerning her pregnancy as to conceal it even from Joseph, and then so communicative that, just arrived among strangers, she

---

[10] In seinem Versuch über die Wundergeschichten des N. T. See Gabler's Neuestes theol. Journal, 7, 4, s. 411.

[11] Exeg. Handb. s. 180 ff. As Paulus supposes an external natural phenomenon so Matthæi imagines a mental vision of angels. Synopse der vier Evangelien, s. 3.

parades the whole history of her expectations? Again the sequel of the narrative contradicts the assumption that the shepherds were informed of the matter by Mary herself, before her delivery. For, according to the gospel history, the shepherds receive the first intelligence of the birth of the Saviour σωτήρ from the angel who appears to them, and who tells them, as a sign of the truth of his communication, that they shall find the babe lying in a manger. Had they already heard from Mary of the approaching birth of the Messiah, the meteoric appearance would have been a confirmation to them of Mary's words, and not the finding of the child a proof of the truth of the apparition. Finally, may we so far confide in the investigations already made as to inquire, whence, if neither a miraculous announcement nor a supernatural conception actually occurred, could Mary have derived the confident anticipation that she should give birth to the Messiah?

In opposition to this natural explanation, so full of difficulties on every side, Bauer announced his adoption of the mythical view [12]; in fact, however, he did not advance one step beyond the interpretation of the Rationalists, but actually repeated Paulus's exposition point for point. To this mixed mythical explanation Gabler justly objected that it, equally with the natural interpretation, multiplies improbabilities: by the adoption of the pure, dogmatic mythus, everything appears simpler; thereby, at the same time, greater harmony is introduced into the early christian history, all the preceding narratives of which ought equally to be interpreted as pure mythi.[13] Gabler, accordingly, explained the narrative as the product of the ideas of the age, which demanded the assistance of angels at the birth of the Messiah. Now had it been known that Mary was delivered in a dwelling belonging to shepherds, it would also have been concluded that angels must have brought the tidings to these good shepherds that the Messiah was born in their manger; and the angels who cease not praising God, must have sung a hymn of praise on the occasion. Gabler thinks it impossible, that a Jewish christian who should have known some of the data of the birth of Jesus, could have thought of it otherwise than as here depicted.[14]

This explanation of Gabler shows, in a remarkable manner, how difficult it is entirely to extricate oneself from the natural explanation, and to rise completely to the mythical; for whilst this theologian believes he treads on pure mythical ground, he still stands with one foot upon that of the natural interpretation. He selects from the account of Luke one incident as historical which, by its connexion with other unhistorical statements and its conformity to the spirit of the primitive christian legend, is proved to be merely mythical; namely, that Jesus was really born in a shepherd's dwelling. He also borrows an assumption from the natural explanation, which the mythical needs not to obtrude on the text: that the shepherds, to whom it is alleged the angels appeared, were the possessors of the manger in which Mary was delivered. The first detail, upon which the second is built, belongs to the same machinery by which Luke, with the help of the census, transported the parents of Jesus from Nazareth to Bethlehem. Now we know what is the fact respecting the census; it crumbles away inevitably before criticism, and with it the datum built entirely upon it, that Jesus was born in a manger. For had not the parents of Jesus been strangers, and had they not come to Bethlehem in company with so large a concourse of strangers as the census might have occasioned, the cause which obliged Mary to accept a stable for her place of

[12] Hebräische Mythologie, 2. Thl. s. 223 ff.
[13] Recension von Bauer's hebr. Mythologie in Gabler's Journal für auserlesene theol. Literatur, 2, 1, s. 58 f.
[14] Neuestes theol. Journal, 7, 4, s. 412 f.

delivery would no longer have existed. But, on the other hand, the incident, that Jesus was born in a stable and saluted in the first instance by shepherds, is so completely in accordance with the spirit of the ancient legend, that it is evident the narrative may have been derived purely from this source. Theophylact, in his time, pointed out its true character, when he says : the angels did not appear to the scribes and pharisees of Jerusalem who were full of all malice, but to the shepherds, in the fields, on account of their simplicity and innocence, and because they by their mode of life were the successors of the patriarchs.[15] It was in the field by the flocks that Moses was visited by a heavenly apparition (Exod. iii. 1 ff.) ; and God took David, the forefather of the Messiah, from his sheepfolds (at Bethlehem), to be the shepherd of his people. Psalm lxxviii. 70 (comp. 1 Sam. xvi. 11). The mythi of the ancient world more generally ascribed divine apparitions to countrymen[16] and shepherds[17] ; the sons of the gods, and of great men were frequently brought up among shepherds.[18] In the same spirit of the ancient legend is the apocryphal invention that Jesus was born in a cave, and we are at once reminded of the cave of Jupiter and of the other gods ; even though the misunderstood passage of Isaiah xxxiii. 16 may have been the immediate occasion of this incident.[19] Moreover the night, in which the scene is laid, —(unless one refers here to the rabbinical representations, according to which, the deliverance by means of the Messiah, like the deliverance from Egypt, should take place by night[20])—forms the obscure background against which the manifested *glory of the Lord* shone so much the more brilliantly, which, as it is said to have glorified the birth of Moses,[21] could not have been absent from that of the Messiah, his exalted antitype.

The mythical interpretation of this section of the gospel history has found an opponent in Schleiermacher.[22] He thinks it improbable that this commencement of the second chapter of Luke is a continuation of the first, written by the same author ; because the frequent opportunities of introducing lyrical effusions—as for example, when the shepherds returned glorifying and praising God, v. 20—are not taken advantage of as in the first chapter ; and here indeed we can in some measure agree with him. But when he adds that a decidedly poetical character cannot be ascribed to this narrative, since a poetical composition would of necessity have contained more of the lyrical, this only proves that Schleiermacher has not justly apprehended the notion of that kind of poetry of which he here treats, namely, the poetry of the mythus. In a word, mythical poetry is objective : the poetical exists in the substance of the narrative, and may therefore appear in the plainest form, free from all the adornments of lyrical effusions ; which latter are rather only the subsequent additions of a more intelligent and artificially elaborated subjective poetry.[23] Undoubtedly this section seems to have been preserved to us more nearly in its original legendary form, whilst the narratives of the first chapter in Luke bear rather the stamp of having been re-wrought by some

---

[15] In Luc. 2. in Suicer, 2, p. 789 f.

[16] Servius ad Verg. Ecl. 10, 26.

[17] Liban. progymn. p. 138, in Wetstein, s. 662.

[18] Thus Cyrus, see Herod. 1, 110 ff. Romulus, see Livy, 1, 4.

[19] Thilo, Codex Apocr. N. T. 1, s. 383 not.

[20] Vid. Schöttgen, 2, s. 531.

[21] Sota, 1, 48 : *Sapientes nostri perhibent, circa horam nativitatis Mosis totam domum repletam fuisse luce* (Wetstein).

[22] Ueber den Lukas, s. 29. f. With whom Neander and others now agree.—L. J. Ch. s. 21 f.

[23] Comp. De Wette, Kritik der mosaischen Geschichte, s. 116 ; George, Mythus u. Sage, s. 33 f.

poetical individual ; but historical truth is not on that account to be sought here any more than there. Consequently the obligation which Schleiermacher further imposes upon himself, to trace out the source of this narrative in the Gospel of Luke, can only be regarded as an exercise of ingenuity. He refuses to recognize that source in Mary, though a reference to her might have been found in the observation, v. 19, *she kept all these sayings in her heart*; wherein indeed he is the more right, since that observation (a fact to which Schleiermacher does not advert) is merely a phrase borrowed from the history of Jacob and his son Joseph.[24] For as the narrative in Genesis relates of Jacob, the father of Joseph, that child of miracle, that when the latter told his significant dreams, and his brethren envied him, *his father observed the saying* : so the narrative in Luke, both here and at verse 51, relates of Mary, that she, whilst others gave utterance aloud to their admiration at the extraordinary occurrences which happened to her child, *kept all these things and pondered them in her heart.* But the above-named theologian points out the shepherds instead of Mary as the source of our narrative, alleging that all the details are given, not from Mary's point of view, but from that of the shepherds.   More truly however is the point of view that of the legend which supersedes both.   If Schleiermacher finds it impossible to believe that this narrative is an air-bubble conglomerated out of *nothing*, he must include under the word *nothing* the Jewish and early christian ideas—concerning Bethlehem, as the necessary birthplace of the Messiah; concerning the condition of the shepherds, as being peculiarly favoured by communications from heaven ; concerning angels, as the intermediate agents in such communications—notions we on our side cannot possibly hold in so little estimation, but we find it easy to conceive that something similar to our narrative might have formed itself out out of them.   Finally, when he finds an adventitious or designed invention impossible, because the Christians of that district might easily have inquired of Mary or of the disciples concerning the truth of the matter : he speaks too nearly the language of the ancient apologists, and presupposes the ubiquity of these persons,[25] already alluded to in the Introduction, who however could not possibly have been in all places rectifying the tendency to form christian legends, wherever it manifested itself.

The notice of the circumcision of Jesus (Luke ii. 21), evidently proceeds from a narrator who had no real advice of the fact, but who assumed as a certainty that, according to Jewish custom, the ceremony took place on the eighth day, and who was desirous of commemorating this important event in the life of an Israelitish boy ;[26] in like manner as Paul (Phil. iii. 5) records his circumcision on the eighth day.   The contrast however between the fulness of detail with which this point is elaborated and coloured in the life of the Baptist, and the barrenness and brevity with which it is stated in reference to Jesus, is striking, and may justify an agreement with the remark of Schleiermacher, that here, at least the author of the first chapter is no longer the originator.   Such being the state of the case, this statement furnishes nothing for our object, which we might not already have known ; only we have till now had no opportunity of observing, distinctly, that the pretended appoint-

---

[24] Gen. xxxvii. 11 (LXX.) :
Ἐζήλωσαν δὲ αὐτὸν οἱ ἀδελφοὶ αὐτοῦ, ὁ δὲ πατὴρ αὐτοῦ διετήρησε τὸ ῥῆμα.—Schöttgen, horae, 1, 262.

Luc. 2, 18 f. :
καὶ πάντες οἱ ἀκούσαντες ἐθαύμασαν — — ἡ δὲ Μαριὰμ πάντα συνετήρει τὰ ῥήματα ταῦτα, συμβάλλουσα ἐν τῇ καρδίᾳ αὐτῆς. 2, 51 : καὶ ἡ μήτηρ αὐτοῦ διετήρει πάντα τὰ ῥήματα ταῦτα ἐν τῇ καρδίᾳ αὐτῆς.

[25] See Introduction.
[26] Perhaps as a precautionary measure to obviate objections on the part of the Jews. (Ammon, Fortbildung, 1, s. 217.)

ment of the name of Jesus before his birth likewise belongs merely to the mythical dress of the narrative. When it is said *his name was called Jesus, which was so named of the angel before he was conceived in the womb*, the importance attached to the circumstance is a clear sign, that a dogmatic interest lies at the bottom of this feature in the narrative ; which interest can be no other than that which gave rise to the statement—in the Old Testament concerning an Isaac and an Ishmael, and in the New Testament concerning a John—that the names of these children were, respectively, revealed to their parents prior to their birth, and on account of which interest the rabbins, in particular, expected that the same thing should occur in relation to the name of the Messiah.[27] Without doubt there were likewise other far more natural reasons which induced the parents of Jesus to give him this name (יֵשׁוּעַ, an abbreviation of יְהוֹשֻׁעַ, ὁ Κύριος σωτηρία) ; a name which was very common among his countrymen ; but because this name agreed in a remarkable manner with the path of life subsequently chosen by him as Messiah and σωτήρ, it was not thought possible that this coincidence could have been accidental. Besides it seemed more appropriate that the name of the Messiah should have been determined by divine command than by human arbitration, and consequently the appointment of the name was ascribed to the same angel who had announced the conception of Jesus.

§ 34.

THE MAGI AND THEIR STAR. THE FLIGHT INTO EGYPT AND THE MURDER OF THE CHILDREN IN BETHLEHEM. CRITICISM OF THE SUPRANATURALISTIC VIEW.

In the Gospel of Matthew also we have a narrative of the Messiah's entrance into the world ; it differs considerably in detail from that of Luke, which we have just examined, but in the former part of the two accounts there is a general similarity (Matt. ii. 1 ff.). The object of both narratives is to describe the solemn introduction of the Messianic infant, the heralding of his birth undertaken by heaven itself, and his first reception among men.[1] In both, attention is called to the new-born Messiah by a celestial phenomenon ; according to Luke, it is an angel clothed in brightness, according to Matthew, it is a star. As the apparitions are different, so accordingly are the recipients ; the angel addresses simple shepherds ; the star is discovered by eastern magi, who are able to interpret for themselves the voiceless sign. Both parties are directed to Bethlehem ; the shepherds by the words of the angel, the magi by the instructions they obtain in Jerusalem ; and both do homage to the infant ; the poor shepherds by singing hymns of praise, the magi by costly presents from their native country. But from this point the two narratives begin to diverge widely. In Luke all proceeds happily ; the shepherds return with gladness in their hearts, the child experiences no molestation, he is presented in the temple on the appointed day, thrives and grows up in tranquillity. In Matthew, on the contrary, affairs take a tragical turn. The inquiry of the wise

---

[27] Pirke R. Elieser, 33 : *Sex hominum nomina dicta sunt, antequam nascerentur: Isaaci nempe, Ismaëlis, Mosis, Salomonis, Josiæ et nomen regis Messiæ.* Bereschith rabba, sect. 1, fol. 3, 3.—(Schöttgen, horae, 2, s. 436) : Sex res prævenerunt creationem mundi : quædam ex illis creatæ sunt, nempe lex et thronus gloriæ ; aliæ ascenderunt in cogitationem (Dei) ut crearentur, nimirum Patriarchæ, Israël, templum, et nomen Messiæ.

[1] Comp. Schneckenburger, über den Ursprung des ersten kanonischen Evangeliums, s. 69 ff.

men in Jerusalem concerning the new-born King of the Jews, is the occasion of a murderous decree on the part of Herod against the children of Bethlehem, a danger from which the infant Jesus is rescued only by a sudden flight into Egypt, whence he and his parents do not return to the Holy Land till after the death of Herod.

Thus we have here a double proclamation of the Messianic child : we might, however, suppose that the one by the angel, in Luke, would announce the birth of the Messiah to the immediate neighbourhood ; the other, by means of the star, to distant lands. But as, according to Matthew, the birth of Jesus became known at Jerusalem, which was in the immediate vicinity, by means of the star ; if this representation be historical, that of Luke, according to which the shepherds were the first to spread abroad with praises to God (v. 17, 20), that which had been communicated to them as glad tidings for all people (v. 10), cannot possibly be correct. So, on the other hand, if it be true that the birth of Jesus was made known in the neighbourhood of Bethlehem as Luke states, by an angelic communication to the shepherds, Matthew must be in error when he represents the first intelligence of the event as subsequently brought to Jerusalem (which is only from two to three hours distant from Bethlehem) by the magi. But as we have recognized many indications of the unhistorical character of the announcement by the shepherds given in Luke, the ground is left clear for that of Matthew, which must be judged of according to its inherent credibility.

Our narrative commences as if it were an admitted fact, that astrologers possessed the power of recognizing a star announcing the birth of the Messiah. That eastern magi should have knowledge of a King of the Jews to whom they owed religious homage might indeed excite our surprise ; but contenting ourselves here with remarking, that seventy years later an expectation did prevail in the east that a ruler of the world would arise from among the Jewish people,[2] we pass on to a yet more weighty difficulty. According to this narrative it appears, that astrology is right when it asserts that the birth of great men and important revolutions in human affairs are indicated by astral phenomena ; an opinion long since consigned to the region of superstition. It is therefore to be explained, how this deceptive science could in this solitary instance prove true, though in no other case are its inferences to be relied on. The most obvious explanation, from the orthodox point of view, is an appeal to the supernatural intervention of God ; who, in this particular instance, in order to bring the distant magi unto Jesus, accommodated himself to their astrological notions, and caused the anticipated star to appear. But the adoption of this expedient involves very serious consequences. For the coincidence of the remarkable sequel with the astrological prognostic could not fail to strengthen the belief, not only of the magi and their fellow-countrymen, but also of the Jews and Christians who were acquainted with the circumstances, in the spurious science of astrology, thereby creating incalculable error and mischief. If therefore it be unadvisable to admit an extraordinary divine intervention,[3] and if the position that in the ordinary course of nature, important occurrences on this earth are attended by changes in the heavenly bodies, be abandoned, the only remaining explanation lies in

---

[2] Joseph. B. J. vi. vi. 4 : Tacit. Histor. v. 13 ; Sueton. Vespas. 4. All the extant allusions to the existence of such a hope at the era of Christ's birth, relate only in an indeterminate manner to a ruler of the world. Virg. Eclog. 4 ; Sueton. Octav. 94.

[3] In saying that it is inadmissible to suppose a divine intervention directly tending to countenance superstition, I refer to what is called *immediate* intervention. In the doctrine of *mediate* intervention, which includes the co-operation of man, there is doubtless a mixture of truth and error. Neander confuses the two. L. J. Ch., s. 29.

the supposition of an accidental coincidence.   But to appeal to chance is in fact either to say nothing, or to renounce the supranaturalistic point of view.

But the orthodox view of this account not only sanctions the false science of astrology, but also confirms the false interpretation of a passage in the prophets.   For as the magi, following their star, proceed in the right direction, so the chief priests and scribes of Jerusalem whom Herod, on learning the arrival and object of the magi, summons before him and questions concerning the birth-place of the King of the Jews, interpret the passage in Micah v. 1 as signifying that the Messiah should be born in Bethlehem ; and to this signification the event corresponds.   Now such an application of the above passage can only be made by forcing the words from their true meaning and from all relation with the context, according to the well-known practice of the rabbins.   For independently of the question whether or not under the word מֹשֵׁל, in the passage cited, the Messiah be intended, the entire context shows the meaning to be, not that the expected governor who was to come forth out of Bethlehem would actually be born in that city, but only that he would be a descendant of David, whose family sprang from Bethlehem.[4]   Thus allowing the magi to have been rightly directed by means of the rabbinical exegesis of the oracle, a false interpretation must have hit on the truth, either by means of divine intervention and accommodation, or by accident.   The judgment pronounced in the case of the star is applicable here also.

After receiving the above answer from the Sanhedrim, Herod summons the magi before him, and his first question concerns the time at which the star appeared (v. 7).   Why did he wish to know this [5]?   The 16th verse tells us, that he might thereby calculate the age of the Messianic child, and thus ascertain up to what age it would be necessary for him to put to death the children of Bethlehem, so as not to miss the one announced by the star.   But this plan of murdering all the children of Bethlehem up to a certain age, that he might destroy the one likely to prove fatal to the interests of his family, was not conceived by Herod until after the magi had disappointed his expectation that they would return to Jerusalem ; a deception which, if we may judge from his violent anger on account of it (v. 16), Herod had by no means anticipated.   Prior to this, according to v. 8, it had been his intention to obtain from the magi, on their return, so close a description of the child, his dwelling and circumstances, that it would be easy for him to remove his infantine rival without sacrificing any other life.   It was not until he had discovered the stratagem of the magi, that he was obliged to have recourse to the more violent measure for the execution of which it was necessary for him to know the time of the star's appearance.[6]   How fortunate for him, then, that he had ascertained this time before he had decided on the plan that made the information important; but how inconceivable that he should make a point which was only indirectly connected with his original project, the subject of his first and most eager interrogation (v. 7) !

Herod, in the second place, commissions the magi to acquaint themselves accurately with all that concerns the royal infant, and to impart their knowledge to him on their return, that he also may go and tender his homage to the child, that is, according to his real meaning, take sure measures for putting

---

[4] Paulus and De Wette, exeg. Handb. in loc.

[5] According to Hoffmann (p. 256), that he might control the assertion of the magi by inquiring of his own astrologers, whether they had seen the star at the same time.   This is not merely unsupported by the text—it is in direct contradiction to it, for we are there told that Herod at once gave terrified credence to the magi.

[6] Fritzsche, in loc. aptly says—*comperto, quasi magos non ad se redituros statim scivisset, orti sideris tempore, etc.*

him to death (v. 8). Such a proceeding on the part of an astute monarch like Herod has long been held improbable.[7] Even if he hoped to deceive the magi, while in conference with them, by adopting this friendly mask, he must necessarily foresee that others would presently awaken them to the probability that he harboured evil designs against the child, and thus prevent them from returning according to his injunction. He might conjecture that the parents of the child on hearing of the ominous interest taken in him by the king, would seek his safety by flight, and finally, that those inhabitants of Bethlehem and its environs who cherished Messianic expectations, would not be a little confirmed in them by the arrival of the magi. On all these grounds, Herod's only prudent measure would have been either to detain the magi in Jerusalem,[8] and in the meantime by means of secret emissaries to dispatch the child to whom such peculiar hopes were attached, and who must have been easy of discovery in the little village of Bethlehem ; or to have given the magi companions who, so soon as the child was found, might at once have put an end to his existence. Even Olshausen thinks that these strictures are not groundless, and his best defence against them is the observation that the histories of all ages present unaccountable instances of forgetfulness—a proof that the course of human events is guided by a supreme hand. When the supernaturalist invokes the supreme hand in the case before us, he must suppose that God himself blinded Herod to the surest means of attaining his object, in order to save the Messianic child from a premature death. But the other side of this divine contrivance is, that instead of the one child, many others must die. There would be nothing to object against such a substitution in this particular case, if it could be proved that there was no other possible mode of rescuing Jesus from a fate inconsistent with the scheme of human redemption. But if it be once admitted, that God interposed supernaturally to blind the mind of Herod and to suggest to the magi that they should not return to Jerusalem, we are constrained to ask, why did not God in the first instance inspire the magi to shun Jerusalem and proceed directly to Bethlehem, whither Herod's attention would not then have been so immediately attracted, and thus the disastrous sequel perhaps have been altogether avoided?[9] The supranaturalist has no answer to this question but the old-fashioned argument that it was good for the infants to die, because they were thus freed by transient suffering from much misery, and more especially from the danger of sinning against Jesus with the unbelieving Jews; whereas now they had the honour of losing their lives for the sake of Jesus, and thus of ranking as martyrs, and so forth.[10]

The magi leave Jerusalem by night, the favourite time for travelling in the east. The star, which they seem to have lost sight of since their departure from home, again appears and goes before them on the road to Bethlehem, until at length it remains stationary over the house that contains the wondrous child and its parents. The way from Jerusalem to Bethlehem lies southward; now the true path of erratic stars is either from west to east, as that of the planets and of some comets, or from east to west, as that of other comets; the orbits of many comets do indeed tend from north to south, but the true motion of all these bodies is so greatly surpassed by their apparent motion

[7] K. Ch. L. Schmidt, exeg. Beiträge, 1, s. 150 f. Comp. Fritzsche and De Wette in loc.
[8] Hoffman thinks that Herod shunned this measure as a breach of hospitality ; yet this very Herod he represents as a monster of cruelty, and that justly, for the conduct attributed to the monarch in chap. ii. of Matthew is not unworthy of his heart, against which Neander superfluously argues (p. 30 f.), but of his head.
[9] Schmidt, ut sup. p. 155 f.
[10] Stark, Synops. bibl. exeg. in N. T., p. 62.

from east to west produced by the rotation of the earth on its axis, that it is imperceptible except at considerable intervals. Even the diurnal movement of the heavenly bodies, however, is less obvious on a short journey than the merely optical one, arising from the observer's own change of place, in consequence of which a star that he sees before him seems, as long as he moves forward, to pass on in the same direction through infinite space ; it cannot therefore stand still over a particular house and thus induce a traveller to halt there also ; on the contrary, the traveller himself must halt before the star will appear stationary. The star of the magi could not then be an ordinary, natural star, but must have been one created by God for that particular exigency, and impressed by him with a peculiar law of motion and rest.[11] Again, this could not have been a true star, moving among the systems of our firmament, for such an one, however impelled and arrested, could never, according to optical laws, appear to pause over a particular house. It must therefore have been something lower, hovering over the earth's surface ; hence some of the Fathers and apocryphal writers [12] supposed it to have been an angel, which, doubtless, might fly before the magi in the form of a star, and take its station at a moderate height above the house of Mary in Bethlehem ; more modern theologians have conjectured that the phenomenon was a meteor.[13] Both these explanations are opposed to the text of Matthew: the former, because it is out of keeping with the style of our Gospels to designate anything purely supernatural, such as an angelic appearance, by an expression that implies a merely natural object, as ἀστήρ (a star) ; the latter, because a mere meteor would not last for so long a time as must have elapsed between the depart ire of the magi from their remote home and their arrival in Bethlehem. Perhaps, however, it will be contended that God created one meteor for the first monition, and another for the second. *

Many, even of the orthodox expositors, have found these difficulties in relation to the star so pressing, that they have striven to escape at any cost from the admission that it preceded the magi in their way towards Bethlehem, and took its station directly over a particular house. According to Süskind, whose explanation has been much approved, the verb προῆγεν (went before) (v. 9), which is in the imperfect tense, does not signify that the star visibly led the magi on their way, but is equivalent to the pluperfect, which would imply that the star had been invisibly transferred to the destination of the magi before their arrival, so that the Evangelist intends to say : the star which the magi had seen in the east and subsequently lost sight of, suddenly made its appearance to them in Bethlehem above the house they were seeking ; it had therefore preceded them.[14] But this is a transplantation of rationalistic artifice into the soil of orthodox exegesis. Not only the word προῆγεν, but the less flexible expression ἕως ἐλθὼν κ. τ. λ. (till it came, etc.) denotes that the transit of the star was not an already completed phenomenon, but one brought to pass under the observation of the magi. Expositors who persist in denying this must, to be consistent, go still farther, and reduce the entire narrative to the standard of merely natural events. So when Olshausen admits that the position of a star could not possibly indicate a single house, that hence the magi must have inquired for the infant's dwelling, and only with child-like simplicity referred the issue as well as the commencement of their journey to a

---

[11] This was the opinion of some of the Fathers, e.g. Euseb. Demonstr. evang. 9, ap. Suicer, 1, s. 559 ; Joann. Damasc. de fide orthod. ii. 7.
[12] Chrysostomus and others ap. Suicer, ut sup. and the Evang. infant. arab. c. vii.
[13] See Kuinöl, Comm. in Matth., p. 23.
[14] Vermischte Aufsätze, s. 8.

heavenly guide,[15]; he deserts his own point of view for that of the rationalists, and interlines the text with explanatory particulars, an expedient which he elsewhere justly condemns in Paulus and others.

The magi then enter the house, offer their adoration to the infant, and present to him gifts, the productions of their native country. One might wonder that there is no notice of the astonishment which it must have excited in these men to find, instead of the expected prince, a child in quite ordinary, perhaps indigent circumstances.[16] It is not fair, however, to heighten the contrast by supposing, according to the common notion, that the magi discovered the child in a stable lying in the manger; for this representation is peculiar to Luke, and is altogether unknown to Matthew, who merely speaks of a *house*, οἰκία, in which the child was found. Then follows (v. 10) the warning given to the magi in a dream, concerning which, as before remarked, it were only to be wished that it had been vouchsafed earlier, so as to avert the steps of the magi from Jerusalem, and thus perchance prevent the whole subsequent massacre.

While Herod awaits the return of the magi, Joseph is admonished by an angelic apparition in a dream to flee with the Messianic child and its mother into Egypt for security (v. 13-15). Adopting the evangelist's point of view, this is not attended with any difficulty; it is otherwise, however, with the prophecy which the above event is said to fulfil, Hosea xi. 1. In this passage the prophet, speaking in the name of Jehovah, says : *When Israel was a child, then I loved him, and called my son out of Egypt.* We may venture to attribute, even to the most orthodox expositor, enough clear-sightedness to perceive that the subject of the first half of the sentence is also the object of the second, namely the people of Israel, who here, as elsewhere, (*e.g.* Exod. iv. 22, Sirach xxxvi. 14), are collectively called the Son of God, and whose past deliverance under Moses out of their Egyptian bondage is the fact referred to : that consequently, the prophet was not contemplating either the Messiah or his sojourn in Egypt. Nevertheless, as our evangelist says, v. 15, that the flight of Jesus into Egypt took place expressly that the above words of Hosea might be fulfilled, he must have understood them as a prophecy relating to Christ—must, therefore, have misunderstood them. It has been pretended that the passage has a twofold application, and, though referring primarily to the Israelitish people, is not the less a prophecy relative to Christ, because the destiny of Israel "after the flesh" was a type of the destiny of Jesus. But this convenient method of interpretation is not applicable here, for the analogy would, in the present case, be altogether external and inane, since the only parallel consists in the bare fact in both instances of a sojourn in Egypt, the circumstances under which the Israelitish people and the child Jesus sojourned there being altogether diverse.[17]

When the return of the magi has been delayed long enough for Herod to become aware that they have no intention to keep faith with him, he decrees the death of all the male children in Bethlehem and its environs up to the age of two years, that being, according to the statements of the magi as to the time of the star's appearance, the utmost interval that could have elapsed since the birth of the Messianic child (16-18). This was, beyond all question, an act of the blindest fury, for Herod might easily have informed himself whether a child who had received rare and costly presents was yet to be found in Bethlehem : but even granting it not inconsistent with the dis-

---

[15] Bibl. Comm. in loc, Hoffmann, s. 261.
[16] Schmidt, exeg. Beiträge, 1, 152 ff.
[17] This is shown in opposition to Olshausen by Steudel in Bengel's Archiv. vii. ii. 425 f. viii. iii. 487.

position of the aged tyrant to the extent that Schleiermacher supposed, it were in any case to be expected that so unprecedented and revolting a massacre would be noticed by other historians than Matthew.[18] But neither Josephus, who is very minute in his account of Herod, nor the rabbins, who were assiduous in blackening his memory, give the slightest hint of this decree. The latter do, indeed, connect the flight of Jesus into Egypt with a murderous scene, the author of which, however, is not Herod, but King Jannæus, and the victims not children, but rabbins.[19] Their story is evidently founded on a confusion of the occurrence gathered from the christian history, with an earlier event; for Alexander Jannæus died 40 years before the birth of Christ. Macrobius, who lived in the fourth century, is the only author who notices the slaughter of the infants, and he introduces it obliquely in a passage which loses all credit by confounding the execution of Antipater, who was so far from a child that he complained of his grey hairs,[20] with the murder of the infants, renowned among the Christians.[21] Commentators have attempted to diminish our surprise at the remarkable silence in question, by reminding us that the number of children of the given age in the petty village of Bethlehem, must have been small, and by remarking that among the numerous deeds of cruelty by which the life of Herod was stained, this one would be lost sight of as a drop in the ocean.[22] But in these observations the specific atrocity of murdering innocent children, however few, is overlooked; and it is this that must have prevented the deed, if really perpetrated, from being forgotten.[23] Here also the evangelist cites (v. 17, 18) a prophetic passage (Jerem. xxxi. 15), as having been fulfilled by the murder of the infants; whereas it originally referred to something quite different, namely the transportation of the Jews to Babylon, and had no kind of reference to an event lying in remote futurity.

While Jesus and his parents are in Egypt, Herod the Great dies, and Joseph is instructed by an angel, who appears to him in a dream, to return to his native country; but as Archelaus, Herod's successor in Judæa, was to be feared, he has more precise directions in a second oracular dream, in obedience to which he fixes his abode at Nazareth in Galilee, under the milder government of Herod Antipas (19–23). Thus in the compass of this single chapter, we have five extraordinary interpositions of God; an anomalous star, and four visions. For the star and the first vision, we have already remarked, one miracle might have been substituted, not only without detriment, but with advantage; either the star or the vision might from the beginning have deterred the magi from going to Jerusalem, and by this means perhaps have averted the massacre ordained by Herod. But that the two last visions are not united in one is a mere superfluity; for the direction to Joseph to proceed to Nazareth instead of Bethlehem, which is made the object of a special vision, might just as well have been included in the first. Such a disregard, even to prodigality, of the *lex parsimoniæ* in relation to the miraculous, one is tempted to refer to human imagination rather than to divine providence.

The false interpretations of Old Testament passages in this chapter are crowned by the last verse, where it is said that by the settlement of the

---

[18] Schmidt, ut sup. p. 156.
[19] Babylon. Sanhedr. f. cvii. 2, ap. Lightfoot, p. 207. Comp. Schöttgen, ii. p. 533. According to Josephus Antiq. xiii. xiii. 5, xiv. 2, they were Jews of each sex and of all ages, and chiefly Pharisees.
[20] Joseph. B. J. i. xxx. 3. Comp. Antiq. xvii. iv. 1.
[21] Macrob. Saturnal. ii. 4 : *Quum audisset (Augustus) inter pueros, quos in Syriâ Herodes rex Judæorum intra bimatum jussit interfici, filium quoque ejus occisum, ait: melius est, Herodis porcum (ὖν) esse quam filium (υἱόν).*
[22] Vid. Wetstein, Kuinöl, Olshausen in loc. Winer d. A. Herodes.
[23] Fritzsche, Comm. in Matt., p. 93 f.

parents of Jesus at Nazareth was fulfilled the saying of the prophets : *He shall be called a Nazarene.* Now this passage is not to be found in the Old Testament, and unless expositors, losing courage, take refuge in darkness by supposing that it is extracted from a canonical [24] or apocryphal [25] book now lost, they must admit the conditional validity of one or other of the following charges against the evangelist. If, as it has been alleged, he intended to compress the Old Testament prophecies that the Messiah would be despised, into the oracular sentence, He shall be called a Nazarene, *i.e.* the citizen of a despised city, [26] we must accuse him of the most arbitrary mode of expression ; or, if he be supposed to give a modification of נזיר (*nasir*) we must tax him with the most violent transformation of the word and the grossest perversion of its meaning, for even if, contrary to the fact, this epithet were applied to the Messiah in the Old Testament, it could only mean either that he would be a Nazarite, [27] which Jesus never was, or that he would be crowned, [28] as Joseph, Gen. xlix. 26, in no case that he would be brought up in the petty town of Nazareth. The most probable interpretation of this passage, and that which has the sanction of the Jewish Christians questioned on the subject by Jerome, is, that the evangelist here alludes to Isa. xi. 1, where the Messiah is called נֵצֶר יִשַׁי (*surculus Jesse*) as elsewhere צֶמַח.[29] But in every case there is the same violence done to the word by attaching to a mere appellative of the Messiah, an entirely fictitious relation to the name of the city of Nazareth.

§ 35.

ATTEMPTS AT A NATURAL EXPLANATION OF THE HISTORY OF THE MAGI. TRANSITION TO THE MYTHICAL EXPLANATION.

To avoid the many difficulties which beset us at every step in interpreting this chapter after the manner of the supranaturalists, it is quite worth our while to seek for another exposition which may suffice to explain the whole according to physical and psychological laws, without any admixture of supernaturalism. Such an exposition has been the most successfully attempted by Paulus.

How could heathen magi, in a remote country of the east, know anything of a Jewish king about to be born ? This is the first difficulty, and it is removed on the above system of interpretation by supposing that the magi were expatriated Jews. But this, apparently, is not the idea of the evangelist. For the question which he puts into the mouth of the magi, "*Where is he that is born King of the Jews ?*" distinguishes them from that people, and as regards the tendency of the entire narrative, the church seems to have apprehended it more correctly than Paulus thinks, in representing the visit of the magi as the first manifestation of Christ to the Gentiles. Nevertheless, as we have above remarked, this difficulty may be cleared away without having recourse to the supposition of Paulus.

Further, according to the natural explanation, the real object of the journey of these men was not to see the new-born king, nor was its cause the star which they had observed in the east ; but they happened to be travelling to Jerusalem perhaps with mercantile views, and hearing far and wide in the land of a new-born king, a celestial phenomenon which they had recently

---

[24] Chrysostom and others.
[25] Vid. Gratz, Comm. zum Ev. Matth. 1, s. 115.
[26] Kuinöl, ad Matth. p. 44 f.
[27] Wetstein, in loc.
[28] Schneckenburger, Beiträge zur Einleitung in das N. T., s. 42.
[29] Gieseler, Studien und Kritiken, 1831, 3. Heft, s. 588 f. Fritzsche, s. 104. Comp. Hieron. ad Jesai. xi. 1.

observed occurred to their remembrance, and they earnestly desired to see the child in question.   By this means, it is true, the difficulty arising from the sanction given to astrology by the usual conception of the story is diminished, but only at the expense of unprejudiced interpretation.   For even if it were admissible unceremoniously to transform magi μάγους into merchants, their purpose in this journey cannot have been a commercial one, for their first inquiry on arriving at Jerusalem is after the new-born king, and they forthwith mention a star, seen by them in the east, as the cause not only of their question, but also of their present journey, the object of which they aver to be the presentation of their homage to the new-born child (v. 2).

The ἀστήρ (star) becomes, on this method of interpretation, a natural meteor, or a comet,[1] or finally, a constellation, that is, a conjunction of planets.[2]   The last idea was put forth by Kepler, and has been approved by several astronomers and theologians.   Is it more easy, on any one of these suppositions, to conceive that the star could precede the magi on their way, and remain stationary over a particular house, according to the representation of the text?   We have already examined the two first hypotheses; if we adopt the third, we must either suppose the verb προάγειν (v. 9) to signify the disjunction of the planets, previously in apparent union,[3] though the text does not imply a partition but a forward movement of the entire phenomenon; or we must call Süskind's pluperfect to our aid, and imagine that the constellation, which the magi could no longer see in the valley between Jerusalem and Bethlehem, again burst on their view over the place where the child dwelt.[4]   For the expression, ἐπάνω οὗ ἦν τὸ παιδίον (v. 9), denotes merely the place of abode, not the particular dwelling of the child and his parents.   This we grant; but when the evangelist proceeds thus: καὶ εἰσελθόντες εἰς τὴν οἰκίαν, (v. 9), he gives the more general expression the precise meaning of dwelling-house, so that this explanation is clearly a vain effort to abate the marvellousness of the evangelical narrative.

The most remarkable supposition adopted by those who regard ἀστήρ as a conjunction of planets, is that they hereby obtain a fixed point in accredited history, to which the narrative of Matthew may be attached.   According to Kepler's calculation, corrected by Ideler, there occurred, three years before the death of Herod, in the year of Rome 747, a conjunction of Jupiter and Saturn in the sign Pisces.   The conjunction of these planets is repeated in the above sign, to which astrologers attribute a special relation to Palestine, about every 800 years, and according to the computation of the Jew Abarbanel (1463) it took place three years before the birth of Moses; hence it is probable enough that the hope of the second great deliverer of the nation would be associated with the recurrence of this conjunction in the time of Herod, and that when the phenomenon was actually observed, it would occasion inquiry on the part of Babylonian Jews.   But that the star mentioned by Matthew was this particular planetary conjunction, is, from our uncertainty as to the year of Christ's birth, and also as to the period of the above astrological calculation, an extremely precarious conjecture; and as, besides, there are certain particulars in the evangelical text, for instance, the words προῆγεν and ἔστη, which do not accord with such an explanation,—so soon as another, more congruous with Matthew's narrative, presents itself, we are justified in giving it the preference.

[1] For both these explanations, see Kuinöl, in loc.
[2] Kepler, in various treatises; Münter, der Stern der Weisen; Ideler, Handbuch der mathemat. und technischen Chronologie, 2. Bd. s. 399 ff.
[3] Olshausen, s. 67.
[4] Paulus, ut sup. s. 202, 221.

The difficulties connected with the erroneous interpretations of passages from the Old Testament are, from the natural point of view, eluded by denying that the writers of the New Testament are responsible for the falsity of these interpretations. It is said that the prophecy of Micah is applied to the Messiah and his birth in Bethlehem by the Sanhedrim alone, and that Matthew has not committed himself to their interpretation by one word of approval. But when the evangelist proceeds to narrate how the issue corresponded with the interpretation, he sanctions it by the authoritative seal of fact. In relation to the passage from Hosea, Paulus and Steudel[5] concur in resorting to a singular expedient. Matthew, say they, wished to guard against the offence which it might possibly give to the Jews of Palestine to learn that the Messiah had once left the Holy Land; he therefore called attention to the fact that Israel, in one sense the first-born of God, had been called out of Egypt, for which reason, he would imply, no one ought to be astonished that the Messiah, the son of God in a higher sense, had also visited a profane land. But throughout the passage there is no trace[6] of such a negative, precautionary intention on the part of the evangelist in adducing this prophecy : on the contrary, all his quotations seem to have the positive object to confirm the Messiahship of Jesus by showing that in him the Old Testament prophecies had their fulfilment. It has been attempted with reference to the two other prophecies cited in this chapter, to reduce the signification of the verb πληρωθῆναι (*to be fulfilled*) to that of mere similitude or applicability ; but the futility of the effort needs no exposure.

The various directions conveyed to the persons of our narrative by means of visions are, from the same point of view, all explained psychologically, as effects of waking inquiries and reflections. This appears, indeed, to be indicated by the text itself, v. 22, according to which Joseph, hearing that Archelaus was master of Judea, feared to go thither, and not until then did he receive an intimation from a higher source in a dream. Nevertheless, on a closer examination we find that the communication given in the dream was something new, not a mere repetition of intelligence received in waking moments. Only the negative conclusion, that on account of Archelaus it was not advisable to settle at Bethlehem, was attained by Joseph when awake ; the positive injunction to proceed to Nazareth was superadded in his dream. To explain the other visions in the above way is a direct interpolation of the text, for this represents both the hostility and death of Herod as being first made known to Joseph by dreams ; in like manner, the magi have no distrust of Herod until a dream warns them against his treachery.

Thus, on the one hand, the sense of the narrative in Matt. ii. is opposed to the conception of its occurrence as natural ; on the other hand, this narrative, taken in its original sense, carries the supernatural into the extravagant, the improbable into the impossible. We are therefore led to doubt the historical character of the narrative, and to conjecture that we have before us something mythical. The first propounders of this opinion were so unsuccessful in its illustration, that they never liberated themselves from the sphere of the natural interpretation, which they sought to transcend. Arabian merchants (thinks Krug, for example) coming by chance to Bethlehem, met with the parents of Jesus, and learning that they were strangers in distress (according to Matthew, the parents of Jesus were not strangers in Bethlehem), made them presents, uttered many good wishes for their child, and pursued their

---

[5] Bengel's Archiv. vii. ii. p. 424.
[6] At a later period, it is true, this journey of Jesus was the occasion of calumnies from the Jews, but those were of an entirely different nature, as will be seen in the following chapter.

journey. When subsequently, Jesus was reputed to be the Messiah, the incident was remembered and embellished with a star, visions, and believing
homage.   To these were added the flight into Egypt and the infanticide ; the
latter, because the above incident was supposed to have had some effect on
Herod, who, on other grounds than those alleged in the text, had caused some
families in Bethlehem to be put to death ; the former, probably because Jesus
had, with some unknown object, actually visited Egypt at a later period.[7]

In this, as in the purely naturalistic interpretation, there remain as so many
garb, the arrival of some oriental travellers, the flight into Egypt, and the
massacre in Bethlehem ; divested, however, of the marvellous garb with which
they are enveloped in the evangelical narrative.   In this unadorned form,
these occurrences are held to be intelligible and such as might very probably
happen, but in point of fact they are more incomprehensible even than when
viewed through the medium of orthodoxy, for with their supernatural embellishments vanishes the entire basis on which they rest.   Matthew's narrative
adequately accounts for the relations between the men of the east and the
parents of Jesus ; this attempt at mythical exposition reduces them to a wonderful chance.   The massacre at Bethlehem has, in the evangelical narrative,
a definite cause ; here, we are at a loss to understand how Herod came
to ordain such an enormity ; so, the journey into Egypt, which had so urgent
a motive according to Matthew, is on this scheme of interpretation totally
inexplicable.   It may indeed be said : these events had their adequate causes
in accordance with the regular course of things, but Matthew has withheld this
natural sequence and given a miraculous one in its stead.   But if the writer
or legend be capable of environing occurrences with fictitious motives and
accessory circumstances, either the one or the other is also capable of fabricating the occurrences themselves, and this fabrication is the more probable,
the more clearly we can show that the legend had an interest in depicting
such occurrences, though they had never actually taken place.

This argument is equally valid against the attempt, lately made from the
supranaturalistic point of view, to separate the true from the false in the evangelical narrative.   In a narrative like this, says Neander, we must carefully
distinguish the kernel from the shell, the main fact from immaterial circumstances, and not demand the same degree of certitude for all its particulars.
That the magi by their astrological researches were led to anticipate the birth
of a Saviour in Judea, and hence journeyed to Jerusalem that they might offer
him their homage is, according to him, the only essential and certain part of
the narrative.   But how, when arrived in Jerusalem, did they learn that the
child was to be born in Bethlehem?   From Herod, or by some other means?
On this point Neander is not equally willing to guarantee the veracity of Matthew's statements, and he regards it as unessential.   The magi, he continues,
in so inconsiderable a place as Bethlehem, might be guided to the child's
dwelling by many providential arrangements in the ordinary course of events ;
for example, by meeting with the shepherds or other devout persons who had
participated in the great event.   When however they had once entered the
house, they might represent the circumstances in the astrological guise with
which their minds were the most familiar.   Neander awards an historical
character to the flight into Egypt and the infanticide.[8]   By this explanation
of the narrative, only its heaviest difficulty, namely, that the star preceded the

---

[7] Ueber formelle oder genetische Erklärungsart der Wunder.   In Henke's Museum, 1, 3,
399 ff.   Similar essays see in the Abhandlungen über die beiden ersten Kapitel des Matthäus u. Lukas, in Henke's Magazin, 5, 1, 171 ff., and in Matthäi, Religionsgl. der Apostel,
2, s. 422 ff.
[8] L. J. Ch., s. 29 ff.

magi on their way and paused above a single house, is in reality thrown over-board ; the other difficulties remain. But Neander has renounced unlimited confidence in the veracity of the evangelist, and admitted that a part of his narrative is unhistorical. If it be asked how far this unhistorical portion ex-tends, and what is its kind—whether the nucleus around which legend has deposited its crystallizations be historical or ideal—it is easy to show that the few and vague data which a less lenient criticism than that of Neander can admit as historical, are far less adapted to give birth to our narrative, than the very precise circle of ideas and types which we are about to exhibit.

§ 36.

THE PURELY MYTHICAL EXPLANATION OF THE NARRATIVE CONCERNING
THE MAGI, AND OF THE EVENTS WITH WHICH IT IS CONNECTED.

Several Fathers of the Church indicated the true key to the narrative con-cerning the magi when, in order to explain from what source those heathen astrologers could gather any knowledge of a Messianic star, they put forth the conjecture that this knowledge might have been drawn from the prophecies of the heathen Balaam, recorded in the Book of Numbers.[1] K. Ch. L. Schmidt justly considers it a deficiency in the exposition of Paulus, that it takes no notice of the Jewish expectation that a star would become visible at the appearance of the Messiah ; and yet, he adds, this is the only thread to guide us to the true origin of this narrative.[2] The prophecy of Balaam (Num. xxiv. 17), *A star shall come out of Jacob*, was the cause—not indeed, as the Fathers supposed, that magi actually recognized a newly-kindled star as that of the Messiah, and hence journeyed to Jerusalem—but that legend repre-sented a star to have appeared at the birth of Jesus, and to have been recog-nized by astrologers as the star of the Messiah. The prophecy attributed to Balaam originally referred to some fortunate and victorious ruler of Israel ; but it seems to have early received a Messianic interpretation. Even if the translation in the Targum of Onkelos, *surget rex ex Jacobo et Messias (unctus) ungetur ex Israele*, prove nothing, because here the word *unctus* is synony-mous with *rex*, and might signify an ordinary king—it is yet worthy of notice that, according to the testimony of Aben Ezra,[3] and the passages cited by Wetstein and Schöttgen, many rabbins applied the prophecy to the Messiah. The name Bar-Cocheba (*son of a star*), assumed by a noted pseudo-Messiah under Hadrian, was chosen with reference to the Messianic interpretation of Balaam's prophecy.

It is true that the passage in question, taken in its original sense, does not speak of a real star, but merely compares to a star the future prince of Israel, and this is the interpretation given to it in the Targum above quoted. But the growing belief in astrology, according to which every important event was signalized by sidereal changes, soon caused the prophecy of Balaam to be understood no longer figuratively, but literally, as referring to a star which was to appear contemporaneously with the Messiah. We have various proofs that a belief in astrology was prevalent in the time of Jesus. The future great-ness of Mithridates was thought to be prognosticated by the appearance of a comet in the year of his birth, and in that of his accession to the throne [4] ;

---

[1] Orig. c. Cels. i. 60. Auctor, op. imperf. in Matth. ap. Fabricius Pseudepigr. V. T., p. 807 ff.
[2] Schmidt's Bibliothek, 3, 1, s. 130.
[3] In loc. Num. (Schöttgen, horæ, ii. p. 152) : *Multi Interpretati sunt hæc de Messiâ.*
[4] Justin. Hist. 37.

and a comet observed shortly after the death of Julius Cæsar, was supposed to have a close relation to that event.[5] These ideas were not without influence on the Jews; at least we find traces of them in Jewish writings of a later period, in which it is said that a remarkable star appeared at the birth of Abraham.[6] When such ideas were afloat, it was easy to imagine that the birth of the Messiah must be announced by a star, especially as, according to the common interpretation of Balaam's prophecy, a star was there made the symbol of the Messiah. It is certain that the Jewish mind effected this combination ; for it is a rabbinical idea that at the time of the Messiah's birth, a star will appear in the east and remain for a long time visible.[7] The narrative of Matthew is allied to this simpler Jewish idea ; the apocryphal descriptions of the star that announced the birth of Jesus, to the extravagant fictions about the star said to have appeared in the time of Abraham.[8] We may therefore state the opinion of K. Ch. L. Schmidt,[9] recently approved by Fritzsche and De Wette, as the nearest approach to truth on the subject of Matthew's star in the east. In the time of Jesus it was the general belief that stars were always the forerunners of great events; hence the Jews of that period thought that the birth of the Messiah would necessarily be announced by a star, and this supposition had a specific sanction in Num. xxiv. 17. The early converted Jewish Christians could confirm their faith in Jesus, and justify it in the eyes of others, only by labouring to prove that in him were realized all the attributes lent to the Messiah by the Jewish notions of their age—a proposition that might be urged the more inoffensively and with the less chance of refutation, the more remote lay the age of Jesus, and the more completely the history of his childhood was shrouded in darkness. Hence it soon ceased to be matter of doubt that the anticipated appearance of a star was really coincident with the birth of Jesus.[10] This being once presupposed, it followed as a matter of course that the observers of this appearance were eastern magi ; first, because none could better interpret the sign than astrologers, and the east was supposed to be the native region of their science ; and secondly, because it must have seemed fitting that the Messianic star which had been seen by the spiritual eye of the ancient magus Balaam, should, on its actual appearance be first recognized by the bodily eyes of later magi.

This particular, however, as well as the journey of the magi into Judea, and their costly presents to the child, bear a relation to other passages in the Old Testament. In the description of the happier future, given in Isaiah, chap. lx., the prophet foretells that, at that time, the most remote people and kings will come to Jerusalem to worship Jehovah, with offerings of gold and incense

---

[5] Sueton. Jul. Cæs. 88.

[6] Jalkut Rubeni, f. xxxii. 3 (ap. Wetstein) : *quâ horâ natus est Abrahamus, pater noster, super quem sit pax, stetit quoddam sidus in oriente et deglutivit quatuor astra, quæ erant in quatuor cæli plagis.* According to an Arabic writing entitled Maallem, this star, prognosticating the birth of Abraham, was seen by Nimrod in a dream. Fabric. Cod. pseudepigr. V. T. i. s. 345.

[7] Testamentum XII. Patriarcharum, test. Levi, 18 (Fabric. Cod. pseud. V. T. p. 584 f.) : καὶ ἀνατελεῖ ἄστρον αὐτοῦ (of the Messianic ἱερεὺς καινὸς) ἐν οὐρανῷ.—φωτίζον φῶς γνώσεως κ. τ. λ. Pesikta Sotarta, f. xlviii. 1 (ap. Schöttgen, ii. p. 531) : *Et prodibit stella ab oriente, quæ est stella Messiæ, et in oriente versabitur dies XV.* Comp. Sohar Genes. f. 74. Schöttgen, ii. 524, and some other passages which are pointed out by Ideler in the Handbuch der Chronologie, 2 Bd. s. 409, Anm. 1, and Bertholdt, Christologia Judæorum, § 14.

[8] Compare with the passages cited Note 7. Protevang. Jac. cap. xxi. : εἴδομεν ἀστέρα παμμεγέθη, λάμψαντα ἐν τοῖς ἄστροις τούτοις καὶ ἀμβλύνοντα αὐτοὺς τοῦ φαίνειν. Still more exaggerated in Ignat. ep. ad Ephes. 19. See the collection of passages connected with this subject in Thilo, cod. apocr. i. p. 390 f.

[9] Exeg. Beiträge, i. s. 159 ff.

[10] Fritzsche in the paraphrase of chap. ii. *Etiam stella, quam judaica disciplina sub Messiæ natale visum iri dicit, quo Jesus nascebatur tempore exorta est.*

and all acceptable gifts.[11] If in this passage the messianic times alone are spoken of, while the Messiah himself is wanting, in Psalm lxxii. we read of a king who is to be feared as long as the sun and moon endure, in whose times the righteous shall flourish, and whom all nations shall call blessed ; this king might easily be regarded as the Messiah, and the Psalm says of him nearly in the words of Isa. lx., that foreign kings shall bring him gold and other presents. To this it may be added, that the pilgrimage of foreign people to Jerusalem is connected with a risen light,[12] which might suggest the star of Balaam. What was more natural, when on the one hand was presented Balaam's messianic star out of Jacob (for the observation of which magian astrologers were the best adapted) ; on the other, a light which was to arise on Jerusalem, and to which distant nations would come, bringing gifts—than to combine the two images and to say : In consequence of the star which had risen over Jerusalem, astrologers came from a distant land with presents for the Messiah whom the star announced ? But when the imagination once had possession of the star, and of travellers attracted by it from a distance, there was an inducement to make the star the immediate guide of their course, and the torch to light them on their way. This was a favourite idea of antiquity : according to Virgil, a star, *stella facem ducens*, marked out the way of Æneas from the shores of Troy to the west [13] ; Thrasybulus and Timoleon were led by celestial fires ; and a star was said to have guided Abraham on his way to Moriah.[14] Besides, in the prophetic passage itself, the heavenly light seems to be associated with the pilgrimage of the offerers as the guide of their course ; at all events the originally figurative language of the prophet would probably, at a later period, be understood literally, in accordance with the rabbinical spirit of interpretation. The magi are not conducted by the star directly to Bethlehem where Jesus was ; they first proceed to Jerusalem. One reason for this might be, that the prophetic passage connects the risen light and the offerers with Jerusalem ; but the chief reason lies in the fact, that in Jerusalem Herod was to be found ; for what was better adapted to instigate Herod to his murderous decree, than the alarming tidings of the magi, that they had seen the star of the great Jewish king?

To represent a murderous decree as having been directed by Herod against Jesus, was the interest of the primitive christian legend. In all times legend has glorified the infancy of great men by persecutions and attempts on their life ; the greater the danger that hovered over them, the higher seems their value ; the more unexpectedly their deliverance is wrought, the more evident is the esteem in which they are held by heaven. Hence in the history of the childhood of Cyrus in Herodotus, of Romulus in Livy,[15] and even later of Augustus in Suetonius,[16] we find this trait ; neither has the Hebrew legend neglected to assign such a distinction to Moses.[17] One point of analogy be-

---

[11] As in Matt. ii. 11 it is said of the magi προσήνεγκαν αὐτῷ—χρυσὸν καὶ λίβανον : so in Isa. lx. 6 (LXX.) : ἥξουσί, φέροντες χρυσίον, καὶ λίβανον οἴσουσι. The third present is in Matt. σμύρνα, in Isa. λίθος τίμιος.

[12] V. 1. und 3 : עָלָיִךְ יְהוָה וּכְבוֹד אוֹרֵךְ בָא כִּי (LXX : Ἰερουσαλήμ) אוֹרִי קוּמִי זָרַח :—וְהָלְכוּ גוֹיִם לְאוֹרֵךְ וּמְלָכִים לְנֹגַהּ זַרְחֵךְ

[13] Æneid. ii. 693 ff.
[14] Wetstein, in loc.
[15] Herod. i. 108 ff. Liv. i. 4.
[16] Octav. 94 :—*ante paucos quam nasceretur menses prodigium Romæ factum publice, quo denuntiabatur, regem populi Romani naturam parturire. Senatum exterritum, censuisse, ne quis illo anno genitus educaretur. Eos, qui gravidas uxores haberent, quo ad se quisque spem traheret, curasse, ne Senatus consultum ad ærarium deferretur.*
[17] Bauer (über das Mythische in der früheren Lebensper. des Moses, in the n. Theol.

tween the narrative in Exod. i. ii, and that in Matthew, is that in both cases the murderous decree does not refer specially to the one dangerous child, but generally to a certain class of children ; in the former, to all new-born males, in the latter to all of and under the age of two years.   It is true that, according to the narrative in Exodus, the murderous decree is determined on without any reference to Moses, of whose birth Pharaoh is not supposed to have had any presentiment, and who is therefore only by accident implicated in its consequences.   But this representation did not sufficiently mark out Moses as the object of hostile design to satisfy the spirit of Hebrew tradition, and by the time of Josephus it had been so modified as to resemble more nearly the legends concerning Cyrus and Augustus, and above all the narrative of Matthew.   According to the later legend, Pharaoh was incited to issue his murderous decree by a communication from his interpreters of the sacred writings, who announced to him the birth of an infant destined to succour the Israelites and humble the Egyptians.[18]   The interpreters of the sacred writings here play the same part as the interpreters of dreams in Herodotus, and the astrologers in Matthew.   Legend was not content with thus signalizing the infancy of the lawgiver alone—it soon extended the same distinction to the great progenitor of the Israelitish nation, Abraham, whom it represented as being in peril of his life from the murderous attempt of a jealous tyrant, immediately after his birth.   Moses was opposed to Pharaoh as an enemy and oppressor ; Abraham held the same position with respect to Nimrod.   This monarch was forewarned by his sages, whose attention had been excited by a remarkable star, that Tharah would have a son from whom a powerful nation would descend.   Apprehensive of rivalry, Nimrod immediately issues a murderous command, which, however, Abraham happily escapes.[19]   What wonder then, that, as the great progenitor and the lawgiver of the nation had their Nimrod and Pharaoh, a corresponding persecutor was found for the restorer of the nation, the Messiah, in the person of Herod ;—that this tyrant was said to have been apprised of the Messiah's birth by wise men, and to have laid snares against his life, from which, however, he happily escapes ?   The apocryphal legend, indeed, has introduced an imitation of this trait, after its own style, into the history of the Forerunner ; he, too, is endangered by Herod's decree, a mountain is miraculously cleft asunder to receive him and his mother, but his father refusing to point out the boy's hiding-place, is put to death.[20]

Jesus escapes from the hostile attempts of Herod by other means than those by which Moses, according to the mosaic history, and Abraham, according to the Jewish legend, elude the decree issued against them ; namely, by a flight out of his native land into Egypt.   In the life of Moses also there occurs a flight into a foreign land ; not, however, during his childhood, but after he had slain the Egyptian, when, fearing the vengeance of Pharaoh, he takes refuge in Midian (Exod. ii. 15).   That reference was made to this flight of the first Goël.in that of the second, our text expressly shows, for the words, which it attributes to the angel, who encourages Joseph to

---

Journ. 13, 3) had already compared the marvellous deliverance of Moses with that of Cyrus and Romulus ; the comparison of the infanticides was added by De Wette, Kritik der Mos. Geschichte, s. 176.

[18] Joseph. Antiq. ii. ix. 2.

[19] Jalkut Rubeni (cont. of the passage cited in Note 6) : *dixerunt sapientes Nimrodi : natus est Tharæ filius hâc ipsâ horâ, ex quo egressurus est populus, qui hæreditabit præsens et futurum seculum ; si tibi placuerit, detur patri ipsius domus argento auroque plena, et occidat ipsum.* Comp. the passage of the Arabic book quoted by Fabric. Cod. pseudepigr. ut sup.

[20] Protev. Jacobi, c. xxii. f.

return out of Egypt into Palestine, are those by which Moses is induced to return out of Midian into Egypt.[21] The choice of Egypt as a place of refuge for Jesus, may be explained in the simplest manner : the young Messiah could not, like Moses, flee *out of* Egypt ; hence, that his history might not be destitute of so significant a feature as a connexion with Egypt, that ancient retreat of the patriarchs, the relation was reversed, and he was made to flee *into* Egypt, which, besides, from its vicinity, was the most appropriate asylum for a fugitive from Judea. The prophetic passage which the evangelist cites from Hosea xi. 1, *Out of Egypt have I called my son*—is less available for the elucidation of this particular in our narrative. For the immediate proofs that the Jews referred this passage to the Messiah are very uncertain ;[22] though, if we compare such passages as Ps. ii. 7, in which the words אַתָּה בְּנִי (*thou art my son*) are interpreted of the Messiah, it cannot appear incredible that the expression לִבְנִי (*my son*) in Hosea was supposed to have a messianic signification.

Against this mythical derivation of the narrative, two objections have been recently urged. First, if the history of the star originated in Balaam's prophecy, why, it is asked, does not Matthew, fond as he is of showing the fulfilment of Old Testament predictions in the life of Jesus, make the slightest allusion to that prophecy ?[23] Because it was not he who wove this history out of the materials furnished in the Old Testament ; he received it, already fashioned, from others, who did not communicate to him its real origin. For the very reason that many narratives were transmitted to him without their appropriate keys, he sometimes tries false ones ; as in our narrative, in relation to the Bethlehem massacre, he quotes, under a total misconception of the passage, Jeremiah's image of Rachel weeping for her children.[24] The other objection is this : how could the communities of Jewish Christians, whence this pretended mythus must have sprung, ascribe so high an importance to the heathen as is implied in the star of the magi ?[25] As if the prophets had not, in such passages as we have quoted, already ascribed to them this importance, which, in fact, consists but in their rendering homage and submission to the Messiah, a relation that must be allowed to correspond with the ideas of the Jewish Christians, not to speak of the particular conditions on which the heathen were to be admitted into the kingdom of the Messiah.

We must therefore abide by the mythical interpretation of our narrative, and content ourselves with gathering from it no particular fact in the life of Jesus, but only a new proof how strong was the impression of his messiahship left by Jesus on the minds of his contemporaries, since even the history of his childhood received a messianic form.[26]

Let us now revert to the narrative of Luke, chap. ii., so far as it runs parallel with that of Matthew. We have seen that the narrative of Matthew

---

[21] Ex. iv. 19, LXX :   Matt. ii. 20 :
βάδιζε, ἄπελθε εἰς Αἴγυπτον, τεθνήκασι γὰρ   ἐγερθεὶς—πορεύου εἰς γῆν Ἰσραήλ· τεθνήκασι
πάντες οἱ ζητοῦντές σου τὴν ψυχήν.   γὰρ οἱ ζητοῦντες τὴν ψυχὴν τοῦ παιδίου.
We may remark that the inappropriate use of the plural in the evangelical passage, can only be explained on the supposition of a reference to the passage in Exod. See Winer, N. T. Gramm. s. 149. Comp. also Exod. iv. 20 with Matt. ii. 14, 21.
[22] Vide e. g. Schöttgen, Horæ, ii. p. 209.
[23] Theile, zur biographie Jesu, § 15, Anm. 9. Hoffmann, s. 269.
[24] Comp. my Streitschriften, i. 1, s. 42 f. ; George, s. 39.
[25] Neander, L. J. Ch. s. 27.
[26] Schleiermacher (Ueber den Lukas, s. 47), explains the narrative concerning the magi as a symbolical one ; but he scorns to take into consideration the passages from the O. T. and other writings, which have a bearing on the subject, and by way of retribution, his exposition at one time rests in generalities, at another, takes a wrong path.

does not allow us to presuppose that of Luke as a series of prior incidents :
still less can the converse be true, namely, that the magi arrived before the
shepherds : it remains then to be asked, whether the two narratives do not
aim to represent the same fact, though they have given it a different garb ?
From the older orthodox opinion that the star in Matthew was an angel, it
was an easy step to identify that apparition with the angel in Luke, and to
suppose that the angels, who appeared to the shepherds of Bethlehem on the
night of the birth of Jesus, were taken by the distant magi for a star vertical
to Judea,[27] so that both the accounts might be essentially correct. Of late,
only one of the Evangelists has been supposed to give the true circumstances,
and Luke has had the preference, Matthew's narrative being regarded as an
embellished edition.

According to this opinion, the angel clothed in heavenly brightness, in
Luke, became a star in the tradition recorded by Matthew, the ideas of angels
and stars being confounded in the higher Jewish theology ; the shepherds
were exalted into royal magi, kings being in antiquity called the shepherds
of their people.[28]   This derivation is too elaborate to be probable, even were
it true, as it is here assumed, that Luke's narrative bears the stamp of historical credibility.   As, however, we conceive that we have proved the
contrary, and as, consequently, we have before us two equally unhistorical
narratives, there is no reason for preferring a forced and unnatural derivation
of Matthew's narrative from that of Luke, to the very simple derivation which
may be traced through Old Testament passages and Jewish notions.   These
two descriptions of the introduction of Jesus into the world, are, therefore,
two variations on the same theme, composed, however, quite independently
of each other.

§ 37.

CHRONOLOGICAL RELATION BEEWEEN THE VISIT OF THE MAGI, TOGETHER
WITH THE FLIGHT INTO EGYPT, AND THE PRESENTATION IN THE TEMPLE
RECORDED BY LUKE.

It has been already remarked, that the narratives of Matthew and Luke
above considered at first run tolerably parallel, but afterwards widely diverge ;
for instead of the tragical catastrophe of the massacre and flight, Luke has
preserved to us the peaceful scene of the presentation of the child Jesus in
the temple.   Let us for the present shut our eyes to the result of the preceding inquiry—the purely mythical character of Matthew's narrative—and ask :
In what chronological relation could the presentation in the temple stand to
the visit of the magi and the flight into Egypt ?

Of these occurrences the only one that has a precise date is the presentation
in the temple, of which it is said that it took place at the expiration of the
period appointed by the law for the purification of a mother, that is, according to Lev. xii. 2–4, forty days after the birth of the child (Luke ii. 22).   The
time of the other incidents is not fixed with the same exactness ; it is merely
said that the magi came to Jerusalem, τοῦ Ἰησοῦ γεννηθέντος ἐν Βηθλεὲμ (Matt.
ii. 1)—how long after the birth the Evangelist does not decide.   As, however,
the participle connects the visit of the magi with the birth of the child, if not
immediately, at least so closely that nothing of importance can be supposed
to have intervened, some expositors have been led to the opinion that the

---

[27] Lightfoot, Horæ, p. 202.
[28] Schneckenburger, Ueber den Ursprung des ersten kanonischen Evangeliums, s. 69 ff.

visit ought to be regarded as prior to the presentation in the temple.[1] Admitting this arrangement, we have to reconcile it with one of two alternatives; either the flight into Egypt also preceded the presentation in the temple; or, while the visit of the magi preceded, the flight followed that event. If we adopt the latter alternative, and thrust the presentation in the temple between the visit of the magi and the flight, we come into collision at once with the text of Matthew and the mutual relation of the facts. The Evangelist connects the command to flee into Egypt with the return of the magi, by a participial construction (v. 13) similar to that by which he connects the arrival of the oriental sages with the birth of Jesus; hence those, who in the one instance hold such a construction to be a reason for placing the events which it associates in close succession, must in the other instance be withheld by it from inserting a third occurrence between the visit and the flight. As regards the mutual relation of the facts, it can hardly be considered probable, that at the very point of time in which Joseph received a divine intimation, that he was no longer safe in Bethlehem from the designs of Herod, he should be permitted to take a journey to Jerusalem, and thus to rush directly into the lion's mouth. At all events, the strictest precautions must have been enjoined on all who were privy to the presence of the messianic child in Jerusalem, lest a rumour of the fact should get abroad. But there is no trace of this solicitous incognito in Luke's narrative; on the contrary, not only does Simeon call attention to Jesus in the temple, unchecked either by the Holy Spirit or by the parents, but Anna also thinks she is serving the good cause, by publishing as widely as possible the tidings of the Messiah's birth (Luke ii. 28 ff. 38). It is true that she is said to have confined her communications to those who were like-minded with herself (ἐλάλει περὶ αὐτοῦ πᾶσι τοῖς προσδεχομένοις λύτρωσιν ἐν Ἱερουσαλὴμ), but this could not hinder them from reaching the ears of the Herodian party, for the greater the excitement produced by such news on the minds of those *who looked for redemption*, the more would the vigilance of the government be aroused, so that Jesus would inevitably fall into the hands of the tyrant who was lying in wait.

Thus in any case, they who place the presentation in the temple after the visit of the magi, must also determine to postpone it until after the return from Egypt. But even this arrangement clashes with the evangelical statement; for.it requires us to insert, between the birth of Jesus and his presentation in the temple, the following events: the arrival of the magi, the flight into Egypt, the Bethlehem massacre, the death of Herod, and the return of the parents of Jesus out of Egypt—obviously too much to be included in the space of forty days. It must therefore be supposed that the presentation of the child, and the first appearance of the mother in the temple, were procrastinated beyond the time appointed by the law. This expedient, however, runs counter to the narrative of Luke, who expressly says, that the visit to the temple took place at the legal time. But in either case the difficulty is the same; the parents of Jesus could, according to Matthew's account, as little think of a journey to Jerusalem after their return from Egypt, as immediately previous to their departure thither. For if Joseph, on his return from Egypt, was warned not to enter Judea, because Archelaus was Herod's successor in that province, he would least of all venture to Jerusalem, the very seat of the redoubted government.

On neither of the above plans, therefore, will the presentation in the temple bear to be placed after the visit of the magi, and the only remaining alterna-

---

[1] Thus, e. g. Augustin de consensu evangelistarum, ii. 5. Storr, opusc. acad. iii. s. 96 ff. Süskind, in Bengel's Archiv. i. 1, s. 216 ff.

tive, which is embraced by the majority of commentators,[2] is to make the incident noticed by Luke, precede both those narrated by Matthew. This is so far the most natural, that in Matthew there is at least an indirect intimation of a considerable interval between the birth of Jesus and the arrival of the magi. For we are told that Herod's decree included all the children in Bethlehem up to the age of two years; we must therefore necessarily infer, that even if Herod, to make sure of his object, exceeded the term fixed by the magi, the star had been visible to these astrologers for more than a year. Now the narrator seems to suppose the appearance of the star to have been cotemporary with the birth of Jesus. Viewing the narratives in this order, the parents of Jesus first journeyed from Bethlehem, where the child was born, to Jerusalem, there to present the legal offerings; they next returned to Bethlehem, where (according to Matt. ii. 1 and 5) they were found by the magi; then followed the flight into Egypt, and after the return from thence, the settlement at Nazareth. The first and most urgent question that here suggests itself is this: What had the parents of Jesus to do a second time in Bethlehem, which was not their home, and where their original business connected with the census must surely have been despatched in the space of forty days? The discussion of this question must be deferred, but we can find an ample substitute for this argument, drawn from the nature of the fact, in one which rests on the words of the evangelical narrative. Luke (v. 39) says, in the most definite manner, that after the completion of the legal observance, the parents of Jesus returned to Nazareth, as to their proper home, not to Bethlehem, which, according to him, was merely a temporary residence.[3] If, then, the magi arrived after the presentation in the temple, they must have met with the parents of Jesus in Nazareth, and not in Bethlehem, as Matthew states. Moreover, had the arrival of the magi really been preceded by the presentation in the temple, together with the attention which must have been excited by the language of Simeon and Anna; it is impossible that at the period of that arrival the birth of the messianic child could have been so much a secret in Jerusalem, that the announcement of it by the magi should be, as Matthew relates, a source of general astonishment.[4]

If, then, the presentation of Jesus in the temple can have taken place neither earlier nor later than the visit of the magi and the flight into Egypt; and if the flight into Egypt can have taken place neither earlier nor later than the presentation in the temple; it is impossible that both these occurrences really happened, and, at the very utmost, only one can be historical.[5]

To escape from this dangerous dilemma, supranaturalism has lately been induced to take a freer position, that by the surrender of what is no longer tenable, the residue may be saved. Neander finds himself constrained to admit, that neither did Luke know anything of what Matthew communicates concerning the childhood of Jesus, nor did the Greek editor of Matthew (to be distinguished from the apostle) know anything of the events detailed by Luke. But, he contends, it does not therefore follow that both the different series of incidents cannot have happened.[6] By giving this turn to the matter,

---

[2] E.g. Hess, Geschichte Jesu, 1, s. 51 ff. Paulus, Olshausen, in loc.

[3] Süskind, ut sup. s. 222.

[4] The same difference as to the chronological relation of the two incidents exists between the two different texts of the apocryphal book: Historia de nativitate Mariæ et de inf. Serv., see Thilo, p. 385, not.

[5] This incompatibility of the two narratives was perceived at an early period by some opponents of Christianity. Epiphanius names one Philosabbatius, together with Celsus and Porphyry (hæres. li. 8).

[6] Neander, L. J. Ch. s. 33, Anm.

the difficulties arising from the words of the Evangelist are certainly avoided ; not so, the difficulties arising from the nature of the facts.   The first Evangelist ranges in close succession the visit of the magi and the flight into Egypt, as though no change of place had intervened ; the author of the third Gospel represents the parents of Jesus as returning with the child, after the presentation in the temple, directly to Nazareth.   We cannot, on this ground, argue from one evangelist against the other ; for it is inadmissible to maintain that certain events never happened, because they were unknown to a remote narrator.   But viewing the two narratives in another light, we perceive how improbable it is that, after the scene in the temple, the birth of the messianic child should be so entirely unknown in Jerusalem as the conduct of Herod on the arrival of the magi implies ; how incredible (reversing the order of the events) that Joseph should be permitted to go to Jerusalem, with the child which Herod had just sought to kill ; how inconceivable, finally, that the parents of Jesus should have returned to Bethlehem after the presentation in the temple (of which more hereafter).   All these difficulties, lying in the nature of the facts, difficulties not less weighty than those connected with the words of the Evangelists, still subsist in Neander's explanation, and prove its inadequacy.

Thus the dilemma above stated remains, and were we compelled to choose under it, we should, in the present stage of our inquiry, on no account decide in favour of Matthew's narrative, and against that of Luke ; on the contrary, as we have recognized the mythical character of the former, we should have no resource but to adhere, with our modern critics,[7] to the narrative of Luke, and surrender that of Matthew.   But is not Luke's narrative of the same nature as that of Matthew, and instead of having to choose between the two, must we not deny to both an historical character?   The answer to this question will be found in the succeeding examination.

§ 38.

THE PRESENTATION OF JESUS IN THE TEMPLE.

The narrative of the presentation of Jesus in the temple (Luke ii. 22) seems, at the first glance, to bear a thoroughly historical stamp.   A double law, on the one hand, prescribing to the mother an offering of purification, on the other, requiring the redemption of the first-born son, leads the parents of Jesus to Jerusalem and to the temple.   Here they meet with a devout man, absorbed in the expectation of the Messiah, named Simeon.   Many expositors hold this Simeon to be the same with the Rabbi Simeon, the son of Hillel, his successor as president of the Sanhedrim, and the father of Gamaliel ; some even identify him with the Sameas of Josephus,[1] and attach importance to his pretended descent from David, because this descent makes him a relative of Jesus, and helps to explain the following scene naturally ; but this hypothesis is improbable, for Luke would hardly have introduced so celebrated a personage by the meagre designation, ἄνθρωπός τις, (a certain man).[2]   Without this hypothesis, however, the scene between the parents of Jesus and Simeon, as also the part played by Anna the prophetess, seems to admit of a very natural explanation.   There is no necessity for supposing, with the

---

[7] Schleiermacher, Ueber den Lukas, s. 47.   Schneckenburger, ut sup.
[1] Antiq. xiv. ix. 4, xv. i. 1 and x. 4.
[2] The Evang. Nicodemi indeed calls him, c. xvi. ὁ μέγας διδάσκαλος, and the Protev. Jacobi, c. xxiv. makes him a priest or even high priest, vid. Varr. ap. Thilo Cod. Apocr. N. T. 1, s. 271, comp. 203.

author of the Natural History,[3] that Simeon was previously aware of the hope
cherished by Mary that she was about to give birth to the Messiah ; we need
only, with Paulus and others, conceive the facts in the following manner.
Animated, like many of that period, with the hope of the speedy advent of
the Messiah, Simeon receives, probably in a dream, the assurance that before
his death he will be permitted to see the expected deliverer of his nation.
One day, in obedience to an irresistible impulse, he visited the temple, and
on this very day Mary brought thither her child, whose beauty at once
attracted his notice ; on learning the child's descent from David, the attention
and interest of Simeon were excited to a degree that induced Mary to disclose
to him the hopes which were reposed on this scion of ancient royalty, with the
extraordinary occurrences by which they had been called into existence.
These hopes Simeon embraced with confidence, and in enthusiastic language
gave utterance to his messianic expectations and forebodings, under the conviction that they would be fulfilled in this child.   Still less do we need the
supposition of the author of the Natural History with respect to Anna, namely,
that she was one of the women who assisted at the birth of the infant Jesus,
and was thus acquainted beforehand with the marvels and the hopes that
had clustered round his cradle ; she had heard the words of Simeon, and
being animated by the same sentiments, she gave them her approval.

Simple as this explanation appears, it is not less arbitrary than we have
already found other specimens of natural interpretation.   The evangelist nowhere says, that the parents of Jesus had communicated anything concerning
their extraordinary hopes to Simeon, before he poured forth his inspired
words ; on the contrary, the point of his entire narrative consists in the idea
that the aged saint had, by virtue of the spirit with which he was filled,
instantaneously discerned in Jesus the messianic child, and the reason why
the co-operation of the Holy Spirit is insisted on, is to make it evident how
Simeon was enabled, without any previous information, to recognise in Jesus
the promised child, and at the same time to foretel the course of his destiny.
Our canonical Gospel refers Simeon's recognition of Jesus to a supernatural
principle resident in Simeon himself ; the *Evangelium infantiæ arabicum* refers
it to something objective in the appearance of Jesus [4]—far more in the spirit
of the original narrative than the natural interpretation, for it retains the
miraculous element.   But, apart from the general reasons against the credibility of miracles, the admission of a miracle in this instance is attended with
a special difficulty, because no worthy object for an extraordinary manifestation
of divine power is discoverable.   For, that the above occurrence during the
infancy of Jesus served to disseminate and establish in more distant circles
the persuasion of his Messiahship, there is no indication ; we must therefore,
with the Evangelist, limit the object of these supernatural communications to
Simeon and Anna, to whose devout hopes was vouchsafed the special reward
of having their eyes enlightened to discern the messianic child.   But that
miracles should be ordained for such occasional and isolated objects, is not
reconcileable with just ideas of divine providence.

Thus here again we find reason to doubt the historical character of the
narrative, especially as we have found by a previous investigation that it is
annexed to narratives purely mythical.   Simeon's real expressions, say some
commentators, were probably these : Would that I might yet behold the new-
born Messiah, even as I now bear this child in my arms !—a simple wish

---

[3] 1 Th. s. 205 ff.
[4] Cap. vi. *Viditque illum Simeon senex instar columnæ lucis refulgentem, cum Domina
Maria virgo, mater ejus, ulnis suis eum gestaret,—et circumdabant eum angeli instar circuli,
celebrantes illum,* etc.   Ap. Thilo, p. 71.

which was transformed *ex eventu* by tradition, into the positive enunciations now read in Luke[5]. But this explanation is incomplete, for the *reason* why such stories became current concerning Jesus, must be shown in the relative position of this portion of the evangelical narrative, and in the interest of the primitive Christian legend. As to the former, this scene at the presentation of Jesus in the temple is obviously parallel with that at the circumcision of the Baptist, narrated by the same evangelist; for on both occasions, at the inspiration of the Holy Spirit, God is praised for the birth of a national deliverer, and the future destiny of the child is prophetically announced, in the one case by the father, in the other by a devout stranger. That this scene is in the former instance connected with the circumcision, in the latter with the presentation in the temple, seems to be accidental; when however the legend had once, in relation to Jesus, so profusely adorned the presentation in the temple, the circumcision must be left, as we have above found it, without embellishment.

As to the second spring in the formation of our narrative, namely, the interest of the Christian legend, it is easy to conceive how this would act. He who, as a man, so clearly proved himself to be the Messiah, must also, it was thought, even as a child have been recognisable in his true character to an eye rendered acute by the Holy Spirit; he who at a later period, by his powerful words and deeds, manifested himself to be the Son of God, must surely, even before he could speak or move with freedom, have borne the stamp of divinity. Moreover if men, moved by the Spirit of God, so early pressed Jesus with love and reverence in their arms, then was the spirit that animated him not an impious one, as his enemies alleged; and if a holy seer had predicted, along with the high destiny of Jesus, the conflict which he had to undergo, and the anguish which his fate would cause his mother,[6] then it was assuredly no chance, but a divine plan, that led him into the depths of abasement on the way to his ultimate exaltation.

This view of the narrative is thus countenanced positively by the nature of the fact,—and negatively by the difficulties attending any other explanation. One cannot but wonder, therefore, how Schleiermacher can be influenced against it by an observation which did not prevent him from taking a similar view of the history of the Baptist's birth, namely, that the narrative is too natural to have been fabricated[7]; and how Neander can argue against it, from exaggerated ideas of the more imposing traits which the mythus would have substituted for our narrative. Far from allowing a purification for the mother of Jesus, and a redemption for himself, to take place in the ordinary manner, Neander thinks the mythus would have depicted an angelic appearance, intended to deter Mary or the priest from an observance inconsistent with the dignity of Jesus.[8] As though even the Christianity of Paul did not maintain that Christ was *born under the law* γενόμενος ὑπὸ νόμον (Gal. iv. 4); how much more then the Judaic Christianity whence these narratives are derived! As though Jesus himself had not, agreeably to this view of his position, submitted to baptism, and according to the Evangelist whose narrative is in question, without any previous expostulation on the part of the

---

[5] Thus E. F. in the treatise, on the two first chapters of Matth. and Luke. In Henke's Mag. 5 bd. s. 169 f. A similar half measure is in Matthäi, Synopse der 4 Evan. s. 3, 5 f.

[6] With the words of Simeon addressed to Mary: καὶ σοῦ δὲ αὐτῆς τὴν ψυχὴν διελεύσεται ῥομφαία (v. 35) comp. the words in the messianic psalm of sorrow, xxii. 21: ῥῦσαι ἀπὸ ῥομφαίας τὴν ψυχήν μου.

[7] Schleiermacher, Ueber den Lukas, s. 37. Compare on the other hand the observations in § 18, with those of the authors there quoted, Note 19.

[8] Neander here (s. 24 f.) mistakes the apocryphal for the mythical, as he had before done the poetical.

Baptist !   Of more weight is Schleiermacher's other observation, that supposing this narrative to be merely a poetical creation, its author would scarcely
have placed by the side of Simeon Anna, of whom he makes no poetical use,
still less would he have characterized her with minuteness, after designating
his principal personage with comparative negligence.   But to represent the
dignity of the child Jesus as being proclaimed by the mouth of two witnesses,
and especially to associate a prophetess with a prophet—this is just the
symmetrical grouping that the legend loves.   The detailed description of
Anna may have been taken from a real person who, at the time when our
narrative originated, was yet held in remembrance for her distinguished piety.
As to the Evangelist's omission to assign her any particular speech, it is to be
observed that her office is to spread abroad the glad news, while that of
Simeon is to welcome Jesus into the temple : hence as the part of the
prophetess was to be performed behind the scenes, her precise words could
not be given.   As in a former instance Schleiermacher supposes the Evangelist
to have received his history from the lips of the shepherds, so here he conceives him to have been indebted to Anna, of whose person he has so vivid
a recollection ; Neander approves this opinion—not the only straw thrown
out by Schleiermacher, to which this theologian has clung in the emergencies
of modern criticism.

At this point also, where Luke's narrative leaves Jesus for a series of years,
there is a concluding sentence on the prosperous growth of the child (v. 40) ;
a similar sentence occurs at the corresponding period in the life of the
Baptist, and both recall the analogous form of expression found in the history
of Samson (Judg. xiii. 24 f.).

§ 39.

RETROSPECT.   DIFFERENCE BETWEEN MATTHEW AND LUKE AS TO THE ORIGINAL RESIDENCE OF THE PARENTS OF JESUS.

In the foregoing examinations we have called in question the historical
credibility of the Gospel narratives concerning the genealogy, birth, and
childhood of Jesus, on two grounds : first, because the narratives taken
separately contain much that will not bear an historical interpretation ; and
secondly, because the parallel narratives of Matthew and Luke exclude each
other, so that it is impossible for both to be true, and one must necessarily be
false ; this imputation however may attach to either, and consequently to
both.   One of the contradictions between the two narratives extends from the
commencement of the history of the childhood to the point we have now
reached ; it has therefore often come in our way, but we have been unable
hitherto to give it our consideration, because only now that we have completely reviewed the scenes in which it figures, have we materials enough on
which to found a just estimate of its consequences.   We refer to the divergency that exists between Matthew and Luke, in relation to the original
dwelling-place of the parents of Jesus.

Luke, from the very beginning of his history, gives Nazareth as the abode of
Joseph and Mary ; here the angel seeks Mary (i. 26) ; here we must suppose
Mary's house οἶκος, to be situated (i. 56) ; from hence the parents of Jesus
journey to Bethlehem on account of the census (ii. 4) : and hither, when
circumstances permit, they return as to their own city πόλις αὐτῶν (v. 39).
Thus in Luke, Nazareth is evidently the proper residence of the parents of
Jesus, and they only visit Bethlehem for a short time, owing to a casual
circumstance.

In Matthew, it is not stated in the first instance where Joseph and Mary resided. According to ii. 1, Jesus was born in Bethlehem, and since no extraordinary circumstances are said to have led his parents thither, it appears as if Matthew supposed them to have been originally resident in Bethlehem. Here he makes the parents with the child receive the visit of the magi ; then follows the flight into Egypt, on returning from which Joseph is only deterred from again seeking Judea by a special divine admonition, which directs him to Nazareth in Galilee (ii. 22). This last particular renders certain what had before seemed probable, namely, that Matthew did not with Luke suppose Nazareth, but Bethlehem, to have been the original dwelling-place of the parents of Jesus, and that he conceived their final settlement at Nazareth to have been the result of unforeseen circumstances.

This contradiction is generally glided over without suspicion. The reason of this lies in the peculiar character of Matthew's Gospel, a character on which a modern writer has built the assertion that this Evangelist does not contradict Luke concerning the original residence of the parents of Jesus, for he says nothing at all on the subject, troubling himself as little about topographical as chronological accuracy. He mentions the later abode of Joseph and Mary, and the birth-place of Jesus, solely because it was possible to connect with them Old Testament prophecies ; as the abode of the parent of Jesus prior to his birth furnished no opportunity for a similar quotation, Matthew has left it entirely unnoticed, an omission which however, in his style of narration, is no proof that he was ignorant of their abode, or that he supposed it to have been Bethlehem.[1] But even admitting that the silence of Matthew on the earlier residence of the parents of Jesus in Nazareth, and on the peculiar circumstances that caused Bethlehem to be his birth-place, proves nothing ; yet the above supposition requires that the exchange of Bethlehem for Nazareth should be so represented as to give some intimation, or at least to leave a possibility, that we should understand the former to be a merely temporary abode, and the journey to the latter a return homeward. Such an intimation would have been given, had Matthew attributed to the angelic vision, that determined Joseph's settlement in Nazareth after his return from Egypt, such communications as the following : Return now into the land of Israel and into your native city Nazareth, for there is no further need of your presence in Bethlehem, since the prophecy that your messianic child should be born in that place is already fulfilled. But as Matthew is alleged to be generally indifferent about localities, we will be moderate, and demand no positive intimation from him, but simply make the negative requisition, that he should not absolutely exclude the idea, that Nazareth was the original dwelling-place of the parents of Jesus. This requisition would be met if, instead of a special cause being assigned for the choice of Nazareth as a residence, it had been merely said that the parents of Jesus returned by divine direction into the land of Israel and betook themselves to Nazareth. It would certainly seem abrupt enough, if without any preamble Nazareth were all at once named instead of Bethlehem : of this our narrator was conscious, and for this reason he has detailed the causes that led to the change (ii. 22). But instead of doing this, as we have shown that he must have done it had he, with Luke, known Nazareth to be the original dwelling-place of the parents of Jesus, his account has precisely the opposite bearing, which undeniably proves that his supposition was the reverse of Luke's. For when Matthew represents Joseph on his return from Egypt as being prevented from going to Judea solely by his fear of Archelaus, he ascribes to him an inclina-

---

[1] Olshausen, bibl. Comm. 1. s. 142 f.

tion to proceed to that province—an inclination which is unaccountable if the affair of the census alone had taken him to Bethlehem, and which is only to be explained by the supposition that he had formerly dwelt there.   On the other hand as Matthew makes the danger from Archelaus (together with the fulfilment of a prophecy) the sole cause of the settlement of Joseph and Mary at Nazareth, he cannot have supposed that this was their original home, for in that case there would have been an independently decisive cause which would have rendered any other superfluous.

Thus the difficulty of reconciling Matthew with Luke, in the present instance, turns upon the impossibility of conceiving how the parents of Jesus could, on their return from Egypt, have it in contemplation to proceed a second time to Bethlehem unless this place had formerly been their home. The efforts of commentators have accordingly been chiefly applied to the task of finding other reasons for the existence of such an inclination in Joseph and Mary.   Such efforts are of a very early date.   Justin Martyr, holding by Luke, who, while he decidedly states Nazareth to be the dwelling-place of the parents of Jesus, yet does not represent Joseph as a complete stranger in Bethlehem (for he makes it the place from which he lineally sprang), seems to suppose that Nazareth was the dwelling-place and Bethlehem the birth-place of Joseph,[2] and Credner thinks that this passage of Justin points out the source, and presents the reconciliation of the divergent statements of our two Evangelists.[3]   But it is far from presenting a reconciliation.   For as Nazareth is still supposed to be the place which Joseph had chosen as his home, no reason appears why, on his return from Egypt, he should all at once desire to exchange his former residence for his birth-place, especially as, according to Justin himself, the cause of his former journey to Bethlehem had not been a plan of settling there, but simply the census—a cause which, after the flight, no longer existed.   Thus the statement of Justin leans to the side of Luke and does not suffice to bring him into harmony with Matthew.   That it was the source of our two evangelical accounts is still less credible ; for how could the narrative of Matthew, which mentions neither Nazareth as a dwelling-place, nor the census as the cause of a journey to Bethlehem, originate in the statement of Justin, to which these facts are essential ?   Arguing generally, where on the one hand, there are two diverging statements, on the other, an insufficient attempt to combine them, it is certain that the latter is not the parent and the two former its offspring, but vice versâ. Moreover, in this department of attempting reconciliations, we have already, in connection with the genealogies, learned to estimate Justin or his authorities.

A more thorough attempt at reconciliation is made in the *Evangelium de nativitate Mariæ*, and has met with much approval from modern theologians. According to this apocryphal book, the house of Mary's parents was at Nazareth, and although she was brought up in the temple at Jerusalem and there espoused to Joseph, she returned after this occurrence to her parents in Galilee.   Joseph, on the contrary, was not only born at Bethlehem, as Justin seems to intimate, but also lived there, and thither brought home his betrothed.[4]   But this mode of conciliation, unlike the other, is favourable to

---

[2] Dial. c. Trypho, 78 : Joseph came from Nazareth, *where he lived*, to Bethlehem, *whence he was*, to be enrolled, ἀνελήλυθει ('Ιωσὴφ) ἀπὸ Ναζαρὲτ, ἔνθα ᾦκει, εἰς Βηθλεὲμ, ὅθεν ἦν, ἀπογράψασθαι.   The words ὅθεν ἦν might however be understood as signifying merely the place of his tribe, especially if Justin's addition be considered : *For his race was of the tribe of Judah, which inhabits that land*, ἀπὸ γὰρ τῆς κατοικούσης τὴν γῆν ἐκείνην φυλῆς 'Ιούδα τὸ γένος ἦν.

[3] Beiträge zur Einleit. in das N. T. 1. s. 217.   Comp. Hoffmann, s. 238 f. 277 ff.

[4] C. I. 8. 10.

Matthew and disadvantageous to Luke. For the census with its attendant circumstances is left out, and necessarily so, because if Joseph were at home in Bethlehem, and only went to Nazareth to fetch his bride, the census could not be represented as the reason why he returned to Bethlehem, for he would have done so in the ordinary course of things, after a few days' absence. Above all, had Bethlehem been his home, he would not on his arrival have sought an inn where there was no room for him, but would have taken Mary under his own roof. Hence modern expositors who wish to avail themselves of the outlet presented by the apocryphal book, and yet to save the census of Luke from rejection, maintain that Joseph did indeed dwell, and carry on his trade, in Bethlehem, but that he possessed no house of his own in that place, and the census recalling him thither sooner than he had anticipated, he had not yet provided one.[5] But Luke makes it appear, not only that the parents of Jesus were not yet settled in Bethlehem, but that they were not even desirous of settling there; that, on the contrary, it was their intention to depart after the shortest possible stay. This opinion supposes great poverty on the part of Joseph and Mary; Olshausen, on the other hand, prefers enriching them, for the sake of conciliating the difference in question. He supposes that they had property both in Bethlehem and Nazareth, and could therefore have settled in either place, but unknown circumstances inclined them, on their return from Egypt, to fix upon Bethlehem until the divine warning came as a preventive. Thus Olshausen declines particularizing the reason why it appeared desirable to the parents of Jesus to settle in Bethlehem; but Heydenreich [6] and others have supplied his omission, by assuming that it must have seemed to them most fitting for him, who was pre-eminently the Son of David, to be brought up in David's own city.

Here, however, theologians would do well to take for their model the honesty of Neander, and to confess with him that of this intention on the part of Joseph and Mary to settle at Bethlehem, and of the motives which induced them to give up the plan, Luke knows nothing, and that they rest on the authority of Matthew alone. But what reason does Matthew present for this alleged change of place? The visit of the magi, the massacre of the infants, visions in dreams—events whose evidently unhistorical character quite disqualifies them from serving as proofs of a change of residence on the part of the parents of Jesus. On the other hand Neander, while confessing that the author of the first Gospel was probably ignorant of the particular circumstances which, according to Luke, led to the journey to Bethlehem, and hence took Bethlehem to be the original residence of the parents of Jesus, maintains that there may be an essential agreement between the two accounts though that agreement did not exist in the consciousness of the writers.[7] But, once more, what cause does Luke assign for the journey to Bethlehem? The census, which our previous investigations have shown to be as frail a support for this statement, as the infanticide and its consequences for that of Matthew. Hence here again it is not possible by admitting the inacquaintance of the one narrator with what the other presents to vindicate the statements of both; since each has against him, not only the ignorance of the other, but the improbability of his own narrative.

But we must distinguish more exactly the respective aspects and elements of the two accounts. As, according to the above observations, the change of residence on the part of the parents of Jesus, is in Matthew so linked with the unhistorical data of the infanticide and the flight into Egypt, that without

[5] Paulus, exeg. Handb. 1, a, s. 178.
[6] Ueber die Unzulässigkeit der mythischen Auffassung u. s. f. 1, s. 101.
[7] L. J. Ch. s. 33.

these every cause for the migration disappears, we turn to Luke's account, which makes the parents of Jesus resident in the same place, both after and before the birth of Jesus.   But in Luke, the circumstance of Jesus being born in another place than where his parents dwelt, is made to depend on an event as unhistorical as the marvels of Matthew, namely the census.   If this be surrendered, no motive remains that could induce the parents of Jesus to take a formidable journey at so critical a period for Mary, and in this view of the case Matthew's representation seems the more probable one, that Jesus was born in the home of his parents and not in a strange place.   Hitherto, however, we have only obtained the negative result, that the evangelical statements, according to which the parents of Jesus lived at first in another place than that in which they subsequently settled, and Jesus was born elsewhere than in the home of his parents, are destitute of any guarantee ; we have yet to seek for a positive conclusion by inquiring what was really the place of his birth.

On this point we are drawn in two opposite directions.   In both Gospels we find Bethlehem stated to be the birth-place of Jesus, and there is, as we have seen, no impediment to our supposing that it was the habitual residence of his parents ; on the other hand, the two Gospels again concur in representing Nazareth as the ultimate dwelling-place of Joseph and his family, and it is only an unsupported statement that forbids us to regard it as their original residence, and consequently as the birth-place of Jesus.   It would be impossible to decide between these contradictory probabilities were both equally strong, but as soon as the slightest inequality between them is discovered, we are warranted to form a conclusion.   Let us first test the opinion, that the Galilean city Nazareth was the final residence of Jesus.   This is not supported barely by the passages immediately under consideration, in the 2nd chapters of Matthew and Luke ;—it rests on an uninterrupted series of data drawn from the Gospels and from the earliest church history.   The Galilean, the Nazarene—were the epithets constantly applied to Jesus.   As Jesus of Nazareth he was introduced by Philip to Nathanael, whose responsive question was, Can any good thing come out of Nazareth?   Nazareth is described, not only as the place where he was brought up, οὗ ἦν τεθραμμένος (Luke iv. 16 f.), but also as his country ; πατρὶς (Matt. xiii. 34, Mark vi. 1).   He was known among the populace as Jesus of Nazareth (Luke xviii. 37.), and invoked under this name by the demons (Mark i. 24).   The inscription on the cross styles him a Nazarene (John xix. 19), and after his resurrection his apostles everywhere proclaimed him as Jesus of Nazareth (Acts ii. 22), and worked miracles in his name (Acts iii. 6).   His disciples too were long called Nazarenes, and it was not until a late period that this name was exclusively applied to a heretical sect. [8]   This appellation proves, if not that Jesus was born in Nazareth, at least that he resided in that place for a considerable time ; and as, according to a probable tradition (Luke iv. 16 f. parall.), Jesus, during his public life, paid but transient visits to Nazareth, this prolonged residence must be referred to the earlier part of his life, which he passed in the bosom of his family.   Thus his family, at least his parents, must have lived in Nazareth during his childhood ; and if it be admitted that they once dwelt there, it follows that they dwelt there always, for we have no historical grounds for supposing a change of residence : so that this one of the two contradictory propositions has as much certainty as we can expect, in a fact belonging to so remote and obscure a period.

Neither does the other proposition, however, that Jesus was born in Beth-

---

[8] Tertull. adv. Marcion iv. 8.   Epiphan. hær. xxix. 1.

lehem, rest solely on the statement of our Gospels; it is sanctioned by an expectation, originating in a prophetic passage, that the Messiah would be born at Bethlehem (comp. with Matt. ii. 5 f., John vii. 42). But this is a dangerous support, which they who wish to retain as historical the Gospel statement, that Jesus was born in Bethlehem, will do well to renounce. For wherever we find a narrative which recounts the accomplishment of a long-expected event, a strong suspicion must arise, that the narrative owes its origin solely to the pre-existent belief that that event would be accomplished. But our suspicion is converted into certainty when we find this belief to be groundless; and this is the case here, for the alleged issue must have confirmed a false interpretation of a prophetic passage. Thus this prophetic evidence of the birth of Jesus in Bethlehem, deprives the historical evidence, which lies in the 2nd chapters of Matthew and Luke, of its value, since the latter seems to be built on the former, and consequently shares its fall. Any other voucher for this fact is however sought in vain. Nowhere else in the New Testament is the birth of Jesus at Bethlehem mentioned; nowhere does he appear in any relation with his alleged birth-place, or pay it the honour of a visit, which he yet does not deny to the unworthy Nazareth; nowhere does he appeal to the fact as a concomitant proof of his messiahship, although he had the most direct inducements to do so, for many were repelled from him by his Galilean origin, and defended their prejudice by referring to the necessity, that the Messiah should come out of Bethlehem, the city of David (John vii. 42).[9] John does not, it is true, say that these objections were uttered in the presence of Jesus;[10] but as, immediately before, he had annexed to a discourse of Jesus a comment of his own, to the effect that the Holy Ghost was not yet given, so here he might very suitably have added, in explanation of the doubts expressed by the people, that they did not yet know that Jesus was born in Bethlehem. Such an observation will be thought too superficial and trivial for an apostle like John: thus much however must be admitted; he had occasion *repeatedly* to mention the popular notion that Jesus was a native of Nazareth, and the consequent prejudice against him; had he then known otherwise, he must have added a corrective remark, if he wished to avoid leaving the false impression, that he also believed Jesus to be a Nazarene. As it is, we find Nathanael, John i. 46, alleging this objection, without having his opinion rectified either mediately or immediately, for he nowhere learns that the *good thing* did not really come out of Nazareth, and the conclusion he is left to draw is, that even out of Nazareth something good can come. In general, if Jesus were really born in Bethlehem, though but fortuitously (according to Luke's representation), it is incomprehensible, considering the importance of this fact to the article of his messiahship, that even his own adherents should always call him the Nazarene, instead of opposing to this epithet, pronounced by his opponents with polemical emphasis, the honourable title of the Bethlehemite.

Thus the evangelical statement that Jesus was born at Bethlehem is destitute of all valid historical evidence; nay, it is contravened by positive historical facts. We have seen reason to conclude that the parents of Jesus lived at Nazareth, not only after the birth of Jesus, but also, as we have no counter evidence, prior to that event, and that, no credible testimony to the contrary existing, Jesus was probably not born at any other place than the home of his parents. With this twofold conclusion, the supposition that Jesus was born at Bethlehem is irreconcileable: it can therefore cost us no further effort to

---

[9] Comp. K. Ch. L. Schmidt, in Schmidt's Bibliothek, 3, 1, s. 123 f.; Kaiser, bibl. Theol. I, s. 230.

[10] On this Heydenreich rests his defence, Ueber die Unzulässigkeit. 1. s. 99.

decide that Jesus was born, not in Bethlehem, but, as we have no trustworthy indications that point elsewhere, in all probability at Nazareth.

The relative position of the two evangelists on this point may be thus stated. Each of their accounts is partly correct, and partly incorrect: Luke is right in maintaining the identity of the earlier with the later residence of the parents of Jesus, and herein Matthew is wrong; again, Matthew is right in maintaining the identity of the birth-place of Jesus with the dwelling-place of his parents, and here the error is on the side of Luke.   Further, Luke is entirely correct in making the parents of Jesus reside in Nazareth before, as well as after, the birth of Jesus, while Matthew has only half the truth, namely, that they were established there after his birth; but in the statement that Jesus was born at Bethlehem both are decidedly wrong.   The source of all the error of their narratives, is the Jewish opinion with which they fell in, that the Messiah must be born at Bethlehem; the source of all their truth, is the fact which lay before them, that he always passed for a Nazarene; finally, the cause of the various admixture of the true and the false in both, and the preponderance of the latter in Matthew, is the different position held by the two writers in relation to the above data.   Two particulars were to be reconciled—the historical fact that Jesus was universally reputed to be a Nazarene, and the prophetic requisition that, as Messiah, he should be born at Bethlehem.   Matthew, or the legend which he followed, influenced by the ruling tendency to apply the prophecies, observable in his Gospel, effected the desired reconciliation in such a manner, that the greatest prominence was given to Bethlehem, the locality pointed out by the prophet; this was represented as the original home of the parents of Jesus, and Nazareth merely as a place of refuge, recommended by a subsequent turn of events.   Luke, on the contrary, more bent on historic detail, either adopted or created that form of the legend, which attaches the greatest important to Nazareth, making it the original dwelling-place of the parents of Jesus, and regarding the sojourn in Bethlehem as a temporary one, the consequence of a casual occurrence.

Such being the state of the case, no one, we imagine, will be inclined either with Schleiermacher,[11] to leave the question concerning the relation of the two narratives to the real facts undecided, or with Sieffert,[12] to pronounce exclusively in favour of Luke.[13]

---

[11] Ueber den Lukas, s. 49.   There is a similar hesitation in Thelte, Biographie Jesu, § 15.
[12] Ueber den Ursprung u. s. w., s. 68 f. u. s. 158.
[13] Comp. Ammon. Fortbildung, 1, s. 194 ff.;   De Wette, exeget. Handb. 1, 2, s. 24 f.; George, s. 84 ff.   That different narrators may give different explanations of the same fact, and that these different explanations may afterwards be united in one book, is proved by many examples in the O. T.   Thus in Genesis, three derivations are given of the name of Isaac; two of that of Jacob (xxv. 26. xxvii. 16), and so of Edom and Beersheba (xxi. 31. xxvi. 33).   Comp. De Wette, Kritik der mos. Gesch., s. 110. 118 ff. and my Streitschriften, 1, 1, s. 83 ff.

CHAPTER V.

THE FIRST VISIT TO THE TEMPLE, AND THE EDUCATION OF JESUS.

§ 40.

JESUS, WHEN TWELVE YEARS OLD, IN THE TEMPLE.

THE Gospel of Matthew passes in silence over the entire period from the return of the parents of Jesus out of Egypt, to the baptism of Jesus by John : and even Luke has nothing to tell us of the long interval between the early childhood of Jesus and his maturity, beyond a single incident—his demeanour on a visit to the temple in his twelfth year (ii. 41–52). This anecdote, out of the early youth of Jesus is, as Hess has truly remarked,[1] distinguished from the narratives hitherto considered, belonging to his childhood, by the circumstance that Jesus no longer, as in the latter, holds a merely passive position, but presents an active proof of his high destination ; a proof which has always been especially valued, as indicating the moment in which the consciousness of that destination was kindled in Jesus.[2]

In his twelfth year, the period at which, according to Jewish usage, the boy became capable of an independent participation in the sacred rites, the parents of Jesus, as this narrative informs us, took him for the first time to the Passover. At the expiration of the feast, the parents bent their way homewards ; that their son was missing gave them no immediate anxiety, because they supposed him to be among their travelling companions, and it was not until after they had accomplished a day's journey, and in vain sought their son among their kinsfolk and acquaintance, that they turned back to Jerusalem to look for him there. This conduct on the part of the parents of Jesus may with reason excite surprise. It seems inconsistent with the carefulness which it has been thought incumbent on us to attribute to them, that they should have allowed the divine child entrusted to their keeping, to remain so long out of their sight ; and hence they have on many sides been accused of neglect and a dereliction of duty, in the instance before us.[3] It has been urged, as a general consideration in vindication of Joseph and Mary, that the greater freedom permitted to the boy is easily conceivable as part of a liberal method of education ;[4] but even according to our modern ideas, it would seem more than liberal for parents to let a boy of twelve years remain out of their sight during so long an interval as our narrative supposes ; how far less reconcileable must it then be with the more rigid views of education held by the

---

[1] Hess, Geschichte Jesu, 1, s. 110.
[2] Olshausen, bibl. Comm. 1, s. 145 f.
[3] Olshausen, ut sup. 1. 150.
[4] Hase, Leben Jesu, § 37.

ancients, not excepting the Jews ? It is remarked however, that viewing the case as an extraordinary one, the parents of Jesus knew their child, and they could therefore very well confide in his understanding and character, so far as to be in no fear that any danger would accrue to him from his unusual free-dom ;[5] but we can perceive from their subsequent anxiety, that they were not so entirely at ease on that head. Thus their conduct must be admitted to be such as we should not have anticipated ; but it is not consequently incredible nor does it suffice to render the entire narrative improbable, for the parents of Jesus are no saints to us, that we should not impute to them any fault.

Returned to Jerusalem, they find their son on the third day in the temple, doubtless in one of the outer halls, in the midst of an assembly of doctors, en-gaged in a conversation with them, and exciting universal astonishment (v. 45 f.). From some indications it would seem that Jesus held a higher position in the presence of the doctors, than could belong to a boy of twelve years. The word καθεζόμενον (*sitting*) has excited scruples, for according to Jewish records, it was not until after the death of the Rabbi Gamaliel, an event long subse-quent to the one described in our narrative, that the pupils of the rabbins sat, they having previously been required to stand [6] when in the school ; but this Jewish tradition is of doubtful authority.[7] It has also been thought a diffi-culty, that Jesus does not merely hear the doctors, but also asks them ques-tions, thus appearing to assume the position of their teacher. Such is indeed the representation of the apocryphal Gospels, for in them Jesus, before he is twelve years old, perplexes all the doctors by his questions,[8] and reveals to his instructor in the alphabet the mystical significance of the characters ;[9] while at the above visit to the temple he proposes controversial questions,[10] such as that touching the Messiah's being at once David's Son and Lord (Matt. xxii. 41), and proceeds to throw light on all departments of knowledge.[11] If the expressions ἐρωτᾶν and ἀποκρίνεσθαι implied that Jesus played the part of a teacher in this scene, so unnatural a feature in the evangelical narrative would render the whole suspicious.[12] But there is nothing to render this interpreta-tion of the words necessary, for according to Jewish custom, rabbinical teach-ing was of such a kind that not only did the masters interrogate the pupils, but the pupils interrogated the masters, when they wished for explanations on any point.[13] We may with the more probability suppose that the writer in-tended to attribute to Jesus such questions as suited a boy, because he, appar-ently not without design, refers the astonishment of the doctors, not to his questions, but to that in which he could best show himself in the light of an intelligent pupil—namely, to his answers. A more formidable difficulty is the statement, that the boy Jesus sat *in the midst of the doctors*, ἐν μέσῳ τῶν διδασ-κάλων. For we learn from Paul (Acts xxii. 3) the position that became a pupil, when he says that he was brought up *at the feet* (παρὰ τοὺς πόδας) of Gamaliel : it being the custom for the rabbins to be placed on chairs, while their pupils sat on the ground,[14] and did not take their places among their masters. It has indeed been thought that ἐν μέσῳ might be so explained as

[5] Heydenreich, über die Unzulässigkeit u. s. f. 1, s. 103.
[6] Megillah, f. 21, apud Lightfoot, in loc.
[7] Vid. Kuinöl, in Luc. p. 353.
[8] Evang. Thomæ, c. vi. ff. Ap. Thilo. p. 288 ff. and Evang. infant. arab. c. xlviii. p. 123, Thilo.
[9] Ibid.
[10] Evang. infant. arab. c. l.
[11] Ibid. c. l. and li. ; comp. ev. Thomæ, c. xix.
[12] Olshausen confesses this, s. 151.
[13] For proofs (e g. Hieros. Taanith, lxvii. 4) see Wetstein and Lightfoot, in loc.
[14] Lightfoot, Horæ, p. 742.

to signify, either that Jesus sat between the doctors, who are supposed to have been elevated on chairs, while Jesus and the other pupils are pictured as sitting on the ground between them,[15] or merely that he was in the company of doctors, that is, in the synagogue ;[16] but according to the strict sense of the words, the expression καθέζεσθαι ἐν μέσῳ τινῶν appears to signify, if not as Schöttgen believes,[17] *in majorem Jesu gloriam*, a place of pre-eminent honour, at least a position of equal dignity with that occupied by the rest.* It need only be asked, would it harmonize with the spirit of our narrative to substitute καθεζόμενον παρὰ τοὺς πόδας τῶν διδασκάλων for καθ. ἐν μέσω τ. δ.? the answer will certainly be in the negative, and it will then be inevitable to admit, that our narrative places Jesus in another relation to the doctors than that of a learner, though the latter is the only natural one for a boy of twelve, however highly gifted.   For Olshausen's position,[18]—that in Jesus nothing was formed from without, by the instrumentality of another's wisdom, because this would be inconsistent with the character of the Messiah, as absolutely self-determined, —contradicts a dogma of the church which he himself advances, namely, that Jesus in his manifestation as man, followed the regular course of human development.   For not only is it in the nature of this development to be gradual, but also, and still more essentially, to be dependent, whether it be mental or physical, on the interchange of reception and influence.   To deny this in relation to the physical life of Jesus—to say, for example, that the food which he took did not serve for the nourishment and growth of his body by real assimilation, but merely furnished occasion for him to reproduce himself from within, would strike every one as Docetism ; and is the analogous proposition in relation to his spiritual development, namely, that he appropriated nothing from without, and used what he heard from others merely as a voice to evoke one truth after another from the recesses of his own mind—is this anything else than a more refined Docetism ?   Truly, if we attempt to form a conception of the conversation of Jesus with the doctors in the temple according to this theory, we make anything but a natural scene of it.   It is not to be supposed that he taught, nor properly speaking that he was taught, but that the discourse of the doctors merely gave an impetus to his power of teaching himself, and was the occasion for an ever-brightening light to rise upon him, especially on the subject of his own destination.   But in that case he would certainly have given utterance to his newly acquired knowledge ; so that the position of a teacher on the part of the boy would return upon us, a position which Olshausen himself pronounces to be preposterous.   At least such an indirect mode of teaching is involved as Ness subscribes to, when he supposes that Jesus, even thus early, made the first attempt to combat the prejudices which swayed in the synagogue, exposing to the doctors, by means of good-humoured questions and requests for explanation, such as are willingly permitted to a boy, the weakness of many of their dogmas.[19]   But even such a position on the part of a boy of twelve, is inconsistent with the true process of human development, through which it behoved the God-Man himself to pass.   Discourse of this kind from a boy must, we grant, have excited the astonishment of all the hearers ; nevertheless the expression ἐξίσταντο πάντες οἱ ἀκούοντες αὐτοῦ (v. 47), looks too much like a panegyrical formula.[20]

---

[15] Paulus, s. 279.
[16] Kuinöl, s. 353 f.
[17] Horæ, ii. p. 886.
[18] Bibl. Comm. p. 151.
[19] Geschichte Jesu, I, s. 112.
[20] In the similar account also which Josephus gives us of himself when fourteen, it is easy to discern the exaggeration of a self-complacent man. Life, 2 : *Moreover, when I was a*

The narrative proceeds to tell us how the mother of Jesus reproached her son when she had found him thus, asking him why he had not spared his parents the anguish of their sorrowful search? To this Jesus returns an answer which forms the point of the entire narrative ; he asks whether they might not have known that he was to be sought nowhere else than in the house of his Father, in the temple? (v. 48 f.) One might be inclined to understand this designation of God as τοῦ πατρὸς generally, as implying that God was the Father of all men, and only in this sense the Father of Jesus. But this interpretation is forbidden, not only by the addition of the pronoun μοῦ, the above sense requiring ἡμῶν (as in Matt. vi. 9), but still more absolutely by the circumstance that the parents of Jesus did not understand these words (v. 50), a decided indication that they must have a special meaning, which can here be no other than the mystery of the Messiahship of Jesus, who as Messiah, was υἱὸς θεοῦ in a peculiar sense.* But that Jesus in his twelfth year had already the consciousness of his Messiahship, is a position which, although it may be consistently adopted from the orthodox point of view, and although it is not opposed to the regular human form of the development of Jesus, which even orthodoxy maintains, we are not here bound to examine. So also the natural explanation, which retains the above narrative as a history, though void of the miraculous, and which accordingly supposes the parents of Jesus, owing to a particular combination of circumstances, to have come even before his birth to a conviction of his Messiahship, and to have instilled this conviction into their son from his earliest childhood,—this too may make it plain how Jesus could be so clear as to his messianic relation to God ; but it can only do so by the hypothesis of an unprecedented coincidence of extraordinary accidents. We, on the contrary, who have renounced the previous incidents as historical, either in the supernatural or the natural sense, are unable to comprehend how the consciousness of his messianic destination could be so early developed in Jesus. For though the consciousness of a more subjective vocation, as that of a poet or an artist, which is dependent solely on the internal gifts of the individual (gifts which cannot long remain latent), may possibly be awakened very early ; an objective vocation, in which the conditions of external reality are a chief co-operator, as the vocation of the statesman, the general, the reformer of a religion, can hardly be so early evident to the most highly endowed individual, because for this a knowledge of cotemporary circumstances would be requisite, which only long observation and mature experience can confer. Of the latter kind is the vocation of the Messiah, and if this is implied in the words by which Jesus in his twelfth year justified his lingering in the temple, he cannot have uttered the words at that period.

In another point of view also, it is worthy of notice that the parents of Jesus are said (v. 50) not to have understood the words which he addressed to them. What did these words signify? That God was his Father, in whose house it behoved him to be. But that her son would in a specific sense be called a υἱὸς θεοῦ had been already made known to Mary by the annunciating angel (Luke i. 32, 35), and that he would have a peculiar relation to the temple she might infer, both from the above title, and from the striking reception which he had met with at his first presentation in the temple, when yet an infant. The parents of Jesus, or at least Mary, of whom it is repeatedly noticed that she carefully kept in her heart the extraordinary communications concerning her son, ought not to have been in the dark a single moment as

child, and about fourteen years of age, I was commended by all for the love I had to learning, on which account the high priests and principal men of the city came there frequently to me together, in order to know my opinion about the accurate understanding of points of the law.

to the meaning of his language on this occasion. But even at the presentation in the temple, we are told that the parents of Jesus marvelled at the discourse of Simeon (v. 33), which is merely saying in other words that they did not understand him. And their wonder is not referred to the declaration of Simeon that their boy would be a cause, not only of the rising again, but of the fall of many in Israel, and that a sword would pierce through the heart of his mother (an aspect of his vocation and destiny on which nothing had previously been communicated to the parents of Jesus, and at which therefore they might naturally wonder); for these disclosures are not made by Simeon until after the wonder of the parents, which is caused only by Simeon's expressions of joy at the sight of the Saviour, who would be the glory of Israel, and a light even to the Gentiles. And here again there is no intimation that the wonder was excited by the idea that Jesus would bear this relation to the heathens, which indeed it could not well be, since this more extended destination of the Messiah had been predicted in the Old Testament. There remains therefore as a reason for the wonder in question, merely the fact of the child's Messiahship, declared by Simeon; a fact which had been long ago announced to them by angels, and which was acknowledged by Mary in her song of praise. We have just a parallel difficulty in the present case, it being as inconceivable that the parents of Jesus should not understand his allusion to his messianic character, as that they should wonder at the declaration of it by Simeon. We must therefore draw this conclusion : if the parents of Jesus did not understand these expressions of their son when twelve years old, those earlier communications cannot have happened ; or, if the earlier communications really occurred, the subsequent expressions of Jesus cannot have remained incomprehensible to them. Having done away with those earlier incidents as historical, we might content ourselves with this later want of comprehension, were it not fair to mistrust the whole of a narrative whose later portions agree so ill with the preceding. For it is the character, not of an historical record, but of a marvellous legend, to represent its personages as so permanently in a state of wonder, that they not only at the first appearance of the extraordinary, but even at the second, third, tenth repetition, when one would expect them to be familiarized with it, continually are astonished and do not understand—obviously with the view of exalting the more highly the divine impartation by this lasting incomprehensibleness. So, to draw an example from the later history of Jesus, the divine decree of his suffering and death is set forth in all its loftiness in the evangelical narratives by the circumstance, that even the repeated, explicit disclosures of Jesus on this subject, remain throughout incomprehensible to the disciples ; as here the mystery of the Messiahship of Jesus is exalted by the circumstance, that his parents, often as it had been announced to them, at every fresh word on the subject are anew astonished and do not understand.

The twofold form of conclusion, that the mother of Jesus kept all these sayings in her heart (v. 51), and that the boy grew in wisdom and stature, and so forth, we have already recognised as a favourite form of conclusion and transition in the heroic legend of the Hebrews; in particular, that which relates to the growth of the boy is almost verbally parallel with a passage relating to Samuel, as in two former instances similar expressions appeared to have been borrowed from the history of Samson.[21]

[21] 1 Sam. ii. 26 (LXX) :
καὶ τὸ παιδάριον Σαμουὴλ ἐπορεύετο μεγαλυνόμενον, καὶ ἀγαθὸν καὶ μετὰ Κυρίου καὶ μετὰ ἀνθρώπων.

Luc. ii. 52 :
καὶ Ἰησοῦς προέκοπτε σοφίᾳ καὶ ἡλικίᾳ, καὶ χάριτι παρὰ θεῷ καὶ ἀνθρώποις.

Compare also what Josephus says Antiq. ii. ix. 6 of the χάρις παιδικὴ of Moses.

§ 41.

THIS NARRATIVE ALSO MYTHICAL. *

Thus here again we must acknowledge the influence of the legend; but as the main part of the incident is thoroughly natural, we might in this instance prefer the middle course, and after disengaging the mythical, seek to preserve a residue of history. We might suppose that the parents of Jesus really took their son to Jerusalem in his early youth, and that after having lost sight of him (probably before their departure), they found him in the temple, where, eager for instruction, he sat at the feet of the rabbins. When called to account, he declared that his favourite abode was in the house of God;[1] a sentiment which rejoiced his parents, and won the approbation of the bystanders. The rest of the story we might suppose to have been added by the aggrandizing legend, after Jesus was acknowledged as the Messiah. Here all the difficulties in our narrative,—the idea of the boy sitting in the midst of the doctors, his claiming God as his father in a special sense, and the departure of the parents without their son, would be rejected; but the journey of Jesus when twelve years old, the eagerness for knowledge then manifested by him, and his attachment to the temple, are retained. To these particulars there is nothing to object negatively, for they contain nothing improbable in itself; but their historical truth must become doubtful if we can show, positively, a strong interest of the legend, out of which the entire narrative, and especially these intrinsically not improbable particulars, might have arisen.

That in the case of great men who in their riper age have been distinguished by mental superiority, the very first presaging movements of their mind are eagerly gleaned, and if they are not to be ascertained historically, are invented under the guidance of probability, is well known. In the Hebrew history and legend especially, we find manifold proofs of this tendency. Thus of Samuel it is said in the old Testament itself, that even as a boy he received a divine revelation and the gift of prophecy (1 Sam. iii.), and with respect to Moses, on whose boyish years the Old Testament narrative is silent, a subsequent tradition, followed by Josephus and Philo, had striking proofs to relate of his early development. As in the narrative before us Jesus shows himself wise beyond his years, so this tradition attributes a like precocity to Moses;[2] as Jesus, turning away from the idle tumult of the city in all the excitement of festival time, finds his favourite entertainment in the temple among the doctors; so the boy Moses was not attracted by childish sports, but by serious occupation, and very early it was necessary to give him tutors, whom, however, like Jesus in his twelfth year, he quickly surpassed.[3]

According to Jewish custom and opinion, the twelfth year formed an epoch in development to which especial proofs of awakening genius were the rather attached, because in the twelfth year, as with us in the fourteenth, the boy was regarded as having outgrown the period of childhood.[4] Accordingly it

---

[1] Gabler neuest. theol. Journal 3, 1, s. 39.

[2] Joseph. Antiq. ii. ix. 6.

[3] Philo, de vita Mosis, Opp. ed. Mangey, Vol. 2. p. 83 f. οὐχ οἷα κομιδῇ νήπιος ἥδετο τωθασμοῖς καὶ γέλωσι καὶ παιδιαῖς—ἀλλ' αἰδῶ καὶ σεμνότητα παραφαίνων, ἀπούσμασι καὶ θεάμασιν, ἃ τὴν ψυχὴν ἔμελλεν ὠφελήσειν προσεῖχε. διδάσκαλοι δ' εὐθὺς, ἀλλαχόθεν ἄλλος, παρῆσαν·—ὧν ἐν οὐ μακρῷ χρόνῳ τὰς δυνάμεις ὑπερέβαλεν, εὐμοιρίᾳ φύσεως φθάνων τὰς ὑφηγήσεις.

[4] Chagiga, ap. Wetstein, in loc. A XII anno filius censetur maturus. So Joma f. lxxxii. 1. Berachoth f. xxiv. 1; whereas Bereschith Rabba lxiii. mentions the 13th year as the critical one.

was believed of Moses that in his twelfth year he left the house of his father, to become an independent organ of the divine revelations.[5] The Old Testament leaves it uncertain how early the gift of prophecy was imparted to Samuel, but he was said by a later tradition to have prophesied from his twelfth year;[6] and in like manner the wise judgments of Solomon and Daniel (1 Kings iii. 23 ff., Susann. 45 ff.) were supposed to have been given when they were only twelve.[7] If in the case of these Old Testament heroes, the spirit that impelled them manifested itself according to common opinion so early as in their twelfth year, it was argued that it could not have remained longer concealed in Jesus; and if Samuel and Daniel showed themselves at that age in their later capacity of divinely inspired seers, Solomon in that of a wise ruler, so Jesus at the corresponding period in his life must have shown himself in the character to which he subsequently established his claim, that namely, of the Son of God and Teacher of Mankind. It is, in fact, the obvious aim of Luke to pass over no epoch in the early life of Jesus without surrounding him with divine radiance, with significant prognostics of the future; in this style he treats his birth, mentions the circumcision at least emphatically, but above all avails himself of the presentation in the temple. There yet remained according to Jewish manners one epoch, the twelfth year, with the first journey to the passover; how could he do otherwise than, following the legend, adorn this point in the development of Jesus as we find that he has done in his narrative? and how could we do otherwise than regard his narrative as a legendary embellishment of this period in the life of Jesus,[8] from which we learn nothing of his real development,[9] but merely something of the exalted notions which were entertained in the primitive church of the early ripened mind of Jesus?

But how this anecdote can be numbered among mythi is found by some altogether inconceivable. It bears, thinks Heydenreich,[10] a thoroughly historical character (this is the very point to be proved), and the stamp of the highest simplicity (like every popular legend in its original form); it contains no tincture of the miraculous, wherein the primary characteristic of a mythus (but not of every mythus) is held to consist; it is so remote from all embellishment that there is not the slightest detail of the conversation of Jesus with the doctors (the legend was satisfied with the dramatic trait, *sitting in the midst of the doctors :* as a dictum, v. 49 was alone important, and towards this the narrator hastens without delay); nay, even the conversation between Jesus and his mother is only given in a fragmentary aphoristic manner (there is no

---

[5] Schemoth R. ap. Wetstein: *Dixit R. Chama: Moses duodenarius avulsus est a domo patris sui etc.*

[6] Joseph. Antiq. v. x. 4 : Σαμούηλος δὲ πεπληρωκὼς ἔτος ἤδη δωδέκατον, προεφήτευς.

[7] Ignat. ep. (interpol.) ad Magnes. c. iii. : Σολομῶν δὲ—δωδεκαετὴς βασιλεύσας, τὴν φοβερὰν ἐκείνην καὶ δυσερμήνευτον ἐπὶ ταῖς γυναιξὶ κρίσιν ἕνεκα τῶν παιδίων ἐποιήσατο.—Δανιὴλ ὁ σοφὸς δωδεκαετὴς γέγονε κάτοχος τῷ θείῳ πνεύματι, καὶ τοὺς μάτην τὴν πολιὰν φέροντας πρεσβύτας συκοφάντας καὶ ἐπιθυμητὰς ἀλλοτρίου κάλλους ἀπήλεγξε. *But Solomon, . . . being king at the age of twelve years, gave that terrible and profound judgment between the woman with respect to the children. . . . Daniel, the wise man, when twelve years old, was possessed by the divine spirit, and convicted those calumniating old men who, carrying gray hairs in vain, coveted the beauty that belonged to another.* This, it is true, is found in a Christian writing, but on comparing it with the above data, we are led to believe that it was drawn from a more ancient Jewish legend.

[8] This Kaiser has seen, bibl. Theol. 1, 234.

[9] Neither do we learn what Hase (Leben Jesu § 37) supposes to be conveyed in this narrative, namely, that as it exhibits the same union with God that constituted the idea of the later life of Jesus, it is an intimation that his later excellence was not the result of conversion from youthful errors, but of the uninterrupted development of his freedom.

[10] Ueber die Unzulässigkeit u. s. f. 1, s. 92.

trace of an omission); finally, the inventor of a legend would have made Jesus speak differently to his mother, instead of putting into his mouth words which might be construed into irreverence and indifference. In this last observation Heydenreich agrees with Schleiermacher, who finds in the behaviour of Jesus to his mother, liable as it is to be misinterpreted, a sure guarantee that the whole history was not invented to supply something remarkable concerning Jesus, in connexion with the period at which the holy things of the temple and the law were first opened to him.[11]

In combating the assertion, that an inventor would scarcely have attributed to Jesus so much apparent harshness towards his mother, we need not appeal to the apocryphal *Evangelium Thomæ*, which makes the boy Jesus say to his foster-father Joseph : *insipientissime fecisti ;* [12] for even in the legend or history of the canonical gospels corresponding traits are to be found. In the narrative of the wedding at Cana, we find this rough address to his mother : τί ἐμοὶ καὶ σοὶ γύναι (John ii. 4) ; and in the account of the visit paid to Jesus by his mother and brethren, the striking circumstance that he apparently wishes to take no notice of his relatives (Matt. xii. 46). If these are real incidents, then the legend had an historical precedent to warrant the introduction of a similar feature, even into the early youth of Jesus ; if, on the other hand, they are only legends, they are the most vivid proofs that an inducement was not wanting for the invention of such features. Where this inducement lay, it is easy to see. The figure of Jesus would stand in the higher relief from the obscure background of his contracted family relations, if it were often seen that his parents were unable to comprehend his elevated mind, and if even he himself sometimes made them feel his superiority—so far as this could happen without detriment to his filial obedience, which, it should be observed, our narrative expressly preserves.

§ 42.

ON THE EXTERNAL LIFE OF JESUS UP TO THE TIME OF HIS PUBLIC APPEARANCE.

What were the external conditions under which Jesus lived, from the scene just considered up to the time of his public appearance ? On this subject our canonical gospels give scarcely an indication.

First, as to his place of residence, all that we learn explicitly is this : that both at the beginning and at the end of this obscure period he dwelt at Nazareth. According to Luke ii. 51, Jesus when twelve years old returned thither with his parents, and according to Matthew iii. 13, Mark i. 9, he, when thirty years old (comp. Luke iii. 23), came from thence to be baptized by John. Thus our evangelists appear to suppose, that Jesus had in the interim resided in Galilee, and, more particularly, in Nazareth. This supposition, however, does not exclude journeys, such as those to the feasts in Jerusalem.

The employment of Jesus during the years of his boyhood and youth seems, from an intimation in our gospels, to have been determined by the trade of his father, who is there called a τέκτων (Matt. xiii. 55). This Greek word, used to designate the trade of Joseph, is generally understood in the sense of *faber*

---

[11] Ueber den Lukas. s. 39 f.
[12] Cap. v. In the Greek text also the more probable reading is καὶ μάλιστα οὐ σοφᾶς, vid. Thilo, p. 287.

lignarius (carpenter) ; [1] a few only, on mystical grounds, discover in it a *faber ferrarius (blacksmith), aurarius (goldsmith),* or *cœmentarius (mason).*[2] The works in wood which he executed are held of different magnitude by different authors : according to Justin and the *Evangelium Thomœ,*[3] they were *ploughs and yokes,* ἄροτρα καὶ ζυγὰ, and in that case he would be what we call a wheelwright ; according to the *Evangelium infantiœ arabicum,*[4] they were doors, milk-vessels, sieves and coffers, and once Joseph makes a throne for the king ; so that here he is represented partly as a cabinet-maker and partly as a cooper. The *Protevangelium Jacobi,* on the other hand, makes him work at *buildings,* οἰκοδομαῖς,[5] without doubt as a carpenter. In these labours of the father Jesus appears to have shared, according to an expression of Mark, who makes the Nazarenes ask concerning Jesus, not merely as in the parallel passage of Matthew : *Is not this the carpenter's son ?* οὐκ οὗτός ἐστιν ὁ τοῦ τέκτονος υἱός ; but *Is not this the carpenter ?* οὐκ οὗτός ἐστιν ὁ τέκτων (vi. 3). It is true that in replying to the taunt of Celsus that the teacher of the Christians was a carpenter by trade, τέκτων ἦν τὴν τέχνην, Origen says, he must have forgotten *that in none of the Gospels received by the churches is Jesus himself called a carpenter,* ὅτι οὐδαμοῦ τῶν ἐν ταῖς ἐκκλησίαις φερομένων εὐαγγελίων τέκτων αὐτὸς ὁ Ἰησοῦς ἀναγέγραπται.[6] The above passage in Mark has, in fact, the various reading, ὁ τοῦ τέκτονος υἱός, which Origen must have taken, unless he be supposed altogether to have overlooked the passage, and which is preferred by some modern critics.[7] But here Beza has justly remarked that *fortasse mutavit aliquis, existimans, hanc artem Christi majestati parum convenire ;* whereas there could hardly be an interest which would render the contrary alteration desirable.[8] Moreover Fathers of the Church and apocryphal writings represent Jesus, in accordance with the more generally accepted reading, as following the trade of his father. Justin attaches especial importance to the fact that Jesus made ploughs and yokes or scales, as symbols of active life and of justice.[9] In the *Evangelium infantiœ Arabicum,* Jesus goes about with Joseph to the places where the latter has work, to help him in such a manner that if Joseph made anything too long or too short, Jesus, by a touch or by merely stretching out his hand, gave to the object its right size, an assistance which was very useful to his foster-father, because, as the apocryphal text naïvely remarks : *nec admodum peritus erat artis fabrilis.*[10]

Apart from these apocryphal descriptions, there are many reasons for believing that the above intimation as to the youthful employment of Jesus is correct. In the first place, it accords with the Jewish custom which prescribed even to one destined to a learned career, or in general to any spiritual occupation, the acquisition of some handicraft ; thus Paul, the pupil of the rabbins, was also a tent-maker, σκηνοποιὸς τὴν τέχνην (Acts xviii. 3). Next, as our previous examinations have shown that we know nothing historical of

---

[1] Hence the title of an Arabian apocryphal work (according to the Latin translation in Thilo, 1, p. 3) : *historia Josephi, fabri lignarii.*
[2] Vid. Thilo, Cod. Apocr. N. T. p. 368 f. not.
[3] Justin. Dial. c. Tryph. 88. According to him Jesus makes these implements, doubtless under the direction of Joseph. In the *Evang. Thomœ* c. xiii. Joseph is the workman.
[4] Cap. xxxviii. ap. Thilo, p. 112 ff.
[5] C. ix. and xiii.
[6] C. Cels. vi. 36.
[7] Fritzsche, in Marc. p. 200.
[8] Vid. Wetstein and Paulus, in loc. ; Winer, Realwörterbuch, 1, s. 665. Note ; Neander, L. J. Chr. s. 46 f. Note.
[9] Ut sup. : ταῦτα γὰρ τὰ τεκτονικὰ ἔργα εἰργάζετο ἐν ἀνθρώποις ὤν, ἄροτρα καὶ ζυγά. διὰ τούτων καὶ τὰ τῆς δικαιοσύνης σύμβολα διδάσκων, καὶ ἐνεργῆ βίον.
[10] Cap. xxxviii.

extraordinary expectations and plans on the part of the parents of Jesus in relation to their son, so nothing is more natural than the supposition that Jesus early practised the trade of his father. Further, the Christians must have had an interest in denying, rather than inventing, this opinion as to their Messiah's youthful occupation, since it often drew down upon them the ridicule of their opponents. Thus Celsus, as we have already mentioned, could not abstain from a reflection on this subject, for which reason Origen will known nothing of any designation of Jesus as a τέκτων in the New Testament ; and every one knows the scoffing question of Libanius about the carpenter's son, a question which seems to have been provided with so striking an answer, only *ex eventu*.[11] It may certainly be said in opposition to this, that the notion of Jesus having been a carpenter, seems to be founded on a mere inference from the trade of the father as to the occupation of the son, whereas the latter was just as likely to apply himself to some other branch of industry ; nay, that perhaps the whole tradition of the carpentry of Joseph and Jesus owes its origin to the symbolical significance exhibited by Justin. As however the allusion in our Gospels to the trade of Joseph is very brief and bare, and is nowhere used allegorically in the New Testament, nor entered into more minutely ; it is not to be contested that he was really a carpenter ; but it must remain uncertain whether Jesus shared in this occupation.

What were the circumstances of Jesus and his parents as to fortune ? The answer to this question has been the object of many dissertations. It is evident that the ascription of pressing poverty to Jesus, on the part of orthodox theologians, rested on dogmatical and æsthetic grounds. On the one hand, they wished to maintain even in this point the *status exinanitionis*, and on the other, they wished to depict as strikingly as possible the contrast between the μορφὴ θεοῦ (*form of God*) and the μορφὴ δούλου (*form of a servant*). That this contrast as set forth by Paul (Phil. ii. 6, ff.), as well as the expression ἐπτώχευσε, which this apostle applies to Christ (2 Cor. viii. 9) merely characterizes the obscure and laborious life to which he submitted after his heavenly pre-existence, and instead of playing the part of king which the Jewish imagination attributed to the Messiah, is also to be regarded as established.[12] The expression of Jesus himself, *The Son of man hath not where to lay his head,* ποῦ τὴν κεφαλὴν κλίνῃ (Matt. viii. 20), may possibly import merely his voluntary renunciation of the peaceful enjoyment of fortune, for the sake of devoting himself to the wandering life of the Messiah. There is only one other particular bearing on the point in question, namely, that Mary presented, as an offering of purification, doves (Luke ii. 24),—according to Lev. xii. 8, the offering of the poor : which certainly proves that the author of this information conceived the parents of Jesus to have been in by no means brilliant circumstances ;[13] but what shall assure us that he also was not induced to make this representation by unhistorical motives? Meanwhile we are just as far from having tenable ground for maintaining the contrary proposition, namely, that Jesus possessed property : at least it is inadmissible to adduce the coat without seam [14] (John xix. 23), until we shall have inquired more closely what kind of relation it has to the subject.

[11] Theodoret. H. E. iii. 23.
[12] Hase, Leben Jesu, § 70 ; Winer, bibl. Realw. i, s. 665.
[13] Winer, ut sup.
[14] This is done by both the above-named theologians.

§ 43.

THE INTELLECTUAL DEVELOPMENT OF JESUS.

Our information concerning the external life of Jesus during his youth is very scanty : but we are almost destitute of any concerning his intellectual development. For the indeterminate phrase, twice occurring in Luke's history of the childhood, concerning the increase of his spiritual strength and his growth in wisdom, tells us no more than we must necessarily have presupposed without it ; while on the expectations which his parents cherished with respect to him before his birth, and on the sentiment which his mother especially then expressed, no conclusion is to be founded, since those expectations and declarations are themselves unhistorical. The narrative just considered, of the appearance of Jesus in the temple at twelve years of age, rather gives us a result—the early and peculiar development of his religious consciousness,—than an explanation of the causes and conditions by which this development was favoured. But we at least learn from Luke ii. 41 (what however is to be of course supposed of pious Israelites), that the parents of Jesus used to go to Jerusalem every year at the Passover. We may conjecture, then, that Jesus from his twelfth year generally accompanied them, and availed himself of this excellent opportunity, amid the concourse of Jews and Jewish proselytes of all countries and all opinions, to form his mind, to become acquainted with the condition of his people and the false principles of the Pharisaic leaders, and to extend his survey beyond the narrow limits of Palestine.[1] *

Whether or in what degree Jesus received the learned education of a rabbin, is also left untold in our canonical Gospels. From such passages as Matt. vii. 29, where it is said that Jesus taught *not as the scribes*, οὐχ ὡς οἱ γραμματεῖς, we can only infer that he did not adopt the method of the doctors of the law, and it does not follow that he had never enjoyed the education of a *scribe* (γραμματεὺς). On the other hand, not only was Jesus called ῥαββὶ and ῥαββουνὶ by his disciples (Matt. xxvi. 25, 49 ; Mark ix. 5, xi. 21, xiv. 45. John iv. 31, ix. 2, xi. 8, xx. 16 : comp. i. 38, 40, 50), and by supplicating sufferers (Mark x. 5), but even the pharisaic ἄρχων Nicodemus (John iii. 2) did not refuse him this title. We cannot, however, conclude from hence that Jesus had received the scholastic instruction of a rabbin ;[2] for the salutation Rabbi, as also the privilege of reading in the synagogue (Luke iv. 16 ff.), a particular which has likewise been appealed to, belonged not only to graduated rabbins, but to every teacher who had given actual proof of his qualifications.[3] The enemies of Jesus explicitly assert, and he does not contradict them, that he had never learned letters : πῶς οὗτος γράμματα οἶδε μὴ μεμαθηκὼς (John vii. 15) ; and the Nazarenes are astonished to find so much wisdom in him, whence we infer that he had not to their knowledge been a student. These facts cannot be neutralized by the discourse of Jesus in which he represents himself as the model of a scribe well instructed unto the kingdom of heaven [4] (Matt. xiii. 52), for the word γραμματεὺς here means a doctor of the law in general, and not directly a doctor qualified in the schools. Lastly, the intimate acquaintance with the doctrinal traditions, and the abuses of the rabbins, which Jesus exhibits,[5] especially in the sermon on the mount and the anti-pharisaic discourse

---

[1] Paulus, exeget. Handb. 1, a, s. 273 ff.
[2] Such, however, are the arguments of Paulus, ut sup. 275 ff.
[3] Comp. Hase, Leben Jesu, § 38 ; Neander, L. J. Chr. s. 45 f.
[4] Paulus, ut sup.
[5] To this Schöttgen appeals, *Christus rabbinorum summus*, in his horæ, ii. p. 890 f.

Matt. xxiii. he might acquire from the numerous discourses of the Pharisees to the people, without going through a course of study under them. Thus the data on our present subject to be found in the Gospels, collectively yield the result that Jesus did not pass formally through a rabbinical school ; on the other hand, the consideration that it must have been the interest of the Christian legend to represent Jesus as independent of human teachers, may induce a doubt with respect to these statements in the New Testament, and a conjecture that Jesus may not have been so entirely a stranger to the learned culture of his nation. But from the absence of authentic information we can arrive at no decision on this point.

Various hypotheses, more or less independent of the intimations given in the New Testament, have been advanced both in ancient and modern times concerning the intellectual development of Jesus : they may be divided into two principal classes, according to their agreement with the natural or the supernatural view. The supernatural view of the person of Jesus requires that he should be the only one of his kind, independent of all external, human influences, self-taught or rather taught of God ; hence, not only must its advocates determinedly reject every supposition implying that he borrowed or learned anything, and consequently place in the most glaring light the difficulties which lay in the way of the natural development of Jesus ; [6] but, the more surely to exclude every kind of reception, they must also be disposed to assign as early an appearance as possible to that spontaneity which we find in Jesus in his mature age. This spontaneous activity is twofold : it is theoretical and practical. As regards the theoretical side, comprising judgment and knowledge, the effort to give as early a date as possible to its manifestation in Jesus, displays itself in the apocryphal passages which have been already partly cited, and which describe Jesus as surpassing his teachers long before his twelfth year, for according to one of them he spoke in his cradle and declared himself to be the Son of God.[7] The practical side, too, of that superior order of spontaneity attributed to Jesus in his later years, namely, the power of working miracles, is attached by the apocryphal gospels to his earliest childhood and youth. The *Evangelium Thomæ* opens with the fifth year of Jesus the story of his miracles,[8] and the Arabian *Evangelium Infantiæ* fills the journey into Egypt with miracles which the mother of Jesus performed by means of the swaddling bands of her infant, and the water in which he was washed.[9] Some of the miracles which according to these apocryphal gospels were wrought by Jesus when in his infancy and boyhood, are analogous to those in the New Testament—cures and resuscitations of the dead ; others are totally diverse from the ruling type in the canonical Gospels—extremely revolting retributive miracles, by which every one who opposes the boy Jesus in any matter whatever is smitten with lameness, or even with death, or else mere extravagancies, such as the giving of life to sparrows formed out of mud.[10]

The natural view of the person of Jesus had an opposite interest, which was also very early manifested both among Jewish and heathen opponents of Christianity, and which consisted in explaining his appearance conformably to the laws of causality, by comparing it with prior and contemporaneous

---

[6] As e. g. Reinhard does, in his Plan Jesu.
[7] Evang. infant. arab. c. i. p. 60 f. ap. Thilo, and the passages quoted § 40 out of the same Gospel and the Evang. Thomæ.
[8] Cap. ii. p. 278, Thilo.
[9] Cap. x. ff.
[10] E. g. Evang. Thomæ, c. iii.–v. Evang. infant. arab. c. xlvi. f. Evang. Thomæ, c. ii. Evang. inf. arab. c. xxxvi.

facts to which it had a relation, and thus exhibiting the conditions on which Jesus depended, and the sources from which he drew. It is true that in the first centuries of the Christian era, the whole region of spirituality being a supernatural one for heathens as well as Jews, the reproach that Jesus owed his wisdom and seemingly miraculous powers, not to himself or to God, but to a communication from without, could not usually take the form of an assertion that he had acquired natural skill and wisdom in the ordinary way of instruction from others.[11] Instead of the natural and the human, the unnatural and the demoniacal were opposed to the divine and the supernatural (comp. Matt. xii. 24), and Jesus was accused of working his miracles by the aid of magic acquired in his youth. This charge was the most easily attached to the journey of his parents with him into Egypt, that native land of magic and secret wisdom, and thus we find it both in Celsus and in the Talmud. The former makes a Jew allege against Jesus, amongst other things, that he had entered into service for wages in Egypt, that he had there possessed himself of some magic arts, and on the strength of these had on his return vaunted himself for a God.[12] The Talmud gives him a member of the Jewish Sanhedrim as a teacher, makes him journey to Egypt with this companion, and bring magic charms from thence into Palestine.[13]

The purely natural explanation of the intellectual development of Jesus could only become prevalent amid the enlightened culture of modern times. In working out this explanation, the chief points of difference are the following : either the character of Jesus is regarded in too circumscribed a view, as the result of only one among the means of culture which his times afforded, or more comprehensively, as the result of all these combined ; again, in tracing this external influence, either the internal gifts and self-determination of Jesus are adequately considered, or they are not.

In any case, the basis of the intellectual development of Jesus was furnished by the sacred writings of his people, of which the discourses preserved to us in the Gospels attest his zealous and profound study. His Messianic ideas seem to have been formed chiefly on Isaiah and Daniel : spiritual religiousness and elevation above the prejudices of Jewish nationality were impressively shadowed forth in the prophetic writings generally, together with the Psalms.

Next among the influences affecting mental cultivation in the native country of Jesus, must be reckoned the three sects under which the spiritual life of his fellow-countrymen may be classified. Among these, the Pharisees, whom Jesus at a later period so strenuously combated, can apparently have had only a negative influence over him ; yet along with their fondness for tradition and legal pedantry, their sanctimoniousness and hypocrisy, by which Jesus was repelled from them, we must remember their belief in angels and in immortality, and their constant admission of a progressive development of the Jewish religion after Moses, which were so many points of union between them and

---

[11] Yet some isolated instances occur, vid. Semler, Baumgarten's Glaubenslehre, 1, s. 42, Anm. 8.

[12] Orig. c. Cels. 1. 28 : καὶ (λέγει) ὅτι οὗτος (ὁ Ἰησοῦς) διὰ πενίαν εἰς Αἴγυπτον μισθαρνήσας, κἀκεῖ δυνάμεων τίνων πειραθείς, ἐφ᾽ αἷς Αἰγύπτιοι σεμνύνονται, ἐπανῆλθεν, ἐν ταῖς δυνάμεσι μέγα φρονῶν, καὶ δι᾽ αὐτὰς θεὸν αὐτὸν ἀνηγόρευσε.

[13] Sanhedr. f. cvii. 2 : R. Josua f. Perachja et יש Alexandrian Aegypti profecti sunt — — יש ex illo tempore magiam exercuit, et Israëlitas ad pessima quævis perduxit. (An important anachronism, as this Josua Ben Perachja lived about a century earlier. See Jost, Geschichte des Isr., 2, s. 80 ff. and 142 of the Appendices.) Schabbath f. civ. 2 : Traditio est, R. Elieserem dixisse ad viros doctos : annon f. Satdae (i.e. Jesus) magiam ex Aegypto adduxit per incisionem in carne suâ factam ? vid. Schöttgen, horæ, ii. p. 697 ff. Eisenmenger, entdecktes Judenthum, 1, s. 149 f.

Jesus. Still as these tenets were only peculiar to the Pharisees in contradistinction to the Sadducees, and, for the rest, were common to all orthodox
Jews, we abide by the opinion that the influence of the Pharisaic sect on the
development of Jesus was essentially negative.

In the discourses of Jesus Sadduceeism is less controverted, nay, he agrees
with it in rejecting the Pharisaic traditions and hypocrisy ; hence a few of the
learned have wished to find him a school in this sect.[14]   But the merely
negative agreement against the errors of the Pharisees,—an agreement which,
moreover, proceeded from quite another principle in Jesus than in the Sadducees,—is more than counterbalanced by the contrast which their religious
indifference, their unbelief in immortality and in spiritual existences, formed
with the disposition of Jesus, and his manner of viewing the world.   That
the controversy with the Sadducees is not prominent in the Gospels, may be
very simply explained by the fact that their sect had very slight influence on
the circle with which Jesus was immediately connected, the adherents of
Sadduceeism belonging to the higher ranks alone.[15]

Concerning one only of the then existing Jewish sects can the question
seriously arise, whether we ought not to ascribe to it a positive influence on
the development and appearance of Jesus—the sect, namely, of the Essenes.[16]
In the last century the derivation of Christianity from Essenism was very much
in vogue ; not only English deists, and among the Germans, Bahrdt and
venturini, but even theologians, such as Stäudlin, embraced the idea.[17]   In
the days of freemasonry and secret orders, there was a disposition to transfer
their character to primitive Christianity.   The concealment of an Essene
lodge appeared especially adapted to explain the sudden disappearance of
Jesus after the brilliant scenes of his infancy and boyhood, and again after
his restoration to life.   Besides the forerunner John, the two men on the
Mount of Transfiguration, and the angels clothed in white at the grave, and on
the Mount of Ascension, were regarded as members of the Essene brotherhood,
and many cures of Jesus and the Apostles were referred to the medical traditions
of the Essenes.   Apart, however, from these fancies of a bygone age, there
are really some essential characteristics which seem to speak in favour of an
intimate relation between Essenism and Christianity.   The most conspicuous
as such are the prohibition of oaths, and the community of goods : with the
former was connected fidelity, peaceableness, obedience to every constituted
authority ; with the latter, contempt of riches, and the custom of travelling
without provisions.   These and other features, such as the sacred meal partaken in common, the rejection of sanguinary sacrifices and of slavery, constitute so strong a resemblance between Essenism and Christianity, that even
so early a writer as Eusebius mistook the Therapeutæ, a sect allied to the
Essenes, for Christians.[18]   But there are very essential dissimilarities which
must not be overlooked.   Leaving out of consideration the *contempt of marriage*, ὑπεροψία γάμου, since Josephus ascribes it to a part only of the Essenes ;
the asceticism, the punctilious observance of the Sabbath, the purifications,
and other superstitious usages of this sect, their retention of the names of the
angels, the mystery which they affected, and their contracted, exclusive devo-

---

[14] E. g. Des Côtes, Schutzschrift für Jesus von Nazaret, s. 128 ff.
[15] Neander, L. J. Chr. s. 39 ff.
[16] Vid. Joseph. B. j. ii. viii. 2–13.   Antiq. xviii. i. 5.   Comp. Philo, *quod omnis probus
liber* and *de vita contemplativa.*
[17] This opinion is judiciously developed by Stäudlin, Geschichte der Sittenlehre Jesu, 1, s.
570 ff. ; and in a romantic manner in the Geschichte des Grossen Propheten von Nazaret, 1.
Band.
[18] H. E. ii. 16 f.

tion to their order, are so foreign, nay so directly opposed to the spirit of Jesus, that, especially as the Essenes are nowhere mentioned in the New Testament, the aid which this sect also contributed to the development of Jesus, must be limited to the uncertain influence which might be exercised over him by occasional intercourse with Essenes.[19]

Did other elements than such as were merely Jewish, or at least confined to Palestine, operate upon Jesus? Of the heathens settled in *Galilee of the Gentiles*, Γαλιλαία τῶν ἐθνῶν, there was hardly much to be learned beyond patience under frequent intercourse with them. On the other hand, at the feasts in Jerusalem, not only foreign Jews, some of whom, as for example the Alexandrian and Cyrenian Jews, had synagogues there (Acts vi. 9), but also devout heathens were to be met with (John xii. 20); and that intercourse with these had some influence in extending the intellectual horizon of Jesus, and spiritualizing his opinions, has, as we have already intimated, all historical probability.[20]

But why do we, in the absence of certain information, laboriously seek after uncertain traces of an influence which cotemporary means of development may have exercised on Jesus? and yet more, why, on the other side, are these labours so anxiously repudiated? Whatever amount of intellectual material may be collected, the spark by which genius kindles it, and fuses its various elements into a consistent whole, is neither easier to explain nor reduced in value. Thus it is with Jesus. Allow him to have exhausted the means of development which his age afforded : a comprehensive faculty of reception is with great men ever the reverse side of their powerful originality; allow him to have owed far more to Essenism and Alexandrianism, and whatever other schools and tendencies existed, than we, in our uncertainty, are in a condition to prove :—still, for the reformation of a world these elements were all too little ; the leaven necessary for this he must obtain from the depth of his own mind.[21]

But we have not yet spoken of an appearance to which our Gospels assign a most important influence in developing the activity of Jesus—that of John the Baptist. As his ministry is first noticed in the Gospels in connexion with the baptism and public appearance of Jesus, our inquiry concerning him, and his relation to Jesus, must open the second part.

---

[19] Comp. Bengel, Bemerkungen über den Versuch. das Christenthum aus dem Essäismus abzuleiten, in Flatt's Magazin, 7, s. 126 ff. ; Neander, L. J. Chr. s. 41 ff.

[20] This is stated with exaggeration by Bahrdt, Briefe über die Bibel, zweites Bändchen, 18ter, 20ster Brief ff. 4tes Bändchen, 49ster Brief.

[21] Comp. Paulus ut sup. 1, a, 273 ff. Planck, Geschichte des Christenthums in der Periode seiner ersten Einführung 1, s. 84. De Wette, bibl. Dogm. § 212. Hase L. J. § 38. Winer, bibl. Realw. s. 677 f. Neander, L. J. Chr. s. 38 ff.

SECOND PART.

HISTORY OF THE PUBLIC LIFE OF JESUS.

CHAPTER I.

RELATIONS BETWEEN JESUS AND JOHN THE BAPTIST.

§ 44.

CHRONOLOGICAL RELATIONS BETWEEN JOHN AND JESUS.

FOR the ministry of John the Baptist, mentioned in all the Gospels, the second and fourth evangelists fix no epoch; the first gives us an inexact one; the third, one apparently precise. According to Matt. iii. 1, John appeared as a preacher of repentance, *in those days*, ἐν ταῖς ἡμέραις ἐκείναις, that is, if we interpret strictly this reference to the previous narrative, about the time when the parents of Jesus settled at Nazareth, and when Jesus was yet a child. We are told, however, in the context, that Jesus came to John for baptism; hence between the first appearance of the Baptist, which was cotemporary with the childhood of Jesus, and the period at which the latter was baptized, we must intercalate a number of years, during which Jesus might have become sufficiently matured to partake of John's baptism. But Matthew's description of the person and work of the Baptist is so concise, the office attributed to him is so little independent, so entirely subservient to that of Jesus, that it was certainly not the intention of the evangelist to assign a long series of years to his single ministry. His meaning incontestably is, that John's short career early attained its goal in the baptism of Jesus.

It being thus inadmissible to suppose between the appearance of John and the baptism of Jesus, that is, between verses 12 and 13 of the 3rd chapter of Matthew, the long interval which is in every case indispensable, nothing remains but to insert it between the close of the second and the beginning of the third chapter, namely, between the settlement of the parents of Jesus at Nazareth and the appearance of the Baptist. To this end we may presume, with Paulus, that Matthew has here introduced a fragment from a history of the Baptist, narrating many particulars of his life immediately preceding his public agency, and very properly proceeding with the words, *in those days*, ἐν ταῖς ἡμέραις ἐκείναις, which connecting phrase Matthew, although he omitted that to which it referred, has nevertheless retained[1]; or we may, with Süskind, apply the words, not to the settlement, but to the subsequent residence of Jesus at Nazareth;[2] or better still, ἐν ταῖς ἡμέραις ἐκείναις, like the corresponding Hebrew expression, בַּיָּמִים הָהֵם e. g., Exod. ii. 11, is probably to be interpreted as relating indeed to the establishment at Nazareth, but so that

---

[1] Exeget. Handbuch. 1 a, s. 46. Schneckenburger agrees with him, über den Ursprung des ersten kanon. Evang., s. 30.
[2] Vermischte Aufsätze, s. 76 ff. Compare Schneckenburger, ut sup.

an event happening thirty years afterwards may yet be said, speaking indefinitely, to occur *in those days*.[3] In neither case do we learn from Matthew concerning the time of John's appearance more than the very vague information, that it took place in the interval between the infancy and manhood of Jesus.

Luke determines the date of John's appearance by various synchronisms, placing it in the time of Pilate's government in Judea ; in the sovereignty of Herod (Antipas), of Philip and of Lysanias over the other divisions of Palestine ; in the high priesthood of Annas and Caiaphas ; and, moreover, precisely in the 15th year of the reign of Tiberius, which, reckoning from the death of Augustus, corresponds with the year 28–29 of our era[4] (iii. 1, 2). With this last and closest demarcation of time all the foregoing less precise ones agree. Even that which makes Annas high priest together with Caiaphas appears correct, if we consider the peculiar influence which, according to John xviii. 13, Acts iv. 6, that ex-high priest retained, even when deposed, especially after the assumption of office by his son-in-law, Caiaphas.

A single exception occurs in the statement about Lysanias, whom Luke makes cotemporary with Antipas and Philip as tetrarch of Abilene. Josephus, it is true, speaks of an Ἀβίλα ἡ Λυσανίου, and mentions a Lysanias as governor of Chalcis in Lebanon, near to which lay the territory of Abila ; so that the same Lysanias was probably master of the latter. But this Lysanias was, at the instigation of Cleopatra, put to death 34 years before the birth of Christ, and a second Lysanias is not mentioned either by Josephus or by any other writer on the period in question.[5] Thus, not only is the time of his government earlier by 60 years than the 15th year of Tiberius, but it is also at issue with the other dates associated with it by Luke. Hence it has been conjectured that Luke here speaks of a younger Lysanias, the descendant of the earlier one, who possessed Abilene under Tiberius, but who, being less famous, is not noticed by Josephus.[6] We cannot indeed prove what Süskind demands for the refutation of this hypothesis, namely, that had such a younger Lysanias existed, Josephus must have mentioned him ; yet that he had more than one inducement to do so, Paulus has satisfactorily shown. Especially, when in relation to the times of the first and second Agrippa he designates Abila, ἡ Λυσανίου, he must have been reminded that he had only treated of the elder Lysanias, and not at all of the younger, from whom, as the later ruler, the country must at that time have derived its second appellation.[7] If, according to this, the younger Lysanias is but an historic fiction, the proposed

---

[3] De Wette and Fritzsche, in loc.

[4] See Paulus, ut sup., s. 336.

[5] I here collect all the passages in Josephus relative to Lysanias, with the parallel passages in Dion Cassius. Antiq. xiii. xvi. 3, xiv. iii. 2, vii. 8.—Antiq. xv. iv. 1. B. j. i. xiii. 1 (Dio Cassius xlix. 32). Antiq. xv. x. 1–3. B. j. i. xx. 4 (Dio Cass. liv. 9). Antiq. xvii. xi. 4. B. j. ii. vi. 3. Antiq. xviii. vi. 10. B. j. ii. ix. 6 (Dio Cass. lix. 8). Antiq. xix. v. 1. B. j. ii. xi. 5. Antiq. xx. v. 2, vii. 1. B. j. ii. xii. 8.

[6] Süskind, vermischte Aufsätze, s. 15 ff. 93 ff.

[7] Tholück thinks he has found a perfectly corresponding example in Tacitus. When this historian, Annal. ii. 42 (A.D. 17), mentions the death of an Archelaus, king of Cappadocia, and yet, Annal. vi. 41 (A.D. 36), cites an Archelaus, also a Cappadocian, as ruler of the Clitæ, the same historical conjecture, says Tholück, is necessary, viz., that there were two Cappadocians named Archelaus. But when the same historian, after noticing the death of a man, introduces another of the same name, under different circumstances, it is no conjecture, but a clear historic datum, that there were two such persons. It is quite otherwise when, as in the case of Lysanias, two writers have each one of the same name, but assign him distinct epochs. Here it is indeed a conjecture to admit two successive persons ; a conjecture so much the less historical, the more improbable it is shown to be that one of the two writers would have been silent respecting the second of the like-named men, had such an one existed.

alternative is but a philological one.[8] For when it is said in the first place: Φιλίππου — τετραρχοῦντος τῆς Ἰτουραίας, κ. τ. λ., and when it follows : καὶ Λυσανίου τῆς Ἀβιληνῆς τετραρχοῦντος : we cannot possibly understand from this, that Philip reigned also over the Abilene of Lysanias. For in that case the word τετραρχοῦντος ought not to have been repeated,[9] and τῆς ought to have been placed before Lysanias, if the author wished to avoid misconstruction. The conclusion is therefore inevitable that the writer himself erred, and, from the circumstance that Abilene, even in recent times, was called, after the last ruler of the former dynasty, ἡ Λυσανίου, drew the inference that a monarch of that name was still existing ; while, in fact, Abilene either belonged to Philip, or was immediately subject to the Romans.[10]

The above chronological notation relates directly to John the Baptist alone ; a similar one is wanting when Luke begins farther on (v. 21 ff.) to speak of Jesus. Of him it is merely said that he was *about thirty years of age*, ὡσεὶ ἐτῶν τριάκοντα, on his public appearance (ἀρχόμενος), but no date is given ; while, in the case of John, there is a contrary omission. Thus even if John commenced his ministry in the 15th year of Tiberius, we cannot thence gather anything as to the time when Jesus commenced his, as it is nowhere said how long John had been baptizing when Jesus came to him on the Jordan ; while, on the other hand, although we know that Jesus, at his baptism, was about 30 years old, this does not help us to ascertain the age of John when he entered on his ministry as Baptist. Remembering, however, Luke i. 26, according to which John was just half a year older than Jesus, and calling to our aid the fact that Jewish usage would scarcely permit the exercise of public functions before the thirtieth year, we might infer that the Baptist could only have appeared half a year before the arrival of Jesus on the banks of the Jordan, since he would only so much earlier have attained the requisite age. But no express law forbade a public appearance previous to the thirtieth year ; and it has been justly questioned whether we can apply to the freer office of a Prophet a restriction which concerned the Priests and Levites, for whom the thirtieth year was fixed for their entrance on regular service [11] (Num. iv. 3, 47. Compare besides 2 Chron. xxxi. 17, where the 20th year is named). This then would not hinder us from placing the appearance of John considerably prior to that of Jesus, even presupposing the averred relation between their ages. Hardly, however, could this be the intention of the Evangelist. For to ascertain so carefully the date of the Forerunner's appearance, and leave that of the Messiah himself undetermined, would be too great an oversight,[12] and we cannot but suppose that his design, in the particulars he gives concerning John, was to fix the time for the appearance of Jesus. To agree with this purpose, he must have understood that Jesus came to the banks of the Jordan and began to teach, shortly after the appearance of John.[13] For that the above chronological determination was originally merely the introduction to a document concerning John, quoted by Luke, is improbable, since its exactness corresponds with the style of him *who had perfect understanding of all things from the very*

---

[8] Michaelis, Paulus, in loc. Schneckenburger, in Ullmann's und Umbreit's Studien, 1833, 4 Heft, s. 1056 ff. Tholück, s. 201 ff.
[9] For, on the authority of a single manuscript to erase, with Schneckenburger and others, the second τετραρχοῦντος, is too evident violence.
[10] Compare with this view, Allgem. Lit. Ztg., 1803, No. 344, s. 552 : De Wette, exeg. Handbuch, in loc.
[11] See Paulus, s. 294.
[12] See Schleiermacher, über den Lukas, s. 62.
[13] Bengel was also of this opinion. Ordo temporum, s. 204 f. ed. 2.

first, παρηκολουθηκότι ἄνωθεν πᾶσιν ἀκριβῶς, and who sought to determine, in like manner, the epoch of the Messiah's birth.

It is not easy, however, to imagine, in accordance with this statement, that John was by so little the predecessor of Jesus, nor is it without reason that the improbability of his having had so short an agency is maintained.   For he had a considerable number of disciples, whom he not only baptized, but taught (Luke xi. 1), and he left behind a party of his peculiar followers (Acts xviii. 25, xix. 3), all which could hardly be the work of a few months.   There needed time, it has been observed, for the Baptist to become so well known, that people would undertake a journey to him in the wilderness ; there needed time for his doctrine to be comprehended, time for it to gain a footing and establish itself, especially as it clashed with the current Jewish ideas ; in a word, the deep and lasting veneration in which John was held by his nation, according to Josephus [14] as well as the evangelists, could not have been so hastily won.[15]

But the foregoing considerations, although they demand, in general, a longer agency for the Baptist, do not prove that the evangelists err in placing the commencement of his ministry shortly before that of Jesus, since they might suppose the required prolongation as a sequel, instead of an introduction, to the appearance of Jesus.   Such a prolongation of the Baptist's ministry, however, is not to be found, at least in the first two Gospels ; for not only do these contain no details concerning John, after the baptism of Jesus, except his sending two disciples (Matt. xi.), which is represented as a consequence of his imprisonment ; but we gather from Matt. iv. 12, Mark i. 14, that during or shortly after the forty days' abode of Jesus in the wilderness, the Baptist was arrested, and thereupon Jesus went into Galilee, and entered on his public career.   Luke, it is true (iv. 14), does not mention the imprisonment of John as the cause of the appearance of Jesus in Galilee, and he seems to regard the commission of the two disciples as occurring while John was at large (vii. 18 ff.) ; and the fourth Evangelist testifies yet more decisively against the notion that John was arrested so soon after the baptism of Jesus ; for in chap. iii. 24, it is expressly stated, that John was actively engaged in his ministry after the first passover, attended by Jesus during His public life.   But on the one hand, as it appears from Luke ix. 9 ; Matt. xiv. 1 ff. ; Mark xiv. 16, that John was put to death long before Jesus, the continuance of his agency after the rise of the latter could not be very protracted (Luke ix. 9 ; Matt. xiv. 1 ff. ; Mark xiv. 16) ; and on the other, that which may be added to the agency of John after the appearance of Jesus, will not make amends for that which is subtracted from it before that epoch.   For, apart from the fact implied by the fourth Evangelist (i. 35), that the Baptist had formed a definite circle of familiar disciples before the appearance of Jesus, it would be difficult to account for the firm footing acquired by his school, if he had laboured only a few months, to be, at their close, eclipsed by Jesus.

There is yet one resource, namely, to separate the baptism of Jesus from the commencement of his ministry, and to say : It was indeed after the first half-year of John's agency that Jesus was so attracted by his fame, as to become a candidate for his baptism ; but for some time subsequently, he either remained among the followers of the Baptist, or went again into retirement, and did not present himself independently until a considerable interval

---

[14] Antiq. xviii. v. 2.
[15] So Cludius, über die Zeit und Lebensdauer Johannis und Jesu.   In Henke's Museum, ii. iii. 502 ff.

had elapsed. By this means we should obtain the requisite extension of John's ministry prior to the more brilliant career of Jesus, without impugning the apparent statement of our evangelists that the baptism of Jesus followed close upon the public appearance of John. But the idea of a long interim, between the baptism of Jesus and the commencement of his ministry, is utterly foreign to the New Testament writers. For that they regard the baptism of Jesus as his consecration to the Messianic office, is proved by the accompanying descent of the spirit and the voice from heaven; the only pause which they allow to intervene, is the six weeks' fast in the wilderness, immediately after which, according to Luke, or after the apparently cotemporary arrest of the Baptist, according to Matthew and Mark, Jesus appears in Galilee. Luke, in particular, by designating (iii. 23) the baptism of Jesus as his ἄρχεσθαι, his assumption of office, and by dating the intercourse of Jesus with his disciples from the βάπτισμα Ἰωάννου (Acts i. 22), evinces his persuasion that the baptism and public manifestation of Jesus were identical.

Thus the gospel narrative is an obstacle to the adoption of the two most plausible expedients for the prolongation of John's ministry, viz., that Jesus presented himself for baptism later, or that his public appearance was retarded longer after his baptism, than has been generally inferred. We are not, however, compelled to renounce either of these suppositions, if we can show that the New Testament writers might have been led to their point of view even without historical grounds. A sufficient motive lies close at hand, and is implied in the foregoing observations. Let the Baptist once be considered, as was the case in the Christian Church (Acts xix. 4), not a person of independent significance, but simply a Forerunner of the Christ; and the imagination would not linger with the mere Precursor, but would hasten forward to the object at which he pointed. Yet more obvious is the interest which primitive Christian tradition must have had in excluding, whatever might have been the fact, any interval between the baptism of Jesus and the beginning of his public course. For to allow that Jesus, by his submission to John's baptism, declared himself his disciple, and remained in that relation for any length of time, was offensive to the religious sentiment of the new church, which desired a Founder instructed by God, and not by man: another turn, therefore, would soon be given to the facts, and the baptism of Jesus would be held to signify, not his initiation into the school of John, but a consecration to his independent office. Thus the diverging testimony of the evangelists does not preclude our adopting the conclusion to which the nature of the case leads us; viz., that the Baptist had been long labouring, anterior to the appearance of Jesus. *

If, in addition to this, we accept the statement of Luke (i. 26 and iii. 23), that Jesus, being only half a year younger than John, was about in his thirtieth year at his appearance, we must suppose that John was in his twentieth year when he began his ministry. There is, as we have seen, no express law against so early an exercise of the prophetic office; neither do I, so decidedly as Cludius,[16] hold it improbable that so young a preacher of repentance should make an impression, or even that he should be taken for a prophet of the olden time—an Elias; I will only appeal to the ordinary course of things as a sanction for presuming, that one who entered so much earlier upon the scene of action was proportionately older, especially when the principles and spirit of his teaching tell so plainly of a mature age as do the discourses of John. There are exceptions to this rule; but the statement of Luke (i. 26), that John was only six months older than Jesus, is insufficient

[16] Cludius, ut sup.

to establish one in this instance, as it accords with the interest of the poetical legend, and must therefore be renounced for the slightest improbability. The result then of our critique on the chronological data Luke iii. 1, 2, comp. 23 and i. 26, is this : if Jesus, as Luke seems to understand, appeared in the fifteenth year of Tiberius, the appearance of John occurred, not in the same year, but earlier; and if Jesus was in his thirtieth year when he began his ministry, the Baptist, so much his predecessor, could hardly be but six months his senior.

§ 45.

APPEARANCE AND DESIGN OF THE BAPTIST. HIS PERSONAL RELATIONS WITH JESUS.

John, a Nazarite, according to our authorities (Matt. iii. 4, ix. 14, xi. 18 ; Luke i. 15), and in the opinion of several theologians,[1] an Essene, is said by Luke (iii. 2) to have been summoned to his public work by the *word of God* ῥῆμα Θεοῦ, which came to him in the wilderness. Not possessing the Baptist's own declaration, we cannot accept as complete the dilemma stated by Paulus,[2] when he says, that we know not whether John himself interpreted some external or internal fact as a divine call, or whether he received a summons from another individual ; and we must add as a third possibility, that his followers sought to dignify the vocation of their Teacher by an expression which recalls to mind the ancient Prophets.

While from the account of Luke it appears that the divine call came to John *in the wilderness,* ἐν τῇ ἐρήμῳ, but that for the purpose of teaching and baptizing he resorted to *the country about Jordan,* περίχωρος τοῦ Ἰορδάνου (ver. 3) ; Matthew (iii. ff.) makes the wilderness of Judea the scene of his labours, as if the Jordan in which he baptized flowed through that wilderness. It is true that, according to Josephus, the Jordan before emptying itself into the Dead Sea traverses a *great wilderness,* πολλὴν ἐρημίαν,[3] but this was not the wilderness of Judea, which lay farther south.[4] Hence it has been supposed that Matthew, misled by his application of the prophecy, *the voice of one crying in the wilderness,* φωνὴ βοῶντος ἐν τῇ ἐρήμῳ, to John, who issued from *the wilderness of Judea,* ἔρημος τῆς Ἰουδαίας, placed there his labours as a preacher of repentance and a baptizer, although their true scene was the blooming valley of the Jordan.[5] In the course of Luke's narrative, however, this evangelist ceases to intimate that John forsook the wilderness after receiving his call, for on the occasion of John's message to Jesus, he makes the latter ask , *Whom went ye out into the wilderness to see ?* Τί ἐξεληλύθατε εἰς τὴν ἔρημον θεάσασθαι (vii. 24). Now as the valley of the Jordan in the vicinity of the Dead Sea was in fact a barren plain, the narrow margin of the river excepted, no greater mistake may belong to Matthew than that of specifying the wilderness as the ἔρημος τῆς Ἰουδαίας ; and even that may be explained away by the supposition, either that John, as he alternately preached and baptized, passed from the wilderness of Judea to the borders

---

[1] Stäudlin, Geschichte der Sittenlehre Jesu, 1, s. 580.   Paulus, exeg. Handb. 1 a, s. 136. Comp. also Creuzer, Symbolik, 4, s. 413 ff.
[2] Ut sup. p. 347.
[3] Bell. jud. iii. x. 7.
[4] See Winer, bibl. Realwörterbuch, A. Wüste.   Schneckenburger, über den Ursprung des ersten kanonischen Evangeliums, s. 39.
[5] Schneckenburger, ut sup., s. 38 f.

of the Jordan,[6] or that the waste tract through which that river flowed, being a continuation of the wilderness of Judea, retained the same name.[7] The baptism of John could scarcely have been derived from the baptism of proselytes,[8] for this rite was unquestionably posterior to the rise of Christianity. It was more analagous to the religious lustrations in practice amongst the Jews, especially the Essenes, and was apparently founded chiefly on certain expressions used by several of the prophets in a figurative sense, but afterwards understood literally. According to these expressions, God requires from the Israelitish people, as a condition of their restoration to his favour, a washing and purification from their iniquity, and he promises that he will himself cleanse them with water (Isaiah i. 16, Ez. xxxvi. 25, comp. Jer. ii. 22). Add to this the Jewish notion that the Messiah would not appear with his kingdom until the Israelites repented,[9] and we have the combination necessary for the belief that an ablution, symbolical of conversion and forgiveness of sins, must precede the advent of the Messiah.

Our accounts are not unanimous as to the signification of John's baptism. They all, it is true, agree in stating *repentance*, μετάνοια, to be one of its essential requirements ; for even what Josephus says of the Baptist, that he admonished the Jews, *practising virtue, just towards each other, and devout towards God, to come to his baptism*, ἀρετὴν ἐπασκοῦντας, καὶ τῇ πρὸς ἀλλήλους δικαιοσύνῃ καὶ πρὸς τὸν Θεὸν εὐσεβείᾳ χρωμένους βαπτισμῷ συνιέναι,[10] has the same sense under a Greek form. Mark and Luke, however, while designating the baptism of John, βάπτισμα μετανοίας, add, εἰς ἄφεσιν ἁμαρτιῶν (i. 4, iii. 3). Matthew has not the same addition ; but he, with Mark, describes the baptized as *confessing their sins*, ἐξομολογούμενοι τὰς ἁμαρτίας αὐτῶν (iii. 6). Josephus, on the other hand, appears in direct contradiction to them, when he gives it as the opinion of the Baptist, that *baptism is pleasing to God, not when we ask pardon for some transgressions, but when we purify the body, after having first purified the mind by righteousness*, οὕτω γὰρ καὶ τὴν βάπτισιν ἀποδεκτὴν αὐτῷ (τῷ Θεῷ) φανεῖσθαι, μὴ ἐπί τίνων ἁμαρτάδων παραιτήσει χρωμένων, ἀλλ᾽ ἐφ᾽ ἁγνείᾳ τοῦ σώματος, ἅτε δὴ ͺκαὶ τῆς ψυχῆς δικαιοσύνῃ προεκκεκαθαρμένης. We might here be led to the supposition that the words *for the remission of sins*, εἰς ἄφεσιν ἁμαρτιῶν, as in Acts ii. 38, and other passages, was commonly used in relation to Christian baptism, and was thence transferred unhistorically to that of John ; but as in the passages quoted from Ezekiel the washing typified not only reformation but forgiveness, the probabilities are in favour of the evangelical statement. Moreover, it is possible to reconcile Josephus and the Evangelists, by understanding the words of the former to mean that the baptism of John was intended to effect a purification, not from particular or merely Levitical transgressions, but of the entire man, not immediately and mysteriously through the agency of water, but by means of the moral acts of reformation.[11]

The several accounts concerning John are farther at variance, as to the relation in which they place his baptism to the *kingdom of heaven*, βασιλεία τῶν οὐρανῶν. According to Matthew, the concise purport of the appeal with which he accompanied his baptism was, *Repent, for the kingdom of heaven is at hand*, μετανοεῖτε᾽ ἤγγικε γὰρ ἡ βασιλεία τῶν οὐρανῶν (iii. 2); according to

---

[6] Winer, ut sup., s. 691.

[7] Paulus, ut sup., s. 301.

[8] Schneckenburger, über das Alter der Jüdischen Proselytentaufe.

[9] Sanhedr. f. xcvii. 2 : *R. Elieser dixit: si Israëlitæ pœnitentiam agunt, tunc per Goëlem liberantur ; sin vero, non liberantur.* Schöttgen, horæ, 2, p. 780 ff.

[10] Antiq. xviii. v. 2.

[11] Thus Paulus, ut sup., s. 314 and 361, Anm.

Luke, the Baptist in the first instance mentions only repentance and remission of sins, but no kingdom of heaven; and it is the conjecture of the people, that he might be the Messiah, by which he is first led to direct them to one who was coming after him (iii. 15 ff.). In Josephus, there is no trace of a relation between the ministry of John and the Messianic idea. Yet we must not therefore conclude that the Baptist himself recognized no such relation, and that its only source was the Christian legend. For the baptism of John, waiving the opinion that it was derived from the baptism of proselytes, is not quite explicable without a reference to the above-mentioned expiatory lustrations of the people—lustrations which were to usher in the times of the Messiah; moreover, the appearance of Jesus is made more comprehensible by the supposition, that John had introduced the idea of the proximity of the Messiah's kingdom. That Josephus should keep back the Messianic aspect of the fact, is in accordance with his general practice, which is explained by the position of his people with respect to the Romans. Besides, in the expression, *to assemble for baptism*, βαπτισμῷ συνιέναι, in his mention of popular *assemblages*, συστρέφεσθαι, and in the fear of Antipas lest John should excite a *revolt*, ἀπόστασις, there lies an intimation of precisely such a religious and political movement as the hope of the Messiah was calculated to produce. That the Baptist should so distinctly foretell the immediate appearance of the Messiah's kingdom must create surprise, and (Luke's reference to a divine call and revelation being held unsatisfactory) might lead to the supposition that the Christian narrator, believing that the true Messiah was actually manifested in the person of Jesus, the cotemporary of John, gave to the language of the latter a definiteness which did not belong to it originally; and while the Baptist merely said, consonantly with the Jewish notion already mentioned : *Repent, that the kingdom of heaven may come*, μετανοεῖτε, ἵνα ἔλθῃ ἡ βασ. τ. οὐρ., a later edition of his words gave γὰρ (*for*) instead of ἵνα (*that*). But such a supposition is needless. In those times of commotion, John might easily believe that he discerned signs, which certified to him the proximity of the Messiah's kingdom; the exact degree of its proximity he left undecided.

According to the Evangelists, the coming of the *kingdom of heaven*, βασιλεία τῶν οὐρανῶν, was associated by John with a Messianic individual to whom he ascribed, in distinction from his own baptism with water, a *baptism with the Holy Ghost and with fire*, βαπτίζειν πνεύματι ἁγίῳ καὶ πυρὶ (Matt. iii. 11 parall.), the outpouring of the Holy Spirit being regarded as a leading feature of the Messianic times (Joel ii. 28 ; Acts ii. 16 ff.). Of this personage he farther predicted, in imagery akin to that used by the prophets on the same subject, that he would winnow the people as wheat (Mal. iii. 2, 3 ; Zech. xiii. 9). The Synoptical Gospels state the case as if John expressly understood this Messianic individual to be Jesus of Nazareth. According to Luke, indeed, the mothers of these two men were cousins, and aware of the destination of their sons. The Baptist while yet unborn acknowledged the divinity of Jesus, and all the circumstances imply that both were early acquainted with their relative position, predetermined by a heavenly communication. Matthew, it is true, says nothing of such a family connexion between John and Jesus ; but when the latter presents himself for baptism, he puts into the mouth of John words which seem to presuppose an earlier acquaintance. His expression of astonishment that Jesus should come to him for baptism, when he had need to be baptized of Jesus, could only arise from a previous knowledge or instantaneous revelation of his character. Of the latter there is no intimation ; for the first visible sign of the Messiahship of Jesus did not occur till afterwards. While in the first and third Gospels (in the second, the facts are so epitomized that the writer's view on the subject is not evident), John and Jesus seem to have been no strangers to each other prior to the baptism ; in the fourth, the Baptist pointedly asserts that he knew not Jesus before the heavenly appearance, which, according to the Synoptical Gospels, was coincident with his baptism (i. 31, 33). Simply considered, this looks like a contradiction. By Luke, the previous acquaintance of the two is stated objectively, as an external matter of fact ; by Matthew, it is betrayed in the involuntary confession of the astonished Baptist ; in the fourth Gospel, on the contrary, their previous unacquaintance is attested subjectively, by his premeditated assertion. It was not, therefore, a very far-fetched idea of the Wolfenbüttel fragmentist, to put down the contradiction to the account of John and Jesus, and to presume that they had in fact long known and consulted each other, but that in public (in order better to play into one another's hands) they demeaned themselves as if they had hitherto been mutual strangers, and each delivered an unbiassed testimony to the other's excellence.[12]

That such premeditated dissimulation might not be imputed to John, and indirectly to Jesus, it has been sought to disprove the existence of the contradiction in question exegetically. What John learned from the heavenly sign was the Messiahship of Jesus ; to this therefore, and not to his person, refer the words, *I knew him not*, κἀγὼ οὐκ ᾔδειν αὐτὸν.[13] But it may be questioned whether such an acquaintance as John must have had with Jesus, presupposing the narrative of Matthew and Luke, was separable from a knowledge of his Messiahship. The connection and intercourse of the two families, as described by Luke, would render it impossible for John not to be early informed how solemnly Jesus had been announced as the Messiah, before and at his birth ; he could not therefore say at a later period that, prior to the sign from heaven, he had not *known*, but only that he had not *believed*, the story of former wonders, one of which relates to himself.[14] It being thus unavoidable to acknowledge that by the above declaration in the fourth Gospel, the Baptist is excluded, not only from a knowledge of the Messiahship of Jesus, but also from a personal acquaintance with him ; it has been attempted to reconcile the first chapter of Luke with this ignorance, by appealing to the distance of residence between the two families, as a preventive to the continuance of their intercourse.[15] But if the journey from Nazareth to the hill country of Judea was not too formidable for the betrothed Mary, how could it be so for the two sons when ripening to maturity? What culpable indifference is hereby supposed in both families to the heavenly communications they had received ! nay, what could be the object of those communications, if they had no influence on the early life and intercourse of the two sons ?[16]

Let it be granted that the fourth Gospel excludes an acquaintance with the

---

[12] Fragment von dem Zwecke Jesu und seiner Jünger, herausgegeben von Lessing, s. 133 ff.

[13] So thinks Semler in his answer to the above Fragments, in loc. ; so think most of the moderns ; Plank, Geschichte des Christenthums in der Periode seiner Einführung, I, K. 7. Winer, bibl. Realwörterbuch, I, s. 691.

[14] Let the reader judge for himself whether Neander's arguments be not forced : " Even if the Baptist could have expected " (say rather must necessarily have known) " from the circumstances of the birth of Jesus, that he was the Messiah, the divine witness in his own mind would eclipse all external testimony, and compared with this divine illumination, all previous knowledge would seem ignorance." p. 68.

[15] Lücke, Commentar zum Evang. Johannis I, s. 362.

[16] Osiander, in despair, answers, that the heavenly communications themselves might contain directions for—keeping the two youths apart ! s. 127.

Messiahship only of Jesus, and that the third presupposes an acquaintance
with his person only, on the part of John; still the contradiction is not removed. For in Matthew, John, when required to baptize Jesus, addresses
him as if he knew him, not generally and personally alone, but specially, in
his character of Messiah. It is true that the words : *I have need to be baptized
of thee, and comest thou to me ?* (iii. 14), have been interpreted, in the true
spirit of harmonizing, as referring to the general superior excellence of Jesus,
and not to his Messiahship.[17] But the right to undertake the baptism which
was to prepare the way for the Messiah's kingdom, was not to be obtained by
moral superiority in general, but was conferred by a special call, such as John
himself had received, and such as could belong only to a prophet, or to the
Messiah and his Forerunner (John i. 19 ff.). If then John attributed to Jesus
authority to baptize, he must have regarded him not merely as an excellent
man, but as indubitably a prophet, nay, since he held him worthy to baptize
himself, as his own superior : that is, since John conceived himself to be the
Messiah's Forerunner, no other than the Messiah himself. Add to this, that
Matthew had just cited a discourse of the Baptist, in which he ascribes to the
coming Messiah a baptism more powerful than his own; how then can we
understand his subsequent language towards Jesus otherwise than thus : " Of
what use is my water baptism to thee, O Messiah? Far more do I need thy
baptism of the Spirit !" [18]

The contradiction cannot be cleared away ; we must therefore, if we would
not lay the burthen of intentional deception on the agents, let the narrators
bear the blame ; and there will be the less hindrance to our doing so, the
more obvious it is how one or both of them might be led into an erroneous
statement.   There is in the present case no obstacle to the reconciliation of
Matthew with the fourth evangelist, farther than the words by which the
Baptist seeks to deter Jesus from receiving baptism ; words which, if uttered
before the occurrence of anything supernatural, presuppose a knowledge of
Jesus in his character of Messiah.   Now the Gospel of the Hebrews, according to Epiphanius, places the entreaty of John that Jesus would baptize him,
as a sequel to the sign from heaven ; [19] and this account has been recently
regarded as the original one, abridged by the writer of our first Gospel, who,
for the sake of effect, made the refusal and confession of the Baptist coincident with the first approach of Jesus.[20]   But that we have not in the Gospel
of the Hebrews the original form of the narrative, is sufficiently proved by its
very tedious repetition of the heavenly voice and the diffuse style of the
whole.   It is rather a very traditional record, and the insertion of John's
refusal after the sign and voice from heaven, was not made with the view of
avoiding a contradiction of the fourth Gospel, which cannot be supposed to
have been recognized in the circle of the Ebionite Christians, but from the
very motive erroneously attributed to Matthew in his alleged transposition,

---

[17] Hess, Geschichte Jesu, 1, s. 117 f.   Paulus, ut sup., s. 366.
[18] Comp. the Fragmentist, ut sup.
[19] Hæres. xxx. 13 : Καὶ ὡς ἀνῆλθεν ἀπὸ τοῦ ὕδατος, ἠνοίγησαν οἱ οὐρανοί, καὶ εἶδε τὸ πνεῦμα
τοῦ Θεοῦ τὸ ἅγιον ἐν εἴδει περιστερᾶς κ. τ. λ. καὶ φωνὴ ἐγένετο, κ. τ. λ. καὶ εὐθὺς περιέλαμψε τὸν
τόπον φῶς μέγα· ὃν ἰδών, φησίν, ὁ Ἰωάννης λέγει αὐτῷ σύ τίς εἶ, Κύριε ; καὶ πάλιν φωνὴ κ. τ. λ.
καὶ τότε, φησίν, ὁ Ἰωάννης παραπεσὼν αὐτῷ ἔλεγε· δέομαι σοῦ Κύριε, σύ με βάπτισον. *And
when he came from the water, the heavens were opened, and he saw the holy spirit of God in
the form of a dove, etc., and a voice was heard, etc., and immediately a great light illuminated
the place ; seeing which, John said to him, Who art thou, Lord ? and again a voice, etc. And
then, John falling at his feet, said to him, I beseech thee, Lord, baptize me.*
[20] Schneckenburger, über den Ursprung des ersten kanonischen Evangeliums, s. 121 f. ;
Lücke, Comm. z. Ev. Joh., 1, s. 361. Usteri, über den Täufer Johannes u. s. w., Studien,
2, 3. s. 446.

namely, to give greater effect to the scene. A simple refusal on the part of the Baptist appeared too weak ; he must at least fall at the feet of Jesus ; and a more suitable occasion could not be given than that of the sign from heaven, which accordingly must be placed beforehand. This Hebrew Gospel, therefore, will not help us to understand how Matthew was led into contradiction with John ; still less will it avail for the explanation of Luke's narrative.

All is naturally explained by the consideration, that the important relation between John and Jesus must have been regarded as existing at all times, by reason of that ascription of pre-existence to the essential which is a characteristic of the popular mind. Just as the soul, when considered as an essence, is conceived more or less clearly as pre-existent ; so in the popular mind, every relation pregnant with consequences is endowed with pre-existence. Hence the Baptist, who eventually held so significant a relation to Jesus, must have known him from the first, as is indistinctly intimated by Matthew, and more minutely detailed by Luke ; according to whom, their mothers knew each other, and the sons themselves were brought together while yet unborn. All this is wanting in the fourth Gospel, the writer of which attributes an opposite assertion to John, simply because in his mind an opposite interest preponderated ; for the less Jesus was known to John by whom he was afterwards so extolled, the more weight was thrown on the miraculous scene which arrested the regards of the Baptist—the more clearly was his whole position with respect to Jesus demonstrated to be the effect, not of the natural order of events, but of the immediate agency of God.

§ 46.

WAS JESUS ACKNOWLEDGED BY JOHN AS THE MESSIAH? AND IN WHAT SENSE?

To the foregoing question whether Jesus was known to John before the baptism, is attached another, namely, What did John think of Jesus and his Messiahship? The evangelical narratives are unanimous in stating, that before Jesus had presented himself for baptism, John had announced the immediate coming of One to whom he stood in a subordinate relation ; and the scene at the baptism of Jesus marked him, beyond mistake, as the personage of whom John was the forerunner. According to Mark and Luke, we must presume that the Baptist gave credence to this sign ; according to the fourth Gospel, he expressly attested his belief (i. 34), and moreover uttered words which evince the deepest insight into the higher nature and office of Jesus (i. 29 ff. 36 ; iii. 27 ff.) ; according to the first Gospel, he was already convinced of these before the baptism of Jesus. On the other hand, Matthew (xi. 2 ff.) and Luke (vii. 18 ff.) tell us that at a later period, the Baptist, on hearing of the ministry of Jesus, despatched some of his disciples to him with the inquiry, whether he (Jesus) was the promised Messiah, or whether another must be expected.

The first impression from this is, that the question denoted an uncertainty on the part of the Baptist whether Jesus were really the Messiah ; and so it was early understood.[1] But such a doubt is in direct contradiction with all the other circumstances reported by the Evangelists. It is justly regarded as

---

[1] Tertull. adv. Marcion, iv. 18. Comp. Bengel, historico-exegetical remarks in Matt. xi. 2-19, in his Archiv. I, iii. p. 754 ff.

psychologically impossible that he whose belief was originated or confirmed by the baptismal sign, which he held to be a divine revelation, and who afterwards pronounced so decidedly on the Messianic call and the superior nature of Jesus, should all at once have become unsteady in his conviction ; he must then indeed have been like a reed shaken by the wind, a comparison which Jesus abnegates on this very occasion (Matt. xi. 7).   A cause for such vacillation is in vain sought in the conduct or fortunes of Jesus at the time ; for the rumour of *the works of Christ*, ἔργα τοῦ Χριστοῦ, which in Luke's idea were miracles, could not awaken doubt in the Baptist, and it was on this rumour that he sent his message.   Lastly, how could Jesus subsequently (John v. 33 ff.) so confidently appeal to the testimony of the Baptist concerning him, when it was known that John himself was at last perplexed about his Messiahship ?[2]

Hence it has been attempted to give a different turn to the facts, and to show that John's inquiry was not made on his own account, but for the sake of his disciples, to overcome in them the doubt with which he was himself untainted.[3]   Hereby it is true, the above-named difficulties are removed ; in particular it is explained why the Baptist should contrive to send this message precisely on hearing of the miracles of Jesus ; he plainly hoping that his disciples, who had not believed his testimony to the Messiahship of Jesus, would be convinced of its truth by beholding the marvellous works of the latter.   But how could John hope that his envoys would chance to find Jesus in the act of working miracles ?   According to Matthew, indeed, they did not so find him, and Jesus appeals (v. 4) only to his former works, many of which they had seen, and of which they might hear wherever he had presented himself.   Luke alone, in giving his evidently second-hand narrative,[4] misconstrues the words of Jesus to require that the disciples of John should have found him in the exercise of his supernatural power.   Further, if it had been the object of the Baptist to persuade his disciples by a sight of the works of Jesus, he would not have charged them with a question which could be answered by the mere words, the authentic declaration of Jesus.   For he could not hope by the assertion of the person whose Messiahship was the very point in debate, to convince the disciples whom his own declaration, in other cases authoritative, had failed to satisfy.   On the whole, it would have been a singular course in the Baptist to lend his own words to the doubts of others, and thereby, as Schleiermacher well observes, to compromise his early and repeated testimony in favour of Jesus.   It is clear that Jesus understood the question proposed to him by the messengers as proceeding from John himself ; (ἀπαγγείλατε Ἰωάννῃ, Matt. xi. 4 ;) and he indirectly complained of the want of faith in the latter by pronouncing those blessed who were not offended in him (ver. 6).[5]

If then it must be granted that John made his inquiry on his own behalf, and not on that of his disciples, and if nevertheless we cannot impute to him a sudden lapse into doubt after his previous confidence ; nothing remains but to take the positive instead of the negative side of the question, and to consider its scepticism as the mere garb of substantial encouragement.[6]   On this

---

[2] See Paulus, Kuinöl, in loc.   Bengel, ut sup., p. 763.
[3] Calvin, Comm. in harm. ex. Matth., Marc. et Luc. in loc.
[4] We agree with Schleiermacher, (über den Lukas, s. 106 f) in thus designating the narrative of the third evangelist, first, on account of the idle repetition of the Baptist's words, ver. 20 ; secondly, on account of the mistake in ver. 18 and 21, of which we shall presently treat, and to which ver. 29, 30, seem to betray a similar one.
[5] Compare Calvin in loc. and Bengel ut sup., s. 753 ff.
[6] Thus most recent commentators : Paulus, Kuinöl, Bengel, Hase, Theile, and even Fritsche.

interpretation, the time which Jesus allowed to escape without publicly manifesting himself as the Messiah, seemed too tedious to John in his imprisonment; he sent therefore to inquire how long Jesus would allow himself to be
waited for, how long he would delay winning to himself the better part of the
people by a declaration of his Messiahship, and striking a decisive blow
against the enemies of his cause—a blow that might even liberate the Baptist
from his prison. But if the Baptist, on the strength of his belief that Jesus
was the Messiah, hoped and sued for a deliverance, perhaps miraculous, by
him from prison, he would not clothe in the language of doubt an entreaty
which sprang out of his faith. Now the inquiry in our evangelical text is one
of unmixed doubt, and encouragement must be foisted in, before it can be
found there. How great a violence must be done to the words is seen by the
way in which Schleiermacher handles them in accordance with this interpretation. The dubitative question, σὺ εἶ ὁ ἐρχόμενος; he changes into the
positive assumption, *thou art he who was to come*; the other still more embarrassing interrogatory, ἢ ἕτερον προσδοκῶμεν; he completely transfigures
thus : *wherefore (seeing that thou performest so great works) do we yet await
thee ?—shall not John with all his authority command, through us, all those who
have partaken of his baptism to obey thee as the Messiah, and be attentive to thy
signs ?* Even if we allow, with Neander, the possibility of truth to this interpretation, a mere summons to action will not accord with the earlier representation of Jesus given by the Baptist. The two enunciations are at issue
as to form ; for if John doubted not the Messiahship of Jesus, neither could
he doubt his better knowledge of the fitting time and manner of his appearance : still farther are they at issue as to matter ; for the Baptist could not
take offence at what is termed the delay of Jesus in manifesting himself as
the Messiah, or wish to animate him to bolder conduct, if he retained his
early view of the destination of Jesus. If he still, as formerly, conceived Jesus
to be *the Lamb of God that taketh away the sins of the world*, ὁ ἀμνὸς τοῦ Θεοῦ,
ὁ αἴρων τὴν ἁμαρτίαν τοῦ κόσμου, no thought could occur to him of a blow to
be struck by Jesus against his enemies, or in general, of a violent procedure to
be crowned by external conquest ; rather, the quiet path which Jesus trod
must appear to him the right one—the path befitting the destination of the
Lamb of God. Thus if the question of John conveyed a mere summons to
action, it contradicted his previous views.

These expedients failing, the original explanation returns upon us ; namely,
that the inquiry was an expression of uncertainty respecting the messianic
dignity of Jesus, which had arisen in the Baptist's own mind ; an explanation
which even Neander allows to be the most natural. This writer seeks to account
for the transient apostacy of the Baptist from the strong faith in which he gave
his earlier testimony, by the supposition that a dark hour of doubt had overtaken the man of God in his dismal prison ; and he cites instances of men
who, persecuted for their Christian faith or other convictions, after having
long borne witness to the truth in the face of death, at length yielded to
human weakness and recanted. But on a closer examination, he has given a
false analogy. Persecuted Christians of the first centuries, and, later, a
Berengarius or a Galileo, were false to the convictions for which they were
imprisoned, and by abjuring which they hoped to save themselves : the
Baptist, to be compared with them, should have retracted his censure of
Herod, and not have shaken his testimony in favour of Christ, which had no
relation to his imprisonment. However that may be, it is evident here that
these doubts cannot have been preceded by a state of certainty.

We come again to the difficulty arising from the statement of Matthew that
John sent his two disciples on hearing of the *works of Christ*, ἀκούσας τὰ

ἔργα τοῦ Χριστοῦ, or as Luke has it, because his disciples *showed him of all these things*, ἀπήγγειλαν περὶ πάντων τούτων. The latter evangelist has narrated, immediately before, the raising of the widow's son, and the healing of the centurion's servant. Could John, then, believe Jesus to be the Messiah before he had performed any messianic works, and be seized with doubt when he began to legitimatize his claim by miracles such as were expected from the Messiah [7]? This is so opposed to all pyschological probability, that I wonder Dr. Paulus, or some other expositor versed in pyschology and not timid in verbal criticism, has not started the conjecture that a negative has slipped out of Matt. xi. 2, and that its proper reading is, ὁ δὲ Ἰωάννης οὐκ ἀκούσας ἐν τῳ δεσμωτηρίῳ τὰ ἔργα τοῦ Χριστοῦ, κ. τ. λ. It might then be conceived, that John had indeed been convinced, at a former period, of the Messiahship of Jesus; now, however, in his imprisonment, the works of Jesus came no longer to his ears, and imagining him inactive, he was assailed with doubt. But had John been previously satisfied of the Messiahship of Jesus, the mere want of acquaintance with his miracles could not have unhinged his faith. The actual cause of John's doubt, however, was the report of these miracles;—a state of the case which is irreconcilable with any previous confidence.

But how could he become uncertain about the Messiahship of Jesus, if he had never recognised it? Not indeed in the sense of beginning to suspect that Jesus was *not* the Messiah; but quite possibly in the sense of beginning to conjecture that a man of such deeds *was* the Messiah.

We have here, not a decaying, but a growing certainty, and this discrimination throws light on the whole purport of the passages in question. John knew nothing of Jesus before, but that he had, like many others, partaken of his baptism, and perhaps frequented the circle of his disciples; and not until after the imprisonment of the Baptist did Jesus appear as a teacher, and worker of miracles. Of this John heard, and then arose in his mind a conjecture, fraught with hope, that as he had announced the proximity of the Messiah's kingdom, this Jesus might be he who would verify his idea.[8] So interpreted, this message of the Baptist excludes his previous testimony; if he had so spoken formerly, he could not have so inquired latterly, and *vice versâ*. It is our task, therefore, to compare the two contradictory statements, that we may ascertain which has more traces than the other, of truth or untruth.

The most definite expressions of John's conviction that Jesus was the Messiah are found in the fourth Gospel, and these suggest two distinct questions: first, whether it be conceivable that John had such a notion of the Messiah as is therein contained; and, secondly, whether it be probable that he believed it realized in the person of Jesus.

With respect to the former, the fourth Gospel makes the Baptist's idea of the Messiah include the characteristics of expiatory suffering, and of a premundane, heavenly existence. It has been attempted, indeed, so to interpret the expressions with which he directs his disciples to Jesus, as to efface the notion of expiatory suffering. Jesus, we are told, is compared to a lamb on account of his meekness and patience; αἴρειν τὴν ἁμαρτίαν τοῦ κόσμου, is to

---

[7] This difficulty occurred to Bengel also, ut sup., p. 769.

[8] The gospel writers, after what they had narrated of the relations between Jesus and the Baptist, of course understood the question to express doubt, whence probably v. 6 (Matt.) and v. 23 (Luke) came in this connection. Supposing these passages authentic, they suggest another conjecture; viz. that Jesus spoke in the foregoing verses of spiritual miracles, and that the Baptist was perplexed by the absence of corporeal ones. The ἀκούσας τὰ ἔργα τ. Χ. must then be set down to the writer's misapprehension of the expressions of Jesus.

be understood either of a patient endurance of the world's malice, or of an endeavour to remove the sins of the world by reforming it; and the sense of the Baptist's words is this : " How moving is it that this meek and gentle Jesus should have undertaken so difficult and painful an office [9] !" But the best critics have shown that even if αἴρειν by itself might bear this interpretation, still ἀμνὸς, not merely with the article but with the addition τοῦ Θεοῦ, must signify, not a lamb in general, but a special, holy Lamb ; and if, as is most probable, this designation has reference to Isa. liii. 7., αἴρειν τὴν ἁμαρτίαν can only be expounded by what is there predicated of the lamb-like servant of God, that he τὰς ἁμαρτίας ἡμῶν φέρει, καὶ περὶ ἡμῶν ὀδυνᾶται (V. 4, LXX.), words which must signify vicarious suffering.[10] Now that the Baptist should have referred the above prophetic passage to the Messiah, and hence have thought of him as suffering, has been recently held more than doubtful.[11]

For so foreign to the current opinion, at least, was this notion of the Messiah, that the disciples of Jesus, during the whole period of their intercourse with him, could not reconcile themselves to it ; and when his death had actually resulted, their trust in him as the Messiah was utterly confounded (Luke xxiv. 20 ff.). How, then, could the Baptist, who, according to the solemn declaration of Jesus, Matt. xi. 11, confirmed by the allusions in the Gospels to his strict ascetic life, ranked below the least in the kingdom of heaven, to which the apostles already belonged—how could this alien discern, long before the sufferings of Jesus, that they pertained to the character of the Messiah, when the denizens were only taught the same lesson by the issue ? Or, if the Baptist really had such insight, and communicated it to his disciples, why did it not, by means of those who left his circle for that of Jesus, win an entrance into the latter—nay, why did it not, by means of the great credit which John enjoyed, mitigate the offence caused by the death of Jesus, in the public at large [12] ? Add to this, that in none of our accounts of the Baptist, with the exception of the fourth Gospel, do we find that he entertained such views of the Messiah's character ; for, not to mention Josephus, the Synoptical Gospels confine his representation of the Messianic office to the spiritual baptism and winnowing of the people. Still it remains possible that a penetrating mind, like that of the Baptist, might, even before the death of Jesus, gather from Old Testament phrases and types the notion of a suffering Messiah, and that his obscure hints on the subject might not be comprehended by his disciples and cotemporaries.

Thus the above considerations are not decisive, and we therefore turn to the expressions concerning the premundane existence and heavenly origin of the Messiah, with the question : Could the Baptist have really held such tenets ? That from the words, John i. 15, 27, 30 : *He that cometh after me is preferred before me; for he was before me,* ὁ ὀπίσω μοῦ ἐρχόμενος ἔμπροσθέν μοῦ γέγονεν, ὅτι πρῶτός μου ἦν, nothing but dogmatical obstinacy can banish the notion of pre-existence, is seen by a mere glance at such expositions as this of Paulus : " He who in the course of time comes after me ; has so appeared in my eyes, ἔμπροσθέν μοῦ, that he (ὅτι—ὥστε, premiss—conclusion !) deserves rather from his rank and character to be called the first." [13] With preponderating arguments more unprejudiced commentators have

[9] Gabler and Paulus.
[10] De Wette, de morte Christi expiatoria, in his Opusc. theol., s. 77 ff.   Lücke, Comm. zum Ev. Joh. 1, s. 347 ff.   Winer, bibl. Realwörterb. 1, s. 693, Anm.
[11] Gabler and Paulus. De Wette.
[12] De Wette, ut sup, p. 76.
[13] Paulus, Leben Jesu, 2 a, die Übers., s. 29. 31.

maintained, that the reason here given why Jesus, who appeared after the Baptist in point of time, had the precedence of him in dignity, is the pre-existence of the former.[14] We have here obviously the favourite dogma of the fourth Evangelist, the eternal pre-existence of the λόγος, present indeed to the mind of that writer, who had just been inditing his proem, but that it was also present to the mind of the Baptist is another question. The most recent expositor allows that the sense in which the Evangelist intends πρῶτος μου, must have been very remote from the Baptist's point of view, at least so far as the λόγος is concerned. The Baptist, he thinks, held the popular Jewish notion of the pre-existence of the Messiah, as the subject of the Old Testament theophanies.[15] There are traces of this Jewish notion in the writings of Paul (e.g. 1 Cor. x. 4. Col. i. 15 f.) and the rabbins[16] ; and allowing that it was of Alexandrian origin, as Bretschneider argues,[17] we may yet ask whether even before the time of Christ, the Alexandrian-judaic theology may not have modified the opinions of the mother country ?[18] Even these expressions then, taken alone, are not conclusive, although it begins to appear suspicious that the Baptist, otherwise conspicuous for exhibiting the practical side of the idea of the Messiah's kingdom, should have ascribed to him by the fourth Evangelist solely, two notions which at that time undoubtedly belonged only to the deepest messianic speculations ; and that the form in which those notions are expressed is too peculiarly that of the writer, not to be put to his account.

We arrive at a more decisive result by taking into examination the passage John iii. 27–36, where John replies to the complaints of his disciples at the rival baptism of Jesus, in a way that reduces all commentators to perplexity. After showing how it lay at the foundation of their respective destinies, which he desired not to overstep, that he must decrease, while Jesus must increase, he proceeds (ver. 31) to use forms of expression precisely similar to those in which the Evangelist makes Jesus speak of himself, and in which he delivers his own thoughts concerning Jesus. Our most recent commentator[19] allows that this discourse of John seems the echo of the foregoing conversation between Jesus and Nicodemus.[20] The expressions in the speech lent to the Baptist are peculiarly those of the apostle John ; for instance, σφραγίζω (to seal), μαρτυρία (testimony), the antithesis of ἄνωθεν and ἐκ τῆς γῆς (from above and of the earth), the phrase ἔχειν ζωὴν αἰώνιον (to have eternal life) ; and the question presents itself : Is it more probable that the Evangelist, as well as Jesus, in whose mouth these expressions are so often put, borrowed them from the Baptist, or that the Evangelist lent them (I will only at present say) to the latter? This must be decided by the fact that the

---

[14] Tholück and Lücke, in loc.
[15] Lücke, ut sup.
[16] See Bertholdt, Christologia Judæorum Jesu apostolorumque ætate, § 23–25.
[17] Probabilia, p. 41.
[18] See Gfrörer, Philo und die Alexandr. Theosophie, part ii. p. 180.
[19] Lücke, ut sup., p. 500.
[20] Compare especially :

Joh. iii. 11 (Jesus to Nicodemus): ἀμὴν, ἀμὴν, λέγω σοι, ὅτι ὃ οἴδαμεν, λαλοῦμεν, καὶ ὃ ἑωράκαμεν, μαρτυροῦμεν· καὶ τὴν μαρτυρίαν ἡμῶν οὐ λαμβάνετε.

V. 18 : ὁ πιστεύων εἰς αὐτὸν οὐ κρίνεται. ὁ δὲ μὴ πιστεύων, ἤδη κέκριται· ὅτι μὴ πεπίστευκεν εἰς τὸ ὄνομα τοῦ μονογενοῦς υἱοῦ τοῦ Θεοῦ.

Joh. iii. 32 (the Baptist) : καὶ ὃ ἑώρακε καὶ ἤκουσε, τοῦτο μαρτυρεῖ· καὶ τὴν μαρτυρίαν αὐτοῦ οὐδεὶς λαμβάνει.

V. 36 : ὁ πιστεύων εἰς τὸν υἱὸν ἔχει ζωὴν αἰώνιον· ὁ δὲ ἀπειθῶν τῷ υἱῷ, οὐκ ὄψεται ζωήν, ἀλλ' ἡ ὀργὴ τοῦ Θεοῦ μένει ἐπ' αὐτόν.

Comp. also the words of the Baptist v. 31, with Joh. iii. 6. 12 f. viii. 23 ; v. 32 with viii. 26 ; v. 33 with vi. 27 ; v. 34 with xii. 49, 50 ; v. 35 with v. 22, 27, x. 28 f. xvii. 2.

ideas, to which the Baptist here gives utterance, lie entirely within the domain of Christianity, and belong specially to the Christianity of the Apostle John. Take for example that antithesis of ἄνω (*from above*), and ἐκ τῆς γῆς (*of the earth*), the designation of Jesus as ἄνωθεν ἐρχόμενος (*he that cometh from above*), as ὃν ἀπέστειλεν ὁ Θεὸς (*he whom God hath sent*), who consequently τὰ ῥήματα τοῦ Θεοῦ λαλεῖ (*speaketh the words of God*), the relation of Jesus to God as the υἱὸς (*son*), whom ὁ πατὴρ ἀγαπᾷ (*the Father loveth*):—what can be characteristic of Christianity, and of the Apostle John's mode of presenting it, if these ideas are not so? and could they belong to the Baptist? *Christianismus ante Christum!* And then, as Olshausen well observes,[21] is it consistent for John, who, even on the fourth Evangelist's own showing, remained separate from Jesus, to speak of the blessedness of a believing union with him? (v. 33 and 36).

Thus much then is certain, and has been acknowledged by the majority of modern commentators : the words v. 31–36 cannot have been spoken by the Baptist. Hence theologians have concluded, that the Evangelist cannot have intended to ascribe them to him, but from v. 31 speaks in his own person.[22] This sounds plausible, if they can only point out any mark of division between the discourse of the Baptist and the addenda of the Evangelist. But none such is to be found. It is true that the speaker from v. 31 uses the third person, and not the first as in v. 30, when referring to the Baptist : but in the former passage the Baptist is no longer alluded to directly and individually, but as one of a class, in which case he must, though himself the speaker, choose the third person. Thus there is no definitive boundary, and the speech glides imperceptibly from those passages which might have been uttered by the Baptist, into those which are altogether incongruous with his position ; moreover from v. 30 Jesus is spoken of in the present tense, as the Evangelist might represent the Baptist to speak during the lifetime of Jesus, but could not in his own person have written after the death of Jesus. In other passages, when presenting his own reflections concerning Jesus, he uses the preterite.[23] Thus, grammatically, the Baptist continues to speak from v. 31, and yet, historically, it is impossible that he should have uttered the sequel ; a contradiction not to be solved, if it be added that, dogmatically, the Evangelist cannot have ascribed to the Baptist words which he never really pronounced. Now if we do not choose to defy the clear rules of grammar, and the sure data of history, for the sake of the visionary dogma of inspiration, we shall rather conclude from the given premises, with the author of the Probabilia, that the Evangelist falsely ascribes the language in question to the Baptist, putting into his mouth a Christology of his own, of which the latter could know nothing. This is no more than Lücke[24] confesses, though not quite so frankly, when he says that the reflections of the Evangelist are here more than equally mixed with the discourse of the Baptist, in such a way as to be undistinguishable. In point of fact, however, the reflections of the Evangelist are easily to be recognized ; but of the fundamental ideas of the Baptist there is no trace, unless they are sought for with a good will which amounts to prejudice, and to which therefore we make no pretension. If then we have a proof in the passages just considered, that the fourth Evangelist did not hesitate to lend to the Baptist messianic and other ideas which were never his ; we may hence conclude retrospectively

---

[21] Bibl. Comm. 2, p. 105.
[22] Paulus, Olshausen, in loc.
[23] E.g. here, v. 32, it is said : τὴν μαρτυρίαν αὐτοῦ οὐδεὶς λαμβάνει, but in the Prolog. v. 11 : καὶ οἱ ἴδιοι αὐτὸν οὐ παρέλαβον. Comp. Lücke, s. 501.
[24] Ut sup.

concerning the passages on which we formerly suspended our decision, that the ideas expressed in them of a suffering and pre-existent Messiah belonged, not to the Baptist, but to the Evangelist.

In giving the above reply to our first question, we have, in strictness, answered the remaining one; for if the Baptist had no such messianic ideas, he could not refer them to the person of Jesus. But to strengthen the evidence for the result already obtained, we will make the second question the object of a special examination. According to the fourth Evangelist the Baptist ascribed to Jesus all the messianic attributes above discussed. If he did this so enthusiastically, publicly, and repeatedly, as we read in John, he could not have been excluded by Jesus from the kingdom of heaven (Matt. xi. 11), nor have been placed below the least of its citizens. For such a confession as that of the Baptist, when he calls Jesus the υἱὸς τοῦ Θεοῦ, who was before him,—such refined insight into the messianic economy, as is shown by his designating Jesus ὁ ἀμνὸς τοῦ Θεοῦ, ὁ αἴρων τὴν ἁμαρτίαν τοῦ κόσμου, Peter himself had not to produce, though Jesus not only receives him into the kingdom of heaven for his confession, Matt. xvi. 16, but constitutes him the rock on which that kingdom was to be founded. But we have something yet more incomprehensible. John, in the fourth gospel, gives it as the object of his baptism, ἵνα φανερωθῇ (Jesus as Messiah) τῷ Ἰσραὴλ (i. 31), and acknowledges it to be the divine ordinance, that by the side of the increasing Jesus, he must decrease (iii. 30); nevertheless after Jesus had begun to baptize by the instrumentality of his disciples, John continues to practise his baptism (iii. 32). Why so, if he knew the object of his baptism to be fulfilled by the introduction of Jesus, and if he directed his followers to him as the Messiah? (i. 36 f.).[25] The continuance of his baptism would be to no purpose; for Lücke's supposition that John's baptism was still of effect in those places where Jesus had not appeared, he himself overthrows by the observation, that at least at the period treated of in John iii. 22 ff., Jesus and John must have been baptizing near to each other, since the disciples of John were jealous of the concourse to the baptism of Jesus. But the continuance of John's baptism appears even to counteract his aim, if that aim were merely to point out Jesus as the Messiah. He thereby detained a circle of individuals on the borders of the Messiah's kingdom, and retarded or hindered their going over to Jesus (and that through his own fault, not theirs alone,[26] for he nullified his verbal direction to Jesus by his contradictory example). Accordingly we find the party of John's disciples still existing in the time of the Apostle Paul (Acts xviii. 24 f., xix. 1 ff.); and, if the Sabæans are to be credited concerning their own history, the sect remains to this day.[27] Certainly, presupposing the averred conviction of the Baptist relative to Jesus, it would seem most natural for him to have attached himself to the latter; this, however, did not happen, and hence we conclude that he cannot have had that conviction.[28]

---

[25] De Wette, de morte Christi expiatoria, in s. Opusc. theol. p. 81; biblische Dogmatik, § 209; Winer, bibl. Realwörterbuch 1, s. 692.

[26] Neander, p. 75. This author erroneously supposes that there is an indication of the Baptist having directed his disciples to Jesus in Acts xviii. 25, where it is said of Apollos: ἐδίδασκεν ἀκριβῶς τὰ περὶ τοῦ Κυρίου, ἐπιστάμενος τὸ βάπτισμα Ἰωάννου. For on comparing the following chapter, we find that Paul had to teach the disciples of John, that by the ἐρχόμενος announced by their master, they were to understand Jesus; whence it is clear that the things of the Lord expounded by Apollos, consisted only in the messianic doctrine, purified by John into an expectation of one who was to come, and that the more accurate instruction which he received from the Christians, Aquila and Priscilla, was the doctrine of its fulfilment in the person of Jesus.

[27] Gesenius, Probeheft der Ersch und Gruber'schen Encyclopädie, d. A. Zabier.

[28] Bretschneider, Probab., s. 46 f.; comp. Lücke, s. 493 f.; De Wette, Opusc. a. a. O.

But chiefly the character and entire demeanour of the Baptist render it impossible to believe that he placed himself on that footing with Jesus, described by the fourth evangelist. How could the man of the wilderness, the stern ascetic, who fed on locusts and wild honey, and prescribed severe fasts to his disciples, the gloomy, threatening preacher of repentance, animated with the spirit of Elias—how could he form a friendship with Jesus, in every thing his opposite? He must assuredly, with his disciples, have stumbled at the liberal manners of Jesus, and have been hindered by them from recognizing him as the Messiah. Nothing is more unbending than ascetic prejudice ; he who, like the Baptist, esteems it piety to fast and mortify the body, will never assign a high grade in things divine to him who disregards such asceticism. A mind with narrow views can never comprehend one whose vision takes a wider range, although the latter may know how to do justice to its inferior ; hence Jesus could value and sanction John in his proper place, but the Baptist could never give the precedence to Jesus, as he is reported to have done in the fourth gospel. The declaration of the Baptist (John iii. 30), that he must decrease, but Jesus must increase, is frequently praised as an example of the noblest and sublimest resignation.[29] The beauty of this representation we grant ; but not its truth. The instance would be a solitary one, if a man whose life had its influence on the world's history, had so readily yielded the ascendant, in his own æra, to one who came to eclipse him and render him superfluous. Such a step is not less difficult for individuals than for nations, and that not from any vice, as egotism or ambition, so that an exception might be presumed (though not without prejudice) in the case of a man like the Baptist ; it is a consequence of that blameless limitation which, as we have already remarked, is proper to a low point of view in relation to a higher, and which is all the more obstinately maintained if the inferior individual is, like John, of a coarse, rugged nature. Only from the divine point of view, or from that of an historian, bent on establishing religious doctrines, could such things be spoken, and the fourth Evangelist has in fact put into the mouth of the Baptist the very same thoughts concerning the relation between him and Jesus, that the compiler of the 2nd book of Samuel has communicated, as his own observation, on the corresponding relation between Saul and David.[30] Competent judges have recently acknowledged that there exists a discrepancy between the synoptical gospels and the fourth, the blame of which must be imputed to the latter : [31] and this opinion is confirmed and strengthened by the fact that the fourth Evangelist transforms the Baptist into a totally different character from that in which he appears in the Synoptical gospels and in Josephus ; out of a practical preacher he makes a speculative christologist ; out of a hard and unbending, a yielding and self-renunciating nature.

The style in which the scenes between John and Jesus (John i. 29 ff. 35 ff.) are depicted, shows them to have originated partly in the free composition of the imagination, partly in a remodelling of the synoptical narratives with a view to the glorification of Jesus. With respect to the former : Jesus is walking, v. 35, near to John ; in v. 29 he is said to come directly to him ; yet on neither occasion is there any account of an interview between the two. Could Jesus really have avoided contact with the Baptist, that there might be no

---

[29] Greiling, Leben Jesu von Nazaret, s. 132 f.
[30] 2 Sam. iii. 1.

וְדָוִד הֹלֵךְ וְחָזֵק

וּבֵית שָׁאוּל הֹלְכִים וְדַלִּים :

John iii. 30.
ἐκεῖνον δεῖ αὐξάνειν.
ἐμὲ δὲ ἐλαττοῦσθαι.

[31] Schulz, die Lehre vom Abendmahl, s. 145.   Winer, Realwörterbuch, I, s. 693.

appearance of preconcerted action? This is Lampe's conjecture; but it is the product of modern reflections, foreign to the time and circumstances of Jesus. Or shall we suppose that the narrator, whether fortuitously or purposely, omitted known details? But the meetings of Jesus and John must have furnished him with peculiarly interesting matter, so that, as Lücke allows,[32] his silence is enigmatical. From our point of view the enigma is solved. The Baptist had, in the Evangelist's idea, pointed to Jesus as the Messiah. This, understood as a visible pointing, required that Jesus should pass by or approach John; hence this feature was inserted in the narrative; but the particulars of an actual meeting being unnecessary, were, though very awkwardly, omitted. The incident of some disciples attaching themselves to Jesus in consequence of the Baptist's direction, seems to be a free version of the sending of two disciples by John from his prison. Thus, as in Matthew xi. 2, and Luke vii. 18, John despatches two disciples to Jesus with the dubitative question. " Art thou *he that should come?*" so in the fourth gospel he likewise sends two disciples to Jesus, but with the positive assertion that he (Jesus) is *the Lamb of God*, ἀμνὸς Θεοῦ; as Jesus in the former case gives to the disciples, after the delivery of their message, the direction : " Go and tell John *the things ye have seen and heard*," ἃ εἴδετε καὶ ἠκούσατε : so in the latter, he gives to the inquiry concerning his abode, the answer : *Come and see*, ἔρχεσθε καὶ ἴδετε. But while in the synoptical gospels the two disciples return to John, in the fourth, they permanently attach themselves to Jesus.

From the foregoing considerations, it is inconceivable that John should ever have held and pronounced Jesus to be the Messiah : but it is easy to show how a belief that he did so might obtain, without historical foundation. According to Acts xix. 4, the Apostle Paul declares what seems sufficiently guaranteed by history, that John baptized εἰς τὸν ἐρχόμενον, and this coming Messiah, adds Paul, to whom John pointed was Jesus (τουτέστιν εἰς Χριστὸν Ἰησοῦν). This was an interpretation of the Baptist's words by the issue ; for Jesus had approved himself to a great number of his cotemporaries, as the Messiah announced by John. There was but a step to the notion that the Baptist himself had, under the ἐρχόμενος, understood the individual Jesus,— had himself the τουτέστιν, κ.τ.λ. in his mind ; a view which, however unhistorical, would be inviting to the early Christians, in proportion to their wish to sustain the dignity of Jesus by the authority of the Baptist, then very influential in the Jewish world.[33] There was yet another reason, gathered from the Old Testament. The ancestor of the Messiah, David, had likewise in the old Hebrew legend a kind of forerunner in the person of Samuel, who by order from Jehovah anointed him to be king over Israel (1 Sam. xvi.), and afterwards stood in the relation of a witness to his claims. If then it behoved the Messiah to have a forerunner, who, besides, was more closely characterized in the prophecy of Malachi as a second Elias, and if, historically, Jesus was

---

[32] Commentar, s. 380.

[33] The passage above quoted from the Acts gives us also some explanation, why the fourth Evangelist of all others should be solicitous to place the Baptist in a more favourable relation to Jesus, than history allows us to conceive. According to v. 1 ff. there were persons in Ephesus who knew only of John's baptism, and were therefore rebaptized by the Apostle Paul in the name of Jesus. Now an old tradition represents the fourth gospel to have been written in Ephesus (Iræneus adv. hær. iii. 1). If we accept this (and it is certainly correct in assigning a Greek locality for the composition of this Gospel), and presuppose, in accordance with the intimation in the Acts, that Ephesus was the seat of a number of the Baptist's followers, all of whom Paul could hardly have converted ; the endeavour to draw them over to Jesus would explain the remarkable stress laid by the fourth Evangelist on the μαρτυρία Ἰωάννου. Storr has very judiciously remarked and discussed this, über den Zweck der Evangelischen Geschichte und der Briefe Johannis, s. 5 ff. 24 f. Compare Hug, Einleitung in das N. T., s. 190 3te Ausg.

preceded by John, whose baptism as a consecration corresponded to an anointing; the idea was not remote of conforming the relation between John and Jesus to that between Samuel and David.

We might have decided with tolerable certainty which of the two incompatible statements concerning the relation between the Baptist and Jesus is to be renounced as unhistorical, by the universal canon of interpretation, that where, in narratives having a tendency to aggrandise a person or a fact (a tendency which the Gospels evince at every step), two contradictory statements are found, that which best corresponds to this aim is the least historical; because if, in accordance with it, the original fact had been so dazzling, it is inconceivable that the other less brilliant representation should afterwards arise; as here, if John so early acknowledged Jesus, it is inexplicable how a story could be fabricated, which reports him to have been in doubt on the same subject at a very late period. We have, however, by a separate examination of the narrative in the fourth gospel, ascertained that it is self-contradictory and contains its own solution; hence our result, found independently of the above canon, serves for its confirmation.

Meanwhile that result is only the negative, that all which turns upon the early acknowledgment of Jesus by John has no claim to be received as historical; of the positive we know nothing, unless the message out of prison may be regarded as a clue to the truth, and we must therefore subject this side of the matter to a separate examination. We will not extend our arguments against the probability of an early and decided conviction on the part of the Baptist, to a mere conjecture awakened in him at a later period that Jesus was the Messiah; and therefore we leave uncontested the proper contents of the narrative. But as regards the form, it is not to be conceived without difficulty. That the Baptist in prison, ἐν τῷ δεσμωτηρίῳ, should have information of the proceedings of Jesus; that he should from that locality send his disciples to Jesus; and that these as we are led to infer, should bring him an answer in his imprisonment.

According to Josephus,[34] Herod imprisoned John from fear of disturbances: allowing this to be merely a joint cause with that given by the Evangelist, it is yet difficult to believe that to a man, one motive of whose imprisonment was to seclude him from his followers, his disciples should have retained free access; although we cannot prove it an impossibility that circumstances might favour the admission of certain individuals. Now that the message was sent from prison we learn from Matthew alone; Luke says nothing of it, although he tells of the message. We might hence, with Schleiermacher,[35] consider Luke's account the true one, and the δεσμωτηρίῳ of Matthew an unhistorical addition. But that critic has himself very convincingly shown, from the tedious amplifications, partly betraying even misunderstanding, which the narrative of Luke contains (vii. 20, 21, 29, 30), that Matthew gives the incident in its original, Luke in a revised form.[36] It would indeed be singular if Matthew had supplied the δεσμωτηρίῳ when it was originally wanting; it is far more natural to suppose that Luke, who in the whole paragraph appears as a reviser, expunged the original mention of the prison.

In judging of Luke's motives for so doing, we are led to notice the difference in the dates given by the evangelists for the imprisonment of John. Matthew, with whom Mark agrees, places it before the public appearance of Jesus in Galilee; for he gives it as the motive for the return of Jesus into that province (Matt. iv. 12; Mark i. 14). Luke assigns no precise date to the

---

[34] Antiq. xviii. v. 2.
[35] Ueber den Lukas, s. 109.
[36] Ibid. p. 106.

arrest of the Baptist (iii. 19 f.), yet it is to be inferred from his silence about the prison, in connexion with the sending of the two disciples, that he regarded it as a later occurrence; but John expressly says, that after the first passover attended by Jesus in his public character, *John was not yet cast into prison* (iii. 24). If it be asked, who is right? we answer that there is something on the face of the account of the first Evangelist, which has inclined many commentators to renounce it in favour of the two last. That Jesus, on the report of John's imprisonment in Galilee by Herod Antipas, should have returned into the dominions of that prince for the sake of safety, is, as Schneckenburger well maintains,[37] highly improbable, since there, of all places, he was the least secure from a similar fate. But even if it be held impossible to dissociate the ἀνεχώρησεν (*he withdrew*) from the cognate idea of seeking security, we may still ask whether, disregarding the mistake in the motive, the fact itself may not be maintained. Matthew and Mark connect with this journey into Galilee after John's imprisonment, the commencement of the public ministry of Jesus; and that this was consequent on the removal of the Baptist, I am quite inclined to believe. For it is in itself the most natural that the exit of the Baptist should incite Jesus to carry on in his stead the preaching of μετανοεῖτέ· ἤγγικε γὰρ ἡ βασιλεία τῶν οὐρανῶν; and the canon cited above is entirely in favour of Matthew. For if it be asked which fiction best accords with the aggrandising spirit of the Christian legend,—that of John's removal before the appearance of Jesus, or that of their having long laboured in conjunction?—the answer must be, the latter. If he to whom the hero of a narrative is superior disappears from the scene before the entrance of the latter, the crowning opportunity for the hero to demonstrate his ascendancy is lost—the full splendour of the rising sun can only be appreciated, when the waning moon is seen above the horizon, growing paler and paler in the presence of the greater luminary. Such is the case in the Gospels of Luke and John, while Matthew and Mark rest satisfied with the less effective representation. Hence, as the least calculated to magnify Jesus, the account of Matthew has the advantage in historical probability.

Thus at the time when the two disciples must have been sent to Jesus, the Baptist was already imprisoned, and we have remarked above, that he could hardly, so situated, transmit and receive messages. But popular legend might be prompted to fabricate such a message, that the Baptist might not depart without at least an incipient recognition of Jesus as the Messiah; so that neither the one nor the other of the two incompatible statements is to be regarded as historical. *

§ 47.

OPINION OF THE EVANGELISTS AND JESUS CONCERNING THE BAPTIST, WITH HIS OWN JUDGMENT ON HIMSELF. RESULT OF THE INQUIRY INTO THE RELATIONSHIP BETWEEN THESE TWO INDIVIDUALS.

The Evangelists apply to John, as the preparer of the Messiah's kingdom, several passages of the Old Testament.

The abode of the preacher of repentance in the wilderness, his activity in preparing the way for the Messiah, necessarily recalled the passage of Isaiah (xl. 3ff. LXX.) : φωνὴ βοῶντος ἐν ἐρήμῳ· ἑτοιμάσατε τὴν ὁδὸν Κυρίῳ κ. τ. λ. This passage, which in its original connection related not to the Messiah and his forerunner, but to Jehovah, for whom a way was to be prepared through

---

[37] Ueber den Ursprung u. s. w. s. 79.

the wilderness toward Judea, that he might return with his people from exile, is quoted by the first three Evangelists as a prophecy fulfilled by the appearance of the Baptist (Matt. iii. 3 ; Mark i. 3 ; Luke iii. 4 ff.). This might be thought a later and Christian application, but there is nothing to controvert the statement of the fourth Evangelist, that the Baptist had himself characterized his destination by those prophetic words.

As the synoptical gospels have unanimously borrowed this passage from the Baptist himself, so Mark has borrowed the application of another prophetic passage to the Baptist from Jesus. Jesus had said (Matt. xi. 10 ; Luke vii. 27) : οὗτος γάρ ἐστι περὶ οὗ γέγραπται· ἰδοὺ ἀποστέλλω τὸν ἄγγελόν μου πρὸ προσώπου σου, ὃς κατασκευάσει τὴν ὁδόν σου ἔμπροσθέν σου·ό. This is he of whom it is written, Behold I send my messenger before thy face, to prepare thy way before thee ; and Mark in the introduction to his Gospel, applies these words of Malachi (iii. 1), together with the above passage from Isaiah, without distinguishing their respective sources, to the forerunner, John. The text is a messianic one ; Jehovah, however, does not therein speak of sending a messenger before the Messiah, but before himself : and it is only in the New Testament citations in all these instances that the second person (σου) is substituted for the first ('פָנָי).

Another notable passage of the same prophet (iii. 23, LXX. iv. 4 : καὶ ἰδοὺ ἐγὼ ἀποστελῶ ὑμῖν Ἠλίαν τὸν Θεσβίτην, πρὶν ἐλθεῖν τὴν ἡμέραν Κυρίου, κ. τ. λ. : Behold, I will send you Elijah the Tishbite before the coming of the day of the Lord, etc.) suggested to the Evangelists the assimilation of John the Baptist to Elias. That John, labouring for the reformation of the people, in the spirit and power of Elias, should prepare the way for the Divine visitation in the times of the Messiah, was according to Luke i. 17, predicted before his birth. In John i. 21, when the emissaries of the Sanhedrim ask, "Art thou Elias?" the Baptist declines this dignity : according to the usual explanation, he only extended his denial to the rude popular notion, that he was the ancient seer corporeally resuscitated, whereas he would have admitted the view of the synoptical gospels, that he had the spirit of Elias. Nevertheless it appears improbable that if the fourth Evangelist had been familiar with the idea of the Baptist as a second Elias, he would have put into his mouth so direct a negative.

This scene, peculiar to the fourth gospel, in which John rejects the title of Elias, with several others, demands a yet closer examination, and must be compared with a narrative in Luke (iii. 15), to which it has a striking similarity. In Luke, the crowd assembled round the Baptist begin to think : Is not this the Christ ? μήποτε αὐτὸς εἴη ὁ Χριστός ; in John, the deputies of the Sanhedrim[1] ask him, Who art thou? σὺ τίς εἶ; which we infer from the Baptist's answer to mean : "Art thou, as is believed, the Messiah ?"[2] According to Luke, the Baptist answers, I indeed baptize you with water ; but one mightier than I cometh, the latchet of whose shoes I am not worthy to unloose. According to John he gives a similar reply ; I baptize with water ; but there standeth one among you whom ye know not ; He it is who coming after me is preferred before me, whose shoes' latchet I am not worthy to unloose : the latter Evangelist adding his peculiar propositions concerning the pre-existence of Jesus, and deferring to another occasion (v. 33) the mention of the Messiah's spiritual baptism, which Luke gives in immediate connexion with the above passage. In Luke, and still more decidedly in John, this whole scene is intro-

---

[1] The expression οἱ Ἰουδαῖοι is thus interpreted by the most learned exegetists. Comp. Paulus, Lücke, Tholuck in loc.

[2] Lücke, Commentar, s. 327.

duced with a design to establish the Messiahship of Jesus, by showing that the Baptist had renounced that dignity, and attributed it to one who should come after him.   If at the foundation of two narratives so similar, there can scarcely be more than one fact,[3] the question is, which gives that fact the most faithfully?   In Luke's account there is no intrinsic improbability ; on the contrary it is easy to imagine, that the people, congregated round the man who announced the Messiah's kingdom, and baptized with a view to it, should, in moments of enthusiasm, believe him to be the Messiah.   But that the Sanhedrim should send from Jerusalem to John on the banks of the Jordan, for the sake of asking him whether he were the Messiah, seems less natural.   Their object could only be what, on a later occasion, it was with respect to Jesus (Matt. xxi. 23 ff.), namely, to challenge the authority of John to baptize, as appears from v. 25.   Moreover, from the hostile position which John had taken towards the sects of the Pharisees and Sadducees (Matt. iii. 7), to whom the members of the Sanhedrim belonged, they must have pre-judged that he was not the Messiah, nor a prophet, and consequently, that he had no right to undertake a βάπτισμα.   But in that case, they could not possibly have so put their questions as they are reported to have done in the fourth gospel.   In the passage from Mathew above cited, they asked Jesus, quite consistently with their impression that he had no prophetic authority : ἐν ποίᾳ ἐξουσίᾳ ταῦτα ποιεῖς ; *By what authority doest thou these things*? but in John, they question the Baptist precisely as if they pre-supposed him to be the Messiah, and when he, apparently to their consternation, has denied this, they tender him successively the dignities of Elias, and of another prophetic forerunner, as if they earnestly wished him to accept one of these titles. Searching opponents will not thus thrust the highest honours on the man to whom they are inimical;—this is the representation of a narrator who wishes to exhibit the modesty of the man, and his subordination to Jesus, by his rejection of those brilliant titles.   To enable him to reject them, they must have been offered ; but this could in reality only be done by well-wishers, as in Luke, where the conjecture that the Baptist was the Messiah is attributed to the people.

Why then did not the fourth Evangelist attribute those questions likewise to the people, from whom, with a slight alteration, they would have seemed quite natural?   Jesus, when addressing the unbelieving Jews in Jerusalem, (John v. 33), appeals to their message to the Baptist, and to the faithful testimony then given by the latter.   Had John given his declaration concerning his relation to Jesus before the common people merely, such an appeal would have been impossible ; for if Jesus were to refer his enemies to the testimony of John, that testimony must have been delivered before his enemies ; if the assertions of the Baptist were to have any diplomatic value, they must have resulted from the official inquiry of a magisterial deputation.   Such a re-modelling of the facts appears to have been aided by the above-mentioned narrative from the synoptical traditions, wherein the high priests and scribes ask Jesus, by what authority he does such things (as the casting out of the buyers and sellers).   Here also Jesus refers to John, asking for their opinion as to the authority of his baptism, only, it is true, with the negative view of repressing their further inquiries (Matt. xxi. 23 ff. parall.) ; but how easily might this reference be made to take an affirmative sense, and instead of the argument, " If ye know not what powers were entrusted to John, ye need not know whence mine are given,"—the following be substituted : "Since ye know what John has declared concerning me, ye must also know what power and

---

[3] Lücke, s. 339.

dignity belong to me ; " whereupon what was originally a question addressed to Jesus, transformed itself into a message to the Baptist.[4]

The judgment of Jesus on the character of John is delivered on two occasions in the synoptical gospels ; first after the departure of John's messengers (Matt. xi. 7 ff.) ; secondly, after the appearance of Elias at the transfiguration (Matt. xvii. 12 ff.), in reply to the question of a disciple. In the fourth gospel, after an appeal to the Baptist's testimony, Jesus pronounces an eulogium on him in the presence of the Jews (v. 35), after referring, as above remarked, to their sending to John. In this passage he calls the Baptist a burning and a shining light, in whose beams the fickle people were for a season willing to rejoice. In one synoptical passage, he declares John to be the promised Elias ; in the other, there are three points to be distinguished. First, with respect to the character and agency of John,—the severity and firmness of his mind, and the pre-eminence which as the messianic forerunner, who with forcible hand had opened the kingdom of heaven, he maintained even over the prophets, are extolled (v. 7–14) ; secondly, in relation to Jesus and the citizens of the *kingdom of heaven*, the Baptist, though exalted above all the members of the Old Testament economy, is declared to be in the rear of every one on whom, through Jesus, the new light had arisen (v. 11). We see how Jesus understood this from what follows (v. 18), when we compare it with Matt. ix. 16 f. In the former passage Jesus describes John as μήτε ἐσθίων μήτε πίνων, *neither eating nor drinking ;* and in the latter it is this very asceticism which is said to liken him to the ἱματίοις and ἀσκοῖς παλαιοῖς, the *old garments* and *old bottles*, with which the new, introduced by Jesus, will not agree. What else then could it be, in which the Baptist was beneath the children of the kingdom of Jesus, but (in connexion with his non-recognition or only qualified acknowledgment of Jesus as Messiah) the spirit of external observance, which still clung to fasting and similar works, and his gloomy asceticism ? And, in truth, freedom from these is the test of transition from a religion of bondage, to one of liberty and spirituality.[5] Thirdly, with respect to the relation in which the agency of John and Jesus stood to their cotemporaries, the same inaptitude to receive the ministrations of both is complained of v. 16 ff., although in v. 12 it is observed, that the violent zeal of some βιασταί had, under the guidance of John, wrested for them an entrance into the kingdom of the Messiah.[6]

In conclusion, we must take a review of the steps by which tradition has gradually annexed itself to the simple historical traits of the relation between John and Jesus. Thus much seems to be historical : that Jesus, attracted by the fame of the Baptist, put himself under the tuition of that preacher, and that having remained some time among his followers, and been initiated into his ideas of the approaching messianic kingdom, he, after the imprisonment of John, carried on, under certain modifications, the same work, never ceasing, even when he had far surpassed his predecessor, to render him due homage.

The first addition to this in the Christian legend, was, that John had taken approving notice of Jesus. During his public ministry, it was known that he had only indefinitely referred to one coming after him ; but it behoved him,

---

[4] Whether the dialogue between John and his complaining disciples (John iii. 25 ff.) be likewise a transmutation of the corresponding scene, Matt. ix. 14 f., as Bretschneider seeks to show, must remain uncertain. Probab., p. 66 ff.

[5] That Jesus, as many suppose, assigns a low rank to the Baptist, because the latter thought of introducing the new order of things by external violence, is not to be detected in the gospels.

[6] For a different explanation see Schneckenburger, Beiträge, s. 48 ff.

at least in a conjectural way, to point out Jesus personally, as that successor. To this it was thought he might have been moved by the fame of the works of Jesus, which, loud as it was, might even penetrate the walls of his prison. Then was formed Matthew's narrative of the message from prison ; the first modest attempt to make the Baptist a witness for Jesus, and hence clothed in an interrogation, because a categorical testimony was too unprecedented.

But this late and qualified testimony was not enough. It was a late one, for prior to it there was the baptism which Jesus received from John, and by which he, in a certain degree, placed himself in subordination to the Baptist ; hence those scenes in Luke, by which the Baptist was placed, even before his birth, in a subservient relation to Jesus.

Not only was it a late testimony which that message contained ; it was but half a one ; for the question implied uncertainty, and ὁ ἐρχόμενος conveyed indecision. Hence in the fourth gospel there is no longer a question about the Messiahship of Jesus, but the most solemn asseverations on that head, and we have the most pointed declarations of the eternal, divine nature of Jesus, and his character as the suffering Messiah.

In a narrative aiming at unity, as does the fourth gospel, these very pointed declarations could not stand by the side of the dubious message, which is therefore only found in this Gospel under a totally reorganized form. Neither does this message accord with that which in the synoptical gospels is made to occur at the baptism of Jesus, and even earlier in his intercourse with John ; but the first three Evangelists, in their loose compositions, admitted, along with the more recent form of the tradition, the less complete one, because they attached less importance to the question of John than to the consequent discourse of Jesus.*

§ 48.

THE EXECUTION OF JOHN THE BAPTIST.

We here take under our examination, by way of appendix, all that has been transmitted to us concerning the tragic end of the Baptist. According to the unanimous testimony of the synoptical Evangelists and Josephus,[1] he was executed, after a protracted imprisonment, by order of Herod Antipas, tetrarch of Galilee ; and in the New Testament accounts he is said to have been beheaded. (Matt. xiv. 3 ff. ; Mark vi. 17 ff. ; Luke ix. 9.)

But Josephus and the Evangelists are at variance as to the cause of his imprisonment and execution. According to the latter, the censure which John had pronounced on the marriage of Herod with his (half) brother's[2] wife, was the cause of his imprisonment, and the revengeful cunning of Herodias, at a court festival, of his death : Josephus gives the fear of disturbances, which was awakened in Herod by the formidable train of the Baptist's followers, as the cause at once of the imprisonment and the execution.[3] If these two accounts be considered as distinct and irreconcilable, it may be doubted which of the two deserves the preference. It is not here as in the case of Herod Agrippa's death, Acts xii. 23, viz., that the New Testament narrative, by intermixing a supernatural cause where Josephus has only a natural one, enables us to prejudge it as unhistorical ; on the contrary, we might here give

---

[1] Antiq. xviii. v. 2.

[2] This former husband of Herodias is named by the Evangelists, Philip, by Josephus, Herod. He was the son of the high priest's daughter, Mariamne, and lived as a private person. V. Antiq. xv. ix. 3 ; xviii. v. 1. 4. B. j. i. xxix. 2, xxx. 7.

[3] Antiq. xviii. v. 4.

the palm to the evangelical narrative, for the particularity of its details. But on the other hand, it must be considered that that very particularity, and especially the conversion of a political into a personal motive, corresponds fully to the development of the legendary spirit among the people, whose imagination is more at home in domestic than in political circles.[4] Meanwhile it is quite possible to reconcile the two narratives. This has been attempted by conjecturing, that the fear of insurrection was the proper cabinet motive for the imprisonment of the Baptist, while the irreverent censure passed on the ruler was thrust forward as the ostensible motive.[5] But I greatly doubt whether Herod would designedly expose the scandalous point touched on by John; it is more likely, if a distinction is to be here made between a private and ostensible cause, that the censure of the marriage was the secret reason, and the fear of insurrection disseminated as an excuse for extreme severity.[6] Such a distinction, however, is not needed; for Antipas might well fear, that John, by his strong censure of the marriage and the whole course of the tetrarch's life, might stir up the people into rebellion against him.

But there is a diversity even between the evangelical narratives themselves, not only in this, that Mark gives the scene at the feast with the most graphic details, while Luke is satisfied with a concise statement (iii. 18–20, ix. 9), and Matthew takes a middle course; but Mark's representation of the relation between Herod and the Baptist differs essentially from that of Matthew. While according to the latter, Herod wished to kill John, but was withheld by his dread of the people, who looked on the Baptist as a prophet (v. 5); according to Mark, it was Herodias who conspired against his life, but could not attain her object, because her husband was in awe of John as a holy man, sometimes heard him gladly, and not seldom followed his counsel (v. 19).[7] Here, again, the individualizing characteristic of Mark's narrative has induced commentators to prefer it to that of Matthew.[8] But in the finishing touches and alterations of Mark we may detect the hand of tradition; especially as Josephus merely says of the people, that *they gave ear to the sound of his words*, ἤρθησαν τῇ ἀκροάσει τῶν λόγων, while he says of Herod, that *having conceived fears of John, he judged it expedient to put him to death*, δείσας κρεῖττον ἡγεῖται (τὸν Ἰωάννην) ἀναιρεῖν. How near lay the temptation to exalt the Baptist, by representing the prince against whom he had spoken, and by whom he was imprisoned, as feeling bound to venerate him, and only, to his remorse, seduced into giving his death-warrant, by his vindictive wife! It may be added, that the account of Matthew is not inconsistent with the character of Antipas, as gathered from other sources.[9]

The close of the evangelical narratives leaves the impression that the dissevered head of John was presented at table, and that the prison was consequently close at hand. But we learn from the passage in Josephus above cited, that the Baptist was confined in Machærus, a fortress on the southern border of Peræa, whereas the residence of Herod was in Tiberias,[10] a day's journey distant from Machærus. Hence the head of John the Baptist

[4] Hase, Leben Jesu, s. 88.
[5] Fritzsche, Comm. in Matth. in loc. Winer, bibl. Realwörterb. 1, s. 694.
[6] Paulus, exeg. Handb. 1, a, s. 361; Schleiermacher, über den Lukas, s. 109.
[7] Vergl. Fritzsche, Comm. in Marc., p. 225.
[8] E.g. Schneckenburger, über den Ursprung des ersten kanonischen Evangeliums, s. 86 f. That the ἐλυπήθη of Matthew, v. 9, is not contradictory to his own narrative, see Fritzsche, in loc.
[9] S. Winer, b. Realwörterb. d. A. Herodes Antipas.
[10] Fritzsche, Commentar. in Matt., p. 491.

could only be presented to Herod after two days' journey, and not while he yet sat at table.   The contradiction here apparent is not to be removed by the consideration, that it is not expressly said in the Gospels that John's head was brought in during the meal, for this is necessarily inferred from the entire narrative.   Not only are the commission of the executioner and his return with the head, detailed in immediate connexion with the incidents of the meal; but only thus has the whole dramatic scene its appropriate conclusion; —only thus is the contrast complete, which is formed by the death-warrant and the feast: in fine, the πίναξ, on which the dissevered head is presented, marks it as the costliest viand which the unnatural revenge of a woman could desire at table.   But we have, as a probable solution, the information of Josephus,[11] that Herod Antipas was then at war with the Arabian king, Aretas, between whose kingdom and his own lay the fortress of Machærus; and there Herod might possibly have resided with his court at that period.

Thus we see that the life of John in the evangelical narratives is, from easily conceived reasons, overspread with mythical lustre on the side which is turned towards Jesus, while on the other its historical lineaments are more visible.

[11] Antiq. xviii. v. 1.

CHAPTER II.

BAPTISM AND TEMPTATION OF JESUS.

§ 49.

WHY DID JESUS RECEIVE BAPTISM FROM JOHN ? *

IN conformity with the evangelical view of the fact, the customary answer given by the orthodox to this question is, that Jesus, by his submission to John's baptism, signified his consecration to the messianic office ; an explanation which is supported by a passage in Justin, according to which it was the Jewish notion, that the Messiah would be unknown as such to himself and others, until Elias as his forerunner should anoint him, and thereby make him distinguishable by all.[1] The Baptist himself, however, as he is represented by the first Evangelist, could not have partaken of this design ; for had he regarded his baptism as a consecration which the Messiah must necessarily undergo, he would not have hesitated to perform it on the person of Jesus (iii. 14).

Our former inquiries have shown that John's baptism related partly εἰς τὸν ἐρχόμενον, its recipients promising a believing preparation for the expected Messiah ; how then could Jesus, if he was conscious of being himself the ἐρχόμενος, submit himself to this baptism ? The usual answer from the orthodox point of view is, that Jesus, although conscious of his Messiahship, yet, so long as it was not publicly attested by God, spoke and acted, not as Messiah, but merely as an Israelite, who held himself bound to obey every divine ordinance relative to his nation.[2] But, here, there is a distinction to be made. Negatively, it became Jesus to refrain from performing any messianic deeds, or using any of the Messiah's prerogatives, before his title was solemnly attested ; even positively, it became him to submit himself to the ordinances which were incumbent on every Israelite ; but to join in a new rite, which symbolized the expectation of another and a future Messiah, could never, without dissimulation, be the act of one who was conscious of being the actual Messiah himself. More recent theologians have therefore wisely admitted, that when Jesus came to John for baptism, he had not a decided conviction of his Messiahship.[3] They indeed regard this uncertainty as only the struggle of modesty. Paulus, for instance, observes that Jesus, notwithstanding he had heard from his parents of his messianic destination, and had felt this first intimation confirmed by many external incidents, as well as by his own spiritual development, was yet not over eager to appro-

---

[1] Dial. c. Tryph. 8, s. 110. der Mauriner Ausg.
[2] Hess. Geschichte Jesu, 1 Bd. s. 118.
[3] Paulus, ut sup., s. 362 ff. 337. Hase, L. J., s. 48, erste Ausg.

priate the honour, which had been as it were thrust upon him. But, if the previous narratives concerning Jesus be regarded as a history, and therefore, of necessity, as a supernatural one; then must he, who was heralded by angels, miraculously conceived, welcomed into the world by the homage of magi and prophets, and who in his twelfth year knew the temple to be his Father's house, have long held a conviction of his Messiahship, above all the scruples of a false modesty. If on the contrary it be thought possible, by criticism, to reduce the history of the childhood of Jesus to a merely natural one, there is no longer anything to account for his early belief that he was the Messiah; and the position which he adopted by the reception of John's baptism becomes, instead of an affected diffidence, a real ignorance of his messianic destiny.—Too modest, continue these commentators, to declare himself Messiah on his own authority, Jesus fulfilled all that the strictest self-judgment could require, and wished to make the decisive experiment, whether the Deity would allow that he, as well as every other, should dedicate himself to the coming Messiah, or whether a sign would be granted, that he himself was the ἐρχόμενος. But to do something seen to be inappropriate, merely to try whether God will correct the mistake, is just such a challenging of the divine power as Jesus, shortly after his baptism, decidedly condemns. Thus it must be allowed that, the baptism of John being a baptism εἰς τὸν ἐρχόμενον, if Jesus could submit himself to it without dissimulation or presumption, he could not at the time have held himself to be that ἐρχόμενος, and if he really uttered the words οὕτω πρέπον ἐστὶ, κ. τ. λ., *Suffer it to be so now*, etc. (which, however, could only be called forth by the refusal of the Baptist—a refusal that stands or falls with his previous conviction of the Messiahship of Jesus), he could only mean by them, that it became him, with every pious Israelite, to devote himself by anticipation to the expected Messiah, in baptism, although the Evangelist, instructed by the issue, put on them a different construction.

But the relation hitherto discussed is only one aspect of John's baptism; the other, which is yet more strongly attested by history, shows it as a βάπτισμα μετανοίας, *a baptism of repentance*. The Israelites, we are told, Matt. iii. 6, were baptized of John, *confessing their sins* : shall we then suppose that Jesus made such a confession? They received the command to repent: did Jesus acknowledge such a command? This difficulty was felt even in the early church. In the Gospel of the Hebrews, adopted by the Nazarenes, Jesus asks his mother and brother, when invited by them to receive John's baptism, wherein he had sinned, that this baptism was needful for him?[4] and an heretical apocryphal work appears to have attributed to Jesus a confession of his own sins at his baptism.[5]

The sum of what modern theologians have contributed towards the removal of this difficulty, consists in the application to Jesus of the distinction between what a man is as an individual, and what he is as a member of the community. He needed, say they, no repentance on his own behalf, but, aware of its necessity for all other men, the children of Abraham not

---

[4] Hieron. adv. Pelagian. iii. 2 : In Evangelio juxta Hebræos—narrat historia : *Ecce mater Domini et fratres ejus dicebant ei : Joannes baptista baptizat in remissionem peccatorum ; eamus et baptizemur ab eo. Dixit autem eis : quid peccavi ut vadam et baptizer ab eo? nisi forte hoc ipsum quod dixi, ignorantia est.*

[5] The author of the *Tractatus de non iterando baptismo* in Cyprian's works, Rigalt., p. 139, says (the passage is also found in Fabric. Cod. apocr. N.T., s. 799 f.) : *Est—liber, qui inscribitur Pauli prædicatio. In quo libro, contra omnes scripturas et de peccato proprio confitentem invenies Christum, qui solus omnino nihil deliquit, et ad accipiendum Joannis baptisma pæne invitum à matre suâ Mariâ esse compulsum.*

excepted, he wished to demonstrate his approval of an institute which confirmed this truth, and hence he submitted to it. But let the reader only take a nearer view of the facts. According to Matt. iii. 6, John appears to have required a confession of sins previous to baptism ; such a confession Jesus, presupposing his impeccability, could not deliver without falsehood ; if he refused, John would hardly baptize him, for he did not yet believe him to be the Messiah, and from every other Israelite he must have considered a confession of sins indispensable. The non-compliance of Jesus might very probably originate the dispute to which Matthew gives a wholly different character ; but certainly, if the refusal of John had such a cause, the matter could scarcely have been adjusted by a mere *suffer it to be so now*, for no confession being given, the Baptist would not have perceived that *all righteousness was fulfilled.* Even supposing that a confession was not required of every baptized person, John would not conclude the ceremony of baptism without addressing the neophyte on the subject of repentance. Could Jesus tacitly sanction such an address to himself, when conscious that he needed no regeneration ? and would he not, in so doing, perplex the minds which were afterwards to believe in him as the sinless one ? We will even abandon the position that John so addressed the neophytes, and only urge that the gestures of those who plunged into the purifying water must have been those of contrition ; yet if Jesus conformed himself to these even in silence, without referring them to his own condition, he cannot be absolved from the charge of dissimulation.

There is then no alternative but to suppose, that as Jesus had not, up to the time of his baptism, thought of himself as the Messiah, so with regard to the μετάνοια (*repentance*), he may have justly ranked himself amongst the most excellent in Israel, without excluding himself from what is predicated in Job iv. 18, xv. 15. There is little historical ground for controverting this ; for the words, *which of you convinceth me of sin ?* (John viii. 46) could only refer to open delinquencies, and to a later period in the life of Jesus. The scene in his twelfth year, even if historical, could not by itself prove a sinless development of his powers.

§ 50.

THE SCENE AT THE BAPTISM OF JESUS CONSIDERED AS SUPERNATURAL AND AS NATURAL.

At the moment that John had completed his baptism of Jesus, the synoptical gospels tell us that the heavens were opened, the Holy Spirit descended on Jesus in the form of a dove, and a voice from heaven designated him the Son of God, in whom the Father was well pleased. The fourth Evangelist (i. 32 ff.) makes the Baptist narrate that he saw the Holy Spirit descend like a dove, and remain on Jesus ; but as in the immediate context John says of his baptism, that it was destined for the manifestation of the Messiah, and as the description of the descending dove corresponds almost verbally with the synoptical accounts, it is not to be doubted that the same event is intended. The old and lost Gospels of Justin and the Ebionites give, as concomitants, a heavenly light, and a flame bursting out of the Jordan ;[1] in the dove and heavenly voice also, they have alterations, hereafter to be

[1] Justin. Mart. dial. c. Tryph. 88 : κατελθόντος τοῦ Ἰησοῦ ἐπὶ τὸ ὕδωρ, καὶ πῦρ ἀνήφθη ἐν τῷ Ἰορδάνῃ, κ. τ. λ. Epiphan. hæres. 30, 13 (after the heavenly voice) : καὶ εὐθὺς περιέλαμψε τὸν τόπον φῶς μέγα.

noticed. For whose benefit the appearance was granted, remains doubtful on a comparison of the various narratives. In John, where the Baptist recites it to his followers, these seem not to have been eye-witnesses; and from his stating that he who sent him to baptize, promised the descent and repose of the Spirit as a mark of the Messiah, we gather that the appearance was designed specially for the Baptist. According to Mark it is Jesus, who, in ascending from the water, sees the heavens open and the Spirit descend. Even in Matthew it is the most natural to refer εἶδε, *he saw*, and ἀνεῴχθησαν αὐτῷ, *were opened to him*, to ὁ Ἰησοῦς, *Jesus*, the subject immediately before; but as it is said, in continuation, that he saw the Holy Spirit ἐρχόμενον ἐπ᾽ αὐτὸν, not ἐφ᾽ αὐτόν (Mark's ἐπ᾽ αὐτὸν, which does not agree with his construction, is explained by his dependence on Matthew), the beholder seems not to be the same as he on whom the Spirit descended, and we are obliged to refer εἶδε and ἀνεῴχθησαν αὐτῷ to the more remote antecedent, namely the Baptist, who, as the heavenly voice speaks of Jesus in the third person, is most naturally to be regarded as also a witness. Luke appears to give a much larger number of spectators to the scene, for according to him, Jesus was baptized ἐν τῷ βαπτισθῆναι ἅπαντα τὸν λαὸν, *when all the people were baptized*, and consequently he must have supposed that the scene described occurred in their presence.[2]

The narrations directly convey no other meaning, than that the whole scene was externally visible and audible, and thus they have been always understood by the majority of commentators. But in endeavouring to conceive the incident as a real one, a cultivated and reflecting mind must stumble at no insignificant difficulties. First, that for the appearance of a divine being on earth, the visible heavens must divide themselves, to allow of his descent from his accustomed seat, is an idea that can have no objective reality, but must be the entirely subjective creation of a time when the dwelling-place of Deity was imagined to be above the vault of heaven. Further, how is it reconcilable with the true idea of the Holy Spirit as the divine, all-pervading Power, that he should move from one place to another, like a finite being, and embody himself in the form of a dove? Finally, that God should utter articulate tones in a national idiom, has been justly held extravagant.[3]

Even in the early church, the more enlightened fathers adopted the opinion, that the heavenly voices spoken of in the biblical history were not external sounds, the effect of vibrations in the air, but inward impressions produced by God in the minds of those to whom he willed to impart himself: thus of the appearance at the baptism of Jesus, Origen and Theodore of Mopsuestia maintain that it was *a vision, and not a reality*, ὀπτασία, οὐ φύσις.[4] To the simple indeed, says Origen, in their simplicity, it is a light thing to set the universe in motion, and to sever a solid mass like the heavens; but those who search more deeply into such matters, will, he thinks, refer to those higher revelations, by means of which chosen persons, even waking, and still more frequently in their dreams, are led to suppose that they perceive something with their bodily senses, while their minds only are affected: so that consequently, the whole appearance in question should

---

[2] See Usteri, über den Täufer Johannes, die Taufe und Versuchung Christi, in the theolog. Studien und Kritiken, 2 Bd. 3 Heft, s. 442 ff., and Bleek, in the same periodical, 1833, 2, s. 428 ff.

[3] Bauer, hebr. Mythologie, 2 s. 225 f. Comp. Gratz, Comm. zum Evang. Matt. i. s. 172 ff.

[4] These are Theodore's words, in Münter's Fragmenta patr. græc. Fasc. I, s. 142. Orig. c. Cels. i. 48. Basil. M. in Suicer's Thesaurus, 2, p. 1479.

be understood, not as an external incident, but as an inward vision sent by God ; an interpretation which has also met with much approbation among modern theologians.

In the first two Gospels and in the fourth, this interpretation is favoured by the expressions, *were opened to him*, ἀνεῴχθησαν αὐτῷ, *he saw*, εἶδε, and *I beheld*, τεθέαμαι, which seem to imply that the appearance was subjective, in the sense intended by Theodore, when he observes that the descent of the Holy Spirit *was not seen by all present, but that, by a certain spiritual contemplation, it was visible to John alone*, οὐ πᾶσιν ὤφθη τοῖς παροῦσιν, ἀλλὰ κατά τινα πνευματικὴν θεωρίαν ὤφθη μόνῳ τῷ Ἰωάννῃ : to John however we must add Jesus, who, according to Mark, participated in the vision. But in opposition to this stands the statement of Luke : the expressions which he uses, ἐγένετο—ἀνεῳχθῆναι—καὶ καταβῆναι—καὶ φωνὴν—γενέσθαι, *it came to pass—was opened—and descended—and a voice came*, bear a character so totally objective and exterior,[5] especially if we add the words, *in a bodily form*, σωματικῷ εἴδει, that (abiding by the notion of the perfect truthfulness of all the evangelical records) the less explicit narratives must be interpreted by the unequivocal one of Luke, and the incident they recount must be understood as something more than an inward revelation to John and Jesus. Hence it is prudent in Olshausen to allow, in concession to Luke, that there was present on the occasion a crowd of persons, who saw and heard something, yet to maintain that this was nothing distinct or comprehensible. By this means, on the one hand, the occurrence is again transferred from the domain, of subjective visions to that of objective phenomena ; while on the other, the descending dove is supposed visible, not to the bodily eye, but only to the open spiritual one, and the words audible to the soul, not to the bodily ear. Our understanding fails us in this pneumatology of Olshausen, wherein there are sensible realities transcending the senses ; and we hasten out of this misty atmosphere into the clearer one of those, who simply tell us, that the appearance was an external incident, but one purely natural.

This party appeals to the custom of antiquity, to regard natural occurrences as divine intimations, and in momentous crises, where a bold resolution was to be taken, to adopt them as guides. To Jesus, spiritually matured into the Messiah, and only awaiting an external divine sanction, and to the Baptist who had already ceded the superiority to the friend of his youth, in their solemn frame of mind at the baptism of the former by the latter, every natural phenomenon that happened at the time, must have been pregnant with meaning, and have appeared as a sign of the divine will. But what the natural appearance actually was, is a point on which the commentators are divided in opinion. Some, with the synoptical writers, include a sound as well as an appearance ; others give, with John, an appearance only. They interpret the opening of the heavens, as a sudden parting of the clouds, or a flash of lightning ; the dove they consider as a real bird of that species, which by chance hovered over the head of Jesus ; or they assume that the lightning or some meteor was compared to a dove, from the manner of its descent. They who include a sound as a part of the machinery in the scene, suppose a clap of thunder, which was imagined by those present to be a Bath Kol, and interpreted into the words given by the first Evangelist. Others, on the contrary, understand what is said of audible words, merely as an explanation of the visible sign, which was regarded as an attestation that Jesus was the Son of God. This last opinion sacrifices the synoptical writers, who undeniably speak of an audible voice, to John, and thus contains a critical

---

[5] As even Lücke confesses, Comm. zum Evang. Joh. i., s. 370, and Bleek, ut sup., s. 437.

doubt as to the historical character of the narratives, which, consistently followed out, leads to quite other ground than that of the naturalistic interpretation. If the sound was mere thunder, and the words only an interpretation put upon it by the bystanders; then, as in the synoptical accounts, the words are evidently supposed to have been audibly articulated, we must allow that there is a traditional ingredient in these records. So far as the appearance is concerned, it is not to be denied that the sudden parting of clouds, or a flash of lightning, might be described as an opening of heaven; but in nowise could the form of a dove be ascribed to lightning or a meteor. The form is expressly the point of comparison in Luke only, but it is doubtless so intended by the other narrators; although Fritszche contends that the words *like a dove*, ὡσεὶ περιστερὰν, in Matthew refer only to the rapid motion. The flight of the dove has nothing so peculiar and distinctive, that, supposing this to be the point of comparison, there would not be in any of the parallel passages a variation, a substitution of some other bird, or an entirely new figure. As, instead of this, the mention of the dove is invariable through all the four gospels, the simile must turn upon something exclusively proper to the dove, and this can apparently be nothing but its form. Hence those commit the least violence on the text, who adopt the supposition of a real dove. Paulus, however, in so doing, incurred the hard task of showing by a multitude of facts from natural history and other sources, that the dove might be tame enough to fly towards a man; [6] how it could linger so long over one, that it might be said, ἔμεινεν ἐπ᾽ αὐτὸν, *it abode upon him*, he has not succeeded in explaining, and he thus comes into collision with the narrative of John, by which he had sustained his supposition of the absence of a voice. [7]

§ 51.

AN ATTEMPT AT A CRITICISM AND MYTHICAL INTERPRETATION OF THE NARRATIVES.

If then a more intelligible representation of the scene at the baptism of Jesus is not to be given, without doing violence to the evangelical text, or without supposing it to be partially erroneous, we are necessarily driven to a critical treatment of the accounts; and indeed, according to De Wette and Schleiermacher, [1] this is the prevalent course in relation to the above point in the evangelical history. From the narrative of John, as the pure source, it is sought to derive the synoptical accounts, as turbid streams. In the former, it is said, there is no opening heaven, no heavenly voice; only the descent of the Spirit is, as had been promised, a divine witness to John that Jesus is the Messiah; but in what manner the Baptist perceived that the Spirit rested on Jesus, he does not tell us, and possibly the only sign may have been the discourse of Jesus.

One cannot but wonder at Schleiermacher's assertion, that the manner in which the Baptist perceived the descending Spirit is not given in the fourth gospel, when here also the expression ὡσεὶ περιστερὰν, *like a dove*, tells it plainly enough; and this particular marks the descent as a visible one, and not a mere inference from the discourse of Jesus. Usteri, indeed, thinks

---

[6] Comp. Eusebius, H. E. vi. 29.
[7] See Paulus, Bauer, Kuinöl, Hase and Theile.
[1] De Wette, bibl. Dogmatik, § 208. Anm. 6, exeg. Handb. 1, 1, s. 34 f. 1, 3, s. 29 f. Schleiermacher, über den Lukas, s. 58 f. Usteri, Bleek, Hase, Kern, Neander.

that the Baptist mentioned the dove, merely as a figure, to denote the gentle, mild spirit which he had observed in Jesus. But had this been all, he would rather have compared Jesus himself to a dove, as on another occasion he did to a lamb, than have suggested the idea of a sensible appearance by the picturesque description, *I saw the Spirit descending from heaven like a dove.* It is therefore not true in relation to the dove, that first in the more remote tradition given by the synoptical writers, what was originally figurative, was received in a literal sense; for in this sense it is understood by John, and if he have the correct account, the Baptist himself must have spoken of a visible dove-like appearance, as Bleek, Neander, and others, acknowledge.

While the alleged distinction in relation to the dove, between the first three evangelists and the fourth, is not to be found; with respect to the voice, the difference is so wide, that it is inconceivable how the one account could be drawn from the other. For it is said that the testimony which John gave concerning Jesus, after the appearance : *This is the Son of God* (John i. 34), taken in connexion with the preceding words : *He that sent me to baptize, the same said unto me,* etc., became, in the process of tradition, an immediate heavenly declaration, such as we see in Matthew : *This is my beloved Son, in whom I am well pleased.* Supposing such a transformation admissible, some instigation to it must be shown. Now in Isaiah xlii. 1, Jehovah says of his servant : הֵן עַבְדִּי אֶתְמָךְ־בּוֹ בְּחִירִי רָצְתָה נַפְשִׁי; words which, excepting those between the parentheses, are almost literally translated by the declaration of the heavenly voice in Matthew. We learn from Matt. xii. 17 ff. that this passage was applied to Jesus as the Messiah; and in it God himself is the speaker, as in the synoptical account of the baptism. Here then was what would much more readily prompt the fiction of a heavenly voice, than the expressions of John. Since, therefore, we do not need a misapprehension of the Baptist's language to explain the story of the divine voice, and since we cannot use it for the derivation of the allusion to the dove; we must seek for the source of our narrative, not in one of the evangelical documents, but beyond the New Testament,—in the domain of cotemporary ideas, founded on the Old Testament, the total neglect of which has greatly diminished the value of Schleiermacher's critique on the New Testament.

To regard declarations concerning the Messiah, put by poets into the mouth of Jehovah, as real, audible voices from heaven, was wholly in the spirit of the later Judaism, which not seldom supposed such vocal communications to fall to the lot of distinguished rabbins,[2] and of the messianic prejudices, which the early Christians both shared themselves, and were compelled, in confronting the Jews, to satisfy. In the passage quoted from Isaiah, there was a divine declaration, in which the present Messiah was pointed to as it were with the finger, and which was therefore specially adapted for a heavenly annunciation concerning him. How could the spirit of Christian legend be slow to imagine a scene, in which these words were audibly spoken from heaven of the Messiah. But we detect a farther motive for such a representation of the case by observing, that in Mark and Luke, the heavenly voice addresses Jesus in the second person, and by comparing the words which, according to the Fathers, were given in the old and lost gospels as those of the voice. Justin, following his *Memoirs of the Apostles,* ἀπομνημονεύματα τῶν ἀποστόλων, thus reports them : υἱός μου εἶ σύ. ἐγὼ σήμερον γεγέννηκα σε ;[3] *Thou art my Son, this day have I begotten thee.* In

---

[2] According to Bava Mezia, f. lix. 1 (in Wetstein, p. 427), R. Elieser appealed to a heavenly sign, in proof that he had tradition in his favour : *tum personuit echo cœlestis : quid vobis cum R. Eliesere? nam ubivis secundum illum obtinet traditio.*

[3] Dial. c. Tryph. 88.

the Gospel of the Hebrews, according to Epiphanius;[4] this declaration was combined with that which our Gospels contain. Clement of Alexandria[5] and Augustin[6] seem to have read the words even in some copies of the latter; and it is at least certain that some of our present manuscripts of Luke have this addition.[7] Here were words uttered by the heavenly voice, drawn, not from Isaiah, but from Psalm ii. 7, a passage considered messianic by Jewish interpreters;[8] in Heb. i. 5, applied to Christ; and, from their being couched in the form of a direct address, containing a yet stronger inducement to conceive it as a voice sent to the Messiah from heaven. If then the words of the psalm were originally attributed to the heavenly voice, or if they were only taken in connexion with the passage in Isaiah (as is probable from the use of the second person, σὺ εἶ, in Mark and Luke, since this form is presented in the psalm, and not in Isaiah), we have a sufficient indication that this text, long interpreted of the Messiah, and easily regarded as an address from heaven to the Messiah on earth, was the source of our narrative of the divine voice, heard at the baptism of Jesus. To unite it with the baptism, followed as a matter of course, when this was held to be a consecration of Jesus to his office.

We proceed to the descent of the Spirit in the form of a dove. In this examination we must separate the descent of the Spirit from the form of the dove, and consider the two particulars apart. That the Divine Spirit was to rest in a peculiar measure on the Messiah, was an expectation necessarily resulting from the notion, that the messianic times were to be those of the outpouring of the Spirit upon all flesh (Joel iii. 1 ff.); and in Isaiah xi. 1 f. it was expressly said of the stem of Jesse, that the spirit of the Lord would rest on it in all its fulness, as the Spirit of wisdom and understanding, of might, and of the fear of the Lord. The communication of the Spirit, considered as an individual act, coincident with the baptism, had a type in the history of David, on whom, when anointed by Samuel, the spirit of Godc came from that day forward (1 Sam. xvi. 13). Further, in the Old Testament phrases concerning the imparting of the Divine Spirit to men, especially in that expression of Isaiah, נוּחַ עַל־, which best corresponds to the μένειν ἐπὶ of John, there already lay the germ of a symbolical representation; for that Hebrew verb is applied also to the halting of armies, or, like the parallel Arabic word, even of animals. The imagination, once stimulated by such an expression, would be the more strongly impelled to complete the picture by the necessity for distinguishing the descent of the Spirit on the Messiah,— in the Jewish view, from the mode in which it was imparted to the prophets (e.g. Isaiah lxi. 1)—in the Christian view, from its ordinary communication to the baptized (e.g. Acts xix. 1 ff).[9] The position being once laid down that the Spirit was to descend on the Messiah, the question immediately occurred: *How* would it descend? This was necessarily decided according to the popular Jewish idea, which always represented the Divine Spirit under some form or other. In the Old Testament, and even in the New (Acts ii. 3), fire is the principal symbol of the Holy Spirit; but it by no means follows that other sensible objects were not similarly used. In an important passage of the Old Testament (Gen. i. 2), the Spirit of God is described as hovering (מְרַחֶפֶת), a word which suggests, as its sensible representation, the movement

---

[4] Hæres. xxx. 13.
[5] Pædagog. i. 6.
[6] De consens. Evangg. ii. 14.
[7] S. Wetstein in loc. des Lukas, and De Wette, Einl. in das N. T., s. 100.
[8] S. Rosenmüller's Schol. in Psalm ii.
[9] Schleiermacher, über den Lukas, s. 57.

of a bird, rather than of fire. Thus the expression רָחַף, Deut. xxxii. 11, is used of the hovering of a bird over its young. But the imagination could not be satisfied with the general figure of a bird ; it must have a specific image, and everything led to the choice of the dove.

In the East, and especially in Syria, the dove is a sacred bird,[10] and it is so for a reason which almost necessitated its association with the Spirit moving on the face of the primitive waters (Gen. i. 2). The brooding dove was a symbol of the quickening warmth of nature ;[11] it thus perfectly represented the function which, in the Mosaic cosmogony, is ascribed to the Spirit of God,—the calling forth of the world of life from the chaos of the first creation. Moreover, when the earth was a second time covered with water, it is a dove, sent by Noah, which hovers over its waves, and which, by plucking an olive leaf, and at length finally disappearing, announces the renewed possibility of living on the earth. Who then can wonder that in Jewish writings, the Spirit hovering over the primeval waters is expressly compared to a dove,[12] and that, apart from the narrative under examination, the dove is taken as a symbol of the Holy Spirit?[13] How near to this lay the association of the hovering dove with the Messiah, on whom the dove-like spirit was to descend, is evident, without our having recourse to the Jewish writings, which designate the Spirit hovering over the waters, Gen. i. 2, as the Spirit of the Messiah,[14] and also connect with him its emblem, the Noachian dove.[15]

When, in this manner, the heavenly voice, and the Divine Spirit down-hovering like a dove, gathered from the cotemporary Jewish ideas, had become integral parts of the Christian legend concerning the circumstances of the baptism of Jesus ; it followed, of course, that the heavens should open themselves, for the Spirit, once embodied, must have a road before it could descend through the vault of heaven.[16]

The result of the preceding inquiries, viz., that the alleged miraculous circumstances of the baptism of Jesus have merely a mythical value, might have been much more readily obtained, in the way of inference from the preceding chapter ; for if, according to that, John had not acknowledged Jesus to be the Messiah, there could have been no appearances at the baptism of Jesus, demonstrative to John of his Messiahship. We have, however, established the mythical character of the baptismal phenomena, without

---

[10] Tibull. Carm. L. 1, eleg. 8, v. 17 f. See the remark of Broeckhuis on this passage ; Creuzer, Symbolik, ii. s. 70 f. ; Paulus, exeg. Handb. 1, a, s. 369.

[11] Creuzer, Symbolik, ii. s. 80.

[12] Chagiga c. ii. : *Spiritus Dei ferebatur super aquas, sicut columba, quæ fertur super pullos suos nec tangit illos.* Ir Gibborim ad Genes. 1, 2, ap. Schöttgen, horæ, i. p. 9.

[13] Targum Koheleth, ii. 12, vox turturis is interpreted as *vox spiritus sancti.* To regard this, with Lücke, as an arbitrary interpretation, seems itself like arbitrariness, in the face of the above data.

[14] Bereschith rabba, s. 2, f. 4, 4, ad Genes. T. 2 (ap. Schöttgen ut sup.) : *intelligitur spiritus regis Messiæ, de quo dicitur,* Jes. xi. 2 : *et quiescet super illum spiritus Domini.*

[15] Sohar. Numer. f. 68. col. 271 f. (in Schöttgen, horæ, 2, p. 537 f.). The purport of this passage rests on the following cabalistic conclusion : If David, according to Ps. lii. 10, is the olive tree ; the Messiah, a scion of David, is the olive leaf : and since it is said of Noah's dove, Gen. viii. 11, that it carried an olive leaf in its mouth ; the Messiah will be ushered into the world by a dove.—Even Christian interpreters have compared the dove at the baptism of Jesus to the Noachian one ; see Suicer, Thesaurus, 2, Art. περιστερὰ, p. 688. It has been customary to cite in this connection, that the Samaritans paid divine honours to a dove under the name of Achima, on Mount Gerizim ; but this is a Jewish accusation, grounded on a wilful misconstruction. See Stäudlin's and Tzschirner's Archiv. für K. G. 1, 3, s. 66. Lücke, 1, s. 367.

[16] See Fritzsche, Comm. in Matt., p. 148.

presupposing the result of the previous chapter ; and thus the two independently obtained conclusions may serve to strengthen each other.

Supposing all the immediate circumstances of the baptism of Jesus unhistorical, the question occurs, whether the baptism itself be also a mere
mythus. Fritzsche seems not disinclined to the affirmative, for he leaves it
undecided whether the first Christians knew historically, or only supposed,
in conformity with their messianic expectations, that Jesus was consecrated
to his messianic office by John, as his forerunner. This view may be supported by the observation, that in the Jewish expectation, which originated
in the history of David, combined with the prophecy of Malachi, there was
adequate inducement to assume such a consecration of Jesus by the Baptist,
even without historical warrant ; and the mention of John's baptism in relation to Jesus (Acts i. 22), in a narrative, itself traditional, proves nothing
to the contrary.* Yet, on the other hand, it is to be considered that the
baptism of Jesus by John furnishes the most natural basis for an explanation
of the messianic project of Jesus. When we have two cotemporaries, of
whom one announces the proximity of the Messiah's kingdom, and the other
subsequently assumes the character of Messiah ; the conjecture arises, even
without positive information, that they stood in a relation to each other—
that the latter owed his idea to the former. If Jesus had the messianic idea
excited in him by John, yet, as is natural, only so far that he also looked forward to the advent of the messianic individual, whom he did not, in the first
instance, identify with himself ; he would most likely submit himself to the
baptism of John. This would probably take place without any striking occurrences ; and Jesus, in no way announced by it as the Baptist's superior,
might, as above remarked, continue for some time to demean himself as his
disciple.

If we take a comparative retrospect of our evangelical documents, the pre-
eminence which has of late been sought for the fourth gospel appears totally
unmerited. The single historical fact, the baptism of Jesus by John, is not
mentioned by the fourth Evangelist, who is solicitous about the mythical
adjuncts alone, and these he in reality gives no more simply than the synoptical writers, his omission of the opening heaven excepted ; for the divine
speech is not wanting in his narrative, if we read it impartially. In the
words, i. 33 : *He that sent me to baptize with water, the same said unto me,
Upon whom thou shalt see the Spirit descending, and remaining on him, the
same is he which baptizeth with the Holy Ghost,* we have not only substantially
the same purport as that conveyed by the heavenly voice in the synoptical
gospels, but also a divine declaration ; the only difference being, that here
John is addressed exclusively, and prior to the baptism of Jesus. This difference originated partly in the importance which the fourth Evangelist attached
to the relation between the Baptist and Jesus, and which required that the
criteria of the messianic individual, as well as the proximity of his kingdom,
should have been revealed to John at his call to baptize ; and it might be
partly suggested by the narrative in 1 Sam. xvi., according to which Samuel,
being sent by Jehovah to anoint a king selected from the sons of Jesse, is
thus admonished by Jehovah on the entrance of David : *Arise and anoint
him, for this is he* (v. 12). The descent of the Spirit, which in David's case
follows his consecration, is, by the fourth Evangelist, made an antecedent
sign of the Messiahship of Jesus.

§ 52.

RELATION OF THE SUPERNATURAL AT THE BAPTISM OF JESUS TO THE
SUPERNATURAL IN HIS CONCEPTION.

At the commencement of this chapter, we enquired into the subjective views of Jesus in his reception of John's baptism, or the idea which he entertained of its relation to his own character. We close this discussion with an inquiry into the objective purpose of the miracles at the baptism of Jesus, or the mode in which they were to subserve the manifestation of his messiahship.

The common answer to such an inquiry is, that Jesus was thereby inducted to his public office, and declared to be the Messiah,[1] *i.e.* that nothing was conferred on him, and that simply the character which he already possessed was manifested to others. But, it may be asked, is such an abstraction intended by our narrators? A consecration to an office, effected by divine co-operation, was ever considered by antiquity as a delegation of divine powers for its fulfilment; hence, in the Old Testament, the kings, as soon as they are anointed, are filled with the spirit of God (1 Sam. x. 6, 10, xvi. 13); and in the New Testament also, the apostles, before entering on their vocation, are furnished with supernatural gifts (Acts ii.). It may, therefore, be beforehand conjectured, that according to the original sense of the Gospels, the consecration of Jesus at his baptism was attended with a supply of higher powers; and this is confirmed by an examination of our narratives. For the synoptical writers all state, that after the baptism, the Spirit led Jesus into the wilderness, obviously marking this journey as the first effect of the higher principle infused at his baptism: and in John, the words μένειν ἐπ᾽ αὐτὸν, applied to the descending Spirit, seem to intimate. that from the time of the baptism there was a relation not previously subsisting, between the πνεῦμα ἅγιον and Jesus.

This interpretation of the marvels at the baptism of Jesus seems in contradiction with the narratives of his conception. If Jesus, as Matthew and Luke state, was conceived by the Holy Ghost; or if, as John propounds, the divine λόγος, *the word*, was made flesh in him, from the beginning of his earthly existence; why did he yet need, at his baptism, a special intromission of the πνεῦμα ἅγιον? Several modern expositors have seen, and sought to solve, this difficulty. Olshausen's explanation consists in the distinction between the potential and the actual; but it is self-contradictory.[2] For if the character of the Χριστὸς which was manifested *actû*, with the ripened manhood of Jesus, at his baptism, was already present *potentiâ* in the child and youth; there must have also been an inward principle of development, by means of which his powers would gradually unfold themselves from within, instead of being first awakened by a sudden illapse of the Spirit from without. This, however, does not preclude the possibility that the divine principle, existing in Jesus, as supernaturally conceived, from the moment of his birth, might need, owing to the human form of its development, some impulse from without; and Lücke[3] has more justly proceeded on this contrast between external impulse and inward development. The λόγος, present in Jesus from his birth, needed, he thinks, however strong might be the inward bent, some external stimulus and vivification, in order to arrive at full activity and mani-

---

[1] Hess, Geschichte Jesu, 1, s. 120.
[2] Bibl. Comm. 1, s. 175 f.
[3] Comm. zum Evang. Joh. 1, s. 378 f.

festation in the world; and that which awakens and guides the divine life-germ in the world is, on apostolic showing, the πνεῦμα ἅγιον. Allowing this, yet the inward disposition and the requisite force of the outward stimulus stand in an inverse relation to each other ; so that the stronger the outward stimulus required, the weaker is the inward disposition ; but in a case where the inward disposition is consummate,—as it must be supposed in Jesus, engendered by the Spirit, or animated by the λόγος,—the exterior impulse ought to be a *minimum*, that is, every circumstance, even the most common, might serve as a determination of the inward tendency. But at the baptism of Jesus we see the *maximum* of exterior impulse, in the visible descent of the divine Spirit ; and although we allow for the special nature of the mes-sianic task, for the fulfilment of which he must be qualified,[4] yet the maximum of inward disposition, which fitted him to be the υἱὸς Θεοῦ, cannot at the same time be supposed as existing in him from his birth : a consequence which Lücke only escapes, by reducing the baptismal scene to a mere inauguration, thus, as has been already shown, contradicting the evangelical records.

We must here give a similar decision to that at which we arrived concern-ing the genealogies ; viz., that in that circle of the early Christian church, in which the narrative of the descent of the πνεῦμα on Jesus at his baptism was formed, the idea that Jesus was generated by the same πνεῦμα cannot have prevailed ; and while, at the present day, the communication of the divine nature to Jesus is thought of as cotemporary with his conception, those Chris-tians must have regarded his baptism as the epoch of such communication. In fact, those primitive Christians whom, in a former discussion, we found to have known nothing, or to have believed nothing, of the supernatural con-ception of Jesus, were also those who connected the first communication of divine powers to Jesus with his baptism in the Jordan. For no other doc-trine did the orthodox fathers of the church more fiercely persecute the ancient Ebionites,[5] with their gnostic fellow-believer Cerinthus,[6] than for this : that the Holy Spirit first united himself with Jesus at his baptism. In the Gospel of the Ebionites it was written that the πνεῦμα not only descended on Jesus in the form of a dove, but entered into him ;[7] and according to Justin, it was the general expectation of the Jews, that higher powers would first be granted to the Messiah, when he should be anointed by his forerunner Elias.[8]

The development of these ideas seems to have been the following. When the messianic dignity of Jesus began to be acknowledged among the Jews, it was thought appropriate to connect his coming into possession of the requisite gifts, with the epoch from which he was in some degree known, and which, from the ceremony that marked it, was also best adapted to represent that anointing with the Holy Spirit, expected by the Jews for their Messiah : and from this point of view was formed the legend of the occurrences at the baptism. But as reverence for Jesus was heightened, and men appeared in the Christian church who were acquainted with more exalted messianic ideas,

---

[4] From the orthodox point of view, it cannot be consistently said, with Hoffmann (p. 301), that for the conviction of his messiahship and the maintenance of the right position, amid so many temptations and adverse circumstances, an internally wrought certainty did not suffice Jesus, and external confirmation by a fact was requisite.

[5] Epiphan. hæres. xxx. 14: ἐπειδὴ γὰρ βούλονται τὸν μὲν Ἰησοῦν ὄντως ἄνθρωπον εἶναι, Χριστὸν δὲ ἐν αὐτῷ γεγενῆσθαι τὸν ἐν εἴδει περιστερᾶς καταβεβηκότα, κ. τ. λ :—*They maintain that Jesus was really man, but that that which descended from heaven in the form of a dove became Christ in him.*

[6] Epiphan. hæres. xxviii. 1.

[7] Epiphan. hæres. xxx. 13 :—περιστερᾶς κατελθούσης καὶ εἰσελθούσης εἰς αὐτὸν :—*of a dove descending and entering into him.*

[8] See the passage above, § 48, note 7.

this tardy manifestation of messiahship was no longer sufficient ; his relation with the Holy Spirit was referred to his conception : and from this point of view was formed the tradition of the supernatural conception of Jesus. Here too, perhaps, the words of the heavenly voice, which might originally be those of Ps. ii. 7, were altered after Isaiah xlii. 1. For the words, σήμερον γεγέννηκα σε, *This day have I begotten thee*, were consistent with the notion that Jesus was constituted the Son of God at his baptism ; but they were no longer suitable to that occasion, when the opinion had arisen that the origin of his life was an immediate divine act. By this later representation, however, the earlier one was by no means supplanted, but, on the contrary, tradition and her recorders being large-hearted, both narratives—that of the miracles at the baptism, and that of the supernatural conception, or the indwelling of the λόγος in Jesus from the commencement of his life, although, strictly, they exclude each other, went forth peaceably side by side, and so were depicted by our Evangelists, not excepting even the fourth. Just as in the case of the genealogies : the narrative of the imparting of the Spirit at the baptism could not arise after the formation of the idea that Jesus was engendered by the Spirit ; but it might be retained as a supplement, because tradition is ever unwilling to renounce any of its acquired treasures.

§ 53.

PLACE AND TIME OF THE TEMPTATION OF JESUS. DIVERGENCIES OF THE EVANGELISTS ON THIS SUBJECT.

The transition from the baptism to the temptation of Jesus, as it is made by the synoptical writers, is attended with difficulty in relation both to place and time.

With respect to the former, it strikes us at once, that according to all the synoptical gospels, Jesus after his baptism was led into the wilderness to be tempted, implying that he was not previously in the wilderness, although, according to Matt. iii. 1, John, by whom he was baptized, exercised his ministry there. This apparent contradiction has been exposed by the most recent critic of Matthew's gospel, for the sake of proving the statement that John baptized in the wilderness to be erroneous.[1] But they who cannot resolve to reject this statement on grounds previously laid down, may here avail themselves of the supposition, that John delivered his preliminary discourses in the wilderness of Judea, but resorted to the Jordan for the purpose of baptizing ; or, if the banks of the Jordan be reckoned part of that wilderness, of the presumption that the Evangelists can only have intended that the Spirit led Jesus farther into the recesses of the wilderness, but have neglected to state this with precision, because their description of the scene at the baptism had obliterated from their imagination their former designation of the locality of John's agency,

But there is, besides, a chronological difficulty : namely, that while, according to the synoptical writers, Jesus, in the plenitude of the Spirit, just communicated to him at the Jordan, betakes himself, in consequence of that communication, for forty days to the wilderness, where the temptation occurs, and then returns into Galilee ; John, on the contrary, is silent concerning the temptation, and appears to suppose an interval of a few days only, between the baptism of Jesus and his journey into Galilee ; thus allowing no space

---

[1] Schneckenburger, über den Ursprung des ersten kanonischen Evang., s. 39.

for a six weeks' residence in the wilderness. The fourth Evangelist commences his narrative with the testimony which the Baptist delivers to the emissaries of the Sanhedrim (i. 19); *the next day* (τῇ ἐπαύριον) he makes the Baptist recite the incident which in the synoptical gospels is followed by the baptism (v. 29): again, *the next day* (τῇ ἐπαύριον) he causes two of his disciples to follow Jesus (v. 35); farther, *the next day* (τῇ ἐπαύριον, v. 44), as Jesus is on the point of journeying into Galilee, Philip and Nathanael join him; and lastly, *on the third day*, τῇ ἡμέρᾳ τῇ τρίτῃ (ii. 1), Jesus is at the wedding in Cana of Galilee. The most natural inference is, that the baptism took place immediately before John's narrative of its attendant occurrences, and as according to the synoptical gospels the temptation followed close on the baptism, both these events must be inserted between v. 28 and 29, as Euthymius supposed. But between that which is narrated down to v. 28, and the sequel from v. 29 inclusive, there is only the interval of a *morrow*, ἐπαύριον, while the temptation requires a period of forty days; hence, expositors have thought it necessary to give ἐπαύριον the wider sense of ὕστερον *afterwards*; this however is inadmissible, because the expression τῇ ἡμέρᾳ τῇ τρίτῃ, *the third day*, follows in connexion with ἐπαύριον, and restricts its meaning to *the morrow*. We might therefore be inclined, with Kuinöl, to separate the baptism and the temptation, to place the baptism after v. 28, and to regard the next day's interview between Jesus and John (v. 29) as a parting visit from the former to the latter : inserting after this the journey into the wilderness and the temptation. But without insisting that the first three Evangelists seem not to allow even of a day's interval between the baptism and the departure of Jesus into the wilderness, yet even later we have the same difficulty in finding space for the forty days. For it is no more possible to place the residence in the wilderness between the supposed parting visit and the direction of the two disciples to Jesus, that is between v. 34 and 35, as Kuinöl attempts, than between v. 28 and 29, since the former as well as the latter passages are connected by τῇ ἐπαύριον, *on the morrow*, Hence we must descend to v. 43 and 44; but here also there is only the interval of a *morrow*, and even chap. ii. 1, we are shut out by an ἡμέρα τρίτη, *third day*, so that, proceeding in this way, the temptation would at last be carried to the residence of Jesus in Galilee, in direct opposition to the statement of the synoptical writers ; while, in further contradiction to them, the temptation is placed at a farther and farther distance from the baptism. Thus neither at v. 29, nor below it, can the forty days' residence of Jesus in the wilderness with the temptation be intercalated : and it must therefore be referred, according to the plan of Lücke and others,[2] to the period before v. 19, which seems to allow of as large an interpolation as can be desired, inasmuch as the fourth Evangelist there commences his history. Now it is true that what follows from v. 19 to 28 is not of a kind absolutely to exclude the baptism and temptation of Jesus as earlier occurrences; but from v. 29 to 34, the Evangelist is far from making the Baptist speak as if there had been an interval of six weeks between the baptism and his narrative of its circumstances.[3] That the fourth Evangelist should have omitted, by chance merely, the history of the temptation, important as it was in the view of the other Evangelists, seems improbable : it is rather to be concluded, either that it was dogmatically offensive to him, so that he omitted it designedly, or that it was not current in the circle of tradition from which he drew his materials.

The period of forty days is assigned by all three of the synoptical writers

[2] Comm. z. Ev. Joh. 1, s. 344.
[3] Comp. de Wette, exeg. Handb. 1, 3, s. 27.

for the residence of Jesus in the wilderness; but to this agreement is annexed the not inconsiderable discrepancy, that, according to Matthew, the temptation by the devil commences after the lapse of the forty days, while, according to the others, it appears to have been going forward during this time; for the words of Mark (i. 13), *he was in the wilderness forty days tempted of Satan,* ἦν ἐν τῇ ἐρήμῳ ἡμέρας τεσσαράκοντα πειραζόμενος ὑπὸ τοῦ Σατανᾶ, and the similar ones of Luke i. 2, can have no other meaning. Added to this, there is a difference between the two latter evangelists; Mark only placing the temptation generally within the duration of forty days, without naming the particular acts of the tempter, which according to Matthew, were subsequent to the forty days; while Luke mentions both the prolonged temptation (πειράζεσθαι) of the forty days, and the three special temptations (πειρασμοὶ) which followed.[4] It has been thought possible to make the three accounts tally by supposing that the devil tempted Jesus during the forty days, as Mark states; that after the lapse of that time he approached him with the three temptations given by Matthew; and that Luke's narrative includes the whole.[5] Further, the temptations have been distinguished into two kinds; that which is only generally mentioned, as continued through the forty days, being considered invisible, like the ordinary attempts of Satan against men; and the three particularized temptations being regarded as personal and visible assaults, resorted to on the failure of the first.[6] But this distinction is evidently built on the air; moreover, it is inconceivable why Luke should not specify one of the temptations of the forty days, and should only mention the three subsequent ones detailed by Matthew. We might conjecture that the three temptations narrated by Luke did not occur after the six weeks, but were given by way of specimen from among the many that took place during that time; and that Matthew misunderstood them to be a sequel to the forty days' temptation.[7] But the challenge to make stones bread must in any case be placed at the end of that period, for it appealed to the hunger of Jesus, arising from a forty days' fast (a cause omitted by Mark alone). Now in Luke also this is the first temptation, and if this occurred at the close of the forty days, the others could not have been earlier. For it is not to be admitted that the separate temptations being united in Luke merely by καὶ, and not by τότε and πάλιν as in Matthew, we are not bound to preserve the order of them, and that without violating the intention of the third Evangelist we may place the second and third temptation before the first. Thus Luke is convicted of a want of historical tact; for after representing Jesus as tempted by the devil forty days, he has no details to give concerning this long period, but narrates later temptations; hence we are not inclined, with the most recent critic of Matthew's Gospel, to regard Luke's as the original, and Matthew's as the traditional and adulterated narrative.[8] Rather, as in Mark the temptation is noticed without farther details than that it lasted forty days, and in Matthew the particular cases of temptation are narrated, the hunger which induced the first rendering it necessary to place them after the forty days; Luke has evidently the secondary statement, for he unites the two previous ones in a manner scarcely tolerable, giving the forty days' process of temptation, and then superfluously bringing forward particular instances as additional facts. It is not on this account to be concluded that Luke wrote after Mark, and in dependence on him; but supposing, on the

---

[4] Compare Fritzsche, Comm. in Marc., s. 23 De Wette, exeg. Handb., 1, 2, s. 33.
[5] Kuinöl, Comm. in Luc., s. 379.
[6] Lightfoot, horæ, p. 243.
[7] Schneckenburger, über den Ursprung des ersten kan. Evang., s. 46.
[8] Ibid.

contrary, that Mark here borrowed from Luke, he extracted only the first and general part of the latter Evangelist's narrative, having ready, in lieu of the farther detail of single temptations, an addition peculiar to himself; namely, that Jesus, during his residence in the wilderness was μετὰ τῶν θηρίων, *with the wild beasts.*

What was Mark's object in introducing the wild beasts, it is difficult to say. The majority of expositors are of opinion that he intended to complete the terrible picture of the wilderness; [9] but to this it is not without reason objected, that the clause would then have been in closer connexion with the words ἦν ἐν τῇ ἐρήμῳ, *he was in the wilderness,* instead of being placed after πειραζόμενος, *tempted.*[10] Usteri has hazarded the conjecture that this particularity may be designed to mark Christ as the antitype of Adam, who, in Paradise, also stood in a peculiar relation to the animals,[11] and Olshausen has eagerly laid hold on this mystical notion; but it is an interpretation which finds little support in the context. Schleiermacher, in pronouncing this feature of Mark's narrative extravagant,[12] doubtless means that this Evangelist here, as in other instances of exaggeration, borders on the style of the apocryphal gospels, for whose capricious fictions we are not seldom unable to suggest a cause or an object, and thus we must rest contented, for the present, to penetrate no farther into the sense of his statement.

With respect to the difference between Matthew and Luke in the arrangement of the several temptations, we must equally abide by Schleiermacher's criticism and verdict, namely, that Matthew's order seems to be the original, because it is founded on the relative importance of the temptations, which is the main consideration,—the invitation to worship Satan, which is the strongest temptation, being made the final one; whereas the arrangement of Luke looks like a later and not very happy transposition, proceeding from the consideration—alien to the original spirit of the narrative—that Jesus could more readily go with the devil from the wilderness to the adjacent mountain and from thence to Jerusalem, than out of the wilderness to the city and from thence back again to the mountain.[13] While the first two Evangelists close their narrative of the temptation with the ministering of angels to Jesus, Luke has a conclusion peculiar to himself, namely, that the devil left Jesus *for a season,* ἄχρι καιροῦ (v. 13), apparently intimating that the sufferings of Jesus were a farther assault of the devil; an idea not resumed by Luke, but alluded to in John xiv. 30.

§ 54.

THE HISTORY OF THE TEMPTATION CONCEIVED IN THE SENSE OF THE EVANGELISTS.

Few evangelical passages have undergone a more industrious criticism, or more completely run through the circle of all possible interpretations, than the history in question. For the personal appearance of the devil, which it seems to contain, was a thorn which would not allow commentators to repose on the most obvious interpretation, but incessantly urged them to new efforts. The series of explanations hence resulting, led to critical comparisons, among

[9] Thus Euthymius, Kuinöl, and others.
[10] Fritzsche, in loc.
[11] Beitrag zur Erklärung der Versuchungsgeschichte, in Ullmann's and Umbreit's Studien, 1834, 4, s. 789.
[12] Ueber den Lukas, s. 56.
[13] Compare Schneckenburger, ut sup., s. 46 f.

which those of Schmidt,[1] Fritzsche,[2] and Usteri,[3] seem to have carried the inquiry to its utmost limits.

The first interpretation that suggests itself on an unprejudiced consideration of the text is this ; that Jesus was led by the Divine Spirit received at his baptism into the wilderness, there to undergo a temptation by the devil, who accordingly appeared to him visibly and personally, and in various ways, and at various places to which he was the conductor, prosecuted his purpose of temptation ; but meeting with a victorious resistance, he withdrew from Jesus, and angels appeared to minister to him. Such is the simple exegesis of the narrative, but viewed as a history it is encumbered with difficulties.

To take the portions of the narrative in their proper order : if the Divine Spirit led Jesus into the wilderness with the design of exposing him to temptation, as Matthew expressly says, ἀνήχθη εἰς τὴν ἔρημον ὑπὸ τοῦ Πνεύματος, πειρασθῆναι (iv. 1), of what use was this temptation ? That it had a vicarious and redeeming value will hardly be maintained, or that it was necessary for God to put Jesus to a trial ; neither can it be consistently shown that by this temptation Jesus was to be made like us, and, according to Heb. iv. 15, tempted in all things like as we are ; for the fullest measure of trial fell to his share in after life, and a temptation, effected by the devil in person, would rather make him *unlike* us, who are spared such appearances.

The forty days' fast, too, is singular. One does not understand how Jesus could hunger after six weeks of abstinence from all food without having hungered long before ; since in ordinary cases the human frame cannot sustain a week's deprivation of nourishment. It is true, expositors[4] console themselves by calling the forty days a round number, and by supposing that the expression of Matthew, νηστεύσας, and even that of Luke, οὐκ ἔφαγεν οὐδέν, are not to be taken strictly, and do not denote abstinence from all food, but only from that which is customary, so that the use of roots and herbs is not excluded. On no supposition, however, can so much be subtracted from the forty days as to leave only the duration of a conceivable fast ; and that nothing short of entire abstinence from all nourishment was intended by the Evangelists Fritzsche has clearly shown, by pointing out the parallel between the fast of Jesus and that of Moses and Elias, the former of whom is said to have eaten no bread and drunk no water for forty days (Exod. xxxiv. 28 ; Deut. ix. 9, 18), and the latter to have gone for the same period in the strength of a meal taken before his journey (1 Kings xix. 8). But such a fast wants the credentials of utility, as well as of possibility. From the context it appears, that the fast of Jesus was prompted by the same Spirit which occasioned his journey to the wilderness, and which now moved him to a holy self-discipline, whereby men of God, under the old dispensation, purified themselves, and became worthy of divine visions. But it could not be hidden from that Spirit, that Satan, in attacking Jesus, would avail himself of this very fast, and make the hunger thence arising an accomplice in his temptation. And was not the fast, in this case, a kind of challenge to Satan, an act of presumption, ill becoming even the best warranted self-confidence?[5]

But the personal appearance of the devil is the great stumbling-block in

[1] Exegetische Beiträge, 1, s. 277 ff.
[2] Comm. in Matth. s. 172 ff.
[3] In the Essay quoted, s. 768.
[4] Thus, e.g., Kuinöl, Comm. in Matth., p. 84. Comp. Gratz, Comm. zum Matth , 1, s. 229. Hoffmann, p. 315.
[5] Usteri, über den Täufer Johannes, die Taufe und Versuchung Christi. In den theol. Studien und Kritiken, zweiten Jahrgangs (1829), drittes Heft, s. 450. De Wette, exeg. Handb., 1, 1, s. 38.

the present narrative.   If, it is said, there be a personal devil, he cannot take a visible form ; and if that were possible, he would hardly demean himself as he is represented to have done in the gospels.   It is with the existence of the devil as with that of angels—even the believers in a revelation are perplexed by it, because the idea did not spring up among the recipients of revelation, but was transplanted by them, during exile, from a profane soil.[6] Moreover, to those who have not quite shut out the lights of the present age, the existence of a devil is become in the highest degree doubtful.

On this subject, as well as on that of angels, Schleiermacher may serve as an interpreter of modern opinion.   He shows that the idea of a being such as the devil, is an assemblage of contradictions : that as the idea of angels originated in a limited observation of nature, so that of the devil originated in a limited observation of self, and as our knowledge of human nature progresses, must recede farther into the background, and the appeal to the devil be henceforth regarded as the resource of ignorance and sloth.[7] Even admitting the existence of a devil, a visible and personal appearance on his part, such as is here supposed, has its peculiar difficulties.   Olshausen himself observes, that there is no parallel to it either in the Old or New Testament.   Farther, if the devil, that he might have some hope of deceiving Jesus, abandoned his own form, and took that of a man, or of a good angel ; it may be reasonably asked whether the passage, 2 Cor. xi. 14, *Satan is transformed into an angel of light*, be intended literally, and if so, whether this fantastic conception can be substantially true ?[8]

As to the temptations, it was early asked by Julian, how the devil could hope to deceive Jesus, knowing, as he must, his higher nature ?[9] And Theodore's answer that the divinity of Jesus was then unknown to the devil, is contradicted by the observation, that had he not then beheld a higher nature in Jesus, he would scarcely have taken the trouble to appear specially to him in person.   In relation to the particular temptations, an assent cannot be withheld from the canon, that, to be credible, the narrative must ascribe nothing to the devil inconsistent with his established cunning.[10] Now the first temptation, appealing to hunger, we grant, is not ill-conceived ; if this were ineffectual, the devil, as an artful tactician, should have had a yet more alluring temptation at hand ; but instead of this, we find him, in Matthew, proposing to Jesus the neck-breaking feat of casting himself down from the pinnacle of the temple—a far less inviting experiment than the metamorphosis of the stones.   This proposition finding no acceptance, there follows, as a crowning effort, a suggestion which, whatever might be the bribe, every true Israelite would instantly reject with abhorrence—to fall down and worship the devil.   So indiscreet a choice and arrangement of temptations has thrown most modern commentators into perplexity.[11] As the three temptations took place in three different and distant places, the question occurs : how did Jesus pass with the devil from one to the other ?   Even the orthodox hold

---

[6] De Wette, bibl. Dogmatik, § 171.   Gramberg, Grundzüge einer Engellehre des A. T., § 5, in Winer's Zeitschrift f. wissenschaftliche Theologie, 1 Bd. s. 182 f.

[7] Glaubenslehre, 1, ss. 44, 45, der zweiten Ausg.

[8] Schmidt, exeg. Beiträge.   Kuinöl, in Matt.

[9] In a fragment of Theodore of Mopsuestia in Münter's Fragm. Patr. Græc. Fasc. 1, p. 99 f.

[10] Paulus.

[11] Hoffmann thinks that the devil, in his second temptation, designedly chose so startling an example as the leap from the temple roof, the essential aim of the temptation being to induce Jesus to a false use of his miraculous power and consciousness of a divine nature. But this evasion leaves the matter where it was, for there is the same absurdity in choosing unfit examples as unfit temptations.

that this change of place was effected quite naturally, for they suppose that Jesus set out on a journey, and that the devil followed him.[12] But the expressions, the devil *takes him—sets him*, παραλαμβάνει—ἵστησιν αὐτὸν ὁ διά- βολος, in Matthew : *taking*, ἀναγαγών, *brought*, ἤγαγεν, *set*, ἔστησεν, in Luke, obviously imply that the transportation was effected by the devil, and moreover, the particular given in Luke, that the devil showed Jesus all the kingdoms of the world in a moment of time, points to something magical ; so that without doubt the Evangelists intended to convey the idea of magical transportations, as in Acts viii. 29, a power of *carrying away*, ἁρπάζειν, is attributed to the *Spirit of the Lord.* But it was early found irreconcilable with the dignity of Jesus that the devil should thus exercise a magical power over him, and carry him about in the air ;[13] an idea which seemed extravagant even to those who tolerated the personal appearance of the devil. The incredibility is augmented, when we consider the sensation which the appearance of Jesus on the roof of the temple must have excited, even supposing it to be the roof of Solomon's Porch only, in which case the gilded spears on the holy of holies, and the prohibition to laymen to tread its roof, would not be an obstacle.[14] The well-known question suggested by the last temptation, as to the situation of the mountain, from whose summit may be seen all the kingdoms of the world, has been met by the information that κόσμος here means no more than Palestine, and βασιλείας, its several kingdoms and tetrarchies ;[15] but this is a scarcely less ludicrous explanation than the one that the devil showed Jesus all the kingdoms of the world on a map ! No answer remains but that such a mountain existed only in the ancient idea of the earth as a plain, and in the popular imagination, which can easily stretch a mountain up to heaven, and sharpen an eye to penetrate infinity.

Lastly, the incident with which our narrative closes, namely, that angels came and ministered to Jesus, is not without difficulty, apart from the above-mentioned doubts as to the existence of such beings. For the expression διηκόνουν can signify no other kind of ministering than that of presenting food ; and this is proved not only by the context, according to which Jesus had need of such tendance, but by a comparison of the circumstances with 1 Kings xix. 5, where an angel brings food to Elijah. But of the only two possible suppositions, both are equally incongruous : that ethereal beings like angels should convey earthly material food, or that the human body of Jesus should be nourished with heavenly substances, if any such exist.

§ 55.

THE TEMPTATION CONSIDERED AS A NATURAL OCCURRENCE EITHER INTERNAL OR EXTERNAL; AND ALSO AS A PARABLE.

The impossibility of conceiving the sudden removals of Jesus to the temple and the mountain, led some even of the ancient commentators to the opinion, that at least the locality of the second and third temptations was not present to Jesus corporeally and externally, but merely in a vision ;[1] while some

---

[12] Hess, Geschichte Jesu, 1, s. 124.
[13] See the author of the discourse *de jejunio et tentationibus Christi*, among Cyprian's works.
[14] Compare Joseph. B. J. v. v. 6, vi. v. 1. Fritzsche, in Matth., s. 164. De Wette, exeg. Handb., 1, 1, s. 40.
[15] The one proposed by Kuinöl, in Matth., p. 90 ; the other by Fritzsche, p. 168.
[1] Theodore of Mopsuestia, ut sup. p. 107, maintained against Julian that the devil had made the image of a mountain, φαντασίαν ὄρους τὸν διάβολον πεποιηκέναι, and according to

modern ones, to whom the personal appearance of the devil was especially offensive, have supposed that the whole transaction with him passed from beginning to end within the recesses of the soul of Jesus. Herewith they have regarded the forty days' fast either as a mere internal representation [2] (which, however, is a most inadmissible perversion of the plainly historic text : νηστεύσας ἡμέρας τεσσαράκοντα ὕστερον ἐπείνασε, Matt. iv. 2), or as a real fact, in which case the formidable difficulties mentioned in the preceding section remain valid. The internal representation of the temptations is by some made to accompany a state of ecstatic vision, for which they retain a supernatural cause, deriving it either from God, or from the kingdom of darkness : [3] others ascribe to the vision more of the nature of a dream, and accordingly seek a natural cause for it, in the reflections with which Jesus was occupied during his waking moments. [4] According to this theory, Jesus, in the solemn mood which the baptismal scene was calculated to produce, reviews his messianic plan, and together with the true means for its execution, he recalls their possible abuses ; an excessive use of miracles and a love of domination, by which man, in the Jewish mode of thinking, became, instead of an instrument of God, a promoter of the plans of the devil. While surrendering himself to such meditations, his finely organized body is overcome by their exciting influence ; he sinks for some time into deep exhaustion, and then into a dream-like state, in which his mind unconsciously embodies his previous thoughts in speaking and acting forms.

To support this transference of the whole scene to the inward nature of Jesus, commentators think that they can produce some features of the evangelical narrative itself. The expression of Matthew (iv. 1), ἀνήχθη εἰς τὴν ἔρημον ὑπὸ τοῦ Πνεύματος, and still more that of Luke (iv. 1), ἤγετο ἐν τῷ Πνεύματι, correspond fully to the forms : ἐγενόμην ἐν πνεύματι, Rev. i. 10, ἀπήνεγκέ με εἰς ἔρημον ἐν πνεύματι, xvii. 3, and to similar ones in Ezekiel ; and as in these passages inward intuition is alone referred to, neither in the evangelical ones, it is said, can any external occurrence be intended. But it has been with reason objected,[5] that the above forms may be adapted either to a real external abduction by the Divine Spirit (as in Acts viii. 39 ; 2 Kings ii. 16), or to one merely internal and visionary, as in the quotation from the Apocalypse, so that between these two possible significations the context must decide ; that in works replete with visions, as are the Apocalypse and Ezekiel, the context indeed pronounces in favour of a merely spiritual occurrence ; but in an historical work such as our gospels, of an external one. Dreams, and especially visions, are always expressly announced as such in the historical books of the New Testament : supposing, therefore, that the temptation was a vision, it should have been introduced by the words εἶδεν ἐν ὁράματι, ἐν ἐκστάσει, as in Acts ix. 12, x. 10 ; or ἐφάνη αὐτῷ κατ᾽ ὄναρ, as in Matt. i. 20, ii. 13. Besides, if a dream had been narrated, the transition to a continuation of the real history must have been marked by a διεγερθεὶς, *being awaked*, as in Matt. i. 24, ii. 14, 21 ; whereby, as Paulus truly says, much labour would have been spared to expositors.

It is further alleged against the above explanations, that Jesus does not

the author of the discourse, already cited, *de jejunio et tentationibus Christi*, the first temptation it is true passed *localiter in deserto*, but Jesus only went to the temple and the mountain as Ezekiel did from Chaboras to Jerusalem—that is, *in spiritu*.

[2] Paulus, s. 379.

[3] See for the former, H. Farmer, Gratz, Comm. zum Ev. Matth. 1, s. 217; for the latter, Olshausen in loc., and Hoffmann (s. 326 f.) if I rightly apprehend him.

[4] Paulus, s. 377 ff.

[5] Fritzsche, in Matth. 155 f. Usteri, Beitrag zur Erklärung der Versuchungsgeschichte, s. 774 f.

seem to have been at any other time subject to ecstasies, and that he nowhere else attaches importance to a dream, or even recapitulates one.[6] To what end God should have excited such a vision in Jesus, it is difficult to conceive, or how the devil should have had power and permission to produce it; especially in Christ. The orthodox, too, should not forget that, admitting the temptation to be a dream, resulting from the thoughts of Jesus, the false messianic ideas which were a part of those thoughts, are supposed to have had a strong influence on his mind.[7]

If, then, the history of the temptation is not to be understood as confined to the soul of Jesus, and if we have before shown that it cannot be regarded as supernatural; nothing seems to remain but to view it as a real, yet thoroughly natural, event, and to reduce the tempter to a mere man. After John had drawn attention to Jesus as the Messiah (thinks the author of the Natural History of the Prophet of Nazareth),[8] the ruling party in Jerusalem commissioned an artful Pharisee to put Jesus to the test, and to ascertain whether he really possessed miraculous powers, or whether he might not be drawn into the interest of the priesthood, and be induced to give his countenance to an enterprise against the Romans. This conception of the διάβολος is in dignified consistency with that of the ἄγγελοι, who appeared after his departure, to refresh Jesus, as an approaching caravan with provisions, or as soft reviving breezes.[9] But this view, as Usteri says, has so long completed its phases in the theological world, that to refute it would be to waste words.

If the foregoing discussions have proved that the temptation, as narrated by the synoptical Evangelists, cannot be conceived as an external or internal, a supernatural or natural occurrence, the conclusion is inevitable, that it cannot have taken place in the manner represented.

The least invidious expedient is to suppose that the source of our histories of the temptation was some real event in the life of Jesus, so narrated by him to his disciples as to convey no accurate impression of the fact. Tempting thoughts, which intruded themselves into his soul during his residence in the wilderness, or at various seasons, and under various circumstances, but which were immediately quelled by the unimpaired force of his will, were, according to the oriental mode of thought and expression, represented by him as a temptation of the devil; and this figurative narrative was understood literally.[10] The most prominent objection to this view, that it compromises the impeccability of Jesus,[11] being founded on a dogma, has no existence for the critic : we can, however, gather from the tenor of the evangelical history, that the practical sense of Jesus was thoroughly clear and just ; but this becomes questionable, if he could ever feel an inclination corresponding to the second temptation in Matthew, or even if he merely chose such a form for communicating a more reasonable temptation to his disciples. Further, in such a narrative Jesus would have presented a confused mixture of fiction and truth out of his life, not to be expected from an ingenuous teacher, as he otherwise appears to be, especially if it be supposed that the tempting thoughts did not really occur to him after his forty days' sojourn in the wilderness, and that this particular is only a portion of the fictitious investi-

---

[6] Ullmann, über die Unsündlichkeit Jesu, in his Studien, I, I, s. 56. Usteri, ut sup., s. 775.
[7] Usteri, s. 776.
[8] I Bd. s. 512 ff.
[9] The former in Henke's n. Magazin 4, 2, s. 352 ; the latter in the natürlichen Geschichte, I, s. 591 ff.
[10] This view is held by Ullmann, Hase, and Neander.
[11] Schleiermacher, über den Lukas, s. 54. Usteri, ut sup., s. 777.

ture ; while if it be assumed, on the contrary, that the date is historical, there remains the forty days' fast, one of the most insurmountable difficulties of the narrative.   If Jesus wished simply to describe a mental exercise in the manner of the Jews, who, tracing the effect to the cause, ascribed evil thoughts to diabolical agency, nothing more was requisite than to say that Satan suggested such and such thoughts to his mind ; and it was quite superfluous to depict a personal devil and a journey with him, unless, together with the purpose of narration, or in its stead, there existed a poetical and diadactic intention.

Such an intention, indeed, is attributed to Jesus by those who hold that the history of the temptation was narrated by him as a parable, but understood literally by his disciples.   This opinion is not encumbered with the difficulty of making some real inward experience of Jesus the basis of the history ;[12] it does not suppose that Jesus himself underwent such temptations, but only that he sought to secure his disciples from them, by impressing on them, as a compendium of messianic and apostolic wisdom, the three following maxims : first, to perform no miracle for their own advantage even in the greatest exigency ; secondly, never to venture on a chimerical undertaking in the hope of extraordinary divine aid ; thirdly, never to enter into fellowship with the wicked, however strong the enticement.[13]   It was long ago observed, in opposition to this interpretation, that the narrative is not easily recognized as a parable, and that its moral is hard to discern.[14]   With respect to the latter objection, it is true that the second temptation would be an ill-chosen image ; but the former remark is the more important one.   To prove that this narrative has not the characteristics of a parable, the following definition has been recently given : a parable, being essentially historical in its form, is only distinguishable from real history when its agents are of an obviously fictitious character.[15]   This is the case where the subjects are mere generalizations, as in the parables of the sower, the king, and others of a like kind ; or when they are, indeed, individualized, but so as to be at once recognized as unhistorical persons, as mere supports for the drapery of fiction, of which even Lazarus, in the parable of the rich man, is an example, though distinguished by a name.   In neither species of parable is it admissible to introduce as a subject a person corporeally present, and necessarily determinate and historical. Thus Jesus could not make Peter or any other of his disciples the subject of a parable, still less himself, for the reciter of a parable is pre-eminently present to his auditors ; and hence he cannot have delivered the history of the temptation, of which he is the subject, to his disciples as a parable.   To assume that the history had originally another subject, for whom oral tradition substituted Jesus, is inadmissible, because the narrative, even as a parable, has no definite significance unless the Messiah be its subject.[16]

If such a parable concerning himself or any other person, could not have been delivered by Jesus, yet it is possible that it was made by some other individual concerning Jesus ; and this is the view taken by Theile, who has recently explained the history of the temptation as a parabolic admonition, directed by some partisan of Jesus against the main features of the worldly

---

[12] If something really experienced by Jesus is supposed as the germ of the parable, this opinion is virtually the same as the preceding.
[13] J. E. C. Schmidt, in seiner Bibliothek, 1, 1, s. 60 f.   Schleiermacher, über den Lukas, s. 54 f.   Usteri, über den Täufer Johannes, die Taufe und Versuchung Christi, in den theol. Studien, 2, 3, s. 456 ff.
[14] K. Ch. L. Schmidt, exeg. Beiträge, 1, s. 339.
[15] Hasert, Bemerkungen über die Ansichten Ullmann's und Usteri's von der Versuchungs-gesch., Studien, 3, 1, s. 74 f.
[16] Hasert, ut sup., s. 76.

messianic hope, with the purpose of establishing the spiritual and moral view of the new economy.[17] Here is the transition to the mythical point of view, which the above theologian shuns, partly because the narrative is not sufficiently picturesque (though it is so in a high degree); partly because it is too pure (though he thus imputes false ideas to the primitive Christians); and partly because the formation of the mythus was too near the time of Jesus (an objection which must be equally valid against the early misconstruction of the parable). If it can be shown, on the contrary, that the narrative in question is formed less out of instructive thoughts and their poetical clothing, as is the case with a parable, than out of Old Testament passages and types, we shall not hesitate to designate it a mythus.

§ 56.

THE HISTORY OF THE TEMPTATION AS A MYTHUS.

Satan, the evil being and enemy of mankind, borrowed from the Persian religion, was by the Jews, whose exclusiveness limited all that was good and truly human to the Israelitish people, viewed as the special adversary of their nation, and hence as the lord of the heathen states with whom they were in hostility.[1] The interests of the Jewish people being centred in the Messiah, it followed that Satan was emphatically his adversary; and thus throughout the New Testament we find the idea of Jesus as the Messiah associated with that of Satan as the enemy of his person and cause. Christ having appeared to destroy the works of the devil (1 John iii. 8), the latter seizes every opportunity of sowing tares among the good seed (Matt. xiii. 39), and not only aims, though unsuccessfully, at obtaining the mastery over Jesus himself (John xiv. 30), but continually assails the faithful (Eph. vi. 11 ; 1 Pet. v. 8). As these attacks of the devil on the pious are nothing else than attempts to get them into his power, that is, to entice them to sin ; and as this can only be done by the indirect suggestion or immediate insinuation of evil, seductive thoughts, Satan had the appellation of ὁ πειράζων, the tempter. In the prologue to the book of Job, he seeks to seduce the pious man from God, by the instrumentality of a succession of plagues and misfortunes : while the ensnaring counsel which the serpent gave to the woman was early considered an immediate diabolical suggestion. (Wisdom ii. 24 ; John viii. 44 ; Rev. xii. 9.)

In the more ancient Hebrew theology, the idea was current that temptation (נִסָּה, LXX. πειράζειν) was an act of God himself, who thus put his favourites, as Abraham (Gen. xxii. 1), and the people of Israel (Exod. xvi. 4, and elsewhere), to the test, or in just anger even instigated men to pernicious deeds. But as soon as the idea of Satan was formed, the office of temptation was transferred to him, and withdrawn from God, with whose absolute goodness it began to be viewed as incompatible (James i. 13). Hence it is Satan, who by his importunity obtains the divine permission to put Job to the severest trial through suffering ; hence David's culpable project of numbering the people, which in the second book of Samuel was traced to the anger of God, is in the later chronicles (1 Chron. xxii. 1) put directly to the account of the

---

[17] Zur Biographie Jesu, § 23.

[1] See Zech. iii. 1, where Satan resists the high priest standing before the angel of the Lord; farther Vajikra rabba, f. cli. 1 (in Bertholdt, Christol. Jud., p. 183), where, according to Rabbi Jochanan, Jehovah said to כלאך המות (i.e. to Satan, comp. Heb. ii. 14 and Lightfoot, horæ, p. 1088) : *Feci quidem t: κοσμοκράτορι, at vero cum populo fœderis negotium nulla in re tibi est.*

devil; and even the well-meant temptation with which, according to Genesis, God visited Abraham, in requiring from him the sacrifice of his son, was in the opinion of the later Jews, undertaken by God at the instigation of Satan.[2] Nor was this enough—scenes were imagined in which the devil personally encountered Abraham on his way to the place of sacrifice, and in which he tempted the people of Israel during the absence of Moses.[3]

If the most eminent men of piety in Hebrew antiquity were thus tempted, in the earlier view, by God, in the later one, by Satan, what was more natural than to suppose that the Messiah, the Head of all the righteous, the representative and champion of God's people, would be the primary object of the assaults of Satan?[4] And we find this actually recorded as a rabbinical opinion,[5] in the material mode of representation of the later Judaism, under the form of a bodily appearance and a personal dialogue.

If a place were demanded where Satan might probably undertake such a temptation of the Messiah, the wilderness would present itself from more than one quarter. Not only had it been from Azazel (Lev. xvi. 8–10), and Asmodeus (Tobit viii. 3), to the demons ejected by Jesus (Matt. xii. 43), the fearful dwelling-place of the infernal powers : it was also the scene of temptation for the people of Israel, that *filius Dei collectivus*.[6] Added to this, it was the habit of Jesus to retire to solitary places for still meditation and prayer (Matt. xiv. 13 ; Mark i. 35 ; Luke vi. 12 ; John vi. 15) ; to which after his consecration to the messianic office he would feel more than usually disposed. It is hence possible that, as some theologians[7] have supposed, a residence of Jesus in the wilderness after his baptism (though not one of precisely forty days' duration) served as the historical foundation of our narrative ; but even without this connecting thread, both the already noticed choice of place and that of time are to be explained by the consideration, that it seemed consonant with the destiny of the Messiah that, like a second Hercules, he should undergo such a trial on his entrance into mature age and the messianic office.

But what had the Messiah to do in the wilderness? That the Messiah, the second Saviour, should like his typical predecessor, Moses, on Mount Sinai, submit himself to the holy discipline of fasting, was an idea the more

---

[2] See the passages quoted by Fabricius in Cod. pseudepigr. V. T., p. 395, from Gemara Sanhedrin.

[3] The same, p. 396. As Abraham went out to sacrifice his son in obedience to Jehovah, *antevertit eum Satanas in via, et tali colloquio cum ipso habito a proposito avertere eum conatus est*, etc. Schemoth, R. 41 (ap. Wetstein in loc. Matth.): *Cum Moses in altum adscenderet, dixit Israëli : post dies XL hora sexta redibo. Cum autem XL illi dies elapsi essent, venit Satanas, et turbavit mundum, dixitque : ubi est Moses, magister vester? mortuus est.* It is worthy of remark that here also the temptation takes place after the lapse of 40 days.

[4] Thus Fritzsche, in Matt. p. 173. His very title is striking, p. 154 : *Quod in vulgari Judæorum opinione erat, fore, ut Satanas salutaribus Messiæ consiliis omni modo, sed sine effectu tamen, nocere studeret, id ipsum Jesu Messiæ accidit. Nam quum is ad exemplum illustrium majorum quadraginta dierum in deserto loco egisset jejunium, Satanas eum convenit, protervisque atque impiis— —consiliis ad impietatem deducere frustra conatus est.*

[5] Schöttgen, horæ, ii. 538, adduces from Fini Flagellum Judæorum, iii. 35, a passage of Pesikta : *Ait Satan : Domine, permitte me tentare Messiam et ejus generationem? Cui inquit Deus : Non habeo ullam adversus eum potestatem. Satanas iterum ait : Sine me, quia potestatem habeo. Respondit Deus : Si in hoc diutius perseverabis, Satan, potius (te) de mundo perdam quam aliquam animam generationis Messiæ perdi permittam.* This passage at least proves that a temptation of the Messiah undertaken by the devil, was not foreign to the circle of Jewish ideas. Although the author of the above quotation represents the demand of Satan to have been denied, others, so soon as the imagination was once excited, would be sure to allow its completion.

[6] Deut. viii. 2 (LXX.) the people are thus addressed : μνησθήσῃ πᾶσαν τὴν ὁδὸν, ἣν ἤγαγέ σε Κύριος ὁ Θεός σου τοῦτο τεσσαρακοστὸν ἔτος ἐν τῇ ἐρήμῳ, ὅπως κακώσῃ σε καὶ πείρασῃ σε καὶ διαγνωσθῇ τὰ ἐν τῇ καρδίᾳ σου, εἰ φυλάξῃ τὰς ἐντολὰς αὐτοῦ ἢ οὔ.

[7] Ziegler, in Gabler's n. theol. Journ., 5, 201 ; Theile, zur Biogr. J., § 23.

inviting, because it furnished a suitable introduction to the first temptation which presupposed extreme hunger. The type of Moses and that of Elias (1 Kings xix. 8), determined also the duration of this fast in the wilderness, for they too had fasted forty days; moreover, the number forty was held sacred in Hebrew antiquity.[8] Above all, the forty days of the temptation of Jesus seem, as Olshausen justly observes, a miniature image of the forty years' trial in the wilderness, endured by the Israelitish people as a penal emblem of the forty days spent by the spies in the land of Canaan (Num. xiv. 34). For, that in the temptations of Jesus there was a special reference to the temptation of Israel in the wilderness, is shown by the circumstance that all the passages cited by Jesus in opposition to Satan are drawn from the re-capitulatory description of the journeyings of the Israelites in Deut. vi. and viii. The apostle Paul too, 1 Cor. x. 6, enumerates a series of particulars from the behaviour of the Israelites in the wilderness, with the consequent judgments of God, and warns Christians against similar conduct, pronouncing, v. 6 and 11, the punishments inflicted on the ancients to be types for the admonition of the living, his cotemporaries, on whom the *ends of the world* were come; *wherefore*, he adds, *let him that thinketh he standeth take heed lest he fall.* It is not probable that this was merely the private opinion of the apostle—it seems rather to have been a current notion that the hard trials of the people led by Moses, as well as of Moses individually, were types of those which awaited the followers of the Messiah in the catastrophe which he was to usher in, and still more emphatically the Messiah himself, who here appears as the antitype of the people, gloriously overcoming all the temptations under which they had fallen.

The Israelites were principally tempted by hunger during their wanderings in the wilderness;[9] hence the first temptation of the Messiah was determined beforehand. The rabbins, too, among the various temptations of Abraham which they recount, generally reckon hunger.[10] That Satan, when prompting Jesus to seek relief from his hunger by an exertion of his own will instead of awaiting it in faith from God, should make use of the terms given in our Evangelists, cannot be matter of surprise if we consider, not only that the wilderness was stony, but that to produce a thing from stones was a proverbial expression, denoting the supply of an object altogether wanting (Matt. iii. 9; Luke xix. 40), and that stone and bread formed a common contrast (Matt. vii. 9). The reply of Jesus to this suggestion is in the same train of ideas on which the entire first act of temptation is constructed; for he quotes the lesson which, according to Deuteronomy viii. 3, the people of Israel tardily learned from the temptation of hunger (a temptation, however, under which they were not resigned, but were provoked to murmur): namely, that man shall not live by bread alone, etc.

But one temptation would not suffice. Of Abraham the rabbins enumerated ten; but this number was too large for a dramatic narrative like that in the gospels, and among lower numbers the sacred three must have the prefer-ence. Thrice during his spiritual contest in Gethsemane Jesus severed him-self from his disciples (Matt. xxvi.); thrice Peter denied his Lord, and thrice Jesus subsequently questioned his love (John xxi.). In that rabbinical pas-sage which represents Abraham as tempted by the devil in person, the patri-arch parries three thrusts from him; in which particular, as well as in the

---

[8] See Wetstein, s. 270; De Wette, Kritik der mos. Geschichte, s. 245; the same in Daub's and Creuzer's Studien, 3, s. 245; v. Bohlen, Genesis, s. 63 f.

[9] Deut. viii. 3, καὶ ἐκάκωσέ σε καὶ ἐλιμαγχόνησε σε, κ. τ. λ.

[10] S. Fabricius, Cod. pseudepigr. V. T., p. 398 ff.

manner in which Old Testament texts are bandied by the parties, the scene is allied to the evangelical one.[11]

The second temptation (in Matthew) was not determined by its relation to the preceding; hence its presentation seems abrupt, and the choice fortuitous or capricious. This may be true with respect to its form, but its substantial meaning is in close connexion with the foregoing temptation, since it also has reference to the conduct of the Jewish people in the wilderness. To them the warning was given in Deut. vi. 16 to tempt God no more as they had tempted him at Massah; a warning which was reiterated 1 Cor. x. 9 to the members of the new covenant, though more in allusion to Num. xxi. 4. To this crying sin, therefore, under which the ancient people of God had fallen, must the Messiah be incited, that by resisting the incitement he might compensate, as it were, for the transgression of the people. Now the conduct which was condemned in them as a *tempting of the Lord,* ἐκπειράζειν Κύριον, was occasioned by a dearth of water, and consisted in their murmurs at this deprivation. This, to later tradition, did not seem fully to correspond to the terms; something more suitable was sought for, and from this point of view there could hardly be a more eligible choice than the one we actually find in our history of the temptation, for nothing can be more properly called a tempting of God than so audacious an appeal to his extraordinary succour, as that suggested by Satan in his second temptation. The reason why a leap from the pinnacle of the temple was named as an example of such presumption, is put into the mouth of Satan himself.

It occurred to the originator of this feature in the narrative, that the passage Ps. xci. 11 was capable of perversion into a motive for a rash act. It is there promised to one dwelling under the protection of Jehovah (a designation under which the Messiah was pre-eminently understood), that *angels should bear him up in their hands, lest at any time he should dash his foot against a stone.* Bearing up in their hands to prevent a fall, seemed to imply a precipitation from some eminence, and this might induce the idea that the divinely-protected Messiah might hurl himself from a height with impunity. But from what height? There could be no hesitation on this point. To the pious man, and therefore to the head of all the pious, is appropriated, according to Ps. xv. 1, xxiv, 3, the distinction of going up to Jehovah's holy hill, and standing within his holy place: hence the pinnacle of the temple, in the presumptuous mode of inference supposed, might be regarded as the height whence the Messiah could precipitate himself unhurt.

The third temptation which Jesus underwent—to worship the devil—is not apparent among the temptations of God's ancient people. But one of the

---

[11] Gemara Sanh., as in note 3. The colloquy between Abraham and Satan is thus continued:

1. *Satanas: Annon tentare te (Deum) in tali re ægre feras? Ecce erudiebas multos— labantem erigebant verba tua—quum nunc advenit ad te (Deus taliter te tentans) nonne ægre ferres* (Job iv. 2-5)?
Cui resp. Abraham: Ego in integritate mea ambulo (Ps. xxvi. 11).

2. *Satanas: Annon timor tuus, spes tua* (Job iv. 6)?
Abraham: Recordare quæso, quis est insons, qui perierit (v. 7)?

3. *Quare, quum videret Satanas, se nihil proficere, nec Abrahamum sibi obedire, dixit ad illum: et ad me verbum furtim ablatum est* (v. 12), *audivi—pecus futurum esse pro holocausto* (Gen. xxii. 7), *non autem Isaacum.*
Cui resp. Abraham: Hæc est pœna mendacis, ut etiam cum vera loquitur, fides ei non habeatur.

I am far from maintaining that this rabbinical passage was the model of our history of the temptation; but since it is impossible to prove, on the other side, that such narratives were only imitations of the New Testament ones, the supposed independent formation of stories so similar shows plainly enough the ease with which they sprang out of the given premises.

most fatal seductions by which the Israelites were led astray in the wilderness was that of idolatry; and the apostle Paul adduces it as admonitory to Christians. Not only is this sin derived immediately from the devil in a passage above quoted;[12] but in the later Jewish idea, idolatry was identical with the worship of the devil (Baruch iv. 7; 1 Cor. x. 20). How, then, could the worship of the devil be suggested to the Messiah in the form of a temptation? The notion of the Messiah as he who, being the King of the Jewish people, was destined to be lord of all other nations, and that of Satan as the ruler of the heathen world[13] to be conquered by the Messiah, were here combined. That dominion over the world which, in the christianized imagination of the period, the Messiah was to obtain by a long and painful struggle, was offered him as an easy bargain if he would only pay Satan the tribute of worship. This temptation Jesus meets with the maxim inculcated on the Israelites, Deut. vi. 13, that God alone is to be worshipped, and thus gives the enemy a final dismissal.

Matthew and Mark crown their history of the temptation with the appearance of angels to Jesus, and their refreshing him with nourishment after his long fast and the fatigues of temptation. This incident was prefigured by a similar ministration to Elijah after his forty days' fast, and was brought nearer to the imagination by the circumstance that the manna which appeased the hunger of the people in the wilderness was named, ἄρτος ἀγγέλων, angels' food (Ps. lxxviii. 25, LXX.; Wisdom xvi. 20).[14]

[12] Note 1.

[13] Bertholdt, Christolog. Judæorum Jesu ætate, § 36, not. 1 and 2; Fritzsche, Comm. in Matth., s. 169 f.

[14] Compare with the above statement the deductions of Schmidt, Fritzsche, and Usteri, as given § 54, notes 1-3, and of De Wette, exeg. Handbuch, 1, 1, s. 41 ff.

CHAPTER III.

LOCALITY AND CHRONOLOGY OF THE PUBLIC LIFE OF JESUS.

§ 57.

DIFFERENCE BETWEEN THE SYNOPTICAL WRITERS AND JOHN, AS TO THE CUSTOMARY SCENE OF THE MINISTRY OF JESUS.

ACCORDING to the synoptical writers, Jesus, born indeed at Bethlehem in Judea, but brought up at Nazareth in Galilee, only absented himself from Galilee during the short interval between his baptism and the imprisonment of the Baptist; immediately after which, he returned thither and began his ministry, teaching, healing, calling disciples, so as to traverse all Galilee; using as the centre of his agency, his previous dwelling-place, Nazareth, alternately with Capernaum, on the north-west border of the lake of Tiberias (Matt. iv. 12–25 parall.). Mark and Luke have many particulars concerning this ministry in Galilee which are not found in Matthew, and those which they have in common with him are arranged in a different order; but as they all agree in the geographical circuit which they assign to Jesus, the account of the first Evangelist may serve as the basis of our criticism. According to him the incidents narrated took place in Galilee, and partly in Capernaum down to viii. 18, where Jesus crosses the Galilean sea, but is scarcely landed on the east side when he returns to Capernaum. Here follows a series of scenes connected by short transitions, such as παράγων ἐκεῖθεν (ix. 9, 27), *passing from thence,* τότε (v. 14), *then,* ταῦτα αὐτοῦ λαλοῦντος (v. 18), *while he spake these things;* expressions which can imply no important change of place, that is, of one province for another, which it is the habit of the writer to mark much more carefully. The passage, ix. 35, περιῆγεν ὁ Ἰησοῦς τὰς πόλεις πάσας—διδάσκων ἐν ταῖς συναγωγαῖς αὐτῶν, is evidently only a repetition of iv. 23, and is therefore to be understood merely of excursions in Galilee. The message of the Baptist (chap. xi.) is also received by Jesus in Galilee, at least such appears to be the opinion of the narrator, from his placing in immediate connexion the complaints of Jesus against the Galilean cities. When delivering the parable in chap. xiii. Jesus is by the sea, doubtless that of Galilee, and, as there is mention of his *house,* οἰκία (v. 1), probably in the vicinity of Capernaum. Next, after having visited his native city Nazareth (xiii. 53) he passes over the sea (xiv. 13), according to Luke ix. 10), into the country of Bethsaida (Julias); whence, however, after the miracle of the loaves, he speedily returns to the western border (xiv. 34). Jesus then proceeds to the northern extremity of Palestine, on the frontiers of Phœnicia (xv. 21); soon, however, returned to the sea of Galilee (v. 29), he takes ship to the eastern side, in the coast of Magdala (v. 39), but again departs northward into the country of Cæsarea Philippi (xvi. 13), in the vicinity of Lebanon, among the lower ridges of which is to be sought the mount of the transfiguration (xvii. 1). After journeying in Galilee for some time longer with his disciples (xvii. 22), and once more visiting Capernaum (v. 24), he leaves Galilee (xix. 1) to travel (as it is most probably explained) [1] through Perea into Judea (a journey which, according to Luke ix. 52, he seems to have made through Samaria) ; xx. 17, he is on his way to Jerusalem ; v. 29, he comes through Jericho ; and xxi. 1, is in the neighbourhood of Jerusalem, which, v. 10, he enters.

Thus, according to the synoptical writers, Jesus, from his return after being baptized by John, to his final journey to Jerusalem, never goes beyond the limits of North Palestine, but traverses the countries west and east of the Galilean sea and the upper Jordan, in the dominions of Herod Antipas and Philip, without touching on Samaria to the south, still less Judea, or the country under the immediate adminstration of the Romans. And within those limits, to be still more precise, it is the land west of the Jordan, and the sea of Tiberias, and therefore Galilee, the province of Antipas, in which Jesus is especially active; only three short excursions on the eastern border of the sea, and two scarcely longer on the northern frontiers of the country, being recorded.

Quite otherwise is the theatre of the ministry of Jesus marked out in the fourth gospel. It is true that here also he goes after his baptism by John into Galilee, to the wedding at Cana (ii. 1), and from thence to Capernaum (v. 12); but in a few days the approaching passover calls him to Jerusalem (v. 13). From Jerusalem he proceeds into the country of Judea (iii. 22), and after some time exercising his ministry there (iv. 1) he returns through Samaria into Galilee (v. 43). Nothing is reported of his agency in this province but a single cure, and immediately on this a new feast summons him to Jerusalem (v. 1), where he is represented as performing a cure, being persecuted, and delivering long discourses, until he betakes himself (vi. 1) to the eastern shore of the sea of Tiberias, and from thence to Capernaum (v. 17, 59). He then itinerates for some time in Galilee (vii. 1), but again leaves it, on occasion of the feast of tabernacles, for Jerusalem (v. 2, 10). To this visit the Evangelist refers many discourses and vicissitudes of Jesus (vii. 10, x. 21), and moreover connects with it the commencement of his public ministry at the feast of dedication, without noticing any intermediate journey out of Jerusalem and Judea (x. 22). After this Jesus again retires into the country of Perea, where he had first been with the Baptist (x. 40), and there remains until the death of Lazarus recalls him to Bethany, near Jerusalem (xi. 1), whence he withdraws to Ephraim, in the vicinity of the wilderness of Judea, until the approach of the passover, which he visited as his last (xii. 1 ff.).

Thus, according to John, Jesus was present at four feasts in Jerusalem, before the final one : was besides once in Bethany, and had been active for a considerable time in Judea and on his journey through Samaria.

Why, it must be asked, have the synoptical writers been silent on this frequent presence of Jesus in Judea and Jerusalem? Why have they represented the matter, as if Jesus, before his last fatal journey to Jerusalem, had not overstepped the limits of Galilee and Perea ? This discrepancy between the synoptical writers and John was long overlooked in the church, and of late it has been thought feasible to deny its existence. It has been said, that Matthew, at the commencement, lays the scene in Galilee and Capernaum,

---

[1] Fritzsche, p. 591.

and pursues his narrative without noticing any journey into Judea until the last ; but that we are not hence to conclude that Matthew was unacquainted with the earlier ministry of Jesus in Judea, for as with this Evangelist the local interest is subordinate to the effort at an appropriate arrangement of his events, many particulars in the former part of his history, which he narrates without indicating any place, may have been known, though not stated by him, to have occurred in the earlier journeys and residences in Judea.[2] But this alleged subordination of the local interest in Matthew, is nothing more than a fiction of the harmonist, as Schneckenburger has recently proved.[3] Matthew very carefully marks (chap. iv.) the beginning and (chap. xix.) the end of the almost exclusive residence of Jesus in Galilee ; all the intervening narration must therefore be regarded as belonging to that residence, unless the contrary be expressed ; and since the Evangelist is on the alert to notice the short excursions of Jesus across the lake and into the north of Galilee, he would hardly pass over in silence the more important, and sometimes prolonged visits to Judea, had they been known or credited by him. Thus much only is to be allowed, that Matthew frequently neglects the more precise statement of localities, as the designation of the spot or neigbourhood in which Jesus laboured from time to time : but in his more general biographical statements, such as the designation of the territories and provinces of Palestine, within the boundaries of which Jesus exercised his ministry, he is as accurate as any other Evangelist.

Expositors must therefore accommodate themselves to the admission of a difference between the synoptical writers and John,[4] and those who think it incumbent on them to harmonize the Gospels must take care lest this difference be found a contradiction ; which can only be prevented by deducng the discrepancy, not from a disparity between the ideas of the Evangelists is to the sphere of the ministry of Jesus, but from the difference of mental aias under which they severally wrote. Some suppose that Matthew, being a Galilean, saw the most interest in Galilean occurrences, and hence confined his narrative to them, though aware of the agency of Jesus at Jerusalem.[5] But what biographer, who had himself accompanied his hero into various provinces, and beheld his labours there, would confine his narration to what he had performed in his (the biographer's) native province ? Such provincial exclusiveness would surely be quite unexampled. Hence others have preferred the supposition that Matthew, writing at Jerusalem, purposely selected from the mass of discourses and actions of Jesus with which he was acquainted, those of which Galilee was the theatre, because they were the least known at Jerusalem, and required narrating more than what had happened within the hearing, and was fresh in the memories of its inhabitants.[6] In opposition to this it has been already remarked,[7] that there is no proof of Matthew's gospel being especially intended for the Christians of Judea and Jerusalem : that even assuming this, a reference to the events which had happened in the reader's own country could not be superfluous : and that, lastly, the like limitation of the ministry of Jesus to Galilee by Mark and Luke cannot be thus accounted for, since these Evangelists obviously did not write for Judea (neither were they Galileans, so that this objection is equally

---

[2] Olshausen, bibl. Comm., 1, s. 189 f.
[3] Schneckenburger, Beiträge, s. 38 f. ; über den Ursprung u. s. f., s. 7 f.
[4] De Wette, Einleitung in das N. T., § 98 u. 106.
[5] Paulus, exeg. Handb., 1, a, s. 39.
[6] Guerike, Beiträge zur Einleitung in das N. T., s. 33 ; Tholuck, Glaubwürdigkeit, s. 303.
[7] Schneckenburger, über den Ursprung u. s. w., s. 9.

valid against the first explanation) ; and were not in so servile a relation to Matthew as to have no access to independent information that might give them a more extended horizon.   It is curious enough that these two attempts to solve the contradiction between the synoptical writers and John, are themselves in the same predicament of mutual contradiction.   For if Matthew has been silent on the incidents in Judea, according to one, on account of his proximity, according to the other, on account of his remoteness, it follows that, two contrary hypotheses being made with equal ease to explain the same fact, both are alike inadequate.

No supposition founded on the local relations of the writers sufficing to explain the difference in question, higher ground must be taken, in a consideration of the spirit and tendency of the evangelical writings.   From this point of view the following proposition has been given :   The cause which determined the difference in the contents of the fourth gospel and that of the synoptical ones, accounts also for their divergency as to the limits they assign to the ministry of Jesus ; in other words, the discourses delivered by Jesus in Jerusalem, and recorded by John, required for their comprehension a more mature development of Christianity than that presented in the first apostolic period ; hence they were not retained in the primitive evangelical tradition, of which the synoptical writers were the organs, and were first restored to the church by John, who wrote when Christianity was in a more advanced stage.[8]   But neither is this attempt at an explanation satisfactory, though it is less superficial than the preceding.   For how could the popular and the esoteric in the teaching of Jesus be separated with such nicety, that the former should be confined to Galilee, and the latter to Jerusalem (the harsh discourse in the synagogue at Capernaum alone excepted) ?   It may be said : in Jerusalem he had a more enlightened public around him, and could be more readily understood than in Galilee.   But the Galileans could scarcely have misunderstood Jesus more lamentably than did the Jews from first to last, according to John's representation, and as in Galilee he had the most undisturbed communion with his disciples, we should rather have conjectured that here would be the scene of his more profound instruction.   Besides, as the synoptical writers have given a plentiful gleaning of lucid and popular discourses from the final residence of Jesus in Jerusalem, there is no ground whatever for believing that his earlier visits were devoid of such, and that his converse on these occasions took throughout a higher tone.   But even allowing that all the earlier discourses of Jesus in Judea and Jerusalem were beyond the range of the first apostolic tradition, *deeds* were performed there, such as the cure of the man who had had an infirmity thirty-eight years, the conferring of sight on the man born blind, and the raising of Lazarus, which, from their imposing rank among the evidences of Christianity, must also have necessitated the mention of those early visits of Jesus to Judea during which they occurred.

Thus it is impossible to explain why the synoptical writers, if they knew of the earlier visits of Jesus to Jerusalem, should not have mentioned them, and it must be concluded that if John be right, the first three Evangelists knew nothing of an essential part of the earlier ministry of Jesus ; if, on the other hand, the latter be right, the author of the fourth gospel, or of the tradition by which he was guided, fabricated a large portion of what he has narrated concerning the ministry of Jesus, or at least assigned to it a false locality.

[8] Kern, über den Ursprung des Evang. Matthäi, in der Tübinger Zeitschrift, 1834, 2tes Heft, s. 198 ff.   Comp. Hug, Einleit. in d. N. T., 2, s. 205 ff. (3te Ausg.).

On a closer examination, however, the relation between John and the synoptical writers is not simply such, that the latter might not know what the former records, but such, that they must have proceeded from positively opposite data. For example, the synoptical writers, Matthew especially, as often as Jesus leaves Galilee, from the time that he takes up his abode there after the Baptist's imprisonment, seldom neglect to give a particular reason ; such as that he wished to escape from the crowd by a passage across the sea (Matt. viii. 18), or that he withdrew into the wilderness of Perea to avoid the snares of Herod (xiv. 13), or that he retired into the region of Tyre and Sidon on account of the offence taken by the scribes at his preaching (xv. 21) : John, on the contrary, generally alleges a special reason why Jesus leaves Judea, and retires into Galilee. Not to contend that his very first journey thither appears to be occasioned solely by the invitation to Cana, his departure again into Galilee after the first passover attended by him in his public character, is expressly accounted for by the ominous attention which the increasing number of his disciples had excited among the Pharisees (iv. 1 ff.). His retirement after the second feast, also, into the country east of the Sea of Tiberias (vi. 1), must be viewed in relation to the ἐζήτουν αὐτὸν οἱ Ἰουδαῖοι ἀποκτεῖναι (v. 18), since immediately after, the Evangelist assigns as a reason for the continuance of Jesus in Galilee, the malignant designs of his enemies, which rendered his abode in Judea perilous to his life (vii. 1). The interval between the Feast of Tabernacles and the Feast of the Dedication seems to have been spent by Jesus in the capital,[9] no unpropitious circumstances compelling him to absent himself (x. 22) ; on the other hand, his journey into Perea (x. 40) and that into Ephraim (xi. 54) are presented as effects of his persecution by the Jews.

Thus precisely the same relation as that which exists between Matthew and Luke, with respect to the original dwelling-place of the parents of Jesus is found between the first three Evangelists and the fourth, with respect to the principal theatre of his ministry. As, in the former instance, Matthew pre-supposes Bethlehem to be the original place of abode, and Nazareth the one subsequently adopted through fortuitous circumstances, while Luke gives the contrary representation ; so in the latter, the entire statement of the synoptical writers turns on the idea that, until his last journey, Galilee was the chosen field of the labours of Jesus, and that he only left it occasionally, from particular motives and for a short time ; while that of John, on the contrary, turns on the supposition, that Jesus would have taught solely in Judea and Jerusalem had not prudence sometimes counselled him to retire into the more remote provinces.[10]

Of these two representations one only can be true. Before they were perceived to be contradictory, the narrative of John was incorporated with that of the synoptical writers ; since they have been allowed to be irreconcilable, the verdict has always been in favour of the fourth Evangelist ; and so prevalent is this custom, that even the author of the Probabilia does not use the difference to the disadvantage of the latter. De Wette numbers it among the objections to the authenticity of Matthew's gospel, that it erroneously limits the ministry of Jesus to Galilee,[11] and Schneckenburger has no more important ground of doubt to produce against the apostolic origin of the first canonical gospel, than the unacquaintance of its author with the extra-Galilean labours of Jesus.[12] If this decision be well founded, it must rest on a careful con-

---

[9] Tholuck, Comm. zum Evang. Joh., p., 207.
[10] Comp. Lücke, ut sup., s. 546.
[11] De Wette, Einleitung in das N. T., § 98.
[12] Schneckenburger, über den Ursprung u. s. f., s. 7. ; Beiträge u. s. f., s. 38 ff.

sideration of the question, which of the two incompatible narratives has the greater corroboration from external sources, and the more internal verisimilitude? We have shown in the introduction that the external evidence or testimony for the authenticity of the fourth gospel and of the synoptical ones, that of Matthew emphatically, is of about equal value : that is, it determines nothing in either case, but leaves the decision to the internal evidence.   In relation to this, the following question must be considered : is it more probable that, although Jesus was actually often in Judea and Jerusalem previous to his last journey, yet at the time and place whence the synoptical gospels arose, all traces of the fact had disappeared : or that, on the contrary, although Jesus never entered Judea for the exercise of his public ministry before his last journey thither, yet at the time and place of the composition of the fourth gospel a tradition of several such visits had been formed?

The above critics seek to show that the first might be the case, in the following manner.   The first gospel, they say,[13] and more or less the two middle ones, contain the tradition concerning the life of Jesus as it was formed in Galilee, where the memory of what Jesus did and said in that province would be preserved with a natural partiality—while, of that part of his life which was spent out of Galilee, only the most critical incidents, such as his birth, consecration, and especially his last journey, which issued in his death, would be retained ; the remainder, including his early journeys to the various feasts, being either unknown or forgotten, so that any fragments of information concerning one or other of the previous residences of Jesus at Jerusalem would be referred to the last, no other being known.

But John himself, in whom our theologians rest all their confidence, expressly mentions (iv. 45) that at the first passover visited by Jesus after his baptism (and probably at others also) the Galileans were present, and apparently in great numbers, since as a consequence of their having witnessed his works in Jerusalem, Jesus found a favourable reception in Galilee.   If we add to this, that most of the disciples who accompanied Jesus in his early journeys to the feasts were Galileans (John iv. 22, ix. 2), it is inconceivable that tidings of the ministry of Jesus at Jerusalem should not from the first reach Galilee.   Once there, could time extinguish them?   We grant that it is in the nature of tradition to fuse and remodel its materials, and as the last journey of Jesus to Jerusalem was pre-eminently memorable, it might absorb the recollections of the previous ones.   But tradition has also another impulse, and it is its strongest; namely to glorify.   It may indeed be said that to circumscribe the early ministry of Jesus by the frontiers of Galilee would serve the purpose of glorifying that province, in which the synoptical tradition had its origin.   But the aim of the synoptical legend was not to glorify Galilee, on which it pronounces severe judgments ;—Jesus is the object round which it would cast a halo, and his greatness is proportionate to the sphere of his influence.   Hence, to show that from the beginning of his ministry he made himself known beyond the Galilean *angulus terræ*, and that he often presented himself on the brilliant theatre of the capital, especially on occasions when it was crowded with spectators and hearers from all regions, was entirely according to the bent of the legend.   If, therefore, there had historically been but one journey of Jesus to Jerusalem, tradition might be tempted to create more by degrees, since it would argue—how could so great a light as Jesus have remained so long under a bushel, and not rather have early and often placed himself on the lofty stand which Jerusalem presented?   Opponents,

---

[13] Schneckenburger, Beiträge, s. 207.   Comp. Gabler's Treatise on the Resurrection of Lazarus, in his Journal für auserlesene theol. Literatur, 3, 2.

too, might object, like the unbelieving brethren of Jesus (John vii. 3, 4), that he who is conscious of the power to perform something truly great, does not conceal himself, but seeks publicity, in order that his capabilities may be recognized ; and to these opponents it was thought the best answer to show that Jesus actually did seek such publicity, and early obtained recognition in an extended sphere. Out of this representation would easily grow the idea which lies at the foundation of the fourth gospel, that not Galilee, but Judea, was the proper residence of Jesus.

Thus, viewed from the point of the possible formation of a legend, the balance inclines in favour of the synoptical writers. But is the result the same when we ascend to the relations and designs of Jesus, and from this point of view inquire, if it be more probable that Jesus visited Jerusalem once only or several times during his public life ?

The alleged difficulty, that the various journeys to the feasts offer the principal means of accounting for the intellectual development of Jesus is easily removed. For those journeys alone would not suffice to explain the mental pre-eminence of Jesus and as the main stress must still be placed on his internal gifts, we cannot pronounce whether to a mind like his, even Galilee might not present enough aliment for their maturing ; besides, an adherence to the synoptical writers would only oblige us to renounce those journeys to the feasts which Jesus took after his public appearance, so that he might still have been present at many feasts previous to his messianic career, without assuming a conspicuous character. It has been held inconceivable that Jesus, so long after his assumption of the messianic character, should confine himself to Galilee, instead of taking his stand in Judea and Jerusalem, which, from the higher culture and more extensive foreign intercourse of their population, were a much more suitable field for his labours ; but it has been long remarked, on the other hand, that Jesus could find easier access to the simple and energetic minds of Galilee, less fettered by priestcraft and Pharisaism, and therefore acted judiciously in obtaining a firm footing there by a protracted ministry, before he ventured to Jerusalem, where, in the centre of priestly and Pharisaic domination, he must expect stronger opposition.

There is a graver difficulty in the synoptical statement, considered in relation to the Mosaic law and Jewish custom. The law rigorously required that every Israelite should appear before Jehovah yearly at the three principal feasts (Exod. xxiii. 14 ff.), and the reverence of Jesus for the Mosaic institutes (Matt. v. 17 ff.) renders it improbable that, during the whole course of his ministry, he should have undertaken but one journey of observance.[14] The Gospel of Matthew, however, be our judgment what it may as to the date and place of its composition, did certainly arise in a community of Jewish Christians, who well knew what the law prescribed to the devout Israelite, and must therefore be aware of the contradiction to the law in which the practice of Jesus was involved, when, during a public ministry of several years' duration, only one attendance at Jerusalem was noticed, or (in case the synoptical writers supposed but a single year's ministry, of which we shall speak below) when he was represented as neglecting two of the great annual feasts. If then, a circle in close proximity to Jewish usage found nothing offensive in the opinion that Jesus attended but one feast, may not this authority remove all hesitation on the subject from our minds ? Besides, on a more careful weighing of the historical and geographical relations, the question suggests itself, whether between the distant, half Gentile Galilee, and Jerusalem, the ecclesiastical bond was so close that the observance of all the feasts could be

---

[14] Hug, Einleit. in das N. T., 2, s. 210.

expected from a Galilean? Even according to the fourth gospel, Jesus omitted attending one passover that occurred in the period of his public career (John vi. 4). There is, however, one point unfavourable to the synoptical writers. That Jesus in his last visit to Jerusalem should, within the short space of the feast day, have brought himself into such decided hostility to the ruling party in the capital, that they contrived his arrest and death, is inexplicable, if we reject the statement of John, that this hostility originated and was gradually aggravated during his frequent previous visits.[15] If it be rejoined, that even in Galilean synagogues there were stationary scribes and Pharisees (Matt. ix. 3, xii. 14), that such as were resident in the capital often visited the provinces (Matt. xv. 1), and that thus there existed a hierarchical nexus by means of which a deadly enmity against Jesus might be propagated in Jerusalem before he had ever publicly appeared there; we then have precisely that ecclesiastical bond between Galilee and Jerusalem which renders improbable on the part of Jesus the non-observance of a series of feasts. Moreover the synoptical writers have recorded an expression of Jesus which tells strongly against their own view. The words : *Jerusalem, Jerusalem—how often would I have gathered thy children together—and ye would not,* have no meaning whatever in Luke, who puts them into the mouth of Jesus before he had even seen Jerusalem during his public ministry (xiii. 34) ; and even from the better arrangement of Matthew (xxiii. 37) it is not to be understood how Jesus, after a single residence of a few days in Jerusalem, could found his reproaches on multiplied efforts to win over its inhabitants to his cause. This whole apostrophe of Jesus has so original a character, that it is difficult to believe it incorrectly assigned to him ; hence to explain its existence, we must suppose a series of earlier residences in Jerusalem, such as those recorded by the fourth Evangelist. There is only one resource,—to pronounce the statement of the synoptical writers unhistorical in the particular of limiting the decisive visit of Jesus to Jerusalem to the few days of the feast, and to suppose that he made a more protracted stay in the capital.[16]

It will be seen from the foregoing discussion, whether, when so much is to be argued *pro* and *contra*, the unhesitating decision of the critics in favour of the fourth Evangelist's statement is a just one. For our own part, we are far from being equally hasty in declaring for the synoptical writers, and are content to have submitted the actual state of the controversy, as to the comparative merits of John and the synoptical writers, to further consideration.*

§ 58.

THE RESIDENCE OF JESUS AT CAPERNAUM.

During the time spent by Jesus in Judea, the capital and its environs recommended themselves as the most eligible theatre for his agency ; and we might have conjectured that in like manner, when in Galilee, he would have chosen his native city, Nazareth, as the centre of his labours. Instead of this we find him, when not travelling, domesticated at Capernaum, as already mentioned ; the synoptical writers designate this place the ἰδία πόλις of Jesus (Matt. ix. 1, comp. Mark ii. 1) ; here, according to them, was the οἶκος, which Jesus was accustomed to inhabit (Mark ii. 1, iii. 20 ; Matt. xiii. 1,

---

[15] Hug, ut supra, s. 211. f.
[16] Compare Weisse, die evang. Geschichte 1, s. 29 ff.

36) probably that of Peter (Mark i. 29 ; Matt. viii. 14, xvii. 25 ; Luke iv. 38). In the fourth gospel, which only mentions very transient visits of Jesus to Galilee, Capernaum is not given as his dwelling-place, and Cana is the place with which he is supposed to have the most connexion. After his baptism he proceeds first to Cana (ii. 1), on a special occasion, it is true ; after this he makes a short stay at Capernaum (v. 12) ; and on his return from his first attendance at the passover, it is again Cana to which he resorts and in which the fourth Evangelist makes him effect a cure (iv. 46 ff.), according to the synoptical writers, performed at Capernaum, and after this we find him once again in the synagogue at Capernaum (vi. 59). The most eminent disciples, also, are said by the writer of the fourth gospel, not as by the synoptical writers, to come from Capernaum, but partly from Cana (xxi. 2) and partly from Bethsaida (i. 45). The latter place, even in the synoptical gospels, is mentioned, with Chorazin, as one in which Jesus had been preeminently active (Matt. xi. 21 ; Luke x. 13).

Why Jesus chose Capernaum as his central residence in Galilee, Mark does not attempt to show, but conducts him thither without comment after his return into Galilee, and the calling of the two pairs of fishermen (i. 21). Matthew (iv. 13 ff.) alleges as a motive, that an Old Testament prophecy (Isa. viii. 23, ix. 1), was thereby fulfilled ; a dogmatical motive, and therefore of no historical value. Luke thinks he has found the reason in a fact, which is more worthy of notice. According to him, Jesus after his return from baptism does not immediately take up his residence in Capernaum, but makes an essay to teach in Nazareth, and after its failure first turns to Capernaum. This Evangelist tells us in the most graphic style how Jesus presented himself at the synagogue on the sabbath-day, and expounded a prophetic passage, so as to excite general admiration, but at the same time to provoke malicious reflections on the narrow circumstances of his family. Jesus, in reply, is made to refer the discontent of the Nazarenes, that he performed no miracles before them as at Capernaum, to the contempt which every prophet meets with in his own country, and to threaten them in Old Testament allusions, that the divine benefits would be withdrawn from them and conferred on strangers. Exasperated by this, they lead him to the brow of the hill, intending to cast him down ; he, however, passes unhurt through the midst of them (iv. 16–30).

Both the other synoptical writers are acquainted with a visit of Jesus to Nazareth ; but they transfer it to a much later period, when Jesus had been long labouring in Galilee, and resident in Capernaum (Matt. xiii. 54 ff. ; Mark vi. 1 ff.). To reconcile their narrative with that of Luke, it has been customary to suppose that Jesus, notwithstanding his first rough reception, as described by Luke, wished to make one more experiment whether his long absence and subsequent fame might not have altered the opinion of the Nazarenes—an opinion worthy of a petty town : but the result was equally unfavourable.[1] The two scenes, however, are too similar to be prevented from mingling with each other. In both instances the teaching of Jesus in the synagogue makes the same impression on the Nazarenes,—that of amazement at the wisdom of the carpenter's son (Luke only giving more details) : in both instances there is a lack of miracles on the part of Jesus, the first two Evangelists presenting more prominently its cause, namely, the unbelief of the Nazarenes, and the third dwelling more on its unfavourable effect : lastly in both instances, Jesus delivers the maxim (the result of his experience), that a prophet is the least esteemed in his own country : and to this Luke appends

---

[1] Paulus, exeg. Handb. 1, 6, s. 463.

a more ample discourse, which irritates the Nazarenes to attempt an act of vlioence, unnoticed by the other Evangelists. But the fact which most decisively shows that the two narratives cannot exist in each other's presence, is that they both claim to relate the first incident of the kind ;[2] for in both, the Nazarenes express their astonishment at the suddenly revealed intellectual gifts of Jesus, which they could not at once reconcile with his known condition.[3] The first supposition that presents itself is, that the scene described by Luke preceded that of Matthew and Mark ; but if so, the Nazarenes could not wonder a second time and inquire, *whence hath this man this wisdom ?* since they must have had proof on that point on the first occasion ; if, on the contrary, we try to give the later date to Luke's incident, it appears unnatural, for the same reason that they should wonder at *the gracious words which proceeded out of his mouth*, neither could Jesus well say, *This day is this scripture fulfilled in your ears*, without severely reflecting on their former insensibility, which had retarded that fulfilment.

These considerations have led the majority of modern commentators to the opinion, that Luke and the other synoptical Evangelists have here given the same history, merely differing in the date, and in the colouring of the facts ;[4] and the only question among them is, which of the two narrations deserves the preference. With respect to the date, that of Luke seems, at the first glance, to have the advantage ; it gives the desiderated motive for the change of residence, and the wonder of the Nazarenes appears most natural on the supposition that then he first assumed the function of a public teacher ; hence Matthew's divergency from Luke has been recently made a serious reproach to hi,m as a chronological error.[5] But there is one particular in all the three narratives which is an obstacle to our referring the incident to so early a period. If Jesus presented himself thus at Nazareth before he had made Capernaum the principal theatre of his agency, the Nazarenes could not utter the words which Jesus imputes to them in Luke : *Whatsoever we have heard done in Capernaum, do also here in thy country* ; nor could they, according to Matthew and Mark, be astonished at the *mighty works* of Jesus,[6] for as he performed few if any miracles at Nazareth, that expression, notwithstanding its perplexing connexion with the σοφία, *the wisdom*, manifested in that city, must refer to works performed elsewhere. If, then, the Nazarenes wondered at the deeds of Jesus at Capernaum, or were jealous of the distinction conferred on that city, Jesus must have previously resided there, and could not have proceeded thither for the first time in consequence of the scene at Nazareth. From this, it is plain that the later chronological position of the narrative is the original one, and that Luke, in placing it earlier, out of mere conjecture, was honest or careless enough to retain the mention of the wonders at Capernaum, though only consistent with the later position.[7] If, with regard to the date of the incident, the advantage is thus on the side of Matthew and Mark, we are left in darkness as to the motive which led Jesus to alter his abode from Nazareth to Capernaum ; unless the circumstance that some of his most confidential disciples had their home there, and the more extensive traffic of the place, may be regarded as inducements to the measure.

The fulness and particularity of Luke's description of the scene, contrasted

---

[2] This Schleiermacher has made evident, über den Lukas, s. 63.
[3] Sieffert, über den Ursprung des ersten kanonischen Evangeliums, s. 89.
[4] Olshausen, Fritzsche, in loc. Hase, Leben Jesu, § 62. Sieffert, ut supra.
[5] Sieffert, ut supra.
[6] What these *mighty works* were can only be made clear when we come to the chapter on the Miracles.
[7] Schleiermacher, ut supra, s. 64.

with the summary style in which it is given by the other two Evangelists, has generally won for the former the praise of superior accuracy.[8] Let us look more closely, and we shall find that the greater particularity of Luke shows itself chiefly in this, that he is not satisfied with a merely general mention of the discourse delivered by Jesus in the synagogue, but cites the Old Testament passage on which he enlarged, and the commencement of its application. The passage is from Isa. lxi. 1, 2, where the prophet announces the return from exile, with the exception of the words *to set at liberty them that are bruised*, ἀποστεῖλαι τεθραυσμένους ἐν ἀφέσει, which are from Isa. lviii. 6. To this passage Jesus gives a messianic interpretation, for he declares it to be fulfilled by his appearance. Why he selected this text from among all others has been variously conjectured. It is known that among the Jews at a later period, certain extracts from the Thorah and the Prophets were statedly read on particular sabbaths and feast days, and it has hence been suggested that the above passage was the selection appointed for the occasion in question. It is true that the chapter from which the words ἀποστεῖλαι κ. τ. λ. are taken, used to be read on the great Day of Atonement, and Bengel has made the supposition, that the scene we are considering occurred on that day, a main pillar of his evangelical chronology.[9] But if Jesus had adhered to the regular course of reading, he would not merely have extracted from the lesson appointed for this feast a few stray words, to insert them in a totally disconnected passage ; and after all, it is impossible to demonstrate that, so early as the time of Jesus, there were prescribed readings, even from the prophets.[10] If then Jesus was not thus circumstantially directed to the passage cited, did he open upon it designedly or fortuitously? Many imagine him turning over the leaves until he found the text which was in his mind :[11] but Olshausen is right in saying that the words ἀναπτύξας τὸ βιβλίον εὗρε τὸν τόπον do not imply that he found the passage after searching for it, but that he alighted on it under the guidance of the Divine Spirit.[12] This, however, is but a poor contrivance, to hide the improbability, that Jesus should fortuitously open on a passage so well adapted to serve as a motto for his first messianic enterprize, behind an appeal to the Spirit, as *deus ex machinâ*. Jesus might very likely have quoted this text with reference to himself, and thus it would remain in the minds of the Evangelists as a prophecy fulfilled in Jesus ; Matthew would probably have introduced it in his own person with his usual form, ἵνα πληρωθῇ, aud would have said that Jesus had now begun his messianic annunciation, κήρυγμα, that the prophecy Isa. lxi. 1 ff. might be fulfilled ; but Luke, who is less partial to this form, or the tradition whence he drew his materials, puts the words into the mouth of Jesus on his first messianic appearance, very judiciously, it is true, but, owing to the chances which it is necessary to suppose, less probably ; so that I am more inclined to be satisfied with the indefinite statement of Matthew and Mark. The other point in which the description of Luke merits the praise of particularity, is his dramatic picture of the tumultuary closing scene ; but this scene perplexes even those who on the whole give the preference to his narrative. It is not to be concealed that the extremely violent expulsion of Jesus by the Nazarenes, seems to have had no adequate provocation :[13] and we cannot with Schleiermacher,[14] expunge

---

[8] Schleiermacher, ut supra, s. 63 f.
[9] Ordo temporum, p. 220 ff. ed. 2.
[10] Paulus, ut supra, 1, b, s. 407.
[11] Paulus, ut supra. Lightfoot, horæ, p. 765.
[12] Bibl. Comm. 1, 470.
[13] Hase, Leben Jesu, § 62.
[14] Ueber den Lukas, s. 93.

the notion that the life of Jesus was threatened, without imputing to the writer a false addition of the words εἰς τὸ κατακρημνίσαι αὐτὸν (v. 29), and thus materially affecting the credibility of his entire narration.   But the still more remarkable clause, διελθὼν διὰ μέσου αὐτῶν ἐπορεύετο (v. 30), is the main difficulty.   It is not to be explained (at least not in accordance with the Evangelist's view) as an effect merely of the commanding glance of Jesus, as Hase supposes ; and Olshausen is again right when he says, that the Evangelist intended to signify that Jesus passed unharmed through the midst of his furious enemies, because his divine power fettered their senses and limbs, because his hour was not yet come (John viii. 20), and because no man could take his life from him until he himself laid it down (John x. 18).[15]   Here again we have a display of the glorifying tendency of tradition, which loved to represent Jesus as one defended from his enemies, like Lot (Gen. xix. 11), or Elisha (2 Kings vi. 18), by a heavenly hand, or better still, by the power of his own superior nature ; unless there be supposed in this case, as in the two examples from the Old Testament, a temporary infliction of blindness, an *illudere per caliginem*, the idea of which Tertullian reprobates.[16]   Thus in this instance also, the less imposing account of the first two Evangelists is to be preferred, namely that Jesus, impeded from further activity by the unbelief of the Nazarenes, voluntarily forsook his ungrateful paternal city.

§ 59.

DIVERGENCIES OF THE EVANGELISTS AS TO THE CHRONOLOGY OF THE LIFE OF JESUS. DURATION OF HIS PUBLIC MINISTRY.

In considering the chronology of the public life of Jesus, we must distinguish the question of its total duration, from that of the arrangement of its particular events.

Not one of our Evangelists expressly tells us how long the public ministry of Jesus lasted; but while the synoptical writers give us no clue to a decision on the subject, we find in John certain data, which seem to warrant one.   In the synoptical gospels there is no intimation how long after the baptism of Jesus his imprisonment and death occurred : nowhere are months and years distinguished ; and though it is once or twice said : μεθ' ἡμέρας ἕξ or δύο (Matt. xvii. 1, xxvi. 2), these isolated fixed points furnish us with no guidance in a sea of general uncertainty.   On the contrary, the many journeys to the feasts by which the narrative of the fourth Evangelist is distinguished from that of his predecessors, furnishes us, so to speak, with chronological abutments, as for each appearance of Jesus at one of these annual feasts, the Passover especially, we must, deducting the first, reckon a full year of his ministry.   We have, in the fourth gospel, after the baptism of Jesus, and apparently at a short interval (comp. i. 29, 35, 44, ii. 1, 12), a passover attended by him (ii. 13).   But the next feast visited by Jesus (v. 1) which is indefinitely designated *a feast of the Jews*, has been the perpetual *crux* of New Testament chronologists.   It is only important in determining the duration of the public life of Jesus, on the supposition that it was a passover ; for in this case it would mark the close of his first year's ministry.   We grant that ἡ ἑορτὴ τῶν Ἰουδαίων, THE *feast of the Jews*, might very probably denote the Passover, which was pre-eminent among their institutions :[1] but it happens that the best

---

[15] Ut supra, 479 ; comp. 2, p. 214.
[16] Adv. Marcion, iv. 8.
[1] Paulus, exeg. Handb. 1, b, s. 788 f.

manuscripts have in the present passage no article, and without it, the above expression can only signify indefinitely one of the Jewish feasts, which the author thought it immaterial to specify.[2]   Thus intrinsically it might mean either the feast of Pentecost,[3] Purim,[4] the Passover,[5] or any other;[6] but in its actual connection it is evidently not intended by the narrator to imply the Passover, both because he would hardly have glanced thus slightly at the most important of all the feasts, and because, vi. 4, there comes another Passover, so that on the supposition we are contesting, he would have passed in silence over a whole year between v. 47, and vi. 1.   For to give the words, ἦν δὲ ἐγγὺς τὸ πάσχα (vi. 4), a retrospective meaning, is too artificial an expedient of Paulus, since, as he himself confesses,[7] this phrase, elsewhere in John, is invariably used with reference to the immediately approaching feast (ii. 13, vii. 2, xi. 55), and must from its nature have a prospective meaning, unless the context indicate the contrary.   Thus not until John vi. 4, do we meet with the second passover, and to this it is not mentioned that Jesus resorted.[8] Then follow the feast of Tabernacles and that of the Dedication, and afterwards, xi. 55, xii. 1, the last passover visited by Jesus.   According to our view of John v. 1, and vi. 4, therefore, we obtain two years for the public ministry of Jesus, besides the interval between his baptism and the first Passover, The same result is found by those who, with Paulus, hold the feast mentioned, v. 1, to be a passover, but vi. 4, only a retrospective allusion ; whereas the ancient Fathers of the Church, reckoning a separate Passover to each of the passages in question, made out three years.   Meanwhile, by this calculation, we only get the minimum duration of the public ministry of Jesus possible according to the fourth gospel, for the writer nowhere intimates that he has been punctilious in naming every feast that fell within that ministry, including those not observed by Jesus, neither, unless we regard it as established that the writer was the apostle John, have we any guarantee that he knew the entire number.

It may be urged in opposition to the calculations, built on the representations of John, that the synoptical writers give no reasons for limiting the term of the public ministry of Jesus to a single year :[9] but this objection rests on a supposition borrowed from John himself, namely that Jesus, Galilean though he was, made it a rule to attend every Passover : a supposition, again, which is overturned by the same writer's own representation.   According to him, Jesus left unobserved the passover mentioned, vi. 4, for from vi. 1, where Jesus is on the east side of the sea of Tiberias, through vi. 17 and 59, where he goes to Capernaum, and vii. 1, where he frequents Galilee, in order to avoid the Jews, to vii. 2 and 10, where he proceeds to Jerusalem on occasion of the feast of Tabernacles, the Evangelist's narrative is so closely consecutive that a journey to the Passover can nowhere be inserted.   Out of the synoptical gospels, by themselves, we gather nothing as to the length of the public ministry of Jesus, for this representation admits of our assigning him either several years of activity, or only one ; their restriction of his intercourse with Jerusalem to his final journey being the sole point in which they control our

---

[2] Lücke, Comm. zum Evang. Joh., 2, s. 6.
[3] Bengel, ordo temporum, p. 219 f.
[4] Hug, Einleit. in das N. T. 2, s. 229 ff.
[5] Paulus, Comm. zum Ev. Joh., s. 279 f.   Exeg. Handb. 1, b, s. 784 ff.
[6] Summaries of the different opinions are given by Hase, L. J., § 53 ; and by Lücke, Comm. z. Ev. Joh., 2, s. 2 ff.
[7] Exeg. Handb. 1, b, s. 785.
[8] See Storr, über den Zweck der evang. Gesch. und der Briefe Johannis, s. 330.
[9] Winer, b. Realw. 1, s. 666.

conclusion. It is true that several Fathers of the Church,[10] as well as some heretics,[11] speak of the ministry of Jesus as having lasted but a single year ; but that the source of this opinion was not the absence of early journeys to the feasts in the synoptical gospels, but an entirely fortuitous association, we learn from those Fathers themselves, for they derive it from the prophetic passage Isa. lxi. 1 f. applied by Jesus (Luke iv.) to himself. In this passage there is mention of *the acceptable year of the Lord*, ἐνιαυτὸς Κυρίου δεκτὸς, which the prophet or, according to the Evangelical interpretation, the Messiah is sent to announce. Understanding this phrase in its strict chronological sense, they adopted from it the notion of a single messianic year, which was more easily reconcilable with the synoptical gospels than with that of John, after whose statement the calculation of the church soon came to be regulated.

In striking contrast with this lowest computation of time, is the tradition, also very ancient, that Jesus was baptized in his thirtieth year, but at the time of his crucifixion was not far from his fiftieth.[12] But this opinion is equally founded on a misunderstanding. *The elders who had conversations with John the disciple of the Lord, in Asia,* πρεσβύτεροι οἱ κατὰ τὴν Ἀσίαν Ἰωάννῃ τῷ τοῦ Κυρίου μαθητῇ συμβεβληκότες,—on whose testimony Irenæus relies when he says, *such is the tradition of John,* παραδεδωκέναι ταῦτα τὸν Ἰωάννην,—had given no information further than that Christ taught, *ætatem seniorem habens.* That this *ætas senior* was the age of from forty to fifty years is merely the inference of Irenæus, founded on what the Jews allege as an objection to the discourse of Jesus, John viii. 57 : *Thou art not yet fifty years old, and hast thou seen Abraham ?* language which according to Irenæus could only be addressed to one, *qui jam quadraginta annos excessit, quinquagesimum autem annum nondum attigit.* But the Jews might very well say to a man a little more than thirty, that he was much too young to have seen Abraham, since he had not reached his fiftieth year, which, in the Jewish idea, completed the term of manhood.[13]

Thus we can obtain no precise information from our gospels as to how long the public labours of Jesus lasted ; all we can gather is, that if we follow the fourth gospel we must not reckon less than two years and something over. But the repeated journeys to the feasts on which this calculation is founded are themselves not established beyond doubt.

Opposed to this minimum, we gain a maximum, if we understand, from Luke iii. 1 ff. and 23, that the baptism of Jesus took place in the fifteenth year of Tiberius, and add to this that his crucifixion occurred under the pro-curatorship of Pontius Pilate. For as Pilate was recalled from his post in the year of Tiberius's death,[14] and as Tiberius reigned rather more than seven years after the fifteenth year of his reign,[15] it follows that seven years are the maximum of the possible duration of the ministry of Jesus after his baptism. But while one of these data, namely, that Jesus was crucified under Pilate, is well attested, the other is rendered suspicious by its association with a chronological error, so that in fact we cannot achieve here even a proximate, still less an accurate solution of our question.

---

[10] Clem. Alex. Stromat. 1, p. 174, Würzb. ed., 340 Sylburg ; Orig. de principp. iv. 5, comp. homil. in Luc. 32.
[11] Iren. adv. hær. i. 1, 5. ii. 35, 38, on the Valentinians. Clem. hom. xvii. 19.
[12] Iren ii. xxii. 5 f. Comp. Credner, Einl. in das N. T. 1, s. 215.
[13] Lightfoot and Tholuck in loc.
[14] Joseph. Antiq. xviii. iv. 2.
[15] Sueton. Tiber. c. lxxiii. Joseph. Antiq. xviii. vi. 10.

§ 60.

THE ATTEMPTS AT A CHRONOLOGICAL ARRANGEMENT OF THE PARTICULAR EVENTS IN THE PUBLIC LIFE OF JESUS.

In attempting a chronological arrangement of the particular events occurring in the interval between the baptism of Jesus and his crucifixion, the peculiar relation of the synoptical writers to John, renders it necessary to give them both a separate and a comparative examination. As to the latter, if its result be a reconciliation of the two accounts, the journeys to the feasts in John must form the panels between which the materials of the synoptical writers must be so inserted, that between each pair of journeys with the incidents at Jerusalem to which they gave rise, would fall a portion of the Galilean history.   For this incorporation to be effected with any certainty, two things would be essential ; first, a notice of the departure of Jesus from Galilee by the first three Evangelists, as often as the fourth speaks of a residence in Jerusalem ; and, secondly, on the part of John, an intimation, if not a narration, between his accounts of the several feasts, of the Galilean occurrences represented by the synoptical writers as an uninterrupted train.   But we have seen that the synoptical writers fail in the required notice ; while it is notorious that John, from the baptism of Jesus to the closing scenes of his life, is only in two or three instances in coincidence with the other Evangelists.   John says (iii. 24) that when Jesus began his ministry, *John was not yet cast into prison* ; Matthew makes the return of Jesus into Galilee subsequent to the imprisonment of the Baptist (iv. 12), hence it has been inferred that that return was from the first passover, and not from the baptism ; [1] but it is undeniable that Matthew places the commencement of the public ministry of Jesus in Galilee, and presupposes no earlier ministry at the feast in Jerusalem, so that the two statements, instead of dovetailing, as has been imagined, are altogether incompatible.   The next, but very dubious point of contact, occurs in the healing of the nobleman's son, according to John iv. 46 ff., or the centurion's servant, according to Matt. viii. 5 ff., and Luke vii. 1 ff., which John places (v. 47) immediately after the return of Jesus from his prolonged residence in Judea and Samaria, during and after the first passover.   It was to be expected, then, that the corresponding narration of the synoptical writers would be preceded by some intimation of the first journey made by Jesus to a feast.   Not only is such an intimation wanting—there is not a single aperture to be found for the insertion of this journey, since, according to the synoptical writers, the cure in question was an immediate sequel to the Sermon on the Mount, which Matthew and Luke represent as the culminating point, of an apparently uninterrupted course of teaching and miracles in Galilee.   Thus neither at this point is the chronology of the first three Evangelists to be eked out by that of the fourth, since they nowhere present a joint on to which the statements of the latter can be articulated.   Another more decided coincidence between the two parties exists in the associated narratives of the miracle of the loaves, and that of walking on the sea, John vi. 1–21, Matt. xiv. 14–36 parall., which John places in the interval immediately preceding the second passover, unvisited by Jesus; but he differs so completely from the synoptical writers in his account of these miracles, both in their introduction and termination, that either he or they must inevitably be wrong.   For while, according to Matthew, Jesus retires from Nazareth

---

[1] Comp. Paulus, Leben Jesu, 1, a, 214 f.

probably, at all events from some part of Galilee, to the opposite side of the sea, where he effects the multiplication of the loaves ; according to John he sets out from Jerusalem. Further, in the first two gospels Jesus proceeds after the miracle of the loaves into a district where he was less known (both Matt. v. 35 and Mark v. 54 expressly stating that the people knew him), whereas in John he goes directly to Capernaum, with which of all places he was the most familiar. We know not here whether to tax the synoptical writers or John with a mistake : and as we cannot pronounce whether he or they have placed this incident too early or too late, we are equally ignorant how much of the synoptical narratives we are to place before, and how much after, the second passover, which John makes nearly cotemporary with the feeding of the five thousand. Here, however, the points of contact between this Evangelist and his predecessors are at an end, until we come to the last journey of Jesus ; and if they are too uncertain to promise even a simple division of the synoptical materials by the two Passovers, how can we hope, by the journeys of Jesus to the *feast of the Jews,* ἑορτὴ τῶν Ἰουδαίων, to the feast of Tabernacles, or to the feast of Dedication, if that be a separate journey, to classify chronologically the uninterrupted series of Galilean occurrences in the first three gospels ? Nevertheless this has been attempted by a succession of theologians down to the present time, with an expenditure of acumen and erudition, worthy of a more fertile subject ; [2] but unprejudiced judges have decided, that as the narrative of the first three Evangelists has scarcely any elements that can give certitude to such a classification, not one of the harmonies of the gospels yet written has any claim to be considered anything more than a tissue of historical conjectures.[3]

It remains to estimate the chronological value of the synoptical writers, apart from John. They are so frequently at variance with each other in the order of events, and it is so seldom that one has all the probabilities on his side, that each of them may be convicted of numerous chronological errors, which must undermine our confidence in their accuracy. It has been maintained that, in the composition of their books, they meditated no precise chronological order,[4] and this is partially confirmed by their mode of narration. Throughout the interval between the baptism of Jesus and the history of the Passion, their narratives resemble a collection of anecdotes, strung together mostly on a thread of mere analogy and association of ideas. But there is a distinction to be made in reference to the above opinion. It is true that from the purport of their narratives, and the indecisiveness and uniformity of their connecting phrases, *we* can detect their want of insight into the more accurate chronological relations of what they record ; but that *the authors* flattered themselves they were giving a chronological narration, is evident from those very connecting phrases, which, however indecisive, have almost always a chronological character, such as καταβάντι ἀπὸ τοῦ ὄρους, παράγων ἐκεῖθεν, ταῦτα αὐτοῦ λαλοῦντος, ἐν αὐτῇ τῇ ἡμέρᾳ, τότε, καὶ ἰδοὺ, etc.[5]

The incidents and discourses detailed by John are, for the most part, peculiar to himself ; he is therefore not liable to the same control in his chronology from independent authors, as are the synoptical writers from each other ; neither is his narration wanting in connectedness and sequence. Hence our

---

[2] See especially the labours of Paulus in the Chronological *Excursus* of his Commentary and his exegetical Manual ; of Hug, in the Einl. z. N. T. 2, s. 2, 233 ff ; and others, given by Winer in his bibl. Realwörterbuch 1, s. 667.
[3] Winer, ut sup. ; comp. Kaiser, biblische Theologie, 1, s. 254. Anm ; die Abhandlung über die verschiedenen Rücksichten u. s. w., in Bertholdt's krit. Journal, 5, s. 239.
[4] Olshausen 1, s. 24 ff.
[5] Schneckenburger's Beiträge, s. 25 ff.

decision on the merits of his chronological order is dependent on the answer to the following question : Is the development and progress of the cause and plan of Jesus, as given by the fourth Evangelist, credible in itself and on comparison with available data, drawn from the other gospels ? The solution to this question is involved in the succeeding inquiry.

CHAPTER IV.

JESUS AS THE MESSIAH. *

---

§ 61.

JESUS, THE SON OF MAN.

In treating of the relation in which Jesus conceived himself to stand to the messianic idea, we can distinguish his dicta concerning his own person from those concerning the work he had undertaken.

The appellation which Jesus commonly gives himself in the Gospels is, *the Son of man*, ὁ υἱὸς τοῦ ἀνθρώπου. The exactly corresponding Hebrew expression בֶּן־אָדָם is in the Old Testament a frequent designation of man in general, and thus we might be induced to understand it in the mouth of Jesus. This interpretation would suit some passages; for example, Matt. xii. 8, where Jesus says : *The Son of man is lord also of the Sabbath day*, κύριος γάρ ἐστι τοῦ σαββάτου ὁ υἱὸς τοῦ ἀνθρώπου,—words which will fitly enough take a general meaning, such as Grotius affixes to them, namely, that man is lord of the Sabbath, especially if we compare Mark (ii. 27), who introduces them by the proposition, *The Sabbath was made for man, and not man for the Sabbath*, τὸ σάββατον διὰ τὸν ἄνθρωπον ἐγένετο, οὐχ ὁ ἄνθρωπος διὰ τὸ σάββατον. But in the majority of cases, the phrase in question is evidently used as a special designation. Thus, Matt. viii. 20, a scribe volunteers to become a disciple of Jesus, and is admonished to count the cost in the words, *The Son of man hath not where to lay his head*, ὁ υἱὸς τοῦ ἀνθρώπου οὐκ ἔχει, ποῦ τὴν κεφαλὴν κλίνῃ : here some particular man must be intended, nay, the particular man into whose companionship the scribe wished to enter, that is, Jesus himself. As a reason for the self-application of this term by Jesus, it has been suggested that he used the third person after the oriental manner, to avoid the *I*.[1] But for a speaker to use the third person in reference to himself, is only admissible, if he would be understood, when the designation he employs is precise, and inapplicable to any other person present, as when a father or a king uses his appropriate title of himself; or when, if the designation be not precise, its relation is made clear by a demonstrative pronoun, which limitation is eminently indispensable if an individual speak of himself under the universal designation *man*. We grant that occasionally a gesture might supply the place of the demonstrative pronoun ; but that Jesus in every instance of his using this habitual expression had recourse to some visible explanatory sign, or that the Evangelists would not, in that case, have supplied

---

* All that relates to the idea of the Messiah as suffering, dying, and rising again, is here omitted, and reserved for the history of the Passion.

[1] Paulus, exeget. Handb. 1, 6, s. 465 ; Fritzsche, in Matth., p. 320.

its necessary absence from a written document by some demonstrative addition, is inconceivable. If both Jesus and the Evangelists held such an elucidation superfluous, they must have seen in the expression itself the key to its precise application. Some are of opinion that Jesus intended by it to point himself out as the ideal man—man in the noblest sense of the word ;[2] but this is a modern theory, not an historical inference, for there is no trace of such an interpretation of the expression in the time of Jesus,[3] and it would be more easy to show, as others have attempted, that the appellation, *Son of Man*, so frequently used by Jesus, had reference to his lowly and despised condition.[4] Apart however from the objection that this acceptation also would require the addition of the demonstrative pronoun, though it might be adapted to many passages, as Matt. viii. 20 ; John i. 51, there are others (such as Matt. xvii. 22, where Jesus, foretelling his violent death, designates himself ὁ υἱὸς τοῦ ἀνθρώπου) which demand the contrast of high dignity with an ignominious fate. So in Matt. x. 23, the assurance given to the commissioned disciples that before they had gone over the cities of Israel the Son of Man would come, could have no weight unless this expression denoted a person of importance ; and that such was its significance is proved by a comparison of Matt. xvi. 28, where there is also a mention of an ἔρχεσθαι, *a coming* of the Son of man, but with the addition ἐν τῇ βασιλείᾳ αὐτοῦ. As this addition can only refer to the messianic kingdom, the υἱὸς τοῦ ἀνθρώπου must be the Messiah.

How so apparently vague an appellation came to be appropriated to the Messiah, we gather from Matt. xxvi. 64 parall., where the Son of man is depicted as coming *in the clouds of heaven*. This is evidently an allusion to Dan. vii. 13 f. where after having treated of the fall of the four beasts, the writer says : *I saw in the night visions, and behold, one like the Son of Man* (כְּבַר אֱנָשׁ ὡς υἱὸς ἀνθρώπου, LXX.) *came with the clouds of heaven, and came to the Ancient of days. And there was given him dominion, and glory, and a kingdom, that all people, nations and languages should serve him : his dominion is an everlasting dominion.* The four beasts (v. 17 ff.) were symbolical of the four great empires, the last of which was the Macedonian, with its offshoot, Syria. After their fall, the kingdom was to be given in perpetuity to the People of God, *the saints of the Most High* : hence, he was to come with *clouds of heaven* could only be, either a personification of the holy people,[5] or a leader of heavenly origin under whom they were to achieve their destined triumph—in a word, the Messiah ; and this was the customary interpretation among the Jews.[6] Two things are predicated of this personage,—that he was like the Son of man, and that he came with the clouds of heaven ; but the *former* particular is his distinctive characteristic, and imports either that he had not a superhuman form, that of an angel for instance, though descending from heaven, or else that the kingdom about to be established presented in its humanity a contrast to the inhumanity of its predecessors, of which ferocious beasts were the fitting emblems.[7] At a later period, it is true, the Jews regarded the coming with the clouds of heaven עִם־עֲנָנֵי שְׁמַיָּא as the more essential attribute of the Messiah, and hence gave him the name Anani, after the Jewish taste of making a merely accessory circumstance the permanent

---

[2] Thus after Herder, Köster e. g. in Immanuel, s, 265.
[3] Lücke, Comm. zum Joh., 1, s. 397 f.
[4] e.g. Grotius.
[5] Abenesra, see Hävernick, ut sup. Comm. zum Daniel, s. 244.
[6] Schöttgen, horæ, ii. s. 63, 73 ; Hävernick, ut sup., s. 243 f.
[7] See for the most important opinions, Hävernick, ut sup., s. 242 f.

epithet of a person or thing.[8] If, then, the expression ὁ υἱὸς τοῦ ἀνθρώπου necessarily recalled the above passage in Daniel, generally believed to relate to the Messiah, it is impossible that Jesus could so often use it, and in connexion with declarations evidently referring to the Messiah, without intending it as the designation of that personage.

That by the expression in question Jesus meant himself, without relation to the messianic dignity, is less probable than the contrary supposition, that he might often mean the Messiah when he spoke of the *Son of Man*, without relation to his own person. When, Matt. x. 23, on the first mission of the twelve apostles to announce the kingdom of heaven, he comforts them under the prospect of their future persecutions by the assurance that they would not *have gone over all the cities of Israel before the coming of the Son of Man*, we should rather, taking this declaration alone, think of a third person, whose speedy messianic appearance Jesus was promising, than of the speaker himself, seeing that he was already come, and it would not be antecedently clear how he could represent his own coming as one still in anticipation. So also when Jesus (Matt. xiii. 37 ff.) interprets the Sower of the parable to be the Son of Man, who at the end of the world will have a harvest and a tribunal, he might be supposed to refer to the Messiah as a third person distinct from himself. This is equally the case, xvi. 27 f., where, to prove the proposition that the loss of the soul is not to be compensated by the gain of the whole world, he urges the speedy coming of the Son of Man, to administer retribution. Lastly, in the connected discourses, Matt. xxiv., xxv. parall., many particulars would be more easily conceived, if the υἱὸς τοῦ ἀνθρώπου whose παρουσία Jesus describes, were understood to mean another than himself.

But this explanation is far from being applicable to the majority of instances in which Jesus uses this expression. When he represents the Son of Man, not as one still to be expected, but as one already come and actually present, for example, in Matt. xviii. 11, where he says: *The Son of Man is come to save that which was lost*; when he justifies his own acts by the authority with which the Son of Man was invested, as in Matt. ix. 6; when, Mark viii. 31 ff. comp. Matt. xvi. 22, he speaks of the approaching sufferings and death of the Son of Man, so as to elicit from Peter the exclamation, οὐ μὴ ἔσται σοι τοῦτο, *this shall not be unto thee*; in these and similar cases he can only, by the υἱὸς τοῦ ἀνθρώπου, have intended himself. And even those passages, which, taken singly, we might have found capable of application to a messianic person, distinct from Jesus, lose this capability when considered in their entire connexion. It is possible, however, either that the writer may have misplaced certain expressions, or that the ultimately prevalent conviction that Jesus was *the Son of Man* caused what was originally said merely of the latter, to be viewed in immediate relation to the former.

Thus besides the fact that Jesus on many occasions called himself the Son of Man, there remains the possibility that on many others, he may have designed another person; and if so, the latter would in the order of time naturally precede the former. Whether this possibility can be heightened to a reality, must depend on the answer to the following question: Is there, in the period of the life of Jesus, from which all his recorded declarations are taken, any fragment which indicates that he had not yet conceived himself to be the Messiah?*

---

[8] Let the reader bear in mind the designation of David's elegy, 2 Sam. i. 17ff. as קֶשֶׁת and the denomination of the Messiah as צֶמַח. Had Schleiermacher considered the nature of Jewish appellatives, he would not have called the reference of υἱὸς τοῦ ἀ. to the passage in Daniel, a strange idea. (Glaubensl., § 99, s. 99, Anm.)

§ 62.

HOW SOON DID JESUS CONCEIVE HIMSELF TO BE THE MESSIAH, AND FIND
RECOGNITION AS SUCH FROM OTHERS ?*

Jesus held and expressed the conviction that he was the Messiah ; this is
an indisputable fact.† Not only did he, according to the Evangelists, receive
with satisfaction the confession of the disciples that he was the Χριστὸς (Matt.
xvi. 16 f.) and the salutation of the people, *Hosanna to the Son of David* (xxi.
15 f.) ; not only did he before a public tribunal (Matt. xxvi. 64, comp. John
xviii. 37) as well as to private individuals (John iv. 26, ix. 37, x. 25) repeatedly declare himself to be the Messiah ; but the fact that his disciples
after his death believed and proclaimed that he was the Messiah, is not to be
comprehended, unless, when living, he had implanted the conviction in their
minds.

To the more searching question, how soon Jesus began to declare himself
the Messiah and to be regarded as such by others, the Evangelists almost
unanimously reply, that he assumed that character from the time of his
baptism.   All of them attach to his baptism circumstances which must have
convinced himself, if yet uncertain, and all others who witnessed or credited
them, that he was no less than the Messiah ; John makes his earliest disciples
recognise his right to that dignity on their first interview (i. 42 ff.), and
Matthew attributes to him at the very beginning of his ministry, in the sermon
on the mount, a representation of himself as the Judge of the world (vii. 21
ff.) and therefore the Messiah.

Nevertheless, on a closer examination, there appears a remarkable divergency on this subject between the synoptical statement and that of John.
While, namely, in John, Jesus remains throughout true to his assertion, and
the disciples and his followers among the populace to their conviction, that
he is the Messiah ; in the synoptical gospels there is a vacillation discernible
—the previously expressed persuasion on the part of the disciples and people
that Jesus was the Messiah, sometimes vanishes and gives place to a much
lower view of him, and even Jesus himself becomes more reserved in his
declarations.   This is particularly striking when the synoptical statement is
compared with that of John ; but even when they are separately considered,
the result is the same.

According to John (vi. 15), after the miracle of the loaves the people were
inclined to constitute Jesus their (messianic) King ; on the contrary, according to the other three Evangelists, either about the same time (Luke ix. 18 f.)
or still later (Matt. xvi. 13 f. ; Mark viii. 27 f.) the disciples could only report,
on the opinions of the people respecting their master, that some said he was
the resuscitated Baptist, some Elias, and others Jeremiah or one of the old
prophets : in reference to that passage of John, however, as also to the
synoptical one, Matt. xiv. 33, according to which, some time before Jesus
elicited the above report of the popular opinion, the people who were with
him in the ship[1] when he had allayed the storm, fell at his feet and worshipped him as the Son of God, it may be observed that when Jesus had
spoken or acted with peculiar impressiveness, individuals, in the exaltation of
the moment, might be penetrated with a conviction that he was the Messiah,
while the general and calm voice of the people yet pronounced him to be
merely a prophet.

---

[1] That the expression οἱ ἐν τῷ πλοίῳ includes more than the disciples, vid. Fritzsche, in
loc.

But there is a more troublesome divergency relative to the disciples. In John, Andrew, after his first interview with Jesus, says to his brother, *we have found the Messiah,* εὑρήκαμεν τὸν Μεσσίαν (i. 42); and Philip describes him to Nathanael as the person foretold by Moses and the prophets (v. 46); Nathanael salutes him as the Son of God and King of Israel (v. 50); and the subsequent confession of Peter appearsmerely a renewed avowal of what had been long a familiar truth.   In the synoptical Evangelists it is only after pro-longed intercourse with Jesus, and shortly before his sufferings, that the ardent Peter arrives at the conclusion that Jesus is the Χριστὸς, ὁ υἱὸς τοῦ θεοῦ τοῦ ζῶντος (Matt. xvi. 16, parall.).   It is impossible that this confession should make so strong an impression on Jesus that, in consequence of it, he should pronounce Peter blessed, and his confession the fruit of immediate divine revelation, as Matthew narrates ; or that, as all the three Evangelists inform us (xvi. 20, viii. 30, ix. 21), he should, as if alarmed, forbid the disciples to promulgate their conviction, unless it represented not an opinion long cherished in the circle of his disciples, but a new light, which had just flashed on the mind of Peter, and through him was communicated to his associates.

There is a third equally serious discrepancy, relative to the declarations of Jesus concerning his Messiahship.   According to John he sanctions the homage which Nathanael renders to him as the Son of God and King of Israel, in the very commencement of his public career, and immediately pro-ceeds to speak of himself under the messianic title, Son of Man (i. 51 f.) : to the Samaritans also after his first visit to the passover (iv. 26, 39 ff.), and to the Jews on the second (v. 46), he makes himself known as the Messiah pre-dicted by Moses.   According to the synoptical writers, on the contrary, he prohibits, in the instance above cited and in many others, the dissemination of the doctrine of his Messiahship, beyond the circle of his adherents.   Farther, when he asks his disciples, *Whom do men say that I am ?* (Matt. xvi. 15) he seems to wish [2] that they should derive their conviction of his Messiahship from his discourses and actions, and when he ascribes the avowed faith of Peter to a revelation from his heavenly Father, he excludes the possibility of his having himself previously made this disclosure to his disciples, either in the manner described by John, or in the more indirect one attributed to him by Matthew in the Sermon on the Mount ; unless we suppose that the dis-ciples had not hitherto believed his assurance, and that hence Jesus referred the new-born faith of Peter to divine influence.

Thus, on the point under discussion the synoptical statement is contra-dictory, not only to that of John, but to itself ; it appears therefore that it ought to be unconditionally surrendered before that of John, which is con-

---

[2] There is a difficulty involved in the form of the question, put by Jesus to his disciples : τίνα με λέγουσιν οἱ ἄνθρωποι εἶναι, τον υἱὸν τοῦ ἀνθρώπου ; i.e. what opinion have the people of me, the Messiah?   This, when compared with the sequel, seems a premature disclosure ; hence expositors have variously endeavoured to explain away its primâ facie meaning.   Some (e.g. Beza) understand the subordinate clause, not as a declaration of Jesus concerning his own person, but as a closer limitation of the question : For whom do the people take me ? for the Messiah?   But this would be a leading question, which, as Fritzsche well observes, would indicate an eagerness for the messianic title, not elsewhere discernible in Jesus. Others, therefore, (as Paulus and Fritzsche,) give the expression υἱὸς τ. ἀ. a general significa-tion, and interpret the question thus : Whom do men say that I, the individual addressing you, am ?   But this explanation has been already refuted in the foregoing section.   If, then, we reject the opinion that the υἱὸς τ. ἀ. is an addition which the exuberant faith of the writer was apt to suggest even in an infelicitous connexion, we are restricted to De Wette's view (exeg. Handb. 1, 1, s. 86 f.), namely, that the expression, ὁ υἱὸς τ. ἀ. was indeed an appellation of the Messiah, but an indirect one, so that it might convey that meaning, as an allusion to Daniel, to Jesus and those already aware of his Messiahship, while to others it was merely the equivalent of, *this man.*

sistent with itself, and one of our critics has justly reproached it with deranging the messianic economy in the life of Jesus.[3] But here again we must not lose sight of our approved canon, that in glorifying narratives, such as our gospels, where various statements are confronted, that is the least probable which best subserves the object of glorification. Now this is the case with John's statement ; according to which, from the commencement to the close of the public life of Jesus, his Messiahship shines forth in unchanging splendour, while, according to the synoptical writers, it is liable to a variation in its light. But though this criterion of probability is in favour of the first three Evangelists, it is impossible that the order in which they make ignorance and concealment follow on plain declarations and recognitions of the Messiahship of Jesus can be correct; and we must suppose that they have mingled and confounded two separate periods of the life of Jesus, in the latter of which alone he presented himself as the Messiah. We find, in fact, that the watchword of Jesus on his first appearance differed not, even verbally, from that of John, who professed merely to be a forerunner ; it is the same *Repent, for the kingdom of heaven is at hand* (Matt. iv. 17) with which John had roused the Jews (iii. 2) ; and indicates in neither the one nor the other an assumption of the character of Messiah, with whose coming the kingdom of heaven was actually to commence, but merely that of a teacher who points to it as yet future.[4] Hence the latest critic of the first gospel justly explains all those discourses and actions therein narrated, by which Jesus explicitly claims to be the Messiah, or, in consequence of which this dignity is attributed to him and accepted, if they occur before the manifestation of himself recorded in John v., or before the account of the apostolic confession (Matt. xvi.), as offences of the writer against chronology or literal truth.[5] We have only to premise, that as chronological confusion prevails throughout, the position of this confession shortly before the history of the Passion, in nowise obliges us to suppose that it was so late before Jesus was recognised as the Messiah among his disciples, since Peter's avowal may have occurred in a much earlier period of their intercourse. This, however, is incomprehensible—that the same reproach should not attach even more strongly to the fourth gospel than to the first, or to the synoptical writers in general. For it is surely more pardonable that the first three Evangelists should give us the pre-messianic memoirs in the wrong place, than that the fourth should not give them at all ; more endurable in the former, to mingle the two periods, than in the latter, quite to obliterate the earlier one.

If then Jesus did not lay claim to the Messiahship from the beginning of his public career, was this omission the result of uncertainty in his own mind ; or had he from the first a conviction that he was the Messiah, but concealed it for certain reasons? In order to decide this question, a point already mentioned must be more carefully weighed. In the first three Evangelists, but not so exclusively that the fourth has nothing similar, when Jesus effects a miracle of healing he almost invariably forbids the person cured to promulgate the event, in these or similar words, ὅρα μηδενὶ εἴπῃς; e.g. the leper, Matt. viii. 4, parall. ; the blind men, Matt. ix. 30 ; a multitude of the healed, Matt. xii. 16 ; the parents of the resuscitated damsel, Mark v. 43 ; above all he enjoins silence on the demoniacs, Mark i. 34, iii. 12 ; and John v. 13, it is said, after the cure of the man at the pool of Bethesda, *Jesus had conveyed himself away, a multitude being in that place.* Thus also he forbade the three

---

[3] Schneckenburger, über den Ursprung u. s. f., s. 28 f.

[4] This distinction of two periods in the public life of Jesus is also made by Fritzsche, Comm. in Matth., s. 213. 536, and Schneckenburger ut sup.

[5] Schneckenburger, ut sup., s. 29.

who were with him on the mount of the Transfiguration, to publish the scene they had witnessed (Matt. xvii. 9) ; and after the confession of Peter, he charges the disciples to tell no man the conviction it expressed (Luke ix. 21). This prohibition of Jesus could hardly, as most commentators suppose,[5] be determined by various circumstantial motives, at one time having relation to the disposition of the person healed, at another to the humour of the people, at another to the situation of Jesus : rather, as there is an essential similarity in the conditions under which he lays this injunction on the people, if we discern a probable motive for it on any occasion, we are warranted in applying the same motive to the remaining cases. This motive is scarcely any other than the desire that the belief that he was the Messiah should not be too widely spread. When (Mark i. 34) Jesus would not allow the ejected demons to speak *because they knew him*, when he charged the multitudes *that they should not make him known* (Matt. xii. 16), he evidently intended that the former should not proclaim him in the character in which their more penetrative, demoniacal glance had viewed him, nor the latter in that revealed by the miraculous cure he had wrought on them—in short, they were not to betray their knowledge that he was the Messiah. As a reason for this wish on the part of Jesus, it has been alleged, on the strength of John vi. 15, that he sought to avoid awakening the political idea of the Messiah's kingdom in the popular mind, with the disturbance which would be its inevitable result.[7] This would be a valid reason ; but the synoptical writers represent the wish, partly as the effect of humility ;[8] Matthew, in connexion with a prohibition of the kind alluded to, applying to Jesus a passage in Isaiah (xlii. 1 f.) where the servant of God is said to be distinguished by his stillness and unobtrusiveness : partly, and in a greater degree, as the effect of an apprehension that the Messiah, at least such an one as Jesus, would be at once proscribed by the Jewish hierarchy.

From all this it might appear that Jesus was restrained merely by external motives, from the open declaration of his Messiahship, and that his own conviction of it existed from the first in equal strength ; but this conclusion cannot be maintained in the face of the consideration above mentioned, that Jesus began his career with the same announcement as the Baptist, an announcement which can scarcely have more than one import—an exhortation to prepare for a coming Messiah. The most natural supposition is that Jesus, first the disciple of the Baptist, and afterwards his successor, in preaching repentance and the approach of the kingdom of heaven, took originally the same position as his former master in relation to the messianic kingdom, notwithstanding the greater reach and liberality of his mind, and only gradually attained the elevation of thinking himself the Messiah. This supposition explains in the simplest manner the prohibition we have been considering, especially that annexed to the confession of Peter. For as often as the thought that he might be the Messiah suggested itself to others, and was presented to him from without, Jesus must have shrunk, as if appalled, to hear confidently uttered that which he scarcely ventured to surmise, or which had but recently become clear to himself. As, however, the Evangelist often put such prohibitions into the mouth of Jesus unseasonably (witness the occasion mentioned, Matt. viii. 4, when, after a cure effected before a crowd of spectators, it was of little avail to enjoin secrecy on the cured),[9] it is prob-

---

[6] Fritzsche, in Matth. p. 309, comp. 352. Olshausen, s. 265.

[7] Fritzsche, p. 352. Olshausen, ut sup.

[8] The opposite view is held by the Fragmentist, who thinks the prohibition was intended to stimulate the popular eagerness.

[9] Fritzsche, s. 309.

able that evangelical tradition, enamoured of the mysteriousness that lay in this incognito of Jesus,[10] unhistorically multiplied the instances of its adoption.*

§ 63.

JESUS, THE SON OF GOD.[†]

In Luke i. 35, we find the narrowest and most literal interpretation of the expression, ὁ υἱὸς τοῦ θεοῦ; namely, as derived from his conception by means of the Holy Ghost. On the contrary, the widest moral and metaphorical sense is given to the expression in Matt. v. 45, where those who imitate the love of God towards his enemies are called the sons of the Father in heaven. There is an intermediate sense which we may term the metaphysical, because while it includes more than mere conformity of will, it is distinct from the notion of actual paternity, and implies a spiritual community of being. In this sense it is profusely employed and referred to in the fourth gospel ; as when Jesus says that he speaks and does nothing of himself, but only what as a son he has learned from the Father (v. 19, xii. 49, and elsewhere), who, moreover, is in him (xvii. 21), and notwithstanding his exaltation over him (xiv. 28), is yet one with him (x. 30). There is yet a fourth sense in which the expression is presented. When (Matt. iv. 3) the devil challenges Jesus to change the stones into bread, making the supposition, *If thou be the Son of God;* when Nathanael says to Jesus, *Thou art the Son of God, the King of Israel* (John i. 49) ; when Peter confesses, *Thou art the Christ, the Son of the living God* (Matt. xvi. 16 ; comp. John vi. 69) ; when Martha thus expresses her faith in Jesus, *I believe that thou art the Christ, the Son of God* (John xi. 27) ; when the high priest adjures Jesus to tell him if he be *the Christ, the Son of God* (Matt. xxvi. 63) : it is obvious that the devil means nothing more than, If thou be the Messiah ; and that in the other passages the υἱὸς τοῦ θεοῦ, united as it is with Χριστὸς and βασιλεὺς, is but an appellation of the Messiah.

In Hos. xi. 1 ; Exod. iv. 22, the people of Israel, and in 2 Sam. vii. 14 ; Ps. ii. 7 (comp. lxxxix. 28), the king of that people, are called the son and the first-born of God. The kings (as also the people) of Israel had this appellation, in virtue of the love which Jehovah bore them, and the tutelary care which he exercised over them (2 Sam. vii. 14) ; and from the second psalm we gather the farther reason, that as earthly kings choose their sons to reign with or under them, so the Israelitish kings were invested by Jehovah, the supreme ruler, with the government of his favourite province. Thus the designation was originally applicable to every Israelitish king who adhered to the principle of the theocracy ; but when the messianic idea was developed, it was pre-eminently assigned to the Messiah, as the best-beloved Son, and the most powerful vicegerent of God on earth.[1]

If, then, such was the original historical signification of the epithet, *Son of God,* as applied to the Messiah, we have to ask : is it possible that Jesus used it of himself in this signification only, or did he use it also in either of the three senses previously adduced? The narrowest, the merely physical import of the term is not put into the mouth of Jesus, but into that of the annunciating angel, Luke i. 35 ; and for this the Evangelist alone is responsible. In the intermediate, metaphysical sense, implying unity of essence

---

[10] Comp. Schleiermacher, über den Lukas, s. 74.
[1] Comp. the excellent treatise of Paulus on the following question in the Einl. zum Leben Jesu, 1, a, s. 28 ff.

and community of existence wit'ı God, it might possibly have been understood by Jesus, supposing him to ł ave remodelled in his own conceptions the theocratic interpretation current among his compatriots. It is true that the abundant expressions having this tendency in the Gospel of John, appear to contradict those of Jesus on an occasion recorded by the synoptical writers (Mark x. 17 f.; Luke xviii. 18 f.), when to a disciple who accosts him as *Good Master*, he replies : *Why callest thou me good ? there is none good but one, that is God.* Here Jesus so tenaciously maintains the distinction between himself and God, that he renounces the predicate of (perfect) goodness, and insists on its appropriation to God alone.[2] Olshausen supposes that this rejection related solely to the particular circumstances of the disciple addressed, who, regarding Jesus as a merely human teacher, ought not from his point of view to have given him a divine epithet, and that it was not intended by Jesus as a denial that he was, according to a just estimate of his character, actually the ἀγαθὸς in whom the one good Being was reflected as in a mirror ; but this is to take for granted what is first to be proved, namely, that the declarations of Jesus concerning himself in the fourth gospel are on a level as to credibility with those recorded by the synoptical writers. Two of these writers cite some words of Jesus which have an important bearing on our present subject : *All things are delivered to me of my Father : and no man knoweth the Son but the Father : neither knoweth any man the Father, but the Son, and he to whomsoever the Son will reveal him,* Matt. xi. 27. Taking this passage in connexion with the one before quoted, we must infer that Jesus had indeed an intimate communion of thought and will with God, but under such limitations, that the attribute of perfect goodness, as well as of absolute knowledge (e.g., of the day and hour of the last day, Mark xiii. 32 parall.) belonged exclusively to God, and hence the boundary line between divine and human was strictly preserved. Even in the fourth gospel Jesus declares, *My Father is greater than I,* ὁ πατήρ μον μείζων μου ἐστὶ (xiv. 28), but this slight echo of the synoptical statement does not remove the difficulty of conciliating the numerous discourses of a totally different tenor in the former, with the rejection of the epithet ἀγαθὸς in the latter. It is surprising, too, that Jesus in the fourth gospel appears altogether ignorant of the theocratic sense of the expression υἱὸς τοῦ θεοῦ, and can only vindicate his use of it in the metaphysical sense, by retreating to its vague and metaphorical application. When, namely (John x. 34 ff.), to justify his assumption of this title, he adduces the scriptural application of the term θεοὶ to other men, such as princes and magistrates, we are at a loss to understand why Jesus should resort to this remote and precarious argument, when close at hand lay the far more cogent one, that in the Old Testament, a theocratic king of Israel, or according to the customary interpretation of the most striking passages, the Messiah, is called the Son of Jehovah, and that therefore he, having declared himself to be the Messiah (v. 25), might consistently claim this appellation.

With respect to the light in which Jesus was viewed as the Son of God by others, we may remark that in the addresses of well-affected persons the title is often so associated as to be obviously a mere synonym of Χριστὸς, and this even in the fourth gospel ; while on the other hand the contentious Ἰουδαῖοι of this gospel seem in their objections as ignorant as Jesus in his defence, of the theocratic, and only notice the metaphysical meaning of the expression.

---

[2] Even if a different reading be adopted for the parallel passage in Matthew (xix. 16 f.), it must remain questionable whether his statement deserves the preference to that of the two other Evangelists.

It is true that, even in the synoptical gospels, when Jesus answers affirma-
tively the question whether he be the Christ, the Son of the living God (Matt.
xxvi. 65, parall.), the high priest taxes him with blasphemy; but he refers
merely to what he considers the unwarranted arrogation of the theocratic
dignity of the Messiah, whereas in the fourth gospel, when Jesus represents
himself as the Son of God (v. 17 f., x. 30 ff.), the Jews seek to kill him for the
express reason that he thereby makes himself ἴσον τῷ θεῷ, nay even ἑαυτὸν
θεὸν. According to the synoptical writers, the high priest so unhesitatingly
considers the idea of the Son of God to pertain to that of the Messiah, that
he associates the two titles as if they were interchangeable, in the question he
addresses to Jesus : on the contrary the Jews in the Gospel of John regard
the one idea as so far transcending the other, that they listen patiently to the
declaration of Jesus that he is the Messiah (x. 25), but as soon as he begins
to claim to be the Son of God, *they take up stones to stone him.* In the
synoptical gospels the reproach cast on Jesus is, that being a *common* man,
he gives himself out for the Messiah ; in the fourth gospel, that being a mere
man, he gives himself out for a *divine* being. Hence Olshausen and others
have justly insisted that in those passages of the latter gospel to which our
remarks have reference, the υἱὸς τοῦ θεοῦ is not synonymous with Messiah,
but is a name far transcending the ordinary idea of the Messiah ;[3] they are
not, however, warranted in concluding that therefore in the first three Evangelists also[4] the same expression imports more than the Messiah. For the
only legitimate interpretation of the high priest's question in Matthew makes
ὁ υἱὸς τοῦ θεοῦ a synonym of ὁ Χριστὸς, and though in the parallel passage of
Luke, the judges first ask Jesus if he be the Christ (xxii. 67)? and when he
declines a direct answer,—predicting that they will behold the Son of man
seated at the right hand of God,—hastily interrupt him with the question, *Art
thou the Son of God ?* (v. 70); yet, after receiving what they consider an
affirmative answer, they accuse him before Pilate as one who pretends to be
Christ, a king (xxiii. 2), thus clearly showing that Son of man, Son of God,
and Messiah, must have been regarded as interchangeable terms. It must
therefore be conceded that there is a discrepancy on this point between the
synoptical writers and John, and perhaps also an inconsistency of the latter
with himself; for in several addresses to Jesus he retains the customary form,
which associated *Son of God* with *Christ* or *King of Israel,* without being
conscious of the distinction between the signification which υἱὸς τ. θ. must
have in such a connexion, and that in which he used it elsewhere—a want of
perception which habitual forms of expression are calculated to induce. We
have before cited examples of this oversight in the fourth Evangelist (John i.
49, vi. 69, xi. 27).

The author of the Probabilia reasonably considers it suspicious that, in the
fourth gospel, Jesus and his opponents should appear entirely ignorant of the
theocratic sense which is elsewhere attached to the expression ὁ υἱὸς τοῦ θεοῦ,
and which must have been more familiar to the Jews than any other, unless
we suppose some of them to have partaken of Alexandrian culture. To such,
we grant, as well as to the fourth Evangelist, judging from his prologue, the
metaphysical relation of the λόγος μονογενὴς to God would be the most
cherished association.

---

[3] Bibl. Comm. 2, s. 130, 253.
[4] Olshausen, ut sup. 1, s. 108 ff.

§ 64.

THE DIVINE MISSION AND AUTHORITY OF JESUS. HIS PRE-EXISTENCE.

The four Evangelists are in unison as to the declaration of Jesus concerning his divine mission and authority. Like every prophet, he is sent by God (Matt. x. 40 ; John v. 23 f., 56 f.), acts and speaks by the authority, and under the immediate guidance of God (John v. 19 ff.), and exclusively possesses an adequate knowledge of God, which it is his office to impart to men (Matt. xi. 27 ; John iii. 13). To him, as the Messiah, all power is given (Matt. xi. 27) ; first, over the kingdom which he is appointed to found and to rule with all its members (John x. 29, xvii. 6) ; next, over mankind in general (John xvii. 2), and even external nature (Matt. xxviii. 18) ; consequently, should the interests of the messianic kingdom demand it, power to effect a thorough revolution in the whole world. At the future commencement of his reign, Jesus, as Messiah, is authorized to awake the dead (John v. 28), and to sit as a judge, separating those worthy to partake of the heavenly kingdom from the unworthy (Matt. xxv. 31 ff. ; John v. 22, 29) ; offices which Jewish opinion attributed to the Messiah,[1] and which Jesus, once convinced of his Messiahship, would necessarily transfer to himself.

The Evangelists are not equally unanimous on another point. According to the synoptical writers, Jesus claims, it is true, the highest human dignity, and the most exalted relation with God, for the present and future, but he never refers to an existence anterior to his earthly career : in the fourth gospel, on the contrary, we find several discourses of Jesus which contain the repeated assertion of such a pre-existence. We grant that when Jesus describes himself as coming down from heaven (John iii. 13, xvi. 28), the expression, taken alone, may be understood as a merely figurative intimation of his superhuman origin. It is more difficult, but perhaps admissible, to interpret, with the Socinian Crell, the declaration of Jesus, *Before Abraham was, I am*, πρὶν ᾿Αβραὰμ γενέσθαι, ἐγώ εἰμι (John viii. 58), as referring to a purely ideal existence in the pre-determination of God ; but scarcely possible to consider the prayer to the Father (John xvii. 5) to confirm the δόξα (*glory*) which Jesus had with Him *before the world was*, πρὸ τοῦ τὸν κόσμον εἶναι, as an entreaty for the communication of a glory predestined for Jesus from eternity. But the language of Jesus, John vi. 62, where he speaks of the Son of man *reascending* ἀναβαίνειν *where he was before* ὅπου ἦν τὸ πρότερον, is in its intrinsic meaning, as well as in that which is reflected on it from other passages, unequivocally significative of actual, not merely ideal, pre-existence.

It has been already conjectured[2] that these expressions, or at least the adaptation of them to a real pre-existence, are derived, not from Jesus, but from the author of the fourth gospel, with whose opinions, as propounded in his introduction, they specifically agree ; for if *the Word was in the beginning with God* (ἐν ἀρχῇ πρὸς τὸν θεόν), Jesus, in whom it was *made flesh*, might attribute to himself an existence before Abraham, and a participation of glory with the Father before the foundation of the world. Nevertheless, we are not warranted in adopting this view, unless it can be shown that neither was the idea of the pre-existence of the Messiah extant among the Jews of Palestine before the time of Jesus, nor is it probable that Jesus attained such a notion, independently of the ideas peculiar to his age and nation.

The latter supposition, that Jesus spoke from his own memory of his pre-

---

[1] Bertholdt, Christol. Judæor. §§ 8. 35, 42.
[2] Bretschneider, Probab., p. 59.

human and pre-mundane existence, is liable to comparison with dangerous parallels in the history of Pythagoras, Ennius, and Apollonius of Tyana, whose alleged reminiscences of individual states which they had experienced prior to their birth,[3] are now generally regarded either as subsequent fables, or as enthusiastic self-delusions of those celebrated men. For the other alternative, that the idea in question was common to the Jewish nation, a presumption may be found in the description, already quoted from Daniel, of the Son of man coming in the clouds of heaven, since the author, possibly, and, at all events, many readers, imagined that personage to be a superhuman being, dwelling beforehand with God, like the angels. But that every one who referred this passage to the Messiah, or that Jesus in particular, associated with it the notion of a pre-existence, is not to be proved ; for, if we exclude the representation of John, Jesus depicts his coming in the clouds of heaven, not as if he had come as a visitant to earth from his home in heaven, but, according to Matt. xxvi. 65 (comp. xxiv. 25), as if he, the earth-born, after the completion of his earthly course, would be received into heaven, and from thence would return to establish his kingdom : thus making the coming from heaven not necessarily include the idea of pre-existence. We find in the Proverbs, in Sirach, and the Book of Wisdom, the idea of a personified and even hypostasized Wisdom of God, and in the Psalms and Prophets, strongly marked personifications of the Divine word ; [4] and it is especially worthy of note, that the later Jews, in their horror of anthropomorphism in the idea of the Divine being, attributed his speech, appearance, and immediate agency, to the *Word* (מימרא) or the *dwelling place* (שכינתא) of Jehovah, as may be seen in the venerable [5] Targum of Onkelos.[6] These expressions, at first mere paraphrases of the name of God, soon received the mystical signification of a veritable hypostasis, of a being at once distinct from, and one with God. As most of the revelations and interpositions of God, whose organ this personified Word was considered to be, were designed in favour of the Israelitish people, it was natural for them to assign to the manifestation which was still awaited from Him, and which was to be the crowning benefit of Israel,—the manifestation, namely, of the Messiah,—a peculiar relation with the Word or Shechina.[7] From this germ sprang the opinion that with the Messiah the Shechina would appear, and that what was ascribed to the Shechina pertained equally to the Messiah : an opinion not confined to the Rabbins, but sanctioned by the Apostle Paul. According to it, the Messiah was, even in the wilderness, the invisible guide and benefactor of God's people (1 Cor. x. 4, 9) ; [8] he was with our first parents in Paradise ; [9] he was the agent in creation (Col. i. 16) ; he even existed before the creation,[10] and prior to his incarnation in Jesus, was in a glorious fellowship with God (Phil. ii. 6).

---

[3] Porphyr. Vita Pythag., 26 f. Jamblich. 14, 63. Diog. Laert. viii. 4 f. 14. Baur, Apollonius von Tyana, pp. 64 f. 98 f. 185 f.

[4] See a notification and exposition of the passages in Lücke, Comm. zum Ev. Joh., 1, s. 211 ff.

[5] Winer, de Onkeloso, p. 10. Comp. De Wette, Einleit. in das A. T., § 58.

[6] Bertholdt, Christol. Judæor., §§ 23–25. Comp. Lücke ut sup., s. 244, note.

[7] Schöttgen, ii. s. 6 f.

[8] Targ. Jes. xvi. 1 : *Iste* (*Messias*) *in deserto fuit rupes ecclesiæ Zionis.* In Bertholdt, ut sup. p. 145.

[9] Sohar chadasch f. lxxxii. 4, ap. Schöttgen, ii. s. 440.

[10] Nezach Israël c. xxxv. f. xlviii. 1. Schmidt, Bibl. für Kritik u. Exegese, 1, s. 38 : משיח מפני תוהו. Sohar Levit. f. xiv. 56. Schöttgen, ii. s. 436 : *Septem* (*lumina condita sunt, antequam mundus conderetur*), *nimirum . . . et lumen Messiæ.* Here we have the pre-existence of the Messiah represented as a real one : for a more ideal conception of it, see Bereschith Rabba, sect. 1, f. iii. 3 (Schöttgen).

As it is thus evident that, immediately after the time of Jesus, the idea of a pre-existence of the Messiah was incorporated in the higher Jewish theology, it is no far-fetched conjecture, that the same idea was afloat when the mind of Jesus was maturing, and that in his conception of himself as the Messiah, this attribute was included. But whether Jesus were as deeply initiated in the speculations of the Jewish schools as Paul, is yet a question, and as the author of the fourth gospel, versed in the Alexandrian doctrine of the λόγος, stands alone in ascribing to Jesus the assertion of a pre-existence, we are unable to decide whether we are to put the dogma to the account of Jesus, or of his biographer.

§ 65.

THE MESSIANIC PLAN OF JESUS. INDICATIONS OF A POLITICAL ELEMENT.

The Baptist pointed to a future individual, and Jesus to himself, as the founder of the kingdom of heaven. The idea of that messianic kingdom belonged to the Israelitish nation ; did Jesus hold it in the form in which it existed among his cotemporaries, or under modifications of his own ?

The idea of the Messiah grew up amongst the Jews in soil half religious, half political : it was nurtured by national adversity, and in the time of Jesus, according to the testimony of the gospels, it was embodied in the expectation that the Messiah would ascend the throne of his ancestor David, free the Jewish people from the Roman yoke, and found a kingdom which would last for ever (Luke i. 32 f., 68 ff. ; Acts i. 6). Hence our first question must be this. Did Jesus include this political element in his messianic plan ?

That Jesus aspired to be a temporal ruler, has at all times been an allegation of the adversaries of Christianity, but has been maintained by none with so much exegetical acumen as by the author of the Wolfenbüttel Fragments,[1] who, be it observed, by no means denies to Jesus the praise of aiming at the moral reformation of his nation. According to this writer, the first indication of a political plan on the part of Jesus is, that he unambiguously announced the approaching messianic kingdom, and laid down the conditions on which it was to be entered, without explaining what this kingdom was, and wherein it consisted,[2] as if he supposed the current idea of its nature to be correct. Now the fact is, that the prevalent conception of the messianic reign had a strong political bias ; hence, when Jesus spoke of the Messiah's kingdom without a definition, the Jews could only think of an earthly dominion, and as Jesus could not have presupposed any other interpretation of his words, he must have wished to be so understood. But in opposition to this it may be remarked, that in the Parables by which Jesus shadowed forth the kingdom of heaven ; in the Sermon on the Mount, in which he illustrates the duties of its citizens ; and lastly, in his whole demeanour and course of action, we have sufficient evidence, that his idea of the messianic kingdom was peculiar to himself. There is not so ready a counterpoise for the difficulty, that Jesus sent the apostles, with whose conceptions he could not be unacquainted, to announce the Messiah's kingdom throughout the land (Matt. x.). These, who disputed which of them should be greatest in the kingdom of their master (Matt. xviii. 1 ; Luke xxii. 24) ; of whom two petitioned for the seats at the right and left of the messianic king (Mark x. 35 ff.) ; who, even after the death and resurrection of Jesus, expected a restoration of the kingdom to Israel (Acts i. 6) ;—these had clearly from the beginning to the end of their inter-

---

[1] Von dem Zweck Jesu und seiner Jünger, s. 108–157.
[2] Comp. Fritzsche, in Matth., s. 114.

course with Jesus, no other than the popular notion of the Messiah ; when, therefore, Jesus despatched them as heralds of his kingdom, it seems necessarily a part of his design, that they should disseminate in all places their political messianic idea.

Among the discourses of Jesus there is one especially worthy of note in Matt. xix. 28 (comp. Luke xxii. 30). In reply to the question of Peter, *We have left all and followed thee ; what shall we have therefore?* Jesus promises to his disciples that in the παλιγγενεσία, *when the Son of man shall sit on his throne, they also shall sit on twelve thrones, judging the twelve tribes of Israel.* That the literal import of this promise formed part of the tissue of the messianic hopes cherished by the Jews of that period, is not to be controverted. It is argued, however, that Jesus spoke figuratively on this occasion, and only employed familiar Jewish images to convey to the apostles an assurance, that the sacrifices they had made here would be richly compensated in their future life by a participation in his glory.[3] But the disciples must have understood the promise literally, when, even after the resurrection of Jesus, they harboured anticipations of worldly greatness ; and as Jesus had had many proofs of this propensity, he would hardly have adopted such language, had he not intended to nourish their temporal hopes. The supposition that he did so merely to animate the courage of his disciples, without himself sharing their views, imputes duplicity to Jesus ;—a duplicity in this case quite gratuitous, since, as Olshausen justly observes, Peter's question would have been satisfactorily answered by any other laudatory acknowledgment of the devotion of the disciples. Hence it appears a fair inference, that Jesus himself shared the Jewish expectations which he here sanctions : but expositors have made the most desperate efforts to escape from this unwelcome conclusion. Some have resorted to an arbitrary alteration of the reading ;[4] others to the detection of irony, directed against the disproportion between the pretensions of the disciples, and their trivial services ;[5] others to different expedients, but all more unnatural than the admission, that Jesus, in accordance with Jewish ideas, here promises his disciples the dignity of being his assessors in his visible messianic judgment, and that he thus indicates the existence of a national element in his notion of the Messiah's kingdom. It is observable, too, that in the Acts (i. 7), Jesus, even after his resurrection, does not deny that he will restore the kingdom to Israel, but merely discourages curiosity as to the times and seasons of its restoration.

Among the actions of Jesus, his last entry into Jerusalem (Matt. xxi. 1 ff.) is especially appealed to as a proof that his plan was partly political. According to the Fragmentist, all the circumstances point to a political design : the time which Jesus chose,—after a sufficiently long preparation of the people in the provinces ; the Passover, which they visited in great numbers ; the animal on which he rode, and by which, from a popular interpretation of a passage in Zechariah, he announced himself as the destined King of Jerusalem ; the approval which he pronounces when the people receive him with a royal greeting ; the violent procedure which he hazards in the temple ; and finally, his severe philippic on the higher class of the Jews (Matt. xxiii.), at the close of which he seeks to awe them into a reception of him as their messianic king, by the threat that he will show himself to them no more in any other guise.

---

[3] Kuinöl, Comm. in Matt., p. 518. Olshausen also, p. 744, understands the discourse symbolically, though he attaches to it a different meaning.

[4] Paulus, exeget. Handb. 2, s. 613 f.

[5] Liebe, in Winer's exeg. Studien, 1, 59 ff.

§ 66.

DATA FOR THE PURE SPIRITUALITY OF THE MESSIANIC PLAN OF JESUS. BALANCE.*

Nowhere in our evangelical narratives is there a trace of Jesus having sought to form a political party. On the contrary, he withdraws from the eagerness of the people to make him a king (John vi. 15); he declares that the messianic kingdom comes not with observation, but is to be sought for in the recesses of the soul (Luke xvii. 20 f.); it is his principle to unite obedience to God with obedience to temporal authority, even when heathen (Matt. xxii. 21); on his solemn entry into the capital, he chooses to ride the animal of peace, and afterwards escapes from the multitude, instead of using their excitement for the purposes of his ambition; lastly, he maintains before his judge, that his kingdom is not *from hence* οὐκ ἐντεῦθεν, *is not of this world* οὐκ ἐκ τοῦ κόσμου τούτου (John xvi. 36), and we have no reason in this instance to question either his or the Evangelist's veracity.

Thus we have a series of indications to counterbalance those detailed in the preceding section. The adversaries of Christianity have held exclusively to the arguments for a political, or rather a revolutionary, project, on the part of Jesus, while orthodox theologians adhere to those only which tell for the pure spirituality of his plan :[1] and each party has laboured to invalidate by hermeneutical skill the passages unfavourable to its theory. It has of late been acknowledged that both are equally partial, and that there is need of arbitration between them.

This has been attempted chiefly by supposing an earlier and a later form of the plan of Jesus.[2] Although, it has been said, the moral improvement and religious elevation of his people were from the first the primary object of Jesus, he nevertheless, in the beginning of his public life, cherished the hope of reviving, by means of this internal regeneration, the external glories of the theocracy, when he should be acknowledged by his nation as the Messiah, and thereby be constituted the supreme authority in the state. But in the disappointment of this hope, he recognised the divine rejection of every political element in his plan, and thenceforth refined it into pure spirituality. It is held to be a presumption in favour of such a change in the plan of Jesus, that there is a gladness diffused over his first appearance, which gives place to melancholy in the latter period of his ministry; that instead of the acceptable year of the Lord, announced in his initiative address at Nazareth, sorrow is the burthen of his later discourses, and he explicitly says of Jerusalem, that he had attempted to save it, but that now its fall, both religious and political, was inevitable, As, however, the evangelists do not keep the events and discourses proper to these distinct periods within their respective limits, but happen to give the two most important data for the imputation of a political design to Jesus (namely the promise of the twelve thrones and the public entrance into the capital), near the close of his life; we must attribute to these writers a chronological confusion, as in the case of the relation which the views of Jesus bore to the messianic idea in general : unless as an alternative it be conceivable, that Jesus uttered during the same period the

---

[1] So Reinhard, über den Plan, welchen der Stifter der christlichen Religion zum Besten der Menschheit entwarf, s. 57 ff. (4te Aufl.).

[2] Paulus, Leben Jesu 1, b, s. 85, 94, 106 ff.; Venturini, 2, s. 310 f.; Hase, Leben Jesu 1 ed. §§ 68, 84. Hase has modified this opinion in his 2nd edition, §§ 49, 50 (comp. theol. Streitschrift, 1, s. 61 ff.), though with apparent reluctance, and he now maintains that Jesus had risen above the political notion of the messianic kingdom before his public appearance.

declarations which seem to indicate, and those which disclaim, a political design.

This, in our apprehension, is not inconceivable ; for Jesus might anticipate a καθίζεσθαι ἐπὶ θρόνους for himself and his disciples, not regarding the means of its attainment as a political revolution, but as a revolution to be effected by the immediate interposition of God. That such was his view may be inferred from his placing that judiciary appearance of his disciples in the παλιγγενεσία ; for this was not a political revolution, any more than a spiritual regeneration,—it was a resurrection of the dead, which God was to effect through the agency of the Messiah, and which was to usher in the messianic times.[3] Jesus certainly expected to restore the throne of David, and with his disciples to govern a liberated people ; in no degree, however, did he rest his hopes on the sword of human adherents (Luke xxii. 38 ; Matt. xxvi. 52), but on the legions of angels, which his heavenly Father could send him (Matt. xxvi. 53).   Wherever he speaks of coming in his messianic glory, he depicts himself surrounded by angels and heavenly powers (Matt. xvi. 27, xxiv. 30 f., xxv. 31 ; John i. 52) ; before the majesty of the Son of man, coming in the clouds of heaven, all nations are to bow without the coercion of the sword, and at the sound of the angel's trumpet, are to present themselves, with the awakened dead, before the judgment-seat of the Messiah and his twelve apostles.   All this Jesus would not bring to pass of his own will, but he waited for a signal from his heavenly Father, who alone knew the appropriate time for this catastrophe (Mark xiii. 32), and he apparently was not disconcerted when his end approached without his having received the expected intimation.   They who shrink from this view, merely because they conceive that it makes Jesus an enthusiast,[4] will do well to reflect how closely such hopes corresponded with the long cherished messianic idea of the Jews,[5] and how easily, in that day of supernaturalism, and in a nation segregated by the peculiarities of its faith, an idea, in itself extravagant, if only it were consistent, and had, in some of its aspects, truth and dignity, might allure even a reasonable man beneath its influence.

With respect to that which awaits the righteous after judgment,—everlasting life in the kingdom of the Father,—it is true that Jesus, in accordance with Jewish notions,[6] compares it to a feast (Matt. viii. 11, xxii. 2 ff.), at which he hopes himself to taste the fruit of the vine (Matt. xxvi. 29), and to celebrate the Passover (Luke xxii. 16) ; but his declaration that in the αἰὼν μέλλων the organic relation between the sexes will cease, and men will be *like the angels* (ἰσάγγελοι, Luke xx. 35 ff.), seems more or less to reduce the above discourses to a merely symbolical significance.

Thus we conclude that the messianic hope of Jesus was not political, nor even merely earthly, for he referred its fulfilment to supernatural means, and to a supermundane theatre (the regenerated earth) : as little was it a purely spiritual hope, in the modern sense of the term, for it included important and unprecedented changes in the external condition of things : but it was the national, theocratic hope, spiritualized and ennobled by his own peculiar moral and religious views.

---

[3] Fritzsche, in Matt., p. 606 f.
[4] De Wette, Bibl. Dogm., § 216.
[5] Bertholdt, Christol. Judæor., §§ 30 ff.
[6] Ibid., § 39.

§ 67.

THE RELATION OF JESUS TO THE MOSAIC LAW.

The Mosaic institutions were actually extinguished in the church of which Jesus was the founder ; hence it is natural to suppose that their abolition formed a part of his design :—a reach of vision, beyond the horizon of the ceremonial worship of his age and country, of which apologists have been ever anxious to prove that he was possessed.[1] Neither are there wanting speeches and actions of Jesus which seem to favour their effort. Whenever he details the conditions of participation in the kingdom of heaven, as in the Sermon on the Mount, he insists, not on the observance of the Mosaic ritual, but on the spirit of religion and morality ; he attaches no value to fasting, praying, and almsgiving, unless accompanied by a corresponding bent of mind (Matt. vi. 1–18); the two main elements of the Mosaic worship, sacrifice and the keeping of sabbaths and feasts, he not only nowhere enjoins, but puts a marked slight on the former, by commending the scribe who declared that the love of God and one's neighbour was *more than whole burnt-offerings and sacrifices*, as one *not far from the kingdom of God* (Mark xii. 23 f.),[2] and he ran counter in action as well as in speech to the customary mode of celebrating the Sabbath (Matt. xii. 1–13 ; Mark ii. 23–28, iii. 1–5 ; Luke vi. 1–10, xiii. 10 ff., xiv. 1 ff. ; John v. 5 ff., vii. 22, ix. 1 ff.), of which in his character of Son of Man he claimed to be Lord. The Jews, too, appear to have expected a revision of the Mosaic law by their Messiah.[3] A somewhat analogous sense is couched in the declarations attributed by the fourth Evangelist to Jesus (ii. 19); Matthew (xxvi. 61) and Mark (xiv. 58) represent him as being accused by false witnesses of saying, *I am able to destroy* (John, *destroy*) *the temple of God* (Mark, *that is made with hands*), *and to build it in three days* (Mark, *I will build another made without hands*). The author of the Acts has something similar as an article of accusation against Stephen, but instead of the latter half of the sentence it is thus added, *and* (he, *i.e.* Jesus) *shall change the customs which Moses delivered us* ; and perhaps this may be regarded as an authentic comment on the less explicit text. In general it may be said that to one who, like Jesus, is so far alive to the absolute value of the internal compared with the external, of the bent of the entire disposition compared with isolated acts, that he pronounces the love of God and our neighbour to be the essence of the law (Matt. xxii. 36 ff.),—to him it cannot be a secret, that all precepts of the law which do not bear on these two points are unessential. But the argument apparently most decisive of a design on the part of Jesus to abolish the Mosaic worship, is furnished by his prediction that the temple, the centre of Jewish worship (Matt. xxiv. 2 parall.), would be destroyed, and that the adoration of God would be freed from local fetters, and become purely spiritual (John iv. 21 ff.).

The above, however, presents only one aspect of the position assumed by Jesus towards the Mosaic law ; there are also data for the belief that he did not meditate the overthrow of the ancient constitution of his country. This side of the question has been, at a former period, and from easily-conceived reasons, the one which the enemies of Christianity in its ecclesiastical form, have chosen to exhibit ;[4] but it is only in recent times that, the theological

---

[1] E.g. Reinhard, Plan Jesu, s. 14 ff.
[2] For an exaggeration in the Ebionite Gospel, vid. Epiphanius, hæres. xxx. 16.
[3] Bertholdt, ut sup. § 31.
[4] This is done the most concisely in the Wolfenbüttel Fragments, von dem Zweck u. s. f., s. 66 ff.

horizon being extended, the unprejudiced expositors of the church [5] have acknowledged its existence.   In the first place, during his life Jesus remains faithful to the paternal law ; he attends the synagogue on the sabbath, journeys to Jerusalem at the time of the feast, and eats of the paschal lamb with his disciples. It is true that he heals on the sabbath, allows his disciples to pluck ears of corn (Matt. xii. 1 ff.), and requires no fasting or washing before meat in his society (Matt. iv. 14, xv. 2).   But the Mosaic law concerning the sabbath simply prescribed cessation from common labour, מְלָאכָה (Exod. xx. 8. ff., xxxi. 12 ff., Deut. v. 12 ff.), including ploughing, reaping (Exod. xxxiv. 21), gathering of sticks (Num. xv. 32 ff.), and similar work, and it was only the spirit of petty observance, the growth of a later age, that made it an offence to perform cures, or pluck a few ears of corn.[6] The washing of hands before eating was but a rabbinical custom ;[7] in the law one general yearly fast was alone prescribed (Lev. xvi. 29 ff., xxiii. 27 ff.) and no private fasting re-quired ; hence Jesus cannot be convicted of infringing the precepts of Moses.[8] In that very Sermon on the Mount in which Jesus exalts spiritual religion so far above all ritual, he clearly presupposes the continuation of sacrifices (Matt. v. 23 f.), and declares that he is not come to destroy the law and the prophets, but to fulfil (Matt. v. 17).   Even if πληρῶσαι, in all probability, refers chiefly to the accomplishment of the Old Testament prophecies, οὐκ ἦλθον καταλῦσαι must at the same time be understood of the conservation of the Mosaic law, since in the context, perpetuity is promised to its smallest letter, and he who represents its lightest precept as not obligatory, is threatened with the lowest rank in the kingdom of heaven.[9]   In accordance with this, the apostles adhered strictly to the Mosaic law, even after the feast of Pentecost ; they went at the hour of prayer into the temple (Acts iii. 1), clung to the syna-gogues and to the Mosaic injunctions respecting food (x. 14), and were unable to appeal to any express declaration of Jesus as a sanction for the procedure of Barnabas and Paul, when the judaizing party complained of their baptizing Gentiles without laying on them the burthen of the Mosaic law.

This apparent contradiction in the conduct and language of Jesus has been apologetically explained by the supposition, that not only the personal obedi-ence of Jesus to the law, but also his declarations in its favour, were a necessary concession to the views of his cotemporaries, who would at once have withdrawn their confidence from him, had he announced himself as the destroyer of their holy and venerated law.[10]   We allow that the obedience of Jesus to the law in his own person, might be explained in the same way as that of Paul, which, on his own showing, was a measure of mere expediency (1 Cor. ix. 20, comp. Acts xvi. 3).   But the strong declarations of Jesus con-cerning the perpetuity of the law, and the guilt of him who dares to violate its lightest precept, cannot possibly be derived from the principle of conces-sion ; for to pronounce that indispensable, which one secretly holds superfluous, and which one even seeks to bring gradually into disuse, would, leaving honesty out of the question, be in the last degree injudicious.

Hence others have made a distinction between the moral and the ritual law, and referred the declaration of Jesus that he wished not to abrogate the law, to the former alone, which he extricated from a web of trivial cere-

---

[5] Especially Fritzsche, in Matt., s. 214 ff.
[6] Winer, bibl. Realwörterb. 2, s. 406 ff.
[7] Comp. Paulus, exeg. Handb. 2, s. 273.
[8] Winer, b. Realw., 1 Bd. s. 426.
[9] Fritzsche, s. 214 ff.
[10] Reinhard, s. 15 ff.   Planck, Geschichte des Christenthums in der Periode seiner Einführung, 1, s. 175 ff.

monies, and embodied in his own example.[11] But such a distinction is not found in those striking passages from the Sermon on the Mount; rather in the νόμος and προφῆται, *the law and the prophets*, we have the most comprehensive designation of the whole religious constitution of the Old Testament,[12] and under the most trivial commandment, and the smallest letter of the law, alike pronounced imperishable, we cannot well understand anything else than the ceremonial precepts.[13]

A happier distinction is that between really Mosaic institutes, and their traditional amplifications.[14] It is certain that the sabbath cures of Jesus, his neglect of the pedantic ablutions before eating, and the like, ran counter, not to Moses, but to later rabbinical requirements, and several discourses of Jesus turn upon this distinction. Matt. xv. 3 ff., Jesus places the commandment of God in opposition to the tradition of the elders, and Matt. xxiii. 23, he declares that where they are compatible, the former may be observed without rejecting the latter, in which case he admonishes the people to do all that the scribes and Pharisees enjoin ; where, on the contrary, either the one or the other only can be respected, he decides that it is better to transgress the tradition of the elders, than the commandment of God as given by Moses (Matt. xv. 3 ff.). He describes the mass of traditional precepts, as a burthen grievous to be borne, which he would remove from the oppressed people, substituting his own light burthen and easy yoke ; whence it may be seen, that with all his forbearance towards existing institutions, so far as they were not positively pernicious, it was his intention that all these *commandments of men*, as plants which his heavenly Father had not planted, should be rooted up (xv. 9, 13). The majority of the Pharisaical precepts referred to externals, and had the effect of burying the noble morality of the Mosaic law under a heap of ceremonial observances ; a gift to the temple sufficed to absolve the giver from his filial duties (xv. 5), and the payment of tithe of anise and cummin superseded justice, mercy, and faith (xxiii. 23). Hence this distinction is in some degree identical with the former, since in the rabbinical institutes it was their merely ceremonial tendency that Jesus censured, while, in the Mosaic law, it was the kernel of religion and morality that he chiefly valued. It must only not be contended that he regarded the Mosaic law as permanent solely in its spiritual part, for the passages quoted, especially from the Sermon on the Mount, clearly show that he did not contemplate the abolition of the merely ritual precepts.

Jesus, supposing that he had discerned morality and the spiritual worship of God to be the sole essentials in religion, must have rejected all which, being merely ritual and formal, had usurped the importance of a religious obligation, and under this description must fall a large proportion of the Mosaic precepts ; but it is well known how slowly such consequences are deduced, when they come into collision with usages consecrated by antiquity. Even Samuel, apparently, was aware that obedience is better than sacrifice (1 Sam. xv. 22), and Asaph, that an offering of thanksgiving is more acceptable to God than one of slain animals (Ps. l.) ; yet how long after were sacrifices retained together with true obedience, or in its stead ! Jesus was more thoroughly penetrated with this conviction than those ancients ; with him, the true commandments of God in the Mosaic law were simply, *Honour thy father and thy mother, Thou shalt not kill*, etc., and above all, *Thou shalt love the Lord thy God with all thy heart, and thy neighbour as thyself*. But

[11] De Wette, Bibl. Dogm., § 210.
[12] Fritzsche, s. 214.
[13] Vid. the Fragmentist, s. 69.
[14] Paulus, exeg. Handb. 1, b, s. 600 f. Leben Jesu, 1, a, s. 296, 312.

his deep-rooted respect for the sacred book of the law, caused him, for the sake of these essential contents, to honour the unessential; which was the more natural, as in comparison with the absurdly exaggerated pedantry of the traditional observances, the ritual of the Pentateuch must have appeared highly simple.   To honour this latter part of the law as of Divine origin, but to declare it abrogated on the principle, that in the education of the human race, God finds necessary for an earlier period an arrangement which is superfluous for a later one, implies that idea of *the law* as *a schoolmaster*, νόμος παιδαγωγὸς (Gal. iii. 24), which seems first to have been developed by the Apostle Paul; nevertheless, its germ lies in the declaration of Jesus, that God had permitted to the early Hebrews, *on account of the hardness of their hearts* (Matt. xix. 8 f.), many things which, in a more advanced state of culture, were inadmissible.

A similar limitation of the duration of the law is involved in the predictions of Jesus (if indeed they were uttered by Jesus, a point which we have to discuss), that the temple would be destroyed at his approaching advent (Matt. xxiv. parall.), and that devotion would be freed from all local restrictions (John iv.); for with these must fall the entire Mosaic system of external worship.   This is not contradicted by the declaration that the law would endure until heaven and earth should pass away (Matt. v. 18), for the Hebrew associated the fall of his state and sanctuary with the end of the old world or dispensation, so that the expressions, so long as the temple stands, and so long as the world stands, were equivalent.[15]   It is true that the words of Jesus, Luke xvi. 16, ὁ νόμος καὶ οἱ προφῆται ἕως Ἰωάννου, seem to imply, that the appearance of the Baptist put an end to the validity of the law; but this passage loses its depreciatory sense when compared with its parallel, Matt. xi. 13.   On the other hand, Luke xvi. 17 controls Matt. v. 18, and reduces it to a mere comparison between the stability of the law, and that of heaven and earth.   The only question then is, in which of the gospels are the two passages more correctly stated?   As given in the first, they intimate that the law would retain its supremacy until, and not after, the close of the old dispensation.   With this agrees the prediction, that the temple would be destroyed; for the spiritualization of religion, and, according to Stephen's interpretation, the abolition of the Mosaic law, which were to be the results of that event, were undoubtedly identified by Jesus with the commencement of the αἰὼν μέλλων of the Messiah.   Hence it appears, that the only difference between the view of Paul and that of Jesus is this: that the latter anticipated the extinction of the Mosaic system as a concomitant of his glorious advent or return to the regenerated earth, while the former believed its abolition permissible on the old, unregenerated earth, in virtue of the Messiah's first advent.[16]

§ 68.

SCOPE OF THE MESSIANIC PLAN OF JESUS.   RELATION TO THE GENTILES.*

Although the church founded by Jesus did, in fact, early extend itself beyond the limits of the Jewish people, there are yet indications which might induce a belief that he did not contemplate such an extension.[1]   When he sends the twelve on their first mission, his command is, *Go not into the way*

[15] Comp. Paulus, exeg. Handb. 1, b, s. 598 f.
[16] Comp. Hase, L. J., s. 84.   Rabbinical notions of the abrogation of the Law in Schöttgen, ii. s. 611 ff.
[1] Thus the Wolfenbüttel Fragmentist, ut sup. s. 72 ff.

of the Gentiles—Go rather to the lost sheep of the house of Israel (Matt. x. 5 f.).
That Matthew alone has this injunction, and not the two other synoptists, is
less probably explained by the supposition that the Hebrew author of the
first gospel interpolated it, than by the opposite one, namely, that it was
wilfully omitted by the Hellenistic authors of the second and third gospels.
For, as the judaizing tendency of Matthew is not so marked that he assigns
to Jesus the intention of limiting the messianic kingdom to the Jews; as, on
the contrary, he makes Jesus unequivocally foretell the calling of the Gentiles
(viii. 11 f., xxi. 33 ff., xxii. 1 ff., xxviii. 19 f.) : he had no motive for fabricating
this particularizing addition ; but the two other Evangelists had a strong one
for its omission, in the offence which it would cause to the Gentiles already
within the fold. Its presence in Matthew, however, demands an explanation,
and expositors have thought to furnish one by supposing the injunction of
Jesus to be a measure of prudence.[2] It is unquestionable that, even if the
plan of Jesus comprehended the Gentiles as well as the Jews, he must at
first, if he would not for ever ruin his cause with his fellow-countrymen,
adopt, and prescribe to the disciples, a rule of national exclusiveness. This
necessity on his part might account for his answer to the Canaanitish woman,
whose daughter he refuses to heal, because he was only sent to the lost sheep
of the house of Israel (Matt. xv. 24), were it not that the boon which he
here denies is not a reception into the messianic kingdom, but a temporal
benefit, such as even Elijah and Elisha had conferred on those who were
not Israelites (1 Kings xvii. 9 ff. ; 2 Kings v. 1 ff.)—examples to which Jesus
elsewhere appeals (Luke iv. 25 ff.). Hence the disciples thought it natural
and unobjectionable to grant the woman's petition, and it could not be
prudential considerations that withheld Jesus, for a time, from compliance.
That an aversion to the Gentiles may not appear to be his motive, it has
been conjectured[3] that Jesus, wishing to preserve an incognito in that country,
avoided the performance of any messianic work. But such a design of concealment is only mentioned by Mark (vii. 25), who represents it as being
defeated by the entreaties of the woman, contrary to the inclinations of
Jesus ; and as this Evangelist omits the declaration of Jesus, that he was not
sent but to the lost sheep of the house of Israel, we must suspect that he
was guided by the wish to supply a less offensive motive for the conduct of
Jesus, rather than by historical accuracy. Had Jesus really been influenced
by the motive which Mark assigns, he must at once have alleged it to his
disciples instead of a merely ostensible one, calculated to strengthen their
already rigid exclusiveness. We should therefore rather listen to the opinion
that Jesus sought, by his repeated refusal, to prove the faith of the woman,
and furnish an occasion for its exhibition,[4] if we could find in the text the
slightest trace of mere dissimulation ; and none of a real change of mind.[5]
Even Mark, bent as he was on softening the features of the incident, cannot
have thought of a dissimulation of this kind ; otherwise, instead of omitting
the harsh words and making the inadequate addition, *and would have no man
know it,* he would have removed the offence in the most satisfactory manner,
by an observation such as, *he said this to prove her* (comp. John vi. 6). Thus
it must be allowed that Jesus in this case seems to share the antipathy of
his countrymen towards the Gentiles, nay, his antipathy seems to be of a
deeper stamp than that of his disciples ; unless their advocacy of the woman

---

[2] Reinhard ; Planck, Geschichte des Christenthums in der Per. seiner Einführung,
I, s. 179 ff.
[3] Paulus, Leben Jesu. 1, a, s. 380 f. Hase, L. J., § 102.
[4] Olshausen, 1, s. 507.
[5] Hase, ut sup.

be a touch from the pencil of tradition, for the sake of contrast and grouping.

This narrative, however, is neutralized by another, in which Jesus is said to act in a directly opposite manner. The centurion of Capernaum, also a Gentile (as we gather from the remarks of Jesus), has scarcely complained of a distress similar to that of the Canaanitish woman, when Jesus himself volunteers to go and heal his servant (Matt. viii. 5). If, then, Jesus has no hesitation, in this instance, to exercise his power of healing in favour of a heathen, how comes it that he refuses to do so in another quite analogous case ? Truly if the relative position of the two narratives in the gospels have any weight, he must have shown himself more harsh and narrow at the later period than at the earlier one. Meanwhile, this single act of benevolence to a Gentile, standing as it does in inexplicable contradiction to the narrative above examined, cannot prove, in opposition to the command expressly given to the disciples, not to go to the Gentiles, that Jesus contemplated their admission as such into the messianic kingdom.

Even the prediction of Jesus that the kingdom of heaven would be taken from the Jews and given to the Gentiles, does not prove this. In the above interview with the centurion of Capernaum, Jesus declares that *many shall come from the east and the west*, and sit down with the patriarchs in *the kingdom of heaven*, while the *children of the kingdom* (obviously the Jews), for whom it was originally designed, will be cast out (Matt. viii. 11 f.). Yet more decidedly, when applying the parable of the husbandmen in the vineyard, he warns his countrymen that *the kingdom of God shall be taken from them, and given to a nation bringing forth the fruits thereof* (Matt. xxi. 43). All this may be understood in the sense intended by the prophets, in their promises that the messianic kingdom would extend to all nations ; namely, that the Gentiles would turn to the worship of Jehovah, embrace the Mosaic religion in its entire form, and afterwards be received into the Messiah's kingdom. It would accord very well with this expectation, that, prior to such a conversion, Jesus should forbid his disciples to direct their announcement of his kingdom to the Gentiles.

But in the discourses concerning his re-appearance, Jesus regards the publication of the gospel to all nations as one of the circumstances that must precede that event (Matt. xxiv. 14 ; Mark xiii. 10) ; and after his resurrection, according to the synoptists, he gave his disciples the command, *Go ye, and teach all nations, baptizing them*, etc. (Matt. xxviii. 19 ; Mark xvi. 15 ; Luke xxiv. 47) ; i.e. go to them with the offer of the Messiah's kingdom, even though they may not beforehand have become Jews. Not only, however, do the disciples, after the first Pentecost, neglect to execute this command, but when a case is thrust on them which offers them an opportunity for compliance with it, they act as if they were altogether ignorant that such a direction had been given by Jesus (Acts x., xi.). The heathen centurion Cornelius, worthy, from his devout life, of a reception into the messianic community, is pointed out by an angel to the Apostle Peter. But because it was not hidden from God, with what difficulty the apostle would be induced to receive a heathen, without further preliminary, into the Messiah's kingdom, he saw it needful to prepare him for such a step by a symbolical vision. In consequence of such an admonition Peter goes to Cornelius ; but to impel him to baptize him and his family, he needs a second sign, the pouring out of the Holy Ghost on these uncircumcised. When, subsequently, the Jewish Christians in Jerusalem call him to account for this reception of Gentiles, Peter appeals in his justification solely to the recent vision, and to the Holy Ghost given to the centurion's family. Whatever judgment we may form of the credibility of this history, it is a memorial of the many deliberations and contentions which it cost the apostles after the departure of Jesus, to convince themselves of the eligibility of Gentiles for a participation in the kingdom of their Christ, and the reasons which at last brought them to a decision. Now if Jesus had given so explicit a command as that above quoted, what need was there of a vision to encourage Peter to its fulfilment? or, supposing the vision to be a legendary investiture of the natural deliberations of the disciples, why did they go about in search of the reflection, that all men ought to be baptized, because before God all men and all animals, as his creatures, are clean, if they could have appealed to an express injunction of Jesus? Here, then, is the alternative: if Jesus himself gave this command, the disciples cannot have been led to the admission of the Gentiles by the means narrated in Acts x., xi.; if, on the other hand, that narrative is authentic, the alleged command of Jesus cannot be historical. Our canon decides for the latter proposition. For that the subsequent practice and pre-eminent distinction of the Christian Church, its accessibility to all nations, and its indifference to circumcision or uncircumcision, should have lain in the mind of its founder, is the view best adapted to exalt and adorn Jesus; while that, after his death, and through the gradual development of relations, the church, which its Founder had designed for the Gentiles only in so far as they became Jews, should break through these limits, is in the simple, natural, and therefore the probable course of things.

§ 69.

RELATION OF THE MESSIANIC PLAN OF JESUS TO THE SAMARITANS. HIS INTERVIEW WITH THE WOMAN OF SAMARIA.

There is the same apparent contradiction in the position which Jesus took, and prescribed to his disciples, towards the inhabitants of Samaria. While in his instructions to his disciples (Matt. x. 5), he forbids them to visit any city of the Samaritans, we read in John (iv.) that Jesus himself in his journey through Samaria laboured as the Messiah with great effect, and ultimately stayed two days in a Samaritan town; and in the Acts (i. 8), that before his ascension he charged the disciples to be his witnesses, not only in Jerusalem and in all Judea, but also in Samaria. That Jesus did not entirely shun Samaria, as that prohibition might appear to intimate, is evident from Luke ix. 52 (comp. xvii. 11), where his disciples bespeak lodgings for him in a Samaritan village, when he has determined to go to Jerusalem; a circumstance which accords with the information of Josephus, that those Galileans who journeyed to the feasts usually went through Samaria.[1] That Jesus was not unfavourable to the Samaritans, nay, that in many respects he acknowledged their superiority to the Jews, is evident from his parable of the Good Samaritan (Luke x. 30 ff.); he also bestows a marked notice on the case of a Samaritan, who, among ten cleansed, was the only one that testified his gratitude (Luke xvii. 16); and, if we may venture on such a conclusion from John iv. 25, and subsequent records,[2] the inhabitants of Samaria themselves had some tincture of the messianic idea.

However natural it may appear that Jesus should avail himself of this susceptible side of the Samaritans, by opportunely announcing to them the

---

[1] Antiq. xx. vi. 1. For some rabbinical rules not quite in accordance with this, see Lightfoot, p. 991.
[2] Bertholdt, Christol. Judæor., § 7.

messianic kingdom ; the aspect which the four Evangelists bear to each other on this subject must excite surprise.   Matthew has no occasion on which Jesus comes in contact with the Samaritans, or even mentions them, except in the prohibition above quoted; Mark is more neutral than Matthew, and has not even that prohibition ; Luke has two instances of contact, one of them unfavourable, the other favourable, together with the parable in which Jesus presents a Samaritan as a model, and his approving notice of the gratitude of one whom he had healed ; John, finally, has a narrative in which Jesus appears in a very intimate and highly favourable relation to the Samaritans.   Are all these various accounts well founded ? If so, how could Jesus at one time prohibit his disciples from including the Samaritans in the messianic plan, and at another time, himself receive them without hesitation ? Moreover, if the chronological order of the Evangelists deserve regard, the ministry of Jesus in Samaria must have preceded the prohibition contained in his instructions to his disciples on their first mission.   For the scene of that mission being Galilee, and there being no space for its occurrence during the short stay which, according to the fourth Evangelist, Jesus made in that province before the first Passover (ii. 1–13), it must be placed after that Passover ; and, as the visit to Samaria was made on his journey, after that visit also.   How, then, could Jesus, after having with the most desirable issue, personally taught in Samaria, and presented himself as the Messiah, forbid his disciples to carry thither their messianic tidings?   On the other hand, if the scenes narrated by John occurred after the command recorded by Matthew, the disciples, instead of wondering that Jesus talked so earnestly with a *woman* (John iv. 27), ought rather to have wondered that he held any converse with a *Samaritan*.[3]

Since then of the two extreme narratives at least, in Matthew and John, neither presupposes the other, we must either doubt the authenticity of the exclusive command of Jesus, or of his connexion with the inhabitants of Samaria.

In this conflict between the gospels, we have again the advantage of appealing to the Book of Acts as an umpire.   Before Peter, at the divine instigation, had received the firstfruits of the Gentiles into the Messiah's kingdom, Philip the deacon, being driven from Jerusalem by the persecution of which Stephen's death was the commencement, journeyed to the city of Samaria, where he preached Christ, and by miracles of all kinds won the Samaritans to the faith, and to the reception of baptism (Acts viii. 5 ff.). This narrative is a complete contrast to that of the first admission of the Gentiles : while in the one there was need of a vision, and a special intimation from the Spirit, to bring Peter into communication with the heathens ; in the other, Philip, without any precedent, unhesitatingly baptizes the Samaritans.   And lest it should be said that the deacon was perhaps of a more liberal spirit than the apostle, we have Peter himself coming forthwith to Samaria in company with John,—an incident which forms another point of opposition between the two narratives; for, while the first admission of the Gentiles makes a highly unfavourable impression on the mother church at Jerusalem, the report that *Samaria had received the word of God* meets with so warm an approval there, that the two most distinguished apostles are commissioned to confirm and consummate the work begun by Philip. The tenor of this proceeding makes it not improbable that there was a precedent for it in the conduct of Jesus, or at least a sanction in his expressions.

---

[3] Some erroneously attribute this meaning to their question ; see in Lücke 1, s. 533.

The narrative in the fourth Gospel (iv.) would form a perfect precedent in the conduct of Jesus, but we have yet to examine whether it bears the stamp of historical credibility. We do not, with the author of the Probabilia, stumble at the designation of the locality, and the opening of the conversation between Jesus and the woman;[4] but from v. 16 inclusively, there are, as impartial expositors confess,[5] many grave difficulties. The woman had entreated Jesus to give her of the water which was for ever to extinguish thirst, and Jèsus immediately says, *Go, call thy husband.* Why so? It has been said that Jesus, well knowing that the woman had no lawful husband, sought to shame her, and bring her to repentance.[6] Lücke, disapproving the imputation of dissimulation to Jesus, conjectures that, perceiving the woman's dulness, he hoped by summoning her husband, possibly her superior in intelligence, to create an opportunity for a more beneficial conversation. But if Jesus, as it presently appears, knew that the woman had not at the time any proper husband, he could not in earnest desire her to summon him; and if, as Lücke allows, he had that knowledge in a supernatural manner, it could not be hidden from him, who knew what was in man, that she would be little inclined to comply with his injunction. If, however, he had a prescience that what he required would not be done, the injunction was a feint, and had some latent object. But that this object was the penitence of the woman there is no indication in the text, for the ultimate effect on her is not shame and penitence, but faith in the prophetic insight of Jesus (v. 19). And this was doubtless what Jesus wished, for the narrative proceeds as if he had attained his purpose with the woman, and the issue corresponded to the design. The difficulty here lies, not so much in what Lücke terms dissimulation,—since this comes under the category of blameless temptation ($\pi\epsilon\iota\rho\acute{a}\zeta\epsilon\iota\nu$), elsewhere occurring,—as in the violence with which Jesus wrests an opportunity for the display of his prophetic gifts.

By a transition equally abrupt, the woman urges the conversation to a point at which the Messiahship of Jesus may become fully evident. As soon as she has recognised Jesus to be a prophet, she hastens to consult him on the controversy pending between the Jews and Samaritans, as to the place appropriated to the true worship of God (v. 20). That so vivid an interest in this national and religious question is not consistent with the limited mental and circumstantial condition of the woman, the majority of modern commentators virtually confess, by their adoption of the opinion, that her drift in this remark was to turn away the conversation from her own affairs.[7] If then the implied query concerning the place for the true worship of God, had no serious interest for the woman, but was prompted by a false shame calculated to hinder confession and repentance, those expositors should remember what they elsewhere repeat to satiety,[8] that in the Gospel of John the answers of Jesus refer not so much to the ostensible meaning of questions, as to the under current of feeling of which they are the indications. In accordance with this method, Jesus should not have answered the artificial question of the woman as if it had been one of deep seriousness; he ought rather to have evaded it, and recurred to the already detected stain on her conscience, which she was now seeking to hide, in order if possible to bring her to a full conviction and open avowal of her guilt. But the fact is that the object of the Evangelist was to show that Jesus had been recognised,

---

[4] Bretschneider, ut sup. s. 47 ff. 97 f.
[5] Lücke, 1, s. 520 ff.
[6] Tholück, in loc.
[7] Lücke and Tholück, in loc. Hase, L. J., 67.
[8] E.g. Tholück, in many passages.

not merely as a prophet, but as the Messiah, and he believed that to turn
the conversation to the question of the legitimate place for the worship of
God, the solution of which was expected from the Messiah,[9] would best
conduce to that end.

Jesus evinces (v. 17) an acquaintance with the past history and present
position of the woman. The rationalists have endeavoured to explain this
by the supposition, that while Jesus sat at the well, and the woman was
advancing from the city, some passer-by hinted to him that he had better
not engage in conversation with her, as she was on the watch to obtain a
sixth husband.[10]   But not to insist on the improbability that a passer-by
should hold a colloquy with Jesus on the character of an obscure woman,
the friends as well as the enemies of the fourth gospel now agree, that every
natural explanation of that knowledge on the part of Jesus, directly counter-
acts the design of the Evangelist.[11] For, according to him, the disclosure
which Jesus makes of his privity to the woman's intimate concerns, is the
immediate cause, not only of her own faith in him, but of that of many
inhabitants of the city (v. 39), and he obviously intends to imply that they
were not too precipitate in receiving him as a prophet, on that ground alone.
Thus in the view of the Evangelist, the knowledge in question was an
effluence of the higher nature of Jesus, and modern supranaturalists adhere
to this explanation, adducing in its support the power which John attributes
to him (ii. 24 f.), of discerning what is in man without the aid of external
testimony.[12]   But this does not meet the case ; for Jesus here not only knows
what is in the woman,—her present equivocal state of mind towards him
who is not her husband,—he has cognizance also of the extrinsic fact that
she has had five husbands, of whom we cannot suppose that each had left
a distinct image in her mind traceable by the observation of Jesus.   That by
means of the penetrative acumen with which he scrutinized the hearts of
those with whom he had to do, Jesus should also have a prophetic insight
into his own messianic destiny, and the fortunes of his kingdom, may under
a certain view of his person appear probable, and in any case must be
deemed in the highest degree dignified ; but that he should be acquainted,
even to the most trivial details, with the adventitious history of obscure
individuals, is an idea that degrades him in proportion to the exaltation of
his prophetic dignity. Such empirical *knowingness* (not omniscience) would
moreover annihilate the human consciousness which the orthodox view supposes to co-exist in Jesus.[13] But the possession of this knowledge, however
it may clash with our conception of dignity and wisdom, closely corresponds
to the Jewish notion of a prophet, more especially of the Messiah ; in the
Old Testament, Daniel recites a dream of Nebuchadnezzar, which that
monarch himself had forgotten (Dan. ii.) ; in the Clementine Homilies, the
true prophet is ὁ πάντοτε πάντα εἰδώς· τὰ μὲν γεγονότα ὡς ἐγένετο, τὰ δὲ γινόμενα
ὡς γίνεται, τὰ δὲ ἐσόμενα ὡς ἔσται ;[14] and the rabbins number such a knowledge of personal secrets among the signs of the Messiah, and observe that
from the want of it, Bar-Cocheba was detected to be a pseudo-Messiah.[15]

Farther on (v. 23) Jesus reveals to the woman what Hase terms the
sublimest principle of his religion, namely, that the service of God consists

---

[9] Comp. Schöttgen, horæ, i. s. 970 f.   Wetstein, s. 863.
[10] Paulus, Leben Jesu, I, a, 187 ; Comment. 4, in loc.
[11] Comp. Olshausen in loc., and Bretschneider, Probab., s. 50.
[12] Olshausen, Lücke, in loc.
[13] Comp. Bretschneider, ut sup. s. 49 f.
[14] Homil. ii. 6, comp. iii. 12.
[15] Schöttgen, horæ, ii. p. 371 f.

in a life of piety; tells her that all ceremonial worship is about to be abolished; and that he is the personage who will effect this momentous change, that is, the Messiah. We have already shown it to be improbable that Jesus, who did not give his disciples to understand that he was the Messiah until a comparatively late period, should make an early and distinct disclosure on the subject to a Samaritan woman. In what respect was she worthy of a communication more explicit than ever fell to the lot of the disciples? What could induce Jesus to send roaming into the futurity of religious history, the contemplation of a woman, whom he should rather have induced to examine herself, and to ponder on the corruptions of her own heart? Nothing but the wish to elicit from her, at any cost, and without regard to her moral benefit, an acknowledgment, not only of his prophetic gifts, but of his Messiahship; to which end it was necessary to give the conversation the above direction. But so contracted a design can never be imputed to Jesus, who, on other occasions, exemplifies a more suitable mode of dealing with mankind: it is the design of the glorifying legend, or of an idealizing biographer.

Meanwhile, continues the narrative (v. 27), the disciples of Jesus returned from the city with provisions, and marvelled that he talked with a woman, contrary to rabbinical rule.[16] While the woman, excited by the last disclosure of Jesus, hastens homeward to invite her fellow-citizens to come and behold the Messiah-like stranger, the disciples entreat him to partake of the food they have procured; he answers, *I have meat to eat that ye know not of* (v. 32). They, misunderstanding his words, imagine that some person has supplied him with food in their absence: one of those carnal interpretations of expressions intended spiritually by Jesus, which are of perpetual recurrence in the fourth gospel, and are therefore suspicious. Then follows a discourse on sowing and reaping (v. 35 ff.), which, compared with v. 37, can only mean that what Jesus has sown, the disciples will reap.[17] We admit that this is susceptible of the general interpretation, that the germ of the kingdom of God, which blossomed and bore fruit under the cultivation of the apostles, was first deposited in the world by Jesus: but it cannot be denied that a special application is also intended. Jesus foresees that the woman, who is hastening towards the city, will procure him an opportunity of sowing the seed of the gospel in Samaria, and he promises the disciples that they at a future time shall reap the fruits of his labours. Who is not here reminded of the propagation of Christianity in Samaria by Philip and the apostles, as narrated in the Acts?[18] That, even abstracting all supernaturalism from our idea of the person of Jesus, he might have foreseen this progress of his cause in Samaria from his knowledge of its inhabitants, is not to be denied; but as the above figurative prediction forms part of a whole more than improbable in an historical point of view, it is equally liable to suspicion, especially as it is easy to show how it might originate without any foundation in fact. According to the prevalent tradition of the early church, as recorded in the synoptical gospels, Jesus laboured personally in Galilee, Judea, and Perea only,—not in Samaria, which, however, as we learn from the Acts, embraced the gospel at no remote period from his death. How natural the tendency to perfect the agency of Jesus, by representing him to have sown the heavenly seed in Samaria, thus extending his ministry through all parts of Palestine; to limit the glory of the apostles and other teachers to that of being the

[16] Lightfoot, p. 1002.
[17] Lücke, I, s. 542.
[18] Lücke, s. 540, note. Bretschneider, s. 52.

mere reapers of the harvest in Samaria; and to put this distinction, on a suitable occasion, into the mouth of Jesus!

The result, then, of our examination of John's Samaritan narrative is, that we cannot receive it as a real history: and the impression which it leaves as a whole tends to the same conclusion. Since Heracleon and Origen,[19] the more ancient commentators have seldom refrained from giving the interview of Jesus with the woman of Samaria an allegorical interpretation, on the ground that the entire scene has a legendary and poetic colouring. Jesus is seated at a well,—that idyllic locality with which the old Hebrew legend associates so many critical incidents; at the identical well, moreover, which a tradition, founded on Gen. xxxiii. 19, xlviii. 22; Josh. xxiv. 32, reported to have been given by Jacob to his son Joseph; hence the spot, in addition to its idyllic interest, has the more decided consecration of national and patriarchal recollections, and is all the more worthy of being trodden by the Messiah. At the well Jesus meets with a woman who has come out to draw water, just as, in the Old Testament, the expectant Eliezer encounters Rebekah with her pitcher, and as Jacob meets with Rachel, the destined ancestress of Israel, or Moses with his future wife. Jesus begs of the woman to let him drink; so does Eliezer of Rebekah; after Jesus has made himself known to the woman as the Messiah, she runs back to the city, and fetches her neighbours: so Rebekah, after Eliezer has announced himself as Abraham's steward, and Rachel, after she has discovered that Jacob is her kinsman, hasten homeward to call their friends to welcome the honoured guest. It is, certainly, not one blameless as those early mothers in Israel, whom Jesus here encounters; for this woman came forth as the representative of an impure people, who had been faithless to their marriage bond with Jehovah, and were then living in the practice of a false worship; while her good-will, her deficient moral strength, and her obtuseness in spiritual things, perfectly typify the actual state of the Samaritans. Thus, the interview of Jesus with the woman of Samaria is only a poetical representation of his ministry among the Samaritans narrated in the sequel; and this is itself a legendary prelude to the propagation of the gospel in Samaria after the death of Jesus.

Renouncing the event in question as unhistorical, we know nothing of any connexion formed by Jesus with the Samaritans, and there remain as indications of his views regarding them, only his favourable notice of an individual from among them (Luke xvii. 16); his unpropitious reception in one of their villages (Luke ix. 53); the prohibition with respect to them, addressed to his disciples (Matt. x. 5); the eulogistic parable (Luke x. 30 ff.); and his valedictory command, that the gospel should be preached in Samaria (Acts i. 8). This express command being subsequent to the resurrection of Jesus, its reality must remain problematical for us until we have examined the evidence for that capital fact; and it is to be questioned whether without it, and notwithstanding the alleged prohibition, the unhesitating conduct of the apostles, Acts viii., can be explained. Are we then to suppose on the part of the apostolic history, a cancelling of hesitations and deliberations that really occurred; or on the part of Matthew, an unwarranted ascription of national bigotry to Jesus; or, finally, on the part of Jesus, a progressive enlargement of view?

[19] Comm. in Joan, tom. 13.

CHAPTER V.

THE DISCIPLES OF JESUS.

§ 70.

THE first two Evangelists agree in stating that Jesus, when walking by the sea of Galilee, called, first, the two brothers Andrew and Peter, and immediately after, James and John, to forsake their fishing nets, and to follow him (Matt. iv. 18–22 ; Mark i. 16–20). The fourth Evangelist also narrates (i. 35–51), how the first disciples came to attach themselves to Jesus, and among them we find Peter and Andrew, and, in all probability, John, for it is generally agreed that the nameless companion of Andrew was that ultimately favourite apostle. James is absent from this account, and instead of his vocation, we have that of Philip and Nathanael. But even when the persons are the same, all the particulars of their meeting with Jesus are variously detailed. In the two synoptical gospels, the scene is the coast of the Galilean sea : in the fourth, Andrew, Peter, and their anonymous friend, unite themselves to Jesus in the vicinity of the Jordan ; Philip and Nathanael, on the way from thence into Galilee. In the former, again, Jesus in two instances calls a pair of brothers ; in the latter, it is first Andrew and his companion, then Peter, and anon Philip and Nathanael, who meet with Jesus. But the most important difference is this : while, in Matthew and Mark, the brethren are called from their fishing immediately by Jesus ; in John, nothing more is said of the respective situations of those who were summoned, than that they *come*, and *are found*, and Jesus himself calls only Philip ; Andrew and his nameless companion being directed to him by the Baptist, Peter brought by Andrew, and Nathanael by Philip.

Thus the two narratives appear to refer to separate events ; and if it be asked which of those events was prior to the other, we must reply that John seems to assign the earlier date to his incidents, for he represents them as taking place before the return of Jesus from the scene of his baptism into Galilee ; while the synoptists place theirs after that journey, especially if, according to a calculation often adopted, we regard the return into Galilee, which they make so important an epoch, as being that from the first Passover, not from the baptism. It is evident, too, from the intrinsic nature of the occurrences reported by the fourth Evangelist, that they could not have succeeded those in Matthew and Mark. For if, as these writers tells us, Andrew and John had alteady followed Jesus, they could not again be in the train of the Baptist, as we see them in the fourth gospel, nor would it have been necessary for that teacher to have directed their attention to Jesus ; neither if Peter had already been called by Jesus himself to become a fisher of men, was there any need for his brother Andrew to bring him to his already elected master. Nevertheless, expositors with one voice declare that the two narratives are equally adapted to precede, or follow, each other. The fourth gospel, say they,[1] recounts merely the first introduction of these men to Jesus ; they did not forthwith become his constant followers, but were first installed by Jesus in their proper discipleship on the occasion which the synoptists have preserved.

Let us test the justness of their view. In the synoptical narrative Jesus says to his future disciples, *Come after me*, δεῦτε ὀπίσω μου, and the result is that they follow him (ἠκολούθησαν αὐτῷ). If we understand from this that the disciples thenceforth constantly followed Jesus, how can we give a different interpretation to the similar expression in the fourth gospel, *Follow me*, ἀκολούθει μοι? It is therefore a laudable consistency in Paulus, to see, in both instances, merely an invitation to a temporary companionship during a walk in the immediate neighbourhood.[2] But this interpretation is incompatible with the synoptical history. How could Peter, at a later period, say so emphatically to Jesus, *We have left all, and followed thee : what shall we have therefore ?*—how could Jesus promise to him and to every one who had forsaken houses, etc., a hundredfold recompense (Matt. xix. 27 ff.), if this forsaking and following had been so transient and interrupted? From these considerations alone it is probable that the ἀκολούθει μοι in John also denotes the commencement of a permanent connexion ; but there are besides the plainest indications that this is the case in the context to the narrative. Precisely as in the synoptical gospels, Jesus appears alone before the scene of the vocation, but after this on every fit occasion the attendance of his disciples is mentioned : so in the fourth gospel, from the time of the occurrence in question, the previously solitary Jesus appears in the company of his disciples (ii. 2, xii. 17, iii. 22, iv. 8, 27, etc.). To say that these disciples, acquired in Peræa, again dispersed themselves after the return of Jesus into Galilee,[3] is to do violence to the gospels out of harmonistic zeal. But even supposing such a dispersion, they could not, in the short time which it is possible to allow for their separation from Jesus, have become so completely strangers to him, that he would have been obliged to re-open an acquaintance with them after the manner narrated by the synoptical writers. Still less probable is it that Jesus, after having distinguished Simon in the most individual manner by the surname Cephas on their first interview, would on a later occasion address to him the summons to be a *fisher of men*—a destination which was common to all the disciples.

The rationalistic commentators perceive a special advantage in their position of the two narratives. It accounts, say they, for what must otherwise be in the highest degree surprising, namely, that Jesus merely in passing, and at the first glance, should choose four fishermen for his disciples, and that among them he should have alighted on the two most distinguished apostles ; that, moreover, these four men, actively employed in their business, should leave it on the instant of their receiving an enigmatical summons from a man with whom they had no intimate acquaintance, and devote themselves to him as his followers. Now on comparing the fourth gospel, we see that Jesus had learned to know these men long before, and that they, too, had had demonstration of his excellence, whence it is easy to understand the felicity of his choice, and their

---

[1] Kuinöl, Comm. in Matth., s. 100 ; Lücke, Comm. z. Joh. 1, s. 388 ; Olshausen, bibl. Comm. 1, s. 197 ; Hase, Leben Jesu, §§ 56, 61.
[2] Leben Jesu, 1, a, s. 212.
[3] Paulus, Leben Jesu, 1, a, s. 213 ; Sieffert, über den Ursprung u. s. f., s. 72.

readiness to follow him. But this apparent advantage is the condemning circumstance in the above position : for nothing can more directly counteract the intention of the first two Evangelists, than to suppose a previous acquaintance between Jesus and the brethren whom he summons to follow him. In both Gospels, great stress is laid on the fact that they *immediately* εὐθέως left their nets, resolved to follow Jesus : the writers must therefore have deemed this something extraordinary, which it certainly was not, if these men had previously been in his train. In relation to Jesus also, the point of the narrative lies in his having, with a prophetic spirit, and at the first glance, selected the right individuals, *not needing that any should testify of man, for he knew what was in man*, according to John ii. 25, and thus presenting one of the characteristics which the Jews expected in their Messiah.

If, then, each of these two diverse narratives professes to describe the first acquaintance of Jesus with his most distinguished disciples, it follows that one only can be correct, while the other is necessarily erroneous.[4] It is our task to inquire which has the more intrinsic proofs of veracity. With respect to the synoptical representation, we share the difficulty which is felt by Paulus, in regarding it as a true account of the first interview between the parties. A penetration into the character of men at the first glance, such as is here supposed to have been evinced by Jesus, transcends all that is naturally possible to the most fortunate and practised knowledge of mankind. The nature of man is only revealed by his words and actions ; the gift of discerning it without these means, belongs to the visionary, or to that species of intuition for which the rabbinical designation of this messianic attribute, *odorando judicare*,[5] is not at all too monstrous. Scarcely less improbable is the unhesitating obedience of the disciples, for Jesus had not yet acquired his Galilean fame ; and to account for this promptitude we must suppose that the voice and will of Jesus had a coercive influence over minds, independently of preparation and motives,[6] which would be to complete the incredibility of the narrative by adding a magical trait to the visionary one already exposed.

If these negative arguments are deemed strong enough to annul the pretensions of the narrative to an historical character, the alternative is to assign to it a mythical interpretation, if we can show on positive grounds that it might have been constructed in a traditional manner without historical foundation. As adequate inducements to the formation of such a legend, we may point, not only to the above cited Jewish notion of the Messiah as the searcher of hearts, but to a specific type of this vocation of the apostles, contained in the narrative (1 Kings xix. 19–21) of the mode in which the prophet Elijah summoned Elisha to become his follower. Here Jesus calls the brethren from their nets and their fishing ; there the prophet calls his future disciple from the oxen and the plough ; in both cases there is a transition from simple physical labour to the highest spiritual office—a contrast which, as is exemplified in the Roman history, tradition is apt either to cherish or to create. Further, the fishermen, at the call of Jesus, forsake their nets and follow him ; so Elisha, when Elijah cast his mantle over him, *left the oxen, and ran after Elijah*. This is one apparent divergency, which is a yet more striking proof of the relation between the two narratives, than is their general similarity. The prophet's disciple entreated that before he attached himself entirely to Elijah, he might be permitted to take leave of his father and mother ; and the prophet does not hesitate to grant him this request, on the understood condition that Elisha should return to him. Similar petitions are offered to Jesus (Luke ix. 59 ff. ;

[4] See Fritzsche, in Matt., p. 189.
[5] Schöttgen, horæ, ii. p. 372.
[6] Paulus, ut sup.

Matt. viii. 21 f.) by some whom he had called, or who had volunteered to follow him ; but Jesus does not accede to these requests : on the contrary, he enjoins the one who wished previously to bury his father, to enter on his discipleship without delay ; and the other, who had begged permission to bid farewell to his friends, he at once dismisses as unfit for the kingdom of God. In strong contrast with the divided spirit manifested by these feeble proselytes, it is said of the apostles, that they, without asking any delay, immediately forsook their occupation, and, in the case of James and John, their father. Could anything betray more clearly than this one feature, that the narrative is an embellished imitation of that in the Old Testament intended to show that Jesus, in his character of Messiah, exacted a more decided adhesion, accompanied with greater sacrifices, than Elijah, in his character of Prophet merely, required or was authorized to require ? [7] The historical germ of the narrative may be this : several of the most eminent disciples of Jesus, particularly Peter, dwelling on the shores of the sea of Galilee, had been fishermen, whence Jesus during their subsequent apostolic agency may have sometimes styled them *fishers of men.* But without doubt, their relation with Jesus was formed gradually, like other human relations, and is only elevated into a marvel through the obliviousness of tradition.

By removing the synoptical narrative we make room for that of John ; but whether we are to receive it as historical, can only be decided by an examination of its matter. At the very outset, it excites no favourable prejudice, that John the Baptist is the one who directs the first two disciples to Jesus ; for if there be any truth in the representation given in a former chapter of the relation between Jesus and the Baptist, some disciples of the latter might, indeed, of their own accord attach themselves to Jesus, formerly their fellow-disciple, but nothing could be farther from the intention of the Baptist than to resign his own adherents to Jesus. This particular seems indebted for its existence to the apologetic interest of the fourth gospel, which seeks to strengthen the cause of Jesus by the testimony of the Baptist. Further, that Andrew, after one evening's intercourse with Jesus, should announce him to his brother with the words, *We have found the Messiah* (i. 42) ; that Philip too, immediately after his call, should speak of him in a similar manner to Nathanael (v. 46) ; is an improbability which I know not how to put strongly enough. We gather from the synoptical statement, which we have above decided to be trustworthy, that some time was necessary for the disciples to recognise Jesus as the Messiah, and openly confess their belief through their spokesman Peter, whose tardy discernment Jesus would have been incorrect in panegyrizing as a divine revelation, if it amounted to no more than what was communicated to him by his brother Andrew at the commencement of his discipleship. Equally unnatural is the manner in which Jesus is said to have received Simon. He accosts him with the words, *Thou art Simon, the son of Jona,*—a mode of salutation which seems, as Bengel has well remarked,[8] to imply that Jesus had a supernatural acquaintance with the name and origin of a man previously unknown to him, analogous to his cognizance of the number of the Samaritan woman's husbands, and of Nathanael's presence under the fig-tree. Jesus then preceeds to bestow on Simon the significant surname of Cephas or Peter. If we are not inclined to degrade the speech of Jesus into buffoonery, by referring this appellation to the bodily organization of the disciple,[9] we must suppose that Jesus at the first glance, with the eye of him who knew hearts, penetrated into the inmost nature of Simon, and discovered not only his general fitness

[7] Paulus, exeg. Handb. 1, b, s. 464.
  Gnomon, in loc.
[9] Paulus, Leben Jesu, 1, a, s. 168.

for the apostleship, but also the special, individual qualities which rendered him comparable to a rock. According to Matthew, it was not until after long intercourse with Jesus, and after he had given many manifestations of his peculiar character, that this surname was conferred on Simon, accompanied by an explanation of its meaning (xvi. 18) : evidently a much more natural account of the matter than that of the fourth Evangelist, who makes Jesus discern at the first glance the future value of Simon to his cause, an *odorando judicare* which transcends the synoptical representation in the same ratio as the declaration, *Thou shalt be called Cephas,* presupposes a more intimate knowledge, than the proposal, *I will make you fishers of men.* Even after a more lengthened conversation with Peter, such as Lücke supposes,[10] Jesus could not pronounce so decidedly on his character, without being a searcher of hearts, or falling under the imputation of forming too precipitate a judgment. It is indeed possible that the Christian legend, attracted by the significance of the name, may have represented Jesus as its author, while, in fact, Simon had borne it from his birth.

The entire narrative concerning Nathanael is a tissue of improbabilities. When Philip speaks to him of a Messiah from Nazareth, he makes the celebrated answer, *Can any good thing come out of Nazareth* (v. 47) ? There is no historical datum for supposing that Nazareth, when Jesus began his ministry, was the object of particular odium or contempt,[11] and there is every probability that the adversaries of Christianity were the first to cast an aspersion on the native city of the Messiah whom they rejected. In the time of Jesus, Nazareth was only depreciated by the Jews, as being a Galilean city— a stigma which it bore in common with many others : but in this sense it could not be despised by Nathanael, for he was himself a Galilean (xxi. 2). The only probable explanation is that a derisive question, which, at the time of the composition of the fourth gospel, the Christians had often to hear from their opponents, was put into the mouth of a cotemporary of Jesus, that by the manner in which he was divested of his doubt, others might be induced to comply with the invitation, *to come and see.* As Nathanael approaches Jesus, the latter pronounces this judgment on his character, *Behold an Israelite indeed in whom is no guile* (v. 48) ! Paulus is of opinion that Jesus might have previously gathered some intimations concerning Nathanael at Cana, where he had just been attending a marriage of some relations.[12] But if Jesus had become acquainted with Nathanael's character in a natural way, he must, in answer to the question *Whence knowest thou me ?* either have reminded him of the occasion on which they had had an earlier interview, or referred to the favourable report of others. Instead of this he speaks of his knowledge that Nathanael had been tarrying under a fig-tree : a knowledge which from its result is evidently intended to appear supernatural. Now to use information, obtained by ordinary means, so as to induce a belief that it has been communicated supernaturally, is charlatanism, if anything deserve the name. As, however, the narrator certainly did not mean to impute such artifice to Jesus, it is undeniably his intention to ascribe to him a supernatural knowledge of Nathanael's character. As little are the words, *When thou wast under the fig-tree, I saw thee,* explained by the exclamation of Paulus, " How often one sees and observes a man who is unconscious of one's gaze ! " Lücke and Tholück are also of opinion, that Jesus observed Nathanael under the fig-tree in a natural manner ; they add, however, the conjecture, that the latter was engaged in some occupation, such as prayer or the study of the law, which

[10] S. 385.
[11] Vid. Lücke, s. 389 f.
[12] Ut sup.

afforded Jesus a key to his character. But if Jesus meant to imply, "How can I fail to be convinced of thy virtue, having watched thee during thy earnest study of the law, and thy fervent prayer under the fig-tree?" he would not have omitted the word προσευχόμενον (*praying*), or ἀναγινώσκοντα (*reading*), for want of which we can extract no other sense from his declaration than this: "Thou mayest be assured of my power to penetrate into thy inmost soul, from the fact that I beheld thee when thou wast in a situation from which all merely human observers were excluded." Here the whole stress is thrown not on any peculiarity in the situation of the person seen, but on the fact that Jesus saw him, whence it is necessarily inferred that he did so by no ordinary, natural means. To imagine that Jesus possessed such a second sight, is, we grant, not a little extravagant; but for that very reason, it is the more accordant with the then existing notions of a prophet, and of the Messiah. A like power of seeing and hearing beyond the limits assigned to human organs, is attributed to Elisha in the Old Testament. When (2 Kings vi. 8, ff.) the king of Syria makes war against Israel, Elisha indicates to the king of Israel every position of the enemy's camp; and when the king of Syria expresses his suspicion that he is betrayed by deserters, he is told that the Israelitish prophet knows all the words that he, the king of Syria, speaks in his private chamber. Thus also (xxi. 32), Elisha knows that Joram has sent out messengers to murder him. How could it be endured that the Messiah should fall short of the prophet in his powers of vision? This particular, too, enables our Evangelist to form a climax, in which Jesus ascends from the penetration of one immediately present (v. 42), to that of one approaching for the first time (v. 48), and finally, to the perception of one out of the reach of human eyesight. That Jesus goes a step farther in the climax, and says, that this proof of his messianic second sight is a trifle compared with what Nathanael has yet to see,—that on him, the Son of man, the angels of God shall descend from the opened heavens (v. 51),—in nowise shows, as Paulus thinks, that there was nothing miraculous in that first proof, for there is a gradation even in miracles.

Thus in the narrative of John we stumble at every step on difficulties, in some instances greater than those with which the synoptical accounts are encumbered: hence we learn as little from the one as the other, concerning the manner in which the first disciples attached themselves to Jesus. I cannot agree with the author of the Probabilia,[13] in deriving the divergency of the fourth Evangelist from his predecessors, from the wish to avoid mentioning the derided fishing trade of the most distinguished apostles; since in chap. xxi., which Bretschneider allows to be by the same hand as the rest of the gospel, he unhesitatingly introduces the obnoxious employment. I rather surmise that the idea of their having received their decisive apostolic call while actually engaged with their fishing-nets, was not afloat in the tradition from which the fourth Evangelist drew; and that this writer formed his scenes, partly on the probably historical report that some disciples of Jesus had belonged to the school of the Baptist, and partly from the wish to represent in the most favourable light the relation between Jesus and the Baptist, and the supernatural gifts of the former.

[13] P. 141.

§ 71.

PETER'S DRAUGHT OF FISHES.

We have hitherto examined only two accounts of the vocation of Peter and his companions ; there is a third given by Luke (v. 1–11). I shall not dilate on the minor points of difference[1] between his narrative and that of the first two Evangelists ; the essential distinction is, that in Luke the disciples do not, as in Matthew and Mark, unite themselves to Jesus on a simple invitation, but in consequence of a plentiful draught of fishes, to which Jesus has assisted Simon. If this feature be allowed to constitute Luke's narrative a separate one from that of his predecessors, we have next to inquire into its intrinsic credibility, and then to ascertain its relation to that of Matthew and Mark.

Jesus, oppressed by the throng of people on the shore of the Galilean sea, enters into a ship, that he may address them with more ease at a little distance from land. Having brought his discourse to a close, he desires Simon, the owner of the boat, to launch out into the deep, and let down his nets for a draught. Simon, although little encouraged by the poor result of the last night's fishing, declares himself willing, and is rewarded by so˙ extraordinary a draught, that Peter and his partners, James and John (Andrew is not here mentioned), are struck with astonishment, the former even with awe, before Jesus, as a superior being. Jesus then says to Simon, *Fear not; from henceforth thou shalt catch men*, and the issue is that the three fishermen forsake all, and follow him.

The rationalistic commentators take pains to show that what is above narrated might occur in a natural way. According to them, the astonishing consequence of letting down the net was the result of an accurate observation on the part of Jesus, assisted by a happy fortuity. Paulus[2] supposes that Jesus at first wished to launch out farther into the deep merely to escape from the crowd, and that it was not until after sailing to some distance, that, descrying a place where the fish were abundant, he desired Peter to let down the net. But he has fallen into a twofold contradiction of the evangelical narrative. In close connexion with the command to launch out into the deep, Jesus adds, *Let down your nets for a draught* ($\epsilon\pi\alpha\nu\acute{\alpha}\gamma\alpha\gamma\epsilon$ $\epsilon\grave{\iota}\varsigma$ $\tau\grave{o}$ $\beta\acute{\alpha}\theta o\varsigma$, $\kappa\alpha\grave{\iota}$ $\chi\alpha\lambda\acute{\alpha}\sigma\alpha\tau\epsilon$ $\tau\grave{\alpha}$ $\delta\acute{\iota}\kappa\tau\upsilon\alpha$, $\kappa.$ $\tau.$ $\lambda.$), as if this were one of his objects in changing the locality ; and if he spoke thus when at a little distance only from the shore, his hope of a successful draught could not be the effect of his having observed a place abundant in fish on the main sea, which the vessel had not yet reached. Our rationalists must therefore take refuge in the opinion of the author of the Natural History of the Great Prophet of Nazareth, who says, Jesus conjectured on general grounds, that under existing circumstances (indicative probably of an approaching storm), fishing in the middle of the sea would succeed better than it had done in the night. But, proceeding from the natural point of view, how could Jesus be a better judge in this matter than the men who had spent half their life on the sea in the employment of fishing ? Certainly if the fishermen observed nothing which could give them hope of a plentiful draught, neither in a natural manner could Jesus ; and the agreement between his words and the result, must, adhering to the natural point of view, be put down wholly to the account of chance. But what senseless audacity, to promise at random a success, which, judging from the occurrences of the past night, was little likely to follow ! It is said, however, that Jesus only desires Peter

---

[1] Storr, üeber den Zweck der ev. Gesch. und der Br. Joh., s. 350.
[2] Exeg. Handb. 1, b, s. 449.

to make another attempt, without giving any definite promise.   But, we must
rejoin, in the emphatic injunction, which Peter's remark on the inauspicious
aspect of circumstances for fishing does not induce him to revoke, there is a
latent promise, and the words, *Let down your nets,* etc., in the present passage,
can hardly have any other meaning than that plainly expressed in the similar
scene, John xxi. 6, *Cast the net on the right side of the ship, and ye shall find.*
When, moreover, Peter retracts his objection in the words, *Nevertheless at thy
word I will let down the net,* ἐπὶ δὲ τῷ ῥήματί σου χαλάσω τὸ δίκτυον, though
ῥῆμα may be translated by *command* rather than by *promise,* in either case he
implies a hope that what Jesus enjoins will not be without result.   If Jesus
had not intended to excite this hope, he must immediately have put an end to
it, if he would not expose himself to disgrace in the event of failure ; and on
no account ought he to have accepted the attitude and expressions of Peter
as his due, if he had only merited them by a piece of lucky advice given at a
venture.

The drift of the narrative, then, obliges us to admit that the writer intended
to signalize a miracle.   This miracle may be viewed either as one of power,
or of knowledge.   If the former, we are to conceive that Jesus by his supernatural power, caused the fish to congregate in that part of the sea where he
commanded Peter to cast in his net.   Now that Jesus should be able, by the
immediate action of his will, to influence men, in the nature of whose minds
his spiritual energy might find a fulcrum, may to a certain extent be conceived,
without any wide deviation from psychological laws ; but that he could thus
influence irrational beings, and those not isolated animals immediately present
to him, but shoals of fish in the depths of the sea, it is impossible to imagine
out of the domain of magic.   Olshausen compares this operation of Jesus to
that of the divine omnipotence in the annual migrations of fish and birds ;[3]
but the comparison is worse than lame,—it lacks all parallelism ; for the latter
is an effect of the divine agency, linked in the closest manner with all the
other operations of God in external nature, with the change of seasons, etc. ;
while the former, even presupposing Jesus to be actually God, would be an
isolated act, interrupting the chain of natural phenomena ; a distinction that
removes any semblance of parallelism between the two cases.   Allowing the
possibility of such a miracle (and from the supranaturalistic point of view,
nothing is in itself impossible), did it subserve any apparent object, adequate
to determine Jesus to so extravagant a use of his miraculous powers ?   Was it
so important that Peter should be inspired by this incident with a superstitious fear, not accordant with the spirit of the New Testament ?   Was this
the only preparation for engrafting the true faith? or did Jesus believe that it
was only by such signs that he could win disciples?   How little faith must he
then have had in the force of mind and of truth ! how much too meanly must
he have estimated Peter, who, at a later period at least (John vi. 68), clung to
his society, not on account of the miracles which he beheld Jesus perform, but
for the sake of *the words of eternal life* which came from his lips !

Under the pressure of these difficulties, refuge may be sought in the other
supposition as the more facile one ; namely, that Jesus, by means of his superhuman knowledge, was merely aware that in a certain place there was then to
be found a multitude of fishes, and that he communicated this information to
Peter.   If by this it be meant that Jesus, through the possession of an omniscience such as is commonly attributed to God, knew at all times, all the fish,
in all seas, rivers and lakes ; there is an end to his human consciousness.   If,
however, it be merely meant that when he crossed any water he became cog-

nizant of its various tribes of fish, with their relative position ; even this would be quite enough to encumber the space in his mind that was due to more weighty thoughts, Lastly, if it be meant that he knew this, not constantly and necessarily, but as often as he wished ; it is impossible to understand how, in a mind like that of Jesus, a desire for such knowledge should arise,— how he,· whose vocation had reference to the depths of the human heart, should be tempted to occupy himself with the fish-frequented depths of the waters.

But before we pronounce on this narrative of Luke, we must consider it in relation to the cognate histories in the first two synoptical gospels. The chronological relation of the respective events is the first point. The supposition that the miraculous draught of fishes in Luke was prior to the vocation narrated by the two other Evangelists, is excluded by the consideration, that the firm attachment which that miracle awakened in the disciples, would render a new call superfluous ; or by the still stronger objection, that if an invitation, accompanied by a miracle, had not sufficed to ally the men to Jesus, he could hardly flatter himself that a subsequent bare summons, unsupported by any miracle, would have a better issue. The contrary chronological position presents a better climax ; but why a second invitation, if the first had succeeded ? For to suppose that the brethren who followed him on the first summons, again left him until the second, is to cut the knot, instead of untying it. Still more complicated is the difficulty, when we take in addition the narrative of the fourth Evangelist : for what shall we think of the connexion between Jesus and his diciples, if it began in the manner described by John ; if, after this, the disciples having from some unknown cause separated from their master, he again called them, as if nothing of the kind had before occurred, on the shore of the Galilean sea ; and if, this invitation also producing no permanent adherence, he for the third time summoned them to follow him, fortifying this final experiment by a miracle? The entire drift of Luke's narrative is such as to exclude, rather than to imply, any earlier and more intimate relation between Jesus and his ultimate disciples. For the indifferent mention of two ships on the shore, whose owners were gone out of them to wash their nets, Simon being unnamed until Jesus chooses to avail himself of his boat, seems, as Schleiermacher has convincingly shown,[4] to convey the idea that the two parties were entire strangers to each other, and that these incidents were preparatory to a relation yet to be formed, not indicative of one already existing : so that the healing of Peter's mother-in-law, previously recounted by Luke, either occurred, like many other cures of Jesus, without producing any intimate connexion, or has too early a date assigned to it by that Evangelist. The latter conjecture is supported by the fact that Matthew places the miracle later.

Thus, it fares with the narrative of Luke, when viewed in relation to that of Matthew and Mark, as it did with that of John, when placed in the same light ; neither will bear the other to precede, or to follow it,—in short, they exclude each other.[5] Which then is the correct narrative ? Schleiermacher prefers that of the Evangelist on whom he has commented, because it is more particular[6] ; and Sieffert[7] has recently asserted with great emphasis, that no one has ever yet doubted the superiority of Luke's narrative, as a faithful picture of the entire occurrence, the number of its special, dramatic, and in-

---

[4] Ueber den Lukas, s. 70.
[5] This, with the legendary character of both narratives, is acknowledged by De Wette, exeg. Handb. 1, 1, s. 37, 1, 2, s. 38 f.
[6] Neander is of the same opinion, L. J., s. 249 f.
[7] Uber den Ursprung des ersten kan. Ev., s. 73.

trinsically authenticated details, advantageously distinguishing it from the account in the first (and second) gospel, which by its omission of the critical incident, the turning point in the narrative (the draught of fishes), is characterized as the recital of one who was not an eye-witness. I have already presented myself elsewhere[8] to this critic, as one hardy enough to express the doubt of which he denies the existence, and I here repeat the question : supposing one only of the two narratives to have been modified by oral tradition, which alternative is more in accordance with the nature of that means of transmission,—that the tangible fact of a draught of fishes should evaporate into a mere saying respecting fishers of men, or that this figurative expression should be condensed into a literal history ? The answer to this question cannot be dubious ; for when was it in the nature of the legend to spiritualize? to change the real, such as the story of a miracle, into the ideal, such as a mere verbal image ? The stage of human culture to which the legend belongs, and the mental faculty in which it originates, demand that it should give a stable body to fleeting thought, that it should counteract the ambiguity and changeableness of words, by affixing them to the permanent and universally understood symbol of action.

It is easy to show how, out of the expression preserved by the first Evangelist, the miraculous story of the third might be formed. If Jesus, in allusion to the former occupation of some of his apostles, had called them fishers of men ; if he had compared the kingdom of heaven to a net cast into the sea, in which all kinds of fish were taken (Matt. xiii. 47) ; it was but a following out of these ideas to represent the apostles as those who, at the word of Jesus, cast out the net, and gathered in the miraculous multitude of fishes.[9] If we add to this, that the ancient legend was fond of occupying its wonder-workers with affairs of fishing, as we see in the story related of Pythagoras by Jamblichus and Porphyry ;[10] it will no longer appear improbable, that Peter's miraculous draught of fishes is but the expression about the fishers of men, transmuted into the history of a miracle, and this view will at once set us free from all the difficulties that attend the natural, as well as the supranatural interpretation of the narrative.

A similar miraculous draught of fishes is recorded in the appendix to the fourth gospel, as having occurred after the resurrection (ch. xxi.). Here again Peter is fishing on the Galilean sea, in company with the sons of Zebedee and some other disciples, and again he has been toiling all night, and has taken nothing.[11] Early in the morning, Jesus comes to the shore, and asks, without their recognising him, if they have any meat? On their answering in the negative, he directs them to cast the net on the right side of the ship, whereupon they have an extremely rich draught, and are led by this sign to recognise Jesus. That this history is distinct from the one given by Luke, is, from its great similarity, scarcely conceivable ; the same narrative has doubtless been placed by tradition in different periods of the life of Jesus.[12]

----

[8] Berliner Jahrbücher für wissenschaftliche Kritik, 1834 Nov. ; now in the Charakteristiken u. Kritiken, s. 264 f.

[9] According to De Wette, the copious draught of fishes was a symbolical miracle, typifying the rich fruits of the apostolic ministry.

[10] Porphyr. vita Pythagoræ, no. 25, ed. Kiessling ; Jamblich. v. P. no. 36. ders. Ausg. It is fair to adduce this history, because, being less marvellous than the gospel narrative, it can hardly be an imitation, but must have arisen independently, and hence it evinces a common tendency of the ancient legend.

[11] Luke v. 5 : δι' ὅλης τῆς νυκτὸς κοπιάσαντες οὐδὲν ἐλάβομεν. John xxi. 3 : καὶ ἐν ἐκείνῃ τῇ νυκτὶ ἐπίασαν οὐδέν.

[12] Comp. de Wette, exeg. Handb., 1, 3, s. 213.

Let us now compare these three fishing histories,—the two narrated of Jesus, and that narrated of Pythagoras,—and their mythical character will be obvious. That which, in Luke, is indubitably intended as a miracle of power, is, in the history of Jamblichus, a miracle of knowledge ; for Pythagoras merely tells in a supernatural manner the number of fish already caught by natural means. The narrative of John holds a middle place, for in it also the number of the fish (153) plays a part; but instead of being predetermined by the worker of the miracle, it is simply stated by the narrator. One legendary feature common to all the three narratives, is the manner in which the multitude and weight of the fishes are described ; especially as this sameness of manner accompanies a diversity in particulars. According to Luke, the multitude is so great that the net is broken, one ship will not hold them, and after they have been divided between the two vessels, both threaten to sink. In the view of the tradition given in the fourth gospel, it was not calculated to magnify the power of the miraculous agent, that the net which he had so marvellously filled should break ; but as here also the aim is to exalt the miracle by celebrating the number and weight of the fishes, they are said to be μεγάλοι (*great*), and it is added that the men *were not able to draw the net for the multitude of fishes* : instead, however, of lapsing out of the miraculous into the common by the breaking of the net, a second miracle is ingeniously made,— that *for all there were so many, yet was not the net broken.* Jamblichus presents a further wonder (the only one he has, besides the knowledge of Pythagoras as to the number of the fish) : namely, that while the fish were being counted, a process that must have required a considerable time, not one of them died. If there be a mind that, not perceiving in the narratives we have compared the finger-marks of tradition, and hence the legendary character of these evangelical anecdotes, still leans to the historical interpretation, whether natural or supernatural ; that mind must be alike ignorant of the true character both of legend and of history, of the natural and the supernatural.

§ 72.

CALLING OF MATTHEW.   CONNEXION OF JESUS WITH THE PUBLICANS.

The first gospel (ix. 9 ff.) tells of *a man named Matthew*, to whom, when sitting at the receipt of custom, Jesus said, *Follow me.*   Instead of Matthew, the second and third gospels have *Levi*, and Mark adds he that was *the son of Alphæus* (Mark ii. 14 ff. ; Luke v. 27 ff.).   At the call of Jesus, Luke says that he left all ; Matthew merely states, that he followed Jesus and prepared a meal, of which many publicans and sinners partook, to the great scandal of the Pharisees.

From the difference of the names it has been conjectured that the Evangelists refer to two different events ; [1] but this difference of the name is more than counterbalanced by the similarity of the circumstances.   In all the three cases the call of the publican is preceded and followed by the same occurrences ; the subject of the narrative is in the same situation ; Jesus addresses him in the same words ; and the issue is the same.[2]   Hence the opinion is pretty general, that the three synoptists have in this instance detailed only one event.   But did they also understand only one person under different names, and was that person the Apostle Matthew ?

[1] Vid. Kuinöl, in Matth., p. 255.
[2] Sieffert, ut sup. p. 55.

This is commonly represented as conceivable on the supposition that Levi was the proper name of the individual, and Matthew merely a surname ;[3] or that after he had attached himself to Jesus, he exchanged the former for the latter.[4] To substantiate such an opinion, there should be some indication that the Evangelists who name the chosen publican Levi, intend under that designation no other than the Matthew mentioned in their catalogues of the apostles (Mark iii. 18 ; Luke vi. 15 ; Acts i. 13). On the contrary, in these catalogues, where many surnames and double names occur, not only do they omit the name of Levi as the earlier or more proper appellation of Matthew, but they leave him undistinguished by the epithet, ὁ τελώνης (*the publican*), added by the first Evangelist in his catalogue (x. 3) ; thus proving that they do not consider the Apostle Matthew to be identical with the Levi summoned from the receipt of custom.[5]

If then the Evangelists describe the vocation of two different men in a precisely similar way, it is improbable that there is accuracy on both sides, since an event could hardly be repeated in its minute particulars. One of the narratives, therefore, is in error ; and the burthen has been thrown on the first Evangelist, because he places the calling of Matthew considerably after the Sermon on the Mount ; while according to Luke (vi. 13 ff.), all the twelve had been chosen before that discourse was delivered.[6] But this would only prove, at the most, that the first gospel gives a wrong position to the history ; not that it narrates that history incorrectly. It is therefore unjust to impute special difficulties to the narrative of the first Evangelist : neither are such to be found in that of Mark and Luke, unless it be thought an inconsistency in the latter to attribute a *forsaking of all*, καταλιπὼν ἅπαντα, to one whom he does not include among the constant followers of Jesus.[7] The only question is, do they not labour under a common difficulty, sufficient to stamp both accounts as unhistorical ?

The close analogy between this call and that of the two pairs of brethren, must excite attention. They were summoned from their nets ; he from the custom-house ; as in their case, so here, nothing further is needed than a simple *Follow me* ; and this call of the Messiah has so irresistible a power over the mind of the called, that the publican, like the fishermen, *leaves all, and follows him*. It is not to be denied, that as Jesus had been for a considerable time exercising his ministry in that country, Matthew must have long known him ; and this is the argument with which Fritzsche repels the accusation of Julian and Porphyry, who maintain that Matthew here shows himself rash and inconsiderate. But the longer Jesus had observed him, the more easily might he have found opportunity for drawing him gradually and quietly into his train, instead of hurrying him in so tumultuary a manner from the midst of his business. Paulus indeed thinks that no call to discipleship, no sudden forsaking of a previous occupation, is here intended, but that Jesus having brought his teaching to a close, merely signified to the friend who had given him an invitation to dinner, that he was now ready to go home with him, and sit down to table.[8] But the meal appears, especially in Luke, to be the consequence, and not the cause, of the summons ; moreover, a modest guest would say to the host who had invited him, *I will follow thee*, ἀκολουθήσω σοι, not *Follow me*, ἀκολούθει μοι ; and in fine, this interpretation renders the whole

---

[3] Kuinöl, ut sup. Paulus, exeg. Handb., 1, b, s. 513. L. J., 1, a, 240.
[4] Bertholdt, Einleitung, 3, s. 1255 f. Fritzsche, s. 340.
[5] Sieffert, s. 56 ; De Wette, exeg. Handb., 1, 1, s. 91.
[6] Sieffert, s. 60.
[7] De Wette, ut sup.
[8] Exeg. Handb., 1, b, s. 510. L. J., 1, a, 240.

anecdote so trivial, that it would have been better omitted.[9] Hence the abruptness and impetuosity of the scene return upon us, and we are compelled to pronounce that such is not the course of real life, nor the procedure of a man who, like Jesus, respects the laws and formalities of human society ; it is the procedure of legend and poetry, which love contrasts, and effective scenes, which aim to give a graphic conception of a man's exit from an old sphere of life, and his entrance into a new one, by representing him as at once discarding the implements of his former trade, leaving the scene of his daily business, and straightway commencing a new life. The historical germ of the story may be, that Jesus actually had publicans among his disciples, and possibly that Matthew was one. These men had truly left the custom-house to follow Jesus ; but only in the figurative sense of this concise expression, not in the literal one depicted by the legend.

It is not less astonishing that the publican should have a great feast in readiness for Jesus immediately after his call. For that this feast was not prepared until the following day,[10] is directly opposed to the narratives, the two first especially. But it is entirely in the tone of the legend to demonstrate the joy of the publican, and the condescension of Jesus, and to create an occasion for the reproaches cast on the latter on account of his intimacy with sinners, by inventing a great feast, given to the publicans at the house of their late associate immediately after his call.

Another circumstance connected with this narrative merits particular attention. According to the common opinion concerning the author of the first gospel, Matthew therein narrates his own call. We may consider it granted that there are no positive indications of this in the narrative ; but it is not so clear that there are no negative indications which render it impossible or improbable. That the Evangelist does not here speak in the first person, nor when describing events in which he had a share in the first person plural, like the author of the Acts of the Apostles, proves nothing ; for Josephus and other historians not less classical, write of themselves in the third person, and the *we* of the pseudo-Matthew in the Ebionite gospel has a very suspicious sound. The use of the expression, ἄνθρωπον, Ματθαῖον λεγόμενον, which the Manicheans made an objection,[11] as they did the above-mentioned circumstance, is not without a precedent in the writings of Xenophon, who in his Anabasis introduces himself as *Xenophon, a certain Athenian*, Ξενοφῶν τις Ἀθηναῖος.[12] The Greek, however, did not fall into this style from absorption in his subject, nor from unaffected freedom from egotism,—causes which Olshausen supposes in the Evangelist ; but either from a wish not to pass for the author, as an old tradition states,[13] or from considerations of taste, neither of which motives will be attributed to Matthew. Whether we are therefore to consider that expression as a sign that the author of the first gospel was not Matthew, may be difficult to decide : [14] but it is certain that this history of the publican's call is throughout less clearly narrated in that gospel than in the third. In the former, we are at a loss to understand why it is abruptly said that Jesus sat at meat in the house, if the Evangelist were himself the hospitable publican, since it would then seem most natural for him to let his joy on account of his call appear in the narrative, by telling, as Luke does, that he immediately made a great feast in his house. To say that he withheld this

[9] Schleiermacher, über den Lukas, s. 76.
[10] Grätz, Comm. z. Matth. 1, s. 470.
[11] Augustin c. Faust. Manich. xvii. 1.
[12] iii. i. 4.
[13] Plutarch. de gloria Atheniens., at the beginning.
[14] Schulz, Ueber das Abendmahl, s. 308.

from modesty, is to invest a rude Galilean of that age with the affectation belonging to the most refined self-consciousness of modern days.

To this feast at the publican's, of which many of the same obnoxious class
partook, the Evangelists annex the reproaches cast at the disciples by the
Pharisees and Scribes, because their master ate with publicans and sinners.
Jesus, being within hearing of the censure, repelled it by the well-known text
on the destination of the physician for the sick, and the Son of Man for
sinners (Matt. ix. 11 ff. parall.). That Jesus should be frequently taunted by
his pharisaical enemies with his too great predilection for the despised class
of publicans (comp. Matt. xi. 19), accords fully with the nature of his position,
and is therefore historical, if anything be so : the answer, too, which is here
put into the mouth of Jesus, is from its pithy and concise character well
adapted for literal transmission. Further, it is not improbable that the reproach
in question may have been especially called forth, by the circumstance that
Jesus ate with publicans and sinners, and went under their roofs. But that
the cavils of his opponents should have been accompaniments of the publican's
dinner, as the evangelical account leads us to infer, especially that of Mark
(v. 16), is not so easily conceivable.[15] For as the feast was *in the house* (ἐν τῇ
οἰκίᾳ), and as the disciples also partook of it, how could the Pharisees utter their
reproaches to them, while the meal was going forward, without defiling themselves by becoming the *guests of a man that was a sinner,*—the very act which
they reprehended in Jesus ? (Luke xix. 7). It will hardly be supposed that
they waited outside until the feast was ended. It is difficult for Schleiermacher
to maintain, even on the representation of Luke taken singly, that the evangelical
narrative only implies, that the publican's feast was the cause of the Pharisees'
censure, and not that they were contemporary.[16] Their immediate' connexion
might easily originate in a legendary manner; in fact, one scarcely knows how
tradition, in its process of transmuting the abstract into the concrete, could
represent the general idea that the Pharisees had taken offence at the friendly
intercourse of Jesus with the publicans, otherwise than thus : Jesus once
feasted in a publican's house, in company with many publicans ; the Pharisees
saw this, went to the disciples and expressed their censure, which Jesus also
heard, and parried by a laconic answer.

After the Pharisees, Matthew makes the disciples of John approach Jesus
with the question, why his disciples did not fast, as they did (v. 14 f.) ; in
Luke (v. 33 ff.) it is still the Pharisees who vaunt their own fasts and those
of John's disciples, as contrasted with the eating aand drinking of the disciples of Jesus ; Mark's account is not clear (v. 18). According to Schleiermacher, every unprejudiced person must perceive in the statement of Matthew
compared with that of Luke, the confusing emendations of a second editor,
who could not explain to himself how the Pharisees came to appeal to the
disciples of John ; whereas, thinks Schleiermacher, the question would have
been puerile in the mouth of the latter; but it is easy to imagine that the
Pharisees might avail themselves of an external resemblance to the disciples
of John when opposing Jesus, who had himself received baptism of that
teacher. It is certainly surprising that after the Pharisees, who were offended
because Jesus ate with publicans, some disciples of John should step forth as
if they had been cited for the purpose, to censure generally the unrestricted
eating and drinking of Jesus and his disciples. The probable explanation is,
that evangelical tradition associated the two circumstances from their intrinsic
similarity, and that the first Evangelist erroneously gave them the additional

---

[15] Comp. de Wette, exeg. Handb. I, 2, p. 134.
[16] Ut sup., p. 77.

connexion of time and place. But the manner in which the third Evangelist fuses the two particulars, appears a yet more artificial combination, and is certainly not historical, because the reply of Jesus could only be directed to John's disciples, or to friendly inquirers : to Pharisees, he would have given another and a more severe answer.[17]

Another narrative, which is peculiar to Luke (xix. 1–10), treats of the same relation as that concerning Matthew or Levi. When Jesus, on his last journey to the feast, passes through Jericho, a *chief among the publicans*, ἀρχιτελώνης, named Zacchæus, that he might, notwithstanding his short stature, get a sight of Jesus among the crowd, climbed a tree, where Jesus observed him, and immediately held him worthy to entertain the Messiah for the night. Here, again, the favour shown to a publican excites the discontent of the more rigid spectators ; and when Zacchæus has made vows of atonement and beneficence, Jesus again justifies himself, on the ground that his office had reference to sinners. The whole scene is very dramatic, and this might be deemed by some an argument for its historical character ; but there are certain internal obstacles to its reception. We are not led to infer that Jesus previously knew Zacchæus, or that some one pointed him out to Jesus by name ;[18] but, as Olshausen truly says, the knowledge of Zacchæus that Jesus here suddenly evinced, is to be referred to his power of discerning what was in men without the aid of testimony. We have before decided that this power is a legendary attribute ; hence the above particular, at least, cannot be historical, and the narrative is possibly a variation on the same theme as that treated of in connexion with the account of Matthew's call, namely, the friendly relation of Jesus to the publicans.

§ 73.

THE TWELVE APOSTLES.

The men whose vocation we have been considering, namely, the sons of Jonas and Zebedee, with Philip and Matthew (Nathanael alone being excepted, form the half of that narrow circle of disciples which appears throughout the New Testament under the name of *the twelve*, οἱ δώδεκα, *the twelve disciples* or *apostles*, οἱ δώδεκα μαθήται or ἀπόστολοι. The fundamental idea of the New Testament writers concerning the twelve, is that Jesus himself chose them (Mark iii. 13 f. ; Luke vi. 13 ; John vi. 70, xv. 16). Matthew does not give us the history of the choice of all the twelve, but he tacitly presupposes it by introducing them as a college already instituted (x. 1). Luke, on the contrary, narrates how, after a night spent on the mountain in vigils and prayer, Jesus selected twelve from the more extensive circle of his adherents, and then descended with them to the plain, to deliver what is called the Sermon on the Mount (vi. 12). Mark also tells us in the same connexion, that Jesus when on a mountain made a voluntary choice of twelve from the mass of his disciples (iii. 13). According to Luke, Jesus chose the twelve immediately before he delivered the Sermon on the Mount, and apparently with reference to it ; but there is no discoverable motive which can explain this mode of associating the two events, for the discourse was not specially addressed to the apostles,[1] neither had they any office to execute during its delivery. Mark's representation, with the exception of the vague tradition from which he sets

[17] De Wette, exeg. Handb. 1, 1, p. 93.
[18] Paulus, exeg. Handb., 3, a, s. 48. Kuinöl, in Luc., p. 632.
[1] Schleiermacher, über den Lukas, s. 85.

out, that Jesus chose the twelve, seems to have been wrought out of his own imagination, and furnishes no distinct notion of the occasion and manner of the choice.[2] Matthew has adopted the best method in merely presupposing, without describing, the particular vocation of the apostles ; and John pursues the same plan, beginning (vi. 67) to speak of *the twelve*, without any previous notice of their appointment.

Strictly speaking, therefore, it is merely presupposed in the gospels, that Jesus himself fixed the number of the apostles.   Is this presupposition correct ?   There certainly is little doubt that this number was fixed during the lifetime of Jesus ; for not only does the author of the Acts represent the twelve as so compact a body immediately after the ascension of their master, that they think it incumbent on them to fill up the breach made by the apostasy of Judas by the election of a new member (i. 15 ff.) ; but the Apostle Paul also notices an appearance of the risen Jesus, specially to *the twelve* (1 Cor. xv. 5).   Schleiermacher, however, doubts whether Jesus himself chose the twelve, and he thinks it more probable that the peculiar relation ultimately borne to him by twelve from amongst his disciples, gradually and spontaneously formed itself.[3]   We have, indeed, no warrant for supposing that the appointment of the twelve was a single solemn act ; on the contrary, the gospels explicitly narrate, that six of them were called singly, or by pairs, and on separate occasions ; but it is still a question whether the number twelve was not determined by Jesus, and whether he did not willingly abide by it as an expedient for checking the multiplication of his familiar companions.   The number is the less likely to have been fortuitous, the more significant it is, and the more evident the inducements to its choice by Jesus.   He himself, in promising the disciples (Matt. xix. 28) *that they shall sit on twelve thrones, judging the twelve tribes of Israel*, gives their number a relation to that of the tribes of his people ; and it was the opinion of the highest Christian antiquity that this relation determined his choice.[4]   If he and his disciples were primarily sent to the *lost sheep of the house of Israel* (Matt. x. 6, xv. 24), it might seem appropriate that the number of the shepherds should correspond to that of the shepherdless tribes (Matt. ix. 36).

The destination of the twelve is only generally intimated in John (xv. 16) ; in Mark, on the contrary, it is particularly, and without doubt accurately, stated.   *He ordained twelve*, it is here said, *that they should be with him*, that is, that he might not be without companionship, aid, and attendance on his journeys ; and accordingly we find them helpful to him in procuring lodgings (Luke ix. 32 ; Matt. xxvi. 17 f.), food (John iv. 8), and other travelling requisites (Matt. xxi. 1 ff.) ; but above all they were in his society to become *scribes well instructed unto the kingdom of heaven* (Matt. xiii. 52).   To this end they had the opportunity of being present at most of the discourses of Jesus, and even of obtaining private elucidations of their meaning (Matt. xiii. 10 ff., 36 ff.) ; of purifying their minds by his severe but friendly discipline (Matt. viii. 26, xvi. 23, xviii. 1 ff. 21 ff. ; Luke ix. 50, 55 f. ; John xiii. 12 ff. etc.), and of elevating their souls by the contemplation of his example (John xiv. 19).   Another motive of Jesus in choosing the twelve, was, according to Mark, *that he might send them forth to preach*, that is, to preach the kingdom of heaven during his life, according to the immediate meaning of Mark ; but the promulgation of his cause after his death, must be supposed as an additional object on the part of Jesus.   (Mark proceeds to enumerate the powers

---

[2] Schleiermacher, über den Lukas, s. 85.
[3] Ut sup., s. 88.
[4] Ep. Barnab. 8, and the Gospel of the Ebionites ap. Epiphanius, hær. xxx. 13.

of healing and of casting out devils ; but on these points we cannot dilate until we reach a future stage of our inquiry.)

It was this latter destination that won for them the distinguished name of *apostles*, ἀπόστολοι (Matt. x. 2 ; Mark vi. 30 ; Luke vii. 13, etc.). It has been doubted whether Jesus himself conferred this name on the twelve, according to Luke vi. 13, and it has been suggested that it was not given them until later, *ex eventu*.[5] But that Jesus should have called them his envoys cannot be improbable, if he really sent them on a journey to announce the approaching kingdom of the Messiah. We grant that it is possible to regard this journey as an event transposed from the period after the death of Jesus to his lifetime, in order that a sort of rehearsal of the subsequent mission of the apostles might pass under the eye of Jesus ; but as it is not improbable that Jesus, perhaps even before he had a full conviction of his own Messiahship, sent out messengers to announce the Messiah's kingdom, we are not warranted to urge such a doubt.

John knows nothing of this mission, recorded by the synoptists. On the other hand, they are ignorant of a circumstance alleged by John, namely, that the disciples baptized during the life of Jesus (iv. 2). According to the synoptical Evangelists, it was not until after the resurrection, that Jesus gave his disciples authority to baptize (Matt. xxviii. 19, parall.). As, however, the rite of baptism was introduced by John, and we have reason to believe that Jesus, for a time, made that teacher his model, it is highly probable that he and his disciples also practised baptism, and hence that the positive statement of the fourth gospel is correct. But the negative statement that *Jesus himself baptised not* (iv. 2), has the appearance of an after-thought, intended to correct the import of the previous passages (iii. 22, iv. 1), and is most probably to be accounted for by the tendency of the fourth gospel to exalt Jesus above the Baptist, and by a corresponding dread of making Jesus exercise the function of the mere forerunner. The question whether Jesus did not baptize at least the apostles, afterwards occasioned much demur in the church.

With the exception of the mission mentioned above, the gospels speak of no important separation between Jesus and his twelve disciples, for there is nothing certain to be gathered from the resumption of their business after his death (John xxi. 2 ff.). No one could detect in our gospels any indications of a repeated interruption to the intercourse of Jesus with his disciples, but theologians, whose harmonistic zeal wished to find room for a second and third vocation ; or expositors, who, in their unwearied application to details, cast about for a means of subsistence for so many indigent men, and thought it necessary to suppose that they were occasionally provided for by a return to their secular labours. As to the subsistence of Jesus and his disciples, we have sufficient sources for it in the hospitality of the East, which, among the Jews, was especially available to the rabbins ; in the companionship of rich women *who ministered unto him of their substance* (Luke viii. 2 f.) ; and finally in the γλωσσόκομον, mentioned, it is true, only by the fourth Evangelist (xii. 6, xiii. 29), which was ample enough to furnish assistance to the poor, as well as to supply the wants of the society, and in which, it is probable, presents from wealthy friends of Jesus were deposited. They who do not hold these means adequate without the labour of the disciples, or who think, on more general grounds, that the total renunciation of their secular employment on the part of the twelve, is improbable, must not try to force their opinion on the Evangelists, who by the stress which they lay on the expression

[5] Schleiermacher, ut sup. s. 87.

of the apostles, *we have left all* (Matt. xix. 27 ff.), plainly intimate the opposite view.

We gather, as to the rank of the twelve disciples of Jesus, that they all belonged to the lower class : four, or perhaps more (John xxi. 2), were fishermen, one a publican, and for the others, it is probable from the degree of cultivation they evince, and the preference always expressed by Jesus for the *poor* πτωχοὺς, and *the little ones*, νηπίους (Matt. v. 3, xi. 5, 25), that they were of a similar grade.

§ 74.

THE TWELVE CONSIDERED INDIVIDUALLY. THE THREE OR FOUR MOST CONFIDENTIAL DISCIPLES OF JESUS.

We have in the New Testament four catalogues of the apostles ; one in each of the synoptical gospels, and one in the Acts (Matt. x. 2–4 ; Mark iii. 6–10 ; Luke vi. 14–16 ; Acts i. 13). Each of these four lists may be divided into three quaternions ; in each corresponding quaternion the first member is the same ; and in the last, the concluding member also, if we except Acts i. 13, where he is absent: but the intermediate members are differently arranged, and in the concluding quaternions there is a difference of names or of persons.

At the head of the first quaternion in all the catalogues, and in Matthew with the prefix πρῶτος (*the first*), stands Simon Peter, the son of Jonas (Matt. xvi. 17) ; according to the fourth gospel, of Bethsaida (i. 45) ; according to the synoptists, resident in Capernaum [1] (Matt. viii. 14, parall.). We hear an echo of the old polemical dispute, when Protestant expositors ascribe this position to mere chance,—an assumption which is opposed by the fact that all four of the catalogues agree in giving the precedence to Peter, though they differ in other points of arrangement ; or when those expositors allege, in explanation, that Peter was first called,[2] which, according to the fourth gospel, was not the case. That this invariable priority is indicative of a certain preeminence of Peter among the twelve, is evident from the part he plays elsewhere in the evangelical history. Ardent by nature, he is always beforehand with the rest of the apostles, whether in speech (Matt. xv. 15, xvi. 16, 22, xvii. 4, xviii. 21, xxvi. 33 ; John vi. 68), or in action (Matt. xiv. 28, xxvi. 58 ; John xviii. 16) ; and if it is not seldom the case that the speech and action are faulty, and that his prompt courage quickly evaporates, as his denial shows, yet he is, according to the synoptical statement, the first who expresses a decided conviction of the Messiahship of Jesus (Matt. xvi. 16, parall.). It is true that of the eulogies and prerogatives bestowed on him on that occasion, that which is implied in his surname is the only one that remains peculiarly his ; for the authority to *bind and to loose*, that is, to forbid and to permit,[3] in the newly-founded Messianic kingdom, is soon after extended to all the apostles (xviii. 18). Yet more decidedly does this preeminence of Peter among the original apostles appear in the Acts, and in the Epistles of Paul.

Next to Peter, the catalogue of the first and third gospels places his brother Andrew ; that of the second gospel and the Acts, James, and after him, John.

---

[1] If ἡ πόλις Ἀνδρέου καὶ Πέτρου, John i. 45, mean the same as ἡ ἰδία πόλις, Matth. ix. 1, that is, the place where they were resident, there exists a contradiction on this point between John and the synoptists.

[2] Comp. Fritzsche, in Matt., p. 358.

[3] Comp. Lightfoot, in loc.

The first and third Evangelists are evidently guided by the propriety of uniting the couples of brethren ; Mark and the author of the Acts, by that of preferring the two apostles next in distinction to Peter to the less conspicuous Andrew, whom they accordingly put last in the quaternion. We have already considered the manner in which these four apostles are signalized in the Christian legend by a special history of their vocation. They appear together in other passages of Mark ; first (i. 29), where Jesus, in company with the sons of Zebedee, enters the house of Simon and Andrew : as, however, the other Evangelists only mention Peter on this occasion, Mark may have added the other names inferentially, concluding that the four fishermen, so recently called, would not be apart from Jesus, and that Andrew had a share in his brother's house, a thing in itself probable.[4]   Again, Mark xiii. 3, our four apostles concur in asking Jesus *privately* (κατ᾽ ἰδίαν) concerning the time of the destruction of the temple, and of his second advent.   But the parallel passages in the other gospels do not thus particularize any of the disciples. Matthew says, *The disciples came to him privately* (xxiv. 3) ; hence it is probable that Mark's limitation is an erroneous one.   Possibly the words κατ᾽ ἰδίαν, being used in the document to which he referred to denote the separation of the twelve from the multitude, appeared to him, from association, an introductory form, of which there are other examples (Matt. xvii. 1 ; Mark ix. 2), to a private conference of Jesus with Peter, James and John, to whom he might add Andrew on account of the fraternity.   Luke, on the other hand, in his account of the miraculous draught of fishes, and the vocation of the fishermen (v. 10), omits Andrew, though he is included in the corresponding narratives, probably because he does not elsewhere appear as one of the select apostles ; for except on the occasions already noticed, he is only mentioned by John (vi. 9, xii. 22), and that in no very important connexion.

The two sons of Zebedee are the only disciples whose distinction rivals that of Peter.   Like him, they evince an ardent and somewhat rash zeal (Luke ix. 54 ; once John is named alone, Mark ix. 38 ; Luke ix. 49) ; and it was to this disposition, apparently, that they owed the surname *Sons of Thunder*, בני רגש υἱοὶ βροντῆς (Mark iii. 17),[5] conferred on them by Jesus. So high did they stand among the twelve, that either they (Mark xi. 35 ff.), or their mother for them (Matt. xx. 20 ff.), thought they might claim the first place in the Messiah's kingdom.   It is worthy of notice that not only in the four catalogues, but elsewhere when the two brothers are named, as in Matt. iv. 21, xvii. 1 ; Mark i. 19, 29, v. 37, ix. 2, x. 35, xiii. 3, xiv. 33 ; Luke v. 10, ix. 54 ; with the exception of Luke viii. 51, ix. 28 ; James is always metioned first, and John is appended to him as *his brother* (ὁ ἀδελφὸς αὐτοῦ). This is surprising ; because, while we know nothing remarkable of James, John is memorable as the favourite disciple of Jesus.   Hence it is supposed that this precedence cannot possibly denote a superiority of James to John, and an explanation has been sought in his seniority.[6]   Nevertheless, it remains a doubt whether so constant a precedence do not intimate a preeminence on the part of James ; at least, if, in the apprehension of the synoptists, John had been as decidedly preferred as he is represented to have been in the fourth gospel, we are inclined to think that they would have named him before his brother James, even allowing him to be the younger. This leads us to a difference between the first three Evangelists and the fourth which requires a closer examination.

---

[4] Comp. Saunier, über die Quellen des Markus, s. 55 f.
[5] Comp. de Wette, in loc.
[6] Paulus, exeg. Handb. 1, b, s. 556.

In the synoptical gospels, as we have observed, Peter, James, and John, form the select circle of disciples whom Jesus admits to certain scenes, which the rest of the twelve were not spiritually mature enough to comprehend; as the transfiguration, the conflict in Gethsemane, and, according to Mark (v. 37), the raising of the daughter of Jairus.[7] After the death of Jesus, also, a James, Peter and John appear as the *pillars* of the church (Gal. ii. 9); this James, however, is not the son of Zebedee, who had been early put to death (Acts xii. 2), but James, the brother of the Lord (Gal. i. 19), who even in the first apostolic council appears to have possessed a predominant authority, and whom many hold to be the second James of the apostolic catalogue given in Acts i.[8] It is observable from the beginning of the Acts, that James the son of Zebedee is eclipsed by Peter and John.   As, then, this James the elder was not enough distinguished or even known in the primitive church, for his early martyrdom to have drawn much lustre on his name, tradition had no inducement, from subsequent events, to reflect an unhistorical splendour on his relation to Jesus ; there is therefore no reason to doubt the statement as to the prominent position held by James, in conjunction with Peter and John, among the twelve apostles.

So much the more must it excite surprise to find, in the fourth gospel the triumvirate almost converted into a monarchy : James, like another Lepidus, is wholly cast out, while Peter and John are in the position of Antony and Octavius, the latter having nearly stripped his rival of all pretensions to an equal rank with himself, to say nothing of a higher.   James is not even named in the fourth gospel ; only in the appendix (xxi. 2) is there any mention of the *sons of Zebedee* ; while several narratives of the vocations of different apostles are given, apparently including that of John himself, no James appears in them, neither is there any speech of his, as of many other apostles, throughout this gospel.

Quite differently does the fourth Evangelist treat Peter.   He makes him one of the first who enter the society of Jesus, and gives him a prominent importance not less often than the synoptists ; he does not conceal that Jesus bestowed on him an honourable surname (i. 43) ; he puts in his mouth (vi. 68 f.) a confession which seems but a new version of the celebrated one in Matt. xvi. 16 ; according to him, Peter once throws himself into the sea that he may more quickly reach Jesus (xxi. 7) ; at the last supper, and in the garden of Gethsemane, he makes Peter more active than even the synoptists represent him (xiii. 6 ff., xviii. 10 f.) ; he accords him the honour of following Jesus into the high priest's palace (xviii. 15), and of being one of the first to visit the grave of Jesus after the resurrection (xx. 3 ff.) ; nay, he even details a special conversation between the risen Jesus and Peter (xxi. 15 ff.). But these advantages of Peter are in the fourth gospel invalidated in a peculiar manner, and put into the shade, in favour of John.   The synoptists tell us that Peter and John were called to the apostleship in the same way, and the former somewhat before the latter ; the fourth Evangelist prefers associating Andrew with the nameless disciple who is taken for John, and makes Peter come to him through the instrumentality of his brother.[9]   He also admits the honourable interpretation of the surname Peter, and the

---

[7] This is probably a mere inference of Mark.   Because Jesus excluded the multitude, and forbade the publication of the event, the Evangelist saw in it one of those secret scenes, to which Jesus was accustomed to admit only the three favoured apostles.

[8] In the ancient church it was thought that Jesus had communicated to these three individuals the γνῶσις, to be mysteriously transmitted.   Vid. in Gieseler, K. G. i, s. 234.

[9] Even Paulus, L. J. 1, a, s. 167 f., remarks that the fourth Evangelist seems to have had a design in noticing this circumstance.

panegyric on Peter's confession ; but this he does in common with Mark and Luke, while the speeches and the action attributed in the fourth gospel to Peter during the last supper and in the garden, are to be classed as only so many mistakes. The more we approach the catastrophe, the more marked is the subordination of Peter to John. At the last supper, indeed, Peter is particularly anxious for the discovery of the traitor : he cannot, however, apply immediately to Jesus (xiii. 23 ff.), but is obliged to make John, *who was leaning on Jesus' bosom*, his medium of communication. While, according to the synoptists, Peter alone followed Jesus into the palace of the high priest; according to the fourth Evangelist, John accompanied him, and under such circumstances, that without him Peter could not have entered,—John, as one known to the high priest, having to obtain admission for him (xviii. 15 f.). In the synoptical gospels, not one of the disciples is bold enough to venture to the cross ; but in the fourth, John is placed under it, and is there established in a new relation to the mother of his dying master : a relation of which we elsewhere find no trace (xix. 26 f.). On the appearance of the risen Jesus at the Galilean sea (xxi.), Peter, as the θερμότερος, casts himself into the sea ; but it is not until after John, as the διορατικώτερος (Euthymius), has recognized the Lord in the person standing on the shore. In the ensuing conversation, Peter is indeed honoured with the commission, *Feed my sheep* ; but this honour is overshadowed by the dubitative question, *Lovest thou me ?* and while the prospect of martyrdom is held up to him, John is promised the distinction of tarrying till Jesus came again, an advantage which Peter is warned not to envy. Lastly, while, according to Luke (xxiv. 12), Peter, first among the apostles, and alone, comes to the vacant grave of his risen master, the fourth gospel (xx. 3), gives him a companion in John, who outruns Peter and arrives first at the grave. Peter goes into the grave before John, it is true ; but it is the latter in whose honour it is recorded, that he *saw and believed*, almost in contradiction to the statement of Luke, that Peter went home *wondering in himself at that which was come to pass*. Thus in the fourth gospel, John, both literally and figuratively, *outruns Peter*, for the entire impression which the attentive reader must receive from the representation there given of the relative position of Peter and John, is that the writer wished a comparison to be drawn in favour of the latter.[10]

But John is moreover especially distinguished in the gospel which bears his name, by the constant epithet, *the beloved disciple, the disciple whom Jesus loved*, ὁ μαθητὴς ὃν ἠγάπα, or ἐφίλει ὁ Ἰησοῦς (xiii. 23, xix. 26, xx. 2, xxi. 7, 20). It is true that we have no absolute proof from the contents of the fourth gospel, whether intrinsically or comparatively considered, that by the above formula, or the more indeterminate one, *the other* ὁ ἄλλος, or *another disciple*, ἄλλος μαθητὴς (x. 15 f., xx, 3, 4, 8), which, as it appears from xx. 2 f., is its equivalent, we are to understand the Apostle John. For neither is the designation in question anywhere used interchangeably with the name of the apostle, nor is there anything narrated in the fourth gospel of the favourite disciple, which in the three first is ascribed to John. Because in xxi. 2 the sons of Zebedee are named among the assistants, it does not follow that the disciple mentioned in v. 7 as the one whom Jesus loved must be John ;

[10] This has not escaped the acumen of Dr. Paulus. In a review of the first volume of the second ed. of Lücke's Comm. zum Johannes, in Lt. Bl. zur allg. Kirchenzeitung, Febr., 1834, no. 18, s. 137 f., he says : "The gospel of John has only preserved the less advantageous circumstances connected with Peter (excepting vi. 68), *such as place him in marked subordination to John* [here the passages above considered are cited]. An adherent of Peter can hardly have had a hand in the Gospel of John." We may add that it seems to have proceeded from an antagonist of Peter, for it is probable that he had such of the school of John, as well as of Paul.

James, or the one of the *two other disciples* mentioned in v. 2, might be meant. Nevertheless, it is the immemorial tradition of the church that the disciple whom Jesus loved was John, nor are all reasons for such a belief extinct even to us; for in the Greek circle from which the fourth gospel sprang, there could scarcely be among the apostles whom it leaves unnamed, one so well known as to be recognized under that description unless it were John, whose residence at Ephesus is hardly to be rejected as a mere fable.

It may appear more doubtful whether the author intended by this title to designate himself, and thus to announce himself as the Apostle John. The conclusion of the twenty-first chapter, v. 24, does certainly make the favourite disciple the testifier and writer of the preceding history ; but we may assume it as granted that this passage is an addition by a strange hand.[11] When, however, in the genuine text of the gospel (xix. 35), the writer says of the effect produced by the piercing of the side of Jesus, *he that saw bear record*, ὁ ἑωρακὼς μεμαρτύρηκε, no other than the favourite disciple can be intended, because he alone among all the disciples (the only parties eligible as witnesses in the case), is supposed to be present at the cross. The probability that the author here speaks of himself is not at all affected by his use of the third person; but the preterite annexed to it may well excite a doubt whether an appeal be not here made to the testimony of John, as one distinct from the writer.[12] This mode of expression, however, may be explained also in accordance with the other supposition,[13] which is supported by the circumstance that the author in i. 14, 16, seems to announce himself as the eye-witness of the history he narrates.

Was that author, then, really the Apostle John, as he apparently wishes us to surmise ? This is another question on which we can only pronounce when we shall have completed our investigation. We will merely allude to the difficulty of supposing that the Apostle John could give so unhistorical a sketch of the Baptist as that in the fourth gospel. But we ask, is it at all probable that the real John would so unbecomingly neglect the well-founded claims of his brother James to a special notice ? and is not such an omission rather indicative of a late Hellenistic author, who scarcely had heard the name of the brother so early martyred ? The designation, *the disciple whom Jesus loved*, which in xxi. 20 has the prolix addition, *who also leaned on his breast at supper*, *and said, Lord which is he that betrayeth thee ?* is not to be considered as an offence against modesty.[14] It is certainly far too laboured and embellished for one who, without any ulterior view, wishes to indicate himself, for such an one would, at least sometimes, have simply employed his name : but a venerator of John, issuing perhaps from one of his schools, might very naturally be induced to designate the revered apostle, under whose name he wished to write, in this half honourable, half mysterious manner.[15]

§ 75.

THE REST OF THE TWELVE, AND THE SEVENTY DISCIPLES.

The second quaternion in all the four catalogues begins with Philip. The three first gospels know nothing more of him than his name. The fourth

---

[11] Vid. Lücke, Comm. zum Joh. 2, s. 708.

[12] Paulus, in his review of Bretschneider's Probabilien, in the Heidelberger Jahrbüchern, 1821, no. 9, s. 138.

[13] Lücke, ut sup. s. 664.

[14] Bretschneider, Probabilia, p. 111 f.

[15] Comp. Paulus, ut sup. s. 137.

alone gives his birth-place, Bethsaida, and narrates his vocation (i. 44 f.); in this gospel he is more than once an interlocutor, but his observations are founded on mistakes (vi. 7, xiv. 8); and he perhaps appears with most dignity, when the Ἕλληνες, who wish to see Jesus, apply immediately to him (xii. 21).

The next in the evangelical lists is Bartholomew ; a name which is nowhere found out of the catalogues. In the synoptical gospels Bartholomew is coupled with Phillip ; in the history of the vocations given by the fourth Evangelist (i. 46), Nathanael appears in company with the latter and (xxi. 2) is again presented in the society of the apostles. Nathanael, however, finds no place among the twelve, unless he be identical with one otherwise named by the synoptists. If so, it is thought that Bartholomew is the most easily adapted to such an alias, as the three first gospels couple him with Philip, just as the fourth, which has no Bartholomew; does Nathanael; to which it may be added that בר תלמי is a mere patronymic, which must have been accompanied by a proper name, such as Nathanael.[1] But we have no adequate ground for such an identification, since the juxtaposition of Bartholomew and Philip is shown to be accidental, by our finding the former (Acts i. 13), as well as the latter (John xxi. 2), linked with different names ; the absence of Bartholomew from the fourth gospel is not peculiar to him among the twelve ; finally, second names as surnames were added to proper as well as to patronymic names, as Simon Peter, Joseph Caiaphas, John Mark, and the like ; so that any other apostle not named by John might be equally well identified with Nathanael, and hence the supposed relation between the two appellations is altogether uncertain.

In the catalogue given in the Acts, Philip is followed, not by Bartholomew, but by Thomas, who in the list of the first gospel comes after Bartholomew, in that of the others, after Matthew. Thomas, in Greek Δίδυμος, appears in the fourth gospel, on one occasion, in the guise of mournful fidelity (xi. 16); on another, in the more noted one of incredulity (xx. 24 ff.) ; and once again in the appendix (xxi. 2). Matthew, the next in the series, is found nowhere else except in the history of his vocation.

The third quaternion is uniformly opened by James the son of Alpheus, of whom we have already spoken. After him comes in both Luke's lists, Simon, whom he calls Zelotes, or the zealot, but whom Matthew and Mark (in whose catalogues he is placed one degree lower) distinguish as the Cannanite ὁ καναντίης (from קנא, to be zealous). This surname seems to mark him as a former adherent of the Jewish sect of zealots for religion,[2] a party which, it is true, did not attain consistence until the latest period of the Jewish state, but which was already in the process of formation. In all the lists that retain the name of Judas Iscariot, he occupies the last place, but of him we must not speak until we enter on the history of the Passion. Luke, in his filling up of the remaining places of this quaternion, differs from the two other Evangelists, and perhaps these also differ from each other ; Luke has a second Judas, whom he styles the brother of James ; Matthew, Lebbeus ; and Mark, Thaddeus. It is true that we now commonly read in Matthew, *Lebbeus, whose surname was Thaddeus* ; but the vacillation in the early readings seems to betray these words to be a later addition intended to reconcile the first two Evangelists ;[3] an attempt which others have made by pointing out a similarity

---

[1] Thus most of the expositors, Fritzsche, Matth., s. 359 ; Winer, Realwörterb. I, s. 163 f. Comp. De Wette, exeg. Handb. I, I, s. 98.

[2] Joseph.. bell. jud. iv. iii. 9.

[3] Comp. Credner, Einleitung I, s. 64 ; De Wette, exeg. Handb. I, I, s. 98 f.

of meaning between the two names, though such a similarity does not exist.[4] But allowing validity to one or other of these harmonizing efforts, there yet remains a discrepancy between Matthew and Mark with their Lebbeus-Thaddeus, and Luke with his Judas, the brother of James   Schleiermacher justly disapproves the expedients, almost all of them constrained and unnatural, which have been resorted to for the sake of proving that here also, we have but one person under two different names.   He seeks to explain the divergency, by supposing, that during the lifetime of Jesus, one of the two men died or left the circle of the apostles, and the other took his place ; so that one list gives the earlier, the other the later member.[5]   But it is scarcely possible to admit that any one of our catalogues was drawn up during the life of Jesus ; and after that period, no writer would think of including a member who had previously retired from the college of apostles ; those only would be enumerated who were ultimately attached to Jesus.   It is the most reasonable to allow that there is a discrepancy between the lists, since it is easy to account for it by the probability that while the number of the apostles, and the names of the most distinguished among them, were well known, varying traditions supplied the place of more positive data concerning the less conspicuous.

Luke makes us acquainted with a circle of disciples, intermediate to the twelve and the mass of the partisans of Jesus.   He tells us (x. 1 ff.) that besides the twelve, Jesus chose *other seventy also*, and sent them two and two before him into all the districts which he intended to visit on his last journey, that they might proclaim the approach of the kingdom of heaven.   As the other Evangelists have no allusion to this event, the most recent critics have not hesitated to make their silence on this head a reproach to them, particularly to the first Evangelist, in his supposed character of apostle.[6]   But the disfavour towards Matthew on this score ought to be moderated by the consideration, that neither in the other gospels, nor in the Acts, nor in any apostolic epistle, is there any trace of the seventy disciples, who could scarcely have passed thus unnoticed, had their mission been as fruitful in consequences, as it is commonly supposed.   It is said, however, that the importance of this appointment lay in its significance, rather than in its effects.   As the number of the twelve apostles, by its relation to that of the tribes of Israel, shadowed forth the destination of Jesus for the Jewish people ; so the seventy, or as some authorities have it, the seventy-two disciples, were representatives of the seventy or seventy-two peoples, with as many different tongues, which, according to the Jewish and early Christian view, formed the sum of the earth's inhabitants,[7] and hence they denoted the universal destination of Jesus and his kingdom.[8]   Moreover, seventy was a sacred number with the Jewish nation ; Moses deputed seventy elders (Num. xi. 16, 25) ; the Sanhedrim had seventy members ;[9] the Old Testament, seventy translators.

Had Jesus, then, under the pressing circumstances that mark his public career, nothing more important to do than to cast about for significant numbers, and to surround himself with inner and outer circles of disciples, regulated by these mystic measures ? or rather, is not this constant preference for sacred numbers, this assiduous development of an idea to which the number of the apostles furnished the suggestion, wholly in the spirit of the primitive

[4] De Wette, ut sup.
[5] Ueber den Lukas, s. 88 f.
[6] Schulz, über das Abendmahl, s. 307. ; Schneckenburger, über den Ursprung, s. 13 f.
[7] Tuf haarez, f. xix. c. iii. ; Clem. hom. xviii. 4 ; Recognit. Clement. ii. 42 ; Epiphan. hær. i. 5.
[8] Schneckenburger, ut sup. ; Gieseler, über Entstehung der schriftl. Evangelien, s. 127 f.
[9] Lightfoot, p. 786.

Christian legend? This, supposing it imbued with Jewish prepossessions, would infer, that as Jesus had respect to the twelve tribes in fixing the number of his apostles, he would extend the parallel by appointing seventy subordinate disciples, corresponding to the seventy elders ; or, supposing the legend animated by the more universal sentiments of Paul, it could not escape the persuasion that to the symbol of the relation of his office to the Israelitish people, Jesus would annex another, significative of its destination for all the kindreds of the earth. However agreeable this class of seventy disciples may have always been to the church, as a series of niches for the reception of men who, without belonging to the twelve, were yet of importance to her, as Mark, Luke and Matthew; we are compelled to pronounce the decision of our most recent critic precipitate, and to admit that the Gospel of Luke, by its acceptance of such a narrative, destitute as it is of all historical confirmation, and of any other apparent source than dogmatical interests, is placed in disadvantageous comparison with that of Matthew. We gather, indeed, from Acts i. 21 f. that Jesus had more than the twelve as his constant companions ; but that these formed a body of exactly seventy, or that that number was selected from them, does not seem adequately warranted [10].

[10] De Wette, exeget. Handb., 1, 1, s. 99 f. 1, 2, s. 61. 1, 3, s. 220 ; Theile, zur Biogr. J., § 24. For the contrary opinion, see Neander, L. J. Chr., s. 498 f.

CHAPTER VI.

THE DISCOURSES OF JESUS IN THE THREE FIRST GOSPELS.*

§ 76.

THE SERMON ON THE MOUNT.

IN reviewing the public life of Jesus, we may separate from the events those discourses which were not merely incidental, but which stand independent and entire. This distinction, however, is not precise, for many discourses, owing to the occurrences that suggested them, may be classed as events ; and many events, from the explanations annexed to them, seem to range themselves with the discourses. The discourses of Jesus given in the synoptical gospels, and those attributed to him in the fourth, differ widely both in form and matter, having only a few isolated sentences in common : they must, therefore, be subjected to a separate examination. Again, there is a dissimilitude between the three first Evangelists : Matthew affects long discourses, and collects into one mass a number of sayings, which in Luke are distributed among various places and occasions ; each of these two Evangelists has also some discourses peculiar to himself. In Mark, the element of discourses exists in a very small proportion. Our purpose will, therefore, be best answered, if we make Matthew's comprehensive discourses our starting point ; ascertain all the corresponding ones in the other gospels ; inquire which amongst them has the best arrangement and representation of these discourses ; and, finally, endeavour to form a judgment as to how far they really proceeded from the lips of Jesus.

The first long discourse in Matthew is that known as the Sermon on the Mount (v.–vii.). The Evangelist, having recorded the return of Jesus after his baptism into Galilee, and the calling of the fishermen, informs us, that Jesus went through all Galilee, teaching and healing ; that great multitudes followed him from all parts of Palestine ; and that for their instruction he ascended a mountain, and delivered the sermon in question (iv. 23 ff.). We seek in vain for its parallel in Mark, but Luke (vi. 20–49) gives a discourse which has the same introduction and conclusion. and presents in its whole tenor the most striking similarity with that of Matthew ; moreover, in both cases, Jesus, at the termination of his discourse, goes to Capernaum, and heals the centurion's servant. It is true that Luke gives a later insertion to the discourse, for previous to it he narrates many journeyings and cures of Jesus, which Matthew places after it ; and while the latter represents Jesus as ascending a mountain, and being seated there during delivery of his discourse, Luke says, almost in contradiction to him, that Jesus *came down and*

---

* All that relates to the sufferings, death, and resurrection of Jesus is here excluded.

stood in the plain. Further, the sermon in Luke contains but a fourth part of that in Matthew, while it has some elements peculiarly its own.

To avoid the unpleasant admission that one of two inspired Evangelists must be in error,—which is inevitable if in relation to the same discourse one of them makes Jesus deliver it on the mountain, the other in the plain ; the one sitting, the other standing ; the one earlier, the other later ; if either the one has made important omissions, or the other as important additions ;—the ancient harmonists pronounced these discourses to be distinct,[1] on the plea that Jesus must frequently have treated of the essential points of his doctrine, and may therefore have repeated word for word certain impressive enunciations. This may be positively denied with respect to long discourses, and even concise maxims will always be reproduced in a new guise and connexion by a gifted and inventive teacher ; to say the least, it is impossible that any but a very barren mind should repeat the same formal exordium, and the same concluding illustration, on separate occasions.

The identity of the discourses being established, the first effort was to conciliate or to explain the divergencies between the two accounts so as to leave their credibility unimpeached. In reference to the different designation of the locality, Paulus insists on the ἐπὶ of Luke, which he interprets to imply that Jesus stood *over* the plain, and therefore on a hill. Tholück, more happily, distinguishes the *level space*, τόπος πεδινὸς, from the plain properly so called, and regards it as a less abrupt part of the mountain. But as one Evangelist makes Jesus ascend the mountain to deliver his discourse, while the other makes him descend for the same purpose, these conciliators ought to admit, with Olshausen, that if Jesus taught in the plain, according to Luke, Matthew has overlooked the descent that preceded the discourse ; or if, as Matthew says, Jesus taught seated on the mountain, Luke has forgotten to mention that after he had descended, the pressure of the crowd induced him to reascend before he commenced his harangue. And without doubt each was ignorant of what he omits, but each knew that tradition associated this discourse with a sojourn of Jesus on a mountain. Matthew thought the mountain a convenient elevation for one addressing a multitude ; Luke, on the contrary, imagined a descent necessary for the purpose : hence the double discrepancy, for he who teaches from a mountain is sufficiently elevated over his hearers to sit, but he who teaches in a plain will naturally stand. The chronological divergencies, as well as the local, must be admitted, if we would abstain from fruitless efforts at conciliation.[2]

The difference as to the length and contents of the discourse is susceptible of three explanations : either the concise record of Luke is a mere extract from the entire discourse which Matthew gives without abridgment ; or Matthew has incorporated many sayings belonging properly to other occasions ; or, lastly, both these causes of variety have concurred. He who, with Tholück, wishes to preserve intact the *fides divina*, or with Paulus, the *fides humana* of the Evangelists, will prefer the first supposition, because to withhold the true is more innocent than to add the false. The above theologians hold that the train of thought in the Sermon on the Mount, as given by Matthew, is closely consecutive, and that this is a proof of its original unity. But any compiler not totally devoid of ability, can give a tolerable appearance of connectedness to sayings which did not originally belong to each other ; and even these commentators are obliged to admit[3] that the alleged consecu-

---

[1] Augustin. de consens. ev. ii. 19. ; Storr, über den Zweck des Evang. u. d. Br. Joh., s. 347 ff. For further references see Tholück's Auslegung der Bergpredigt, Einl., § 1.
[2] Comp. De Wette, exeg. Handb., I, 1, s. 47 ff. I, 2, s. 44.
[3] Tholück, s. 24 ; Paulus, exeg. Handb., I, b, s. 584.

tiveness extends over no more than half the sermon, for from vi. 19 it is a string of more or less isolated sentences, some of them very unlikely to have been uttered on the occasion. More recent criticism has therefore decided that the shorter account of Luke presents the discourse of Jesus in its original form, and that Matthew has taken the licence of incorporating with this much that was uttered by Jesus at various times, so as to retain the general sketch —the exordium, peroration, and essential train of thought; while between these compartments he inserted many sayings more or less analogous borrowed from elsewhere.[4] This view is especially supported by the fact that many of the sentences, which in Matthew make part of the Sermon on the Mount, are in Mark and Luke dispersed through a variety of scenes. Compelled to grant this, yet earnestly solicitous to avert from the Evangelist an imputation that might invalidate his claim to be considered an eye-witness, other theologians maintain that Matthew did not compile the discourse under the idea that it was actually spoken on a single occasion, but with the clearest knowledge that such was not the case.[5] It is with justice remarked in opposition to this, that when Matthew represents Jesus as ascending the mountain before he begins his discourse, and descending after its close, he obviously makes these two incidents the limits of a single address; and that when he speaks of the impression which the discourse produced on the multitude, whose presence he states as the inducement to its delivery, he could not but intend to convey the idea of a continuous harangue.[6] As to Luke's edition of the sermon, there are parts in which the interrupted connexion betrays deficiencies, and there are additions which do not look genuine;[7] it is also doubtful whether he assigns a more appropriate connexion to the passages in the position of which he differs from Matthew;[8] and hence, as we shall soon see more fully, he has in this instance no advantage over his predecessor.

The assemblage to whom the Sermon on the Mount was addressed, might from Luke's account be supposed a narrow circle, for he states that the choice of the apostles immediately preceded the discourse, and that at its commencement Jesus *lifted up his eyes on his disciples,* and he does not, like Matthew, note the *multitude,* ὄχλους, as part of the audience. On the other hand, Matthew also mentions that before the sermon the disciples gathered round Jesus and were taught by him; and Luke represents the discourse as being delivered *in the audience of the people* (vii. 1); it is therefore evident that Jesus spoke to the crowd in general, but with a particular view to the edification of his disciples.[9] We have no reason to doubt that a real harangue of Jesus, more than ordinarily solemn and public, was the foundation of the evangelical accounts before us.

Let us now proceed to an examination of particulars. In both editions, the Sermon on the Mount is opened by a series of beatitudes; in Luke, however, not only are several wanting which we find in Matthew, but most of those common to both are in the former taken in another sense than in the latter.[10] The *poor,* πτωχοὶ, are not specified as in Matthew by the addition, *in spirit,* τῷ πνεύματι; they are therefore not those who have a deep consciousness of inward poverty and misery, but the literally poor; neither is the

---

[4] Schulz, vom Abendmahl, s. 313 f. ; Sieffert, s. 74 ff. ; Fritzsche, s. 301.
[5] Olshausen, Bibl. Comm., 1, s. 197 ; Kern, in der Tüb. Schrift, 1834, 2, s. 33.
[6] Schulz, ut sup. s. 315 ; Schneckenburger, Beiträge, s. 26 ; Credner, Einleit., 1, s. 69.
[7] Schleiermacher, über den Lukas, s. 89 f.
[8] Tholück, p. 11, and my Review of the writings of Sieffert and others in the Jahrbuch f. wiss. Kritik, Nov. 1834 ; now in my Charakteristiken u. Kritiken, s. 252 ff.
[9] Comp. Tholück, ut sup. s. 25 ff. ; De Wette, exeget. Handb., 1, 1, s. 49.
[10] Storr, Ueber den Zweck u. s. w., s. 348 f. Olshausen.

hunger of the πεινῶντες (*hungering*) referred to τὴν δικαιοσύνην (*righteousness*) ; it is therefore not spiritual hunger, but bodily ; moreover, the adverb νῦν, *now*, definitely marks out *those who hunger and those who weep*, the πεινῶντες and κλαίοντες. Thus in Luke the antithesis is not, as in Matthew, between the present sorrows of pious souls, whose pure desires are yet unsatisfied, and their satisfaction about to come ; but between present suffering and future well-being in general.[11]   This mode of contrasting the αἰὼν οὗτος and the αἰὼν μέλλων, *the present age* and *the future*, is elsewhere observable in Luke, especially in the parable of the rich man ; and without here inquiring which of the two representations is probably the original, I shall merely remark, that this of Luke is conceived entirely in the spirit of the Ebionites,—a spirit which has of late been supposed discernible in Matthew.   It is a capital principle with the Ebionites, as they are depicted in the Clementine Homilies, that he who has his portion in the present age, will be destitute in the age to come ; while he who renounces earthly possessions, thereby accumulates heavenly treasures.[12]   The last beatitude relates to those who are persecuted for the sake of Jesus.   Luke in the parallel passage has, *for the Son of man's sake ;* hence the words *for my sake* in Matthew, must be understood to refer to Jesus solely in his character of Messiah.[13]

The beatitudes are followed in Luke by as many *woes* οὐαί, which are wanting in Matthew.   In these the opposition established by the Ebionites between this world and the other, is yet more strongly marked ; for woe is denounced on the rich, the full, and the joyous, simply as such, and they are threatened with the evils corresponding to their present advantages, under the new order of things to be introduced by the Messiah ; a view that reminds us of the Epistle of James, v. 1 ff.   The last woe is somewhat stiffly formed after the model of the last beatitude, for it is evidently for the sake of the contrast to the true prophets, so much calumniated, that the false prophets are said, without any historical foundation, to have been spoken well of by all men.   We may therefore conjecture, with Schleiermacher,[14] that we are indebted for these maledictions to the inventive fertility of the author of the third gospel. He added this supplement to the beatitudes, less because, as Schleiermacher supposes, he perceived a chasm, which he knew not how to fill, than because he judged it consistent with the character of the Messiah, that, like Moses of old, he should couple curses with blessings.   The Sermon on the Mount is regarded as the counterpart of the law, delivered on Mount Sinai ; but the introduction, especially in Luke, reminds us more of a passage in Deuteronomy, in which Moses commands that on the entrance of the Israelitish people into the promised land, one half of them shall take their stand on Mount Gerizim, and pronounce a manifold blessing on the observers of the law, the other half on Mount Ebal, whence they were to fulminate as manifold a curse on its transgressors.   We read in Josh. viii. 33 ff. that this injunction was fulfilled.[15]

With the beatitudes, Matthew suitably connects the representation of the

---

[11] De Wette, exeg. Handb., 1, 2, s. 44 f. ; Neander. L. J. Chr., s. 155 f., Anm.

[12] Homil. xv. 7 ; comp. Credner in Winer's Zeitschrift f. wiss. Theologie, 1, s. 298 f. ; Schneckenburger, über das Evangelium der Aegyptier, § 6.

[13] Schneckenburger, über den Ursprung, s. 29.

[14] Ut sup. s. 90, Neander agrees with him, ut sup.

[15] The Rabbins also attached weight to these Mosaic blessings and curses, vid. Lightfoot, p. 255.   As here we have eight blessings, they held that Abraham had been blessed *benedictionibus septem* (Baal Turim, in Gen. xii. Lightfoot, p. 256) ; David, Daniel with his three companions, and the Messiah, *benedictionibus sex*. (Targ. Ruth. 3. ibid.) They also counted together with the twenty *beatitudines* in the Psalms, as many *væ* in Isaiah. (Midrasch Tehillim in Ps. i. ib.).

disciples as *the salt of the earth*, and *the light of the world* (v. 13 ff.). In Luke, the discourse on the salt is, with a rather different opening, introduced in another place (xiv. 34 f.), where Jesus admonishes his hearers to ponder the sacrifices that must be made by those who would follow him, and rather to abstain from the profession of discipleship than to maintain it dishonourably; and to this succeeds aptly enough the comparison of such degenerate disciples to salt that has lost its savour. Thus the dictum accords with either context, and from its aphoristical conciseness would be likely to recur, so that it may have been really spoken in both discourses. On the contrary, it cannot have been spoken in the sequence in which it is placed by Mark (ix. 50): for the idea that every one shall be salted with fire (in allusion to hell), has no internal connexion with the comparison of the true disciples of Jesus to salt, denoting their superiority: the connexion is merely external, resulting from the verbal affinity of ἁλίζειν and ἅλας,—it is the connexion of the dictionary.[16] The altered sequel which Mark gives to the apothegm (*have salt in yourselves, and be at peace with one another*) might certainly be united to it without incongruity, but it would accord equally well with quite a different train of thought. The apothegm on the light which is not to be hidden, as the salt is not to be without savour, is also wanting in the Sermon on the Mount as given by Luke; who, however, omitting the special application to the disciples, has substantially the same doctrine in two different places. We find it first (viii. 16) immediately after the interpretation of the parable of the sower, where it also occurs in Mark (iv. 21), It must be admitted that there is no incoherence in associating the shining of the light with the fructification of the seed; still, a judicious teacher will pause on the interpretation of a parable, and will not disturb its effect by a hasty transition to new images. At any rate there is no intrinsic connexion between the shining of the inward light, and the declaration appended to it by Luke, that all secrets shall be made manifest. We have here a case which is of frequent recurrence with this Evangelist; that, namely, of a variety of isolated sayings being thrown confusedly together between two independent discourses or narratives. Thus between the parable of the sower and the narrative of the visit paid to Jesus by his mother and brethren, the apothegm on the light is inserted on account of its internal analogy with the parable; then, because in this apothegm there occurs the opposition between concealment and manifestation, it suggested to the writer the otherwise heterogeneous discourse on the revelation of all secrets; whereupon is added, quite irrelevantly to the context, but with some relation to the parable, the declaration, *Whosoever hath, to him shall be given.* In the second passage on the manifestation of the light (xi. 33), the subject has absolutely no connexion, unless we interpolate one,[17] with that of the context, which turns on the condemnation of the cotemporaries of Jesus by the Ninevites. The fact is, that here again, between the discourses against the demand for signs and those at the Pharisee's dinner, we have a chasm filled up with disjointed fragments of harangues.

At v. 17 ff. follows the transition to the main subject of the sermon; the assurance of Jesus that he came not to destroy the law and the prophets, but to fulfil, etc. Now as Jesus herein plainly presupposes that he is himself the Messiah, to whom was ascribed authority to abolish a part of the law, this declaration cannot properly belong to a period in which, if Matt. xvi. 13 ff. be rightly placed, he had not yet declared himself to be the Messiah. Luke

---

[16] Schneckenburger, Beiträge, s. 58. Neander tries to show, very artificially, a real connection of thought, s. 157, Anm.

[17] Olshausen in loc. The true reading is indicated by Schneckenburger, Beiträge, s. 58; Tholück, ut sup. s. 11.

(xvi. 17) inserts this declaration together with the apparently contradictory one, that the law and the prophets were in force until the coming of John. These are two propositions that we cannot suppose to have been uttered consecutively ; and the secret of their conjunction in Luke's gospel lies in the word νόμος, *law,* which happens to occur in both.[18] It is to be observed that between the parable of the steward and that of the rich man, we have another of those pauses in which Luke is fond of introducing his fragments.

So little, it appears from v. 20, is it the design of Jesus to inculcate a disregard of the Mosaic law, that he requires a far stricter observance of its precepts than the Scribes and Pharisees, and he makes the latter appear in contrast to himself as the underminers of the law. Then follows a series of Mosaic commandments, on which Jesus comments so as to show that he penetrates into the spirit of the law, instead of cleaving to the mere letter, and especially discerns the worthlessness of the rabbinical glosses (48). This section, in the order and completeness in which we find it in Matthew, is wanting in Luke's Sermon on the Mount ; a decisive proof that the latter has deficiencies. For not only does this chapter contain the fundamental thought of the discourse as given by Matthew, but the desultory sayings which Luke gives, concerning the love of enemies, mercifulness and beneficence, only acquire a definite purpose and point of union in the contrast between the spiritual interpretation of the law given by Jesus, and the carnal one given by the doctors of the time. The words, too, with which Luke makes Jesus proceed after the last woe : *But I say unto you,* and those at v. 39, *And he spake a parable unto them,* have been correctly pointed out as indicative of chasms.[19] As regards the isolated parallel passages, the admonition to a quick reconciliation with an adversary (v. 25 f.), is, to say the least, not so easily brought into connexion with the foregoing matter in Luke (xii. 58) as in Matthew.[20] It is still worse with the passage in Luke which is parallel with Matt. v. 32 ; this text (relative to divorce), which in Matthew is linked in the general chain of ideas, is in Luke (xvi. 18) thrust into one of the apertures we have noticed, between the assurance of the perpetuity of the law and the parable of the rich man. Olshausen tries to find a thread of connexion between the passage and the one preceding it, by interpreting *adultery,* μοιχεύειν, allegorically, as faithlessness to the divine law ; and Schleiermacher[21] attaches it to the succeeding parable by referring it to the adulterous Herod : but such interpretations are altogether visionary.[22] Probably tradition had apprized the Evangelist that Jesus, after the foregoing declaration as to the perpetuity of the Mosaic law, had enunciated his severe principle on the subject of divorce, and hence he gave it this position, not knowing more of its original connexion. In Matt. xix. 9, we find a reiteration of this principle on an occasion very likely to call it forth. The exhortations to patience and submissiveness, form, in Matthew, the spiritual interpretation of the old rule, *an eye for an eye,* etc., and are therefore a following out of the previous train of thought. In Luke (vi. 29), they are introduced with much less precision by the command concerning love to enemies : which command is also decidedly better given in Matthew as the rectification of the precept, *Thou shalt love thy neighbour, and hate thine enemy* (43 ff.). Again : the observation that to love friends is nothing more than bad men can do, is, in Matthew, made, in order to controvert the traditional perversion of the Mosaic injunction to love one's neighbour, into a

---

[18] This cause is overlooked by Schleiermacher, s. 205 ; comp. De Wette, in loc.
[19] Schleiermacher, ut sup. s. 90. Tholück, s. 21.
[20] Tholück, s. 12, 187 ; De Wette, in loc.
[21] Ut sup. 206 f.
[22] Comp. De Wette, exeg. Handb. 1, 2, s. 86.

permission to hate enemies : in Luke, the observation follows the rule, *What-soever ye would that men should do to you*, etc., which in Matthew occurs farther on (vii. 12) without any connexion.   On the whole, if the passage in Luke from vi. 2–36, be compared with the corresponding one in Matthew, there will be found in the latter an orderly course of thought ; in the former, considerable confusion.[23]

The warnings against Pharisaic hypocrisy (vi. 1–6) are without a parallel in Luke ; but he has one of the model prayer, which recent criticism has turned not a little to the disadvantage of Matthew.   The ancient harmonists, it is true, had no hesitation in supposing that Jesus delivered this prayer twice,— in the connexion in which it is given by Matthew, as well as under the circumstances narrated by Luke (xi. ff.).[24]   But if Jesus had already in the Sermon on the Mount given a model prayer, his disciples would scarcely have requested one afterwards, as if nothing of the kind had occurred ; and it is still more improbable that Jesus would repeat the same formulary, without any recollection that he had delivered it to these disciples long before.   Hence our most recent critics have decided that Luke alone has preserved the natural and true occasion on which this prayer was communicated, and that like many other fragments, it was interpolated in Matthew's Sermon on the Mount by the writer.[25]   But the vaunted naturalness of Luke's representation, I, for one, cannot discover.   Apart from the improbability, admitted even by the above critics, that the disciples of Jesus should have remained without any direction to pray until the last journey, in which Luke places the scene ; it is anything but natural that Jesus should abstain from giving his disciples the exemplar which was in his mind until they sought for it, and that then he should forthwith fall into prayer.   He had, doubtless, often prayed in their circle from the commencement of their intercourse ; and if so, their request was superfluous, and must, as in John xiv. 9, have produced only an admonition to recollect what they had long seen and heard in his society.   The account of Luke seems to have been framed on mere conjecture ; it was known that the above prayer proceeded from Jesus, and the further question as to the motive for its communication, received the gratuitous answer : without doubt his disciples had asked him for such an exemplar.   Without, therefore, maintaining that Matthew has preserved to us the connexion in which this prayer was originally uttered by Jesus, we are not the less in doubt whether it has a more accurate position in Luke.[26]   With regard to the elements of the prayer, it is impossible to deny what Wetstein says : *tota hæc oratio ex formulis Hebræorum concinnata est ;*[27] but Fritzsche's observation is also just, that desires of so general a nature might be uttered in the prayers of various persons, even in similar phraseology, without any other cause than the broad uniformity of human feeling.[28]   We may add that the selection and allocation of the petitions in the prayer are entirely original, and bear the impress of that religious consciousness which Jesus possessed and sought to impart to his followers.[29] Matthew inserts after the conclusion of the prayer two propositions, which are properly the corollary of the third petition, but which seem inaptly placed, not only because they are severed by the concluding petition from the passage to which they have reference, but because they have no point of coincidence

[23] De Wette, exeg. Handb. 1, 1, s. 48.
[24] Orig. de orat. xviii. and Hess, Gesch. Jesu, 2, s. 48 f.
[25] Schleiermacher, ut sup. s. 173; Olshausen, 1, s. 235; Sieffert, s. 78 ft. Neander, s. 235 f. note.
[26] Comp. De Wette, exeg. Handb. 1, 1, s. 69. 1, 2, s. 65.
[27] N.T. 1, 323.   The parallels may be seen in Wetstein and Lightfoot.
[28] Comm. in Matt., p. 265.
[29] Comp. De Wette, 1, 1, s. 69 ff. ; Neander, s. 237 ff.

with the succeeding censures and admonitions which turn on the hypocrisy of the Pharisaic fasts. Mark, however, has still more infelicitously appended these propositions to the discourse of Jesus on the efficacy of believing prayer (xi. 25).[30]

At vi. 19, the thread of strict connexion is broken, according to the admission of Paulus, and so far all expositors are bound to agree with him. But his position, that notwithstanding the admitted lack of coherence in the succeeding collection of sentences, Jesus spoke them consecutively, is not equally tenable ; on the contrary, our more recent critics have all the probabilities on their side when they suppose, that in this latter half of the Sermon on the Mount Matthew has incorporated a variety of sayings uttered by Jesus on different occasions. First stands the apothegm on earthly and heavenly treasures (19–21), which Luke, with more apparent correctness, inserts in a discourse of Jesus, the entire drift of which is to warn his adherents against earthly cares (xii. 33 f.). It is otherwise with the next sentence, on the eye being the light of the body. Luke annexes this to the apothegm already mentioned on the light that is to be exhibited ; now as the *light* λύχνος, placed on a candlestick, denotes something quite distinct from what is intended by the comparison of the eye to a *light*, λύχνος, the only reason for combining the two apothegms lies in the bare word λύχνος : a rule of association which belongs properly to the dictionary, and which, beyond it, is worse than none. Then follows, also without any apparent connexion, the apothegm on the two masters, appended by Luke to the parable of the steward, with which it happens to have the word *Mammon*, μαμωνᾶς, in common. Next comes, in Matthew v. 25–34, a dissuasion from earthly solicitude, on the ground that natural objects flourish and are sustained without anxiety on their part ; in Luke, this doctrine is consistently united with the parable (found only in the third gospel) of the man who, in the midst of amassing earthly treasures, is summoned away by death (xii. 22 ff.).[31] The warning not to be blind to our own faults while we are sharp-sighted and severe towards those of others (vii. 1–5), would, if we rejected the passage from v. 19, of chap. vi. to the end, form a suitable continuation to the previous admonition against Pharisaic sanctimoniousness (vi. 16–18), and might, therefore, have belonged to the original body of the discourse.[32] This is the more probable because Luke has the same warning in his Sermon on the Mount (37 f. 41 f.), where it happens to assort very well with the preceding exhortation to mercifulness ; but at v. 39 and 40, and part of 38, it is interrupted by subjects altogether irrelevant. The text, *With what measure ye mete*, etc., is very inappropriately interposed by Mark (iv. 24), in a passage similar in kind to one of Luke's intermediate miscellanies. V. 6, in Matthew, is equally destitute of connexion and parallel ; but the succeeding assurances and arguments as to the efficacy of prayer (v. 7–11), are found in Luke xi. 9, very fitly associated with another parable peculiar to that Evangelist : that of the friend awaked at midnight. The apothegm, *What ye would that men should do unto you*, etc., is quite iso-lated in Matthew ; in Luke, it has only an imperfect connexion.[33] The following passage (v. 13 f.) on the *strait gate* στενὴ πύλη, is introduced in Luke (xiii. 23) by the question addressed to Jesus : *Are there few that be saved ?* εἰ ὀλίγοι οἱ σωζόμενοι; which seems likely enough to have been conceived by

---

[30] Comp. De Wette, 1, 2, s. 176.
[31] From vi. 19 to the end of the chapter even Neander finds no orderly association, and conjectures that the editor of the Greek Gospel of Matthew was the compiler of this latter half of the discourse (p. 169, note).
[32] Neander, ut sup. ; De Wette, in loc.
[33] De Wette, 1, 2, s. 45.

one who knew that Jesus had uttered such a saying as the above, but was at a loss for an occasion that might prompt the idea; moreover, the image is far less completely carried out in Luke than in Matthew, and is blended with parabolical elements.[34] The apothegm on the tree being known by its fruits (v. 16–20), appears in Luke (vi. 43 ff.), and even in Matthew, farther on (xii. 33 ff.), to have a general application, but in Matthew's Sermon on the Mount, it has a special relation to the false prophets; in Luke, it is in the last degree misplaced. The denunciation of those who say to Jesus, *Lord, Lord,* but who, on account of their evil deeds will be rejected by him at the day of judgment (21–23), decidedly presupposes the Messiahship of Jesus, and cannot therefore, have well belonged to so early a period as that of the Sermon on the Mount; hence it is more appropriately placed by Luke (xiii. 25 ff.). The peroration of the discourse is, as we have mentioned, common to both Evangelists.

The foregoing comparison shows us that the discourses of Jesus, like fragments of granite, could not be dissolved by the flood of oral tradition; but they were not seldom torn from their natural connexion, floated away from their original situation, and deposited in places to which they did not properly belong. Relative to this effect, there is this distinction between the three first Evangeliists; Matthew, like an able compiler, though far from being sufficiently informed to give each relic in its original connexion, has yet for the most part succeeded in judiciously associating analogous materials; while the two other Evangelists have left many small fragments just where chance threw them, in the intervals between longer discourses. Luke has laboured in some instances to combine these fragments artificially, but he could not thus compensate for the absence of natural connexion.

§ 77.

INSTRUCTIONS TO THE TWELVE. LAMENTATIONS OVER THE GALILEAN CITIES. JOY OVER THE CALLING OF THE SIMPLE.

The first gospel (x.) reports another long discourse as having been delivered by Jesus, on the occasion of his sending out the twelve to preach the kingdom of heaven. Part of this discourse is peculiar to the first gospel; that portion of it which is common to the two other synoptists is only partially assigned by them to the same occasion, Luke introducing its substance in connexion with the mission of the seventy (x. 2 ff.), and in a subsequent conversation with the disciples (xii. 2 ff.). Some portion of the discourse is also found repeated both in Matthew and the other Evangelists, in the prophetic description given by Jesus of his second advent.

In this instance again, while the older harmonists have no hesitation in supposing a repetition of the same discourse,[1] our more recent critics are of opinion that Luke only has the true occasions and the original arrangement of the materials, and that Matthew has assembled them according to his own discretion.[2] Those expositors who are apologetically inclined, maintain that Matthew was not only conscious of here associating sayings uttered at various times, but presumed that this would be obvious to his readers.[3] On the other hand, it is justly observed that the manner in which the discourse is

---

[34] De Wette in loc. des Lukas.

[1] E.g. Hess, Gesch. Jesu, i, s. 545.

[2] Schulz, ut sup. s. 308, 314; Sieffert, s. 80 ff.

[3] Olshausen, in loc. The latter bold assertion in Kern, über den Ursprung des Evang. Matth., s. 63.

introduced by the words : *These twelve Jesus sent forth, and commanded them* (v. 5) ; and closed by the words : *when Jesus made an end of commanding his twelve disciples,* etc. (xi. 1) ; proves clearly enough that it was the intention of the Evangelist to give his compilation the character of a continuous harangue.[4]

Much that is peculiar to Matthew in this discourse, appears to be merely an amplification on thoughts which are also found in the corresponding passages of the two other synoptists ; but there are two particulars in the opening of the instructions as detailed by the former, which differ specifically from anything presented by his fellow Evangelists. These are the limitation of the agency of the disciples to the Jews (v. 5, 6), and the commission (associated with that to announce the kingdom of heaven and heal the sick, of which Luke also speaks, ix. 2), to raise the dead : a surprising commission, since we know of no instances previous to the departure of Jesus, in which the apostles raised the dead ; and to suppose such when they are not narrated, after the example of Olshausen, is an expedient to which few will be inclined.

All that the synoptists have strictly in common in the instructions to the twelve, are the rules for their external conduct ; how they were to journey, and how to behave under a variety of circumstances (Matt. v. 9–11, 14 ; Mark vi. 8–11 ; Luke ix. 3–5). Here, however, we find a discrepancy ; according to Matthew and Luke, Jesus forbids the disciples to take with them, not only gold, a scrip, and the like, but even *shoes,* ὑποδήματα, and a *staff,* ῥάβδον ; according to Mark, on the contrary, he merely forbids their taking more than a *staff* and *sandals,* εἰ μὴ ῥάβδον μόνον and σανδάλια. This discrepancy is most easily accounted for by the admission, that tradition only preserved a reminiscence of Jesus having signified the simplicity of the apostolic equipment by the mention of the staff and shoes, and that hence one of the Evangelists understood that Jesus had interdicted all travelling requisites except these ; the other, that these also were included in his prohibition. It was consistent with Mark's love of the picturesque to imagine a wandering apostle furnished with a staff, and therefore to give the preference to the former view.

It is on the occasion of the mission of the seventy, that Luke (x. 2) puts into the mouth of Jesus the words which Matthew gives (ix. 37 f.) as the motive for sending forth the twelve, namely, the apothegm, *The harvest truly is ready, but the labourers are few* ; also the declaration that the labourer is worthy of his hire (v. 7, comp. Matt. x. 10) ; the discourse on the apostolic salutation and its effect (Matt. v. 12 f. ; Luke v. 5 f.) ; the denunciation of those who should reject the apostles and their message (Matt. v. 15 ; Luke v. 12) ; and finally, the words, *Behold, I send you forth as lambs,* etc. (Matt. v. 16 ; Luke v. 3). The sequence of these propositions is about equally natural in both cases. Their completeness is alternately greater in the one than in the other ; but Matthew's additions generally turn on essentials, as in v. 16 ; those of Luke on externals, as in v. 7, 8, and in v. 4, where there is the singular injunction to salute no man by the way, which might appear an unhistorical exaggeration of the urgency of the apostolic errand, did we not know that the Jewish greetings of that period were not a little ceremonious.[5] Sieffert observes that the instructions which Jesus gave—according to Matthew, to the twelve, according to Luke, to the seventy—might, so far as their tenor is concerned, have been imparted with equal fitness on either

---

[4] Schulz, s. 315.
[5] Vid. De Wette, Archäol., § 265, and in loc.

occasion ; but I doubt this, for it seems to me improbable that Jesus should, as Luke states, dismiss his more confidential disciples with scanty rules for their outward conduct, and that to the seventy he should make communications of much greater moment and pathos.[6] The above critic at length decides in favour of Luke, whose narrative appears to him more precise, because it distinguishes the seventy from the twelve. We have already discussed this point, and have found that a comparison is rather to the advantage of Matthew. The blessing pronounced on him who should give even a cup of cold water to the disciples of Jesus (v. 42), is at least more judiciously inserted by Matthew as the conclusion of the discourse of instructions, than in the endless confusion of the latter part of Mark ix. (v. 41), where ἐάν (*if*), and ὃς ἄν (*whosoever*), seem to form the only tie between the successive propositions.

The case is otherwise when we regard those portions of the discourse which Luke places in his twelfth chapter, and even later, and which in Matthew are distinguishable as a second part of the same discourse. Such are the directions to the apostles as to their conduct before tribunals (Matt. x. 19 f. ; Luke xii. 11); the exhortation not to fear those who can only kill the body (Matt. v. 28 ; Luke v. 4 f.); the warning against the denial of Jesus (Matt. v. 32 f. ; Luke v. 8 f.); the discourse on the general disunion of which he would be the cause (Matt. v. 34 ff. ; Luke v. 51 ff.) ; a passage to which Matthew, prompted apparently by the enumeration of the members of a family, attaches the declaration of Jesus that these are not to be valued above him, that his cross must be taken, etc., which he partly repeats on a subsequent occasion, and in a more suitable connexion (xvi. 24 f.) ; further, predictions which recur in the discourse on the Mount of Olives, relative to the universal persecution of the disciples of Jesus (v. 17 f. 22, comp. xxiv. 9, 13); the saying which Luke inserts in the Sermon on the Mount (vi. 40), and which also appears in John (xv. 20), that the disciple has no claim to a better lot than his master (v. 24 f.) ; lastly, the direction, which is peculiar to the discourse in Matthew, to flee from one city to another, with the accompanying consolation (v. 23). These commands and exhortations have been justly pronounced by critics [7] to be unsuitable to the first mission of the twelve, which, like the alleged mission of the seventy, had no other than happy results (Luke ix. 10, x. 17); they presuppose the troublous circumstances which supervened after the death of Jesus, or perhaps in the latter period of his life. According to this, Luke is more correct than Matthew in assigning these discourses to the last journey of Jesus ; [8] unless, indeed, such descriptions of the subsequent fate of the apostles and other adherents of Jesus were produced *ex eventu*, after his death, and put into his mouth in the form of prophecies ; a conjecture which is strongly suggested by the words, *He who taketh not up his cross*, etc. (v. 38).[9]

The next long discourse of Jesus in Matthew (chap. xi.) we have already considered, so far as it relates to the Baptist. From v. 20–24, there follow complaints and threatenings against the Galilean cities, in which *most of his mighty works were done*, and which, nevertheless, *believed not*. Our modern critics are perhaps right in their opinion that these apostrophes are less suitable to the period of his Galilean ministry, in which Matthew places

---

[6] Comp. De Wette, exeg. Handb. I, I, s. 99.
[7] Schulz, s. 308 ; Sieffert, s. 82 ff.
[8] The satisfactory connexion which modern criticism finds throughout the 12th chap. of Luke, I am as little able to discover as Tholück, Auslegung der Bergpredigt, s. 13 f., who has strikingly exposed the partiality of Schleiermacher for Luke, to the prejudice of Matthew.
[9] Vid. De Wette in loc.

them, than to that in which they are introduced by Luke (x. 13 ff.); namely, when Jesus had left Galilee, and was on his way to Judea and Jerusalem, with a view to his final experiment.[10]   But a consideration of the immediate context seems to reverse the probability.   In Matthew, the description of the ungracious reception which Jesus and John had alike met with, leads very naturally to the accusations against those places which had been the chief theatres of the ministry of the former; but it is difficult to suppose, according to Luke, that Jesus would speak of his past sad experience to the seventy, whose minds must have been entirely directed to the future, unless we conceive that he chose a subject so little adapted to the exigencies of those whom he was addressing, in order to unite the threatened judgment on the Galilean cities, with that which he had just denounced against the cities that should reject his messengers.   But it is more likely that this association proceeded solely from the writer, who, by the comparison of a city that should prove refractory to the disciples of Jesus, to Sodom, was reminded of the analogous comparison to Tyre and Sidon, of places that had been disobedient to Jesus himself, without perceiving the incongruity of the one with the circumstances which had dictated the other.[11]

The *joy*, ἀγαλλίασις, expressed by Jesus (v. 25–27) on account of the insight afforded to *babes*, νηπίοις, is but loosely attached by Matthew to the preceding maledictions.   As it supposes a change in the mental frame of Jesus, induced by pleasing circumstances, Luke (x. 17, 21 ff.), would have all the probabilities on his side, in making the return of the seventy with satisfactory tidings the cause of the above expression; were it not that the appointment of the seventy, and consequently their return, are altogether problematical; besides, it is possible to refer the passage in question to the return of the twelve from their mission.   Matthew connects with this rejoicing of Jesus his invitation to the *weary and heavy laden* (v. 28–30).   This is wanting in Luke, who, instead, makes Jesus turn to his disciples *privately*, and pronounce them blessed in being privileged to see and hear things which many prophets and kings yearned after in vain (23 f.): an observation which does not so specifically agree with the preceding train of thought, as the context assigned to it by Matthew, and which is moreover inserted by the latter Evangelist in a connexion (xiii. 16 f.) that may be advantageously confronted with that of Luke.

§ 78.

THE PARABLES.*

According to Matthew (chap. xiii.), Jesus delivered seven parables, all relating to the βασιλεία τῶν οὐρανῶν.   Modern criticism, however, has doubted whether Jesus really uttered so many of these symbolical discourses on one occasion.[1]   The parable, it has been observed, is a kind of problem, to be solved by the reflection of the hearer; hence after every parable a pause is requisite, if it be the object of the teacher to convey real instruction, and not to distract by a multiplicity of ill-understood images.[2]   It will, at least, be admitted, with Neander, that parables on the same or closely-related subjects can only be spoken consecutively, when, under manifold forms, and from

[10] Schleiermacher, über den Lukas, s. 169 f.; Schneckenburger, über den Ursprung u. s. f., s. 32 f.
[11] Comp. De Wette, exeg. Handb., 1, 1, s. 110. 1, 2, s. 62.
[1] Schulz, über das Abendmahl, s. 314.
[2] Olshausen, bibl. Comm. 1, s. 437.

various points of view, they lead to the same result.[3] Among the seven parables in question, those of the mustard-seed and the leaven have a common fundamental idea, differently shadowed forth—the gradual growth and ultimate prevalence of the kingdom of God: those of the net and the tares represent the mingling of the good with the bad in the kingdom of God; those of the treasure and the pearl inculcate the inestimable and all-indemnifying value of the kingdom of God; and the parable of the sower depicts the unequal susceptibility of men to the preaching of the kingdom of God. Thus there are no less than four separate fundamental ideas involved in this collection of parables—ideas which are indeed connected by their general relation to the kingdom of God, but which present this object under aspects so widely different, that for their thorough comprehension a pause after each was indispensable. Hence, it has been concluded, Jesus would not merit the praise of being a judicious teacher, if, as Matthew represents, he had spoken all the above parables in rapid succession.[4] If we suppose in this instance, again, an assemblage of discourses similar in kind, but delivered on different occasions, we are anew led to the discussion as to whether Matthew was aware of the latter circumstance, or whether he believed that he was recording a continuous harangue. The introductory form, *And he spake many things to them in parables* (v. 3): καὶ ἐλάλησεν αὐτοῖς πολλὰ ἐν παραβολαῖς, and the concluding one, *when Jesus had finished these parables* (v. 53): ὅτε ἐτέλεσεν ὁ Ἰησοῦς τὰς παραβολὰς ταύτας, seem to be a clear proof that he did not present the intermediate matter as a compilation. Mark, indeed, narrates (iv. 10), that at the close of the first parable, the disciples being again, κατα μόνας, *in private*, with Jesus, asked him for its interpretation; and hence it has been contended[5] that there was an interruption of the discourse at this point; but this cannot serve to explain the account of Matthew, for he represents the request of the disciples as being preferred on the spot, without any previous retirement from the crowd; thus proving that he did not suppose such an interruption. The concluding form which Matthew inserts after the fourth parable (v. 34 f.), might, with better reason, be adduced as intimating an interruption, for he there comprises all the foregoing parables in one address by the words, *All these things spake Jesus in parables*, etc., ταῦτα πάντα ἐλάλησεν ὁ Ἰησοῦς ἐν παραβολαῖς κ. τ. λ., and makes the pause still more complete by the application of an Old Testament prophecy; moreover, Jesus is here said (36) to change his locality, to dismiss the multitude to whom he had hitherto been speaking on the shore of the Galilean sea, and enter *the house*, εἰς τὴν οἰκίαν, where he gives three new parables, in addition to the interpretation which his disciples had solicited of the second. But that the delivery of the last three parables was separated from that of the preceding ones by a change of place, and consequently by a short interval of time, very little alters the state of the case. For it is highly improbable that Jesus would without intermission tax the memory of the populace, whose minds it was so easy to overburthen, with four parables, two of which were highly significant; and that he should forthwith overwhelm his disciples, whose power of comprehension he had been obliged to aid in the application of the first two parables, with three new ones, instead of ascertaining if they were capable of independently expounding the third and fourth. Further, we have only to look more closely at Matthew's narrative, in order to observe that he has fallen quite involuntarily on the interruption at v. 34 ff. If it were his intention to communicate a series of parables, with

---

[3] L. J. Chr., s. 175.
[4] Schneckenburger, über den Ursprung u. s. f., s. 33.
[5] Olshausen, s. 438.

the explanations that Jesus privately gave to his disciples of the two which were most important, and were therefore to be placed at the head of the series, there were only three methods on which he could proceed. First, he might make Jesus, immediately after the enunciation of a parable, give its interpretation to his disciples in the presence of the multitude, as he actually does in the case of the first parable (10–23). But the representation is beset with the difficulty of conceiving how Jesus, surrounded by a crowd, whose expectation was on the stretch, could find leisure for a conversation aside with his disciples.[6] This inconvenience Mark perceived, and therefore chose the second resource that was open to him—that of making Jesus with his disciples withdraw after the first parable into *the house*, and there deliver its interpretation. But such a proceeding would be too great a hindrance to one who proposed publicly to deliver several parables one after the other; for if Jesus returned to the house immediately after the first parable, he had left the scene in which the succeeding ones could be conveniently imparted to the people. Consequently, the narrator in the first gospel cannot, with respect to the interpretation of the second parable, either repeat his first plan, or resort to the second; he therefore adopts a third, and proceeding uninterruptedly through two further parables, it is only at their close that he conducts Jesus to the house, and there makes him impart the arrear of interpretation. Herewith there arose in the mind of the narrator a sort of rivalry between the parables which he had yet in reserve, and the interpretation, the arrear of which embarrassed him; as soon as the former were absent from his recollection, the latter would be present with its inevitably associated form of conclusion and return homeward; and when any remaining parables recurred to him, he was obliged to make them the sequel of the interpretation. Thus it befel with the three last parables in Matthew's narration; so that he was reduced almost against his will to make the disciples their sole participants, though it does not appear to have been the custom of Jesus thus to clothe his private instructions; and Mark (v. 33 f.) plainly supposes the parables which follow the interpretation of the second, to be also addressed to the people.[7]

Mark, who (iv. 1) depicts the same scene by the sea-side, as Matthew, has in connexion with it only three parables, of which the first and third correspond to the first and third of Matthew, but the middle one is commonly deemed peculiar to Mark.[8] Matthew has in its place the parable wherein the kingdom of heaven is likened to a man who sowed good seed in his field; but while men slept, the enemy came and sowed tares among it, which grew up with the wheat. The servants know not from whence the tares come, and propose to root them up; but the master commands them to let both grow together until the harvest, when it will be time enough to separate them. In Mark, Jesus compares the kingdom of heaven to a man who casts seed into the ground, and while he sleeps and rises again, the seed passes, he knows not how, from one stage of development to another: *and when it is ripe, he puts in the sickle, because the harvest is come.* In this parable there is wanting what constitutes the dominant idea in that of Matthew, the tares, sown by the enemy; but as, nevertheless, the other ideas, of sowing, sleeping, growing one knows not how, and harvest, wholly correspond, it may be questioned whether Mark does not here merely give the same parable in a different version, which he preferred to that of Matthew, because it seemed

---

[6] Schleiermacher, s. 120.

[7] Fritzsche, Comm. in Marc., s. 120, 128, 134; De Wette, in loc.

[8] Comp. Saunier, über die Quellen des Markus, s. 74; Fritzsche ut sup.; De Wette in loc.

more intermediate between the first parable of the sower, and the third of the mustard-seed.

Luke, also, has only three of the seven parables given in Matt. xiii. ; namely, those of the sower, the mustard-seed, and the leaven ; so that the parables of the buried treasure, the pearl, and the net, as also that of the tares in the field, are peculiar to Matthew. The parable of the sower is placed by Luke (viii. 4 ff.) somewhat earlier, and in other circumstances, than by Matthew, and apart from the two other parables which he has in common with the first Evangelist's series. These he introduces later, xiii. 18–21 ; a position which recent critics unanimously acknowledge as the correct one.[9] But this decision is one of the most remarkable to which the criticism of the present age has been led by its partiality to Luke. For if we examine the vaunted connectedness of this Evangelist's passages, we find that Jesus, having healed a woman *bowed down by a spirit of infirmity*, silences the punctilious ruler of the synagogue by the argument about the ox and ass, after which it is added (v. 17), *And when he had said these things, all his adversaries were ashamed ; and all the people rejoiced for all the glorious things that were done by him.* Surely so complete and marked a form of conclusion is intended to wind up the previous narrative, and one cannot conceive that the sequel went forward in the same scene ; on the contrary, the phrases, *then said he*, and *again he said*, by which the parables are connected, indicate that the writer had no longer any knowledge of the occasion on which Jesus uttered them, and hence inserted them at random in this indeterminate manner, far less judiciously than Matthew, who at least was careful to associate them with analogous materials.[10]

We proceed to notice the other evangelical parables,[11] and first among them, those which are peculiar to one Evangelist. We come foremost in Matthew to the parable of the servant (xviii. 23 ff) who, although his lord had forgiven him a debt of ten thousand talents, had no mercy on his fellow-servant who owed him a hundred ; tolerably well introduced by an exhortation to placability (v. 15), and the question of Peter, *How oft shall my brother sin against me, and I forgive him ?* Likewise peculiar to Matthew is the parable of the labourers in the vineyard (xx. 1 ff.), which suitably enough forms a counterpoise to the foregoing promise of a rich recompense to the disciples. Of the sentences which Matthew appends to this parable (v. 16), the first, *So the last shall be first, and the first last*, by which he had also prefaced it (xix. 30), is the only one with which it has any internal connexion ; the other, *for many are called, but few chosen*, rather gives the moral of the parable of the royal feast and the wedding garment, in connexion with which Matthew actually repeats it (xxii. 14). It was well adapted, however, even torn from this connexion, to circulate as an independent apothegm, and as it appeared fitting to the Evangelist to annex one or more short sentences to the end of a parable, he might be induced, by some superficial similarity to the one already given, to place them in companionship. Farther, the parable of the two sons sent into the vineyard, is also peculiar to Matthew (xxi. 28 ff.), and is not ill-placed in connexion with the foregoing questions and retorts between Jesus and the Pharisees ; its anti-Pharisaic significance is also well brought out by the sequel (31 f.).

Among the parables which are peculiar to Luke, that of the two debtors (vii. 41 ff.) ; that of the good Samaritan (x. 30 ff.) ; that of the man whose

[9] Schleiermacher, ut. sup. s. 192 ; Olshausen, 1, s. 431 ; Schneckenburger, ut sup. s. 33.
[10] Comp. De Wette, exeg. Handb., 1, 2, s. 73 f.
[11] Analogies to these parables and apothegms are given out of the rabbinical literature by Wetstein, Lightfoot, and Schöttgen, in loc.

accumulation of earthly treasure is interrupted by death (xii. 16 ff. comp. Wis. xi. 17 ff.); and also the two which figure the efficacy of importunate prayer (xi. 5 ff., xviii. 2 ff.); have a definite, clear signification, and with the exception of the last, which is introduced abruptly, a tolerably consistent connexion. We may learn from the two last parables, that it is often necessary entirely to abstract particular features from the parables of Jesus, seeing that in one of them God is represented by a lukewarm friend, in the other by an unjust judge. To the latter is annexed the parable of the Pharisee and Publican (9–14), of which only Schleiermacher, on the strength of a connexion, fabricated by himself between it and the foregoing, can deny the antipharisaic tendency.[12] The parables of the lost sheep, the piece of silver, and the prodigal son (Luke xv. 3–32), have the same direction. Matthew also has the first of these (xviii. 12 ff.), but in a different connexion, which determines its import somewhat differently, and without doubt, as will presently be shown, less correctly. It is easy to imagine that these three parables were spoken in immediate succession, because the second is merely a variation of the first, and the third is an amplification and elucidation of them both. Whether, according to the opinion of modern criticism, the two succeeding parables also belong with the above to one continuous discourse,[13] must be determined by a closer examination of their contents, which are in themselves noteworthy.

The parable of the unjust steward, notoriously the *crux interpretum*, is yet without any intrinsic difficulty. If we read to the end of the parable, including the moral (v. 9), we gather the simple result, that the man who without precisely using unjust means to obtain riches, is yet in the sight of God an *unprofitable servant*, δοῦλος ἀχρεῖος (Luke xvii. 10), and, in the employment of the gifts intrusted to him by God, a *steward of injustice*, οἰκονόμος τῆς ἀδικίας, may best atone for this pervading unfaithfulness by lenity and beneficence towards his fellow-men, and may by their intervention procure a place in heaven. It is true that the beneficence of the fictitious steward is a fraud; but we must abstract this particular, as, in the case of two previous parables, we have to abstract the lukewarmness of the friend, and the injustice of the judge : nay, the necessity for such an abstraction is intimated in the narrative itself, for from v. 8 we gather that what the steward did in a worldly spirit is, in the application, to be understood in a more exalted sense of the *children of light*. Certainly, if we suppose the words, *He that is faithful in that which is least*, etc. (10–12) to have been uttered in their present connexion, it appears as if the steward were set forth as a model, deserving in some sense or other the praise of faithfulness ; and when (v. 13) it is said that no servant can serve two masters, the intended inference seems to be that this steward had held to the rightful one. Hence we have expositions such as that of Schleiermacher, who under the master understands the Romans ; under the debtors, the Jewish people ; under the steward, the publicans, who were generous to the latter at the expense of the former ; thus, in the most arbitrary manner, transforming the master into a violent man, and justifying the steward.[14] Olshausen carries the perversion of the parable to the extreme, for he degrades the master, who, by his judicial position evidently announces himself as the representative of God, into ἄρχων τοῦ κόσμου τούτου, *the prince of this world*, while he exalts the steward into the image of a man who applies the riches of this world to spiritual objects. But as in the moral (v. 9) the parable has a consistent ending ; and as inaccurate association is by no means

---

[12] Ueber den Lukas, s. 220.
[13] Schleiermacher, ut sup. s. 202 ff. Olshausen in loc.
[14] Ut sup.

unexampled in Luke ; it is not admissible to concede to the following verses any influence over the interpretation of the parable, unless a close relation of idea can be made manifest. Now the fact is, that the very opposite, namely, the most perplexing diversity, exists. Moreover, it is not difficult to show what might have seduced Luke into a false association. In the parable there was mention of the *mammon of unrighteousness*, μαμωνᾶς τῆς ἀδικίας ; this suggested to him the saying of Jesus, that he who proves faithful in the ἀδίκῳ μαμωνᾷ, *the unrighteous mammon*, as that which is least, may also have the true riches committed to his trust. But the word *mammon* having once taken possession of the writer's mind, how could he avoid recollecting the well-known aphorism of Jesus on God and Mammon, as two incompatible masters, and adding it (v. 13), however superfluously, to the preceding texts ? [15] That by this addition the previous parable was placed in a thoroughly false light, gave the writer little concern, perhaps because he had not seized its real meaning, or because, in the endeavour completely to disburthen his evangelical meaning, he lost all solicitude about the sequence of his passages. It ought, in general, to be more considered, that those of our Evangelists who, according to the now prevalent opinion, noted down oral traditions, must, in the composition of their writings, have exerted their memory to an extent that would repress the activity of reflection ; consequently the arrangement of the materials in their narratives is governed by the association of ideas, the laws of which are partly dependent on external relations ; and we need not be surprised to find many passages, especially from the discourses of Jesus, ranged together for the sole cause that they happen to have in common certain striking consonant words.

If from hence we glance back on the position, that the parable of the unjust steward must have been spoken in connexion with the foregoing one of the prodigal son, we perceive that it rests merely on a false interpretation. According to Schleiermacher, it is the defence of the publicans against the Pharisees, that forms the bond ; but there is no trace of publicans and Pharisees in the latter parable. According to Olshausen, the compassionate love of God, represented in the foregoing parable, is placed in juxtaposition with the compassionate love of man, represented in the succeeding one ; but simple beneficence is the sole idea on which the latter turns, and a parallel between this and the manner in which God meets the lost with pardon, is equally remote from the intention of the teacher and the nature of the subject. The remark (v. 14) that the Pharisees heard all these things, and, being covetous, derided Jesus, does not necessarily refer to the individuals mentioned xv. 2, so as to imply that they had listened to the intermediate matter as one continuous discourse ; and even if that were the case, it would only show the view of the writer with respect to the connectedness of the parables ; a view which, in the face of the foregoing investigation, cannot possibly be binding on us.[16]

---

[15] Schneckenburger has decided, Beiträge, No. V. where he refutes Olshausen's interpretation of the parable, that this verse does not really belong to its present position, while with respect to the preceding verses from v. 9, he finds it possible to hold the contrary opinion. De Wette also considers that v. 13 is the only one decidedly out of place. He thinks it possible, by supplying an intermediate proposition, which he supposes the writer to have omitted, and which led from the *prudent* use of riches to faithfulness in preserving those entrusted to us, to give a sufficient connexion to v. 9 and 10–12, without necessarily referring the idea of faithfulness to the conduct of the steward. The numerous attempts, both ancient and modern, to explain the parable of the steward without a critical dislocation of the associated passages, are only so many proofs that it is absolutely requisite to a satisfactory interpretation.

[16] Comp. de Wette, exeg. Handb. 1, 2, s. 80.

We have already discussed the passage from v. 15 to 18; it consists of disconnected sayings, and to the last, on adultery, is annexed the parable of the rich man, in a manner which, as we have already noticed, it is attempted in vain to show as a real connexion. It must, however, be conceded to Schleiermacher, that if we separate them, the alternative, namely, the common application of the parable to the penal justice of God, is attended with great difficulties.[17] For there is no indication throughout the parable, of any actions on the part of the rich man and Lazarus, that could, according to our notions, justify the exaltation of the one to a place in Abraham's bosom, and the condemnation of the other to torment; the guilt of the one appears to lie in his wealth, the merit of the other in his poverty. It is indeed generally supposed of the rich man, that he was immoderate in his indulgence, and that he had treated Lazarus unkindly.[18] But the latter is nowhere intimated; for the picture of the beggar lying at the door of the rich man, is not intended in the light of a reproach to the latter, because he might easily have tendered his aid, and yet neglected to do so; it is designed to exhibit the contrast, not only between the earthly condition of the two parties, but between their proximity in this life, and their wide separation in another. So the other particular, that the beggar was eager for the crumbs that fell from the rich man's table, does not imply that the rich man denied him this pittance, or that he ought to have given him more than the mere crumbs; it denotes the deep degradation of the earthly lot of Lazarus compared with that of the rich man, in opposition to their reversed position after death, when the rich man is fain to entreat for a drop of water from the hand of Lazarus. On the supposition that the rich man had been wanting in compassion towards Lazarus, the Abraham of the parable could only reply in the following manner : "Thou hadst once easy access to Lazarus, and yet thou didst not relieve him ; how then canst thou expect him to traverse a long distance to give thee alleviation ? " The sumptuous life of the rich man, likewise, is only depicted as a contrast to the misery of the beggar ; for if he had been supposed guilty of excess, Abraham must have reminded him that he had taken too much of the good things of this life, not merely that he had received his share of them. Equally groundless is it, on the other hand, to suppose high moral excellencies in Lazarus, since there is no intimation of such in the description of him, which merely regards his outward condition,—neither are such ascribed to him by Abraham ; his sole merit is, the having received evil in this life. Thus, in this parable the measure of future recompense is not the amount of good done, or wickedness perpetrated, but of evil endured, and fortune enjoyed,[19] and the aptest motto for this discourse is to be found in the Sermon on the Mount, according to Luke's edition : *Blessed be ye poor, for yours is the kingdom of God ! Woe to you that are rich ! for ye have received your consolation* ; a passage concerning which we have already remarked, that it accords fully with the Ebionite view of the world. A similar estimation of external poverty is ascribed to Jesus by the other synoptists, in the narrative of the rich young man, and in the aphorisms on the camel and the needle's eye (Matt. xix. 16 ff. ; Mark x. 17 ff. ; comp. Luke xviii. 18 ff.). Whether this estimation belong to Jesus himself, or only to the synoptical tradition concerning him, it was probably generated by the notions of the Essenes.[20] We have hitherto considered the contents of the parable down

---

[17] Ut sup. s. 208.   [18] Vid. Kuinöl, in loc.
[19] Comp. De Wette, 1, 2, s. 86 f.
[20] On the Essenes as *contemners of riches* (καταφρονητὰς πλούτου), comp. Joseph., b. j. ii. viii. 3 ; Credner, über Essener und Ebioniten, in Winer's Zeitschrift, 1, s. 217 ; Gfrörer, Philo, 2, s. 311.

to v. 27 : from whence to the conclusion the subject is, the writings of the Old Testament as the adequate and only means of grace.

In conclusion, we turn to a group of parables, among which some, as relating to the death and return of Christ, ought, according to our plan, to be excepted from the present review; but so far as they are connected with the rest, it is necessary to include them.   They are the three parables of the rebellious husbandmen in the vineyard (Matt. xxi. 33 ff. parall.), of the talents or minæ (Matt. xxv. 14 ff. ; Luke xix. 12 ff.), and the marriage feast (Matt. xxii. 2 ff. ; Luke xiv. 16 ff.).   Of these the parable of the husbandmen in all the accounts, that of the talents in Matthew, and that of the marriage feast in Luke, are simple parables, unattended with difficulty.   Not so the parable of the minæ in Luke, and of the marriage feast in Matthew.   That the former is fundamentally the same with that of the talents in Matthew, is undeniable, notwithstanding the many divergencies.   In both are found the journey of a master ; the assembling of the servants to entrust them with a capital, to be put into circulation ; after the return of the master, a reckoning in which three servants are signalized, two of them as active, the third as inactive, whence the latter is punished, and the former rewarded ; and in the annunciation of this issue the words of the master are nearly identical in the two statements.   The principal divergency is, that besides the relation between the master who journeys into a far country and his servants, in Luke there is a second relation between the former and certain rebellious citizens ; and accordingly, while in Matthew the master is simply designated ἄνθρωπος, a *man*, in Luke he is styled ἄνθρωπος εὐγενής, a *nobleman*, and a *kingdom* is assigned to him, the object of his journey being to *receive for himself a kingdom* : an object of which there is no mention in Matthew.   The subjects of this personage, it is further said, hated him, and after his departure renounced their allegiance.   Hence at the return of the lord, the rebellious citizens, as well as the slothful servant, are punished ; but in their case the retribution is that of death : the faithful servants, on the other hand, are not only rewarded generally by an entrance into the joy of their Lord, but royally, by the gift of a number of cities.   There are other divergencies of less moment between Luke and Matthew ; such as, that the number of servants is undetermined by the one, and limited to ten by the other ; that in Matthew they receive talents, in Luke minæ ; in the one unequal sums, in the other equal ; in the one, they obtain unequal profits from unequal sums by an equal expenditure of effort, and are therefore equally rewarded ; in the other, they obtain unequal profits from equal sums by an unequal expenditure of effort, and are therefore unequally rewarded.

Supposing this parable to have proceeded from the lips of Jesus on two separate occasions, and that Matthew and Luke are right in their respective arrangements, he must have delivered it first in the more complex form given by Luke, and then in the simple one given by Matthew ;[21] since the former places it before, the latter after the entrance into Jerusalem.   But this would be contrary to all analogy.   The first presentation of an idea is, according to the laws of thought, the most simple ; with the second new relations may be perceived, the subject may be viewed under various aspects, and brought into manifold combinations.   There is, therefore, a foundation for Schleiermacher's opinion, that contrary to the arrangement in the Gospels, Jesus first delivered the parable in the more simple form, and amplified it on a subsequent occasion.[22]   But for our particular case this order is not less inconceivable than

---

[21] Thus Kuinöl, Comm. in Luc., p. 635.
[22] Ueber den Lukas, 239 f.   Neander agrees with him, L. J. Chr., p. 188.

the other.   The author of a composition such as a parable, especially when it exists only in his mind and on his lips, and is not yet fixed in writing, remains the perfect master of his materials even on their second and more elaborate presentation; the form which he had previously given to them is not rigid and inflexible, but pliant, so that he can adapt the original thoughts and images to the additional ones, and thus give unity to his production. Hence, had he who gave the above parable the form which it has in Luke, been its real author, he would, after having transformed the master into a king, and inserted the particulars respecting the rebellious citizens, have intrusted arms to the servants instead of money (comp. Luke xxii. 36),[23] and would have made them show their fidelity rather by conflict with the rebels, than by increasing their capital; or in general would have introduced some relation between the two classes of persons in the parable, the servants and the citizens; instead of which, they are totally unconnected throughout, and form two ill-cemented divisions.[24]   This shows very decisively that the parable was not enriched with these additional particulars by the imagination of its author, but that it was thus amplified by another in the process of transmission.   This cannot have been effected in a legendary manner, by the gradual filling up of the original sketch, or the development of the primitive germ; for the idea of rebellious citizens could never be evolved from that of servants and talents, but must have been added from without, and therefore have previously existed as part of an independent whole.   This amounts to the position that we have here an example of two originally distinct parables, the one treating of servants and talents, the other of rebellious citizens, flowing together in consequence of their mutually possessing the images of a ruler's departure and return.[25]   The proof of our proposition must depend on our being able easily to disentangle the two parables; and this we can effect in the most satisfactory manner, for by extracting v. 12, 14, 15, and 27, and slightly modifying them, we get in a rather curtailed but consistent form, the parable of the rebellious citizens, and we then recognise the similarity of its tendency with that of the rebellious husbandmen in the vineyard.[26]

A similar relation subsists between the form in which the parable of the marriage feast is given by Luke (xiv. 16 ff.), and that in which it is given by Matthew (xxii. 2 ff.); only that in this case Luke, as in the other, Matthew, has the merit of having preserved the simple original version.   On both sides, the particulars of the feast, the invitation, its rejection, and the consequent bidding of other guests, testify the identity of the two parables; but, on the other hand, the host who in Luke is merely *a certain man*, ἄνθρωπός τις, is in Matthew *a king*, βασιλεύς, whose feast is occasioned by the marriage of his son; the invited guests, who in Luke excuse themselves on various pleas to the messenger only once sent out to them, in Matthew refuse to come on the first invitation, and on the second more urgent one some go to their occupations, while others maltreat and kill the servants of the king, who immediately sends forth his armies to destroy those murderers, and burn up their city. Nothing of this is to be found in Luke; according to him, the host merely causes the poor and afflicted to be assembled in place of the guests first

---

[23] This is a reply to Neander's objection, p. 191, note.
[24] How Paulus, exeg. Handb. 3, a, p. 76, can pronounce the more complex form of the parable in Luke as not only the most fully developed but the best wound up, I am at a loss to understand.
[25] Comp. De Wette, 1, 1, s. 208 f.
[26] V. 12. Ἄνθρωπός τις εὐγενὴς ἐπορεύθη εἰς χώραν μακρὰν, λαβεῖν ἑαυτῷ βασιλείαν, καὶ ὑποστρέψαι.   14. οἱ δὲ πολῖται αὐτοῦ ἐμίσουν αὐτὸν, καὶ ἀπέστειλαν πρεσβείαν ὀπίσω αὐτοῦ, λέγοντες· οὐ θέλομεν τοῦτον βασιλεῦσαι ἐφ' ἡμᾶς.   15. καὶ ἐγένετο ἐν τῷ ἐπανελθεῖν αὐτὸν

invited, a particular which Matthew also appends to his fore-mentioned incidents.   Luke closes the parable with the declaration of the host, that none
of the first bidden guests shall partake of his supper ; but Matthew proceeds
to narrate how, when the house was full, and the king had assembled his
guests, one was discovered to be without a wedding garment, and was
forthwith carried away into outer darkness.

The maltreatment and murder of the king's messengers are features in the
narrative of Matthew which at once strike us as inconsistent—as a departure
from the original design.   Disregard of an invitation is sufficiently demonstrated by the rejection of it on empty pretexts such as Luke mentions ; the
maltreatment and even the murder of those who deliver the invitation, is an
exaggeration which it is less easy to attribute to Jesus than to the Evangelist.
The latter had immediately before communicated the parable of the rebellious
husbandmen ; hence there hovered in his recollection the manner in which
they were said to have used the messengers of their lord, beating one, killing
and stoning others (λαβόντες τοὺς δούλους αὐτοῦ ὃν μὲν ἔδειραν, ὃν δὲ ἀπέκτειναν,
ὃν δὲ ἐλιθοβόλησαν), and he was thus led to incorporate similar particulars into
the present parable (κρατήσαντες τοὺς δούλους αὐτοῦ ὕβρισαν καὶ ἀπέκτειναν),
overlooking the circumstance that what might have been perpetrated with
sufficient motive against servants who appeared with demands and authority
to enforce them, had in the latter case no motive whatever.   That hereupon,
the king, not satisfied with excluding them from the feast, sends out his
armies to destroy them and burn up their city, necessarily follows from the
preceding incidents, but appears, like them, to be the echo of a parable
which presented the relation between the master and the dependents, not in
the milder form of a rejected invitation, but in the more severe one of an
insurrection ; as in the parable of the husbandmen in the vineyard, and that
of the rebellious citizens, which we have above separated from the parable of
the minæ.   Yet more decidedly does the drift of the last particular in Matthew's parable, that of the wedding garment, betray that it was not originally
associated with the rest.   For if the king had commanded that all, *both bad
and good*, who were to be found in the highways, should be bidden to the
feast, he could not wonder that they had not all wedding attire.   To assume
that those thus suddenly summoned went home to wash, and adjust their
dress, is an arbitrary emendation of the text.[27]   Little preferable is the supposition that, according to oriental manners, the king had ordered a caftan to
be presented to each guest, and might therefore justly reproach the meanest
for not availing himself of the gift ;[28] for it is not to be proved that such a
custom existed at the period,[29] and it is not admissible to presuppose it
merely because the anger of the king appears otherwise unfounded.   But the
addition in question is not only out of harmony with the imagery, but with
the tendency of this parable.   For while hitherto its aim had been to exhibit
the national contrast between the perversity of the Jews, and the willingness
of the Gentiles : it all at once passes to the moral one, to distinguish between
the worthy and the unworthy.   That after the Jews had contemned the invitation to partake of the kingdom of God, the heathens would be called into
it, is one complete idea, with which Luke very properly concludes his parable ;

λαβόντα τὴν βασιλείαν, καὶ εἶπε φωνηθῆναι αὐτῷ τοὺς δούλους—(καὶ εἶπεν αὐτοῖς·)   27. —τοὺς
ἐχθρούς μου ἐκείνους, τοὺς μὴ θελήσαντάς με βασιλεῦσαι ἐπ' αὐτοὺς, ἀγάγετε ὧδε καὶ κατασφάξατε
ἔμπροσθέν μου.
[27] Fritzsche, p. 656. This remark serves to refute De Wette's vindication of the above
particular in his exeg. Handb.
[28] Paulus. exeg. Handb. 3, a, s. 210 ; Olshausen, bibl. Comm. 1, s. 811.
[29] Vid. Fritzsche, ut sup.

that he who does not prove himself worthy of the vocation by a corresponding disposition, will be again cast out of the kingdom, is another idea, which appears to demand a separate parable for its exhibition. Here again it may be conjectured that the conclusion of Matthew's parable is the fragment of another, which, from its also referring to a feast, might in tradition, or in the memory of an individual, be easily mingled with the former, preserved in its purity by Luke.[30] This other parable must have simply set forth, that a king had invited various guests to a wedding feast, with the tacit condition that they should provide themselves with a suitable dress, and that he delivered an individual who had neglected this observance to his merited punishment. Supposing our conjectures correct, we have here a still more compound parable than in the former case: a parable in which, 1stly, the narrative of the ungrateful invited parties (Luke xiv.) forms the main tissue, but so that, 2ndly, a thread from the parable of the rebellious husbandmen is interwoven ; while, 3rdly, a conclusion is stitched on, gathered apparently from an unknown parable on the wedding garment.

This analysis gives us an insight into the procedure of evangelical tradition with its materials, which must be pregnant with results.

§ 79.

MISCELLANEOUS INSTRUCTIONS AND CONTROVERSIES OF JESUS.

As the discourses in Matthew xv. 1–20 have been already considered, we must pass on to xviii. 1 ff., Mark ix. 33 ff., Luke ix. 46 ff., where various discourses are connected with the exhibition of a little child, occasioned by a contention for pre-eminence among the disciples. The admonition to become as a little child, and to humble one's self as a little child, in Matthew, forms a perfectly suitable comment on the symbolical reproof (v. 3, 4,) ; but the connexion between this and the following declaration of Jesus, that whosoever receives one such little child in his name, receives him, is not so obvious. For the child was set up to teach the disciples in what they were to imitate it, not how they were to behave towards it, and how Jesus could all at once lose sight of his original object, it is difficult to conceive. But yet more glaring is the irrelevance of the declaration in Mark and Luke ; for they make it follow immediately on the exhibition of the child, so that, according to this, Jesus must, in the very act, have forgotten its object, namely, to present the child to his ambitious disciples as worthy of imitation, not as in want of reception.[1] Jesus was accustomed to say of his disciples, that whosoever received them, received him, and in him, the Father who had sent him (Matt. x. 40 ff. ; Luke x. 16 ; John xiii. 20). Of children he elsewhere says merely, that whosoever does not receive the kingdom of heaven as a little child cannot enter therein (Mark x. 15 ; Luke xviii. 17). This declaration would be perfectly adapted to the occasion in question, and we may almost venture to conjecture that ὃς ἐὰν μὴ δέξηται τὴν βασιλείαν τῶν οὐρανῶν ὡς παιδίον, was the original passage, and that the actual one is the result of its confusion with Matthew x. 40, ὃς ἐὰν δέξηται παιδίον τοιοῦτον ἓν ἐπὶ τῷ ὀνόματί μου.

Closely connected by the word ἀποκριθεὶς, *answering*, with the sentences

---

[30] From the appendix to Schneckenburger's Beiträgen, I see that a reviewer in the Theol. Literaturblatt, 1831, No. 88, has also conjectured that we have here a blending of two originally distinct parables.

[1] Comp. De Wette, 1, 1, s. 152.

just considered, Mark (ix. 38 f.) and Luke (ix. 49 f.) introduce the information which John is said to give to Jesus, that the disciples having seen one casting out devils in the name of Jesus, without attaching himself to their society, had forbidden him. Schleiermacher explains the connexion thus : because Jesus had commanded the reception of children *in his name*, John was led to the confession, that he and his associates had hitherto been so far from regarding the performance of an act in the name of Jesus as the point of chief importance, that they had interdicted the use of his name to one who followed not with them.[2] Allowing this explanation to be correct, we must believe that John, arrested by the phrase, *in my name* (which yet is not prominent in the declaration of Jesus, and which must have been thrown still further into the background by the sight of the child set up in the midst), drew from it the general inference, that in all actions the essential point is to perform them *in the name of Jesus* ; and with equal rapidity, leaped to the remote reflection, that the conduct of the disciples towards the exorcist was in contradiction with this rule. But all this supposes the facility of combination which belongs to a Schleiermacher, not the dulness which still characterized the disciples. Nevertheless, the above critic has unquestionably opened on the true vein of connexion between the preceding apothegm and this ἀπόκρισις of John ; he has only failed to perceive that this connexion is not intrinsic and original, but extrinsic and secondary. It was quite beyond the reach of the disciples to apply the words *in my name*, by a train of deductions, to an obliquely connected case in their own experience ; but, according to our previous observations, nothing could be more consistent with the habit of association that characterizes the writer of the evangelical tradition in the third gospel, whence the second Evangelist seems to have borrowed, than that he should be reminded by the striking phrase, *in my name*, in the preceding discourse of Jesus, of an anecdote containing the same expression, and should unite the two for the sake of that point of external similarity alone.[3]

To the exhortation to receive such little children, Matthew annexes the warning against ̗*offending one of these little ones*, σκανδαλίζειν ἕνα τῶν μικρῶν τούτων, an epithet which, in x. 42, is applied to the disciples of Jesus, but in this passage, apparently, to children.[4] Mark (v. 42) has the same continuation, notwithstanding the interruption above noticed, probably because he forsook Luke (who here breaks off the discourse, and does not introduce the admonition against offences until later, xvii. 1 f., and apart from any occasion that might prompt it), and appealed to Matthew.[5] Then follows in Matthew (v. 8 f.) and Mark (v. 43 f.) a passage which alone ought to open the eyes of commentators to the mode in which the synoptists arrange the sayings of Jesus. To the warning against the *offending*, σκανδαλίζειν, of the little ones, and the woe pronounced on those by whom *offences come*, τὸ σκάνδαλον ἔρχεται, they annex the apothegm on the *offending*, σκανδαλίζειν, of the hand, eye, etc. Jesus could not proceed thus,—for the injunctions : Mislead not the little ones ! and, Let not your sensuality mislead you ! have nothing in common but the word *mislead*. It is easy, however, to account for their association by the writer of the first gospel.[6] The word σκανδαλίζειν recalled to his mind all the discourses of Jesus containing a similar expression that had come to his knowledge, and although he had previously presented the admonitions con-

[2] Ueber den Lukas, s. 153 f.
[3] Comp. De Wette, in loc.
[4] Vid. Fritsche and De Wette, in loc.
[5] Saunier, über die Quellen des Markus, s. 111.
[6] Comp. De Wette, in loc., Matt.

cerning seduction by the members, in a better connexion, as part of the Sermon on the Mount, he could not resist the temptation of reproducing them here, for the sake of this slight verbal affinity with the foregoing text. But at v. 10 he resumes the thread which he had dropped at v. 7, and adds a further discourse on the *little ones*, μικροὺς. Matthew makes Jesus confirm the value of the little ones by the declaration, that the Son of man was come to seek the lost, and by the parable of the lost sheep (v. 11–14). It is not, however, evident why Jesus should class the μικροὺς with the ἀπολωλὸς (*lost*) ; and both the declaration and the parable seem to be better placed by Luke, who introduces the former in the narrative of the calling of Zaccheus (xix. 10), and the latter, in a reply to the objections of the Pharisees against the amity of Jesus with the publicans (xv. 3 ff.). Matthew seems to have placed them here, merely because the discourse on the little ones reminded him of that on the lost—both exemplifying the mildness and humility of Jesus.

Between the moral of the above parable (v. 14) and the following rules for the conduct of Christians under injuries (v. 15 ff.), there is again only a verbal connexion, which may be traced by means of the words, ἀπόληται, should perish, and ἐκέρδησας, *thou hast gained*; for the proposition : God wills not that one of these little ones should perish, might recall the proposition : We should endeavour to win over our brother, by showing a readiness to forgive. The direction to bring the offender before the *church*, ἐκκλησία, is generally adduced as a proof that Jesus intended to found a church. But he here speaks of the ἐκκλησία as an institution already existing : hence we must either refer the expression to the Jewish synagogue, an interpretation which is favoured by the analogy of this direction with Jewish precepts ; or if, according to the strict meaning of the word and its connexion, ἐκκλησία must be understood as the designation of the Christian community, which did not then exist, it must be admitted that we have here, at least in the form of expression, an anticipation of a subsequent state of things.[7] The writer certainly had in view the new church, eventually to be founded in the name of Jesus, when, in continuation, he represented the latter as imparting to the body of the disciples the authority to bind and to loose, previously given to Peter, and thus to form a messianic religious constitution. The declarations concerning the success of unanimous prayer, and the presence of Jesus among two or three gathered together in his name, accord with this prospective idea.[8]

The next discourse that presents itself (Matt. xix. 3–12, Mark x. 2–12), though belonging, according to the Evangelists, to the last journey of Jesus, is of the same stamp with the disputations which they, for the most part, assign to the last residence of Jesus in Jerusalem. Some Pharisees propose to Jesus the question, at that time much discussed in the Jewish schools,[9] whether it be lawful for a man to put away his wife for every cause. To avoid a contradiction between modern practice and the dictum of Jesus, it has been alleged that he here censures the species of divorce which was the only one known at that period, namely, the arbitrary dismissal of a wife ; but not the judicial separation resorted to in the present day.[10] But this very argument involves the admission, that Jesus denounced all the forms of divorce known to him ; hence the question still remains whether, if he could have had cognizance of the modern procedure in dissolving matrimony, he would have held it right to limit his general censure. Of the succeeding declaration,

---

[7] Vid. de Wette, exeg. Handb. 1, 1, p. 155.
[8] Analogous passages from Jewish writings are given in Wetstein, Lightfoot, Schöttgen, in loc.
[9] Bemidbar R. ad. Num. v. 30, in Wetstein, p. 303.
[10] E.g. Paulus, L. J. 1, b, s. 46.

prompted by a question of the disciples,[11] namely, that celibacy may be practised for the kingdom of heaven's sake, Jesus himself says, that it cannot be understood by all, but only by those *to whom it is given* (v. 11). That the doctrine of Jesus may not run counter to modern opinion, it has been eagerly suggested, that his panegyric on celibacy had relation solely to the circumstances of the coming time, or to the nature of the apostolic mission, which would be impeded by family ties.[12] But there is even less intimation of this special bearing in the text, than in the analogous passage 1 Cor. vii. 25 ff.,[13] and, adhering to a simple interpretation, it must be granted that we have here one of the instances in which ascetic principles, such as were then prevalent, especially among the Essenes,[14] manifest themselves in the teaching of Jesus, as represented in the synoptical gospels.

The controversial discourses which Matthew, almost throughout in agreement with the other synoptists, places after the entrance of Jesus into Jerusalem (xxi. 23–27 ; xxii. 15–46),[15] are certainly pre-eminently genuine fragments, having precisely the spirit and tone of the rabbinical dialectics in the time of Jesus. The third and fifth among them are particularly worthy of note, because they exhibit Jesus as an interpreter of Scripture. With respect to the former, wherein Jesus endeavours to convince the Sadducees that there will be a resurrection of the dead, from the Mosaic designation of God as the God of Abraham, of Isaac, and of Jacob, maintaining that he is not the God of the dead, but of the living (Matt. xxii. 31–33 parall.): Paulus admits that Jesus here argues subtilly, while he contends that the conclusion is really involved in the premises. But in the expression אֱלֹהֵי־אַבְרָהָם *the God of Abraham*, etc., which had become a mere formula, nothing more is implied than that Jehovah, as he had been the protecting Deity of these men, would for ever continue such to their posterity. An individual relation subsisting between Jehovah and the patriarchs after their death, is nowhere else alluded to in the Old Testament, and could only be discovered in the above form by rabbinical interpreters, at a time when it was thought desirable, at any cost, to show that the idea of immortality, which had become prevalent, was contained in the law ; where, however, it is not to be met with by unprejudiced eyes. We find the relation of God to Abraham, Isaac, and Jacob, adduced as a guarantee of immortality elsewhere in rabbinical argumentations, all of which could hardly have been modelled on this one of Jesus.[16] If we look into the most recent commentaries, we nowhere find a candid confession as to the real character of the argumentation in question. Olshausen has wonders to tell of the deep truth contained in it, and thinks that he can deduce from it, in the shortest way, the authenticity and divinity of the Pentateuch. Paulus sees the validity of the proof between the lines of the text ; Fritzsche is silent. Wherefore these evasions? Why is the praise of having seen clearly, and spoken openly, in this matter, abandoned to the Wolfenbüttel Fragmentist ? [17]

---

[11] For probable doubts as to the correctness of the position given to this discourse of Jesus, vid. Neander, L. J. Chr., s. 525, Anm.

[12] Paulus, ib. s. 50, exeg. Handb. 2, s. 599.

[13] In this passage, it is true that celibacy is at first recommended as good for *the present distress*; but the Apostle does not rest there ; for at v. 32 ff. he adds, *He that is unmarried careth for the things of the Lord—he that is married for the things of the world* :—a motive to celibacy which must be equally valid under all circumstances, and which affords us a glimpse into the fundamental asceticism of Paul's views. Comp. Rückert's Commentary in loc.

[14] Vid. Gfrörer, Philo, 2, s. 310 f.

[15] A concise elucidation of them may be found in Hase, L. J. § 129.

[16] Vid. Gemara Hieros. Berac. f. v. 4, in Lightfoot, p. 423, and R. Manasse Ben Isr. in Schöttgen, i. p. 180.

[17] See his 4th Fragment, Lessing's 4ten Beitrag, s. 434 ff.

What spectres and double-sighted beings, must Moses and Jesus have been, if they mixed with their cotemporaries without any real participation in their opinions and weaknesses, their joys and griefs : if, mentally dwelling apart from their age and nation, they conformed to these relations only externally and by accommodation, while, internally and according to their nature, they stood among the foremost ranks of the enlightened in modern times ! Far more noble were these men, nay, they would then only engage our sympathy and reverence, if, in a genuinely human manner, struggling with the limitations and prejudices of their age, they succumbed to them in a hundred secondary matters, and only attained perfect freedom in relation to the one point by which each was destined to contribute to the advancement of mankind.

A controversial question concerning the Messiah is proposed (v. 41–46) to the Pharisees by Jesus, namely, How can the same personage be at once the Lord and the son of David ? Paulus maintains that this is a model of interpretation in conformity with the text ;[18] an assertion which is no good augury that his own possesses that qualification. According to him, Jesus, in asking how David could call the Messiah, *Lord*, when in the general opinion he was his son, intended to apprise the Pharisees, that in this Psalm it is not David who is speaking of the Messiah, but another poet who is speaking of David as his lord, so that to suppose this warlike psalm a messianic one, is a mistake. Why, asks Paulus, should not Jesus have found out this interpretation, since it is the true one ? But this is the grand error of his entire scheme of interpretation—to suppose that what is truth in itself, or more correctly, for us, must, even to the minutest details, have been truth for Jesus and the apostles. The majority of ancient Jewish interpreters apply this psalm to the Messiah ;[19] the apostles use it as a prophecy concerning Christ (Acts ii. 34 f. ; 1 Cor. xv. 25); Jesus himself, according to Matthew and Mark, adds ἐν πνεύματι to Δαβὶδ καλεῖ αὐτὸν Κύριον, thus plainly giving his approval to the notion that it is David who there speaks, and that the Messiah is his subject : how then can it be thought that he held the contrary opinion ? It is far more probable, as Olshausen has well shown, that Jesus believed the psalm to be a messianic one : while, on the other hand, Paulus is equally correct in maintaining that it originally referred, not to the Messiah, but to some Jewish ruler, whether David or another. Thus we find that Jesus here gives a model of interpretation, in conformity, not with the text, but with the spirit of his time : a discovery which, if the above observations be just, ought to excite no surprise. The solution of the enigma which Jesus here proposes to the Pharisees, lay without doubt, according to his idea, in the doctrine of the higher nature of the Messiah ; whether he held that, in virtue of this, he might be styled the Lord of David, while, in virtue of his human nature, he might also be regarded as his son ; or whether he wished to remove the latter notion as erroneous.[20] The result, however, and perhaps also the intention of Jesus with respect to the Pharisees, was merely to convince them that he was capable of retaliating on them, in their own way, by embarrassing them with captious questions, and that with better success than they had obtained in their attempts to entrap him. Hence the Evangelists place this passage at the close of the disputations prompted by the Pharisees, and Matthew adds, *Neither durst any man from that day forth ask him any more questions :* a concluding form which is more suitable here than after the lesson ad-

---

[18] L. J. i, b, s. 115 ff.
[19] Vid. Wetstein, in loc. Hengstenberg, Christol. 1, a, s. 140 f. ; also Paulus himself, exeg. Handb. 3, a, s. 283 f.
[20] Comp. De Wette, in loc.

ministered to the Sudducees, where it is placed by Luke (xx. 40), or than after
the discussion on the greatest commandment, where it is introduced by Mark
(xii. 34).

Immediately before this question of Jesus, the first two Evangelists narrate
a conversation with a *lawyer*, νομικὸς, or *scribe*, γραμματεὺς, concerning the
greatest commandment. (Matt. xxii. 34 ff. ; Mark xii. 28 ff.) Matthew
annexes this conversation to the dispute with the Sadducees, as if the
Pharisees wished, by their question as to the greatest commandment, to
avenge the defeat of the Sadducees. It is well known, however, that these
sects were not thus friendly ; on the contrary, we read in the Acts (xxiii. 7),
that the Pharisees were inclined to go over to the side of one whom they had
previously persecuted, solely because he had had the address to take the position of an opponent towards the Sadducees. We may here quote Schneckenburger's observation,[21] that Matthew not seldom (iii. 7, xvi. 1) places
the Pharisees and Sadducees side by side in a way that represents, not their
real hostility, but their association in the memory of tradition, in which one
opposite suggested another. In this respect, Mark's mode of annexing this
conversation to the foregoing, is more consistent ; but all the synoptists seem
to labour under a common mistake in supposing that these discussions,
grouped together in tradition on account of their analogy, followed each other
so closely in time, that one colloquy elicited another. Luke does not give
the question concerning the greatest commandment in connexion with the
controversies on the resurrection and on the Messiah ; but he has a similar
incident earlier, in his narrative of the journey to Jerusalem (x. 25 ff.). The
general opinion is that the first two Evangelists recount the same occurrence
and the third, a distinct one.[22] It is true that the narrative of Luke differs
from that of Matthew and Mark, in several not immaterial points, The first
difference, which we have already noticed, relates to chronological position,
and this has been the chief inducement to the supposition of two events.
The next difference lies in the nature of the question, which, in Luke, turns on
the rule of life calculated to insure the inheritance of eternal life, but, in the
other Evangelists, on the greatest commandment. The third difference is in
the subject who pronounces this commandment, the first two synoptists representing it to be Jesus, the third, the lawyer. Lastly, there is a difference
as to the issue, the lawyer in Luke putting a second, self-vindicatory, question,
which calls forth the parable of the good Samaritan ; while in the two other
Evangelists, he retires either satisfied, or silenced by the answer to the first.
Meanwhile, even between the narrative of Matthew and that of Mark, there
are important divergencies. The principal relates to the character of the
querist, who in Matthew proposes his question with a view to *tempt* Jesus
(πειράζων) ; in Mark, with good intentions, because he had perceived that
Jesus had answered the Sadducees well. Paulus, indeed, although he elsewhere (Luke x. 25) considers the act of tempting (ἐκπειράζων) as the putting
a person to the proof to subserve interested views, pronounces that the word
πειράζων in this instance can only be intended in a good sense. But the sole
ground for this interpretation lies, not in Matthew, but in Mark, and in the
unfounded supposition that the two writers could not have a different idea of
the character and intention of the inquiring doctor of the law. Fritzsche has
correctly pointed out the difficulty of conciliating Matthew and Mark as lying,
partly in the meaning of the word πειράζων, and partly in the context, it being
inadmissible to suppose one among a series of malevolent questions, friendly,

[21] Ueber den Ursprung u. s. f., s. 45, 47.
[22] Paulus and Olshausen, in loc.

without any intimation of the distinction on the part of the writer. With this important diversity is connected the minor one, that while in Matthew, the scribe, after Jesus has recited the two commandments, is silent, apparently from shame, which is no sign of a friendly disposition on his part towards Jesus; in Mark, he not only bestows on Jesus the approving expression, *Well, Master, thou hast said the truth*, but enlarges on his doctrine so as to draw from Jesus the declaration that he has *answered discreetly*, and is, *not far from the kingdom of God*. It may be also noticed that while in Matthew Jesus simply repeats the commandment of love, in Mark he prefaces it by the words, *Hear, O Israel, the Lord thy God is one Lord*. Thus, if it be held that the differences between the narrative of Luke, and that of the two other Evangelists, entail a necessity for supposing that they are founded on two separate events; the no slighter differences between Mark and Matthew must in all consistency be made a reason for supposing a third. But it is so difficult to credit the reality of three occurrences essentially alike, that the other alternative, of reducing them to one, must, prejudice apart, be always preferred. The narratives of Matthew and Mark are the most easily identified; but there are not wanting points of contact between Matthew and Luke, for in both the *lawyer* νομικὸς appears as a tempter (πειράζων), and is not impressed in favour of Jesus by his answer; nor even between Luke and Mark, for these agree in appending explanatory remarks to the greatest commandment, as well as in the insertion of forms of assent, such as, *Thou hast answered right, Thou hast said the truth*. Hence it is evident that to fuse only two of their narratives is a half measure, and that we must either regard all three as independent, or all three as identical: whence again we may observe the freedom which was used by the early Christian legend, in giving various forms to a single fact or idea—the fundamental fact in the present case being, that, out of the whole Mosaic code, Jesus had selected the two commandments concerning the love of God and our neighbour as the most excellent.[23]

We come now to the great anti-pharisaic discourse, which Matthew gives (xxiii.) as a sort of pitched battle after the skirmishing of the preceding disputations. Mark (xii. 38 ff.) and Luke (xx. 45 ff.) have also a discourse of Jesus against the *scribes*, γραμματεῖς, but extending no farther than a few verses. It is however highly probable, as our modern critics allow,[24] that Jesus should launch out into fuller invectives against that body of men under the circumstances in which Matthew places that discourse, and it is almost certain that such sharp enunciations must have preceded the catastrophe; so that it is not admissible to control the account of the first Evangelist by the meagre one of the two other synoptists,[25] especially as the former is distinguished by connectedness and unity. It is true that much of what Matthew here presents as a continuous address, is assigned by Luke to various scenes and occasions, and it would hence follow that the former has, in this case again, blended the original elements of the discourse with kindred matter, belonging to the discourses of various periods,[26] if it could be shown that the arrangement of Luke is the correct one: a position which must therefore be examined. Those parts of the anti-pharisaic harangue which Luke has in common with Matthew, are, excepting the couple of verses which he places in the same connexion as Matthew, introduced by him as concomitant with

[23] Comp. De Wette, exeg. Handb., 1, 1, s. 186.
[24] Sieffert, über den Ursprung des ersten Ev., s. 117 f.
[25] Comp. De Wette, 1, 1, s. 189.
[26] Schulz, über das Abendmahl, s. 313 f. ; Schneckenburger, über den Ursprung, s. 54.

two entertainments to which he represents Jesus as being invited by Pharisees (xi. 37 ff. ; xiv. 1 ff.)—a politeness on their pa;t which appears in no other gospel. The expositors of the present day, almost with one voice, concur in admiring the naturalness and faithfulness with which Luke has preserved to us the original occasions of these discourses.[27] It is certainly natural enough that, in the second entertainment, Jesus, observing the efforts of the guests to obtain the highest places for themselves, should take occasion to admonish them against assuming the precedence at feasts, even on the low ground of prudential considerations ; and this admonition appears in a curtailed form, and without any special cause in the final anti-pharisaic discourse in Matthew, Mark, and even in Luke again (xx. 46). But it is otherwise with the discourse which Luke attaches to the earlier entertainment in the Pharisee's house. In the very commencement of this repast, Jesus not only speaks of the *ravening*, ἁρπαγή, and *wickedness*, πονηρία, with which the Pharisees fill the cup and platter, and honours them with the title of *fools*, ἄφρονες, but breaks forth into a denunciation of *woe*, οὐαὶ, against them and the scribes and doctors of the law, threatening them with retribution for all the blood that had been shed by their fathers, whose deeds they approved. We grant that Attic urbanity is not to be expected in a Jewish teacher, but even according to the oriental standard, such invectives uttered at table against the host and his guests, would be the grossest dereliction of what is due to hospitality. This was obvious to Schleiermacher's acute perception ; and he therefore supposes that the meal passed off amicably, and that it was not until its close, when Jesus was again out of the house, that the host expressed his surprise at the neglect of the usual ablutions by Jesus and his disciples, and that Jesus answered with so much asperity.[28] But to assume that the writer has not described the meal itself and the incidents that accompanied it, and that he has noticed it merely for the sake of its connexion with the subsequent discourse, is an arbitrary mode of overcoming the difficulty. For the text runs thus : *And he went in and sat down to meat. And when the Pharisee saw it, he marvelled that he had not first washed before dinner. And the Lord said unto him*, εἰσελθὼν δὲ ἀνέπεσεν· ὁ δὲ Φαρισαῖος ἰδὼν ἐθαύμασεν, ὅτι οὐ πρῶτον ἐβαπτίσθη—· εἶπε δὲ ὁ Κύριος πρὸς αὐτόν. It is manifestly impossible to thrust in between these sentences the duration of the meal, and it must have been the intention of the writer to attach *he marvelled* ἐθαύμασεν to *he sat down to meat* ἀνέπεσεν, and *he said* εἶπεν to *he marvelled* ἐθαύμασεν. But if this could not really have been the case, unless Jesus violated in the grossest manner the simplest dictates of civility, there is an end to the vaunted accuracy of Luke in his allocation of this discourse : and we have only to inquire how he could be led to give it so false a position. This is to be discovered by comparing the manner in which the two other synoptists mention the offence of the Pharisees, at the omission of the ablutions before meals by Jesus and his disciples : a circumstance to which they annex discourses different from those given by Luke. In Matthew (xv. 1 ff.), scribes and Pharisees from Jerusalem ask Jesus why his disciples do not observe the custom of washing before meat? It is thus implied that they knew of this omission, as may easily be supposed, by report. In Mark (vii. 1 ff.), they look on (ἰδόντες,) while some disciples of Jesus eat with unwashen hands, and call them to account for this irregularity. Lastly, in Luke, Jesus himself

---

[27] Schleiermacher, über den Lukas, s. 182, 196 f. ; Olshausen, in loc., and the writers mentioned in the foregoing note.
[28] Ut sup. 180.

dines with a Pharisee, and on this occasion it is observed that he neglects the usual washings. This is an evident climax : hearing, witnessing, taking food together. Was it formed, in the descending gradation, from Luke to Matthew, or, in the ascending one, from Matthew to Luke ? From the point of view adopted by the recent critics of the first gospel, the former mode will be held the most probable, namely, that the memory of the original scene, the repast in the Pharisee's house, was lost in the process of tradition, and is therefore wanting in the first gospel. But, apart from the difficulty of conceiving that this discourse was uttered under the circumstances with which it is invested by Luke, it is by no means in accordance with the course of tradition, when once in possession of so dramatic a particular as a feast, to let it fall again, but rather to supply it, if lacking. The general tendency of the legend is to transform the abstract into the concrete, the mediate into the immediate, hearsay into vision, the spectator into the participator ; and as the offence taken against Jesus by the Pharisees referred, among other things, to the usages of the table, nothing was more natural than for legend to associate the origin of the offence with a particular place and occasion, and for this purpose to imagine invitations given to Jesus by Pharisees—invitations which would be historically suspicious, if for no other reason than that Luke alone knows anything of them. Here, then, we again find Luke in his favourite employment of furnishing a frame to the discourses of Jesus which tradition had delivered to him ; a procedure much farther removed from historic faithfulness, than the effort of Matthew to give unity to discourses gathered from different periods, without adding matter of his own. The formation of the climax above displayed, can only be conceived, in accordance with the general relation between the synoptists, in the following manner : Mark, who in this instance evidently had Matthew before him, enriched his account with the dramatic expression ἰδόντες ; while Luke, independent of both, has added a repast, δεῖπνον, whether presented to him by a more developed tradition, or invented by his own more fertile imagination. Together with this unhistorical position, the proportions themselves seem to be disfigured in Luke (xi. 39–41, 49), and the observation of the lawyer, *Master, thus saying thou reproachest us also* (xi. 45), too much resembles an artificial transition from the philippic against the Pharisees, to that against the doctors of the law.[29]

Another passage in this discourse has been the subject of much discussion. It is that (v. 35) in which Jesus threatens his cotemporaries, that all the innocent blood shed from that of Abel to that of Zacharias, the son of Barachias, slain in the temple, will be required of their generation. The Zacharias of whom such an end is narrated 2 Chron. xxiv. 20 ff. was a son, not of Barachias, but of Jehoiada. On the other hand, there was a Zacharias, the son of Baruch, who came to a similar end in the Jewish war.[30] Moreover, it appears unlikely that Jesus would refer to a murder which took place 850 B.C. as the last. Hence it was at first supposed that we have in v. 35 a prophecy, and afterwards, a confusion of the earlier with the later event ; and the latter notion has been used as an accessory proof that the first gospel is a posterior compilation.[31] It is, however, equally probable, that the Zacharias, son of Jehoiada, whose death is narrated in the Chronicles, has been confounded with the prophet Zechariah, who was a son of Barachias (Zech. i. 1 ; LXX. ;

[29] Comp. De Wette, exeg. Handb. 1, 1, s. 189. 1, 2, s. 67, 76.
[30] Joseph., b. j. iv. v. 4.
[31] Eichhorn, Einleitung in das N.T., 1, s. 510 ff. ; Hug, Einl. in das N.T., 2, s. 10 ff. ; Credner, Einl., 1, s. 207.

Baruch, in Josephus, is not the same name) ;[32] especially as a Targum, evidently in consequence of a like confusion with the prophet who was a grandson of Iddo, calls the murdered Zechariah a son of Iddo.[33]   The murder of a prophet, mentioned by Jeremiah (xxvi. 23), was doubtless subsequent to that of Zechariah, but in the Jewish order of the canonical books, Jeremiah precedes the Chronicles ; and to oppose a murder revealed in the first canonical book, to one recorded in the last, was entirely in the style of Jewish parlance.[34]

After having considered all the discourses of Jesus given by Matthew, and compared them with their parallels, with the exception of those which had come before us in previous discussions, or which have yet to come before us in our examination of single incidents in the public ministry, or of the history of the passion : it might appear requisite to the completeness of our criticism, that we should also give a separate investigation to the connexion in which the two other synoptists give the discourses of Jesus, and from this point review the parallels in Matthew.   But we have already cast a comparative glance over the most remarkable discourses in Luke and Mark, and gone through the parables which are peculiar to each ; and as to the remainder of what they offer in the form of discourses, it will either come under our future consideration, or if not, the point of view from which it is to be criticised, has been sufficiently indicated in the foregoing investigations.

[32] Vid. Theile, über Zacharias Barachias Sohn, in Winer's und Engelhardt's neuem krit. Journ., 2, s. 401 ff. ; De Wette, in loc.
[33] Targum Thren. ii. 20, in Wetstein, s. 491.
[34] Comp. De Wette, in loc.

CHAPTER VII.

DISCOURSES OF JESUS IN THE FOURTH GOSPEL.

§ 80.

CONVERSATION OF JESUS WITH NICODEMUS.

THE first considerable specimen which the fourth gospel gives of the teaching of Jesus, is his conversation with Nicodemus (iii. 1–21). In the previous chapter (23–25) it is narrated, that during the first passover attended by Jesus after his entrance on his public ministry, he had won many to faith in him by the *miracles, σημεῖα,* which he performed, but that he did not commit himself to them because he saw through them : he was aware, that is, of the uncertainty and impurity of their faith. Then follows in our present chapter, as an example, not only of the adherents whom Jesus had found even thus early, but also of the wariness with which he tested and received them, a more detailed account how Nicodemus, a ruler of the Jews and a Pharisee, applied to him, and how he was treated by Jesus.

It is through the Gospel of John alone that we learn anything of this Nicodemus, who in vii. 50 f. appears as the advocate of Jesus, so far as to protest against his being condemned without a hearing, and in xix. 39 as the partaker with Joseph of Arimathea of the care of interring Jesus. Modern criticism, with reason, considers it surprising that Matthew (with the other synoptists) does not even mention the name of this remarkable adherent of Jesus, and that we have to gather all our knowledge of him from the fourth gospel ; since the peculiar relation in which Nicodemus stood to Jesus, and his participation in the care of his interment, must have been as well known to Matthew as to John. This difficulty has been numbered among the arguments which are thought to prove that the first gospel was not written by the Apostle Matthew, but was the product of a tradition considerably more remote from the time and locality of Jesus.[1] But the fact is that the common fund of tradition on which all the synoptists drew had preserved no notice of this Nicodemus. With touching piety the Christian legend has recorded in the tablets of her memory, the names of all the others who helped to render the last honours to their murdered master—of Joseph of Arimathea and the two Marys (Matt. xxvii. 57–61 parall.) ; why then was Nicodemus the only neglected one—he who was especially distinguished among those who tended the remains of Jesus, by his nocturnal interview with the teacher sent from God, and by his advocacy of him among the chief priests and Pharisees? It is so difficult to conceive that the name of this man, if he had really assumed such a position, would have vanished from the popular evangelical tradition,

---

[1] Schulz, über das Abendmahl, s. 321.

without leaving a single trace, that one is induced to inquire whether the contrary supposition be not more capable of explanation : namely, that such a relation between Nicodemus and Jesus might have been fabricated by tradition, and adopted by the author of the fourth gospel without having really subsisted.

John xii. 42, it is expressly said that *many among the chief rulers* believed on Jesus, but concealed their faith from dread of excommunication by the Pharisees, because *they loved the praise of men more than the praise of God.*[2] That towards the end of his career *many* people of rank believed in Jesus, even in secret only, is not very probable, since no indication of it appears in the Acts of the Apostles ; for that the advice of Gamaliel (Acts v. 34 ff.) did not originate in a positively favourable disposition towards the cause of Jesus, seems to be sufficiently demonstrated by the spirit of his disciple Saul. Moreover the synoptists make Jesus declare in plain terms that the secret of his Messiahship had been revealed only to *babes,* and hidden from the *wise* and *prudent* (Matt. xi. 25 ; Luke x. 21), and Joseph of Arimathea is the only individual of the ruling class whom they mention as an adherent of Jesus. How, then, if Jesus did not really attach to himself any from the upper ranks, came the case to be represented differently at a later period? In John vii. 48 f. we read that the Pharisees sought to disparage Jesus by the remark that none of the rulers or of the Pharisees, but only the ignorant populace, believed on him ; and even later adversaries of Christianity, for example, Celsus, laid great stress on the circumstance that Jesus had had as his disciples ἐπιρρήτους ἀνθρώπους, τελώνας καὶ ναύτας τοὺς πονηροτάτους.[3] This reproach was a thorn in the side of the early church, and though as long as her members were drawn only from the people, she might reflect with satisfaction on the declarations of Jesus, in which he had pronounced the *poor,* πτωχοὺς, and *simple, νηπίους,* blessed : yet so soon as she was joined by men of rank and education, these would lean to the idea that converts like themselves had not been wanting to Jesus during his life. But, it would be objected, nothing had been hitherto known of such converts. Naturally enough, it might be answered ; since fear of their equals would induce them to conceal their relations with Jesus. Thus a door was opened for the admission of any number of secret adherents among the higher class (John xii. 42 f.). But, it would be further urged, how could they have intercourse with Jesus unobserved? Under the veil of the night, would be the answer ; and thus the scene was laid for the interviews of such men with Jesus (xix. 39). This, however, would not suffice ; a representative of this class must actually appear on the scene : Joseph of Arimathea might have been chosen, his name being still extant in the synoptical tradition ; but the idea of him was too definite, and it was the interest of the legend to name more than one eminent friend of Jesus. Hence a new personage was devised, whose Greek name Νικόδημος seems to point him out significantly as the representative of the dominant class.[4] That this development of the legend is confined to the fourth gospel, is to be explained, partly by the generally admitted lateness of its origin, and partly on the ground that in the evidently more cultivated circle in which it arose, the limitation of the adherents of Jesus to the

---

[2] This " secret information " is very welcome to Dr. Paulus, because it gives a useful hint " as to many occurrences in the life of Jesus, the causes of which are not obvious " (L. J. 1, b, s. 141) ; that is Paulus, like Bahrdt and Venturini, though less openly, is fond of using such secret and influential allies as *deus ex machinâ,* for the explanation of much that is miraculous in the life of Jesus (the transfiguration, residence after the resurrection, etc.).

[3] Orig. c. Cels. i. 62.

[4] Let the reader bear in mind the kindred names Nicolaus and Nicolaitans.

common people would be more offensive, than in the circle in which the synoptical tradition was formed. Thus the reproach which modern criticism has cast on the first gospel, on the score of its silence respecting Nicodemus, is turned upon the fourth, on the score of its information on the same subject.

These considerations, however, should not create any prejudice against the ensuing conversation, which is the proper object of our investigations. This may still be in the main genuine; Jesus may have held such a conversation with one of his adherents, and our Evangelist may have embellished it no further than by making this interlocutor a man of rank. Neither will we, with the author of the Probabilia, take umbrage at the opening address of Nicodemus, nor complain, with him, that there is a want of connexion between that address and the answer of Jesus.[5] The requisition of a *new birth* (γεννηθῆναι ἄνωθεν), as a condition of entrance into the kingdom of heaven, does not differ essentially from the summons with which Jesus opens his ministry in the synoptical gospels, *Repent ye, for the kingdom of heaven is at hand.* New birth, or new creation, was a current image among the Jews, especially as denoting the conversion of an idolater into a worshipper of Jehovah. It was customary to say of Abraham, that when, according to the Jewish supposition, he renounced idolatry for the worship of the true God, he became a new creature (בריה חדשה).[6] The proselyte, too, in allusion to his relinquishing all his previous associations, was compared to a new-born child.[7] That such phraseology was common among the Jews at that period, is shown by the confidence with which Paul applies, as if it required no explanation, the term *new creation*, καινὴ κτίσις, to those truly converted to Christ. Now, if Jesus required, even from the Jews, as a condition of entrance into the messianic kingdom, the *new birth* which they ascribed to their heathen proselytes, Nicodemus might naturally wonder at the requisition, since the Israelite thought himself, as such, unconditionally entitled to that kingdom: and this is the construction which has been put upon his question v. 4.[8] But Nicodemus does not ask, How canst thou say that a Jew, or a child of Abraham, must be born again? His ground of wonder is that Jesus appears to suppose it possible for a *man* to be born again, and that *when he is old*. It does not, therefore, astonish him that spiritual new birth should be expected in a Jew, but corporeal new birth in a man. How an oriental, to whom figurative speech in general—how a Jew, to whom the image of the new birth in particular must have been familiar—how especially a *master of Israel*, in whom the misconstruction of figurative phrases cannot, as in the apostles (e.g. Matt. xv. 15 f. ; xvi. 7), be ascribed to want of education—could understand this expression literally, has been matter of extreme surprise to expositors of all parties, as well as to Jesus (v. 10). Hence some have supposed that the Pharisee really understood Jesus, and only intended by his question to test the ability of Jesus to interpret his figurative expression

---

[5] Prob., p. 44. Bretschneider is right, however, in declaring against Kuinöl's method of supplying a connexion between the discourses in John, by the insertion of propositions and intermediate discourses, supposed to have been omitted. Lücke judiciously admits (1, p. 446) that if, in John, something appears to be wanting between two consecutive expressions of Jesus, we are yet to suppose that there was an immediate connexion between them in the mind of the Evangelist, and it is this connexion which it is the task of exegesis to ascertain. In truth the discourses in the fourth gospel are never entirely wanting in connexion (apart from the exceptions to be noticed in § 81), though that connexion is sometimes very latent.
[6] Bereschith R., sect. 39 f. xxxviii. 2. Bammidbar R., s. 11 f. ccxi. 2. Tanchuma f. v. 2, in Schöttgen, i. s. 704. Something similar is said of Moses, from Schemoth R., ib.
[7] Jevamoth f. lxii. 1, xcii. 1, in Lightfoot, p. 984.
[8] E.g. Knapp, comm. in colloq. Christi cum Nicod. in loc.

into a simple proposition : [9] but Jesus does not treat him as a hypocrite, as in that case he must have done—he continues to instruct him, as one really *ignorant* οὐ γινώσκοντα (v. 10). Others give the question the following turn : This cannot be meant in a physical sense, how then otherwise ? [10] But the true drift of the question is rather the contrary : By these words I can only understand physical new birth, but how is this possible ? Our wonder at the ignorance of the Jewish doctor, therefore, returns upon us ; and it is heightened when, after the copious explanation of Jesus (v. 5–8), that the new birth which he required was a *spiritual birth*, γεννηθῆναι ἐκ τοῦ πνεύματος, Nicodemus has made no advance in comprehension, but asks with the same obtuseness as before (v. 9), *How can these things be ?* By this last difficulty Lücke is so straitened, that, contrary to his ordinary exegetical tact, he refers the continued amazement of Nicodemus (as other expositors had referred his original question) to the circumstance that Jesus maintained the necessity of new birth even for Israelites. But, in that case, Nicodemus would have inquired concerning the necessity, not the possibility, of that birth ; instead of asking, *How can* these things be ? he would have asked, *Why must* these things be ? This inconceivable mistake in a Jewish doctor is not then to be explained away, and our surprise must become strong suspicion so soon as it can be shown, that legend or the Evangelist had inducements to represent this individual as more simple than he really was. First, then, it must occur to us, that in all descriptions and recitals, contrasts are eagerly exhibited ; hence in the representation of a colloquy in which one party is the teacher, the other the taught, there is a strong temptation to create a contrast to the wisdom of the former by exaggerating the simplicity of the latter. Further, we must remember the satisfaction it must give to a Christian mind of that age, to place a master of Israel in the position of an unintelligent person, by the side of the Master of the Christians. Lastly, it is, as we shall presently see more clearly, the constant method of the fourth Evangelist in detailing the conversations of Jesus, to form the knot and the progress of the discussion, by making the interlocutors understand literally what Jesus intended figuratively.

In reply to the second query of Nicodemus, Jesus takes entirely the tone of the fourth Evangelist's prologue (v. 11–13).[11] The question hence arises, whether the Evangelist borrowed from Jesus, or lent to him his own style. A previous investigation has decided in favour of the latter alternative.[12] But this inquiry referred merely to the form of the discourses ; in relation to their matter, its analogy with the ideas of Philo, does not authorize us at once to conclude that the writer here puts his Alexandrian doctrine of the Logos into the mouth of Jesus ; [13] because the expressions, *We speak that we do know*, etc. ὃ οἴδαμεν λαλοῦμεν κ. τ. λ., and, *No man hath ascended up to heaven*, etc. οὐδεὶς ἀναβέβηκεν κ. τ. λ., have an analogy with Matt. xi. 27 ; and the idea of the pre-existence of the Messiah which is here propounded, is, as we have seen, not foreign to the Apostle Paul.

V. 14 and 15 Jesus proceeds from the more simple things of the earth, ἐπιγείοις, the communications concerning the new birth, to the more difficult

---

[9] Paulus, Comm. 4, s. 183. L. J. 1, a, s. 176.

[10] Lücke and Tholück, in loc.

[11] III. 11 : ὃ ἑωράκαμεν μαρτυροῦμεν καὶ τὴν μαρτυρίαν ἡμῶν οὐ λαμβάνετε. 13 · καὶ οὐδεὶς ἀναβέβηκεν εἰς τὸν οὐρανὸν, εἰ μὴ ὁ ἐκ τοῦ οὐρανοῦ καταβὰς, ὁ υἱὸς τοῦ ἀνθρώπου ὁ ὢν ἐν τῷ οὐρανῷ.

I. 18 : θεὸν οὐδεὶς ἑώρακε πώποτε. ὁ μονογενὴς υἱὸς, ὁ ὢν εἰς τὸν κόλπον τοῦ πατρὸς ἐκεῖνος ἐξηγήσατο.

11 : —καὶ οἱ ἴδιοι αὐτὸν οὐ παρέλαβον.

[12] Sup. § 46.

[13] This is informed in the Probabilia, p. 46.

things of heaven, ἐπουρανίοις, the announcement of the destination of the Messiah to a vicarious death. The Son of Man, he says, must *be lifted up* (ὑψωθῆναι, which, in John's phraseology, signifies crucifixion, with an allusion to a glorifying exaltation), in the same way, and with the same effect, as the brazen serpent Num. xxi. 8, 9. Here many questions press upon us. Is it credible, that Jesus already, at the very commencement of his public ministry, foresaw his death, and in the specific form of crucifixion? and that long before he instructed his disciples on this point, he made a communication on the subject to a Pharisee? Can it be held consistent with the wisdom of Jesus as a teacher, that he should impart such knowledge to Nicodemus? Even Lücke[14] puts the question why, when Nicodemus had not understood the more obvious doctrine, Jesus tormented him with the more recondite, and especially with the secret of the Messiah's death, which was then so remote? He answers: it accords perfectly with the wisdom of Jesus as a teacher, that he should reveal the sufferings appointed for him by God as early as possible, because no instruction was better adapted to cast down false worldly hopes. But the more remote the idea of the Messiah's death from the conceptions of his cotemporaries, owing to the worldliness of their expectations, the more impressively and unequivocally must Jesus express that idea, if he wished to promulgate it ; not in an enigmatical form which he could not be sure that Nicodemus would understand. Lücke continues : Nicodemus was a man open to instruction ; one of whom good might be expected. But in this very conversation, his dulness of comprehension in *earthly things*, ἐπίγεια, had evinced that he must have still less capacity for *heavenly things*, ἐπουράνια ; and, according to v. 12, Jesus himself despaired of enlightening him with respect to them. Lücke, however, observes, that it was a practice with Jesus to follow up easy doctrine which had not been comprehended, by difficult doctrine which was of course less comprehensible ; that he purposed thus to give a spur to the minds of his hearers, and by straining their attention, engage them to reflect. But the examples which Lücke adduces of such proceeding on the part of Jesus, are all drawn from the fourth gospel. Now the very point in question is, whether that gospel correctly represents the teaching of Jesus ; consequently Lücke argues in a circle. We have seen a similar procedure ascribed to Jesus in his conversation with the woman of Samaria, and we have already declared our opinion that such an overburthening of weak faculties with enigma on enigma, does not accord with the wise rule as to the communication of doctrine, which the same gospel puts into the mouth of Jesus, xvi. 12. It would not stimulate, but confuse, the mind of the hearer, who persisted in a misapprehension of the well-known figure of the new birth, to present to him the novel comparison of the Messiah and his death, to the brazen serpent and its effects; a comparison quite incongruous with his Jewish ideas.[15] In the first three Gospels Jesus pursues an entirely different course. In these, where a misconstruction betrays itself on the part of the disciples, Jesus (except where he breaks off altogether, or where it is evident that the Evangelist unhistorically associates a number of metaphorical discourses) applies himself with the assiduity of an earnest teacher to the thorough explanation of the difficulty, and not until he has effected this does he proceed, step by step, to convey further instruction (e.g. Matt. xiii. 10 ff., 36 ff., xv. 16, xvi. 8 ff.).[16] This

---

[14] Ut sup. p. 476.

[15] Comp. Bretschneider, ut sup.

[16] De Wette adduces as examples of a similar procedure on the part of Jesus in the synoptical gospels, Matt. xix. 21, xx. 22 f. But these two cases are of a totally different kind from the one under consideration in John. We have here to treat of a want of com-

is the method of a wise teacher ; on the contrary, to leap from one subject to another, to overburthen and strain the mind of the hearer, a mode of instruction which the fourth Evangelist attributes to Jesus, is wholly inconsistent with that character. To explain this inconsistency, we must suppose that the writer of the fourth gospel thought to heighten in the most effective manner the contrast which appears from the first, between the wisdom of the one party and the incapacity of the other, by representing the teacher as overwhelming the pupil, who put unintelligent questions on the most elementary doctrine, with lofty and difficult themes, beneath which his faculties are laid prostrate.

From v. 16, even those commentators who pretend to some ability in this department, lose all hope of showing that the remainder of the discourse may have been spoken by Jesus.   Not only does Paulus make this confession, but even Olshausen, with a concise statement of his reasons.[17]   At the above verse, any special reference to Nicodemus vanishes, and there is commenced an entirely general discourse on the destination of the Son of God, to confer a blessing on the world, and on the manner in which unbelief forfeits this blessing.   Moreover, these ideas are expressed in a form, which at one moment appears to be a reminiscence of the Evangelist's introduction, and at another has a striking similarity with passages in the first Epistle of John.[18]   In particular, the expression, *the only begotten Son*, ὁ μονογενὴς υἱὸς, which is repeatedly (v. 16 and 18) attributed to Jesus as a designation of his own person, is nowhere else found in his mouth, even in the fourth gospel; this circumstance, however, marks it still more positively as a favourite phrase of the Evangelist (i. 14–18), and of the writer of the Epistles (1 John iv. 9).   Further, many things are spoken of as past, which at the supposed period of this conversation with Nicodemus were yet future.   For even if the words, *he gave*, ἔδωκεν, refer not to the giving over to death, but to the sending of the Messiah into the world ; the expressions, *men loved darkness* ἠγάπησαν οἱ ἄνθρωποι τὸ σκότος, and, *their deeds were evil*, ἦν πονηρὰ αὐτῶν τὰ ἔργα (v. 19), as Lücke also remarks, could only be used after the triumph of darkness had been achieved in the rejection and execution of Jesus : they belong then to the Evangelist's point of view at the time when he wrote, not to that of Jesus when on the threshold of his public ministry.   In general the whole of this discourse attributed to Jesus, with its constant use of the third person to designate the supposed speaker ; with its dogmatical terms *only begotten, light,* and the like, applied to Jesus ; with its comprehensive view of the crisis and its results, which the appearance of Jesus produced, is far too objective for us to believe that it came from the lips of Jesus.   Jesus could not speak thus

---

prehension, in the face of which it is surprising that Jesus instead of descending to its level, chooses to elevate himself to a still less attainable altitude.   In the passages quoted from the synoptists, on the other hand, we have examples of an excessive self-valuation, too high an estimate of their ability to promote the cause of Jesus, on the part of the rich young man and of the sons of Zebedee, and Jesus with perfect propriety checks their egotistic ardour by the abrupt presentation of a higher demand.   These instances could only be parallel with that of Nicodemus, if the latter had piqued himself on his enlightenment, and Jesus, by a sudden flight into a higher region, had sought to convince him of his ignorance.

[17] Bibl. Comm. 2, s. 96.

[18] III. 19 : αὕτη δέ ἐστιν ἡ κρίσις, ὅτι τὸ φῶς ἐλήλυθεν εἰς τὸν κόσμον, καὶ ἠγάπησαν οἱ ἄνθρωποι μᾶλλον τὸ σκότος ἢ τὸ φῶς.

III. 16 : οὕτω γὰρ ἠγάπησεν ὁ θεὸς τὸν κόσμον, ὥστε τὸν υἱὸν αὐτοῦ τὸν μονογενῆ ἔδωκεν, ἵνα πᾶς ὁ πιστεύων εἰς αὐτὸν, μὴ ἀπόληται ἀλλ' ἔχῃ ζωὴν αἰώνιον.

I. 9 : ἦν τὸ φῶς τὸ ἀληθινὸν, τὸ φωτίζον πάντα ἄνθρωπον, ἐρχόμενον εἰς τὸν κόσμον.
5 : καὶ τὸ φῶς ἐν τῇ σκοτίᾳ φαίνει, καὶ ἡ σκοτία αὐτὸ οὐ κατέλαβεν.

1 John iv. 9 : ἐν τούτῳ ἐφανερώθη ἡ ἀγάπη τοῦ θεοῦ ἐν ἡμῖν, ὅτι τὸν υἱὸν αὐτοῦ τὸν μονογενῆ ἀπέσταλκεν ὁ θεὸς εἰς τὸν κόσμον, ἵνα ζήσωμεν δι' αὐτοῦ.

of himself, but the Evangelist might speak thus of Jesus. Hence the same expedient has been adopted, as in the case of the Baptist's discourse already considered, and it has been supposed that Jesus is the speaker down to v. 16, but that from that point the Evangelist appends his own dogmatic reflections.[19] But there is again here no intimation of such a transition in the text ; rather, the connecting word *for*, γὰρ (v. 16), seems to indicate a continuation of the same discourse. No writer, and least of all the fourth Evangelist (comp. vii. 39, xi. 51 f., xii. 16, xxxiii. 37 ff.), would scatter his own observations thus undistinguishingly, unless he wished to create a misapprehension.[20]

If then it be established that the evangelist, from v. 16 to the end of the discourse, means to represent Jesus as the speaker, while Jesus can never have so spoken, we cannot rest satisfied with the half measure adopted by Lücke, when he maintains that it is really Jesus who continues to speak from the above passage, but that the Evangelist has inwoven his own explanations and amplifications more liberally than before. For this admission undermines all certainty as to how far the discourse belongs to Jesus, and how far to the Evangelist; besides, as the discourse is distinguished by the closest uniformity of thought and style, it must be ascribed either wholly to Jesus or wholly to the Evangelist. Of these two alternatives the former is, according to the above considerations, impossible ; we are therefore restricted to the latter, which we have observed to be entirely consistent with the manner of the fourth Evangelist.

But not only on the passage v. 16–21 must we pass this judgment : v. 14 has appeared to us out of keeping with the position of Jesus ; and the behaviour of Nicodemus, v. 4 and 9, altogether inconceivable. Thus in the very first sample, when compared with the observations which we have already made on John iii. 22 ff., iv. 1 ff., the fourth gospel presents to us all the peculiarities which characterize its mode of reporting the discourses of Jesus. They are usually commenced in the form of dialogue, and so far as this extends, the lever that propels the conversation is the striking contrast between the spiritual sense and the carnal interpretation of the language of Jesus ; generally, however, the dialogue is merged into an uninterrupted discourse, in which the writer blends the person of Jesus with his own, and makes the former use concerning himself, language which could only be used by John concerning Jesus.

§ 81.

THE DISCOURSES OF JESUS, JOHN V.–XII.

In the fifth chapter of John, a long discourse of Jesus is connected with a cure wrought by him on the sabbath (19–47). The mode in which Jesus at

---

[19] Paulus and Olshausen, in loc.

[20] Tholück (Glaubwürdigkeit, s. 335) adduces as examples of a similar unobserved fusion of a discourse quoted from a foreign source, with the writer's own matter, Gal. ii. 14 ff. Euseb., H. E. iii. 1, 39. Hieron. Comm. in Jes. 53. But such instances in an epistle, a commentary or an historical work interspersed with reasoning and criticism are not parallel with those in an historical narrative of the nature of our fourth gospel. In works of the former kind, the reader expects the author to reason, and hence, when the discourse of another party has been introduced, he is prepared at the slightest pause to see the author again take up the argument. It is quite different with a work like our fourth gospel. The introduction, it is true, is put forth as the author's own reasoning, and it is there quite natural that after a brief quotation from the discourse of another, v. 15, he should, at v. 16, resume the character of speaker without any express intimation. But when once he has entered on his narrative, which is strictly a recital of what has been done, and what has been said, all that he annexes without any mark of distinction (as e.g. xii. 37) to a discourse explicitly ascribed to another, must be considered as a continuation of that discourse.

v. 17 defends his activity on the sabbath, is worthy of notice, as distinguished from that adopted by him in the earlier gospels. These ascribe to him, in such cases, three arguments : the example of David, who ate the shew-bread; the precedent of the sabbatical labours of the priests in the temple, quoted also in John vii. 23 (Matt. xii. 3 ff. parall.); and the course pursued with respect to an ox, sheep, or ass, that falls into the pit (Matt. xii. 11, parall.), or is led out to watering on the sabbath (Luke xiii. 18) : all which arguments are entirely in the practical spirit that characterizes the popular teaching of Jesus. The fourth Evangelist, on the contrary, makes him argue from the uninterrupted activity of God, and reminds us by the expression which he puts into the mouth of Jesus, *My Father worketh hitherto,* ὁ πατήρ ἕως ἄρτι ἐργάζεται, of a principle in the Alexandrian metaphysics, viz. *God never ceases to act,* ποιῶν ὁ θεὸς οὐδέποτε παύεται : [1] a metaphysical proposition more likely to be familiar to the author of the fourth gospel than to Jesus. In the synoptical gospels, miracles of healing on the sabbath are followed up by declarations respecting the nature and design of the sabbatical institution, a species of instruction of which the people were greatly in need ; but in the present passage, a digression is immediately made to the main theme of the gospel, the person of Christ and his relation to the Father. The perpetual recurrence of this theme in the fourth gospel has led its adversaries, not without reason, to accuse it of a tendency purely theoretic, and directed to the glorification of Jesus. In the matter of the succeeding discourse there is nothing to create a difficulty, nothing that Jesus might not have spoken, for it treats, with the strictest coherence, of things which the Jews expected of the Messiah, or which Jesus attributed to himself, according to the synoptists also : as, for instance, the raising of the dead, and the office of judging the world. But this consistency in the matter only heightens the difficulty connected with the form and phraseology in which it is expressed. For the discourse, especially its latter half (from v. 31), is full of the closest analogies with the first epistle of John, and with passages in the gospel in which either the author speaks, or John the Baptist.[2] One means of explaining the former resemblance is to suppose, that the Evangelist formed his style by closely imitating that of Jesus. That this is possible, is not to be disputed ; but it

---

[1] Philo. Opp. ed. Mang. i. 44. apud Gfrörer, i. p. 122.

[2] Joh. v. 20 : ὁ γὰρ πατὴρ φιλεῖ τὸν υἱὸν καὶ πάντα δείκνυσιν αὐτῷ, ἃ αὐτὸς ποιεῖ.

24 : ὁ τὸν λόγον μου ἀκούων—μεταβέβηκεν ἐκ τοῦ θανάτου εἰς τὴν ζωήν.

32 : καὶ οἶδα, ὅτι ἀληθής ἐστιν ἡ μαρτυρία, ἣν μαρτυρεῖ περὶ ἐμοῦ.

34 : ἐγὼ δὲ οὐ παρὰ ἀνθρώπου τὴν μαρτυρίαν λαμβάνω.

36 : ἐγὼ δὲ ἔχω μαρτυρίαν μείζω τοῦ Ἰωάννου.

37 : καὶ ὁ πέμψας με πατήρ, αὐτὸς μεμαρτύρηκε περὶ ἐμοῦ.

Ib. : οὔτε τὴν φωνὴν αὐτοῦ ἀκηκόατε πώποτε, οὔτε τὸ εἶδος αὐτοῦ ἑωράκατε.

38 : καὶ τὸν λόγον αὐτοῦ οὐκ ἔχετε μένοντα ἐν ὑμῖν.

40 : καὶ οὐ θέλετε ἐλθεῖν πρός με, ἵνα ζωὴν ἔχητε.

42 : ὅτι τὴν ἀγάπην τοῦ θεοῦ οὐκ ἔχετε ἐν ἑαυτοῖς.

44 : πῶς δύνασθε ὑμεῖς πιστεύειν, δόξαν παρὰ ἀλλήλων λαμβάνοντες, καὶ τὴν δόξαν τὴν παρὰ τοῦ μόνου θεοῦ οὐ ζητεῖτε ;

John iii. 35 (the Baptist) : ὁ γὰρ πατὴρ ἀγαπᾷ τὸν υἱὸν καὶ πάντα δέδωκεν ἐν τῇ χειρὶ αὐτοῦ.

1 Joh. iii. 14 : ἡμεῖς οἴδαμεν, ὅτι μεταβεβήκαμεν ἐκ τοῦ θανάτου εἰς τὴν ζωήν.

Joh. xix. 35 : καὶ ἀληθινή ἐστιν αὐτοῦ ἡ μαρτυρία, κἀκεῖνος οἶδεν, ὅτι ἀληθῆ λέγει. Comp. xxi. 24. 1 Joh. 3, 12.

1 Joh. v. 9 : εἰ τὴν μαρτυρίαν τῶν ἀνθρώπων λαμβάνομεν, ἡ μαρτυρία τοῦ θεοῦ, μείζων ἐστίν· ὅτι αὕτη ἐστιν ἡ μαρτυρία τοῦ θεοῦ, ἣν μεμαρτύρηκε περὶ τοῦ υἱοῦ αὐτοῦ.

Joh. i. 18 : θεὸν οὐδεὶς ἑώρακε πώποτε. Comp. 1 Joh. iv. 12.

1 Joh. i. 10 : καὶ ὁ λόγος αὐτοῦ οὐκ ἐστιν ἐν ὑμῖν.

1 Joh. v. 12 : ὁ μὴ ἔχων τὸν υἱὸν τοῦ θεοῦ ζωὴν οὐκ ἔχει.

1 Joh. ii. 15 : οὐκ ἔστιν ἡ ἀγάπη τοῦ πατρὸς ἐν αὐτῷ.

Joh. xi. 43 : ἠγάπησαν γὰρ τὴν δόξαν τῶν ἀνθρώπων μᾶλλον, ἤπερ τὴν δόξαν τοῦ θεοῦ.

is equally certain that it could proceed only from a mind destitute of originality and self-confidence,—a character which the fourth Evangelist in nowise exhibits   Further, as in the other gospels Jesus speaks in a thoroughly different tone and style, it would follow, if he really spoke as he is represented to have done by John, that the manner attributed to him by the synoptists is fictitious. Now, that this manner did not originate with the Evangelists is plain from the fact, that each of them is so little master of his matter. Neither could the bulk of the discourses have been the work of tradition, not only because they have a highly original cast, but because they bear the impress of the alleged time and locality. On the contrary, the fourth Evangelist, by the ease with which he disposes his materials, awakens the suspicion that they are of his own production ; and some of his favourite ideas and phrases, such as, *The Father showeth the Son all that himself doeth*,[3] and those already quoted, seem to have sprung from an Hellenistic source, rather than from Palestine. But the chief point in the argument is, that in this gospel John the Baptist speaks, as we have seen, in precisely the same strain as the author of the gospels, and his Jesus. It cannot be supposed, that not only the Evangelist, but the Baptist, whose public career was prior to that of Jesus, and whose character was strongly marked, modelled his expressions with verbal minuteness on those of Jesus. Hence only two cases are possible : either the Baptist determined the style of Jesus and the Evangelist (who indeed appears to have been the Baptist's disciple) ; or the Evangelist determined the style of the Baptist and Jesus. The former alternative will be rejected by the orthodox, on the ground of the higher nature that dwelt in Christ ; and we are equally disinclined to adopt it, for the reason that Jesus, even though he may have been excited to activity by the Baptist, yet appears as a character essentially distinct from him, and original ; and for the still more weighty consideration, that the style of the Evangelist is much too feeble for the rude Baptist,—too mystical for his practical mind. There remains, then, but the latter alternative, namely, that the Evangelist has given his own style both to Jesus and to the Baptist : an explanation in itself more natural than the former, and supported by a multitude of examples from all kinds of historical writers. If however the Evangelist is thus responsible for the form of this discourse, it is still possible that the matter may have belonged to Jesus, but we cannot pronounce to what extent this is the case, and we have already had proof that the Evangelist, on suitable opportunities, very freely presents his own reflections in the form of a discourse from Jesus.

In chap. vi., Jesus represents himself, or rather his Father, v. 27 ff., as the giver of the spiritual manna. This is analogous to the Jewish idea above quoted, that the second Goël, like the first, would provide manna ;[4] and to the invitation of Wisdom in the Proverbs, ix. 5, *Come, eat of my bread : ἔλθετε, φάγετε τῶν ἐμῶν ἄρτων.* But the succeeding declaration, that he is himself *the bread of life that cometh down from heaven, ἄρτος ὁ ζῶν ὁ ἐκ τοῦ οὐρανοῦ καταβὰς* (v. 33 and 35) appears to find its true analogy only in the idea of Philo, that the *divine word, λόγος θεῖος,* is *that which nourishes the soul, τὸ τρέφον τὴν ψυχήν.*[5] From v. 51, the difficulty becomes still greater. Jesus proceeds to represent his flesh as the bread from heaven, which he will give for the life of the world, and *to eat the flesh of the Son of Man, and to drink his blood,* he pronounces to be the only means of attaining *eternal life.* The

---

[3] Vid. the passages compared by Gfrörer, 1, s. 194, from Philo, *de linguarum confusione.*
[4] Sup. § 14.
[5] De profugis, Opp. Mang., i. s. 566, Gfrörer, 1, s. 202. What is farther said of the λόγος : ἀφ' οὗ πᾶσαι παιδεῖαι καὶ σοφίαι ῥέουσιν ἀέννοι may be compared with John iv. 14, vi. 35, vii. 38.

similarity of these expressions to the words which the synoptists and Paul attribute to Jesus, at the institution of the Lord's Supper, led the older commentators generally to understand this passage as having reference to the Sacramental supper, ultimately to be appointed by Jesus.[6] The chief objection to this interpretation is, that before the institution of the supper, such an allusion would be totally unintelligible. Still the discourse might have some sense, however erroneous, for the hearers, as indeed it had, according to the narrator's statement ; and the impossibility of being understood is not, in the fourth gospel, so shunned by Jesus, that that circumstance alone would suffice to render this interpretation improbable. It is certainly supported by the analogy between the expressions in the discourse, and the words associated with the institution of the supper, and this analogy has wrung from one of our recent critics the admission, that even if Jesus himself, in uttering the above expressions, did not refer to the supper, the Evangelist, in choosing and conveying this discourse of Jesus might have had that institution in his mind, and might have supposed that Jesus here gave a premonition of its import.[7] In that case, however, he could scarcely have abstained from modifying the language of Jesus ; so that, if the choice of the expression *eat the flesh*, etc., can only be adequately explained on the supposition of a reference to the Lord's Supper, we owe it, without doubt, to the Evangelist alone. Having once said, apparently in accordance with Alexandrian ideas, that Jesus had described himself as *the bread of life*, how could he fail to be reminded of the *bread*, which in the Christian community was partaken of as the body of Christ, together with a beverage, as his blood ? He would the more gladly seize the opportunity of making Jesus institute the supper prophetically, as it were ; because, as we shall hereafter see, he knew nothing definite of its historical institution by Jesus.[8]

The discourse above considered, also bears the form of a dialogue, and it exhibits strikingly the type of dialogue which especially belongs to the fourth gospel : that, namely, in which language intended spiritually, is understood carnally. In the first place (v. 34), the Jews (as the woman of Samaria in relation to the water) suppose that by *the bread which cometh down from heaven*, Jesus means some material food, and entreat him evermore to supply them with such. Such a misapprehension was certainly natural ; but one would have thought that the Jews, before they carried the subject farther, would have indignantly protested against the assertion of Jesus (v. 32), that Moses had not given them heavenly bread. When Jesus proceeds to call himself *the bread from heaven*, the Jews in the synagogue at Capernaum murmur that he, the son of Joseph, whose father and mother they knew, should arrogate to himself a descent from heaven (v. 41) ; a reflection which the synoptists with more probability attribute to the people of Nazareth, the native city of Jesus, and to which they assign a more natural cause. That the Jews should not understand (v. 53) how Jesus could give them his flesh to eat is very conceivable ; and for that reason, as we have observed, it is the less so that Jesus should express himself thus unintelligibly. Neither is it surprising that this *hard saying*, σκληρὸς λόγος, should cause many disciples to fall away from him, nor easy to perceive how Jesus could, in the first instance, himself give reason for the secession, and then, on its occurrence, feel so much displeasure as is implied in v. 61 and 67. It is indeed said, that Jesus wished to sift his disciples, to remove from his society the super-

---

[6] See Lücke's History of the interpretation of this passage in his Comm. 2, Appendix B, p. 727 ff.

[7] Hase, L. J. § 99.

[8] Comp. Bretschneider, Probab., pp. 56, 88 ff.

ficial believers, the earthly-minded, whom he could not trust; but the measure which he here adopted was one calculated to alienate from him even his best and most intelligent followers. For it is certain that the twelve, who on other occasions knew not what was meant by the leaven of the Pharisees (Matt. xvi. 7), or by the opposition between what goes into the mouth, and what comes out of it (Matt. xv. 15), would not understand the present discourse; and the *words of eternal life*, for the sake of which they remained with him (v. 68), were assuredly not the words of this sixth chapter.[9]

The further we read in the fourth gospel, the more striking is the repetition of the same ideas and expressions. The discourses of Jesus during the Feast of Tabernacles, ch. vii. and viii. are, as Lücke has remarked, mere repetitions and amplifications of the oppositions previously presented (especially in ch. v.), of the coming, speaking, and acting, of Jesus, and of God (vii. 17, 28 f., viii. 28 f., 38, 40, 42, compare with v. 30, 43, vi. 38); of being *from above*, εἶναι ἐκ τῶν ἄνω, and *from beneath*, ἐκ τῶν κάτω (viii. 23, comp. iii. 31); of bearing witness of one's self, and receiving witness from God (viii. 13–19, comp. v. 31–37); of light and darkness (viii. 12, comp. iii. 10, ff., also xii. 35 f.); of true and false judgment (viii. 15 f., comp. v. 30). All that is new in these chapters, is quickly repeated, as the mention of the departure of Jesus whither the Jews cannot follow him (vii. 33 f., viii. 21, comp. xiii. 33, xiv. 2 ff., xvi. 16 ff.); a declaration, to which are attached, in the first two instances, very improbable misapprehensions or perversions on the part of the Jews, who, although Jesus had said, *I go unto him that sent me*, are represented as imagining, at one time, that he purposed journeying to the *dispersed among the Gentiles*, at another, that he meditated suicide. How often, again, in this chapter are repeated the asseverations, that he seeks not his own honour, but the honour of the Father (vii. 17 f., viii. 50, 54); that the Jews neither know whence he came, nor the father who sent him (vii. 28, viii. 14, 19, 54); that whosoever believeth in him shall have eternal life, shall not see death, while whosoever believeth not must die in his sins, having no share in eternal life (viii. 21, 24, 51, comp. iii. 36, vi. 40). —The ninth chapter, consisting chiefly of the deliberations of the Sanhedrim with the man born blind, whom Jesus had restored to sight, has of course the form of conversation, but as Jesus is less on the scene than heretofore, there is not the usual amount of artificial contrast; in its stead, however, there is, as we shall presently find, another evidence of artistic design in the narrator.

The tenth chapter commences with the well-known discourse on the Good Shepherd; a discourse which has been incorrectly called a parable.[10] Even the briefest among the other parables of Jesus, such as that of the leaven and of the mustard-seed, contain the outline of a history that develops itself, having a commencement, progress, and conclusion. Here, on the contrary, there is no historical development; even the particulars that have an historical character are stated generally, as things that are wont to happen, not as things that once happened, and they are left without further limitation; moreover, the *door* usurps the place of the Shepherd, which is at first the principal image; so that we have here, not a parable, but an allegory. Therefore this

---

[9] In relation to this chapter, I entirely approve the following remark in the Probabilia (p. 56): *videretur—Jesus ipse studuisse, ut verbis illuderet Judæis, nec ab iis intelligeretur, sed reprobaretur. Ita vero nec egit, nec agere potuit, neque si ita docuisset, tanta effecisset, quanta illum effecisse historia testatur.* Comp. De Wette, exeg. Handb., 1, 3, s. 6.

[10] E. g. by Tholück and Lücke. The latter, however, allows that it is rather an incipient than a complete parable. Olshausen also remarks, that the discourses of the Shepherd and the Vine are rather comparisons than parables; and Neander shows himself willing to distinguish the parable presented by the synoptists as a species, under the genus similitude, to which the παροιμίαι of John belong.

passage at least—(and we shall find no other, for the similitude of the vine, ch. xv., comes, as Lücke confesses, under the same category as the one in question)—furnishes no argument against the allegation by which recent critics have justified their suspicions as to the authenticity of the fourth gospel ; namely, that its author seems ignorant of the parabolic mode of teaching which, according to the other Evangelists, was habitual with Jesus. It does not however appear totally unknown to the fourth Evangelist that Jesus was fond of teaching by parables, for he attempts to give examples of this method, both in ch. x. and xv., the first of which he expressly styles a *parable,* παροιμία. But it is obvious that the parabolic form was not accordant with his taste, and that he was too deficient in the faculty of depicting external things, to abstain from the intermixture of reflections, whence the parable in his hand became an allegory.

The discourses of Jesus at the Feast of Tabernacles extend to x. 18. From v. 25, the Evangelist professes to record sayings which were uttered by Jesus three months later, at the Feast of Dedication. When, on this occasion, the Jews desire from him a distinct declaration whether he be the Messiah, his immediate reply is, that he has already told them this sufficiently, and he repeats his appeal to the testimony of the Father, as given in the *works,* ἔργα, done by Jesus in his name (as in v. 36). Hereupon he observes that his unbelieving interrogators are not of his sheep, whence he reverts to the allegory of the shepherd, which he had abandoned, and repeats part of it word for word.[11] But Jesus had not recently abandoned this allegory ; for since its delivery three months are supposed to have elapsed, and it is certain that in the interim much must have been spoken, done, and experienced by Jesus, that would thrust this figurative discourse into the background of his memory, so that he would be very unlikely to recur to it, and in no case would he be able to repeat it, word for word. He who had just quitted the allegory was the Evangelist, to whom three months had not intervened between the inditing of the first half of this chapter, and that of the second. He wrote at once what, according to his statement, was chronologically separated by a wide interval ; and hence the allegory of the shepherd might well leave so distinct an echo in his memory, though not in that of Jesus. If any think that they can solve this difficulty by putting only the *verbal* similarity of the later discourse to the earlier one to the account of the Evangelist, such an opinion cannot be interdicted to them. For others, this instance, in connexion with the rest, will be a positive proof that the discourses of Jesus in the fourth gospel are to a great extent the free compositions of the Evangelist.

The same conclusion is to be drawn from the discourse with which the fourth Evangelist represents Jesus as closing his public ministry (xii. 44–50). This discourse is entirely composed of reminiscences out of previous chapters,[12] and, as Paulus expresses it,[13] is a mere echo of some of the principal apophthegms of Jesus occurring in the former part of the gospel. One cannot easily consent to let the ministry of Jesus close with a discourse so little original, and the majority of recent commentators are of opinion that it is the intention

---

[11] x. 27: τὰ πρόβατα τὰ ἐμὰ τῆς φωνῆς μου ἀκούει,
κἀγὼ γινώσκω αὐτά·
28: καὶ ἀκολουθοῦσί μοι.

x. 3 : καὶ τὰ πρόβατα τῆς φωνῆς αὐτοῦ ἀκούει.
14 : καὶ γινώσκω τυ ἐμα
4 : καὶ τὰ πρόβατα αὐτῷ ἀκολουθεῖ.

Also κἀγω ζωὴν αἰώνιον δίδωμι αὐτοῖς corresponds to ἐγὼ ἦλθον, ἵνα ζωὴν ἔχωσι, v. 10, and καὶ οὐχ ἁρπάσει τις αὐτὰ ἐκ τῆς χειρός μου is the counterpart of what is said v. 12 of the hireling who allows the sheep to be scattered.
[12] Comp. v. 44 with vii. 17 ; v. 46 with viii. 12 ; v. 47 with iii. 17 ; v. 48 with iii. 18, v. 45 ; v. 49 with viii. 28 ; v. 50 with vi. 40, vii. 17, viii. 28.
[13] L. J., b, s. 142.

of the Evangelist here to give us a mere epitome of the teaching of Jesus.[14] According to our view also, the Evangelist is the real speaker ; but we must contend that his introductory words, *Jesus cried and said*, Ἰησοῦς δὲ ἔκραξε καὶ εἶπεν, are intended to imply that what follows is an actual harangue, from the lips of Jesus. This commentators will not admit, and they can appeal, not without a show of reason, to the statement of the Evangelist, v. 36, that Jesus withdrew himself from the public eye, and to his ensuing observations on the obstinate unbelief of the Jews, in which he seems to put a period to the public career of Jesus ; whence it would be contrary to his plan to make Jesus again step forward to deliver a valedictory discourse. I will not, with the older expositors, oppose to these arguments the supposition that Jesus, after his withdrawal, returned to pronounce these words in the ears of the Jews ; but I hold fast to the proposition that by the introduction above quoted, the Evangelist can only have intended to announce an actual harangue. It is said, indeed, that the aorist in ἔκραξε and εἶπε has the signification of the pluperfect, and that we have here a recapitulation of the previous discourses of Jesus, notwithstanding which the Jews had not given him credence. But to give this retrospective signification there ought to be a corresponding indication in the words themselves, or in the context, whereas this is far less the case than e.g. in John xviii. 24. Hence the most probable view of the question is this : John had indeed intended to close the narrative of the public ministry of Jesus at v. 36, but his concluding observations, v. 37 ff., with the categories of *faith*, πίστις, and *unbelief*, ἀπιστία, reminded him of discourses which he had already recorded, and he could not resist the temptation of making Jesus recapitulate them with additional emphasis in a parting harangue.

§ 82.

ISOLATED MAXIMS OF JESUS, COMMON TO THE FOURTH GOSPEL AND THE SYNOPTICAL ONES.

The long discourses of Jesus above examined are peculiar to the fourth gospel ; it has only a few brief maxims to which the synoptists present parallels. Among the latter, we need not give a special examination to those which are placed by John in an equally suitable connexion, with that assigned to them by the other Evangelists (as xii. 25, comp. with Matt. x. 39, xvi. 25 ; and xiii. 16, comp. with Matt. x. 24) ; and as the passage ii. 19 compared with Matt. xxvi. 61, must be reserved until we treat of the history of the Passion, there remain to us only three passages for our present consideration. The first of these is iv. 44, where the Evangelist, after having mentioned that Jesus departed from Samaria into Galilee, adds, *For Jesus himself testified that a prophet has no honour in his own country*, αὐτὸς γὰρ ὁ Ἰ. ἐμαρτύρησεν, ὅτι προφήτης ἐν τῇ ἰδίᾳ πατρίδι τιμὴν οὐκ ἔχει. We find the same idea in Matthew xiii. 57 (Mark vi. 4 ; Luke iv. 24), *A prophet is not without honour, save in his own country and in his own house*, οὐκ ἔστι προφήτης ἄτιμος, εἰ μὴ ἐν τῇ πατρίδι αὐτοῦ καὶ ἐν τῇ οἰκίᾳ αὐτοῦ. But while in the latter case it stands in a highly appropriate connexion, as a remark prompted by the ungracious reception which Jesus met with in his native city, and which caused him to leave it again : in John, on the contrary, it is given as a motive for the return of Jesus into his own country, Galilee, where, moreover, he is immediately said to be warmly received. The experience stated in the above sentence would rather have disinclined than induced Jesus to undertake a journey into Galilee ;

---

[14] Lücke, Tholück, Paulus, in loc.

hence the expedient of translating γὰρ by *although*, is the best adapted to the
necessity of the case, and has even been embraced by Kuinöl, except that,
unhappily, it is an open defiance of the laws of language.   Unquestionably,
if Jesus knew that the prophet held this unfavourable position in his *native
country*, πατρίς, it is not probable that he would regard it as a reason for going
thither.   Some expositors, therefore, have been induced to understand πατρίς,
not as the province, but in a narrower sense, as the native city, and to supply,
after the statement that Jesus went into Galilee, the observation, which they
assume the Evangelist to have omitted, that he avoided his native city,
Nazareth, for the reason given in the ensuing verse.   But an ellipsis such as
this explanation requires us to suppose, belongs not less to the order of
impossibilities than the transmutation of γὰρ into *though*.   The attempt to
introduce the desiderated statement that Jesus did not visit his own πατρίς
into the present passage has been therefore renounced : but it has yet been
thought possible to discover there an intimation that he did not soon return
thither ; a delay for which the maxim, ὅτι προφήτης κ. τ. λ. might consistently
be quoted as a reason.[2]   But to render this interpretation admissible, the
entire period of the absence of Jesus from Galilee must have been mentioned
immediately before the notice of his return ; instead of this, however, only the
short time that Jesus had tarried in Samaria is given (v. 45), so that in
ludicrous disproportion of cause and effect, the fear of the contempt of his
fellow country men would on the above supposition, be made the reason for
delaying his return into Galilee, not until after a residence of some months in
Judea, but until after the lapse of two days spent in Samaria.   So long,
therefore, as Galilee and Nazareth are admitted to be the πατρίς of Jesus, the
passage in question cannot be vindicated from the absurdity of representing,
that Jesus was instigated to return thither by the contempt which he knew to
await him.   Consequently, it becomes the interest of the expositor to recollect,
that Matthew and Luke pronounce Bethlehem to be the birthplace of Jesus,
whence it follows that Judea was his native country, which he now forsook on
account of the contempt he had there experienced.[3]   But according to iv. 1,
comp. ii. 23, iii. 26 ff., Jesus had won a considerable number of adherents in
Judea, and could not therefore complain of a lack of *honour*, τιμή ; moreover
the enmity of the Pharisees, hinted at in iv. 1, was excited by the growing
consequence of Jesus in Judea, and was not at all referrible to such a cause
as that indicated in the maxim : ὅτι προφήτης κ. τ. λ.   Further, the entrance
into Galilee is not connected in our passage with a departure from Judea, but
from Samaria ; and as, according to the import of the text, Jesus departed
from Samaria and went into Galilee, because he had found that a prophet has
no honour in his own country, Samaria might rather seem to be pointed out
as his native country, in conformity with the reproach cast on him by the
Jews, viii. 48 ; though even this supposition would not give consistency to the
passage, for in Samaria also Jesus is said, iv. 39, to have had a favourable
reception.   Besides, we have already seen,[4] that the fourth Evangelist knows
nothing of the birth of Jesus in Bethlehem, but on all occasions presupposes
him to be a Galilean and a Nazarene.   From the above considerations we

---

[1] Cyril, Erasmus.   Tholück's expedient, which Olshausen approves, is to give ἐμαρτύρησεν
the signification of the pluperfect, and to understand γὰρ as an explicative.   But I do not see
how this can be of any avail, for γὰρ and οὖν (v. 45) would still form a relation of agreement
between two propositions, which one would have expected to be opposed to each other by
μὲν and δέ.

[2] Paulus, Comm. 4, s. 251, 56.

[3] This idea is so entirely in the spirit of the ancient harmonists, that I can scarcely believe
Lücke to be the first to whom it had occurred (Comm. 1, s. 545 f.).

[4] Vid. sup. § 39.

obtain only the negative result, that it is impossible to discover any consistent relation between the maxim in question and the context. A positive result,— namely, how the maxim came to occupy its actual position, notwithstanding this want of relation, will perhaps be obtained when we have examined the two other passages belonging to the present head of our inquiry. The declaration xiii. 20, *He that receiveth you receiveth me, and he that receiveth me receiveth him that sent me,* has an almost verbal parallel in Matt. x. 40. In John, it is preceded by the prediction of the betrayal of Jesus, and his explanation to his disciples that he had told them this before it came to pass, in order that when his prediction was fulfilled, they might believe in him as the Messiah. What is the connexion between these subjects and the above declaration, or between the latter and its ensuing context, where Jesus recurs to his betrayer? It is said that Jesus wished to impress on his disciples the high dignity of a messianic missionary, a dignity which the betrayer thought lightly of losing ; [5] but the negative idea of loss, on which this supposition turns, is not intimated in the text. Others are of opinion that Jesus, observing the disciples to be disheartened by the mention of the betrayer, sought to inspire them with new courage by representing to them their high value ; [6] but in that case he would hardly have reverted immediately after to the traitor. Others, again, conjecture that some intermediate sentences have been omitted by the writer ; [7] but this expedient is not much happier than that of Kuinöl, who supposes the passage to be a gloss taken from Matt. x. 40, united originally to v. 16 of chap. xiii. of John, but by some chance transposed to the end of the paragraph. Nevertheless, the indication of v. 16 is an useful way-mark. This verse, as well as v. 20, has a parallel in the discourse of instructions in Matthew (x. 24) ; if a few fragments of this discourse had reached the author of the fourth gospel through the medium of tradition, it is very probable that one of them would bring the others to his recollection. In v. 16 there is mention of the *sent,* ἀπόστολος, and of *him who sent him,* πέμψας αὐτὸν ; so in v. 20, of those whom Jesus will send, and of Him who sent Jesus. It is true, that the one passage has a humiliating, the other an encouraging tendency, and their affinity lies, therefore, not in the sense, but in the words ; so that as soon as the fourth Evangelist puts down, from memory, traditional sayings of Jesus, we see him subject to the same law of association as the synoptists. It would have been the most natural arrangement to place v. 20 immediately after v. 16 ; but the thought of the traitor was uppermost in the mind of the writer, and he could easily postpone the insertion of an apophthegm that had only a verbal connexion with his previous matter.

Our third passage, xiv. 31, lies yet farther within the domain of the history of the Passion than the one last examined, but as, like this, it can be viewed quite independently, we shall not be anticipating if we include it in our present chapter. In the above passage, the words *Arise, let us go hence,* ἐγείρεσθε, ἄγωμεν ἐντεῦθεν, remind us of those by which Jesus, Matt. xxvi. 46 ; Mark xiv. 42, summons his disciples to join him in encountering the traitor : *Rise, let us be going,* ἐγείρεσθε ἄγωμεν. The position of the words in John is perplexing, because the summons to depart has no effect ; Jesus, as if he had said nothing of the kind, immediately continues (xv. 1), *I am the true vine,* etc., and does not take his departure with his disciples until after he has considerably prolonged his discourse. Expositors of every hue have been singularly unanimous in explaining the above words by the supposition, that Jesus certainly

[5] Paulus, L. J. 1, b, s. 158.
[6] Lücke, 2, s 478.
[7] Tholück, in loc.

intended at the moment to depart and betake himself to Gethsemane, but love for his disciples, and a strong desire to impart to them still further admonition and comfort, detained him; that hence, the first part of the summons, *Arise*, was executed, but that, standing in the room in which he had supped, he pursued his discourse, until, later (xviii. 1), he also put into effect the words, *let us go hence.*[8] It is possible that the circumstances were such; it is also possible that the image of this last evening, with all its details, might be engraven so deeply and accurately in the memory of a disciple, that he might narrate how Jesus arose, and how touchingly he lingered. But one who wrote under the influence of a recollection thus lively, would note the particulars which were most apparent; the rising to depart and the delay,— not the mere words, which without the addition of those circumstances are altogether unintelligible. Here again, then, the conjecture arises that a reminiscence of the evangelical tradition presented itself to the writer, and that he inserted it just where it occurred to him, not, as it happened, in the best connexion; and this conjecture assumes probability so soon as we discover what might have reminded him of the above expression. In the synoptical parallels the command, *Rise, let us be going*, is connected with the announcement, *Behold the hour is at hand, and the Son of man is betrayed into the hands of sinners—behold he is at hand that doth betray me*; with the announcement, that is, of the hostile power which is approaching, before which, however, Jesus exhibits no fear, but goes to encounter the danger with the decision implied in that command. In John's gospel, also, Jesus, in the passage under our notice, had been speaking of a hostile power when he said, *The Prince of this world cometh and hath nothing in me.* It makes little difference that in John it is the power that dwells in the betrayer, and in those led by him, while, in the synoptical gospels, it is the betrayer who is impelled by that power, that is said to approach. If the author of the fourth gospel knew by tradition that Jesus had united with the announcement of an approaching danger the words, *Rise, let us be going*, this expression would be likely to occur to him on the mention of the prince of this world; and as in that stage of his narrative he had placed Jesus and his disciples in the city and within doors, so that a considerable change of place was necessary before they could encounter the enemy, he added to ἄγωμεν (*let us go*), ἐντεῦθεν (*hence*). As, however, this traditional fragment had intruded itself unawares into the train of thought, which he designed to put as a farewell discourse into the mouth of Jesus, it was immediately lost sight of, and a free course was given to the stream of valedictory instruction, not yet exhausted.

If, from the point of view now attained, we glance back on our first passage, iv. 44, it is easy to see how the Evangelist might be led to insert in so unsuitable a connexion the testimony of Jesus as to the treatment of a prophet in his own country. It was known to him traditionally, and he appears to have applied it to Galilee in general, being ignorant of any unfavourable contact of Jesus with the Nazarenes. As, therefore, he knew of no special scene by which this observation might have been prompted, he introduced it where the simple mention of Galilee suggested it, apparently without any definite idea of its bearing.

The result of the above investigation is this: the fourth Evangelist succeeds in giving connectedness to his materials, when he presents his own thoughts in the form of discourses delivered by Jesus; but he often fails lamentably in that particular, when he has to deal with the real traditional sayings of Jesus.

---

[8] Paulus, L. J. 1, b, s. 175; Lücke, Tholück, Olshausen, in loc.; Hug, Einl. in das N. T. 2, s. 209.

In the above instances, when he has the same problem before him as the synoptists, he is as unfortunate in its solution as they ; nay, he is in a yet more evil case, for his narrative is not homogeneous with the common evangelical tradition, and presented few places where a genuine traditional relic could be inserted. Besides, he was accustomed to cast his metal, liquid from his own invention, and was little skilled in the art of adapting independent fragments to each other, so as to form an harmonious mosaic.

§ 83.

THE MODERN DISCUSSIONS ON THE AUTHENTICITY OF THE DISCOURSES IN THE GOSPEL OF JOHN. RESULT.

The foregoing examination of the discourses of Jesus in the fourth gospel, has sufficiently prepared us to form a judgment on the controversy of which they have recently been the subject. Modern criticism views these discourses with suspicion, partly on account of their internal contexture, which is at variance with certain generally received rules of historical probability, and partly on account of their external relation to other discourses and narratives. On the other hand, this gospel has had numerous defenders.

With respect to the internal contexture of the above discourses, there arises a twofold question : Does it correspond to the laws, first of verisimilitude, and secondly, of memory ?

It is alleged by the friends of the fourth gospel that its discourses are distinguished by a peculiar stamp of truth and credibility ; that the conversations which it represents Jesus as holding with men of the most diverse disposition and capacity, are faithful delineations of character, satisfying the strictest demands of psychological criticism.[1] In opposition to this, it is maintained to be in the highest degree improbable, that Jesus should have adopted precisely the same style of teaching to persons differing widely in their degrees of cultivation ; that he should have spoken to the Galileans in the synagogue at Capernaum not more intelligibly than to a *master of Israel* ; that the matter of his discourses should have turned almost entirely on one doctrine—the dignity of his person ; and that their form should have been such as to seem selected with a view to perplex and repel his hearers. Neither, it is further urged, do the interlocutors express themselves in conformity with their position and character. The most educated Pharisee has no advantage in intelligence over a Samaritan woman of the lowest grade ; the one, as well as the other, can only put a carnal interpretation on the discourse which Jesus intends spiritually ; their misconstructions, too, are frequently so glaring, as to transcend all belief, and so uniform that they seem to belong to a standing set of features with which the author of the fourth gospel has chosen, for the sake of contrast, to depict those whom he brings into conversation with Jesus.[2] Hence, I confess, I understand not what is the meaning of verisimilitude in the mind of those who ascribe it to the discourses of Jesus in the Gospel of John.

As to the second point, regarding the powers of memory, it is pretty generally agreed that discourses of the kind peculiar to John's gospel,—in contradistinction to the apophthegms and parables, either isolated or strung together, in the synoptical gospels,—namely, series of dependent propositions,

---

[1] Wegscheider, Einl. in das Evang. Joh., s. 271 ; Tholück Comm. s. 37 f.
[2] Thus Eckermann, theol. Beiträge, 5, 2, s. 228 ; (Vogel) der Evangelist Johannes und seine Ausleger vor dem jüngsten Gericht, 1, s. 28 ff. ; Wegscheider, s. 281 ; Bretschneider, Probabil., 33, 45, apud Wegscheider, ut sup. s. 281 ; Bretschneider, Probab., p. 33, 45.

or prolonged dialogues, are among the most difficult to retain and reproduce with accuracy.[3] Unless such discourses were reduced to writing at the moment of their delivery, all hope of their faithful reproduction must be abandoned. Hence Dr. Paulus once actually entertained the idea, that in the judgment-halls of the temple or the synagogues at Jerusalem, there were stationed a sort of shorthand writers, whose office it was to draw up verbal processes, and that from their records the Christians, after the death of Christ, made transcripts.[4] In like manner, Bertholdt was of opinion, that our Evangelist, during the lifetime of Jesus, took down most of the discourses of Jesus in the Aramæan language, and made these notes the foundation of his gospel, composed at a much later period.[5] These modern hypotheses are clearly unhistorical ; [6] nevertheless, their propounders were able to adduce many reasons in their support. The prophetic declarations of Jesus relative to his death and resurrection, said Bertholdt, are more indefinite in John than in the synoptical gospels, a sure sign that they were recorded before their fulfilment, for otherwise the writer's experience of the event would have reflected more clearness on the predictions. To this we may add the kindred argument, by which Henke thought it possible to establish the genuineness of the discourses in John : namely, that the fourth Evangelist not seldom appends explanatory remarks, often indeed erroneous, to the obscure expressions of Jesus, thus proving that he was scrupulously conscientious in reporting the discourses, for otherwise he would have mingled his comments with their original matter.[7] But it is with justice objected, that the obscurity of the predictions in the fourth gospel is in perfect harmony with the mystical spirit that pervades the work,*and as, besides, the author, together with his fondness for the obscure and enigmatical, indisputably possessed taste, he must have been conscious that a prophecy would only be the more piquant and genuine-looking, the more darkly it was delivered : hence, though he put those predictions into the mouth of Jesus long after the events to which they refer, he might yet choose to give them an indefinite form. This observation helps to explain why the Evangelist, when elucidating some obscure expressions of Jesus, adds that his disciples did not understand them until after his resurrection, or after the out-pouring of the Holy Spirit (ii. 22, vii. 39) ; for the opposition of the darkness in which the disciples at one time groped, to the light which ultimately arose on them, belongs to that order of contrasts with which this gospel abounds. Another argument, adopted by Bertholdt and approved by Tholück, is, that in the discourses of the fourth gospel there sometimes occur observations, which, having no precise meaning in themselves, nor any connexion with the rest of the discourse, must have been occasioned by some external circumstance, and can only be accounted for on the supposition of prompt, nay, of immediate reduction to writing ; and among their examples the passage, *Arise, let us go hence* (xiv. 31), is one of the most important. But the origin of such digressive remarks has been above explained in a manner that renders the hypothesis of instantaneous notetaking superfluous.

Thus commentators had to excogitate some other means of certifying the

---

[3] De Wette, Einl. in das N. T., § 105 ; Tholück, Comm. z. Joh., s. 38 f. ; Glaubwürdig-keit, s. 344 ff. ; Lücke, 1, s. 198 f.

[4] Commentar, 4, s. 275 f.

[5] Verosimilia de origine evangelii Joannis, opusc. p. 1 ff., Einleit. in das N. T., s. 1302 ff. This opinion is approved by Wegscheider, ut sup. p. 270 ff. and also Hug, 2. 263 f., and Tholück, Comm. p. 38, think the supposition of early notes not to be altogether rejected.

[6] Lücke, 1, s. 192 f.

[7] Henke, programm. quo illustratur Johannes apostolus nonnullorum Jesu apophthegma-tum et ipse interpres.

[8] Bretschneider, Probab., p. 14 f.

genuineness of the discourses of Jesus in the fourth gospel. The general argument, so often adduced, founded on what a good memory might achieve, especially among men of simple lives, unusued to writing, lies in the region of abstract possibility, where, as Lücke remarks,[9] there may always be nearly as much said against as for a theory. It has been thought more effectual to adopt an argument resting on a narrower basis, and to appeal to the individual distinctions of the Apostle John,—to his intimate and peculiar relation to Jesus as the favourite disciple,—to his enthusiasm for his master, which must surely have strengthened his memory, and have enabled him to preserve in the most lively recollection all that came from the lips of his divine friend.[10] Although this peculiar relation of John to Jesus rests on the authority of John's gospel alone, we might, without reasoning in a circle, draw from it conclusions as to the credibility of the discourses communicated by him, were the faults of which his gospel is accused only such as proceed from the inevitable fading of the memory ; because the positive notices of that relation could never flow from this negative cause. As, however, the suspicion which has arisen to the prejudice of the fourth Evangelist has gone far beyond those limits, even to the extent of taxing him with free invention, no fact resting on the word of John can be used in support of the discourses which he communicates. But neither the above relation, if admitted, nor the remark that John apparently attached himself to Jesus in early youth, when impressions sink deepest, and from the time of his master's death lived in a circle where the memory of his words and deeds was cherished,[11] suffices to render it probable that John could retain in his mind long series of ideas, and complicated dialogues, until the period in which the composition of his gospel must be placed. For critics are agreed that the tendency of the fourth gospel, its evident aim to spiritualize the common faith of Christians into the Gnosis, and thus to crush many errors which had sprung up, is a decisive attestation that it was composed at a period when the church had attained a degree of maturity, and consequently in the extreme old age of the apostle.[12]

Hence the champions of the discourses in question are fain to bring forward, as a forlorn hope, the supernatural assistance of the Paraclete, which was promised to the disciples, and which was to restore all that Jesus had said to their remembrance. This is done by Tholück with great confidence,[13] by Lücke with some diffidence,[14] which Tholück's Anzeiger severely censures, but which we consider laudable, because it implies a latent consciousness of the circle that is made, in attempting to prove the truthfulness of the discourses in John, by a promise which appears nowhere but in those discourses ;[15] and of the inadequacy of an appeal, in a scientific inquiry, to a popular notion, such as that of the aid of the Holy Spirit. The consciousness of this inadequacy shows itself indirectly in Tholück, for he ekes out the assistance of the Paraclete by early notes ; and in Lücke also, for he renounces the verbal authenticity of the discourses in John, and only contends for their substantial veracity on grounds chiefly connected with the relation which they bear to other discourses.

[9] Ut sup. p. 199.
[10] Wegscheider, p. 286 ; Lücke, p. 195 f.
[11] Wegscheider, p. 285 ; Lücke, ut sup.
[12] Lücke, s. 124 f. 175. Kern, über den Ursprung des Evang. Matthäi, in der Tüb. Zeitschrift, 1834, 2, s. 109.
[13] S. 39.
[14] S. 197. "But lastly, why should we fear to adduce," etc.
[15] The aid promised to the disciples when brought before rulers and tribunals, Matt. x. 19 f., is quite distinct from a bringing to remembrance of the discourses of Jesus (John xiv. 26).

The external relation of the discourses of Jesus in John's gospel is also twofold ; for they may be compared both with those discourses which the synoptists put into the mouth of Jesus, and with the manner in which the author of the fourth gospel expresses himself when he is avowedly the speaker.

As a result of the former comparison, critics have pointed out the important difference that exists between the respective discourses in their matter, as well as in their form.   In the first three gospels, Jesus closely adapts his teaching to the necessities of his shepherdless people, contrasting, at one time, the corrupt institutions of the Pharisees with the moral and religious precepts of the Mosaic law ; at another, the carnal messianic hopes of the age with the purely spiritual nature of his kingdom, and the conditions of entrance therein. In the fourth gospel, on the contrary, he is perpetually dilating, and often in a barren, speculative manner, on the doctrine of his person and higher nature : so that in opposition to the diversified doctrinal and practical materials of the synoptical discourses, we have in John a one-sided dogmatism.[16]   That this opposition does not hold invariably, and that in the discourses of the synoptical gospels there are passages which have more affinity with those of John, and vice versâ, must be granted to judicious critics ; [17] but the important preponderance of the dogmatical element on the one side, and of the practical on the other, is a difficulty that demands a thorough explanation.   In answer to this requisition, it is common to adduce the end which John is supposed to have had in view in the composition of his gospel : namely, to furnish a supplement to the first three gospels, and to supply their omissions.   But if Jesus taught first in one style, then in another, how was it that the synoptists selected almost exclusively the practical and popular, John, nearly without exception, the dogmatic and speculative portions of his discourse ?   This is accounted for in a manner intrinsically probable.   In the oral tradition, it is observed, on which the first three gospels were founded, the simple and popular, the concise and sententious discourses of Jesus, being the most easy of retention, would alone be propagated, while his more profound, subtle and diffuse discourses would be lost.[18]   But according to the above supposition, the fourth Evangelist came as a gleaner after the synoptists : now it is certain that all the discourses of Jesus having a practical tendency had not been preserved by them ; hence, that the former has almost invariably avoided giving any relic of such discourses, can only be explained by his preference for the dogmatic and speculative vein : a preference which must have had both an objective and a subjective source, the necessities of his time and circumstances, and the bent of his own mind.   This is admitted even by critics who are favourable to the authenticity of the fourth gospel,[19] with the reservation, that the preference betrays itself only negatively, by omission, not positively, by addition.

There is a further difference between the synoptical gospels and the fourth, as to the form of teaching adopted by Jesus ; in the one, it is aphoristic and parabolic, in the other, dialectic.[20]   We have seen that the parable is altogether wanting in the fourth gospel, and it is natural to ask why, since Luke, as well as Matthew, has many admirable parables peculiar to himself, John has not been able to make a rich gleaning, even after those two predecessors ? It is true that isolated apothegms and sentences, similar to the synoptical ones, are not entirely absent from the fourth gospel : but, on the other hand,

[16] Bretschneider, Probab., p. 2, 3, 31 ff.
[17] De Wette, Einl. in das N. T., § 103 ; Hase, L. J., § 7.
[18] Lücke, ut sup. pp. 336, 337.   Kern, ut sup.
[19] Tholück, ut sup.
[20] Bretschneider, ut sup.

it must be admitted that the prevailing aphoristic and parabolic form of in
struction, ascribed to Jesus by the synoptists, is more suited to the character
of a popular teacher of Palestine, than the dialectic form which he is made to
adopt by John.[21]

But the relation of the discourses of Jesus in the gospel of John, to the
Evangelist's own style of thinking and writing, is decisive.   Here we find a
similarity,[22] which, as it extends to the discourses of a third party, namely, the
Baptist, cannot be explained by supposing that the disciple had formed his
style on that of the master,[23] but requires us to admit that the Evangelist has
lent his own style to the principal characters in his narrative.   The latest
commentator on John has not only acknowledged this with regard to the
colouring of the expression ; he even thinks that in the matter itself he can
here and there detect the explanatory amplifications of the Evangelist, who, to
use his own phrase, has had a hand in the composition of the longer and more
difficult discourses.[24]   But since the Evangelist does not plainly indicate his
additions, what is to assure us that they are not throughout interwoven with
the ideas of Jesus, nay, that all the discourses which he communicates are not
entirely his own productions ?   The style furnishes no guidance, for this is
everywhere the same, and is admitted to be the Evangelist's own ; neither does
the sense, for in it also there is no essential difference whether the Evangelist
speaks in his own name or in that of Jesus : where then is the guarantee that
the discourses of Jesus are not, as the author of the Probabilia maintains, free
inventions of the fourth Evangelist ?

Lücke adduces some particulars, which on this supposition would be in his
opinion inexplicable.[25]   First, the almost verbal agreement of John with the
synoptists in isolated sayings of Jesus.   But as the fourth Evangelist was within the pale of the Christian community, he must have had at his command a
tradition, from which, though drawing generally on his own resources, he
might occasionally borrow isolated, marked expressions, nearly unmodified.
Another argument of Lücke is yet more futile.   If, he says, John had really
had the inclination and ability to invent discourses for Jesus, he would have
been more liberal in long discourses ; and the alternation of brief remarks
with prolonged addresses, is not to be explained on the above supposition.
But this would follow only if the author of the fourth gospel appeared to be a
tasteless writer, whose perception did not tell him, that to one occasion a
short discourse was suitable, to another a long one, and that the alternation of
diffuse harangues with concise sentences was adapted to produce the best
impression.   Of more weight is the observation of Paulus, that if the fourth
Evangelist had given the rein to his invention in attributing discourses to
Jesus, he would have obtruded more of his own views, of which he has given
an abstract in his prologue ; whereas the scrupulousness with which he abstains from putting his doctrine of the Logos into the mouth of Jesus, is a
proof of the faithfulness with which he confined himself to the materials presented by his memory or his authorities.[26]   But the doctrine of the Logos is
substantially contained in the succeeding discourse of Jesus ; and that the
form in which it is propounded by the evangelist in his preface, does not also

---

[21] De Wette, ut sup. § 105.

[22] Comp. Schulze, der schriftst. Charakter und Werth des Johannes. 1803.

[23] Stronck—de doctrinâ et dictione Johannis apostoli, ad Jesu magistri doctrinam diction-
emque exacte composita. 1797.

[24] Lücke, Comm. z. Joh. 1, p. 200.

[25] Ut. sup p. 199.

[26] In his review of the 2nd Ed. of Lücke's Commentar., in the Litt. Blatt der allgem.
Kirchenzeitung 1834, no. 18.

reappear, is sufficiently explained by the consideration, that he must have known that form to be altogether foreign to the teaching of Jesus.

We therefore hold it to be established, that the discourses of Jesus in John's gospel are mainly free compositions of the Evangelist; but we have admitted that he has culled several sayings of Jesus from an authentic tradition, and hence we do not extend this proposition to those passages which are countenanced by parallels in the synoptical gospels. In these compilations we have an example of the vicissitudes which befal discourses, that are preserved only in the memory of a second party. Severed from their original connexion, and broken up into smaller and smaller fragments, they present when reassembled the appearance of a mosaic, in which the connexion of the parts is a purely external one, and every transition an artificial juncture. The discourses of Jesus in John present just the opposite appearance. Their gradual transitions, only rendered occasionally obscure by the mystical depths of meaning in which they lie,—transitions in which one thought develops itself out of another, and a succeeding proposition is frequently but an explanatory amplification of the preceding,[27]—are indicative of a pliable, unresisting mass, such as is never presented to a writer by the traditional sayings of another, but such as proceeds from the stores of his own thought, which he moulds according to his will. For this reason the contributions of tradition to these stores of thought (apart from the sayings which are also found in the earlier gospels) were not so likely to have been particular, independent dicta of Jesus, as rather certain ideas which formed the basis of many of his discourses, and which were modified and developed according to the bent of a mind of Alexandrian or Greek culture. Such are the correlative ideas of πατήρ and υἱός (*father* and *son*), φῶς and σκότος (*light* and *darkness*), ζωή and θάνατος (*life* and *death*), ἄνω and κάτω (*above* and *beneath*), σάρξ and πνεῦμα (*flesh* and *spirit*); also some symbolical expressions, as ἄρτος τῆς ζωῆς (*bread of life*), ὕδωρ ζῶν (*water of life*). These and a few other ideas, variously combined by an ingenious author, compose the bulk of the discourses attributed to Jesus by John; a certain uniformity necessarily attending this elemental simplicity.*

[27] This peculiarity of the discourses in John cannot be better described than by Erasmus in his Epist. ad Ferdinandum, prefatory to his Paraphrase : *habet Johannes suum quoddam dicendi genus, ita sermonem velut ansulis ex sese cohærentibus contexens, nonnunquam ex contrariis, nonnunquam ex similibus, nonnunquam ex iisdem, subinde repetitis,——ut orationis quodque membrum semper excipiat prius, sic ut prioris finis sit initium sequentis, etc.*

CHAPTER VIII.

EVENTS IN THE PUBLIC LIFE OF JESUS, EXCLUDING THE MIRACLES.

—————

§ 84.

GENERAL COMPARISON OF THE MANNER OF NARRATION THAT DISTIN-
GUISHES THE SEVERAL EVANGELISTS. *

IF, before proceeding to the consideration of details, we compare the general character and tone of the historical narration in the various gospels, we find differences, first, between Matthew and the two other synoptists; secondly, between the three first evangelists collectively and the fourth.

Among the reproaches which modern criticism has heaped on the gospel of Matthew, a prominent place has been given to its want of individualized and dramatic life; a want which is thought to prove that the author was not an eye-witness, since an eye-witness is ordinarily distinguished by the precision and minuteness of his narration.[1] Certainly, when we read the indefinite designation of times, places and persons, the perpetually recurring τότε, *then*, παράγων ἐκεῖθεν, *departing from thence*, ἄνθρωπος, *a man*, which characterize this gospel; when we recollect its wholesale statements, such as that Jesus went through all the cities and villages (ix. 35, xi. 1, comp. iv. 23); that they brought to him all sick people, and that he healed them all (iv. 24 f., xiv. 35 f., comp. xv. 29 ff.); and finally, the bareness and brevity of many isolated narratives : we cannot disapprove the decision of this criticism, that Matthew's whole narrative resembles a record of events which, before they were committed to writing, had been long current in oral tradition, and had thus lost the impress of particularity and minuteness. But it must be admitted, that this proof, taken alone, is not absolutely convincing; for in most cases we may verify the remark, that even an eye-witness may be unable graphically to narrate what he has seen.[2]

But our modern critics have not only measured Matthew by the standard of what is to be expected from an eye-witness, in the abstract; they have also compared him with his fellow-evangelists. They are of opinion, not only that John decidedly surpasses Matthew in the power of delineation, both in their few parallel passages and in his entire narrative, but also that the two other synoptists, especially Mark, are generally far clearer and fuller in their style of narration.[3] This is the actual fact, and it ought not to be any longer evaded. With respect to the fourth Evangelist, it is true that, as one would

---

[1] Schulz, über das Abendmahl, s. 303 ff. ; Sieffert, über den Urspr. des ersten kanon. Evang. s. 58, 73, u. s. ; Schneckenburger, über den Urspr. s. 73.

[2] Olshausen, b. Comm. 1. s. 15.

[3] See the above named critics, passim ; and Hug. Einl. in das N. T. 2, s. 212.

have anticipated, he is not devoid of general, wholesale statements, such as, that Jesus during the feast did many miracles, that hence many believed on him (ii. 23), with others of a similar kind (iii. 22, vii. 1) : and he not seldom designates persons indecisively. Sometimes, however, he gives the names of individuals whom Matthew does not specify (xii. 3, 4, comp with Matt. xxvi. 7, 8; and xviii. 10 with Matt. xxvi. 51 ; also vi. 5 ff. with Matt. xiv. 16 f.) ; and he generally lets us know the district or country in which an event happened. His careful chronology we have already noticed ; but the point of chief importance is that his narratives (e.g. that of the man born blind, and that of the resurrection of Lazarus) have a dramatic and life-like character, which we seek in vain in the first gospel. The two intermediate Evangelists are not free from indecisive designations of time (e.g. Mark viii. 1 ; Luke v. 17, viii. 22); of place (Mark iii. 13 ; Luke vi. 12) ; and of persons (Mark x. 17 ; Luke xiii. 23) ; nor from statements that Jesus went through all cities, and healed all the sick (Mark i. 32 ff., 38 f.; Luke iv. 40 f.) ; but they often give us the details of what Matthew has only stated generally. Not only does Luke associate many discourses of Jesus with special occasions concerning which Matthew is silent, but both he and Mark notice the office or names of persons, to whom Matthew gives no precise designation (Matt. ix. 18 ; Mark v. 22 ; Luke viii. 41; Matt. xix. 16; Luke xviii. 18; Matt. xx. 30 ; Mark x. 46). But it is chiefly in the lively description of particular incidents, that we perceive the decided superiority of Luke, and still more of Mark, over Matthew. Let the reader only compare the narrative of the execution of John the Baptist in Matthew and Mark (Matt. xiv. 3 ; Mark vi. 17), and that of the demoniac or demoniacs of Gadara (Matt. viii. 28 ff. parall.).

These facts are, in the opinion of our latest critics, a confirmation of the fourth Evangelist's claim to the character of an eye-witness, and of the greater proximity of the second and third Evangelists to the scenes they describe, than can be attributed to the first. But, even allowing that one who does not narrate graphically cannot be an eye-witness, this does not involve the proposition that whoever does narrate graphically must be an eye-witness. In all cases in which there are extant two accounts of a single fact, the one full, the other concise, opinions may be divided as to which of them is the original.[4] When these accounts have been liable to the modifications of tradition, it is important to bear in mind that tradition has two tendencies : the one, to sublimate the concrete into the abstract, the individual into the general ; the other, not less essential, to substitute arbitrary fictions for the historical reality which is lost.[5] If then we put the want of precision in the narrative of the first Evangelist to the account of the former function of the legend, ought we at once to regard the precision and dramatic effect of the other gospels, as a proof that their authors were eye-witnesses? Must we not rather examine whether these qualities be not derived from the second function of the legend?[6] The decision with which the other inference is drawn, is in fact merely an after-taste of the old orthodox opinion, that all our gospels proceed immediately from eye-witnesses, or at least through a medium incapable of error. Modern criticism has limited this supposition, and admitted the possibility that one or the other of our gospels may have been affected by oral tradition. Accordingly it maintains, not without probability, that a gospel in which the descriptions are throughout destitute of colouring and life, cannot be the pro-

---

[4] Comp. Saunier, über die Quellen des Markus, s. 42 ff.

[5] Kern, über den Urspr. des Ev. Matt. ut sup. s. 70 f.

[6] I say, *examine whether*—not, *consider it decided that*—so that the accusation of opponents, that I use both the particularity and the brevity of narratives as proofs of their mythical character, falls to the ground of itself.

duction of an eye-witness, and must have suffered from the effacing fingers of tradition.   But the counter proposition, that the other gospels, in which the style of narration is more detailed and dramatic, rest on the testimony of eye-witnesses, would only follow from the supposed necessity that this must be the case with some of our gospels.   For if such a supposition be made with respect to several narratives of both the above kinds, there is no question that the more graphic and vivid ones are with preponderant probability to be referred to eye-witnesses.   But this supposition has merely a subjective foundation.   It was an easier transition for commentators to make from the old notion that all the gospels were immediately or mediately autoptical narratives, to the limited admission that perhaps one may fall short of this character, than to the general admission that it may be equally wanting to all.   But, according to the rigid rules of consequence, with the orthodox view of the scriptural canon, falls the assumption of pure ocular testimony, not only for one or other of the gospels, but for all ; the possibility of the contrary must be presupposed in relation to them all, and their pretensions must be estimated according to their internal character, compared with the external testimonies.   From this point of view—the only one that criticism can consistently adopt—it is as probable, considering the nature of the external testimonies examined in our Introduction, that the three last Evangelists owe the dramatic effect in which they surpass Matthew, to the embellishments of a more mature tradition, as that this quality is the result of a closer communication with eye-witnesses.

That we may not anticipate, let us, in relation to this question, refer to the results we have already obtained.   The greater particularity by which Luke is distinguished from Matthew in his account of the occasions that suggested many discourses of Jesus, has appeared to us often to be the result of subsequent additions ; and the names of persons in Mark (xiii. 3 comp. v. 37 ; Luke viii. 51) have seemed to rest on a mere inference of the narrator.   Now, however, that we are about to enter on an examination of particular narratives, we will consider, from the point of view above indicated, the constant forms of introduction, conclusion, and transition, already noticed, in the several gospels.   Here we find the difference between Matthew and the other synoptists, as to their more or less dramatic style, imprinted in a manner that can best teach us how much this style is worth.

Matthew (viii. 16 f.) states in general terms, that on the evening after the cure of Peter's mother-in-law, many demoniacs were brought to Jesus, all of whom, together with others that were sick, he healed.   Mark (i. 32) in a highly dramatic manner, as if he himself had witnessed the scene, tells, that on the same occasion, the whole city was gathered together at the door of the house in which Jesus was ; at another time, he makes the crowd block up the entrance (ii. 2) ; in two other instances, he describes the concourse as so great, that Jesus and his disciples could not take their food (iii. 20, vi. 31) ; and Luke on one occasion states, that the people even gathered together in innumerable multitudes so that *they trode one upon another* (xii. 1).   All highly vivid touches, certainly : but the want of them can hardly be prejudicial to Matthew, for they look thoroughly like strokes of imagination, such as abound in Mark's narrative, and often, as Schleiermacher observes,[7] give it almost an apocryphal appearance.   In detailed narratives, of which we shall presently notice many examples, while Matthew simply tells what Jesus said on a certain occasion, the two other Evangelists are able to describe the glance with which his words were accompanied (Mark iii. 5, x. 21 ; Luke vi. 10).

---

7 Ueber den Lukas, s. 74, and elsewhere.

On the mention of a blind beggar of Jericho, Mark is careful to give us his name, and the name of his father (x. 46). From these particulars we might already augur, what the examination of single narratives will prove : namely, that the copiousness of Mark and Luke is the product of the second function of the legend, which we may call the function of embellishment. Was this embellishment gradually wrought out by oral tradition, or was it the arbitrary addition of our Evangelists ? Concerning this, there may be a difference of opinion, and a degree of probability in relation to particular passages is the nearest approach that can be made to a decision. In any case, not only must it be granted, that a narrative adorned by the writer's own additions is more remote from primitive truth than one free from such additions ; but we may venture to pronounce that the earlier efforts of the legend are rapid sketches, tending to set off only the leading points whether of speech or action, and that at a later period it aims rather to give a symmetrical effect to the whole, including collateral incidents; so that, in either view, the closest approximation to truth remains on the side of the first gospel.

While the difference as to the more or less dramatic style of concluding and connecting forms, lies chiefly between Matthew and the other synoptists ; another difference with respect to these forms, exists between all the synoptists and John. While most of the synoptical anecdotes from the public life of Jesus are wound up by a panegyric, those of John generally terminate, so to speak, polemically. It is true that the three first Evangelists sometimes mention, by way of conclusion, the offence that Jesus gave to the narrow-hearted, and the machinations of his enemies against him (Matt. viii. 34, xii. 14, xxi. 46, xxvi. 3 f. ; Luke iv. 28 f., xi. 53 f.) ; and, on the other hand, the fourth Evangelist closes some discourses and miracles by the remark, that in consequence of them, many believed on Jesus (ii. 23, iv. 39, 53, vii. 31, 40 f., viii. 30, x. 42, xi. 45). But in the synoptical gospels, throughout the period previous to the residence of Jesus in Jerusalem, we find forms implying that the fame of Jesus had extended far and wide (Matt. iv. 24, ix. 26, 31 ; Mark i. 28, 45, v. 20, vii. 36 ; Luke iv. 37, v. 15, vii. 17, viii. 39) ; that the people were astonished at his doctrine (Matt. vii. 28 ; Mark i. 22, xi. 18 ; Luke xix. 48), and miracles (Matt. viii. 27, ix. 8, xiv. 33, xv. 31), and hence followed him from all parts (Matt. iv. 25, viii. 1, ix. 36, xii. 15, xiii. 2, xiv. 13). In the fourth gospel, on the contrary, we are continually told that the Jews sought to kill Jesus (v. 18, vii. 1) ; the Pharisees wish to take him, or send out officers to seize him (vii. 30, 32, 44 ; comp. viii. 20, x. 39) ; stones are taken up to cast at him (viii. 59, x. 31) ; and even in those passages where there is mention of a favourable disposition on the part of the people, the Evangelist limits it to one portion of them, and represents the other as inimical to Jesus (vii. 11–13). He is especially fond of drawing attention to such circumstances, as that before the final catastrophe all the guile and power of the enemies of Jesus were exerted in vain, because his hour was not yet come (vii. 30, viii. 20) ; that the emissaries sent out against him, overcome by the force of his words, and the dignity of his person, retired without fulfilling their errand (vii. 32, 44 ff.) ; and that Jesus passed unharmed through the midst of an exasperated crowd (viii. 59, x. 39 ; comp. Luke iv. 30). The writer, as we have above remarked, certainly does not intend us in these instances to think of a natural escape, but of one in which the higher nature of Jesus, his invulnerability so long as he did not choose to lay down his life, was his protection. And this throws some light on the object which the fourth Evangelist had in view, in giving prominence to such traits as those just enumerated : they helped him to add to the number of the contrasts, by which, throughout his works, he aims to exalt the person of Jesus. The profound wisdom of Jesus, as the divine Logos, appeared the more resplendent, from its opposition to the rude unapprehensiveness of the Jews; his goodness wore a more touching aspect, confronted with the inveterate malice of his enemies; his appearance gained in impressiveness, by the strife he excited among the people; and his power, as that of one who had life in himself, commanded the more reverence, the oftener his enemies and their instruments tried to seize him, and, as if restrained by a higher power, were not able to lay hands on him,—the more marvellously he passed through the ranks of adversaries prepared to take away his life. It has been made matter of praise to the fourth Evangelist, that he alone presents the opposition of the pharisaic party to Jesus, in its rise and gradual progress: but there are reasons for questioning whether the course of events described by him, be not rather fictitious than real. Partially fictitious, it evidently is; for he appeals to the supernatural for a reason why the Pharisees so long effected nothing against Jesus: whereas the synoptists preserve the natural sequence of the facts by stating as a cause, that the Jewish hierarchy feared the people, who were attached to Jesus as a prophet (Matt. xxi. 46; Mark xii. 12; Luke xx. 19). If then the fourth Evangelist was so far guided by his dogmatical interest, that for the escape of Jesus from the more early snares and assaults of his enemies, he invented such a reason as best suited his purpose; what shall assure us that he has not also, in consistency with the characteristics which we have already discerned in him, fabricated, for the sake of that interest, entire scenes of the kind above noticed? Not that we hold it improbable, that many futile plots and attacks of the enemies of Jesus preceded the final catastrophe of his fate:—we are only dubious whether these attempts were precisely such as the gospel of John describes.

§ 85.

ISOLATED GROUPS OF ANECDOTES. IMPUTATION OF A LEAGUE WITH BEELZEBUB, AND DEMAND OF A SIGN.

In conformity with the aim of our criticism, we shall here confine our attention to those narratives, in which the influence of the legend may be demonstrated. The strongest evidence of this influence is found where one narrative is blended with another, or where the one is a mere variation of the other: hence, chronology having refused us its aid, we shall arrange the anecdotes about to be considered according to their mutual affinity.

To begin with the more simple form of legendary influence: Schulz has already complained, that Matthew mentions two instances, in which a league with Beelzebub was imputed to Jesus, and a sign demanded from him; circumstances which in Mark and Luke happen only once.[1] The first time the imputation occurs (Matt. ix. 32 ff.), Jesus has cured a dumb demoniac; at this the people marvel, but the Pharisees observe, *He casts out demons through the prince* (ἄρχων) *of the demons.* Matthew does not here say that Jesus returned any answer to this accusation. On the second occasion (xii. 22 ff.), it is a blind and dumb demoniac whom Jesus cures; again the people are amazed, and again the Pharisees declare that the cure is effected by the help of Beelzebub, the ἄρχων of the demons, whereupon Jesus immediately exposes the absurdity of the accusation. That it should have been alleged against Jesus more than once when he cast out demons, is in itself probable. It is

---

[1] Ut sup. s. 311.

however suspicious that the demoniac who gives occasion to the assertion of the Pharisees, is in both instances dumb (in the second only, blindness is added). Demoniacs were of many kinds, every variety of malady being ascribed to the influence of evil spirits ; why, then, should the above imputation be not once attached to the cure of another kind of demoniac, but twice to that of a dumb one ? The difficulty is heightened if we compare the narrative of Luke (xi. 14 f.), which, in its introductory description of the circumstances, corresponds not to the second narrative in Matthew, but to the first ; for as there, so in Luke, the demoniac is only dumb, and his cure and the astonishment of the people are told with precisely the same form of expression :—in all which points, the second narrative of Matthew is more remote from that of Luke. But with this cure of the dumb demoniac, which Matthew represents as passing off in silence on the part of Jesus, Luke connects the very discourse which Matthew appends to the cure of the one both blind and dumb ; so that Jesus must on both these successive occasions, have said the same thing. This is a very unlikely repetition, and united with the improbability, that the same accusation should be twice made in connexion with a dumb demoniac, it suggests the question, whether legend may not here have doubled one and the same incident ? How this can have taken place, Matthew himself shows us, by representing the demoniac as, in the one case, simply dumb, in the other, blind also. Must it not have been a striking cure which excited, on the one hand, the astonishment of the people, on the other, this desperate attack of the enemies of Jesus ? Dumbness alone might soon appear an insufficient malady for the subject of the cure, and the legend, ever prone to enhance, might deprive him of sight also. If then, together with this new form of the legend, the old one too was handed down, what wonder that a compiler, more conscientious than critical, such as the author of the first gospel, adopted both as distinct histories, merely omitting on one occasion the discourse of Jesus, for the sake of avoiding repetition.[2]

Matthew, having omitted (ix. 34) the discourse of Jesus, was obliged also to defer the demand of a sign, which required a previous rejoinder on the part of Jesus, until his second narration of the charge concerning Beelzebub ; and in this point again the narrative of Luke, who also attaches the demand of a sign to the accusation, is parallel with the later passage of Matthew.[3] But

---

[2] Schleiermacher (s. 175) does not perceive the connexion of the discourse on the blasphemy against the Holy Ghost, in Matthew (xii. 31 f.), though it links on excellently to the foregoing expression, ἐγὼ ἐν πνεύματι θεοῦ ἐκβάλλω τὰ δαιμόνια (v. 28). It is more easy, however, to understand this difficulty, than that he should think (s. 185 f.) that discourse better introduced in Luke (xii. 10). For here, between the preceding proposition, that whosoever denies the Son of Man before men, shall be denied before the angels of God, and the one in question, the only connexion is that the expression ἀρνεῖσθαι τὸν υἱὸν τοῦ ἀνθρώπου brought to the writer's recollection the words εἰπεῖν λόγον εἰς τὸν υἱὸν τοῦ ἀνθρώπου. One proof of this is that between the latter passage and the succeeding declaration, that the necessary words would be given to the disciples, when before the tribunal, by the πνεῦμα ἅγιον, the connexion consists just as superficially in the expression πνεῦμα ἅγιον. What follows in Matthew (v. 33–37), had been partly given already in the Sermon on the Mount, but stands here in a better connexion than Schleiermacher is willing to admit.

[3] Luke makes the demand of a sign follow immediately on the accusation, and then gives in succession the answers of Jesus to both. This representation modern criticism holds to be far more probable than that of Matthew, who gives first the accusation and its answer, then the demand of a sign and its refusal ; and this judgment is grounded on the difficulty of supposing, that after Jesus had given a sufficiently long answer to the accusation, the very same people who had urged it would still demand a sign (Schleiermacher, s. 175 ; Schneckenburger, über den Urspr. s. 52 f.). But on the other hand, it is equally improbable that Jesus, after having some time ago delivered a forcible discourse on the more important point, the accusation concerning Beelzebub, and even after an interruption which had led him to a totally irrelevant declaration (Luke xi. 27 f.), should revert to the less important point,

Matthew not only has, with Luke, a demand of a sign in connexion with the above charge ; he has also another, after the second feeding of the multitude (xvi. 1 ff.), and this second demand Mark also has (viii. 11 f.), while he omits the first. Here the Pharisees come to Jesus (according to Matthew, in the unlikely companionship of Sadducees), and tempt him by asking for *a sign from heaven*, σημεῖον ἐκ τοῦ οὐρανοῦ. To this Jesus gives an answer, of which the concluding proposition, *a wicked and adulterous generation seeketh after a sign ; and there shall no sign be given unto it, but the sign of the prophet Jonas*, γενεὰ πονηρὰ καὶ μοιχαλὶς σημεῖον ἐπιζητεῖ, καὶ σημεῖον οὐ δοθήσεται αὐτῇ, εἰ μὴ τὸ σημεῖον Ἰωνᾶ τοῦ προφήτου, in Matthew, agrees word for word with the opening of the earlier refusal. It is already improbable enough, that Jesus should have twice responded to the above requisition with the same enigmatical reference to Jonah ; but the words (v. 2, 3) which, in the second passage of Matthew, precede the sentence last quoted, are totally unintelligible. For why Jesus, in reply to the demand of his enemies that he would show them a sign from heaven, should tell them that they were indeed well versed in the natural signs of the heavens, but were so much the more glaringly ignorant of the spiritual signs of the messianic times, is so far from evident, that the otherwise unfounded omission of v. 2 and 3, seems to have arisen from despair of finding any connexion for them.[4] Luke, who also has (xii. 54 f.), in words only partly varied, this reproach of Jesus that his cotemporaries understood better the signs of the weather than of the times, gives it another position, which might be regarded as the preferable one ; since after speaking of the fire which he was to kindle, and the divisions which he was to cause, Jesus might very aptly say to the people : You take no notice of the unmistakable prognostics of this great revolution which is being prepared by my means, so ill do you understand the signs of the times.[5] But on a closer examination, Luke's arrangement appears just as abrupt here, as in the case of the two parables (xiii. 18).[6] If from hence we turn again to Matthew, we easily see how he was led to his mode of representation. He may have been induced to double the demand of a sign, by the verbal variation which he met with, the required sign being at one time called simply a σημεῖον, at another a σημεῖον ἐκ τοῦ οὐρανοῦ. And if he knew that Jesus had exhorted the Jews to study the signs of the times, as they had hitherto studied the appearance of the heavens, the conjecture was not very remote, that the Jews had given occasion for this admonition by demanding a *sign from heaven*, σημεῖον ἐκ τοῦ οὐρανοῦ. Thus Matthew here presents us, as Luke often does elsewhere, with a fictitious introduction to a discourse of Jesus ; a proof of the pro-

namely, the demand of a sign. The discourse on the departure and return of the unclean spirit, is in Matthew (v. 43-45) annexed to the reply of Jesus to this demand ; but in Luke (xi. 24 ff.) it follows the answer to the imputation of a league with Beelzebub, and this may at first seem to be a more suitable arrangement. But on a closer examination, it will appear very improbable that Jesus should conclude a defence, exacted from him by his enemies, with so calm and purely theoretical a discourse, which supposes an audience, if not favourably prepossessed, at least open to instruction ; and it will be found that here again there is no further connexion than that both discourses treat of the expulsion of demons. By this single feature of resemblance, the writer of the third gospel was led to sever the connexion between the answer to the oft-named accusation, and that to the demand of a sign, which accusation and demand, as the strongest proofs of the malevolent unbelief of the enemies of Jesus, seem to have been associated by tradition. The first Evangelist refrained from this violence, and reserved the discourse on the return of the unclean spirit, which was suggested by the suspicion cast on the expulsion of demons by Jesus, until he had communicated the answer by which Jesus parries the demand of a sign.

4 Vid. Griesbach, Comm. crit. in loc.
5 Comp. Schleiermacher, s. 190 f.
6 De Wette, exeg. Handb. i. 1. s. 139.

position, advanced indeed, but too little regarded by Sieffert:[7] that it is in the nature of traditional records, such as the three first gospels, that one particular should be best preserved in this narrative, another in that ; so that first one, and then the other, is at a disadvantage, in comparison with the rest.

§ 86.

VISIT OF THE MOTHER AND BRETHREN OF JESUS. THE WOMAN WHO PRONOUNCES THE MOTHER OF JESUS BLESSED.

All the synoptists mention a visit of the mother and brethren of Jesus, on being apprised of which Jesus points to his disciples, and declares that they who do the will of God are his mother and his brethren (Matt. xii. 46 ff. ; Mark iii. 31 ff. ; Luke viii. 19 ff.). Matthew and Luke do not tell us the object of this visit, nor, consequently, whether this declaration of Jesus, which appears to imply a disowning of his relatives, was occasioned by any special circumstance. On this subject Mark gives us unexpected information ; he tells us (v. 21) that while Jesus was teaching among a concourse of people, who even prevented him from taking food, his relatives, under the idea that he was beside himself, went out to seize him, and take him into the keeping of his family.[1] In describing this incident, the Evangelist makes use of the expression, ἔλεγον ὅτι ἐξέστη (*they said, he is beside himself*), and it was merely this expression, apparently, that suggested to him what he next proceeds to narrate : οἱ γραμματεῖς ἔλεγον, ὅτι Βεελζεβοὺλ ἔχει κ. τ. λ. (*the scribes said, he hath Beelzebub*, etc., comp. John x. 20). With this reproach, which however he does not attach to an expulsion of demons, he connects the answer of Jesus ; he then recurs to the relatives, whom he now particularizes as the mother and brethren of Jesus, supposing them to have arrived in the meantime ; and he makes their announcement call forth from Jesus the answer of which we have above spoken.

These particulars imparted by Mark are very welcome to commentators, as a means of explaining and justifying the apparent harshness of the answer which Jesus returns to the announcement of his nearest relatives, on the ground of the perverted object of their visit. But, apart from the difficulty that, on the usual interpretation of the accounts of the childhood of Jesus, it is not to be explained how his mother could, after the events therein described, be thus mistaken in her son, it is very questionable whether we ought to accept this information of Mark's. In the first place, it is associated with the obvious exaggeration, that Jesus and his disciples were prevented even from taking food by the throng of people ; and in the second place, it has in itself a strange appearance, from its want of relation to the context. If these points are considered, it will scarcely be possible to avoid agreeing with the opinion of Schleiermacher, that no explanation of the then existing relations of Jesus with his family is to be sought in this addition ; that it rather belongs to those exaggerations to which Mark is so prone, as well in his introductions to isolated incidents, as in his general statements.[2] He wished to make it understood why Jesus returned an ungracious answer to the announcement of his relatives ; for this purpose he thought it necessary to give their visit an object of which Jesus did not approve, and as he knew that the Pharisees had

[7] Ueber den Urspr. s. 115.
[1] For the proof of this interpretation, see Fritzsche, comm. in Marc. p. 97 ff.
[2] Ueber den Lukas, s. 121.

pronounced him to be under the influence of Beelzebub, he attributed a similar opinion to his relatives.

If we lay aside this addition of Mark's, the comparison of the three very similar narratives presents no result as it regards their matter ;[3] but there is a striking difference between the connexions in which the Evangelists place the event. Matthew and Mark insert it after the defence against the suspicion of diabolical aid, and before the parable of the sower ; whereas Luke makes the visit considerably prior to that imputation, and places the parable even before the visit. It is worthy of notice, however, that Luke has, after the defence against the accusation of a league with Beelzebub, in the position which the two other Evangelists give to the visit of the relatives of Jesus, an incident which issues in a declaration, precisely similar to that which the announcement calls forth. After the refutation of the Pharisaic reproach, and the discourse on the return of the unclean spirit, a woman in the crowd is filled with admiration, and pronounces the mother of Jesus blessed, on which Jesus, as before on the announcement of his mother, replies ; *Yea, rather blessed are they who hear the word of God and keep it !*[4] Schleiermacher here again prefers the account of Luke : he thinks this little digression on the exclamation of the woman especially evinces a fresh and lively recollection, which has inserted it in its real place and circumstances ; whereas Matthew, confounding the answer of Jesus to the ejaculation of the woman, with the very similar one to the announcement of his relatives, gives to the latter the place of the former, and thus passes over the scene with the woman.[5] But how the woman could feel herself hurried away into so enthusiastic an exclamation, precisely on hearing the abstruse discourse on the return of the expelled demons, or even the foregoing reprehensible reply to the Pharisees, it is difficult to understand, and the contrary conjecture to that of Schleiermacher might rather be established ; namely, that in the place of the announcement of the relatives, the writer of the third gospel inserted the scene with the woman, from its having a like termination. The evangelical tradition, as we see from Matthew and Mark, whether from historical or merely accidental motives, had associated the above visit and the saying about the spiritual relatives, with the discourse of Jesus on the accusation of a league with Beelzebub, and on the return of the unclean spirit ; and Luke also, when he came to the conclusion of that discourse, was reminded of the anecdote of the visit and its point—the extolling of a spiritual relationship to Jesus. But he had already mentioned the visit ;[6] he therefore seized on the scene with the woman, which presented a

---

[3] Schneckenburger (über den Ur. s. 54) finds an attempt at dramatic effect in the εἶπέ τις, and the ἐκτείνας τὴν χεῖρα of Matthew, as compared with the εἶπον and περιβλεψάμενος κύκλῳ of Mark. This is a remarkable proof of the partial acumen which plays so distinguished a part to the disadvantage of Matthew in modern criticism. For who does not see that if Matthew had εἶπον, it would be numbered among the proofs that his narrative is wanting in dramatic life ? As for the words ἐκτείνας τὴν χεῖρα, there is nothing to be discovered in them which could give to them more than to the περιβλεψάμενος of Mark, the stamp of artificiality ; we might as well attribute the latter expression to Mark's already discovered fondness for describing the action of the eyes, and consequently regard it as an addition of his own.

[4] Answer to the announcement, viii. 21 : μήτηρ μοῦ καὶ ἀδελφοί μοῦ οὗτοί εἰσιν οἱ τὸν λόγον τοῦ θεοῦ ἀκούοντες καὶ ποιοῦντες αὐτόν.   Answer to the woman, xi. 28 : μενοῦνγε μακάριοι (sc. οὐχ ἡ μήτηρ μοῦ, ἀλλ') οἱ ἀκούοντες τὸν λόγον τοῦ θεοῦ καὶ φυλάσσοντες αὐτόν·

[5] Ut sup s. 177 f.

[6] That which decided the Evangelist to place the visit after the parable of the sower, was probably not, as Schleiermacher thinks, a real chronological connexion. On the contrary, we recognize the usual characteristic of his arrangement, in the transition from the concluding sentence in the explanation of the parable : *these are they who having heard the word, keep it, and bring forth fruit with patience*, to the similar expression of Jesus on the occasion of the visit : *those who hear the word of God and do it.*

similar termination. From the strong resemblance between the two anecdotes, I can scarcely believe that they are founded on two really distinct incidents ; rather, it is more likely that the memorable declaration of Jesus, that
he preferred his spiritual before his bodily relatives, had in the legend received
two different settings or frames. According to one, it seemed the most
natural that such a depreciation of his kindred should be united with an actual
rejection of them ; to another, that the exaltation of those who were spiritually near to him, should be called forth by a blessing pronounced on those
who were nearest to him in the flesh. Of these two forms of the legend,
Matthew and Mark give only the first ; Luke, however, had already disposed
of this on an earlier occasion ; when, therefore, he came to the passage where,
in the common evangelical tradition, that anecdote occurred, he was induced
to supply its place by the second form.

§ 87.

CONTENTIONS FOR PRE-EMINENCE AMONG THE DISCIPLES.   THE LOVE OF
JESUS FOR CHILDREN.

The three first Evangelists narrate several contentions for pre-eminence
which arose among the disciples, with the manner in which Jesus composed
these differences.   One such contention, which is said to have arisen among
the disciples after the transfiguration, and the first prediction of the passion,
is common to all the gospels (Matt. xviii. 1 ff. ; Mark ix. 33 ff. ; Luke ix.
46 ff.).   There are indeed divergencies in the narratives, but the identity of
the incident on which they are founded is attested by the fact, that in all of
them, Jesus sets a little child before his disciples as an example ; a scene
which, as Schleiermacher remarks,[1] would hardly be repeated.   Matthew and
Mark concur in mentioning a dispute about pre-eminence, which was excited
by the two sons of Zebedee.   These disciples (according to Mark), or their
mother for them (according to Matthew), petitioned for the two first places
next to Jesus in the messianic kingdom (Matt. xx. 20 ff. ; Mark x. 35 ff.).[2]
Of such a request on the part of the sons of Zebedee, the third Evangelist
knows nothing ; but apart from this occasion, there is a further contention for
pre-eminence, on which discourses are uttered, similar to those which the two
first Evangelists have connected with the above petition.   At the last supper
of which Jesus partook with his disciples before his passion, Luke makes the
latter fall into a φιλονεικία (dispute) which among them shall be the greatest ;
a dispute which Jesus seeks to quell by the same reasons, and partly with the
same words, that Matthew and Mark give in connexion with the ἀγανάκτησις,
(indignation), excited in the disciples generally by the request of the sons of
Zebedee.   Luke here reproduces a sentence which he, in common with Mark,
had previously given almost in the same form, as accompanying the presentation of the child ; and which Matthew has, not only on the occasion of

[1] Ut sup. s. 152.
[2] Schulz (üb. d. Abendm. s. 320) speaks consistently with the tone of the recent criticism
on Matthew when he asserts, that he does not doubt *for a moment* that every *observant*
reader will, *without hesitation*, prefer the representation of Mark, who, without mentioning
the mother, confines the whole transaction to Jesus and the two apostles. But so far as historical probability is concerned, I would ask, why should not a woman, who was one of the
female companions of Jesus (Matt. xxvii. 56), have ventured on such a petition ? As regards
psychological probability, the sentiment of the church, in the choice of the passage for St.
James's day, has usually decided in favour of Matthew ; for so solemn a prayer, uttered on
the spur of the moment, is just in character with a woman, and more especially a mother
devoted to her sons.

Salome's prayer, but also in the great anti-pharisaic discourse (comp. Luke xxii. 26; Mark ix. 35 ; Luke ix. 48 ; Matt. xx. 26 f., xxiii. 11). However credible it may be that with the worldly messianic hopes of the disciples, Jesus should often have to suppress disputes among them on the subject of their future rank in the Messiah's kingdom, it is by no means probable that, for example, the sentence, *Whosoever will be great among you, let him be the servant of all :* should be spoken, 1st, on the presentation of the child ; 2ndly, in connexion with the prayer of the sons of Zebedee ; 3rdly, in the anti-pharisaic discourse, and 4thly, at the last supper. There is here obviously a traditional confusion, whether it be (as Sieffert in such cases is fond of supposing) that several originally distinct occurrences have been assimilated by the legend, i.e. the same discourse erroneously repeated on various occasions ; or that out of one incident the legend has made many, i.e. has invented various occasions for the same discourse. Our decision between these two possibilities must depend on the answer to the following question : Have the various facts, to which the analogous discourses on humility are attached, the dependent appearance of mere frames to the discourses, or the independent one of occurrences that carry their truth and significance in themselves ?

It will not be denied that the petition of the sons of Zebedee, is in itself too specific and remarkable to be a mere background to the ensuing discourse ; and the same judgment must be passed on the scene with the child : so that we have already two cases of contention for pre-eminence subsisting in themselves. If we would assign to each of these occurrences its appropriate discourses, the declarations which Matthew connects with the presentation of the child : *Unless ye become as this child,* etc., and *Whosoever shall humble himself as this child,* etc., evidently belong to this occasion. On the other hand, the sentences on ruling and serving in the world and in the kingdom of Jesus, seem to be a perfectly suitable comment on the petition of the sons of Zebedee, with which Matthew associates them : also the saying about the first and the last, the greatest and the least, which Mark and Luke give so early as at the scene with the child, Matthew seems rightly to have reserved for the scene with the sons of Zebedee. It is otherwise with the contention spoken of by Luke (xxii. 24 ff.). This contention originates in no particular occasion, nor does it issue in any strongly marked scene (unless we choose to insert here the washing of the disciples' feet, described by John, who, for the rest, mentions no dispute ;—of which scene, however, we cannot treat until we come to the history of the Passion). On the contrary, this contention is ushered in merely by the words, ἐγένετο δὲ καὶ φιλονεικία ἐν αὐτοῖς,—nearly the same by which the first contention is introduced, ix. 46,—and leads to a discourse from Jesus, which, as we have already noticed, Matthew and Mark represent him to have delivered in connexion with the earlier instances of rivalry ; so that this passage of Luke has nothing peculiarly its own, beyond its position, at the last supper. This position, however, is not very secure ; for that immediately after the discourse on the betrayer, so humiliating to the disciples, pride should so strongly have taken possession of them, is as difficult to believe, as it is easy to discover, by a comparison of v. 23 and 24, how the writer might be led, without historical grounds, to insert here a contention for pre-eminence. It is clear that the words καὶ αὐτοὶ ἤρξαντο συζητεῖν πρὸς ἑαυτοὺς, τὸ, τίς ἄρα εἴη ἐξ αὐτῶν ὁ τοῦτο μέλλων πράσσειν ; suggested to him the similar ones, ἐγένετο δὲ καὶ φιλονεικία ἐν αὐτοῖς, τὸ, τίς αὐτῶν δοκεῖ εἶναι μείζων ; that is, the disputes about the betrayer called to his remembrance the disputes about pre-eminence. One such dispute indeed, he had already mentioned, but had only connected with it, one sentence excepted, the discourses occasioned by the exhibition of the child ; he had yet in reserve those which the

two first Evangelists attach to the petition of the sons of Zebedee, an occasion
which seems not to have been present to the mind of the third Evangelist,
whence he introduces the discourses pertaining to it here, with the general
statement that they originated in a contention for pre-eminence, which broke
out among the disciples.   Meanwhile the chronological position, also, of the
two first-named disputes about rank, has very little probability ; for in both
instances, it is after a prediction of the passion, which, like the prediction of
the betrayal, would seem calculated to suppress such thoughts of earthly
ambition.[3]   We therefore welcome the indication which the evangelical narrative itself presents, of the manner in which the narrators were led unhistorically to such an arrangement.   In the answer of Jesus to the prayer of Salome,
the salient point was the suffering that awaited him and his disciples ; hence
by the most natural association of ideas, the ambition of the two disciples, the
antidote to which was the announcement of approaching trial, was connected
with the prediction of the passion.   Again, on the first occasion of rivalry, the
preceding prediction of the passion leads in Mark and Luke to the observation, that the disciples did not understand the words of Jesus, and yet feared
to ask him concerning them, whence it may be inferred that they debated
and disputed on the subject among themselves ; here, then, the association
of ideas caused the Evangelists to introduce the contention for pre-eminence,
also carried on in the absence of Jesus.   This explanation is not applicable
to the narrative of Matthew, for there, between the prediction of the passion
and the dispute of the disciples, the anecdote of the coin angled for by Peter,
intervenes.

With the above contentions for pre-eminence, another anecdote is indirectly
connected by means of the child which is put forward on one of those occasions.   Children are brought to Jesus that he may bless them ; the disciples
wish to prevent it, but Jesus speaks the encouraging words, *Suffer little children to come unto me*, and adds that only for children, and those who resemble
children, is the kingdom of heaven destined (Matt. xix. 13 ff. ; Mark x. 13 ff. ;
Luke xviii. 15 ff.).   This narrative has many points of resemblance to that of
the child placed in the midst of the disciples.   Firstly, in both, Jesus presents
children as a model, and declares that only those who resemble children can
enter the kingdom of God ; secondly, in both, the disciples appear in the
light of opposition to children ; and, thirdly, in both, Mark says, that Jesus
took the children in his arms (ἐναγκαλισάμενος).   If these points of resemblance be esteemed adequate ground for reducing the two narratives to one,
the latter must, beyond all question, be retained as the nearest to truth, because the saying of Jesus, *Suffer little children*, etc., which from its retaining
this original form in all the narratives, bears the stamp of genuineness, could
scarcely have been uttered on the other occasion ; whereas, the sentences on
children as patterns of humility, given in connexion with the contention about
rank, might very well have been uttered under the circumstances above described, in retrospective allusion to previous contentions about rank.   Nevertheless, this might rather be the place for supposing an assimilation of originally diverse occurrences, since it is at least evident, that Mark has inserted the
expression ἐναγκαλισάμενος in both, simply on account of the resemblance
between the two scenes.

[3] Compare Schleiermacher, ut sup. s. 283.

§ 88.

THE PURIFICATION OF THE TEMPLE.

Jesus, during his first residence in Jerusalem, according to John (ii. 14 ff.), according to the synoptists, during his last (Matt. xxi. 12 ff. parall.), undertook the purification of the temple. The ancient commentators thought, and many modern ones still think,[1] that these were separate events, especially as, besides the chronological difference, there is some divergency between the three first Evangelists and the fourth in their particulars. While, namely, the former, in relation to the conduct of Jesus, merely speak in general terms of an *expulsion*, ἐκβάλλειν, John says that he made a *scourge of small cords*, φραγέλλιον ἐκ σχοινίων, for this purpose : again, while according to the former, he treats all the sellers alike, he appears, according to John, to make some distinction, and to use the sellers of doves somewhat more mildly ; moreover, John does not say that he drove out the buyers, as well as the sellers. There is also a difference as to the language used by Jesus on the occasion ; in the synoptical gospels, it is given in the form of an exact quotation from the Old Testament ; in John, merely as a free allusion. But, above all, there is a difference as to the result : in the fourth gospel, Jesus is immediately called to account ; in the synoptical gospels, we read nothing of this, and according to them, it is not until the following day that the Jewish authorities put to Jesus a question, which seems to have reference to the purification of the temple (Matt. xxi. 23 ff.), and to which Jesus replies quite otherwise than to the remonstrance in the fourth gospel. To explain the repetition of such a measure, it is remarked that the abuse was not likely to cease on the first expulsion, and that on every revival of it, Jesus would feel himself anew called on to interfere ; that, moreover, the temple purification in John is indicated to be an earlier event than that in the synoptical gospels, by the circumstance, that the fourth Evangelist represents Jesus as being immediately called to account, while his impunity in the other case appears a natural consequence of the heightened consideration which he had in the meantime won.

But allowing to these divergencies their full weight, the agreement between the two narratives preponderates. We have in both the same abuse, the same violent mode of checking it, by *casting out* (ἐκβάλλειν) the people, and *overthrowing* (ἀναστρέφειν) the tables ; nay, virtually, the same language in justification of this procedure, for in John, as well as in the other gospels, the words of Jesus contain a reference, though not a verbally precise one, to Isa. lvi. 7 ; Jer. vii. 11. These important points of resemblance must at least extort such an admission as that of Sieffert,[2] namely, that the two occurrences, originally but little alike, were assimilated by tradition, the features of the one being transferred to the other. But thus much seems clear ; the synoptists know as little of an earlier event of this kind, as in fact of an earlier visit of Jesus to Jerusalem : and the fourth Evangelist seems to have passed over the purification of the temple after the last entrance of Jesus into the metropolis, not because he presumed it to be already known from the other gospels, but because he believed that he must give an early date to the sole act of the kind with which he was acquainted. If then each of the Evangelists knew only of one purification of the temple, we are not warranted either by the slight divergencies in the description of the event, or by the important difference in its chronological position, to suppose that there were

---

[1] Paulus and Tholuck, in loc. ; Neander, L. J. Chr., s. 388, Anm.
[2] Ueber den Urspr. s. 108 ff.

two ; since chronological differences are by no means rare in the gospels, and are quite natural in writings of traditional origin.   It is therefore with justice that our most modern interpreters have, after the example of some older ones, declared themselves in favour of the identity of the two histories.[3]

On which side lies the error?   We may know beforehand how the criticism of the present day will decide on this question : namely, in favour of the fourth gospel.   According to Lücke, the scourge, the diversified treatment of the different classes of traders, the more indirect allusion to the Old Testament passage, are so many indications that the writer was an eye and ear witness of the scene he describes ; while as to chronology, it is well known that this is in no degree regarded by the synoptists, but only by John, whence, according to Sieffert,[4] to surrender the narrative of the latter to that of the former, would be to renounce the certain for the uncertain.   As to John's dramatic details, we may match them by a particular peculiar to Mark, *And they would not suffer that any man should carry any vessel through the temple* (v. 16), which besides has a support in the Jewish custom which did not permit the court of the temple to be made a thoroughfare.[5]   If, nevertheless, this particular is put to the account of Mark's otherwise ascertained predilection for arbitrary embellishment,[6] what authorizes us to regard similar artistic touches from the fourth Evangelist, as necessary proofs of his having been an eye-witness?   To appeal here to his character of eye-witness as a recognized fact,[7] is too glaring a *petitio principii*, at least in the point of view taken by a comparative criticism, in which the decision as to whether the artistic details of the fourth Evangelist are mere embellishments, must depend solely on intrinsic probability.   Although the different treatment of the different classes of men is in itself a probable feature, and the freer allusion to the Old Testament is at least an indifferent one ; it is quite otherwise with the most striking feature in the narrative of John.   Origen has set the example of objecting to the twisting and application of the scourge of small cords, as far too violent and disorderly a procedure.[8]   Modern interpreters soften the picture by supposing that Jesus used the scourge merely against the cattle[9] (a supposition, however, opposed to the text, which represents *all* πάντας as being driven out by the scourge) ; yet still they cannot avoid perceiving the use of a scourge at all to be unseemly in a person of the dignity of Jesus, and only calculated to aggravate the already tumultuary character of the proceeding.[10]   The feature peculiar to Mark is encumbered with no such difficulties, and while it is rejected, is this of John to be received?   Certainly not, if we can only find an indication in what way the fourth Evangelist might be led to the free invention of such a particular.   Now it is evident from the quotation v. 17, which is peculiar to him, that he looked on the act of Jesus as a demonstration of holy zeal—a sufficient temptation to exaggerate the traits of zealousness in his conduct.

In relation to the chronological difference, we need only remember how the fourth Evangelist antedates the acknowledgment of Jesus as the Messiah by the disciples, and the conferring of the name of Peter on Simon, to be freed from the common assumption of his pre-eminent chronological accuracy,

---

[3] Lücke, I. s. 435 ff. ; De Wette, exeg. Handb. i. 1, s. 174 f. ; i. 3, s. 40.
[4] Ut sup. s. 109 ; comp. Schneckenburger, s. 26 f.
[5] Lightfoot, s. 632, from Bab. Jevamoth, f. vi. 2.
[6] Lücke, s. 438.
[7] Lücke, s. 437 ; Sieffert, s. 110.
[8] Comm. in Joh. tom. 10, § 17 ; Opp. 1, p. 322, ed. Lommatzsch.
[9] Kuinöl, in loc.
[10] Bretschneider, Probab. p. 43.

which is alleged in favour of his position of the purification of the temple. For this particular case, however, it is impossible to show any reason why the occurrence in question would better suit the time of the first than of the last passover visited by Jesus, whereas there are no slight grounds for the opposite opinion. It is true that nothing in relation to chronology is to be founded on the improbability that Jesus should so early have referred to his death and resurrection, as he must have done, according to John's interpretation of the saying about the destruction and rebuilding of the temple;[11] for we shall see, in the proper place, that this reference to the death and resurrection, owes its introduction into the declaration of Jesus to the Evangelist alone. But it is no inconsiderable argument against John's position of the event, that Jesus, with his prudence and tact, would hardly have ventured thus early on so violent an exercise of his messianic authority.[12] For in that first period of his ministry he had not given himself out as the Messiah, and under any other than messianic authority, such a step could then scarcely have been hazarded ; moreover, he in the beginning rather chose to meet his cotemporaries on friendly ground, and it is therefore hardly credible that he should at once, without trying milder means, have adopted an appearance so antagonistic. But to the last week of his life such a scene is perfectly suited. Then, after his messianic entrance into Jerusalem, it was his direct aim in all that he did and said, to assert his messiahship, in defiance of the contradiction of his enemies ; then, all lay so entirely at stake, that nothing more was to be lost by such a step.

As regards the nature of the event, Origen long ago thought it incredible, that so great a multitude should have unresistingly submitted to a single man, —one, too, whose claims had ever been obstinately contested : his only resource in this exigency is to appeal to the superhuman power of Jesus, by virtue of which he was able suddenly to extinguish the wrath of his enemies, or to render it impotent ; and hence Origen ranks this expulsion among the greatest miracles of Jesus.[13] Modern expositors decline the miracle,[14] but Paulus is the only one among them who has adequately weighed Origen's remark, that in the ordinary course of things the multitude would have opposed themselves to a single person. Whatever may be said of the surprise caused by the suddenness of the appearance of Jesus[15] (if, as John relates, he made himself a scourge of cords, he would need some time for preparation), of the force of right on his side[16] (on the side of those whom he attacked, however, there was established usage) ; or, finally, of the irresistible impression produced by the personality of Jesus[17] (on usurers and cattle-dealers—on brute men, as Paulus calls them ?) : still, such a multitude, certain as it might be of the protection of the priesthood, would not have unresistingly allowed themselves to be driven out of the temple by a single man. Hence Paulus is of opinion that a number of others, equally scandalized by the sacrilegious traffic, made common cause with Jesus, and that to their united strength the buyers

---

[11] English Commentators, ap. Lücke, 1, s. 435 f., Anm.
[12] Eng. Comm. ap Lücke. According to Neander (s. 387, Anm.), Jesus, after his last entrance into Jerusalem, when the enthusiasm of the populace was on his side, must have shunned every act that could be interpreted into a design of using external force, and thus creating distusbances. But he must equally have shunned this at the beginning, as at the end, of his career, and the proceeding in the temple was rather a provocation of external force against himself, than a use of it for his own purposes.
[13] Comm. in Joh. Tom. 10. 16, p. 321 f., ed. Lommatzch.
[14] Lücke, in loc.
[15] Lücke, s. 413.
[16] Ib. and Tholück, in loc.
[17] Olshausen, 1, s. 785.

and sellers were compelled to yield.[18]   But this supposition is fatal to the entire incident, for it makes Jesus the cause of an open tumult ; and it is not easy either to reconcile this conduct with his usual aversion to everything revolutionary, or to explain the omission of his enemies to use it as an accusation against him.   For that they held themselves bound in conscience to admit that the conduct of Jesus was justifiable in this case, is the less credible, since, according to a rabbinical authority,[19] the Jews appear to have been so far from taking umbrage at the market in the court of the Gentiles (and this is all we are to understand by the word ἱερὸν),[20] that the absence of it seemed to them like a melancholy desolation of the temple.   According to this, it is not surprising that Origen casts a doubt on the historical value of this narrative, by the expression, εἴγε καὶ αὐτὴ γεγένηται (*if it really happened*), and at most admits that the Evangelist, in order to present an idea allegorically, καὶ γεγενημένῳ συνέχρήσατο πράγματι (*also borrowed the form of an actual occurrence*).[21]

But in order to contest the reality of this history, in defiance of the agreement of all the four Evangelists, the negative grounds hitherto adduced must be seconded by satisfactory positive ones, from whence it might be seen how the primitive Christian legend could be led to the invention of such a scene, apart from any historical foundation.   But these appear to be wanting.   For our only positive data in relation to this occurrence are the passages cited by the synoptists from Isaiah and Jeremiah, prohibiting that the temple should be made a den of robbers ; and the passage from Malachi iii. 1–3, according to which it was expected that in the messianic times Jehovah would suddenly come to his temple, that no one would stand before his appearing, and that he would undertake a purification of the people and the worship.   Certainly these passages seem to have some bearing on the irresistible reforming activity of Jesus in the temple, as described by our Evangelists ; but there is so little indication that they had reference in particular to the market in the outer court of the temple, that it seems necessary to suppose an actual opposition on the part of Jesus to this abuse, in order to account for the fulfilment of the above prophecies by him being represented under the form of an expulsion of buyers and sellers.*

§ 89.

NARRATIVES OF THE ANOINTING OF JESUS BY A WOMAN.

An occasion on which Jesus was anointed by a woman as he sat at meat, is mentioned by all the Evangelists (Matt. xxvi. 6 ff. ; Mark xiv. 3 ff. ; Luke vii. 36 ff. ; John xii. 1 ff.), but with some divergencies, the most important of which lie between Luke and the other three.   First, as to the chronology ; Luke places the incident in the earlier period of the life of Jesus, before his departure from Galilee, while the other three assign it to the last week of his life ; secondly, as to the character of the woman who anoints Jesus : she is, according to Luke, a *woman who was a sinner*, γυνὴ ἁμαρτωλὸς ; according to the two other synoptists, a person of unsullied reputation ; according to John, who is more precise, Mary of Bethany.   From the second point of difference it follows, that in Luke the objection of the spectators turns on the admission

[18] Comm. 4, s. 164.
[19] Hieros. Joh. tobh. f. lxi. 3, ap. Lightfoot, p. 411.
[20] Lücke, Comm. 1, s. 410.
[21] Ut sup., comp. also Woolston, Disc. 1.

of so infamous a person, in the other gospels, on the wastefulness of the woman; from both, it follows, that Jesus in his defence dwells, in the former, on the grateful love of the woman, as contrasted with the haughty indifference of the Pharisees, in the latter, on his approaching departure, in opposition to the constant presence of the poor. There are yet the minor differences, that the place in which the entertainment and the anointing occur, is by the two first and the fourth Evangelists called Bethany, which according to John xi. 1, was a κώμη (*town*), by Lukea πόλις (*city*), without any more precise designation; further, that the objection, according to the three former, proceeds from the disciples, according to Luke, from the entertainer. Hence the majority of commentators distinguish two anointings, of which one is narrated by Luke the other by the three remaining Evangelists.[1]

But it must be asked, if the reconciliation of Luke with the other three Evangelists is despaired of, whether the agreement of the latter amongst themselves is so decided, and whether we must not rather proceed, from the distinction of two anointings, to the distinction of three, or even four? To four certainly it will scarcely extend; for Mark does not depart from Matthew, except in a few touches of his well-known dramatic manner; but between these two Evangelists on the one side, and John on the other, there are differences which may fairly be compared with those between Luke and the rest. The first difference relates to the house in which the entertainment is said to have been given; according to the two first Evangelists, it was the house of Simon the leper, a person elsewhere unnoticed; the fourth does not, it is true, expressly name the host, but since he mentions Martha as the person who waited on the guests, and her brother Lazarus as one of those who sat at meat, there is no doubt that he intended to indicate the house of the latter as the locality of the repast.[2] Neither is the time of the occurrence precisely the same, for according to Matthew and Mark the scene takes place after the solemn entrance of Jesus into Jerusalem, only two days at the utmost before the passover; according to John, on the other hand, before the entrance, as early as six days prior to the passover.[3] Further, the individual whom John states to be that Mary of Bethany so intimately united to Jesus, is only known to the two first evangelists as *a woman*, γυνή;[4] neither do they represent her as being, like Mary, in the house, and one of the host's family, but as coming, one knows not whence, to Jesus, while he reclined at table. Moreover, the act of anointing is in the fourth gospel another than in the two first. In the latter, the woman pours her ointment of spikenard on the head of Jesus; in John, on the contrary, she anoints his feet, and dries them with her hair,[5] a difference which gives the whole scene a new character. Lastly, the two synoptists are not aware that it was Judas who gave utterance to the censure against the woman; Matthew attributing it to the disciples, Mark, to the spectators generally.[6]

Thus between the narrative of John, and that of Matthew and Mark, there is scarcely less difference than between the account of these three collectively, and that of Luke: whoever supposes two distinct occurrences in the one case, must, to be consistent, do so in the other; and thus, with Origen, hold, at

---

[1] Thus Paulus, exeg. Handb. 1, b, s. 766; L. J. 1, a, s. 292; Tholück, Lücke, Olshausen, in loc.; Hase, L. J. § 96, Anm.

[2] This difference struck Origen, who has given a critical comparison of these four narratives, to which, in point of acumen, there is no parallel in more modern commentaries. See his *in Matth. Commentarior. series*, Opp. ed. de la Rue, 3, s. 892 ff.

[3] Origenes, ut sup.

[4] Ib.

[5] Ib.

[6] Ib.

least conditionally, that there were three separate anointings. So soon, however, as this consequence is more closely examined, it must create a difficulty, for how improbable is it that Jesus should have been expensively anointed three times, each time at a feast, each time by a woman, that woman being always a different one ; that moreover Jesus should, in each instance, have had to defend the act of the woman against the censures of the spectators ! [7] Above all, how is it to be conceived that after Jesus, on one and even on two earlier occasions, had so decidedly given his sanction to the honour rendered to him, the disciples, or one of them, should have persisted in censuring it? [8]

These considerations oblige us to think of reductions, and it is the most natural to commence with the narratives of the two first synoptists and of John, for these agree not only in the place, Bethany, but also, generally, in the time of the event, the last week of the life of Jesus ; above all, the censure and the reply are nearly the same on both sides. In connexion with these similarities the differences lose their importance, partly from the improbability that an incident of this kind should be repeated ; partly from the probability, that in the traditional propagation of the anecdote such divergencies should have insinuated themselves. But if in this case the identity of the occurrences be admitted, in consideration of the similarities, and in spite of the dissimilarities ; then, on the other hand, the divergencies peculiar to the narrative of Luke can no longer hinder us from pronouncing it to be identical with that of the three other Evangelists, provided that there appear to be only a few important points of resemblance between the two. And such really exist, for Luke now strikingly accords with Matthew and Mark, in opposition to John : now, with the latter, in opposition to the former. Luke gives the entertainer the same name as the two first synoptists, namely, Simon, the only difference being, that the former calls him *a Pharisee*, while the latter style him *the leper*. Again, Luke agrees with the other synoptists in opposition to John, in representing the woman who anoints Jesus as a nameless individual, not belonging to the house ; and further, in making her appear with a *box of ointment*, ἀλάβαστρον μύρου, while John speaks only of a *pound of ointment*, λίτρα μύρου, without specifying the vessel. On the other hand, Luke coincides in a remarkable manner with John, and differs from the two other Evangelists, as to the mode of the anointing. While, namely, according to the latter, the ointment is poured on the head of Jesus, according to Luke, the woman, *who was a sinner*, as, according to John, Mary, anoints the feet of Jesus ; and even the striking particular, that she dried them with her hair,[9] is given by both in nearly the same words ; excepting that in Luke, where the woman is described as a sinner, it is added that she bathed the feet of Jesus with her tears, and kissed them. Thus, without doubt, we have here but one history under three various forms ; and this seems to have been the real conclusion of Origen, as well as recently of Schleiermacher.

In this state of the case, the effort is to escape as cheaply as possible, and to save the divergencies of the several Evangelists at least from the appearance of contradiction. First, with regard to the differences between the two first Evangelists and the last, it has been attempted to reconcile the discrepant dates by the supposition, that the meal at Bethany was held really, as John informs us, six days before Easter ; but that Matthew, after whom Mark wrote, has no contradictory date ; that rather he has no date at all ; for though he inserts the narrrative of the meal and the anointing after the declaration of

---

[7] Comp. Schleiermacher, über den Lukas, s. 111.
[8] Origenes and Schleiermacher. Winer, N. T. Gramm., s. 149.
[9] Luke vii. 38 : τοὺς πόδας αὐτοῦ—ταῖς   John xii. 3 : ἐξέμαξε ταῖς θριξὶν αὐτῆς τοὺς
θριξὶ τῆς κεφαλῆς αὐτῆς ἐξέμασσε.   πόδας αὐτοῦ.

Jesus, *that after two days is the feast of the Passover,* ὅτι μετὰ δύο ἡμέρας τὸ πάσχα γίνεται, this does not prove that he intended to place it later as to time, for it is probable that he gave it this position simply because he wished to note here, before coming to the betrayal by Judas, the occasion on which the traitor first embraced his black resolve, namely, the repast at which he was incensed by Mary's prodigality, and embittered by the rebuke of Jesus.[10] But in opposition to this, modern criticism has shown that, on the one hand, in the mild and altogether general reply of Jesus there could lie nothing personally offensive to Judas ; and that, on the other hand, the two first gospels do not name Judas as the party who censured the anointing, but the disciples or the bystanders generally : whereas, if they had noted this scene purely because it was the motive for the treachery of Judas, they must have especially pointed out the manifestation of his feeling.[11]   There remains, consequentiy, a chronological contradiction in this instance between the two first synoptists and John : a contradiction which even Olshausen admits.[12]

It has been attempted in a variety of ways to evade the farther difference as to the person of the host.   As Matthew and Mark speak only of the *house of Simon the leper,* οἰκία Σίμωνος τοῦ λεπροῦ, some have distinguished the owner of the house, Simon, from the giver of the entertainment, who doubtless was Lazarus, and have supposed that hence, in both cases without error, the fourth Evangelist mentions the latter, the two first synoptists the former.[13] But who would distinguish an entertainment by the name of the householder, if he were not in any way the giver of the entertainment ?   Again, since John does not expressly call Lazarus the host, but merely one of the συνανακειμένων *(those sitting at the table),* and since the inference that he was the host is drawn solely from the circumstance that his sister Martha *served,* διηκόνει ; others have regarded Simon as the husband of Martha, either separated on account of his leprosy, or already deceased, and have supposed that Lazarus then resided with his widowed sister :[14] an hypothesis which it is more easy to reconcile with the narratives than the former, but which is unsupported by any certain information.

We come next to the divergency relative to the mode of anointing ; accordto the two first Evangelists, the ointment was poured ¡on the head of Jesus ; according to the fourth, on his feet.   The old, trivial mode of harmonizing the two statements, by supposing that both the head and the feet were anointed, has recently been expanded into the conjecture that Mary indeed intended only to anoint the feet of Jesus (John), but as she accidentally broke the vessel (συντρίψασα, Mark), the ointment flowed over his head also (Matt.).[15] This attempt at reconciliation falls into the comic, for as we cannot imagine how a woman who was preparing to anoint the feet of Jesus could

[10] Kuinöl, Comm. in Matt., p. 687.
[11] Sieffert, über den Ursprung, s. 125 f.
[12] Bibl. Comm. 2, s. 277.
[13] Vid. Kuinöl, ut sup. p. 688 ; also Tholück, s. 228.
[14] Paulus, exeg. Handb. 2, s. 582 ; 3, b, s. 466.
[15] Schneckenburger, über den Ursprung, u. s. f., s. 60.   There is no trace in Mark's account that the words συντρίψασα τὸ ἀλάβαστρον signify an accidental fracture; nor, on the other hand can they, without the harshest ellipsis, be understood to imply merely the removal of that which stopped the opening of the vessel, as Paulus and Fritzsche maintain. Interpreted without violence, they can only mean a breaking of the vessel itself.   Is it asked with Paulus (Ex. Handb. 3. b. s. 471) : To what purpose destroy a costly vessel ? or with Fritzsche (in Marc. p. 602) : To what purpose risk wounding her own hand, and possibly the head of Jesus also ?   These are questions which have a bearing on the matter considered as the act of the woman, but not as a narrative of Mark ; for that to him, the destruction of a precious vessel should appear suited to the noble prodigality of the woman, is in perfect accordance with the exaggerating style which we have often observed in him.

bring the vessel of ointment over his head, we must suppose that the ointment spirted upwards like an effervescing draught.   So that here also the contradiction remains, and not only between Matthew and John, where it is admitted even by Schneckenburger, but also between the latter Evangelist and Mark.

The two divergencies relative to the person of the woman who anoints Jesus, and to the party who blames her, were thought to be the most readily explained.   That what John ascribes to Judas singly, Matthew and Mark refer to all the disciples or spectators, was believed to be simply accounted for by the supposition, that while the rest manifested their disapprobation by gestures only, Judas vented his in words.[16]   We grant that the word ἔλεγον (*they said*), preceded as it is in Mark by the words ἀγανακτοῦντες πρὸς ἑαυτοὺς (*having indignation within themselves*), and followed, as in Matthew, by the words Ἰγνοὺς δὲ ὁ ησοῦς (*but Jesus knowing*), does not necessarily imply that all the disciples gave audible expression to their feelings ; as, however, the two first Evangelists immediately after this meal narrate the betrayal by Judas, they would certainly have named the traitor on the above occasion, had he, to their knowledge, made himself conspicuous in connection with the covetous blame which the woman's liberality drew forth.   That John particularizes the woman, whose name is not given by the synoptists, as Mary of Bethany, is, in the [ordinary view, only an example how the fourth Evangelist supplies the omissions of his predecessors.[17]   But as the two first synoptists attach so much importance to the deed of the woman, that they make Jesus predict the perpetuation of her memory on account of it—a particular which John has not—they would assuredly have also given her name had they known it ; so that in any case we may conclude thus much : they knew not who the woman was, still less did they conceive her to be Mary of Bethany.

Thus if the identity only of the last Evangelist's narrative with that of the two first be acknowledged, it must be confessed that we have, on the one side or the other, an account which is inaccurate, and disfigured by tradition. It is, however, not only between these, but also between Luke and his fellow Evangelists collectively, that they who suppose only one incident to be the foundation of their narratives, seek to remove as far as possible the appearance of contradiction.   Schleiermacher, whose highest authority is John, but who will on no account renounce Luke, comes in this instance, when the two so widely diverge, into a peculiar dilemma, from which he must have thought that he could extricate himself with singular dexterity, since he has not evaded it, as he does others of a similar kind, by the supposition of two fundamental occurrences.   It is true that he finds himself constrained to concede, in favour of John, that Luke's informant could not in this case have been an eyewitness ; whence minor divergencies, as for instance those relative to the locality, are to be explained.   On the other hand, the apparently important differences that, according to Luke, the woman is a sinner, according to John, Mary of Bethany ; that according to the former, the host, according to the latter, the disciples, make objections ; and that the reply of Jesus is in the respective narrations totally different—these, in Schleiermacher's opinion, have their foundation in the fact that the occurrence may be regarded from two points of view.   The one aspect of the occurrence is the murmuring of the disciples, and this is given by Matthew ; the other, namely, the relations of Jesus with the pharisaic host, is exhibited by Luke ; and John confirms both representations.   The most decided impediment to the reconciliation of Luke with the other evangelists, his designation of the woman as *a sinner*, ἁμαρτωλὸς,

---

[16] Kuinöl, in Matth., p. 689.
[17] Paulus, exeg. Handb. 3 b, s. 466, and many others.

Schleiermacher invalidates, by calling it a false inference of the narrator from the address of Jesus to Mary, *Thy sins are forgiven thee,* ἀφέωνταί σοι αἱ ἁμαρτίαι. This Jesus might say to Mary in allusion to some error, unknown to us, but such as the purest are liable to, without compromising her reputation with the spectators, who were well acquainted with her character; and it was only the narrator who erroneously concluded from the above words of Jesus, and from his further discourse, that the woman concerned was a sinner in the ordinary sense of the word, whence he has incorrectly amplified the thoughts of the host, v. 39.[18] It is not, however, simply of *sins,* ἁμαρτίαι, but of *many sins,* πολλαὶ ἁμαρτίαι, that Jesus speaks in relation to the woman; and if this also be an addition of the narrator, to be rejected as such because it is inconsistent with the character of Mary of Bethany, then has the entire speech of Jesus from v. 40–48, which turns on the opposition between forgiving and loving little and much, been falsified or misrepresented by the Evangelist: and on the side of Luke especially, it is in vain to attempt to harmonize the discordant narratives.

If, then, the four narratives can be reconciled only by the supposition that several of them have undergone important traditional modifications: the question is, which of them is the nearest to the original fact? That modern critics should unanimously decide in favour of John, cannot suprise us after our previous observations; and as little can the nature of the reasoning by which their judgment is supported. The narrative of John, say they (reasoning in a circle), being that of an eyewitness, must be at once supposed the true one,[19] and this conclusion is sometimes rested for greater security on the false premiss, that the more circumstantial and dramatic narrator is the more accurate reporter—the eye-witness.[20] The breaking of the box of ointment, in Mark, although a dramatic particular, is readily rejected as a mere embellishment; but does not John's statement of the quantity of spikenard as a pound, border on exaggeration? and ought not the extravagance which Olshausen, in relation to this disproportionate consumption of ointment, attributes to Mary's love, to be rather referred to the Evangelist's imagination, which would then also have the entire credit of the circumstance, that *the house was filled with the odour of the ointment?* It is worthy of notice, that the estimate of the value of the perfume at 300 denarii, is given by John and Mark alone; as also at the miraculous feeding of the multitude, it is these two Evangelists who rate the necessary food at 200 denarii. If Mark only had this close estimate, how quickly would it be pronounced, at least by Schleiermacher, a gratuitous addition of the narrator! What then is it that, in the actual state of the case, prevents the utterance of this opinion, even as a conjecture, but the prejudice in favour of the fourth gospel? Even the anointing of the head, which is attested by two of the synoptists, is, because John mentions the feet instead of the head, rejected as unusual, and incompatible with the position of Jesus at a meal:[21] whereas the anointing of the feet with precious oil was far less usual; and this the most recent commentator on the fourth gospel admits.[22]

But peculiar gratitude is rendered to the eye-witness John, because he has rescued from oblivion the names, both of the anointing woman, and of the censorious disciple.[23] It has been supposed that the synoptists did in fact

---

[18] Ueber den Lukas, s. 111 ff.
[19] Sieffert, ut sup. s. 123 f.
[20] Schulz, ut sup. s. 320 f.
[21] Schneckenburger, ut sup. s. 60.
[22] Lücke, 2, s. 417; comp. Lightfoot, horæ, p. 468, 1081.
[23] Schulz, ut sup.

know the name of the woman, but withheld it from the apprehension that danger might possibly accrue to the family of Lazarus, while John, writing later, was under no such restraint;[24] but this expedient rests on mere assumptions.   Our former conclusion therefore subsists, namely, that the earlier Evangelists knew nothing of the name of the woman ; and the question arises, how was this possible?   Jesus having expressly promised immortal renown to the deed of the woman, the tendency must arise to perpetuate her name also, and if this were identical with the known and oft-repeated name of Mary of Bethany, it is not easy to understand how the association of the deed and the name could be lost in tradition, and the woman who anointed Jesus become nameless.   It is perhaps still more incomprehensible, supposing the covetous blame cast upon the woman to have been really uttered by him who proved the betrayer, that this should be forgotten in tradition, and the expression of blame attributed to the disciples generally. When a fact is narrated of a person otherwise unknown, or even when the person being known, the fact does not obviously accord with his general character, it is natural that the name should be lost in tradition ; but when the narrated word or work of a person agrees so entirely with his known character, as does the covetous and hypocritical blame in question with the character of the traitor, it is difficult to suppose that the legend would sever it from his name.   Moreover, the history in which this blame occurs, verges so nearly on the moment of the betrayal (especially according to the position given to it by the two first Evangelists), that had the blame really proceeded from Judas, the two facts would have been almost inevitably associated. Nay, even if that expression of latent cupidity had not really belonged to Judas, there must have been a temptation eventually to ascribe it to him, as a help to the delineation of his character, and to the explanation of his sub-sequent treachery.   Thus the case is reversed, and the question is whether, instead of praising John that he has preserved to us this precise information, we ought not rather to give our approbation to the synoptists, that they have abstained from so natural but unhistorical a combination.   We can arrive at no other conclusion with respect to the designation of the woman who anoints Jesus as Mary of Bethany.   On the one hand, it is inconceivable that the deed, if originally hers, should be separated from her celebrated name ; on the other, the legend, in the course of its development, might naturally come to attribute to one whose spiritual relations with Jesus had, according to the third and fourth gospels, early obtained great celebrity in the primitive church, an act of devoted love towards him, which originally belonged to another and less known person.

But from another side also we find ourselves induced to regard the narratives of Matthew and Mark, who give no name to the woman, rather than that of John, who distinguishes her as Mary of Bethany, as the parent stem of the group of anecdotes before us.   Our position of the identity of all the four narratives must, to be tenable, enable us also to explain how Luke's representation of the facts could arise.   Now, supposing the narrative of John to be the nearest to the truth, it is not a little surprising that in the legend, the anointing woman should doubly descend from the highly honoured Mary, sister of Lazarus, to an unknown, nameless individual, and thence even to a notorious sinner ; it appears far more natural to give the intermediate position to the indifferent statement of the synoptists, out of whose equivocal nameless woman might equally be made, either in an ascending scale, a Mary ; or, in a descending one, a sinner.

[24] Thus Grotius and Herder.

The possibility of the first transformation has been already shown : it must next be asked, where could be an inducement, without historical grounds, gradually to invest the anointing woman with the character of a sinner? In the narrative itself our only clue is a feature which the two first synoptists have not, but which John has in common with Luke; namely, that the woman anointed the feet of Jesus. To the fourth Evangelist, this tribute of feeling appeared in accordance with the sensitive, devoted nature of Mary, whom he elsewhere also (xi. 32), represents as falling at the feet of Jesus; but by another it might be taken, as by Luke, for the gesture of contrition; an idea which might favour the conception of the woman as a sinner—might *favour*, we say, not *cause* : for a cause, we must search elsewhere.*

§ 90.

THE NARRATIVES OF THE WOMAN TAKEN IN ADULTERY, AND OF MARY AND MARTHA.†

In the Gospel of John (viii. 1–11), †the Pharisees and scribes bring a woman taken in adultery to Jesus, that they may obtain his opinion as to the procedure to be observed against her; whereupon Jesus, by appealing to the consciences of the accusers, liberates the woman, and dismisses her with an admonition. The genuineness of this passage has been strongly contested, nay, its spuriousness might be regarded as demonstrated, were it not that even the most thorough investigations on the subject [1] indirectly betray a design, which Paulus openly avows, of warding off the dangerous surmises as to the origin of the fourth gospel, which are occasioned by the supposition that this passage, encumbered as it is with improbabilities, is a genuine portion of that gospel. For in the first place, the scribes say to Jesus : *Moses in the law commanded us that such should be stoned* : now in no part of the Pentateuch is this punishment prescribed for adultery, but simply death, the mode of inflicting it being left undetermined (Lev. xx. 10 ; Deut. xxii. 22) ; nor was stoning for adultery a latter institution of the Talmud, for according to the canon : *omne mortis supplicium, in scripturâ absolute positum esse strangulationem,*[2] the punishment appointed for this offence in the Talmud is strangulation.[3] Further, it is difficult to discover what there was to ensnare Jesus in the question proposed to him ;[4] the scribes quoted to him the commandment of the law, as if they would warn him, rather than tempt him, for they could not expect that he would decide otherwise than agreeably to the law. Again, the decision of Jesus is open to the stricture, that if only he who is conscious of perfect purity were authorized to judge and punish, all social order would be at an end. The circumstance of Jesus writing on the ground has a legendary and mystical air, for even if it be not correctly explained by the gloss of Jerome : *eorum videlicet, qui accusabant, et omnium mortalium peccata,* it yet seems to imply something more mysterious than a mere manifestation of contempt for the accusers. Lastly, it is scarcely conceivable that every one of those men who dragged the woman before Jesus, zealous for the law, and adverse to his cause as they are supposed to be, should have had so tender a conscience, as on the appeal of Jesus to retire without prosecuting their design, and leave the woman behind them uninjured; this rather

---

[1] Ap. Wetstein, Paulus, Lücke, in loc.
[2] Maimonides on Sanhedr. 7, 1.
[3] Mischna, tr. Sanhedr. c. 10.
[4] For a thorough discussion of this and the following points, vid. Paulus and Lücke in loc.

appears to belong merely to the legendary or poetical embellishment of the scene.   Yet however improbable it may appear, from these observations, that the occurrence happened precisely as it is here narrated, this, as Bret- schneider justly maintains,[5] proves nothing against the genuineness of the passage, since it is arguing in a circle to assume the apostolic composition of the fourth gospel, and the consequent impossibility that a narrative containing contradictions should form a portion of it, prior to an examination of its several parts.   Nevertheless, on the other hand, the absence of the passage in the oldest authorities is so suspicious, that a decision on the subject cannot be hazarded.

In any case, the narrative of an interview between Jesus and a woman of the above character must be very ancient, since, according to Eusebius, it was found in the Gospel of the Hebrews, and in the writings of Papias.[6]   It was long thought that the woman mentioned in the Hebrew gospel and by Papias was identical with the adulteress in John ; but against this it has been justly observed, that one who had the reproach of *many* sins, must be distinct from her who was detected in the *one* act of adultery.[7]   I wonder, however, that no one has, to my knowledge, thought, in connexion with the passage of Eusebius, of the woman in Luke of whom Jesus says that her *many sins,* ἁμαρτίαι πολλαί, are forgiven.   It is true that the word διαβληθείσης does not fully agree with this idea, for Luke does not speak of actual expressions of the Pharisee in disparagement of the woman, but merely of the unfavourable thoughts which he had concerning her ; and in this respect the passage in Eusebius would agree better with the narrative of John, which has an express denunciation, a διαβάλλειν.

Thus we are led on external grounds, by the doubt whether an ancient notice refer to the one or the other of the two narratives, to a perception of their affinity,[8] which is besides evident from internal reasons.   In both we have a woman, a sinner, before Jesus ; in both, this woman is regarded with an evil eye by Pharisaic sanctimoniousness, but is taken into protection by Jesus, and dismissed with a friendly πορεύου, *go.*   These were precisely the features, the origin of which we could not understand in the narrative of Luke, viewed as a mere variation of the history of the anointing given by the other Evan- gelists.   Now, what is more natural than to suppose that they were transferred into Luke's history of the anointing, from that of the forgiven sinner ?   If the Christian legend possessed, on the one side, a woman who had anointed Jesus, who was on this account reproached, but was defended by Jesus ; and on the other side a woman who was accused before him of many sins, but whom he pardoned ; how easily, aided by the idea of an anointing of the feet of Jesus, which bears the interpretation of an act of penitence, might the two histories flow together—the anointing woman become also a sinner, and the sinner also an anointer ?   Then, that the scene of the pardon was an entertainment, was a feature also drawn from the history of the anointing : the entertainer must be a Pharisee, because the accusation of the woman ought to proceed from a Pharisee party, and because, as we have seen, Luke has a predilection for Pharisaic entertainments.   Lastly, the dis- course of Jesus may have been borrowed, partly from the original narrative of the woman who was a sinner, partly from analogous occasions.   If these

---

[5] Probab., p. 72 ff.
[6] Euseb. H. E. iii. 39 : ἐκτέθειται δὲ (ὁ Παπίας) καὶ ἄλλην ἱστορίαν περὶ γυναικὸς ἐπὶ πολλαῖς ἁμαρτίαις διαβληθείσης ἐπὶ τοῦ Κυρίου, ἣν τὸ καθ' Ἑβραίους εὐαγγέλιον περιέχει.
[7] Lücke, 2, s. 217.   Paulus, Comm. 4, s. 410.
[8] Elsewhere also the two were confounded, vid. Fabricii Cod. apocryph. N. T. 1, s. 357, not.

conjectures be correct, the narratives are preserved unmixed, on the one hand, by the two first Evangelists ; on the other, by the fourth, or whoever was the author of the passage on the adulteress ; for if the latter contains much that is legendary, it is at least free from any admixture of the history of the anointing.

Having thus accounted for one modification of the narrative concerning the anointing woman, namely, her degradation into a sinner, by the influence of another and somewhat similar anecdote, which was current in the first age of Christianity, we may proceed to consider, experimentally, whether a like external influence may not have helped to produce the opposite modification of the unknown into Mary of Bethany : a modification which, for the rest, we have already seen to be easy of explanation.   Such an influence could only proceed from the sole notice of Mary (with the exception of her appearance at the resurrection of Lazarus) which has been preserved to us, and which is rendered memorable by the declaration of Jesus, *One thing is needful, and Mary hath chosen*, etc. (Luke x. 38 ff.).   We have, in fact, here as well as there, Martha occupied in serving (John xii. 2, καὶ ἡ Μάρθα διηκόνει; Luke x. 40, ἡ δὲ Μάρθα περιεσπᾶτο περὶ πολλὴν διακονίαν); here, Mary sitting at the feet of Jesus, there, anointing his feet ; here, blamed by her sister, there by Judas, for her useless conduct, and in both cases, defended by Jesus.   It is surely unavoidable to say, if once the narrative of the anointing of Jesus by a woman were current together with that of Mary and Martha, it was very natural, from the numerous points of resemblance between them, that they should be blended in the legend, or by some individual, into one story ; that the unknown woman who anointed the feet of Jesus, who was blamed by the spectators, and vindicated by Jesus, should be changed into Mary, whom tradition had depicted in a similar situation ; the task of serving at the meal with which the anointing was connected attributed to Mary's sister, Martha ; and finally, her brother Lazarus made a partaker of the meal :—so that here the narrative of Luke on the one side, and that of the two synoptists on the other, appear to be pure anecdotes, that of John a mixed one.

Further, in Luke's narrative of the visit of Jesus to the two sisters, there is no mention of Lazarus, with whom, however, according to John (xi. and xii.), Mary and Martha appear to have dwelt ; nay, Luke speaks precisely as if the presence or existence of this brother, whom indeed neither he nor either of the other synoptists anywhere notices, were entirely unknown to him.   For had he known anything of Lazarus, or had he thought of him as present, he could not have said : *A certain woman, named Martha, received him into her house*; he must at least have named her brother also, especially as, according to John, the latter was an intimate friend of Jesus.   This silence is remarkable, and commentators have not succeeded in finding a better explanation of it than that given in the Natural History of the Prophet of Nazareth, where the shortly subsequent death of Lazarus is made available for the supposition that he was, about the time of that visit of Jesus, on a journey for the benefit of his health.[9]   Not less striking is another point relative to the locality of this scene.   According to John, Mary and Martha dwelt in Bethany, a small town in the immediate vicinity of Jerusalem ; whereas Luke, when speaking of the visit of Jesus to these sisters, only mentions a *certain town*, κώμην τινὰ, which is thought, however, to be easily reconciled with the statement of John, by the observation, that Luke assigns the visit to the journey of Jesus to Jerusalem, and to one travelling thither out of Galilee, Bethany would lie in the way. But it would lie quite at the end of this way, so that the visit of Jesus must fall at the close of his journey, whereas Luke places it soon after the departure out of Galilee, and separates it from the entrance into Jerusalem by a multitude of incidents filling eight entire chapters. Thus much then is clear : the author or editor of the third gospel was ignorant that that visit was paid in Bethany, or that Mary and Martha dwelt there, and it is only that Evangelist who represents Mary as the anointing woman, who also names Bethany as the home of Mary : the same place where, according to the two first synoptists, the anointing occurred. If Mary were once made identical with the anointing woman, and if the anointing were known to have happened in Bethany, it would naturally follow that this town would be represented as Mary's home. Hence it is probable that the anointing woman owes her name to the current narrative of the visit of Jesus to Martha and Mary, and that Mary owes her home to the narrative of the meal at Bethany.

We should thus have a group of five histories, among which the narrative given by the two first synoptists of the anointing of Jesus by a woman, would form the centre, that in John of the adulteress, and that in Luke of Mary and Martha, the extremes, while the anointing by the sinner in Luke, and that by Mary in John, would fill the intermediate places. It is true that all the five narratives might with some plausibility be regarded as varied editions of one historical incident ; but from the essential dissimilarity between the three to which I have assigned the middle and extreme places, I am rather of opinion that these are each founded on a special incident, but that the two intermediate narratives are secondary formations which owe their existence to the intermixture of the primary ones by tradition.

CHAPTER IX.

MIRACLES OF JESUS.

§ 91.

JESUS CONSIDERED AS A WORKER OF MIRACLES.

THAT the Jewish people in the time of Jesus expected miracles from the Messiah is in itself natural, since the Messiah was a second Moses and the greatest of the prophets, and to Moses and the prophets the national legend attributed miracles of all kinds: by later Jewish writings it is rendered probable ;[1] by our gospels, certain. When Jesus on one occasion had (without natural means) cured a blind and dumb demoniac, the people were hereby led to ask : *Is not this the son of David ?* (Matt. xii. 23), a proof that a miraculous power of healing was regarded as an attribute of the Messiah. John the Baptist, on hearing of the *works* of Jesus (ἔργα), sent to him with the inquiry, *Art thou he that should come* (ἐρχόμενος)? Jesus, in proof of the affirmative, merely appealed again to his miracles (Matt. xi. 2 ff. parall.). At the Feast of Tabernacles, which was celebrated by Jesus in Jerusalem, many of the people believed on him, saying, in justification of their faith, *When Christ cometh, will he do more miracles than these which this man hath done ?* (John vii. 31).

But not only was it predetermined in the popular expectation that the Messiah should work miracles in general,—the particular kinds of miracles which he was to perform were fixed, also in accordance with Old Testament types and declarations. Moses dispensed meat and drink to the people in a supernatural manner (Exod. xvi. 17) : the same was expected, as the rabbins explicitly say, from the Messiah. At the prayer of Elisha, eyes were in one case closed, in another, opened supernaturally (2 Kings vi.) : the Messiah also was to open the eyes of the blind. By this prophet and his master, even the dead had been raised (1 Kings xvii. ; 2 Kings iv.) : hence to the Messiah also power over death could not be wanting.[2] Among the prophecies, Isa. xxxv. 5, 6 (comp. xlii. 7) was especially influential in forming this portion of the messianic idea. It is here said of the messianic times: *Then shall the eyes of the blind be opened and the ears of the deaf unstopped ; then shall the lame man leap as a hart, and the tongue of the dumb shall sing.* These words, it is true, stand in Isaiah in a figurative connexion, but they were early understood literally, as is evident from the circumstance that Jesus describes his miracles

---

[1] See the passages quoted in the first volume, Introd. § 14, notes 9, 10, to which may be added 4 Esdr. xiii. 50 (Fabric. Cod. pseudepigr. V. T. ii. p. 286), and Sohar Exod. fol. iii. col. 12 (Schöttgen, horæ, ii. p. 541, also in Bertholdt's Christol. § 33, note 1).

[2] See the rabbinical passages quoted in the 1st vol. ut sup.

to the messengers of John (Matt. xi. 5) with an obvious allusion to this prophetic passage.

Jesus, in so far as he had given himself out and was believed to be the Messiah, or even merely a prophet, had to meet this expectation when, according to several passages already considered (Matt. xii. 38, xvi. 1, parall.), his Pharisaic enemies required *a sign* from him; when, after the violent expulsion of the traders and money-changers from the temple, the Jews desired from him *a sign* that should legitimate such an assumption of authority (John ii. 18); and when the people in the synagogue at Capernaum, on his requiring faith in himself as the sent of God, made it a condition of this faith that he should show them *a sign* (John vi. 30).

According to the gospels, Jesus more than satisfied this demand made by his cotemporaries on the Messiah.   Not only does a considerable part of the evangelical narratives consist of descriptions of his miracles ; not only did his disciples after his death especially call to their own remembrance and to that of the Jews the δυνάμεις (*miracles*) σημεῖα (*signs*) and τέρατα (*wonders*) wrought by him (Acts ii. 22 ; comp. Luke xxiv. 19): but the people also were, even during his life, so well satisfied with this aspect of his character that many believed on him in consequence (John ii. 23 ; comp. vi. 2), contrasted him with the Baptist who gave no sign (John x. 41), and even believed that he would not be surpassed in this respect by the future Messiah (John vii. 31).   The above demands of a sign do not appear to prove that Jesus had performed no miracles, especially as several of them occur immediately after important miracles, e. g. after the cure of a demoniac, Matt. xii. 38 ; and after the feeding of the five thousand, John vi. 30.   This position indeed creates a difficulty, for how the Jews could deny to these two acts the character of proper *signs* it is not easy to understand ; the power of expelling demons, in particular, being rated very highly (Luke x. 17).   The sign demanded on these two occasions must therefore be more precisely defined according to Luke xi. 16 (comp. Matt. xvi. 1 ; Mark viii. 11), as a *sign from heaven*, σημεῖον ἐξ οὐρανοῦ, and we must understand it to be the specifically messianic *sign of the Son of Man in heaven*, σημεῖον τοῦ υἱοῦ τοῦ ἀνθρώπου ἐν τῷ οὐρανῷ (Matt. xxiv. 30).   If however it be preferred to sever the connexion between these demands of a sign and the foregoing miracles, it is possible that Jesus may have wrought numerous miracles, and yet that some hostile Pharisees, who had not happened to be eyewitnesses of any of them, may still have desired to see one for themselves.

That Jesus censures the seeking for miracles (John iv. 48) and refuses to comply with any one of the demands for a sign, does not in itself prove that he might not have voluntarily worked miracles in other cases, when they appeared to him to be more seasonable.   When in relation to the demand of the Pharisees, Mark viii. 12, he declares that there shall be no sign given *to this generation* τῇ γενεᾷ ταύτῃ, or Matt. xii. 39 f., xvi. 4; Luke xi. 29 f., that there shall no sign be given to it but *the sign of Jonah the prophet*, it would appear that by this *generation*, γενεὰ, which in Matthew and Luke he characterizes as *evil and adulterous*, he could only mean the Pharisaic part of his cotemporaries who were hostile to him, and that he intended to declare, that to these should be granted either no sign at all, or merely the sign of Jonas, that is, as he interprets it in Matthew, the miracle of his resurrection, or as modern expositors think, the impressive manifestation of his person and teaching.   But if we take the words οὐ δοθήσεται αὐτῇ in the sense that his enemies were to obtain no sign from him, we encounter two difficulties : on the one hand, things must have chanced singularly if among the many miracles wrought by Jesus in the greatest publicity, not one fell under the observation of Pharisees (moreover Matt. xii. 24 f. parall. contradicts this, for there Pharisees are plainly supposed to be present at the cure of the blind and dumb demoniac) : on the other hand, if signs personally witnessed are here intended, the enemies of Jesus certainly did not see his resurrection, or his person after he was risen. Hence the above declaration cannot well mean merely that his enemies should be excluded from an actual sight of his miracles. There is yet another expedient, namely, to suppose that the expression οὐ δοθήσεται αὐτῇ refers to a sign which should conduce to the good of the subject of which it is predicated : but all the miracles of Jesus happened equally with his original mission and his resurrection at once for the benefit of that subject and the contrary, namely, in their object for its benefit, in their result not so. Nothing therefore remains but to understand the γενεὰ of the cotemporaries of Jesus generally, and the δίδοσθαι to refer to observation generally, mediate or immediate : so that thus Jesus would appear to have here repudiated the working of miracles in general.

This is not very consistent with the numerous narratives of miracles in the gospels, but it accords fully with the fact that in the preaching and epistles of the apostles, a couple of general notices excepted (Acts ii. 22, x. 38 f.), the miracles of Jesus appear to be unknown, and everything is built on his resurrection : on which the remark may be ventured that it could neither have been so unexpected nor could it have formed so definite an epoch, if Jesus had previously raised more than one dead person, and had wrought the most transcendent miracles of all kinds. This then is the question : Ought we, on account of the evangelical narratives of miracles, to explain away that expression of Jesus, or doubt its authenticity; or ought we not, rather, on the strength of that declaration, and the silence of the apostolic writings, to become distrustful of the numerous histories of miracles in the gospels ?

This can only be decided by a close examination of these narratives, among which, for a reason that will be obvious hereafter, we give the precedence to the expulsions of demons.*

§ 92.

THE DEMONIACS, CONSIDERED GENERALLY.

While in the fourth gospel, the expressions δαιμόνιον ἔχειν *to have a demon*, and δαιμονιζόμενος, *being a demoniac*, appear nowhere except in the accusations of the Jews against Jesus, and as parallels to μαίνεσθαι, *to be mad* (viii. 48 f., x. 20 f.; comp. Mark iii. 22, 30 ; Matt. xi. 18), the synoptists may be said to represent demoniacs as the most frequent objects of the curative powers of Jesus. When they describe the commencement of his ministry in Galilee, they give the demoniacs δαιμονιζομένους [1] a prominent place among the sufferers whom Jesus healed (Matt. iv. 24 ; Mark i. 34), and in all their summary notices of the ministry of Jesus in certain districts, demoniacs play a chief part (Matt. viii. 16 f. ; Mark i. 39, iii. 11 f. ; Luke vi. 18). The power to cast out devils is before anything else imparted by Jesus to his disciples (Matt. x. 1, 8 ; Mark iii. 15, vi. 7 ; Luke ix. 1), who to their great joy succeed in using it according to their wishes (Luke x. 17, 20 ; Mark vi. 13).

Besides these summary notices, however, several cures of demoniacs are narrated to us in detail, so that we can form a tolerably accurate idea of their peculiar condition. In the one whose cure in the synagogue at Capernaum is

---

[1] That the σεληνιαζόμενοι associated with them by Matthew are only a particular species of demoniacs, whose malady appeared to be governed by the changes of the moon, is proved by Matt. xvii. 14 ff. where a δαιμόνιον is expelled from a σεληνιαζόμενος.

given by the Evangelists as the first of this kind (Mark i. 23 ff. ; Luke iv. 33 ff.), we find, on the one hand, a disturbance of the self-consciousness, causing the possessed individuals to speak in the person of the demon, which appears also in other demoniacs, as for example, the Gadarenes (Matt. viii. 29 f. parall.) ; on the other hand, spasms and convulsions with savage cries. This spasmodic state has, in the demoniac who is also called a lunatic (Matt. xvii. 14 ff. parall.), reached the stage of manifest epilepsy ; for sudden falls, often in dangerous places, cries, gnashing of the teeth, and foaming, are known symptoms of that malady.[2] The other aspect of the demoniacal state, namely, the disturbance of the self-consciousness, amounts in the demoniac of Gadara, by whose lips a demon, or rather a plurality of these evil spirits, speaks as a subject, to misanthropic madness, with attacks of maniacal fury against himself and others.[3] Moreover, not only the insane and epileptic, but the dumb (Matt. ix. 32 ; Luke xi. 14 ; Matt. xii. 22, the *dumb demoniac* is also *blind*) and those suffering from a gouty contraction of the body (Luke xiii. 11 ff.), are by the evangelists designated more or less precisely as demoniacs.

The idea of these sufferers presupposed in the gospels and shared by their authors, is that a wicked, unclean spirit ($\delta\alpha\iota\mu\acute{o}\nu\iota\sigma\nu$, $\pi\nu\epsilon\hat{v}\mu\alpha$ $\acute{\alpha}\kappa\acute{\alpha}\theta\alpha\rho\tau\sigma\nu$), or several have taken possession of them (hence their condition is described by the expressions $\delta\alpha\iota\mu\acute{o}\nu\iota\sigma\nu$ $\check{\epsilon}\chi\epsilon\iota\nu$, $\delta\alpha\iota\mu\sigma\nu\acute{\iota}\zeta\epsilon\sigma\theta\alpha\iota$, *to have a demon, to be a demoniac*), speak through their organs (thus Matt. viii. 31, $\sigma\acute{\iota}$ $\delta\alpha\acute{\iota}\mu\sigma\nu\epsilon\varsigma$ $\pi\alpha\rho\epsilon\kappa\acute{\alpha}\lambda\sigma\nu\nu$ $\alpha\mathring{v}\tau\grave{o}\nu$ $\lambda\acute{\epsilon}\gamma\sigma\nu$-$\tau\epsilon\varsigma$), and put their limbs in motion at pleasure (thus Mark ix. 20, $\tau\grave{o}$ $\pi\nu\epsilon\hat{v}\mu\alpha$ $\acute{\epsilon}\sigma\pi\acute{\alpha}\rho\alpha\xi\epsilon\nu$ $\alpha\mathring{v}\tau\grave{o}\nu$), until, forcibly expelled by a cure, they depart from the patient ($\acute{\epsilon}\kappa\beta\acute{\alpha}\lambda\lambda\epsilon\iota\nu$, $\acute{\epsilon}\xi\acute{\epsilon}\rho\chi\epsilon\sigma\theta\alpha\iota$). According to the representation of the Evangelists, Jesus also held this view of the matter. It is true that when, as a means of liberating the possessed, he addresses the demons within them (as in Mark ix. 25 ; Matt. viii. 32 ; Luke iv. 35), we might with Paulus [4] regard this as a mode of entering into the fixed idea of these more or less insane persons, it being the part of a physical physician, if he would produce any effect, to accommodate himself to this idea, however strongly he may in reality be convinced of its groundlessness. But this is not all ; Jesus, even in his private conversations with his disciples, not only says nothing calculated to undermine the notion of demoniacal possession, but rather speaks repeatedly on a supposition of its truth ; as e. g. in Matt. x. 8, where he gives the commission, *Cast out devils* ; in Luke x. 18 ff. ; and especially in Matt. xvii. 21, parall., where he says, *This kind goeth not out but by prayer and fasting.* Again, in a purely theoretical discourse, perhaps also in the more intimate circle of his disciples, Jesus gives a description quite accordant with the idea of his cotemporaries of the departure of the unclean spirit, his wandering in the wilderness, and his return with a reinforcement (Matt. xii. 43 ff.). With these facts before us, the attempt made by generally unprejudiced inquirers, such as Winer,[5] to show that Jesus did not share the popular opinion on demoniacal possession, but merely accommodated his language to their understanding, appears to us a mere adjustment of his ideas by our own. A closer examination of the last-mentioned passage will suffice to remove every thought of a mere accommodation on the part of Jesus. It is true that commentators have sought to evade all that is conclusive in this passage, by interpreting it figuratively, or even as a parable,[6] in every explanation of which (if we set

---

[2] Compare the passages of ancient physicians, ap. Winer, bibl. Realwörterb. 1, s. 191.
[3] Rabbinical and other passages, ap. Winer, ut sup. s. 192.
[4] Exeg. Handb. 1, b, s. 475 ; comp. Hase, L. J. s. 60.
[5] Ut sup. s. 191.
[6] Grätz, Comm. z. Matth. 1, s. 615.

aside such as that given by O¹;hausen [7] after Calmet), the essential idea is, that superficial conversion to the cause of Jesus is followed by a relapse into aggravated sin.[8] But. I would fain know, what justifies us in abandoning the literal interpretation of this discourse ? In the propositions themselves there is no indication of a figurative meaning, nor is it rendered probable by the general style of teaching used by Jesus, for he nowhere else presents moral relations in the garb of demoniacal conditions ; on the contrary, whenever he speaks, as here, of the departure of evil spirits, e. g. in Matt. xvii. 21, he evidently intends to be understood literally. But does the context favour a figurative interpretation ? Luke (xi. 24 ff.) places the discourse in question after the defence of Jesus against the Pharisaic accusation, that he cast out devils by Beelzebub : a position which is undoubtedly erroneous, as we have seen, but which is a proof that he at least understood Jesus to speak literally—of real demons. Matthew also places the discourse near to the above accusation and defence, but he inserts between them the demand of a sign, together with its refusal, and he makes Jesus conclude with the application, *Even so shall it be also unto this wicked generation.* This addition, it is true, gives the discourse a figurative application to the moral and religious condition of his cotemporaries, but only thus : Jesus intended the foregoing description of the expelled and returning demon literally, though he made a secondary use of this event as an image of the moral condition of his cotemporaries. At any rate Luke, who has not the same addition, gives the discourse of Jesus, to use the expression of Paulus, as a warning against demoniacal relapses. That the majority of theologians in the present day, without decided support on the part of Matthew, and in decided contradiction to Luke, advocate the merely figurative interpretation of this passage, appears to be founded in an aversion to ascrible to Jesus so strongly developed a demonology, as lies in his words literally understood. But this is not to be avoided, even leaving the above passage out of consideration. In Matt. xii. 25 f. 29, Jesus speaks of a kingdom and household of the devil, in a manner which obviously outsteps the domain of the merely figurative : but above all, the passage already quoted, Luke x. 18–20, is of such a nature as to compel even Paulus, who is generally so fond of lending to the hallowed personages of primitive Christian history the views of the present age, to admit that the kingdom of Satan was not merely a symbol of evil to Jesus, and that he believed in actual demoniacal possession. For he says very justly, that as Jesus here speaks, not to the patient or to the people, but to those who themselves, according to his instructions, cured demoniacs, his words are not to be explained as a mere accommodation, when he confirms their belief that *the spirits are subject* unto them, and describes their capability of curing the malady in question, as a power over the *power of the enemy.*[9] In answer also to the repugnance of those with whose enlightenment a belief in demoniacal possession is inconsistent, to admit that Jesus held that belief, the same theologian justly observes that the most distinguished mind may retain a false idea, prevalent among his cotemporaries, if it happen to lie out of his peculiar sphere of thought.[10]

Some light is thrown on the evangelical conception of the demoniacs, by the opinions on this subject which we find in writers more or less cotempor-

---

[7] B. Comm. 1, s. 424. According to this, the passage relates to the Jewish people, who before the exile were possessed by the devil in the form of idolatry, and afterwards in the worst form of Pharisaism.

[8] Thus Fritzsche, in Matt., p. 447.

[9] Exeg. Handb. 2, s. 566.

[10] Ut sup. 1, b. s. 483. 2, s. 96.

ary. The general idea that evil spirits had influence on men, producing melancholy, insanity, and epilepsy, was early prevalent among the Greeks [11] as well as the Hebrews ; [12] but the more distinct idea that evil spirits entered into the human body and took possession of its members was not developed until a considerably later period, and was a consequence of the dissemination of the Oriental, particularly the Persian pneumatology among both Hebrews and Greeks.[13]   Hence we find in Josephus the expressions δαιμόνια τοῖς ζῶσιν εἰσδυόμενα,[14] ἐγκαθεζόμενα [15] (demons entering into the living, settling themselves there), and the same ideas in Lucian [16] and Philostratus.[17]

Of the nature and origin of these spirits nothing is expressly stated in the gospels, except that they belong to the household of Satan (Matt. xii. 26 ff. parall.), whence the acts of one of them are directly ascribed to Satan (Luke xiii. 16).   But from Josephus,[18] Justin Martyr,[19] and Philostratus,[20] with whom rabbinical writings agree,[21] we learn that these demons were the disembodied souls of wicked men ; and modern theologians have not scrupled to attribute this opinion on their origin to the New Testament also.[22]   Justin and the rabbins more nearly particularize, as spirits that torment the living, the souls of the giants, the offspring of those angels who allied themselves to the daughters of men ; the rabbins further add the souls of those who perished in the deluge, and of those who participated in building the tower of Babel ;[23] and with this agree the Clementine Homilies, for, according to them also, these souls of the giants, having become demons, seek to attach themselves, as the stronger, to human souls, and to inhabit human bodies.[24]   As, however, in the continuation of the passage first cited, Justin endeavours to convince the heathens of immortality from their own ideas, the opinion which he there expresses, of demons being the souls of the departed in general, can scarcely be

---

[11] Hence the words δαιμονᾶν, κακοδαιμονᾶν were used as synonymous with μελαγχολᾶν μαίνεσθαι. Hippocrates had to combat the opinion that epilepsy was the effect of demoniacal influence. Vid. Wetstein, s. 282 ff.

[12] Let the reader compare the רוּחַ רָעָה מֵאֵת יְהֹוָה, which made Saul melancholy, 1 Sam. xvi. 14. Its influence on Saul is expressed by בְּעֵתְתוּ.

[13] Vid. Creuzer, Symbolik, 3, s. 69 f. ; Baur, Apollonius von Tyana und Christus, s. 144.

[14] Bell. jud. vii. vi. 3.

[15] Antiq. vi. xi. 2. On the state of Saul.

[16] Philopseud., 16.

[17] Vitæ Apollon. iv. 20, 25, comp. Baur, ut sup. s. 38 f. 42.   Even Aristotle speaks of δαιμονί τινι γενομένοις κατόχοις. de mirab. 166, ed. Bekk.

[18] Ut sup., bell. j. : τὰ γὰρ καλούμενα δαιμόνια—πονηρῶν ἐστιν ἀνθρώπων πνεύματα, τοῖς ζῶσιν εἰσδυόμενα καὶ κτείνοντα τοὺς βοηθείας μὴ τυγχάνοντας.

[19] Apoll. i. 18.

[20] Ut sup. iii. 38.

[21] Vid. Eisenmenger, entdecktes Judenthum, 2, s. 427.

[22] Paulus, exeg. Handb. 2, s. 39 ; L. J. 1, a, s. 217.   He appeals in support of this to Matt. xiv. 2, where Herod, on hearing of the miracles of Jesus, says : It is John the Baptist, he is risen from the dead.   In this expression Paulus finds the rabbinical opinion of the עִיבּוּר, which is distinct from that of the גִלְגוּל, or transmigration of souls properly so called, (that is, the passage of disembodied souls into the bodies of infants, while in the process of formation), and according to which the soul of a dead person might unite itself to that of a living one, and add to its power (vid. Eisenmenger 2, s. 85 ff.)   But, as Fritzsche and others have shown, the word ἠγέρθη refers to an actual resurrection of the Baptist, and not to this rabbinical notion ; which, moreover, even were it implied, is totally different from that of demoniacal possession.   Here it would be a good spirit who had entered into a prophet for the strengthening of his powers, as according to a later Jewish idea the soul of Seth was united to that of Moses, and again the souls of Moses and Aaron to that of Samuel (Eisenmenger, ut sup.) ; but from this it would by no means follow, that it was possible for wicked spirits to enter into the living.

[23] Justin, Apol. ii. 5., Eisenmenger, ut sup.

[24] Homil. viii. 18 f., ix. 9 f.

regarded as his, especially as his pupil Tatian expressly declares himself against it;[25] while Josephus affords no criterion as to the latent idea of the New Testamant, since his Greek education renders it very uncertain whether he presents the doctrine of demoniacal possession in its original Jewish, or in a Grecian form. If it must be admitted that the Hebrews owed their doctrine of demons to Persia, we know that the Deves of the Zend mythology were originally and essentially wicked beings, existing prior to the human race; of these two characteristics, Hebraism as such might be induced to expunge the former, which pertained to Dualism, but could have no reason for rejecting the latter. Accordingly, in the Hebrew view, the demons were the fallen angels of Gen. vi., the souls of their offspring the giants, and of the great criminals before and immediately after the deluge, whom the popular imagination gradually magnified into superhuman beings. But in the ideas of the Hebrews, there lay no motive for descending beyond the circle of these souls, who might be conceived to form the court of Satan. Such a motive was only engendered by the union of the Græco-roman culture with the Hebraic: the former had no Satan, and consequently no retinue of spirits devoted to his service, but it had an abundance of Manes, Lemures, and the like,—all names for disembodied souls that disquieted the living. Now, the combination of these Græco-roman ideas with the above-mentioned Jewish ones, seems to have been the source of the demonology of Josephus, of Justin, and also of the later rabbins; but it does not follow that the same mixed view belongs to the New Testament. Rather, as this Græcised form of the doctrine in question is nowhere positively put forth by the evangelical writers, while on the contrary the demons are in some passages represented as the household of Satan: there is nothing to contravene the inference to be drawn from the unmixedly Jewish character of thought which reigns in the synoptical gospels on all other subjects (apart from Christian modifications); namely, that we must attribute to them the pure and original Jewish conception of the doctrine of demons.

It is well known that the older theology, moved by a regard for the authority of Jesus and the Evangelists, espoused the belief in the reality of demoniacal possession. The new theology, on the contrary, especially since the time of Semler,[26] in consideration of the similarity between the condition of the demoniacs in the New Testament and many naturally diseased subjects of our own day, has begun to refer the malady of the former also to natural causes, and to ascribe the evangelical supposition of supernatural causes to the prejudices of that age. In modern days, on the occurrence of epilepsy, insanity, and even a disturbance of the self-consciousness resembling the condition of the possessed described in the New Testament, it is no longer the custom to account for them by the supposition of demoniacal influence: and the reason of this seems to be, partly that the advancement in the knowledge of nature and of mind has placed at command a wider range of facts and analogies, which may serve to explain the above conditions naturally: partly that the contradiction, involved in the idea of demoniacal possession, is beginning to be at least dimly perceived. For—apart from the difficulties which the notion of the existence of a devil and demons entails—whatever theory may be held as to the relation between the self-consciousness and the bodily organs, it remains absolutely inconceivable how the union between the two could be so far dissolved, that a foreign self-consciousness could gain an

---

[25] Orat. contra Græcos, 16.

[26] See his *Commentatio de dæmoniacis quorum in N. T. fit mentio,* and his minute consideration of demoniacal cases. So early as the time of Origen, physicians gave natural explanations of the state of those supposed to be possessed. Orig. in Matth. xvii. 15.

entrance, thrust out that which belonged to the organism, and usurp its place. Hence for every one who at once regards actual phenomena with enlightened eyes, and the New Testament narratives with orthodox ones, there results the contradiction, that what now proceeds from natural causes, must in the time of Jesus have been caused supernaturally.

In order to remove this inconceivable difference between the conditions of one age and another, avoiding at the same time any imputation on the New Testament, Olshausen, whom we may fairly take as the representative of the mystical theology and philosophy of the present day, denies both that all states of the kind in question have now a natural cause, and that they had in the time of Jesus invariably a supernatural cause. With respect to our own time he asks, if the apostles were to enter our mad-houses, how would they name many of the inmates?[27] We answer, they would to a certainty name many of them demoniacs, by reason of their participation in the ideas of their people and their age, not by reason of their apostolic illumination ; and the official who acted as their conductor would very properly endeavour to set them right : whatever names therefore they might give to the inmates of our asylums, our conclusions as to the naturalness of the disorders of those in-mates would not be at all affected. With respect to the time of Jesus, this theologian maintains that the same forms of disease were, even by the Jews, in one case held demoniacal, in another not so, according to the difference in their origin : for example, one who had become insane through an organic disorder of the brain, or dumb through an injury of the tongue, was not looked on as a demoniac, but only those, the cause of whose condition was more or less psychical. Of such a distinction in the time of Jesus, Olshausen is manifestly bound to give us instances. Whence could the Jews of that age have acquired their knowledge of the latent natural causes of these con-ditions—whence the criterion by which to distinguish an insanity or imbecility originating in a malformation of the brain, from one purely psychical ? Was not their observation limited to outward phenomena, and those of the coarsest character? The nature of their distinctions seems to be this : the state of an epileptic with his sudden falls and convulsions, or of a maniac in his delirium, especially if, from the reaction of the popular idea respecting himself he speaks in the person of another, seems to point to an external influence which governs him ; and consequently, so soon as the belief in demoniacal possession existed among the people, all such states were referred to this cause, as we find them to be in the New Testament : whereas in dumbness and gouty contraction or lameness, the influence of an external power is less decidedly indicated, so that these afflictions were at one time ascribed to a possessing demon, at another not so. Of the former case we find an example in the dumb persons already mentioned, Matt. ix. 32, xii. 22, and in the woman who was *bowed down*, Luke xiii. 11 ; of the latter, in the man *who was deaf and had an impediment* in his speech, Mark vii. 32 ff., and in the many paralytics mentioned in the gospels. The decision for the one opinion or the other was however certainly not founded on an investigation into the origin of the disease, but solely on its external symptoms. If then the Jews, and with them the Evangelists, referred the two chief classes of these condi-tions to demoniacal influence, there remains for him who believes himself bound by their opinion, without choosing to shut out the lights of modern science, the glaring inconsistency of considering the same diseases as in one age natural, in another supernatural.

But the most formidable difficulty for Olshausen, in his attempted media-

---

[27] B. Comm. 1, s. 296, Anm.

tion between the Judaical demonology of the New Testament and the intelligence of our own day, arises from the influence of the latter on his own mind—an influence which renders him adverse to the idea of personal demons. This theologian, initiated in the philosophy of the present age, endeavours to resolve the host of demons, which in the New Testament are regarded as distinct individuals, into a system of emanations, forming the continuity of a single substance, which indeed sends forth from itself separate powers, not, however, to subsist as independent individuals, but to return as accidents into the unity of the substance. This cast of thought we have already observed in the opinions of Olshausen concerning angels, and it appears still more decidedly in his demonology. Personal demons are too repugnant, and as Olshausen himself expresses it,[28] the comprehension of two subjects in one individual is too inconceivable to find a ready acceptation. Hence it is everywhere with vague generality that a kingdom of evil and darkness is spoken of; and though a personal prince is given to it, its demons are understood to be mere effluxes and operations, by which the evil principle manifests itself. But the most vulnerable point of Olshausen's opinion concerning demons is this : it is too much for him to believe that Jesus asked the name of the demon in the Gadarene ; since he himself doubts the personality of those emanations of the kingdom of darkness, it cannot, he thinks, have been thus decidedly supposed by Christ ;—hence he understands the question, *What is thy name ?* (Mark v. 9) to be addressed, not to the demon, but to the man,[29] plainly in opposition to the whole context, for the answer, *Legion,* appears to be in no degree the result of a misunderstanding, but the right answer—the one expected by Jesus.

If, however, the demons are, according to Olshausen's opinion, impersonal powers, that which guides them and determines their various functions is the law which governs the kingdom of darkness in relation to the kingdom of light. On this theory, the worse a man is morally, the closer must be the connexion between him and the kingdom of evil, and the closest conceivable connexion—the entrance of the power of darkness into the personality of the man, *i.e.* possession—must always occur in the most wicked. But historically this is not so : the demoniacs in the gospels appear to be sinners only in the sense that all sick persons need forgiveness of sins ; and the greatest sinners (Judas for example) are spared the infliction of possession. The common opinion, with its personal demons, escapes this contradiction. It is true that this opinion also, as we find for instance, in the Clementine Homilies, firmly maintains it to be by sin only that man subjects himself to the ingress of the demon ;[30] but here there is yet scope for the individual will of the demon, who often, from motives not to be calculated, passes by the worst, and holds in chase the less wicked.[31] On the contrary, if the demons are considered, as by Olshausen, to be the actions of the power of evil in its relation to the power of goodness; this relation being regulated by laws, everything arbitrary and accidental is excluded. Hence it evidently costs that theologian some pains to disprove the consequence, that according to his theory the possessed must always be the most wicked. Proceeding from the apparent contest of two powers in the demoniacs, he adopts the position that the state of demoniacal possession does not appear in those who entirely

[28] S. 295 f.
[29] S. 302, after the example of Paulus, exeg. Handb. 1, b, s. 474.
[30] Homil. viii. 19.
[31] Thus Asmodeus chooses Sara and her husband as objects of torment and destruction, not because either the former or the latter were particularly wicked, but because Sara's beauty attracted him. Tob. vi. 12-15.

give themselves up to evil, and thus maintain an internal unity of disposition, but only in those in whom there exists a struggle against sin.[32] In that case, however, the above state, being reduced to a purely moral phenomenon, must appear far more frequently ; every violent inward struggle must manifest itself under this form, and especially those who ultimately give themselves up to evil must, before arriving at this point, pass through a period of conflict, that is of possession. Olshausen therefore adds a physical condition, namely, that the preponderance of evil in the man must have weakened his corporeal organization, particularly the nervous system, before he can become susceptible of the demoniacal state. But since such disorders of the nervous system may occur without any moral fault, who does not see that the state which it is intended to ascribe to demoniacal power as its proper source, is thus referred chiefly to natural causes, and that therefore the argument defeats its own object ? Hence Olshausen quickly turns away from this side of the question, and lingers on the comparison of the δαιμονιζόμενος (*demoniac*) with the πονηρὸς (*wicked*) ; whereas he ought rather to compare the former with the epileptic and insane, for it is only by this means that any light can be thrown on the nature of possession. This shifting of the question from the ground of physiology and psychology to that of morality and religion, renders the discussion concerning the demoniacs one of the most useless which Olshausen's work contains.[33]

Let us then relinquish the ungrateful attempt to modernize the New Testament conception of the demoniacs, or to judaize our modern ideas ;—let us rather, in relation to this subject, understand the statements of the New Testament as simply as they are given, without allowing our investigations to be restricted by the ideas therein presented, which belonged to the age and nation of its writers.[34]

The method adopted for the cure of the demoniacal state was, especially among the Jews, in conformity with what we have ascertained to have been the idea of its nature. The cause of the malady was not supposed to be, as in natural diseases, an impersonal object or condition, such as an impure fluid, a morbid excitement or debility, but a self-conscious being ; hence it was treated, not mechanically or chemically, but logically, *i.e.* by words. The demon was enjoined to depart ; and to give effect to this injunction, it was coupled with the names of beings who were believed to have power over demons. Hence the main instrument against demoniacal possession was conjuration,[35] either in the name of God, or of angels, or of some other potent being, *e.g.* the Messiah (Acts xix. 13), with certain forms which were said to be derived from Solomon.[36] In addition to this, certain roots,[37] stones,[38] fumigations and amulets [39] were used, in obedience to traditions likewise believed to have been handed down from Solomon. Now as the cause of the malady was not seldom really a psychical one, or at least one lying in the nervous system, which may be acted on to an incalculable extent by moral instrumentality, this psychological treatment was not altogether illusory ! for by exciting in the patient the belief that the demon by which he

---

[32] S. 294.
[33] It fills s. 289–298.
[34] I have endeavoured to present helps towards a scientific conception of the states in question in several essays, which are now incorporated in my Charakteristiken u. Kritiken. Comp. Wirth, Theorie des Somnambulismus. S. 311 ff.
[35] See note 16, the passage quoted from Lucian.
[36] Joseph., Antiq. viii. ii. 5.
[37] Joseph., ut sup.
[38] Gittin, f. lxvii. 2.
[39] Justin Mart. dial. c. Tryph. lxxxv.

was possessed, could not retain his hold before a form of conjuration, it might often effect the removal of the disorder. Jesus himself admits that the Jewish exorcists sometimes succeeded in working such cures (Matt. xii. 27). But we read of Jesus that without conjuration by any other power, and without the appliance of any further means, he expelled the demons by his word. The most remarkable cures of this kind, of which the gospels inform us, we are now about to examine.

§ 93.

CASES OF THE EXPULSION OF DEMONS BY JESUS, CONSIDERED SINGLY.

Among the circumstantial narratives which are given us in the three first gospels of cures wrought by Jesus on demoniacs, three are especially remarkable : the cure of a demoniac in the synagogue at Capernaum, that of the Gadarenes possessed by a multitude of demons, and lastly, that of the lunatic whom the disciples were unable to cure.

In John the conversion of water into wine is the first miracle performed by Jesus after his return from the scene of his baptism into Galilee ; but in Mark (i. 23 ff.) and Luke (iv. 33 ff.) the cure of a demoniac in the synagogue of Capernaum has this position. Jesus had produced a deep impression by his teaching, when suddenly, a demoniac who was present, cried out in the character of the demon that possessed him, that he would have nothing to do with him, that he knew him to be the Messiah who was come to destroy them—the demons ; whereupon Jesus commanded the demon to hold his peace and come out of the man, which happened amid cries and convulsions on the part of the demoniac, and to the great astonishment of the people at the power thus exhibited by Jesus.

Here we might, with rationalistic commentators, represent the case to ourselves thus : the demoniac, during a lucid interval, entered the synagogue, was impressed by the powerful discourse of Jesus, and overhearing one of the audience speak of him as the Messiah, was seized with the idea that the unclean spirit by which he was possessed, could not maintain itself in the presence of the holy Messiah ; whence he fell into a paroxysm, and expressed his awe of Jesus in the character of the demon. When Jesus perceived this, what was more natural than that he should make use of the man's persuasion of his power, and command the demon to come out of him, thus laying hold of the maniac by his fixed idea ; which according to the laws of mental hygiene, might very probably have a favourable effect. It is under this view that Paulus regards the occasion as that on which the thought of using his messianic fame as a means of curing such sufferers, first occurred to Jesus.[1]

But many difficulties oppose themselves to this natural conception of the case. The demoniac is supposed to learn that Jesus was the Messiah from the people in the synagogue. On this point the text is not merely silent, but decidedly contradicts such an opinion. The demon, speaking through the man, evidently proclaims his knowledge of the Messiahship of Jesus, in the words, οἶδά σε τίς εἶ κ. τ. λ., not as information casually imparted by man, but as an intuition of his demoniacal nature. Further, when Jesus cries, *Hold thy peace!* he refers to what the demon had just uttered concerning his messiahship ; for it is related of Jesus that he suffered not the demons to speak because they knew him (Mark i. 34 ; Luke iv. 41), or because they

---

[1] Exeg. Handb. i. 6, s. 422 ; L. J. I, a, s. 128.

made him known (Mark iii. 12). If then Jesus believed that by enjoining silence on the demon he could hinder the promulgation of his messiahship, he must have been of opinion, not that the demoniac had heard something of it from the people in the synagogue, but contrariwise that the latter might learn it from the demoniac; and this accords with the fact, that at the time of the first appearance of Jesus, in which the Evangelists place the occurrence, no one had yet thought of him as the Messiah.

If it be asked, how the demoniac could discover that Jesus was the Messiah, apart from any external communication, Olshausen presses into his service the preternaturally heightened activity of the nervous system, which, in demoniacs as in somnambules, sharpens the presentient power, and produces a kind of clear-sightedness, by means of which such a man might very well discern the importance of Jesus as regarded the whole realm of spirits. The evangelical narrative, it is true, does not ascribe that knowledge to a power of the patient, but of the demon dwelling within him, and this is the only view consistent with the Jewish ideas of that period. The Messiah was to appear, in order to overthrow the demoniacal kingdom ($\dot{\alpha}\pi o\lambda\acute{\epsilon}\sigma\alpha\iota$ $\dot{\eta}\mu\hat{\alpha}s$, comp. 1 John iii. 8 ; Luke x. 18 f.)[2] and to cast the devil and his angels into the lake of fire (Matt. xxv. 41 ; Rev. xx. 10)[3] : it followed of course that the demons would recognize him who was to pass such a sentence on them.[4] This however might be deducted as an admixture of the opinion of the narrator, without damage to the rest of the narrative ; but it must first be granted admissible to ascribe so extensive a presentient power to demoniacal subjects. Now, as it is in the highest degree improbable that a nervous patient, however intensely excited, should recognize Jesus as the Messiah, at a time when he was not believed to be such by any one else, perhaps not even by himself ; and as on the other hand this recognition of the Messiah by the demon so entirely agrees with the popular ideas ;—we must conjecture that on this point the evangelical tradition is not in perfect accordance with historical truth, but has been attuned to these ideas.[5] There was the more inducement to this, the more such a recognition of Jesus on the part of the demons would redound to his glory. As when adults disowned him, praise was prepared for him out of the mouth of babes (Matt. xxi. 16)—as he was convinced that if men were silent, the very stones would cry out (Luke xix. 40) : so it must appear fitting, that when his people whom he came to save would not acknowledge him, he should have the involuntary homage of demons, whose testimony, since they had only ruin to expect from him, must be impartial, and from their higher spiritual nature was to be relied on.

In the above history of the cure of a demoniac, we have a case of the simplest kind ; the cure of the possessed Gadarenes on the contrary (Matt. viii. 28 ff. ; Mark v. 1 ff. ; Luke viii. 26 ff.) is a very complex one, for in this instance we have, together with several divergencies of the Evangelists, instead of one demon, many, and instead of a simple departure of these demons, their entrance into a herd of swine.

After a stormy passage across the sea of Galilee to its eastern shore, Jesus

---

[2] Bibl. Comm. i. 296.

[3] Comp. Bertholdt, Christol. Jud. §§ 36–41.

[4] According to Pesikta in Jalkut Schimoni ii. f. lvi. 3 (s. Bertholdt, p. 185). Satan recognizes in the same manner the pre-existing Messiah at the foot of the throne of God with terror, as he *qui me et omnes gentiles in infernum præcipitaturus est.*

[5] Fritzsche, in Marc., p. 35 : *In multis evangeliorum locis homines legas a pravis dæmonibus agitatos, quum primum conspexerint Jesum, eum Messiam esse, a nemine unquam de hac re commonitos, statim intelligere. In qua re hac nostri scriptores ducti sunt sententia, consentaneum esse. Satanæ satellites facile cognovisse Messiam, quippe insignia de se supplicia aliquando sumturum.*

meets, according to Mark and Luke, a demoniac who lived among the tombs,[6] and was subject to outbreaks of terrific fury against himself[7] and others ; according to Matthew, there were two. It is astonishing how long harmonists have resorted to miserable expedients, such as that Mark and Luke mention only one because he was particularly distinguished by wildness, or Matthew two, because he included the attendant who guarded the maniac,[8] rather than admit an essential difference between the two narratives. Since this step has been gained, the preference has been given to the statement of the two intermediate Evangelists, from the consideration that maniacs of this class are generally unsociable ; and the addition of a second demoniac by Matthew has been explained by supposing that the plurality of the demons spoken of in the narratives became in his apprehension a plurality of demoniacs.[9] But the impossibility that two maniacs should in reality associate themselves, or perhaps be associated merely in the original legend, is not so decided as to furnish in itself a ground for preferring the narrative in Mark and Luke to that in Matthew. At least if it be asked, which of the two representations could the most easily have been formed from the other by tradition, the probability on both sides will be found equal. For if according to the above supposition, the plurality of demons might give rise to the idea of a plurality of demoniacs, it may also be said, conversely : the more accurate representation of Matthew, in which a plurality of demoniacs as well as of demons was mentioned, did not give prominence to the specifically extraordinary feature in the case, namely, that one man was possessed by many demons ; and as, in order to exhibit this, the narrative when reproduced must be so expressed as to make it clear that many demons inhabited one man, this might easily occasion by degrees the opposition of the demoniac in the singular to the plural number of the demons. For the rest, the introduction of Matthew's narrative is concise and general, that of the two others circumstantially descriptive ; another difference from which the greater originality of the latter has been deduced.[10] But it is quite as probable that the details which Luke and Mark have in common, namely, that the possessed would wear no clothing, broke all fetters, and wounded himself with stones, are an arbitrary enlargement on the simple characteristic, *exceeding fierce*, which Matthew gives, with the consequence that no one could pass by that way,—as that the latter is a vague abridgment of the former.

This scene between Jesus and the demoniac or demoniacs opens, like the other, with a cry of terror from the latter, who, speaking in the person of the possessing demon, exclaims that he wishes to have nothing to do with Jesus, the Messiah, from whom he has to expect only torment. Two hypotheses have been framed, to explain how the demoniac came at once to recognize Jesus as the Messiah : according to one, Jesus was even then reputed to be the Messiah on the Peræan shore ;[11] according to the other, some of those who had come across the sea with Jesus had said to the man (whom on account of his fierceness no one could come near !) that the Messiah had just

---

[6] A favourite resort of maniacs, vid. Lightfoot and Schöttgen, in loc., and of unclean spirits, vid. rabbinical passages, ap. Wetstein.

[7] The notion that the cutting himself with stones which Mark ascribes to the demoniac, was an act of penance in lucid moments, belongs to the errors to which Olshausen is led by his false opinion of a moral and religious point of view in relation to these phenomena. It is well known, however, that the paroxysms of such disorders are precisely the occasions on which a self-destructive fury is manifested.

[8] Vid. the collection of such explanations, ap. Fritzsche, in Matt., p. 327.

[9] Thus Schulz, über das Abendmahl, s. 309 ; Paulus, in loc. Hase, L. J. § 75.

[10] Schulz, ut sup.

[11] Schleiermacher, über den Lukas, s. 127.

landed at such a spot : [12] but both are alike groundless, for it is plain that in this narrative, as in the former, the above featu.e is a product of the Jewish-Christian opinion respecting the relation of the demons to the Messiah.[13] Here, however, another difference meets us. According to Matthew, the possessed, when they see Jesus, cry : *What have we to do with thee ? Art thou come to torment us ?*—according to Luke, the demoniac falls at the feet of Jesus and says beseechingly, *Torment me not* ; and lastly, according to Mark, he runs from a distance to meet Jesus, falls at his feet and adjures him by God not to torment him.   Thus we have again a climax : in Matthew, the demoniac, stricken with terror, deprecates the unwelcome approach of Jesus ; in Luke, he accosts Jesus, when arrived, as a suppliant ; in Mark, he eagerly runs to meet Jesus, while yet at a distance.   Those commentators who here take Mark's narrative as the standard one, are obliged themselves to admit, that the hastening of a demoniac towards Jesus whom he all the while dreaded, is somewhat of a contradiction ; and they endeavour to relieve themselves of the difficulty, by the supposition that the man set off to meet Jesus in a lucid moment, when he wished to be freed from the demon, but being heated by running,[14] or excited by the words of Jesus,[15] he fell into the paroxysm in which, assuming the character of the demon, he entreated that the expulsion might be suspended.   But in the closely consecutive phrases of Mark, *Seeing*— *he ran*—*and worshipped*—*and cried*—*and said,* ἰδὼν—ἔδραμε—καὶ προσεκύνησε—καὶ κράξας—εἶπε· there is no trace of a change in the state of the demoniac, and the improbability of his representation subsists, for one really possessed, if he had recognized the Messiah at a distance, would have anxiously avoided, rather than have approached him ; and even setting this aside, it is impossible that one who believed himself to be possessed by a demon inimical to God, should adjure Jesus by God, as Mark makes the demoniac do.[16] If then his narrative cannot be the original one, that of Luke, which is only so far the simpler that it does not represent the demoniac as running towards Jesus and adjuring him, is too closely allied to it to be regarded as the nearest to the fact.   That of Matthew is without doubt the purest, for the terror-stricken question, *Art thou come to destroy us before the time ?* is better suited to a demon, who, as the enemy of the Messiah's kingdom, could expect no forbearance from the Messiah than the entreaty for clemency in Mark and Luke ; though Philostratus, in a narrative which might be regarded as an imitation of this evangelical one, has chosen the latter form.[17]

From the course of the narratives hitherto, it would appear that the demons, in this as in the first narrative, addressed Jesus in the manner described, before anything occurred on his part ; yet the two intermediate Evangelists go on to state, that Jesus had commanded the unclean spirit to come out of the man.   When did Jesus do this?   The most natural answer would be : before the man spoke to him.   Now in Luke the address of the demoniac is so closely connected with the word προσέπεσε, *he fell down,* and then again with ἀνακράξας, *having cried out,* that it seems necessary to place the command of Jesus before the cry and the prostration, and hence to consider it as their cause.   Yet Luke himself rather gives the mere sight of Jesus as the cause of

---

[12] Paulus, L. J. 1, a, s. 232.
[13] Vid. Fritzsche, in Matt., p. 329.
[14] Natürliche Geschichte, 2, 174.
[15] Paulus, exeg. Handb. 1, 473 ; Olshausen, s. 302.
[16] This even Paulus, s. 474, and Olshausen, s. 303, find surprising.
[17] It is the narrative of the manner in which Apollonius of Tyana unmasked a demon (empusa), vit. Ap. iv. 35; ap. Baur, s. 145.

those demonstrations on the part of the demoniac, so that his representation leaves us in perplexity as to where the command of Jesus should find its place. The case is still worse in Mark, for here a similar dependence of the successive phrases thrusts back the command of Jesus even before the word ἔδραμε, *he ran*, so that we should have to imagine rather strangely that Jesus cried to the demon, ἔξελθε, *Come out*, from a distance. Thus the two intermediate Evangelists are in an error with regard either to the consecutive particulars that precede the command or to the command itself, and our only question is, where may the error be most probably presumed to lie? Here Schleiermacher himself admits, that if in the original narrative an antecedent command of Jesus had been spoken of, it would have been given in its proper place, before the prayer of the demons, and as a quotation of the precise words of Jesus ; whereas the supplementary manner in which it is actually inserted, with its abbreviated and indirect form (in Luke ; Mark changes it after his usual style, into a direct address), is a strong foundation for the opinion that it is an explanatory addition furnished by the narrator from his own conjecture.[18] And it is an extremely awkward addition, for it obliges the reader to recast his conception of the entire scene. At first the pith of the incident seems to be, that the demoniac had instantaneously recognized and supplicated Jesus ; but the narrator drops this original idea, and reflecting that the prayer of the demon must have been preceded by a severe command from Jesus, he corrects his previous omission, and remarks that Jesus had given his command in the first instance.

To their mention of this command, Mark and Luke annex the question put by Jesus to the demon : *What is thy name?* In reply, a multitude of demons make known their presence, and give as their name, *Legion*. Of this episode Matthew has nothing. In the above addition we have found a supplementary explanation of the former part of the narrative : what if this question and answer were an anticipatory introduction to the sequel, and likewise the spontaneous production of the legend or the narrator? Let us examine the reasons that render it probable : the wish immediately expressed by the demons to enter the herd of swine, does not in Matthew presuppose a multitude of demons in each of the two possessed, since we cannot know whether the Hebrews were not able to believe that even two demons only could possess a whole herd of swine : but a later writer might well think it requisite to make the number of the evil spirits equal the number of the swine. Now, what a herd is in relation to animals, an army or a division of an army is in relation to men and superior beings, and as it was required to express a large division, nothing could more readily suggest itself than the Roman legion, which term in Matt. xxvi. 53, is applied to angels, as here to demons. But without further considering this more precise estimate of the Evangelists, we must pronounce it inconceivable that several demons had set up their habitation in one individual. For even if we had attained so far as to conceive how one demon by a subjection of the human consciousness could possess himself of a human organization, imagination would still fail us to conceive that many personal demons could at once possess one man. For as possession means nothing else, than that the demon constitutes himself the subject of the consciousness, and as consciousness can in reality have but one focus, one

---

[18] Ut sup. s. 128. When, however, he accounts for this incorrect supplement of Luke's by supposing that his informant, being engaged in the vessel, had remained behind, and thus had missed the commencement of the scene with the demoniac, this is too laboured an exercise of ingenuity, and presupposes the antiquated opinion, that there was the most immediate relation possible between the evangelical histories and the facts which they report.

central point : it is under every condition absolutely inconceivable that several demons should at the same time take possession of one man. Manifold possession could only exist in the sense of an alternation of possession by various demons, and not as here in that of a whole army of them dwelling at once in one man, and at once departing from him.

All the narratives agree in this, that the demons (in order, as Mark says, not to be sent out of the country, or according to Luke, into the *deep*) entreated of Jesus permission to enter into the herd of swine feeding near ; that this was granted them by Jesus ; and that forthwith, owing to their influence, the whole herd of swine (Mark, we must not ask on what authority, fixes their number at about two thousand) were precipitated into the sea and drowned. If we adopt here the point of view taken in the gospel narratives, which throughout suppose the existence of real demons, it is yet to be asked : how can demons, admitting even that they can take possession of men,—how, we say, can they, being at all events intelligent spirits, have and obtain the wish to enter into brutal forms ? Every religion and philosophy which rejects the transmigration of souls, must, for the same reason, also deny the possibility of this passage of the demons into swine ; and Olshausen is quite right in classing the swine of Gadara in the New Testament with Balaam's ass in the Old, as a similar *scandal and stumbling block*.[19] This theologian, however, rather evades than overcomes the difficulty, by the observation that we are here to suppose, not an entrance of the individual demons into the individual swine, but merely an influence of all the evil spirits on the swine collectively. For the expression, εἰσελθεῖν εἰς τοὺς χοίρους, *to enter into the swine*, as it stands opposed to the expression, ἐξελθεῖν ἐκ τοῦ ἀνθρώπου, *to go out of the man*, cannot possibly mean otherwise than that the demons were to assume the same relation to the swine which they had borne to the possessed man ; besides, a mere influence could not preserve them from banishment out of the country or into the deep, but only an actual habitation of the bodies of the animals : so that the scandal and stumbling block remain. Thus the prayer in question cannot possibly have been offered by real demons, though it might by Jewish maniacs, sharing the ideas of their people. According to these ideas it is a torment to evil spirits to be destitute of a corporeal envelopment, because without a body they cannot gratify their sensual desires ;[20] if therefore they were driven out of men they must wish to enter into the bodies of brutes, and what was better suited to an impure spirit πνεῦμα ἀκάθαρτον, than an impure animal ζῶον ἀκάθαρτον, like a swine ?[21] So far, therefore, it is possible that the Evangelists might correctly represent the fact, only, in accordance with their national ideas, ascribing to the demons what should rather have been referred to the madness of the patient. But when it is further said that the demons actually entered the swine, do not the Evangelists affirm an evident impossibility? Paulus thinks that the Evangelists here as everywhere else identify the possessed men with the possessing demons, and hence attribute to the latter the entrance into the swine, while in fact it was only the former, who, in obedience to their fixed idea, rushed upon the herd.[22] It is true that Matthew's expression ἀπῆλθον εἰς τοὺς χοίρους, taken alone, might be understood of a mere rushing towards the swine ; not only however,

---

[19] S. 305, Anm.

[20] Clem. Hom. ix. 10.

[21] Fritzsche, in Matth., p. 332. According to Eisenmenger, 2, 447 ff., the Jews held that demons generally had a predilection for impure places, and in Jalkut Rubeni f. x. 2. (Wetstein) we find this observation : *Anima idololatrarum, quæ venit a spiritu immundo, vocatur porcus*.

[22] Ut sup. s. 474, 485. Winer, b. Realw. 1, s. 192.

as Paulus himself must admit, does the word εἰσελθόντες in the two other Evangelists distinctly imply a real entrance into the swine ; but also Matthew has like them before the word ἀπῆλθον, *they entered*, the expression ἐξελθόντες οἱ δαίμονες, *the demons coming out* (sc. ἐκ τῶν ἀνθρώπων *out of the men*) : thus plainly enough distinguishing the demons who entered the swine from the men.[23] Thus our Evangelists do not in this instance merely relate what actually happened, in the colours which it took from the false lights of their age ; they have here a particular, which cannot possibly have happened in the manner they allege.

A new difficulty arises from the effect which the demons are said to have produced in the swine. Scarcely had they entered them, when they compelled the whole herd to precipitate themselves into the sea. It is reasonably asked, what then did the demons gain by entering into the animals, if they immediately destroyed the bodies of which they had taken possession, and thus robbed themselves of the temporary abode for which they had so earnestly entreated?[24] The conjecture, that the design of the demons in destroying the swine, was to incense the minds of their owners against Jesus, which is said to have been the actual result,[25] is too far-fetched ; the other conjecture that the demoniacs, rushing with cries on the herd, together with the flight of their keepers, terrified the swine and chased them into the water,[26]—even if it were not opposed as we have seen to the text,—would not suffice to explain the drowning of a herd of swine amounting to 2,000, according to Mark ; or only a numerous herd, according to the general statement of Matthew. The expedient of supposing that in truth it was only a part of the herd that was drowned,[27] has not the slightest foundation in the evangelical narrative. The difficulties connected with this point are multiplied by the natural reflection that the drowning of the herd would involve no slight injury to the owners, and that of this injury Jesus was the mediate author. The orthodox, bent on justifying Jesus, suppose that the permission to the demons to enter into the swine was necessary to render the cure of the demoniac possible, and, they argue, brutes are assuredly to be killed that man may live ;[28] but they do not perceive that they thus, in a manner most inconsistent with their point of view, circumscribe the power of Jesus over the demoniacal kingdom. Again, it is supposed, that the swine probably belonged to Jews, and that Jesus intended to punish them for their covetous transgression of the law,[29] that he acted with divine authority, which often sacrifices individual good to higher objects, and by lightning, hail and inundations causes destruction to the property of many men,[30] in which case, to accuse God of injustice would be absurd.[31] But to adopt this expedient is to confound, in a way the most inadmissible on the orthodox system, Christ's state of humiliation with his state of exaltation : it is to depart, in a spirit of mysticism, from the wise doctrine of Paul, that he was *made under the law*, γενόμενος ὑπὸ νόμον (Gal. iv. 4), and that he *made himself of no reputation* ἑαυτόν ἐκένωσε (Phil. ii. 7): it is to make Jesus a being altogether foreign to us, since in relation to the moral estimate of his actions, it lifts him above the standard of humanity. Nothing remains, therefore, but to take the naturalistic supposition of the

[23] Fritzsche, in Matth., s. 330.
[24] Paulus, ut sup. s. 475 f.
[25] Olshausen, s. 307.
[26] Paulus, s. 474.
[27] Paulus, s. 485 ; Winer, ut sup.
[28] Olshausen, ut sup.
[29] Ibid.
[30] Ullmann, über die Unsündlichkeit Jesu, in seinen Studien, 1, 1, s. 51 f.
[31] Olshausen, ut sup.

rushing of the demoniacs among the swine, and to represent the consequent destruction of the latter as something unexpected by Jesus, for which therefore he is not responsible : [32] in the plainest contradiction to the evangelical account, which makes Jesus, even if not directly cause the issue, foresee it in the most decided manner.[33]   Thus there appears to attach to Jesus the charge of an injury done to the property of another, and the opponents of Christianity have long ago made this use of the narrative.[34]   It must be admitted that Pythagoras in a similar case acted far more justly, for when he liberated some fish from the net, he indemnified the fishermen who had taken them.[35]

Thus the narrative before us is a tissue of difficulties, of which those relating to the swine are not the slightest.   It is no wonder therefore that commentators began to doubt the thorough historical truth of this anecdote earlier than that of most others in the public life of Jesus, and particularly to sever the connexion between the destruction of the swine and the expulsion of the demons by Jesus.   Thus Krug thought that tradition had reversed the order of these two facts.   The swine according to him were precipitated into the sea before the landing of Jesus, by the storm which raged during his voyage, and when Jesus subsequently wished to cure the demoniac, either he himself or one of his followers persuaded the man that his demons were already gone into those swine and had hurled them into the sea ; which was then believed and reported to be the fact.[36]   K. Ch. L. Schmidt makes the swine-herds go to meet Jesus on his landing ; during which interim many of the untended swine fall into the sea ; and as about this time Jesus had commanded the demon to depart from the man, the bystanders imagine that the two events [37] stood in the relation of cause and effect.   The prominent part which is played in these endeavours at explanation, by the accidental coincidence of many circumstances, betrays that maladroit mixture of the mythical system of interpretation with the natural which characterizes the earliest attempts, from the mythical point of view.   Instead of inventing a natural foundation, for which we have nowhere any warrant, and which in no degree explains the actual narrative in the gospels, adorned as it is with the miraculous ; we must rather ask, whether in the probable period of the formation of the evangelical narratives, there are not ideas to be found from which the story of the swine in the history before us might be explained ?

We have already adduced one opinion of that age bearing on this point, namely, that demons are unwilling to remain without bodies, and that they have a predilection for impure places, whence the bodies of swine must be best suited to them : this does not however explain why they should have precipitated the swine into the water.   But we are not destitute of information that will throw light on this also.   Josephus tells us of a Jewish conjuror who cast out demons by forms and means derived from Solomon, that in order to convince the bystanders of the reality of his expulsions, he set a vessel of water in the neighbourhood of the possessed person, so that the departing demon must throw it down and thus give ocular proof to the spectators that he was out of the man.[38]   In like manner it is narrated of Apollonius of Tyana, that he commanded a demon which possessed a young man, to

[32] Paulus.
[33] Ullmann.
[34] E. g. Woolston, Disc. 1, p. 32 ff.
[35] Jamblich. vita Pythag. no. 36. ed. Kiessling.
[36] In the Abhandlung über genetische oder formelle Erklärungsart der Wunder in Henke's Museum, 1, 3, s. 410 ff.
[37] Exeg. Beiträge, 2, 109 ff.
[38] Antiq. viii. ii. 5.

depart with a visible sign, whereupon the demon entreated that he might overturn a statue that stood near at hand ; which to the great astonishment of the spectators actually ensued in the very moment that the demon went out of the youth.[39] If then the agitation of some near object, without visible contact, was held the surest proof of the reality of an expulsion of demons : this proof could not be wanting to Jesus ; nay, while in the case of Eleazar, the object being only *a little* (μικρὸν) removed from the exorciser and the patient, the possibility of deception was not altogether excluded, Matthew notices in relation to Jesus, more emphatically than the two other Evangelists, the fact that the herd of swine was feeding a *good way off* (μακρὰν), thus removing the last remnant of such a possibility. That the object to which Jesus applied this proof, was from the first said to be a herd of swine, immediately pro- needed from the Jewish idea of the relation between unclean spirits and animals, but it furnished a welcome opportunity for satisfying another ten- dency of the legend. Not only did it behove Jesus to cure ordinary demo- niacs, such as the one in the history first considered; he must have succeeded in the most difficult cures of this kind. It is the evident object of the present narrative, from the very commencement, with its startling description of the fearful condition of the Gadarene, to represent the cure as one of extreme difficulty. But to make it more complicated, the possession must be, not simple, but manifold, as in the case of Mary Magdalene, *out of whom were cast seven demons* (Luke viii. 2), or in the demoniacal relapse in which the expelled demon returns with seven worse than himself (Matt. xii. 45) ; whence the number of the demons was here made, especially by Mark, to exceed by far the probable number of a herd. As in relation to an inanimate object, as a vessel of water or a statue, the influence of the expelled demons could not be more clearly manifested by any means, than by its falling over contrary to the law of gravity ; so in animals it could not be more surely attested in any way, than by their drowning themselves contrary to their instinctive desire of life. Only by this derivation of our narrative from the confluence of various ideas and interests of the age, can we explain the above noticed contradiction, that the demons first petition for the bodies of the swine as a habitation, and immediately after of their own accord destroy this habitation. The petition grew, as we have said, out of the idea that demons shunned incorporeality, the destruction, out of the ordinary test of the reality of an exorcism ;—what wonder if the combination of ideas so heterogeneous produced two contra- dictory features in the narrative ?

The third and last circumstantially narrated expulsion of a demon has the peculiar feature, that in the first instance the disciples in vain attempt the cure, which Jesus then effects with ease. The three synoptists (Matt. xvii. 14 ff. ; Mark ix. 14 ff. ; Luke ix. 37 ff.) unanimously state that Jesus having descended with his three most confidential disciples from the Mount of the Transfiguration, found his other disciples in perplexity, because they were unable to cure a possessed boy, whom his father had brought to them.

In this narrative also there is a gradation from the greatest simplicity in Matthew, to the greatest particularity of description in Mark ; and here again this gradation has led to the conclusion that the narrative of Matthew is the farthest from the fact, and must be made subordinate to that of the two other Evangelists.[40] In the introduction of the incident in Matthew, Jesus, having descended from the mountain, joins the multitude (ὄχλος), whereupon the father of the boy approaches, and on his knees entreats Jesus

---

[39] Philostr. v. Ap. iv. 20; ap. Baur, ut sup. s. 39.
[40] Schulz. s. 319.

to cure his child ; in Luke, the *multitude* (ὄχλος) meet Jesus ; lastly, in Mark, Jesus sees around the disciples a great multitude, among whom were scribes disputing with them ; the people, when they see him, run towards him and salute him, he inquires what is the subject of dispute, and on this the father of the boy begins to speak. Here we have a climax in relation to the conduct of the people; in Matthew, Jesus appears to join them by accident; in Luke, they come to meet him; and in Mark, they run towards him to salute him. The last Evangelist has the singular remark : *And straightway all the people, when they saw him, were greatly amazed.* What could there possibly be so greatly to amaze the people in the arrival of Jesus with some disciples ? This remains, in spite of all the other means of explanation that have been devised, so thorough a mystery, that I cannot find so absurd as Fritzsche esteems it, the idea of Euthymius, that Jesus having just descended from the Mount of Transfiguration, some of the heavenly radiance which had there shone around him was still visible, as on Moses when he came down from Sinai (Exod. xxxiv. 29 f.). That among this throng of people there were scribes who arraigned the disciples on the ground of their failure, and involved them in a dispute, is in and by itself quite natural ; but connected as it is with the exaggerations concerning the behaviour of the multitude, this feature also becomes suspicious, especially as the other two Evangelists have it not ; so that if it can be shown how the narrator might be led to insert it by a mental combination of his own, we shall have sufficient warrant for renouncing it. Shortly before (viii. 11), on the occasion of the demand of a sign from Jesus by the Pharisees, Mark says, ἤρξαντο συζητεῖν αὐτῷ, *they began to question with him*, apparently on the subject of his ability to work miracles ; and so here when the disciples show themselves unable to perform a miracle, he represents the scribes (the majority of whom belonged to the Pharisaic sect), as συζητοῦντας τοῖς μαθηταῖς, *questioning with the disciples*. In the succeeding description of the boy's state there is the same gradation as to particularity, except that Matthew is the one who alone has the expression σεληνιάζεται (*is lunatic*), which it is unfair to make a reproach to him, [41] since the reference of periodical disorders to the moon was not uncommon in the time of Jesus.[42] Mark alone calls the spirit that possessed the dumb boy (v. 17), and *deaf* (v. 25). The emission of inarticulate sounds by epileptics during their fits, might be regarded as the dumbness of the demon, and their incapability of noticing any words addressed to them, as his deafness.

When the father has informed Jesus of the subject of dispute and of the inability of the disciples to relieve the boy, Jesus breaks forth into the exclamation, *O faithless and perverse generation*, etc. On a comparison of the close of the narrative in Matthew, where Jesus, when his disciples ask him why they could not cast out the demon, answers; *Because of your unbelief*, and proceeds to extol the power of faith, even though no larger than a grain of mustard seed, as sufficient to remove mountains (v. 19 ff.): it cannot be doubted that in this expression of dissatisfaction Jesus apostrophizes his disciples, in whose inability to cast out the demon, he finds a proof of their still deficient faith.[43] This concluding explanation of the want of power in the disciples, by their unbelief, Luke omits : and Mark not only imitates him in this, but also interweaves (v. 21–24), a by-scene between Jesus and the father, in which he first gives an amplified description of the symptoms of

---

[41] As Schulz appears to do, ut sup.
[42] See the passages quoted by Paulus, exeg. Handb. 1, b, s. 569, and by Winer, 1, s. 191 f.
[43] Thus Fritzsche, in loc.

the child's malady, drawn partly from Matthew, partly from his own resources, and then represents the father, on being required to believe, as confessing with tears the weakness of his faith, and his desire that it may be strengthened. Taking this together with the mention of the disputative scribes, we cannot err in supposing the speech of Jesus, *O faithless generation*, etc., in Mark and also in Luke to refer to the people, as distinguished from the disciples; in Mark, more particularly to the father, whose unbelief is intimated to be an impediment to the cure, as in another case (Matt. ix. 2), the faith of relatives appears to further the desired object. As however both the Evangelists give this aspect to the circumstances, because they do not here give the explanation of the inefficiency of the disciples by their unbelief, together with the declaration concerning the power of faith to remove mountains : we must inquire whether the connexion in which they place these discourses is more suitable than this in which they are inserted by Matthew. In Luke the declaration : *If ye have faith as a grain of mustard seed*, etc. (neither he nor Mark has, *Because of your unbelief*), occurs xvii. 5, 6, with only the slight variation, that instead of the mountain a tree is named ; but it is here destitute of any connexion either with the foregoing or the following context, and has the appearance of a short stray fragment, with an introduction, no doubt fictitious (of the same kind as Luke xi. 1, xiii. 23), in the form of an entreaty from the disciples : *Lord, increase our faith*. Mark gives the sentence on the faith which removes mountains as the moral of the history of the cursed fig tree, where Matthew also has it a second time. But to this history the declaration is totally unsuitable, as we shall presently see ; and if we are unwilling to content ourselves with ignorance of the occasion on which it was uttered, we must accept its connexion in Matthew as the original one, for it is perfectly appropriate to a failure of the disciples in an attempted cure. Mark has sought to make the scene more effective by other additions, beside this episode with the father ; he tells us that the people ran together that they might observe what was passing, that after the expulsion of the demon the boy was *as one dead, insomuch that many said, he is dead ;* but that Jesus, taking him by the hand, as he does elsewhere with the dead (Matt. ix. 25), lifts him up and restores him to life.

After the completion of the cure, Luke dismisses the narrative with a brief notice of the astonishment of the people ; but the two first synoptists pursue the subject by making the disciples, when alone with Jesus, ask him why they were not able to cast out the demon ? In Matthew the immediate reply of Jesus accounts for their incapability by their unbelief; but in Mark, his answer is, *This kind goeth not out but by prayer and fasting*, which Matthew also adds after the discourse on unbelief and the power of faith. This seems to be an unfortunate connexion of Matthew's ; for if fasting and praying were necessary for the cure, the disciples, in case they had not previously fasted, could not have cast out the demon even if they had possessed the firmest faith.[44] Whether these two reasons given by Jesus for the inability of the disciples can be made consistent by the observation, that fasting and prayer are means of strengthening faith ;[45] or whether we are are to suppose with Schleiermacher an association of two originally unrelated passages, we will not here attempt to decide. That such a spiritual and corporeal discipline on the part of the exorcist should have effect on the possessed, has been held surprising : it has been thought with Porphyry,[46] that it would rather be to the purpose that the patient should observe this discipline, and hence it has

[44] Schleiermacher, s. 150.
[45] Köster, Immanuel, s. 197 ; Fritzsche, in loc.
[46] De abstinent. ii. p. 204 and 417 f. ; Vid. Winer, 1, s. 191.

been supposed that the προσευχὴ καὶ νηστεία, *prayer and fasting*, were pre-scribed to the demoniac as a means of making the cure radical.[47] But this is evidently in contradiction to the text. For if fasting and praying on the part of the patient were necessary for the success of the cure, it must have been gradual and not sudden, as all cures are which are attributed to Jesus in the gospels, and as this is plainly enough implied to be by the words, καὶ ἐθεραπεύθη ὁ παῖς ἀπὸ τῆς ὥρας ἐκείνης, *and the child was cured from that very hour*, in Matthew, and the word ἰάσατο, *he cured*, placed between ἐπετίμησε κ. τ. λ. *Jesus rebuked the unclean spirit*, and ἀπέδωκε κ. τ. λ. *delivered him again to his father*, in Luke. It is true Paulus turns the above expression of Matthew to his advantage, for he understands it to mean that from that time forward the boy, by the application of the prescribed discipline, gradually recovered. But we need only observe the same form of expression where it elsewhere occurs as the final sentence in narratives of cures, to be convinced of the impossibility of such an interpretation. When, for example, the story of the woman who had an issue of blood closes with the remark (Matt. ix. 22) καὶ ἐσώθη ἡ γυνὴ ἀπὸ ὥρας ἐκείνης, this will hardly be translated, *et exinde mulier paulatim servabatur* : it can only mean : *servata est (et servatam se præbuit) ab illo temporis momento*. Another point to which Paulus appeals as a proof that Jesus here commenced a cure which was to be consummated by degrees, is the expression of Luke, ἀπέδωκεν αὐτὸν τῷ πατρὶ αὐτοῦ, *he delivered him again to his father*, which, he argues, would have been rather superfluous, if it were not intended to imply a recommendation to special care. But the more immediate signification of ἀποδίδωμι is not to deliver or give up, but to give back ; and therefore in the above expression the only sense is : *puerum, quem sanandum acceperat, sanatum reddidit*, that is, the boy who had fallen into the hands of a strange power—of the demon—was re-stored to the parents as their own. Lastly, how arbitrary is it in Paulus to take the expression ἐκπορεύεται, *goeth out* (Matt. v. 21), in the closer significa-tion of a total departure, and to distinguish this from the preliminary departure which followed on the bare word of Jesus (v. 18) ! Thus in this case, as in every other, the gospels present to us, not a cure which was protracted through days and weeks, but a cure which was instantaneously completed by one miracle : hence the *fasting and prayer* cannot be regarded as a prescrip-tion for the patient.

With this whole history must be compared an analogous narrative in 2 Kings iv. 29 ff. Here the prophet Elisha attempts to bring a dead child to life, by sending his staff by the hands of his servant Gehazi, who is to lay it on the face of the child ; but this measure does not succeed, and Elisha is obliged in his own person to come and call the boy to life. The same relation that exists in this Old Testament story between the prophet and his servant, is seen in the New Testament narrative between the Messiah and his disciples : the latter can do nothing without their master, but what was too difficult for them, he effects with certainty. Now this feature is a clue to the tendency of both narratives, namely, to exalt their master by exhibiting the distance between him and his most intimate disciples ; or, if we compare the evan-gelical narrative before us with that of the demoniacs of Gadara, we may say : the latter case was made to appear one of extreme difficulty in itself ; the former, by the relation in which the power of Jesus, which is adequate to the occasion, is placed to the power of the disciples, which, however great in other instances, was here insufficient.

Of the other more briefly narrated expulsions of demons, the cure of a

---

[47] Paulus, exeg. Handb. 2, s. 471 f.

dumb demoniac and of one who was blind also, has been already sufficiently examined in connexion with the accusation of a league with Beelzebub: as also the cure of the woman who was bowed down, in our general considerations on the demoniacs. The cure of the possessed daughter of the Canaanitish woman (Matt. xv. 22 ff.; Mark vii. 25 ff.) has no further peculiarity than that it was wrought by the word of Jesus at a distance: a point of which we shall speak later.

According to the evangelical narratives, the attempt of Jesus to expel the demon succeeded in every one of these cases. Paulus remarks that cures of this kind, although they contributed more than anything else to impress the multitude with veneration for Jesus, were yet the easiest in themselves, and even De Wette sanctions a psychological explanation of the cures of demoniacs, though of no others.[48] With these opinions we cannot but agree; for if we regard the real character of the demoniacal state as a species of madness accompanied by a convulsive tendency of the nervous system, we know that psychical and nervous disorders are most easily wrought upon by psychical influence;—an influence to which the surpassing dignity of Jesus as a prophet, and eventually even as the Messiah himself, presented all the requisite conditions. There is, however, a marked gradation among these states, according as the psychical derangement has more or less fixed itself corporeally, and the disturbance of the nervous system has become more or less habitual, and shared by the rest of the organization. We may therefore lay down the following rule: the more strictly the malady was confined to mental derangement, on which the word of Jesus might have an immediate moral influence, or in a comparatively slight disturbance of the nervous system, on which he would be able to act powerfully through the medium of the mind, the more possible was it for Jesus *by his word* λόγῳ (Matt viii. 16), and *instantly* παραχρῆμα (Luke xiii. 13), to put an end to such states: on the other hand, the more the malady had already confirmed itself, as a bodily disease, the more difficult is it to believe that Jesus was able to relieve it in a purely psychological manner and at the first moment. From this rule results a second: namely, that to any extensive psychological influence on the part of Jesus the full recognition of his dignity as a prophet was requisite; whence it follows that at times and in districts where he had long had that reputation, he could effect more in this way than where he had it not.

If we apply these two measures to the cures in the gospels, we shall find that the first, viz., that of the demoniac in the synagogue at Capernaum, is not, so soon as we cease to consider the Evangelist's narrative of it circumstantially correct, altogether destitute of probability. It is true that the words attributed to the demon seem to imply an intuitive knowledge of Jesus; but this may be probably accounted for by the supposition that the widely-spread fame of Jesus in that country, and his powerful discourse in the synagogue, had impressed the demoniac with the belief, if not that Jesus was the Messiah, as the Evangelists say, at least that he must be a prophet: a belief that would give effect to his words. As regards the state of this demoniac we are only told of his fixed idea (that he was possessed), and of his attacks of convulsions; his malady may therefore have been of the less rooted kind, and accessible to psychological influence. The cure of the Gadarenes is attended with more difficulty in both points of view. Firstly, Jesus was comparatively little known on the eastern shore; and secondly, the state of these demoniacs is described as so violent and deep-seated a mania, that a word from Jesus

---

[48] Paulus, exeg. Handb. 1, b, s. 438; L. J. I, a, s. 223; De Wette, bibl. Dogm. § 222, Anm. c.

could hardly suffice to put an end to it.   Here therefore the natural explanation of Paulus will not suffice, and if we are to regard the narrative as having
any foundation in fact, we must suppose that the description of the demoniac's
state, as well as other particulars, has been exaggerated by the legend.   The
same judgment must be passed in relation to the cure of the boy who was
lunatic, since an epilepsy which had existed from infancy (Mark v. 21) and the
attacks of which were so violent and regular, must be too deeply rooted in the
system for the possibility of so rapid and purely psychological a cure to be
credible.   That even dumbness and a contraction of many years' duration,
which we cannot with Paulus explain as a mere insane imagination that speech
or an erect carriage was not permitted,[49]—that these afflictions should disappear at a word, no one who is not committed to dogmatical opinions can
persuade himself.   Lastly, least of all is it to be conceived, that even without
the imposing influence of his presence, the miracle-worker could effect a cure
at a distance, as Jesus is said to have done on the daughter of the Canaanitish
woman.

Thus in the nature of things there is nothing to prevent the admission, that
Jesus cured many persons who suffered from supposed demoniacal insanity or
nervous disorder, in a psychical manner, by the ascendancy of his manner
and words (if indeed Venturini[50] and Kaiser[51] are not right in their conjecture,
that patients of this class often believed themselves to be cured, when in fact
the crisis only of their disorder had been broken by the influence of Jesus ;
and that the Evangelists state them to have been cured because they learned
nothing further of them, and thus knew nothing of their probable relapse).
But while granting the possibility of many cures, it is evident that in this field
the legend has not been idle, but has confounded the easier cases, which alone
could be cured psychologically, with the most difficult and complicated, to
which such a treatment was totally inapplicable.[52]   Is the refusal of a sign on
the part of Jesus reconcilable with such a manifestation of power as we have
above defined,—or must even such cures as can be explained psychologically,
but which in his age must have seemed miracles, be denied in order to make
that refusal comprehensible ?   We will not here put this alternative otherwise
than as a question.

If in conclusion we cast a glance on the gospel of John, we find that it does
not even mention demoniacs and their cure by Jesus.   This omission has not
seldom been turned to the advantage of the Apostle John, the alleged author,
as indicating a superior degree of enlightenment.[53]   If however this apostle
did not believe in the reality of possession by devils, he must have had, as the
author of the fourth gospel, according to the ordinary view of his relation to
the synoptical writers, the strongest motives for rectifying their statements,
and preventing the dissemination of what he held to be a false opinion, by
setting the cures in question in a true light.   But how could the Apostle John
arrive at the rejection of the opinion that the above diseases had their foundation in demoniacal possession ?   According to Josephus it was at that period
a popular Jewish opinion, from which a Jew of Palestine who, like John, did
not visit a foreign land until late in life, would hardly be in a condition to

---

[49] Exeg. Handb. in loc.
[50] Natürliche Geschichte, 2, s. 429.
[51] Bibl. Theol. 1, s. 196.
[52] Among the transient disorders on which Jesus may have acted psychologically, we may
perhaps number the fever of Peter's mother-in-law, which Jesus is said to have cured, Matt.
viii. 14 ff. parall.
[53] It is so more or less by Eichhorn, in the allg. Bibliothek, 4, s. 435 ; Herder, von Gottes
Sohn u. s. f., s. 20 ; Wegscheider, Einl. in das Evang. Joh., s. 313 ; De Wette, bibl. Dogm.,
§ 269.

liberate himself; it was, according to the nature of things and the synoptical accounts, the opinion of Jesus himself, John's adored master, from whom the favourite disciple certainly would not be inclined to swerve even a hair's breadth. But if John shared with his cotemporaries and with Jesus himself the notion of real demoniacal possession, and if the cure of demoniacs formed the principal part, nay, perhaps the true foundation of the alleged miraculous powers of Jesus: how comes it that the Apostle nevertheless makes no mention of them in his gospel? That he passed over them because the other Evangelists had collected enough of such histories, is a supposition that ought by this time to be relinquished, since he repeats more than one history of a miracle which they had already given; and if it be said that he repeated these because they needed correction,—we have seen, in our examination of the cures of demoniacs, that in many a reduction of them to their simple historical elements would be very much in place. There yet remains the supposition that, the histories of demoniacs being incredible or offensive to the cultivated Greeks of Asia Minor, among whom John is said to have written, he left them out of his gospel for the sake of accommodating himself to their ideas. But we must ask, could or should an apostle, out of mere accommodation to the refined ears of his auditors, withhold so essential a feature of the agency of Jesus? Certainly this silence, supposing the authenticity of the three first gospels, rather indicates an author who had not been an eye-witness of the ministry of Jesus; or, according to our view, at least one who had not at his command the original tradition of Palestine, but only a tradition modified by Hellenistic influence, in which the expulsions of demons, being less accordant with the higher culture of the Greeks, were either totally suppressed or kept so far in the background that they might have escaped the notice of the author of the gospel.

§ 94.

CURES OF LEPERS.

Among the sufferers whom Jesus healed, the leprous play a prominent part, as might have been anticipated from the tendency of the climate of Palestine to produce cutaneous disease. When, according to the synoptical writers, Jesus directs the attention of the Baptist's messengers to the actual proofs which he had given of his Messiahship (Matt. ix. 5), he adduces among these, the cleansing of lepers; when, on the first mission of the disciples, he empowers them to perform all kinds of miracles, the cleansing of lepers is numbered among the first (Matt. x. 8), and two cases of such cures are narrated to us in detail.

One of these cases is common to all the synoptical writers, but is placed by them in two different connexions: namely, by Matthew, immediately after the delivery of the Sermon on the Mount (viii. 1 ff.); by the other Evangelists, at some period, not precisely marked, at the beginning of the ministry of Jesus in Galilee (Mark i. 40 ff.; Luke v. 12 ff.). According to the narratives, a leper comes towards Jesus, and falling on his knees, entreats that he may be cleansed; this Jesus effects by a touch, and then directs the leper to present himself to the priest in obedience to the law, that he may be pronounced clean (Lev. xiv. 2 ff.). The state of the man is in Matthew and Mark described simply by the word λεπρὸς, *a leper*; but in Luke more strongly, by the words, πλήρης λέπρας, *full of leprosy*. Paulus, indeed, regards the being thus replete with leprosy as a symptom that the patient was curable (the eruption and peeling of the leprosy on the entire skin being indicative of the healing crisis) ; and accordingly, that commentator represents the incident to himself in the following manner. The leper applied to Jesus in his character of Messiah for an opinion on his state, and, the result being favourable, for a declaration that he was clean (εἰ θέλεις, δύνασαί με καθαρίσαι), which might either spare him an application to the priest, or at all events give him a consolatory hope in making that application. Jesus expressing himself ready to make the desired examination (θέλω), stretched out his hand, in order to feel the patient, without allowing too near an approach while he was possibly still capable of communicating contagion ; and after a careful examination, he expressed, as its result, the conviction that the patient was no longer in a contagious state (καθαρίσθητι), whereupon quickly and easily (εὐθέως) the leprosy actually disappeared.[1]

Here, in the first place, the supposition that the leper was precisely at the crisis of healing is foreign to the text, which in the two first Evangelists speaks merely of leprosy, while the πλήρης λέπρας, of the third can mean nothing else than the Old Testament expression מְצֹרָע כַּשֶּׁלֶג (Exod. iv. 6 ; Num. xii. 10 ; 2 Kings v. 27), which, according to the connexion in every instance, signifies the worst stage of leprosy. That the word καθαρίζειν in the Hebraic and Hellenistic use of the Greek language, might also mean merely *to pronounce clean* is not to be denied, only it must retain the signification throughout the passage. But that after having narrated that Jesus had said, *Be thou clean*, καθαρίσθητι, Matthew should have added καὶ εὐθέως ἐκαθαρίσθη κ. τ. λ. in the sense that thus the sick man was actually pronounced clean by Jesus, is, from the absurd tautology such an interpretation would introduce, so inconceivable, that we must here, and consequently throughout the narrative, understand the word καθαρίζεσθαι of actual cleansing. It is sufficient to remind the reader of the expressions λεπροὶ καθαρίζονται, *the lepers are cleansed* (Matt. xi. 5), and λεπροὺς καθαρίζετε, *cleanse the lepers* (Matt. x. 8), where neither can the latter word signify merely to pronounce clean, nor can it have another meaning than in the narrative before us. But the point in which the natural interpretation the most plainly betrays its weakness, is the disjunction of θέλω, *I will*, from καθαρίσθητι, *be thou clean*. Who can persuade himself that these words, united as they are in all the three narratives, were separated by a considerable pause—that θέλω was spoken during or more properly before the manipulation, καθαρίσθητι after, when all the Evangelists represent the two words as having been uttered by Jesus without separation, whilst he touched the leper? Surely, if the alleged sense had been the original one, at least one of the Evangelists, instead of the words ἥψατο αὐτοῦ ὁ Ἰησοῦς λέγων· θέλω, καθαρίσθητι, *Jesus touched him, saying, I will, be thou clean*, would have substituted the more accurate expression, ὁ Ἰ. ἀπεκρίνατο· θέλω, καὶ ἁψάμενος αὐτοῦ εἶπε· καθαρίσθητι, *Jesus answered, I will ; and having touched him, said : be thou clean*. But if καθαρίσθητι was spoken in one breath with θέλω, so that Jesus announces the cleansing simply as a result of his will without any intermediate examination, the former word cannot possibly signify a mere declaration of cleanness, to which a previous examination would be requisite, and it must signify an actual making clean. It follows, therefore, that the word ἅπτεσθαι in this connexion is not to be understood of an exploratory manipulation, but, as in all other narratives of the same class, of a curative touch.

In support of his natural explanation of this incident, Paulus appeals to the rule, that invariably the ordinary and regular is to be presupposed in a narra-

---

[1] Exeg. Handb., I, b, s. 698 ff.

tive where the contrary is not expressly indicated. [2] But this rule shares the ambiguity which is characteristic of the entire system of natural interpretation, since it leaves undecided what is ordinary and regular in our estimation, and what was so in the ideas of the author whose writings are to be explained. Certainly, if I have a Gibbon before me, I must in his narratives presuppose only natural causes and occurrences when he does not expressly convey the contrary, because to a writer of his cultivation, the supernatural is at the utmost only conceivable as a rare exception. But the case is altered when I take up an Herodotus, in whose mode of thought the intervention of higher powers is by no means unusual and out of rule ; and when I am considering a collection of anecdotes which are the product of Jewish soil, and the object of which is to represent an individual as a prophet of the highest rank —as a man in the most intimate connexion with the Deity, to meet with the supernatural is so completely a thing of course, that the rule of the rationalists must here be reversed, and we must say : where, in such narratives, importance is attached to results which, regarded as natural, would have no importance whatever,—*there*, supernatural causes must be expressly excluded, if we are not to presuppose it the opinion of the narrator that such causes were in action. Moreover, in the history before us, the extraordinary character of the incident is sufficiently indicated by the statement, that the leprosy left the patient immediately on the word of Jesus. Paulus, it is true, contrives, as we have already observed, to interpret this statement as implying a gradual, natural healing, on the ground that $\varepsilon\vartheta\acute{\varepsilon}\omega\varsigma$, the word by which the Evangelists determine the time of the cure, signifies, according to the different connexions in which it may occur, in one case *immediately*, in another merely *soon*, and *unobstructedly*. Granting this, are we to understand the words $\varepsilon\vartheta\acute{\varepsilon}\omega\varsigma\ \acute{\varepsilon}\xi\acute{\varepsilon}\beta\alpha\lambda\varepsilon\nu$ $\alpha\grave{\upsilon}\tau\grave{o}\nu$, which follow in close connexion in Mark (v. 43), as signifying that soon and without hindrance Jesus sent the cleansed leper away ? Or is the word to be taken in a different sense in two consecutive verses ?

We conclude, then, that in the intention of the evangelical writers the instantaneous disappearance of the leprosy in consequence of the word and touch of Jesus, is the fact on which their narratives turn. Now to represent the possibility of this to one's self is quite another task than to imagine the instantaneous release of a man under the grasp of a fixed idea, or a permanently invigorating impression on a nervous patient. Leprosy, from the thorough derangement of the animal fluids of which it is the symptom, is the most obstinate and malignant of cutaneous diseases ; and that a skin corroded by this malady should by a word and touch instantly become pure and healthy, is, from its involving the immediate effectuation of what would require a long course of treatment, so inconceivable, [3] that every one who is free from certain prejudices (as the critic ought always to be) must involuntarily be reminded by it of the realm of fable. And in the fabulous region of Oriental and more particularly of Jewish legend, the sudden appearance and disappearance of leprosy presents itself the first thing. When Jehovah endowed Moses, as a preparation for his mission into Egypt, with the power of working all kinds of signs, amongst other tokens of this gift he commanded him to put his hand into his bosom, and when he drew it out again, it was covered with leprosy ; again he was commanded to put it into his bosom, and on drawing it out a second time it was once more clean (Exod iv. 6, 7). Subsequently, on account of an attempt at rebellion against Moses, his sister Miriam was suddenly stricken with leprosy, but on the intercession of Moses was soon

---

[2] Ut sup. s. 705, and elsewhere.
[3] Compare Hase, L. J., § 86.

healed (Num. xii. 10 ff.). Above all, among the miracles of the prophet Elisha the cure of a leper plays an important part, and to this event Jesus himself refers (Luke iv. 27.) The Syrian general, Naaman, who suffered from leprosy, applied to the Israelitish prophet for his aid ; the latter sent to him the direction to wash seven times in the river Jordan, and on Naaman's observance of this prescription the leprosy actually disappeared but was subsequently transferred by the prophet to his deceitful servant Gehazi (2 Kings v.). I know not what we ought to need beyond these Old Testament narratives to account for the origin of the evangelical anecdotes. What the first Goël was empowered to do in the fulfilment of Jehovah's commission, the second Goël must also be able to perform, and the greatest of prophets must not fall short of the achievements of any one prophet. If then, the cure of leprosy was without doubt included in the Jewish idea of the Messiah ; the Christians, who believed the Messiah to have really appeared in the person of Jesus, had a yet more decided inducement to glorify his history by such traits, taken from the Mosaic and prophetic legend ; with the single difference that, in accordance with the mild spirit of the New Covenant (Luke ix. 55 f.) they dropped the punitive side of the old miracles.

Somewhat more plausible is the appeal of the rationalists to the absence of an express statement, that a miraculous cure of the leprosy is intended in the narrative of the ten lepers, given by Luke alone (xvii. 12 ff.). Here neither do the lepers expressly desire to be cured, their words being only, *Have mercy on us* ; nor does Jesus utter a command directly referring to such a result, for he merely enjoins them to show themselves to the priests : and the rationalists avail themselves of this indirectness in his reply, as a help to their supposition, that Jesus, after ascertaining the state of the patients, encouraged them to subject themselves to the examination of the priests, which resulted in their being pronounced clean, and the Samaritan returned to thank Jesus for His encouraging advice. [4] But mere advice does not call forth so ardent a demonstration of gratitude as is here described by the words ἔπεσεν ἐπὶ πρόσωπον, *he fell down on his face ;* still less could Jesus desire that because his advice had had a favourable issue, all the ten should have returned, and returned to glorify God—for what ? that he had enabled Jesus to give them such good advice ? No : a more real service is here presupposed ; and this the narrative itself implies, both in attributing the return of the Samaritan to his discovery that he was healed (ἰδὼν ὅτι ἰάθη), and in making Jesus indicate the reason why thanks were to be expected from all, by the words : οὐχὶ οἱ δέκα ἐκαθαρίσθησαν ; *Were there not ten cleansed ?* Both these expressions can only by an extremely forced interpretation be made to imply, that because the lepers saw the correctness of the judgment of Jesus in pronouncing them clean, one of them actually returned to thank him, and the others ought to have returned. But that which is most decisive against the natural explanation is this sentence : *And as they went they were cleansed,* ἐν τῷ ὑπάγειν αὐτοὺς ἐκαθαρίσθησαν. If the narrator intended, according to the above interpretation, merely to say : the lepers having gone to the priest, and showed themselves to him, were pronounced clean : he must at least have said : πορευθέντες ἐκαθαρίσθησαν, *having made the journey they were cleansed,* whereas the deliberate choice of the expression ἐν τῷ ὑπάγειν (*while in the act of going*), incontestibly shows that a healing effected during the journey is intended. Thus here also we have a miraculous cure of leprosy, which is burdened with the same difficulties as the former anecdote ; the origin of which is, however, as easily explained.

But in this narrative there is a peculiarity which distinguishes it from the

---

[4] Paulus, L. J. 1, b, s. 68.

former. Here there is no simple cure, nay, the cure does not properly form the main object of the narrative : this lies rather in the different conduct of the cured, and the question of Jesus, *were there not ten cleansed*, etc. (v. 17), forms the point of the whole, which thus closes altogether morally, and seems to have been narrated for the sake of the instruction conveyed.[5] That the one who appears as a model of thankfulness happens to be a Samaritan, cannot pass without remark, in the narrative of the Evangelist who alone has the parable of the Good Samaritan. As there two Jews, a priest and a Levite, show themselves pitiless, while a Samaritan, on the contrary, proves exemplarily compassionate : so here, nine unthankful Jews stand contrasted with one thankful Samaritan. May it not be then (in so far as the sudden cure of these lepers cannot be historical) that we have here, as well as there, a parable pronounced by Jesus, in which he intended to represent gratitude, as in the other case compassion, in the example of a Samaritan ? It would then be with the present narrative as some have maintained it to be with the history of the temptation. But in relation to this we have both shown, and given the reason, that Jesus never made himself immediately figure in a parable, and this he must have done if he had given a narrative of ten lepers once healed by him. If then we are not inclined to relinquish the idea that something originally parabolic is the germ of our present narrative, we must represent the case to ourselves thus: from the legends of cures performed by Jesus on lepers, on the one hand ; and on the other, from parables in which Jesus (as in that of the compassionate Samaritan) presented individuals of this hated race as models of various virtues, the Christian legend wove this narrative, which is therefore partly an account of a miracle and partly a parable.

§ 95.

CURES OF THE BLIND.

One of the first places among the sufferers cured by Jesus is filled (also agreeably to the nature of the climate [1]) by the blind, of whose cure again we read not only in the general descriptions which are given by the Evangelists (Matt. xv. 30 f. ; Luke vii. 21), and by Jesus himself (Matt. xi. 5), of his messianic works, but also in some detailed narratives of particular cases. We have indeed more of these cures than of the kind last noticed, doubtless because blindness, as a malady affecting the most delicate and complicated of organs, admitted a greater diversity of treatment. One of these cures of the blind is common to all the synoptical writers ; the others (with the exception of the blind and dumb demoniac in Matthew, whom we need not here reconsider) are respectively peculiar to the first, second, and fourth Evangelists.

The narrative common to all the three synoptical writers is that of a cure of blindness wrought by Jesus at Jericho, on his last journey to Jerusalem (Matt. xx. 29 parall.) : but there are important differences both as to the object of the cure, Matthew having two blind men, the two other Evangelists only one ; and also as to its locality, Luke making it take place on the entrance of Jesus into Jericho, Matthew and Mark on his departure out of Jericho. Moreover the touching of the eyes, by which, according to the first evangelist, Jesus effected the cure, is not mentioned by the two other narrators, Of these differences the latter may be explained by the observation, that though Mark and Luke are silent as to the touching, they do not there-

---

[5] Schleiermacher, über den Lukas, s. 215.
[1] Vid. Winer, Realw., Art. Blinde.

fore deny it: the first, relative to the number cured, presents a heavier difficulty. To remove this it has been said by those who give the prior authority
to Matthew, that one of the two blind men was possibly more remarkable
than the other, on which account he alone was retained in the first tradition ;
but Matthew, as an eye-witness, afterwards supplied the second blind man.
On this supposition Luke and Mark do not contradict Matthew, for they nowhere deny that another besides their single blind man was healed; neither
does Matthew contradict them, for where there are two, there is also one. [2]
But when the simple narrator speaks of one individual in whom something
extraordinary has happened, and even, like Mark, mentions his name, it is
plain that he tacitly contradicts the statement that it happened in two individuals—to contradict it expressly there was no occasion. Let us turn then
to the other side and, taking the singular number of Mark and Luke as the
original one, conjecture that the informant of Matthew (the latter being
scarcely on this hypothesis an eye-witness) probably mistook the blind man's
guide for a second blind man.[3] Hereby a decided contradiction is admitted,
while to account for it an extremely improbable cause is superfluously invented. The third difference relates to the place ; Matthew and Mark have
ἐκπορευομένων ἀπὸ, as *they departed from*, Luke, ἐν τῷ ἐγγίζειν εἰς Ἱεριχὼ, as
they came nigh to Jericho. If there be any whom the words themselves fail to
convince that this difference is irreconcilable, let them read the forced attempts to render these passages consistent with each other, which have been
made by commentators from Grotius down to Paulus.

Hence it was a better expedient which the older harmonists [4] adopted, and
which has been approved by some modern critics.[5] In consideration of the
last-named difference, they here distinguished two events, and held that Jesus
cured a blind man first on his entrance into Jericho (according to Luke), and
then again on his departure from that place (according to Matthew and Luke).
Of the other divergency, relative to the number, these harmonists believed
that they had disencumbered themselves by the supposition that Matthew
connected in one event the two blind men, the one cured on entering and
the other on leaving Jericho, and gave the latter position to the cure of both.
But if so much weight is allowed to the statement of Matthew relative to the
locality of the cure, as to make it, in conjunction with that of Mark, a reason
for supposing two cures, one at each extremity of the town, I know not why
equal credit should not be given to his numerical statement, and Storr appears to me to proceed more consistently when, allowing equal weight to both
differences, he supposes that Jesus on his entrance into Jericho, cured one
blind man (Luke) and subsequently on his departure two (Matthew).[6] The
claim of Matthew is thus fully vindicated, but on the other hand that of Mark
is denied. For if the latter be associated with Matthew, as is here the case,
for the sake of his locality, it is necessary to do violence to his numerical
statement, which taken alone would rather require him to be associated with
Luke ; so that to avoid impeaching either of his statements, which on this
system of interpretation is not admissible, his narrative must be equally de-
tached from that of both the other Evangelists. Thus we should have three
distinct cures of the blind at Jericho : 1st, the cure of one blind man on the
entrance of Jesus, 2nd, that of another on his departure, and 3rd, the cure of
two blind men, also during the departure ; in all, of four blind men. Now to

[2] Gratz, Comm z. Matth. 2, s. 323.
[3] Paulus, exeg. Handb. 3, a, s. 44.
[4] Schulz, Anmerkungen zu Michaelis, 2, s. 105.
[5] Sieffert, ut sup. s. 104.
[6] Ueber den Zweck der evang. Geschichte und der Briefe Joh., s. 345.

separate the second and third cases is indeed difficult. For it will not be maintained that Jesus can have gone out by two different gates at the same time, and it is nearly as difficult to imagine that having merely set out with the intention of leaving Jericho, he returned again into the town, and not until afterwards took his final departure. But, viewing the case more generally, it is scarcely an admissible supposition, that three incidents so entirely similar thus fell together in a group. The accumulation of cures of the blind is enough to surprise us ; but the behaviour of the companions of Jesus is incomprehensible ; for after having seen in the first instance, on entering Jericho, that they had acted in opposition to the designs of Jesus by rebuking the blind man for his importunity, since Jesus called the man to him, they nevertheless repeated this conduct on the second and even on the third occasion. Storr, it is true, is not disconcerted by this repetition in at least two incidents of this kind, for he maintains that no one knows whether those who had enjoined silence on going out of Jericho were not altogether different persons from those who had done the like on entering the town : indeed, supposing them to be the same, such a repetition of conduct which Jesus had implicitly disapproved, however unbecoming, was not therefore impossible, since even the disciples who had been present at the first miraculous feeding, yet asked, before the second, whence bread could be had for such a multitude? —but this is merely to argue the reality of one impossibility from that of another, as we shall presently see when we enter on the consideration of the two miraculous feedings. Further, not only the conduct of the followers of Jesus, but also almost every feature of the incident must have been repeated in the most extraordinary manner. In the one case as in the other, the blind men cry, *Have mercy upon us*, (or *me*,) *thou son of David* ; then (after silence has been enjoined on them by the spectators) Jesus commands that they should be brought to him : he next asks what they will that he should do to them ; they answer, that we may receive our sight ; he complies with their wish, and they gratefully follow him. That all this was so exactly repeated thrice, or even twice, is an improbability amounting to an impossibility ; and we must suppose, according to the hypothesis adopted by Sieffert in such cases, a legendary assimilation of different facts, or a traditionary variation of a single occurrence. If, in order to arrive at a decision, it be asked : what could more easily happen, when once the intervention of the legend is presupposed, than that one and the same history should be told first of one, then of several, first of the entrance, then of the departure ? it will not be necessary to discuss the other possibility, since this is so incomparably more probable that there cannot be even a momentary hesitation in embracing it as real. But in thus reducing the number of the facts, we must not with Sieffert stop short at two, for in that case not only do the difficulties with respect to the repetition of the same incident remain, but we fall into a want of logical sequency in admitting one divergency (in the number) as unessential, for the sake of removing another (in the locality). If it be further asked, supposing only one incident to be here narrated, which of the several narratives is the original one ? the statements as to the locality will not aid us in coming to a decision ; for Jesus might just as well meet a blind man on entering as on leaving Jericho. The difference in the number is more likely to furnish us with a basis for a decision, and it will be in favour of Mark and Luke, who have each only one blind man ; not, it is true, for the reason alleged by Schleiermacher,[7] namely, that Mark, by his mention of the blind man's name, evinces a more accurate acquaintance with the circumstances ; for Mark, from his propensity to individualize out of his own imagination, ought least of all to

[7] Ut sup. s. 237.

be trusted with respect to names which are given by him alone.   Our decision is founded on another circumstance.

It seems probable that Matthew was led to add a second blind man by his
recollection of a previous cure of two blind men narrated by him alone (ix.
27 ff.).   Here, likewise, when Jesus is in the act of departure,—from the
place, namely, where he had raised the ruler's daughter,—two blind men
follow him (those at Jericho are sitting by the way side), and in a similar
manner cry for mercy of the Son of David, who here also, as in the other
instance, according to Matthew, immediately cures them by touching their
eyes.   With these similarities there are certainly no slight divergencies ; nothing is here said of an injunction to the blind men to be silent, on the part of
the companions of Jesus ; and, while at Jericho Jesus immediately calls the
blind men to him, in the earlier case, they come in the first instance to him
when he is again in the house ; further, while there he asks them, what they
will have him to do to them ? here he asks, if they believe him able to cure
them ?   Lastly, the prohibition to tell what had happened, is peculiar to the
earlier incident.   The two narratives standing in this relation to each other,
an assimilation of them might have taken place thus : Matthew transferred
the two blind men and the touch of Jesus from the first anecdote to the
second ; the form of the appeal from the blind men, from the second to the
first.

The two histories, as they are given, present but few data for a natural
explanation.   Nevertheless the rationalistic commentators have endeavoured
to frame such an explanation.   When Jesus in the earlier occurrence asked
the blind men whether they had confidence in his power, he wished, say they,
to ascertain whether their trust in him would remain firm during the operation, and whether they would punctually observe his further prescriptions ; [8]
having then entered the house, in order to be free from interruption, he
examined, for the first time, their disease, and when he found it curable
(according to Venturini [9] it was caused by the fine dust of that country), he
assured the sufferers that the result should be according to the measure of
their faith.   Hereupon Paulus merely says briefly, that Jesus removed the
obstruction to their vision ; but he also must have imagined to himself something similar to what is described in detail by Venturini, who makes Jesus
anoint the eyes of the blind men with a strong water prepared beforehand,
and thus cleanse them from the irritating dust, so that in a short time their
sight returned.   But this natural explanation has not the slightest root in
the text ; for neither can the *faith* ($\pi i\sigma\tau\iota s$) required from the patient imply
anything else than, as in all similar cases, trust in the miraculous power of
Jesus, nor can the word $\eta\psi\alpha\tau o$, *he touched*, signify a surgical operation, but
merely that touch which appears in so many of the evangelical curative
miracles, whether as a sign or a conductor of the healing power of Jesus ;
of further prescriptions for the completion of the cure there is absolutely
nothing.   It is not otherwise with the cure of the blind at Jericho, where,
moreover, the two middle Evangelists do not even mention the touching of
the eyes.

If then, according to the meaning of the narrators, the blind instantaneously
receive their sight as a consequence of the simple word or touch of Jesus,
there are the same difficulties to be encountered here as in the former case
of the lepers.   For a disease of the eyes, however slight, as it is only engendered gradually by the reiterated action of the disturbing cause, is still

---

[8] Paulus, L. J. 1, a, s. 249.
[9] Natürl. Gesch. des Propheten von Naz. 2, s. 216.

less likely to disappear on a word or a touch ; it requires very complicated treatment, partly surgical, partly medical, and this must be pre-eminently the case with blindness, supposing it to be of a curable kind.   How should we represent to ourselves the sudden restoration of vision to a blind eye by a word or a touch ? as purely miraculous and magical ?   That would be to give up thinking on the subject.   As magnetic ?   There is no precedent of magnetism having influence over a disease of this nature.   Or, lastly, as psychical ? But blindness is something so independent of the mental life, so entirely corporeal, that the idea of its removal at all, still less of its sudden removal by means of a mental operation, is not to be entertained.   We must therefore acknowledge that an historical conception of these narratives is more than merely difficult to us ; and we proceed to inquire whether we cannot show it to be probable that legends of this kind should arise unhistorically.

We have already quoted the passage in which, according to the first and third gospels, Jesus in reply to the messengers of the Baptist who had to ask him whether he were the ἐρχόμενος (*he that should come*), appeals to his works. Now he here mentions in the very first place the cure of the blind, a significant proof that this particular miracle was expected from the Messiah, his words being taken from Isa. xxxv. 5, a prophecy interpreted messianically; and in a rabbinical passage above cited, among the wonders which Jehovah is to perform in the messianic times, this is enumerated, that he *oculos cæcorum aperiet, id quod per Elisam fecit.*[10]   Now Elisha did not cure a positive blindness, but merely on one occasion opened the eyes of his servant to a perception of the supersensual world, and on another, removed a blindness which had been inflicted on his enemies in consequence of his prayer (2 Kings vi. 17–20).   That these deeds of Elisha were conceived, doubtless with reference to the passage of Isaiah, as a real opening of the eyes of the blind, is proved by the above rabbinical passage, and hence cures of the blind were expected from the Messiah.[11]   Now if the Christian community, proceeding as it did from the bosom of Judaism, held Jesus to be the messianic personage, it must manifest the tendency to ascribe to him every messianic predicate, and therefore the one in question.

The narrative of the cure of a blind man at Bethsaida, and that of the cure of *a man that was deaf and had an impediment in his speech*, which are both peculiar to Mark (viii. 22 ff., vii. 32 ff.), and which we shall therefore consider together, are the especial favourites of all rationalistic commentators. If, they exclaim, in the other evangelical narratives of cures, the accessory circumstances by which the facts might be explained were but preserved as they are here, we could prove historically that Jesus did not heal by his mere word, and profound investigators might discover the natural means by which

---

[10] Vid. vol. i. p. 81, note.
[11] Elsewhere also we find proof that in those times the power of effecting miraculous cures, especially of blindness, was commonly ascribed to men who were regarded as favourites of the Deity.   Thus Tacitus, Hist. iv. 81, and Suetonius, Vespas. vii. tell us, that in Alexandria a blind man applied to Vespasian, shortly after he was made emperor, alleging that he did so by the direction of the god Serapis, with the entreaty that he would cure him of his blindness by wetting his eyes with his spittle.   Vespasian complied, and the result was that the blind man immediately had his sight restored.   As Tacitus attests the truth of this story in a remarkable manner, Paulus is probably not wrong in regarding the affair as the contrivance of adulatory priests, who to procure for the emperor the fame of a miracle-worker, and by this means to secure his favour on behalf of their god, by whose counsel the event was occasioned, hired a man to simulate blindness.   Ex. Handb. 2, s. 56 f.   However this may be, we see from the narrative what was expected, even beyond the limits of Palestine, of a man who, as Tacitus here expresses himself concerning Vespasian, enjoyed *favor e cælis* and an *inclinatio numinum.*

his cures were effected![12] And in fact chiefly on the ground of these narratives, in connexion with particular features in other parts of the second gospel, Mark has of late been represented, even by theologians who do not greatly favour this method of interpretation, as the patron of the naturalistic system.[13]

In the two cures before us, it is at once a good augury for the rationalistic commentators that Jesus takes both the patients apart from the multitude, for no other purpose, as they believe, than that of examining their condition medically, and ascertaining whether it were susceptible of relief. Such an examination is, according to these commentators, intimated by the Evangelist himself, when he describes Jesus as putting his fingers into the ears of the deaf man, by which means he discovered that the deafness was curable, arising probably from the hardening of secretions in the ear, and hereupon, also with the finger, he removed the hindrance to hearing. Not only are the words, *he put his fingers into his ears*, ἔβαλε τοὺς δακτύλους εἰς τὰ ὦτα, interpreted as denoting a surgical operation, but the words, *he touched his tongue*, ἥψατο τῆς γλώσσης, are supposed to imply that Jesus cut the ligament of the tongue in the degree necessary to restore the pliancy which the organ had lost. In like manner, in the case of the blind man, the words, *when he had put his hands upon him*, ἐπιθεὶς τὰς χεῖρας αὐτῷ, are explained as probably meaning that Jesus by pressing the eyes of the patient removed the crystalline lens which had become opaque. A further help to this mode of interpretation is found in the circumstance that both to the tongue of the man who had an impediment in his speech, and to the eyes of the blind man, Jesus applied spittle. Saliva has in itself, particularly in the opinion of ancient physicians,[14] a salutary effect on the eyes ; as, however, it in no case acts so rapidly as instantaneously to cure blindness and a defect in the organs of speech, it is conjectured, with respect to both instances, that Jesus used the saliva to moisten some medicament, probably a caustic powder; that the blind man only heard the spitting and saw nothing of the mixture of the medicaments, and that the deaf man, in accordance with the spirit of the age, gave little heed to the natural means, or that the legend did not preserve them. In the narrative of the deaf man the cure is simply stated, but that of the blind man is yet further distinguished, by its representing the restoration of his sight circumstantially, as gradual. After Jesus had touched the eyes of the patient as above mentioned, he asked him *if he saw aught* ; not at all, observes Paulus, in the manner of a miracle-worker, who is sure of the result, but precisely in the manner of a physician, who after performing an operation endeavours to ascertain if the patient is benefited. The blind man answers that he sees, but first indistinctly, so that men seem to him like trees. Here apparently the rationalistic commentator may triumphantly ask the orthodox one : if divine power for the working of cures stood at the command of Jesus, why did he not at once cure the blind man perfectly? If the disease presented an obstacle which he was not able to overcome, is it not clear from thence that his power was a finite, ordinarily human power? Jesus once more puts his hands on the eyes of the blind man, in order to aid the effect of the first operation, and only then is the cure completed.[15]

---

[12] These are nearly the words of Paulus, exeg. Handb. 2, s. 312, 391.

[13] De Wette, Beitrag zur Charakteristik des Evangelisten Markus, in Ullmann's und Umbreit's Studien, 1, 4, 789 ff. Comp. Köster, Immanuel, f. 72. On the other hand : comp. De Wette's exeg. Handb. 1, 2, s. 148 f.

[14] Pliny, H. N. xxviii. 7, and other passages in Wetstein.

[15] Paulus, ut sup. s. 312 f. 392 ff. ; Natürliche Geschichte, 3, s. 31 ff. 216 f. ; Köster, Immanuel, s. 188 ff.

The complacency of the rationalistic commentators in these narratives of Mark, is liable to be disturbed by the frigid observation, that, here also, the circumstances which are requisite to render the natural explanation possible are not given by the Evangelists themselves, but are interpolated by the said commentators. For in both cures Mark furnishes the saliva only; the efficacious powder is infused by Paulus and Venturini: it is they alone who make the introduction of the fingers into the ears first a medical examination and then an operation ; and it is they alone who, contrary to the signification of language, explain the words ἐπιτιθέναι τὰς χεῖρας ἐπὶ τοὺς ὀφθαλμοὺς, *to lay the hands upon the eyes*, as implying a surgical operation on those organs. Again, the circumstance that Jesus takes the blind man aside, is shown by the context (vii. 36, viii. 26) to have reference to the design of Jesus to keep the miraculous result a secret, not to the desire to be undisturbed in the application of natural means : so that all the supports of the rationalistic explanation sink beneath it, and the orthodox one may confront it anew. This regards the touch and the spittle either as a condescension towards the sufferers, who were thereby made more thoroughly sensible to whose power they owed their cure ; or as a conducting medium for the spiritual power of Christ, a medium with which he might nevertheless have dispensed.[16]   That the cure was gradual, is on this system accounted for by the supposition, that Jesus intended by means of the partial cure to animate the faith of the blind man, and only when he was thus rendered worthy was he completely cured ;[17] or it is conjectured that, owing to the malady being deep-seated, a sudden cure would perhaps have been dangerous.[18]

But by these attempts to interpret the evangelical narratives, especially in the last particular, the supernaturalistic theologians, who bring them forward, betake themselves to the same ground as the rationalists, for they are equally open to the charge of introducing into the narratives what is not in the remotest degree intimated by the text.   For where, in the procedure of Jesus towards the blind man, is there a trace that his design in the first instance was to prove and to strengthen the faith of the patient?   In that case, instead of the expression, *He asked him if he saw aught*, which relates only to his external condition, we must rather have read, as in Matt. ix. 28, *Believe ye that I am able to do this ?*   But what shall we say to the conjecture that a sudden cure might have been injurious !   The curative act of a worker of miracles is (according to Olshausen's own opinion) not to be regarded as the merely negative one of the removal of a disease, but also as the positive one of an impartation of new and fresh strength to the organ affected, whence the idea of danger from an instantaneous cure when wrought by miraculous agency, is not to be entertained. Thus no motive is to be discovered which could induce Jesus to put a restraint on the immediate action of his miraculous power, and it must therefore have been restricted, independently of his volition, by the force of the deep-seated malady.   This, however, is entirely opposed to the idea of the gospels, which represent the miraculous power of Jesus as superior to death itself ; it cannot therefore have been the meaning of our Evangelists.   If we take into consideration the peculiar characteristics of Mark as an author, it will appear that his only aim is to give dramatic effect to the scene.   Every sudden result is difficult to bring before the imagination : he who wishes to give to another a vivid idea of a rapid movement, first goes through it slowly, and a quick result is perfectly conceivable only when the narrator has shown the process in detail.

[16] For the former explanation, Hess, Geschichte Jesu, 1, s, 390 f.; for the latter, Olshausen, b, Comm. 1. s. 510.

[17] Kuinöl, in Marc., p. 110.

[18] Olshausen, s. 509.

Consequently a writer whose object it is to assist as far as may be the imagination of his reader, will wherever it is possible exhibit the propensity to render the immediate mediate, and when recording a sudden result, still to bring forward the successive steps that led to it.[19] So here Mark, or his informant, supposed that he was contributing greatly to the dramatic effect, when he inserted between the blindness of the man and the entire restoration of his sight, the partial cure, or the seeing men as trees, and every reader will say, from his own feeling, that this object is fully achieved.   But herein, as others also have remarked,[20] Mark is so far from manifesting an inclination to the natural conception of such miracles, that he, on the contrary, not seldom labours to aggrandize the miracle, as we have partly seen in the case of the Gadarene, and shall yet have frequent reason to remark.   In a similar manner may also be explained why Mark in these narratives which are peculiar to him (and elsewhere also, as in vi. 13, where he observes that the disciples anointed the sick with oil), mentions the application of external means and manifestations in miraculous cures.   That these means, the saliva particularly, were not in the popular opinion of that age naturally efficacious causes of the cure, we may be convinced by the narrative concerning Vespasian quoted above, as also by passages of Jewish and Roman authors, according to which saliva was believed to have a magical potency, especially against diseases of the eye.[21]   Hence Olshausen perfectly reproduces the conception of that age when he explains the touch, saliva, and the like, to be conductors of the superior power resident in the worker of miracles.   We cannot indeed make this opinion ours, unless with Olshausen we proceed upon the supposition of a parallelism between the miraculous power of Jesus and the agency of animal magnetism : a supposition which, for the explanation of the miracles of Jesus, especially of the one before us, is inadequate and therefore superfluous.   Hence we put this means merely to the account of the Evangelist.   To him also we may then doubtless refer the taking aside of the blind man, the exaggerated description of the astonishment of the people, (ὑπερπερισσῶς ἐξεπλήσσοντο ἅπαντες, vii. 37,) and the strict prohibition to tell any man of the cure.   This secrecy gave the affair a mysterious aspect, which, as we may gather from other passages, was pleasing to Mark. We have another trait belonging to the mysterious in the narratives of the cure of the deaf man, where Mark says, *And looking up to heaven he sighed* (vii. 34). What cause was there for sighing at that particular moment?   Was it the misery of the human race,[22] which must have been long known to Jesus from many melancholy examples?   Or shall we evade the difficulty by explaining the expression as implying nothing further than silent prayer or audible speech?[23]   Whoever knows Mark will rather recognise the exaggerating narrator in the circumstance that he ascribes to Jesus a deep emotion, on an occasion which could not indeed have excited it, but which, being accompanied by it, had a more mysterious appearance.   But above all, there appears to me to be an air of mystery in this, that Mark gives the authoritative word with which Jesus opened the ears of the deaf man in its original Syriac form, ἐφφαθά, as on the resuscitation of the daughter of Jairus, this Evangelist alone has the words ταλιθὰ κοῦμι (v. 41).   It is indeed said that these expressions are anything rather than magical forms ;[24] but that Mark chooses to give these authoritative words in a language foreign to his readers, to whom he is obliged

---

[19] Comp. De Wette, Kritik der Mosaischen Geschichte, s. 36 f.
[20] Fritzsche, Comm. in Marc., p. xliii.
[21] Vid. ap. Wetstein and Lightfoot, John ix. 6.
[22] Thus Fritzsche, after Euthymius, in Marc., p. 304.
[23] The former is the supposition of Kuinöl, the latter of Schott.
[24] Hess, Gesch. Jesu, 1, s. 391, Anm. 1.

at the same time to explain them, nevertheless proves that he must have attributed to this original form a special significance, which, as it appears from the context, can only have been a magical one. This inclination to the mysterious we may now retrospectively find indicated in the application of those outward means which have no relation to the result ; for the mysterious consists precisely in the presentation of infinite power through a finite medium, in the combination of the strongest effect with apparently inefficacious means.

If we have been unable to receive as historical the simple narrative given by all the synoptical writers of the cure of the blind man at Jericho, we are still less prepared to award this character to the mysterious description, given by Mark alone, of the cure of a blind man at Bethsaida, and we must regard it as a product of the legend, with more or less addition from the evangelical narrator. The same judgment must be pronounced on his narrative of the cure of the deaf man who had an impediment in his speech κωφὸς μογιλάλος ; for, together with the negative reasons already adduced against its historical credibility, there are not wanting positive causes for its mythical origin, since the prophecy relating to the messianic times, τότε ὦτα κωφῶν ἀκούσονται—τρανὴ δὲ ἔσται γλῶσσα μογιλάλων, the ears of the deaf shall be unstopped, the tongue of the dumb shall sing (Isa. xxxv. 5, 6), was in existence, and according to Matt. xi. 5, was interpreted literally.

If the narratives of Mark which we have just considered, seem at the first glance to be favourable to the natural explanation, the narrative of John, chap. ix., must, one would think, be unfavourable and destructive to it ; for here the question is not concerning a blind man, whose malady having originated accidentally, might be easier to remove, but concerning a man born blind. Nevertheless, as the expositors of this class are sharp-sighted, and do not soon lose courage, they are able even here to discover much in their favour. In the first place, they find that the condition of the patient is but vaguely described, however definite the expression, blind from his birth, τυφλὸν ἐκ γενετῆς may seem to sound. The statement of time which this expression includes, Paulus, it is true, refrains from overthrowing (though his forbearance is unwilling and in fact incomplete) : hence he has the more urgent necessity for attempting to shake the statement as to quality. Τυφλὸς is not to signify total blindness, and as Jesus tells the man to go to the pool of Siloam, not to get himself led thither, he must have still had some glimmering of eye-sight, by means of which he could himself find the way thither. Still more help do the rationalistic commentators find for themselves in the mode of cure adopted by Jesus. He says beforehand (v. 4) he must work the works of him that sent him while it is day, ἕως ἡμέρα ἐστὶν, for in the night no man can work ; a sufficient proof that he had not the idea of curing the blind man by a mere word, which he might just as well have uttered in the night—that, on the contrary, he intended to undertake a medical or surgical operation, for which certainly daylight was required. Further, the clay, πηλὸς, which Jesus made with his spittle, and with which he anointed the eyes of the blind man, is still more favourable to the natural explanation than the expression πτύσας having spit, in a former case, and hence it is a fertile source of questions and conjectures. Whence did John know that Jesus took nothing more than spittle and dust to make his eye-salve, Was he himself present, or did he understand it merely from the narrative of the cured blind man ? The latter could not : with his then weak glimmering of sight, correctly see what Jesus took : perhaps Jesus while he mixed a salve out of other ingredients accidentally spat upon the ground, and the patient fell into the error of supposing that the spittle made part of the salve. Still more : while or before Jesus put something on the eyes, did he not also remove something by extraction or friction, or otherwise effect a change in the state of these organs? This would be an essential fact which might easily be mistaken by the blind man and the spectators for a merely accessory circumstance. Lastly, the washing in the pool of Siloam which was prescribed to the patient was perhaps continued many days—was a protracted cure by means of the bath—and the words ἦλθε βλέπων *he came seeing*, do not necessarily imply that he came thus after his first bath, but that at a convenient time after the completion of his cure, he came again seeing.[25]

But, to begin at the beginning, the meaning here given to ἡμέρα and νύξ is too shallow even for Venturini,[26] and especially clashes with the context (v. 5), which throughout demands an interpretation of the words with reference to the speedy departure of Jesus.[27] As to the conjecture that the clay was made of medicinal ingredients of some kind or other, it is the more groundless, since it cannot be said here, as in the former case, that only so much is stated as the patient could learn by his hearing or by a slight glimmering of light, for, on this occasion, Jesus undertook the cure, not in private, but in the presence of his disciples. Concerning the further supposition of previous surgical operations, by which the anointing and washing, alone mentioned in the text, are reduced to mere accessories, nothing more is to be said, than that by this example we may see how completely the spirit of natural explanation despises all restraints, not scrupling to pervert the clearest words of the text in support of its arbitrary combinations. Further, when, from the circumstance that Jesus ordered the blind man to go to the pool of Siloam, it is inferred that he must have had a share of light, we may remark, in opposition to this, that Jesus merely told the patient *whither* he should go (ὕπαγεν); *how* he was to go, whether alone or with a guide, he left to his own discretion. Lastly, when the closely connected words *he went his way, therefore, and washed and came seeing,* ἀπῆλθεν οὖν καὶ ἐνίψατο καὶ ἦλθε βλέπων (v. 7 ; comp. v. 11) are stretched out into a process of cure lasting several weeks, it is just as if the words *veni, vidi, vici*, were translated thus : After my arrival I reconnoitred for several days, fought battles at suitable intervals, and finally remained conqueror.

Thus here also the natural explanation will not serve us, and we have still before us the narrative of a man born blind, miraculously cured by Jesus. That the doubts already expressed as to the reality of the cures of the blind, apply with increased force to the case of a man born blind, is self-evident. And they are aided in this instance by certain special critical reasons. Not one of three first Evangelists mentions this cure. Now, if in the formation of the apostolic tradition, and in the selection which it made from among the miracles of Jesus, any kind of reason was exercised, it must have taken the shape of the two following rules : first, to choose the greater miracles before those apparently less important; and secondly, those with which edifying discourses were connected, before those which were not thus distinguished. In the first respect, it is plain that the cure of a man blind from his birth, as the incomparably more difficult miracle, was by all means to be chosen rather than that of a man in whom blindness had supervened, and it is not to be conceived why, if Jesus really gave sight to a man born blind, nothing of this should have entered into the evangelical tradition, and from thence into the synoptical gospels. It is true that with this consideration of the magnitude of the miracles, a regard to the edifying nature of the discourses connected with them might not seldom come into collision, so that a less striking, but from the conversations which it caused, a more instructive miracle, might be preferred to one more striking, but presenting less of the

[25] Paulus, Comm. 4, s. 472.
[26] Natürliche Gesch. 3, s. 215.
[27] Vid. Tholuck and Lücke, in loc.

latter kind of interest.   But the cure of the blind man in John is accompanied
by very remarkable conversations, first, of Jesus with the disciples, then, of the
cured man with the magistrates, and lastly of Jesus with the cured man, such
as there is no trace of in the synoptical cures of the blind ; conversations in
which, if not the entire course of the dialogue, at least some aphoristic pearls
(as v. 4, 5, 39), were admirably suited to the purpose of three first Evangelists.
These writers, therefore, could not have failed to introduce the cure of the
man born blind into their histories, instead of their less remarkable and less
edifying cures of the blind, if the former had made a part of the evangelical
tradition whence they drew.   It might possibly have remained unknown to the
general Christian tradition, if it had taken place at a time and under circumstances which did not favour its promulgation—if it had been effected in a remote corner of the country, without further witnesses.   But Jesus performed
this miracle in Jerusalem, in the circle of his disciples ; it made a great sensation in the city, and was highly offensive to the magistracy, hence the affair must
have been known if it had really occurred ; and as we do not find it in the common evangelical tradition, the suspicion arises that it perhaps never did occur.
   But it will be said, the writer who attests it is the Apostle John. This, however, is too improbable, not only on account of the incredible nature of the contents of the narrative, which could thus hardly have proceeded from an eye-
witness, but also from another reason.   The narrator interprets the name
of the pool, Siloam, by the Greek ἀπεσταλμένος (v. 7) ; a false explanation,
for one who is sent is called שָׁלֻיחַ, whereas שִׁלֹחַ according to the most probable
interpretation signifies a waterfall.[28]   The Evangelist, however, chose the above
interpretation, because he sought for some significant relation between the
name of the pool, and the sending thither of the blind man, and thus seems to
have imagined that the pool had by a special providence received the name of
Sent, because at a future time the Messiah, as a manifestation of his glory, was
to send thither a blind man.[29]   Now, we grant that an apostle might give a
grammatically incorrect explanation, in so far as he is not held to be inspired,
and that even a native of Palestine might mistake the etymology of Hebrew
words, as the Old Testament itself shows ; nevertheless, such a play upon words
looks more like the laboured attempt of a writer remote from the event, than
of an eye-witness.   The eye-witness would have had enough of important
matters in the miracle which he had beheld, and the conversation to which he
had listened ; only a remote narrator could fall into the triviality of trying
to extort a significant meaning from the smallest accessory circumstance.
Tholuck and Lücke are highly revolted by this allegory, which, as the latter
expresses himself, approaches to absolute folly, hence they are unwilling to
admit that it proceeded from John, and regard it as a gloss.   As, however, all
critical authorities, except one of minor importance, present this particular,
such a position is sheer arbitrariness, and the only choice left us is either
with Olshausen, to edify ourselves by this interpretation as an apostolic one,[30]
or, with the author of the Probabilia, to number it among the indications that
the fourth gospel had not an apostolic origin.[31]
   The reasons which might prevent the author of the fourth gospel, or the
tradition whence he drew, from resting contented with the cures of the blind
narrated by the synoptical writers, and thus induce the one or the other to
frame the history before us, are already pointed out by the foregoing remarks.

[28] Vid. Paulus and Lücke, in loc.
[29] Thus Euthymius and Paulus, in loc.
[30] B. Comm. 2, s. 230, where, however, he refers the ἀπεσταλμένος to the outflow of the
spirit proceeding from God.
[31] S. 93.

The observation has been already made by others, that the fourth Evangelist has fewer miracles than the synoptical writers, but that this deficiency in number is compensated by a superiority in magnitude.[32] Thus while the other Evangelists have simple paralytics cured by Jesus, the fourth gospel has one who had been lame thirty-eight years ; while, in the former, Jesus resuscitates persons who had just expired, in the latter, he calls back to life one who had lain in the grave four days, in whom therefore it might be presumed that decomposition had begun ; and so here, instead of a cure of simple blindness, we have that of a man born blind,—a heightening of the miracle altogether suited to the apologetic and dogmatic tendency of this gospel. In what way the author, or the particular tradition which he followed, might be led to depict the various details of the narrative, is easily seen. The act of spitting, πτύειν, was common in magical cures of the eyes ; clay, πηλὸς, was a ready substitute for an eye-salve, and elsewhere occurs in magical proceedings ; [33] the command to wash in the pool of Siloam may have been an imitation of Elisha's order, that the leper Naaman should bathe seven times in the river Jordan. The conversations connected with the cure partly proceed from the tendency of the Gospel of John already remarked by Storr, namely, to attest and to render as authentic as possible both the cure of the man, and the fact of his having been born blind, whence the repeated examination of the cured man, and even of his parents ; partly they turn upon the symbolical meaning of the expressions, *blind* and *seeing*, *day* and *night*,—a meaning which it is true is not foreign to the synoptical writers, but which specifically belongs to the circle of images in favour with John.

§ 96.

CURES OF PARALYTICS. DID JESUS REGARD DISEASES AS PUNISHMENTS ? *

An important feature in the history of the cure of the man born blind has been passed over, because it can only be properly estimated in connexion with a corresponding one in the synoptical narratives of the cure of a paralytic (Matt. ix. 1 ff. ; Mark ii. 1 ff. ; Luke v. 17 ff.), which we have in the next place to consider. Here Jesus first declares to the sick man : ἀφέωνταί σοί αἱ ἁμαρτίαι σου, *thy sins are forgiven thee*, and then as a proof that he had authority to forgive sins, he cures him. It is impossible not to perceive in this a reference to the Jewish opinion, that any evil befalling an individual, and especially disease, was a punishment of his sins ; an opinion which, presented in its main elements in the Old Testament (Lev. xxvi. 14 ff. ; Deut. xxviii. 15 ff. ; 2 Chron. xxi. 15, 18 f.) was expressed in the most definite manner by the later Jews.[1] Had we possessed that synoptical narrative only, we must have believed that Jesus shared the opinion of his cotemporary fellow-countrymen on this subject, since he proves his authority to forgive sins (as the cause of disease) by an example of his power to cure disease (the consequence of sin). But, it is said, there are other passages where Jesus directly contradicts this Jewish opinion ; whence it follows, that what he then says to the paralytic was a mere accommodation to the ideas of the sick man, intended to promote his cure.[2]

The principal passage commonly adduced in support of this position, is the introduction to the history of the man born blind, which was last con-

---

[32] Köster, Immanuel, s. 79 ; Bretschneider, Probab., s. 122.
[33] Wetstein, in loc.
[1] Nedarim f. xli. 1. (Schöttgen, 1, p. 93) : *Dixit R. Chija fil. Abba : nullus ægrotus a morbo suo sanatur, donec ipsi omnia peccata remissa sint.*
[2] Hase, L. J. § 73. Fritzsche, in Matt., p. 335.

sidered (John ix. 1–3). Here the disciples, seeing on the road the man whom they knew to have been blind from his birth, put to Jesus the question, whether his blindness was the consequence of his own sins, or of those of his parents? The case was a peculiarly difficult one on the Jewish theory of retribution. With respect to diseases which attach themselves to a man in his course through life, an observer who has once taken a certain bias, may easily discover or assume some peculiar delinquencies on the part of this man as their cause. With respect to inborn diseases, on the contrary, though the old Hebraic opinion (Exod. xx. 5; Deut. v. 9; 2 Sam. iii. 29), it is true, presented the explanation that by these the sins of the fathers were visited on their posterity: yet as, for human regulations, the Mosaic law itself ordained that each should suffer for his own sins alone (Deut. xxiv. 16; 2 Kings xiv. 6); and as also, in relation to the penal justice of the Divine Being, the prophets predicted a similar dispensation (Jer. xxxi. 30; Ezek. xviii. 19 f.); rabbinical acumen resorted to the expedient of supposing, that men so afflicted might probably have sinned in their mother's womb,[3] and this was doubtless the notion which the disciples had in view in their question v. 2. Jesus says, in answer, that neither for his own sin nor for that of his parents, did this man come into the world blind; but in order that by the cure which he, as the Messiah, would effect in him, he might be an instrument in manifesting the miraculous power of God. This is generally understood as if Jesus repudiated the whole opinion, that disease and other evils were essentially punishments of sin. But the words of Jesus are expressly limited to the case before him; he simply says, that this particular misfortune had its foundation, not in the guilt of the individual, but in higher providential designs. The supposition that his expressions had a more general sense, and included a repudiation of the entire Jewish opinion, could only be warranted by other more decided declarations from him to that effect. As, on the contrary, according to the above observations, a narrative is found in the synoptical gospels which, simply interpreted, implies the concurrence of Jesus in the prevalent opinion, the question arises: which is easier, to regard the expression of Jesus in the synoptical narratives as an accommodation, or that in John as having relation solely to the case immediately before him?—a question which will be decided in favour of the latter alternative by every one who, on the one hand, knows the difficulties attending the hypothesis of accommodation as applied to the expressions of Jesus in the gospels, and on the other, is clear-sighted enough to perceive, that in the passage in question in the fourth gospel, there is not the slightest intimation that the declaration of Jesus had a more general meaning.

It is true that according to correct principles of interpretation, one Evange-list ought not to be explained immediately by another, and in the present case it is very possible that while the synoptical writers ascribe to Jesus the common opinion of his age, the more highly cultivated author of the fourth gospel may make him reject it: but that he also confined the rejection of the current opinion on the part of Jesus to that single case, is proved by the manner in which he represents Jesus as speaking on another occasion. When, namely, Jesus says to the man who had been lame thirty-eight years (John v.) and had just been cured, μηκέτι ἁμάρτανε, ἵνα μὴ χεῖρόν τί σοι γένηται (v. 14), *Sin no more, lest a worse thing come unto thee*; this is equivalent to his saying to the paralytic whom he was about to cure, ἀφέωνταί σοι αἱ

---

[3] Sanhedr. f. xci. 2, and Bereschith Rabba f. xxxviii. 1. (Lightfoot, p. 1050): *Antonius interrogavit Rabbi (Judam): a quonam tempore incipit malus affectus prævalere in homine? an a tempore formationis ejus (inutero), an a tempore processionis ejus (ex utero)? Dicit ei Rabbi: a tempore formationis ejus.*

ἁμαρτίαι σου, *thy sins are forgiven thee* : in the one case disease is removed, in the other threatened, as a punishment of sin. But here again the expositors, to whom it is not agreeable that Jesus should hold an opinion which they reject, find a means of evading the direct sense of the words. Jesus, say they, perceived that the particular disease of this man was a natural consequence of certain excesses, and warned him from a repetition of these as calculated to bring on a more dangerous relapse.[4] But an insight into the natural connexion between certain excesses and certain diseases as their consequence, is far more removed from the mode of thinking of the age in which Jesus lived, than the notion of a positive connexion between sin in general and disease as its punishment; hence, if we are nevertheless to ascribe the former sense to the words of Jesus, it must be very distinctly conveyed in the text. But the fact is that in the whole narrative there is no intimation of any particular excess on the part of the man ; the words μηκέτι ἁμάρτανε, relate only to sin in general, and to supply a conversation of Jesus with the sick man, in which he is supposed to have acquainted the former with the connexion between his sufferings and a particular sin,[5] is the most arbitrary fiction. What exposition ! for the sake of evading a result which is dogmatically unwelcome, to extend the one passage (John ix.) to a generality of meaning not really belonging to it, to elude the other (Matt. ix.) by the hypothesis of accommodation, and forcibly to affix to a third (John v.) a modern idea ; whereas if the first passage be only permitted to say no more than it actually says, the direct meaning of the other two may remain unviolated !

But another passage, and that a synoptical one, is adduced in vindication of the superiority of Jesus to the popular opinion in question. This passage is Luke xiii. 1 ff., where Jesus is told of the Galileans whom Pilate had caused to be slain while they were in the act of sacrificing, and of others who were killed by the falling of a tower. From what follows, we must suppose the informants to have intimated their opinion that these calamities were to be regarded as a divine visitation for the peculiar wickedness of the parties so signally destroyed. Jesus replied that they must not suppose those men to have been especially sinful ; they themselves were in no degree better, and unless they repented would meet with a similar destruction. Truly it is not clear how in these expressions of Jesus a repudiation of the popular notion can be found. If Jesus wished to give his voice in opposition to this, he must either have said : you are equally great sinners, though you may not perish bodily in the same manner; or : do you believe that those men perished on account of their sins? No ! the contrary may be seen in you, who, notwithstanding your wickedness, are not thus smitten with death. On the contrary, the expressions of Jesus as given by Luke can only have the following sense : that those men have already met with such calamities is no evidence of their peculiar wickedness, any more than the fact that you have been hitherto spared the like, is an evidence of your greater worth ; on the contrary, earlier or later, similar judgments falling on you will attest your equal guilt :—whereby the supposed law of the connexion between the sin and misfortune of every individual is confirmed, not overthrown. This vulgar Hebrew opinion concerning sickness and evil, is indeed in contradiction with that esoteric view, partly Essene, partly Ebionite, which we have found in the introduction to the Sermon on the Mount, the parable of the rich man, and elsewhere, and according to which the righteous in this generation are the suffering, the poor and the sick ; but both opinions are clearly to be seen in the discourses of Jesus by an unprejudiced exegesis, and the contradiction

---

[4] Paulus Comm. 4, s. 264 ; Lücke, 2, s. 22.
[5] This is done by Tholuck, in loc.

which we find between them authorizes us neither to put a forced construction on the one class of expressions, nor to deny them to have really come from Jesus, since we cannot calculate how he may have solved for himself the opposition between two ideas of the world, presented to him by different sides of the Jewish culture of that age.

As regards the above-mentioned cure, the synoptical writers make Jesus in his reply to the messengers of the Baptist, appeal to the fact that the lame walked (Matt. xi. 5), and at another time the people wonder when, among other miracles, they see *the maimed to be whole and the lame to walk* (Matt. xv. 31). In the place of the *lame*, χωλοὶ, *paralytics*, παραλυτικοὶ, are elsewhere brought forward (Matt. iv. 24), and especially in the detailed histories of cures relating to this kind of sufferers (as Matt. ix. 1 ff. parall., viii. 5, parall.), παραλυτικοὶ, and not χωλοὶ, are named. The sick man at the pool of Bethesda (John v. 5) belongs probably to the χωλοῖς spoken of in v. 3 ; there also ξηροὶ, *withered*, are mentioned, and in Matt. xii. 9 ff. parall. we find the cure of a man who had a withered hand. As however the three last named cures will return to us under different heads, all that remains here for our examination is the cure of the paralytic Matt. ix. 1 ff. parall.

As the definitions which the ancient physicians give of paralysis, though they all show it to have been a species of lameness, yet leave it undecided whether the lameness was total or partial ;[6] and as, besides, no strict adherence to medical technicalities is to be expected from the Evangelists, we must gather what they understand by paralytics from their own descriptions of such patients. In the present passage, we read of the paralytic that he was borne on a *bed* κλίνη, and that to enable him to arise and carry his bed was an unprecedented wonder παράδοξον, whence we must conclude that he was lame, at least in the feet. While here there is no mention of pains, or of an acute character of disease, in another narrative (Matt. viii. 6) these are evidently presupposed when the centurion says that his servant is *sick* of the *palsy*, *grievously tormented*, βέβληται—παραλυτικὸς, δεινῶς βασανιζόμενος ; so that under paralytics in the gospels we have at one time to understand a lameness without pain, at another a painful, gouty disease of the limbs.[7]

In the description of the scene in which the paralytic (Matt. ix. 1 ff. parall.) is brought to Jesus, there is a remarkable gradation in the three accounts. Matthew says simply, that as Jesus, after an excursion to the opposite shore, returned to Capernaum, there was brought to him a paralytic, stretched on a bed. Luke describes particularly how Jesus, surrounded by a great multitude, chiefly Pharisees and scribes, taught and healed in a certain house, and how the bearers, because on account of the press they could not reach Jesus, let the sick man down to him through the roof. If we call to mind the structure of oriental houses, which had a flat roof, to which an opening led from the upper story ;[8] and if we add to this the rabbinical manner of speaking, in which to the *via per portum* (דרך פתחים) was opposed the *via per tectum* (דרך גגין) as a no less ordinary way for reaching the ὑπερῷον *upper story* or *chamber*,[9] we cannot under the expression καθιέναι διὰ τῶν κεράμων, *to let down through the tiling*, understand anything else than that the bearers—who, either by means of stairs leading thither directly from the street, or from the roof of a neighbouring house, gained access to the roof of the house in which Jesus was,—let down the sick man with his bed, apparently by cords, through the opening already existing in the roof. Mark, who, while with Matthew he

---

[6] See the examples in Wetstein, N. T. 1, s. 284, and in Wahl's Clavis.
[7] Comp. Winer, Realw., and Fritzsche, in Matt. p. 194.
[8] Winer, ut sup. Art. Dach.
[9] Lightfoot, p. 601.

places the scene at Capernaum, agrees with Luke in the description of the great crowd and the consequent ascent to the roof, goes yet further than Luke, not only in determining the number of the bearers to be four, but also in making them, regardless of the opening already existing, uncover the roof and let down the sick man through an aperture newly broken.

If we ask here also in which direction, upwards or downwards, the climax may most probably have been formed, the narrative of Mark, which stands at the summit, has so many difficulties that it can scarcely be regarded as nearest the truth. For not only have opponents asked, how could the roof be broken open without injury to those beneath?[10] but Olshausen himself admits that the disturbance of the roof, covered with tiles, partakes of the extravagant.[11] To avoid this, many expositors suppose that Jesus taught either in the inner court,[12] or in the open air in front of the house,[13] and that the bearers only broke down a part of the parapet in order to let down the sick man more conveniently. But both the phrase, διὰ τῶν κεράμων, in Luke, and the expressions of Mark, render this conception of the thing impossible, since here neither can στέγη mean parapet, nor ἀποστεγάζω the breaking of the parapet, while ἐξορύττω can only mean the breaking of a hole. Thus the disturbance of the roof subsists, but this·is further rendered improbable on the ground that it was altogether superfluous, inasmuch as there was a door in every roof. Hence help has been sought in the supposition that the bearers indeed used the door previously there, but because this was too narrow for the bed of the patient, they widened it by the removal of the surrounding tiles.[14] Still, however, there remains the danger to those below, and the words imply an opening actually made, not merely widened.

But dangerous and superfluous as such a proceeding would be in reality, it is easy to explain how Mark, wishing further to elaborate the narrative of Luke, might be led to add such a feature. Luke had said that the sick man was let down, so that he descended in the midst before Jesus, ἔμπροσθεν τοῦ Ἰησοῦ. How could the people precisely hit upon this place, unless Jesus accidentally stood under the door of the roof, except by breaking open the roof above the spot where they knew him to be (ἀπεστέγασαν τὴν στέγην ὅπου ἦν)?[15] This trait Mark the more gladly seized because it was adapted to place in the strongest light the zeal which confidence in Jesus infused into the people, and which was to be daunted by no labour. This last interest seems to be the key also to Luke's departure from Matthew. In Matthew, who makes the bearers bring the paralytic to Jesus in the ordinary way, doubtless regarding the laborious conveyance of the sick man on his bed as itself a proof of their faith, it is yet less evident wherein Jesus sees their faith. If the original form of the history was that in which it appears in the first gospel, the temptation might easily arise to make the bearers devise a more conspicuous means of evincing their faith, which, since the scene was already described as happening in a great crowd, might appear to be most suitably found in the uncommon way in which they contrived to bring their sick man to Jesus.

But even the account of Matthew we cannot regard as a true narrative or a fact. It has indeed been attempted to represent the result as a natural one,

---

10 Woolston, Disc. 4.
11 I, s. 310 f.
12 Köster, Immanuel, s. 166, Anm. 66.
13 This appears to be the meaning of Paulus, L. J. 1, a, s. 238. Otherwise exeg. Handb. I, b, s. 505.
14 Thus Lightfoot, Kuinöl, Olshausen, in loc.
15 Vid. Fritzsche, in Marc., p. 52.

by explaining the state of the man to be a nervous weakness, the worst symptom of which was the idea of the sick man that his disease must continue as a punishment of his sin ; [16] reference has been made to analogous cases of a rapid psychical cure of lameness ; [17] and a subsequent use of long-continued curative means has been supposed.[18]   But the first and last expedients are purely arbitrary ; and if in the alleged analogies there may be some truth, yet it is always incomparably more probable that histories of cures of the lame and paralytic in accordance with messianic expectation, should be formed by the legend, than that they should really have happened.   In the passage of Isaiah already quoted (xxxv. 6), it was promised in relation to the messianic time : *then shall the lame man leap as a hart,* τότε ἁλεῖται ὡς ἔλαφος ὁ χωλὸς, and in the same connexion, v. 3, the prophet addresses to the *feeble knees* γόνατα παραλελυμένα the exhortation, *Be strong,* ἰσχύσατε, which, with the accompanying particulars, must have been understood literally, of a miracle to be expected from the Messiah, since Jesus, as we have already mentioned, among other proofs that he was the ἐρχόμενος adduced this : χωλοὶ περιπατοῦσι, *the lame walk.*

§ 97.

INVOLUNTARY CURES.

Occasionally in their general statements concerning the curative power of Jesus, the synoptical writers remark, that all kinds of sick people only sought to touch Jesus, or to lay hold on the hem of his garment, in order to be healed, and that immediately on this slight contact, a cure actually followed (Matt. xiv. 36 ; Mark iii. 10, vi. 56 ; Luke vi. 19). In these cases Jesus operated, not, as we have hitherto always seen, with a precise aim towards any particular sufferer, but on entire masses, without taking special notice of each individual ; his power of healing appears not here, as elsewhere, to reside in his will, but in his body and its coverings ; he does not by his own voluntary act dispense its virtues, but is subject to have them drawn from him without his consent.

Of this species of cure again a detailed example is preserved to us, in the history of the woman who had an issue of blood, which all the synoptical writers give, and interweave in a peculiar manner with the history of the re-suscitation of the daughter of Jairus, making Jesus cure the woman on his way to the ruler's house (Matt. ix. 20 ff. ; Mark v. 25 ff. ; Luke viii. 43 ff.).   On comparing the account of the incident in the several Evangelists, we might in this instance be tempted to regard that of Luke as the original, because it seems to offer an explanation of the uniform connexion of the two histories. As, namely, the duration of the woman's sufferings is fixed by all the narrators at twelve years, so Luke, whom Mark follows, gives twelve years also as the age of the daughter of Jairus ; a numerical similarity which might be a suffi-cient inducement to associate the two histories in the evangelical tradition. But this reason is far too isolated by itself to warrant a decision, which can only proceed from a thorough comparison of the three narratives in their various details.   Matthew describes the woman simply as γυνὴ αἱμορροοῦσα δώδεκα ἔτη, which signifies that she had for twelve years been subject to an important loss of blood, probably in the form of excessive menstruation.

---

[16] Paulus, exeg. Handb. 1, b, s. 498, 501.
[17] Bengel, Gnomon, 1, 245, ed. 2.   Paulus, s. 502, again takes an obvious fable in Livy ii. 36 for a history, capable of a natural explanation.
[18] Paulus, ut sup. s. 501.

Luke, the reputed physician, shows himself here in no degree favourable to his professional brethren, for he adds that the woman had spent all her living on physicians without obtaining any help from them. Mark, yet more un-favourable, says that she had *suffered many things of many physicians, and was nothing bettered, but rather grew worse.* Those who surround Jesus when the woman approaches him are, according to Matthew, his disciples, according to Mark and Luke, a thronging multitude. After all the narrators have de-scribed how the woman, as timid as she was believing, came behind Jesus and touched the hem of his garment, Mark and Luke state that she was imme-diately healed, but that Jesus, being conscious of the egress of curative power, asked *who touched me?* The disciples, astonished, ask in return, how he can distinguish a single touch amidst so general a thronging and pressure of the crowd. According to Luke, he persists in his assertion; according to Mark, he looks inquiringly around him in order to discover the party who had touched him : then, according to both these Evangelists, the woman approaches trembling, falls at His feet and confesses all, whereupon Jesus gives her the tranquillizing assurance that her faith has made her whole. Matthew has not this complex train of circumstances; he merely states that after the touch Jesus looked round, discovered the woman, and announced to her that her faith had wrought her cure.

This difference is an important one, and we neen not greatly wonder that it induced Storr to suppose two separate cures of women afflicted in the same manner.[1] To this expedient he was yet more decidedly determined by the still wider divergencies in the narrative of the resuscitation of the daughter of Jairus, a narrative which is interlaced with the one before us; it is, however, this very interlacement which renders it totally impossible to imagine that Jesus, twice, on both occasions when he was on his way to restore to life the daughter of a Jewish ruler ($ἄρχων$), cured a woman who had had an issue of blood twelve years. While, on this consideration, criticism has long ago decided for the singleness of the fact on which the narratives are founded, it has at the same time given the preference to those of Mark and Luke as the most vivid and circumstantial.[2] But, in the first place, if it be admitted that Mark's addition $ἀλλὰ μᾶλλον εἰς τὸ χεῖρον ἐλθοῦσα$, *but rather grew worse,* is merely a finishing touch from his own imagination to the expression $οὐκ ἴσχυσεν ὑπ' οὐδενὸς θεραπευθῆναι$ *neither could be healed of any,* which he found in Luke ; there seems to be the same reason for regarding this particular of Luke's as an inference of his own by which he has amplified the simple statement $αἱμορροοῦσα δώδεκα ἔτη$, which Matthew gives without any addition. If the woman had been ill twelve years, she must, it was thought, during that period have frequently had recourse to physicians : and as, when contrasted with the inefficiency of the physicians, the miraculous power of Jesus, which in-stantaneously wrought a cure, appeared in all the more brilliant a light; so in the legend, or in the imagination of the narrators, there grew up these additions. What if the same observation applied to the other differences? That the woman according to Matthew also, only touched Jesus from behind, implied the effort and the hope to remain concealed; that Jesus immediately looked round after her, implied that he was conscious of her touch. This hope on the part of the woman became the more accountable, and this con-sciousness on the part of Jesus the more marvellous, the greater the crowd that surrounded Jesus and pressed upon him ; hence the companionship of the disciples in Matthew is by the other two Evangelists changed into a *thronging*

[1] Ueber den Zweck der evang. Geschichte und der Briefe Joh., s. 351 f.
[2] Schulz, ut sup. s. 317 ; Olshausen, 1, s. 322.

of the *multitude* (βλέπεις τὸν ὄχλον συνθλίβοντά σε). Again, Matthew mentions that Jesus looked round after the woman touched him ; on this circumstance the supposition might be founded that he had perceived her touch in a peculiar manner ; hence the scene was further worked up, and we are shown how Jesus, though pressed on all sides, had yet a special consciousness of that particular touch by the healing power which it had drawn from him ; while the simple feature ἐπιστραφεὶς καὶ ἰδὼν αὐτὴν, *he turned him about, and when he saw her*, in Matthew, is transformed into an inquiry and a searching glance around upon the crowd to discover the woman, who then is represented as coming forward, trembling, to make her confession.   Lastly, on a comparison of Matt. xiv. 36, the point of this narrative, even as given in the first gospel, appears to lie in the fact that simply to touch the clothes of Jesus had in itself a healing efficacy.   Accordingly, in the propagation of this history, there was a continual effort to make the result follow immediately on the touch, and to represent Jesus as remaining, even after the cure, for some time uncertain with respect to the individual who had touched him, a circumstance which is in contradiction with that superior knowledge elsewhere attributed to Jesus. Thus, under every aspect, the narrative in the first gospel presents itself as the earlier and more simple, that of the second and third as a later and more embellished formation of the legend.

As regards the common substance of the narratives, it has in recent times been a difficulty to all theologians, whether orthodox or rationalistic, that the curative power of Jesus should have been exhibited apart from his volition. Paulus and Olshausen agree in the opinion,[3] that the agency of Jesus is thus reduced too completely into the domain of physical nature ; that Jesus would then be like a magnetiser who in operating on a nervous patient is conscious of a diminution of strength, or like a charged electrical battery, which a mere touch will discharge.   Such an idea of Christ, thinks Olshausen, is repugnant to the Christian consciousness, which determines the fulness of power resident in Jesus to have been entirely under the governance of his will ; and this will to have been guided by a knowledge of the moral condition of the persons to be healed.   It is therefore supposed that Jesus fully recognized the woman even without seeing her, and considering that she might be spiritually won over to him by this bodily succour, he consciously communicated to her an influx of his curative power ; but in order to put an end to her false shame and constrain her to a confession, he behaved as if he knew not who had touched him.   But the Christian consciousness, in cases of this kind, means nothing else than the advanced religious culture of our age, which cannot appropriate the antiquated ideas of the Bible.   Now this consciousness must be neutral where we are concerned, not with the dogmatical appropriation, but purely with the exegetical discovery of the biblical ideas.   The interference of this alleged Christian consciousness is the secret of the majority of exegetical errors, and in the present instance it has led the above named commentators astray from the evident sense of the text.   For the question of Jesus in both the more detailed narratives τίς ὁ ἁψάμενός μου ; *who touched me ?* repeated as it is in Luke, and strengthened as it is in Mark by a searching glance around, has the appearance of being meant thoroughly in earnest ; and indeed it is the object of these two Evangelists to place the miraculous nature of the curative power of Jesus in a particularly clear light by showing that the mere touching of his clothes accompanied by faith, no previous knowledge on his part of the person who touched, nor so much as a word

[3] Exeg. Handb. 1, b, s. 524 f. ; bibl. Comm. 1, s. 324 f. ; comp. Köster, Immanuel, s. 201 ff.

from him, being requisite, was sufficient to obtain a cure.   Nay, even originally, in the more concise account of Matthew, the expressions προσελθοῦσα
ὄπισθεν ἥψατο *having come behind him, she touched*, and ἐπιστραφεὶς καὶ ἰδὼν
αὐτὴν *he turned him about, and when he saw her*, clearly imply that Jesus knew
the woman only after she had touched him.   If then, it is not to be proved
that Jesus had a knowledge of the woman previous to her cure and a special
will to heal her ; nothing remains for those who will not admit an involuntary
exhibition of curative power in Jesus, but to suppose in him a constant
general will to cure, with which it was only necessary that faith on the part of
the diseased person should concur, in order to produce an actual cure.   But
that, notwithstanding the absence of a special direction of the will to the cure
of this woman on the part of Jesus, she was restored to health, simply by her
faith, without even touching his clothes, is assuredly not the idea of the
Evangelists.   On the contrary, it is their intention to substitute for an individual act of the will on the part of Jesus, the touch on the part of the sick
person ; this it is which, instead of the former, brings into action the latent
power of Jesus : so that the materialistic character of the representation is not
in this way to be avoided.

A step further was necessary to the rationalistic interpretation, which not
only with modern supranaturalism regards as incredible the unconscious efflux
of curative power from Jesus, but also denies in general any efflux of such
power, and yet wishes to preserve unattainted the historical veracity of the
Evangelists.   According to this system, Jesus was led to ask who touched
him, solely because he felt himself held back in his progress ; the assertion
that consciousness of a departure of power, δύναμις ἐξελθοῦσα, was the cause
of his question, is a mere inference of the two narrators, of whom the one,
Mark, actually gives it as his own observation ; and it is only Luke who
incorporates it with the question of Jesus.   The cure of the woman was
effected by means of her exalted confidence, in consequence of which when
she touched the hem of Jesus she was seized with a violent shuddering in her
whole nervous system, which probably caused a sudden contraction of the
relaxed vessels ; at the first moment she could only believe, not certainly
know that she was cured, and only by degrees, probably after the use of
means recommended to her by Jesus, did the malady entirely cease.[4]   But
who can represent to himself the timid touch of a sick woman whose design
was to remain concealed, and whose faith rendered her certain of obtaining
a cure by the slightest touch, as a grasp which arrested the progress of Jesus,
pressed upon as he was, according to Mark and Luke, by the crowd?   Further, what a vast conception of the power of confidence is demanded by the
opinion, that it healed a disease of twelve years' duration without the concurrence of any real force on the part of Jesus!   Lastly, if the Evangelists are
supposed to have put into the mouth of Jesus an inference of their own (that
healing efficacy had gone out of him)—if they are supposed to have described
a gradual cure as an instantaneous one ; then, with the renunciation of these
particulars all warrant for the historical reality of the entire narrative falls to
the ground, and at the same time all necessity for troubling ourselves with
the natural interpretation.

In fact, if we only examine the narrative before us somewhat more closely,
and compare it with kindred anecdotes, we cannot remain in doubt as to its
proper character.   As here and in some other passages it is narrated of Jesus,
that the sick were cured by the bare touch of his clothes : so in the Acts we

---

[4] Paulus, exeg. Handb. 1, b, s. 524 f. 530.   L. J. 1, a, s. 244 f. ; Venturini, 2, s. 204 ff. ;
Köster, ut sup.

are told that the *handkerchiefs* σουδάρια and *aprons* σιμικίνθια of Paul cured all kinds of sick persons to whom they were applied (xix. 11 f.), and that the very shadow of Peter was believed to have the same efficacy (v. 15) ; while the apocryphal gospels represent a mass of cures to have been wrought by means of the swaddling bands of the infant Jesus, and the water in which he was washed.[5] In reading these last histories, every one knows that he is in the realm of fiction and legend ; but wherein are the cures wrought by the pocket-handkerchiefs of Paul to be distinguished from those wrought by the swaddling bands of Jesus, unless it be that the latter proceeded from a child, the former from a man ? It is certain that if the story relative to Paul were not found in a canonical book, every one would deem it fabulous, and yet the credibility of the narratives should not be concluded from the assumed origin of the book which contains them, but on the contrary, our judgment of the book must be founded on the nature of its particular narratives. But again, between these cures by the pocket-handkerchiefs and those by the touch of the hem of the garment, there is no essential distinction. In both cases we have the contact of objects which are in a merely external connexion with the worker of the miracle ; with the single difference, that this connexion is with regard to the pocket-handkerchiefs an interrupted one, with regard to the clothes a continuous one; in both cases again, results which, even according to the orthodox view, are only derived from the spiritual nature of the men in question, and are to be regarded as acts of their will in virtue of its union with the divine, are reduced to physical effects and effluxes. The subject thus descends from the religious and theological sphere to the natural and physical, because a man with a power of healing resident in his body, and floating as an atmosphere around him, would belong to the objects of natural science, and not of religion. But natural science is not able to accredit such a healing power by sure analogies or clear definitions ; hence these cures, being driven from the objective to the subjective region, must receive their explanation from psychology. Now psychology, taking into account the power of imagination and of faith, will certainly allow the possibility that without a real curative power in the reputed miracle-worker, solely by the strong confidence of the diseased person that he possesses this power, bodily maladies which have a close connexion with the nervous system may be cured : but when we seek for historical vouchers for this possibility, criticism, which must here be called to aid, will soon show that a far greater number of such cures has been invented by the faith of others, than has been performed by the parties alleged to be concerned. Thus it is in itself by no means impossible, that through strong faith in the healing power residing even in the clothes and handkerchiefs of Jesus and the apostles, many sick persons on touching these articles were conscious of real benefit ; but it is at least equally probable, that only after the death of these men, when their fame in the church was ever on the increase, anecdotes of this kind were believingly narrated, and it depends on the nature of the accounts, for which of the two alternatives we are to decide. In the general statement in the Gospels and the Acts, which speak of whole masses having been cured in the above way, this accumulation at any rate is traditional. As to the detailed history which we have been examining, in its representation that the woman had suffered twelve years from a very obstinate disease, and one the least susceptible of merely psychical influence, and that the cure was performed by power consciously emitted from Jesus, instead of by the imagination of the patient : so large a portion betrays itself to be mythical that we can no longer discern any historical elements, and must regard the whole as legendary.

[5] Vid. Evangelium infantiæ arabicum, ap. Fabricius and Thilo.

It is not difficult to see what might give rise to this branch of the evangelical miraculous legend, in distinction from others. The faith of the popular mind, dependent on the senses, and incapable of apprehending the divine through the medium of thought alone, strives perpetually to draw it down into material existence. Hence, according to a later opinion, the saint must continue to work miracles when his bones are distributed as relics, and the body of Christ must be present in the transubstantiated host ; hence also, according to an idea developed much earlier, the curative power of the men celebrated in the New Testament must be attached to their body and its coverings. The less the church retained of the words of Jesus, the more tenaciously she clung to the efficacy of his mantle, and the further she was removed from the free spiritual energy of the apostle Paul, the more consolatory was the idea of carrying home his curative energy in a pocket-handkerchief.

§ 98.

CURES AT A DISTANCE.

The cures performed at a distance are, properly speaking, the opposite of these involuntary cures. The latter are effected by mere corporeal contact without a special act of the will ; the former solely by the act of the will without corporeal contact, or even local proximity. But there immediately arises this objection : if the curative power of Jesus was so material that it dispensed itself involuntarily at a mere touch, it cannot have been so spiritual that the simple will could convey it over considerable distances ; or conversely, if it was so spiritual as to act apart from bodily presence, it cannot have been so material as to dispense itself independently of the will. Since we have pronounced the purely physical mode of influence in Jesus to be improbable, free space is left to us for the purely spiritual, and our decision on the latter will therefore depend entirely on the examination of the narratives and the facts themselves.

As proofs that the curative power of Jesus acted thus at a distance, Matthew and Luke narrate to us the cure of the sick servant of a centurion at Capernaum, John that of the son of a *nobleman* βασιλικὸς, at the same place (Matt. viii. 5 ff. ; Luke vii. 1 ff. ; John iv. 46 ff.) ; and again Matthew (xv. 22 ff.), and Mark (vii. 25 ff.), that of the daughter of the Canaanitish woman. Of these examples, as in the summary narration of the last there is nothing peculiar, we have here to consider the two first only. The common opinion is, that Matthew and Luke do indeed narrate the same fact, but John one distinct from this, since his narrative differs from that of the two others in the following particulars : firstly, the place from which Jesus cures, is in the synoptical gospels the place where the sick man resides, Capernaum,—in John a different one, namely, Cana ; secondly, the time at which the synoptists lay the incident, namely, when Jesus is in the act of returning home after his Sermon on the Mount, is different from that assigned to it in the fourth gospel, which is immediately after the return of Jesus from the first passover and his ministry in Samaria ; thirdly, the sick person is according to the former the slave, according to the latter the son of the suppliant ; but the most important divergencies are those which relate, fourthly, to the suppliant himself, for in the first and third gospels he is a military person (an ἑκατόνταρχος), in the fourth a person in office at court (βασιλικὸς), according to the former (Matt. v. 10 ff.), a Gentile, according to the latter without doubt a Jew ; above all, the synoptists make Jesus eulogize him as a pattern of the most fervent, humble faith, because, in the conviction that Jesus could cure at a distance, he prevented him from going to his house; whereas in John, on the contrary, he is blamed for his weak faith which required signs and wonders, because he thought the presence of Jesus in his house necessary for the purpose of the cure.[1]

These divergencies are certainly important enough to be a reason, with those who regard them from a certain point of view, for maintaining the distinction of the fact lying at the foundation of the synoptical narratives from that reported by John : only this accuracy of discrimination must be carried throughout, and the diversities between the two synoptical narratives themselves must not be overlooked. First, even in the designation of the person of the patient they are not perfectly in unison ; Luke calls him δοῦλος ἔντιμος, *a servant who was dear* to the centurion ; in Matthew, the latter calls him ὁ παῖς μοῦ, which may equally mean either a *son* or a *servant*, and as the centurion when speaking (v. 9) of his servant, uses the word δοῦλος, while the cured individual is again (v. 13) spoken of as ὁ παῖς αὐτοῦ, it seems most probable that the former sense was intended. With respect to his disease, the man is described by Matthew as παραλυτικὸς δεινῶς βασανιζόμενος *a paralytic grievously tormented* ; Luke is not only silent as to this species of disease, but he is thought by many to presuppose a different one, since after the indefinite expression κακῶς ἔχων, *being ill*, he adds, ἤμελλε τελευτᾶν, *was ready to die*, and paralysis is not generally a rapidly fatal malady.[2] But the most important difference is one which runs through the entire narrative, namely, that all which according to Matthew the centurion does in his own person, is in Luke done by messengers, for here in the first instance he makes the entreaty, not personally, as in Matthew, but through the medium of the Jewish elders, and when he afterwards wishes to prevent Jesus from entering his house, he does not come forward himself, but commissions some friends to act in his stead. To reconcile this difference, it is usual to refer to the rule : *quod quis per alium facit*, etc.[3] If then it be said, and indeed no other conception of the matter is possible to expositors who make such an appeal, —Matthew well knew that between the centurion and Jesus everything was transacted by means of deputies, but for the sake of brevity, he employed the figure of speech above alluded to, and represented him as himself accosting Jesus : Storr is perfectly right in his opposing remark, that scarcely any historian would so perseveringly carry that metonymy through an entire narrative, especially in a case where, on the one hand, the figure of speech is by no means so obvious as when, for example, that is ascribed to a general which is done by his soldiers ; and where, on the other hand, precisely this point, whether the person acted for himself or through others, is of some consequence to a full estimate of his character.[4] With laudable consistency, therefore, Storr, as he believed it necessary to refer the narrative of the fourth gospel to a separate fact from that of the first and third, on account of the important differences ; so, on account of the divergencies which he found between the two last, pronounces these also to be narratives of two separate events. If any one wonder that at three different times so entirely similar a cure should have happened at the same place (for according to John also, the patient lay and was cured at Capernaum), Storr on his side wonders how it can be regarded as in the least improbable that in Capernaum at two different

[1] See the observations of Paulus, Lücke, Tholuck, and Olshausen, in loc.
[2] Schleiermacher, über den Lukas, s. 92.
[3] Augustin, de consens. evang. i. 20 ; Paulus, exeg. Handb. 1, b, s. 709 ; Köster, Immanuel, s. 63.
[4] Ueber den Zweck Jesu, u. s. f., s. 351.

periods two centurions should have had each a sick servant, and that again at another time a nobleman should have had a sick son at the same place ; that the second centurion (Luke) should have heard the history of the first, have applied in a similar manner to Jesus, and sought to surpass his example of humility, as the first centurion (Matthew), to whom the earlier history of the nobleman (John) was known, wished to surpass the weak faith of the latter ; and lastly, that Jesus cured all the three patients in the same manner at a distance. But the incident of a distinguished official person applying to Jesus to cure a dependent or relative, and of Jesus at a distance operating on the latter in such a manner, that about the time in which Jesus pronounced the curative word, the patient at home recovered, is so singular in its kind that a threefold repetition of it may be regarded as impossible, and even the supposition that it occurred twice only, has difficulties ; hence it is our task to ascertain whether the three narratives may not be traced to a single root.

Now the narrative of the fourth Evangelist which is most generally held to be distinct, has not only an affinity with the synoptical narratives in the outline already given ; but in many remarkable details either one or the other of the synoptists agrees more closely with John than with his fellow synoptist. Thus, while in designating the patient as παῖς, Matthew may be held to accord with the υἱὸς of John, at least as probably as with the δοῦλος of Luke ; Matthew and John decidedly agree in this, that according to both the functionary at Capernaum applies in his own person to Jesus, and not as in Luke by deputies. On the other hand, the account of John agrees with that of Luke in its description of the state of the patient ; in neither is there any mention of the paralysis of which Matthew speaks, but the patient is described as near death, in Luke by the words ἤμελλε τελευτᾷν, in John by ἤμελλεν ἀποθνήσκειν, in addition to which it is incidentally implied in the latter, v. 52, that the disease was accompanied by a *fever*, πυρετὸς. In the account of the manner in which Jesus effected the cure of the patient, and in which his cure was made known, John stands again on the side of Matthew in opposition to Luke. While namely, the latter has not an express assurance on the part of Jesus that the servant was healed, the two former make him say to the officer, in very similar terms, the one, ὕπαγε, καὶ ὡς ἐπίστευσας γενηθήτω σοι, *Go thy way, and as thou hast believed so shall it be done unto thee*, the other, πορεύου, ὁ υἱός σου ζῇ, *Go thy way, thy son liveth* ; and the conclusion of Matthew also, καὶ ἰάθη ὁ παῖς αὐτοῦ ἐν τῇ ὥρᾳ ἐκείνῃ, has at least in its form more resemblance to the statement of John, that by subsequent inquiry the father ascertained it to be ἐν ἐκείνῃ τῇ ὥρᾳ, *at the same hour* in which Jesus had spoken the word that his son had begun to amend, than to the statement of Luke, that the messengers when they returned found the sick man restored to health. In another point of this conclusion, however, the agreement with John is transferred from Matthew again to Luke. In both Luke and John, namely, a kind of embassy is spoken of, which towards the close of the narrative comes out of the house of the officer ; in the former it consists of the centurion's friends, whose errand it is to dissuade Jesus from giving himself unnecessary trouble ; in the latter, of servants who rejoicingly meet their master and bring him the news of his son's recovery. Unquestionably where three narratives are so thoroughly entwined with each other as these, we ought not merely to pronounce two of them identical and allow one to stand for a distinct fact, but must rather either distinguish all, or blend all into one. The latter course was adopted by Semler, after older examples,[5]

---

[5] Vid. Lücke, 1, s. 552.

and Tholuck has at least declared it possible. But with such expositors the next object is so to explain the divergencies of the three narratives, that no one of the Evangelists may seem to have said anything false. With respect to the rank of the applicant, they make the βασιλικὸς in John a military officer, for whom the ἑκατόνταρχος of the two others would only be a more specific designation ; as regards the main point, however, namely, the conduct of the applicant, it is thought that the different narrators may have represented the event in different periods of its progress ; that is, John may have given the earlier circumstance, that Jesus complained of the originally weak faith of the suppliant, the synoptists only the later, that he praised its rapid growth. We have already shown how it has been supposed possible, in a yet easier manner, to adjust the chief difference between the two synoptical accounts relative to the mediate or immediate entreaty. But this effort to explain the contradictions between the three narratives in a favourable manner is altogether vain. There still subsist these difficulties : the synoptists thought of the applicant as a centurion, the fourth Evangelist as a courtier ; the former as strong, the latter as weak in faith ; John and Matthew imagined that he applied in his own person to Jesus ; Luke, that out of modesty he sent deputies.[6]

Which then represents the fact in the right way, which in the wrong ? If we take first the two synoptists by themselves, expositors with one voice declare that Luke gives the more correct account. First of all, it is thought improbable that the patient should have been, as Matthew says, a paralytic, since in the case of a disease so seldom fatal the modest centurion would scarcely have met Jesus to implore his aid immediately on his entrance into the city :[7] as if a very painful disease such as is described by Matthew did not render desirable the quickest help, and as if there were any want of modesty in asking Jesus before he reached home to utter a healing word. Rather, the contrary relation between Matthew and Luke seems probable from the observation, that the miracle, and consequently also the disease of the person cured miraculously, is never diminished in tradition but always exaggerated ; hence the tormented paralytic would more probably be heightened into one *ready to die*, μέλλων τελευτᾷν, than the latter reduced to a mere sufferer. But especially the double message in Luke is, according to Schleiermacher, a feature very unlikely to have been invented. How if, on the contrary, it very plainly manifested itself to be an invention ? While in Matthew the centurion, on the offer of Jesus to accompany him, seeks to prevent him by the objection : *Lord, I am not worthy that thou shouldest come under my roof*, in Luke he adds by the mouth of his messenger, *wherefore neither thought I myself worthy to come unto thee*, by which we plainly discover the conclusion on which the second embassy was founded. If the man declared himself unworthy that Jesus should come to him, he cannot, it was thought, have held himself worthy to come to Jesus ; an exaggeration of his humility by which the narrative of Luke again betrays its secondary character. The first embassy seems to have originated in the desire to introduce a previous recommendation of the centurion as a motive for the promptitude with which Jesus offered to enter the house of a Gentile. The Jewish elders, after having informed Jesus of the case of disease, add *that he was worthy for whom he should do this, for he loveth our nation and has built us a synagogue* : a recommendation the tenor of which is not unlike what Luke (Acts x. 22) makes the

---

[6] Fritzsche, in Matth. p. 310 : *discrepat autem Lucas ita a Matthæi narratione, ut centurionem non ipsum venisse ad Jesum) sed per legatos cum eo egisse tradat ; quibus dissidentibus pacem obtrudere, boni nego interpretis esse.*

[7] Schleiermacher, ut sup. s. 92 f.

messengers of Cornelius say to Peter to induce him to return with them, namely, that the centurion was a *just man, and one that feareth God, and in good report among all the nation of the Jews.* That the double embassy cannot have been original, appears the most clearly from the fact, that by it the narrative of Luke loses all coherence. In Matthew all hangs well together : the centurion first describes to Jesus the state of the sufferer, and either leaves it to Jesus to decide what he shall next do, or before he prefers his request Jesus anticipates him by the offer to go to his house, which the centurion declines in the manner stated. Compare with this his strange conduct in Luke : he first sends to Jesus by the Jewish elders the request that he will come and heal his servant, but when Jesus is actually coming, repents that he has occasioned him to do so, and asks only for a miraculous word from Jesus. The supposition that the first request proceeded solely from the elders and not from the centurion [8] runs counter to the express words of the Evangelist, who by the expressions : ἀπέστειλε—πρεσβυτέρους—ἐρωτῶν αὐτὸν, *he sent—the elders—beseeching him,* represents the prayer as coming from the centurion himself ; and that the latter by the word ἐλθὼν meant only that Jesus should come into the neighbourhood of his house, but when he saw that Jesus intended actually to enter his house, declined this as too great a favour,—is too absurd a demeanour to attribute to a man who otherwise appears sensible, and of whom for this reason so capricious a change of mind as is implied in the text of Luke, was still less to be expected. The whole difficulty would have been avoided, if Luke had put into the mouth of the first messengers, as Matthew in that of the centurion, only the entreaty, direct or indirect, for a cure in general ; and then after Jesus had offered to go to the house where the patient lay, had attributed to the same messengers the modest rejection of this offer. But on the one hand, he thought it requisite to furnish a motive for the resolution of Jesus to go into the Gentile's house ; and on the other, tradition presented him with a deprecation of this personal trouble on the part of Jesus : he was unable to attribute the prayer and the deprecation to the same persons, and he was therefore obliged to contrive a second embassy. Hereby, however, the contradiction was only apparently avoided, since both embassies are sent by the centurion. Perhaps also the centurion who was unwilling that Jesus should take the trouble to enter his house, reminded Luke of the messenger who warned Jairus not to trouble the master to enter his house, likewise after an entreaty that he would come into the house ; and as the messenger says to Jairus, according to him and Mark, μὴ σκύλλε τὸν διδάσκαλον, *trouble not the master* (Luke viii. 49), so here he puts into the mouth of the second envoys, the words, κύριε μὴ σκύλλου, *Lord, trouble not thyself,* although such an order has a reason only in the case of Jairus, in whose house the state of things had been changed since the first summons by the death of his daughter, and none at all in that of the centurion whose servant still remained in the same state.

Modern expositors are deterred from the identification of all the three narratives, by the fear that it may present John in the light of a narrator who has not apprehended the scene with sufficient accuracy, and has even mistaken its main drift.[9] Were they nevertheless to venture on a union, they would as far as possible vindicate to the fourth gospel the most original account of the facts ; a position of which we shall forthwith test the security, by an examination of the intrinsic character of the narratives. That the suppliant is according to the fourth Evangelist a βασιλικὸς, while according to the two others he is an ἑκατόνταρχος, is an indifferent particular from which

8 Kuinöl, in Matt., p. 221 f.
9 Tholuck, in loc. ; Hase, § 68, Anm. 2.

we can draw no conclusion on either side ; and it may appear to be the same with the divergency as to the relation of the diseased person to the one who entreats his cure. If, however, it be asked with reference to the last point, from which of the three designations the other two could most easily have arisen ? it can scarcely be supposed that the υἱὸς of John became in a descending line, first the doubtful term παῖς, and then δοῦλος ; and even the reverse ascending order is here less probable than the intermediate alternative, that out of the ambiguous παῖς (=עֶבֶד) there branched off in one direction the sense of *servant*, as in Luke ; in the other, of *son*, as in John. We have already remarked, that the description of the patient's state in John, as well as in Luke, is an enhancement on that in Matthew, and consequently of later origin. As regards the difference in the locality, from the point of view now generally taken in the comparative criticism of the gospels, the decision would doubtless be, that in the tradition from which the synoptical writers drew, the place from which Jesus performed the miracles was confounded with that in which the sick person lay, the less noted Cana being absorbed in the celebrated Capernaum ; whereas John, being an eye-witness, retained the more correct details. But the relation between the Evangelists appears to stand thus only when John is assumed to have been an eye-witness ; if the critic seeks, as he is bound to do, to base his decision solely on the intrinsic character of the narratives, he will arrive at a totally different result. Here is a narrative of a cure performed at a distance, in which the miracle appears the greater, the wider the distance between the curer and the cured. Would oral tradition, in propagating this narrative, have the tendency to diminish that distance, and consequently the miracle, so that in the account of John, who makes Jesus perform the cure at a place from which the nobleman does not reach his son until the following day, we should have the original narrative, in that of the synoptists on the contrary, who represent Jesus as being in the same town with the sick servant, the one modified by tradition ? Only the converse of this supposition can be held accordant with the nature of the legend, and here again the narrative of John manifests itself to be a traditional one. Again, the preciseness with which the hour of the patient's recovery is ascertained in the fourth gospel has a highly fictitious appearance. The simple expression of Matthew, usually found at the conclusion of histories of cures : *he was healed in the self-same hour*, is dilated into an inquiry on the part of the father as to the hour in which the son began to amend, an answer from the servants that yesterday at the seventh hour the fever left him, and lastly the result, that in the very hour in which Jesus had said, Thy son liveth, the recovery took place. This is a solicitous accuracy, a tediousness of calculation, that seems to bespeak the anxiety of the narrator to establish the miracle, rather than to show the real course of the event. In representing the βασιλικὸς as conversing personally with Jesus, the fourth gospel has preserved the original simplicity of the narrative better than the third ; though as has been remarked, the servants who come to meet their master in the former seem to be representatives of Luke's second embassy. But in the main point of difference, relative to the character of the applicant, it might be thought that, even according to our own standard, the preference must be given to John before the two other narrators. For if that narrative is the more legendary, which exhibits an effort at aggrandizement or embellishment, it might be said that the applicant whose faith is in John rather weak, is in Luke embellished into a model of faith. It is not, however, on embellishment in general that legend or the inventive narrator is bent, but on embellishment in subservience to their grand object, which in the gospels is the glorification of Jesus ; and viewed in this light, the embellishment will in

two respects be found on the side of John. First, as this Evangelist continually aims to exhibit the pre-eminence of Jesus, by presenting a contrast to
it in the weakness of all who are brought into communication with him, so
here this purpose might be served by representing the suppliant as weak rather
than strong in faith. The reply, however, which he puts into the mouth of
Jesus, *Unless ye see signs and wonders ye will not believe,* has proved too
severe, for which reason it reduces most of our commentators to perplexity.
Secondly, it might seem unsuitable that Jesus should allow himself to be
diverted from his original intention of entering the house in which the patient
was, and thus appear to be guided by external circumstances ; it might be
regarded as more consistent with his character that he should originally resolve to effect the cure at a distance instead of being persuaded to this by
another. If then, as tradition said, the suppliant did nevertheless make a
kind of remonstrance, this must have had an opposite drift to the one in the
synoptical gospels, namely, to induce Jesus to a journey to the house where
the patient lay.

In relation to the next question, the possibility and the actual course of the
incident before us, the natural interpretation seems to find the most pliant
material in the narrative of John. Here, it is remarked, Jesus nowhere says
that he will effect the patient's cure, he merely assures the father that his son
is out of danger (ὁ υἱός σου ζῇ), and the father, when he finds that the favourable turn of his son's malady coincides with the time at which he was conversing with Jesus, in no way draws the inference that Jesus had wrought
the cure at a distance. Hence, this history is only a proof that Jesus by
means of his profound acquaintance with semeiology, was able, on receiving
a description of the patient's state, correctly to predict the course of his
disease ; that such a description is not here given is no proof that Jesus had
not obtained it ; while further this proof of knowledge is called a σημεῖον
(v. 54) because it was a sign of a kind of skill in Jesus which John had not
before intimated, namely, the ability to predict the cure of one dangerously
ill.[10]   But, apart from the misinterpretation of the word σημεῖον, and the interpolation of a conversation not intimated in the text ; this view of the
matter would place the character and even the understanding of Jesus in the
most equivocal light. For if we should pronounce a physician imprudent,
who in the case of a patient believed to be dying of fever, should even from
his own observation of the symptoms, guarantee a cure, and thus risk his
reputation : how much more rashly would Jesus have acted, had he, on the
mere description of a man who was not a physician, given assurance that a
disease was attended with no danger ? We cannot ascribe such conduct to
him, because it would be in direct contradiction with his general conduct, and
the impression which he left on his cotemporaries. If then Jesus merely
predicted the cure without effecting it, he must have been assured of it in a
more certain manner than by natural reasoning,—he must have known it in a
supernatural manner. This is the turn given to the narrative by one of the
most recent commentators on the gospel of John. He puts the question,
whether we have here a miracle of knowledge or of power ; and as there is no
mention of an immediate effect from the words of Jesus, while elsewhere in
the fourth gospel the superior knowledge of Jesus is especially held up to our
view, he is of opinion that Jesus, by means of his higher nature, merely knew
that at that moment the dangerous crisis of the disease was past.[11]   But if
our gospel frequently exhibits the superior knowledge of Jesus, this proves
nothing to the purpose, for it just as frequently directs our attention to his

---

[10] Paulus, Comm. 4, s. 253 f. ; Venturini, 2, s. 140 ff. ; comp. Hase, § 68.
[11] Lücke, 1, s. 550 f.

superior power. Further, where the supernatural knowledge of Jesus is concerned, this is plainly stated (as i. 49, ii. 25, vi. 64), and hence if a supernatural cognizance of the already effected cure of the boy had been intended,
John would have made Jesus speak on this occasion as he did before to
Nathanael, and tell the father that he already saw his son on his bed in an
ameliorated state.   On the contrary, not only is there no intimation of the
exercise of superior knowledge, but we are plainly enough given to understand that there was an exercise of miraculous power.   When the sudden
cure of one *at the point of death* is spoken of, the immediate question is,
What brought about this unexpected change? and when a narrative which
elsewhere makes miracles follow on the word of its hero, puts into his mouth
an assurance that the patient lives, it is only the mistaken effort to diminish
the marvellous, which can prevent the admission, that in this assurance the
author means to give the cause of the cure.

In the case of the synoptical narratives, the supposition of a mere prediction will not suffice, since here the father (Matt. v. 8) entreats the exercise of
healing power, and Jesus (v. 13), accedes to this entreaty.   Hence every way
would seem to be closed to the natural interpretation (for the distance of
Jesus from the patient made all physical or psychical influence impossible), if
a single feature in the narrative had not presented unexpected help.   This
feature is the comparison which the centurion institutes between himself and
Jesus.   As he need only speak a word in order to see this or that command
performed by his soldiers and servants, so, he concludes, it would cost Jesus
no more than a word to restore his servant to health.   Out of this comparison
it has been found possible to extract an intimation that as on the side of the
centurion, so on that of Jesus, human proxies were thought of.   According to
this, the centurion intended to represent to Jesus, that he need only speak a
word to one of his disciples, and the latter would go with him and cure his
servant, which is supposed to have forthwith happened.[12]   But as this would
be the first instance in which Jesus had caused a cure to be wrought by his
disciples, and the only one in which he commissions them immediately to
perform a particular cure, how could this peculiar circumstance be silently
presupposed in the otherwise detailed narrative of Luke?   Why, since this
narrator is not sparing in spinning out the rest of the messenger's speech,
does he stint the few words which would have explained all—the simple addition after εἰπὲ λόγῳ, *speak the word*, of ἑνὶ τῶν μαθητῶν, *to one of thy disciples*,
or something similar?   But, above all, at the close of the narrative, where
the result is told, this mode of interpretation falls into the greatest perplexity,
not merely through the silence of the narrator, but through his positive statement.   Luke, namely, concludes with the information that when the friends
of the centurion returned into the house, they found the servant already
recovered.   Now, if Jesus had caused the cure by sending with the messengers one or more of his disciples, the patient could only begin gradually to
be better after the disciples had come into the house with the messengers;
he could not have been already well on their arrival.   Paulus indeed supposes that the messengers lingered for some time listening to the discourse of
Jesus, and that thus the disciples arrived before them; but how the former
could so unnecessarily linger, and how the Evangelist could have been silent
on this point as well as on the commission of the disciples, he omits to explain.   Whether instead of the disciples, we hold that which corresponds on
the side of Jesus to the soldiers of the centurion to be demons of disease,[13]

---

[12] Paulus, exeg. Handb. 1, b, s. 710 f. ; Natürliche Geschichte, 2 s. 285 ff.
[13] Clem. homil. ix. 21 ; Fritzsche, in Matth., 313.

ministering angels,[14] or merely the word and the curative power of Jesns ;[15] in any case there remains to us a miracle wrought at a distance.

This kind of agency on the part of Jesus is, according to the admission even of such commentators as have not generally any repugnance to the miraculous, attended with special difficulty, because from the want of the personal presence of Jesus, and its beneficial influence on the patient, we are deprived of every possibility of rendering the cure conceivable by means of an analogy observable in nature.[16] According to Olshausen, indeed, this distant influence has its analogies; namely, in animal magnetism.[17] I will not directly contest this, but only point out the limits within which, so far as my knowledge extends, this phenomenon confines itself in the domain of animal magnetism. According to our experience hitherto, the cases in which one person can exert an influence over another at a distance are only two : first, the magnetizer or an individual in magnetic relation to him can act thus on the somnambule, but this distant action must always be preceded by immediate contact,—a preliminary which is not supposed in the relation of Jesus to the patient in our narrative ; secondly, such an influence is found to exist in persons who are themselves somnambules, or otherwise under a disordered state of the nerves : neither of which descriptions can apply to Jesus. If thus such a cure of distant persons as is ascribed to Jesus in our narratives, far outsteps the extreme limits of natural causation, as exhibited in magnetism and the kindred phenomena ; then must Jesus have been, so far as the above narratives can lay claim to historical credit, a supernatural being. But before we admit him to have been so really, it is worth our while as critical inquirers, to examine whether the narrative under consideration could not have arisen without any historical foundation ; especially as by the very fact of the various forms which it has taken in the different gospels it shows itself to contain legendary ingredients. And here it is evident that the miraculous cures of Jesus by merely touching the patient, such as we have examples of in that of the leper, Matt. viii. 3, and in that of the blind men, Matt. ix. 29, might by a natural climax rise, first into the cure of persons when in his presence, by a mere word, as in the case of the demoniacs, of the lepers, Luke xvii. 14, and other sufferers ; and then into the cure even of the absent by a word ; of which there is a strongly marked precedent in the Old Testament. In 2 Kings v. 9 ff. we read that when the Syrian general Naaman came before the dwelling of the prophet Elisha that he might be cured of his leprosy, the prophet came not out to meet him, but sent to him by a servant the direction to wash himself seven times in the river Jordan. At this the Syrian was so indignant that he was about to return home without regarding the direction of the prophet. He had expected, he said, that the prophet would come to him, and calling on his God, strike his hand over the leprous place ; that without any personal procedure of this kind, the prophet merely directed him to go to the river Jordan and wash, discouraged and irritated him, since if water were the thing required, he might have had it better at home than here in Israel. By this Old Testament history we see what was ordinarily expected from a prophet, namely, that he should be able to cure when present by bodily contact ; that he could do so without contact, and at a distance, was not presupposed. Elisha effected the cure of the leprous general in the latter manner (for the washing was not the cause of cure here, any more than in John ix., but the miraculous power of the prophet, who saw fit to annex its influence to this external act), and hereby proved himself a highly distin-

---

[14] Wetstein, N. T. 1, p. 349 ; comp. Olshausen, in loc.
[15] Köster, Immanuel, s. 195, Anm.
[16] Lücke, 1, s. 550.   [17] Bibl. Comm. 1, s. 268.

guished prophet: ought then the Messiah in this particular to fall short of the prophet? Thus our New Testament narrative is manifested to be a necessary reflection of that Old Testament story. As, there, the sick person will not believe in the possibility of his cure unless the prophet comes out of his house; so here according to one edition of the story the applicant likewise doubts the possibility of a cure, unless Jesus will come into his house; according to the other editions, he is convinced of the power of Jesus to heal even without this; and all agree that Jesus, like the prophet, succeeded in the performance of this especially difficult miracle.

§ 99.

CURES ON THE SABBATH.

Jesus, according to the gospels, gave great scandal to the Jews by not seldom performing his curative miracles on the sabbath. One example of this is common to the three synoptical writers, two are peculiar to Luke, and two to John.

In the narrative common to the three synoptical writers, two cases of supposed desecration of the sabbath are united; the plucking of the ears of corn by the disciples (Matt. xii. 1 parall.), and the cure of the man with the withered hand by Jesus (v. 9 ff. parall.). After the conversation which was occasioned by the plucking of the corn, and which took place in the fields, the two first Evangelists continue as if Jesus went from this scene immediately into the synagogue of the same place, to which no special designation is given, and there, on the occasion of the cure of the man with the withered hand, again held a dispute on the observance of the sabbath, It is evident that these two histories were originally united only on account of the similarity in their tendency; hence it is to the credit of Luke, that he has expressly separated them chronologically by the words ἐν ἑτέρῳ σαββάτῳ, on another Sabbath.[1] The further inquiry, which narrative is here the more original? we may dismiss with the observation, that if the question which Matthew puts into the mouth of the Pharisees, Is it lawful to heal on the sabbath days? is held up as a specimen of invented dialogue;[2] we may with equal justice characterize in the same way the question lent to Jesus by the two intermediate Evangelists; while their much praised[3] description of Jesus calling to the man to stand forth in the midst, and then casting reproving glances around, may be accused of having the air of dramatic fiction.

The narratives all agree in representing the affliction under which the patient laboured, as a χεὶρ ξηρὰ, or ἐξηραμμένη. Indefinite as this expression is, it is treated too freely when it is understood, as by Paulus, to imply only that the hand was injured by heat,[4] or even by a sprain, according to Venturini's supposition.[5] For when, in order to determine the signification in which this term is used in the New Testament we refer, as it is proper to do, to the Old Testament, we find (1 Kings xiii. 4) a hand which, on being stretched out, ἐξηράνθη (וַתִּיבַשׁ), described as incapable of being drawn back again, so that we must understand a lameness and rigidity of the hand; and on a comparison of Mark ix. 18, where the expression ξηραίνεσθαι to be withered or wasted away is applied to an epileptic, a drying up and shrinking of that

[1] Schleiermacher, über den Lukas, s. 80 f.
[2] Schneckenburger, über den Ursprung, u. s. f., s. 50.
[3] Schleiermacher, ut sup.
[4] Exeg. Handb. 2, s. 48 ff.
[5] Natürliche Geschichte, 2, s. 421.

member.[6] Now from the narrative before us a very plausible argument may be drawn in favour of the supposition, that Jesus employed natural means in the treatment of this and other diseases. Only such cures, it is said, were prohibited on the sabbath as were attended with any kind of labour; thus, if the Pharisees, as it is here said, expected Jesus to transgress the sabbatical laws by effecting a cure, they must have known that he was not accustomed to cure by his mere word, but by medicaments and surgical operations.[7] As, however, a cure merely by means of a conjuration otherwise lawful, was forbidden on the sabbath, a fact which Paulus himself elsewhere adduces;[8] as moreover there was a controversy between the schools of Hillel and Schammai, whether it were permitted even to administer consolation to the sick on the sabbath;[9] and as again, according to an observation of Paulus, the more ancient rabbins were stricter on the point of sabbatical observance than those whose writings on this subject have come down to us;[10] so the cures of Jesus, even supposing that he used no natural means, might by captious Pharisees be brought under the category of violations of the sabbath. The principal objection to the rationalistic explanation, namely, the silence of the Evangelists as to natural means, Paulus believes to be obviated in the present case by conceiving the scene thus: at that time, and in the synagogue, there was indeed no application of such means; Jesus merely caused the hand to be shown to him, that he might see how far the remedies hitherto prescribed by him (which remedies however are still a bare assumption) had been serviceable, and he then found that it was completely cured; for the expression ἀποκατεστάθη, used by all the narrators, implies a cure completed previously, not one suddenly effected in the passing moment. It is true that the context seems to require this interpretation, since the outstretching of the hand prior to the cure would appear to be as little possible, as in 1 Kings xiii. 4, the act of drawing it back : nevertheless the Evangelists give us only the word of Jesus as the source of the cure; not natural means, which are the gratuitous addition of expositors.[11]

Decisive evidence, alike for the necessity of viewing this as a miraculous cure, and for the possibility of explaining the origin of the anecdote, is to be obtained by a closer examination of the Old Testament narrative already mentioned, 1 Kings xiii. 1 ff. A prophet out of Judah threatened Jeroboam, while offering incense on his idolatrous altar, with the destruction of the altar and the overthrow of his false worship; the king with outstretched hand commanded that this prophet of evil should be seized, when suddenly his hand dried up so that he could not draw it again towards him, and the altar was rent. On the entreaty of the king, however, the prophet besought Jehovah for the restoration of the hand, and its full use was again granted.[12] Paulus also refers to this narrative in the same connexion, but only for the purpose of applying to it his natural method of explanation; he observes that Jeroboam's anger may have produced a transient convulsive rigidity of the muscles and so forth, in the hand just stretched out with such impetuosity. But who does not see that

---

[6] Winer, b. Realw. 1, s. 796.
[7] Paulus, ut sup. s. 49, 54 ; Köster, Immanuel, s. 185 f.
[8] Ut sup. s. 83, ex Tract. Schabbat.
[9] Schabbat, f. 12, ap. Schöttgen, i. p. 123.
[10] See the passage last cited.
[11] Fritzsche, in Matt., p. 427 ; in Marc., p. 79.
[12] 1 Kings xiii. 4, LXX : καὶ ἰδοὺ ἐξηράνθη ἡ χεὶρ αὐτοῦ.   Matth. xii. 10 : καὶ ἰδοὺ ἄνθρωπος ἦν τὴν χεῖρα ἔχων ξηράν (Mark, ἐξηραμμένην.)

6 : καὶ ἐπέστρεψε τὴν χεῖρα τοῦ βασιλέως πρὸς αὐτὸν, καὶ ἐγένετο καθὼς τὸ πρότερον.   13 : τότε λέγει τῷ ἀνθρώπῳ· ἔκτεινον τὴν χεῖρά σου· καὶ ἐξέτεινε· καὶ ἀποκατεστάθη ὑγιὴς ὡς ἡ ἄλλη.

we have here a legend designed to glorify the monotheistic order of prophets, and to hold up to infamy the Israelitish idolatry in the person of its founder Jeroboam? The man of God denounces on the idolatrous altar quick and miraculous destruction; the idolatrous king impiously stretches forth his hand against the man of God; the hand is paralyzed, the idolatrous altar falls asunder into the dust, and only on the intercession of the prophet is the king restored. Who can argue about the miraculous and the natural in what is so evidently a mythus? And who can fail to perceive in our evangelical narrative an imitation of this Old Testament legend, except that agreeably to the spirit of Christianity the withering of the hand appears, not as a retributive miracle, but as a natural disease, and only its cure is ascribed to Jesus; whence also the outstretching of the hand is not, as in the case of Jeroboam, the criminal cause of the infliction, continued as a punishment, and the drawing of it back again a sign of cure; but, on the contrary, the hand which had previously been drawn inwards, owing to disease, can after the completion of the cure be again extended. That, in other instances, about that period, the power of working cures of this kind was in the East ascribed to the favourites of the gods, may be seen from a narrative already adduced, in which, together with the cure of blindness, the restoration of a diseased hand is attributed to Vespasian.[13]

But this curative miracle does not appear independently and as an object by itself: the history of it hinges on the fact that the cure was wrought on the Sabbath, and the point of the whole lies in the words by which Jesus vindicates his activity in healing on the Sabbath against the Pharisees. In Luke and Mark this defence consists in the question, *Is it lawful to do good on the sabbath days, or to do evil, to save life or to destroy it?* in Matthew, in a part of this question, together with the aphorism on saving the sheep which might fall into the pit on the sabbath. Luke, who has not this saying on the present occasion, places it (varied by the substitution of ὄνος ἢ βοῦς, *an ass or an ox* for πρόβατον *sheep*, and of φρέαρ, *well* or *pit* for βόθυνος, *ditch*) in connexion with the cure of an ὑδρωπικὸς *a man who had the dropsy* (xiv. 5); a narrative which has in general a striking similarity to the one under consideration. Jesus takes food in the house of one of the chief Pharisees, where, as in the other instance in the synagogue, he is watched (here, ἦσαν παρατηρούμενοι, there, παρετήρουν). A dropsical person is present; as, there, a man with a withered hand. In the synagogue, according to Matthew, the Pharisees ask Jesus, εἰ ἔξεστι τοῖς σάββασι θεραπεύειν; *Is it lawful to heal on the sabbath days?* According to Mark and Luke, Jesus asks them whether it be *lawful to save life*, etc.: so, here, he asks them, εἰ ἔξεστι τῷ σαββάτῳ θεραπεύειν; *Is it lawful to heal on the sabbath?* whereupon in both histories the interrogated parties are silent (in that of the withered hand, Mark: οἱ δὲ ἐσιώπων; in that of the dropsical patient, Luke: οἱ δὲ ἡσύχασαν). Lastly, in both histories we have the saying about the animal fallen into a pit, in the one as an epilogue to the cure, in the other (that of Matthew) as a prologue. A natural explanation, which has not been left untried even with this cure of the dropsy,[14] seems more than usually a vain labour, where, as in this case, we have before us no particular narrative, resting on its own historical basis, but a mere variation on the theme of the sabbath cures, and the text on the endangered domestic animal, which might come to one (Matthew) in connexion with the cure of a withered hand, to another (Luke) with the cure of a dropsical patient, and to a third in a different connexion still; for there is yet a third story of a miraculous cure with which a similar saying is associated. Luke,

---

[13] Tacit. Hist. iv. 81.
[14] Paulus, exeg. Handb. 2, s. 341 f.

namely, narrates (xiii. 10 ff.) the cure of a woman bowed down by demoniaca
influence, as having been performed by Jesus on the sabbath; when to the
indignant remonstrance of the ruler of the synagogue, Jesus replies by
asking, whether every one does not loose his ox or ass from the stall on the
sabbath, and lead him away to watering? a question which is undeniably a
variation of the one given above.   So entirely identical does this history appear with the one last named, that Schleiermacher comes to this conclusion :
since in the second there is no reference to the first, and since consequently
the repetition is not excused by confession, the two passages Luke xiii. 10,
and xiv. 5, cannot have been written one after the other by the same author.[15]

Thus we have here, not three different incidents, but only three different
frames in which legend has preserved the memorable and thoroughly popular
aphorism on the domestic animal, to be rescued or tended on the sabbath.
Yet, unless we would deny to Jesus so original and appropriate an argument,
there must lie at the foundation a cure of some kind actually performed by
him on the sabbath; not, however, a miraculous one.   We have seen that
Luke unites the saying with the cure of a demoniacal patient: now it might
have been uttered by Jesus on the occasion of one of those cures of demoniacs of which, under certain limitations, we have admitted the natural possibility.   Or, when Jesus in cases of illness among his followers applied the
usual medicaments without regard to the sabbath, he may have found this
appeal to the practical sense of men needful for his vindication.   Or lastly,
if there be some truth in the opinion of rationalistic commentators that Jesus,
according to the oriental and more particularly the Essene custom, occupied
himself with the cure of the body as well as of the soul, he may, when com-
plying with a summons to the former work on the sabbath, have had occasion
for such an apology.   But in adopting this last supposition, we must not,
with these commentators, seek in the particular supernatural cures which the
gospels narrate, the natural reality; on the contrary, we must admit that this
is totally lost to us, and that the supernatural has usurped its place.[16] Further, it cannot have been cures in general with which that saying of Jesus was
connected; but any service performed by him or his disciples which might
be regarded as a rescuing or preservation of life, and which was accompanied
by external labour, might in his position with respect to the Pharisaic party,
furnish an occasion for such a defence.

Of the two cures on the sabbath narrated in the fourth gospel, one has
already been considered with the cures of the blind; the other (v. 1 ff.) might
have been numbered among the cures of paralytics, but as the patient is
not so designated, it was admissible to reserve it for our present head.   In
the porches of the pool of Bethesda in Jerusalem, Jesus found a man who,
as it subsequently appears, had been lame for thirty-eight years; this sufferer
he enables by a word to stand up and carry home his bed, but, as it was the
sabbath, he thus draws down on himself the hostility of the Jewish hierarchy.   Woolston [17] and many later writers have thought to get clear of this
history in a singular manner, by the supposition that Jesus here did not cure
a real sufferer but merely unmasked a hypocrite.[18]   The sole reason which
can with any plausibility be urged in favour of this notion, is that the cured

---

[15] Ut sup. s. 196.
[16] Winer (bibl. Realw. 1, s. 796) says : We should be contented to refrain from seeking a
natural explanation *in individual cases* (of the cures of Jesus), and ever bear in mind that the
banishment of the miraculous out of the agency of Jesus can never be effected *so long as the
gospels are regarded historically.*
[17] Disc. 3.
[18] Paulus, Comm. 4, s. 263 ff. L. J. 1, a, s. 298.

man points out Jesus to his enemies as the one who had commanded him to carry his bed on the sabbath (v. 15; comp. 11 ff.), a circumstance which is only to be explained on the ground that Jesus had enjoined what was unwelcome.   But that notification to the Pharisees might equally be given, either with a friendly intention, as in the case of the man born blind (John ix. 11, 25), or at least with the innocent one of devolving the defence of the alleged violation of the sabbath on a stronger than himself.[19]   The Evangelist at least gives it as his opinion that the man was really afflicted, and suffered from a wearisome disease, when he describes him as *having had an infirmity thirty-eight years*, τριάκοντα καὶ ὀκτὼ ἔτη ἔχων ἐν τῇ ἀσθενείᾳ (v. 5): for the forced interpretation once put on this passage by Paulus, referring the thirty-eight years to the man's age, and not to the duration of his disease, he has not even himself ventured to reproduce.[20]   On this view of the incident it is also impossible to explain what Jesus says to the cured man on a subsequent meeting (v. 14): *Behold thou art made whole ; sin no more lest a worse thing come unto thee.*   Even Paulus is compelled by these words to admit that the man had a real infirmity, though only a trifling one :—in other words he is compelled to admit the inadequacy of the idea on which his explanation of the incident is based, so that here again we retain a miracle, and that not of the smallest.

In relation to the historical credibility of the narrative, it may certainly be held remarkable that so important a sanative institution as Bethesda is described to be by John, is not mentioned either by Josephus or the rabbins, especially if the popular belief connected a miraculous cure with this pool :[21] but this affords nothing decisive,   It is true that in the description of the pool there lies a fabulous popular notion, which appears also to have been received by the writer (for even if v. 4 be spurious, something similar is contained in the words κίνησις τοῦ ὕδατος, v. 3, and ταραχθῇ, v. 7).   But this proves nothing against the truth of the narrative, since even an eye-witness and a disciple of Jesus may have shared a vulgar error.   To make credible, however, such a fact as that a man who had been lame eight-and-thirty years, so that he was unable to walk, and completely bed-ridden, should have been perfectly cured by a word, the supposition of psychological influence will not suffice, for the man had no knowledge whatever of Jesus, v. 13 ; nor will any physical analogy, such as magnetism and the like, serve the purpose : but if such a result really happened, we must exalt that by which it happened above all the limits of the human and the natural.   On the other hand. it ought never to have been thought a difficulty[22] that from among the multitude of the infirm waiting in the porches of the pool, Jesus selected one only as the object of his curative power, since the cure of him whose sufferings had been of the longest duration was not only particularly adapted, but also sufficient, to glorify the miraculous power of the Messiah.   Nevertheless, it is this very trait which suggests a suspicion that the narrative has a mythical character. On a great theatre of disease, crowded with all kinds of sufferers, Jesus, the exalted and miraculously gifted physician, appears and selects the one who is afflicted with the most obstinate malady, that by his restoration he may present the most brilliant proof of his miraculous power.   We have already remarked that the fourth gospel, instead of extending the curative agency of Jesus over large masses and to a great variety of diseases, as the synoptical gospels do, concentrates it on a few cases which proportionately gain in in-

---

[19] Vid. Lücke and Tholuck, in loc.
[20] Comp. with Comm. 4, s. 290, his Leben Jesu, 1, a, s. 298.
[21] Bretschneider, Probab., s. 69.
[22] As by Hase, L. J. § 92.

tensity : thus here, in the narrative of the cure of a man who had been lame thirty-eight years, it has far surpassed all the synoptical accounts of cures performed on persons with diseased limbs, among whom the longest sufferer is described in Luke xiii. 11, only as a woman who had had a spirit of infirmity eighteen years. Without doubt the fourth Evangelist had received some intimation (though, as we have gathered from other parts of his history, it was far from precise) of cures of this nature performed by Jesus, especially of that wrought on the paralytic, Matt. ix. 2 ff. parall., for the address to the patient, and the result of the cure are in this narrative in John almost verbally the same as in that case, especially according to Mark's account.[23]   There is even a vestige in this history of John, of the circumstance that in the synoptical narrative the cure appears in the light of a forgiveness of sins : for as Jesus in the latter consoles the patient, before the cure, with the assurance, *thy sins are forgiven thee*, so in the former, he warns him, after the cure, in the words, *sin no more*, etc.   For the rest, this highly embellished history of a miraculous cure was represented as happening on the sabbath, probably because the command to take up the bed which it contained appeared the most suitable occasion for the reproach of violating the sabbath.

§ 100.

RESUSCITATIONS OF THE DEAD.

The Evangelists tell us of three instances in which Jesus recalled the dead to life.   One of these is common to the three synoptists, one belongs solely to Luke, and one to John.

The instance which is common to the three first Evangelists is the resuscitation of a girl, and is in all the three gospels united with the narrative of the woman who had an issue of blood (Matt. ix. 18 f. 23—26 ; Mark v. 22 ff. ; Luke viii. 41 ff.).   In the more precise designation of the girl and her father, the synoptical writers vary.   Matthew introduces the father generally as ἄρχων εἷς *a certain ruler*, without any name ; the two others as a *ruler of the synagogue named Jairus :* the latter moreover describes the girl as being twelve years old, and Luke states that she was the only child of her father ; particulars of which Matthew is ignorant.   A more important difference is, that according to Matthew the ruler in the first instance speaks of his daughter to Jesus as being dead, and intreats him to restore her to life ; whereas according to the two other Evangelists, he left her while yet living, though on the point of death, that he might fetch Jesus to avert her actual decease, and first when Jesus was on the way with him, people came out of his house with the information that his daughter had in the meantime expired, so that to trouble Jesus further was in vain.   The circumstances of the resuscitation also are differently described, for Matthew knows not that Jesus, as the other Evangelists state, took with him only his three most confidential disciples as witnesses.   Some theologians, Storr for example, have thought these divergencies so important, that they have supposed two different cases in which, among other similar circumstances, the daughter, in one case of a civil ruler (Matthew), in the other, of a ruler of the synagogue named Jairus (Mark and

---

[23] Mark ii. 9: (τί ἐστιν, εὐκοπώτερον, εἰπεῖν———) ἔγειραι, καὶ ἆρόν σου τὸν κράββατον καὶ περιπάτει ;

11 :—ἔγειρα καὶ ἆρον τὸν κράββατόν σου καὶ ὕπαγε εἰς τὸν οἶκόν σου.

12 : καὶ ἠγέρθη εὐθέως, καὶ ὥρας τὸν κράββατον ἐξῆλθεν ἐναντίον πάντων.

John v. 8 : ἔγειραι, ἆρον τὸν κράββατόν σου, καὶ περιπάτει.

9 : καὶ εὐθέως ἐγένετο ὑγιὴς ὁ ἄνθρωπος, καὶ ἦρε τὸν κράββατον αὐτοῦ καὶ περιεπάτει.

Luke), was raised from the dead by Jesus.[1] But that, as Storr supposes, and as it is inevitable to suppose on his view, Jesus not only twice resuscitated a girl, but also on both these occasions, healed a woman with an issue immediately before, is a coincidence which does not at all gain in probability by the vague observation of Storr, that it is quite possible for very similar things to happen at different times. If then it must be admitted that the Evangelists narrate only one event, the weak attempt to give perfect agreement to their narratives should be forborne. For neither can the expression of Matthew ἄρτι ἐτελεύτησε mean, as Kuinöl maintains,[2] *est morti proxima*, nor can that of Mark, ἐσχάτως ἔχει, or of Luke ἀπέθνησκε, imply that death had already taken place : not to mention that according to both, the fact of the death is subsequently announced to the father as something new.[3]

Our more modern critics have wisely admitted a divergency between the accounts in doing which they have unanimously given the palm of superior accuracy to the intermediate Evangelists. Some are lenient towards Matthew, and only attribute to his mode of narration a brevity which might belong even to the representation of an eye-witness ;[4] while others regard this want of particularity as an indication that the first gospel had not an apostolic origin.[5] Now that Mark and Luke give the name of the applicant, on which Matthew is silent, and also that they determine his rank more precisely than the latter, will just as well bear an unfavourable construction for them, as the usual favourable one ; since the designation of persons by name, as we have before remarked, is not seldom an addition of the later legend. For example, the woman with the issue first receives the name of Veronica in the tradition of John Malala ;[6] the Canaanitish woman that of Justa in the Clementine Homilies :[7] and the two thieves crucified with Jesus, the names of Gestas and Demas in the Gospel of Nicodemas.[8] Luke's μονογενής (*one only daughter*) only serves to make the scene more touching, and the ἐτῶν δώδεκα *twelve years of age*, he, and after him Mark, might have borrowed from the history of the woman with the issue. The divergency that, according to Matthew, the maiden is spoken of in the first instance as dead, according to the two others as only dying, must have been considered very superficially by those who have thought it possible to turn it in accordance with our own rule to the disadvantage of Matthew, on the ground that his representation serves to aggrandize the miracle. For in both the other gospels the death of the girl is subsequently announced, and its being supposed in Matthew to have occurred a few moments earlier is no aggrandizement of the miracle. Nay, it is the reverse ; for the miraculous power of Jesus appears greater in the former, not indeed objectively, but subjectively, because it is heightened by contrast and surprise. There, where Jesus is in the first instance intreated to restore the dead to life, he does no more than what was desired of him ; here, on the contrary, where supplicated only for the cure of a sick person, he actually brings that person to life again, he does more than the interested parties seek or understand. There, where the power of awaking the dead is presupposed

---

[1] Ueber den Zweck des Evang. und der Briefe Joh., s. 351 ff.
[2] Comm. in Matth. p. 263. Observe his argumentation : *verba* [N.B. *Matthaei*]: ἄρτι ἐτελεύτησεν, *non possunt latine reddi : jam mortua est : nam, auctore* [N.B. *Luca*] *patri adhuc cum Christo colloquenti nuntiabat servus, filiam jam exspirasse ; ergo* [*auctore Matthaeo?*] *nondum mortua erat, cum pater ad Jesum accederet.*
Compare, on the subject of these vain attempts at reconciliation, Schleiermacher, über den Lukas, s. 132, and Fritzsche, in Matth., p. 347 f.
[4] Olshausen, in loc.
[5] Schleiermacher, ut sup. s. 131 ff. ; Schulz, über d. Abendmahl, s. 316 f.
[6] Vid. Fabricius, Cod. Apocr. N. T. 2, p. 449 ff.
[7] Homil. ii. 19.   [8] Cap. x.

by the father to belong to Jesus, the extraordinary nature of such a power is less marked than here, where the father at first only presupposes the power of healing the sick, and when death has supervened, is diverted from any further hope. In the description of the arrival and the conduct of Jesus in the house where the corpse lay, Matthew's brevity is at least clearer than the diffuse accounts of the two other Evangelists. Matthew tells us that Jesus, having reached the house, put forth the minstrels already assembled for the funeral, together with the rest of the crowd, on the ground that there would be no funeral there ; this is perfectly intelligible. But Mark and Luke tell us besides that he excluded his disciples also, with the exception of three, from the scene about to take place, and for this it is difficult to discover a reason. That a greater number of spectators would have been physically or psychologically an impediment to the resuscitation, can only be said on the supposition that the event was a natural one. Admitting the miracle, the reason for the exclusion can only be sought in the want of fitness in the excluded parties, whom, however, the sight of such a miracle would surely have been the very means to benefit. But we must not omit to observe that the two later synoptists, in opposition to the concluding statement of Matthew that the fame of this event went abroad in the whole land, represent Jesus as enjoining the strictest silence on the witnesses : so that on the whole it rather appears that Mark and Luke regarded the incident as a mystery, to which only the nearest relatives and the most favoured disciples were admitted. Lastly, the difference on which Schulz insists as favourable to the second and third Evangelists, namely, that while Matthew makes Jesus simply take the maiden by the hand, they have preserved to us the words which he at the same time uttered, the former even in the original language ;—can either have no weight at all, or it must fall into the opposite scale. For that Jesus, if he said anything when recalling a girl to life, made use of some such words as ἡ παῖς ἐγείρου, *maiden, I say unto thee, arise,* the most remote narrator might imagine, and to regard the ταλιθὰ κοῦμι of Mark as an indication that this Evangelist drew from a peculiarly original source, is to forget the more simple supposition that he translated these words from the Greek of his informant for the sake of presenting the life-giving word in its original foreign garb, and thus enhancing its mysteriousness, as we have before observed with reference to the ἐφφαθὰ in the cure of the deaf man. After what we have seen we shall willingly abstain from finding out whether the individual who originally furnished the narrative in Luke were one of the three confidential disciples, and whether the one who originally related it, also put it into writing : a task to which only the acumen of Schleiermacher is equal.[9]

In relation to the facts of the case, the natural interpretation speaks with more than its usual confidence, under the persuasion that it has on its side the assurance of Jesus himself, that the maiden was not really dead, but merely in a sleep-like swoon ; and not only rationalists, like Paulus, and semi-rationalists, like Schleiermacher, but also decided supranaturalists, like Olshausen, believe, on the strength of that declaration of Jesus, that this was no resuscitation of the dead.[10] The last-named commentator attaches especial importance to the antithesis in the speech of Jesus, and because the words οὐκ ἀπέθανε, *is not dead,* are followed by ἀλλὰ καθεύδει, *but sleepeth,* is of opinion that the former expression cannot be interpreted to mean merely, she is not

---

[9] Ut sup. s. 129.
[10] Paulus, exeg. Handb. 1, b, s. 526, 31 f. ; Schleiermacher, ut sup. s. 132 ; Olshausen, 1, s. 327. Even Neander does not express himself decidedly against this interpretation of the words of Jesus ; while with regard to the girl's real condition, he thinks the supposition of a merely apparent death probable. L. J. Chr., s. 343. Comp. 338 f.

dead, since I have resolved to restore her to life; strange criticism,—
for it is precisely this addition which shows that she was only not dead
in so far as it was in the power of Jesus to recall her to life. Reference
is also made to the declaration of Jesus concerning Lazarus, John xi. 14,
Λάζαρος ἀπέθανε, *Lazarus is dead*, which is directly the reverse of the passage
in question, οὐκ ἀπέθανε τὸ κοράσιον, *the damsel is not dead*. But Jesus had
before said of Lazarus, αὕτη ἡ ἀσθένεια οὐκ ἔστι πρὸς θάνατον, *this sickness is not
unto death* (v. 4), and Λάζαρος ὁ φίλος ἡμῶν κεκοίμηται, *our friend Lazarus
sleepeth* (v. 11). Thus in the case of Lazarus also, who was really dead, we
have just as direct a denial of death, and affirmation of mere sleep, as in the
narrative before us. Hence Fritzsche is undoubtedly right when he paraphrases the words of Jesus in our passage as follows : *puellam ne pro mortua
habetote, sed dormire existimatote quippe in vitam mox redituram.* Moreover,
Matthew subsequently (xi. 5) makes Jesus say, νεκροὶ ἐγείρονται, *the dead are
raised up* ; and as he mentions no other instance of resuscitation by Jesus,
he must apparently have had this in his mind.[11]

But apart from the false interpretation of the words of Jesus, this view of
the subject has many difficulties. That in many diseases conditions may present themselves which have a deceptive resemblance to death, or that in the
indifferent state of medical science among the Jews of that age especially, a
swoon might easily be mistaken for death is not to be denied. But how was
Jesus to know that there was such a merely apparent death in this particular
case? However minutely the father detailed to him the course of the disease,
nay, even if Jesus were acquainted beforehand with the particular circumstances of the girl's illness (as the natural explanation supposes) : we must
still ask, how could he build so much on this information, as, without having
seen the girl, and in contradiction to the assurance of the eye-witnesses,
decidedly to declare that she was not dead, according to the rationalistic
interpretation of his words? This would have been rashness and folly to boot,
unless Jesus had obtained certain knowledge of the true state of the case in a
supernatural way :[12] to admit which, however, is to abandon the naturalistic
point of view. To return to the explanation of Paulus; between the expressions, ἐκράτησε τῆς χειρὸς αὐτῆς, *he took her by the hand*, and ἠγέρθη τὸ
κοράσιον, *the maid arose*, expressions which are closely enough connected in
Matthew, and are still more inseparably linked by the words εὐθέως and
παραχρῆμα in the other two gospels, he inserts a course of medical treatment,
and Venturini can even specify the different restoratives which were applied.[13]
Against such arbitrary suppositions, Olshausen justly maintains that in the
opinion of the evangelical narrator the life-giving word of Jesus (and we might
add, the touch of his hand, furnished with divine power) was the means of
restoring the girl to life.

In the case cf resuscitation narrated by Luke alone (vii. 11 ff.) the natural
explanation has not such a handle as was presented by the declaration of
Jesus in the narrative just considered. Nevertheless, the rationalistic commentators take courage, and rest their hopes mainly on the circumstance that
Jesus *speaks* to the young man lying in the coffin (v. 14). Now, say they, no
one would speak to a dead person, but only to such an one as is ascertained
or guessed to be capable of hearing.[14] But this rule would prove that all the
dead whom Christ will raise at the last day are only apparently dead, as otherwise they could not hear his voice, which it is expressly said they will do

---

[11] Comp. de Wette, exeg. Handb. 1, 1, s. 95 ; Weisse, die ev. Geschichte, 1, s. 503.
[12] Comp. Neander. L. J., s. 342.
[13] Natürliche Geschichte, 2, s. 212.
[14] Paulus, exeg. Handb. 1, b, s. 716, Anm. and 719 f.

(John v. 28 ; comp. 1 Thess. iv. 16) ; it would therefore prove too much. Certainly one who is spoken to must be supposed to hear, and in a certain sense to be living ; but in the present instance this holds only in so far as the voice of him who quickens the dead can penetrate even to the ears from which life has departed.   We must indeed admit the possibility that with the bad custom which prevailed among the Jews of burying their dead a few hours after their decease, a merely apparent corpse might easily be carried to the grave ; [15] but all by which it is attempted to show that this possibility was here a reality, is a tissue of fictions.   In order to explain how Jesus, even without any intention to perform a miracle, came to join the funeral procession, and how the conjecture could occur to him that the individual about to be buried was not really dead, it is first imagined that the two processions, that of the funeral and that of the companions of Jesus, met precisely under the gate of the city, and as they impeded each other, halted for a while :— directly in opposition to the text, which makes the bearers first stand still when Jesus touches the bier.   Affected by the peculiar circumstances of the case, which he had learned during the pause in his progress, Jesus, it is said, approached the mother, and not with any reference to a resurrection which he intended to effect, but merely as a consolatory address, said to her, *Weep not*.[16]   But what an empty, presuming comforter would he be, who, when a mother was about to consign her only son to the grave, should forbid her even the relief of tears, without offering to her either real help by recalling the departed one, or ideal, by suggesting grounds for consolation !   Now the latter Jesus does not attempt : hence unless we would allow him to appear altogether heartless, he must be supposed to have resolved on the former, and for this he in fact makes every preparation, designedly touching the bier, and causing the bearers to stand still.   Here, before the reanimating word of Jesus, the natural explanation inserts the circumstance that Jesus observed some sign of life in the youth, and on this, either immediately or after a previous application of medicaments,[17] spoke the words, which helped completely to awake him.   But setting aside the fact that those intervening measures are only interpolated into the text, and that the strong words : νεανίσκε, σοὶ λέγω, ἐγέρθητι, *Young man, I say unto thee arise !* resemble rather the authoritative command of a miracle worker than the attempt of a physician to restore animation ; how, if Jesus were conscious that the youth was alive when he met him, and was not first recalled to life by himself, could he with a good conscience receive the praise which, according to the narrative, the multitude lavished on him as a great prophet on account of this deed?   According to Paulus, he was himself uncertain how he ought to regard the result ; but if he were not convinced that he ought to ascribe the result to himself, it was his duty to disclaim all praise on account of it ; and if he omitted to do this, his conduct places him in an equivocal light, in which he by no means appears in the other evangelical histories, so far as they are fairly interpreted.   Thus here also we must acknowledge that the Evangelist intends to narrate to us a miraculous resuscitation of the dead, and that according to him, Jesus also regarded his deed as a miracle.[18]

In the third history of a resurrection, which is peculiar to John (chap. xi.), the resuscitated individual is neither just dead nor being carried to his grave, but has been already buried several days.   Here one would have thought there was little hope of effecting a natural explanation ; but the arduousness

---

[15] Ibid, ut sup. s. 723.   Comp. De Wette, exeg. Handb. 1, 2, s. 47.
[16] Thus Hase also, L. J. § 87.
[17] Venturini, 2, s. 293.
[18] Comp. Schleiermacher, ut sup. s. 103 f.

of the task has only stimulated the ingenuity and industry of the rationalists in developing their conception of this narrative. We shall also see that together with the rigorously consequent mode of interpretation of the rationalists,—which, maintaining the historical integrity of the evangelical narrative throughout, assumes the responsibility of explaining every part naturally, there has appeared another system, which distinguishes certain features of the narrative as additions after the event, and is thus an advance towards the mythical explanation.

The rationalistic expositors set out here from the same premises as in the former narrative, namely, that it is in itself possible for a man who has lain in a tomb four days to come to life again, and that this possibility is strengthened in the present instance by the known custom of the Jews ; propositions which we shall not abstractedly controvert. From this they proceed to a supposition which we perhaps ought not to let pass so easily,[19] namely, that from the messenger whom the sisters had sent with the news of their brother's illness, Jesus had obtained accurate information of the circumstances of the disease ; and the answer which he gave to the messenger, *This sickness is not unto death* (v. 4), is said to express, merely as an inference which he had drawn from the report of the messenger, his conviction that the disease was not fatal. Such a view of his friend's condition would certainly accord the best with his conduct in remaining two days in Peræa after the reception of the message (v. 6) ; since, according to that supposition, he could not regard his presence in Bethany as a matter of urgent necessity. But how comes it that after the lapse of these two days, he not only resolves to journey thither (v. 8), but also has quite a different opinion of the state of Lazarus, nay, certain knowledge of his death, which he first obscurely (v. 10) and then plainly (v. 14) announces to his disciples? Here the thread of the natural explanation is lost, and the break is only rendered more conspicuous by the fiction of a second messenger,[20] after the lapse of two days, bringing word to Jesus that Lazarus had expired in the interim. For the author of the gospel at least cannot have known of a second messenger, otherwise he must have mentioned him, since the omission to do so gives another aspect to the whole narrative, obliging us to infer that Jesus had obtained information of the death of Lazarus in a supernatural manner. Jesus, when he had resolved to go to Bethany, said to the disciples, *Lazarus sleepeth, but I go that I may awake him out of sleep* (κεκοίμηται—ἐξυπνίσω—v. 11) ; this the naturalists explain by the supposition that Jesus must in some way have gathered from the statements of the messengers who announced the death of Lazarus, that the latter was only in a state of lethargy. But we can as little here as in the former case impute to Jesus the foolish presumption of giving, before he had even seen the alleged corpse, the positive assurance that he yet lived.[21] From this point of view, it is also a difficulty that Jesus says to his disciples (v. 15) *I am glad for your sakes that I was not there, to the intent ye may believe* (ἵνα πιστεύσητε). Paulus explains these words to imply that Jesus feared lest the death, had it happened in his presence, might have shaken their faith in him; but, as Gabler [22] has remarked, πιστεύω cannot mean merely the negative : *not to lose faith*, which would rather have been expressed by a phrase such as : ἵνα μὴ ἐκλείπῃ ἡ πίστις ὑμῶν, *that your faith fail not* (see Luke xxii. 32) ; and moreover we

---

[19] Paulus, Comp. 4, s. 535 ff. ; L. J. 1, b, s. 55 ff.
[20] In the translation of the text in his *Leben Jesu*, 2, b, s, 46, Paulus appears to suppose, beside the message mentioned in the gospel, *three* subsequent messages.
[21] Comp. C. Ch. Flatt, etwas zur Vertheidigung des Wunders der Wiederbelebung des Lazarus, in Süskind's Magazin, 14tes Stück, s. 93 ff.
[22] Journal für auserlesene theol. Literatur, 3, 2, s. 261, Anm.

nowhere find that the idea which the disciples formed of Jesus as the Messiah was incompatible with the death of a man, or, more correctly, of a friend, in his presence.

From the arrival of Jesus in Bethany the evangelical narrative is somewhat more favourable to the natural explanation. It is true that Martha's address to Jesus (v. 21 f.), *Lord, if thou hadst been here, my brother had not died, but I know that even now, whatsoever thou wilt ask of God, he will give it thee,* ἀλλὰ καὶ νῦν οἶδα, ὅτι, ὅσα ἂν αἰτήσῃ τὸν θεόν, δώσει σοι ὁ θεός, appears evidently to express the hope that Jesus may be able even to recall the dead one to life. However, on the assurance of Jesus which follows, *Thy brother shall rise again,* ἀναστήσεται ὁ ἀδελφός σου, she answers despondingly, Yes, at the last day. This is certainly a help to the natural explanation, for it seems retrospectively to give to the above declaration of Martha (v. 22) the general sense, that even now, although he has not preserved the life of her brother, she believes Jesus to be him to whom God grants all that he desires, that is, the favourite of the Deity, the Messiah. But the expression which Martha there uses is not πιστεύω but οἶδα, and the turn of phrase : I know that this will happen if thou only willest it to be so, is a common but indirect form of petition, and is here the more unmistakable, because the object of the entreaty is clearly indicated by the foregoing antithesis. Martha evidently means, Thou hast not indeed prevented the death of our brother, but even now it is not too late, for at thy prayer God will restore him to thee and us. Martha's change of mind, from the hope which is but indirectly expressed in her first reply (v. 24) to its extinction in the second, cannot be held very surprising in a woman who here and elsewhere manifests a very hasty disposition, and it is in the present case sufficiently explained by the form of the foregoing assurance of Jesus (v. 23). Martha had expected that Jesus would reply to her indirect prayer by a decided promise of its fulfilment, and when he answers quite generally and with an expression which it was usual to apply to the resurrection at the last day (ἀναστήσεται), she gives a half-impatient half-desponding reply.[23] But that general declaration of Jesus, as well as the yet more indefinite one (v. 25 f.), *I am the resurrection and the life,* is thought favourable to the rationalistic view : Jesus, it is said, was yet far from the expectation of an extraordinary result, hence he consoles Martha merely with the general hope that he, the Messiah, would procure for those who believed in him a future resurrection and a life of blessedness. As however Jesus had before (v. 11) spoken confidently to his disciples of awaking Lazarus, he must then have altered his opinion in the interim—a change for which no cause is apparent. Further, when (v. 40) Jesus is about to awake Lazarus, he says to Martha, *Said I not unto thee that if thou wouldst believe thou shouldst see the glory of God?* evidently alluding to v. 23, in which therefore he must have meant to predict the resurrection which he was going to effect. That he does not declare this distinctly, and that he again veils the scarcely uttered promise in relation to the brother (v. 25) in general promises for the believing, is the effect of design, the object of which is to try the faith of Martha, and extend her sphere of thought.[24]

When Mary at length comes out of the house with her companions, her weeping moves Jesus himself to tears. To this circumstance the natural interpretation appeals with unusual confidence, asking whether if he were already certain of his friend's resurrection, he would not have approached his grave with the most fervent joy, since he was conscious of being able to call

[23] Flatt, ut sup. 102 f. ; De Wette, in loc. ; Neander, s. 351 f.
[24] Flatt, ut sup. ; Lücke, Tholuck and De Wette, in loc.

him again living from the grave in the next moment ?   In this view the words
ἐνεβριμήσατο (v. 33) and ἐμβριμώμενος (v. 38) are understood of a forcible
repression of the sorrow caused by the death of his friend, which subsequently
found vent in tears (ἐδάκρυσεν).   But both by its etymology, according to
which it signifies *fremere in aliquem* or *in se*, and by the analogy of its use in
the New Testament, where it appears only in the sense of *increpare aliquem*
(Matt. ix. 30; Mark i. 43, xiv. 5), ἐμβριμᾶσθαι is determined to imply an
emotion of anger, not of sorrow ; where it is united, not with the dative of
another person, but with τῷ πνεύματι and ἐν ἑαυτῷ, it must be understood of a
silent, suppressed displeasure.   This sense would be very appropriate in v.
38, where it occurs the second time ; for in the foregoing observation of the
Jews, *Could not this man, who opened the eyes of the blind, have caused that
even this man should not have died?* there lies an intimation that they were
scandalized, the prior conduct of Jesus perplexing them as to his present
demeanour, and vice versâ.   But where the word ἐμβριμᾶσθαι is first used
v. 33, the general weeping seems to have been likely to excite in Jesus a
melancholy, rather than an angry emotion : yet even here a strong disapproval
of the want of faith (ὀλιγοπιστία) which was manifested was not impossible.
That Jesus then himself broke out into tears, only proves that his indignation
against the faithless generation around him dissolved into melancholy, not
that melancholy was his emotion from the beginning.   Lastly, that the Jews
(v. 36) in relation to the tears which Jesus shed, said among themselves,
Behold, how he loved him! appears to be rather against than for those who
regard the emotion of Jesus as sorrow for the death of his friend, and
sympathy with the sisters ; for, as the character of the narrative of John in
general would rather lead us to expect an opposition between the real import
of the demeanour of Jesus, and the interpretation put upon it by the spectators, so in particular *the Jews* in this gospel are always those who either misunderstand or pervert the words and actions of Jesus.   It is true that the
mild character of Jesus is urged, as inconsistent with the harshness which
displeasure on his part at the very natural weeping of Mary and the rest
would imply ; [25] but such a mode of thinking is by no means foreign to the
Christ of John's gospel.   He who gave to the βασιλικὸς, when preferring the
inoffensive request that he would come to his house and heal his son, the
rebuke, *Except ye see signs and wonders ye will not believe*; he who, when
some of his disciples murmured at the hard doctrines of the sixth chapter,
assailed them with the cutting question, *Doth this offend you ?* and *Will ye
also go away ?* (vi. 61, 67); he who repulsed his own mother, when at the
wedding at Cana she complained to him of the want of wine, with the harsh
reply, *What have I to do with thee, Woman ?* (ii. 4)—who thus was always
the most displeased when men, not comprehending his higher mode of
thought or action, showed themselves desponding or importunate,—would
here find peculiar reason for this kind of displeasure.   If this be the true
interpretation of the passage, and if it be not sorrow for the death of Lazarus
which Jesus here exhibits, there is an end to the assistance which the natural
explanation of the entire event is thought to derive from this particular
feature ; meanwhile, even on the other interpretation, a momentary emotion
produced by sympathy with the mourners is quite reconcilable with the foreknowledge of the resurrection.[26]   And how could the words of the Jews v. 37,
serve, as rationalistic commentators think, to excite in Jesus the hope that
God would now perhaps perform something extraordinary for him ?   The

[25] Lücke, 2, s. 388.
[26] Flatt, ut sup. s. 104 f. ; Lücke, ut sup.

Jews did not express the hope that he could awake the dead, but only the conjecture that he might perhaps have been able to preserve his friend's life ; Martha therefore had previously said more when she declared her belief that even now the Father would grant him what he asked ; so that if such hopes were excited in Jesus from without, they must have been excited earlier, and especially before the weeping of Jesus, to which it is customary to appeal as the proof that they did not yet exist.

Even supranaturalists admit tnat the expression of Martha when Jesus commanded that the stone should be taken away from the grave, Κύριε, ἤδη ὄζει (v. 39), is no proof at all that decomposition had really commenced, nor consequently that a natural resuscitation was impossible, since it may have been a mere inference from the length of time since the burial.[27] But more weight must be attached to the words with which Jesus, repelling the objections of Martha, persists in having the tomb opened (v. 40): *Said I not unto thee that if thou wouldst believe thou shouldst see the glory of God?* How could he say this unless he was decidedly conscious of his power to resuscitate Lazarus ? According to Paulus, this declaration only implied generally that those who have faith will, in some way or other, experience a glorious manifestation of the divinity. But what glorious manifestation of the divinity was to be seen here, on the opening of the grave of one who had been buried four days, unless it were his restoration to life? and what could be the sense of the words of Jesus, as opposed to the observation of Martha, that her brother was already within the grasp of decay, but that he was empowered to arrest decay ? But in order to learn with certainty the meaning of the words τὴν δόξαν τοῦ θεοῦ in our present passage we need only refer to v. 4, where Jesus had said that the sickness of Lazarus was not *unto death*, πρὸς θάνατον, but *for the glory of God*, ὑπὲρ τῆς δόξης τοῦ θεοῦ. Here the first member of the anti-thesis, *not unto death*, clearly shows that the δόξα τοῦ θεοῦ signifies the glorifi-cation of God by the life of Lazarus, that is, since he was now dead, by his resurrection : a hope which Jesus could not venture to excite in the most critical moment, without having a superior assurance that it would be fulfilled.[28] After the opening of the grave, and before he says to the dead man, *Come forth !* he thanks the Father for having heard his prayer. This is adduced, in the rationalistic poirt of view, as the most satisfactory proof that he did not first recall Lazarus to life by those words, but on looking into the grave found him already alive again. Truly, such an argument was not to be expected from theologians who have some insight into the character of John's gospel. These ought to have remembered how common it is in this gospel, as for example in the expression *glorify thy son*, to represent that which is yet to be effected or which is only just begun, as already performed ; and in the present instance it is especially suited to mark the certainty of obtaining fulfilment, that it is spoken of as having already happened. And what inven-tion does it further require to explain, both how Jesus could perceive in Lazarus the evidences of returning life, and how the latter could have come to life again ! Between the removal of the stone, says Paulus, and the thanksgiving of Jesus, lies the critical interval when the surprising result was accomplished ; then must Jesus, yet some steps removed from the grave, have discerned that Lazarus was living. By what means ? and how so quickly and unhesitatingly ? and why did he and no one else discern it ? He may have discerned it by the movements of Lazarus, it is conjectured. But how easily might he deceive himself with respect to a dead body lying in a dark cavern :

[27] Flatt, s. 106 ; Olshausen, 2, s. 269.
[28] Flatt, s. 97 f.

how precipitate was he, if without having examined more nearly, he so quickly and decidedly declared his conviction that Lazarus lived! Or, if the movements of the supposed corpse were strong and not to be mistaken, how could they escape the notice of the surrounding spectators? Lastly, how could Jesus in his prayer represent the incident about to take place as a sign of his divine mission, if he was conscious that he had not effected, but only discovered, the resuscitation of Lazarus? As arguments for the natural possibility of a return of life in a man who had been interred four days, the rationalistic explanation adduces our ignorance of the particular circumstances of the supposed death, the rapidity of interment among the Jews, afterwards the coolness of the cave, the strong fragrance of the spices, and lastly, the reanimating draught of warm air, which on the rolling away of the stone streamed into the cave. But all these circumstances do not produce more than the lowest degree of possibility, which coincides with the highest degree of improbability: and with this the certainty with which Jesus predicts the result must remain irreconcilable.[29]

These decided predictions are indeed the main hindrance to the natural interpretation of this chapter; hence it has been sought to neutralize them, still from the rationalistic position, by the supposition that they did not proceed from Jesus, but may have been added *ex eventu* by the narrator. Paulus himself found the words ἐξυπνίσω αὐτὸν (v. 11) quite too decided, and therefore ventured the conjecture that the narrator, writing with the result in his mind, had omitted a qualifying *perhaps*, which Jesus had inserted.[30] This expedient has been more extensively adopted by Gabler. Not only does he partake the opinion of Paulus as to the above expression, but already in v. 4, he is inclined to lay the words ὑπὲρ τῆς δόξης τοῦ θεοῦ *for the glory of God*, to the account of the Evangelist: again v. 15, he conjectures that in the words χαίρω δι' ὑμᾶς, ἵνα πιστεύσητε, ὅτι οὐκ ἤμην ἐκεῖ, *I am glad for your sakes that I was not there, to the intent ye may believe*, there is a slight exaggeration resulting from John's knowledge of the issue; lastly, even in relation to the words of Martha v. 22, ἀλλὰ καὶ νῦν οἶδα κ. τ. λ. he admits the idea of an addition from the pen of the writer.[31] By the adoption of this expedient, the natural interpretation avows its inability by itself to cope with the difficulties in John's narrative. For if, in order to render its application possible, it is necessary to expunge the most significant passages, it is plain that the narrative in its actual state does not admit of a natural explanation. It is true that the passages, the incompatibility of which with the rationalistic mode of explanation is confessed by their excision, are very sparingly chosen; but from the above observations it is clear, that if all the features in this narrative which are really opposed to the natural view of the entire event were ascribed to the Evangelist, it would in the end be little short of the whole that must be regarded as his invention. Thus, what we have done with the two first narratives of resuscitations, is with the last and most remarkable history of this kind, effected by the various successive attempts at explanation themselves, namely, to reduce the subject to the alternative : that we either receive the event as supernatural, according to the representation of the evangelical narrative ; or,

---

[29] Compare on this subject, especially Flatt and Lücke.

[30] Comm. 4, s. 437 ; in the L. J. 1, b, s. 57, and 2, b, s. 46, this conjecture is no longer employed.

[31] Ut sup. s. 272 ff. Even Neander shows himself not disinclined to such a conjecture as far as regards v. 4 (s. 349). As Gabler believes that these expressions cannot have come from Jesus, but only from John, so Dieffenbach, in Bertholdt's Krit. Journal, 5. s. 7 ff., maintains that they cannot have proceeded from John, and as he holds that the rest of the gospel is the production of that apostle, he pronounces those passages to be interpolations.

if we find it incredible as such, deny that the narrative has an historical character.

In order, in this dilemma, to arrive at a decision, with respect to all the three narratives, we must refer to the peculiar character of the kind of miracles which we have now before us.   We have hitherto been ascending a ladder of miracles ; first, cures of mental disorders, then, of all kinds of bodily maladies, in which, however, the organization of the sufferer was not so injured as to cause the cessation of consciousness and life ; and now, the revivification of bodies, from which the life has actually departed.   This progression in the marvellous is, at the same time, a gradation in inconceivability.   We have indeed been able to represent to ourselves how a mental derangement, in which none of the bodily organs were attacked beyond the nervous system, which is immediately connected with mental action, might have been removed, even in a purely psychical manner, by the mere word, look, and influence of Jesus : but the more deeply the malady appeared to have penetrated into the entire corporeal system, the more inconceivable to us was a cure of this kind. Where in insane persons the brain was disturbed to the extent of raging madness, or where in nervous patients the disorder was so confirmed as to manifest itself in periodical epilepsy ; there we could scarcely imagine how permanent benefit could be conferred by that mental influence ; and this was yet more difficult where the disease had no immediate connection with the mind, as in leprosy, blindness, lameness, etc.   And yet, up to this point, there was always something present, to which the miraculous power of Jesus could apply itself ; there was still a consciousness in the objects, on which to make an impression —a nervous life to be stimulated.   Not so with the dead.   The corpse from which life and consciousness have flown has lost the last fulcrum for the power of the miracle worker ; it perceives him no longer—receives no impression from him ; for the very capability of receiving impressions must be conferred on him anew.   But to confer this, that is, to give life in the proper sense, is a creative act, and to think of this as being exercised by a man, we must confess to be beyond our power.

But even within the limits of our three histories of resurrections, there is an evident climax.   Woolston has remarked with justice, that it seems as if each of these narratives were intended to supply what was wanting in the preceding.[32]   The daughter of Jairus is restored to life on the same bed on which she had just expired ; the youth of Nain, when already in his coffin, and on his way to interment ; lastly, Lazarus, after four days' abode in the tomb.   In the first history, a word was the only intimation that the maiden had fallen under the powers of the grave ; in the second, the fact is imprinted on the imagination also, by the picture of the young man being already carried out of the city towards his grave ; but in the third, Lazarus, who had been some time inclosed in the grave, is depicted in the strongest manner as an inhabitant of the nether world : so that, if the reality of the death could be doubted in the first instance, this would become more difficult in the second, and in the third, as good as impossible.[33]   With this gradation, there is a corresponding increase in the difficulty of rendering the three events conceivable ; if, indeed, when the fact itself is inconceivable, there can exist degrees of inconceivableness between its various modifications.   If, however, the resurrection of a dead person in general were possible, it must rather be possible in the case of one just departed, and yet having some remains of vital warmth, than in that of a corpse, cold and being carried to the grave ; and again, in

[32] Disc. 5.
[33] Bretschneider, Probab., s. 61.

this, rather than in the case of one who had already lain four days in the grave, and in which decay is supposed to have commenced, nay, with respect to which, this supposition, if not confirmed, is at least not denied.

But, setting aside the miraculous part of the histories in question, each succeeding one is both intrinsically more improbable, and externally less attested, than the foregoing. As regards the internal improbability, one element of this, which indeed lies in all, and therefore also in the first, is especially conspicuous in the second. As a motive by which Jesus was induced to raise the young man at Nain, the narrative mentions compassion for the mother (v. 13). Together with this we are to include, according to Olshausen, a reference to the young man himself. For, he observes, man as a conscious being can never be treated as a mere instrument, which would be the case here, if the joy of the mother were regarded as the sole object of Jesus in raising the youth.[34] This remark of Olshausen demands our thanks, not that it removes the difficulty of this and every other resuscitation of the dead, but that it exhibits that difficulty in the clearest light. For the conclusion, that what in itself, or according to enlightened ideas, is not allowable or fitting, cannot be ascribed to Jesus by the Evangelists, is totally inadmissible. We should rather (presupposing the purity of the character of Jesus) conclude that when the evangelical narratives ascribe to him what is not allowable, they are incorrect. Now that Jesus, in his resuscitations of the dead, made it a consideration whether the persons to be restored to life might, from the spiritual condition in which they died, derive advantage from the restoration or the contrary, we find no indication; that, as Olshausen supposes, the corporeal awakening was attended with a spiritual awakening, or that such a result was expected, is nowhere said. These resuscitated individuals, not excepting even Lazarus, recede altogether from our observation after their return to life, and hence Woolston was led to ask why Jesus rescued from the grave precisely these insignificant persons, and not rather John the Baptist, or some other generally useful man. Is it said, he knew it to be the will of Providence that these men, once dead, should remain so? But then, it should seem, he must have thought the same of all who had once died, and to Woolston's objection there remains no answer but this : as it was positively known concerning celebrated men, that the breach which their deaths occasioned was never filled up by their restoration to life, legend could not annex the resurrections which she was pleased to narrate to such names, but must choose unknown subjects, in relation to which she was not under the same control.

The above difficulty is common to all the three narratives, and is only rendered more prominent in the second by an accidental expression : but the third narrative is full of difficulties entirely peculiar to itself, since the conduct of Jesus throughout, and, to a considerable extent, that of the other parties, is not easily to be conceived. When Jesus receives the information of the death of Lazarus, and the request of the sisters implied therein, that he would come to Bethany, he remains still two days in the same place, and does not set out toward Judea till after he is certain of the death. Why so ? That it was not because he thought the illness attended with no danger, has been already shown; on the contrary, he foresaw the death of Lazarus. That indifference was not the cause of the delay, is expressly remarked by the Evangelist (v. 5). What then ? Lücke conjectures that Jesus was then occupied with a particularly fruitful ministry in Peræa, which he was not willing to interrupt for the sake of Lazarus, holding it his duty to postpone his less important call as a worker of miracles and a succouring friend, to his higher

[34] I, s. 276 f.

call as a teacher.[35] But he might here have very well done the one, and not have left the other undone ; he might either have left some disciples to carry forward his work in that country, or remaining there himself, have still cured Lazarus, whether through the medium of a disciple, or by the power of his will at a distance. Moreover, our narrator is entirely silent as to such a cause for the delay of Jesus. This view of it, therefore, can be listened to only on the supposition that no other motive for the delay is intimated by the Evangelist, and even then as nothing more than a conjecture. Now another motive is clearly indicated, as Olshausen has remarked, in the declaration of Jesus, v. 15, that he is glad he was not present at the death of Lazarus, because, for the object of strengthening the faith of the disciples, the resurrection of his friend would be more effectual than his cure. Thus Jesus had designedly allowed Lazarus to die, that by his miraculous restoration to life, he might procure so much the more faith in himself. Tholuck and Olshausen on the whole put the same construction on this declaration of Jesus; but they confine themselves too completely to the moral point of view, when they speak of Jesus as designing, in his character of teacher, to perfect the spiritual condition of the family at Bethany and of his disciples ; [36] since, according to expressions, such as ἵνα δοξασθῇ ὁ υἱὸς τ. θ. (v. 4), his design was rather the messianic one of spreading and confirming faith in himself as the Son of God, though principally, it is true, within that narrow circle. Here Lücke exclaims : by no means ! never did the Saviour of the needy, the noblest friend of man, act thus arbitrarily and capriciously ; [37] and De Wette also observes, that Jesus in no other instance designedly brings about or increases his miracles.[38] The former, as we have seen, concludes that something external, preoccupation elsewhere, detained Jesus ; a supposition which is contrary to the text, and which even De Wette finds inadequate, though he points out no other expedient. If then these critics are correct in maintaining that the real Jesus cannot have acted thus ; while, on the other hand, they are incorrect in denying that the author of the fourth gospel makes his Jesus act thus : nothing remains but with the author of the Probabilia,[39] from this incongruity of the Christ in John's gospel with the Christ alone conceivable as the real one, to conclude that the narrative of the fourth Evangelist is unhistorical.

The alleged conduct of the disciples also, v. 12 f., is such as to excite surprise. If Jesus had represented to them, or at least to the three principal among them, the death of the daughter of Jairus as a mere sleep, how could they, when he said of Lazarus, *he sleeps, I will awake him,* κεκοίμηται, ἐξυπνίσω αὐτὸν, think that he referred to a natural sleep? One would not awake a patient out of a healthy sleep; hence it must have immediately occurred to the disciples that here sleep (κοίμησις) was spoken of in the same sense as in the case of the maiden. That, instead of this, the disciples understand the deep expressions of Jesus quite superficially, is entirely in the fourth Evangelist's favourite manner, which we have learned to recognise by many examples. If tradition had in any way made known to him, that to speak of death as a sleep was part of the customary phraseology of Jesus, there would immediately spring up in his imagination, so fertile in this kind of antithesis, a misunderstanding corresponding to that figure of speech.[40]

---

[35] Comm. 2, s. 376. Also Neander, s. 346.
[36] Tholuck, s. 202 ; Olshausen, 2, s. 260.
[37] Ut sup.
[38] Andachtsbuch, 1, s. 292 f. Exeg. Handb. 1, 3, s. 134.
[39] S. 59 f. 79.
[40] Comp. de Wette, exeg. Handb. 1, 3, s. 135.

The observation of the Jews, v. 37, is scarcely conceivable, presupposing the truth of the synoptical resuscitations of the dead. The Jews appeal to the cure of the man born blind (John ix.), and draw the inference, that he who had restored sight to this individual, must surely have been able to avert the death of Lazarus. How came they to refer to this heterogeneous and inadequate example, if there lay before them, in the two resuscitations of the dead, miracles more analogous, and adapted to give hope even in this case of actual death? It is certain that the Galilean resuscitations were prior to this of Lazarus, since Jesus after this period went no more into Galilee; neither could those events remain unknown in the capital,[41] especially as we are are expressly told that the fame of them *went abroad into all that land, throughout all Judæa, and throughout all the country round about.* To the real Jews therefore these cases must have been well known; and as the fourth Evangelist makes his Jews refer to something less to the point, it is probable that he knew nothing of the above events: for that the reference belongs to him, and not to the Jews themselves, is evident from the fact, that he makes them refer to the very cure which he had last narrated.

A formidable difficulty lies also in the prayer which is put into the mouth of Jesus, v. 41 f. After thanking the Father for hearing his prayer, he adds, that for himself he knew well that the Father heard him always, and that he uttered this special thanksgiving only for the sake of the people around him, in order to obtain their belief in his divine mission. Thus he first gives his address a relation to God, and afterwards reduces this relation to a feigned one, intended to exist only in the conceptions of the people. Nor is the sense of the words such as Lücke represents it, namely, that Jesus for his own part would have prayed in silence, but for the benefit of the people uttered his prayer aloud (for in the certainty of fulfilment there lies no motive for silent prayer); they imply that for himself he had no need to thank the Father for a single result, as if surprised, since he was sure beforehand of having his wish granted, so that the wish and the thanks were coincident; that is, to speak generally, his relation to the Father did not consist in single acts of prayer, fulfilment, and thanks, but in a continual and permanent interchange of these reciprocal functions, in which no single act of gratitude in and by itself could be distinguished in this manner. If it may be admitted that in relation to the necessities of the people, and out of sympathy with them, such an isolated act could have taken place on the part of Jesus; yet, if there be any truth in this explanation, Jesus must have been entirely borne away by sympathy, must have made the position of the people his own, and thus in that moment have prayed from his own impulse, and on his own behalf.[42] But, here, scarcely has he begun to pray when the reflection arises that he does this from no need of his own; he prays therefore from no lively feeling, but out of cold accommodation, and this must be felt difficult to conceive, nay, even revolting. He who in this manner prays solely for the edification of others, ought in no case to tell them that he prays from their point of view, not from his own; since an audible prayer cannot make any impression on the hearers, unless

---

[41] This is what Neander maintains, L. J. Chr., s. 354. He objects that the fourth Evangelist must in any case have known of resuscitations of the dead by Jesus, even supposing the narrative in question to be an unhistorical exaggeration. But this objection is refuted by the observation, that, as an inducement to the formation of such a narrative, the general tradition that Jesus had raised the dead would be sufficient, and an acquaintance with particular instances as exemplars was not at all requisite.
[42] This argument applies also to De Wette, who, while acknowledging that such an idea would be unsuitable in the *mouth* of Jesus, supposes nevertheless that it was really in his *mind*.

they suppose the speaker's whole soul to be engaged.   How then could Jesus make his prayer ineffective by this addition ?   If he felt impelled to lay before God a confession of the true state of the case, he might have done this in silence ; that he uttered the confession aloud, and that we in consequence read it, could only happen on a calculation of advantage to later Christendom, to the readers of the gospel.   While the thanksgiving was, for obvious reasons, needful to awake the faith of the spectators, the more developed faith which the fourth gospel presupposes, might regard it as a difficulty ; because it might possibly appear to proceed from a too subordinate, and more particularly, a too little constant relation between the Father and the Son.   Consequently the prayer which was necessary for the hearers, must be annulled for readers of a later period, or its value restricted to that of a mere accommodation. But this consideration cannot have been present in the mind of Jesus : it could belong only to a Christian who lived later.   This has been already felt by one critic, who has hence proposed to throw v. 42 out of the text, as an unauthenticated addition by a latter hand.[43]   But as this judgment is destitute of any external reason, if the above passage could not have been uttered by Jesus, we must conclude that the Evangelist only lent the words to Jesus in order to explain the preceding, v. 41 ; and to this opinion Lücke has shown himself not altogether disinclined.[44]   Assuredly we have here words, which are only lent to Jesus by the Evangelist : but if it be so with these words, what is our security that it is so *only* with these ?   In a gospel in which we have already detected many discourses to be merely lent to the alleged speakers— in a narrative which presents historical improbabilities at all points,—the difficulty contained in a single verse is not a sign that that verse does not belong to the rest, but that the whole taken together does not belong to the class of historical compositions.[45]

As regards the gradation in the external testimony to the three narratives, it has already been justly observed by Woolston, that only the resurrection of the daughter of Jairus, in which the miraculous is the least marked, appears in three Evangelists ; the two others are each related by one Evangelist only : [46] and as it is far less easy to understand the omission in the other gospels in relation to the resurrection of Lazarus, than in relation to the raising of the youth at Nain, there is here again a complete climax.

That the last-named event is mentioned by the author of Luke's gospel alone ;—especially that Matthew and Mark have it not instead of the resuscitation of the daughter of Jairus, or together with that narrative,—is a difficulty in more than one respect.[47]   Even viewed generally as a resuscitation of a dead person, one would have thought, as there were few of such miracles according to our gospels, and as they are highly calculated to carry conviction, it could not have been too much trouble to the Evangelists to recount it as a second instance ; especially as Matthew has thought it worth while, for example, to narrate three cures of blindness, which nevertheless were of far less importance, and of which, therefore, he might have spared two, inserting instead of them either one or the other of the remaining resuscitations of the dead.   But admitting that the two first Evangelists had some reason, no longer to be discovered, for not giving more than one history of a resurrection, they ought, one must think, to have chosen that of the youth at Nain far rather

[43] Dieffenbach, über einige wahrscheinliche Interpolationen im Evangelium Johannis, in Bertholdt's krit. Journal, 5, s. 8 f.
[44] Comm. z. Joh., 1te Aufl., 2, s. 310.
[45] Thus the author of the Probabilia also argues, p. 61.
[46] Disc. 5.
[47] Comp. Schleiermacher, über den Lukas, s. 103 ff.

than that of the daughter of Jairus, because the former, as we have above observed, was a more indubitable and striking resurrection. As nevertheless they give only the latter, Matthew at least can have known nothing of the others ; Mark, it is true, probably had it before him in Luke, but he had, as early as iii. 7, or 20, leaped from Luke vi. 12 (17) to Matt. xii. 15 ; and only at iv. 35 (21 ff.) returns to Luke viii. 22 (16 ff.) ; [48] thus passing over the resurrection of the youth (Luke vii. 11 ff.). But now arises the second question : how can the resurrection of the youth, if it really happened, have remained unknown to the author of the first gospel? Even apart from the supposition that this gospel had an apostolic origin, this question is fraught with no less difficulty than the former. Besides the people, there were present many of his disciples, $\mu\alpha\theta\eta\tau\alpha\grave{\iota}$ $\grave{\iota}\kappa\alpha\nu o\grave{\iota}$; the place, Nain, according to the account which Josephus gives of its position relative to Mount Tabor, cannot have been far from the ordinary Galilean theatre of the ministry of Jesus ; [49] lastly, the fame of the event, as was natural, was widely disseminated (v. 17). Schleiermacher is of opinion that the authors of the first sketches from the life of Jesus, not being within the apostolic circle, did not generally venture to apply to the much occupied apostles, but rather sought the friends of Jesus of the second order, and in doing so they naturally turned to those places where they might hope for the richest harvests,—to Capernaum and Jerusalem ; events which, like the resuscitation in question, occurred in other places, could not so easily become common property. But first, this conception of the case is too subjective, making the promulgation of the most important deeds of Jesus, dependent on the researches of amateurs and collectors of anecdotes, who went about gleaning, like Papias, at a later period ; secondly, (and these two objections are essentially connected,) there lies at its foundation the erroneous idea that such histories were fixed, like inert bodies once fallen to the ground, in the places to which they belonged, guarded there as lifeless treasures, and only exhibited to those who took the trouble to resort to the spot : instead of which, they were rather like the light-winged inhabitants of the air, flying far away from the place which gave them birth, roaming everywhere, and not seldom losing all association with their original locality. We see the same thing happen daily ; inumerable histories, both true and false, are represented as having occurred at the most widely different places. Such a narrative, once formed, is itself the substance, the alleged locality, the accident : by no means can the locality be the substance, to which the narrative is united as the accident, as it would follow from Schleiermacher's supposition. Since then it cannot well be conceived that an incident of this kind, if it really happened, could remain foreign to the general tradition, and hence unknown to the author of the first gospel : the fact of this author's ignorance of the incident gives rise to a suspicion that it did not really happen.

But this ground of doubt falls with incomparably greater weight, on the narrative of the resurrection of Lazarus in the fourth gospel. If the authors or collectors of the three first gospels knew of this, they could not, for more than one reason, avoid introducing it into their writings. For, first, of all the resuscitations effected by Jesus, nay, of all his miracles, this resurrection of Lazarus, if not the most wonderful, is yet the one in which the marvellous presents itself the most obviously and strikingly, and which therefore, if its historical reality can be established, is a pre-eminently strong proof of the extraordinary endowments of Jesus as a divine messenger ; [50] whence the

[48] Saunier, über die quellen des Markus, s. 66 ff.
[49] Comp. Winer bibl. Realw. d. A.
[50] Let the reader recollect the well-known expression of Spinoza.

Evangelists, although they had related one or two other instances of the kind, could not think it superfluous to add this also.   But, secondly, the resurrection of Lazarus had, according to the representation of John, a direct influence in the development of the fate of Jesus ; for we learn from xi. 47 ff., that the increased resort to Jesus, and the credit which this event procured him, led to that consultation of the Sanhedrim in which the sanguinary counsel of Caiaphas was given and approved.   Thus the event had a double importance —pragmatical as well as dogmatical ; consequently, the synoptical writers could not have failed to narrate it, had it been within their knowledge. Nevertheless, theologians have found out all sorts of reasons why those Evangelists, even had the fact been known to them, should refrain from its narration.   Some have been of opinion that at the time of the composition of the three first gospels, the history was still in every mouth, so that to make a written record of it was superfluous ; [51] others, on the contrary, have conjectured that it was thought desirable to guard against its further publication, lest danger should accrue to Lazarus and his family, the former of whom, according to John xii. 10, was persecuted by the Jewish hierarchy on account of the miracle which had been preformed in him ; a caution for which there was no necessity at the later period at which John wrote his gospel.[52]   It is plain that these two reasons nullify each other, and neither of them is in itself worthy of a serious refutation ; yet as similar modes of evading a difficulty are still more frequently resorted to than might be supposed, we ought not to think some animadversion on them altogether thrown away.   The proposition, that the resurrection of Lazarus was not recorded by the synoptists because it was generally known in their circle, proves too much ; since on this rule, precisely the most important events in the life of Jesus, his baptism, death, and resurrection, must have remained unwritten.   Moreover, writings, which like our gospels, originate in a religious community, do not serve merely to make known the unknown ; it is their office also to preserve what is already known.   In opposition to the other explanation, it has been remarked by others, that the publication of this history among those who were not natives of Palestine, as was the case with those for whom Mark and Luke wrote, could have done no injury to Lazarus ; and even the author of the first gospel, admitting that he wrote in and for Palestine, could hardly have withheld a fact in which the glory of Christ was so peculiarly manifested, merely out of consideration to Lazarus, who, supposing the more improbable case that he was yet living at the time of the composition of the first gospel, ought not, Christian as he doubtless was, to refuse to suffer for the name of Christ ; and the same observation would apply to his family.   The most dangerous time for Lazarus according to John xii. 10, was that immediately after his resurrection, and a narrative which appeared so long after, could scarcely have heightened or renewed this danger ; besides, in the neighbourhood of Bethany and Jerusalem whence danger was threatened to Lazarus, the event must have been so well-known and remembered that nothing was to be risked by its publication.[53]

[51] Whitby, Annot. in loc.

[52] Thus Grotius and Herder ; Olshausen also adopts this explanation under the form of conjecture, 2, s. 256 f., Anm.

[53] See these arguments dispersed in Paulus and Lücke on this chapter ; in Gabler, ut sup. p. 238 ff. ; and Hase, L. J. § 119.—A new reason why Matthew in particular is silent on the resurrection of Lazarus, has been excogitated by Heydenreich (über die Unzulässigkeit der mythischen Auffassung, 2tes Stück, s. 42). The Evangelist, he says, omitted it, because it required to be represented and treated with a tenderness and liveliness of feeling, of which he did not think himself capable.   Hence, the modest man chose to avoid the history altogether rather than to deprive it by his manner of narration, of its proper pathos and sublimity.—Idle modesty truly !

It appears then that the resurrection of Lazarus, since it is not narrated by the synoptists, cannot have been known to them ; and the question arises, how was this ignorance possible ? Hase gives the mysterious answer, that the reason of this omission lies hid in the common relations under which the synoptists in general were silent concerning all the earlier incidents in Judæa ; but this leaves it uncertain, at least so far as the expressions go, whether we ought to decide to the disadvantage of the fourth gospel or of its predecessors. The latest criticism of the gospel of Matthew has cleared up the ambiguity in Hase's answer after its usual manner, determining the nature of those common relations which he vaguely adduces, thus : Every one of the synoptists, by his ignorance of a history which an apostle must have known, betrays himself to be no apostle.[54] But this renunciation of the apostolic origin of the first gospel, does not by any means enable us to explain the ignorance of its author and his compeers of the resurrection of Lazarus. For besides the remarkable character of the event, its occurrence in the very heart of Judæa, the great attention excited by it, and its having been witnessed by the apostles,—all these considerations render it incomprehensible that it should not have entered into the general tradition, and from thence into the synoptical gospels. It is argued that these gospels are founded on Galilean legends, i.e. oral narratives and written notices by the Galilean friends and companions of Jesus ; that these were not present at the resurrection of Lazarus, and therefore did not include it in their memoirs ; and that the authors of the first gospels, strictly confining themselves to the Galilean sources of information, likewise passed over the event.[55] But there was not such a wall of partition between Galilee and Judæa, that the fame of an event like the resurrection of Lazarus could help sounding over from the one to the other. Even if it did not happen during a feast time, when (John iv. 45) many Galileans might be eye-witnesses, yet the disciples, who were for the greater part Galileans, were present (v. 16), and must, so soon as they returned into Galilee after the resurrection of Jesus, have spread abroad the history throughout this province, or rather, before this, the Galileans who kept the last passover attended by Jesus, must have learned the event, the report of which was so rife in the city. Hence even Lücke finds this explanation of Gabler's unsatisfactory ; and on his own side attempts to solve the enigma by the observation, that the original evangelical tradition, which the synoptists followed, did not represent the history of the Passion mainly in a pragmatical light, and therefore gave no heed to this event as the secret motive of the murderous resolve against Jesus, and that only John, who was initiated into the secret history of the Sanhedrim, was in a condition to supply this explanatory fact.[56] This view of the case would certainly appear to neutralize one reason why the synoptists must have noticed the event in question, namely, that drawn from its pragmatical importance ; but when it is added, that as a miracle regarded in itself, apart from its more particular circumstances, it might easily be lost among the rest of those narratives from which we have in the three first gospels a partly accidental selection,—we must reply, that the synoptical selection of miracles appears to be an accidental one only when that is at once assumed which ought first to be proved : namely, that the miracles in the fourth gospel are historical : and unless the selection be casual to a degree inconsistent with the slightest intelligence in the compilers, such a miracle cannot have been overlooked.[57]

[54] Schneckenburger, über den Urspr., s. 10.
[55] Gabler, ut sup. s. 240 f. ; also Neander, s. 357.
[56] Comm. z. Joh. 2, s. 402.
[57] Comp. De Wette, exeg. Handb. 1, 3, s. 139. In Schleiermacher's Lectures on the

It has doubtless been these and similar considerations, which have led the latest writers on the controversy concerning the first gospel, to complain of the one-sidedness with which the above question is always answered to the disadvantage of the synoptists, especially Matthew, as if it were forgotten that an answer dangerous to the fourth gospel lies just as near at hand.[58] For our own part, we are not so greatly alarmed by the fulminations of Lücke, as to be deterred from the expression of our opinion on the subject. This theologian, even in his latest editions, reproaches those who, from the silence of the synoptical writers, conclude that this narrative is a fiction and the gospel of John not authentic, with an unparalleled lack of discernment, and a total want of insight into the mutual relations of our gospels (that is, into those relations viewed according to the professional conviction of theologians, which is unshaken even by the often well-directed attacks of the author of the Probabilia). We, nevertheless, distinctly declare that we regard the history of the resurrection of Lazarus, not only as in the highest degree improbable in itself, but also destitute of external evidence ; and this whole chapter, in connexion with those previously examined, as an indication of the unauthenticity of the fourth gospel.

If it is thus proved that all the three evangelical histories of resuscitations are rendered more or less doubtful by negative reasons : all that is now wanting to us is positive proof, that the tradition of Jesus having raised the dead might easily be formed without historical foundation. According to rabbinical,[59] as well as New Testament passsages (e.g. John v. 28 f., vi. 40, 44 ; 1 Cor. xv. ; 1 Thess. iv. 16), the resuscitation of the dead was expected of the Messiah at his coming. Now the παρουσία, the appearance of the Messiah Jesus on earth, was in the view of the early church broken by his death into two parts ; the first comprised his preparatory appearance, which began with his human birth, and ended with the resurrection and ascension ; the second was to commence with his future advent on the clouds of heaven, in order to open the αἰὼν μέλλων, *the age to come*. As the first appearance of Jesus had wanted the glory and majesty expected in the Messiah, the great demonstrations of messianic power, and in particular the general resurrection of the dead, were assigned to his second, and as yet future appearance on earth. Nevertheless, as an immediate pledge of what was to be anticipated, even in the first advent some fore-splendours of the second must have been visible in single instances ; Jesus must, even in his first advent, by awaking some of the dead, have guaranteed his authority one day to awake all the dead ; he must, when questioned as to his messiahship, have been able to

Life of Jesus (if I may be permitted to refer to a work not yet printed), the silence in question is explained in the following manner. The synoptical Evangelists in general were ignorant of the relations of Jesus with the family of Bethany, because perhaps the apostles did not wish an intimate personal connection of this kind to pass into the general tradition, from which those Evangelists drew ; and ignorance of the relations of Jesus with the family in general, of course included ignorance of this particular fact connected with them. But what motive could the apostles have for such reserve ? Are we to infer secret, or even, with Venturini, tender ties? Must not such a private relation in the case of Jesus have presented much to edify us ? The intimations which John and Luke afford us on this subject contain in fact much of this description, and from the narrative which the latter gives of the visit of Jesus to Martha and Mary, we see also that the apostles, in furnishing their accounts, were by no means averse to allow something of these relations to appear, so far as they could retain a general interest. Now in this light, the resurrection of Lazarus, as a pre-eminent miracle, was incomparably more valuable than that visit with its single aphorism "One thing is needful," and involved less of the private relations of Jesus with the family of Bethany ; the supposed effort to keep these secret, could not therefore have hindered the promulgation of the resurrection of Lazarus.

[58] Kern, über den Ursprung des Evang. Matth., Tübing. Zeitschrift, 1834, 2, s. 110.
[59] Bertholdt. Christol. Jud. § 35.

adduce among other criteria the fact that the dead were raised up by him (Matt. xi. 5), and he must have imparted the same power to his disciples (Matt. xi. 8, comp. Acts ix. 40, xx. 10); but especially as a close prefiguration of the hour *in which all that are in their graves shall hear his voice, and shall come forth* (John v. 28 f.), he must have *cried with a loud voice, Come forth !* to one who *had lain in the grave four days* (John xi. 17, 43). For the origination of detailed narratives of single resuscitations, there lay, besides, the most appropriate types in the Old Testament. The prophets Elijah and Elisha (1 Kings xvii. 17 ff. ; 2 Kings iv. 18 ff.) had awaked the dead, and to these instances Jewish writings appealed as a type of the messianic time.[60] The object of the resuscitation was with both these prophets a child, but a boy, while in the narrative common to the synoptists we have a girl ; the two prophets revived him while he lay on the bed, as Jesus does the daughter of Jairus ; both entered alone into the chamber of death, as Jesus excludes all save a few confidential friends ; only, as it is fitting, the Messiah needs not the laborious manipulations by which the prophets attained their object. Elijah in particular raised the son of a widow, as Jesus did at Nain ; he met the widow of Zarephath at the gate (but before the death of her son) as Jesus met the widow of Nain, under the gate of the city (after the death of her son); lastly, it is in both instances told in the same words how the miracle-worker restored the son to the mother.[61] Even one already laid in his grave, like Lazarus, was restored to life by the prophet Elisha ; with this difference, however, that the prophet himself had been long dead, and the contact of his bones reanimated a corpse which was accidentally thrown upon them (2 Kings xiii. 21). There is yet another point of similarity between the resuscitations of the dead in the Old Testament and that of Lazarus ; it is that Jesus, while in his former resuscitation he utters the authoritative word without any preliminary, in that of Lazarus offers a prayer to God, as Elisha, and more particularly Elijah, are said to have done. While Paulus extends to these narratives in the Old Testament, the natural explanation which he has applied to those in the New, theologians of more enlarged views have long ago remarked, that the resurrections in the New Testament are nothing more than mythi, which had their origin in the tendency of the early Christian church, to make her Messiah agree with the type of the prophets, and with the messianic ideal.[62]

---

[60] See the passages quoted from Tanchuma, Vol. I. § 14.

[61] 1 Kings xvii. 23, LXX. καὶ ἔδωκεν αὐτὸ τῇ μητρὶ αὐτοῦ, Luke vii. 15 : καὶ ἔδωκεν αὐτὸν τῇ μητρὶ αὐτοῦ.

[62] Thus the author of the Abhandlung über die verschiedenen Rücksichten, in welchen der Biograph Jesu arbeiten kann, in Bertholdt's krit. Journ., 5, s. 237 f., Kaiser, bibl. Theol. 1, s. 202.—A resuscitation strikingly similar to that of the young man at Nain is narrated by Philostratus, of Apollonius of Tyana. " As according to Luke, it was a young man, the only son of a widow, who was being carried out of the city ; so, in Philostratus, it is a young maiden already betrothed, whose bier Apollonius meets. The command to set down the bier, the mere touch, and a few words, are sufficient here, as there, to bring the dead to life " (Baur, Apollonius v. Tyana und Christus, s. 145). I should like to know whether Paulus, or any other critic, would be inclined to explain this naturally ; if, however, it ought to be regarded as an imitation of the evangelical narrative (a conclusion which can hardly be avoided), we must have a preconceived opinion of the character of the books of the New Testament, to evade the consequence, that the resuscitations of the dead which they contain are only less designed imitations of those in the Old Testament ; which are themselves to be derived from the belief of antiquity, that a victorious power over death was imparted to the favourites of the gods (Hercules, Esculapius, etc.), and more immediately, from the Jewish idea of a prophet.

§ 101.

ANECDOTES HAVING RELATION TO THE SEA.*

As in general, at least according to the representations of the three first Evangelists the country around the Galilean sea was the chief theatre of the ministry of Jesus ; so a considerable number of his miracles have an immediate reference to the sea. One of this class, the miraculous draught of fishes granted to Peter, has already presented itself for our consideration ; besides this, there are the miraculous stilling of the storm which had arisen on the sea while Jesus slept, in the three synoptists ; Matthew, Mark, and John ; the summary of most of those, the walking of Jesus on the sea, likewise during a storm, in incidents which the appendix to the fourth gospel places after the resurrection ; and lastly, the anecdote of the coin that was to be angled for by Peter, in Matthew.

The first-named narrative (Matt. viii. 23 ff. parall.) is intended, according to the Evangelist's own words, to represent Jesus to us as him whom *the winds and the sea obey*, οἱ ἄνεμοι καὶ ἡ θάλασσα ὑπακούουσιν. Thus, to follow out the gradation in the miraculous which has been hitherto observed, it is here presupposed, not merely that Jesus could act on the human mind and living body in a psychological and magnetic manner ; or with a revivifying power on the human organism when it was forsaken by vitality ; nay, not merely as in the history of the draught of fishes earlier examined, that he could act immediately with determinative power, on irrational yet animated existences, but that he could act thus even on inanimate nature. The possibility of finding a point of union between the alleged supernatural agency of Jesus, and the natural order of phenomena, here absolutely ceases : here, at the latest, there is an end to miracles in the wider and now more favoured sense ; and we come to those which must be taken in the narrowest sense, or to the miracle proper.† The purely supranaturalistic view is therefore the first to suggest itself. Olshausen has justly felt, that such a power over external nature is not essentially connected with the destination of Jesus for the human race and for the salvation of man ; whence he was led to place the natural phenomenon which is here controlled by Jesus in a relation to sin, and therefore to the office of Jesus. Storms, he says, are the spasms and convulsions of nature, and as such the consequences of sin, the fearful effects of which are seen even on the physical side of existence.[1] But it is only that limited observation of nature which in noting the particular forgets the general, that can regard storms, tempests, and similar phenomena (which in connexion with the whole have their necessary place and beneficial influence) as evils and departure from original law : and a theory of the world in which it is seriously upheld, that before the fall there were no storms and tempests, as, on the other hand, no beasts of prey and poisonous plants, partakes—one does not know whether to say, of the fanatical, or of the childish. But to what purpose, if the above explanation will not hold, could Jesus be gifted with such a power over nature ? As a means of awakening faith in him, it was inadequate and superfluous : because Jesus found individual adherents without any demonstration of a power of this kind, and general acceptance even this did not procure him. As little can it be regarded as a type of the original dominion of man over external nature, a dominion which he is destined to re-attain ; for the value of this dominion consists precisely in this, that it is a mediate one, achieved by the progressive reflection and the united efforts of

[1] Bibl. Comm. 1, s. 287.

ages, not an immediate and magical dominion, which costs no more than a word.   Hence in relation to that part of nature of which we are here speaking the compass and the steam-vessel are an incomparably truer realization of man's dominion over the ocean, than the allaying of the waves by a mere word.   But the subject has another aspect, since the dominion of man over nature is not merely external and practical, but also immanent or theoretical, that is, man even when externally he is subjected to the might of the elements, yet is not internally conquered by them ; but, in the conviction that the powers of physical nature can only destroy in him that which belongs to his physical existence, is elevated in the self-certainty of the spirit above the possible destruction of the body.   This spiritual power, it is said, was exhibited by Jesus, for he slept tranquilly in the midst of the storm, and when awaked by his trembling disciples, inspired them with courage by his words.   But for courage to be shown, real danger must be apprehended : now for Jesus, supposing him to be conscious of an immediate power over nature, danger could in no degree exist : therefore he could not here give any proof of this theoretical power.

In both respects the natural explanation would find only the conceivable and the desirable attributed to Jesus in the evangelical narrative ; namely, on the one hand, an intelligent observation of the state of the weather, and on the other, exalted courage in the presence of real peril.   When we read that Jesus *commanded the winds* ἐπιτιμᾷν τοῖς ἀνέμοις, we are to understand simply that he made some remark on the storm, or some exclamations at its violence : and his calming of the sea we are to regard only as a prognostication, founded on the observation of certain signs, that the storm would soon subside.   His address to the disciples is said to have proceeded, like the celebrated saying of Cæsar, from the confidence that a man who was to leave an impress on the world's history, could not so lightly be cut short in his career by an accident. That those who were in the ship regarded the subsidence of the storm as the effect of the words of Jesus, proves nothing, for Jesus nowhere confirms their inference.[2]   But neither does he disapprove it, although he must have observed the impression which, in consequence of that inference, the result had made on the people ;[3] he must therefore, as Venturini actually supposes, have designedly refrained from shaking their high opinion of his miraculous power, in order to attach them to him the more firmly.   But, setting this altogether aside, was it likely that the natural presages of the storm should have been better understood by Jesus, who had never been occupied on the sea, than by Peter, James, and John, who had been at home on it from their youth upwards ?[4]

It remains then that, taking the incident as it is narrated by the Evangelists, we must regard it as a miracle ; but to raise this from an exegetical result to a real fact, is, according to the above remarks extremely difficult : whence there arises a suspicion against the historical character of the narrative.   Viewed more nearly however, and taking Matthew's account as the basis, there is nothing to object to the narrative until the middle of v. 26.   It might really have happened that Jesus in one of his frequent passages across the Galilean sea, was sleeping when a storm arose ; that the disciples awaked him with alarm, while he, calm and self-possessed, said to them, *Why are ye fearful, O ye of little faith?*   What follows—the commanding of the waves, which

---

[2] Thus Paulus, exeg. Handb., 1, b, s. 468 ff. ; Venturini, 2, s. 166 ff ; Kaiser, bibl. Theol., 1, s. 197.   Hase, also, § 74, thinks this view probable.
[3] Neander, L. J. Chr., s. 363, who for the rest here offers but a weak defence against the natural explanation.
[4] Hase, ut sup.

Mark, with his well-known fondness for such authoritative words, reproduces as if he were giving the exact words of Jesus in a Greek translation (σιώπα, πεφίμωσο !)—might have been added in the propagation of the anecdote from one to another. There was an inducement to attribute to Jesus such a command over the winds and the sea, not only in the opinion entertained of his person, but also in certain features of the Old Testament history. Here, in poetical descriptions of the passage of the Israelites through the Red Sea, Jehovah is designated as he who *rebuked the Red Sea*, ἐπετίμησε τῇ ἐρυθρᾷ θαλάσσῃ (Psa. cvi. 9 ; LXX. comp. Nahum i. 4), so that it retreated. Now, as the instrument in this partition of the Red Sea was Moses, it was natural to ascribe to his great successor, the Messiah, a similar function ; accordingly we actually find from rabbinical passages, that a drying up of the sea was expected to be wrought by God in the messianic times, doubtless through the agency of the Messiah, as formerly through that of Moses.[5] That instead of drying up the sea Jesus is said only to produce a calm, may be explained, on the supposition that the storm and the composure exhibited by Jesus on the occasion were historical, as a consequence of the mythical having combined itself with this historical element ; for, as according to this, Jesus and his disciples were on board a ship, a drying up of the sea would have been out of place.

Still it is altogether without any sure precedent, that a mythical addition should be engrafted on the stem of a real incident, so as to leave the latter totally unmodified. And there is one feature, even in the part hitherto assumed to be historical, which, more narrowly examined, might just as probably have been invented by the legend as have really happened. That Jesus, before the storm breaks out, is sleeping, and even when it arises, does not immediately awake, is not his voluntary deed, but chance ;[6] it is this very chance, however, which alone gives the scene its full significance, for Jesus sleeping in the storm is by the contrast which he presents, a not less emblematical image than Ulysses sleeping when, after so many storms, he was about to land on his island home. Now that Jesus really slept at the time that a storm broke out, may indeed have happened by chance in one case out of ten ; but in the nine cases also, when this did not happen, and Jesus only showed himself calm and courageous during the storm, I am inclined to think that the legend would so far have understood her interest, that, as she had represented the contrast of the tranquillity of Jesus with the raging of the elements to the intellect, by means of the words of Jesus, so she would depict it for the imagination, by means of the image of Jesus sleeping in the ship (or as Mark has it,[7] on a pillow in the hinder part of the ship). If then that which may possibly have happened in a single case, must certainly have been invented by the legend in nine cases ; the expositor must in reason prepare himself for the undeniable possibility, that we have before us one of the nine cases, instead of that single case.[8] If then it be granted that nothing further remains as an historical foundation for our narrative, than that Jesus exhorted his disciples to show the firm courage of faith in opposition to the raging waves of the sea,

---

[5] Vid. Vol. I, § 14, note 9.

[6] Neander alters the fact, when he describes Jesus as falling asleep in the midst of the fury of the storm and the waves, and thus manifesting a tranquillity of soul which no terror of nature could disturb (s. 362). Luke says expressly, *as they sailed he fell asleep : and there came down a storm, etc.*, πλεόντων δὲ αὐτῶν ἀφύπνωσε· καὶ κατέβη λαίλαψ κ. τ. λ., and according to the representation of the other Evangelists also, the sleeping of Jesus appears to have preceded the breaking out of the storm, since otherwise the timorous disciples would not have awaked him—they would rather not have allowed him to go to sleep.

[7] Comp Saunier, über die Quellen des Markus, s. 82.

[8] This may serve as an answer to Tholuck's accusation, Glaubwürdigkeit, s. 110.

it is certainly possible that he may once have done this in a storm at sea ; but just as he said : if ye have faith as a grain of mustard seed, ye may say to this mountain, Be thou removed, and cast into the sea (Matt. xxi. 21), or to this tree, Be thou plucked up by the root, and be thou planted in the sea (Luke xvii. 6), and both shall be done (καὶ ὑπήκουσεν ἂν ὑμῖν, Luke): so he might, not merely on the sea, but in any situation, make use of the figure, that to him who has faith, winds and waves shall be obedient at a word (ὅτι καὶ τοῖς ἀνέμοις ἐπιτάσσει καὶ τῷ ὕδατι, καὶ ὑπακούουσιν αὐτῷ, Luke). If we now take into account what even Olshausen remarks, and Schneckenburger has shown,[9] that the contest of the kingdom of God with the world was in the early times of Christianity commonly compared to a voyage through a stormy ocean ; we see at once, how easily legend might come to frame such a narrative as the above, on the suggestions afforded by the parallel between the Messiah and Moses, the expressions of Jesus, and the conception of him as the pilot who steers the little vessel of the kingdom of God through the tumultuous waves of the world. Setting this aside, however, and viewing the matter only generally, in relation to the idea of a miracle-worker, we find a similar power over storms and tempests, ascribed, for example, to Pythagoras.[10]

We have a more complicated anecdote connected with the sea, wanting in Luke, but contained in John vi. 16 ff., as well as in Matt. xiv. 22 ff., and Mark vi. 45 ff., where a storm overtakes the disciples when sailing by night, and Jesus appears to their rescue, walking towards them on the sea. Here, again, the storm subsides in a marvellous manner on the entrance of Jesus into the ship ; but the peculiar difficulty of the narrative lies in this, that the body of Jesus appears so entirely exempt from a law which governs all other human bodies without exception, namely, the law of gravitation, that he not only does not sink under the water, but does not even dip into it ; on the contrary, he walks erect on the waves as on firm land. If we are to represent this to ourselves, we must in some way or other, conceive the body of Jesus as an ethereal phantom, according to the opinion of the Docetæ ; a conception which the Fathers of the Church condemned as irreligious, and which we must reject as extravagant. Olshausen indeed says, that a superior corporeality, impregnated with the powers of a higher world, such an appearance need not create surprise :[11] but these are words to which we can attach no definite idea. If the spiritual activity of Jesus which refined and perfected his corporeal nature, instead of being conceived as that which more and more completely emancipated his body from the psychical laws of passion and sensuality, is understood as if by its means the body was exempted from the physical law of gravity :—this is a materialism of which, as in a former case, it is difficult to decide whether it be more fantastical or childish. If Jesus did not sink in the water, he must have been a spectre, and the disciples in our narrative would not have been wrong in taking him for one. We must also recollect that on his baptism in the river Jordan, Jesus did not exhibit this property, but was submerged like an ordinary man. Now had he at that time also the power of sustaining himself on the surface of the water, and only refrained from using it ? and did he thus increase or reduce his specific gravity by an act of his will ? or are we to suppose, as Olshausen would

[9] Ueber den Ursprung, u. s. f., s. 68 f.
[10] According to Jamblich. vita Pyth, 135, ed. Kiessling, there were narrated of Pythagoras, ἀνέμων βιαίων χαλαζῶν τε χύσεως παραυτίκα κατευνήσεις καὶ κυμάτων ποταμίων τε καὶ θαλασσίων ἀπευδιασμοὶ πρὸς εὐμαρῆ τῶν ἑταίρων διάβασιν, instantaneous tranquillizings of violent winds and hailstorms, and soothings of the waves of rivers and seas, to afford easy transit to his companions. Comp. Porphyr. v. p. 29 same ed.
[11] Ut sup. s. 491.

perhaps say, that at the time of his baptism he had not attained so far in the process of subtilizing his body, as to be freely borne up by the water, and that he only reached this point at a later period ? These are questions which Olshausen justly calls absurd : nevertheless they serve to open a glimpse into the abyss of absurdities in which we are involved by the supranaturalistic interpretation, and particularly by that which this theologian gives of the narrative before us.

To avoid these, the natural explanation has tried many expedients. The boldest is that of Paulus, who maintains that the text does not state that Jesus walked on the water ; and that the miracle in this passage is nothing but a philological mistake, since περιπατεῖν ἐπὶ τῆς θαλάσσης is analogous to the expression στρατοπεδεύειν ἐπὶ τῆς θαλάσσης, Exod. xiv. 2, and signifies to walk, as the other to encamp, over the sea, that is, on the elevated sea-shore.[12] According to the meaning of the words taken separately, this explanation is possible : its real applicability in this particular instance, however, must be determined by the context. Now this represents the disciples as having rowed twenty-five or thirty furlongs (John), or as being in the midst of the sea (Matthew and Mark), and then it is said that Jesus came towards the ship, and so near that he could speak to them, περιπατῶν ἐπὶ τῆς θαλάσσης. How could he do this if he remained on the shore ? To obviate this objection, Paulus conjectures that the disciples in that stormy night probably only skirted the shore ; but the words ἐν μέσῳ τῆς θαλάσσης, *in the midst of the sea*, though not, we grant, to be construed with mathematical strictness, yet, even taken according to the popular mode of speaking, are too decidedly opposed to such a supposition for it to be worth our further consideration. But this mode of interpretation encounters a fatal blow in the passage where Matthew says of Peter, that *having come down out of the ship he walked on the water*, καταβὰς ἀπὸ τοῦ πλοίου περιεπάτησεν ἐπὶ τὰ ὕδατα (v. 29) ; for as it is said shortly after that Peter began *to sink* (καταποντίζεσθαι), walking merely on the shore cannot have been intended here ; and if not here, neither can it have been intended in the former instance relating to Jesus, the expressions being substantially the same.[13]

But if Peter, in his attempt *to walk upon the waters*, περιπατεῖν ἐπὶ τὰ ὕδατα, began to sink, may we not still suppose that both he and Jesus merely swam in the sea, or waded through its shallows ? Both these suppositions have actually been advanced.[14] But the act of wading must have been expressed by περιπατεῖν διὰ τῆς θαλάσσης, and had that of swimming been intended, one or other of the parallel passages would certainly have substituted the precise expression for the ambiguous one : besides, it must be alike impossible either to swim from twenty-five to thirty furlongs in a storm, or to wade to about the middle of the sea, which certainly was beyond the shallows ; a swimmer could not easily be taken for a spectre ; and, lastly, the prayer of Peter for special permission to imitate Jesus, and his failure in it from want of faith, point to something supernatural.[15]

The reasoning on which the natural mode of interpretation rests here, as elsewhere, has been enunciated by Paulus in connexion with this passage in a form which reveals its fundamental error in a particularly happy manner. The question, he says, in such cases is always this : which is more probable,

---

[12] Paulus, Memorabilien, 6, Stuck, No. V. ; exeg. Handb. 2, s. 238 ff.
[13] Against the extremely arbitrary expedient which Paulus has here adopted, see Storr, Opusc. acad. 3, p. 288.
[14] The former by Bolten, Bericht des Matthäus, in loc ; the latter in Henke's neuem Magazin, 6, 2, s. 327 ff.
[15] Comp. Paulus and Fritzsche, in loc.

that the evangelical writer should use an expression not perfectly exact, or that there should be a departure from the course of nature? It is evident that the dilemma is falsely stated, and should rather be put thus: Is it more probable that the author should express himself inaccurately (rather, in direct contradiction to the supposed sense), or that he should mean to narrate a departure from the course of nature? For only what he means to narrate is the immediate point of inquiry; what really happened is, even according to the distinction of the judgment of a writer from the fact that he states, on which Paulus everlastingly insists, an altogether different question. Because according to our views a departure from the course of nature cannot have taken place, it by no means follows, that a writer belonging to the primitive age of Christianity could not have credited and narrated such a case; [16] and therefore to abolish the miraculous, we must not explain it away from the narrative, but rather inquire whether the narrative itself, either in whole or in part, must not be excluded from the domain of history. In relation to this inquiry, first of all, each of our three accounts has peculiar features which in an historical light are suspicious.

The most striking of these features is found in Mark v. 48, where he says of Jesus that he came walking on the sea towards the disciples, *and would have passed by them*, καὶ ἤθελε παρελθεῖν αὐτούς, but that he was constrained by their anxious cries to take notice of them. With justice Fritzsche interprets Mark's meaning to be, that it was the intention of Jesus, supported by divine power, to walk across the whole sea as on firm land. But with equal justice Paulus asks, Could anything have been more useless and extravagant than to perform so singular a miracle without any eye to witness it? We must not however on this account, with the latter theologian, interpret the words of Mark as implying a natural event, namely, that Jesus, being on the land, was going to pass by the disciples who were sailing in a ship not far from the shore, for the miraculous interpretation of the passage is perfectly accordant with the spirit of our Evangelist. Not contented with the representation of his informant, that Jesus, on this one occasion, adopted this extraordinary mode of progress with special reference to his disciples, he aims by the above addition to convey the idea of walking on the water being so natural and customary with Jesus, that without any regard to the disciples, whenever a sheet of water lay in his road, he walked across it as unconcernedly as if it had been dry land. But such a mode of procedure, if habitual with Jesus, would presuppose most decidedly a subtilization of his body such as Olshausen supposes; it would therefore presuppose what is inconceivable. Hence this particular of Mark's presents itself as one of the most striking among those by which the second Evangelist now and then approaches to the exaggerations of the apocryphal gospels.[17] *

In Matthew, the miracle is in a different manner, not so much heightened as complicated; for there, not only Jesus, but Peter also makes an experiment in walking on the sea, not indeed altogether successful. This trait is rendered suspicious by its intrinsic character, as well as by the silence of the two other narrators. Immediately on the word of Jesus, and in virtue of the faith which he has in the beginning, Peter actually succeeds in walking on the water for some time, and only when he is assailed by fear and doubt does he begin to sink. What are we to think of this? Admitting that Jesus, by means

---

[16] See the excellent passage in Fritzsche, Comm. in Matth., p. 505.

[17] Mark's inclination to exaggerate shows itself also in his concluding sentence, v. 51, (comp. vii. 37): *and they were sore amazed in themselves beyond measure and wondered;* which will scarcely be understood to import, as Paulus supposes (2, s. 266), a disapproval of the excessive astonishment.

of his etherealized body, could walk on the water, how could he command Peter, who was not gifted with such a body, to do the same? or if by a mere word he could give the body of Peter a dispensation from the law of gravitation, can he have been a man? and if a God, would he thus lightly cause a suspension of natural laws at the caprice of a man? or, lastly, are we to suppose that faith has the power instantaneously to lessen the specific gravity of the body of a believer? Faith is certainly said to have such a power in the figurative discourse of Jesus just referred to, according to which the believer is able to remove mountains and trees into the sea,—and why not also himself to walk on the sea? The moral that as soon as faith falters, power ceases, could not be so aptly presented by either of the two former figures as by the latter, in the following form: as long as a man has faith he is able to walk unharmed on the unstable sea, but no sooner does he give way to doubt than he sinks, unless Christ extend to him a helping hand. The fundamental thought, then, of Matthew's episodical narrative is, that Peter was too confident in the firmness of his faith, that by its sudden failure he incurred great danger, but was rescued by Jesus; a thought which is actually expressed in Luke xxii. 31 f., where Jesus says to Simon: *Satan hath desired to have you that he may sift you as wheat; but I have prayed for thee that thy faith fail not.* These words of Jesus have reference to Peter's coming denial; this was the occasion when his faith, on the strength of which he had just before offered to go with Jesus to prison and to death, would have wavered, had not the Lord by his intercession, procured him new strength. If we add to this the above-mentioned habit of the early Christians to represent the persecuting world under the image of a turbulent sea, we cannot fail, with one of the latest critics, to perceive in the description of Peter courageously volunteering to walk on the sea, soon, however, sinking from faintheartedness; but borne up by Jesus, an allegorical and mythical representation of that trial of faith which this disciple who imagined himself so strong, met so weakly, and which higher assistance alone enabled him to surmount.[18]

But the account of the fourth gospel also is not wanting in peculiar features, which betray an unhistorical character. It has ever been a cross to harmonists, that while according to Matthew and Mark, the ship was only in the middle of the sea when Jesus reached it: according to John, it immediately after arrived at the opposite shore; that while, according to the former, Jesus actually entered into the ship, and the storm thereupon subsided: according to John, on the contrary, the disciples did indeed wish to take him into the ship, but their actually doing so was rendered superfluous by their immediate arrival at the place of disembarkation. It is true that here also abundant methods of reconciliation have been found. First, the word ἤθελον, *they wished*, added to λαβεῖν, *to receive*, is said to be a mere redundancy of expression; then, to signify simply the joyfulness of the reception, as if it had been said, ἐθέλοντες ἔλαβον; then, to describe the first impression which the recognition of Jesus made on the disciples, his reception into the ship, which really followed, not being mentioned.[19] But the sole reason for such an interpretation lies in the unauthorized comparison with the synoptical accounts: in the narrative of John, taken separately, there is no ground for it, nay, it is excluded. For the succeeding sentence: εὐθέως τὸ πλοῖον ἐγένετο ἐπὶ τῆς γῆς, εἰς ἣν ὑπῆγον, *immediately the ship was at the land whither they went*, though it is united, not by δὲ but by καὶ, can nevertheless only be taken antithetically, in the sense that the reception of Jesus into the ship, notwith-

[18] Schneckenburger, über den Ursprung u. s. f., s. 68 f.; Weisse, die evang. Geschichte, I, s. 521.
[19] Vid. Lücke and Tholuck.

standing the readiness of the disciples, did not really take place, because they were already at the shore. In consideration of this difference, Chrysostom held that there were two occasions on which Jesus walked on the sea. He says that on the second occasion, which John narrates, Jesus did not enter into the ship, *in order that the miracle might be greater* ἵνα τὸ θαῦμα μεῖζον ἐργάσηται.[20] This view we may transfer to the Evangelist, and say : if Mark has aggrandized the miracle, by implying that Jesus intended to walk past the disciples across the entire sea ; so John goes yet farther, for he makes him actually accomplish this design, and without being taken into the ship, arrive at the opposite shore.[21] Not only, however, does the fourth Evangelist seek to aggrandize the miracle before us, but also to establish and authenticate it more securely. According to the synoptists, the sole witnesses were the disciples, who saw Jesus come towards them, walking on the sea : John adds to these few immediate witnesses, a multitude of mediate ones, namely, the people who were assembled when Jesus performed the miracle of the loaves and fishes. These, when on the following morning they no longer find Jesus on the same spot, make the calculation, that Jesus cannot have crossed the sea by ship, for he did not get into the same boat with the disciples, and no other boat was there (v. 22) ; while, that he did not go by land, is involved in the circumstance that the people when they have forthwith crossed the sea, find him on the opposite shore (v. 25), whither he could hardly have arrived by land in the short interval. Thus in the narrative of the fourth gospel, as all natural means of passage are cut off from Jesus, there remains for him only a supernatural one, and this consequence is in fact inferred by the multitude in the astonished question which they put to Jesus, when they find him on the opposite shore : *Rabbi, when camest thou hither?* As this chain of evidence for the miraculous passage of Jesus depends on the rapid transportation of the multitude, the Evangelist hastens to procure *other boats* ἄλλα πλοιάρια for their service (v. 23). Now the multitude who take ship (v. 22, 26 ff.) are described as the same whom Jesus had miraculously fed, and these amounted (according to v. 10) to about 5000. If only a fifth, nay, a tenth of these passed over, there needed for this, as the author of the Probabilia has justly observed, a whole fleet of ships, especially if they were fishing boats ; but even if we suppose them vessels of freight, these would not all have been bound for Capernaum, or have changed their destination for the sake of accommodating the crowd. This passage of the multitude, therefore, appears only to have been invented,[22] on the one hand, to confirm by their evidence the walking of Jesus on the sea ; on the other, as we shall presently see, to gain an opportunity for making Jesus, who according to the tradition had gone over to the opposite shore immediately after the multiplication of the loaves, speak yet further with the multitude on the subject of this miracle.

After pruning away these offshoots of the miraculous which are peculiar to the respective narratives, the main stem is still left, namely, the miracle of Jesus walking on the sea for a considerable distance, with all its attendant improbabilities as above exposed. But the solution of these accessory particulars, as it led us to discover the causes of their unhistorical origin, has facilitated the discovery of such causes for the main narrative, and has thereby

---

[20] Homil. in Joann. 43.

[21] In De Wette's objection, that the opinion of an exaggeration of the miracle in John, is discountenanced by the addition that they were immediately at the land (ex. Handb. 1, 3, s. 79), there appears to me only a misunderstanding ; but his assertion that in John t'e manner in which Jesus goes over the sea is not represented as a miracle (s. 78), is to me thoroughly incomprehensible.

[22] Bretschneider, Probab., p. 81.

rendered possible the solution of this also. We have seen, by an example already adduced, that it was usual with the Hebrews and early Christians, to represent the power of God over nature, a power which the human spirit when united to him was supposed to share, under the image of supremacy over the raging waves of the sea. In the narrative of the Exodus this supremacy is manifested by the sea being driven out of its place at a sign, so that a dry path is opened to the people of God in its bed ; in the New Testament narrative previously considered, the sea is not removed out of its place, but only so far laid to rest that Jesus and his disciples can cross it in safety in their ship : in the anecdote before us, the sea still remains in its place as in the second, but there is this point of similarity to the first, that the passage is made on foot, not by ship, yet as a necessary consequence of the other particular, on the surface of the sea, not in its bed. Still more immediate inducements to develop in such a manner the conception of the power of the miracle-worker over the waves, may be found both in the Old Testament, and in the opinions prevalent in the time of Jesus. Among the miracles of Elisha, it is not only told that he divided the Jordan by a stroke of his mantle, so that he could go through it dry shod (2 Kings ii. 14), but also that he caused a piece of iron which had fallen into the water to swim (2 Kings vi. 6) ; an ascendancy over the law of gravitation which it would be imagined the miracle-worker might be able to evince in relation to his own body also, and thus to exhibit himself, as it is said of Jehovah, Job ix. 8, LXX., περιπατῶν ὡς ἐπ᾽ ἐδάφους ἐπὶ θαλάσσης, *walking upon the sea as upon a pavement.* In the time of Jesus much was told of miracle-workers who could walk on the water. Apart from conceptions exclusively Grecian,[23] the Greco-oriental legend feigned that the hyperborean Abaris possessed an arrow, by means of which he could bear himself up in the air, and thus traverse rivers, seas, and abysses,[24] and popular superstition attributed to many wonder-workers the power of walking on water.[25] Hence the possibility that with all these elements and inducements existing, a similar legend should be formed concerning Jesus, appears incomparably stronger, than that a real event of this kind should have occurred :—and with this conclusion we may dismiss the subject.

The *manifestation* φανέρωσις of Jesus *at the sea of Tiberias* ἐπὶ τῆς θαλάσσης τῆς Τιβεριάδος narrated John xxi. has so striking a resemblance to the sea anecdotes hitherto considered, that although the fourth gospel places it in the period after the resurrection, we are induced, as in an earlier instance we brought part of it under notice in connexion with the narrative of Peter's draught of fishes, so here to institute a comparison between its other features, and the narrative of Jesus walking on the sea. In both cases, Jesus is perceived by the disciples in the twilight of early morning ; only in the latter instance he does not, as in the former, walk on the sea, but stands on the shore, and the disciples are in consternation, not because of a storm, but because of the fruitlessness of their fishing. In both instances they are afraid of him ; in the one, they take him for a spectre, in the other, not one of them ventures to ask him who he is, *knowing that it is the Lord.* But especially the scene with Peter, peculiar to the first gospel, has its corresponding one in the present passage. As, there, when Jesus walking on the sea makes himself known to his disciples, Peter entreats permission to go to him on the water : so here, as soon as Jesus is recognized standing on the shore, Peter throws himself into the water that he may reach him the shortest way by

[23] See the passages in Wetstein, p. 417 f.
[24] Jamblich, vita Pythagoræ, 136 ; comp. Porphyr. 29.
[25] Lucian. Philopseudes, 13.

swimming. Thus, that which in the earlier narrative was the miraculous act of walking on the sea, becomes in the one before us, in relation to Jesus, the simple act of standing on the shore, in relation to Peter, the natural act of swimming; so that the latter history sounds almost like a rationalistic paraphrase of the former : and there have not been wanting those who have maintained that at least the anecdote about Peter in the first gospel, is a traditional transformation of the incident in John xxi. 7 into a miracle.[26] Modern criticism is restrained from extending this conjecture to the anecdote of Jesus walking on the sea, by the fact that the supposed apostolic fourth gospel itself has this feature in the earlier narrative (vi. 16 ff.). But from our point of view it appears quite possible, that the history in question either came to the author of this gospel in the one form, and to the author of the appendix in the other ; or that it came to the one author of both in a double form, and was inserted by him in separate parts of his narrative. Meanwhile, if the two histories are to be compared, we ought not at once to assume that the one, John xxi., is the original, the other, Matt. xiv. parall., the secondary ; we must first ask which of the two bears intrinsic marks of one or the other character. Now certainly if we adhere to the rule that the more miraculous narrative is the later, that in John xxi appears, in relation to the manner in which Jesus approaches the disciples, and in which Peter reaches Jesus, to be the original. But this rule is connected in the closest manner with another ; namely, that the more simple narrative is the earlier, the more complex one the later, as the conglomerate is a later formation than the homogeneous stone ; and according to this rule, the conclusion is reversed, and the narrative in John xxi. is the more traditional, for in it the particulars mentioned above are interwoven with the miraculous draught of fishes, while in the earlier narrative they form in themselves an independent whole. It is indeed true, that a greater whole may be broken up into smaller parts ; but such fragments have not at all the appearance of the separate narratives of the draught of fishes and the walking on the sea, since these, on the contrary, leave the impression of being each a finished whole. From this interweaving with the miracle of the draught of fishes,—to which we must add the circumstance that the entire circle of events turns upon the risen Jesus, who is already in himself a miracle,—it is apparent how, contrary to the general rule, the oft-named particulars could lose their miraculous character, since by their combination with other miracles they were reduced to mere accessories, to a sort of natural scaffolding. If then the narrative in John xxi. is entirely secondary, its historical value has already been estimated with that of the narratives which furnished its materials.

If, before we proceed further, we take a retrospect of the series of sea-anecdotes hitherto examined, we find, it is true, that the two extreme anecdotes are altogether dissimilar, the one relating mainly to fishing, the other to a storm ; nevertheless, on a proper arrangement, each of them appears to be connected with the preceding by a common feature. The narrative of the call of the fishers of men (Matt. iv. 18 ff. par.) opens the series ; that of Peter's draught of fishes (Luke v. 1 ff.) has in common with this the saying about the fishers of men, but the fact of the draught of fishes is peculiar to it ; this fact reappears in John xxi., where the circumstances of Jesus standing on the shore in the morning twilight. and the swimming of Peter towards him, are added ; these two circumstances are in Matt. xiv. 22 ff. parall. metamorphosed into the act of walking on the sea on the part of Jesus and of Peter, and at the same time a storm, and its cessation on the

[26] Schneckenburger, über den Urspr., s. 68.

entrance of Jesus into the ship, are introduced; lastly, in Matt. viii. 23 ff. parall., we have an anecdote single in its kind, namely, that of the stilling of the storm by Jesus.

We come to a history for which a place is less readily found in the foregoing series, in Matt. xvii. 24 ff. It is true that here again there is a direction of Jesus to Peter to go and fish, to which, although it is not expressly stated, we must suppose that the issue corresponded: but first, it is only one fish which is to be caught, and with an angle; and secondly, the main point is, that in its mouth is to be found a piece of gold to serve for the payment of the temple tribute for Jesus and Peter, from the latter of whom this tax had been demanded. This narrative as it is here presented has peculiar difficulties, which Paulus well exhibits, and which Olshausen does not deny. Fritzsche justly remarks, that there are two miraculous particulars presupposed: first, that the fish had a coin in its mouth; secondly, that Jesus had a foreknowledge of this. On the one hand, we must regard the former of these particulars as extravagant, and consequently the latter also; and on the other, the whole miracle appears to have been unnecessary. Certainly, that metals and other valuables have been found in the bodies of fish is elsewhere narrated,[27] and is not incredible; but that a fish should have a piece of money in its mouth, and keep it there while it snapped at the bait—this even Dr. Schnappinger[28] found inconceivable. Moreover, the motive of Jesus for performing such a miracle could not be want of money, for even if at that time there was no store in the common fund, still Jesus was in Capernaum, where he had many friends, and where consequently he could have obtained the needful money in a natural way. To exclude this possibility, we must with Olshausen confound borrowing with begging, and regard it as inconsistent with the *decorum divinum* which must have been observed by Jesus. Nor after so many proofs of his miraculous power, could Jesus think this additional miracle necessary to strengthen Peter's belief in his messiahship.

Hence we need not wonder that rationalistic commentators have attempted to free themselves at any cost from a miracle which even Olshausen pronounces to be the most difficult in the evangelical history, and we have only to see how they proceed in this undertaking. The pith of the natural explanation of the fact lies in the interpretation of the word εὑρήσεις, *thou shalt find*, in the command of Jesus, not of an immediate discovery of a stater in the fish, but of a mediate acquisition of this sum by selling what was caught.[29] It must be admitted that the above word may bear this signification also; but if we are to give it this sense instead of the usual one, we must in the particular instance have a clear intimation to this effect in the context. Thus, if it were said in the present passage: Take the first fine fish, carry it to the market, κἀκεῖ εὑρήσεις στατῆρα, *and there thou shalt find a stater*, this explanation would be in place; as however instead of this, the word εὑρήσεις is preceded by ἀνοίξας τὸ στόμα αὐτοῦ, *when thou hast opened his mouth*,—as, therefore, no place of sale, but a place inside the fish, is mentioned, as that on the opening of which the coin is to be obtained,—we can only understand an immediate discovery of the piece of money in this part of the fish.[30] Besides, to what purpose would the opening of the fish's mouth be mentioned, unless the desideratum were to be found there? Paulus sees in this only the injunction to release the fish from the hook without delay, in order to keep

[27] See the examples in Wetstein, in loc.
[28] Die h. Schrift des n. Bundes, 1, s. 314, 2te Aufl.
[29] Paulus, ex. Handb. 2, 502 ff.   Comp. Hase, L. J. § 111.
[30] Comp. Storr, in Flatt's Magazin, 2, s. 68 ff.

it alive, and thus to render it more saleable. The order to open the mouth of the fish might indeed, if it stood alone, be supposed to have the extraction of the hook as its object and consequence ; but as it is followed by εὑρήσεις στατῆρα, *thou shalt find a stater*, it is plain that this is the immediate end of opening the mouth. The perception that, so long as the opening of the fish's mouth is spoken of in this passage, it will be inferred that the coin was to be found there, has induced the rationalistic commentators to try whether they could not refer the word στόμα, *mouth*, to another subject than the fish, and no other remained than the fisher, Peter. But as στόμα appeared to be connected with the fish by the word αὐτοῦ, which immediately followed it, Dr. Paulus, moderating or exaggerating the suggestion of a friend, who proposed to read ἀνθευρήσεις, instead of—αὐτοῦ, εὑρήσεις—allowed αὐτοῦ to remain, but took it adverbially, and translated the passage thus : thou hast then only to open thy mouth to offer the fish for sale, and thou wilt on the spot (αὐτοῦ) receive a stater as its price. But, it would still be asked, how could a single fish fetch so high a price in Capernaum, where fish were so abundant ? Hence Paulus understands the words, τὸν ἀναβάντα πρῶτον ἰχθὺν ἆρον, *take up the fish that first cometh up*, collectively thus : continue time after time to take the fish that first comes to thee, until thou hast caught as many as will be worth a stater.

If the series of strained interpretations which are necessary to a natural explanation of this narrative throw us back on that which allows it to contain a miracle ; and if this miracle appear to us, according to our former decision, both extravagant and useless, nothing remains but to presume that here also there is a legendary element. This view has been combined with the admission, that a real but natural fact was probably at the foundation of the legend : namely, that Jesus once ordered Peter to fish until he had caught enough to procure the amount of the temple tribute ; whence the legend arose that the fish had the tribute money in its mouth.[31] But, in our opinion, a more likely source of this anecdote is to be found in the much-used theme of a catching of fish by Peter, on the one side, and on the other, the well-known stories of precious things having been found in the bodies of fish. Peter, as we learn from Matt. iv., Luke v., John xxi., was the fisher in the evangelical legend to whom Jesus in various forms, first symbolically, and then literally, granted the rich draught of fishes. The value of the capture appears here in the shape of a piece of money, which, as similar things are elsewhere said to have been found in the belly of fishes, is by an exaggeration of the marvel said to be found in the mouth of the fish. That it is the stater, required for the temple tribute, might be occasioned by a real declaration of Jesus concerning his relation to that tax ; or conversely, the stater which was accidentally named in the legend of the fish angled for by Peter, might bring to recollection the temple tribute, which amounted to that sum for two persons, and the declaration of Jesus relative to this subject.

With this tale conclude the sea anecdotes.

§ 102.

THE MIRACULOUS MULTIPLICATION OF THE LOAVES AND FISHES.

As, in the histories last considered, Jesus determined and mitigated the motions of irrational and even of inanimate existences ; so, in the narratives which we are about to examine, he exhibits the power of multiplying not only

[31] Kaiser, bibl. Theol. 1, s. 200. Comp. Hase, ut sup.

natural objects, but also productions of nature which had been wrought upon by art.

That Jesus miraculously multiplied prepared articles of food, feeding a great multitude of men with a few loaves and fishes, is narrated to us with singular unanimity by all the Evangelists (Matt. xiv. 13 ff. ; Mark vi. 30 ff. ; Luke ix. 10 ff. ; John vi. 1 ff.).   And if we believe the two first, Jesus did not do this merely once ; for in Matt. xv. 32 ff. ; Mark viii. 1 ff. we read of a second multiplication of loaves and fishes, the circumstances of which are substantially the same as those of the former.   It happens somewhat later ; the place is rather differently described, and the length of time during which the multitude stayed with Jesus is differently stated ; moreover, and this is a point of greater importance, the proportion between the stock of food and the number of men is different, for, on the first occasion, five thousand men are satisfied with five loaves and two fishes, and, on the second, four thousand with seven loaves and a few fishes ; on the first twelve baskets are filled with the fragments, on the second only seven.   Notwithstanding this, not only is the substance of the two histories exactly the same—the satisfying of a multitude of people with disproportionately small means of nourishment ; but also the description of the scene in the one, entirely corresponds in its principal features to that in the other.   In both instances, the locality is a solitary region in the vicinity of the Galilean sea ; Jesus is led to perform the miracle because the people have lingered too long with him ; he manifests a wish to feed the people from his own stores, which the disciples regard as impossible ; the stock of food at his disposal consists of loaves and fishes ; Jesus makes the people sit down, and, after giving thanks, distributes the provisions to them through the medium of the disciples ; they are completely satisfied, and yet a disproportionately great quantity of fragments is afterwards collected in baskets ; lastly, in the one case as in the other, Jesus after thus feeding the multitude, crosses the sea.

This repetition of the same event creates many difficulties.   The chief of these is suggested by the question : Is it conceivable that the disciples, after they had themselves witnessed how Jesus was able to feed a great multitude with a small quantity of provision, should nevertheless on a second occasion of the same kind, have totally forgotten the first, and have asked, *Whence should we have so much bread in the wilderness as to feed so great a multitude?* To render such an obliviousness on the part of the disciples probable, we are reminded that they had, in just as incomprehensible a manner, forgotten the declarations of Jesus concerning his approaching sufferings and death, when these events occurred ;[1] but it is equally a pending question, whether after such plain predictions from Jesus, his death could in fact have been so unexpected to the disciples.   It has been supposed that a longer interval had elapsed between the two miracles, and that during this there had occurred a number of similar cases, in which Jesus did not think fit to afford miraculous assistance :[2] but, on the one hand, these are pure fictions ; on the other, it would remain just as inconceivable as ever, that the striking similarity of the circumstances

----

[1] Olshausen, 1, s. 512.   This theologian, in the note on the same page, observes, that according to the words, *We have taken no bread*, Matt. xvi. 7, the disciples, even after the second feeding, were not alive to the fact, that there was no necessity for providing themselves with food for the body in the neighbourhood of the Son of Man.   But this instance is not to the point, for the circumstances are here altogether different.   That from the miraculous feeding of the people when they were accidentally belated in the wilderness, the disciples did not draw the same convenient conclusion with the biblical commentator, can only redound to their honour.

[2] Ibid.

preceding the second feeding of the multitude to those preceding the first, should not have reminded even one of the disciples of that former event. Paulus therefore is right in maintaining, that had Jesus once already fed the multitude by a miracle, the disciples, on the second occasion, when he expressed his determination not to send the people away fasting, would confidently have called upon him for a repetition of the former miracle.

In any case then, if Jesus on two separate occasions fed a multitude with disproportionately small provision, we must suppose, as some critics have done, that many features in the narrative of the one incident were transferred to the other, and thus the two, originally unlike, became in the course of oral tradition more and more similar ; the incredulous question of the disciples especially having been uttered only on the first occasion, and not on the second.[3] It may seem to speak in favour of such an assimilation, that the fourth Evangelist, though in his numerical statement he is in accordance with the first narrative of Matthew and Mark, yet has, in common with the second, the circumstances that the scene opens with an address of Jesus and not of the disciples, and that the people come to Jesus on a mountain. But if the fundamental features be allowed to remain,—the wilderness, the feeding of the people, the collection of the fragments,—it is still, even without that question of the disciples, sufficiently improbable that the scene should have been repeated in so entirely similar a manner.   If, on the contrary, these general features be renounced in relation to one of the histories, it is no longer apparent, how the veracity of the evangelical narratives as to the *manner* in which the second multiplication of loaves and fishes took place can be questioned on all points, and yet their statement as to the *fact* of its occurrence be maintained as trustworthy, especially as this statement is confined to Matthew and his imitator Mark.

Hence later critics have, with more[4] or less[5] decision, expressed the opinion, that here one and the same fact has been doubled, through a mistake of the first Evangelist, who was followed by the second. They suppose that several narratives of the miraculous feeding of the multitude were current which presented divergencies from each other, especially in relation to numbers, and that the author of the first gospel, to whom every additional history of a miracle was a welcome prize, and who was therefore little qualified for the critical reduction of two different narratives of this kind into one, introduced both into his collection.   This fully explains how on the second occasion the disciples could again express themselves so incredulously : namely, because in the tradition whence the author of the first gospel obtained the second history of a miraculous multiplication of loaves and fishes, it was the first and only one, and the Evangelist did not obliterate this feature because, apparently, he incorporated the two narratives into his writing just as he read or heard them.   Among other proofs that this was the case, may be mentioned the constancy with which he and Mark, who copied him, not only in the account of the events, but also in the subsequent allusion to them (Matt. xvi. 9 f. ; Mark viii. 19 f.), call the baskets in the first feeding, κόφινοι, in the second σπυρίδες.[6] It is indeed correctly maintained, that the Apostle Matthew could not possibly take one event for two, and relate a new history which

---

[3] Gratz, Comm. z. Matth. 2, s. 90 f. ; Sieffert, über den Ursprung, s 97.
[4] Thiesz, Krit. Commentar, 1, s. 168 ff. ; Schulz. über das Abendmahl, s. 311.   Comp. Fritzsche, in Matth., p. 523.
[5] Schleiermacher, über den Lukas, s. 145 ; Sieffert, ut sup. s. 95 ff. ; Hase, § 97. Neander is undecided, L. J. Chr., s. 372 ff., Anm.
[6] Comp. Saunier, ut sup. s. 105.

never happened : [7] but this proposition does not involve the reality of the second miraculous feeding of the multitude, unless the apostolic origin of the first gospel be at once presupposed, whereas this yet remains to be proved. Paulus further objects, that the duplication of the history in question could be of no advantage whatever to the design of the Evangelist ; and Olshausen, developing this idea more fully, observes that the legend would not have left the second narrative as simple and bare as the first.   But this argument, that a narrative cannot be fictitious, because if it were so it would have been more elaborately adorned, may very properly be at once dismissed, since its limits being altogether undefined, it might be repeated under all circumstances, and in the end would prove fable itself not sufficiently fabulous.   But, in this case particularly, it is totally baseless, because it presupposes the narrative of the first feeding of the multitude to be historically accurate ; now, if we have already in this a legendary production, the other edition of it, namely, the second history of a miraculous feeding, needs not to be distinguished by special traditionary features.   But not only is the second narrative not embellished as regards the miraculous, when compared with the first ; it even diminishes the miracle, for, while increasing the quantity of provision, it reduces the number of those whom it satisfied : and this retrogression in the marvellous is thought the surest proof that the second feeding of the multitude really occurred ; for, it is said, he who chose to invent an additional miracle of this kind, would have made it surpass the first, and instead of five thousand men would have given, not four, but ten thousand.[8]   This argument, also, rests on the unfounded assumption that the first narrative is of course the historical one ; though Olshausen himself has the idea that the second might with probability be regarded as the historical basis, and the first as the legendary copy, and then the fictitious would have the required relation to the true—that of exaggeration.   But when in opposition to this, he observes, how improbable it is that an unscrupulous narrator would place the authentic fact, being the less imposing, last, and eclipse it beforehand by the false one,—that such a writer would rather seek to outdo the truth, and therefore place his fiction last, as the more brilliant,—he again shows that he does not comprehend the mythical view of the biblical narratives, in the degree necessary for forming a judgment on the subject.   For there is no question here of an unscrupulous narrator, who would designedly surpass the true history of the miraculous multiplication of the loaves and fishes, and least of all is Matthew pronounced to be such a narrator : on the contrary, it is held that with perfect honesty, one account gave five thousand, another four, and that, with equal honesty, the first Evangelist copied from both ; and for the very reason that he went to work innocently and undesignedly, it was of no importance to him which of the two histories stood first and which last, the more important or the less striking one ; but he allowed himself to be determined on this point by accidental circumstances, such as that he found the one connected with incidents which appeared to him the earlier, the other with such as he supposed to be the later.   A similar instance of duplication occurs in the Pentateuch in relation to the histories of the feeding of the Israelites with quails, and of the production of water out of the rock, the former of which is narrated both in Exod. xvi. and Num. xi., the latter in Exod. xvii. and again in Num. xx., in each instance with an alteration in time, place, and other circumstances.[9] Meanwhile, all this yields us only the negative result that the double narratives

---

[7] Paulus, ex. Handb. 2, s. 315 ; Olshausen, ut sup.
[8] Olshausen, s. 513.
[9] See the proof in De Wette, Kritik der mos. Gesch., s. 220 ff., 314 ff.

of the first gospels cannot have been founded on two separate events. To determine which of the two is historical, or whether either of them deserves that epithet, must be the object of a special inquiry.

To evade the pre-eminently magical appearance which this miracle presents, Olshausen gives it a relation to the moral state of the participants, and supposes that the miraculous feeding of the multitude was effected through the intermediation of their spiritual hunger. But this is ambiguous language, which, on the first attempt to determine its meaning, vanishes into nothing. For in cures, for example, the intermediation here appealed to consists in the opening of the patient's mind to the influence of Jesus by faith, so that when faith is wanting, the requisite fulcrum for the miraculous power of Jesus is also wanting : here therefore the intermediation is real. Now if the same kind of intermediation took place in the case before us, so that on those among the multitude who were unbelieving the satisfying power of Jesus had no influence, then must the satisfaction of hunger here (as, in the above cases, the cure) be regarded as something effected by Jesus directly in the body of the hungry persons, without any antecedent augmentation of the external means of nourishment. But such a conception of the matter, as Paulus justly remarks, and as even Olshausen intimates, is precluded by the statement of the Evangelists, that real food was distributed among the multitude ; that each enjoyed as much as he wanted ; and that at the end the residue was greater than the original store. It is thus plainly implied that there was an external and objective increase of the provisions, as a preliminary to the feeding of the multitude. Now, this cannot be conceived as effected by means of the faith of the people in a real manner, in the sense that that faith co-operated in producing the multiplication of the loaves. The intermediation which Olshausen here supposes, can therefore have been only a teleological one, that is, we are to understand by it, that Jesus undertook to multiply the loaves and fishes for the sake of producing a certain moral condition in the multitude. But an intermediation of this kind affords me not the slightest help in forming a conception of the event ; for the question is not *why*, but *how* it happened. Thus all which Olshausen believes himself to have done towards rendering this miracle more intelligible, rests on the ambiguity of the expression, *intermediation* ; and the inconceivableness of an immediate influence of the will of Jesus on irrational nature, remains chargeable upon this history as upon those last examined.

But there is another difficulty which is peculiar to the narrative before us. We have here not merely, as hitherto, a modification or a direction of natural objects, but a multiplication of them, and that to an enormous extent. Nothing, it is true, is more familiar to our observation than the growth and multiplication of natural objects, as presented to us in the parable of the sower, and the grain of mustard seed, for example. But, first, these phenomena do not take place without the co-operation of other natural agents, as earth, water, air, so that here, also, according to the well-known principle of physics, there is not properly speaking an augmentation of the substance, but only a change in the accidents ; secondly, these processes of growth and multiplication are carried forward so as to pass through their various stages in corresponding intervals of time. Here, on the contrary, in the multiplication of the loaves and fishes by Jesus, neither the one rule nor the other is observed : the bread in the hand of Jesus is no longer, like the stalk on which the corn grew, in communication with the maternal earth, nor is the multiplication gradual, but sudden.

But herein, it is said, consists the miracle, which in relation to the last point especially, may be called the acceleration of a natural process. That which comes to pass in the space of three quarters of a year, from seed-time to har-

vest, was here effected in the minutes which were required for the distribution
of the food ; for natural developments are capable of acceleration, and to how
great an extent we cannot determine.[10]   It would, indeed, have been an acceleration of a natural process, if in the hand of Jesus a grain of corn had borne
fruit a hundred-fold, and brought it to maturity, and if he had shaken the
multiplied grain out of his hands as they were filled again and again, that the
people might grind, knead, and bake it, or eat it raw from the husk in the wilderness where they were ;—or if he had taken a living fish, suddenly called
forth the eggs from its body, and converted them into full-grown fish, which
then the disciples or the people might have boiled or roasted, this, we should
say, would have been an acceleration of a natural process.   But it is not corn
that he takes into his hand, but bread ; and the fish also, as they are distributed
in pieces, must have been prepared in some way, perhaps, as in Luke xxiv.
42, comp. John xxi. 9, broiled or salted.   Here then, on both sides, the production of nature is no longer simple and living, but dead and modified by
art : so that to introduce a natural process of the above kind, Jesus must, in
the first place, by his miraculous power have metamorphosed the bread into
corn again, the roasted fish into raw and living ones ; then instantaneously
have effected the described multiplication ; and lastly, have restored the
whole from the natural to the artificial state.   Thus the miracle would be
composed, 1st, of a revivification, which would exceed in miraculousness all
other instances in the gospels ; secondly, of an extremely accelerated natural
process ; and thirdly, of an artificial process, effected invisibly, and likewise
extremely accelerated, since all the tedious proceedings of the miller and
baker on the one hand, and of the cook on the other, must have been accomplished in a moment by the word of Jesus.   How then can Olshausen deceive
himself and the believing reader, by the agreeably sounding expression, *accelerated natural process*, when this nevertheless can designate only a third part of
the fact of which we are speaking ? [11]

But how are we to represent such a miracle to ourselves, and in what stage
of the event must it be placed ?   In relation to the latter point, three opinions
are possible, corresponding to the number of the groups that act in our narrative ; for the multiplication may have taken place either in the hands of Jesus,
or in those of the disciples who dispensed the food, or in those of the people
who received it.   The last idea appears, on the one hand, puerile even to extravagance, if we are to imagine Jesus and the apostles distributing, with
great carefulness, that there might be enough for all, little crumbs which in
the hands of the recipients swelled into considerable pieces : on the other
hand, it would have been scarcely a possible task, to get a particle, however
small, for every individual in a multitude of five thousand men, out of five
loaves, which, according to Hebrew custom, and particularly as they were
carried by a boy, cannot have been very large ; and still less out of two fishes.
Of the two other opinions I think, with Olshausen, the one most suitable is
that which supposes that the food was augmented under the creative hands of
Jesus, and that he time after time dispensed new quantities to the disciples.
We may then endeavour to represent the matter to ourselves in two ways :
first we may suppose that as fast as one loaf or fish was gone, a new one came
out of the hands of Jesus, or secondly, that the single loaves and fishes grew,
so that as one piece was broken off, its loss was repaired, until on a calcula-

---

[10] Thus Olshausen, in loc. after Pfenninger.   Comp. Hase, § 97.
[11] This lamentable observation of mine, according to Olshausen, has its source in something worse than intellectual incapacity, namely, in my total disbelief in a living God : otherwise assuredly it would not have appeared so great a difficulty to me that the Divine causality should have superseded human operations (s. 479, der 3ten Aufl.).

tion the turn came for the next loaf or fish. The first conception appears to be opposed to the text, which as it speaks of fragments ἐκ τῶν πέντε ἄρτων, *of the five loaves* (John vi. 13), can hardly be held to presuppose an increase of this number ; thus there remains only the second, by the poetical description of which Lavater has done but a poor service to the orthodox view.[12] For this miracle belongs to the class which can only appear in any degree credible so long as they can be retained in the obscurity of an indefinite conception : [13] no sooner does the light shine on them, so that they can be examined in all their parts, than they dissolve like the unsubstantial creations of the mist. Loaves, which in the hands of the distributors expand like wetted sponges,— broiled fish, in which the severed parts are replaced instantaneously, as in the living crab gradually,—plainly belong to quite another domain than that of reality.

What gratitude then do we not owe to the rationalistic interpretation, if it be true that it can free us, in the easiest manner, from the burden of so un-heard-of a miracle ? If we are to believe Dr. Paulus,[14] the Evangelists had no idea that they were narrating anything miraculous, and the miracle was first conveyed into their accounts by expositors. What they narrate is, according to him, only thus much : that Jesus caused his small store of provisions to be distributed, and that in consequence of this the entire multitude obtained enough to eat. Here, in any case, we want a middle term, which would dis-tinctly inform us, how it was possible that, although Jesus had so little food to offer, the whole multitude obtained enough to eat. A very natural middle term however is to be gathered, according to Paulus, out of the historical combination of the circumstances. As, on a comparison with John vi. 4, the multitude appear to have consisted for the greater part of a caravan on its way to the feast, they cannot have been quite destitute of provisions, and prob-ably a few indigent persons only had exhausted their stores. In order then to induce the better provided to share their food with those who were in want, Jesus arranged that they should have a meal, and himself set the example of imparting what he and his disciples could spare from their own little store ; this example was imitated, and thus the distribution of bread by Jesus having led to a general distribution, the whole multitude were satisfied. It is true that this natural middle term must be first mentally interpolated into the text ; as, however, the supernatural middle term which is generally received is just as little stated expressly, and both alike depend upon inference, the reader can hardly do otherwise than decide for the natural one. Such is the reasoning of Dr. Paulus : but the alleged identity in the relation of the two middle terms to the text does not in fact exist. For while the natural explan-ation requires us to suppose a new distributing subject (the better provided among the multitude), and a new distributed object (their provisions), to-gether with the act of distributing these provisions : the supranatural explan-ation contents itself with the subject actually present in the text (Jesus and his disciples), with the single object there given (their little store), and the described distribution of this ; and only requires us to supply from our imagin-ation the means by which this store could be made sufficient to satisfy the hunger of the multitude, namely its miraculous augmentation under the hands of Jesus (or of his disciples). How can it be yet maintained that neither of the two middle terms is any more suggested by the text than the other ? That the miraculous multiplication of the loaves and fishes is not expressly men-

---

[12] Jesus Messias, 2, Bd. No. 14, 15 and 20.
[13] For this reason Neander (s. 377) passes over the miracle with a few entirely general re-marks.
[14] Exeg. Handb. 2, s. 205 ff.

tioned, is explained by the consideration that the event itself is one of which no clear conception can be formed, and therefore it is best conveyed by the result alone.   But how will the natural theologian account for nothing being said of the distribution, called forth by the example of Jesus, on the part of those among the multitude who had provisions ?   It is altogether arbitrary to insert that distribution between the sentences, *He gave them to the disciples, and the disciples to the multitude* (Matt. xiv. 19), and, *they did all eat and were filled* (v. 20) ; while the words, καὶ τοὺς δύο ἰχθύας ἐμέρισε πᾶσι, *and the two fishes divided he among them all* (Mark vi. 41), plainly indicate that only the two fishes—and consequently only the five loaves—were the object of distribution for all.[15]   But the natural explanation falls into especial embarrassment when it comes to the baskets which, after all were satisfied, Jesus caused to be filled with the fragments that remained.   The fourth Evangelist says : συνήγαγον οὖν, καὶ ἐγέμισαν δώδεκα κοφίνους κλασμάτων ἐκ τῶν πέντε ἄρτων τῶν κριθίνων, ἃ ἐπερίσσευσε τοῖς βεβρωκόσιν, *therefore they gathered them together, and filled twelve baskets with the fragments of the five barley loaves, which remained over and above unto them that had eaten* (vi. 13).   This seems clearly enough to imply that out of those identical five loaves, after five thousand men had been satisfied by them, there still remained fragments enough to fill twelve baskets, —more, that is, than the amount of the original store.   Here, therefore, the natural expositor is put to the most extravagant contrivances in order to evade the miracle.   It is true, when the synoptists simply say that the remnants of the meal were collected, and twelve baskets filled with them, it might be thought from the point of view of the natural explanation, that Jesus, out of regard to the gift of God, caused the fragments which the crowd had left from their own provisions to be collected by his disciples.   But as, on the one hand, the fact that the people allowed the remains of the repast to lie, and did not appropriate them, seems to indicate that they treated the nourishment presented to them as the property of another ; so, on the other hand, Jesus, when, without any preliminary, he directs his disciples to gather them up, appears to regard them as his own property.   Hence Paulus understands the words ἦραν κ. τ. λ. of the synoptists, not of a collection first made after the meal, of that which remained when the people had been satisfied, but of the overplus of the little store belonging to Jesus and the disciples, which the latter, after reserving what was necessary for Jesus and themselves, carried round as an introduction and inducement to the general repast.   But how, when the words ἔφαγον καὶ ἐχορτάσθησαν πάντες, *they did all eat and were filled*, are immediately followed by καὶ ἦραν, *and they took up*, can the latter member of the verse refer to the time prior to the meal?   Must it not then have necessarily been said at least ἦραν γὰρ, *for they took up* ?   Further, how, after it had just been said that the people did eat and were filled, can τὸ περισσεῦσαν, *that which remained*, especially succeeded as it is in Luke by αὐτοῖς, *to them*, mean anything else than what the people had left ?   Lastly, how is it possible that out of five loaves and two fishes, after Jesus and his disciples had reserved enough for themselves, or even without this, there could in a natural manner be twelve baskets *filled* for distribution among the people? But still more strangely does the natural explanation deal with the narrative of John.   Jesus here adds, as a reason for gathering up the fragments, ἵνα μή τι ἀπόληται, *that nothing be lost* ; hence it appears impossible to divest the succeeding statement that they filled twelve baskets with the remains of the five loaves, of its relation to the time after the meal ; and in this case, it would be impossible to get clear of a miraculous multiplication of the loaves.   Paulus therefore, although

---

[15] Olshausen, in loc.

the words συνήγαγον οὖν καὶ ἐγεμισαν δώδεκα κοφίνους κ. τ. λ., *therefore they gathered them together and filled twelve baskets*, etc., form a strictly coherent whole, chooses rather to detach συνήγαγον οὖν, and, by a still more forced construction than that which he employed with the synoptical text, makes the narrative pass all at once, without the slightest notice, into the pluperfect, and thus leap back to the time before the meal.

Here, then, the natural explanation once more fails to fulfil its task : the text retains its miracle, and if we have reason to think this incredible, we must inquire whether the narrative of the text deserves credence. The agreement of all the four Evangelists is generally adduced in proof of its distinguished credibility : but this agreement is by no means so perfect, There are minor differences, first between Matthew and Luke ; then between these two and Mark, who in this instance again embellishes ; and lastly, between the synoptists collectively and John, in the following points : according to the synoptists, the scene of the event is a *desert place*, according to John, a *mountain* ; according to the former, the scene opens with an address from the disciples, according to John, with a question from Jesus (two particulars in which, as we have already remarked, the narrative of John approaches that of the second feeding in Matthew and Mark) ; lastly, the words which the three first Evangelists put into the mouth of the disciples indefinitely, the fourth in his individualizing manner ascribes to Philip and Andrew, and the same Evangelist also designates the bearer of the loaves and fishes as a *boy* (παιδάριον). These divergencies however may be passed over as less essential, that we may give our attention only to one, which has a deeper hold. While, namely, according to the synoptical accounts, Jesus had been long teaching the people and healing their sick, and was only led to feed them by the approach of evening, and the remark of the disciples that the people needed refreshment : in John, the first thought of Jesus, when he lifts up his eyes and sees the people gathering round him, is that which he expresses in his question to Philip : *Whence shall we buy bread that these may eat?* or rather, as he asked this merely to *prove* Philip, well knowing himself *what he would do*, he at once forms the resolution of feeding the multitude in a miraculous manner. But how could the design of feeding the people arise in Jesus immediately on their approach? They did not come to him for this, but for the sake of his teaching and his curative power. He must therefore have conceived this design entirely of his own accord, with a view to establish his miraculous power by so signal a demonstration. But did he ever thus work a miracle without any necessity, and even without any inducement,—quite arbitrarily, and merely for the sake of working a miracle? I am unable to describe strongly enough how impossible it is that eating should here have been the first thought of Jesus, how impossible that he could thus obtrude his miraculous repast on the people. Thus in relation to this point, the synoptical narrative, in which there is a reason for the miracle, must have the preference to that of John, who, hastening towards the miracle, overlooks the requisite motive for it, and makes Jesus create instead of awaiting the occasion for its performance. An eye-witness could not narrate thus ; [16] and if, therefore, the account of that gospel to which the greatest authority is now awarded, must be rejected as unhistorical ; so, with respect to the other narratives, the difficulties of the fact itself are sufficient to cast a doubt on their historical credibility, especially if in addition to these negative grounds we can discover positive reasons which render it probable that our narrative had an unhistorical origin.

---

[16] Against Neander's attempt at reconciliation, compare De Wette, exeg. Handb. 1, 3, s. 77.

Such reasons are actually found both within the evangelical history itself, and beyond it in the Old Testament history, and the Jewish popular belief. In relation to the former source, it is worthy of remark, that in the synoptical gospels as well as in John, there are more or less immediately appended to the feeding of the multitude by Jesus with literal bread, figurative discourses of Jesus on bread and leaven : namely, in the latter, the declarations concerning the bread of heaven, and the bread of life which Jesus gives (John vi. 27 ff.) ; in the former, those concerning the false leaven of the Pharisees and Sadducees, that is, their false doctrine and hypocrisy.[17]   (Matt. xvi. 5 ff. ; Mark viii. 14 ff. ; comp. Luke xii. 1) ; and on both sides, the figurative discourse of Jesus is erroneously understood of literal bread.   It would not then be a very strained conjecture, that as in the passages quoted we find the disciples and the people generally, understanding literally what Jesus meant figuratively ; so the same mistake was made in the earliest Christian tradition.   If, in figurative discourses, Jesus had sometimes represented himself as him who was able to give the true bread of life to the wandering and hungering people, perhaps also placing in opposition to this, the leaven of the Pharisees : the legend, agreeably to its realistic tendency, may have converted this into the fact of a miraculous feeding of the hungry multitude in the wilderness by Jesus.   The fourth Evangelist makes the discourse on the bread of heaven arise out of the miracle of the loaves : but the relation might very well have been the reverse, and the history owe its origin to the discourse, especially as the question which introduces John's narrative, *Whence shall we buy bread that these may eat ?* may be more easily conceived as being uttered by Jesus on the first sight of the people, if he alluded to feeding them with the word of God (comp. John iv. 32 ff.), to appeasing their spiritual hunger (Matt. v. 6), in order to exercise ($\pi\epsilon\iota\rho\acute{a}\zeta\omega\nu$) the higher understanding of his disciples, than if he really thought of the satisfaction of their bodily hunger, and only wished to try whether his disciples would in this case confide in his miraculous power.   The synoptical narrative is less suggestive of such a view ; for the figurative discourse on the leaven could not by itself originate the history of the miracle. Thus the gospel of John stands alone with reference to the above mode of derivation, and it is more agreeable to the character of this gospel to conjecture that it has applied the narrative of a miracle presented by tradition to the production of figurative discourses in the Alexandrian taste, than to suppose that it has preserved to us the original discourses out of which the legend spun that miraculous narrative.

If then we can discover, beyond the limits of the New Testament, very powerful causes for the origination of our narrative, we must renounce the attempt to construct it out of materials presented by the gospels themselves.

---

[17] This indication has been recently followed up by Weisse.   He finds the key to the history of the miraculous multiplication of the loaves, in the question addressed by Jesus to the disciples when they misunderstand his admonition against the leaven of the Pharisees and Sadducces.   He asks them whether they did not remember how many baskets they had been able to fill from the five and again from the seven loaves, and then adds, *How is it that ye do not understand that I spake it not to you concerning bread,* etc. (Matt. xvi. 11).   Now, says Weisse, the parallel which Jesus here institutes between his discourse on the leaven, and the history of the feeding of the multitude, shows that the latter also is only to be interpreted parabolically (s. 511 ff.).   But the form of the question of Jesus : πόσους κοφίνους (σπυρίδας) ἐλάβετε ; *how many baskets ye took up,* presupposes a real event ; we can form no conception, as we have already remarked in relation to the history of the temptation, of a parable in which Jesus and his disciples would have played a principal part ; moreover, the inference which Jesus would convey is, according to the text, not that because the present narrative was figurative, so also must be the interpretation of the subsequent discourse, but that after the earlier proof how superfluous was any solicitude about physical bread where Jesus was at hand, it was absurd to understand his present discourse as relating to such.

And here the fourth Evangelist, by putting into the mouth of the people a reference to the manna, that bread of heaven which Moses gave to the fathers in the wilderness (v. 31), reminds us of one of the most celebrated passages in the early history of the Israelites (Exod. xvi.), which was perfectly adapted to engender the expectation that its antitype would occur in the Messianic times ; and we in fact learn from rabbinical writings, that among those functions of the first Goël which were to be revived in the second, a chief place was given to the impartation of bread from heaven.[18] If the Mosaic manna presents itself as that which was most likely to be held a type of the bread miraculously augmented by Jesus ; the fish which Jesus also multiplied miraculously, may remind us that Moses gave the people, not only a substitute for bread in the manna, but also animal food in the quails (Exod. xvi. 8, xii. 13 ; Num. xi. 4 ff.). On comparing these Mosaic narratives with our evangelical ones, there appears a striking resemblance even in details. The locality in both cases is the wilderness ; the inducement to the miracle here as there, is fear lest the people should suffer from want in the wilderness, or perish from hunger ; in the Old Testament history, this fear is expressed by the people in loud murmurs, in that of the New Testament, it results from the shortsightedness of the disciples, and the benevolence of Jesus. The direction of the latter to his disciples that they should give the people food, a direction which implies that he had already formed the design of feeding them miraculously, may be paralleled with the command which Jehovah gave to Moses to feed the people with manna (Exod. xvi. 4), and with quails (Exod. xvi. 12 ; Num. xi. 18–20). But there is another point of similarity which speaks yet more directly to our present purpose. As, in the evangelical narrative, the disciples think it an impossibility that provision for so great a mass of people should be procured in the wilderness, so, in the Old Testament history, Moses replies doubtingly to the promise of Jehovah to satisfy the people with flesh (Num. xi. 21 f.). To Moses, as to the disciples, the multitude appears too great for the possibility of providing sufficient food for them ; as the latter ask, whence they should have so much bread in the wilderness, so Moses asks ironically whether they should slay the flocks and the herds (which they had not). And as the disciples object, that not even the most impoverishing expenditure on their part would thoroughly meet the demand, so Moses, clothing the idea in another form, had declared, that to satisfy the people as Jehovah promised, an impossibility must happen (the fish of the sea be gathered together for them) ; objections which Jehovah there, as here Jesus, does not regard, but issues the command that the people should prepare for the reception of the miraculous food.

But though these two cases of a miraculous supply of nourishment are thus analogous, there is this essential distinction, that in the Old Testament, in relation both to the manna and the quails, it is a miraculous procuring of food not previously existing which is spoken of, while in the New Testament it is a miraculous augmentation of provision already present, but inadequate ; so that the chasm between the Mosaic narrative and the evangelical one is too great for the latter to have been derived immediately from the former. If we search for an intermediate step, a very natural one between Moses and the Messiah is afforded by the prophets. We read of Elijah, that through him and for his sake, the little store of meal and oil which he found in the possession of the widow of Zarephath was miraculously replenished, or rather was made to suffice throughout the duration of the famine (1 Kings xvii. 8–16). This species of miracle is developed still further, and with a greater

---

[18] Vid. Vol. I. § 14.

resemblance to the evangelical narrative, in the history of Elisha (2 Kings iv. 42 ff.). As Jesus fed five thousand men in the wilderness with five loaves and two fishes, so this prophet, during a famine, fed a hundred men with twenty loaves, (which like those distributed by Jesus in John, are called barley loaves,) together with some ground corn (בְּכַרְמֶל, LXX. παλάθας) ; a disproportion between the quantity of provisions and the number of men, which his servant, like the disciples in the other instance, indicates in the question : *What! should I set this before a hundred men?* Elisha, like Jesus, is not diverted from his purpose, but commands the servant to give what he has to the people ; and as in the New Testament narrative great stress is laid on the collection of the remaining fragments, so in the Old Testament it is specially noticed at the close of this story, that notwithstanding so many had eaten of the store, there was still an overplus.[19] The only important difference here is, that on the side of the evangelical narrative, the number of the loaves is smaller, and that of the people greater ; but who does not know that in general the legend does not easily imitate, without at the same time surpassing, and who does not see that in this particular instance it was entirely suited to the position of the Messiah, that his miraculous power, compared with that of Elisha, should be placed, as it regards the need of natural means, in the relation of five to twenty, but as it regards the supernatural performance, in that of five thousand to one hundred? Paulus indeed, in order to preclude the inference, that as the two narratives in the Old Testament are to be understood mythically, so also is the strikingly similar evangelical narrative, extends to the former the attempt at a natural explanation which he has pursued with the latter, making the widow's cruse of oil to be replenished by the aid of the scholars of the prophets, and the twenty loaves suffice for one hundred men by means of a praiseworthy moderation ;[20] a mode of explanation which is less practicable here than with the New Testament narrative, in proportion as, by reason of the greater remoteness of these anecdotes, they present fewer critical (and, by reason of their merely mediate relation to Christianity, fewer dogmatical) motives for maintaining their historical veracity.

Nothing more is wanting to complete the mythical derivation of this history of the miraculous feeding of the multitude, except the proof, that the later Jews also believed of particularly holy men, that by their means a small amount of provision was made sufficient, and of this proof the disinterested industry of Dr. Paulus as a collector, has put us in possession. He adduces a rabbinical statement that in the time of a specially holy man, the small quantity of shew-bread more than sufficed for the supply of the priests.[21] To be consequent, this commentator should try to explain this story also naturally,—by the moderation of the priests, for instance : but it is not in the canon, hence he can unhesitatingly regard it as a fable, and he only so far admits its striking similarity to the evangelical narrative as to observe, that in consequence of the Jewish belief in such augmentations of food, attested by that rabbinical statement, the New Testament narrative may in early times

---

[19] 2 Kings iv. 43, LXX.: τί δῶ τοῦτο ἐνώπιον ἑκατὸν ἀνδρῶν ;
Ibid. v. 44 : καὶ ἔφαγον, καὶ κατέλιπον κατὰ τὸ ῥῆμα Κυρίου.

John vi. 9 : ἀλλὰ ταῦτα τί ἐστιν εἰς τοσούτους ;
Matt. xiv. 20 : καὶ ἔφαγον πάντες, καὶ ἐχορτάσθησαν, καὶ ἦραν τὸ περισσεῦον τῶν κλασμάτων, κ. τ. λ.

[20] Exeg. Handb. 2, s. 237 f.

[21] Joma f. 39, 1 : *Tempore Simeonis justi benedictio erat super duos panes pentecostales et super decem panes προθέσεως, ut singuli sacerdotes, qui pro rata parte acciperent quantitatem olivæ, ad satietatem comederent, imo ut adhuc reliquiæ superessent.*

have been understood by judaizing Christians in the same (miraculous) sense. But our examination has shown that the evangelical narrative was designedly composed so as to convey this sense, and if this sense was an element of the popular Jewish legend, then is the evangelical narrative without doubt a product of that legend.[22].

§ 103.

JESUS TURNS WATER INTO WINE.

Next to the history of the multiplication of the loaves and fishes, may be ranged the narrative in the fourth gospel (ii. 1 ff.), of Jesus at a wedding in Cana of Galilee turning water into wine. According to Olshausen, both miracles fall under the same category, since in both a substratum is present, the substance of which is modified.[1] But he overlooks the logical distinction, that in the miracle of the loaves and fishes, the modification is one of quantity merely, an augmentation of what was already existing, without any change of its quality (bread becomes *more* bread, but remains *bread*); whereas at the wedding in Cana the substratum is modified in quality—out of a certain substance there is made not merely more of the same kind, but something else (out of water, wine) ; in other words, a real transubstantiation takes place. It is true there are changes in quality which are natural results, and the instantaneous effectuation of which by Jesus would be even more easy to conceive, than an equally rapid augmentation of quantity ; for example, if he had suddenly changed must into wine, or wine into vinegar, this would only have been to conduct in an accelerated manner the same vegetable substratum, the vinous juice, through various conditions natural to it. The miracle would be already heightened if Jesus had imparted to the juice of another fruit, the apple for instance, the quality of that of the grape, although even in this his agency would have been within the limits of the same kingdom of nature. But here, where water is turned into wine, there is a transition from one kingdom of nature to another, from the elementary to the vegetable ; a miracle which as far exceeds that of the multiplication of the loaves, as if Jesus had hearkened to the counsel of the tempter, and turned stones into bread.[2]

To this miracle, as to the former, Olshausen, after Augustine,[3] applies his definition of an accelerated natural process, by which we are to understand that we have here simply the occurrence, in an accelerated manner, of that which is presented yearly in the vine in a slow process of development. This mode of viewing the matter would have some foundation, if the substratum on which Jesus operated had been the same out of which wine is wont to be naturally produced ; if he had taken a vine in his hand, and suddenly caused it to bloom, and to bear ripe grapes, this might have been called an accelerated natural process. Even then indeed we should still have no wine, and if Jesus were to produce this also from the vine which he took into his hand, he must add an operation which would be an invisible substitute for the winepress, that is, an accelerated artificial process ; so that

---

[22] Comp. De Wette, ex Handb. 1, 1, s. 133 f.

[1] Bibl. Comm. 2, s. 74.

[2] Neander is of opinion that an analogy may be found for this miracle yet more easily than for that of the loaves—in the mineral springs, the water of which is rendered so potent by natural agencies, that it produces effects which far exceed those of ordinary water, and in part resemble those of wine ! (s. 369.)

[3] In Joann. tract. 8 : *Ipse vinum fecit in nuptiis, qui omni anno hoc facit in vitibus.*

on this supposition the category of the accelerated natural process would already be insufficient.   In fact, however, we have no vine as a substratum for this production of wine, but water, and in this case we could only speak with propriety of an accelerated natural process, if by any means, however gradual, wine were ever produced out of water.   Here it is urged, that certainly out of water, out of the moisture produced in the earth by rain and the like, the vine draws its sap, which in due order it applies to the production of the grape, and of the wine therein contained ; so that thus yearly, by means of a natural process, wine does actually come out of water.[4]   But apart from the fact that water is only one of the elementary materials which are required for the fructification of the vine, and that to this end, soil, air, and light, must concur ; it could not be said either of one, or of all these elementary materials together, that they produce the grape or the wine, nor, consequently, that Jesus, when he produced wine out of water, did the same thing, only more quickly, which is repeated every year as a gradual process : on the contrary, here again there is a confusion of essentially distinct logical categories.   For we may place the relation of the product to the producing agent, which is here treated of, under the category of power and manifestation, or of cause and effect : never can it be said that water is the power or the cause, which produces grapes and wine, for the power which gives existence to them is strictly the vegetable individuality of the vine-plant, to which water, with the rest of the elementary agencies, is related only as the solicitation to the power, as the stimulus to the cause.   That is, without the co-operation of water, air, etc., grapes certainly cannot be produced, any more than without the vine plant ; but the distinction is, that in the vine the grape, in itself or in its germ, is already present, and water, air, etc., only assist in its development ; whereas in these elementary substances, the grape is present neither *actu* nor *potentiâ ;* they can in no way produce the fruit out of themselves, but only out of something else—the vine.   To turn water into wine is not then to make a cause act more rapidly than it would act in a natural way, but it is to make the effect appear without a cause, out of a mere accessory circumstance ; or, to refer more particularly to organic nature, it is to call forth the organic product without the producing organism, out of the simple inorganic materials, or rather out of one of these materials only.   This is about the same thing as to make bread out of earth without the intervention of the corn plant, flesh out of bread without a previous assimilation of it by an animal body, or in the same immediate manner, blood out of wine. If the supranaturalist is not here contented with appealing to the incomprehensibleness of an omnipotent word of Jesus, but also endeavours, with Olshausen, to bring the process which must have been contained in the miracle in question nearer to his conception, by regarding it in the light of a natural process ; he must not, in order to render the matter more probable, suppress a part of the necessary stages in that process, but exhibit them all. They would then present the following series : 1st, to the water, as one only of the elementary agents, Jesus must have added the power of the other elements above named ; 2ndly (and this is the chief point), he must have procured, in an equally invisible manner, the organic individuality of the vine ; 3rdly, he must have accelerated, to the degree of instantaneousness, the natural process resulting from the reciprocal action of these objects upon one another, the blooming and fructification of the vine, together with the ripening of the grape ; 4thly, he must have caused the artificial process of pressing,

---

[4] Thus Augustine, ut sup. approved by Olshausen : *sicut enim, quod miserunt ministri in hydrias in vinum conversum est opere Domini, sic et quod nubes fundunt, in vinum convertitur ejusdem opere Domini.*

and so forth, to occur invisibly and suddenly ; and lastly, he must again have accelerated the further natural process of fermentation, so as to render it momentary.   Thus, here again, the designation of the miracle as an accelerated natural process, would apply to two stages only out of five, the other three being such as cannot possibly be brought under this point of view, though the two first, especially the second, are of greater importance even than belonged to the stages which were neglected in the application of this view to the history of the miraculous feeding : so that the definition of an accelerated natural process is as inadequate here as there.[5]   As, however, this is the only, or the extreme category, under which we can bring such operations nearer to our conception and comprehension ; it follows that if this category be shown to be inapplicable, the event itself is inconceivable.

Not only, however, has the miracle before us been impeached in relation to possibility, but also in relation to utility and fitness.   It has been urged both in ancient[6] and modern[7] times, that it was unworthy of Jesus that he should not only remain in the society of drunkards, but even further their intemperance by an exercise of his miraculous power.   But this objection should be discarded as an exaggeration, since, as expositors justly observe, from the words *after men have well drunk*, ὅταν μεθυσθῶσι (v. 10), which *the ruler of the feast* ἀρχιτρίκλινος uses with reference to the usual course of things at such feasts, nothing can with certainty be deduced with respect to the occasion in question.   We must however still regard as valid an objection, which is not only pointed out by Paulus and the author of the Probabilia,[8] but admitted even by Lücke and Olshausen to be at the first glance a pressing difficulty : namely, that by this miracle Jesus did not, as was usual with him, relieve any want, any real need, but only furnished an additional incitement to pleasure ; showed himself not so much helpful as courteous ; rather, so to speak, performed a miracle of luxury, than of true beneficence.   If it be here said that it was a sufficient object for the miracle to confirm the faith of the disciples,[9] which according to v. 11 was its actual effect ; it must be remembered that, as a general rule, not only had the miracles of Jesus, considered with regard to their form, i.e. as extraordinary results, something desirable as their consequence, for instance, the faith of the spectators ; but also, considered with regard to their matter, i.e. as consisting of cures, multiplications of loaves, and the like, were directed to some really beneficent end. In the present miracle this characteristic is wanting, and hence Paulus is not wrong when he points out the contradiction which would lie in the conduct of Jesus, if towards the tempter he rejected every challenge to such miracles as, without being materially beneficent, or called for by any pressing necessity, could only formally produce faith and astonishment, and yet in this instance performed a miracle of that very nature.[10]

The supranaturalist was therefore driven to maintain that it was not faith in general which Jesus here intended to produce, but a conviction entirely special, and only to be wrought by this particular miracle.   Proceeding on this supposition, nothing was more natural than to be reminded by the opposition of water and wine on which the miracle turns, of the opposition between him who baptized with water (Matt. iii. 11), who at the same time

---

[5] Even Lücke, 1, s. 405, thinks the analogy with the above natural process deficient and unintelligible, and does not know how to console himself better than by the consideration, that a similar inconvenience exists in relation to the miracle of the loaves.
[6] Chrysost. hom. in Joann. 21.
[7] Woolston, Disc. 4.
[8] P. 42.
[9] Tholuck, in loc.
[10] Comm. 4, s. 151 f.

came neither eating nor drinking (Luke i. 15 ; Matt. xi. 18), and him who, as he baptized with the Holy Ghost and with fire, so he did not deny himself the ardent, animating fruit of the vine, and was hence reproached with being a *wine-bibber* οἰνοπότης (Matt. xi. 19) ; especially as the fourth gospel, in which the narrative of the wedding at Cana is contained, manifests in a peculiar degree the tendency to lead over the contemplation from the Baptist to Jesus. On these grounds Herder,[11] and after him some others,[12] have held the opinion, that Jesus by the above miraculous act intended to symbolize to his disciples, several of whom had been disciples of the Baptist, the relation of his spirit and office to those of John, and by this proof of his superior power, to put an end to the offence which they might take at his more liberal mode of life. But here the reflection obtrudes itself, that Jesus does not avail himself of this symbolical miracle, to enlighten his disciples by explanatory discourses concerning his relation to the Baptist ; an omission which even the friends of this interpretation pronounce to be surprising.[13] How needful such an exposition was, if the miracle were not to fail of its special object, is evident from the fact, that the narrator himself, according to v. 11, understood it not at all in this light, as a symbolization of a particular maxim of Jesus, but quite generally, as a *manifestation* φανέρωσις of his glory.[14] Thus if that special lesson were the object of Jesus in performing the miracle before us, then the author of the fourth gospel, that is, according to the supposition of the above theologians, his most apprehensive pupil, misunderstood him, and Jesus delayed in an injudicious manner to prevent this misunderstanding ; or if both these conclusions are rejected, there still subsists the difficulty, that Jesus, contrary to the prevailing tendency of his conduct, sought to attain the general object of proving his miraculous power, by an act for which apparently he might have substituted a more useful one.

Again, the disproportionate quantity of wine with which Jesus supplies the guests, must excite astonishment. Six vessels, each containing from two to three μετρητὰς, supposing the Attic μετρητὴς, corresponding to the Hebrew *bath*, to be equivalent to $1\frac{1}{2}$ Roman *amphoræ*, or twenty-one Wirtemberg measures,* would yield 252–378 measures.[15] What a quantity for a company who had already drunk freely ! What enormous vessels ! exclaims Dr. Paulus, and leaves no effort untried to reduce the statement of measures in the text. With a total disregard of the rules of the language, he gives to the preposition ἀνὰ a collective meaning, instead of its proper distributive one, so as to make the six *water pots* (ὑδρίαι) contain, not each, but altogether, from two to three μετρητὰς ; and even Olshausen consoles himself, after Semler, with the fact, that it is nowhere remarked that the water in all the vessels was turned into wine. But these are subterfuges ; they to whom the supply of so extravagant and dangerous a quantity of wine on the part of Jesus is incredible, must conclude that the narrative is unhistorical.

Peculiar difficulty is occasioned by the relation in which this narrative places Jesus to his mother, and his mother to him. According to the express statement of the Evangelist, the turning of water into wine was the *beginning*

---

[11] Von Gottes Sohn u. s. f. nach Johannes Evangelium, s. 131 f.

[12] C. Ch. Flatt, über die Verwandlung des Wassers in Wein, in Süskind's Magazin, 14. Stück, s. 86 f. ; Olshausen, ut sup. s. 75 f. ; comp. Neander, L. J. Chr., s. 372.

[13] Olshausen, ut sup.

[14] Lücke also thinks this symbolical interpretation too far-fetched, and too little supported by the tone of the narrative, s. 406. Comp. De Wette, ex. Handb. 1, 3, s. 37.

* [A Wirtemburg wine Maas, or measure, is equal to about $3\frac{1}{4}$ pints English, or more exactly 3·32.—Tr.]

[15] Wurm, de ponderum, mensurarum etc. rationibus, ap. Rom. et Græc., p. 123, 126. Comp. Lücke, in loc.

of the miracles of Jesus, ἀρχὴ τῶν σημείων; and yet his mother reckons so confidently on his performing a miracle here, that she believes it only necessary to point out to him the deficiency of wine, in order to induce him to afford supernatural aid; and even when she receives a discouraging answer, she is so far from losing hope, that she enjoins the servants to be obedient to the directions of her son (v. 3, 5). How is this expectation of a miracle on the part of the mother of Jesus to be explained? Are we to refer the declaration of John, that the metamorphosis of the water was the first miracle of Jesus, merely to the period of his public life, and to presuppose as real events, for his previous years, the apocryphal miracles of the Gospels of the Infancy? Or, believing that Chrysostom was right in regarding this as too uncritical,[16] are we rather to conjecture that Mary, in consequence of her conviction that Jesus was the Messiah, a conviction wrought in her by the signs that attended his birth, expected miracles from him, and as perhaps on some earlier occasions, so now on this, when the perplexity was great, desired from him a proof of his power?[17]   Were only that early conviction of the relatives of Jesus that he was the Messiah somewhat more probable, and especially the extraordinary events of the childhood, by which it is supposed to have been produced, better accredited! Moreover, even presupposing the belief of Mary in the miraculous power of her son, it is still not at all clear how, notwithstanding his discouraging answer, she could yet confidently expect that he would just on this occasion perform his first miracle, and feel assured that she positively knew that he would act precisely so as to require the assistance of the servants.[18]   This decided knowledge on the part of Mary, even respecting the manner of the miracle about to be wrought, appears to indicate an antecedent disclosure of Jesus to her, and hence Olshausen supposes that Jesus had given his mother an intimation concerning the miracle on which he had resolved. But when could this disclosure have been made? Already as they were going to the feast? Then Jesus must have foreseen that there would be a want of wine, in which case Mary could not have apprised him of it as of an unexpected embarrassment. Or did Jesus make the disclosure after her appeal, and consequently in connexion with the words : *What have I to do with thee, woman,* etc.? But with this answer, it is impossible to conceive so opposite a declaration to have been united; it would therefore be necessary, on Olshausen's view, to imagine that Jesus uttered the negative words aloud, the affirmative in an undertone, merely for Mary : a supposition which would give the scene the appearance of a comedy. Thus it is on no supposition to be understood how Mary could expect a miracle at all, still less precisely such an one. The first difficulty might indeed be plausibly evaded, by maintaining that Mary did not here apply to Jesus in expectation of a miracle, but simply that she might obtain her son's advice in the case, as she was wont to do in all difficult circumstances :[19] his reply however shows that he regarded the words of his mother as a summons to perform a miracle, and moreover the direction which Mary gave to the servants remains on this supposition totally unexplained.

The answer of Jesus to the intimation of his mother (v. 4) has been just as often blamed with exaggeration[20] as justified on insufficient grounds.   How-

[16] Homil. in Joann. in loc.
[17] Tholuck, in loc.
[18] This argument is valid against Neander also, who appeals to the faith of Mary chiefly as a result of the solemn inauguration at the baptism (s. 370).
[19] Hess, Gesch. Jesu, 1, s. 135. Comp. also Calvin, in loc.
[20] E.g. by Woolston, ut sup.

ever truly it may be urged that the Hebrew phrase, מַה־לִּי וָלָךְ, to which the
Greek τί ἐμοὶ καὶ σοὶ corresponds, appears elsewhere as an expression of
gentle blame, e.g. 2 Sam. xvi. 10 ; [21] or that with the entrance of Jesus on his
special office his relation to his mother as regarded his actions was dissolved : [22] it nevertheless remains undeniable, that it was fitting for Jesus to
be modestly apprised of opportunities for the exercise of his miraculous
power, and if one who pointed out to him a case of disease and added an
entreaty for help, did not deserve reprehension, as little and even less did
Mary, when she brought to his knowledge a want which had arisen, with a
merely implied entreaty for assistance.   The case would have been different
had Jesus considered the occasion not adapted, or even unworthy to have a
miracle connected with it ; he might then have repelled with severity the
implied summons, as an incitement to a false use of miraculous power (instanced in the history of the temptation) ; as, on the contrary, he immediately
after showed by his actions that he held the occasion worthy of a miracle, it
is absolutely incomprehensible how he could blame his mother for her information, which perhaps only came to him a few moments too soon.[23]

Here again it has been attempted to escape from the numerous difficulties
of the supranatural view, by a natural interpretation of the history.   The
commentators who advance this explanation set out from the fact, that it was
the custom among the Jews to make presents of oil or wine at marriage
feasts.   Now Jesus, it is said, having brought with him five new disciples as
uninvited guests, might foresee a deficiency of wine, and wished out of
pleasantry to present his gift in an unexpected and mysterious manner.   The
δόξα (glory) which he manifested by this proceeding, is said to be merely his
humanity, which in the proper place did not disdain to pass a jest ; the πίστις,
(faith) which he thereby excited in his disciples, was a joyful adherence to a
man who exhibited none of the oppressive severity which had been anticipated in the Messiah.   Mary was aware of her son's project, and warned him
when it appeared to her time to put it in execution ; but he reminded her
playfully not to spoil his jest by over-haste.   His causing water to be drawn,
seems to have belonged to the playful deception which he intended ; that all
at once wine was found in the vessels instead of water, and that this was regarded as a miraculous metamorphosis, might easily happen at a late hour of
the night, when there had already been considerable drinking ; lastly, that
Jesus did not enlighten the wedding party as to the true state of the case,
was the natural consequence of his wish not himself to dissipate the delusion
which he had playfully caused.[24]   For the rest, how the plan was effected, by
what arrangements on the part of Jesus the wine was conveyed in the place
of the water, this, Paulus thinks, is not now to be ascertained ; it is enough
for us to know that all happened naturally.   As however, according to the
opinion of this expositor, the Evangelist was aware, in a general manner, that
the whole occurrence was natural, why has he given us no intimation to that
effect ?   Did he wish to prepare for the reader the same surprise that Jesus
had prepared for the spectators ? still he must afterwards have solved the
enigma, if he did not intend the delusion to be permanent.   Above all, he
ought not to have used the misleading expression, that Jesus by this act
manifested forth his glory (τὴν δόξαν αὐτοῦ, v. 11), which, in the phraseology
of this gospel, can only mean his superior dignity ; he ought not to have
called the incident a sign (σημεῖον), by which something supernatural is im-

[21] Flatt, ut sup. s. 90 ; Tholuck, in loc.
[22] Olshausen, in loc.
[23] Comp. also the Probabilia, p. 41 f.
[24] Paulus, Comm. 4, s. 150 ff. ; L. J. 1, a, s. 169 ff. ; Natürliche Gesch. 2, s. 61 ff.

plied ; lastly, he ought not, by the expression, *the water that was made wine* (τὸ ὕδωρ οἶνον γεγενημένον, v. 9), and still less by the subsequent designation of Cana as the place *where he made the water wine* (ὅπου ἐποίησεν ὕδωρ οἶνον), to have occasioned the impression, that he approved the miraculous conception of the event.[25] The author of the Natural History sought to elude these difficulties by the admission, that the narrator himself, John, regarded the event as a miracle, and meant to describe it as such. Not to mention, however, the unworthy manner in which he explains this error on the part of the Evangelist,[26] it is not easy to conceive of Jesus that he should have kept his disciples in the same delusion as the rest of the guests, and not have given to them at least an explanation concerning the real course of the event. It would therefore be necessary to suppose that the narrator of this event was not one of the disciples of Jesus : a supposition which goes beyond the sphere of this system of interpretation. But even admitting that the narrator himself, whoever he may have been, was included in the same deception with those who regarded the affair as a miracle, in which case his mode of representation and the expressions which he uses would be accounted for ; still the procedure of Jesus, and his mode of acting, are all the more inconceivable, if no real miracle were on foot. Why did he with refined assiduity arrange the presentation of the wine, so that it might appear to be a miraculous gift? Why, in particular, did he cause the vessels in which he intended forthwith to present the wine, to be filled beforehand with water, the necessary removal of which could only be a hindrance to the secret execution of his plan ? unless indeed it be supposed, with Woolston, that he merely imparted to the water the taste of wine, by pouring into it some liquor. Thus there is a double difficulty ; on the one hand, that of imagining how the wine could be introduced into the vessels already filled with water ; on the other, that of freeing Jesus from the suspicion of having wished to create the appearance of a miraculous transmutation of the water. It may have been the perception of these difficulties which induced the author of the Natural History entirely to sever the connexion between the water which was poured in, and the wine which subsequently appeared, by the supposition that Jesus had caused the water to be fetched, because there was a deficiency of this also, and Jesus wished to recommend the beneficial practice of washing before and after meals, but that he afterwards caused the wine to be brought out of an adjoining room where he had placed it :—a conception of the matter which requires us either to suppose the intoxication of all the guests, and especially of the narrator, as so considerable, that they mistook the wine brought out of the adjoining room, for wine drawn out of the water vessels ; or else that the deceptive arrangements of Jesus were contrived with very great art, which is inconsistent with the straightforwardness of character elsewhere ascribed to him.

In this dilemma between the supranatural and the natural interpretations, of which, in this case again, the one is as insufficient as the other, we should be reduced, with one of the most recent commentators on the fourth gospel, to wait "until it pleased God, by further developments of judicious Christian reflection, to evolve a solution of the enigma to the general satisfaction ; "[27] did we not discern an outlet in the fact, that the history in question is found in John's gospel alone. Single in its kind as this miracle is, if it were also the first performed by Jesus, it must, even if all the twelve were not then with Jesus, have yet been known to them all ; and even if among the rest of the

---

[25] Compare on this point, Flatt, ut sup. s. 77 ff. and Lücke, in loc.
[26] He makes the word μεθύσκεσθαι, v. 10, refer to John also.
[27] Lücke, s. 407.

Evangelists there were no apostle, still it must have passed into the general Christian tradition, and from thence into the synoptical memoirs : consequently, as John alone has it, the supposition that it arose in a region of tradition unknown to the synoptists, seems easier than the alternative, that it so early disappeared out of that from which they drew ; the only question is, whether we are in a condition to show how such a legend could arise without historical grounds.   Kaiser points for this purpose to the extravagant spirit of the oriental legend, which has ever been so fertile in metamorphoses : but this source is so wide and indefinite, that Kaiser finds it necessary also to suppose a real jest on the part of Jesus,[28] and thus remains uneasily suspended between the mythical and the natural explanations, a position which cannot be escaped from, until there can be produced points of mythical connexion and origin more definite and exact.   Now in the present case we need halt neither at the character of eastern legend in general, nor at metamorphoses in general, since transmutations of this particular element of water are to be found within the narrower circle of the ancient Hebrew history.   Besides some narratives of Moses procuring for the Israelites water out of the flinty rock in the wilderness (Exod. xvii. 1 ff. ; Num. xx. 1 ff.)—a bestowal of water which, after being repeated in a modified manner in the history of Samson (Judges xv. 18 f.), was made a feature in the messianic expectations ;[29]—the first transmutation of water ascribed to Moses, is the turning of all the water in Egypt into blood, which is enumerated among the so-called plagues (Exod. vii. 17 ff.).   Together with this *mutatio in deterius*, there is in the history of Moses a *mutatio in melius*, also effected in water, for he made bitter water sweet, under the direction of Jehovah (Exod. xiv. 23 ff.[30]) ; as at a later era, Elisha also is said to have made unhealthy water good and innoxious (2 Kings ii. 19 ff.[31]).   As, according to the rabbinical passage quoted, the *bestowal* of water, so also, according to this narrative in John, the *transmutation* of water appears to have been transferred from Moses and the prophets to the Messiah, with such modifications, however, as lay in the nature of the case.   If namely, on the one hand, a change of water for the worse, like that Mosaic transmutation into blood—if a miracle of this retributive kind might not seem well suited to the mild spirit of the Messiah as recognised in Jesus : so on the other hand, such a change for the better as, like the removal of bitterness or noxiousness, did not go beyond the *species* of water, and did not, like the change into blood, alter the substance of the water itself, might appear insufficient for the Messiah ; if then the two conditions be united, a change of water for the better, which should at the same time be a specific alteration of its substance, must almost of necessity be a change into wine.   Now this is narrated by John, in a manner not indeed in accordance with reality, but which must be held all the more in accordance with the spirit of his gospel.   For the harshness of Jesus towards his mother is, historically considered, incredible ; but it is entirely in the spirit of the fourth gospel, to place in relief the exaltation of Jesus as the divine Logos by such demeanour towards suppliants (as in John iv. 48), and even towards his mother.[32]   Equally in the spirit of this gospel is it also, to exhibit the firm

---

[28] Bibl. Theol. 1, s. 200.

[29] In the passages cited Vol. I. § 14, out of Midrasch Koheleth, it is said among other things : *Goël primus—ascendere fecit puteum : sic quoque Goël postremus ascendere faciet aquas*, etc.

[30] A natural explanation of this miracle is given by Josephus in a manner worthy of notice, Antiq. iii. 1, 2.

[31] We may also remind the reader of the transmutation of water into oil, which Eusebius (H. E. vi. 9.) narrates of a Christian bishop.

[32] Compare the Probabilia, ut sup.

faith which Mary maintains notwithstanding the negative answer of Jesus, by making her give the direction to the servants above considered, as if she had a preconception even of the manner in which Jesus would perform his miracle, a preconception which is historically impossible.[33]

§ 104.

JESUS CURSES A BARREN FIG-TREE.

The anecdote of the fig-tree which Jesus caused to wither by his word, because when he was hungry he found no fruit on it, is peculiar to the two first gospels (Matt. xxi. 18 ff. ; Mark xi. 12 ff.), but is narrated by them with divergencies which must affect our view of the fact. One of these divergencies of Mark from Matthew, appears so favourable to the natural explanation, that, chiefly in consideration of it, a tendency towards the natural view of the miracles of Jesus has been of late ascribed to this Evangelist ; and for the sake of this one favourable divergency, he has been defended in relation to the other rather inconvenient one, which is found in the narrative before us.

If we were restricted to the manner in which the first Evangelist states the consequence of the curse of Jesus : *and immediately the fig-tree withered away* καὶ ἐξηράνθη παραχρῆμα ἡ συκῆ, it would be difficult here to carry out a natural explanation ; for even the forced interpretation of Paulus, which makes the word παραχρῆμα (*immediately*) only exclude further human accession to the fact, and not a longer space of time, rests only on an unwarranted transference of Mark's particulars into the narrative of Matthew.   In Mark, Jesus curses the fig-tree on the morning after His entrance into Jerusalem, and not till the following morning the disciples remark, in passing, that the tree is withered. Through this interim, which Mark leaves open between the declaration of Jesus and the withering of the tree, the natural explanation of the whole narrative insinuates itself, taking its stand on the possibility, that in this interval the tree might have withered from natural causes. Accordingly, Jesus is supposed to have remarked in the tree, besides the lack of fruit, a condition from which he prognosticated that it would soon wither away, and to have uttered this prediction in the words : No one will ever again gather fruit from thee.   The heat of the day having realized the prediction of Jesus with unexpected rapidity, and the disciples remarking this the next morning, they then first connected this result with the words of Jesus on the previous morning, and began to regard them as a curse : an interpretation which, indeed, Jesus does not confirm, but impresses on the disciples, that if they have only some self-reliance, they will be able, not only to predict such physiologically evident results, but also to know and effect things far more difficult.[1]   But even admitting Mark's statement to be the correct one, the natural explan-

---

[33] De Wette thinks the analogies adduced from the Old Testament too remote ; according to him, the metamorphosis of wine into water by Bacchus, instanced by Wetstein, would be nearer to the subject, and not far from the region of Greek thought, out of which the gospel of John arose.   The most analogous mythical derivation of the narrative would be to regard this supply of wine as the counterpart to the supply of bread, and both as corresponding to the bread and wine in the last supper.   But, he continues, the mythical view is opposed, 1, by the not yet overthrown authenticity of the fourth gospel ; 2, by the fact that the narrative bears less of a legendary than a subjective impress, by the obscurity that rests upon it, and its want of one presiding idea, together with the abundance of practical ideas worthy of Jesus which it embodies.   By these observations De Wette seems to intimate his approval of a natural explanation, built on the self-deception of John ; an explanation which is encumbered with the difficulties above noticed.

[1] Paulus, exeg. Handb. 3, a, s. 157 ff.

ation still remains impossible. For the words of Jesus in Mark (v. 14) : μηκέτι ἐκ σοῦ εἰς τὸν αἰῶνα μηδεὶς καρπὸν φάγοι, *No man eat fruit of thee here-after for ever*, if they had been meant to imply a mere conjecture as to what would probably happen, must necessarily have had a potential signification given to them by the addition of ἂν; and in the expression of Matthew : μηκέτι ἐκ σοῦ καρπὸς γένηται, *Let no fruit grow on thee henceforward for ever*, the command is not to be mistaken, although Paulus would only find in this also the expression of a possibility. Moreover the circumstance that Jesus addresses the tree itself, as also the solemn εἰς τὸν αἰῶνα, *for ever*, which he adds, speaks against the idea of a mere prediction, and in favour of a curse ; Paulus perceives this fully, and hence with unwarrantable violence he interprets the words λέγει αὐτῇ *he saith to it*, as if they introduced a saying merely in reference to the tree, while he depreciates the expression εἰς τὸν αἰῶνα, by the translation : *in time to come.* But even if we grant that the Evangelists, owing to their erroneous conception of the incident, may have somewhat altered the words of Jesus, and that he in reality only prognosticated the withering of the tree ; still, when the prediction was fulfilled, Jesus did nevertheless ascribe the result to his own supernatural influence. For in speaking of what he has done in relation to the fig-tree, he uses the verb ποιεῖν (v. 21 Matt.) ; which cannot except by a forced interpretation, be referred to a mere prediction. But more than this, he compares what he has done in relation to the fig-tree, with the removal of mountains ; and hence, as this, according to every possible interpretation, is an act of causation, so the other must be regarded as an influence on the tree. In any case, when Peter spoke of the fig-tree as having been cursed by Jesus (v. 21 Mark), either the latter must have contra-dicted the construction thus put on his words, or his silence must have implied his acquiescence. If then Jesus in the issue ascribes the withering of the tree to his influence, he either by his address to it designed to produce an effect, or he ambitiously misused the accidental result for the sake of deluding his disciples ; a dilemma, in which the words of Jesus, as they are given by the Evangelists, decidedly direct us to the former alternative.

Thus we are inexorably thrown back from the naturalistic attempt at an explanation, to the conception of the supranaturalists, pre-eminently difficult as this is in the history before us. We pass over what might be said against the physical possibility of such an influence as is there presupposed ; not, indeed, because, with Hase, we could comprehend it through the medium of natural magic,[2] but because another difficulty beforehand excludes the inquiry, and does not allow us to come to the consideration of the physical possibility. This decisive difficulty relates to the moral possibility of such an act on the part of Jesus. The miracle he here performs is of a punitive character. Another example of the kind is not found in the canonical accounts of the life of Jesus ; the apocryphal gospels alone, as has been above remarked, are full of such miracles. In one of the synoptical gospels there is, on the contrary, a passage often quoted already (Luke ix. 55 f.), in which it is declared, as the profound conviction of Jesus, that the employment of miraculous power in order to execute punishment or to take vengeance, is contrary to the spirit of his vocation ; and the same sentiment is attributed to Jesus by the Evangelist, when he applies to him the words of Isaiah : *He shall not break a bruised reed*, etc. (Matt. xii. 20). Agreeably to this principle, and to his prevalent mode of action, Jesus must rather have given new life to a withered tree, than have made a green one wither ; and in order to compre-hend his conduct on this occasion, we must be able to show reasons which

[2] L. J. § 128.

he might possibly have had, for departing in this instance from the above principle, which has no mark of unauthenticity. The occasion on which he enunciated that principle was when, on the refusal of a Samaritan village to exercise hospitality towards Jesus and his disciples, the sons of Zebedee asked him whether they should not rain down fire on the village, after the example of Elijah. Jesus replied by reminding them of the nature of the spirit to which they belonged, a spirit with which so destructive an act was incompatible. In our present case Jesus had not to deal with men who had treated him with injustice, but with a tree which he happened not to find in the desired state. Now, there is here no special reason for departing from the above rule ; on the contrary, the chief reason which in the first case might possibly have moved Jesus to determine on a judicial miracle, is not present in the second. The moral end of punishment, namely, to bring the punished person to a conviction and acknowledgment of his error, can have no existence in relation to a tree ; and even punishment in the light of retribution is out of the question when we are treating of natural objects destitute of volition.[3] For one to be irritated against an inanimate object, which does not happen to be found just in the desired state, is with reason pronounced to be a proof of an uncultivated mind ; to carry such indignation to the destruction of the object is regarded as barbarous, and unworthy of a reasonable being ; and hence Woolston is not wrong in maintaining, that in any other person than Jesus, such an act would be severely blamed.[4] It is true that when a natural object is intrinsically and habitually defective, it may very well happen, that it may be removed out of the way, in order to put a better in its place ; a measure, however, for which, in every case, only the owner has the adequate motive and authority (comp. Luke xiii. 7). But that this tree, because just at that time it presented no fruit, would not have borne any in succeeding years, was by no means self-evident :—nay, the contrary is implied in the narrative, since the form in which the curse of Jesus is expressed, that fruit shall never more grow on the tree, presupposes, that without this curse the tree might yet have been fruitful.

Thus the evil condition of the tree was not habitual but temporary ; still further, if we follow Mark, it was not even objective, or existing intrinsically in the tree, but purely subjective, that is, a result of the accidental relation of the tree to the momentary wish and want of Jesus. For according to an addition which forms the second feature peculiar to Mark in this narrative, it was not then the time of figs (v. 13) ; it was not therefore a defect, but, on the contrary, quite in due order, that this tree, as well as others, had no figs on it, and Jesus (in whom it is already enough to excite surprise that he expected to find figs on the tree so out of season) might at least have reflected, when he found none, on the groundlessness of his expectation, and have forborne so wholly unjust an act as the cursing of the tree. Even some of the fathers stumbled at this addition of Mark's and felt that it rendered the conduct of Jesus enigmatical ;[5] and to descend to later times, Woolston's

---

[3] Augustin. de verbis Domini in ev. sec. Joann., sermo 44 : *Quid arbor fecerat, fructum non afferendo ? quæ culpa arboris infæcunditas ?*

[4] Disc. 4.

[5] Orig. Comm. in Matt., Tom. xvi. 29 : Ὁ δὲ Μάρκος ἀναγράψας τὰ κατὰ τὸν τόπον, ἀπεμφαῖνόν τι ὡς πρὸς τὸ ῥητὸν προσέθηκε, ποιήσας, ὅτι—οὐ γὰρ ἦν καιρὸς σύκων.—Εἴποι γὰρ ἄν τις· εἰ μὴ ὁ καιρὸς σύκων ἦν, πῶς ἦλθεν ὁ Ἰ. ὡς εὑρήσων τι ἐν αὐτῇ, καὶ πῶς δικαίως εἶπεν αὐτῇ· μηκέτι εἰς τὸν αἰῶνα ἐκ σοῦ μηδεὶς καρπὸν φάγῃ ; comp. Augustin ut sup. *Mark, in relating this event, adds something which seems not to tally well with his statement, when he observes that it was not the season for figs. It might be urged : if it was not the season for figs, why should Jesus go and look for fruit on the tree, and how could he, with justice, say to it, Let no man eat fruit of thee for ever ?*

ridicule is not unfounded, when he says that if a Kentish countryman were to seek for fruit in his garden in spring, and were to cut down the trees which had none, he would be a common laughing-stock. Expositors have attempted to free themselves from the difficulty which this addition introduces, by a motley series of conjectures and interpretations. One the one hand, the wish that the perplexing words did not stand in the text, has been turned into the hypothesis that they may probably be a subsequent gloss.[6] On the other hand, as, if an addition of this kind must stand there, the contrary statement, namely, that it was then the time of figs, were rather to be desired, in order to render intelligible the expectation of Jesus, and his displeasure when he found it deceived ; it has been attempted in various ways to remove the negative out of the proposition. One expedient is altogether violent, οὗ being read instead of οὐ, a point inserted after ἦν, and a second ἦν supplied after σύκων, so that the translation runs thus : *ubi enim tum versabatur* (Jesus), *tempus ficuum erat* ; [7] another expedient, the transformation of the sentence into an interrogatory one, *nonne enim*, etc., is absurd.[8] A third expedient is to understand the words καιρὸς σύκων as implying the time of the fig-gathering, and thus to take Mark's addition as a statement that the figs were not yet gathered, i.e. were still on the trees,[9] in support of which interpretation, appeal is made to the phrase καιρὸς τῶν καρπῶν (Matt. xxi. 34). But this expression strictly refers only to the *antecedent* of the harvest, the existence of the fruits in the fields or on the trees ; when it stands in an affirmative proposition, it can only be understood as referring to the *consequent*, namely, the possible gathering of the fruit, in so far as it also includes the *antecedent*, the existence of the fruits in the field : hence ἔστι καιρὸς καρπῶν can only mean thus much : the (ripe) fruits stand in the fields, and are therefore ready to be gathered. In like manner, when the above expression stands in a negative proposition, the *antecedent*, the existence of the fruits in the field, on the trees, etc., is primarily denied, that of the *consequent* only secondarily and by implication ; thus οὐκ ἔστι καιρὸς σύκων, means : the figs are not on the trees, and therefore not ready to be gathered ; by no means the reverse : they are not yet gathered, and therefore are still on the trees. But this unexampled figure of speech, by which, while according to the words the *antecedent* is denied, according to the sense only the *consequent* is denied, and the *antecedent* affirmed, is not all which the above explanation entails upon us ; it also requires the admission of another figure which is sometimes called synchisis, sometimes hyperbaton. For, as a statement that the figs were then still on the trees, the addition in question does not show the reason why Jesus found none on that tree, but why he expected the contrary ; it ought therefore, say the advocates of this explanation, to stand, not after *he found nothing but leaves*, but after *he came, if haply he might find any thing thereon ;* a transposition, however, which only proves that this whole explanation runs counter to the text. Convinced, on the one hand, that the addition of Mark denies the prevalence of circumstances favourable to the existence of figs on that tree, but, on the other hand, still labouring to justify the expectation of Jesus, other expositors have sought to give to that negation, instead of the general sense, that it was not the right season of the year for figs, a fact of which Jesus must unavoidably have been aware, the particular sense, that special circumstances only not necessarily known to Jesus, hindered the fruitfulness of the tree. It would have been a hindrance altogether special,

---

[6] Toupii emendd. in Suidam, 1, p. 330 f.
[7] Heinsius and others, ap. Fritzsche, in loc.
[8] Maji Obs., ib.
[9] Dahme, in Henke's n. Magazin, 2. Bd. 2. Heft, s. 252. Kuinöl, in Marc, p. 150 f.

if the soil in which the tree was rooted had been an unfruitful one ; hence, according to some, the words καιρὸς σύκων actually signify *a soil favourable to figs*.[10] Others with more regard to the verbal meaning of καιρὸς, adhere it is true to the interpretation of it as *favourable time*, but instead of understanding the statement of Mark universally, as referring to a regular, annual season, in which figs were not to be obtained, they maintain it to mean that that particular year was from some incidental causes unfavourable to figs.[11] But the immediate signification of καιρὸς is the right, in opposition to the wrong season, not a favourable season as opposed to an unfavourable one. Now, when any one, even in an unproductive year, seeks for fruits at the time in which they are wont to be ripe, it cannot be said that it is the wrong season for fruit ; on the contrary, the idea of a bad year might be at once conveyed by the statement, that *when the time for fruit came*, ὅτε ἦλθεν ὁ καιρὸς τῶν καρπῶν, there was none to be found. In any case, if the whole course of the year were unfavourable to figs, a fruit so abundant in Palestine, Jesus must almost as necessarily have known this as that it was the wrong season ; so that the enigma remains, how Jesus could be so indignant that the tree was in a condition which, owing to circumstances known to him, was inevitable.

But let us only remember who it is to whom we owe that addition. It is Mark, who, in his efforts after the explanatory and the picturesque, so frequently draws on his own imagination ; and in doing this, as it has been long ago perceived, and as we also have had sufficient opportunities of observing on our way, he does not always go to work in the most considerate manner. Thus, here, he is arrested by the first striking particular that presents itself, namely, that the tree was without fruit, and hastens to furnish the explanation, that it was not the time for figs, not observing that while he accounts physically for the barrenness of the tree, he makes the conduct of Jesus morally inexplicable. Again, the above-mentioned divergency from Matthew in relation to the time within which the tree withered, far from evincing more authentic information,[12] or a tendency to the natural explanation of the marvellous on the part of Mark, is only another product of the same dramatising effort as that which gave birth to the above addition. The idea of a tree suddenly withering at a word, is difficult for the imagination perfectly to fashion ; whereas it cannot be called a bad dramatic contrivance, to lay the process of withering behind the scenes, and to make the result be first noticed by the subsequent passers by. For the rest, in the assertion that it was then (a few days before Easter) no time for figs, Mark is so far right, as it regards the conditions of climate in Palestine, that at so early a time of the year the new figs of the season were not yet ripe, for the early fig or boccore is not ripe until the middle or towards the end of June ; while the proper fig, the kermus, ripens only in the month of August. On the other hand, there might about Easter still be met with here and there, hanging on the tree, the third fruit of the fig-tree, the late kermus, which had remained from the previous autumn, and through the winter :[13] as we read in Josephus that a part of Palestine (the shores of the Galilean sea, more fruitful, certainly, than the country around Jerusalem, where the history in question occurred, *produces figs uninterruptedly during ten months of the year*, σῦκον δέκα μησὶν ἀδιαλείπτως χορηγεῖ.[14]

---

[10] Vid. Kuinöl, in loc.
[11] Paulus, exeg. Handb., 3, a, s. 175 ; Olshausen, b, Comm. 1, s. 782.
[12] As Sieffert thinks, Ueber den Urspr., s. 113 ff. Compare my reviews, in the Charakteristiken und Kritiken, s. 272.
[13] Vid. Paulus, ut sup. s. 168 f. ; Winer, b. Realw. d. A. Feigenbaum.
[14] Bell. Jud. III. x. 8.

But even when we have thus set aside this perplexing addition of Mark's, that the tree was not really defective, but only appeared so to Jesus in consequence of an erroneous expectation : there still subsists, even according to Matthew, the incongruity that Jesus appears to have destroyed a natural object on account of a deficiency which might possibly be merely temporary. He cannot have been prompted to this by economical considerations, since he was not the owner of the tree ; still less can he have been actuated by moral views, in relation to an inanimate object of nature ; hence the expedient has been adopted of substituting the disciples as the proper object on which Jesus here intended to act, and of regarding the tree, and what Jesus does to it, as a mere means to his ultimate design. This is the symbolical interpretation, by which first the fathers of the church, and of late the majority of orthodox theologians among the moderns, have thought to free Jesus from the charge of an unsuitable action. According to them, anger towards the tree which presented nothing to appease his hunger, was not the feeling of Jesus, in performing this action ; his object not simply the extermination of the unfruitful plant : on the contrary, he judiciously availed himself of the occasion of finding a barren tree, in order to impress a truth on his disciples more vividly and indelibly than by words. This truth may either be conceived under a special form, namely, that the Jewish nation which persisted in rendering no pleasing fruit to God and to the Messiah, would be destroyed ; or under the general form, that every one who was as destitute of good works as this tree was of fruit, had to look forward to a similar condemnation.[15]   Other commentators however with reason maintain, that if Jesus had had such an end in view in the action, he must in some way have explained himself on the subject ; for if an elucidation was necessary when he delivered a parable, it was the more indispensable when he performed a symbolical action, in proportion as this, without such an indication of an object lying beyond itself, was more likely to be mistaken for an object in itself ; [16] it is true that, here as well as elsewhere, it might be supposed, that Jesus probably enlarged on what he had done, for the instruction of his disciples, but that the narrators, content with the miracle, have omitted the illustrative discourse. If however Jesus gave an interpretation of his act in the alleged symbolical sense, the Evangelists have not merely been silent concerning this discourse, but have inserted a false one in its place ; for they represent Jesus, after his procedure with respect to the tree, not as being silent, but as giving, in answer to an expression of astonishment on the part of his disciples, an explanation which is not the above symbolical one, but a different, nay, an opposite one. For when Jesus says to them that they need not wonder at the withering of the fig-tree, since with only a little faith they will be able to effect yet greater things, he lays the chief stress on his agency in the matter, not on the condition and the fate of the tree as a symbol : therefore, if his design turned upon the latter, he would have spoken to his disciples so as to contravene that design ; or rather, if he so spoke, that cannot have been his design. For the same reason, falls also Sieffert's totally unsupported hypothesis, that Jesus, not indeed after, but before that act, when on the way to the fig-tree, had held a conversation with his disciples on the actual condition and future lot of the Jewish nation, and that to this conversation the symbolical cursing of the tree was a mere key-stone, which explained itself : for all comprehension of the act in question which that

---

[15] Ullman, über die Unsündlichkeit Jesu, in his Studien, 1, s. 50 ; Sieffert, ut sup. s. 115 ff. ; Olshausen, 1, s. 783 f. ; Neander, L. J. Chr., s. 378.
[16] Paulus, ut sup. s. 170 ; Hase, L. J. § 128 ; also Sieffert, ut sup.

introduction might have facilitated, must, especially in that age when there was so strong a bias towards the miraculous, have been again obliterated by the subsequent declaration of Jesus, which regarded only the miraculous side of the fact. Hence Ullmann has judged rightly in preferring to the symbolical interpretation, although he considers it admissible, another which had previously been advanced : [17] namely, that Jesus by this miracle intended to give his followers a new proof of his perfect power, in order to strengthen their confidence in him under the approaching perils. Or rather, as a special reference to coming trial is nowhere exhibited, and as the words of Jesus contain nothing which he had not already said at an earlier period (Matt. xvii. 20; Luke xvii. 6), Fritzsche is more correct in expressing the view of the Evangelists quite generally, thus : Jesus used his displeasure at the unfruitfulness of the tree, as an occasion for performing a miracle, the object of which was merely the general one of all his miracles, namely to attest his Messiahship.[18]   Hence Euthymius speaks entirely in the spirit of the narrators, as described by Fritzsche,[19] when he forbids all investigation into the special end of the action, and exhorts the reader only to look at it in general as a miracle.[20]   But it by no means follows from hence that we too should refrain from all reflection on the subject, and believingly receive the miracle without further question ; on the contrary, we cannot avoid observing, that the particular miracle which we have now before us, does not admit of being explained as a real act of Jesus, either upon the general ground of performing miracles, or from any peculiar object or motive whatever.   Far from this, it is in every respect opposed both to his theory and his prevailing practice, and on this account, even apart from the question of its physical possibility, must be pronounced more decidedly, than any other, to be such a miracle as Jesus cannot really have performed.

It is incumbent on us, however, to adduce positive proof of the existence of such causes as, even without historical foundation, might give rise to a narrative of this kind.   Now in our usual source, the Old Testament, we do, indeed, find many figurative discourses and narratives about trees, and fig-trees in particular ; but none which has so specific an affinity to our narrative, that we could say the latter is an imitation of it.   But we need not search long in the New Testament, before we find, first in the mouth of the Baptist (Matt. iii. 10), then in that of Jesus (vii. 19), the apothegm of the tree, which, because it bears no good fruit, is cut down and cast into the fire ; and further on (Luke xiii. 6 ff.) this theme is dilated into the fictitious history of a man who for three years in vain seeks for fruit on a fig-tree in his vine-yard, and on this account determines to cut it down, but that the gardener intercedes for another year's respite.   It was already an idea of some fathers of the church, that the cursing of the fig-tree was only the parable of the barren fig-tree carried out into action.[21]   It is true that they held this opinion in the sense of the explanation before cited, namely, that Jesus himself, as he had previously exhibited the actual condition and the approaching catastrophe

---

[17] Heydenreich, in the Theol. Nachrichten, 1814, Mai., s. 121 ff.

[18] Comm. in Matt. p. 637.

[19] Comm., in Marc. p. 481 : *Male—vv. dd. in eo hæserunt, quod Jesus sine ratione innocentem ficum aridam reddidisse videretur, mirisque argutiis usi sunt, ut aliquod hujus rei consilium fuisse ostenderent.   Nimirum apostoli, evangelistæ et omnes primi temporis Christiani, qua erant ingeniorum simplicitate, quid quantumque Jesus portentose fecisse diceretur, curavunt tantummodo, non quod Jesu in edendo miraculo consilium fuerit, subtiliter et argute quæsiverunt.*

[20] Μὴ ἀκριβολογοῦ διατί τετιμώρηται τὸ φυτὸν, ἀναίτιον ὄν· ἀλλὰ μόνον ὅρα τὸ θαῦμα, καὶ θαύμαζε τὸν θαυματουργόν.

[21] Ambrosius, Comm. in Luc, in loc. Neander adopts this opinion, ut sup.

of the Jewish people in a figurative discourse, intended on the occasion in question to represent them by a symbolical action ; which, as we have seen, is inconceivable. Nevertheless, we cannot help conjecturing, that we have before us one and the same theme under three different modifications : first, in the most concentrated form, as an apothegm; then expanded into a parable ; and lastly realized as a history. But we do not suppose that what Jesus twice described in words, he at length represented by an action ; in our opinion, it was tradition which converted what it met with as an apothegm and a parable into a real incident. That in the real history the end of the tree is somewhat different from that threatened in the apothegm and parable, namely, withering instead of being cut down, need not amount to a difficulty. For had the parable once become a real history, with Jesus for its subject, and consequently its whole didactic and symbolical significance passed into the external act, then must this, if it were to have any weight and interest, take the form of a miracle, and the natural destruction of the tree by means of the axe must be transformed into an immediate withering on the word of Jesus. It is true that there seems to be the very same objection to this conception of the narrative which allows its inmost kernel to be symbolical, as to the one above considered ; namely, that it is contravened by the words of Jesus which are appended to the narrative. But on our view of the gospel histories we are warranted to say, that with the transformation of the parable into a history, its original sense also was lost, and as the miracle began to be regarded as constituting the pith of the matter, that discourse on miraculous power and faith, was erroneously annexed to it. Even the particular circumstance that led to the selection of the saying about the removal of the mountain for association with the narrative of the fig-tree, may be shown with probability. The power of faith, which is here represented by an effectual command to a mountain : *Be thou removed and be thou cast into the sea*, is elsewhere (Luke xvii. 6) symbolized by an equally effectual command to a species of fig-tree (συκάμινος) : *Be thou plucked up by the root, and be thou planted in the sea*. Hence the cursing of the fig-tree, so soon as its withering was conceived to be an effect of the miraculous power of Jesus, brought to mind the tree or the mountain which was to be transported by the miraculous power of faith, and this saying became appended to that fact. Thus, in this instance, praise is due to the third gospel for having preserved to us the parable of the barren συκῆ, and the apothegm of the συκάμινος to be transplanted by faith, distinct and pure, each in its original form and significance ; while the two other synoptists have transformed the parable into a history, and have misapplied the apothegm (in a somewhat altered form) to a false explanation of that pretended history.[22]

[22] Conceptions of the narrative in the main accordant with that here given, may be found in De Wette, exeg. Handb., 1, 1, s. 176 f. ; 1, 2, s. 174 f., and Weisse, die evang. Gesch., 1, s. 576 f.

CHAPTER X.

THE TRANSFIGURATION OF JESUS, AND HIS LAST JOURNEY TO JERUSALEM.

§ 105.

THE TRANSFIGURATION OF JESUS CONSIDERED AS A MIRACULOUS EXTERNAL EVENT.

THE history of the transfiguration of Jesus on the mountain could not be ranged with the narratives of miracles which we have hitherto examined ; not only because it relates to a miracle which took place *in* Jesus instead of a miracle performed *by* him ; but also because it has the character of an epoch in the life of Jesus, which on the score of resemblance could only be associated with the baptism and resurrection. Hence Herder has correctly designated these three events as the three luminous points in the life of Jesus, which attest his heavenly mission.[1]

According to the impression produced by the first glance at the synoptical narrative (Matt. xvii. 1 ff. ; Mark ix. 2 ff. ; Luke ix. 28 ff.)—for the history is not found in the fourth gospel—we have here a real, external, and miraculous event. Jesus, six or eight days after the first announcement of his passion, ascends a mountain with his three most confidential disciples, who are there witnesses how all at once his countenance, and even his clothes, are illuminated with supernatural splendour ; how two venerable forms from the realm of spirits, Moses and Elias, appear talking with him ; and lastly, how a heavenly voice, out of the bright cloud, declares Jesus to be the Son of God, to whom they are to give ear.

These few points in the history give rise to a multitude of questions, by the collection of which Gabler has done a meritorious service.[2] In relation to each of the three phases of the event—the light, the apparition of the dead, and the voice—both its possibility, and the adequacy of its object, may be the subject of question. First, whence came the extraordinary light with which Jesus was invested ? Let it be remembered that a *metamorphosis* of Jesus is spoken of (μεταμορφώθη ἔμπροσθεν αὐτῶν) : now this would appear to imply, not a mere illumination from without, but an irradiation from within, a transient effulgence, so to speak, of the beams of the divine glory through the veil of humanity. Thus Olshausen regards this event as an important crisis in the process of purification and glorification, through which he supposes the corporeality of Jesus to have passed, during his whole life up to the

---

[1] Vom Erlöser der Menschen nach unsern drei ersten Evangelien, s. 114.
[2] In a treatise on the history of the Transfiguration, in his neuesten theol. Journal, 1. Bd. 5. Stück, s. 517 ff. Comp. Bauer, hebr. Mythol. 2, s. 233 ff.

time of his ascension.[3] But without here dilating further on our previous arguments, that either Jesus was no real man, or the purification which he underwent during his life, must have consisted in something else than the illumination and subtilization of his body; it is in no case to be conceived how his clothes, as well as his body, could participate in such a process of transfiguration. If, on this account, it be rather preferred to suppose an illumination from without, this would not be a metamorphosis, which however is the term used by the Evangelists : so that no consistent conception can be formed of this scene, unless indeed we choose, with Olshausen, to include both modes, and think of Jesus as both radiating, and irradiated. But even supposing this illumination possible, there still remains the question, what purpose could it serve? The answer which most immediately suggests itself is : to glorify Jesus ; but compared with the spiritual glory which Jesus created for himself by word and deed, this physical glorification, consisting in the investing of his body with a brilliant light, must appear very insignificant, nay, almost childish. If it be said that, nevertheless, such a mode of glorifying Jesus was necessary for the maintenance of weak faith : we reply that in that case, it must have been effected in the presence of the multitude, or at least before the entire circle of the disciples, not surely before just the select three who were spiritually the strongest ; still less would these few eye-witnesses have been prohibited from communicating the event precisely during the most critical period, namely, until after the resurrection.—These two questions apply with enhanced force to the second feature in our history, the apparition of the two dead men. Can departed souls become visible to the living? and if, as it appears, the two men of God presented themselves in their former bodies, only transfigured, whence had they these—according to biblical ideas —before the universal resurrection? Certainly in relation to Elijah, who went up to heaven without laying aside his body, this difficulty is not so great; Moses, however, died, and his corpse was buried. But further, to what end are we to suppose that these two illustrious dead appeared? The evangelical narrative, by representing the forms as *talking with Jesus*, συλλαλοῦντες τῷ Ἰ., seems to place the object of their appearance in Jesus ; and if Luke be correct, it had reference more immediately to the approaching sufferings and death of Jesus. But they could not have made the first announcement of these events to him, for, according to the unanimous testimony of the synoptists, he had himself predicted them a week before (Matt. xvi. 21 parall.). Hence it is conjectured, that Moses and Elias only informed Jesus more minutely concerning the particular circumstances and conditions of his death :[4] but, on the one hand, it is not accordant with the position which the gospels assign to Jesus in relation to the ancient prophets, that he should have needed instruction from them ; and on the other hand, Jesus had already foretold his passion so circumstantially, that the more special revelations from the world of spirits could only have referred to the particulars of his being delivered to the Gentiles, and the spitting in his face, of which he does not speak till a subsequent occasion (Matt. xx. 19 ; Mark x. 34). If, however, it be suggested, that the communication to be made to Jesus consisted not so much in information, as in the conferring of strength for his approaching sufferings : we submit that at this period there is not yet any trace of a state of mind in Jesus, which might seem to demand assistance of this kind ; while for his later sufferings this early strengthening did not suffice, as is evident from the fact, that in Gethsemane a new impartation is necessary.

[3] Bibl. Comm. i, s. 534 f.
[4] Olshausen, ut sup. s. 537.

Thus we are driven, though already in opposition to the text, to try whether we cannot give the appearance a relation to the disciples ; but first, the object of strengthening faith is too general to be the motive of so special a dispensation ; secondly, Jesus, in the parable of the rich man, must on this supposition have falsely expounded the principle of the divine government in this respect, for he there says that he who will not hear the writings of Moses and the prophets,—and how much more he who will not hear the present Christ ? —would not be brought to believe, though one should return to him from the dead : whence it must be inferred that such an apparition, at least to that end, is not permitted by God. The more special object, of convincing the disciples that the doctrine and fate of Jesus were in accordance with Moses and the prophets, had been already partly attained ; and it was not completely attained until after the death and resurrection of Jesus, and the outpouring of the Spirit : the transfiguration not having formed any epoch in their enlightenment on this subject.—Lastly, the voice out of the bright cloud (without doubt the *Shechinah*) is, like that at the baptism, a divine voice : but what an anthropomorphic conception of the Divine Being must that be, which admits the possibility of real, audible speech on his part ! Or if it be said, that a communication of God to the spiritual ear, is alone spoken of here,[5] the scene of the transfiguration is reduced to a vision, and we are suddenly transported to a totally different point of view.

§ 106.

THE NATURAL EXPLANATION OF THE NARRATIVE IN VARIOUS FORMS.

It has been sought to escape from the difficulties of the opinion which regards the transfiguration of Jesus as not only a miraculous, but also an external event, by confining the entire incident to the internal experience of the parties concerned. In adopting this position, the miraculous is not at once relinquished ; it is only transferred to the internal workings of the human mind, as being thus more simple and conceivable. Accordingly it is supposed, that by divine influence the spiritual nature of the three apostles, and probably also of Jesus himself, was exalted to a state of ecstasy, in which they either actually entered into intercourse with the higher world, or were able to shadow forth its forms to themselves in the most vivid manner ; that is, the event is regarded as a vision.[1] But the chief support of this interpretation, namely, that Matthew himself, by the expression ὅραμα, *vision* (v. 9), describes the event as merely subjective and visionary, gives way so soon as it is remembered, that neither is there anything in the signification of the word ὅραμα which determines it to refer to what is merely mental, nor is it exclusively so applied even in the phraseology of the New Testament, for we also find it, as in Acts vii. 31, used to denote something perceived externally.[2] As regards the fact itself, it is improbable, and at least without scriptural precedent, that several persons, as, here, three or four, should have had the same very complex vision ;[3] to which it may be added, that on this view of the subject also, the whole difficult question recurs concerning the utility of such a miraculous dispensation.

---

[5] Olshausen, 1, s. 539 ; comp. s. 178.
[1] Thus Tertull. adv. Marcion, iv. 22 ; Herder, ut sup. 115 f., with whom also Gratz agrees. Comm. z. Matth. 2, s. 163 f., 169.
[2] Comp. Fritzsche, in Matth., p. 552 ; Olshausen, 1, s. 523.
[3] Olshausen, ut sup.

To avoid the above difficulty, others, still confining the event to the internal experience of the parties, regard it as the product of a natural activity
of soul, and thus explain the whole as a dream.[4] During or after a prayer
offered by Jesus, or by themselves, in which mention was made of Moses and
Elias, and their advent as messianic forerunners desired, the three disciples,
according to this interpretation, slept, and (the two names mentioned by Jesus
yet sounding in their ears) dreamed that Moses and Elias were present, and
that Jesus conversed with them : an illusion which continued during the first
confused moments after their awaking.   As the former explanation rests on
the ὅραμα of Matthew, so it is alleged in support of this, that Luke describes
the disciples as *heavy with sleep*, βεβαρημένοι ὕπνῳ, and only towards the end
of the scene as *fully awake*, διαγρηγορήσαντες (v. 32).   The hold which the
third Evangelist here presents to the natural explanation, has been made a
reason for assigning to his narrative an important superiority over that of the
two other Evangelists ; recent critics pronouncing that by this and other
particulars, which bring the event nearer to natural possibility, the account in
Luke evinces itself to be the original, while that of Matthew, by its omission
of those particulars, is proved to be the traditionary one, since with the eagerness for the miraculous which characterized that age, no one would fabricate
particulars calculated to diminish the miracle, as is the case with the sleepiness of the disciples.[5]   This mode of conclusion we also should be obliged to
adopt, if in reality the above features could only be understood in the spirit
of the natural interpretation.   But we have only to recollect how in another
scene, wherein the sufferings, which according to Luke were announced at
the transfiguration, began to be accomplished, and wherein, according to the
same Evangelist, Jesus likewise held communication with a heavenly apparition, namely, in Gethsemane, the disciples, in all the synoptical gospels, again
appear *asleep*, καθεύδοντες (Matt. xxvi. 40 parall.).   If it be admitted, that the
merely external, formal resemblance of the two scenes, might cause a narrator
to convey the trait of the slumber into the history of the transfiguration, there
is a yet stronger probability that the internal import of the trait might appear
to him appropriate to this occasion also, for the sleeping of the disciples at
the very moment when their master was going through his most critical experience, exhibits their infinite distance from him, their inability to attain his
exalted level ; the prophet, the recipient of a revelation, is among ordinary
men like a watcher among the sleeping : hence it followed, of course, that as
in the deepest suffering, so here also in the highest glorification of Jesus, the
disciples should be represented as heavy with sleep.   Thus this particular, so
far from furnishing aid to the natural explanation, is rather intended by a
contrast to heighten the miracle which took place in Jesus.   We are, therefore, no longer warranted in regarding the narrative in Luke as the original
one, and in building an explanation of the event on his statement; on the
contrary, we consider that addition, in connexion with the one already mentioned (v. 31), a sign that his account is a traditionary and embellished one,[6]
and must rather adhere to that of the two other Evangelists.
Not only, however, does the interpretation which sees in the transfiguration
only a natural dream of the apostles, fail as to its main support, but it has

---

[4] Rau, symbola ad illustrandam Evv. de metamorphosi J. Chr. narrationem ; Gabler, ut
sup. s. 539 ff. ; Kuinöl, Comm. z. Matth. p. 459 ff. ; Neander, L. J. Chr. s. 474 f.
[5] Schulz, über das Abendmahl, s. 319 ; Schleiermacher, über den Lukas, s. 148 f. ; comp.
also Köster, Immanuel, s. 60 f.
[6] Bauer has discerned this, ut sup. s. 237 ; Fritzsche, p. 556 ; De Wette, exeg. Handb.
1, 2, s. 56 f. ; Weisse, die evang. Gesch. 1, s. 536 ; and Paulus also partly, exeg. Handb.
2, s. 447 f.

besides a multitude of internal difficulties. It presupposes only the three disciples to have been dreaming, leaving Jesus awake, and thus not included in the illusion. But the whole tenor of the evangelical narrative implies that Jesus as well as the disciples saw the appearance; and what is still more decisive, had the whole been a mere dream of the disciples, he could not afterwards have said to them : *Tell the vision to no man,* since by these words he must have confirmed in them the belief that they had witnessed something special and miraculous. Supposing however that Jesus had no share in the dream, it still remains altogether unexampled, that three persons should in a natural manner have had the same dream at the same time. This the friends of the above interpretation have perceived, and hence have supposed that the ardent Peter, who indeed is the only speaker, alone had the dream, but that the narrators, by a synecdoche attributed to all the disciples what in fact happened only to one. But from the circumstance that Peter here, as well as elsewhere, is the spokesman, it does not follow that he alone had the vision, and the contrary can by no figure of speech be removed from the clear words of the Evangelists. But the explanation in question still more plainly betrays its inadequacy. Not only does it require, as already noticed, that the audible utterance of the name of Moses and Elias on the part of Jesus, should be blended with the dream of the disciples ; but it also calls in the aid of a storm, which by its flashes of lightning is supposed to have given rise in them to the idea of supernatural splendour, by its peals of thunder, to that of conversation and heavenly voices, and to have held them in this delusion even for some time after they awaked. But, according to Luke, it was on the waking of the disciples ($\delta\iota\alpha\gamma\rho\eta\gamma\rho\rho\dot{\eta}\sigma\alpha\nu\tau\epsilon\varsigma$ δὲ εἶδον κ. τ. λ.) that they saw the two men standing by Jesus : this does not look like a mere illusion protracted from a dream into waking moments ; hence Kuinöl introduces the further supposition, that, while the disciples slept, there came to Jesus two unknown men, whom they, in awaking, connected with their dream, and mistook for Moses and Elias. By giving this turn to the circumstances, all those occurrences which on the interpretation based on the supposition of a dream, should be regarded as mere mental conceptions, are again made external realities : for the idea of supernatural brilliancy is supposed to have been produced by a flash of lightning, the idea of voices, by thunder, and lastly, the idea of two persons· in company with Jesus, by the actual presence of two unknown individuals. All this the disciples could properly perceive only when they were awake ; and hence the supposition of a dream falls to the ground as superfluous.

Therefore, since this interpretation, by still retaining a thread of connexion between the alleged character of the event and a mental condition, has the peculiar difficulty of making three partake in the same dream, it is better entirely to break this thread, and restore all to the external world : so that we now have a natural external occurrence before us, as in the first instance we had a supernatural one. Something objective presented itself to the disciples ; thus it is explained how it could be perceived by several at once : they deceived themselves when awake as to what they saw ; this was natural, because they were all born within the same circle of ideas, were in the same frame of mind, and in the same situation. According to this opinion, the essential fact in the scene on the mountain, is a secret interview which Jesus had preconcerted, and with a view to which he took with him the three most confidential of his disciples. Who the two men were with whom Jesus held this interview, Paulus does not venture to determine ; Kuinöl conjectures that they were secret adherents of the same kind as Nicodemus ; according to Venturini, they were Essenes, secret allies of Jesus. Before these were arrived, Jesus prayed, and the disciples, not being invited to join, slept; for the sleep noticed by Luke, though it were dreamless, is gladly retained in this interpretation, since a delusion appears more probable in the case of persons just awaking. On hearing strange voices talking with Jesus, they awake, see Jesus, who probably stood on a higher point of the mountain than they, enveloped in unwonted brilliancy, proceeding from the first rays of morning, which, perhaps reflected from a sheet of snow, fell on Jesus, but were mistaken by them in the surprise of the moment for a supernatural illumination; they perceive the two men, whom, for some unknown reasons, the drowsy Peter, and after him the rest, take for Moses and Elias; their astonishment increases when they see the two unknown individuals disappear in a bright morning cloud, which descends as they are in the act of departing, and hear one of them pronounce out of the cloud the words: οὗτος ἐστιν κ. τ. λ., which they under these circumstances unavoidably regard as a voice from heaven.[7] This explanation, which even Schleiermacher is inclined to favour,[8] is supposed, like the former, to find a special support in Luke, because in this Evangelist the assertion that the two men are Moses and Elias, is much less confidently expressed than in Matthew and Mark, and more as a mere notion of the drowsy Peter. For while the two first Evangelists directly say: ὤφθησαν αὐτοῖς Μωσῆς καὶ Ἡλίας (*there appeared unto them Moses and Elias*), Luke more warily, as it seems, speaks of ἄνδρες δύο, οἵτινες ἦσαν Μωσῆς καὶ Ἡλίας (*two men, who were Moses and Elias*), the first designation being held to contain the objective fact, the second its subjective interpretation. But this interpretation is obviously approved by the narrator, from his choice of the word οἵτινες ἦσαν, instead of ἔδοξαν εἶναι; that he first speaks of *two men*, and afterwards give s ₜhem their names, cannot have been to leave another interpretation open to the reader, but only to imitate the mysteriousness of the extraordinary scene, by the indefiniteness of his first expression. While this explanation has thus as little support in the evangelical narratives as those previously considered, it has at the same time no fewer difficulties in itself. The disciples must have been so far acquainted with the appearance of the morning beams on the mountains of their native land, as to be able to distinguish them from a heavenly glory; how they came to have the idea that the two unknown individuals were Moses and Elias, is not easy to explain on any of the former views, but least of all on this;—why Jesus, when Peter, by his proposal about the building of the three tabernacles, gave him to understand the delusion of the disciples, did not remove it, is incomprehensible, and this difficulty has induced Paulus to resort to the supposition, that Jesus did not hear the address of Peter;—the whole conjecture about secret allies of Jesus has justly lost all repute; and lastly, the one of those allies who spoke the words to the disciples out of the cloud, must have permitted himself to use an unworthy mystification.

§ 107.

THE HISTORY OF THE TRANSFIGURATION CONSIDERED AS A MYTHUS.

Thus here, as in every former instance, after having run through the circle of natural explanations, we are led back to the supernatural; in which, however, we are precluded from resting by difficulties equally decisive. Since

---

[7] Paulus, exeg. Handb., 2, 436 ff.; L. J. 1, b, s. 7 ff.; Natürliche Geschichte, 3, s. 256 ff.
[8] Ut sup.

then the text forbids a natural interpretation, while it is impossible to maintain as historical the supernatural interpretation which it sanctions, we must apply ourselves to a critical examination of its statements. These are indeed said to be especially trustworthy in the narrative before us, the fact being narrated by three Evangelists, who strikingly agree even in the precise determination of the time, and being moreover attested by the Apostle Peter (2 Pet. i. 17). [1] The agreement as to the time (the *eight days* ἡμέραι ὀκτὼ of Luke meaning, according to the usual reckoning, the same as the *six days* ἡμέραι ἓξ of the other Evangelists) is certainly striking ; and besides this, all the three narrators concur in placing immediately after the transfiguration the cure of the demoniacal boy, which the disciples had failed to effect. But both these points of agreement may be accounted for, by the origin of the synoptical gospels from a fixed fund of evangelical tradition, in relation to which, we need not be more surprised that it has grouped together many anecdotes in a particular manner without any objective reason, than that it has often preserved expressions in which it might have varied, through all the three editions. [2] The attestation of the history by the three synoptists is, however, very much weakened, at least on the ordinary view of the relation which the four gospels bear to each other, by the silence of John ; since it does not appear why this Evangelist should not have included in his history an event which was so important, and which moreover accorded so well with his system, nay, exactly realized the declaration in his prologue (v. 14) : *We beheld his glory, the glory as of the only begotten of the Father.* The worn-out reason, that he might suppose the event to be sufficiently known through his predecessors, is, over and above its general invalidity, particularly unavailable here, because no one of the synoptists was in this instance an eye-witness, and consequently there must be many things in their narratives which one who, like John, had participated in the scene, might rectify and explain. Hence another reason has been sought for this and similar omissions in the fourth gospel ; and such an one has been supposed to be found in the anti-gnostic, or, more strictly, the anti-docetic tendency which has been ascribed to the gospel, in common with the epistles, bearing the name of John. It is, accordingly, maintained that in the history of the transfiguration, the splendour which illuminated Jesus, the transformation of his appearance into something more than earthly, might give countenance to the opinion that his human form was nothing but an unsubstantial veil, through which at times his true, superhuman nature shone forth ; that his converse with the spirits of ancient prophets might lead to the conjecture, that he was himself perhaps only a like spirit of some Old Testament saint revisiting the earth ; and that, rather than give nourishment to such erroneous notions, which began early to be formed among gnosticising Christians, John chose to suppress this and similar histories. [3] But besides that it does not correspond with the apostolic *plainness of speech* (παῤῥησία) to suppress important facts in the evangelical history, on account of their possible abuse by individuals, John, if he were guided by the above consideration must at least have proceeded with some consistency, and have excluded from the circle of his accounts all narratives which, in an equal degree with the one in question, were susceptible of a docetic misinterpretation. Now, here, every one must at once be reminded of the history of the walking of Jesus on the sea, which is at least equally calculated with the history of the transfiguration, to produce the idea that the body of Jesus was a mere phantom, but which John nevertheless records. It is true that the relative importance of events

---

[1] Paulus, exeg. Handb., s. 446 ; Gratz, 2, s. 165 f.
[2] Comp. De Wette, Einleitung in das N. T. § 79.
[3] Thus Schneckenburger, Beiträge, s. 62 ff.

might introduce a distinction ; so that of two narratives with an equally strong docetic aspect, John might include the one on account of its superior weight, while he omitted the less important. But no one will contend that the walking of Jesus on the sea surpasses, or even equals, in importance the history of the transfiguration. John, if he were intent on avoiding what wore a docetic appearance, must on every consideration have suppressed the first history before all others. As he has not done so, the above principle cannot have influenced him, and consequently can never be advanced as a reason for the designed omission of a history in the fourth gospel ; rather it may be concluded, and particularly in relation to the event in question, that the author knew nothing, or at least nothing precise, of that history. [4] It is true that this conclusion can form an objection to the historical character of the narrative of the transfiguration, to those only who suppose the fourth gospel to be the work of an apostle ; so that from this silence we cannot argue against the truth of the narrative. On the other hand, the agreement of the synoptists proves nothing in its favour, since we have already been obliged to pronounce unhistorical more than one narrative in which three, nay, all four gospels agree. Lastly, as regards the alleged testimony of Peter, from the more than doubtful genuineness of the second Epistle of Peter, the passage which certainly refers to our history of the transfiguration is renounced as a proof of its historical truth even by orthodox theologians. [5]

On the other hand besides the difficulties previously enumerated, lying in the miraculous contents of the narrative, we have still a further ground for doubt in relation to the historical validity of the transfiguration : namely, the conversation which, according to the two first Evangelists, the disciples held with Jesus immediately after. In descending from the mountain, the disciples ask Jesus : τί οὖν οἱ γραμματεῖς λέγουσιν, ὅτι Ἠλίαν δεῖ ἐλθεῖν πρῶτον ; *Why then say the scribes that Elias must first come?* (Matt. v. 10). This sounds just as if something had happened, from which they necessarily inferred that Elias would not appear ; and not in the least as if they were coming directly from a scene in which he had actually appeared ; for in the latter case they would not have asked a question, as if unsatisfied, but must rather have indicated their satisfaction by the remark, εἰκότως οὖν οἱ γραμματεῖς λέγουσιν κ. τ. λ. *Truly then do the scribes say, etc.* [6] Hence, expositors interpret the question of the disciples to refer, not to the absence of an appearance of Elias in general, but to the absence of a certain concomitant in the scene which they had just witnessed. The doctrine of the scribes, namely, had taught them to anticipate that Elias on his second appearance would exert a reforming influence on the life of the nation ; whereas in the appearance which they had just beheld he had presently vanished again without further activity. [7] This explanation would be admissible if the words ἀποκαταστήσει πάντα (*will restore all things*) stood in the question of the disciples ; instead of this, however, it stands in both narratives (Matt. v. 11 ; Mark v. 12) only in the answer of Jesus : so that the disciples, according to this supposition, must, in the most contradictory manner, have been silent as to what they really missed, the *restoration of all things*, and only have mentioned that which after the foregoing appearance they could not have missed, namely, the *coming* of Elias.

---

[4] Neander, because he considers the objective reality of the transfiguration doubtful, also finds the silence of the fourth Evangelist a difficulty in this instance (s. 475 f.).

[5] Olshausen, s. 533, Anm.

[6] Vid. Rau, in the Programme quoted in Gabler, neuestes theolog. Journal, 1, 3, s. 506 ; De Wette, in loc. Matth.

[7] Fritzsche, in Matth., p. 553 ; Olshausen, 1, s. 541. Still less satisfactory expedients in Gabler, ut sup. and in Matthäi, Religionsgl. der Apostel, 2, s. 596.

As, however, the question of the disciples presupposes no previous appearance of Elias, but, on the contrary, expresses the feeling that such an appearance was wanting, so the answer which Jesus gives them has the same purport. For when he replies : the scribes are right in saying that Elias must come before the Messiah ; but this is no argument against my Messiahship, since an Elias has already preceded me in the person of the Baptist,—when he thus seeks to guard his disciples against the doubt which might arise from the expectation of the scribes, by pointing out to them the figurative Elias who had preceded him,—it is impossible that an appearance of the actual Elias can have previously taken place ; otherwise Jesus must in the first place have referred to this appearance, and only in the second place to the Baptist.[8] Thus the immediate connexion of this conversation with that appearance cannot be historical, but is rather owing solely to this point of similarity ;— that in both mention is made of Elias.[9] But not even at an interval, and after the lapse of intermediate events, can such a conversation have been preceded by an appearance of Elias ; for however long afterwards, both Jesus and the three eye-witnesses among his disciples must have remembered it, and could never have spoken as if such an appearance had not taken place. Still further, an appearance of the real Elias cannot have happened even *after* such a conversation, in accordance with the orthodox idea of Jesus. For he, too, explicitly declares his opinion that the literal Elias was not to be expected, and that the Baptist was the promised Elias ; if therefore, nevertheless, an appearance of the real Elias did subsequently take place, Jesus must have been mistaken ; a consequence which precisely those who are most concerned for the historical reality of the transfiguration, are the least in a position to admit. If then the appearance and the conversation directly exclude each other, the question is, which of the two passages can better be renounced ? Now the purport of the conversation is so confirmed by Matt. xi. 14, comp. Luke i. 17, while the transfiguration is rendered so improbable by all kinds of difficulties, that there cannot be much doubt as to the decision. According to this, it appears here as in some former cases, that two narratives proceeding from quite different presuppositions, and having arisen also in different times, have been awkwardly enough combined : the passage containing the conversation proceeding from the probably earlier opinion, that the prophecy concerning Elias had its fulfilment in John ; whereas the narrative of the transfiguration doubtless originated at a later period, when it was not held sufficient that in the messianic time of Jesus, Elias should only have appeared figuratively, in the person of the Baptist,—when it was thought fitting that he should also have shown himself personally and literally, if in no more than a transient appearance before a few witnesses (a public and more influential one being well known not to have taken place).[10]

In order next to understand how such a narrative could arise in a legendary manner, the first feature to be considered, on the examination of which that of all the rest will most easily follow, is the sun-like splendour of the countenance of Jesus, and the bright lustre of his clothes. To the oriental, and more particularly to the Hebrew imagination, the beautiful, the majestic, is the luminous ; the poet of the Song of Songs compares his beloved to the hues of morning, to the moon, to the sun (vi. 9) ; the holy man supported by the blessing of God, is compared to the sun going forth in his might (Judg. v. 31) ; and above all the future lot of the righteous is likened to the splen-

---

[8] This even Paulus admits, 2, s. 442.
[9] Schleiermacher, über den Lukas, s. 149.
[10] This is an answer to Weisse's objection, s. 539.

dour of the sun and the stars (Dan. xii. 3; Matt. xiii. 43).[11] Hence, not only does God appear clothed in light, and angels with resplendent countenances and shining garments (Ps. l. 2, 3; Dan. vii. 9 f., x. 5, 6; Luke xxiv. 4; Rev. i. 13 ff.), but also the pious of Hebrew antiquity, as Adam before the fall, and among subsequent instances, more particularly Moses and Joshua, are represented as being distinguished by such a splendour;[12] and the later Jewish tradition ascribes celestial splendour even to eminent rabbins in exalted moments.[13] But the most celebrated example of this kind is the luminous countenance of Moses, which is mentioned, Exod. xxxiv. 29 ff., and as in other points, so in this, a conclusion was drawn from him in relation to the Messiah, *a minori ad majus*. Such a mode of arguing is indicated by the Apostle Paul, 2 Cor. iii. 7 ff., though he opposes to Moses, *the minister of the letter*, διάκονος τοῦ γράμματος, not Jesus, but, in accordance with the occasion of his epistle, the apostles and Christian teachers, *ministers of the spirit*, διακόνους τοῦ πνεύματος, and the *glory*, δόξα, of the latter, which surpassed the glory of Moses, is an object of *hope*, ἐλπίς, to be attained only in the future life. But especially in the Messiah himself, it was expected that there would be a splendour which would correspond to that of Moses, nay, outshine it; and a Jewish writing which takes no notice of our history of the transfiguration, argues quite in the spirit of the Jews of the first Christian period, when it urges that Jesus cannot have been the Messiah, because his countenance had not the splendour of the countenance of Moses, to say nothing of a higher splendour.[14] Such objections, doubtless heard by the early Christians from the Jews, and partly suggested by their own minds, could not but generate in the early church a tendency to introduce into the life of Jesus an imitation of that trait in the life of Moses, nay, in one respect to surpass it, and instead of a shining countenance that might be covered with a veil, to ascribe to him a radiance, though but transitory, which was diffused even over his garments.

That the illumination of the countenance of Moses served as a type for the transfiguration of Jesus, is besides proved by a series of particular features. Moses obtained his splendour on Mount Sinai: of the transfiguration of Jesus also the scene is a mountain; Moses, on an earlier ascent of the mountain, which might easily be confounded with the later one, after which his countenance became luminous, had taken with him, besides the seventy elders, three confidential friends, Aaron, Nadab, and Abihu, to participate in the vision of Jehovah (Exod. xxiv. 1, 9-11); so Jesus takes with him his three most confidential disciples, that, so far as their powers were adequate, they might be witnesses of the sublime spectacle, and their immediate object was, according to Luke v. 28, *to pray*, προσεύξασθαι: just as Jehovah calls Moses with the three companions and the elders, to come on the mountain, that they might worship at a distance. As afterwards, when Moses ascended Sinai with Joshua, the *glory of the Lord*, δόξα Κυρίου, covered the mountain as a

[11] Comp. Jalkut Simeoni, p. 2 f. x. 3, (ap. Wetstein, p. 435): *Facies justorum futuro tempore similes erunt soli et lunæ, cælo et stellis, fulguri, etc.*

[12] Bereschith Rabba, xx. 29, (ap. Wetstein): *Vestes lucis vestes Adami primi.* Pococke, ex Nachmanide (ibid.): *Fulgida facta fuit facies Mosis instar solis, Josuæ instar lunæ*; *quod idem affirmarunt veteres de Adamo.*

[13] In Pirke Elieser, ii. there is, according to Wetstein, the following statement: *inter docendum radios ex facie ipsius, ut olim e Mosis facie, prodiisse, adeo ut non dignosceret quis, utrum dies esset an nox.*

[14] Nizzachon vetus, p. 40, ad Exod. xxxiv. 33 (ap. Wetstein): *Ecce Moses magister noster felicis memoriæ, qui homo merus erat, quia Deus de facie ad faciem cum eo locutus est, vultum tam lucentem retulit, ut Judæi vererentur accedere: quanto igitur magis de ipsa divinitate hoc tenere oportet, atque Jesu faciem ob uno orbis cardine ad alterum fulgorem diffundere conveniebat? At non præditus fuit ullo splendore, sed reliquis mortalibus fuit simillimus. Qua propter constat, non esse in eum credendum.*

cloud, νεφέλη, (v. 15 f. LXX.) ; as Jehovah called to Moses out of the cloud, until at length the latter entere1 into the cloud (v. 16-18) : so we have in our narrative a *bright cloud,* νεφέλη φωτὸς, which overshadows Jesus and the heavenly forms, *a voice out of the cloud,* φωνὴ ἐκ τῆς νεφέλης, and in Luke an *entering,* εἰσελθεῖν, of the three into the cloud. The first part of the address pronounced by the voice out of the cloud, consists of the messianic declaration, composed out of Ps. ii. 7, and Isa. xlii. 1, which had already sounded from heaven at the baptism of Jesus ; the second part is taken from the words with which Moses, in the passage of Deuteronomy quoted earlier (xviii. 15), according to the usual interpretation, announces to the people the future Messiah, and admonishes them to obedience towards him.[15]

By the transfiguration on the mount Jesus was brought into contact with his type Moses, and has it had entered into the anticipation of the Jews that the messianic time, according to Isa. lii. 6 ff., would have not merely one, but several forerunners,[16] and that among others the ancient lawgiver especially would appear in the time of the Messiah : [17] so no moment was more appropriate for his appearance than that in which the Messiah was being glorified on a mountain, as he had himself once been. With him was then naturally associated the prophet, who, on the strength of Mal. iii. 23, was the most decidedly expected to be a messianic forerunner, and, indeed, according to the rabbins, to appear contemporaneously with Moses. If these two men appeared to the Messiah, it followed as a matter of course that they conversed with him ; and if it were asked what was the tenor of their conversation, nothing would suggest itself so soon as the approaching sufferings and death of Jesus, which had been announced in the foregoing passage, and which besides, as constituting emphatically the messianic mystery of the New Testament, were best adapted for the subject of such a conversation with beings of another world : whence one cannot but wonder how Olshausen can maintain that the mythus would never have fallen upon this theme of conversation. According to this, we have here a mythus,[18] the tendency of which is twofold : first, to exhibit in the life of Jesus an enhanced repetition of the glorification of Moses ; and secondly, to bring Jesus as the Messiah into contact with his two forerunners,—by this appearance of the lawgiver and the prophet, of the founder and the reformer of the theocracy, to represent Jesus as the perfecter of the kingdom of God, and the fulfilment of the law and the prophets ; and besides this, to show a confirmation of his messianic dignity by a heavenly voice.[19]

---

[15] From this parallel with the ascent of the mountain by Moses may perhaps be derived the interval—the ἡμέραι ἐξ—by which the two first Evangelists separate the present event from the discourses detailed in the foregoing chapter. For the history of the adventures of Moses on the mountain begins with a like statement of time, it being said that after the cloud had covered the mountain *six days*, Moses was called to Jehovah (v. 16). Although the point of departure was a totally different one, this statement of time might be retained for the opening of the scene of transfiguration in the history of Jesus.

[16] Vide Bertholdt, Christologia Judæorum, § 15, s. 60 ff.

[17] Debarim Rabba, iii. (Wetstein) : *Dixit Deus S. B. Mosi : per vitam tuam, quemadmodum vitam tuam posuisti pro Israelitis in hoc mundo, ita tempore futuro, quando Eliam f· ·ophetam ad ipsos mittam, vos quo eodem tempore venietis.* Comp. Tanchuma f. xlii. 1, ap. 'chöttgen 1, s. 149.

[18] 1. narrative is pronounced to be a mythus by De Wette, Kritik der mos. Gesch. s. 250 ; comp. exeg. Handb., 1, 1, s. 146 f. ; Bertholdt, Christologia Jud. § 15, not. 17 ; Credner, Einleitung in das N. T. 1, s. 241 ; Schulz, über das Abendmahl, s. 319, at least admits that there is more or less of the mythical in the various evangelical accounts of the transfiguration, and Fritzsche, in Matt. p. 448 f. and 456 adduces the mythical view of this event not without signs of approval. Compare also Kuinöl, in Matth., p. 459, and Gratz, 2, s. 161 ff.

[19] Plato also in the Symposion (p. 223, B. ff. Steph.), glorifies his Socrates by arranging

Before we part with our subject, this example may serve to shows with peculiar clearness, how the natural system of interpretation, while it seeks to preserve the historical certainty of the narratives, loses their ideal truth—sacrifices the essence to the form : whereas the mythical interpretation, by renouncing the historical body of such narratives, rescues and preserves the idea which resides in them, and which alone constitutes their vitality and spirit. Thus if, as the natural explanation would have it, the splendour around Jesus was an accidental, optical phenomenon, and the two appearances either images of a dream or unknown men, where is the significance of the incident? where the motive for preserving in the memory of the church an anecdote so void of ideas, and so barren of inference, resting on a common delusion and superstition? On the contrary, while according to the mythical interpretation, I do not, it is true, see in the evangelical narrative any real event,—I yet retain a sense, a purpose in the narrative, know to what sentiments and thoughts of the first Christian community it owes its origin, and why the authors of the gospels included so important a passage in their memoirs.[20]

§ 108.

DIVERGING ACCOUNTS CONCERNING THE LAST JOURNEY OF JESUS TO JERUSALEM.

Shortly after the transfiguration on the mountain, the Evangelists make Jesus enter on the fatal journey which conducted him to his death. With respect to the place from whence he set out on this journey, and the route which he took, the evangelical accounts differ. The synoptists agree as to the point of departure, for they all represent Jesus as setting out from Galilee (Matt. xix. 1 ; Mark x. 1 ; Luke ix. 51 ; in this last passage, Galilee is not indeed expressly named, but we necessarily infer it to be the supposed locality from what precedes, in which only Galilee and districts in Galilee are spoken of, as well as from the journey through Samaria, mentioned in the succeeding passage) :[1] but concerning the route which Jesus chose from thence to Judæa, they appear to be at variance. It is true that the statements of two of them

in a natural manner, and in a comic spirit, a similar group to that which the Evangelists here present in a supernatural manner, and in a tragic spirit. After a bacchanalian entertainment, Socrates outwatches his friends, who lie sleeping around him : as here the disciples around their master ; with Socrates there are awake two noble forms alone, the tragic and the comic poet, the two elements of the early Grecian life, which Socrates united in himself : as, with Jesus, the lawgiver and prophet, the two pillars of the Old Testament economy, which in a higher manner were combined in Jesus ; lastly, as in Plato both Agathon and Aristophanes at length sleep, and Socrates remains alone in possession of the field : so in the gospel, Moses and Elias at last vanish, and the disciples see Jesus left alone.

[20] Weisse, not satisfied with the interpretation found by me in the mythus, and labouring besides to preserve an historical foundation for the narrative, understands it as a figurative representation in the oriental manner, by one of the three eye-witnesses, of the light which at that time arose on them concerning the destination of Jesus, and especially concerning his relation to the Old Testament theocracy and to the messianic prophecies. According to him, the high mountain symbolizes the height of knowledge which the disciples then attained ; the metamorphosis of the form of Jesus, and the splendour of his clothes, are an image of their intuition of the spiritual messianic idea ; the cloud which overshadowed the appearance, signifies the dimness and indefiniteness in which the new knowledge faded away, from the inability of the disciples yet to retain it; the proposal of Peter to build tabernacles, is the attempt of this apostle at once to give a fixed dogmatical form to the sublime intuition. Weisse is fearful (s. 543) that this his conception of the history of the transfiguration may also be pronounced mythical : I think not ; it is too manifestly allegorical.

[1] Schleiermacher, über den Lukas, s. 160.

on this point are so obscure, that they might appear to lend some aid to the harmonizing exegesis. Mark says in the clearest and most definite manner that Jesus took his course through Peræa ; but his statement, *He came into the coasts of Judæa on the further side of Jordan,* ἔρχεται εἰς τὰ ὅρια τῆς Ἰουδαίας διὰ τοῦ πέραν τοῦ Ἰορδάνου, is scarcely anything more than the mode in which he judged it right to explain the hardly intelligible expression of Matthew, whom he follows in this chapter. What it precisely is which the latter intends by the words, *He departed from Galilee, and came into the coasts of Judæa beyond Jordan,* μετῆρεν ἀπὸ τῆς Γαλιλαίας καὶ ἦλθεν εἰς τὰ ὅρια τῆς Ἰουδαίας πέραν τοῦ Ἰορδάνου, is in fact not at all evident. For if the explanation : he came into that part of Judæa which lies on the opposite side of the Jordan,[2] clashes alike with geography and grammar, so the interpretation to which the comparison of Mark inclines the majority of commentators, namely, that Jesus came into Judæa through the country on the farther side of the Jordan,[3] is, even as modified by Fritzsche, not free from grammatical difficulty. In any case, however, thus much remains : that Matthew, as well as Mark, makes Jesus take the most circuitous course through Peræa, while Luke, on the other hand, appears to lead him the more direct way through Samaria. It is true that his expression, xvii. 11, where he says that Jesus, on his journey to Jerusalem, *passed through the midst of Samaria and Galileee,* διήρχετο διὰ μέσου Σαμαρείας καὶ Γαλιλαίας, is scarcely clearer than the one just cited from Matthew. According to the customary meaning of words, he seems to state that Jesus first crossed Samaria, and then Galilee, in order to arrive at Jerusalem. But this is an inversion of the true order ; for if he set out from a place in Galilee, he must first traverse the rest of Galilee, and not until then could he enter Samaria. Hence the words διέρχεσθαι διὰ μέσου κ. τ. λ. have been interpreted to mean a progress along the boundary between Galilee and Samaria,[4] and Luke has been reconciled with the two first Evangelists by the supposition, that Jesus journeyed along the Galilean-Samarian frontier, until he reached the Jordan, that he then crossed this river, and so proceeded through Peræa towards Judæa and Jerusalem. But this latter supposition does not agree with Luke ix. 51 ff. ; for we learn from this passage that Jesus, after his departure from Galilee, went directly to a Samaritan village, and here made an unfavourable impression, *because his face was as though he would go to Jerusalem,* ὅτι τὸ πρόσωπον αὐτοῦ ἦν πορευόμενον εἰς Ἱερουσαλήμ. Now this seems clearly to indicate that Jesus took his way directly from Galilee, through Samaria, to Judæa. We shall therefore be on the side of probability, if we judge this statement to be an artificial arrangement of words, to which the writer was led by his desire to introduce the narrative of the ten lepers, one of whom was a Samaritan ;[5] and consequently admit that there is here a divergency between the synoptical gospels.[6] Towards the end of the journey of Jesus, they are once more in unison, for according to their unanimous statement, Jesus arrived at Jerusalem from Jericho (Matt. xx. 29, parall.) ; a place which, we may observe, lay more in the direct road for a Galilean coming through Peræa, than for one coming through Samaria.

Thus there is indeed a difference between the synoptists with regard to the way taken by Jesus ; but still they agree as to the first point of departure, and

---

[2] Kuinöl and Gratz, in loc.
[3] Thus e.g. Lightfoot, in loc.
[4] Wetstein, Olshausen, in loc., Schleiermacher, ut sup. s. 164, 214.
[5] Vid. De Wette, in loc.
[6] Fritzsche, in Marc. p. 415 : *Marcus Matthæi,* xix. 1, *se auctoritati h. l. adstringit, dicitque, Jesum e Galilæa* (cf. ix. 33) *profectum esse per Peraeam. Sed auctore Luca,* xvii. 11, *in Judæam contendit per Samariam itinere brevissimo.*

the last stage of the road; the account of John, however, diverges from them in both respects. According to him, it is not Galilee from whence Jesus sets out to attend the last passover, for so early as before the feast of tabernacles of the previous year, he had left that province, apparently for the last time (vii. 1, 10); that between this feast and that of the dedication (x. 22) he had returned thither, is at least not stated; after the latter feast, however, he betook himself to Peræa, and remained there (x. 40) until the illness and death of Lazarus recalled him into Judæa, and into the immediate vicinity of Jerusalem, namely, to Bethany (xi. 8 ff.). On account of the machinations of his enemies, he quickly withdrew from thence again, but, because he intended to be present at the coming Passover, he retired no further than to the little city of Ephraim, near to the wilderness (xi. 54); and from this place, no mention being made of a residence in Jericho (which, besides, did not lie in the way from Ephraim, according to the situation usually assigned to the latter city), he proceeded to Jerusalem to the feast.

So total a divergency necessarily gave unwonted occupation to the harmonists. According to them, the departure from Galilee mentioned by the synoptists, is not the departure to the last Passover, but to the feast of dedication;[7] though Luke, when he says, *when the time came that he should be received up*, ἐν τῷ συμπληροῦσθαι τὰς ἡμέρας τῆς ἀναλήψεως αὐτοῦ (ix. 51), incontrovertibly marks it as the departure to that feast on which the sufferings and death of Jesus awaited him, and though all the synoptists make the journey then begun end in that triumphal entry into Jerusalem which, according to the fourth gospel also, took place immediately before the last passover.[8] If, according to this, the departure from Galilee narrated by the synoptists is regarded as that to the feast of dedication, and the entrance into Jerusalem which they mention as that to the subsequent passover; they must have entirely passed over all which, on this supposition, lay between these two points, namely, the arrival and residence of Jesus in Jerusalem during the feast of dedication, his journey from thence into Peræa, from Peræa to Bethany, and from Bethany to Ephraim. If from this it should appear to follow that the synoptists were ignorant of all these particulars: our harmonists urge, on the contrary, that Luke makes Jesus soon after his journey out of Galilee, encounter scribes, who try to put him to the proof (x. 25 ff.); then shows him in Bethany in the vicinity of Jerusalem (x. 38 ff.); hereupon removes him to the frontiers of Samaria and Galilee (xvii. 11); and not until then, makes him proceed to the passover in Jerusalem (xix. 29 ff.): all which plainly enough indicates, that between that departure out of Galilee, and the final entrance into Jerusalem, Jesus made another journey to Judæa and Jerusalem, and from thence back again.[9] But, in the first place, the presence of the scribes proves absolutely nothing; and in the second, Luke makes no mention of Bethany, but only of a visit to Mary and Martha, whom the fourth Evangelist places in that village: from which, however, it does not follow that the third also supposed them to dwell there, and consequently imagined Jesus when at their home, to be in the vicinity of Jerusalem. Again, from the fact that so very long after his departure (ix. 51–xvii. 11), Jesus first appears on the frontier between Galilee and Samaria, it only follows that we have before us no orderly progressive narrative. But, according to this harmonizing view, even Matthew was aware of those intermediate events, and has indicated them for the more attentive reader: the one member of his sentence, *he departed from Galilee*, μετῆρεν ἀπὸ τῆς Γαλιλαίας, intimates the journey of Jesus to the

---

[7] Paulus, 2, s. 293, 554. Comp. Olshausen, 1, s. 583.
[8] Schleiermacher, ut sup. s. 159.
[9] Paulus, 2, s. 294 ff.

feast of dedication, and thus forms a separate whole ; the other, *and came into the coasts of Judæa beyond Jordan*, καὶ ἦλθεν εἰς τὰ ὅρια τῆς Ἰουδαίας πέραν τοῦ Ἰορδάνου, refers to the departure of Jesus from Jerusalem into Peræa (John x. 40), and opens a new period. In adopting this expedient, however, it is honourably confessed that without the data gathered from John, no one would have thought of such a dismemberment of the passage in Matthew.[10] In opposition to such artifices, no way is open to those who presuppose the accuracy of John's narrative, but that adopted by the most recent criticism ; namely, to renounce the supposition that Matthew, who treats of the journey very briefly, was an eye-witness ; and to suppose of Luke, whose account of it is very full, that either he or one of the collectors of whose labours he availed himself, mingled together two separate narratives, of which one referred to the earlier journey of Jesus to the feast of dedication, the other to his last journey to the passover, without suspecting that between the departure of Jesus out of Galilee, and his entrance into Jerusalem, there fell yet an earlier residence in Jerusalem, together with other journeys and adventures.[11]

We may now observe how in the course of the narrative concerning the last journey or journeys to Jerusalem, the relation between the synoptical gospels and that of John is in a singular manner reversed. As in the first instance, we discovered a great blank on the side of the former, in their omission of a mass of intermediate events which John notices ; so now, towards the end of the account of the journey, there appears on the side of the latter, a similar, though smaller blank, for he gives no intimation of Jesus having come through Jericho on his way to Jerusalem. It may indeed be said, that John might overlook this passage through Jericho, although, according to the synoptists, it was distinguished by a cure of the blind, and the visit to Zacchæus ; but, it is to be asked, is there in his narrative room for a passage through Jericho ? This city does not lie on the way from Ephraim to Jerusalem, but considerably to the eastward ; hence help is sought in the supposition that Jesus made all kinds of minor excursions, in one of which he came to Jericho, and from hence went forward to Jerusalem.[12]

In any case a remarkable want of unity prevails in the evangelical accounts of the last journey of Jesus ; for according to the common, synoptical tradition, he journeyed out of Galilee by Jericho (and, as Matthew and Mark say, through Peræa, as Luke says, through Samaria) ; while according to the fourth gospel, he must have come hither from Ephraim : statements which it is impossible to reconcile.

§ 109.

DIVERGENCIES OF THE GOSPELS, IN RELATION TO THE POINT FROM WHICH JESUS MADE HIS ENTRANCE INTO JERUSALEM.

Even concerning the close of the journey of Jesus—concerning the last station before he reached Jerusalem, the Evangelists are not entirely in unison. While from the synoptical gospels it appears, that Jesus entered Jerusalem on the same day on which he left Jericho, and consequently without halting long at any intervening place (Matt. xx. 34, xxi. 1 ff. parall.) : the fourth gospel makes him go from Ephraim only so far as Bethany, spend the night there, and enter Jerusalem only on the following day (xii. 1, 12 ff.). In order

---

[10] Paulus, ut sup. 295 f., 584 f.
[11] Schleiermacher, ut sup. s. 161 f. ; Sieffert, über den Urspr., s. 104 ff. With the former agrees, in relation to Luke, Olshausen, ut sup.
[12] Tholuck, Comm. z. Joh., s. 227 ; Olshausen, I, s. 771 f.

to reconcile the two accounts it is said : we need not wonder that the synop-tists, in their summary narrative, do not expressly touch upon the spending of the night in Bethany, and we are not to infer from this that they intended to deny it ; there exists, therefore, no contradiction between them and John, but what they present in a compact form, he exhibits in detail.[1] But while Matthew does not even name Bethany, the two other synoptists mention this place in a way which decidedly precludes the supposition that Jesus spent the night there. They narrate that when Jesus *came near to Bethphage and Bethany*, ὡς ἤγγισεν εἰς Βηθφαγῆ καὶ Βηθανίαν, he caused an ass to be fetched from the next village, and forthwith rode on this into the city. Between events so connected it is impossible to imagine a night interposed ; on the contrary, the narrative fully conveys the impression that immediately on the message of Jesus, the ass was surrendered by its owner, and that immediately after the arrival of the ass, Jesus prepared to enter the city. Moreover, if Jesus intended to remain in Bethany for the night, it is impossible to discover his motive in sending for the ass. For if we are to suppose the village to which he sent to be Bethany, and if the animal on which he purposed to ride would not be required until the following morning, there was no need for him to send forward the disciples, and he might conveniently have waited until he arrived with them in Bethany ; the other alternative, that before he had reached Bethany, and ascertained whether the animal he required might not be found there, he should have sent beyond this nearest village to Bethphage, in order there to procure an ass for the following morning, is altogether destitute of probability ; and yet Matthew, at least, says decidedly that the ass was procured in Bethphage. To this it may be added, that according to the representation of Mark, when Jesus arrived in Jerusalem, the *evening* ὀψία, had already commenced (xi. 11), and consequently it was only possible for him to take a cursory survey of the city and the temple, after which he again returned to Bethany. It is not, certainly, to be proved that the fourth gospel lays the entrance in the morning ; but it must be asked, why did not Jesus, when he only came from so near a place as Bethany, set out earlier from thence, that he might have time to do something worth speaking of in Jerusalem ? The late arrival of Jesus in the city, as stated by Mark, is evi-dently to be explained only by the longer distance from Jericho thither ; if he came from Bethany merely, he would scarcely set out so late, as that after he had only looked round him in the city, he must again return to Bethany, in order on the following day to set out earlier, which nothing had hindered him from doing on this day. It is true that, in deferring the arrival of Jesus in Jerusalem until late in the evening, Mark is not supported by the two other synoptists, for these represent Jesus as undertaking the purification of the temple on the day of his arrival, and Matthew even makes him perform cures, and give answers to the high priests and scribes (Matt. xxi. 12 ff.) : but even without this statement as to the hour of entrance, the arrival of Jesus near to the above villages, the sending of the disciples, the bringing of the ass, and the riding into the city, are too closely consecutive, to allow of our inserting in the narrative of the synoptists a night's residence in Bethany.

If then it remains, that the three first Evangelists make Jesus proceed directly from Jericho, without any stay in Bethany, while the fourth makes him come to Jerusalem from Bethany only, they must, if they are mutually correct, speak of two separate entrances ; and this has been recently main-tained by several critics.[2] According to them, Jesus first (as the synoptists

---

[1] Tholuck and Olshausen, ut sup.
[2] Paulus, exeg. Handb. 3, a, s. 92 ff., 98 ff. ; Schleiermacher, über den Lukas, s. 244 f.

relate) proceeded directly to Jerusalem with the caravan going to the feast, and on this occasion there happened, when he made himself conspicuous by mounting the animal, an unpremeditated demonstration of homage on the part of his fellow-travellers, which converted the entrance into a triumphal progress. Having retired to Bethany in the evening, on the following morning (as John relates) a great multitude went out to meet him, in order to convey him into the city, and as he met with them on the way from Bethany, there was a repetition on an enlarged scale of the scene on the foregoing day, —this time preconcerted by his adherents. This distinction of an earlier entrance of Jesus into Jerusalem before his approach was known in the city, and a later, after it was learned that he was in Bethany, is favoured by the difference, that according to the synoptical narrative, the people who render homage to him are only *going before* προάγοντες, and *following* ἀκολουθοῦντες (Matt. v. 9), while according to that of John, they are *meeting* him ὑπαντήσαντες (v. 13, 18). If however it be asked : why then among all our narrators, does each give only one entrance, and not one of them show any trace of a second? The answer in relation to John is, that this Evangelist is silent as to the first entrance, probably because he was not present on the occasion, having possibly been sent to Bethany to announce the arrival of Jesus.[3] As, however, according to our principles, if it be assumed of the author of the fourth gospel, that he is the apostle named in the superscription, the same assumption must also be made respecting the author of the first : we ask in vain, whither are we then to suppose that *Matthew* was sent on the second entrance, that he knew nothing to relate concerning it ? since with the repeated departure from Bethany to Jerusalem, there is no conceivable cause for such an errand. In relation to John indeed it is a pure invention ; not to insist, that even if the two Evangelists were not personally present, they must yet have learned enough of an event so much talked of in the circle of the disciples, to be able to furnish an account of it. Above all, as the narrative of the synoptists does not indicate that a second entrance had taken place after the one described by them : so that of John is of such a kind, that before the entrance which it describes, it is impossible to conceive another. For according to this narrative, the day before the entrance which it details (consequently, according to the given supposition, on the day of the synoptical entrance), many Jews went from Jerusalem to Bethany, because they had heard of the arrival of Jesus, and now wished to see him and Lazarus whom he had restored to life (v. 9, comp. 12). But how could they learn on the day of the synoptical entrance, that Jesus was at Bethany ? On that day Jesus did indeed pass either by or through Bethany, but he proceeded directly to Jerusalem, whence, according to all the narratives, he could have returned to Bethany only at so late an hour in the evening, that Jews who now first went from Jerusalem, could no longer hope to be able to see him.[4] But why should they take the trouble to seek Jesus in Bethany, when they had on that very day seen him in Jerusalem itself? Surely in this case it must have been said—not merely, that they came *not for Jesus' sake* ONLY, *but that they might see Lazarus also*, οὐ διὰ τὸν Ἰησοῦν μόνον ἀλλ᾽ ἵνα καὶ τὸν Λάζαρον ἴδωσι,—but rather that they had indeed seen Jesus himself in Jerusalem, but as they wished to see Lazarus also, they came therefore to Bethany : whereas the Evangelist represents these people as coming from Jerusalem partly to see Jesus ; he cannot therefore have supposed that Jesus might have been seen in Jerusalem on that very day. Further, when it is said in John,

---

[3] Schleiermacher, ut sup.
[4] Comp. Lücke, 2, s. 432, Anm.

that on the following day it was heard in Jerusalem that Jesus was coming (v.
12), this does not at all seem to imply that Jesus had already been there the
day before, but rather that the news had come from Bethany, of his intention
to enter on this day.   So also the reception which is immediately prepared
for him, alone has its proper significance when it is regarded as the glorification of his first entrance into the metropolis; it could only have been
appropriate on his second entrance, if Jesus had the day before entered unobserved and unhonoured, and it had been wished to repair this omission on
the following day—not if the first entrance had already been so brilliant.
Moreover, on the second entrance every feature of the first must have been
repeated, which, whether we refer it to a preconceived arrangement on the
part of Jesus, or to an accidental coincidence of circumstances, still remains
improbable.   With respect to Jesus, it is not easy to understand how he
could arrange the repetition of a spectacle which, in the first instance significant, if acted a second time would be flat and unmeaning;[5] on the other
hand, circumstances must have coincided in an unprecedented manner, if on
both occasions there happened the same demonstrations of homage on the
part of the people, with the same expressions of envy on the part of his
opponents; if, on both occasions, too, there stood at the command of Jesus
an ass, by riding which he brought to mind the prophecy of Zechariah.   We
might therefore call to our aid Sieffert's hypothesis of assimilation, and suppose that the two entrances, originally more different, became thus similar by
traditional intermixture : were not the supposition that two distinct events lie
at the foundation of the evangelical narratives, rendered improbable by another circumstance.

On the first glance, indeed, the supposition of two entrances seems to find
support in the fact, that John makes his entrance take place the day after the
meal in Bethany, at which Jesus was anointed under memorable circumstances ; whereas the two first synoptists (for Luke knows nothing of a meal
at Bethany in this period of the life of Jesus) make their entrance precede
this meal : and thus, quite in accordance with the above supposition, the
synoptical entrance would appear the earlier, that of John the later.   This
would be very well, if John had not placed his entrance so early, and the
synoptists their meal at Bethany so late, that the former cannot possibly have
been subsequent to the latter.   According to John, Jesus comes six days
before the passover to Bethany, and on the following day enters Jerusalem
(xiii. 1, 12); on the other hand, the meal at Bethany, mentioned by the
synoptists (Matt. xxvi. 6 ff. parall.), can have been at the most but two days
before the passover (v. 2) ; so that if we are to suppose the synoptical entrance
prior to the meal and the entrance in John, there must then have been after
all this, according to the synoptists, a second meal in Bethany.   But between
the two meals thus presupposed, as between the two entrances, there would
have been the most striking resemblance even to the minutest points; and
against the interweaving of two such double incidents, there is so strong a
presumption, that it will scarcely be said there were two entrances and two
meals, which were originally far more dissimilar, but, from the transference
of features out of the one incident into the other by tradition, they have become as similar to each other as we now see them : on the contrary, here if
anywhere, it is easier, when once the authenticity of the accounts is given up,
to imagine that tradition has varied one incident, than that it has assimilated
two.[6]

[5] Hase, L. J. § 124.
[6] Comp. De Wette, exeg. Handb. 1, 1, s. 172.

§ 110.

MORE PARTICULAR CIRCUMSTANCES OF THE ENTRANCE. ITS OBJECT AND HISTORICAL REALITY.

While the fourth gospel first makes the multitude that streamed forth to meet Jesus render him their homage, and then briefly states that Jesus mounted a young ass which he had obtained; the synoptists commence their description of the entrance with a minute account of the manner in which Jesus came by the ass. When, namely, he had arrived in the neighbourhood of Jerusalem, towards Bethphage and Bethany, at the Mount of Olives, he sent two of his disciples into the village lying before them, telling them that when they came there they would find—Matthew says, *an ass tied, and a colt with her*; the two others, *a colt whereon never man sat*—which they were to loose and bring to him, silencing any objections of the owner by the observation, *the Lord hath need of him* (or *them*). This having been done, the disciples spread their clothes, and placed Jesus—on both the animals, according to Matthew; according to the two other synoptists, on the single animal.

The most striking part of this account is obviously the statement of Matthew, that Jesus not only required two asses, though he alone intended to ride, but that he also actually sat on them both. It is true that, as is natural, there are not wanting attempts to explain the former particular, and to do away with the latter. Jesus, it is said, caused the mother animal to be brought with the colt, on which alone he intended to ride, in order that the young and still sucking animal might by this means be made to go more easily;[1] or else the mother, accustomed to her young one, followed of her own accord:[2] but a young animal, yet unweaned, would scarcely be given up by its owner to be ridden. A sufficient motive on the part of Jesus in sending for the two animals, could only be that he intended to ride both, which Matthew appears plainly enough to say; for his words imply, not only that the clothes were spread, but also that Jesus was placed on the two animals (ἐπάνω αὐτῶν). But how are we to represent this to ourselves? As an alternate mounting of the one and the other, Fritzsche thinks:[3] but this, for so short a distance would have been a superfluous inconvenience. Hence commentators have sought to rid themselves of the singular statement. Some, after very weak authorities, and in opposition to all critical principles, read in the words relative to the spreading of the clothes, ἐπ᾽ αὐτὸν (τὸν πῶλον), *upon it* (*the colt*), instead of ἐπάνω αὐτῶν, *upon them*; and then in the mentioning that Jesus placed himself thereon, refer the ἐπάνω αὐτῶν to the clothes which were spread on one of the animals.[4] Others, thinking to escape the difficulty without an alteration of the reading, characterize Matthew's statement as an *enallage numeri*,[5] by which, according to Winer's explanation, it is meant that the Evangelist, using an inaccurate mode of expression, certainly speaks of both the animals, but only in the sense in which we say of him who springs from one of two horses harnessed together, that he springs from the horses.[6] Admitting this expedient to be sufficient, it again becomes incomprehensible why Jesus, who

---

[1] Paulus, 3, a, s. 115; Kuinöl, in Matth., p. 541.
[2] Olshausen, 1, s. 776.
[3] Comm. in Matth., p. 630. His expedient is approved by De Wette, exeg. Handb. 1, 1, s. 173.
[4] Paulus, ut sup. s. 143 f.
[5] Glassius, phil. sacr., p. 172. Thus also Kuinöl and Gratz, in loc.
[6] N. T. Gramm., s. 149.

according to this only meant to use one animal, should have sent for two.
The whole statement becomes the more suspicious, when we consider that it
is given by the first Evangelist alone ; for in order to reconcile the others
with him it will not suffice to say, as we ordinarily read, that they name only
the foal as being that on which Jesus rode, and that while omitting the ass
as an accessory fact, they do not exclude it.

But how was Matthew led into this singular statement ? Its true source
has been pointed out, though in a curious manner, by those who conjecture, that Jesus in his instructions to the two disciples, and Matthew in
his original writing, following the passage of Zechariah (ix. 9), made use of
several expressions for the one idea of the ass, which expressions were by the
Greek translator of the first gospel misconstrued to mean more than one
animal.[7]   Undoubtedly it was the accumulated designations of the ass in the
above passage : חֲמוֹר וְעַיִר בֶּן־אֲתֹנוֹת, ὑποζύγιον καὶ πῶλον νέον, LXX. which
occasioned the duplication of it in the first gospel ; for the *and* which in the
Hebrew was intended in an explanatory sense, was erroneously understood
to denote an addition, and hence instead of : *an ass, that is, an ass's foal*,
was substituted : *an ass together with an ass's foal*.[8]   But this mistake cannot
have originated with the Greek translator, who, if he had found throughout
Matthew's narrative but one ass, would scarcely have doubled it purely on the
strength of the prophetic passage, and as often as his original spoke of one
ass, have added a second, or introduced the plural number instead of the
singular ; it must rather have been made by one whose only written source
was the prophetic passage, out of which, with the aid of oral tradition, he
spun his entire narrative, *i.e.* the author of the first gospel ; who hereby, as
recent criticism correctly maintains, irrecoverably forfeits the reputation of an
eye-witness ? [9]

If the first gospel stands alone in this mistake, so, on the other hand, the
two intermediate Evangelists have a feature peculiar to themselves, which it
is to the advantage of the first to have avoided.   We shall merely point out
in passing the prolixity with which Mark and Luke (though they, as well as
Matthew, make Jesus describe to the two disciples, how they would find the
ass, and wherewith they were to satisfy the owner), yet do not spare themselves or the reader the trouble of almost verbally repeating every particular
as having occurred (Mark v. 4 ff. ; Luke v. 32 ff.) ; whereas Matthew, with
more judgment, contents himself with the observation, *and the disciples went
and did as Jesus commanded them*.   This, as affecting merely the form of the
narrative, we shall not dwell on further.   But it concerns the substance, that,
according to Mark and Luke, Jesus desired an animal *whereon yet never man
sat*, ἐφ᾽ ὃ οὐδεὶς πώποτε ἀνθρώπων ἐκάθισε : a particular of which Matthew
knows nothing.   One does not understand how Jesus could designedly increase the difficulty of his progress, by the choice of a hitherto unridden
animal, which, unless he kept it in order by divine omnipotence (for the
most consummate human skill would not suffice for this on the first riding),
must inevitably have occasioned much disturbance to the triumphal procession, especially as we are not to suppose that it was preceded by its
mother, this circumstance having entered into the representation of the first
Evangelist only.   To such an inconvenience Jesus would assuredly not have
exposed himself without a cogent reason : such a reason however appears to
lie sufficiently near in the opinion of antiquity, according to which, to use

---

[7] Eichhorn, allgem. Bibliothek, 5, s. 896 f. ; comp. Bolten, Bericht des Matthäus, s.
317 f.
[8] Vide Fritzsche, in loc.   This is admitted by Neander also, s. 550, Anm.
[9] Schulz, über das Abendmahl, s. 310 f. ; Sieffert, über den Urspr., s. 107 f.

Wetstein's expression, *animalia, usibus humanis nondum mancipata, sacra habebantur*; so that thus Jesus, for his consecrated person, and the high occasion of his messianic entrance, may have chosen to use only a sacred animal. But regarded more closely, this reason will appear frivolous, and absurd also; for the spectators had no means of knowing that the ass had never been ridden before, except by the unruliness with which he may have disturbed the peaceful progress of the triumphal train.[10] If we are thus unable to comprehend how Jesus could seek an honour for himself in mounting an animal which had never yet been ridden; we shall, on the contrary, find it easy to comprehend how the primitive Christian community might early believe it due to his honour that he should ride only on such an animal, as subsequently that he should lie only in an unused grave. The authors of the intermediate gospels did not hesitate to receive this trait into their memoirs, because they indeed, in writing, would not experience the same inconvenience from the undisciplined animal, which it must have caused to Jesus in riding.

The two difficulties already considered belong respectively to the first Evangelist, and the two intermediate ones: another is common to them all, namely, that which lies in the circumstance that Jesus so confidently sends two disciples for an ass which they would find in the next village, in such and such a situation, and that the issue corresponds so closely to his prediction. It might here appear the most natural, to suppose that he had previously bespoken the ass, and that consequently it stood ready for him at the hour and place appointed;[11] but how could he have thus bespoken an ass in Bethphage, seeing that he was just come from Jericho? Hence even Paulus in this instance finds something else more probable: namely, that about the time of the feasts, in the villages lying on the high road to Jerusalem, many beasts of burden stood ready to be hired by travellers; but in opposition to this it is to be observed, that Jesus does not at all seem to speak of the first animal that may happen to present itself, but of a particular animal. Hence we cannot but be surprised that Olshausen describes it as only the probable idea of the narrator, that to the Messiah making his entrance into Jerusalem, the providence of God presented everything just as he needed it; as also that the same expositor, in order to explain the ready compliance of the owners of the animal, finds it necessary to suppose that they were friends of Jesus; since this trait rather serves to exhibit the as it were magical power which resided in the name of the *Lord*, at the mention of which the owner of the ass unresistingly placed it at his disposal, as subsequently the inhabitant of the room gave it up at a word from the Master (Matt. xxvi. 18 parall.). To this divine providence in favour of the Messiah, and the irresistible power of his name, is united the superior knowledge by means of which Jesus here clearly discerns a distant fact which might be available for the supply of his wants.

Now admitting this to be the meaning and design of the Evangelists, such a prediction of an accidental circumstance might certainly be conceived as

---

[10] That the above motive will not suffice to explain the conduct of Jesus, Paulus has also felt; for only the despair on his part of finding a more real and special motive, can account for his becoming in this solitary instance mystical, and embracing the explanation of Justin Martyr, whom he elsewhere invariably attacks, as the author of the perverted ecclesiastical interpretations of the Bible. According to Justin, the ass designated ὑποζύγιον (*that is under the yoke*), is a symbol of the Jews; the ass never yet ridden, of the Gentiles (Dial. c. Tryph. 53); and Paulus, adopting this idea, endeavours to make it probable that Jesus, by mounting an animal which had never before been ridden, intended to announce himself as the founder and ruler of a new religious community. Exeg. Handb. 3, a, s. 116 ff.

[11] Natürliche Gesch. 3, s. 566 f.; Neander, L. J. Chr., s. 550, Anm.

the effect of a magnetic clairvoyance.[12]　But, on the one hand, we know full well the tendency of the primitive Christian legend to create such proofs of the superior nature of her Messiah (witness the calling of the two pairs of brethren; but the instance most analogous has been just alluded to, and is hereafter to be more closely examined, namely, the manner in which Jesus causes the room to be bespoken for his last supper with the twelve); on the other hand, the dogmatic reasons drawn from prophecy, for displaying the far-seeing of Jesus here as precisely the knowledge of an ass being tied at a certain place, are clearly obvious; so that we cannot abstain from the conjecture, that we have here nothing more than a product of the tendency which characterized the Christian legend, and of the effort to base Christian belief on ancient prophecy.　In considering, namely, the passage quoted in the first and fourth gospels from Zechariah, where it is merely said that the meek and lowly king will come riding on an ass, in general; it is usual to overlook another prophetic passage, which contains more precisely the *tied* ass of the Messiah.　This passage is Gen. xlix. 11, where the dying Jacob says to Judah concerning the Shiloh, שִׁילֹה, *Binding his foal unto the vine, and his ass's colt unto the choice vine,* δεσμεύων πρὸς ἄμπελον τὸν πῶλον αὐτοῦ καὶ τῇ ἕλικι τὸν πῶλον τῆς ὄνου αὐτοῦ.　Justin Martyr understands this passage also, as well as the one from Zechariah, as a prediction relative to the entrance of Jesus, and hence directly asserts that the foal which Jesus caused to be fetched was bound to a vine.[13]　In like manner the Jews not only held the general interpretation that the Shiloh was the Messiah, as may be shown already in the Targum,[14] but also combined the passage relative to the binding of the ass with that on the riding of it into Jerusalem.[15]　That the above prophecy of Jacob is not cited by any one of our Evangelists, only proves, at the utmost, that it was not verbally present to their minds when they were writing the narrative before us: it can by no means prove that the passage was not an element in the conceptions of the circle in which the anecdote was first formed.　The transmission of the narrative through the hands of many who were not aware of its original relation to the passage in Genesis, may certainly be argued from the fact that it no longer perfectly corresponds to the prophecy.　For a perfect agreement to exist, Jesus, after he had, according to Zechariah, ridden into the city on the ass, must on dismounting, have bound it to a vine, instead of causing it to be unbound in the next village (according to Mark, from a door by the way-side) as he actually does.　By this means, however, there was obtained, together with the fulfilment of those two prophecies, a proof of the supernatural knowledge of Jesus, and the magical power of his name; and in relation to the former point, it might be remembered in particular, that Samuel also had once proved his gifts as a seer by the prediction, that as Saul was returning homeward, two men would meet him with the information that the asses of Kis his father were found (1 Sam. x. 2).　The narrative in the fourth gospel, having no connection with the Mosaic passage, says nothing of the ass being tied, or of its being fetched by the disciples, and merely states with reference to the passage of Zechariah alone: *Jesus, having found a young ass, sat thereon* (v. 14).[16]

---

[12] Weisse, s. 573.

[13] Apol. i. 32 : τὸ δὲ δεσμεύων πρὸς ἄμπελον τὸν πῶλον αὐτοῦ—σύμβολον δηλωτικὸν ἦν τῶν γενησομένων τῷ Χριστῷ καὶ τῶν ὑπ' αὐτοῦ πραχθησομένων.　πῶλος γάρ τις ὄνου εἱστήκει ἔν τινι εἰσόδῳ κώμης πρὸς ἄμπελον δεδεμένος ὃν ἐκέλευσεν ἀγαγεῖν αὐτῷ κ. τ. λ.　*Binding his colt to a vine—was a symbol indicative of what would happen to Christ ; for there stood at the entrance of a certain village, bound to a vine, an ass's colt, which he ordered them to bring to him,* etc.

[14] Vid. Schöttgen, horæ, ii. p. 146.

[15] Midrasch Rabba, f. xcviii.

[16] On account of this silence of the fourth Evangelist, even Neander (ut sup.) is in this

The next feature that presents itself for our consideration, is the homage which is rendered to Jesus by the populace. According to all the narrators except Luke, this consisted in cutting down the branches of trees, which, according to the synoptists, were strewed in the way, according to John (who with more particularity mentions palm branches), were carried by the multitude that met Jesus; further, according to all except John, in the spreading of clothes in the way. To this were added joyous acclamations, of which all have, with unimportant modifications, the words εὐλογημένος ὁ ἐρχόμενος ἐν ὀνόματι Κυρίου, *Blessed be he that cometh in the name of the Lord*; all except Luke the ὡσαννὰ, *Hosanna ;* and all, the greeting as King, or Son of David. The first, from Ps. cxviii. 26, בָּרוּךְ הַבָּא בְּשֵׁם יְהוָֹה, was, it is true, a customary form of salutation to persons visiting the feasts, and even the second, הוֹשִׁיעָה נָּא, taken from the preceding verse of the same psalm, was a usual cry at the feast of tabernacles and the passover;[17] but the addition τῷ υἱῷ Δαυὶδ, *to the Son of David*, and ὁ βασιλεὺς τοῦ Ἰσραήλ, *the King of Israel*, shows that the people here applied these general forms to Jesus especially as the Messiah, bid him welcome in a pre-eminent sense, and wished success to his undertaking. In relation to the parties who present the homage, Luke's account is the most circumscribed, for he so connects the spreading of the clothes in the way (v. 36) with the immediately preceding context, that he appears to ascribe it, as well as the laying of the clothes on the ass, solely to the disciples, and he expressly attributes the acclamations to the *whole multitude of the disciples* only (ἅπαν τὸ πλῆθος τῶν μαθητῶν); whereas Matthew and Mark make the homage proceed from the accompanying mass of people. This difference, however, can be easily reconciled; for when Luke speaks of the *multitude of the disciples*, πλῆθος τῶν μαθητῶν, this means the wider circle of the adherents of Jesus, and, on the other hand, the *very great multitude* πλεῖστος ὄχλος in Matthew, only means all those who were favourable to him among the multitude. But while the synoptists remain within the limits of the company who were proceeding to the feast, and who were thus the fellow-travellers of Jesus, John, as above noticed, makes the whole solemnity proceed from those who go out of Jerusalem to meet Jesus (v. 13), while he represents the multitude who are approaching with Jesus as testifying to the former the resurrection of Lazarus, on account of which, according to John, the solemn escort of Jesus into Jerusalem was prepared (v. 17 f.). This cause we cannot admit as authentic, inasmuch as we have found critical reasons for doubting the resurrection of Lazarus : but with the alleged cause, the fact itself of the escort is shaken; especially if we reflect, that the dignity of Jesus might appear to demand that the inhabitants of the city of David should have gone forth to bring him in with all solemnity, and that it fully harmonizes with the prevailing characteristics of the representation of the fourth gospel, to describe, before the arrival of Jesus at the feast, how intently the expectations of the people were fixed upon him (vii. 11 ff., xi. 56).

The last trait in the picture before us, is the displeasure of the enemies of Jesus at the strong attachment to him, exhibited by the people on this occasion. According to John (v. 19), the Pharisees said to each other : we see from this that the (lenient) proceedings which we have hitherto adopted are of no avail; all the world is following him (we must interpose, with forcible measures). According to Luke (v. 39 f.), some Pharisees addressed Jesus as if they expected him to impose silence on his disciples ; on which

---

instance inclined to admit, that a more simple event, owing to the disproportionate importance subsequently attached to it, was unhistorically modified.

[17] Comp. Paulus, in loc.

he answers, that if these were silent, the stones would cry out. While in Luke and John this happens during the progress, in Matthew it is only after Jesus has arrived with the procession in the temple, and when the children, even here, continue to cry, Hosanna to the Son of David, that the high priests and scribes direct the attention of Jesus to the impropriety, as it appears to them, whereupon he repulses them with a sentence out of Ps. viii. 3. (*Out of the mouth of babes and sucklings thou hast perfected praise*) (v. 15 f.); a sentence which in the original obviously relates to Jehovah, but which Jesus thus applies to himself. The lamentation of Jesus over Jerusalem, connected by Luke with the entrance, will come under our consideration further on.

John, and more particularly Matthew by his phrase τοῦτο δὲ ὅλον γέγονεν, ἵνα πληρωθῇ κ. τ. λ., *All this was done that it might be fulfilled*, etc. (v. 4), unequivocally express the idea that the design, first of God, inasmuch as he ordained this scene, and next of the Messiah, as the participant in the Divine counsels, was, by giving this character to the entrance, to fulfil an ancient prophecy. If Jesus saw in the passage of Zechariah (ix. 9),[18] a prophecy concerning himself as the Messiah, this cannot have been a knowledge resulting from the higher principle within him ; for, even if this prophetic passage ought not to be referred to an historical prince, as Uzziah,[19] or John Hyrcanus,[20] but to a messianic individual,[21] still the latter, though a pacific, must yet be understood as a temporal prince, and moreover as in peaceful possession of Jerusalem—thus as one altogether different from Jesus. But it appears quite possible for Jesus to have come to such an interpretation in a natural way, since at least the rabbins with decided unanimity interpret the passage of Zechariah of the Messiah.[22] Above all, we know that the contradiction which appeared to exist between the insignificant advent here predicted of the Messiah, and the brilliant one which Daniel had foretold, was at a later period commonly reconciled by the doctrine, that according as the Jewish people showed themselves worthy or the contrary, their Messiah would appear in a majestic or a lowly form.[23] Now even if this distinction did not exist in the time of Jesus, but only in general a reference of the passage Zech. ix. 9 to the Messiah : still Jesus might imagine that now, on his first appearance, the prophecy of Zechariah must be fulfilled in him, but hereafter, on his second appearance, the prophecy of Daniel. But there is

---

[18] The citation given by Matthew is a combination of a passage from Isaiah with that of Zechariah. For the words *Tell ye the daughter of Zion*, εἴπατε τῇ θυγατρὶ Σιών, are from Isa. lxii. 11 ; the rest from Zechariah ix. 9, where the LXX. has with some divergency : ἰδοὺ ὁ βασιλεύς σου ἔρχεταί σοι δίκαιος καὶ σώζων αὐτὸς πραῢς καὶ ἐπιβεβηκὼς ἐπὶ ὑποζύγιον καὶ πῶλον νέον.

[19] Hitzig, über die Abfassungszeit der Orakel, Zach. ix.–xiv. in the Theol. Studien, 1830, 1, s. 36 ff. refers the preceding verse to the warlike deeds of this king, and the one in question to his pacific virtues.

[20] Paulus, exeg. Handb. 3, a, s. 121 ff.

[21] Rosenmüller, Schol. in V. T. 7, 4, s. 274 ff.

[22] In the passage cited Introd., § 14, from Midrasch Coheleth, the description, *pauper et insidens asino* in Zechariah, is in the very first instance referred to the *Goël postremus*. This ass of the Messiah was held identical with that of Abraham and Moses, vid. Jalkut Rubeni f. lxxix. 3, 4, ap. Schöttgen, i. s. 169; comp. Eisenmenger, entdecktes Judenthum, 2, s. 697 f.

[23] Sanhedrin f. xcviii. 1 (ap. Wetstein) : *Dixit R. Alexander : R. Josua f. Levi duobus inter se collatis locis tanquam contrariis visis objecit : scribitur Dan. vii. 13 : et ecce cum nubibus cœli velut filius hominis venit. Et scribitur Zach. ix. 9 : pauper et insidens asino. Verum hæc duo loca ita inter se conciliari possunt : nempe, si justitia sua mereantur Israëlitæ, Messias veniet cum nubibus cœli : si autem non mereantur, veniet pauper, et vehetur asino.*

a third possibility; namely, that either an accidental riding into Jerusalem on an ass by Jesus was subsequently interpreted by the Christians in this manner, or that, lest any messianic attribute should be wanting to him, the whole narrative of the entrance was freely composed after the two prophecies and the dogmatic presupposition of a superhuman knowledge on the part of Jesus.

THIRD PART.

HISTORY OF THE PASSION, DEATH AND
RESURRECTION OF JESUS.

CHAPTER I.

RELATION OF JESUS TO THE IDEA OF A SUFFERING AND DYING MESSIAH; HIS DISCOURSES ON HIS DEATH, RESURRECTION, AND SECOND ADVENT.

---

§ III.

DID JESUS IN PRECISE TERMS PREDICT HIS PASSION AND DEATH?

ACCORDING to the gospels, Jesus more than once, and while the result was yet distant,[1] predicted to his disciples that sufferings and a violent death awaited him. Moreover, if we trust the synoptical accounts, he did not predict his fate merely in general terms, but specified beforehand the place of his passion, namely, Jerusalem ; the time, namely, the approaching passover ; the persons from whom he would have to snffer, namely, the chief priests, scribes and Gentiles ; the essential form of his passion, namely, crucifixion, in consequence of a judicial sentence ; and even its accessory circumstances, namely, scourging, reviling, and spitting (Matt. xvi. 21, xvii. 12, 22 f., xx. 17 ff., xxvi. 12 with the parall., Luke xiii. 33). Between the synoptics and the author of the fourth gospel, there exists a threefold difference in relation to this subject. Firstly and chiefly, in the latter the predictions of Jesus do not appear so clear and intelligible, but are for the most part presented in obscure figurative discourses, concerning which the narrator himself confesses that the disciples understood them not until after the issue (ii. 22). In addition to a decided declaration that he will voluntarily lay down his life (x. 15 ff.), Jesus in this gospel is particularly fond of alluding to his approaching death under the expressions ὑψοῦν, ὑψοῦσθαι, *to lift up, to be lifted up*, in the application of which he seems to vacillate between his exaltation on the cross, and his exaltation to glory (iii. 14, viii. 28, xii. 32) ; he compares his approaching exaltation with that of the brazen serpent in the wilderness (iii. 14), as, in Matthew, he compares his fate with that of Jonah (xii. 40) ; on another occasion, he speaks of going away whither no man can follow him (vii. 33 ff., viii. 21 f.), as, in the synoptists, of a taking away of a bridegroom, which will plunge his friends into mourning (Matt. ix. 15 parall.), and of a cup, which he must drink, and which his disciples will find it hard to partake of with him (Matt. xx. 22 parall.). The two other differences are less marked, but are still observable. One of them is, that while in John the allusions to the violent death of Jesus run in an equal degree through the whole gospel ; in the synoptists, the repeated and definite announcements of his death are found only towards the

---

[1] His predictions concerning particular circumstances of his passion, uttered shortly before its occurrence, in the last days days of his life, can only be considered farther on, in the history of those days.

end, partly immediately before, partly during, the last journey; in earlier chapters there occurs, with the exception of the obscure discourse on the sign of Jonah (which we shall soon see to be no prediction of death), only the intimation of a removal (doubtless violent) of the bridegroom. The last difference is, that while according to the three first Evangelists, Jesus imparts those predictions (again with the single exception of the above intimation, Matt. ix. 15) only to the confidential circle of his disciples; in John, he utters them in the presence of the people, and even of his enemies.

In the critical investigation of these evangelical accounts, we shall proceed from the special to the general, in the following manner. First we shall ask : Is it credible that Jesus had a foreknowledge of so many particular features of the fate which awaited him? and next : Is even a general foreknowledge and prediction of his sufferings, on the part of Jesus, probable? in which inquiry, the difference between the representation of John and that of the synoptists, will necessarily come under our consideration.

There are two modes of explaining how Jesus could so precisely foreknow the particular circumstances of his passion and death ; the one resting on a supernatural, the other on a natural basis. The former appears adequate to solve the problem by the simple position, that before the prophetic spirit, which dwelt in Jesus in the richest plenitude, his destiny must have lain unfolded from the beginning. As, however, Jesus himself, in his announcements of his sufferings, expressly appealed to the Old Testament, the prophecies of which concerning him must be fulfilled in all points (Luke xviii. 31, comp. xxii. 37, xxiv. 25 ff. ; Matt. xxvi. 54) : so the orthodox view ought not to despise this help, but must give to its explanation the modification, that Jesus continually occupied with the prophecies of the Old Testament, may have drawn those particularities out of them, by the aid of the spirit that dwelt within him.[2] According to this, while the knowledge of the time of his passion remains consigned to his prophetic presentiment, unless he be supposed to have calculated this out of Daniel, or some similar source ; Jesus must have come to regard Jerusalem as the scene of his suffering and death, by contemplating the fate of earlier prophets as a type of his own, the Spirit telling him, that where so many prophets had suffered death, there, à fortiori, must the Messiah also suffer (Luke xiii. 33) ; that his death would be the sequel of a formal sentence, he must have gathered from Isa. liii. 8, where a *judgment* מִשְׁפָּט is spoken of as impending over the servant of God, and from v. 12, where it is said that he was *numbered with the transgressors*, ἐν τοῖς ἀνόμοις ἐλογίσθη (comp. Luke xxii. 37) ; that his sentence would proceed from the rulers of his own people, he might perhaps have concluded from Ps. cxviii. 22, where the *builders*, οἰκοδομοῦντες who reject the corner-stone, are, according to apostolic interpretation (Acts iv. 11), the Jewish rulers ; that he would be delivered to the Gentiles, he might infer from the fact, that in several plaintive psalms, which are susceptible of a messianic interpretation, the persecuting parties are represented as רְשָׁעִים, i. e. heathens; that the precise manner of his death would be crucifixion, he might have deduced, partly from the type of the brazen serpent which was suspended on a pole, Num. xxi. 8 f. (comp. John iii. 14), partly from the piercing of the hands and feet, Ps. xxii. 17, LXX. ; lastly, that he would be the object of scorn and personal maltreatment, he might have concluded from passages such as v. 7 ff. in the Psalm above quoted, Isa. l. 6, etc. Now if the spirit which dwelt in Jesus, and which, according to the orthodox opinion, revealed to him the reference of these prophecies and types to his ultimate destiny, was a spirit of truth : this refer-

---

[2] Comp. Olshausen, bibl. Comm., 1, s. 528.

ence to Jesus must admit of being proved to be the true and original sense of those Old Testament passages. But, to confine ourselves to the principal passages only, a profound grammatical and historical exposition has convincingly shown, for all who are in a condition to liberate themselves from dogmatic presuppositions, that in none of these is there any allusion to the sufferings of Christ. Instead of this, Isa. l. 6, speaks of the ill usage which the prophets had to experience ; [3] Isa. liii. of the calamities of the prophetic order, or more probably of the Israelitish people ;[4] Ps. cxviii. of the unexpected deliverance and exaltation of that people, or of one of their princes ;[5] while Ps. xxii. is the complaint of an oppressed exile.[6] As to the 17th verse of this Psalm, which has been interpreted as having reference to the crucifixion of Christ, even presupposing the most improbable interpretation of כארי by *perfoderunt*, this must in no case be understood literally, but only figuratively, and the image would be derived, not from a crucifixion, but from a chase, or a combat with wild beasts ;[7] hence the application of this passage to Christ is now only maintained by those with whom it would be lost labour to contend. According to the orthodox view, however, Jesus, in a supernatural manner, by means of his higher nature, discovered in these passages a pre-intimation of the particular features of his passion ; but, in that case, since such is not the true sense of these passages, the spirit that dwelt in Jesus cannot have been the spirit of truth, but a lying spirit. Thus the orthodox expositor, so far as he does not exclude himself from the light dispensed by an unprejudiced interpretation of the Old Testament, is driven, for the sake of his own interest, to adopt the natural opinion ; namely, that Jesus was led to such an interpretation of Old Testament passages, not by divine inspiration, but by a combination of his own.

According to this opinion,[8] there was no difficulty in foreseeing that it would be the ruling sacerdotal party to which Jesus must succumb, since, on the one hand, it was pre-eminently embittered against Jesus, on the other, it was in possession of the necessary power ; and equally obvious was it that they would make Jerusalem the theatre of his judgment and execution, since this was the centre of their strength ; that after being sentenced by the rulers of his people, he would be delivered to the Romans for execution, followed from the limitation of the Jewish judicial power at that period ; that crucifixion was the death to which he would be sentenced, might be conjectured from the fact that with the Romans this species of death was a customary infliction, especially on rebels ; lastly, that scourging and reviling would not be wanting, might likewise be inferred from Roman custom, and the barbarity of judicial proceedings in that age.—But viewing the subject more nearly, how could Jesus so certainly know that Herod, who had directed a threatening attention to his movements (Luke xiii. 31), would not forestall the sacerdotal party, and add to the murder of the Baptist, that of his more important follower ? And even if he felt himself warranted in believing that real danger threatened him from the side of the hierarchy only (Luke xiii. 33) ; what was his guarantee that one of their tumultuary attempts to murder him would not at last succeed (comp. John viii. 39, x. 31), and that he would not, as Stephen did at a later period, without any further formalities, and without a previous delivery to the Romans, find his death in quite

---

[3] Gesenius, Jesaias, iii. 137 ff. ; Hitzig, Comm. zu. Jes., s. 550.
[4] Gesenius, ut sup. s. 158 ff. ; Hitzig, s. 577 ff. ; Vatke, bibl. Theol. 1, s. 528 ff.
[5] De Wette, Comm. zu den Psalmen, s. 514 ff. ; 3te Aufl.
[6] Ibid. s. 224 ff.
[7] Paulus, exeg. Handb. 3, b, s. 677 ff., and De Wette in loc.
[8] See this view developed by Fritzsche, Comm. in Marc., p. 381 f.

another manner than by the Roman punishment of crucifixion? Lastly, how could he so confidently assert that the very next plot of his enemies, after so many failures, would be successful, and that the very next journey to the pass-over would be his last?—But the natural explanation also can call to its aid the Old Testament passages, and say: Jesus, whether by the application of a mode of interpretation then current among his countrymen, or under the guidance of his own individual views, gathered from the passages already quoted, a precise idea of the circumstances attendant on the violent end which awaited him as the Messiah.[9] But if in the first place it would be difficult to prove, that already in the lifetime of Jesus all these various passages were referred to the Messiah ; and if it be equally difficult to conceive that Jesus could independently, prior to the issue, discover such a reference ; so it would be a case undistinguishable from a miracle, if the result had actually corre-sponded to so false an interpretation ; moreover, the Old Testament oracles and types will not suffice to explain all the particular features in the predic-tions of Jesus, especially the precise determination of time.

If then Jesus cannot have had so precise a foreknowledge of the circum-stances of his passion and death, either in a supernatural or a natural way : he cannot have had such a foreknowledge at all : and the minute predictions which the Evangelists put into his mouth must be regarded as a *vaticinium post eventum*.[10] Commentators who have arrived at this conclusion, have not failed to extol the account of John, in opposition to that of the synoptists, on the ground that precisely those traits in the predictions of Jesus which, from their special character, he cannot have uttered, are only found in the synop-tists, while John attributes to Jesus no more than indefinite intimations, and distinguishes these from his own interpretation, made after the issue ; a plain proof that in his gospel alone we have the discourses of Jesus unfalsified, and in their original form.[11] But, regarded more nearly, the case does not stand so that the fourth Evangelist can only be taxed with putting an erroneous interpretation on the otherwise unfalsified declarations of Jesus : for in one passage, at least, he has put into his mouth an expression which, obscurely, it is true, but still unmistakably, determines the manner of his death as crucifixion ; and consequently, he has here altered the words of Jesus to correspond with the result. We refer to the expression ὑψωθῆναι, *to be lifted up* : in those passages of the fourth gospel where Jesus speaks in a passive sense of the Son of Man being lifted up, this expression might possibly mean his exaltation to glory, although in iii. 14, from the comparison with the ser-pent in the wilderness, which was well known to have been elevated on a pole, even this becomes a difficulty ; but when, as in viii. 28, he represents the exaltation of the Son of Man as the act of his enemies (ὅταν ὑψώσητε τὸν υἱὸν τ. ἀ.), it is obvious that these could not lift him up immediately to glory, but only to the cross ; consequently, if the result above stated be admitted as valid, John must himself have framed this expression, or at least have distorted the Aramæan words of Jesus, and hence he essentially falls under the same category with the synoptical writers. That the fourth Evangelist, though the passion and death of Jesus were to him past events, and therefore clearly pre-sent to his mind, nevertheless makes Jesus predict them in obscure expres-sions,—this has its foundation in the entire manner of this writer, whose fond-

---

[9] Vid. Fritzsche, ut sup.
[10] Paulus, exeg. Handb. 2, s. 415 ff. ; Ammon, bibl. Theol. 2, s. 377 f. ; Kaiser, bibl. Theol. 1, s. 246. Fritzsche also, ut sup. and Weisse, 1, s. 423, partly admit this.
[11] Bertholdt, Einleitung in d. N. T. 1305 ff. ; Wegscheider, Einl. in das Evang. Johannis, s. 271 f.

ness for the enigmatical and mysterious here happily met the requirement, to give an unintelligible form to prophecies which were not understood.

There were sufficient inducements for the Christian legend thus to put into the mouth of Jesus, after the event, a prediction of the particular features of his passion, especially of the ignominious crucifixion. The more the Christ crucified became *to the Jews a stumbling-block, and to the Greeks foolishness* (1 Cor. i. 23), the more need was there to remove this offence by every possible means ; and as, among subsequent events, the resurrection especially served as a *retrospective* cancelling of that shameful death ; so it must have been earnestly desired to take the sting from that offensive catastrophe *beforehand* also, and this could not be done more effectually than by such a minute prediction. For as the most unimportant fact, when prophetically announced, gains importance, by thus being made a link in the chain of a higher know-ledge : so the most ignominious fate, when it is predicted as part of a divine plan of salvation, cases to be ignominious ; above all, when the very person over whom such a fate impends, also possesses the prophetic spirit, which enables him to foresee and foretell it, and thus not only suffers, but participates in the divine prescience of his sufferings, he manifests himself as the *ideal* power over those suffering. But the fourth Evangelist has gone still farther on this track ; he believes it due to the honour of Jesus to represent him as also the *real* power over his sufferings, as not having his life taken away by the vio-lence of others, but as resigning it voluntarily (x. 17 f.) : a representation which indeed already finds some countenance in Matt. xxvi. 53, where Jesus asserts the possibility of praying to the Father for legions of angels, in order to avert his sufferings.

§ 112.

THE PREDICTIONS OF JESUS CONCERNING HIS DEATH IN GENERAL ; THEIR RELATION TO THE JEWISH IDEA OF THE MESSIAH : DECLARATIONS OF JESUS CONCERNING THE OBJECT AND EFFECTS OF HIS DEATH.

If in this manner we subtract from the declarations of Jesus concerning his approaching fate, attributed to him in the gospels, all which regards the particular circumstances of this catastrophe ; there still remains on the part of Jesus the general announcement, that suffering and death awaited him, and also that this part of his career was a fulfilment of the Old Testament prophecies relative to the Messiah. As, however, the principal passages cited from the Old Testament, which treat of suffering and death, are only by mistake referred to the Messiah, while others, as Dan. ix. 26 ; Zech. xii. 10, have not this signification :[1] the orthodox, above all, must again beware of attributing so false an interpretation of these prophecies, to the supernatural principle in Jesus. That instead of this, Jesus might possibly, by a purely natural combination, have educed the general result, that since he had made the hierarchy of his nation his implacable enemies, he had, in so far as he was resolved not to swerve from the path of his destination, the worst to fear from their revenge and authority (John x. 11 ff.) ; that from the fate of former prophets (Matt. v. 12, xxi. 33 ff. ; Luke xiii. 33 f.), and isolated passages bearing such an interpretation, he might prognosticate a similar end to his own career, and accordingly predict to his followers that earlier or later a violent death awaited him—this it would be a needless overstraining of

[1] Daniel, übersetzt und erklärt von Bertholdt, 2, s. 541 ff., 660 ff. ; Rosenmüller, Schol. in V. T. 7, 4, p. 339 ff.

the supranaturalistic view any longer to deny, and the rational mode of considering the subject should be admitted.[2]

It may appear surprising if, after this admission, we still put the question, whether, according to the New Testament representation, it be probable that Jesus *actually* uttered such a prediction? since, certainly, a general announcement of his violent death is the least which the evangelical accounts appear to contain, but our meaning in the question is this: is the sequel, especially the conduct of the disciples, so described in the gospels, as to be reconcilable with a prior disclosure of Jesus relative to the sufferings which awaited him? Now the express statements of the Evangelists do not merely tend to show that the disciples did not understand the discourses of Jesus on his coming death, in the sense that they did not know how to adjust these facts in their own minds, or to make them tally with their preconceived ideas concerning the Messiah,—a difficulty which drew from Peter the first time that Jesus announced his death, the exclamation : *Be it far from thee, Lord, this shall not be unto thee ;*—for we find the words of Mark (ix. 32), *But they understood not that saying,* οἱ δὲ ἠγνόουν τὸ ῥῆμα, thus amplified in Luke: *and it was hid from them, that they perceived it not,* καί ἦν παρακεκαλυμμένον ἀπ᾽ αὐτῶν ἵνα μὴ αἴσθωνται αὐτό (ix. 45); and the latter Evangelist on another occasion says: *and they understood none of these things, and this saying was hid from them, neither knew they the things that were spoken,* καὶ αὐτοὶ οὐδὲν τούτων συνῆκαν, καὶ ἦν τὸ ῥῆμα τοῦτο κεκρυμμένον ἀπ᾽ αὐτῶν, καὶ οὐκ ἐγίνωσκον τὰ λεγόμενα (xviii. 34): expressions which appear to imply that the disciples absolutely did not understand what the words of Jesus meant. In accordance with this, the condemnation and execution of Jesus fall upon them as a blow for which they are entirely unprepared, and consequently annihilate all the hopes which they had fixed on him as the Messiah (Luke xxiv. 20 f., *The chief priests and our rulers have crucified him. But we trusted that it had been he which should have redeemed Israel*). But had Jesus spoken of his death to the disciples with such perfect *openness* (παῤῥησίᾳ, Mark viii. 32), they must necessarily have understood his clear words and detailed discourses, and had he besides shown them that his death was foreshadowed in the messianic prophecies of the Old Testament, and was consequently a part of the Messiah's destination (Luke xviii. 31, xxii. 37), they could not, when his death actually ensued, have so entirely lost all belief in his messiahship. It is true that the Wolfenbüttel Fragmentist is wrong in his attempt to show in the conduct of Jesus, as described by the Evangelists, indications that his death was unexpected even to himself; but, looking merely at the conduct of the disciples, it is difficult to avoid the conclusion which that writer draws, namely, that to judge by that conduct, Jesus cannot have made any antecedent disclosure to his disciples concerning his death ; on the contrary, they appear to the very last moment to have held the common opinion on this matter, and only to have adopted the characteristics of suffering and death into their conception of the Messiah, after the death of Jesus had unexpectedly come upon them.[3] At all events we have before us the following dilemma : either the statements of the Evangelists as to the inability of the disciples to understand the predictions of Jesus, and their surprise at his death, are unhistorically exaggerated; or the decided declarations of Jesus concerning the death which awaited him, were composed *ex eventu*, nay, it becomes doubtful whether he even in general predicted his death as a part of his messianic destiny. On both sides, the legend might be led into

[2] De Wette, de morte Christi expiatoria, in his Opusc. Theol., p. 130 ; Hase, L. J. § 106.
[3] Vom Zweck Jesu und seiner Junger, s. 114 ff. 153 f.

unhistorical representations. For the fabrication of a prediction of his death in general, there were the same reasons which we have above shown to be an adequate motive for attributing to him a prognostication of the particular features of his passion : to the fiction of so total a want of comprehension in the disciples, an inducement might be found, on the one hand, in the desire to exhibit the profoundness of the mystery of a suffering Messiah revealed by Jesus, through the inability of the disciples to understand it; on the other, in the fact that in the evangelical tradition the disciples were likened to unconverted Jews and heathens, to whom anything was more intelligible than the death of the Messiah.

In order to decide between these alternatives, we must first examine whether, prior to the death of Jesus, and independently of that event, the messianic ideas of the age included the characteristics of suffering and death. If already in the lifetime of Jesus it was the Jewish opinion that the Messiah must die a violent death, then it is highly probable that Jesus imbibed this idea as a part of his convictions, and communicated it to his disciples ; who, in that case, could so much the less have remained uninstructed on this point, and overwhelmed by the actual result, in the degree alleged by the Evangelists. If, on the contrary, that idea was not diffused among his countrymen before the death of Jesus, it still remains possible that Jesus might arrive at that idea by his private reflection ; but it is a prior possibility that the disciples were the first to adopt the characteristics of suffering and death into their conception of the Messiah, after they had been taught by the issue.

The question whether the idea of a suffering and dying Messiah was already diffused among the Jews in the time of Jesus, is one of the most difficult points of discussion among theologians, and one concerning which they are the least agreed. And the difficulty of the question does not lie in the interests of party, so that it might be hoped that with the rise of impartial investigation, the subject would cease to be perplexed ; for, as Stäudlin has aptly shown,[4] both the orthodox and the rationalistic interest may alternately tend in each direction, and we in fact find theologians of both parties on both sides.[5] The difficulty lies in the deficiency of information, and in the uncertainty of that which we do possess. If the Old Testament contained the doctrine of a suffering and dying Messiah, it might certainly thence be inferred with more than mere probability, that this doctrine existed among the Jews in the time of Jesus : as, however, according to the most recent researches, the Old Testament, while it does indeed contain the doctrine of an expiation of the sins of the people to take place at the messianic era (Ezek. xxxvi. 25, xxxvii. 23 ; Zech. xiii. 1 ; Dan. ix. 24), has no trace of this expiation being effected by the suffering and death of the Messiah [6]: there is no decision of the question before us to be expected from this quarter. The apocryphal books of the Old Testament lie nearer to the time of Jesus ; but as these are altogether silent concerning the Messiah in general,[7] there can be no discussion as to their containing that special feature. Again, if we turn to Philo and Josephus, the two authors who wrote soonest after the

---

[4] Ueber den Zweck und die Wirkungen des Todes Jesu, in der Göttingischen Bibliothek, I, 4, s. 252 ff.
[5] See the list in De Wette, ut sup. s. 6 ff. The most important voices for the existence of the idea in question in the time of Jesus, have been noticed by Stäudlin in the above treatise, I, s. 233 ff., and by Hengstenberg, Christologie des A. T., I, a, s. 270 ff., b, s. 290 ff. ; for the opposite opinion, by De Wette, ut sup. p. 1 ff.
[6] Comp. De Wette, bibl. Dogm, § 201 f. ; Baumgarten Crusius, bibl. Theol. § 54.
[7] Vid. De Wette, ut sup. § 189 ff.

period in question, we find the latter silent as to the messianic hopes of his nation ;[8] and though the former does indeed speak of messianic times, and a messiah-like hero, he says nothing of sufferings on his part.[9] Thus there remain, as sources of information on this point, only the New Testament and the later Jewish writings.

In the New Testament, almost everything is calculated to give the impression, that a suffering and dying Messiah was unthought-of among the Jews who were contemporary with Jesus.   To the majority of the Jews, we are told, the doctrine of a crucified Messiah was a σκανδαλὸν, and the disciples were at a loss to understand Jesus in his repeated and explicit announcements of his death.   This does not look as if the doctrine of a suffering Messiah had been current among the Jews of that period; on the contrary, these circumstances accord fully with the declaration which the fourth Evangelist puts into the mouth of the Jewish *multitude*, ὄχλος (xii. 34), namely, that they had heard in the *law* (νόμος) *that Christ abideth for ever*, ὅτι ὁ Χριστὸς μένει εἰς τὸν αἰῶνα.[10]   Indeed, for a general acceptation of the idea of a suffering Messiah among the Jews of that period, even those theologians who take the affirmative side in this argument do not contend ; but, admitting that the hope of a worldly Messiah whose reign was to endure for ever, was the prevalent one, they only maintain (and herein the Wolfenbüttel Fragmentist agrees with them)[11], that a less numerous party,—according to Stäudlin, the Essenes; according to Hengstenberg, the better and more enlightened part of the people in general—held the belief that the Messiah would appear in a humble guise, and only enter into glory through suffering and death.   In support of this they appeal especially to two passages ; one out of the third, and one out of the fourth gospel.   When Jesus is presented as an infant in the temple at Jerusalem, the aged Simeon, among other prophecies, particularly concerning the opposition which her son would have to encounter, says to Mary : *Yea, a sword shall pierce through thine own soul also* (Luke ii. 35) ; words which seem to describe her maternal sorrow at the death of her son, and consequently to represent the opinion, that a violent death awaited the Messiah, as one already current before Christ.   Still more plainly is the idea of a suffering Messiah contained in the words which the fourth gospel makes the Baptist utter on seeing Jesus : *Behold the Lamb of God which taketh away the sin of the world* (i. 29) ! This, viewed in its relation to Isa. liii., would in the mouth of the Baptist likewise tend to prove, that the idea of expiatory suffering on the part of the Messiah was in existence before the time of Jesus.   But both these passages have been above shown to be unhistorical, and from the fact that the primitive Christian legend was led, a considerable time after the issue, to attribute to persons whom it held divinely inspired, a foreknowledge of the divine decree with respect to the death of Jesus, it can by no means be concluded, that this insight really existed prior to the death of Jesus.   In conclusion, it is urged, that at least the Evangelists and apostles refer to the idea of a suffering and dying Messiah in the Old Testament ; whence it is thought warrantable to conclude, that this interpretation of the Old Testament passages connected with our present subject, was not unprecedented among the Jews. Certainly Peter (Acts iii. 18 f. ; 1 Pet. i. 11 f.) and Paul (Acts xxvi. 22 f. ;

[8] Comp. De Wette, ut sup. § 193.

[9] Gfrörer, Philo, 1, s. 495 ff.

[10] A passage to this effect out of the *law* (νόμος) properly so called, would be difficult to find : De Wette, de morte, p. 72, refers to Isa. ix. 5 ; Lücke, in loc. to Ps. cx. 4 ; Dan. vii. 14, ii. 44.

[11] Vom Zweck Jesu und seiner Jünger, s. 179 f.

1 Cor. xv. 3) appeal to Moses and the prophets as annunciators of the death of Jesus, and Philip, in his interview with the Ethiopian eunuch, interprets a passage in Isa. liii. of the sufferings of the Messiah : but as those teachers of the church spoke and wrote all this after the event, we have no assurance that they did not assign to certain Old Testament passages a relation to the sufferings of the Messiah, solely in consquence of that event, and not by adopting a mode of interpretation previously current among their Jewish cotemporaries.[12]

If, according to this, the opinion that the idea in question already existed among the countrymen of Jesus during his lifetime, has no solid foundation in the New Testament; we must proceed to inquire whether that idea may not be found in the later Jewish writings. Among the earliest writings of this class now extant, are the Chaldee paraphrases of Onkelos and Jonathan ; and the *Targum* of the latter, who, according to rabbinical tradition, was a pupil of Hillel the elder,[13] is commonly cited as presenting the idea of a suffering Messiah, because it refers the passage, Isa. lii. 13–liii. 12, to the Messiah. But with respect to the interpretation of this passage in the *Targum of Jonathan*, it is the singular fact, that while the prophecies which it contains are in general interpreted messianically, yet so often as suffering and death are spoken of, either these ideas are avoided with marked design, and for the most part by some extremely forced expedient, or are transferred to a different subject, namely, the people of Israel : a significant proof that to the author, suffering and violent death appeared irreconcilable with the idea of the Messiah.[14] But this, we are told, is the commencement of that aberration from the true sense of the sacred text, into which the later Jews were seduced by their carnal disposition, and their hostility to Christianity : the more ancient interpreters, it is said, discovered in this passage of Isaiah a suffering and dying Messiah. It is true that Abenezra, Abarbanel and others, testify that many ancient teachers referred Isa. liii. to the Messiah :[15] but some of their statements leave it by no means clear that those more ancient interpretations are not as partial as that of Jonathan ; and in relation to all of them it remains uncertain, whether the interpreters of whom they speak reach as far back as the age of Jonathan, which is highly improbable with respect to those parts of the book *Sohar*, wherein the passage in question is referred to a suffering Messiah.[16] The writing which, together with that of Jonathan, may be regarded as the nearest to the time

---

[12] Vid. De Wette, de morte Chr. p. 73 f.

[13] Comp. Gesenius, Jesaias 2, Th. s. 66 ; De Wette, Einleitung in das A. T. § 59, 3te Ausg.

[14] Literal translation according to Hitzig, lii. 14 :—As many were *amazed* at him, so disfigured, not human, was *his* appearance, and *his* form not that of the children of men, etc.

liii. 4 :—But he *bore* our infirmities, and *charged himself with* our sorrows, and we esteemed *him* stricken, smitten of God and afflicted.

Targum of Jonathan : *Quemadmodum per multos dies ipsum exspectârunt Israëlitae, quorum contabuit inter gentes adspectus et splendor (et evanuit) e filiis hominum, etc.*

Idcirco pro delictis nostris ipse depre- cabitur, et iniquitates nostræ propter eum condonabuntur, licet nos reputati simus contusi, plagis affecti et afflicti.

Origen also relates, c. Celsus, i. 55, how a person esteemed *a wise man among the Jews,* λεγόμενος παρὰ ᾽Ιουδαίοις σοφὸς, maintained, in opposition to his Christian interpretation of the passage in Isaiah, *that this was prophesied concerning the whole nation, which had been dispersed and afflicted, in order that many might become proselytes,* ταῦτα πεπροφητεῦσθαι ὡς περὶ ἑνὸς τοῦ ὅλου λαοῦ, καὶ γενομένου ἐν τῇ διασπορᾷ, καὶ πληγέντος, ἵνα πολλοὶ προσήλυτοι γένωνται.

[15] Vid. Schöttgen, 2, s. 182 f. ; Eisenmenger, entdecktes Judenthum, 2, s. 758.

[16] Ap. Schöttgen, 2 s. 181 f.

of Jesus, namely, the apocryphal fourth book of Esdras, drawn up, according to the most probable computation, shortly after the destruction of Jerusalem under Titus,[17] does indeed mention the death of the Messiah : not however as a painful one, but only as a death which, after the long duration of the messianic kingdom, was to precede the general resurrection.[18] The idea of great calamities, the birth-throes, as it were, of the Messiah (חבלי המשיח, comp. ἀρχὴ ὠδίνων, Matt. xxiv. 8), which would usher in the messianic times, was undoubtedly disseminated before Christ;[19] and equally early there appears to have been placed in the front of these ills, which were to press upon the people of Israel in particular, the *Antichrist*, ἀντίχριστος, whom the *Christ*, Χριστὸς would have to oppose (2 Thess. ii. 3 ff.):[20] but since he was to annihilate this adversary in a supernatural manner, *with the spirit of his mouth*, τῷ πνεύματι τοῦ στόματος αὐτοῦ, this involved no suffering for the Messiah. Nevertheless, there are to be found passages in which a suffering of the Messiah is spoken of, and in which this suffering is even represented as vicarious, on behalf of the people :[21] but first, this is only a suffering, and no death of the Messiah ; secondly, it befals him either before his descent into earthly life, in his pre-existence,[22] or during the concealment in which he keeps himself from his birth until his appearance as Messiah :[23] lastly, the antiquity of these ideas is doubtful, and according to certain indications, they could only be dated after the destruction of the Jewish state by Titus.[24] Meanwhile, Jewish writings are by no means destitute of passages, in which it is directly asserted that a Messiah would perish in a violent manner : but these passages relate, not to the proper Messiah, the offspring of David, but to another, from among the posterity of Joseph and Ephraim, who was appointed to hold a subordinate position in relation to the former.   This Messiah *ben Joseph* was to precede the Messiah *ben David*, to unite the ten tribes of the former kingdom of Israel with the two tribes of the kingdom of Judah, but after this to perish by the sword in the battle with Gog and Magog : a catastrophe to which Zech. xii. 10 was referred.[25] But of this second, dying Messiah, any certain traces are wanting before the Babylonian *Gemara*, which was compiled in the fifth and sixth centuries after Christ, and the book *Sohar*, the age of which is extremely doubtful.[26]

Although, according to this, it cannot be proved, and is even not probable, that the idea of a suffering Messiah already existed among the Jews in the time of Jesus : it is still possible that, even without such a precedent, Jesus himself, by an observation of circumstances, and a comparison of them with Old Testament narratives and prophecies, might come to entertain the belief that suffering and death were a part of the office and destination of the Messiah ; and if so, it would be more natural that he should embrace this conviction gradually in the course of his public ministry, and that he should

---

[17] De Wette, de morte Chr. expiatoria, ut sup. s. 50.
[18] vii. 29.
[19] Schöttgen, 2, s. 509 ff. ; Schmidt, Christologische Fragmente, in his Bibliothek, I, s. 24 ff. ; Bertholdt, Christol. Jud., § 13.
[20] Schmidt, ut sup. ; Bertholdt, ut sup., § 16.
[21] Pesikta in Abkath Rochel, ap. Schmidt, s. 48 f.
[22] Sohar, P. II. lxxxv. 2, ap. Schmidt, § 47 f.
[23] Gemara Sanhedrin, f. xcviii. 1 ; ap. De Wette, de morte Chr., p. 95 f., and ap. Hengstenberg, s. 292.
[24] Sohar, P. II. f. lxxx.ii. 2 ; ap. De Wette, s. 94 : *Cum Israëlitæ essent in terra sancta, per cultus religiosos et sacrificia quæ faciebanto, omnes illos morbos et pœnas e mundo, sustulerunt ; nunc vero Messias debet auferre eas ab hominibus.*
[25] Vid. Bertholdt, ut sup. § 17.
[26] De Wette, de morte Chr., p. 112 ; comp. 53 ff.

chiefly have confined his communications on the subject to his intimate friends, than that he should have had this conviction from the beginning, and have expressed it before indifferent persons, nay enemies. The latter is the representation of John; the former, of the synoptists.*

In relation also to the declarations of Jesus concerning the object and effects of his death, we can, as above in relation to the announcement of the death itself, distinguish a more natural, from a more supranatural point of view. When Jesus in the fourth gospel likens himself to the true shepherd, who lays down his life for the sheep (x. 11, 15): this may have the perfectly natural sense, that he is determined not to swerve from his office of shepherd and teacher, even though, in the prosecution of it, death should threaten him (the moral necessity of his death);[27] the foreboding expression in the same gospel (xii. 24), that *except a corn of wheat fall into the ground and die, it abideth alone, but if it die it bringeth forth much fruit*, admits of an equally rational explanation, as a figurative representation of the victorious power which martyrdom gives to an idea and conviction (the moral efficacy of his death);[28] lastly, that which is so often repeated in the Gospel of John,—namely, that it is good for the disciples that Jesus should go away, for without his departure the *comforter*, παράκλητος will not come to them, who will glorify him in them,—may be supposed to express the perfectly natural consideration of Jesus, that without the removal of his sensible presence, the hitherto so material ideas of his disciples would not be spiritualized (the psychological efficacy of his death).[29] The words of Jesus at the institution of the sacramental supper, belong more to the supranaturalistic mode of view. For if that which the intermediate Evangelists make him say on this occasion—that the cup presented is *the blood of the new testament*, τὸ αἷμα τῆς καινῆς διαθήκης (Mark xiv. 24), and *the new testament in his blood*, ἡ καινὴ διαθήκη ἐν τῷ αἵματι αὐτοῦ (Luke xxii. 20),—might appear to signify no more than that, as by the bloody sacrifice at Sinai was sealed the covenant of this ancient people with God, so by his (the Messiah's) blood would be sealed in a higher sense the community of the new covenant, gathering round him: in the account of Matthew, on the contrary, when he makes Jesus add, that his blood will be shed for many *for the remission of sins*, εἰς ἄφεσιν ἁμαρτιῶν, the idea of the covenant sacrifice is blended with that of expiatory sacrifice : and also in the two other Evangelists by the addition : *which is shed for many*, or *for you*, τὸ περὶ πολλῶν, ὑπὲρ ὑμῶν ἐκχυνόμενον, the transition is made from the covenant sacrifice to the expiatory sacrifice. Further, when in the first gospel (xx. 28) Jesus says, he must *give his life a ransom for many*, δοῦναι τὴν ψυχὴν αὐτοῦ λύτρον ἀντὶ πολλῶν, this is doubtless to be referred to Isa. liii., where, according to a notion current among the Hebrews (Isa. xliii. 3 ; Prov. xxi. 18), the death of the servant of God is supposed to have a propitiatory relation to the rest of mankind.

Thus Jesus might by psychological reflection come to the conviction that such a catastrophe would be favourable to the spiritual development of his disciples, and that it was indispensable for the spiritualizing of their messianic ideas, nay, in accordance with national conceptions, and by a consideration of Old Testament passages, even to the idea that his messianic death would have an expiatory efficacy. Still, what the synoptists make Jesus say of his death, as a sin offering, might especially appear to belong rather to the system which was developed after the death of Jesus ; and what the fourth Evangelist puts into his mouth concerning the Paraclete, to have been conceived *ex*

---

[27] Hase, L. J. § 108.
[28] Ibid.
[29] Ibid. and § 109.

eventu : so that, again, in these expressions of Jesus concerning the object of his death, there must be a separation of the general from the special.

§ 113.

PRECISE DECLARATIONS OF JESUS CONCERNING HIS FUTURE RESURRECTION.

According to the evangelical accounts, Jesus predicted his resurrection in words not less clear than those in which he announced his death, and also fixed the time of its occurrence with singular precision. As often as he said to his disciples, the Son of Man will be crucified, he added : *And the third day he shall rise again*, καὶ τῇ τρίτῃ ἡμέρᾳ ἀναστήσεται, or ἐγερθήσεται (Matt. xvi. 21, xvii. 23, xx. 19 parall. comp. xvii. 9, xxvi. 32 parall.).

But of this announcement also it is said, that the disciples understood it not ; so little, that they even debated among themselves *what the rising from the dead should mean*, τί ἐστι τὸ ἐκ νεκρῶν ἀναστῆναι (Mark ix. 10); and in consistency with this want of comprehension, they, after the death of Jesus, exhibit no trace of a recollection that his resurrection had been foretold to them, no spark of hope that this prediction would be fulfilled. When the friends of Jesus had taken down his body from the cross, and laid it in the grave, they undertook (John xix. 40)—or the women reserved to themselves (Mark xvi. 1 ; Luke xxiii. 56)—the task of embalming him, which is only performed in the case of those who are regarded as the prey of corruption ; when, on the morning which, according to the mode of reckoning in the New Testament, opened the day which had been predetermined as that of the resurrection, the women went to the grave, they were so far from thinking of a predicted resurrection, that they were anxious about the probable difficulty of rolling away the stone from the grave (Mark xvi. 3); when Mary Magdalene, and afterwards Peter, found the grave empty, their first thought, had the resurrection been predicted, must have been, that it had now actually taken place : instead of this, the former conjectures that the body may have been stolen (John xx. 2), while Peter merely wonders, without coming to any definite conjecture (Luke xxiv. 12); when the women told the disciples of the angelic apparition which they had witnessed, and discharged the commission given them by the angel, the disciples partly regarded their words as *idle tales*, λῆρος (Luke xxiv. 11), and were partly moved to fear and astonishment (ἐξέστησαν ἡμᾶς, Luke xxiv. 22 ff.); when Mary Magdalene, and subsequently the disciples going to Emmaus, assured the eleven, that they had themselves seen the risen one, they met with no credence (Mark xvi. 11, 13), and Thomas still later did not believe even the assurance of his fellow-apostles (John xx. 25); lastly, when Jesus himself appeared to the disciples in Galilee, all of them did not even then cast off doubt (οἱ δὲ ἐδίστασαν, Mark xxviii. 17). All this we must, with the Wolfenbüttel Fragmentist,[1] find incomprehensible, if Jesus had so clearly and decidedly predicted his resurrection.

It is true, that as the conduct of the disciples, after the death of Jesus, speaks against such a prediction on the part of Jesus, so the conduct of his enemies appears to speak for it. For when, according to Matt. xxvii. 62 ff., the chief priests and Pharisees entreat Pilate to set a watch at the grave of Jesus, they allege as a reason for their request, that Jesus while yet alive had said : *After three days I will rise again*, μετὰ τρεῖς ἡμέρας ἐγείρομαι. But this

---

[1] See his animated and impressive treatise, vom Zweck, u. s. f., s. 121 ff. Comp. Briefe über den Rationalismus, s. 224 ff., and De Wette, exeg. Handb. 1, 1, s. 143.

narrative of the first gospel, which we can only estimate at a future point in our investigation, at present decides nothing, but only falls to one side of the dilemma, so that we must now say : if the disciples really so acted after the death of Jesus, then neither can he have decidedly foretold his resurrection, nor can the Jews in consideration of such a prediction have placed a watch at his grave; or, if the two latter statements be true, the disciples cannot have so acted.

It has been attempted to blunt the edge of this dilemma, by attributing to the above predictions, not the literal sense, that the deceased Jesus would return out of the grave, but only the figurative sense that his doctrine and cause, after having been apparently crushed, would again expand and flourish.[2] As the Old Testament prophets, it was said, represent the restoration of the Israelitish people to renewed prosperity, under the image of a resurrection from the dead (Isa. xxvi. 19 ; Ezek. xxxvii.) ; as they mark the short interval within which, under certain conditions, this turn of things was to be expected, by the expression : in two or three days will Jehovah revive the smitten one, and raise the dead (Hos. vi. 2),[3] a statement of time which Jesus also uses indefinitely for a short interval (Luke xiii. 32) : so by the declaration that he will *rise on the third day after his death*, τῇ τρίτῃ ἡμέρᾳ ἀναστῆναι, he intends to say no more than that even though he may succumb to the power of his enemies and be put to death, still the work which he has begun will not come to an end, but will in a short time go forward with a fresh impetus. This merely figurative mode of speaking adopted by Jesus, the apostles, after Jesus had actually risen in the body, understood literally, and regarded them as prophecies of his personal resurrection. Now that in the prophetic passages adduced, the expressions קוּם הָיָה and הֵקִיץ have only the alleged figurative sense, is true ; but these are passages the whole tenor of which is figurative, and in which, in particular, the depression and death which precede the revivification are themselves to be understood only in a figurative sense. Here, on the contrary, all the foregoing expressions : παραδίδοσθαι, κατακρίνεσθαι, σταυροῦσθαι, ἀποκτείνεσθαι κ. τ. λ. (*to be delivered, condemned, crucified, killed*, etc.) are to be understood literally ; hence all at once, with the words ἐγερθῆναι and ἀναστῆναι, to enter on a figurative meaning, would be an unprecedented abruptness of transition ; not to mention that passages such as Matt. xxvi. 32, where Jesus says : *After I am risen again I will go before you into Galilee*, μετὰ τὸ ἐγερθῆναί με προάξω ὑμᾶς εἰς τὴν Γαλιλαίαν, can have no meaning at all unless ἐγείρεσθαι be understood literally. In this closely consecutive series of expressions, which must be taken in a purely literal sense, there is then no warrant, and even no inducement, to understand the statement of time which is connected with them, otherwise than also literally, and in its strictly etymological meaning. Thus if Jesus really used these words, and in the same connexion in which they are given by the Evangelists, he cannot have meant to announce by them merely the speedy victory of his cause ; his meaning must have been, that he himself would return to life in three days after his violent death.[4]

As however Jesus, judging from the conduct of his disciples after his death, cannot have announced his resurrection in plain words : other commentators have resigned themselves to the admission, that the Evangelists, after the

---

[2] Thus especially Herder, vom Erlöser der Menschen, s. 133 ff. Briefe über den Rationalismus, s. 227. Comp. Küinol, Comm. in Matth., p. 444 f.

[3] LXX. : ὑγιάσει ἡμᾶς μετὰ δύο ἡμέρας· ἐν τῇ ἡμέρᾳ τῇ τρίτῃ ἐξαναστησόμεθα, καὶ ζησόμεθα ἐνώπιον αὐτοῦ.

[4] Comp. Süskind, einige Bemerkungen über die Frage, ob Jesus seine Auferstehung bestimmt vorhergesagt habe? in Flatt's Magazin, 7, s. 203 ff.

issue, gave to the discourses of Jesus a definiteness which, as uttered by him, they did not possess; that they have not merely understood literally, what Jesus intended figuratively, of the revival of his cause after his death, but in accordance with their erroneous interpretation, have so modified his words that, as we now read them, we must certainly understand them in a literal sense;[5] yet that not all the discourses of Jesus are altered in this manner; here and there his original expressions still remain.

§ 114.

FIGURATIVE DISCOURSES, IN WHICH JESUS IS SUPPOSED TO HAVE ANNOUNCED HIS RESURRECTION.

According to the fourth gospel, Jesus, at the very commencement of his ministry, in figurative language, referred his enemies, the Jews, to his future resurrection (ii. 19 ff.). On his first messianic visit to Jerusalem, and when, after the abuse of the market in the temple had provoked him to that exhibition of holy zeal of which we have formerly spoken, the Jews require a sign from him, by which he should legitimatize his claim to be considered a messenger of God, who had authority to adopt such violent measures, Jesus gives them this answer, *Destroy this temple, and after three days I will raise it up*, λύσατε τὸν ναὸν τοῦτον, καὶ ἐν τρισὶν ἡμέραις ἐγερῶ αὐτόν. The Jews took these words in the sense, which, since they were spoken in the temple, was the most natural, and urged, in reply to Jesus, that as it had taken forty years to build this temple, he would scarcely be able, if it were destroyed, to rebuild it in three days; but the Evangelist informs us, that this was not the meaning of Jesus, and that he here spoke (though indeed the disciples were not aware of this until after his resurrection), of the *temple of his body*, ναὸς τοῦ σώματος αὐτοῦ : i.e. under the destruction and rebuilding of the temple, he alluded to his death and resurrection. Even if we admit, what however the most moderate expositors deny,[1] that Jesus could properly (as he is also represented to have done in Matthew xii. 39 ff.) when the Jews asked him for a visible and immediate sign, refer them to his resurrection as the greatest, and for his enemies the most overwhelming miracle in his history : still he must have done this in terms which it was possible for them to understand (as in the above passage of Matthew, where he expresses himself quite plainly). But the expressions of Jesus, as here given, could not possibly be understood in this sense. For when one who is in the temple, speaks of the destruction of this temple, every one will refer his words to the building itself. Hence Jesus, when he uttered the words, *this temple*, τὸν ναὸν τοῦτον, must have pointed to his body with his finger; as, indeed, is generally presupposed by the friends of this interpretation.[2] But, in the first place, the Evangelist says nothing of such a gesture, notwithstanding that it lay in his interest to notice this, as a support of his interpretation. In the second place, Gabler has with justice remarked, how ill-judged and ineffective it would have been, by the addition of a mere gesture to give a totally new meaning to a speech, which verbally, and therefore logically, referred to the temple. If, however, Jesus used this expedient, the motion of his finger could not have been unobserved; the Jews must rather have demanded from him how he could be so arrogant as to call his body *the temple*, ναὸς; or even if not so, still, pre-

---

[5] Paulus, ut sup. 2, s. 415 ff. ; Hase, L. J. § 109.
[1] E.g. Lücke, 1, s. 426 ; comp., on the contrary, Tholuck, in loc.
[2] Vid. Tholuck, ut sup.

supposing that action, the disciples could not have remained in the dark concerning the meaning of his words, until after the resurrection.[3]

By these difficulties modern exegetists have felt constrained to renounce John's explanation of the words of Jesus, as erroneous and made *ex eventu*, and to attempt to penetrate, independently of the Evangelist's explanation, into the sense of the enigmatical saying which he attributes to Jesus.[4] The construction put upon it by the Jews, who refer the words of Jesus to a real destruction and rebuilding of the national sanctuary, cannot be approved without imputing to Jesus an extravagant example of vain-glorious boasting, at variance with the character which he elsewhere exhibits. If on this account search be made for some figurative meaning which may possibly be assigned to the declaration, there presents itself first a passage in the same gospel (iv. 21 ff.) where Jesus announces to the woman of Samaria, that the time is immediately coming, in which the Father will no longer be worshipped exclusively in Jerusalem (ἐν Ἱεροσολύμοις), but will, as a Spirit, receive spiritual worship. Now in the present passage also, the destruction of the temple might, it is said, have signified the abolition of the temple-service at Jerusalem, supposed to be the only valid mode of worship. This interpretation is confirmed by a narrative in the Acts (vi. 14). Stephen, who, as it appears, had adopted the above expressions of Jesus, was taxed by his accusers with declaring, *that Jesus of Nazareth shall destroy this place, and shall change the customs which Moses delivered,* ὅτι Ἰησοῦς ὁ Ναζωραῖος οὗτος καταλύσει τὸν τόπον τοῦτον, καὶ ἀλλάξει τὰ ἔθη, ἃ παρέδωκε Μωϋσῆς : in which words a change of the Mosaic religious institutions, without doubt a spiritualization of them, is described as a sequel to the destruction of the temple. To this may be added a passage in the synoptical gospels. Nearly the same words which in John are uttered by Jesus himself, appear in the two first gospels (Matt. xxvi. 60 f. ; Mark xiv. 57 f.) as the accusation of false witnesses against him ; and here Mark, in addition, designates the temple which is to be destroyed, as one *made with hands,* χειροποίητος, and the new one which is to be built, as *another, made without hands,* ἄλλος, ἀχειροποίητος, whereby he appears to indicate the same contrast between a ceremonial and a spiritual religious system. By the aid of these passages, it is thought, the declaration in John may be explained thus : the sign of my authority to purify the temple, is my ability in a short time to introduce in the place of the Jewish ceremonial worship, a spiritual service of God ; i.e. I am authorized to reform the old system, in so far as I am qualified to found a new one. It is certainly a trivial objection to this explanation, that in John the object is not changed, as in Mark, where the temple which is to be built is spoken of as *another* (ἄλλος), but instead of this, is indicated by the word αὐτὸς, as the same with the one destroyed ;[5] since, indeed, the Christian system of religion in relation to the Jewish, may, just as the risen body of Jesus in relation to the dead one, be conceived as at once identical and different, inasmuch as in both cases the substance is the same, while the transitory accidents only are supposed to be removed. But it is a more formidable objection which attaches itself to the determination of time, ἐν τρισὶν ἡμέραις. That this expression is also used indefinitely and proverbially, in the sense of a short

[3] Henke, *Joannes apostolus nonnullorum Jesu apophthegmatum in evang. suo et ipse interpres.* In Pott's and Ruperti's Sylloge Comm. theol. 1, s. 9 ; Gabler, Recension des Henke'schen Programms im neuesten theol. Journal, 2, 1, s. 88 ; Lücke, in loc.

[4] Thus, besides Henke in the above Programm, Herder, von Gottes Sohn nach Johannes Evang., s. 135 f. ; Paulus, Comm. 4, s. 165 f. ; L. J. 1, a, s. 173 f. ; Lücke, and De Wette, in loc.

[5] Storr, in Flatt's Magazin, 4, s. 199.

interval of time in general, is not adequately proved by the two passages which are usually appealed to with this view ; for in them the third day, by being placed in connexion with the second and first (Hos. vi. 2 : מִיָּמִים בַּיּוֹם הַשְּׁלִישִׁי ; Luke xiii. 32 : σήμερον καὶ αὔριον καὶ τῇ τρίτῃ) is announced as a merely relative and proximate statement, whereas in our passage it stands alone, and thus presents itself as an absolute and precise determination of time.[6]

Thus alike invited and repelled by both explanations,[7] theologians take refuge in a double sense, which holds the middle place either between the interpretation of John and the symbolical one last stated,[8] or between the interpretation of John and that of the Jews ; [9] so that Jesus either spoke at once of his body which was to be killed and again restored to life, and of the modification of the Jewish religion which was to be effected, chiefly by means of that death and resurrection ; or, in order to repel the Jews, he challenged them to destroy their real temple, and on this condition, never to be fulfilled, promised to build another, still, however, combining with this ostensible sense for the multitude, an esoteric sense, which was only understood by the disciples after the resurrection, and according to which ναὸς denoted his body. But such a challenge addressed to the Jews, together with the engagement appended to it, would have been an unbecoming manifestation of petulance, and the latent intimation to the disciples, a useless play on words ; besides that, in general, a double meaning either of the one or the other kind is unheard of in the discourse of a judicious man.[10] As, in this manner, the possibility of explaining the passage in John might be entirely despaired of, the author of the Probabilia appeals to the fact that the synoptists call the witnesses, who allege before the judgment seat that Jesus had uttered that declaration, ψευδομάρτυρας, *false witnesses* ; whence he concludes, that Jesus never said what John here attributes to him, and thus gains an exemption from the explanation of the passage, since he regards it as a figment of the fourth Evangelist, whose object was both to explain the calumniations of the accusers, and also to nullify them by a mystical interpretation of his words.[11] But, on the one hand, it does not follow, from the fact that the synoptists call the witnesses false, that, in the opinion of the Evangelists, Jesus had never said anything whatever of that whereof they accused him ; for he might only have said it somewhat differently (λύσατε, not λύσω), or have intended it in a different sense (figuratively instead of literally) : on the other hand, if he said nothing at all of this kind, it is difficult to explain how the false witnesses should come to choose that declaration, and especially the remarkable phrase, ἐν τρισὶν ἡμέραις.

If, according to this, on every interpretation of the expression, except the inadmissible one relative to the body of Jesus, the words ἐν τρισὶν ἡμέραις form a difficulty : a resource might be found in the narrative of the Acts, as being free from that determination of time. For here Stephen is only accused of saying, ὅτι Ἰ. ὁ Ναζ. οὗτος καταλύσει τὸν τόπον τοῦτον (τὸν ἅγιον), καὶ ἀλλάξει τὰ ἔθη ἃ παρέδωκε Μωϋσῆς. What is *false* in this allegation (for the witnesses against Stephen also are described as μάρτυρες ψευδεῖς), might be the

---

[6] Tholuck and Olshausen, in loc.
[7] Hence Neander remains suspended in indecision between the two, s. 395 f.
[8] Thus Kern, die Hauptthatsachen der evang. Gesch., Tüb. Zeitschrift, 1836, 2, s. 128.
[9] Thus Olshausen.
[10] Kern says, indeed, that a similar doubleness of meaning is found elsewhere in significant discourse ; but he refrains from adducing an example.
[11] Probab., p. 23 ff.

second proposition, which speaks in literal terms of a changing of the institutes of Moses, and instead of this, Stephen, and before him Jesus, may very probably have said in the figurative signification above developed, καὶ πάλιν οἰκοδομήσει (—σω) αὐτὸν, or καὶ ἄλλον (ἀχειροποίητον) οἰκοδομήσει (—σω). Meanwhile, this expedient is not at all needful, so far as any insurmountable difficulty in the words ἐν τρισὶν ἡμέραις, is concerned. As the number 3 is used proverbially, not only in connexion with 2 or 4 (Prov. xxx. 15, 18, 21, 29 ; Wis. xxiii. 21, xxvi. 25), but also by itself (Wis. xxv. 1, 3) ; so the expression, *in three days*, if it were once, in combination with the second and first day, become common as an indefinite statement of time, might probably at length be applied in the same sense when standing alone. Whether the expression should signify a long or a short period would then depend on the connexion : here, in opposition to the construction of a great and elaborate building, to the real, natural erection of which, as the Jews directly remark, a long series of years was required, the expression can only be understood as denoting the shortest time.[12] A prediction, or even a mere intimation of the resurrection, is therefore not contained in these words.

As, here, Jesus is said to have intimated his resurrection beforehand, by the image of the destroying and rebuilding of the temple, so, on another occasion, he is supposed to have quoted the type of the prophet Jonah with the same intention (Matt. xii. 39 ff., comp. xvi. 4 ; Luke xi 29 ff.). When the scribes and Pharisees desired to see a sign from him, Jesus is said to have repulsed their demand by the reply, that to so evil a *generation* γενεὰ no sign shall be given, but *the sign of the prophet Jonah*, τὸ σημεῖον Ἰωνᾶ τοῦ προφήτου, which, in the first passage of Matthew, Jesus himself explains thus : as Jonah was three days and three nights *in the belly of the whale*, ἐν τῇ κοιλίᾳ τοῦ κήτους, so also the Son of man will pass three days and three nights in the *heart of the earth*, ἐν τῇ καρδίᾳ τῆς γῆς. In the second passage, in which Matthew attributes this declaration to Jesus, he does not repeat the above interpretation ; while Luke, in the parallel passage, explains it simply thus : *For as Jonah was a sign to the Ninevites, so shall also the Son of man be to this generation.* Now against the possibility of Jesus having himself given the interpretation of the sign of Jonah which Matthew puts into his mouth, v. 40, a variety of objections may be urged. It is indeed scarcely a tenable argument, that Jesus cannot have spoken of three days and three nights, which he would pass in the heart of the earth, because he only lay in the grave one day and two nights :[13] since the phraseology of the New Testament decidedly has the peculiarity of designating the abode of Jesus in the grave as of three days' duration, because it touched upon the evening of the day before the Sabbath, and the morning of the day after it ; and if this one day, together with two nights, were once taken for three whole days, it would only be a round way of expressing this completeness, to add to the days the nights also, which, besides, would naturally follow in the comparison with the three days and three nights of Jonah.[14] But if Jesus gave the explanation of the sign of Jonah which Matthew attributes to him, this would have been so clear a prediction of his resurrection, that for the same reasons which, according to the above observations, are opposed to the literal predictions of that event, we must conclude that Jesus cannot have given this explanation. At all events it must have led the disciples who, according to v. 49, were present, to question Jesus, and in that case it is not to be understood why he did not make the subject perfectly clear, and thus announce his resurrection in plain

[12] Comp. Neander, s. 396, Anm.
[13] Paulus, exeg. Handb. in loc.
[14] Comp. Fritzsche and Olshausen, in loc.

words. But if he cannot have done this, because then the disciples could
not have acted after his death as they are said to have done in the evangelical
accounts : neither can he, by that comparison of the fate which awaited him
with that of Jonah, have called forth from his disciples a question, which, if
proposed to him, he must have answered ; but which, judging from the sequel,
he cannot have answered.

On these grounds, modern critics have pronounced the explanation of the
σημεῖον Ἰωνᾶ in Matthew to be an interpretation made *post eventum* by the
Evangelist, and by him falsely attributed to Jesus.[15]   According to them,
Jesus indeed directed the attention of the Pharisees to the *sign of Jonah*, but
only in the sense in which Luke makes him explain it : namely, that as Jonah
himself, by his mere appearance and preaching of repentance, without miracles, had sufficed as a sign from God to the Ninevites ; so his own cotemporaries, instead of craving for miracles, should be satisfied with his person and
preaching.   This interpretation is the only one which accords with the tenor
of the discourse of Jesus—even in Matthew, and more particularly with the
parallel between the relation of the Ninevites to Jonah, and that of the queen
of the south to Solomon.   As it was the *wisdom of Solomon*, σοφία Σολομῶνος,
by which the latter felt herself attracted from the ends of the earth : so, in
Jonah, even according to the expression of Matthew, it was solely his *preaching*, κήρυγμα, which brought the Ninevites to repentance.   It might be supposed that the future tense in Luke : οὕτως ἔσται καὶ ὁ υἱὸς τ. ἀ. τῇ γενεᾷ
ταύτῃ (σημεῖον), *So shall also the Son of Man be to this generation (a sign)*,
cannot be referred to Jesus and his preaching as manifested at that moment,
but only to something future, as his resurrection : but this in reality points
either to the future *judgment* κρίσις, in which it will be made manifest, that as
Jonah was reckoned a sign to the Ninevites, so was the Son of Man to the
Jews then living ; or to the fact that when Jesus spoke these words, his
appearance had not yet attained its consummation, and many of its stages lay
yet in futurity.   Nevertheless, it must have been at an early period, as we see
from the first gospel, that the fate of Jonah was placed in a typical relation to
the death and resurrection of Jesus, since the primitive church anxiously
searched through the Old Testament for types and prophecies of the offensive
catastrophe which befel their Messiah.

There are still some expressions of Jesus in the fourth gospel, which have
been understood as latent prophecies of the resurrection.   The discourse on
the *corn of wheat*, xii. 24, it is true, too obviously relates to the work of Jesus
as likely to be furthered by his death, to be here taken into further consideration.   But in the farewell discourses in John there are some declarations,
which many are still inclined to refer to the resurrection.   When Jesus says :
*I will not leave you comfortless, I will come unto you ; yet a little time, and the
world sees me no more, but ye see me ; a little while, and ye shall not see me,
and again a little while and ye shall see me*, etc. (xiv. 18 ff., xvi. 16 ff.) ; many
believe that these expressions—with the relation between μικρὸν καὶ πάλιν
μικρὸν, *a little while, and again a little while* ; the opposition between
ἐμφανίζειν ἡμῖν (τοῖς μαθηταῖς) καὶ οὐχὶ τῷ κόσμῳ, *manifest to you (the disciples)
and not to the world* ; the words πάλιν ὄψομαι and ὄψεσθε, *I shall see you
again, and ye shall see*, which appear to indicate a strictly personal interview
—can be referred to nothing else than the resurrection, which was precisely
such a reappearance after a short removal, and moreover a personal reappearance granted to the friends of Jesus alone.[16]   But this promised reappearance

[15] Paulus, exeg. Handb. 2, s. 97 ff.   Schulz, über das Abendm., s. 317 f.
[16] Süskind, ut sup. s. 184 ff.

is at the same time described by Jesus in a manner which will not suit the days of the resurrection. If the words *because I live*, ὅτι ἐγὼ ζῶ (xiv. 19), denote his resurrection, we are at a loss to know what can be meant by the succeeding clause, *ye shall live also*, καὶ ὑμεῖς ζήσεσθε. Again, Jesus says that on that reappearance his disciples will know his relation to the Father, and will no more need to ask anything of him (xiv. 20, xvi. 23): yet even on the very last day of their intercourse with him after the resurrection, they ask a question of him (Acts i. 6), and one which from the point of view of the fourth gospel is altogether senseless. Lastly, when he promises that to him who loves him, he and the Father will come, and make their abode with him, it is perfectly clear that Jesus here speaks not of a corporeal return, but of his spiritual return, through the παράκλητος.[17] Nevertheless, even this explanation has its difficulties, since, on the other hand, the expressions *ye shall see me*, ὄψεσθέ με, and *I shall see you*, ὄψομαι ὑμᾶς, will not entirely suit that purely spiritual return : hence we must defer the solution of this apparent contradiction until we can give a more complete elucidation of the discourses in which these expressions occur. In the meantime we merely observe, that the farewell discourses in John, being admitted, even by the friends of the fourth gospel, to contain an intermixture of the Evangelist's own thoughts, are the last source from which to obtain a proof on this subject.

After all, there might seem to be a resource in the supposition, that though Jesus did not indeed speak of his future resurrection, it was not the less foreknown by him. Now if he had a foreknowledge of his resurrection, either he obtained it in a supernatural manner, by means of the prophetic spirit, the higher principle that dwelt within him—by means of his divine nature, if that be preferred : or he knew it in a natural manner, by the exercise of his human reason. But a supernatural foreknowledge of that event, as well as of his death, is inconceivable, owing to the relation in which Jesus places it to the Old Testament. Not merely in passages such as Luke xviii. 31 (which, as prophecies, can no longer have an historical value for us after the result of our last inquiry), does Jesus represent his resurrection, together with his passion and death, as a fulfilment of *all things that are written by the prophets concerning the Son of man*, πάντων τῶν γεγραμμένων διὰ τῶν προφητῶν τῷ υἱῷ τοῦ ἀνθρώπου ; but even after the issue, he admonishes his disciples that they ought to believe *all that the prophets have spoken*, ἐπὶ πᾶσιν οἷς ἐλάλησαν οἱ προφῆται, namely, that *Christ ought to have suffered these things and to enter into his glory*, ταῦτα ἔδει παθεῖν τὸν Χριστὸν, καὶ εἰσελθεῖν εἰς τὴν δόξαν αὐτοῦ (Luke xxiv. 25 f.). According to the sequel of the narrative, Jesus forthwith expounded to these disciples (going to Emmaus) all the passages of scripture relating to himself, *beginning at Moses and all the prophets*, ἀρξάμενος ἀπὸ Μωσέως καὶ ἀπὸ πάντων τῶν προφητῶν, to which farther on (v. 44) the *psalms* are added ; but no single passage is given us as having been interpreted by Jesus of his resurrection, except that it would follow from Matt. xii. 39 f., that he regarded the fate of the prophet Jonah as a type of his own ; and regarding the subsequent apostolic interpretation as an echo of that of Jesus, it might be concluded, that he, as afterwards the apostles, found such prophecies chiefly in Ps. xvi. 8 ff. (Acts ii. 25 ff., xiii. 35); Isa. liii. (Acts viii. 32 ff.); Isa. lv. 3 (Acts xiii. 34), and possibly also in Hos. vi. 2. But the fate of Jonah has not even an external similarity to that of Jesus ; and the book which narrates his history carries its object so completely in itself, that whoever may ascribe to it or to one of its particulars, a typical relation to events in futurity, assuredly mistakes its true sense and the design of its author.

---

[17] Vid. Lücke, in loc.

Isa. lv. 3 is so obviously irrelevant that one can scarcely conceive how the passage could be brought into special connexion with the resurrection of Jesus. Isa. liii. refers decidedly to a collective subject perpetually restored to life in new members. Hosea vi. has a figurative reference, not to be mistaken, to the people and state of Israel. Lastly, the principal passage, Ps. xvi. can only be interpreted of a pious man, who by the help of Jehovah hopes to escape from the danger of death, not in the sense that he, like Jesus, would rise again from the grave, but that he would not be laid there—that is, obviously, not for the present, and with the understanding, that when his time should come, he must pay the tribute of nature : [18] which, again, will not apply to Jesus. Thus if a supernatural principle in Jesus—a prophetic spirit —caused him to discover a pre-intimation of his resurrection in these Old Testament histories and passages ; then, as no one of them really contained such a pre-intimation, the spirit in him cannot have been the spirit of truth, but must have been a lying spirit, the supernatural principle in him, not a divine, but a demoniacal principle. If, in order to avoid this consequence, supranaturalists who are accessible to a rational interpretation of the Old Testament, resort to their only remaining expedient, of regarding the foreknowledge of Jesus concerning his resurrection as purely natural and human : we must reply, that the resurrection, conceived as a miracle, was a secret of the divine counsels, to penetrate into which, prior to the issue, was an impossibility to a human intelligence ; while viewed as a natural result, it was a chance the last to be calculated upon, apart from the supposition of an apparent death planned by Jesus and his colleagues.

Thus the foreknowledge, as well as the prediction of the resurrection, was attributed to Jesus only after the issue ; and in fact, it was an easy matter, with the groundless arbitrariness of Jewish exegesis, for the disciples and the anthors of the New Testament to discover in the Old, types and prophecies of the resurrection. Not that they did this with crafty design, according to the accusation of the Wolfenbüttel Fragmentist, and others of his class : but as he who has looked at the sun, long sees its image wherever he may turn his gaze ; so they, blinded by their enthusiasm for the new Messiah, saw him on every page of the only book they read, the Old Testament, and in the conviction that Jesus was the Messiah, founded in the genuine feeling that he had satisfied their deepest need—a conviction and a feeling which we also still honour—they laid hold on supports which have long been broken, and which can no longer be made tenable by the most zealous efforts of an exegesis which is behind the age.

§ 115.

THE DISCOURSES OF JESUS ON HIS SECOND ADVENT. CRITICISM OF THE DIFFERENT INTERPRETATIONS.

Not only did Jesus, according to the evangelical accounts, predict that he should return to life three days after his death ; but also that at a later period, in the midst of the calamities which would issue in the destruction of the temple in Jerusalem, he should come in the clouds of heaven, to close the present period of the world, and by a general judgment, open the future age (Matt. xxiv. and xxv. ; Mark. xiii. ; Luke xvii. 22–37, xxi. 5–36).

As Jesus for the last time went out of the temple (Luke has not this circumstance), and his disciples (Luke says indefinitely, *some*) admiringly drew

---

[18] Vid. de Wette, Comm. über die Psalmen, s. 178.

his attention to the magnificent building, he assured them that all which they then looked on, would be destroyed from its foundations (Matt. xxiv. 1, 2, parall.). On the question of the disciples, when this would happen, and what would be the sign of the Messiah's coming, which in their idea was associated with such a crisis (v. 3), Jesus warns them not to be deceived by persons falsely giving themselves out to be the Messiah, and by the notion that the expected catastrophe must follow immediately on the first prognostics ; for wars and rumours of war, risings of nation against nation and kingdom against kingdom, famine, pestilence, and earthquakes in divers places, would be only the beginning of the sorrows which were to precede the advent of the Messiah (v. 4–8). They themselves, his adherents, must first suffer hatred, persecution, and the sword ; perfidy, treachery, deception by false prophets, lukewarmness and general corruption of morals, would prevail among men ; but at the same time the news of the Messiah's kingdom must be promulgated through the whole world.   Only after all this, could the end of the present period of the world arrive, until when, he who would partake of the blessedness of the future must endure with constancy (v. 9–14). A nearer presage of this catastrophe would be the fulfilment of the oracle of Daniel (ix. 27), the standing of the abomination of desolation in the holy place (according to Luke xxi. 20, the encompassing of Jerusalem with armies). When this should take place, it would be high time for the most precipitate flight (according to Luke, because the devastation of Jerusalem would be at hand, an event which he more nearly particularizes in the address of Jesus to the city, xix. 43 f. : *thine enemies shall cast a trench about thee, and compass thee round, and keep thee in on every side, and shall lay thee even with the ground, and thy children within thee; and they shall not leave in thee one stone upon another*).   At this juncture, all who should have hindrances to rapid departure would be deserving of compassion, and it would be in the highest degree desirable that the recommended flight should not fall in an unfavourable season; for then would commence unexampled tribulation (according to Luke, v. 24, consisting chiefly in many of the people of Israel perishing by the sword, in others being carried away captive, and in Jerusalem being trodden down of the Gentiles for a predetermined period) : a tribulation which only the merciful abridgment of its duration by God, for the sake of the elect, could render supportable (v. 15–22).   At this time would arise false prophets and Messiahs, seeking to delude by miracles and signs, and promising to show the Messiah in this or that place : whereas a Messiah who was concealed anywhere, and must be sought out, could not be the true one ; for his advent would be like the lightning, a sudden and universal revelation, of which the central point would be Jerusalem, the object of punishment on account of its sin (v. 23–28).   Immediately after this time of tribulation, the darkening of the sun and moon, the falling of the stars, and the shaking of all the powers of heaven would usher in the appearance of the Messiah, who, to the dismay of the dwellers on the earth, would come with great glory in the clouds of heaven, and immediately send forth his angels to gather together his elect from all the corners of the earth (v. 29–31).   By the fore-named signs the approach of the described catastrophe would be as certainly discernible as the approach of summer by the budding of the fig-tree ; the existing generation would, by all that was true, live to witness it, though its more precise period was known to God only (v. 32–36).   But, after the usual manner of mankind (what follows, Mark and Luke partly have not at all, partly not in this connexion), they would allow the advent of the Messiah, as formerly the deluge, to overtake them in thoughtless security (v. 37–39) : and yet it would be an extremely critical period, in which those who stood in the closest relation to each other, would be delivered over to entirely opposite destinies (v. 40, 41). Hence watchfulness would be requisite, as in all cases where the period of a decisive issue is uncertain : an admonition which is then illustrated by the image of the master of the house and the thief (v. 43, 44) ; of the servant to whom his lord, when about to travel, entrusted the rule of his house (v. 45–51) ; of the wise and foolish virgins (xxv. 1–13) : and lastly, of the talents (v. 14–30). Hereupon follows a description of the solemn judgment, which the Messiah would hold over all nations, and in which, according as the duties of humanity were observed or neglected, he would award blessedness or misery (v. 31–46).[1]

Thus in these discourses Jesus announces that *shortly* (εὐθέως, xxiv. 29), after that calamity, which (especially according to the representation in Luke's gospel) we must identify with the destruction of Jerusalem and its temple, and within the term of the cotemporary generation (ἡ γενεὰ αὕτη, v. 34), he would visibly make his second advent in the clouds, and terminate the existing dispensation. Now as it will soon be eighteen centuries since the destruction of Jerusalem, and an equally long period since the generation cotemporary with Jesus disappeared from the earth, while his visible return and the end of the world which he associated with it, have not taken place : the announcement of Jesus appears so far to have been erroneous. Already in the first age of Christianity, when the return of Christ was delayed longer than had been anticipated, there arose, according to 2 Peter iii. 3 f., scoffers, asking : *where is the promise of his coming? for since the fathers fell asleep, all things continue as they were from the beginning of the creation.* In modern times, the inference which may apparently be drawn from the above consideration, to the disadvantage of Jesus and the apostles, has been by no one more pointedly expressed than by the Wolfenbüttel Fragmentist. No promise throughout the whole scriptures, he thinks, is on the one hand more definitely expressed, and on the other, has turned out more flagrantly false, than this, which yet forms one of the main pillars of Christianity. And he does not see in this a mere error, but a premeditated deception on the part of the apostles (to whom, and not to Jesus himself, he attributes that promise, and the discourses in which it is contained) ; a deception induced by the necessity of alluring the people on whose contributions they wished to subsist, by the promise of a speedy reward : and discernible by the boldness of their attempts to evade the doubts springing from the protracted delay of the return of Christ : Paul, for example, in the second epistle to the Thessalonians, sheltering himself in obscure phrases ; and Peter, in his second epistle, resorting to the preposterous expedient of appealing to the divine mode of reckoning time, in which a thousand years are equal to one day.[2] *

Such inferences from the discourse before us would inflict a fatal wound on

---

[1] Compare, on the import and connexion of this discourse, Fritzsche, in Matth., p. 695 ff; De Wette, exeg. Handb., I, 1, s. 197 ff ; Weizel, die unchristliche Unsterblichkeitslehre, in the theol. Studien und Kritiken, 1836, s. 599 ff.—In agreement with these commentators I append the following division of the passage in Matthew :

I. Signs of the *end*, τέλος, xxiv. 4–14.

   a. More remote signs, *the beginning of sorrows*, ἀρχὴ ὠδίνων, 4–8.

   b. More immediate signs, the actual sorrows, 9–14.

II. The *end*, τέλος, itself, xxiv. 15–25, 46.

   a. Its commencement with the destruction of Jerusalem, and the great *tribulation* θλῖψις which accompanies it, 15–28.

   b. Its culminating point : the advent of the Messiah, together with the assembling of his elect, 29–31. (Here follow retrospective observations and warnings, xxiv. 32–xxv. 30.)

   c. Close of the τέλος with the messianic judgment, 31–46.

[2] Vom Zweck Jesu und seiner Jünger, s. 184, 201 ff., 207 ff.

Christianity ; hence it is natural that exegetists should endeavour by all means to obviate them.* And as the whole difficulty consists in Jesus having apparently placed an event now long past, in immediate chronological connexion with one still future, three expedients are possible : either to deny that Jesus in part spoke of something now past, and to allege that he spoke solely of what is still future ; or to deny that a part of his discourse relates to something still future, and thus to refer the entire prediction to what is already lying in the past ; or lastly, to admit that the discourse of Jesus does indeed partly refer to something which is still future to us, but either to deny that he places the two series of events in immediate chronological succession, or to maintain that he has also noticed what is intermediate.

Some of the Fathers of the Church, as Irenæus and Hilary—yet living in the primitive expectation of the return of Christ, and at the same time not so practised in regular exegesis, as to be incapable of overlooking certain difficulties attendant on a desirable interpretation—referred the entire prediction, from its commencement in Matt. xxiv. to its end in Matt. xxv., to the still future return of Christ to judgment.[3] But as this interpretation admits that Jesus in the commencement of his discourse uses the destruction of Jerusalem as a type of the final catastrophe, it virtually nullifies itself. For what does that admission signify, but that the discourse of Jesus, in the first instance, produces the impression that he spoke of the destruction of Jerusalem, i.e. of something now past, and that only more extended reflection and combination can give it a relation to something still lying in futurity ?

To modern rationalism, based as it was on naturalistic principles, the hope of the second advent of Christ was in every form annihilated. Hence, not scrupling at any exegetical violence for the sake of removing from scripture what was discordant with its preconceived system, it threw itself on the opposite side, and hazarded the attempt to refer the discourses in question, in their entire tenor, solely to the destruction of Jerusalem, and the events which immediately preceded and followed it.[4] According to this interpretation, the *end* spoken of is only the cessation of the Judeo-Gentile economy of the world ; what is said of the advent of Christ in the clouds, is only a figurative description of the promulgation and triumph of his doctrine ; the assembling of the nations to judgment, and the sending of some into blessedness, and others into condemnation, is an image of the happy consequences which would result from embracing the doctrine and cause of Jesus, and the evil consequences attendant on indifference or hostility to them. But in this explanation there is a want of similarity between the symbols and the ideas represented, which is not only unprecedented in itself, but particularly inconceivable in this case ; since Jesus is here addressing minds of Jewish culture, and must therefore be aware that what he said of the Messiah's advent in the clouds, of the judgment, and the end of the existing period of the world, would be understood in the most literal sense.

It thus appears that the discourse of Jesus will not as a whole, admit of being referred either to the destruction of the Jewish state, or to the events at the end of the world ; it would therefore be necessarily referred to something distinct from both, if this twofold impossibility adhered alike to all its parts. But the case is not so ; for while, on the one hand, what is said Matt. xxiv. 2, 3, 15 ff. of the devastation of the temple, cannot be referred to the end of the

---

[3] The former *adv. hæres.* v. 25 ; the latter, Comm. in Matth. in loc. Compare on the different interpretations of this passage the list in Schott, *Commentarius in eos J. Chr. sermones, qui de reditu ejus ad judicium—agunt,* p. 73 ff.

[4] Bahrdt., Uebersetzung des N. T., 1, s. 1103, 3te Ausg. ; Eckermann, Handb. der Glaubenslehre, 2, s. 579, 3, s. 427, 437, 709 ff ; and others in Schott, ut sup.

world : on the other hand, what is predicted xxv. 31 ff. of the judgment to be held by the Son of Man, will not suit the destruction of Jerusalem. As, according to this, in the earlier part of the discourse of Jesus, the destruction of Jerusalem is the predominant subject, but in the subsequent part, the end of all things : it is possible to make a division, so as to refer the former to the more proximate event, the latter to the more remote one. This is the middle path which has been taken by the majority of modern exegetists, and here the only question is : where is the partition to be made? As it must present a space of time within which the whole period from the destruction of Jerusalem to the last day may be supposed to fall, and which therefore would include many centuries, it must, one would think, be plainly indicated, so as to be easily and unanimously found. It is no good augury for the plan, that this unanimity does not exist,—that, on the contrary, the required division is made in widely different parts of the discourse of Jesus.

Thus much on the one hand appeared to be decided : that at least the close of the 25th chapter, from v. 31, with its description of the solemn tribunal which the Messiah, surrounded by his angels, would hold over all nations, cannot be referred to the time of the destruction of Jerusalem. Hence many theologians believed that they could fix the boundary here, retaining the relation to the end of the Jewish state until xxv. 30, and at this point making the transition to the end of the world.[5] On the very first glance at this explanation, it must appear strange that the great chasm which it supposes to exist between v. 30 and 31, is marked simply by a δέ. Moreover, not only are the darkening of the sun and moon, earthquakes, and falling of the stars, understood as a mere image of the subversion of the Jewish state and worship; but when xxiv. 31, it is said of the Messiah, that he will *come in the clouds*, this is supposed to mean, invisibly ; *with power*—only observable by the effects he produces ; *with great glory*—with such as consists in the conclusions which may be drawn from those effects ; while the *angels* who gather together the nations by the sound of the trumpet, are supposed to represent the apostles preaching the gospel.[6] Quite erroneously, appeal is made, in support of this merely figurative meaning, to the prophetic pictures of the divine day of judgment, Isa. xiii. 9 ff., xxiv. 18 ff.; Jer. iv. 23 f. ; Ezek. xxxii. 7 ff. ; Joel iii. 3 ff. ; Amos viii. 9 ; farther, to descriptions[7] such as Judges v. 20 ; Acts ii., xvii. ff. In those prophetic passages, real eclipses of the sun and moon, earthquakes, and the like, are intended, and are described as prodigies which will accompany the predicted catastrophe ; the song of Deborah, again, celebrates a real participation of heaven in the battle against Sisera, a participation which in the narrative, iv. 15, is ascribed to God himself, in the song, to his heavenly hosts ; lastly, Peter expects, that the outpouring of the spirit will be succeeded by the appearances in the heavens, promised among the signs of the *great day of the Lord*.

The attempt to effect a division near the end of the discourse, at xxv. 30, failing, from its rendering much that goes before incapable of explanation ; the next expedient is to retreat as far towards the commencement as possible, by considering how far it is inevitable to recognise a relation to the immediate future. The first resting place is after xxiv. 28 ; for what is said, up to this point, of war and other calamities, of the abomination in the temple, of the

---

[5] This is the opinion of Lightfoot, in loc., Flatt, *Comm. de notione vocis βασιλεία τῶν οὐρανῶν*, in Velthusen's und A. Sammlung 2, 461 ff. ; Jahn, Erklärung der Weissagungen Jesu von der Zerstörung Jerusalem u. s. w., in Bengel's Archiv. 2, 1, s. 79 ff., and others, cited in Schott, s. 75 f.

[6] Thus especially Jahn, in the treatise above cited.

[7] Kern, Hauptthatsachen der evang. Geschichte, Tüb. Zeitschr. 1836, 2, s. 140 ff.

necessity for speedy flight, in order to escape unprecedented misery, cannot
be divested of a reference to the destruction of Jerusalem without the greatest
violence : while what follows concerning the appearance of the Son of Man
in the clouds, etc., just as imperatively demands an application to the last
day.[8] But in the first place, it appears incomprehensible how the enormous
interval, which on this explanation also is supposed to fall between the one
portion of the discourse and the other, can be introduced between two verses,
of all others, which Matthew connects by an adverb expressive of the shortest
possible time (εὐθέως). It has been sought to remove this inconvenience by
the assertion that εὐθέως does not here signify the quick succession of the one
incident on the other, but only the unexpected occurrence of an event, and
that consequently, what is here said amounts merely to this : suddenly, at
some period (how distant is undetermined) after the calamities attendant on
the destruction of Jerusalem, the Messiah will visibly appear. Such an interpretation of εὐθέως is, as Olshausen correctly perceives, merely a desperate
resource : but even were it otherwise, it would afford no real aid, since not
only does Mark in his parallel passage, v. 24, by the words, *in those days,
after that tribulation,* ἐν ἐκείναις ταῖς ἡμέραις μετὰ τὴν θλίψιν ἐκείνην, place the
events which he proceeds to mention in uninterrupted chronological succession
with those which he had before detailed; but also, shortly after this point in
each of the narratives (Matt. v. 34 parall.), we find the assurance that all this
will be witnessed by the existing generation.   As thus the opinion, that from
v. 29, everything relates to the return of Christ to judge the world, was
threatened with annihilation by v. 34 ; the word γενεὰ, as the Wolfenbüttel
Fragmentist[9] complains, was put to the torture, that it might cease to bear
witness against this mode of division.   At one time it is made to signify the
Jewish nation ;[10] at another the adherents of Jesus ;[11] and of both the one
and the other Jesus is supposed to say that it will (how many generations
hence being left uncertain) be still in existence on the arrival of that catastrophe.   So to explain the verse in question, that it may not contain a
determination of time, is even maintained to be necessary on a consideration
of the context, v. 35 : for as in this Jesus declares it impossible to determine
the period of that catastrophe, he cannot immediately before have given such
a determination, in the assurance that his cotemporaries would yet live to see
all of which he had been speaking.   But this alleged necessity so to interpret
the word γενεὰ, has long been dissipated by the distinction between an inexact
indication of the space of time, beyond which the event will not be deferred
(γενεὰ), and the precise determination of the epoch (ἡμέρα καὶ ὥρα) at which it
will occur ; the former Jesus gives, the latter he declares himself unable to
give.[12]   But the very possibility of interpreting γενεὰ in the above manner
vanishes, when it is considered, that in connexion with a verb of time, and
without anything to imply a special application, γενεὰ cannot have any other
than its original sense : i.e. *generation, age ;* that in a passage aiming to
determine the signs of the Messiah's advent, it would be very unsuitable to
introduce a declaration which, instead of giving any information concerning
the arrival of that catastrophe, should rather treat of the duration of the
Jewish nation, or of the Christian community, of which nothing had previously
been said; that, moreover, already at v. 33, in the words ὑμεῖς ὅταν ἴδητε
πάντα ταῦτα, γινώσκετε κ. τ. λ., YE, *when ye shall* SEE *all these things, know,*

  8 Thus Storr, Opusc. acad. 3, s. 34 ff. ; Paulus, exeg. Handb. 3, a, s. 346 f. 402 f.
  9 Ut sup. s. 188.
  10 Storr, ut sup. s. 39, 116 ff.
  11 Paulus, in loc.
  12 Vid. Kuinöl in Matt., s. 649.

etc., it is presupposed that the parties addressed would witness the approach of the event in question ; and lastly, that in another passage (Matt. xvi. 28 parall.) the certainty of living to see the coming of the Son of man is asserted not simply of *this generation*, γενεὰ αὕτη, but of *some standing here*, τινες τῶν ὧδε ἑστηκότων, whereby it is shown in the most decisive manner, that in the present passage also, Jesus intended by the above expression the race of his cotemporaries, who were not to have become extinct before that catastrophe should occur.[13]   Unable to deny this, and yet anxious to separate as widely as possible the end of the world here announced, and the age of Jesus, others would find in the declaration before us nothing more than this : the events hitherto described will *begin* to be fulfilled in the present age, though their complete fulfilment may yet be deferred many centuries.[14]   But when already at v. 8 the subject is said to be the *beginning* of the tribulation, while from v. 14 we have a description of the end of the present period of the world, which that tribulation would introduce, and it is here (v. 34) said, the existing generation shall not pass away, ἕως ἂν πάντα ταῦτα γένηται, *until all these things be fulfilled* : we must inevitably understand by πάντα ταῦτα, *all these things*, not merely the beginning, but also the last-mentioned events at the end of the world.

Thus there is still at v. 34 something which must be referred to an event very near to the time of Jesus : hence the discourse of Jesus cannot from so early a point as v. 29, refer to the end of the world, an epoch so far distant ; and the division must be made somewhat farther on, after v. 35 or 42.[15]   But on this plan, expressions are thrown into the first part of the discourse, which resist the assigned application to the time of the destruction of Jerusalem ;— the glorious advent of Christ in the clouds, and the assembling of all nations by angels (v. 30 f.) must be regarded as the same extravagant figures, which formerly forbade our acceptance of another mode of division.

Thus the declaration v. 34 which, together with the preceding symbolical discourse on the fig tree (v. 32 f.), and the appended asseveration (v. 35), must refer to a very near event, has, both before and after it, expressions which can only relate to the more distant catastrophe : hence it has appeared to some as a sort of oasis in the discourse, having a sense isolated from the immediate context.   Schott, for instance, supposes that, up to v. 26, Jesus had been speaking of the destruction of Jerusalem ; that at v. 27 he does indeed make a transition to the events at the end of the present period of the world ; but that at v. 32, he reverts to the original subject, the destruction of Jerusalem ; and only at v. 36 proceeds again to speak of the end of the world.[16]   But this is to hew the text in pieces, out of desperation.   Jesus cannot possibly have spoken with so little order and coherence ; still less can he have so linked his sentences together as to give no intimation of such abrupt transitions.

---

[13] Comp. the Wolfenbüttel Fragmentist, ut sup. s. 190 ff.   Schott, ut sup. s. 127 ff.

[14] Kern, ut sup. s. 141 f.   That Jesus conceived the epoch at which he spoke to be separated from the end of the world by a far longer interval than would elapse before the destruction of Jerusalem, Kern thinks he can prove in the shortest way from v. 14, of the 24th chapter of Matthew, where Jesus says, *And this gospel of the kingdom shall be preached in all the world for a witness unto all nations, and then shall the end come.*   For such a promulgation of Christianity, he thinks, it is " beyond contradiction " that a far longer space of time than these few lustrums would be requisite.   As it happens, the apostle Paul himself presents the contradiction, when he represents the gospel as having been already preached to that extent before the destruction of Jerusalem, e.g. Col. i. 5 : τοῦ εὐαγγελίου, (6) τοῦ παρόντος—ἐν παντὶ τῷ κόσμῳ—(23)—τοῦ κηρυχθέντος ἐν πάσῃ τῇ κτίσει τῇ ὑπὸ τὸν οὐρανὸν. Comp. Rom. x. 13.

[15] The former is chosen by Süskind, vermischte Aufsätze, s. 90 ff. ; the latter by Kuinöl, in Matth., p. 653 ff.

[16] See his Commentarius, in loc.

Nor is this imputed to him by the most recent critics. According to them, it is the Evangelist who has joined together, not in the best order, distinct and heterogeneous declarations of Jesus. Matthew, indeed, admits Schulz, imagined that these discourses were spoken without intermission, and only arbitrariness and violence can in this respect sever them from each other ; but hardly did Jesus himself deliver them in this consecutive manner, and with this imprint of unity.[17] The various phases of his coming, thinks Sieffert, his figurative appearance at the destruction of Jerusalem, and his literal appearance at the last day, though they may not have been expressly discriminated, were certainly not positively connected by Jesus ; but subjects which he spoke of in succession were, from their obscurity, confused together by the Evangelist.[18] And as in this instance there recurs the difference between Matthew and Luke, that what Matthew represents as being spoken on a single occasion, Luke distributes into separate discourses ; to which it is also to be added, that much of what Matthew gives, Luke either has not, or has it in a different form : therefore Schleiermacher[19] believed himself warranted to rectify the composition of Matthew by that of Luke, and to maintain that while in Luke the two separate discourses, xvii. 22 ff. and xxi. 5 ff., have each their appropriate connexion and their indubitable application, in Matthew (chap. xxiv. and xxv.), by the blending of those two discourses, and the introduction of portions of other discourses, the connexion is destroyed, and the application obscured. According to this, the discourse, Luke xxi., taken alone, contains nothing which outsteps the reference to the capture of Jerusalem and the accompanying events. Yet here also (v. 27) we find the declaration, *Then shall they see the Son of Man coming in a cloud,* τότε ὄψονται τὸν υἱὸν τοῦ ἀνθρώπου ἐρχόμενον ἐν νεφέλῃ ; and when Schleiermacher explains this as a mere image representing the revelation of the religious significance of the political and natural events before described, he falls into a violence of interpretation which overturns his entire opinion as to the mutual relation of these accounts. If, then, in the connexion of the end of all things with the destruction of Jerusalem, Matthew by no means stands alone, but is countenanced by Luke—to say nothing of Mark, whose account in this instance is an extract from Matthew : we may, it is true, conclude, that as in other discourses of Jesus, so perhaps in this also, many things which were uttered at different times are associated ; but there is nothing to warrant the supposition, that precisely what relates to the two events, which in our idea are so remote from each other, is the foreign matter, especially since we see, from the unanimous representation of the remaining New Testament writings, that the primitive church expected, as a speedy issue, the return of Christ, together with the end of the present period of the world (1 Cor. x. 11, xv. 51 ; Phil. iv. 5 ; 1 Thess. iv. 15 ff. ; James v. 8 ; 1 Pet. iv. 7 ; 1 John ii. 18 ; Rev. i. 1, 3, iii. 11, xxii. 7, 10, 12, 20).

Thus it is impossible to evade the acknowledgment, that in this discourse, if we do not mutilate it to suit our own views, Jesus at first speaks of the destruction of Jerusalem, and farther on and until the close, of his return at the end of all things, and that he places the two events in immediate connexion. There remains, therefore, but one expedient for vindicating the correctness of his announcement, namely, on the one hand, to assign the coming of which he speaks to the future, but, on the other hand, to bring it at the same time into the present—instead of a merely future, to make it a

---

[17] Ueber das Abendmahl, s. 315 f.
[18] Ueber den Ursprung des ersten kanon. Evangel., s. 119 ff. Also Weisse, ut sup.
[19] Ueber den Lukas, s. 215 ff., 265 ff. Here also his opinion is approved by Neander, s. 562.

perpetual coming. The whole history of the world, it is said, since the first appearance of Christ, is an invisible return on his part, a spiritual judgment which he holds over mankind. Of this, the destruction of Jerusalem (in our passage until v. 28) is only the first act; in immediate succession (εὐθέως, v. 29 ff.) comes the revolution effected among mankind by the publication of the gospel; a revolution which is to be carried on in a series of acts and epochs, until the end of all things, when the judgment gradually effected in the history of the world, will be made known by an all-comprehending, final revelation.[20] But the famous utterance of the poet,* spoken from the inmost depth of modern conviction, is ill-adapted to become the key of a discourse, which more than any other has its root in the point of view proper to the ancient world. To regard the judgment of the world, the coming of Christ, as something successive, is a mode of conception in the most direct opposition to that of the New Testament. The very expressions by which it designates that catastrophe, as *that day* or *the last day*, ἐκείνη or ἐσχάτη ἡμέρα, show that it is to be thought of as momentary; the συντέλεια τοῦ αἰῶνος, *end of the age* (v. 3), concerning the signs of which the apostles inquire, and which Jesus elsewhere (Matt. xiii. 39) represents under the image of the harvest, can only be the final close of the course of the world, not something which is gradually effected during this course; when Jesus compares his coming to lightning (xxiv. 27), and to the entrance of the thief in the night (v. 43), he represents it as one sudden event, and not as a series of events.[21] If we consider in addition to this the extravagant figures, which it is not less necessary to suppose on this interpretation, than on the above-mentioned reference of the 24th chapter to the destruction of Jerusalem,[22] it will appear necessary to abstain from this expedient, as from all the previous ones.†

Thus the last attempt to discover in the discourse before us the immense interval which, looking from our position in the present day, is fixed between the destruction of Jerusalem and the end of all things, having failed; we are taught practically that that interval lies only in our own conception, which we are not justified in introducing into the text. And when we consider that we owe our idea of that interval only to the experience of many centuries, which have elapsed since the destruction of Jerusalem: it cannot be difficult to us to imagine how the author of this discourse, who had not had this experience, might entertain the belief that shortly after the fall of the Jewish sanctuary, the world itself, of which, in the Jewish idea, that sanctuary was the centre, would also come to an end, and the Messiah appear in judgment.

---

[20] Olshausen, bibl. Comm. 1, s. 865 ; Kern, ut sup. s. 138 ff. Comp. Steudel Glaubensl. s. 479 ff.

[* " Die Weltgeschichte ist das Weltgericht : " Schiller. TR.]

[21] Comp. especially Weizel, die Zeit des jüngsten Tags u. s. f. in den Studien der evang. Geistlichkeit Würtembergs, 9, 2, s. 140 ff., 154 ff.

[22] According to Kern, the appearing of the Son of Man in the clouds, signifies "the manifestation of everything which forms so great an epoch in the development of the history of mankind, that from it, the agency of Christ, who is the governing power in the history of mankind, may be as clearly recognised as if the sign of Christ were seen in the heavens. The mourning of all the tribes of the earth is to be understood of the sorrow with which men will be visited, owing to the *judgment*, κρίσις, which accompanies the propagation of the kingdom of Christ, as consisting in an expulsion of ungodliness out of the world, and the annihilation of the old man." Still further does Weisse allow himself to be carried away by the allegorizing propensity : Christ "commiserates those who are with child and who give suck, i.e. those who would still labour and produce in the old order of things ; he further pities those whose flight falls in the winter, i.e. in a rude, inhospitable period, which bears no fruit for the spirit." (Die evang. Gesch. 2, s. 592.)

§ 116.

ORIGIN OF THE DISCOURSES ON THE SECOND ADVENT.

The result just obtained involves a consequence, to avoid which has been the object of all the futile attempts at explanation hitherto examined : if, namely, Jesus conceived and declared that the fall of the Jewish sanctuary would be shortly followed by his visible return and the end of the world, while it is now nearly 1800 years since the one catastrophe, and yet the other has not arrived ; it follows that in this particular he was mistaken. Hence expositors, who so far yield to exegetical evidence, as to agree with us in the above conclusion concerning the meaning of the discourse before us, seek from dogmatical considerations to evade this legitimate consequence

Hengstenberg, as is well known, has advanced, in relation to the history of the Hebrew prophets, the following theory, which has met with approval from other expositors. To the spiritual vision of these men, he says, future things presented themselves not so much through the medium of time as of space— as it were, in great pictures ; and thus, as is the case in paintings or perspective views, the most distant object often appeared to them to stand immediately behind the nearest, foreground and background being intermingled with each other : and this theory of a perspective vision we are to apply to Jesus, especially in regard to the discourse in question.[1] But we may here cite the appropriate remark of Paulus,[2] that as one, who in a perspective externally presented, does not know how to distinguish distances, labours under an optical delusion, i.e. errs : so likewise in an internal perspective of ideas, if such there be, the disregard of distances must be pronounced an error ; consequently this theory does not show that the above men did not err, but rather explains how they easily might err.

Even Olshausen considers this theory, which he elsewhere adopts, insufficient in the present case to remove all appearance of error on the part of Jesus ; and he therefore seeks to derive special grounds of justification, from the particular nature of the event predicted.[3] In the first place he regards it as indispensable to the full moral influence of the doctrine of Christ's return, that this catastrophe should be regarded as possible, nay probable, at any moment. This consideration may indeed justify such enunciations as Matt. xxiv. 37 ff., where Jesus admonishes to watchfulness, because no one can know how soon the decisive moment may arrive ; but by no means such as xxiv. 34, where he declares that within the term of the existing generation, all will be fulfilled. For one whose mind is in a healthy state, conceives the possible as possible, the probable as probable ; and if he wishes to abide by the truth, he so exhibits them to others : he, on the contrary, by whom the merely possible or probable is conceived as the real, is under a mistake ; and he who, without so conceiving it himself, yet for a moral or religious object, so represents it to others, permits himself to use a pious fraud. Olshausen further avails himself of a position already noticed, namely, that the opinion that the advent of Christ is at hand, is a true one, inasmuch as the entire history of the world is a coming of Christ ; though not so as to exclude his final coming at the end of all things. But if it is proved that Jesus represented his literal, final coming as near at hand, while, in fact, only his figurative perpetual coming occurred in the period indicated : he has confused these two

[1] Hengstenberg, Christologie des A. T., 1, a, s. 305 ff.
[2] Exeg. Handb. 3, a, s. 403. Comp. also Kern, Hauptthatsachen, ut sup. s. 137.
[3] Bibl. Comm. 1, s. 865 ff.

modes of his coming. The last argument which Olshausen adduces—that because the acceleration or delay of the return of Christ depends on the conduct of men, consequently on their free-will, his prophecy is only to be understood conditionally—stands or falls with the first ; for to represent something conditional as unconditional is to create a false impression.

Sieffert, likewise, regards the grounds on which Olshausen seeks to free the assertions of Jesus concerning his return from the imputation of error, as inadequate ; nevertheless he holds it an impossibility to the Christian consciousness, to ascribe an erroneous expectation to Jesus.[4]   In no case would this furnish a warrant, arbitrarily to sever from each other those elements in the discourse of Jesus which refer to the nearer event, from those which in our view refer to the more remote one : rather, if we had reasons for holding such an error on the part of Jesus inconceivable, we must deny in general that the discourses on the second advent, in which those two sets of materials are so inextricably interwoven, originated with him.   But, looking from the orthodox point of view, the question is not : what will it satisfy the Christian consciousness of the present day to believe or not to believe concerning Christ ? but, what stands written concerning Christ ? and to this the above consciousness must accommodate itself as it best may.   Considering the subject rationally, however, a feeling resting on presuppositions, such as the so-called Christian consciousness, has no voice in matters of science ; and as often as it seeks to intermeddle with them, is to be reduced to order by the simple reprimand : *mulier taceat in ecclesiâ !*[5]

But have we no other grounds for questioning that Jesus really uttered the predictions contained in Matt. xxiv. and xxv. parall.? In pursuing this inquiry, we may first take our stand on the assertion of supranaturalistic theologians, that what Jesus here predicts, he could not know in the natural way of reasonable calculation, but only in a supernatural manner.[6]   Even the main fact, that the temple would be destroyed and Jerusalem laid waste, could not, according to this opinion, be so certainly foreknown.   Who could conjecture, it is asked, that the Jews would carry their frantic obstinacy so far as to render such an issue inevitable ?   Who could calculate, that precisely such emperors, would send such procurators, as would provoke insurrection by their baseness and pusillanimity ?   Still more remarkable is it, that many particular incidents which Jesus foretold actually occurred.   The wars, pestilence, earthquakes, famines, which he prophesied, may be shown in the history of the succeeding times ; the persecution of his followers really took place ; the prediction that there would be false prophets, and even such as would, by promises of miracles, allure the people into the wilderness (Matt. xxiv, 11, 24 ff. parall.), may be compared with a strikingly similar passage from Josephus, describing the last times of the Jewish state ;[7] the *encompassing of Jerusalem with armies*, mentioned by Luke, with the *trench*, χάραξ, which he elsewhere (xix. 43 f.) speaks of as being cast about the city, may be recognized in the circumstance recorded by Josephus, that Titus caused Jerusalem to be enclosed by a wall ;[8] lastly it may also excite astonishment that the declarations, *there shall not be left one stone upon another*, οὐκ ἀφεθήσεται λίθος ἐπὶ λίθῳ, in relation to

---

[4] Ueber den Ursprung u. s. f., s. 119.   Weisse advances a similar opinion, ut sup.

[5] Compare also my Streitschriften, 1, 1, conclusion.

[6] Comp. e.g. Gratz, Comm. zum Matth. 2, 444 ff.

[7] Antiq. xx. viii. 6 (comp. bell. jud. ii. xiii. 4.) : *And now these impostors and deceivers persuaded the multitude to follow them into the wilderness, and pretended that they would exhibit manifest wonders and signs that should be performed by the providence of God. And many that were prevailed on by them, suffered the punishments of their folly ; for Felix brought them back, and then punished them.*

[8] Bell. jud. v. xii. 1, 2.

the temple, and *they shall lay thee even with the ground*, ἐδαφιοῦσί σε, (Luke xix. 44), in relation to the city, were fulfilled to the letter.[9] When on the orthodox point of view, from the impossibility of foreseeing such particulars in a natural manner, it is concluded that Jesus had a supernatural insight into the future ; this conclusion is here attended not only with the same difficulty as above, in connection with the announcement of his death and resurrection, but with another also. In the first place, according to Matthew (xxiv. 15), and Mark (xiii. 14), Jesus represented the first stage of the catastrophe as a fulfilment of the prophecy of Daniel concerning an *abomination of desolation*, and consequently referred Dan. ix. 27 (comp. xi. 31, xii. 11) to an event at the destruction of Jerusalem by the Romans. For what Paulus maintains,—namely, that Jesus here only borrows an expression from Daniel, without regarding that declaration of the prophet as a prophecy concerning something which in his time (the time of Jesus) was still future— is here rendered especially inconceivable by the addition : *let him that readeth understand.* Now it may be regarded as an established point in the modern criticism and explanation of the Old Testament, that the above passages in Daniel have reference to the desecration of the temple by Antiochus Epiphanes ;[10] consequently, the interpretation of them which the Evangelists here lend to Jesus is a false one. But to proceed to the difficulty which is peculiar to the prophecy in Matt. xxiv., xxv. : only one side of it, that relating to Jerusalem, has been fulfilled ; the other, that relating to the return of Jesus and the end of the world, remains unfulfilled. Such a half-true prophecy as this cannot have been drawn by Jesus from his higher nature, and he must have been left in this matter to his human faculties. But that he should be able, by means of these, to foresee a result, dependent on so many fortuities as was the destruction of Jerusalem, with its particular circumstances, appears inconceivable ; and hence the conjecture arises, that these discourses, in the definiteness which they now possess, were not uttered prior to the issue, consequently not by Jesus, but that they may have been put into his mouth as prophecies *after* the issue. Thus Kaiser, for example, is of opinion that Jesus threatened a terrible fate to the temple and the nation by means of the Romans, conditionally, in case the nation did not accept salvation from the Messiah, and described this fate in prophetic types; but that the unconditional form and the more precise delineations were given to his discourse *post eventum.* Credner also infers, from the circumstances, that incidents accompanying the destruction of Jerusalem are put into the mouth of Jesus as prophecies, that the three first gospels cannot have been composed before this event.[11] It must certainly be supposed that the prophecy, as we have it in the two first gospels, was formed immediately after or even during the issue, since here the appearance of the Messiah is predicted as an event that would immediately succeed the fall of Jerusalem, which in later years could no longer be the expectation. As this immediate chronological connexion of the two catastrophes is not so expressly made by Luke, it has been supposed that this Evangelist gives the prophecy as it was modified by experience, that the Messiah's advent and the end of the world had in nowise followed close on the destruction of Jerusalem.[12]

In opposition to these two opinions, that the prophecy in question had a

---

[9] More ample comparisons of the results mentioned by Josephus and others, with the prophecy, see in Credner, Einleit. in das N. T. I, s. 207.

[10] Bertholdt, Daniel übersetzt und erklärt, 2, s. 668 ff. ; Paulus, exeg. Handb. 3, a, s. 340 f. ; De Wette, Einleit. in das A. T., § 254 ff.

[11] Kaiser, bibl. Theol. I, s. 247 ; Credner, Einl. in das N. T. I, s. 206 f.

[12] De Wette, Einl. in das N. T., § 97, 101. Exeg. Handb. I, I, s. 204, I, 2, s. 103.

supernatural source, and that it was only made after the issue ; it is sought, in a third quarter, to show that what is here predicted, Jesus might really have known in a natural way.[13] While, on the one hand, it is held in the highest degree astonishing that the result should have so closely corresponded with the most minute features of the prophecy of Jesus ; on the other hand, there are expositors by whom this correspondence is called in question. *The encompassing of Jerusalem with armies*, say they, is precisely what Titus, according to Josephus, pronounces impossible to be effected ;[14] it is predicted that a *trench* χάραξ would be cast about the city, while Josephus informs us, that after the first attempt at forming an *embankment* χῶμα had been rendered useless, by an act of incendiarism on the part of the besieged,[15] Titus desisted from his scheme ; of false Messiahs, arising in the interval between the death of Jesus and the destruction of Jerusalem, history says nothing ; the commotions among nations, and the natural phenomena, in that period, are far from being so important as they are here represented ; but above all, in these prophecies, especially as they are given in Matthew and Mark, it is not the destruction of Jerusalem which is predicted, but solely that of the temple : plain divergencies of the prophecy from the result, which would not exist, if either a supernatural glance into the future, or a *vaticinium post eventum* were concerned.

According to these theologians, we are on the wrong track in seeking the counterpart of these prophecies forwards, in the result ; since it was backwards, on types presented in the past, that the authors looked.   A mass of such types was furnished by the Jewish conception of the circumstances which would precede the advent of the Messiah.   False prophets and Messiahs, war, famine and pestilence, earthquakes and commotions in the heavens, prevalent corruption of manners, persecution of the faithful servants of Jehovah, were held to be the immediate harbingers of the messianic kingdom. Moreover, in the prophets there are descriptions of the tribulation which would presage and accompany the day of the coming of Jehovah (Isa. xiii. 9 ff., Joel i. 15, ii. 1 ff. 10 ff., iii. 3 ff., iv. 15 f. ; Zeph. i. 14 ff. ; Hagg. ii. 7 ; Zech. xiv. 1 ff. ; Mal. iii. 1 ff), or which would precede the messianic kingdom of the saints (Dan. vii.–xii.), as also expressions in later Jewish writings,[16] so analogous with our evangelical prediction, as to put it beyond question, that the description which it gives of the time of the Messiah's advent is drawn from a circle of ideas which had long been current among the Jews.

Another question is, whether the principal feature in the picture before us, the destruction of the temple and the devastation of Jerusalem, as introductory to the coming of the Messiah, may also be shown to have made part of the popular conception in the time of Jesus.   In Jewish writings we find the notion, that the birth of the Messiah would coincide with the destruction of the sanctuary :[17] but this idea was obviously first formed after the fall of the temple, in order that a fountain of consolation might spring out of the lowest depth of misery.   Josephus finds in Daniel, together with what relates to Antiochus, a prophecy of the annihilation of the Jewish state by the Romans :[18] but as this is not the primary object in any of the visions in

---

[13] Paulus, Fritzsche, De Wette in loc.

[14] B. j. V. xii. 1 : *To encompass the whole city round with his army, was not very easy, by reason of its magnitude and the difficulty of the situation ; and on other accounts dangerous.*

[15] B. j. V xi. 1 ff., xii. 1.

[16] Vid. Schöttgen, 2, s. 509 ff. ; Bertholdt, § 13 ; Schmidt, Biblioth. 1, s. 24 ff.

[17] Vid. Schöttgen, 2, s. 525 f.

[18] Antiq. X. xi. 7.   After having interpreted the little horn of Antiochus, he briefly

Daniel, Josephus might first make this interpretation after the issue, in which case it would prove nothing as to the time of Jesus. Nevertheless, it is conceivable, that already in the time of Jesus, the Jews might attribute to the prophecies of Daniel a reference to events yet future, although these prophecies in fact related to a far earlier period ; and they might do so on the same grounds as those on which the Christians of the present age still look forward to the full realization of Matt. xxiv. and xxv. As immediately after the fall of the kingdom made of iron mixed with clay, and of the horn that speaks blasphemies and makes war against the saints, the coming of the Son of man in the clouds, and the commencement of the everlasting kingdom of the saints, is prophesied, while this result had not by any means succeeded the defeat of Antiochus : there was an inducement still to look to the future, not only for the heavenly kingdom, but also, since they were made immediately to precede it, for the calamities caused by the kingdom of iron and clay ; among which calamities, by analogy with what was predicted of the horn, the desecration of the temple was conspicuous. But while the prophecy in Daniel includes only the desecration of the temple and the interruption of the worship, together with (the partial [19]) destruction of the city : in the discourse before us complete destruction is predicted to the temple—and likewise to the city, not merely in Luke, where the expressions are very marked, but undoubtedly in the two other Evangelists also, as appears to be indicated by the exhortation to hasty flight from the city ;—which prediction of total destruction, as it is not contained in the type, can apparently have been gathered only from the result. But in the first place, the description in Daniel with the expressions שָׁמֵם and הִשְׁחִית (ix. 26 f., xii. 11), which the LXX. translates by ἐρήμωσις, desolation, and διαφθείρω, I destroy, may easily be also understood of a total destruction ; and secondly, if once, in connexion with the sins of the nation, the temple and city had been destroyed and the people carried away captive, every enthusiastic Israelite, to whom the religious and moral condition of his fellow-countrymen appeared corrupt and irremediable, might thenceforth expect and predict a repetition of that former judgment. According to this, even those particulars in which, as we have seen in the foregoing section, Luke surpasses his fellow-narrators in definiteness, are not of a kind to oblige us to suppose, either a supernatural foreknowledge, or a vaticinium post eventum : on the contrary, all may be explained by a close consideration of what is narrated concerning the first destruction of Jerusalem in 2 Kings xxv. ; 2 Chron. xxxvi. ; and Jer. xxxix. 52.

There is only one point which Jesus, as the author of this discourse, could not have gathered from any types, but must have drawn entirely from himself : namely, the declaration that the catastrophe which he described would arrive within the present generation. This prediction we must hesitate to derive from a supernatural knowledge, for the reason, already noticed, that it is only

adds : *In the very same manner Daniel also wrote concerning the government of the Romans, and that our country should be made desolate by them.* He doubtless supposed that the fourth, iron monarchy, Dan. ii. 40, represented the Romans, since, besides attributing it to a dominion over all the earth, he explains its destruction by the stone as something still future, Ant. X. x. 4 : *Daniel did also declare the meaning of the stone to the King ; but I do not think proper to relate it, since I have only undertaken to describe things past or things present, but not things that are future.* Now Daniel ii. 44 interprets the stone to mean the heavenly kingdom, which would destroy the iron one, but would itself endure for ever,—a messianic particular, on which Josephus does not choose to dilate. But that, correctly interpreted, the iron legs of the image signify the Macedonian empire, and the feet of iron mixed with clay, the Syrian empire which sprang out of the Macedonian, see De Wette, Einleit. in das N. T., § 254.

[19] Vid. Joseph., Antiq. xii. v.

half fulfilled : while the other side of the fact, the striking fulfilment of at least the one half of the prophecy, might incline us to distrust the supposition of a merely natural calculation, and to regard this determination of time as a feature introduced into the discourse of Jesus after the issue.   Meanwhile, it is clear from the passages cited at the conclusion of the last section, that the apostles themselves expected the return of Christ to take place within their lifetime ; and it is not improbable that Jesus also believed that this event, together with the ruin of the city and temple, which according to Daniel was to precede it, was very near at hand.   The more general part of the expectation, namely, the appearing at some future time in the clouds of heaven, to awake the dead, to sit in judgment, and to found an everlasting kingdom, would necessarily, from a consideration of Daniel, where such a coming is ascribed to the Son of man, be contemplated by Jesus as a part of his own destiny, so soon as he held himself to be the Messiah ; while, with regard to the time, it was natural that he should not conceive a very long interval as destined to elapse between his first messianic coming in humiliation, and his second, in glory.*

One objection to the genuineness of the synoptical discourses on the second advent, is yet in reserve ; it has, however, less weight in our point of view than in that of the prevalent criticism of the gospels.   This objection is derived from the absence of any detailed description of the second advent of Jesus in the Gospel of John.[20]   It is true that the fundamental elements of the doctrine of Christ's return are plainly discoverable in the fourth gospel also.[21] Jesus therein ascribes to himself the offices of the future judgment, and the awaking of the dead (John v. 21–30) ; which last is not indeed numbered among the concomitants of the advent of Christ in the synoptical gospels, but not seldom appears in that connexion elsewhere in the New Testament (e.g. 1 Cor. xv. 23 ; 1 Thess. iv. 16).   When Jesus, in the fourth gospel, sometimes denies that he is come into the world for judgment (iii. 17, viii. 15, xii. 47), this refers only to his first presence on earth, and is limited by opposite declarations, in which he asserts that he is come into the world for judgment (ix. 39, comp. viii. 16), to the sense that the object of his mission is not to condemn but to save, and that his judgment is not individual or partial ; that it consists, not in an authoritative sentence proceeding subjectively from himself, but in an objective act proceeding from the intrinsic tendency of things, a doctrine which is significantly expressed in the declaration, that him who hears his word without believing *he* judges not, but *the word, which he has spoken, shall judge him in the last day* (ὁ λόγος, ὃν ἐλάλησα, κρινεῖ αὐτὸν ἐν τῇ ἐσχάτῃ ἡμέρᾳ, xii. 48).   Further, when the Jesus of John's gospel says of the believer : οὐ κρίνεται, *he is not judged*, εἰς κρίσιν οὐκ ἔρχεται, *he shall not come into judgment* (iii. 18, v. 24), this is to be understood of a judgment with a condemnatory issue ; when on the contrary, it is said of the unbeliever : ἤδη κέκριται, *he is judged already* (iii. 18), this only means that the assigning of the merited lot to each is not reserved until the future judgment at the end of all things, since each one in his inward disposition bears within himself the fate which is his due.   This does not exclude a future solemn act of judgment, wherein that which has at present only a latent existence will be made matter of awful revelation ; for in the very passage last quoted we find the consignment to condemnation, and elsewhere the awarding of future blessedness (v. 28 f., vi. 39 f., 54), associated with the last day and the resurrection.

[20] Vid. Hase, L. J., § 130.
[21] The passages bearing on this subject are collected and explained in Schott, *Commentarius*, etc., p. 364 ff.   Comp. Lücke, in loc. and Weizel, urchristl. Unsterblichkeitslehre, in the Theol. Studien, 1836, s. 626 ff.

In like manner, Jesus says in Luke also, in the same connexion in which he describes his return as a still future, external catastrophe, xvii. 20 f. : *The kingdom of God cometh not with observation ; neither shall they say, lo here ! or, lo there ! for behold the kingdom of God is within you.* A certain interpretation of the words uttered by the Jesus of John's gospel, supposes him even to intimate that his return was not far distant. The expressions already mentioned in the farewell discourses, in which Jesus promises his disciples not to leave them comfortless, but, after having gone to the Father, shortly (xvi. 16) to come again to them (xiv. 3, 18), are not seldom understood of the return of Christ at the last day ; [22] but when we hear Jesus say of this same return, that he will therein reveal himself only to his disciples, and not to the world (xiv. 19, comp. 22), it is impossible to think of it as the return to judgment, in which Jesus conceived that he should reveal himself to good and bad without distinction. There is a particularly enigmatical allusion to the coming of Christ in the appendix to the fourth gospel, chap. xxi. On the question of Peter as to what will become of the apostle John, Jesus here replies, *If I will that he tarry till I come, what is that to thee ?* (v. 22) whence, as it is added, the Christians inferred that John would not die, since they supposed the *coming* (ἔρχεσθαι) here spoken of, to be the final return of Christ, in which those who witnessed it were to be changed, without tasting death (1 Cor. xv. 51 f.). But, adds the author correctively, Jesus did not say, the disciple would not die, but only, if he willed that he should tarry till he came, what was that to Peter ? Hereby the Evangelist may have intended to rectify the inference in two ways. Either it appeared to him erroneous to identify the remaining until Jesus came, with not dying, i.e. to take the coming of which Jesus here spoke for the last, which would put an end to death ; and in that case he must have understood by it an invisible coming of Christ, possibly in the destruction of Jerusalem : [23] or, he held it erroneous that what Jesus had only said hypothetically—even if he willed the given case, that was no concern of Peter's—should be understood categorically, as if such had really been the will of Jesus ; in which case the ἔρχομαι would retain its customary sense.[24]

If, according to this, all the main features of the doctrine of the second advent are put into the mouth of Jesus in the fourth gospel also, still we nowhere find anything of the detailed, graphic description of the external event, which we read in the synoptical gospels. This relation between the two representations, creates no slight difficulty on the ordinary view of the origin of the gospels, and especially that of the fourth. If Jesus really spoke of his return so fully and solemnly as the synoptists represent him to have done, and treated of the right knowledge and observation of the signs as something of the highest importance ; it is inconceivable that the author of the fourth gospel could pass over all this, if he were an immediate disciple of Jesus. The usual mode of accounting for such an omission, by the supposition that he believed this part of the teaching of Jesus to be sufficiently known from the synoptical gospels, or from oral tradition, is the more inadequate here in proportion as all which bears a prophetic character, especially when relating to events at once so much longed for and dreaded, is exposed to misinterpretation ; as we may see from the rectification just noticed, which the author of John xxi. found it necessary to apply to the opinion of his contemporaries concerning the promise given by Jesus to John. Thus, in the present case, an explanatory word would have been highly seasonable and useful, especi-

---

[22] Vid. Tholuck, in loc.
[23] Comp. Tholuck, ut sup.
[24] Thus Lücke, and also Tholuck, in loc. ; Schott, p. 409.

ally as the representation of the first gospel, which made the end of all things follow immediately on the destruction of Jerusalem, must be the more an occasion of doubt and offence the nearer the latter event came, and in a still greater degree when it was past.   And who was more capable of affording such enlightenment than the favourite disciple, particularly if, according to Mark xiii. 3, he was the only Evangelist who had been present at the discourse of Jesus on this subject?   Hence, here again, a special reason for his silence is sought in the alleged destination of his gospel for non-judaical, idealizing Gnostics, whose point of view those descriptions would not have suited, and were therefore omitted.[25]   But precisely in relation to such readers, it would have been a culpable compliance, a confirmation in their idealizing tendency, had John, out of deference to them, suppressed the real side of the return of Christ.   The apostle must rather have withstood the propensity of these people to evaporate the external, historical part of Christianity, by giving due prominence to it ; as, in his epistle, in opposition to their Docetism, he lays stress on the corporeality of Jesus : so, in opposition to their idealism, he must have been especially assiduous to exhibit in the return of Christ the external facts by which it would be signalized.   Instead of this, he himself speaks nearly like a Gnostic, and constantly aims, in relation to the return of Christ, to resolve the external and the future into the internal and the present.   Hence there is not so much exaggeration, as Olshausen supposes, in the opinion of Fleck, that the representation of the doctrine of Jesus concerning his return in the synoptical gospels, and that given in the fourth, exclude each other ; [26] for if the author of the fourth gospel be an apostle, the discourses on the second advent which the three first Evangelists attribute to Jesus, cannot have been so delivered by him, and vice versâ.   We, however, as we have said, cannot avail ourselves of this argument, having long renounced the pre-supposition that the fourth gospel had an apostolic origin. But, on our point of view, we can fully explain the relation which the representation of the fourth gospel bears to that of the synoptists.   In Palestine, where the tradition recorded by the three first gospels was formed, the doctrine of a solemn advent of the Messiah which was there prevalent, and which Jesus embraced, was received in its whole breadth into the Christian belief : whereas in the Hellenistic-theosophic circle in which the fourth gospel arose, this idea was divested of its material envelopment, and the return of Christ became the ambiguous medium between a real and an ideal, a present and a future event, which it appears in the fourth gospel.

[25] Olshausen, 1, s. 870.
[26] Fleck, de regno divino, p. 483.

CHAPTER II.

MACHINATIONS OF THE ENEMIES OF JESUS; TREACHERY OF JUDAS; LAST SUPPER WITH HIS DISCIPLES.

§ 117.

DEVELOPMENT OF THE RELATION OF JESUS TO HIS ENEMIES.

In the three first gospels the principal enemies of Jesus are the Pharisees and scribes,[1] who saw in him the most ruinous opponent of their institutions; together with the chief priests and elders, who, as the heads of the external temple-worship and the hierarchy founded upon it, could have no friendly feeling towards one who on every opportunity represented as the main point, the internal service of God with the devotion of the mind. Elsewhere we find among the enemies of Jesus the Sadducees (Matt. xvi. 1, xxii. 23 ff. parall. comp. Matt. xvi. 6 ff. parall.), to whose materialism much in his opinions must have been repugnant; and the Herodian party (Mark iii. 6; Matt. xxii. 16 parall.) who, having been unfavourable to the Baptist, were naturally so to his successor. The fourth gospel, though it sometimes mentions the chief priests and Pharisees, the most frequently designates the enemies of Jesus by the general expression: οἱ Ἰουδαῖοι, *the Jews*; an expression which proceeds from a later, Christian point of view.

The four Evangelists unanimously relate, that the more defined machinations of the Pharisaic-hierarchical party against Jesus, took their rise from an offence committed by the latter against the prevalent rules concerning the observation of the sabbath. When Jesus had cured the man with the withered hand, it is said in Matthew: *the Pharisees went out, and held a council against him, how they might destroy him* (xii. 14, comp. Mark iii. 6; Luke vi. 11); and in like manner John observes, on the occasion of the Sabbath cure at the pool of Bethesda: *therefore did the Jews persecute Jesus*, and after mentioning a declaration of Jesus, proceeds thus: *therefore the Jews sought the more to kill him* (v. 16, 18).

But immediately after this commencing point, the synoptical account of the relation in question diverges from that of John. In the synoptists, the next offence is given by the neglect of washing before meals on the part of Jesus and his disciples, with the sharp invectives which, when called to account on the subject, he launched forth against the spirit of petty observance, and the hypocrisy and spirit of persecution with which it was united in the Pharisees and lawyers; after all which it is said, that the latter conceived a deep animosity against him, and tried to sift him and entrap him by dangerous questions, in order to obtain grounds of accusation against him (Luke xi. 37–54,

---

[1] Winer's bibl. Realwörterb.

599

comp. Matt. xv. 1 ff. ; Mark vii. 1 ff.). On his last journey to Jerusalem, the Pharisees gave Jesus a warning against Herod (Luke xiii. 31), which apparently had no other object than to induce him to leave the country. The next important cause of offence to the hierarchical party, was the striking homage paid to Jesus by the people on his entrance into Jerusalem, and the purification of the temple which he immediately undertook : but they were still withheld from any violent measures towards him by the strength of his interest with the people (Matt. xxi. 15 f. ; Mark ix. 18 ; Luke xix. 39, 47 f.), which was the sole reason why they did not possess themselves of his person, after the severe manner in which he had characterized them, in the parable of the husbandmen of the vineyard (Matt. xxi. 45 f. parall.). After these events, it scarcely needed the anti-Pharisaic discourse Matt. xxiii. to make the chief priests, the scribes and elders, *i.e.* the Sanhedrim, assemble in the palace of the high priest, shortly before the passover, for a consultation, *that they might take Jesus by subtlety and kill him* (Matt. xxvi. 3 ff. parall.).

In the fourth gospel, also, the great number of the adherents of Jesus among the people is sometimes, it is true, described as the reason why his enemies desired to seize him (vii. 32, 44, comp. iv. 1 ff.), and his solemn entrance into Jerusalem embitters them here also (xii. 19) ; sometimes their murderous designs are mentioned without any motive being stated (vii. 1, 19, 25, viii. 40) : but the main cause of offence in this gospel, lies in the declarations of Jesus concerning his exalted dignity. Even on the occasion of the cure of the lame man on the Sabbath, what chiefly irritated the Jews was that Jesus justified it by appealing to the uninterrupted agency of God as his Father, which in their opinion was a blasphemous *making of himself equal with God*, ἴσον ἑαυτὸν ποιεῖν τῷ θεῷ (v. 18) ; when he spoke of his divine mission, they sought to lay hold on him (vii. 30, comp. viii. 20) ; on his asserting that he was before Abraham, they took up stones to cast at him (viii. 59) ; they did the same when he declared that he and the Father were one (x. 31), and when he asserted that the Father was in him and he in the Father, they again attempted to seize him (x. 39). But that which, according to the fourth gospel, turns the scale, and causes the hostile party to take a formal resolution against Jesus, is the resuscitation of Lazarus. When this act was reported to the Pharisees, they and the chief priests convened a council of the Sanhedrim, in which the subject of deliberation was, that if Jesus continued to perform so many *signs*, σημεῖα, all would at length adhere to him, and then the Roman power would be exerted to the destruction of the Jewish nation ; whereupon the high priest Caiaphas pronounced the momentous decision, that it was better for one man to die for the people than for the whole nation to perish. His death was now determined upon, and it was enjoined on every one to point out his abode, that he might be arrested (xi. 46 ff.).

With regard to this difference modern criticism observes, that we should not at all comprehend the tragical turn of the fate of Jesus from the synoptical accounts, and that John alone opens to us a glance into the manner in which, step by step, the breach between the hierarchical party and Jesus was widened ; in short, that in this point also the representation of the fourth gospel shows itself a pragmatical one, which that of the other gospels is not.[2] But what it is in which the Gospel of John exhibits superiority in gradation and progress, it is difficult to see, since the very first definite statement concerning the incipient enmity (v. 18) contains the extreme of the offence (ἴσον ἑαυτὸν ποιῶν τῷ θεῷ, *making himself equal with God*) and the extreme of the

---

[2] Schneckenburger, über den Urspr., s. 9 f. Lücke, 1, s. 133, 159, 2, s. 402.

enmity (ἐζήτουν αὐτὸν ἀποκτεῖναι, *they sought to kill him*); so that all which is narrated further concerning the hostility of the Jews is mere repetition, and the only fact which presents itself as a step towards more decided measures is the resolution of the Sanhedrim, chap. xi. This species of gradation, however, is not wanting in the synoptical account also: here we have the transition from the indefinite *laying wait* for Jesus, and the *communing what might be done to him* (Luke xi. 54, vi. 11), or as it is more precisely given in Matthew (xii. 14), and in Mark (iii. 6), the *taking counsel how they might destroy him*, to the definite resolve as to the manner (δόλῳ) and the time (μὴ ἐν τῇ ἑορτῇ Matt. xxvi. 4 f. parall.).—But it is especially made a reproach to three first Evangelists, that in passing over the resurrection of Lazarus, they have omitted that incident which gave the final impulse to the fate of Jesus.[3] If we, on the contrary, in virtue of the above result of our criticism of this miraculous narrative, must rather praise the synoptists, that they do not represent as the turning point in the fate of Jesus, an incident which never really happened : so the fourth Evangelist, by the manner in which he relates the murderous resolve to which it was the immediate inducement, by no means manifests himself as one whose authority can be held by us a sufficient warrant for the truth of his narrative. The circumstance that he ascribes to the high priest the gift of prophecy (without doubt in accordance with a superstitious idea of his age[4]), and regards his speech as a prediction of the death of Jesus, would certainly not by itself prove that he could not have been an apostle and eye-witness.[5] But it has with justice been held a difficulty, that our Evangelist designates Caiaphas as the *high priest of that year*, ἀρχιερεὺς τοῦ ἐνιαυτοῦ ἐκείνου (xi. 49), and thus appears to suppose that this dignity, like many Roman magistracies, was an annual one; whereas it was originally held for life, and even in that period of Roman ascendancy, was not a regular annual office, but was transferred as often as it pleased the arbitrariness of the Romans. To conclude on the authority of the fourth gospel, in opposition to the general custom, and notwithstanding the silence of Josephus, that Annas and Caiaphas, by a private agreement, held the office for a year by turns,[6] is an expedient to which those may resort whom it pleases; to take ἐνιαυτοῦ indefinitely for χρόνου,[7] is, from the twofold repetition of the same expression, v. 51 and xviii. 13, inadmissible; that at that period the high priesthood was frequently transferred from one to another, and some high priests were not allowed to remain in their office longer than a year,[8] did not justify our author in designating Caiaphas as the high priest of a particular year, when in fact he filled that post for a series of years, and certainly throughout the duration of the public agency of Jesus; lastly, that John intended to say that Caiaphas was high priest in the year in which Jesus died, without thereby excluding earlier and later years, in which he also held the office,[9] is an equally untenable position. For if the time in which an incident occurs is described as a certain year, this mode of expression must imply, that either the incident the date of which is to be determined, or the fact by which that date is to be determined, is connected with the term of a year. Thus either the author of the fourth gospel must have been of the opinion, that from the death of Jesus, to which this decision of Caiaphas was the initiative step, a

---

[3] Comp. besides the critics above cited, Hug, Enleit. in das N. T. 2, s. 215.
[4] For the most correct views on this point see Lücke, 2, s. 407 ff.
[5] As the author of the Probabilia thinks, s. 94.
[6] Hug, ut sup. s. 221.
[7] Kuinöl, in loc.
[8] Paulus, Comm. 4, s. 579 f.
[9] Lücke, in loc.

plenitude of spiritual gifts, including the gift of prophecy to the high priest of that period, was dispensed throughout that particular year,[10] and no longer; or, if this be a far-fetched explanation, he must have imagined that Caiaphas was high priest for the term of that year only.   Lücke concludes that as, according to Josephus, the high priest of that period held his office for ten years successively, therefore John cannot have meant, by the expression ἀρχιερεὺς τοῦ ἐνιαυτοῦ ἐκείνου, that the office of high priest was an annual one; whereas the author of the Probabilia, on the ground that the evidence of this meaning in the words of the gospel, is far more certain than that John is its author, reverses this proposition, and concludes, that as the fourth gospel here presents an idea concerning the duration of the office of high priest which could not be entertained in Palestine, therefore its author cannot have been a native of Palestine.[11]

Of the further statements also, as to the points in which Jesus gave offence to the hierarchy of his nation, those which the synoptists have alone, or in common with John, are credible; those which are peculiar to the latter, not so.   Among those which are common to both sides, the solemn entrance of Jesus into Jerusalem, and the strong attachment of the people to him, were equally natural causes of offence with his discourses and actions in opposition to the sabbatical institutions, in whatever the latter may have consisted: on the contrary, the manner in which, according to the fourth gospel, the Jews take offence at the declarations of Jesus concerning himself as the Son of God, is, according to our earlier analysis,[12] as inconceivable, as it is consistent with the common order of things that the polemical tone towards the Pharisees which the first Evangelists all lend to Jesus, should irritate the party attacked.   Thus no new or more profound insight into the causes and motives of the reaction against Jesus, is to be obtained from the fourth gospel: but the information which the synoptists have preserved to us fully suffices to make that fact intelligible.

§ 118.

JESUS AND HIS BETRAYER.

Although it had been resolved in the council of the chief priests and elders, that the feast time should be allowed to pass over before any measures were taken against Jesus, because any act of violence against him in these days might easily excite an insurrection, on the part of his numerous adherents among the visitants to the feast (Matt. xxvi. 5; Mark xiv. 2): yet this consideration was superseded by the facility with which one of his disciples offered to deliver him into their hands.   Judas, surnamed Ἰσκαριώτης, doubtless on account of his origin from the Jewish city of Kerioth[1] (Josh. xv. 25), went, according to the synoptists, a few days before the passover, to the heads of the priesthood, and volunteered to deliver Jesus quietly into their hands, for which service they promised him money, according to Matthew, thirty pieces of silver (ἀργύρια, Matt. xxvi. 14 ff. parall.).   Of such an antecedent transac-

---

[10] Lightfoot, in loc.
[11] Probabil., ut sup.
[12] Vol. II. § 62.*

[1] Olshausen gives us more precise information concerning the descent of the traitor, when he says (bibl. Comm. 2, s. 458 Anm.): "Perhaps the passage, Gen. xlix. 17, *Dan shall be a serpent, an adder in the path, that biteth the horse's heels, so that his rider shall fall backward*, is a prophetic intimation of the treachery of Judas, whence we might conclude that he was of the tribe of Dan."

tion between Judas and the enemies of Jesus, the fourth gospel not only says nothing, but appears moreover to represent the matter as if Judas had not formed the determination of betraying Jesus to the priesthood, until the last supper, and had then promptly put it into execution. The same *entering* (εἰσελθεῖν) of Satan into Judas, which Luke (xxii. 3) places before his first interview with the chief priests, and before any preparation had been made for Jesus and his disciples to eat the passover together, is represented by the author of the fourth gospel as occurring at this meal, before Judas left the company (xiii. 27): a proof, as it appears, that in the opinion of this Evangelist, Judas now made his first traitorous visit. He does indeed observe, before the meal (xiii. 2), that the *devil had put it into the heart* of Judas to betray Jesus, and this τοῦ διαβόλου βεβληκότος εἰς τὴν καρδίαν is commonly regarded as the parallel of Luke's εἰσῆλθε σατανᾶς (*Satan entered* into him), being understood to imply the formation of the treacherous resolve, in consequence of which Judas went to the chief priests : but if he had previously been in treaty with them, the betrayal was already completed, and it is then not easy to perceive what can be meant by the words εἰσῆλθεν εἰς αὐτὸν ὁ σατανᾶς on the occasion of the last meal, since the summoning of those who were to seize Jesus was no new diabolical resolution, but only the execution of that which had already been embraced. The expression in John v. 27 only obtains an entirely consistent sense in distinction from v. 2, when the βάλλειν εἰς τὴν καρδίαν in the latter, is understood of the rising of the thought, the εἰσελθεῖν in the former, of the ripening of this thought into resolution, the supposition that Judas had pledged himself to the chief priests before the meal being thus excluded.[2] In this manner, however, the statement of the synoptists that Judas, some time before the perpetration of his treacherous act, made a bargain with the enemies of Jesus, stands in contradiction with that of John, that he only put himself in league with them immediately before the deed ; and here Lücke decides in favour of John, maintaining it to be after his departure from the last supper (xiii. 30), that Judas made that application to the chief priests which the synoptists (Matt. xxvi. 14 f. parall.) place before the meal.[3] But this decision of Lücke's is founded solely on deference to the presupposed authority of John ; for even if, as he remarks, Judas could very well obtain an interview with the priests when night had commenced : still, regarding the matter apart from any presuppositions, the probability is beyond comparison stronger on the side of the synoptists, who allow some time for the affair, than on that of John, according to whom it is altogether sudden, and Judas, truly as if he were possessed, rushes out when it is already night to treat with the priests, and immediately hurry to the deed.

Concerning the motives which induced Judas to league himself with the enemies of Jesus, we learn from the three first gospels no more than that he received money from the chief priests. This would indicate that he was actuated by covetousness, especially according to the narrative in Matthew, where Judas, before he promises to betray Jesus, puts the question, *What will ye give me?* Clearer light is thrown on this subject by the statement of the fourth gospel (xii. 4 ff.), that on the occasion of the meal in Bethany, Judas was indignant at the anointing, as an unnecessary expenditure,—that he carried the purse, and acted the thief in that office ; whence it might be supposed that the avarice of Judas, no longer satisfied by his peculations on the funds of the society, hoped to reap a more considerable harvest by

[2] That, according to the account in John, Judas first went to the chief priests from the meal, is acknowledged by Lightfoot also (horæ, p. 465), but he on this account regards the meal described by John as earlier than the synoptical one.

[3] Comm. z. Joh. 2, s. 484.

betraying Jesus to the rich and powerful sacerdotal party. We must hold ourselves under obligation to the author of the fourth gospel, that by the preservation of these particulars, which are wanting in the other Evangelists, he has made the act of Judas somewhat more comprehensible,—so soon as his statements are shown to have an historical foundation. We have shown above, however, how improbable it is that, had that censure really proceeded from Judas, the legend should have lost this trait;[4] how probable, on the other hand, a legendary origin of it, it is easy to discern. The meal at Bethany stood in the evangelical tradition near to the end of the life of Jesus, an end brought about by the treachery of Judas;—how easily might the thought arise in some one, that the narrow-minded censure of a noble prodigality could only come from the covetous Judas? That the censure at the same time turned upon the propriety of selling the ointment for the benefit of the poor, could in the mouth of Judas be only a pretext, behind which he concealed his selfishness: but advantage to himself from the sale of the ointment could not be expected by him, unless he allowed himself to purloin some of the money saved; and this again he could not do unless he were the purse-bearer. If it thus appear possible for the statement that Judas was a *thief and had the bag*, to have had an unhistorical origin: we have next to inquire whether there are any reasons for supposing that such was actually the case.

Here we must take into consideration another point on which the synoptists and John differ, namely, the foreknowledge of Jesus that Judas would betray him. In the synoptical gospels, Jesus first manifests this knowledge at the last supper, consequently at a time in which the deed of Judas had virtually been perpetrated; and apparently but a short time before, Jesus had so little presentiment that one of the twelve would be lost to him, that he promised them all, without exception, the honour of sitting on twelve thrones of judgment in the palingenesia (Matt. xix. 28). According to John, on the contrary, Jesus declares shortly before the time of the last passover but one, consequently a year before the result, that one of the twelve is *a devil*, διάβολος, meaning, according to the observation of the Evangelist, Judas, as his future betrayer (vi. 70); for, as it had been observed shortly before (v. 64), *Jesus knew from the beginning,—who should betray him*. According to this, Jesus knew from the commencement of his acquaintance with Judas, that this disciple would prove a traitor; and not merely did he foresee this external issue, but also, since he knew what was in man (John ii. 25), he must have penetrated the motives of Judas, namely, covetousness and love of money. And, if so, would he have made him purse-bearer, i.e. placed him in a position in which his propensity to seek gain by any means, even though dishonest, must have had the most abundant nourishment? Would he have made him a thief by giving him opportunity, and thus, as if designedly, have brought up in him a betrayer for himself? Considered simply in an economical point of view, who entrusts a purse to one of whom he knows that he robs it? Then, in relation to the idea of Jesus as a moral teacher, who places the weak in a situation which so constantly appeals to his weak point, as to render it certain that he will sooner or later give way to the temptation? No truly: Jesus assuredly did not so play with the souls immediately entrusted to him, did not exhibit to them so completely the opposite of what he taught them to pray for, *lead us not into temptation* (Matt. vi. 13), as to have made Judas, of whom he foreknew that he would become his betrayer out of covetousness, the purse-bearer of his society; or, if he gave him this office, he cannot have had such a foreknowledge.

4 Vol. II. § 89.

In order to arrive at a decision in this alternative, we must consider that foreknowledge separately, and inquire whether, apart from the treasurership of Judas, it be probable or not? We shall not enter on the question of the psychological possibility, because there is always freedom of appeal to the divine nature of Jesus; but with regard to the moral possibility it is to be asked, whether presupposing that foreknowledge, it be justifiable in Jesus to have chosen Judas among the twelve, and to have retained him within this circle? As it was only by this vocation that his treachery as such could be rendered possible; so Jesus appears, if he foresaw this treachery, to have designedly drawn him into the sin. It is urged that intercourse with Jesus afforded Judas the possibility of escaping that abyss :[5] but Jesus is supposed to have foreseen that this possibility would not be realized. It is further said that even in other circles the evil implanted in Judas would not the less have developed itself in a different form : a proposition which has a strong tinge of fatalism. Again, when it is said to be of no avail to a man that the evil, the germ of which lies within him, should not be developed, this appears to lead to consequences which are repudiated by the apostle Paul, Rom. iii. 8, vi. 1 f. And regarding the subject in relation to feeling merely,—how could Jesus endure to have a man, of whom he knew that he would be his betrayer, and that all instruction would be fruitless to him, as his constant attendant throughout the whole period of his public life? Must not the presence of such a person have every hour interfered with his confidential intercourse with the rest of the twelve? Assuredly they must have been weighty motives, for the sake of which Jesus imposed on himself anything so repugnant and difficult. Such motives or objects must either have had relation to Judas, and thus have consisted in the design to make him better—which however was precluded by the decided foreknowledge of his crime ; or they must have had relation to Jesus himself and his work, i.e. Jesus had the conviction that if the work of redemption by means of his death were to be effected, there must be one to betray him.[6] But for the purpose of redemption, according to the Christian theory, the death of Jesus was the only indispensable means : whether this should be brought about by a betrayal, or in any other way, was of no moment, and that the enemies of Jesus must, earlier or later, have succeeded in getting him into their power without the aid of Judas, is undeniable. That the betrayer was indispensable in order to bring about the death of Jesus exactly at the passover, which was a type of himself [7]—with such trivialities it will scarcely be attempted to put us off in these days.

If then we are unable to discover any adequate motive which could induce Jesus advertently to receive and retain in his society his betrayer in the person of Judas : it appears decided that he cannot beforehand have known him to be such. Schleiermacher, in order that he may not infringe on the authority of John by denying this foreknowledge, prefers doubting that Jesus chose the twelve purely by his own act, and supposes that this circle was rather formed by the voluntary adherence of the disciples : since it would be more easy to justify the conduct of Jesus, if he merely refrained from rejecting Judas when he spontaneously offered himself than if he drew him to himself by free choice.[8] But hereby the authority of John is still endangered, for it is he who makes Jesus say to the twelve : *Ye have not chosen me, but I have chosen you* (xv. 16, comp. vi. 76) ; moreover, even dismissing the idea of a decided act of election, still for any one to remain constantly with Jesus there needed his

[5] See these and the following reasons in Olshausen, 2, s. 458 ff.
[6] Olshausen, ut sup.
[7] Such an argument may be gathered from what Olshausen says, 2, s. 387, 388.
[8] Ueber den Lukas, s. 88.

permission and sanction, and even these he could not, acting humanly, give to a man of whom he knew that, by means of this relation to himself, he would be enabled to mature the blackest crime.   It is said, however, that Jesus put himself entirely into the Divine point of view, and admitted Judas into his society, for the sake of the possibility of reformation which he yet foreknew would never be realised ; but this would be a Divine inhumanity,—not the conduct of the God-man.   If, according to this, it is extremely difficult to maintain as historical the statement of the fourth gospel, that Jesus from the beginning knew Judas to be his betrayer : so it is equally easy to discern what even without historical foundation might lead to such a representation.

It would be natural to suppose, that the fact of Jesus being betrayed by one of his own disciples, would be injurious to him in the eyes of his enemies, even if we did not know that Celsus, in the character of a Jew, reproached Jesus *that he was betrayed by one of those whom he called his disciples*, ὅτι ὑφ' ὧν ὠνόμαζε μαθητῶν προὐδόθη, as a proof that he was less able to attach his followers to himself than every robber-chief.[9]   Now as the injurious consequences to be drawn from the ignominious death of Jesus, appeared to be most completely obviated by the assertion that he had long foreknown his death : so, the arguments against Jesus derived from the treachery of Judas, might seem to be most effectually repelled by the statement, that he had penetrated into the character of the traitor from the first, and could have escaped what his treason prepared for him ; since this would involve the inference that he had exposed himself to the effects of his faithlessness by his own free will, and out of higher considerations.[10]   This method included a second advantage, which attaches to the enunciator of every prediction alleged to be fulfilled, and which the fourth Evangelist naïvely makes his Jesus express, when, after the exposure of the betrayer, he puts into his mouth the words : *Now I tell you before it come, that when it is come to pass, ye may believe that I am he* (xiii. 19)—In fact, the best motto for every *vaticinium post eventum*.   These two objects were the more completely attained, the earlier the period in the life of Jesus to which this foreknowledge was referred ; whence it is to be explained why the author of the fourth gospel, not satisfied with the ordinary representation, that Jesus predicted his betrayal by Judas at the last supper, placed his knowledge on this subject in the commencement of the connexion between him and Judas.[11]

This early knowledge on the part of Jesus concerning the treachery of Judas being dismissed as unhistorical, there would be room for the statement that Judas carried the purse of the society ; since this particular only appeared incompatible with the above foreknowledge, while, if Jesus was in general mistaken in Judas, he might, under this error, have entrusted the funds to him.   But by the proof that the representation of John, in relation to the knowledge of Jesus concerning his betrayer, is a fictitious one, its credibility in this matter is so shaken, that no confidence can be placed in the other statement.   If the author of the fourth gospel has embellished the relation between Jesus and Judas on the side connected with Jesus, he can scarcely

---

[9] Orig. c. Cels., ii. 11 f.
[10] Comp. Probabil., p. 130.
[11] Still farther back we find, not the knowledge of Jesus concerning his betrayer, but an important meeting between them, in the apocryphal *Evangelium infantiæ arabicum*, c. xxxv. ap. Fabricius 1, p. 197 f., ap. Thilo, 1, p. 108 f.   Here a demoniacal boy, who in his attacks bit violently at everything around him, is brought to the child Jesus, attempts to bite him, and because he cannot reach him with his teeth gives him a blow on the right side, whereupon the child Jesus weeps, while Satan comes out of the boy in the form of a furious dog.   *Hic autem puer, qui Jesum percussit et ex quo Satanas sub forma canis exivit, fuit Judas Ischariotes, qui illum Judæis prodidit.*

have left the side of Judas unadorned ; if he has introduced the fact, that Jesus *was betrayed*, by making Jesus foresee this part of his destiny, his other statement, that Judas had beforehand exhibited his avarice by a dishonest use of the common purse, may easily be only an introduction to the fact, that Jesus was betrayed *by Judas*.

But even though we renounce the information given by John concerning the character and motives of Judas : we still retain, in the forementioned statement of the synoptists, the most decided intimation that the chief motive of his deed was covetousness.

§ 119.

DIFFERENT OPINIONS CONCERNING THE CHARACTER OF JUDAS, AND THE MOTIVES OF HIS TREACHERY.

From the earliest to the latest times there have been persons, who have held opinions at issue with this view of the New Testament writers concerning the motives of Judas, and with their entirely reprobatory judgment upon them (comp. Acts i. 16 ff.) ; and this divergency has arisen partly out of an exaggerated supranaturalism, and partly out of a rationalistic bias.

An over-strained supranaturalism, proceeding from the point of view presented in the New Testament itself, namely, that the death of Jesus, decreed in the Divine plan of the world for the salvation of mankind, might even regard Judas, by whose treachery the death of Jesus was brought about, as a blameless instrument in the hand of Providence, a co-operator in the redemption of mankind. He might be placed in this light by the supposition that he had knowledge of that Divine decree, and that its fulfilment was the object at which he aimed in betraying Jesus. We actually find this mode of viewing the subject on the part of the gnostic sect of the Cainites, who, according to the ancient writers on heresies, held that Judas had liberated himself from the narrow Jewish opinions of the other disciples and attained to the gnosis, and accordingly betrayed Jesus because he knew that by his death the kingdom of the inferior spirits who ruled the world would be overthrown.[1] Others in the early church admitted that Judas betrayed Jesus out of covetousness ; maintaining, however, that he did not anticipate the death of Jesus as a consequence of his betrayal, but supposed that he would, as he had often previously done, escape from his enemies by an exertion of his supernatural power :[2] an opinion which forms the transition to the modern methods of justifying the traitor.

As the above mentioned supranaturalistic exaltation of Judas by the Cainites immediately proceeded from their antagonistic position with respect to Judaism, in virtue of which they had made it a principle to honour all who were blamed by the Jewish authors of the Old Testament, and the judaizing authors of the New, and vice versâ : so Rationalism especially in its first indignation at the long subjection of the reason to the fetters of authority,

---

[1] Iren. adv. hær. I. 35 : *Judam proditorem—solum præ ceteris cognoscentem veritatem perfecisse proditionis mysterium, per quem et terrena et cælestia omnia dissoluta dicunt.* Epiphan. xxxviii. 3 : *Some Cainites say, that Judas betrayed Jesus because he regarded him as a wicked man* πονηρὸν, *who meant to destroy the good law :* ἄλλοι δὲ τῶν αὐτῶν, οὐχὶ φασιν, ἀλλὰ ἀγαθὸν αὐτὸν ὄντα παρέδωκε κατὰ τὴν ἐπουράνιον γνῶσιν ἔγνωσαν γάρ, φησιν, οἱ ἄρχοντες, ὅτι, ἐὰν ὁ Χριστὸς παραδοθῇ σταυρῷ, κενοῦται αὐτῶν ἡ ἀσθενὴς δύναμις· καὶ τοῦτό, φησι γνούς ὁ Ἰούδας, ἔσπευσε καὶ πάντα ἐκίνησεν ὥστε παραδοῦναι αὐτὸν, ἀγαθὸν ἔργον ποιήσας ἡμῖν εἰς σωτηρίαν. καὶ δεῖ ἡμᾶς ἐπαινεῖν καὶ ἀποδιδόναι αὐτῷ τὸν ἔπαινον, ὅτι δι' αὐτοῦ κατεσκευάσθη ἡμῖν ἡ τοῦ σταυροῦ σωτηρία καὶ ἡ διὰ τῆς τοιαύτης ὑποθέσεως τῶν ἄνω ἀποκάλυψις.

[2] Theophylact, in Matth. xxvii. 4.

felt a certain delight both in divesting of their nimbus those biblical personages who according to its views had been too zealously deified by orthodoxy,
and also in defending and elevating those who were condemned or depreciated by the latter.   Hence, in the Old Testament, the exaltation of
Esau over Jacob, of Saul over Samuel ; in the New, of Martha over Mary,
the eulogiums on the doubting Thomas, and now the apology even for the
traitor Judas.   According to some, he became a criminal out of injured
honour : the manner in which Jesus reproved him at the meal at Bethany,
and, in general, the inferior degree of regard which he experienced in comparison with other disciples, converted his love for his teacher into hatred and
revenge.[3] Others have preferred the conjecture preserved by Theophylact,
that Judas may have hoped to see Jesus this time also escape from his
enemies.   Some have taken up this idea in the supranaturalistic sense, supposing
it to be the expectation of Judas that Jesus would set himself at liberty by an
exertion of his miraculous power ;[4] others consistently with their point of
view have supposed that Jndas may probably have expected that if Jesus were
taken prisoner the people would raise an insurrection in his favour and set
him at liberty.[5]   These opinions represent Judas as one who, in common with
the other disciples, conceived the messianic kingdom as an earthly and
political one, and hence was discontented that Jesus so long abstained from
availing himself of the popular favour, in order to assume the character of the
messianic ruler.   Instigated either by attempts at bribery on the part of the
Sanhedrim, or by the humour of their plan to seize Jesus in secret after the
feast, Judas sought to forestall this project, which must have been fatal to
Jesus, and to bring about his arrest before the expiration of the feast time, in
which he might certainly hope to see Jesus liberated by an insurrection, by
which means he would be compelled at last to throw himself into the arms of
the people, and thus take the decisive step towards the establishment of his
dominion.   When he heard Jesus speak of the necessity of his being captured,
and of his rising again in three days, he understood these expressions as an
intimation of the concurrence of Jesus in his plan ; under this mistake, he
partly failed to hear, and partly misinterpreted, his additional admonitory
discourse ; and especially understood the words : *What thou doest, do
quickly,* as an actual encouragement to the execution of his design.   He took
the thirty pieces of silver from the priests either to conceal his real intentions
under the appearance of covetousness, and thus to lull every suspicion on
their part ; or, because, while he expected an exaltation to one of the first
places in the kingdom of his master, he was not unwilling to combine with it
even that small advantage.   But Judas had miscalculated in two points :
first, in not considering that after the feasting of the paschal night, the people
would not be early on the alert for an insurrection ; secondly, in overlooking
the probability, that the Sanhedrim would hasten to deliver Jesus into the
hands of the Romans, from whom a popular insurrection would hardly
suffice to deliver him.   Thus Judas is supposed to be either an honest man
misunderstood,[6] or a deluded one, who however was of no common character,
but exhibited even in his despair the wreck of apostolic greatness ;[7] or, he
is supposed, by evil means, indeed, to have sought the attainment of an

---

[3] Kaiser, bibl. Theol. I, s. 249.   Klopstock gives a similar representation in his Messias.
[4] K. Ch. L. Schmidt, exeg. Beiträge, I, Thl. 2ter Versuch, s. 18 ff. ; comp. Schmidt's
Bibliothek, 3, I, s. 163 ff.
[5] Paulus, exeg. Handb. 3, b, s. 451 ff. L. J. I, b, s. 143 ff. ; Hase, L. J., § 132.   Comp.
Theile, zur Biographie Jesu, § 33.
[6] Schmidt, ut sup.
[7] Hase.

object, which was nevertheless good.[8] Neander imagines the two opposite opinions concerning Jesus, the supernatural and the natural, to have presented themselves to the mind of Judas in the form of a dilemma, so that he reasoned thus : if Jesus is the Messiah, a delivery into the hands of his enemies will, owing to his supernatural power, in no way injure him, but will, on the contrary, serve to accelerate his glorification : if, on the other hand, he is not the Messiah, he deserves destruction. According to this, the betrayal was merely a test, by which the doubting disciple meant to try the messiahship of his master.[9]

Among these views, that which derives the treachery of Judas from wounded ambition, is the only one which can adduce a positive indication in its favour : namely, the repulse which the traitor drew on himself from Jesus at the meal in Bethany. But against such an appeal to this reproof we have already, on another occasion, applied the remark of the most recent criticism, that its mildness, especially as compared with the far more severe rebuke administered to Peter, Matt. xvi. 23, must forbid our attributing to it such an effect as the rancour which it is supposed to have engendered in Judas ; [10] while that in other instances he was less considered than his fellow-disciples, we have nowhere any trace.

All the other conjectures as to what was properly the motive of the deed of Judas, can only be supported by negative grounds, i.e. grounds which make it improbable in general that his project had a bad aim, and in particular, that his motive was covetousness ; a positive proof, that he intended to further the work of Jesus, and especially that he was actuated by violent political views of the Messiah's kingdom, is not to be discovered.—That Judas had in general no evil designs against Jesus is argued chiefly from the fact, that after the delivery of Jesus to the Romans, and the inevitableness of his death had come to his knowledge, he fell into despair ; this being regarded as a proof that he had expected an opposite result. But not only does the unfortunate result of crime, as Paulus thinks, but also its fortunate result, that is, its success, " exhibit that which had before been veiled under a thousand extenuating pretexts, in all the blackness of its real form." Crime once become real, once passed into act, throws off the mask which it might wear while it remained merely ideal, and existed in thought alone ; hence, as little as the repentance of many a murderer, when he sees his victim lie before him, proves that he did not really intend to commit the murder ; so little can the anguish of Judas, when he saw Jesus beyond rescue, prove that he had not beforehand contemplated the death of Jesus as the issue of his deed.

But, it is further said, covetousness cannot have been the motive of Judas ; for if gain had been his object, he could not be blind to the fact that the continued charge of the purse in the society of Jesus, would yield him more than the miserable thirty pieces of silver (from 20 to 25 thalers,* of our money), a sum which among the Jews formed the compensation for a wounded slave, being four months' wages. But these thirty pieces of silver are in vain sought for in any other narrator than Matthew. John is entirely silent as to any reward offered to Judas by the priests ; Mark and Luke speak indefinitely of *money* ἀργύριον, which they had promised him ; and Peter in the Acts (i. 18) merely mentions a *reward*, μισθὸς, which Judas obtained. Matthew, however, who alone has that definite sum, leaves us at the same time in no doubt as to the historical value of his statement. After relating the end of Judas (xxvii. 9 f.), he cites a passage from Zechariah (xi. 12 f. ; he ascribes it by mistake

8 Paulus.   9 Neander, L. J. Chr., s. 578 f.
10 Vol. II. § 88 ; comp. Hase, ut sup.
[* The German Thaler (Rixthaler) is equivalent to about three shillings. TR.]

to Jeremiah), wherein likewise thirty pieces of silver appear as a price at which some one is valued. It is true that in the prophetic passage the thirty pieces of silver are not given as purchase money, but as hire; he to whom they are paid is the prophet, the representative of Jehovah, and the smallness of the sum is an emblem of the slight value which the Jews set upon the divine benefits so plentifully bestowed on them.[11] But how easily might this passage, where there was mention of a shamefully low price (ironically *a goodly price* אֶדֶר הַיְקָר), at which the Israelites had rated the speaker in the prophecy, remind a Christian reader of his Messiah, who, in any case, had been sold for a paltry price compared with his value, and hence be led to determine by this passage, the price which was paid to Judas for betraying Jesus.[12] Thus the *thirty pieces of silver*, τριάκοντα ἀργύρια, present no support to those who would prove that it could not be the reward which made Judas a traitor; for they leave us as ignorant as ever how great or how small was the reward which Judas received. Neither can we, with Neander, conclude that the sum was trifling from Matt. xxvii. 6 ff.; Acts i. 18, where it is said that a *field*, ἀγρὸς or χωρίον, was purchased with the reward assigned to the treachery of Judas; since, even apart from the historical value of that statement, hereafter to be examined, the two expressions adduced may denote a larger or a smaller piece of land, and the additional observations of Matthew, that it was destined *to bury strangers in*, εἰς ταφὴν τοῖς ξένοις will not allow us to think of a very small extent. How the same theologian can discover in the statement of the two intermediate Evangelists, that the Jewish rulers had promised Judas *money*, ἀργύριον, an intimation that the sum was small, it is impossible to conceive.—Far more weighty is the observation above made with a different aim, that Jesus would scarcely have appointed and retained as purse-bearer one whom he knew to be covetous even to dishonesty; whence Neander directly infers that the fourth Evangelist, when he derived the remark of Judas at the meal in Bethany from his covetousness, put a false construction upon it, in consequence of the idea which ultimately prevailed respecting Judas, and especially added the accusation, that Judas robbed the common fund, out of his own imagination.[13] But in opposition to this it is to be asked, whether in Neander's point of view it be admissible to impute to the apostle John, who is here understood to be the author of the fourth gospel, so groundless a calumny—for such it would be according to Neander's supposition; and, in our point of view, it would at least be more natural to conclude, that Jesus indeed knew Judas to be fond of money, but did not until the last believe him to be dishonest, and hence did not consider him unfit for the post in question. Neander observes in conclusion: if Judas could be induced by money to betray Jesus, he must have long lost all true faith in him. This indeed follows of necessity, and must be supposed in every view of the subject; but this extinction of faith could of itself only lead him to *go back*, ἀπελθεῖν εἰς τὰ ὀπίσω (John vi. 66); in order to prompt him to meditate treachery there must be a further, special incitement, which, intrinsically, might just as well be covetousness, as the views which are attributed to him by Neander and others.

That covetousness, considered as such an immediate motive, suffices to explain the deed of Judas, I will not maintain; I only contend that any other motives are neither stated nor anywhere intimated in the gospels, and that consequently every hypothesis as to their existence is built on the air.[14]

---

[11] Rosenmüller, Schol. in V. T. 7, 4, s. 318 ff.

[12] Even Neander thinks this a possible origin of the above statement in the first gospel, s. 574, Anm.

[13] L. J. Chr., s. 573.   [14] Comp. also Fritzsche, in Matth., p. 759 f.

§ 120.

PREPARATION FOR THE PASSOVER.

On the first day of unleavened bread, in the evening of which the paschal lamb was to be slain, consequently, the day before the feast properly speaking, which however commenced on that evening, *i.e.* the 14th of Nisan, Jesus, according to the two first Evangelists, in compliance with a question addressed to Him by the disciples, sent—Matthew leaves it undecided which and how many, Mark says, two disciples, whom Luke designates as Peter and John—to Jerusalem (perhaps from Bethany), to bespeak a place in which he might partake of the passover with them, and to make the further arrangements (Matt. xxvi. 17 ff. parall.). The three narrators do not altogether agree as to the directions which Jesus gave to these disciples. According to all, he sends them to a man of whom they had only to desire, in the name of their *master* διδάσκαλος, a place in which to celebrate the passover, in order at once to have their want supplied : but first, this locality is more particularly described by the two intermediate Evangelists than by Matthew, namely as *a large upper room*, which was already *furnished and prepared* for the reception of guests ; and secondly, the manner in which they were to find the owner, is described by the former otherwise than by the latter. Matthew makes Jesus merely say to the disciples, that they were to go *to such a man*, πρὸς τὸν δεῖνα : the others, that, being come into the city, they would meet a man *bearing a pitcher of water*, whom they were to follow into the house which he should enter, and there make their application to the owner.

In this narrative there have been found a multitude of difficulties, which Gabler has assembled in a special treatise.[1] At the very threshold of the narrative it occasions surprise, that Jesus should not have thought of any preparation for the passover until the last day, nay, that he should even then have needed to be reminded of it by the disciples, as the two first Evangelists tell us : for owing to the great influx of people at the time of the passover (2,700,000, according to Josephus),[2] the accommodations in the city were soon disposed of, and the majority of the strangers were obliged to encamp in tents before the city. It is the more remarkable, then, that, notwithstanding all this the messengers of Jesus find the desired chamber disengaged, and not only so, but actually kept in reserve by the owner and prepared for a repast, as if he had had a presentiment that it would be bespoken by Jesus. And so confidently is this reckoned on by Jesus that he directs his disciples to ask the owner of the house,—not *whether* he can obtain from him a room in which to eat the passover, but merely—*where* the guest-chamber appropriated to this purpose may be ? or, if we take Matthew's account, he directs them to say to him that he will eat the passover at his house ; to which it must be added that, according to Mark and Luke, Jesus even knows what kind of chamber will be assigned him, and in what part of the house it is situated. But the way in which, according to these two Evangelists, the two disciples were to find their way to the right house, is especially remarkable. The words ὑπάγετε εἰς τὴν πόλιν πρὸς τὸν δεῖνα in Matthew (v. 18), sound as if Jesus had named the person to whom the disciples were to go, but that the narrator either would not or could not repeat it : whereas in the two other Evangelists, Jesus indicates the house into which they were to enter, by means of

[1] Ueber die Anordnung des letzten Paschamahls Jesu, in his neust. theol. Journal, 2, 5, s. 441 ff.
[2] Bell. jud. vi. ix. 3.

a person whom they would meet carrying a vessel of water.   Now how could Jesus in Bethany, or wherever else he might be, foreknow this accidental circumstance, unless, indeed, it had been pre-concerted that at this particular time a servant from the house should appear with a vessel of water, and thus await the messengers of Jesus ?   To the rationalistic expositors everything in our narrative appeared to point to a preconcerted arrangement; and this being presupposed, they believed that all its difficulties would at once be solved.   The disciples, dispatched so late, could only find a room disengaged if it had been previously bespoken by Jesus; he could only direct them to address the owner of the house so categorically, if he had already previously made an arrangement with him ; this would explain the precise knowledge of Jesus as to the locality, and, lastly, (the point from which this explanation sets out), his certainty that the disciples would meet a man carrying water from that particular house.   This circumlocutory manner of indicating the house, which might have been avoided by the simple mention of the owner's name, is supposed to have been adopted by Jesus, that the place where he intended to keep the passover might not be known before the time to the betrayer, who would otherwise perhaps have surprised him there, and thus have disturbed the repast.[3]

But such is not at all the impression produced by the evangelical narrative. Of a preconcerted arrangement, of a previous bespeaking of the apartment, it says nothing ; on the contrary, the words, *they found as he had said unto them,* in Mark and Luke, seem intended to convey the idea that Jesus was able to predict everything as they afterwards actually found it ; a solicitous foresight is nowhere indicated, but rather a miraculous foreknowledge.   Here, in fact, as above in the procuring of the animal for the entrance into Jerusalem, we have a twofold miracle : first, the fact that everything stands ready to supply the wants of Jesus, and that no one is able to withstand the power of his name ; secondly, the ability of Jesus to take cognizance of distant circumstances, and to predict the merest fortuities.[4]   It must create surprise that, forcibly as this supranaturalistic conception of the narrative before us urges itself upon the reader, Olshausen himself seeks to elude it, by arguments which would nullify most of the histories of miracles, and which we are accustomed to hear only from rationalists.   To the impartial expositor, he says,[5] the narrative does not present the slightest warrant for a miraculous interpretation (we almost fancy ourselves transported into the commentary of Paulus) ; if the narrators intended to recount a miracle, they must have expressly observed that no previous arrangement had been made (precisely the rationalistic demand—if a cure were meant to be recognised as a miracle, the application of natural means must have been expressly denied) ; moreover the object of such a miracle is not to be discerned, a strengthening of the faith of the disciples was not then necessary, nor was it to be effected by this unimportant miracle, after the more exalted ones which had preceded it :— grounds on which the thoroughly similar narrative of the procuring of the ass for the entrance, which Olshausen upholds as a miracle, would be equally excluded from the sphere of the supernatural.

The present narrative, indeed, is so strikingly allied to the earlier one just

---

[3] Thus Gabler, ut sup. ; Paulus, exeg. Handb., 3, b, s. 781 ; Kern, Hauptthatsachen, Tüb. Zeitschr. 1836, 3, s. 3 f. ; Neander, s. 583.

[4] Beza, in Matth. xxvi. 18, correctly, save that he supposes too special a reference to the approaching sufferings of Jesus, thus represents the object of this prediction : *ut magis ac magis intelligerent discipuli, nihil temere in urbe magistro eventurum, sed quæ ad minutissimas usque circumstantias penitus perspecta haberet.*

[5] Bibl. Comm. 2, s. 385 f.   Comp. in opposition to this De Wette, in loc.

mentioned, that in relation to their historical reality, the same judgment must be passed on both. In the one as in the other, Jesus has a want, the speedy supply of which is so cared for by God, that Jesus foreknows to the minutest particular the manner in which it is to be supplied; in the one he needs a guest chamber, as in the other an animal on which to ride; in the one as in the other, he sends out two disciples, to bespeak the thing required; in the one he gives them as a sign by which to find the right house—a man carrying water whom they are to meet, as in the other they have a sign in the circumstance of the ass being tied where two roads meet; in the one as in the other, he directs his disciples simply to mention him to the owner, in the one case as the *master*, διδάσκαλος, in the other, as the *lord*, κύριος, in order to ensure unhesitating compliance with his demand; in both instances the result closely corresponds to his prediction. In the narrative more immediately under our consideration, as in the earlier one, there is wanting an adequate object, for the sake of which so manifold a miracle should have been ordained; while the motive which might occasion the development of the miraculous narrative in the primitive Christian legend is obvious. An Old Testament narrative, to which we have already had occasion to refer in connexion with the earlier miracle, is still more strikingly recalled by the one before us. After disclosing to Saul that he was destined to be King of Israel, Samuel, as a sign of the truth of this more remote announcement, foretells whom Saul will meet on his return homewards : namely, first two men with the information that his father's asses are found; then three others, who will be carrying animals for sacrifice, bread and wine, and will offer him some of the bread, etc. (1 Sam. x. 1 ff.) : whence we see by what kind of predictions the Hebrew legend made its prophets attest their inspiration.

As regards the relation of the gospels to each other, the narrative of Matthew is commonly placed far below that of the two other synoptists, and regarded as the later and more traditional.[6] The circumstance of the man carrying water, especially, is held to have belonged to the original fact, but to have been lost in tradition before the narrative reached Matthew, who inserted in its place the enigmatical ὑπάγετε πρὸς τὸν δεῖνα, *go to such a man*. But we have seen, on the contrary, that the δεῖνα presents no difficulty; while the circumstance of the water-bearer is in the highest degree enigmatical.[7] Still less is the omission of Matthew to designate the two commissioned disciples as Peter and John, an indication that the narrative of the third gospel is the more original one. For when Schleiermacher says that this trait might easily be lost in the course of transmission through several hands, but that it could scarcely have been added by a later hand,—the latter half of his proposition, at least, is without foundation. There is little probability that Jesus should have assigned so purely economical an office to the two most eminent disciples; whereas it is easy to conceive that in the first instance it was simply narrated, as by Matthew, that Jesus sent *the disciples* or *some disciples*, that hereupon the number was fixed at *two*, perhaps from the narrative of the procuring of the ass, and that at length, as the appointment had relation to a task which was ultimately of high importance,—the preparing of the last meal of Jesus,—these places were filled by the two chief apostles, so that in this instance even Mark appears to have kept nearer to the original fact, since he has not adopted into his narrative the names of the two disciples, which are presented by Luke.

[6] Schulz, über das Abendmahl, s. 321 ; Schleiermacher, über den Lukas, s. 280 ; Weisse, die evang. Gesch., s. 600 f.

[7] Vid. Theile, über die letzte Mahlzeit Jesu, in Winer's and Engelhardt's neuem krit. Journal, 2, s. 169, Anm., and zur Biographie Jesu, § 31.

§ 121.

DIVERGENT STATEMENTS RESPECTING THE TIME OF THE LAST SUPPER.

Not only does the fourth Evangelist omit all mention of the above arrangements for the paschal meal; he also widely diverges from the synoptists in relation to the meal itself. Independently of the difference which runs throughout the description of the scene, and which can only be hereafter considered, he appears, in regard to the time of the meal, to represent it as occurring before the passover, as decidedly as it is represented by the synoptists to be the paschal meal itself.

When we read in the latter, that the day on which the disciples were directed by Jesus to prepare for the meal, was already *the first day of unleavened bread*, ἡ πρώτη τῶν ἀζύμων, *when the passover must be killed*, ἐν ᾗ ἔδει θύεσθαι τὸ πάσχα (Matt. xxvi. 17 parall.): we cannot suppose the meal in question to have been any other than the paschal ; further, when the disciples ask Jesus, *Where wilt thou that we prepare for thee to eat the passover?* ποῦ θέλεις ἑτοιμάσωμέν σοι φαγεῖν τὸ πάσχα ; when it is hereupon said of the disciples, that they *made ready the passover*, ἡτοίμασαν τὸ πάσχα (Matt. v. 19 parall.), and of Jesus, that *when evening was come, he sat down with the twelve*, ὀψίας γενομένης ἀνέκειτο μετὰ τῶν δώδεκα (v. 20) : the meal to which they here sat down appears to be marked out even to the superfluity as the paschal, even if Luke (xxii. 15) did not make Jesus open the repast with the words : *With desire I have desired to eat this passover with you*, ἐπιθυμίᾳ ἐπεθύμησα τοῦτο τὸ πάσχα φαγεῖν μεθ' ὑμῶν.—When, on the other hand, the fourth gospel commences its narrative of the last meal with the statement of time : *before the feast of the passover*, πρὸ δὲ τῆς ἑορτῆς τοῦ πάσχα, (xiii. 1) ; the *supper*, δεῖπνον, which is mentioned immediately after (v. 2), appears also to happen before the passover ; especially as throughout John's description of this evening, which, especially in relation to the discourses accompanying the meal, is very ample, there is not any notice or even allusion, to indicate that Jesus was on this occasion celebrating the passover. Further, when Jesus after the meal addresses the traitor with the summons, *what thou doest, do quickly*, this is misunderstood by the rest of the disciples to mean, *Buy those things that we have need of against the feast*, εἰς τὴν ἑορτήν (v. 29). Now the requirements for the feast related chiefly to the paschal meal, and consequently the meal just concluded cannot have been the paschal. Again, it is said, xviii. 28, that on the following morning, the Jews would not enter the Gentile prætorium, *lest they should be defiled ; but that they might eat the passover*, ἵνα μὴ μιανθῶσιν, ἀλλ' ἵνα, φάγωσι τὸ πάσχα : whence it would seem that the paschal meal was yet in prospect. To this it may be added that this same succeeding day, on which Jesus was crucified, is called the *preparation of the passover*, παρασκευὴ τοῦ πάσχα, i.e. the day on the evening of which the paschal lamb was to be eaten ; moreover, when it is said of the second day after the meal in question, being that which Jesus passed in the grave : *that sabbath day was an high day*, ἦν γὰρ μεγάλη ἡ ἡμέρα ἐκείνου τοῦ σαββάτου (xix. 31) ; this peculiar solemnity appears to have proceeded from the circumstance, that on that sabbath fell the first day of the passover, so that the paschal lamb was not eaten on the evening on which Jesus was arrested, but on the evening of his burial.

These divergencies are so important, that many expositors, in order to prevent the Evangelists from falling into contradiction with each other, have here also tried the old expedient of supposing that they do not speak of the same thing—that John intends to describe an altogether different repast from that of the synoptists. According to this view, the δεῖπνον of John was an ordinary evening meal, doubtless in Bethany ; on this occasion Jesus washed the disciples' feet, spoke of the betrayer, and after Judas had left the company, added other discourses of a consoling and admonitory tendency, until at length, on the morning of the 14th of Nisan, he summoned the disciples to depart from Bethany and proceed to Jerusalem, in the words : *Arise, let us go hence* (xiv. 31). Here the synoptical account may be interposed, since it represents the two disciples as being sent forward to Jerusalem to prepare for the paschal meal, and then records its celebration, concerning which John is silent, and only takes up the thread of the narrative at the discourses delivered after the paschal meal (xv. 1 ff.).[1] But this attempt to avoid contradiction by referring the respective narratives to totally different events, is counteracted by the undeniable identity of many features in the two meals. Independently of isolated particulars which are found alike in both accounts, it is plain that John, as well as the synoptists, intends to describe the last meal of which Jesus partook with his disciples. This is implied in the introduction to John's narrative ; for the proof which is there said to be given of Jesus having loved his own *unto the end*, εἰς τέλος, may be the most suitably referred to his last moments of companionship with them. In like manner, the discourses after the meal point to the prospect of immediate separation ; and the meal and discourses are, in John also, immediately followed by the departure to Gethsemane and the arrest of Jesus. It is true that, according to the above opinion, these last-named incidents are connected only with those discourses which were delivered on the occasion of the later meal, omitted by John (xv. 17) : but that between xiv. 31 and xv. 1 the author of the fourth gospel intentionally omitted the whole incident of the paschal meal, is a position which, although it might appear to explain with some plausibility the singular ἐγείρεσθε, ἄγωμεν ἐντεῦθεν, *Arise, let us go hence*, no one will now seriously maintain. But even admitting such an ellipsis, there still remains the fact that Jesus (xiii. 38) foretells to Peter his denial with this determination of time : οὐ μὴ ἀλέκτωρ φωνήσῃ, *the cock shall not crow*, which he could only make use of at the last meal, and not, as is here presupposed, at an earlier one.[2]

Thus this expedient must be relinquished, and it must be admitted that all the Evangelists intend to speak of the same meal, namely, the last of which Jesus partook with his disciples. And in making this admission, the fairness which we owe to every author, and which was believed to be due in a peculiar degree to the authors of the Bible, appeared to demand an enquiry whether, although they represent one and the same event with great divergencies in several respects, yet nevertheless both sides may not be correct. To obtain an affirmative result of this inquiry it must be shown, as regards the time, either that the three first Evangelists, as well as the fourth, do not intend to describe a paschal meal, or that the latter, as well as the former, does so intend.

In an ancient Fragment[3] it is sought to solve the problem in the first method, by denying that Matthew places the last meal of Jesus at the proper time for the paschal meal, the evening of the 14th of Nisan, and his passion on the first day of the feast of the passover, the 15th of Nisan ; but one does

---

[1] Thus Lightfoot, horæ, p. 463 ff. ; Hess, Geschichte Jesu, 2, s. 273 ff. ; also Venturini 3, s. 634 ff.
[2] An insufficient outlet from this difficulty is pointed out by Lightfoot, p. 482 f.
[3] Fragm. ex Claudii Apollinaris libro de Paschate, in Chron. Paschal. ed. du Fresne. Paris, 1688, p. 6 f. præf.

not see how the express indications respecting the passover in the synoptists can be neutralized.

Hence it has been a far more general attempt in recent times, to draw John to the side of the other Evangelists.[4]   His expression *before the feast of the passover*, πρὸ τῆς ἑορτῆς τοῦ πάσχα (xiii. 1), was thought to be divested of its difficulty by the observation that it is not immediately connected with the *supper* δεῖπνον, but only with the statement that Jesus knew that his hour was come, and that he loved his own unto the end ; it is only in the succeeding verse that there is any mention of the meal, to which therefore that determination of time does not refer.   But to what then can it refer ? to the knowledge that his hour was come ? this is only an incidental remark ; or to the love which endured to the end ? but to this so special a determination of time can only refer, if an external proof of love be intended, and such an one is presented in his conduct at the meal, which consequently remains the point to which that determination of the day must apply.   It is therefore conjectured further that the words πρὸ τῆς ἑορτῆς were used out of accommodation to the Greeks for whom John wrote : since that people did not, like the Jews, begin their day with the evening, the meal taken at the beginning of the first day of the passover, would appear to them to be taken on the evening before the passover.   But what judicious writer, if he supposes a misconstruction possible on the part of the reader, chooses language which can only serve to encourage that misconstruction?   A still more formidable difficulty is presented by xviii. 28, where the Jews, on the morning after the imprisonment of Jesus, will not enter the judgment hall *lest they should be defiled, but that they may eat the passover*, ἀλλ' ἵνα φάγωσι τὸ πάσχα.   Nevertheless it was supposed that passages such as Deut. xvi. 1, 2, where all the sacrifices to be killed during the time of the passover are denoted by the expression פֶּסַח, authorise the interpretation of τὸ πάσχα in this place of the remaining sacrifices to be offered during the paschal week, and especially of the Chagiga, which was to be consumed towards the end of the first feast day.   But as Mosheim has correctly remarked, from the fact that the paschal lamb, together with the rest of the sacrifices to be offered during the feast of the passover was designated πάσχα, it by no means follows that these can be so designated with the exclusion of the paschal lamb.[5]   On the other hand, the friends of the above view have sought to show the necessity of their mode of interpretation, by observing that for the eating of the passover which was celebrated late in the evening, consequently at the commencement of the succeeding day, the entering of a Gentile house in the morning, being a defilement which lasted only through the current day, would have been no disqualification ; but that it would have been such for the partaking of the Chagiga, which was eaten in the afternoon, consequently on the same day on which the defilement was contracted ; so that only this, and not the passover, can have been intended.   But first, we do not know whether entrance into a Gentile house was a defilement for the day merely ; secondly, if such were the case, the Jews, by a defilement contracted in the morning, would still have disqualified themselves from participating in the preparatory proceedings, which fell on the afternoon of the 14th of Nisan ; as, for example, the slaying of the lamb in the outer court of the temple.   Lastly, in order to interpret the passage xix. 14 in consistency with their own view, the harmonists understand the *preparation of the passover*, παρασκευὴ τοῦ πάσχα, to mean the day of preparation for the sabbath in the Easter week ; a violence of interpretation which at least finds no countenance

---

[4] See especially Tholuck and Olshausen, in loc. ; Kern, Hauptthatsachen, Tüb. Zeitschr. 1836, 3, s. 5 ff.
[5] Diss. de verâ notione coenæ Domini, annexed to Cudworth, syst. intell., p. 22, not. 1.

in xix. 31, where the παρασκευή is said to be the preparation for the sabbath, since from this passage it only appears, that the Evangelist conceived the first day of the passover as occurring that year on the sabbath.[6]

These difficulties, which resist the reference of the narrative in John to a real paschal meal, appeared to be obviated by a presupposition derived from Lev. xxiii. 5 ; Num. ix. 3 ; and a passage in Josephus ;[7] namely, that the paschal lamb was eaten, not on the evening from the 14th to the 15th, but on that from the 13th to the 14th of Nisan, so that between the paschal meal and the first feast day, the 15th of Nisan, there fell a working day, the 14th. On this supposition, it would be correct that the day following the last paschal meal taken by Jesus, should be called, as in John xix. 14, *the preparation of the passover*, παρασκευή τοῦ πάσχα, because it was actually a day of preparation for the feast day ; it would also be correct that the following sabbath should be called μεγάλη (xix. 31), since it would coincide with the first day of the feast.[8] But the greatest difficulty, which lies in John xviii. 28, remains unsolved ; for on this plan the words, *that they might eat the passover, ἵνα φάγωσι τὸ πάσχα*, must, since the paschal meal would be already past, be understood of the unleavened bread, which was eaten also during the succeeding feast days : an interpretation which is contrary to all the usages of language. If to this it be added, that the supposition of a working day falling between the passover and the first feast day, has no foundation in the Pentateuch and Josephus, that it is decidedly opposed to later custom, and is in itself extremely improbable ; this expedient cannot but be relinquished.[9]

Perceiving the impossibility of effecting the reconciliation of the synoptists with John by this simple method, other expositors have resorted to a more artificial expedient. The appearance of the Evangelists having placed the last meal of Jesus on different days, is alleged to have its truth in the fact, that either the Jews or Jesus celebrated the passover on another than the usual day. The Jews, say some, in order to avoid the inconvenience arising from the circumstance, that in that year the first day of the passover fell on a Friday, so that two consecutive days must have been solemnized as a sabbath, deferred the paschal meal until the Friday evening, whence on the day of the crucifixion they had still to beware of defilement ; Jesus, however, adhering strictly to the law, celebrated it at the prescribed time, on the Thursday evening : so that the synoptists are right when they describe the last meal of Jesus as an actual celebration of the passover ; and John also is right when he represents the Jews as, the day after, still looking forward to the eating of the paschal lamb.[10] In this case, Mark would be wrong in his statement, that on the day *when they killed the passover*, ὅτε τὸ πάσχα ἔθυον (v. 12), Jesus also caused it to be prepared ; but the main point is, that though in certain cases the passover was celebrated in a later month, it was still on the 15th day ; there is nowhere any trace of a transference to a later day of the same month. —It has therefore been a more favourite supposition that Jesus anticipated the usual time of eating the passover. From purely personal motives, some have thought, foreseeing that at the proper time of the paschal supper he should be already lying in the grave, or at least not sure of life until that period, he, like

---

[6] See these counter observations particularly in Lücke and de Wette, in loc. ; in Sieffert über den Ursprung, s. 127 ff., and Winer, bibl. Realwörterb. 2, s. 238 ff.

[7] Antiq. II. xiv. 16.

[8] Fritzsche, vom Osterlamm ; more recently, Rauch, in the theol. Studien und Kritiken, 1832, 3, s. 537 f.

[9] Comp. De Wette, theol. Studien und Krit. 1834, 4, s. 939 f. ; Tholuck, Comm. z. Joh. s. 245 f. ; Winer, ut sup.

[10] Calvin, in Matth. xxvi. 17.

those Jews who were prevented from journeying to the feast, and like all the Jews of the present day, without a sacrificed lamb, and with mere substitutes for it, celebrated a *commemorative passover*, πάσχα μνημονευτικὸν.[11]   But in the first place, Jesus would not then, as Luke says, have kept the passover on the day *on which the passover must be killed*, ἐν ᾗ ἔδει θύεσθαι τὸ πάσχα; and secondly, in the merely commemorative celebration of the passover, though the prescribed locality (Jerusalem) is dispensed with, the regular time (the evening from the 14th to the 15th Nisan) is inviolably observed : whereas in the case of Jesus the reverse would hold, and he would have celebrated the passover at the usual place, but at an unusual time, which is without example. To shield the alleged transposition of the passover by Jesus from the charge of being unprecedented and arbitrary, it has been maintained that an entire party of his cotemporaries joined in celebrating the passover earlier than the great body of the nation.   It is known that the Jewish sect of the Caraites or Scripturalists differed from the Rabbinites or Traditionalists especially in the determination of the new moon, maintaining that the practice of the latter in fixing the new moon according to astronomical calculation was an innovation, whereas they, true to the ancient, legal practice, determined it according to an empirical observation of the phase of the new luminary.   Now in the time of Jesus, we are told, the Sadducees, from whom the Caraites are said to have sprung, determined the time of the new moon, and with it that of the festival of the passover, which was dependent upon it, differently from the Pharisees ; and Jesus, as the opponent of tradition and the friend of scripture, favoured their practice in this matter.[12]   But not to insist that the connexion of the Caraites with the ancient Sadducees is a mere conjecture ; it was a well-founded objection put forth by the Caraites, that the determination of the new moon by calculation did not arise until after the destruction of the temple by the Romans ; so that at the time of Jesus such a difference cannot have existed ; nor is there besides any indication to be discovered that at that time the passover was celebrated on different days by different parties.[13]   Supposing, however, that the above difference as to the determining of the new moon already prevailed in the time of Jesus, the settling of it according to the phase, which Jesus is supposed to have followed, would rather have resulted in a later than an earlier celebration of the passover ; whence some have actually conjectured that more probably Jesus followed the astronomical calculation.[14]

Besides what may thus be separately urged against every attempt at an amicable adjustment of the differences between the Evangelists, as to the time of the last supper; there is one circumstance which is decisive against all, and which only the most recent criticism has adequately exposed.   With respect, namely, to this contradiction, the case is not so that among passages for the most part harmonious, there appear only one or two statements of an apparently inconsistent sense, of which it might be said that the author had here used an inaccurate expression, to be explained from the remaining passages : but, that *all* the chronological statements of the synoptists tend to show that Jesus must have celebrated the passover, *all* those of John, on the contrary, that he cannot have celebrated it.[15]   Thus there stand opposed to each other two differing series of evangelical passages, which are manifestly based on two different views of the fact on the part of the narrators : hence, as Sieffert re-

---

[11] Grotius, in Matth. xxvi. 18.
[12] Iken, Diss. philol. theol., vol. 2, p. 416 ff.
[13] Vid. Paulus, exeg. Handb. 3, a, s. 486 ff.
[14] Michaelis, Anm. zu Joh. 13.
[15] Sieffert, ut sup. ; Hase, L. J., § 124 ; De Wette, exeg. Handb. 1, 3, s. 149 ff ; Theile, zur Biographie Jesu, § 31.

marks, to persist in disputing the existence of a divergency between the Evangelists, can no longer be regarded as scientific exposition, but only as unscientific arbitrariness and obstinacy.

Modern criticism is therefore constrained to admit, that on one side or the other there is an error; and, setting aside the current prejudices in favour of the fourth gospel, it was really an important reason which appeared to necessitate the imputation of this error to the synoptists.   The ancient Fragmentist, attributed to Apollinaris, mentioned above, objects to the opinion that Jesus *suffered on the great day of unleavened bread,* τῇ μεγάλῃ ἡμέρᾳ τῶν ἀζύμων ἔπαθεν, that this would have been *contrary to the law* ἀσύμφωνος τῷ νόμῳ ; and in recent times also it has been observed, that the day following the last meal of Jesus is treated on all sides so entirely as a working day, that it cannot be supposed the first day of the passover, nor, consequently, the meal of the previous evening, the paschal meal.   Jesus does not solemnize the day, for he goes out of the city, an act which was forbidden on the night of the passover; nor do his friends, for they begin the preparations for his burial, and only leave them unfinished on account of the arrival of the next day, the sabbath ; still less do the members of the Sanhedrim keep it sacred, for they not only send their servants out of the city to arrest Jesus, but also personally undertake judicial proceedings, a trial, sentence, and accusation before the Procurator ; in general, there appears, throughout, only the fear of desecrating the following day, which commenced on the evening of the crucifixion, and nowhere any solicitude about the current one :   clear signs that the synoptical representation of the meal as a paschal one, is a later error, since in the remaining narrative of the synoptists themselves, there is evidence, not easy to be mistaken, of the real fact, that Jesus was crucified before the passover.[16] These observations are certainly of weight.   It is true that the first, relative to the conduct of Jesus, might perhaps be invalidated by the contradiction existing between the Jewish decisions as to the law cited ;[17] while the last and strongest may be opposed by the fact, that trying and giving sentence on the sabbaths and feast days was not only permitted among the Jews, but there was even a larger place for the administration of justice on such days, on account of the greater concourse of people ; so, also, according to the New Testament itself, the Jews sent out officers to seize Jesus on the *great day* ἡμέρα μεγάλη of the Feast of Tabernacles (John vii. 44 f.), and at the Feast of Dedication they were about to stone him (John x. 31), while Herod caused Peter to be imprisoned during the *days of unleavened bread* ; though indeed he intended to defer the public sentencing and execution until after the passover (Acts xii. 2 f.).   In proof that the crucifixion of Jesus might take place on the feast of the passover, it is urged that the execution was performed by Roman soldiers ; and that moreover, even according to Jewish custom, it was usual to reserve the execution of important criminals for a feast time, in order to make an impression on a greater multitude.[18]   But only thus much is to be proved : that during the feast time, and thus during the passover, on the five intermediate and less solemn days, criminals were tried and executed,—not that this was admissible also on the first and last days of the passover, which

---

[16] Theile, in Winer's Krit. Journal, 2, s. 157 ff. ; Sieffert and Lücke, ut sup.

[17] Pesachin f. lxv. 2, ap. Lightfoot, p. 654 : *Paschate primo tenetur quispiam ad pernoctationem.   Gloss. : Paschatizans tenetur ad pernoctandum in Hierosolyma nocte prima.*   On the other hand, Tosaphoth ad tr. Pesachin 8 : *In Paschate Aegyptiaco dicitur : nemo exeat—usque ad mane.   Sed sic non fuit in sequentibus generationibus,—quibus comedebatur id uno loco et pernoctabant in alio.*   Comp. Schneckenburger, Beiträge, s. 9.

[18] Tract. Sanhedr. f. lxxxix. 1, ap. Schöttgen, i. p. 221 ; comp. Paulus, ut sup. s. 492.

ranked as sabbaths ;[19] and thus we read in the Talmud that Jesus was crucified on the ערב פסח, i.e. the evening before the passover.[20]   It would be
another thing if, as Dr. Baur strives to prove, the execution of criminals, as a
sanguinary expiation for the people, belonged to the essential significance of
the passover, as a feast of expiation, and hence the custom, noticed by the
Evangelists, of liberating a prisoner at the feast had been only the reverse
side to the execution of another, presenting the same relation as that between
the two goats and the two sparrows in the Jewish offerings of atonement and
purification.[21]

It is certainly very possible that the primitive Christian tradition might be
led even unhistorically to associate the last supper of Jesus with the paschal
lamb, and the day of his death with the feast of the passover. As the
Christian supper represented in its form, the passover, and in its import, the
death of Jesus : it was natural enough to unite these two points—to place the
execution of Jesus on the first day of the passover, and to regard his last
meal, at which he was held to have founded the Christian supper, as the
paschal meal. It is true that presupposing the author of the first gospel to
have been an apostle and a participator in the last meal of Jesus, it is difficult
to explain how he could fall into such a mistake. At least it is not enough
to say, with Theile, that the more the last meal partaken with their master
transcended all paschal meals in interest to the disciples, the less would they
concern themselves as to the time of it, whether it occurred on the evening of
the passover, or a day earlier.[22] For the first Evangelist does not leave this
undetermined, but speaks expressly of a paschal meal, and to this degree a
real participator, however long he might write after that evening, could not
possibly deceive himself. Thus on the above view, the supposition that the
first Evangelist was an eye-witness must be renounced, and he must be held,
in common with the two intermediate ones, to have drawn his materials from
tradition.[23] The difficulty arising from the fact, that all the synoptists, and
consequently all those writers who have preserved to us the common evangelical tradition, agree in such an error,[24] may perhaps be removed by the
observation, that just as generally as in the Judæo-Christian communities, in
which the evangelical tradition was originally formed, the Jewish passover
was still celebrated, so generally must the effort present itself to give that
feast a Christian import, by referring it to the death and the last meal of
Jesus.

But it is equally easy, presupposing the correctness of the synoptical determination of time, to conceive how John might be led erroneously to place the
death of Jesus on the afternoon of the 14th of Nisan, and his last meal on
the previous evening. If, namely, this Evangelist found in the circumstance
that the legs of the crucified Christ were not broken, a fulfilment of the words
Not a bone of him shall be broken, ὀστοῦν οὐ συντριβήσεται αὐτῷ (Exod. xii.
46) : this supposed relation between the death of Jesus and the paschal
lamb might suggest to him the idea, that at the same time in which the
paschal lambs were killed, on the afternoon of the 14th of Nisan, Jesus

[19] Fritzsche, in Matth., p. 763 f. ; comp. 755 ; Lücke, 2, s. 614.
[20] Sanhedr. f. xliii. 1, ap. Schöttgen, ii. p. 700.
[21] Ueber die ursprüngliche Bedeutung des Passahfestes u. s. w., Tübinger, Zeitschrift f.
Theol. 1832, 1, s. 90 ff.
[22] Ut sup. s. 167 ff.
[23] Sieffert, ut sup. s. 144 ff. ; Lücke, s. 628 ff. ; Theile, zur Biogr. Jesu, § 31 ; De Wette,
exeg. Handb. 1, 3, s. 149 ff. ; comp. Neander, L. J. Chr., s. 580 ff. Anm.
[24] Fritzsche, in Matth., p. 763 ; Kern, über den Urspr. des Ev. Matth. in der Tüb. Zeitschrift, 1834, 2, s. 98.

suffered on the cross and gave up the ghost ;[25] in which case the meal taken the evening before was not the paschal meal.[26]

Thus we can conceive a possible cause of error on both sides, and since the internal difficulty of the synoptical determination of time, namely, the manifold violations of the first day of the passover, is in some degree removed by the observations above cited, and is counterpoised by the agreement of three Evangelists : our only course is to acknowledge an irreconcilable contradiction between the respective accounts, without venturing a decision as to which is the correct one.

§ 122.

DIVERGENCIES IN RELATION TO THE OCCURRENCES AT THE LAST MEAL OF JESUS.

Not only in relation to the time of the last meal of Jesus, but also in relation to what passed on that occasion, there is a divergency between the Evangelists. The chief difference lies between the synoptists and the fourth gospel : but, on a stricter comparison, it is found that only Matthew and Mark closely agree, and that Luke diverges from them considerably, though on the whole he is more accordant with his predecessors than with his successor.

Besides the meal itself, the following features are common to all the accounts : that, during the meal, the coming betrayal by Judas is spoken of; and that, during or after the meal, Jesus predicts to Peter his denial. As minor differences we may notice, that in John, the mode of indicating the traitor is another and more precise than that described by the other Evangelists, and has a result of which the latter are ignorant ; and that, further, in the fourth gospel the meal is followed by prolonged farewell discourses, which are not found in the synoptists : but the principal difference is, that while according to the synoptists Jesus instituted the Lord's supper at this final meal, in John he instead of this washes the disciples' feet.

The three synoptists have in common the instituting of the Lord's supper, together with the announcement of the betrayal, and the denial ; but there exists a divergency between the two first and the third as to the order of these occurrences, for in the former the announcement of the betrayal stands first, in the latter, the instituting of the Supper; while the announcement of Peter's denial, in Luke, apparently takes place in the room in which the repast had been held, in the two other Evangelists, on the way to the Mount of Olives. Again, Luke introduces some passages which the two first Evangelists either do not give at all, or not in this connexion : the contention for pre-eminence and the promise of the twelve thrones, have in their narratives a totally different position ; while what passes in Luke on the subject of the swords is in them entirely wanting.

In his divergency from the two first Evangelists, Luke makes some approximation to the fourth. As John, in the washing of the disciples' feet, presents a symbolical act having reference to ambitious contention for pre-eminence, accompanied by discourses on humility : so Luke actually mentions a contention for pre-eminence, and appends to it discourses not entirely without affinity with those in John ; further, it is in common with John that Luke makes the observations concerning the betrayer occur at the opening of the

---

[25] Comp. Suicer, thesaur. 2, s. 613.
[26] Another view as to the cause of the error in the fourth gospel is given in the Probabilia, s. 100 ff. ; comp. Weisse, die evang. Gesch. 1, s. 446 f. Anm.

repast, and after a symbolical act ; and lastly, that he represents the announcement of Peter's denial as having been delivered in the room where the repast
had been held.

The greatest difficulty here naturally arises from the divergency, that the
institution of the Lord's supper, unanimously recorded by the synoptists, is
wanting in John, who in its stead relates a totally different act of Jesus,
namely, the washing of the disciples' feet. Certainly, by those who, in similar
cases, throughout the whole previous course of the evangelical narrative, have
found a sufficient resource in the supposition, that it was the object of John
to supply the omissions of the earlier gospels, the present difficulty is sur-
mounted as well, or as ill, as any other. John, it is said, saw that the institution of the Supper was already narrated in the three first Evangelists in a
way which fully agreed with his own recollection ; hence he held a repetition
of it superfluous.[1] But if, among the histories already recorded in the three
first gospels, the fourth Evangelist really intended to reproduce only those in
the representation of which he found something to rectify or supply : why
does he give another edition of the history of the miraculous feeding, in
which he makes no emendation of any consequence, and at the same time
omit the institution of the Lord's supper? For here the divergencies between
the synoptists in the arrangement of the scene, and the turn given to the
words of Jesus, and more especially the circumstance that they, according to
his representation, erroneously, make that institution occur on the evening of
the passover, must have appeared to him a reason for furnishing an authentic
account. In consideration of this difficulty, the position that the author of
the fourth gospel was acquainted with the synoptical writings, and designed to
complete and rectify them, is now, indeed, abandoned ; but it is still maintained that he was acquainted with the common oral tradition, and supposed
it known to his readers also, and on this ground, it is alleged, he passed over
the institution of the Supper as a history generally known.[2] But that it should
be the object of an evangelical writing to narrate only the less known,
omitting the known, is an idea which cannot be consistently entertained.
Written records imply a mistrust of oral tradition ; they are intended not
merely as a supplement to this, but also as a means of fixing and preserving it,
and hence the capital facts, being the most spoken of, and therefore the most
exposed to misrepresentation, are precisely those which written records can
the least properly omit. Such a fact is the founding of the Lord's supper,
and we find, from a comparison of the different New Testament accounts, that
the expressions with which Jesus instituted it must have early received
additions or mutilations ; consequently, it is the last particular which John
should have omitted. But, it is further said, the narrating of the institution
of the Lord's supper was of no importance to the object of the fourth gospel.[3]
How so ? With regard to its general object, the convincing of its readers
that *Jesus is the Christ the Son of God* (xx. 31), was it of no importance to
communicate a scene in which he appears as the founder of a *new covenant*,
καινὴ διαθήκη ? and in relation to the special object of the passage in question,
namely, the exhibiting of the love of Jesus as a love which endured unto the
end (xiii. 1), would it have contributed nothing to mention how he offered
his body and blood as meat and drink to his followers, and thus realized his
words in John vi. ? But, it is said, John here as elsewhere, only concerns
himself with the more profound discourses of Jesus, for which reason he
passes over the institution of the Supper, and begins his narrative with the

---

[1] Paulus, 3, b, s. 499; Olshausen, 2, s. 294.
[2] Lücke, 2, s. 484 f. ; Neander, L. J. Chr., s. 583, Anm.
[3] Olshausen, ut sup.

discourse connected with the washing of the disciples' feet.[4] Nothing, however, but the most obdurate prejudice in favour of the fourth gospel, can make this discourse on humility appear more profound than what Jesus says of the partaking of his body and blood, when instituting the Lord's supper.

But the main point is that harmonists should show us in what part of John's narrative, if we are to believe that he presupposed Jesus to have instituted the Supper at this last meal, he can have made the alleged omission—that they should indicate the break at which that incident may be suitably introduced. On looking into the different commentaries, there appears to be more than one place excellently adapted to such an insertion. According to Olshausen, the end of the 13th chapter, after the announcement of Peter's denial, presents the interval in which the institution of the Supper must be supposed to occur ; herewith the repast closed, and the succeeding discourses from xiv. 1 were uttered by Jesus after the general rising from table, and while standing in the chamber.[5] But, here, it appears as if Olshausen, for the sake of obtaining a resting place between xiii. 38 and xiv. 1, had resigned himself to the delusion of supposing that the words *Arise, let us go hence*, at which he makes Jesus rise from table and deliver the rest of his discourse standing, are found at the end of the 13th chapter, whereas they do not occur until the end of the 14th. Jesus had been speaking of going whither his disciples could not follow him, and had just rebuked the rashness of Peter, in volunteering to lay down life for his sake, by the prediction of his denial : here, at xiv. 1 ff., he calms the minds of the disciples, whom this prediction had disturbed, exhorting them to faith, and directing their attention to the blessed effects of his departure.—Repelled by the firm coherence of this part of the discourse, other commentators, e.g. Paulus, retreat to xiii. 30, and are of opinion that the institution of the Supper may be the most fitly introduced after the withdrawal of Judas, for the purpose of putting his treachery into execution, since this circumstance might naturally excite in Jesus those thoughts concerning his death which lie at the basis of the institution.[6] But even rejecting the opinion of Lücke and others, that ὅτε ἐξῆλθε, *when he went out*, should be united to λέγει ὁ Ἰησοῦς, *Jesus said*, it is unquestionable that the words of Jesus v. 31, *Now is the Son of man glorified*, etc., and what he says farther on (v. 33) of his speedy departure, have an immediate reference to the retiring of Judas. For the verb δοξάζειν in the fourth gospel always signifies the glorification of Jesus, to which he is to be led by suffering ; and with the departure of the apostate disciple to those who brought suffering and death on Jesus, his glorification and his speedy death were decided.—The verses 31-33 being thus inseparably connected with v. 30 ; the next step is to carry the institution of the Supper somewhat lower, and place it where this connexion may appear to cease : accordingly, Lücke makes it fall between v. 33 and 34, supposing that after Jesus (v. 31-33) had composed the minds of the disciples, disturbed and shocked by the departure of the traitor, and had prepared them for the sacred meal, he, at v. 34 f., annexes to the distribution of the bread and wine the new commandment of love. But, as it has been elsewhere remarked,[7] since at v. 36 Peter asks Jesus, in allusion to v. 33, whither he will go, it is impossible that the Supper can have been instituted after the declaration of Jesus v. 33 ; for otherwise Peter would have interpreted the expression *I go*, ὑπάγω, by the *body given* σῶμα διδόμενον and the *blood shed* αἷμα ἐκ χυνόμενον, or in any case would

[4] Sieffert, über den Urspr., s. 152.
[5] Bibl. Comm. 2, s. 310, 381 f.
[6] Paulus, exeg. Handb. 3, b, s. 497.
[7] Meyer, Comm. über den Joh., in loc.

rather have felt prompted to ask the meaning of these latter expressions.—
Acknowledging this, Neander retreats a verse, and inserts the Supper between
v. 32 and 33; [8] but he thus violently severs the obvious connexion between
the words εὐθὺς δοξάσει αὐτὸν *shall straightway glorify him* in the former
verse, and the words ἔτι μικρὸν μεθ᾽ ὑμῶν εἰμι *yet a little while I am with you*
in the latter.—It is, therefore, necessary to retreat still farther than Neander,
or even Paulus : but as from v. 30 up to v. 18, the discourse turns uninterruptedly on the traitor, and this discourse again is inseparably linked to the
washing of the disciples' feet and the explanation of that act, there is no
place at which the institution of the Supper can be inserted until the beginning of the chapter.   Here, however, according to one of the most recent
critics, it may be inserted in a way which perfectly exonerates the author of
the gospel from the reproach of misleading his reader by an account which is
apparently continuous, while it nevertheless passes over the Supper.   For,
says this critic, from the very commencement John does not profess to narrate anything of the meal itself, or what was concomitant with it, but only
what occurred after the meal ; inasmuch as the most natural interpretation of
δείπνου γενομένου is : *after the meal was ended*, while the words ἐγείρεται ἐκ τοῦ
δείπνου, *he riseth from supper*, plainly show that the washing of the disciples'
feet was not commenced until after the meal. [9]   But after the washing of the
feet is concluded, it is said of Jesus, that he sat down again (ἀναπεσὼν πάλιν
v. 12), consequently the meal was not yet ended when he commenced that
act, and by the words *he riseth from supper*, it is meant that he rose to wash
the disciples' feet from the yet unfinished meal, or at least after the places
had been taken preparatory to the meal.   Again, δείπνου γενομένου does not
mean : *after a meal was ended*, any more than the words τοῦ ᾽Ι. γενομένου ἐν
Βηθανίᾳ (Matt. xxvi. 6) mean : *after Jesus had been in Bethany* : as the latter
expression is intended by Matthew to denote the time during the residence
of Jesus in Bethany, so the former is intended by John to denote the course
of the meal itself. [10]   Hence he thereby professes to inform us of every remarkable occurrence connected with that meal, and in omitting to mention
the institution of the Lord's supper, which was one of its features, he incurs
the reproach of having given a deficient narrative, nay of having left out precisely what is most important.—Instead of this highest extremity of John's
account, Kern has recently taken the lowest, and has placed the institution
of the Supper after the words, *Arise, let us go hence*, xiv. 31 ; [11] whereby he
assigns to it the improbable and indeed unworthy position, of an act only
occurring to Jesus when he is preparing to depart.

Thus, viewing the subject generally, there is no conceivable motive why
John, if he spoke of this last evening at all, should have omitted the institution of the Lord's supper ; while, on descending to a particular consideration, there is in the course of his narrative no point where it could be
inserted : hence nothing remains but to conclude that he does not mention
it because it was unknown to him.   But as a means of resisting this conclusion, theologians, even such as acknowledge themselves unable to explain
the omission of the institution, rely on the observation, that a rite so universally prevalent in the primitive church as was the Lord's supper, cannot
possibly have been unknown to the fourth Evangelist, whoever he may have
been. [12]   Certainly, he knew of the Lord's supper as a Christian rite, for this

---

[8] L. J. Chr., s. 587, Anm.
[9] Sieffert, s. 152 ff.
[10] Comp. Lücke, s. 468.
[11] Die Hauptthatsachen der evang. Gesch. Tüb. Zeitschr. 1836, 3, s. 12.
[12] Hase, L. J., § 133 ; Kern, Hauptthatsachen, s. 11 ; Theile, zur Biographie Jesu, § 31.

may be inferred from his 6th chapter, and unavoidably he must have known of it; it may, however, have been unknown to him under what circumstances Jesus formally instituted this observance. The referring of so revered an usage to the authority of Jesus himself was an object of interest to this Evangelist; but from unacquaintance with the synoptical scene, and also from a partiality for the mysterious, which led him to put into the mouth of Jesus expressions unintelligible at the moment, and only to be explained by the issue, he effected this purpose, not by making Jesus actually institute the rite, but by attributing to him obscure expressions about the necessity of eating his flesh and drinking his blood, which, being rendered intelligible only by the rite of the Lord's supper introduced into the church after his death, might be regarded as an indirect institution of that rite.

As John omits the institution of the Lord's supper, so the synoptists omit the washing of the disciples' feet: but it cannot be maintained with equal decision that they were therefore ignorant of this incident; partly on account of its inferior importance and the more fragmentary character of this part of the synoptical narrative; and partly because, as has been above remarked, the contention for pre-eminence in Luke v. 24 ff. has appeared to many expositors to be connected with the washing of the disciples' feet, as the inducement to that action on the part of Jesus.[13] But as regards this contention for pre-eminence, we have shown above, that being unsuited to the tenor of the scene before us, it may owe its position only to a fortuitous association of ideas in the narrator:[14] while the washing of the disciples' feet, in John, might appear to be a legendary development of a synoptical discourse on humility. In Matthew (xx. 26 ff.) Jesus admonishes his disciples that he among them who would be great must be the *minister* διάκονος of the others, just as he himself came not to *be ministered unto but to minister* διακονηθῆναι, ἀλλὰ διακονῆσαι; and in Luke (xxii. 27) he expresses the same thought in the question: *Whether is greater, he that sitteth at meat or he that that serveth?* τίς γὰρ μείζων; ὁ ἀνακείμενος, ἢ ὁ διακονῶν; and adds, *but I am among you as he that serveth,* ἐγὼ δέ εἰμι ἐν μέσῳ ὑμῶν ὡς ὁ διακονῶν. Now it is certainly probable that Jesus might see fit to impress this lesson on the disciples through the medium of their senses, by an actual *serving* διακονεῖν among them, while they played the part of those sitting at meat (ἀνακείμενοι); but it is equally probable, since the synoptists are silent respecting such a measure, that either the legend, before it reached the fourth Evangelist, or this writer himself, spun the fact out of the dictum.[15] Nor is it necessary to suppose that the above declaration came to him as having been uttered at the last meal of Jesus, in accordance with the representation of Luke; for it naturally resulted from the expressions ἀνακεῖσθαι (*to recline at meat*), and διακονεῖν (*to serve*), that this symbolizing of the relation which they denote should be attached to a meal, and this meal might on easily conceivable grounds appear to be the most appropriately represented as the last.

According to Luke's representation, Jesus on this occasion addresses the disciples as those who had continued with him in his temptations, and as a reward for this fidelity promises them that they shall sit with him at table in his kingdom, and seated on thrones, judge the twelve tribes of Israel (v. 28–30). This appears incongruous with a scene in which he had immediately before announced his betrayal by one of the twelve, and in which he

---

[13] Sieffert, s. 153; Paulus and Olshausen, in loc. For the opposite opinion comp. De Wette, 1, 1, s. 222, 1, 2, s. 107.

[14] Vol. II. § 83.

[15] The conjecture as to the origin of this anecdote in the Probabilia, s. 70 f. is too farfetched.

Immediately after predicted his denial by another ; at a time, moreover, in which the *temptations* πειρασμοὶ properly so called, were yet future. After what we have already observed in relation to the entire character of the scene in Luke, we can hardly seek the reason for the insertion of this fragment of a discourse, in anything else than a fortuitous association of ideas, in which the contention about rank among the disciples might suggest the rank promised to them by Jesus, and the discourse on sitting at table and serving, the promise that the disciples should sit at table with Jesus in his messianic kingdom.[16]

In the succeeding conversation Jesus says to his disciples figuratively, that now it will be necessary to buy themselves swords, so hostilely will they be met on all sides, but is understood by them literally, and is shown two swords already in the possession of the society. Concerning this passage I am inclined to agree with Schleiermacher, who is of opinion that Luke introduced it here as a prelude to Peter's use of the sword in the ensuing narrative.[17]

The other divergencies in relation to the last meal will come under review in the course of the following investigations.

§ 123.

ANNOUNCEMENT OF THE BETRAYAL AND THE DENIAL.

In the statement that Jesus from the beginning knew who would be his betrayer, the fourth gospel stands alone ; but all four of the Evangelists concur in testifying that at his last meal he predicted his betrayal by one of his disciples.

But in the first place there is this difference : while according to Matthew and Mark the discourse respecting the betrayer opens the scene, and in particular precedes the institution of the Lord's supper (Matt. xxvi. 21 ff.; Mark xiv. 18 ff.) ; Luke represents Jesus as not speaking of the betrayer until after the commencement of the meal, and the institution of the commemorative rite (xxii. 21 ff.) ; and in John what relates to the betrayer goes forward during and after the washing of the disciples' feet (xiii. 10–30). The intrinsically trivial question, which Evangelist is here right, is extremely important to theologians, because its decision involves the answer to another question, namely, whether the betrayer also partook of the ritual Supper. It neither appeared consistent with the idea of that supper as a feast of the most intimate love and union, that a virtual alien like Judas should participate in it, nor did it seem to accord with the love and compassion of the Lord, that he should have permitted an unworthy disciple by this participation to aggravate his guilt.[1] So undesirable a view of the facts was believed to be avoided by following the arrangement of Matthew and Mark, and making the designation of the betrayer precede the institution of the Supper : for as it was known from John, that as soon as Judas saw himself detected and exposed, he withdrew from the company, it would thence appear that Jesus did not institute the Supper until after the retirement of the traitor.[2] But this expedient is founded on nothing but an inadmissible incorporation of the narrative of John with that of the synoptists. For the withdrawal of Judas is mentioned only by the fourth Evangelist ; and he alone needs the supposition of such a circumstance, because, according to him, Judas now first entered into his

---

[16] Comp. De Wette, in loc.
[17] Ueber den Lukas, s. 275.
[1] Olshausen, 2, s. 380.
[2] Thus Lücke, Paulus, Olshausen.

transactions with the enemies of Jesus, and thus, in order to come to terms with them, and obtain the requisite force, needed a somewhat longer time. In the synoptists there is no trace of the betrayer having left the company ; on the contrary, everything in their narrative appears to imply that Judas, first on the general departure from the room in which the repast had been taken, instead of going directly to the garden, went to the chief priests, of whom he at once, the agreement having been made beforehand, received the necessary force for the arrest of Jesus. Thus whether Luke or Matthew be right in the arrangement of the scene, all the synoptists intimate that Judas did not leave the company before the general departure, and consequently that he partook of the ritual Supper.

But also as to the manner in which Jesus pointed out his betrayer, there exists no slight divergency between the Evangelists. In Luke Jesus only makes the brief remark that the hand of his betrayer is with him on the table, whereupon the disciples ask among themselves, who it can be that is capable of such a deed ? In Matthew and Mark he says, first, that one of those, who are present will betray him ; and when the disciples individually ask him, Lord, is it I ? he replies : *he that dippeth his hand with me in the dish* ; until at last, after a woe has been denounced on the traitor, according to Matthew, Judas also puts that question, and receives an affirmative answer. In John, Jesus alludes to the betrayer during and after the washing of the disciples' feet, in the observations, that not all the disciples present are clean, and that on the contrary the scripture must be fulfilled : *he that eateth bread with me, hath lifted up his heel against me.* Then he says plainly, that one of them will betray him ; the disciples look inquiringly at each other, wondering of whom he speaks, when Peter prompts John, who is lying next to Jesus, to ask who is the traitor ? Jesus replies, he to whom he shall give a sop, which he immediately does to Judas, with an admonition to hasten the execution of his project ; whereupon Judas leaves the company.

Here again the harmonists are at once ready to incorporate the different scenes with each other, and render them mutually consistent. According to them, Jesus, on the question of each disciple whether he were the traitor, first declared aloud that one of his companions at table would betray him (Matthew) ; hereupon John asked in a whisper which of them he meant, and Jesus also in a whisper made the answer, he to whom he should give the sop (John) ; then Judas, likewise in a whisper, asked whether it were he, and Jesus in the same manner replied in the affirmative (Matthew) ; lastly, after an admonition from Jesus to be speedy, the betrayer left the company (John).[3] But that the question and answer interchanged between Jesus and Judas were spoken in a whisper, Matthew, who alone communicates them, gives no intimation, nor is this easily conceivable without presupposing the improbable circumstance, that Judas reclined on the one side of Jesus, as John did on the other : if, however, the colloquy were uttered aloud, the disciples could not, as John narrates, have so strangely misunderstood the words, *what thou doest, do quickly,*—and the supposition of a stammering question on the side of Judas, and a low-toned answer from Jesus, cannot be seriously held a satisfactory explanation.[4] Nor is it probable that Jesus, after having already made the declaration : he who dippeth with me in the dish will betray me, would for the more precise indication of the traitor have also given him a sop ; it is rather to be supposed that these are but two different modes of reporting the same particular. But when once this is admitted, as it is by Paulus and

<hr>

[3] Kuinöl, in Matth., p. 707.
[4] This is Olshausen's expedient, **2**, s. 402. Against it see Sieffert, s. 148. f.

Olshausen, so much is already renounced either in relation to the one narrative or the other, that it is inconsistent to resort to forced suppositions, in order to overcome the difficulty involved in the explicit answer which Matthew makes Jesus give to the traitor; and it should rather be allowed that we have before us two divergent accounts, of which the one was not so framed that its deficiencies might be supplied by the other.

Having, with Sieffert and Fritzsche, attained this degree of insight, the only remaining question is : to which of the two narratives must we give the preference as the original? Sieffert has answered this question very decidedly in favour of John ; not merely, as he maintains, because he shares in the prejudice which attributes to that Evangelist the character of an eye-witness ; but also because his narrative is in this part, by its intrinsic evidence of truthfulness, and the vividness of its scenes, advantageously distinguished from that of Matthew, which presents no indications of an autoptical origin. For example, while John is able to describe with the utmost minuteness the manner in which Jesus indicated his betrayer : the narrative of the first gospel is such as to induce the conjecture that its author had only received the general information, that Jesus had personally indicated his betrayer.[5] It certainly cannot be denied, that the direct answer which Jesus gives to Judas in Matthew (v. 25) has entirely the appearance of having been framed, without much fertility of imagination, to accord with the above general information ; and in so far it must be regarded as inferior to the more indirect, and therefore more probable mode of indicating the traitor, in John. But in relation to another feature, the result of the comparison is different. In the two first Evangelists Jesus says : *he who has dipped* or *who dippeth with me*, ὁ ἐμβάψας or ἐμβαπτόμενος μετ᾽ ἐμοῦ : in John, *he to whom I shall give a sop when I have dipped it*, ᾧ ἐγὼ βάψας τὸ ψωμίον ἐπιδώσω ; a difference in which the greater preciseness of the indication, and consequently the inferior probability, is on the side of the fourth gospel. In Luke, Jesus designates the traitor merely as one of those who are sitting at meat with him ; and as regards the expression ὁ ἐμβάψας κ. τ. λ. in Matthew and Mark, the interpretation given of it by Kuinöl and Henneberg,[6] who suppose it to mean one of the party at table, leaving it uncertain which, is not so mistaken as Olshausen represents it to be. For, first, to the question of the several disciples, is it I? Jesus might see fit to return an evasive answer ; and secondly, the above answer, as Kuinöl has correctly remarked, stands in the relation of an appropriate climax to the previous declaration : *one of you shall betray me* (v. 21), since it presents that aggravating circumstance of the betrayal, fellowship at table. Even if the authors of the two first gospels understood the expression in question to imply, that Judas in particular dipped his hand in the dish with Jesus, and hence supposed this second declaration to have indicated him personally : still the parallel passage in Luke, and the words εἰς ἐκ τῶν δώδεκα, *one of the twelve*, which in Mark precede ὁ ἐμβαπτόμενος, show that originally the second expression was merely an amplification of the former, though from the wish to have a thoroughly unequivocal designation of the betrayer on the part of Jesus, it was early interpreted in the other more special sense. When, however, a legendary exaggeration of the preciseness of the indication is once admitted, the manner in which the fourth gospel describes that indication must be included in the series of progressive representations, and according to Sieffert, it must have been the original from which all the rest proceeded. But if we beforehand renounce the affirmative reply to Judas, σὺ εἶπας, *thou hast said,*

---

[5] Ut sup. s. 147 ff.
[6] Comm. über die Gesch. des Leidens und Todes Jesu, in loc.

in Matthew, the mode of designation in John is the most definite of all; for the intimation : one of my companions at table, is comparatively indefinite, and even the expression : he who dippeth with me in the dish, is a less direct sign of the traitor, than if Jesus had himself dipped the morsel and presented it to him. Now is it in the spirit of the ancient legend, if Jesus really gave the more precise designation, to lose its hold of this, and substitute one less precise, so as to diminish the miracle of the foreknowledge exhibited by Jesus?. Assuredly not; but rather the very reverse holds true. Hence we conclude that Matthew, together with the unhistorically precise, has yet at the same time preserved the historically less precise ; whereas John has entirely lost the latter and has retained only the former.

After thus renouncing what is narrated of a personal designation of the traitor by Jesus, as composed *post eventum*, there yet remains to us the general precognition and prediction on the part of Jesus, that one of his disciples and companions at table would betray him. But even this is attended with difficulties. That Jesus received any external notification of treason brooding against him in the circle of his confidential friends, there is no indication in the gospels : he appears to have gathered this feature of his destiny also out of the scriptures alone. He repeatedly declares that by his approaching betrayal the scripture will be fulfilled (John xiii. 18, xvii. 12 ; comp. Matt. xxvi. 24 parall.), and in the fourth gospel (xiii. 18), he cites as this *scripture*, γραφὴ, the words : *He that eateth bread with me, hath lifted up his heel against me*, ὁ τρώγων μετ᾽ ἐμοῦ τὸν ἄρτον ἐπῆρεν ἐπ ἐμὲ τὴν πτέρναν αὐτοῦ, from Ps. xli. 10. This passage in the Psalms refers either to the well-known perfidious friends of David, Ahithophel and Mephibosheth, or, if the Psalm be not the composition of David, to some unknown individuals who stood in a similar relation to the poet.[7] There is so little trace of a messianic significance, that even Tholuck and Olshausen acknowledge the above to be the original sense. But according to the latter, in the fate of David was imaged that of the Messiah; according to the former, David himself, under a divine impulse often used expressions concerning himself, which contained special allusions to the fate of Jesus. When, however, Tholuck adds : David himself, under the influence of inspiration, did not always comprehend this more profound sense of his expressions ; what is this but a confession that by the interpretation of such passages as relating to Christ there is given to them another sense than that in which their author originally intended them? Now that Jesus deduced from this passage of the 41st Psalm, that it would be his lot to be betrayed by a friend, in the way of natural reflection, is the more inconceivable, because there is no indication to be discovered that this Psalm was interpreted messianically among the Jews : while that such an interpretation was a result of the divine knowledge in Jesus is impossible, because it is a false interpretation. It is rather to be supposed, that the passage in question was applied to the treachery of Judas only after the issue. It is necessary to figure to ourselves the consternation which the death of the Messiah must have produced in the minds of his first adherents, and the solicitous industry with which they endeavoured to comprehend this catastrophe ; and to remember that to a mind of Jewish culture, to comprehend a fact or doctrine was not to reconcile it with consciousness and reason, but to bring it into harmony with scripture. In seeking such a result, the primitive Christians found predicted in the oracles of the Old Testament, not only the death of the Messiah, but also his falling by means of the perfidy of one of his friends, and even the subsequent fate and end of this traitor (Matt. xxvii. 9 f. ;

---

[7] See De Wette, in loc.

Acts i. 20) ; and as the most striking Old Testament authority for the betrayal, there presented itself the above passage from Ps. xli., where the author complains of maltreatment from one of his most intimate friends. These vouchers from the Old Testament might be introduced by the writers of the evangelical history either as reflections from themselves or others by way of appendix to their narrative of the result, as is done by the authors of the first gospel and the Acts, where they relate the end of Judas : or, what would be more impressive, they might put them into the mouth of Jesus himself before the issue, as is done by the author of the fourth gospel in the present instance. The Psalmist had meant by לַחְמִי אִ֥יֶשׁ one who *generally* was *accustomed* to eat bread with him : but this expression might easily come to be regarded as the designation of one *in the act* of eating bread with the subject of the prophecy : and hence it seemed appropriate to choose as the scene for the delivery of the prediction, a meal of Jesus with his disciples, and for the sake of proximity to the end of Jesus to make this meal the last. For the rest, the precise words of the psalm were not adhered to, for instead of ὁ τρώγων μετ᾽ ἐμοῦ τὸν ἄρτον, *he who eateth bread with me*, was substituted either the synonymous phrase μετ᾽ ἐμοῦ ἐπὶ τῆς τραπέζης, *with me on the table*, as in Luke ; or, in accordance with the representation of the synoptists that this last was a paschal meal, an allusion to the particular sauce used on that occasion : ὁ ἐμβαπτόμενος μετ ἐμοῦ εἰς τὸ τρυβλίον, *he who dippeth with me in the dish*, as in Mark and Matthew. This, at first entirely synonymous with the expression ὁ τρώγων κ. τ. λ., as a designation of some one of his companions at table, was soon, from the desire for a personal designation, misconstrued to mean that Judas accidentally dipped his hand into the dish at the same moment with Jesus, and at length the morsel dipped into the dish by Judas at the same time with Jesus, was by the fourth Evangelist converted into the sop presented by Jesus to his betrayer.

There are other parts also of this scene in John, which, instead of having a natural character, as Sieffert maintains, must rather be pronounced artificial. The manner in which Peter has to use the intervention of the disciple leaning on Jesus' bosom, in order to obtain from the latter a more definite intimation concerning the betrayer, besides being foreign to the synoptists, belongs to that unhistorical colouring which, as we have above shown, the fourth gospel gives to the relation of the two apostles. Moreover, to disguise an indication of Judas in the evil character of the traitor, beneath an action of friendliness, as that of giving him the sop, must retain something untruthful and revolting, whatever may be imagined of objects which Jesus might have in view, such as the touching of the traitor with compunction even at that hour. Lastly, the address, *What thou doest, do quickly*, after all that can be done to soften it,[8] is still harsh,—a kind of braving of the impending catastrophe; and rather than resort to any refinements in order to justify these words as spoken by Jesus, I prefer agreeing with the author of the Probabilia, who sees in them the effort of the fourth Evangelist to improve on the ordinary representation, according to which Jesus foreknew the betrayal and refrained from preventing it, by making him even challenge the traitor to expedite his undertaking.[9]

Besides the betrayal, Jesus is said to have predicted the denial by Peter, and to have fixed the precise time of its occurrence, declaring that before the cock should crow (Mark says twice) on the following morning, Peter would

---

[8] Vid. Lücke and Tholuck, in loc.

[9] P. 62 : *reliqui quidem narrant evangelistæ servatorem scivisse proditionis consilium, nec impedivisse ; ipsum vero excitâsse Judam ad proditionem nemo eorum dicit, neque convenit hoc Jesu.*

deny him thrice (Matt. xxvi. 33 ff. parall.): which prediction, according to the gospels, was exactly accomplished.   It is here observed on the side of Rationalism, that the extension of the prophetic gift to the cognizance of such merely accessory circumstances as the crowing of cocks, must excite astonishment ; as also that Jesus, instead of warning, predicts the result as inevitable : [10] a feature which calls to mind the Fate of the Greek tragedy, in which a man, in spite of his endeavour to avoid what the oracle has predicted of him, nevertheless fulfils its inexorable decree.   Paulus will not admit either οὐ φωνήσει σήμερον ἀλέκτωρ, or ἀπαρνεῖσθαι, or τρὶς, to have been spoken in their strict verbal signification, but gives to the entire speech of Jesus only this indecisive and problematical sense : so easily to be shaken is the imagined firmness of this disciple, that between the present moment and the early morning, events may arise which would cause him more than once to stumble and be unfaithful to his master.   But this is not the right mode of removing the difficulty of the evangelical narrative.   The words attributed to Jesus so closely agree with the subsequent event, that the idea of a merely fortuitous coincidence is not to be here entertained.   Occurring as they do in a tissue of prophecies *post eventum*, we must rather suppose that after Peter had really denied Jesus more than once during that night, the announcement of such a result was put into the mouth of Jesus, with the common marking of time by the crowing of the cock,[11] and the reduction of the instances of denial to three.   That this determination of time and number was permanent in the evangelical tradition (except that Mark, doubtless arbitrarily, for the sake of balancing the *thrice* denying by another number, speaks of the *twice* crowing of the cock), appears to be explained without any great difficulty by the familiarity of the expressions early chosen, and the ease with which they could be retained in the memory.

Just as little claim to be regarded as a real prophecy has the announcement of Jesus to the rest of his disciples that they will all of them be offended because of him in the coming night, that they will forsake him and disperse (Matt. xxvi. 31 parall., comp. John xvi. 32) ; especially as the Evangelists themselves, in the words : *For it is written, I will smite the shepherd, and the sheep of the flock shall be scattered abroad*, point out to us the Old Testament passage (Zech. xiii. 7), which, first sought out by the adherents of Jesus for the satisfaction of their own difficulties as to the death of their master, and the melancholy consequences which immediately ensued, was soon put into the mouth of Jesus as a prophecy of these consequences.

§ 124.

THE INSTITUTION OF THE LORD'S SUPPER.

It was at the last meal, according to the synoptists, with whom the Apostle Paul also agrees (1 Cor. xi. 23 ff.), that Jesus gave to the unleavened bread and the wine which, agreeably to the custom of the paschal feast,[1] he, as head of the family, had to distribute among his disciples, a relation to his speedily approaching death.   During the repast, we are told, he took bread, and after giving thanks, broke it and gave it to his disciples with the declaration : *This is my body*, τοῦτό ἐστι τὸ σῶμά μου, to which Paul and Luke add : *which is given* or *broken for you*, τὸ ὑπὲρ ὑμῶν διδόμενον or κλώμενον ; in like manner,

---

[10] Paulus, exeg. Handb. 3, b, s. 538.   L. J. 1, b, s. 192.   Hase, L. J., § 137.
[11] Comp. Lightfoot and Paulus, in loc.
[1] Comp. on this subject especially, Lightfoot, horæ, p. 474 ff., and Paulus, exeg. Handb. 3, b, s. 511 ff.

according to Paul and Luke after supper, he presented to them a cup of wine with the words : *This is my blood of the new testament*, τοῦτό ἐστι τὸ αἷμά μου, τὸ τῆς καινῆς διαθήκης, or, according to Paul and Luke : *the new testament in my blood, which is shed for many*, or *for you*, καινὴ διαθήκη ἐν τῷ αἵματί μου, τὸ περὶ πολλῶν, or ὑπὲρ ὑμῶν, ἐκχυνόμενον, to which Matthew adds : *for the remission of sins*, εἰς ἄφεσιν ἁμαρτιῶν, and Paul, what he and Luke previously give in reference to the bread : *Do this*, τοῦτο ποιεῖτε (Paul, with the wine, *as oft as ye drink it*, ὁσάκις ἂν πίνητε), *in remembrance of me*, εἰς τὴν ἐμὴν ἀνάμνησιν. The controversy between the different confessions as to the meaning of these words,—whether they signify a transmutation of bread and wine into the body and blood of Christ, or a presence of the body and blood of Christ with and beneath those elements, or lastly, the symbolizing of the body and blood of Christ by bread and wine,—may be pronounced obsolete, and ought not to be any longer pursued, at least exegetically, because it is founded on a misplaced distinction. It is only when transmitted to a modern age, and to the occidental mind, in which the forms of thought are more abstract, that what the ancient oriental understood by the words, τοῦτό ἐστι, divides itself into the above variety of possible significations ; and if we would obtain a correct conception of the idea which originally suggested the expression, we must cease to discriminate thus. To explain the words in question as implying a transmutation of the substance, is to go too far, and to be too definite ; to understand them of an existence *cum et sub specie, etc.*, is too much of a refinement ; while to translate them : *this signifies*, is too limited and meagre an interpretation. To the writers of our gospels, the bread in the commemorative supper *was* the body of Christ : but had they been asked, whether the bread were transmuted, they would have denied it ; had they been spoken to of a partaking of the body with and under the form of bread, they would not have understood it ; had it been inferred that consequently the bread merely signified the body, they would not have been satisfied.

Thus to dispute farther on this point is a fruitless labour : it is a more interesting question, whether Jesus merely intended this peculiarly significant distribution of bread and wine as a parting demonstration of attachment to his disciples, or whether he designed that it should be celebrated by his disciples in memory of him after his departure. If we had only the account of the two first Evangelists,—this is admitted even by orthodox theologians,[2]—there would be no solid ground for the latter supposition ; but the words, *Do this in rememberance of me*, which are added by Paul and Luke, appear decisive of the fact that Jesus purposed the founding of a commemorative meal, which, according to Paul, the Christians were to celebrate, *until he should come*, ἄχρις οὗ ἂν ἔλθῃ. Concerning this very addition, however, it has been of late conjectured that it may not have been originally uttered by Jesus, but that in the celebration of the Lord's supper in the primitive church, the presiding member of the community, in distributing the elements, may have exhorted the rest to continue the repetition of this meal in remembrance of Christ, and that from this primitive Christian ritual the above words were added to the address of Jesus.[3] This conjecture should not be opposed by an exaggerated estimate of the authority of the Apostle Paul, such as that of Olshausen, who infers from the words, *I have received of the Lord*, παρέλαβον ἀπὸ τοῦ Κυρίου, that he here delivers an immediate revelation from Christ, nay, that Christ himself speaks through him : since, as even Süskind has admitted, and as

---

[2] Süskind, in the treatise : Hat Jesus das Abendmahl als einen mnemonischen Ritus angeordnet ? in his Magazin 11, s. 1 ff.

[3] Paulus, exeg. Handb, 3, b, s. 527.

Schulz has recently shown in the most convincing manner,[4] the phrase παραλαμβάνειν ἀπό τινος cannot signify an immediate reception, but only a mediate transmission from the individual specified. If, however, Paul had not that addition from Jesus himself, still Süskind thinks himself able to prove that it must have been communicated, or at least confirmed, by an apostle, and is of opinion, in the manner of his school, that by a series of abstract distinctions, he can define certain boundary lines which must in this case prevent the intrusion of an unhistorical tradition. But the severe attention to evidence which characterizes our own day, ought not to be expected from an infant religious society, between the distant portions of which there was not yet any organized connexion, or for the most part any other than oral communication. On the other hand, however, we must not be induced to regard the words τοῦτο ποιεῖτε κ. τ. λ. as a later addition to the address of Jesus, on false grounds, such as, that it would have been repugnant to the humility of Jesus to found a rite in remembrance of himself;[5] nor must we rate too highly the silence of the two first Evangelists, in opposition to the testimony of Paul.

Perhaps this point may be decided by means of another more general question, namely, what led Jesus to make this peculiarly significant distribution of bread and wine among his disciples? Orthodox theologians seek to remove as far as possible from the person of Jesus, as divine, all progress, and especially a gradual or sudden origination of plans and resolutions not previously present in his mind : hence, according to them, there lay in Jesus from the beginning, together with the foreknowledge of his destiny, and his entire plan, the design to institute this supper, as a commemorative rite to be observed by his church; and this opinion may at least appeal for support, to the allusions implying that he already contemplated the institution a year beforehand, attributed to Jesus in the sixth chapter of the fourth gospel.

This is certainly an insecure support, for, as a previous enquiry has shown, those allusions, totally unintelligible before the institution of the Supper, cannot have proceeded from Jesus, but only from the Evangelist.[6] Further, as, viewing the subject generally, it appeared to annul the reality of the human nature in Jesus, to suppose that all lay foreseen and prepared in him from the first, or at least from the commencement of his mature age ; Rationalism has maintained, on the contrary, that the idea of the symbolical act and words in question did not arise in Jesus until the last evening. According to this view, at the sight of the broken bread and the outpoured wine, Jesus had a foreboding of his near and violent death ; he saw in the former an image of his body which was to be put to death, and in the latter of his blood which was to be shed ; and this momentary impression was communicated by him to his disciples.[7] But such a tragical impression could only be felt by Jesus if he contemplated his death as a near event. That he did so with a greater distinctness at the last meal, is thought to be proved by the assurance which, according to all the synoptists, he gave to his disciples, that he would no more drink of the fruit of the vine until he drank it new in the kingdom of his Father ; whence, as there is no ground for supposing a vow of abstinence on his part, he must have foreseen that his end would arrive within the next few days. If, however, we observe how in Luke this assurance in relation to the wine is preceded by the declaration of Jesus, that he will no more eat the passover until it be fulfilled in the kingdom of God, it appears probable that

[4] Ueber das Abendmahl, s. 217 ff.
[5] Kaiser, bibl. Theol. 2, a, s. 39 ; Stephani, das h. Abendmahl, s. 61.
[6] Vol. II. § 81.
[7] Paulus, ut sup. s. 519 ff. ; Kaiser, ut sup. s. 37 ff.

originally the *fruit of the vine* also was understood not as wine in general, but as specially the beverage of the passover ; of which a trace may perhaps be discovered in the expression of Matthew and Mark—*this fruit of the vine*, τουτου του γεννήματος τῆς ἀμπέλου. Meals in the messianic kingdom were, in accordance with the ideas of the age, often spoken of by Jesus, and he may have expected that in that kingdom the Passover would be observed with peculiar solemnity. When therefore he declares that he will no more partake of this meal in the present *age*, αἰὼν, but only in the future ; first, this does not apply to eating and drinking in general, and hence does not mean that his sojourn in this pre-messianic world was to have an end within the next few days, but only within the space of a year ; nor, secondly, does it necessarily involve the idea that this change was to be introduced by his death, for he might even yet expect that the kingdom of the Messiah would commence during his life.

Meanwhile, to deny every presentiment of his end on the part of Jesus in these last days of his life, is on the one hand, not warranted by our previous examination ; and on the other, would compel us to doubt the institution of the ritual Supper by Jesus, which we can hardly do in opposition to the testimony of Paul. It is moreover easily conceivable, that the continually increasing involvement of his relation to the Jewish hierarchy, might at length bring to Jesus the conviction that his death was inevitable, and that in a moment of emotion he might even fix the next passover as the term which he should not survive. Thus each of the supposed cases appears possible : either that, owing to a thought suggested by the impressiveness of the moment, at the last passover which he celebrated with his disciples, he made bread and wine the symbols of his body which was to be slain and his blood which was to be shed ; or that for some time previously he had embraced the design of bequeathing such a commemorative meal to his adherents, in which case he may very probably have uttered the words preserved by Paul and Luke. But before this intimation of the death of Jesus had been duly appropriated by the disciples, and received into their conviction, they were overtaken by the actual catastrophe, for which, therefore, they might be regarded as wholly unprepared.*

CHAPTER III.

RETIREMENT TO THE MOUNT OF OLIVES, ARREST, TRIAL, CONDEMNATION AND CRUCIFIXION OF JESUS.

---

§ 125.

AGONY OF JESUS IN THE GARDEN.

ACCORDING to the synoptical narratives, Jesus, immediately after the conclusion of the meal and the singing of the *Hallel*, it being his habit during this feast time to spend the night out of Jerusalem (Matt. xxi. 17 ; Luke xxii. 39), went to the Mount of Olives, into a *garden* χωρίον (in John, κῆπος) called Gethsemane (Matt. xxvi. 30, 36 parall.). John, who gives the additional particular that the garden lay over the brook Kedron, does not represent him as departing thither until after a long series of valedictory discourses (xiv.–xvii.), of which we shall hereafter have to speak again. While John makes the arrest of Jesus follow immediately on the arrival of Jesus in the garden, the synoptists insert between the two that scene which is usually designated the agony of Jesus.

Their accounts of this scene are not in unison. According to Matthew and Mark, Jesus takes with him his three most confidential disciples, Peter and the sons of Zebedee, leaving the rest behind, is seized with fearfulness and trembling, tells the three disciples that he is sorrowful even unto death, and admonishing them to remain wakeful in the mean time, removes to a distance from them also, that he may offer a prayer for himself, in which, with his face bent to the earth, he entreats that the cup of suffering may pass from him, but still resigns all to the will of his Father. When he returns to the disciples, he finds them sleeping, again admonishes them to watchfulness, then removes from them a second time, and repeats the former prayer, after which he once more finds his disciples asleep. For the third time he retires to repeat the prayer, and returning, for the third time finds the disciples sleeping, but now awakes them, in order to meet the coming betrayer. Of the number three, which thus doubly figures in the narrative of the two first Evangelists, Luke says nothing ; according to him, Jesus retires from all the disciples, after admonishing them to watch, for the distance of about a stone's cast, and prays kneeling, once only, but nearly in the same words as in the other gospels, then returns to the disciples and awakes them, because Judas is approaching with the multitude. But, on the other hand, Luke in his single scene of prayer, has two circumstances which are foreign to the other narrators, namely, that while Jesus was yet praying, and immediately before the most violent mental struggle, an angel appeared to strengthen him, and that during the *agony* ἀγωνία which ensued, the sweat of Jesus *was as it were great drops of blood falling to the ground.*

From the earliest times this scene in Gethsemane has been a stumbling-block, because Jesus therein appears to betray a weakness and fear of death which might be considered unworthy of him. Celsus and Julian, doubtless having in their minds the great examples of a dying Socrates and other heathen sages, expressed contempt for the fear of death exhibited by Jesus ; [1] Vanini boldly extolled his own demeanour in the face of execution as superior to that of Jesus ; [2] and in the *Evangelium Nicodemi*, Satan concludes from this scene that Christ is a mere man.[3] The supposition resorted to in this apocryphal book, that the trouble of Jesus was only assumed in order to encourage the devil to enter into a contest with him,[4] is but a confession of inability to reconcile a real truth of that kind with the ideal of Jesus. Hence appeal has been made to the distinction between the two natures in Christ ; the sorrowfulness and the prayer for the removal of the cup having been ascribed to the human nature, the resignation to the will of the Father, to the divine.[5] As however, in the first place, this appeared to introduce an inadmissible division in the nature of Jesus ; and in the second place, even a fear experienced by his human nature in the prospect of approaching bodily sufferings appeared unworthy of him : his consternation was represented as being of a spiritual and sympathetic character—as arising from the wickedness of Judas, the danger which threatened his disciples, and the fate which was impending over his nation.[6] The effort to free the sorrow of Jesus from all reference to physical suffering, or to his own person, attained its highest pitch in the ecclesiastical tenet, that Jesus by substitution was burthened with the guilt of all mankind, and vicariously endured the wrath of God against that guilt.[7] Some have even supposed that the devil himself wrestled with Jesus.[8]

But such a cause for the trouble of Jesus is not found in the text ; on the contrary, here as elsewhere (Matt. xx. 22 f. parall.), the *cup* ποτήριον for the removal of which Jesus prays, must be understood of his own bodily sufferings and death. Moreover, the above ecclesiastical opinion is founded on an unscriptural conception of the vicarious office of Jesus. It is true that even in the conception of the synoptists, the suffering of Jesus is a vicarious one for the sins of many ; but the substitution consists, according to them, not in

---

[1] Orig. c. Cels. ii. 24 : λέγει (ὁ Κέλσος)· τί οὖν ποτνιᾶται, καὶ ὀδύρεται, καὶ τὸν τοῦ ὀλέθρου φόβον εὔχεται παραδραμεῖν, λέγων κ. τ. λ. : *He says* (i.e. *Celsus*) : *Why then does he supplicate help, and bewail himself, and pray for escape from the fear of death, saying*, etc. Julian, in a Fragment of Theodore of Mopsuestia, ap. Münter, Fragm. Patr. græc. Fasc. I, p. 121 : ἀλλὰ καὶ τοιαῦτα προσεύχεταί, φήσιν, ὁ Ἰ., οἷα ἄθλιος ἄνθρωπος, συμφορὰν φέρειν εὐκόλως οὐ δυνάμενος, καὶ ὑπ᾽ ἀγγέλου, θεὸς ὤν, ἐνισχύεται. *Jesus, says he, also presents such petitions as a wretched mortal would offer, when unable to bear a calamity with serenity ; and although divine, he is strengthened by an angel.*

[2] Gramond. hist. Gall. ab. exc. Henr. IV. L. iii. p. 211 : *Lucilius Vanini—dum in patibulum trahitur—Christo illudit in hæc eadem verba : illi in extremis præ timore imbellis sudor : ego imperterritus morior.*

[3] Evang. Nicod. c. xx. ap. Thilo, I, s. 702 ff. : ἐγὼ γὰρ οἶδα, ὅτι ἄνθρωπός ἐστι, καὶ ἤκουσα αὐτοῦ λέγοντος· ὅτι περίλυπός ἐστιν ἡ ψυχή μου ἕως θανάτου.

[4] Ibid. s. 706. Hades replies to Satan : εἰ δὲ λέγεις, ὅτι ἤκουσας αὐτοῦ φοβουμένου τὸν θάνατον, παίξων σε καὶ γελῶν ἔφη τοῦτο, θέλων, ἵνα σε ἁρπάσῃ ἐν χειρὶ δυνατῇ.

[5] Orig. c. Cels. ii. 25.

[6] Hieron. Comm. in Matth. in loc. : *Contristabatur non timore patiendi, qui ad hoc venerat, ut pateretur, sed propter infelicissimum Judam, et scandalum omnium apostolorum, et rejectionem populi Judæorum, et eversionem miseræ Hierusalem.*

[7] Calvin, Comm. in harm. evangg. Matth. xxvi. 37 : *Non—mortem horruit simpliciter, quatenus transitus est e mundo sed quia formidabile Dei tribunal illi erat ante oculos, judex ipse incomprehensibili vindicta armatus, peccata vero nostra, quorum onus illi erat impositum, sua ingenti mole eum premebant.* Comp. Luther's Hauspostille, die erste Passionspredigt.

[8] Lightfoot, p. 884 f.

Jesus having immediately borne these sins and the punishment due to mankind on account of them, but in a personal suffering being laid upon him on account of those sins, and in order to remove their punishment. Thus, as on the cross, it was not directly the sins of the world, and the anger of God in relation to them, which afflicted him, but the wounds which he received, and his whole lamentable situation, wherein he was indeed placed for the sins of mankind : so, according to the idea of the Evangelists, in Gethsemane also, it was not immediately the feeling of the misery of humanity which occasioned his dismay, but the presentiment of his own suffering, which, however, was encountered in the stead of mankind.

From the untenable ecclesiastical view of the agony of Jesus, a descent has in more modern times been made to coarse materialism, by reducing what it was thought hopeless to justify ethically, as a mental condition, to a purely physical one, and supposing that Jesus was attacked by some malady in Gethsemane ;[9] an opinion which Paulus, with a severity which he should only have more industriously applied to his own explanations, pronounces to be altogether unseemly and opposed to the text, though he does not regard as improbable Heumann's hypothesis, that in addition to his inward sorrow, Jesus had contracted a cold in the clayey ground traversed by the Kedron.[10] On the other hand, the scene has been depicted in the colours of modern sentimentalism, and the feelings of friendship, the pain of separation, the thoughts of parting, have been assigned as the causes which so lacerated the mind of Jesus :[11] or a confused blending of all the different kinds of sorrow, selfish and sympathetic, sensual and spiritual, has been presupposed.[12] Paulus explains εἰ δυνατόν ἐστι, παρελθέτω τὸ ποτήριον (if it be possible, let this cup pass from me) as the expression of a purely moral anxiety on the part of Jesus, as to whether it were the will of God that he should give himself up to the attack immediately at hand, or whether it were not more accordant with the Divine pleasure, that he should yet escape from this danger : thus converting into a mere inquiry of God, what is obviously the most urgent prayer.

While Olshausen falls back on the ecclesiastical theory, and authoritatively declares that the supposition of external corporeal suffering having called forth the anguish of Jesus, ought to be banished as one which would annihilate the essential characteristics of his mission ; others have more correctly acknowledged that in that anguish the passionate wish to be delivered from the terrible sufferings in prospect, the horror of sensitive nature in the face of annihilation, are certainly apparent.[13]   With justice also it is remarked, in opposition to the reproach which has been cast on Jesus, that the speedy conquest over rebellious nature removes every appearance of sinfulness ;[14] that, moreover, the shrinking of physical nature at the prospect of annihilation belongs to the essential conditions of life ;[15] nay, that the purer the human nature in an individual, the more susceptible is it in relation to suffering and annihilation ;[16] that the conquest over suffering intensely appreciated is greater than a stoical or even a Socratic insensibility.[17]

---

[9] Thiess, Krit. Comm. s. 418 ff.
[10] Ut sup. s. 549, 554 f., Anm.
[11] Schuster, zur Erläuterung des N. T., in Eichhorn's Biblioth. 9, s. 1012 ff.
[12] Hess, Gesch. Jesu, 2, s. 322 ff. ; Kuinöl, in Matth., p. 719.
[13] Ullmann, über die Unsündlichkeit Jesu, in his Studien, 1, s. 61.   Hasert, ib. 3, 1, s. 66 ff.
[14] Ullmann, ut sup.
[15] Hasert, ut sup.
[16] Luther, in der Predigt vom Leiden Christi im Garten.
[17] Ambrosius in Luc., Tom. x. 56.

With more reason, criticism has attacked the peculiar representation of the third gospel. The strengthening angel has created no little difficulty to the ancient church on dogmatical grounds,—to modern exposition on critical grounds. An ancient scholium on the consideration, *that he who was adored and glorified with fear and trembling by all the celestial powers, did not need the strengthening of the angel,* ὅτι τῆς ἰσχύος τοῦ ἀγγέλου οὐκ ἐπεδέετο ὁ ὑπὸ πάσης ἐπουρανίου δυνάμεως φόβῳ καὶ τρόμῳ προσκυνούμενος καὶ δοξαζόμενος, interprets the ἐνισχύειν ascribed to the angel as a *declaring strong,* i.e. as the offering of a doxology ;[18] while others, rather than admit that Jesus could need to be strengthened by an angel, transform the ἄγγελος ἐνισχύων into an evil angel, who attempted to use force against Jesus.[19] The orthodox also, by founding a distinction between the state of humiliation and privation in Christ and that of his glorification, or in some similar way, have long blunted the edge of the dogmatical difficulty : but in place of this a critical objection has been only so much the more decidedly developed. In consideration of the suspicion which, according to our earlier observations, attaches to every alleged angelic appearance, it has been sought to reduce the angel in this narrative first into a man,[20] and then into an image of the composure which Jesus regained.[21] But the right point in the angelic appearance for criticism to grapple with, is indicated by the circumstance that Luke is the only Evangelist from whom we learn it.[22] If, according to the ordinary presupposition, the first and fourth gospels are of apostolic origin ; why this silence as to the angel on the part of Matthew, who is believed to have been in the garden, why especially on the part of John, who was among the three in the nearer neighbourhood of Jesus ? If it be said : because sleepy as they were, and at some distance, and moreover under cover of the night, they did not observe him : it must be asked, whence are we to suppose that Luke received this information ?[23] That, assuming the disciples not to have themselves observed the appearance, Jesus should have narrated it to them on that evening, there is, from the intense excitement of those hours and the circumstance that the return of Jesus to his disciples was immediately followed by the arrival of Judas, little probability; and as little, that he communicated it to them in the days after the resurrection, and that nevertheless this information appeared worthy of record to none but the third Evangelist, who yet received it only at second hand. As in this manner there is every presumption against the historical character of the angelic appearance ; why should not this also, like all appearances of the same kind which have come under our notice, especially in the history of the infancy of Jesus, be interpreted by us mythically ? Gabler has been before us in advancing the idea, that in the primitive Christian community the rapid transition from the most violent mental conflict to the most tranquil resignation, which was observable in Jesus on that night, was explained, agreeably to the Jewish mode of thought, by the intervention of a strengthening angel, and that this explanation may have mingled itself with the narrative : Schleiermacher, too, finds it the most probable that this moment, described by Jesus himself as one of hard trial, was early glorified in hymns by angelic appearances, and that this embellish-

---

[18] In Matthaei's N. T., p. 447.
[19] Lightfoot, ut sup.
[20] Venturini, 3, 677, and conjecturally Paulus also, s. 561.
[21] Eichhorn, allg. Bibl. 1, s. 628 ; Thiess, in loc.
[22] Comp. on this subject and the following, Gabler, neust. theol. Journal, 1, 2, s. 109 ff. 3, s. 217 ff.
[23] Comp. Julian, ap. Theod. of Mopsuestia in Münter's Fragm. Patr. 1, p. 121 f.

ment, originally intended in a merely poetical sense, was received by the narrator of the third gospel as historical.[24]

The other feature peculiar to Luke, namely, the bloody sweat, was early felt to be no less fraught with difficulty than the strengthening by the angel. At least it appears to have been this more than anything else, which occasioned the exclusion of the entire addition in Luke, v. 43 and 44, from many ancient copies of the gospels. For as the orthodox, who according to Epiphanius[25] rejected the passage, appear to have shrunk the most from the lowest degree of fear which is expressed by the bloody sweat: so to the docetic opinions of some who did not receive this passage,[26] this was the only particular which could give offence. Thus in an earlier age, doubts were raised respecting the fitness of the bloody sweat of Jesus on dogmatical considerations : while in more modern times this has been done on physiological grounds. It is true that authorities are adduced for instances of bloody sweat from Aristotle[27] down to the more recent investigators of nature ;[28] but such a phenomenon is only mentioned as extremely rare, and as a symptom of decided disease. Hence Paulus points to the ὡσεὶ (*as it were*), as indicating that it is not directly a bloody sweat which is here spoken of, but only a sweat which might be compared to blood : this comparison, however, he refers only to the thick appearance of the drops, and Olshausen also agrees with him thus far, that a red colour of the perspiration is not necessarily included in the comparison. But in the course of a narrative which is meant as a prelude to the sanguinary death of Jesus, it is the most natural to take the comparison of the sweat to drops of blood, in its full sense. Further, here, yet more forcibly than in relation to the angelic appearance, the question suggests itself: how did Luke obtain this information ? or to pass by all questions which must take the same form in this instance as in the previous one, how could the disciples, at a distance and in the night, discern the falling of drops of blood? According to Paulus indeed it ought not to be said that the sweat fell, for as the word καταβαίνοντες, *falling*, refers not to ἱδρὼς, *sweat*, but to the θρόμβοι αἵματος, *drops of blood*, which are introduced merely for the purpose of comparison, it is only meant that a sweat as thick and heavy as falling drops of blood stood on the brow of Jesus. But whether it be said : the sweat fell like drops of blood to the earth, or : it was like drops of blood falling to the earth, it comes pretty much to the same thing ; at least the comparison of a sweat standing on the brow to blood falling on the earth would not be very apt, especially if together with the falling, we are to abstract also the colour of the blood, so that of the words, *as it were drops of blood falling on the ground*, ὡσεὶ θρόμβοι αἵματος καταβαίνοντες εἰς τὴν γῆν, only ὡσεὶ θρόμβοι, *as it were drops*, would properly have any decided meaning. Since then we can neither comprehend the circumstance, nor conceive what historical authority for it the narrator could have had, let us, with Schleiermacher, rather take this feature also as a poetical one construed historically by the Evangelist, or better still, as a mythical one, the origin of which may be easily explained from the tendency to perfect the conflict in the garden as a prelude to the sufferings of Jesus on the cross, by showing that not merely the psychical aspect of that suffering was fore-

---

[24] Ueber den Lukas, s. 288 ; comp. De Wette, in loc. and Theile, zur. Biogr. Jesu, § 32. Neander also appears willing silently to abandon this trait and the following one.
[25] Ancoratus, 31.
[26] Vid. Wetstein, s. 807.
[27] De part. animal. iii. 15.
[28] Vid. ap. Michaelis, not. in loc., and Kuinöl, in Luc., p. 691 f.

shadowed in the mental trouble, but also its physical aspect, in the bloody sweat.

As a counterpoise to this peculiarity of Luke, his two predecessors have, as we have said, the twofold occurrence of the number three,—the three disciples taken apart, and the three retirements and prayers of Jesus. It has indeed been contended that so restless a movement hither and thither, so rapid an alternation of retirement and return, is entirely suited to the state of mind in which Jesus then was,[29] and also, that in the repetition of the prayer there is correctly shown an appropriate gradation; a more and more complete resignation to the will of the Father.[30] But that the two narrators count the retirements of Jesus, marking them by the expressions ἐκ δευτέρου and ἐκ τρίτου, at once shows that the number three was a point of importance to them ; and when Matthew, though he certainly gives in the second prayer an expression somewhat different from that of the first, in the third makes Jesus only repeat *the same words*, τὸν αὐτὸν λόγον, and when Mark does this even the second time,—this is a significant proof that they were embarrassed how to fill up the favourite number three with appropriate matter. According to Olshausen, Matthew, with his three acts of this conflict, must be right in opposition to Luke, because these three attacks made on Jesus through the medium of fear, correspond to the three attacks through the medium of desire, in the history of the temptation. This parallel is well founded ; it only leads to an opposite result to that deduced by Olshausen. For which is more probable ; that in both cases the threefold repetition of the attack had an objective ground, in a latent law of the kingdom of spirits, and hence is to be regarded as really historical ; or that it had merely a subjective ground in the manner of the legend, so that the occurrence of this number here, as certainly as above in the history of the temptation, points to something mythical ? [31]

If then we subtract the angel, the bloody sweat, and the precisely threefold repetition of the retirement and prayer of Jesus, as mythical additions, there remains so far, as an historical kernel, the fact, that Jesus on that evening in the garden experienced a violent access of fear, and prayed that his sufferings might be averted, with the reservation nevertheless of an entire submission to the will of God : and at this point of the inquiry, it is not a little surprising, on the ordinary view of the relation between our gospels, that even this fundamental fact of the history in question, is wanting in the Gospel of John.

§ 126.

RELATION OF THE FOURTH GOSPEL TO THE EVENTS IN GETHSEMANE. THE FAREWELL DISCOURSES IN JOHN, AND THE SCENE FOLLOWING THE ANNOUNCEMENT OF THE GREEKS.

The relation of John to the synoptical narratives just considered has, when regarded more closely, two aspects : first, he has not what the synoptists present ; and secondly, instead of this he has something which it is difficult to reconcile with their statements.

As regards the first and negative side, it has to be explained how, on the ordinary supposition concerning the author of the fourth gospel and the correctness of the synoptical account, it happens that John, who according to the

---

[29] Paulus, ut sup. s. 549.
[30] Theile, in Winer's and Engelhardt's krit. Journal, 2, s. 353 ; Neander, L. J. Chr., s. 616 f.
[31] Comp. Weisse, die evang. Gesch. 1, s. 611.

two first gospels was one of the three whom Jesus took with him, to be the more immediate witnesses of his conflict, passes in silence over the whole event? It will not suffice to appeal to his sleepiness during the scene; for, if this was a hindrance to its narration, all the Evangelists must have been silent on the subject, and not John alone. Hence the usual expedient is tried here also, and he is said to have omitted the scene because he found it already presented with sufficient care in the writings of the synoptists.[1] But between the two first synoptists and the third there is here so important a divergency, as to demand most urgently that John, if he took their accounts into consideration, should speak a mediating word in this difference. If however, John had not the works of his predecessors lying before him, he might still, it is said, suppose that history to be sufficiently familiar to his readers as a part of evangelical tradition.[2] But as this tradition was the source of the divergent representations of the synoptists, it must itself have early begun to exhibit variations, and to narrate the fact first in one way, then in another: consequently on this view also there was a call on the author of the fourth gospel to rectify these wavering accounts. Hence of late an entirely new supposition has been adopted, namely, that John omits the events in Gethsemane lest, by the mention of the strengthening angel, he should give any furtherance to the Ebionitish opinion that the higher nature in Christ was an angel, which united itself with him at baptism; and now as it might be inferred, again departed from him before the hour of suffering.[3] But—not to urge that we have already found any hypothesis of this nature inadequate to explain the omissions in the Gospel of John—if this Evangelist wished to avoid any indication of a close relation between Jesus and angels, he must also have excluded other passages from his gospel: above all, as Lücke remarks,[4] the declaration concerning the ascending and descending of angels upon him, i. 52; and also the idea, given indeed only as the conjecture of some bystanders, that *an angel spake to him*, ἄγγελος αὐτῷ λελάληκεν, xii. 29. If, however, he on any ground whatever, found special matter of hesitation in the appearance of the angel in the garden: this would only be a reason for omitting the intervention of the angel, with Matthew and Mark, and not for excluding the whole scene, which was easily separable from this single particular.

If the mere absence of the incident from the narrative of John is not to be explained, the difficulty increases when we consider what this Evangelist communicates to us instead of the scene in the garden, concerning the mental condition of Jesus during the last hours previous to his arrest. In the same place which the synoptists assign to the agony in the garden, John, it is true, has nothing, for he makes the capture of Jesus follow at once on his arrival in the garden: but immediately before, at and after the last meal, he has discourses inspired by a state of mind, which could hardly have as a sequel scenes like those which according to the synoptical narratives occurred in the garden. In the farewell discourses in John, namely, xiv.–xvii. Jesus speaks precisely in the tone of one who has already inwardly triumphed over approaching suffering; from a point of view in which death is quenched in the beams of the glory which is to come after; with a divine peace which is cheerful in the certainty of its immovability: how is it possible that immediately after, this peace should give place to the most violent mental emotion, this tranquillity, to a trouble even unto death, and that from victory achieved he should sink again into doubtful contest, in which he needed strengthening

---

[1] Olshausen, 2, s. 429.
[2] Lücke, 2, s. 591.
[3] Schneckenburger, Beiträge, s. 65 f.
[4] Comm. I, s. 177 f.

by an angel?   In those farewell discourses, he appears throughout as one who from the plenitude of his inward serenity and confidence, comforts his trembling friends : and yet he now seeks spiritual aid from the drowsy disciples, for he requests them to watch with him ; there, he is so certain of the salutary effects of his approaching death, as to assure his followers, that it is well for them that he should go away, else the *Comforter* παράκλητος would not come to them : here, he again doubts whether his death be really the will of the Father ; there, he exhibits a consciousness which under the necessity of death, inasmuch as it comprehends that necessity, recovers freedom, so that his will to die is one with the divine will that he should die : here, these two wills are so at variance, that the subjective, submissively indeed, but painfully, bows to the absolute.   And these two opposite states of mind are not even separated by any intervening incident of an appalling character, but only by the short space of time which elapsed during the walk from Jerusalem to the Mount of Olives, across the Kedron : just as if, in that brook, as in another Lethe, Jesus had lost all remembrance of the foregoing discourses.

It is true that we are here referred to the alternation of mental states, which naturally becomes more rapid in proportion as the decisive moment approaches ;[5] to the fact that not seldom in the life of believers there occurs a sudden withdrawal of the higher sustenance of the soul, an abandonment of them by God, which alone renders the victory nevertheless achieved truly great and admirable.[6]   But this latter opinion at once betrays its unintelligent origin from a purely imaginative species of thought (to which the soul can appear like a lake, ebbing or flowing according as the floodgates of the conducting canals are opened or closed), by the contradictions in which it is on all sides involved.   The triumph of Christ over the fear of death is said only to appear in its true magnitude, when we consider, that while a Socrates could only conquer because he remained in the full possession of his mental energies, Christ was able to triumph over all the powers of darkness, even when forsaken by God and the fulness of his spirit, by his merely human *soul* ψυχή :—but is not this the rankest Pelagianism, the most flagrant contradiction of the doctrine of the church, as of sound philosophy, which alike maintain that without God, man can do no good thing, that only by his armour can man repel the shafts of the wicked one?   To escape from thus contradicting the results of sober reflection, the imaginative thinker is driven to contradict himself, by supposing that in the strengthening angel (which, incidentally, contrary to the verbal significance of the text, is reduced to a merely internal vision of Jesus) there was imparted to Jesus, when wrestling in the extremity of his abandonment, an influx of spiritual strength ; so that he thus would not, as it was at first vaunted, have conquered without, but only with Divine aid ; if, in accordance with Luke, the angel be supposed to have appeared prior to the last, most violent part of the conflict, in order to strengthen Jesus for this ultimate trial.   But rather than fall into so evident a self-contradiction, Olshausen prefers covertly to contradict the text, and hence transposes the order of the incidents, assuming, without further preliminary, that the strengthening came after the third prayer, consequently after the victory had been already gained, whence he is driven to the extreme arbitrariness of interpreting the phrase : καὶ γενόμενος ἐν ἀγωνίᾳ ἐκτενέστερον προσηύχετο, *and being in an agony he prayed*, as the pluperfect—*he had prayed*.

But setting aside this figurative representation of the cause which produced

---

[5] Lücke, 2, s. 392 ff.
[6] Olshausen, 2, s. 429 f.

the sudden change of mood in Jesus ; such a change is in itself burthened with many difficulties. Correctly speaking, what here took place in Jesus was not a mere change, but a relapse of the most startling kind. In the so-called sacerdotal prayer, John xvii. especially, Jesus had completely closed his account with the Father ; all fear in relation to what awaited him lay so far behind the point which he had here attained, that he spent not a single word on his own suffering, and only spoke of the afflictions which threatened his friends ; the chief subject of his communion with the Father was the glory into which he was about to enter, and the blessedness which he hoped to have obtained for his followers : so that his departure to the scene of his arrest has entirely the character of an accessory fact, merely consummating by external realization what was already inwardly and essentially effected. Now if Jesus after this closing of his account with God, once more opened it ; if after having held himself already victor, he once more sank into anxious conflict : must he not have laid himself open to the remonstrance : why didst thou not, instead of indulging in vain anticipations of glory, rather occupy thyself betimes with earnest thoughts of the coming trial, that by such a preparation, thou mightest spare thyself perilous surprise on its approach ? why didst thou utter the words of triumph before thou hadst fought, so as to be obliged with shame to cry for help at the on-coming of the battle ? In fact after the assurance of already achieved victory expressed in the farewell discourses, and especially in the final prayer, the lapse into such a state of mind as that described by the synoptists, would have been a very humiliating declension, which Jesus could not have foreseen, otherwise he would not have expressed himself with so much confidence ; and which, therefore, would prove that he was deceived in himself, that he held himself to be stronger than he actually found himself, and that he had given utterance to this too high self-valuation, not without a degree of presumption. Those who regard this as inconsistent with the equally judicious and modest character which Jesus manifests on other occasions, will find themselves urged to the dilemma, that either the farewell discourses in John, at least the final prayer, or else the events in Gethsemane, cannot be historical.

It is to be regretted that in coming to a decision in this case, theologians have set out rather from dogmatical prejudices than from critical grounds. Usteri's assertion, at least, that the representation given in John of the state of mind of Jesus in his last hours is the only correct one, while that of the synoptists is unhistorical,[7] is only to be accounted for by that author's then zealous adherence to the paragraphs of Schleiermacher's *Dogmatik*, wherein the idea of the impeccability of Jesus is carried to an extent which excludes even the slightest degree of conflict ; for that, apart from such presuppositions, the representation given in John of the last hours of Jesus, is the more natural and appropriate, it might be difficult to prove. On the contrary, Bretschneider might rather appear to be right, when he claims the superiority in naturalness and intrinsic evidence of truth for the synoptists :[8] were it not that our confidence in the decisions of this writer is undermined, by his dislike for the dogmatical and metaphysical purport of the discourses assigned to this period in John—a dislike which appears to indicate that his entire polemic against John originated in the discordance between his own critical philosophy of reflection, and the speculative doctrine of the fourth gospel.

John, indeed, as even the author of the Probabilia remarks, has not wholly passed over the anxiety of Jesus in relation to his approaching death ; he has

[7] Commentatio critica, qua Evangelium Joannis genuinum esse—ostenditur, p. 57 ff.
[8] Probab., p. 33 ff.

only assigned to it an earlier epoch, John xii. 27 ff. The scene with which John connects it takes place immediately after the entrance of Jesus into Jerusalem, when certain Greeks, doubtless proselytes of the gate, who had come among the multitude to the feast, wished to have an interview with him. With all the diversity of the circumstances and of the event itself, there is yet a striking agreement between what here occurs and what the synoptists place in the last evening of the life of Jesus, and in the seclusion of the garden. As Jesus here declares to his disciples, *my soul is troubled even unto death,* περίλυπός ἐστιν ἡ ψυχή μου ἕως θανάτου (Matt. xxvi. 38): so there he says : *Now is my soul troubled,* νῦν ἡ ψυχή μου τετάρακται (John xii, 27); as he here prays, *that if it be possible, this hour may pass from him,* ἵνα, εἰ δυνατόν ἐστι, παρέλθῃ ἀπ᾽ αὐτοῦ ἡ ὥρα (Mark xiv. 35): so there he entreats : *Father, save me from this hour,* πάτερ, σῶσόν με ἐκ τῆς ὥρας ταύτης (John xii. 27); as here he calms himself by the restriction : *nevertheless, not as I will, but as thou wilt,* ἀλλ᾽ οὐ τί ἐγὼ θέλω, ἀλλὰ τί σύ (Mark xiv. 36): so there, by the reflection : *but for this cause came I to this hour,* ἀλλὰ διὰ τοῦτο ἦλθον εἰς τὴν ὥραν ταύτην (John xii. 27); lastly, as here an *angel* appears *strengthening* Jesus, ἄγγελος ἐνισχύων (Luke xxii. 43) : so there something happens which occasions the bystanders to observe that *an angel spake to him,* ἄγγελος αὐτῷ λελάληκεν (John xii. 29). This similarity has induced many of the more modern theologians to pronounce the incident in John xii. 27 ff., and that in Gethsemane identical; and after this admission the only question was, on which side the reproach of inaccurate narration, and more especially of erroneous position, ought to fall.

Agreeably to the tendency of the latest criticism of the gospels, the burthen of error in this matter has been more immediately cast on the synoptists. The true occasion of the mental conflict of Jesus is said to be found only in John, namely, in the approach of those Greeks who intimated to him through Philip and Andrew their wish for an interview with him. These persons doubtless wished to make the proposal that he should leave Palestine and carry forward his work among the foreign Jews ; such a proposal held out to him the enticement of escape from the threatening danger, and this for some moments placed him in a state of doubt and inward conflict, which however ended by his refusing to admit the Greeks to his presence.[9] Here we have the effects of a vision rendered so acute by a double prejudice, both critical and dogmatical, as to read statements between the lines of the text; for of such an intended proposal on the part of the Greeks, there is no trace in John ; and yet, even allowing that the Evangelist knew nothing of the plan of the Greeks from these individuals themselves, there must have been some intimation in the discourse of Jesus that his emotion had reference to such a proposal. Judging from the context, the request of the Greeks had no other motive than that the solemn entrance of Jesus, and the popular rumour concerning him, had rendered them curious to see and know the celebrated man; and this desire of theirs was not connected with the emotion which Jesus experienced on the occasion, otherwise than that it led Jesus to think of the speedy propagation of his kingdom in the Gentile world, and of its indispensable condition, namely, his death. Here, however, the idea of his death is only mediately and remotely presented to the soul of Jesus ; hence it is the more difficult to conceive how it could affect him so strongly, as that he should feel himself urged to beseech the Father for delivery from this hour ; and if he were ever profoundly moved by the presentiment of death, the

---

[9] Goldhorn, über das Schweigen des Joh. Evangeliums über den Seelenkampf Jesu in Gethsemane, in Tzschirner's Magazin. f. christl. Prediger, 1, 2, s. 1 ff.

synoptists appear to place this fear in a more suitable position, 'in immediate proximity to the commencement of his sufferings. The representation of John is also deficient in certain circumstances, presented by the synoptists, which appear to vindicate the trouble of Jesus. In the solitude of the garden and the gloom of night, such an ebullition of feeling is more conceivable; and its unrepressed utterance to his most intimate and worthy friends is natural and justifiable. But according to John that agitation seized Jesus in the broad daylight, in a concourse of people ; a situation in which it is ordinarily more easy to maintain composure, or in which at least it is usual, from the possibility of misconstruction, to suppress the more profound emotions.

Hence it is more easy to agree with Theile's opinion, that the author of the fourth gospel has inserted the incident, correctly placed by the synoptists, in a false position.[10] Jesus having said, as an introduction to the answer which he returned to the request of the Greeks, that they might see the man who had been so glorified by his entrance into the city : Yes, the hour of my glorification is come, but of glorification by death (xii. 23 f.) : this led the narrator astray, and induced him, instead of giving the real answer of Jesus to the Greeks together with the result, to make Jesus dilate on the intrinsic necessity of his death, and then almost unconsciously to interweave the description of the internal conflict which Jesus had to experience in virtue of his voluntary sacrifice, whence he subsequently, in its proper place, omits this conflict. There is nothing strange in Theile's opinion, except that he supposes it possible for the Apostle John to have made such a transposition. That the scene in Gethsemane, from his having been asleep while it was passing, was not deeply imprinted on his mind, and that it was besides thrust into the background of his memory by the crucifixion which shortly followed, might have been considered explanatory of an entire omission, or a merely summary account of the scene on his part, but by no means of an incorrect position. If notwithstanding his sleepiness at the time, he had taken any notice of the event, he must at least have retained thus much—that that peculiar state of mind in Jesus befel him close upon the commencement of his sufferings, in the night and in privacy : how could he ever so far belie his memory as to make the scene take place at a much earlier period, in the open day, and among many people ? Rather than thus endanger the authenticity of the Gospel of John, others, alleging the possibility that such a state of mind might occur more than once in the latter part of the life of Jesus, deny the identity of the two scenes.[11]

Certainly, between the synoptical representation of the mental conflict of Jesus and that given in John, besides the external difference of position, there exist important internal divergencies ; the narrative in John containing features which have no analogy with anything in the synoptical account of the events in Gethsemane. It is true that the petition of Jesus in John for for deliverance from *this hour*, is perfectly in unison with his prayer in the synoptists : but, on the other hand, there is no parallel to the additional prayer in John : *Father, glorify thy name,* πάτερ, δόξασόν σου τὸ ὄνομα (xii. 28) : further, though in both accounts an angel is spoken of, yet there is no trace in the synoptists of the heavenly voice which in the fourth gospel occasions the belief that an angel is concerned. Such heavenly voices are not found in the three first gospels elsewhere than at the baptism and again at the transfiguration ; of which latter scene the prayer of Jesus in John :

[10] Vid. the Review of Usteri's Comm. crit., in Winer's and Engelhardt's n. krit. Jour. nal, 2, s. 359 ff.

[11] Hase, L. J., § 134 ; Lücke, 2, s. 591 f., Anm.

Father, glorify thy name, may remind us.   In the synoptical description of the transfiguration, it is true the expressions δόξα, *glory* and δοξάζειν, *to glorify,* are not found : but the Second Epistle to Peter represents Jesus as receiving in the transfiguration *honour and glory,* τιμὴν καὶ δόξαν, and the heavenly voice as coming from the *excellent glory,* μεγαλοπρεπὴς δόξα (i. 17 f.).   Thus in addition to the two narratives already considered, there presents itself a third as a parallel ; since the scene in John xii. 27 ff. is on the one side, by the trouble of spirit and the angel, allied to the occurrences in Gethsemane, while on the other side, by the prayer for glorification and the confirmatory voice from heaven, it has some affinity with the history of the transfiguration. And here two cases are possible : either that the narrative of John is the simple root, the separation of which into its constituent elements has given rise in a traditional manner to the two synoptical anecdotes of the transfiguration and the agony in the garden ; or that these last are the original formations, from the fusing and intermingling of which in the legend the narrative of John is the mixed product : between which cases only the intrinsic character of the narratives can decide.   That the synoptical narratives of the transfiguration and the agony in the garden are clear pictures, with strongly marked features, can by itself prove nothing ; since, as we have sufficiently shown, a narrative of legendary origin may just as well possess these characteristics as one of a purely historical nature.   Thus if the narrative in John were merely less clear and definite, this need not prevent it from being regarded as the original, simple sketch, from which the embellishing hand of tradition had elaborated those more highly coloured pictures.   But the fact is that the narrative in John is wanting not only in definiteness, but in agreement with the attendant circumstances and with itself.   We have no intimation what was the answer of Jesus to the Greeks, or what became of those persons themselves ; no appropriate motive is given for the sudden anguish of Jesus and his prayer for glorification.   Such a mixture of heterogeneous parts is always the sign of a secondary product, of an alluvial conglomeration ; and hence we seem warranted to conclude, that in the narrative of John the two synoptical anecdotes of the transfiguration and the agony in the garden are blended together.   If, as is apparently the case, the legend when it reached the fourth Evangelist presented these two incidents in faded colours,[12] and in indistinct outline : it would be easy for him, since his idea of *glorification* (δοξάζειν) had the double aspect of suffering and exaltation, to confuse the two ; what he gathered from the narrative of the agony in the garden, of a prayer of Jesus to the Father, he might connect with the heavenly voice in the history of the transfiguration, making this an answer to the prayer ; to the voice, the more particular import of which, as given by the synoptists, was unknown to him, he gave, in accordance, with his general notion of this incident as a *glory* δόξα conferred on Jesus, the import : *I have both glorified and will glorify again,* καὶ ἐδόξασα, καὶ πάλιν δοξάσω, and to make it correspond with this divine response, he had to unite with the prayer of Jesus for deliverance that for glorification also ; the strengthening angel, of which the fourth Evangelist had perhaps also heard something, was included in the opinion of the people as to the source of the heavenly voice ; in regard to the time, John placed his narrative about midway between the transfiguration and the agony in the garden, and from ignorance of the original circumstances the choice in this respect was infelicitous.

If we here revert to the question from which we set out, whether we are rather

---

[12] Against the offence which it has pleased Tholuck (Glaubw. s. 41) to take at this expression (*Verwischen*), comp. the Aphorismen zur Apologie des Dr. Strauss und seines Werkes, s. 69 f.

to retain the farewell discourses in John as thoroughly historical, and renounce the synoptical representation of the scene in Gethsemane, or vice
versâ : we shall be more inclined, considering the result of the inquiry just
instituted, to embrace the latter alternative. The difficulty, that it is scarcely
conceivable how John could accurately remember these long discourses of
Jesus, Paulus has thought to solve, by the conjecture, that the apostle,
probably on the next Sabbath, while Jesus lay in the grave, recalled to his
mind the conversations of the previous evening, and perhaps also wrote them
down.[13] But in that period of depression, which John also shared, he would
be scarcely in a condition to reproduce these discourses without obscuring
their peculiar hue of unclouded serenity ; on the contrary, as the author of
the Wolfenbüttel fragments observes, had the narrative of the words and deeds
of Jesus been committed to writing by the Evangelists in the couple of days
after the death of Jesus, when they had no longer any hope, all promises
would have been excluded from their gospels.[14] Hence even Lücke, in consideration of the mode of expression in the farewell discourses, and particularly in the final prayer, being so peculiarly that of John, has relinquished
the position that Jesus spoke in the very words which John puts into his
mouth, i.e. the authenticity of these discourses in the strictest sense ; but
only to maintain the more firmly their authenticity in the wider sense, i.e. the
genuineness of the substantial thoughts.[15] Even this, however, has been
attacked by the author of the Probabilia, for he asks, with especial reference to chap. xvii., whether it be conceivable that Jesus in the anticipation
of violent death, had nothing of more immediate concern than to commune
with God on the subject of his person, the works he had already achieved,
and the glory to be expected ? and whether it be not rather highly probable that
the prayer flowed only from the mind of the writer, and was intended by him as
a confirmation of his doctrine of Jesus as the incarnate *word* λόγος, and of the
dignity of the apostles ?[16] This representation is so far true that the final
prayer in question resembles not an immediate outpouring of soul, but a
product of reflection—is rather a discourse *on* Jesus than a discourse *from*
him. It presents everywhere the mode of thought of one who stands far in
advance of the circumstances of which he writes, and hence already sees the
form of Jesus in the glorifying haze of distance ; an illusion which he heightens
by putting his own thoughts, which had sprung from an advanced development of the Christian community, into the mouth of its Founder prior to its
actual existence. But in the preceding farewell discourses also there are
many thoughts which appear to have taken their shape from an experience
of the event. Their entire tone may be the most naturally explained by the
supposition, that they are the work of one to whom the death of Jesus was
already a past event, the terrors of which had melted away in its blessed
consequences, and in the devotional contemplation of the church. In particular, apart from what is said of the return of Christ, that era in the Christian
cause which is generally called the outpouring of the Holy Spirit, is predicted in the declarations concerning the Paraclete, and the judgment
which he would hold over the world (xiv. 16 ff. 25, xv. 26, xvi. 7 ff. 13 ff.),
with a distinctness which seems to indicate light borrowed from the issue.
    In relation, however, to the fact that the farewell discourses involve the
decided foreknowledge of the immediately approaching result, the sufferings
and death of Jesus (xiii. 18 ff., 33, 38, xiv. 30 f. xvi. 5 ff. 16, 32 f.), the

---

[13] L. J. 1, b, s. 165 f.
[14] Vom Zweck J. und seiner Jünger, s. 124.
[15] 2, s. 588 f.
[16] Ut sup.

narrative of John stands on the same ground with the synoptical one, since this also rests on the presupposition of the most exact prescience of the hour and moment when the sufferings will commence.   It was not only at the last meal and on the departure to the Mount of Olives, that this foreknowledge was shown, according to the three first gospels, for in them as well as in John, Jesus predicts that the denial of Peter will take place before the cock crow; not only does the agony in the garden rest on the foreknowledge of the impending sufferings, but at the end of this conflict Jesus is able to say that now, at this very minute, the betrayer is in the act of approaching (Matt. xxvi. 45 f.).   Paulus, it is true, maintains that Jesus saw from a distance the troop of guards coming out of the city, which, as they had torches, was certainly possible from a garden on the Mount of Olives: but without being previously informed of the plans of his enemies, Jesus could not know that he was the object of pursuit; and at any rate the Evangelists narrate the words of Jesus as a proof of his supernatural knowledge.   But if according to our previous inquiry, the foreknowledge of the catastrophe in general could not proceed from the higher principle in Jesus, neither could that of the precise moment when it would commence; while that he in a natural way, by means of secret friends in the Sanhedrim, or otherwise, was apprised of the fatal blow which the Jewish rulers with the help of one of his disciples were about to aim at him in the coming night, we have no trace in our Evangelical accounts, and we are therefore not authorized to presuppose anything of the kind.   On the contrary, as the above declaration of Jesus is given by the narrators as a proof of his higher knowledge, either we must receive it as such, or, if we cannot do this, we must embrace the negative inference, that they are here incorrect in narrating such a proof; and the positive conclusion on which this borders is, not that that knowledge was in fact only a natural one, but, that the evangelical narrators must have had an interest in maintaining a supernatural knowledge of his approaching sufferings on the part of Jesus; an interest the nature of which has been already unfolded.

The motive also for heightening the prescience into a real presentiment, and thus for creating the scene in Gethsemane, is easy of discovery.   On the one hand, there cannot be more a obvious proof that a foreknowledge of an event or condition has existed, than its having risen to the vividness of a presentiment; on the other hand, the suffering must appear the more awful, if the mere presentiment extorted from him who was destined to that suffering, anguish even to bloody sweat, and prayer for deliverance.   Further, the sufferings of Jesus were exhibited in a higher sense, as voluntary, if before they came upon him externally, he had resigned himself to them internally; and lastly, it must have gratified primitive Christian devotion, to withdraw the real crisis of these sufferings from the profane eyes to which he was exposed on the cross, and to enshrine it as a mystery only witnessed by a narrow circle of the initiated.   As materials for the formation of this scene, besides the description of the sorrow and the prayer which were essential to it, there presented itself first the image of a *cup* ποτήριον, used by Jesus himself as a designation of his sufferings (Matt. xx. 22 f.); and secondly, Old Testament passages, in Psalms of lamentation, xlii. 6, 12, xliii. 5, where in the LXX. the ψυχὴ περίλυπος (*soul exceeding sorrowful*) occurs, and in addition to this the expression ἕως θανάτου (*unto death*) the more naturally suggested itself, since Jesus was here really about to encounter death.   This representation must have been of early origin, because in the Epistle to the Hebrews (v. 7) there is an indubitable allusion to this scene.—Thus Gabler said too little when he pronounced the angelic appearance, a mythical garb of the fact that Jesus in the deepest sorrow of that night suddenly felt an accession of mental strength ; since rather, the entire scene in Gethsemane, because it rests on presuppositions destitute of proof, must be renounced.

Herewith the dilemma above stated falls to the ground, since we must pronounce unhistorical not only one of the two, but both representations of the last hours of Jesus before his arrest. The only degree of distinction between the historical value of the synoptical account and that of John is, that the former. is a mythical product of the first era of traditional formation, the latter of the second,—or more corrctly, the one is a product of the second order, the other of the third. The representation common to the synoptists and to John, that Jesus foreknew his sufferings even to the day and hour of their arrival, is the first modification which the pious legend gave to the real history of Jesus ; the statement of the synoptists , that he even had an antecedent experience of his sufferings, is the second step of the mythical ; while, that although he foreknew them, and also in one instance had a foretaste of them (John xii. 27 ff.), he had yet long beforehand completely triumphed over them, and when they stood immediately before him, looked them in the face with unperturbed serenity—this representation of the fourth gospel is the third and highest grade of devotional, but unhistorical embellishment.

§ 127.

ARREST OF JESUS.

In strict accordance with the declaration of Jesus that even now the betrayer is at hand, Judas while he is yet speaking approaches with an armed force (Matt. xxvi. 47 parall., comp. John xvii. 3). This band, which according to the synoptists came from the chief priests and elders, was according to Luke led by the *captains of the temple* στρατηγοῖς τοῦ ἱεροῦ, and hence was probably a detachment of the soldiers of the temple, to whom, judging from the word ὄχλος, and from *staves* ξύλοι being mentioned among the weapons, was apparently joined a tumultuous crowd : according to the representation of John, who, together with the *servants* or *officers of the chief priests and Pharisees*, ὑπηρέταις τῶν ἀρχιερέων καὶ Φαρισαίων, speaks of a *band* σπεῖρα, and a *captain* χιλίαρκος, without mentioning any tumultuary force, it appears as if the Jewish magistrates had procured as a support a detachment of Roman soldiery.[1]

According to the three first Evangelists, Judas steps forth and kisses Jesus, in order by this preconcerted sign to indicate him to the approaching band as the individual whom they were to seize : according to the fourth gospel, on the contrary, Jesus advances apparently out of the garden (ἐξελθὼν) to meet them, and presents himself as the person whom they seek. In order to reconcile this divergency, some have conceived the occurrences thus : Jesus, to prevent his disciples from being taken, first went towards the multitude, and made himself known ; hereupon Judas stepped forth, and indicated him by the kiss.[2] But had Jesus already made himself known, Judas might have spared the kiss ; for that the people did not believe the assertion of Jesus that he was the man whom they sought, and still waited for its confirmation by the kiss of the bribed disciple, is a supposition incompatible with the

---

[1] Vid. Lücke, in loc. ; Hase, L. J., § 135.
[2] Paulus, exeg. Handb. 3, b, s. 567.

statement of the fourth gospel that the words *I am he*, made so strong an impression on them that *they went backward and fell to the ground*. Hence others have inverted the order of the scene, imagining that Judas first stepped forward and distinguished Jesus by the kiss, and that then, before the crowd could press into the garden, Jesus himself advanced and made himself known.[3] But if Judas had already indicated him by the kiss, and he had so well understood the object of the kiss as is implied in his answer to it, Luke v. 48 : there was no need for him still to make himself known, seeing that he was already made known ; to do so for the protection of the disciples was equally superfluous, since he must have inferred from the traitor's kiss, that it was intended to single him out and carry him away from his followers ; if he did so merely to show his courage, this was almost theatrical : while, in general, the idea that Jesus, between the kiss of Judas, and the entrance of the crowd, which was certainly immediate, advanced towards the latter with questions and answers, throws into his demeanour a degree of hurry and precipitancy so ill suited to his circumstances, that the Evangelists can scarcely have meant such an inference to be drawn. It should therefore be acknowledged that neither of the two representations is designed as a supplement to the other,[4] since each has a different conception of the manner in which Jesus was made known, and in which Judas was active in the affair. That Judas was *guide to them that took Jesus*, ὁδηγὸς τοῖς συλλαβοῦσι τὸν Ἰησοῦν (Acts i. 16), all the Evangelists agree. But while according to the synoptical account the task of Judas includes not only the pointing out of the place, but also the distinguishing of the person by the kiss, John makes the agency of Judas end with the indication of the place, and represents him after the arrival on the spot as standing inactive among the crowd (εἱστήκει δὲ καὶ Ἰούδας—μετ’ αὐτῶν, v. 5). Why John does not assign to Judas the task of personally indicating Jesus, it is easy to see : because, namely, he would have Jesus appear, not as one delivered up, but as delivering himself up, so that his sufferings may be manifested in a higher degree as undertaken voluntarily. We have only to remember how the earliest opponents of Christianity imputed the retirement of Jesus out of the city into the distant garden, as an ignominious flight from his enemies,[5] in order to find it conceivable that there arose among the Christians at an early period the inclination to transcend the common evangelical tradition in representing his demeanour on his arrest in the light of a voluntary self-resignation.

In the synoptists the kiss of Judas is followed by the cutting question of Jesus to the traitor ; in John, after Jesus has uttered the ἐγώ εἰμι, *I am he*, it is stated that under the influence of these commanding words, the multitude who had come out to seize him went backward and fell to the ground, so that Jesus had to repeat his declaration and as it were encourage the people to seize him. Of late it has been denied that there was any miracle here : the impression of the personality of Jesus, it is said, acted psychologically on those among the crowd who had already often seen and heard Jesus ; and in support of this opinion reference is made to the examples of this kind in the life

---

[3] Lücke, 2, s. 599 ; Hase, ut sup. ; Olshausen, 2. s. 435.

[4] How can Lücke explain the omission of the kiss of Judas in the Gospel of John from its having been too notorious a fact ? and how can he adduce as an analogous instance the omission of the transaction between the betrayer and the Sanhedrim by John ? for this, as something passing behind the scenes, might very well be left out, but by no means an incident which, like that kiss, happened so conspicuously in the foreground and centre of the scene.

[5] So says the Jew of Celsus, Orig. c. Cels. ii. 9 : ἐπειδὴ ἡμεῖς ἐλέγξαντες αὐτὸν καὶ καταγνόντες ἠστιοῦμεν κολάζεσθαι, κρυπτόμενος μὲν καὶ διαδιδράσκων ἐπονειδιστότατα ἑάλω. *When we, having convicted and condemned him, had determined that he should suffer punishment ; concealing himself, and endeavouring to escape, he experienced a most shameful capture.*

of Marius, Coligny, and others.[6] But neither in the synoptical account, account, according to which there needed the indication of Jesus by the kiss, nor in that of John, according to which there needed the declaration of Jesus, *I am he*, does Jesus appear to be known to the crowd, at least in such a manner as to exercise any profound influence over them; while the above examples only show that sometimes the powerful impression of a man's personality has paralyzed the murderous hands of an individual or of a few, but not that a whole detachment of civil officers and soldiers has been made, not merely to draw back, but to fall to the ground. It answers no purpose for Lücke to make first a few fall down and then the whole crowd, except that of rendering it impossible to imagine the scene with gravity. Hence we turn to the old theologians, who here unanimously acknowledge a miracle. The Christ who by word of his mouth cast down the hostile multitude, is no other than he who according to 2 Thess. ii. 8, shall consume the Antichrist *with the spirit of his mouth*, i.e. not the historical Christ, but the Christ of the Jewish and primitive Christian imagination. The author of the fourth gospel especially, who had so often remarked how the enemies of Jesus and their creatures were unable to lay hands on him, because his hour was not yet come (vii. 30, 32, 44 ff., viii. 20), had an inducement, now, when the hour was come, to represent the ultimately successful attempt as also failing at the first in a thoroughly astounding manner; especially as this fully accorded with the interest by which he is governed throughout the description of this whole scene—the demonstrating that the capture of Jesus was purely an act of his own free will. When Jesus lays the soldiers prostrate by the power of his word, he gives them a proof of what he could do, if to liberate himself were his object; and when he allows himself to be seized immediately after, this appears as the most purely voluntary self-sacrifice. Thus in the fourth gospel Jesus gives a practical proof of that power, which in the first he only expresses by words, when he says to one of his disciples: *Thinkest thou that I cannot now pray to my Father, and he shall presently give me twelve legions of angels* (v. 53)?

After this, the author of the fourth gospel very inappropriately holds up the solicitude which Jesus manifested that his disciples should not be taken captive with him, as a fulfilment of the declaration of Jesus (xvii. 12), that he had lost none of those intrusted to him by the Father; a declaration which was previously more suitably referred to the spiritual preservation of his disciples. As the next feature in the scene, all the Evangelists agree, that when the soldiers began to lay hands on Jesus, one of his disciples drew his sword, and cut off the ear of the high priest's servant, an act which met with a reproof from Jesus. Still Luke and John have each a peculiar trait. Not to mention that both particularize the ear as the right ear, while their two predecessors had left this point undetermined; the latter not only gives the name of the wounded servant, but states that the disciple who wounded him was Peter. Why the synoptists do not name Peter, it has been sought to

---

[6] Lücke, 2, s. 597 f.; Olshausen, 2, s. 435; Tholuck, s. 299. The reference to the murderer of Coligny is, however, unwarranted, as any one will find who will look into the book incorrectly cited by Tholuck: *Serrani commentatorium de statu religionis et reip. in regno Galliæ*, L. x. p. 32, b. The murderer was not in the least withheld from the prosecution of his design by the firmness of the noble old man. Comp. also Schiller, Werke, 1 Bd. s. 382 f., 384; Ersch and Gruber's Encyclopädie, 7 Band, s. 452 f. Such inaccuracies in the department of modern history cannot indeed excite surprise in a writer who elsewhere (Glaubwürdigkeit, s. 437) speaks of the duke of Orleans, Louis Philippe's father, as the brother of Louis XVI. How can a knowledge so diversified as that of Dr. Tholuck be always quite accurate.

explain in different ways. The supposition that they wished to avoid compromising the apostle, who at the time of the composition of their gospels was
yet living,[7] belongs to the justly exploded fictions of an exegesis framed on
the false principle of supplying conjecturally all those links in the chain of
natural causation which are wanting in the gospels. That these Evangelists
elsewhere for the most part omit names,[8] is too sweeping an accusation as
regards Matthew, though he does indeed leave unnamed indifferent persons,
such as Jairus, or Bartimæus ; but that the real Matthew, or even the common
evangelical tradition, thus early and generally should have lost the name from
an anecdote of Peter, so thoroughly accordant with the part played by this
apostle, can scarcely be considered very probable. To me, the reverse would
be much more conceivable, namely, that the anecdote was originally current
without the mention of any name (and why should not a less distinguished
adherent of Jesus—for from the synoptists it is not necessarily to be inferred
that it was one of the twelve—whose name was therefore the more readily forgotten, have had courage and rashness enough to draw his sword at that
crisis ?), but a later narrator thought such a mode of conduct particularly
suited to the impetuous character of Peter, and hence ascribed it to him by a
combination of his own. On this supposition, we need not appeal, in support of the possibility that John could know the servant's name, to his acquaintance with the household of the high priest,[9] any more than to a
peculiar acquaintance of Mark with some inhabitants of Jericho, in explanation of his obtaining the name of the blind man.

The distinctive trait in Luke's account of this particular is, that Jesus heals
the servant's ear, apparently by a miracle. Olshausen here makes the com-
placent remark, that this circumstance best explains how Peter could escape
uninjured—astonishment at the cure absorbed the general attention : while
according to Paulus, Jesus by touching the wounded ear ($\dot{a}\psi\dot{a}\mu\epsilon\nu os$) only
meant to examine it, and then told what must be done for the purpose of
healing ($\dot{\iota}\dot{a}\sigma a\tau o$ $a\dot{v}\tau\dot{o}\nu$) ; had he cured it by a miracle there must have been
some notice of the astonishment of the spectators. Such pains-taking inter-
pretations are here especially needless, since the fact that Luke stands alone
in giving the trait in question, together with the whole tenor of the scene,
tells us plainly enough what opinion we are to form on the subject. Should
Jesus, who had removed by his miraculous power so much suffering of which
he was innocent, leave uncured suffering which one of his disciples out of
attachment to him, and thus indirectly he himself, had caused ? This must
soon have been found inconceivable, and hence to the stroke of the sword of
Peter was united a miraculous cure on the part of Jesus—the last in the evangelical history.

Here, immediately before he is led away, the synoptists place the remonstrance which Jesus addressed to those who had come to take him prisoner :
that though, by his daily public appearance in the temple he had given the
best opportunity for them to lay hands upon him, yet—a bad augury for the
purity of their cause—they came to a distance to seek him with as many
preparations, as against a thief ? In the fourth gospel, he is made to say
something similar to Annas, to whose inquiries concerning his disciples and
his doctrine, he replies by referring him to the publicity of his entire agency,
to his teaching in the temple and synagogue (xviii. 20 f.). Luke, as if he had
gathered from both, that Jesus had said something of this kind to the high
priest, and also at the time of his arrest, represents the chief priests and elders

---

[7] Paulus, exeg. Handb. 3, b, s. 570.
[8] Ibid.
[9] As Lücke, Tholuck and Olshausen, in loc.

themselves as being present in the garden, and Jesus as here speaking to them in the above manner, which is certainly a mere blunder.[10]

According to the two first Evangelists, all the disciples now fled. Here Mark has the special particular, that a young man with a linen cloth cast about his naked body, when he was in danger of being seized, left the linen cloth and fled naked. Apart from the industrious conjectures of ancient and even modern expositors, as to who this young man was ; this information of Mark's has been regarded as a proof of the very early origin of this gospel, on the ground that so unimportant an anecdote, and one moreover to which no name is attached, could have no interest except for those who stood in close proximity to the persons and events.[11] But this inference is erroneous ; for the above trait gives even to us, at this remote distance of time, a vivid idea of the panic and rapid flight of the adherents of Jesus, and must therefore have been welcome to Mark, from whatever source he may have received it, or how late soever he may have written.

§ 128.

EXAMINATION OF JESUS BEFORE THE HIGH PRIEST.

From the place of arrest the synoptists state Jesus to have been led to the high priest, whose name, Caiaphas, is, however, only mentioned by Matthew ; while John represents him as being led in the first instance to Annas, the father-in-law of the existing high priest ; and only subsequently to Caiaphas (Matt. xxvi. 57 ff. parall. ; John xviii. 12 ff.). The important rank of Annas renders this representation of John as conceivable as the silence of the synoptists is explicable, on the ground that the ex-high priest had no power of deciding in this cause. But it is more surprising that, as must be believed from the first glance, the fourth Evangelist merely gives some details of the transaction with Annas, and appears entirely to pass by the decisive trial before the actual high priest, except that he states Jesus to have been led away to Caiaphas. There was no more ready expedient for the harmonists than the supposition, which is found e.g. in Euthymius, that John, in consistency with the supplementary character of his gospel, perserved the examination before Annas as being omitted by the synoptists, while he passed by that before Caiaphas, because it was described with sufficient particularity by his predecessors.[1] This opinion, that John and the synoptists speak of two entirely distinct trials, has a confirmation in the fact that the tenor of the respective trials is totaly different. In that which the synoptists describe, according to Matthew and Mark, the false witnesses first appear against Jesus ; the high priest then asks him if he really pretends to be the Messiah, and on receiving an affirmative answer, declares him guilty of blasphemy, and worthy of death, whereupon follows maltreatment of his person. In the trial depicted by John, Jesus is merely questioned concerning his disciples and his doctrine, he appeals to the publicity of his conduct, and after having been maltreated for this reply by an attendant (ὑπηρέτης), is sent away without the passing of any sentence. That the fourth Evangelist should thus give no particulars concerning the trial before Caiaphas is the more surprising, since in the one before Annas, if it be this which he narrates, according to his own representation nothing was decided, and consequently the grounds for the

[10] Schleiermacher, über den Lukas, s. 290.
[11] Paulus, exeg. Handb. 3, b, s. 576.
[1] Paulus, ut sup. s. 577 ; Olshausen, 2, s. 244.

condemnation of Jesus by the Jewish authorities, and the sentence itself, are altogether wanting in his gospel.   To explain this by the supplementary object of John is to impute to him too irrational a mode of procedure ; for if he omitted facts because the other Evangelists had already given them, without intimating that he did so purely for that reason, he could only reckon on introducing confusion, and entailing on himself the suspicion of having given a false narrative, He can hardly have had the opinion. that the trial before Annas was the principal one, and that therefore it was allowable to omit the other, since he reports no judgment as having been passed in the former ; but if he knew the trial before Caiaphas to have been the principal one, and yet gave no more particular information concerning it, this also was a highly singular course for him to take.

Thus the very simplest view of the case seems at once to point to the attempt to discover in the account of the fourth gospel indications that it also is to be understood of the trial before Caiaphas.   What affords the strongest presumption of the identity of the two trials is the identity of an incident concomitant with both, John as well as the synoptists making Peter deny Jesus during the trial detailed.   It is further remarkable that after Annas has been spoken of, at v. 13, as the father-in-law of Caiaphas, there follows at v. 14, a more precise designation of Caiaphas as the author of the fatal counsel, recorded in John xi. 50, although apparently the Evangelist proceeds to narrate a trial held, not before Caiaphas, but before Annas.   Moreover in the description of the trial itself, there is mention throughout of the palace and of questions from the *high priest*, a title which John nowhere else applies to Annas, but only to Caiaphas.   But that in accordance with the above supposition, the Evangelist from v. 15, should be describing something which passed before Caiaphas, appears impossible from v. 24, for it is there first said that Annas sent Jesus to Caiaphas, so that he must until then have been before Annas.   With ready thought this difficulty was first met by removing the 24th verse to the place where it was wanted, namely, after v. 13, and laying the blame of its present too late position on the negligence of transcribers. [2]   As, however, this transposition, being destitute of any critical authority, must appear an arbitrary and violent expedient for getting rid of the difficulty, it was next tried whether the statement in v. 24, without being actually moved from its place, might not receive such an interpretation as to come in point of sense after v. 13 ; i.e., the word ἀπέστειλεν was taken as a pluperfect, and it was supposed that John intended here to supply retrospectively what he had forgotten to observe at v. 13, namely, that Annas immediately sent Jesus to Caiaphas, so that the trial just described was conducted by the latter. [3]   As the general possibility of such an *enallage temporum* is admissible, the only question is whether it be accordant with the style of the present writer, and whether it be intimated in the context.   In the latter respect it is certainly true that if nothing important had occurred in the presence of Annas, the Evangelist, in annexing to his notice of the relationship of Annas to Caiaphas the more precise designation of the latter, might be drawn on to speak without further preface of the trial before Caiaphas, and might afterwards, by way of appendix, at some resting place, as here at the close of the transactions of the high priest with Jesus, intimate the transition which he had made.   An accurate Greek writer certainly in this case, if he did not use the pluperfect, would at least have made evident the explanatory reference to what had preceded, by the addition of a γὰρ to the

[2] Thus e.g. Erasmus, in loc.
[3] Thus Winer, N. T. Gramm., § 41, 5 ; Tholuck and Lücke, in loc.

aorist. Our Evangelist, however, in whom the characteristic of the Hellen-istic writers to connect their propositions but loosely, in accordance with the genius of the Hebrew language, is very strongly marked, might perhaps have introduced that supplementary observation even without a particle, or, accor-ding to the ordinary reading, by οὖν, which is not merely indicative that a subject is continued, but also that it is resumed.[4] If these considerations be held to establish that he also intended to narrate the trial before Caiaphas : it is clear from the aspect of his account taken by itself, as well as from the previous comparison with the synoptical one, that his narrative cannot be complete.

We turn, therefore, to the account of the synoptists, and among them also, namely, between the two first and the third, we find numerous divergencies. According to the former, when Jesus was brought into the palace of the high priest, the scribes and elders were already assembled, and while it was still night proceeded to hold a trial, in which first witnesses appeared, and then the high priest addressed to him the decisive question, on the answer to which the assembly declared him worthy of death (in John also the trial goes forward in the night, but there is no intimation of the presence of the great council). According to the representation of the third gospel, on the other hand, Jesus throughout the night is merely kept under guard in the high priest's palace, and maltreated by the underlings ; and when at the break of day the Sanhedrim assembles, no witnesses appear, but the high priest pre-cipitates the sentence by the decisive question. Now, that in the depth of the night, while Judas was gone out with the guard, the members of the council should have assembled themselves for the reception of Jesus, might be regarded as improbable, and in so far, the preference might be given to the represen-tation of the third gospel, which makes them assemble at daybreak only :[5] were it not that Luke himself neutralizes this advantage by making the high priests and elders present at the arrest ; a zeal which might well have driven them straightway to assemble for the sake of accelerating the conclusion. But in the account of Matthew and Mark also there is this singularity, that after they have narrated to us the whole trial together with the sentence, they yet (xxvii. 1 and xv. 1) say : *when the morning was come, they took counsel,* πρωΐας δὲ γενομένης συμβούλιον ἔλαβον, thus making it appear, if not that the members of the Sanhedrim reassembled in the morning, which could hardly be, seeing that they had been together the whole night ; yet that they now first came to a definite resolution against Jesus, though, according to these same Evangelists, this had already been done in the nocturnal council.[6] It may be said that to the sentence of death already passed in the night, was added in the morning the resolution to deliver Jesus to Pilate : but according to the then existing state of the law, this followed as a matter of course, and needed no special resolution. That Luke and John omit the production of the false witnesses, is to be regarded as a deficiency in their narrative. For from the coincidence of John ii. 19 and Acts vi. 14 with Matthew and Mark, it is highly probably that the declaration about the destruction and rebuilding of the temple was really uttered by Jesus ; while that that declaration should be used as an article of accusation against him on his trial was an almost necessary result. The absence of this weighty point in Luke, Schleiermacher explains by the circumstance, that the author of this passage in the third gospel had indeed followed the escort which conducted Jesus from the garden, but had with most others been excluded from the palace of the high priest,

[4] Winer, Gramm., § 57, 4.
[5] Thus Schleiermacher, über den Lukas, s. 295.
[6] Schleiermacher, ut sup. ; comp. Fritzsche, in loc. Matth.

and consequently narrated what occurred there merely from hearsay. But, not to anticipate future points, the single trait of the cure of the servant's ear suffices to preclude our attributing to the author of this portion of Luke's gospel so close a proximity to the fact. It rather appears that the above declaration came to the third Evangelist under the form of an article of accusation against Stephen, instead of Jesus ; while the fourth has it only as a declaration from Jesus, and not as an article of accusation against him. This subject having however necessarily come under our observation at an earlier point of our inquiry, it is needless to pursue it further here. [7]

When Jesus made no answer to the allegations of the witnesses, he was asked, according to the two first Evangelists, by the high priest,—in the third gospel, without the above cause, by the Sanhedrim,—whether he actually maintained that he was the Messiah (the Son of God)? To this question, according to the two former, he at once replies in the affirmative, in the words σύ εἶπας, *thou hast said*, and ἐγώ εἰμι, *I am*, and adds that hereafter or immediately (ἀπ' ἄρτι) they would see the Son of man sitting on the right hand of the divine power, and coming in the clouds of heaven ; according to Luke, on the other hand, he first declares that his answer will be of no avail, and then adds that hereafter the Son of man shall sit on the right hand of the power of God ; whereupon all eagerly ask : Art thou then the Son of God? and he replies in the affirmative. Thus Jesus here expresses the expectation that by his death he will at once enter into the glory of sitting as Messiah at the right hand of God, according to Ps. cx. 1, which he had already, Matt. xxii. 44, interpreted of the Messiah. For even if he at first perhaps thought of attaining his messianic glorification without the intervention of death, because this intervention was not presented to him by the ideas of the age ; if it was only at a later period, and as a result of circumstances, that the foreboding of such a necessity began to arise and gradually to acquire distinctness in his mind ; now, a prisoner, forsaken by his adherents, in the presence of the rancorously hostile Sanhedrim, it must, if he would retain the conviction of his messiahship, become a certainty to him, that he could enter into his messianic glorification by death alone. When, according to the two first Evangelists, Jesus adds to the *sitting on the right hand of power*, the *coming in the clouds of heaven*, he predicts, as on an earlier occasion, his speedy advent, and in this instance he decidedly predicts it as a return. Olshausen maintains that the ἀπ' ἄρτι of Matthew ought to be referred only to καθήμενον κ. τ. λ., because it would not suit ἐρχόμενον κ. τ. λ., since it is not to be conceived that Jesus could then have represented himself as about to come in the clouds : a purely dogmatical difficulty, which does not exist in our point of view, but which cannot in any point of view warrant such an offence against grammatical interpretation as this of Olshausen. On the above declaration of Jesus, according to Matthew and Mark the high priest rends his clothes, declaring Jesus convicted of blasphemy, and the council pronounces him guilty of death ; and in Luke also, all those assembled observe that now there is no need of any further witness, since the criminal declaration has been uttered by Jesus in their own hearing.*

To the sentence is then added in the two first Evangelists the maltreatment of Jesus, which John, who here mentions no sentence, represents as following the appeal of Jesus to the publicity of his work, while Luke places it before the trial ; more probably because it was not any longer precisely known when this maltreatment occurred, than because it was repeated at various times and under various circumstances. In John the maltreatment is said to proceed

<hr />

[7] Vol. II. § 67.   Vol. III. § 114.

from an *attendant*, ὑπηρέτης, in Luke, from *the men that held Jesus*, ἄνδρες συνέχοντες τὸν Ἰ. ; in Mark, on the contrary, those who began to spit in the face of Jesus (καὶ ἤρξαντό τινες ἐμπτύειν αὐτῷ) must have been some of those (πάντες) who had just before condemned him, since he distinguishes the ὑπηρέτας, *servants*, from them ; and in Matthew also, who, without introducing a new nominative proceeds merely with τότε ἤρξαντο, *then began they*, it is plainly the members of the Sanhedrim themselves who descend to such unworthy conduct : which Schleiermacher justly considers improbable, and in so far prefers the representation of Luke to that of Matthew.[8] In John the maltreatment consists in a *blow on the cheek with the palm of the hand*, ῥάπισμα, which an attendant gives Jesus on account of a supposed insolent answer to the high priest ; in Matthew and Mark, in spitting on the face (ἐνέπτυσαν εἰς τὸ πρόσωπον αὐτοῦ), and blows on the head and cheek, to which it is added, in Luke also, that he was blindfolded, then struck on the face, and scoffingly asked to attest his messianic second sight by telling who was the giver of the blow.[9] According to Olshausen, the spirit of prophecy did not scorn to predict these rudenesses in detail, and at the same time to describe the state of mind which the Holy One of God opposed to the unholy multitude. He correctly adduces in relation to this scene Isa. l. 6 f.; (LXX.) : *I gave my back to the smiters, and my cheeks to them that plucked off the hair : I hid not my face from shame and spitting*, etc., τὸν νῶτόν μου δέδωκα εἰς μάστιγας, τὰς δὲ σιαγόνας μου εἰς ῥαπίσματα, τὸ δὲ πρόσωπόν μου οὐκ ἀπέστρεψα ἀπὸ αἰσχύνης ἐμπτυσμάτων κ. τ. λ. (comp. Mic. iv. 14) ; and for the manner in which Jesus bore all this, the well-known passage Isa. liii. 7, where the servant of God is represented as enduring maltreatment in silence. But the interpretation of these passages in Isaiah as prophecies concerning the Messiah is equally opposed to the context in both instances : [10] consequently the agreement of the result with these passages must either have been the effect of human design, or purely accidental. Now it is certain that the servants and soldiers in their maltreatment had not the intention of causing prophecies to be fulfilled in Jesus ; and it will hardly be chosen to suppose that Jesus affected silence with this view ; while to deduce from mere chance a coincidence which certainly, as Olshausen says, extends to minutiæ, is always unsatisfactory. Probable as it is from the rude manners of that age, that Jesus was maltreated when a prisoner, and moreover that amongst other things he received just such insults as are described by the Evangelists : it is yet scarcely to be denied, that their descriptions are modelled on prophecies which, when once Jesus appeared as a sufferer and maltreated person, were applied to him ; and however consistent it may be with the character of Jesus that he should have borne this maltreatment patiently, and repelled improper questions by a dignified silence : the Evangelists would scarcely have noticed this so often and so solicitously,[11] if it had not been their intention thus to exhibit the fulfilment of Old Testament oracles.

[8] Ut sup.

[9] Matthew does not mention the blindfolding, and appears to imagine that Jesus named the person who maltreated him, whom he saw, but did not otherwise know.

[10] Vid. Gesenius, in loc.

[11] Matth. xxvi. 63 ; comp. Mark xiv. 61 : ὁ δὲ Ἰ. ἐσιώπα.
Matth. xxvii. 12 : οὐδὲν ἀπεκρίνατο.
Matth. xxvii. 14 ; comp. Mark xv. 5 : καὶ οὐκ ἀπεκρίνατο αὐτῷ πρὸς οὐδὲ ἐν ῥῆμα, ὥστε θαυμάζειν τὸν ἡγεμόνα λίαν.
Luke xxiii. 9 : αὐτὸς δὲ οὐδὲν ἀπεκρίνατο αὐτῷ.
John xix. 9 : ὁ δὲ Ἰ. ἀπόκρισιν οὐκ ἔδωκεν αἰτῷ.

§ 129.

THE DENIAL OF PETER.

The two first Evangelists state, that at the moment in which Jesus was led away from the garden, all the disciples forsook him and fled ; but in their accounts, as well as in those of Luke and John, Peter is said to have followed him at a distance, and to have obtained admission with the escort into the court of the high priest's palace : while, according to the synoptists, it is Peter alone who gives this proof of courage and attachment to Jesus, which however soon enough issues in the deepest humiliation for him ; the fourth Evangelist gives him John for a companion, and moreover represents the latter as the one who, by means of his acquaintance with the high priest, procures admittance for Peter into his palace ; a divergency which, with the whole peculiar relation in which this gospel places Peter with respect to John, has been already considered.[1]

According to all the Evangelists, it was in this *court*, αὐλή, that Peter, intimidated by the inauspicious turn in the fortunes of Jesus, and the high priest's domestics by whom he was surrounded, sought to allay the repeatedly expressed suspicion that he was one of the followers of the arrested Galilean, by reiterated asseverations that he knew him not.   But, as we have already intimated, in relation to the owner of this habitation, there exists an apparent divergency between the fourth gospel and the synoptists.   In John, to judge from the first glance at his narrative, the first denial (xviii. 17) happens during the trial before Annas, since it stands after the statement that Jesus was led to Annas (v. 13), and before the verse in which he is said to have been sent to Caiaphas (v. 24), and only the two further acts of denial (v. 25–27), in so far as they follow the last-named statement, and as immediately after them the delivery to Pilate is narrated (v. 28), appear in John also to have occurred during the trial before Caiaphas and in his palace.   But to this supposition of a different locality for the first denial and the two subsequent ones, there is a hindrance in the account of the fourth gospel itself.   After the mention of the first denial, which happened at the door of the palace (of Annas apparently), it is said that the night being cold the servants and officers had made a fire of coals, *and Peter stood with them and warmed himself*, ἦν δὲ καὶ μετ᾿ αὐτῶν ὁ Πέτρος ἑστὼς καὶ θερμαινόμενος (v. 18).   Now, when farther on, the narrative of the second and third denial is opened with nearly the same words : *And Simon Peter stood and warmed himself*, ἦν δὲ Σίμων Πέτρος ἑστὼς καὶ θερμαινόμενος (v. 25): this cannot be understood otherwise than as an allusion to the previously noticed circumstances of the fire of coals, and of Peter's standing by it to warm himself, and hence it must be inferred that the Evangelist intended to represent the second and third denial as having occurred by the same fire, consequently, on the above supposition, likewise in the house of Annas.   It is true that the synoptists speak of a fire in the court of the palace of Caiaphas also (Mark v. 54 ; Luke v. 55), at which Peter warmed himself (here, however, sitting, as in John standing) : but it does not thence follow that John also imagined a similar fire to have been in the court of the actual high priest, and according to the supposition on which we have hitherto proceeded, he only mentions such a fire in the house of Annas. They who regard as too artificial an expedient the conjecture of Euthymius, that the dwellings of Annas and Caiaphas perhaps had a common court, and that consequently Peter could remain standing by the same fire after Jesus had been led away from the former to the latter, prefer the supposition that the second and third denial occurred, according to John, not after, but during the leading away of Jesus from Annas to Caiaphas.[2] Thus on the presupposition that John narrates a trial before Annas, the difference between the gospels in relation to the locality of the denial remains a total one ; and in this irreconcilable divergency, some have decided in favour of John, on the ground that the scattered disciples had only fragmentary information concerning this scene,—that Peter himself being a stranger in Jerusalem did not know in which palace he had, to his misfortune, entered ; but that he, and after him the first Evangelists, supposed the denials to have taken place in the court of Caiaphas ; whereas John, from his more intimate acquaintance with the city and the high priest's palace, was able to rectify this mistake.[3] But even admitting the incredible supposition that Peter erroneously believed himself to have denied Jesus in the palace of Caiaphas, still John, who in these days was in the society of Peter, would certainly at once have corrected his assertion, so that such an erroneous opinion could not have become fixed in his mind. Hence it might be preferred to reverse the attempt, and to vindicate the synoptists at the expense of John : were it not that the observations contained in the foregoing section (according to which John, after having merely mentioned that Jesus was led away to Annas, may speak from v. 15 of what occurred in the palace of Caiaphas), present a possible solution of this contradiction also.

In relation to the separate acts of denial, all the Evangelists agree in stating that there were three of them, in accordance with the prediction of Jesus ; but in the description of the several instances they are at variance. First, as it regards place and persons ; according to John the first denial is uttered on the very entrance of Peter, to *a damsel that kept the door*, παιδίσκη θυρωρός (v. 17) ; in the synoptists, in the inner court, where Peter sat at the fire, to *a damsel*, παιδίσκη (Matt. v. 69 f. parall.). The second takes place, in John (v. 25), and also in Luke, where at least notices no change of position (v. 58), at the fire : in Matthew (v. 71) and Mark (v. 68 ff.), after Peter was gone out into the *porch*, πυλῶν, προαύλιον ; further, in John it is made to several persons ; in Luke, to one ; in Matthew to another damsel than the one to whom he made the first denial ; in Mark, to the same. The third denial happened, according to Matthew and Mark, who mention no change of place after the second, likewise in the porch ; according to Luke and John, since they likewise mention no change of place, undoubtedly still in the inner court, at the fire ; further, according to Matthew and Mark, to many bystanders, according to Luke to one : according to John, to one who happens to be a relative of the servant who had been wounded in the garden. As regards the conversation which passed on this occasion, the suspicious queries are at one time addressed to Peter himself, at another to the bystanders, in order to point him out to their observation, and in the two first instances they are given by the different Evangelists with tolerable agreement, as merely expressing the opinion that he appeared to be one of the adherents of the man recently taken prisoner. But in the third instance, where the parties render a motive for their suspicion, they according to the synoptists mention his Galilean dialect as a proof of its truth ; while in John the relative of Malchus appeals to his recollection of having seen Peter in the garden. Now the former mode of accounting for the suspicion is as natural as the second, together with the designation of the individual who adduced it as a

<hr/>

[2] Thus Schleiermacher, über den Lukas, s. 289 ; Olshausen, 2, s. 445.
[3] Thus Paulus, ut sup. s. 577 f.

relative of Malchus, appears artificial, and fabricated for the sake of firmly interweaving into the narrative the connexion of the sword-stroke given in the garden with the name of Peter.[4] In the answers of Peter there is the divergency, that according to Matthew he already the second time fortifies his denial by an oath, while according to Mark this is not the case until the third denial, and in the two other Evangelists this circumstance is not mentioned at all; moreover, Matthew, to preserve a gradation, adds on the third denial that Peter began to *curse* καταναθεματίζειν as well as to *swear* ὀμνύειν, a representation which when compared with the other gospels may appear exaggerated.

So to adjust these very differently narrated denials in such a manner that no Evangelist may be taxed with having given an incorrect or even a merely inexact account, was no light labour for the harmonists. Not only did the older, supranaturalistic expositors, such as Bengel, undertake this task, but even recently, Paulus has given himself much trouble to bring the various acts of denial recounted by the Evangelists into appropriate order, and thus to show that they have a natural sequence. According to him, Peter denies the Lord,

1. Before the portress (1st denial in John);
2. Before several standing at the fire (2nd in John);
3. Before a damsel at the fire (1st in the synoptists);
4. Before one who has no particular designation (2nd in Luke);
5. On going out into the porch, before a damsel (2nd in Matthew and Mark. Out of this denial Paulus should in consistency have made two, since the damsel, who points out Peter to the bystanders, is according to Mark the same as the one in No. 3, but according to Matthew another);
6. Before the relative of Malchus (3rd in John);
7. Before one who professes to detect him by his Galilean dialect (3rd in Luke), and who forthwith
8. is seconded by several others, to whom Peter yet more strongly affirms that he knows not Jesus (3rd in Matthew and Mark).

Meanwhile by such a discrimination of the accounts out of respect to the veracity of the Evangelists, there was incurred the danger of impeaching the yet more important veracity of Jesus; for he had spoken of a threefold denial: whereas, on the plan of discrimination, according to the more or less consequent manner in which it is carried out, Peter would have denied Jesus from 6 to 9 times. The old exegesis found help in the canon: *abnegatio ad plures plurium interrogationes facta uno paroxysmo, pro unâ numeratur.*[5] But even granting such a mode of reckoning admissible, still, as each of the four narrators for the most part notices a greater or less interval between the separate denials which he recounts; in each instance, denials related by different Evangelists, e.g. one narrated by Matthew, one by Mark, and so forth, must have occurred in immediate succession: a supposition altogether arbitrary. Hence of late it has been a more favourite expedient to urge that the *thrice* τρὶς in the mouth of Jesus was only a round number intended to express a repeated denial, as also that Peter, once entangled in the confusion to a supposed necessity for falsehood, would be more likely to repeat his asseverations to 6 or 7 than merely to three inquirers.[6] But even if, according to Luke (v. 59 f.), the interval from the first denial to the last be estimated as more than an hour, still such a questioning from all kinds of people on all

---

[4] Comp. Weisse, die evang. Geschichte, 1, s. 609.
[5] Bengel, in the Gnomon.
[6] Paulus, ut sup. s. 578.

sides, as well as the ultimate impunity of Peter amid so general a suspicion, is extremely improbable; and when expositors describe the state of mind of Peter during this scene as a complete stupefaction,[7] they rather present the condition which befals the reader who has to arrange his ideas in such a crowd of continually repeated questions and answers having an identical meaning—like the incessant and lawless beating of a watch out of order. Olshausen has justly discarded the attempt to remove such differences as a fruitless labour: nevertheless he, on the one hand, immediately proceeds to a forced reconciliation of the divergencies at some points of the narrative; and on the other, he maintains that there were precisely three denials, whereas Paulus again has evinced a more correct discernment in pointing out the premeditated effort of the Evangelists to show that the denial was threefold. What on that evening happened repeatedly (not, however, eight or nine times), was represented as having happened precisely three times, in order to furnish the closest fulfilment to the prediction of Jesus, which was understood in its strictest literality.

The termination, and as it were the catastrophe, of the whole history of the denial is, in all the narratives, according to the prediction of Jesus, introduced by the crowing of the cock. In Mark, it crows after the first denial (v. 68), and then a second time after the third; in the other Evangelists only once, after the last act of denial. While John concludes his account with this particular, Matthew and Mark proceed to tell us that on hearing the cock crow, Peter remembered the words of Jesus and wept; but Luke has an additional feature peculiar to himself, namely, that on the crowing of the cock Jesus turned and looked at Peter, whereupon the latter, remembering the prediction of Jesus, broke out into bitter weeping. Now according to the two first Evangelists, Peter was not in the same locality with Jesus: for he is said to have been *without* ἔξω (Matt. v. 69) or *beneath* κάτω (Mark v. 66) *in the court* ἐν τῇ αὐλῇ, and it is thus implied that Jesus was in an inner or upper apartment of the palace: it must be asked, therefore, how could Jesus hear the denial of Peter, and thereupon turn to look at him? In relation to the latter part of the difficulty, the usual answer is that Jesus was at that moment being led from the palace of Annas to that of Caiaphas, and looked significantly at the weak disciple in passing.[8] But of such a removal of Jesus Luke knows nothing; and his expression, *the Lord turned and looked on Peter*, καὶ στραφεὶς ὁ Κύριος ἐνέβλεψε τῷ Πέτρῳ, would not so well imply that Jesus looked at Peter in passing, as that he turned round to do so when standing; besides, the above supposition will not explain how Jesus became aware that his disciple had denied him, since in the tumult of this evening he could not well, as Paulus thinks, have heard when in a room of the palace the loud tones of Peter in the court. It is true that the express distinction of the places in which Jesus and Peter were is not found in Luke, and according to him Jesus also might have had to remain some time in the court: but first, the representation of the other Evangelists is here more probable: secondly, Luke's own narrative of the denial does not previously create the impression that Jesus was in the immediate vicinity. But hypotheses for the explanation of that look of Jesus might have been spared, had a critical glance been directed to the origin of the incident. The unaccountable manner in which Jesus, who in the whole previous occurrence is kept behind the scene, here all on a sudden casts a glance upon it, ought itself, together with the silence of the other Evangelists, to have been taken as an indication of the real character of this feature in Luke's nar-

---

[7] Hess, Geschichte Jesu, 2, s. 343.

[8] Paulus and Olshausen, in loc.; Schleiermacher, ut sup. 289; Neander, s. 622, Anm.

rative. When also it is added, that as Jesus looked on Peter the latter remembered the words which Jesus had earlier spoken to him concerning his coming denial ; it might have been observed that the glance of Jesus is nothing else than the sensible image of Peter's remorseful recollection. The narrative of John, which is in this case the simplest, exhibits the fulfilment of the prediction of Jesus objectively, by the crowing of the cock ; the two first Evangelists add to this the subjective impression, which this coincidence made on Peter ; while Luke renders this again objective, and makes sorrowful remembrance of the words of the master, with the force of a penetrating glance, pierce the inmost soul of the disciple.[9]

§ 130.

THE DEATH OF THE BETRAYER.

On hearing that Jesus was condemned to death, Judas, according to the first gospel (xxvii. 3 ff.), was smitten with remorse, and hastened to the chief priests and elders to return to them the thirty pieces of silver, with the declaration that he had betrayed an innocent person. When however the latter scornfully retorted that on him alone rested all responsibility for that deed, Judas, after casting down the money in the temple, impelled by despair, went away and hanged himself. Hereupon the Sanhedrists, holding it unlawful to put the money returned by Judas into the treasury, since it was the price of blood, bought with it a potter's field as a burying place for strangers. To this particular the Evangelist appends two remarks : first, that from this mode of purchase, the piece of ground was called the *field of blood* up to his time : and secondly, that by this course of things an ancient prophecy was fulfilled.—The rest of the Evangelists are silent concerning the end of Judas ; but on the other hand we find in the Acts of the Apostles (i. 16 ff.) some information on this subject which in several points diverges from that of Matthew. Peter, when about to propose the completion of the apostolic number by the choice of a new colleague, thinks proper, by way of preliminary to remind his hearers of the manner in which the vacancy in the apostolic circle had arisen, i.e. of the treachery and the end of Judas ; and in relation to the latter he says, that the betrayer purchased himself a field with the reward of his crime, but fell headlong, and burst asunder in the midst, so that all his bowels gushed out, which being known in all Jerusalem, the piece of ground was called ἀκελδαμὰ, i.e. *the field of blood.* In addition to this, the narrator makes Peter observe that these occurrences were a fulfilment of two passages in the Psalms.

Between these two accounts there exists a double divergency : the one pertaining to the manner of the death of Judas, the other to the statement when and by whom the piece of ground was bought. As regards the former, Matthew declares that Judas laid violent hands on himself out of remorse and despair : whereas in the Acts nothing is said of remorse on the part of the traitor, and his death has not the appearance of suicide, but of an accident, or more accurately, of a calamity decreed by heaven as a punishment ; further, in Matthew he inflicts death on himself by the cord : according to the representation of Peter, it is a fall which puts an end to his life by causing a horrible rupture of the body.

How active the harmonists of all times have been in reconciling these divergencies, may be seen in Suïcer [1] and Kuinöl : here we need only briefly adduce the principal expedients for this purpose. As the divergency lay

---

[9] Comp. de Wette, in loc.
[1] Thesaurus, vid. ἀπάγχω.

chiefly in the words ἀπήγξατο, *he hanged himself,* in Matthew, and πρηνὴς γενόμενος, *falling headlong,* in Luke, the most obvious resource was to see whether one of these expressions could not be drawn to the side of the other. This has been tried with ἀπήγξατο in various ways ; this word being interpreted at one time as signifying only the torments of a guilty conscience,[2] at another, a disease consequent on these,[3] at another, any death chosen out of melancholy and despair ;[4] and to this it has been thought that the statement πρηνὴς γενόμενος κ. τ. λ. in the Acts added the more precise information, that the kind of death to which Judas was driven by an evil conscience and despair was precipitation from a steep eminence. Others on the contrary have sought to accommodate the meaning of πρηνὴς γενόμενος to ἀπήγξατο, understanding it merely to express as a circumstance what ἀπήγξατο expresses as an act : and accordingly maintaining that if the latter should be rendered *se suspendit,* the former should be translated by *suspensus.*[5] From repugnance to the obvious violence of this attempt, others, sparing the natural meaning of the expressions on both sides, have reconciled the divergent accounts by the supposition that Matthew narrates an earlier, the author of the Acts a later, stage of the events which marked the end of Judas. Some of the ancient commentators indeed separated these two stages so widely as to see in Matthew's statement (ἀπήγξατο) only an unsuccessful attempt at self-destruction, which from the bough whereon he suspended himself having broken, or from some other cause, Judas outlived, until the judgment of heaven overtook him in the πρηνὴς γενόμενος, *falling headlong.*[6] But since Matthew evidently intends in his expression ἀπήγξατο to narrate the last moments of the traitor : the two epochs, the account of which is supposed to be respectively given by Matthew and the Acts, have in later times been placed in closer proximity, and it has been held that Judas attempted to hang himself to a tree on an eminence, but as the rope gave way or the branch broke, he was precipitated into the valley over steep cliffs and sharp bushes, which lacerated his body.[7] The author of a treatise on the fate of Judas in Schmidt's Bibliothek[8] has already remarked as a surprising circumstance, how faithfully according to this opinion, the two narrators have shared the information between them : for it is not the case that one gives the less precise statement, the other the more precise ; but that one of them narrates precisely the first part of the incident without touching on the second, the other, the second without intruding on the first ; and Hase justly maintains that each narrator knew only the state of the fact which he has presented, since otherwise he could not have omitted the other half.[9]

After thus witnessing the total failure of the attempts at reconciliation in relation to the first difference ; we have now to inquire whether the other, relative to the acquisition of the piece of ground, can be more easily adjusted. It consists in this : according to Matthew, it is the members of the Sanhedrim

---

[2] Grotius.
[3] Heinsius.
[4] Perizonius.
[5] Thus the Vulgate and Erasmus. See in opposition to all these interpretations, Kuinöl, in Matth., p. 473 ff.
[6] Œcumenius, on the Acts, I.: ὁ Ἰούδας οὐκ ἐναπέθανε τῇ ἀγχόνῃ, ἀλλ᾽ ἐπεβίω, κατενεχθεὶς πρὸ τοῦ ἀποπνιγῆναι. Comp. Theophylact, on Matth. xxvii. and a Schol. Ἀπολιναρίου ap. Matthæi.
[7] Thus, after Casaubon, Paulus, 3, b, s. 457 f.; Kuinöl, in Matth. 747 f.; Winer, b. Realw. Art. Judas, and with some indecision Olshausen, 2, s. 455 f. Even Fritzsche is become so weary on the long way to these last chapters of Matthew, that he contents himself with this reconciliation, and, on the presupposition of it, maintains that the two accounts concur *amicissime.*
[8] 2 Band, 2 Stück, s. 248 f.
[9] L. J., § 132. Comp. Theile, zur Biographie Jesu, § 33.

who, after the suicide of Judas, purchase a field with the money which he had
left behind (from a potter moreover—a particular which is wanting in the Acts);
whereas, according to the Acts, Judas himself purchases the piece of ground,
and on this very spot is overtaken by sudden death ; and from this difference there results another, namely, that according to the latter account, it was
the blood of the betrayer shed on the piece of ground, according to the former,
the blood of Jesus cleaving to the purchase money, which caused the ground
to be named *the field of blood*, ἀγρὸς or χωρίον αἵματος. Now here Matthew's
manner of expressing himself is so precise, that it cannot well be twisted so as
to favour the other narrative ; but the word ἐκτήσατο (*he purchased* or *acquired*)
in the Acts presents inviting facilities for its adaptation to Matthew. By the
reward of treachery, Judas acquired a field—such, it is said, is the meaning in
the Acts—not immediately, but mediately ; since by returning the money he
gave occasion for the purchase of a piece of ground ; not for himself, but for
the Sanhedrim or the public good.[10] But however numerous the passages
adduced in which κτᾶσθαι has the signification : to acquire for another, still in
such instances it is necessary that the other party for whom one acquires
should be specified or intimated, and when this is not the case, as in the passage in the Acts, it retains the original meaning : to acquire for one's self.[11]
This Paulus felt, and hence gave the facts the following turn : the terrible fall
of Judas into a lime pit was the cause of this piece of ground being purchased
by the Sanhedrim, and thus Peter might very well say of Judas ironically, that
in death by the fall of his corpse he had appropriated to himself a fine
property.[12] But in the first place this interpretation is in itself strained ; and
in the second, the passage cited by Peter from the Psalms : *let his habitation be
desolate*, γενηθήτω ἡ ἔπαυλις αὐτοῦ ἔρημος, shows that he thought of the piece of
ground as the real property of Judas, and as being judicially doomed to desolation as the scene of his death.

According to this, neither the one difference nor the other admits of a favourable reconciliation ; indeed the existence of a real divergency was admitted
even by Salmasius, and Hase thinks that he can explain this discrepancy,
without endangering the apostolic origin of the two statements, from the
violent excitement of those days, in consequence of which only the general
fact that Judas committed suicide was positively known, and concerning the
more particular circumstances of the event, various reports were believed.
But in the Acts nothing is said of suicide, and that two apostles, Matthew and
Peter (if the first gospel be supposed to proceed from the former, the discourse
in the Acts from the latter), should have remained so entirely in the dark concerning the death of their late colleague, a death which took place in their immediate vicinity, that one of them represented him as dying by accident, the
other voluntarily, is difficult to believe. That therefore only one of the two
accounts can be maintained as apostolic, has been correctly perceived by the
author of the above-mentioned treatise in Schmidt's Bibliothek. And in
choosing between the two he has proceeded on the principle that the narrative
the least tending to glorification is the more authentic ; whence he gives the
preference to the account in the Acts before that in the first gospel, because
the former has not the glorifying circumstances of the remorse of Judas, and
his confession of the innocence of Jesus. But, it is ever the case with two contradictory narratives, not only that if one stands it excludes the other, but also
that if one falls it shakes the other : hence, if the representation of the facts
which is attested by the authority of the Apostle Matthew be renounced, there

---

[10] Vid. Kuinöl, in Matth., p. 748.
[11] Vid. Schmidt's Biblioth., ut sup. s. 251 f.
[12] Paulus, 3, b, s. 457 f. ; Fritzsche, p. 799.

is no longer any warrant for the other, which professedly rests on the testimony of the Apostle Peter.

If then we are to treat the two narratives on the same footing, namely as legends, with respect to which it is first to be discovered how far their historical nucleus extends, and how far they consist of traditional deposits ; we must, in order to be clear on the subject, consider the data which form the roots of the two narratives. Here we find one which is common to both, with two others of which each has one peculiarly to itself. The datum common to both narratives is, that there was in Jerusalem a piece of ground which was called *the field of blood*, ἀγρὸς or χωρίον αἵματος, or in the original tongue, according to the statement of the Acts, ἀκελδαμὰ. As this information is concurrently given by two narratives in other respects totally divergent, and as, besides, the author of the first gospel appeals to the actual practice of his day in proof that the field was called by this name : we cannot well doubt the existence of a piece of ground so named. That it really had a relation to the betrayer of Jesus is less certain, since our two narratives give different accounts of this relation : the one stating that Judas himself bought the property, the other that it was not purchased until after his death, with the thirty pieces of silver. We can therefore draw no further conclusion than that the primitive Christian legend must have early attributed to that field of blood a relation to the betrayer. But the reason wherefore this relation took various forms is to be sought in the other datum from which our narratives proceed, namely, in the Old Testament passages, which the authors cite (from different sources, however), as being fulfilled by the fate of Judas.

In the passage of the Acts, Ps. lxix. 25, and Ps. cix. 8, are quoted in this manner. The latter is a psalm which the first Christians from among the Jews could not avoid referring to the relation of Judas to Jesus. For not only does the author, alleged to be David, but doubtless a much later individual,[13] dilate from the opening of the psalm on such as speak falsely and insidiously against him, and return him hatred for his love, but from v. 6, where the curses commence, he directs himself against a particular person, so that the Jewish expositors thought of Doeg, David's calumniator with Saul, and the Christians just as naturally of Judas. From this psalm is gathered the verse which, treating of the transfer of one office to another, appeared perfectly to suit the case of Judas. The other psalm, it is true, speaks more vaguely of such as hate and persecute the author without cause, yet this also is ascribed to David, and is so similar to the other in purport and style, that it might be regarded as its parallel, and if curses might be applied to the betrayer out of the former, they might be so out of the latter.[14] Now if Judas had actually bought with the wages of his treachery a piece of land, which from being the scene of his horrible end, subsequently remained waste : it was a matter of course to refer to him precisely those passages in this psalm which denounce on the enemies the desolation of their *habitation* ἔπαυλις. As, however, from the divergency of Matthew, the fact that Judas himself bought that piece of ground and came to his end upon it, is doubtful : while it can scarcely be supposed that the piece of land on which the betrayer of Jesus met his end would be so abhorrent to the Jews that they would let it lie waste as a land of blood ; it is more probable that this name had another origin no longer to be discovered, and was interpreted by the Christians in accordance with their own ideas ; so that we must not derive the application of the passage in the Psalms, and the naming of that waste piece of land, from

---

[13] Vid. De Wette, in loc.

[14] In other parts of the N. T. also we find passages from this psalm messianically applied : as v. 4, John xv. 25, v. 9 ; John ii. 17 ; and John xix. 28 f., probably v. 21.

an actual possession of it by Judas, but on the contrary, we must refer to those two causes the existence of the legend, which ascribes such a possession to Judas. For if the two psalms in question were once applied to the betrayer, and if in one of them the desolation of his ἔπαυλις (LXX.) was denounced, he must have previously been in possession of such an ἔπαυλις, and this it was thought, he would probably have purchased with the reward of his treason. Or rather, that out of the above psalms the desolation of the ἔπαυλις was a particular specially chosen, appears to have been founded on the natural presupposition, that the curse would be chiefly manifested in relation to something which he had acquired by the wages of his iniquity ; added to the circumstance that among the objects anathematized in the psalm, the one most capable of being bought was the ἔπαυλις. This conception of the facts was met in the most felicitous manner by the ἀκελδαμὰ lying near Jerusalem, which, the less was known of the origin of its name and of the horror attached to it, might the more easily be applied by the primitive Christian legend to its own purposes, and regarded as the *desolate habitation*, ἔπαυλις ἠρημωμένη, of the betrayer.

Instead of these passages from the Psalms, the first gospel cites as being fulfilled by the last acts of Judas, a passage which it attributes to Jeremiah, but to which nothing corresponding is to be found except in Zech. xi. 12 f., whence it is now pretty generally admitted that the Evangelist substituted one name for the other by mistake.[15] How Matthew might be led by the fundamental idea of this passage—an unreasonably small price for the speaker in the prophecy—to an application of it to the treachery of Judas, who for a paltry sum had as it were sold his master, has been already shown.[16] Now the prophetic passage contains a command from Jehovah to the author of the prophecy, to cast the miserable sum with which he had been paid, into the house of the Lord, and also אֶל־הַיּוֹצֵר, which, it is added, was done. The person who casts down the money is in the prophecy the same with the speaker, and consequently with him who is rated at the low price, because the sum here is not purchase money but hire, and hence is received by the person so meanly estimated, who alone can cast it away again : in the application of the Evangelist, on the contrary, the sum being considered as purchase money, another than the one so meanly estimated was to be thought of as receiving and casting away the sum. If the one sold for so paltry a price was Jesus : he who received the money and finally rejected it could be no other than his betrayer. Hence it is said of the latter, that *he cast down the pieces of silver in the temple* ἐν τῷ ναῷ corresponding to the phrase וַיַּשְׁלִיךְ אֹתוֹ בֵּית יְהֹוָה in the prophetic passage, although these very words happen to be absent from the extremely mutilated citation of Matthew. But in apposition to the בֵּית יְהֹוָה, wherein the money was cast, there stood besides אֶל־הַיּוֹצֵר. The LXX. translates : εἰς τὸ χωνευτήριον, *into the melting furnace*; now, it is with reason conjectured that the pointing should be altered thus : אֶל־הַיּוֹצֵר, and the word rendered : *into the treasury* ;[17] the author of our gospel adhered to the literal translation by κεραμεύς *potter*. But what the potter had to do here,—why the money should be given to him, must at first have been as incomprehensible to him as it is to us when we adhere to the common reading. Here however there occurred to his recollection the field of blood, to which, as we gather from the Acts, the Christian legend gave a relation to Judas, and

---

[15] Still for other conjectures see Kuinöl, in loc.
[16] § 119.
[17] Hitzig, in Ullmann's and Umbreit's Studien, 1830, 1, s. 35 ; Gesenius, Wörterbuch ; comp. Rosenmüller's Scholia in V. T. 7, 4, s. 320 ff.

hence resulted the welcome combination, that it was probably that field for which the thirty pieces of silver were to be given to the *potter.* As, however, it was impossible to conceive the potter as being in the temple when receiving the money, and yet according to the prophetic passage the pieces of silver were cast into the temple : a separation was made between the casting into the temple and the payment to the potter. If the former must be ascribed to Judas, if he had thus once cast away the money, he himself could no longer purchase the piece of ground from the potter, but this must be done by another party, with the money which Judas had cast away. Who this party must be followed of course : if Judas gave up the money, he would give it up to those from whom he had received it ; if he cast it into the temple, it would fall into the hands of the rulers of the temple : thus in both ways it would revert to the Sanhedrim. The object of the latter in purchasing the ground was perhaps drawn from the use to which that waste place was actually appropriated. Lastly, if Judas cast away again the reward of his treachery, this, it must be inferred, could only be out of remorse. To make Judas manifest remorse, and thus win from the traitor himself a testimony to the innocence of Jesus, was as natural to the conception of the primitive Christian community, as to convert Pilate, and to make Tiberius himself propose in the Roman senate the deification of Christ,[18] But how would the remorse of Judas further manifest itself? A return to the right on his part, was not only unattested by any facts, but was besides far too good a lot for the traitor : hence repentance must have become in him despair, and he must have chosen the end of the well-known traitor in the history of David, Ahithophel, of whom it is said, 2 Sam. xvii. 23 : ἀνέστη καὶ ἀπῆλθεν—καὶ ἀπήγξατο, *he arose, and went—and hanged himself,* as of Judas here : ἀνεχώρησε καὶ ἀπελθὼν ἀπήγξατο, *he departed, and went and hanged himself.*

A tradition referred to Papias appears to be allied to the narrative in the Acts rather than to that of Matthew. Œcumenius, quoting the above collector of traditions, says, that Judas, as an awful example of impiety, had his body distended to such a degree, that a space where a chariot could pass was no longer sufficiently wide for him, and that at last being crushed by a chariot, he burst asunder and all his bowels were pressed out.[19] The latter statement doubtless arose from a misconstruction of the ancient legend ; for the chariot was not originally brought into immediate contact with the body of Judas, but was merely used as a measure of his size, and this was afterwards erroneously understood as if a chariot in passing had crushed the swollen body of Judas. Hence, not only in Theophylact and in an ancient *Scholium,*[20] without any distinct reference to Papias, but also in a *Catena* with an express citation of his ἐξηγήσεις, we actually find the fact narrated without that addition.[21] The monstrous swelling of Judas, spoken of in this passage, might, it

---

18 Tertull. Apologet. c. xxi. : *Ea omnia super Christo Pilatus, et ipse jam pro sua conscientia Christianus, Cæsari tum Tiberio nunciavit.* c. v. : *Tiberius ergo, cujus tempore nomen Christianum in seculum introit, annunciatum sibi ex Syria Palæstina, quod illic veritatem illius Divinitatis revelaverat, detulit ad Senatum cum prærogativa suffragii sui. Senatus, quia non ipse probaverat, respuit.* For further details on this subject, see Fabricius, Cod. Apocr. N. T. 1, p. 214 ff., 298 ff. ; comp. 2, p. 505.
19 Œcumen. ad Act. i. : τοῦτο δὲ σαφέστερον ἱστορεῖ Παπίας, ὁ Ἰωάννου τοῦ ἀποστόλου μαθητής· μέγα ἀσεβείας ὑπόδειγμα ἐν τούτῳ τῷ κόσμῳ περιεπάτησεν Ἰούδας. Πρησθεὶς γὰρ ἐπὶ τοσοῦτον τὴν σάρκα, ὥστε μὴ δύνασθαι διελθεῖν, ἁμάξης ῥᾳδίως διερχομένης, ὑπὸ τῆς ἁμάξης ἐπιεσθη, ὥστε τὰ ἔγκατα αὐτοῦ ἐκκενωθῆναι.
20 Vid. sup.
21 In Münter's Fragm. Patr. 1, p. 17 ff. For the rest the passage is of very similar tenor with that of Œcumenius, and is partly an exaggeration of it : τοῦτο δὲ σαφέστερον ἱστορεῖ Παπίας, ὁ Ἰωάννου μαθητὴς, λέγων οὕτως ἐν τῷ τετάρτῳ τῆς ἐξηγήσεως τῶν κυριακῶν λόγων· μέγα δὲ ἀσεβείας ὑπόδειγμα ἐν τούτῳ τῷ κόσμῳ περιεπάτησεν ὁ Ἰούδας· πρησθεὶς ἐπὶ τοσοῦτον τὴν

is supposed, originally be only an explanation of the displacing and protrusion of the viscera, and in like manner the dropsy into which Theophylact represents him as falling might be regarded as an explanation of this swelling: when, however, in Ps. cix., applied in the Acts to Judas, amongst other maledictions, we read : וַתָּבֹא (קְלָלָה) בְּמֵעָיו כַּמַּיִם בְּקִרְבּוֹ LXX: εἰσῆλθεν (ἡ κατάρα) ὡσεὶ ὕδωρ εἰς τὰ ἔγκατα αὐτοῦ, *so let it (cursing) come into his bowels like water* (v. 18) : it appears possible that the *dropsical disease*, νόσος ὑδερικὴ, may have been also taken from this passage; as also one of the features in the monstrous description which Papias gives of the condition of Judas, namely, that from the enormous swelling of his eyelids he could no longer see the light of day, might remind us of v. 23 in the other psalm applied to Judas, where, among the curses this is enumerated : *Let their eyes be darkened that they see not*, σκοτισθήτωσαν οἱ ὀφθαλμοὶ αὐτῶν τοῦ μὴ βλέπειν, a hindrance to sight, which when once the swollen body of Judas was presupposed, must necessarily assume the form of a swelling up of the eyelids.   If then the tradition which is allied to the account in Acts i. developed its idea of the end of Judas chiefly in correspondence with the ideas presented in these two psalms ; and if in that passage of the Acts itself the account of the connexion of Judas with the piece of ground is derived from the same source : it is no farfetched conjecture that what is said in the Acts concerning the end of the betrayer may have had a similar origin.   That he died an early death may be historical ; but even if not so, in Psalm cix. in the very same verse (v. 8), which contains the transfer of the *office*, ἐπισκοπὴ, to another, an early death is predicted for the betrayer in the words : *Let his days be few*, γενηθήτωσαν αἱ ἡμέραι αὐτοῦ ὀλίγαι, and it might also be believed that the death by falling headlong also was gathered from Ps. lxix. 22, where it is said : *Let their table become a snare before them*, γενηθήτω ἡ τράπεζα αὐτῶν—εἰς σκάνδαλον (לְמוֹקֵשׁ).

Thus we scarcely know with certainty concerning Judas even so much as that he came to a violent and untimely death, for if, as was natural, after his departure from the community of Jesus, he retired, so far as the knowledge of its members was concerned, into an obscurity in which all historical information as to his further fate was extinguished : the primitive Christian legend might without hindrance represent as being fulfilled in him all that the prophecies and types of the Old Testament threatened to the false friend of the Son of David, and might even associate the memory of his crime with a well-known desecrated place in the vicinity of Jerusalem.[22]

σάρκα, ὥστε μηδὲ ὁπόθεν ἅμαξα ῥᾳδίως διέρχεται, ἐκεῖνον δύνασθαι διελθεῖν, ἀλλὰ μηδὲ αὐτὸν μόνον τὸν ὄγκον τῆς κεφαλῆς αὐτοῦ· τὰ μὲν γὰρ βλέφαρα τῶν ὀφθαλμῶν αὐτοῦ (Cod. Venet. : φασὶ τοσοῦτον ἐξοιδῆσαι, ὡς αὐτὸν μὲν καθόλου τὸ φῶς μὴ βλέπειν) μηδὲ ὑπὸ ἰατροῦ διόπτρας ὀφθῆναι κ. τ. λ.   Μετὰ πολλὰς δὲ βασάνους καὶ τιμωρίας ἐν ἰδίῳ, φασὶ, χωρίῳ τελευτήσαντος κ. τ. λ.   *Papias, the disciple of John, gives a clearer account of this (in the fourth section of his exegesis of our Lord's words) as follows : Judas moved about in this world a terrible example of impiety, being swollen in body to such a degree that where a chariot could easily pass he was not able to find a passage, even for the bulk of his head.   His eyelids, they say, were so swelled out that he could not see the light, nor could his eyes be made visible even by the physician's dioptra*, etc.   *After suffering many torments and judgments, dying, as they say, in his own field*, etc.

[22] Comp. De Wette, exeg. Handb. 1, 1, s. 231 f. ; 1, 4, s. 10 f.

§ 131.

JESUS BEFORE PILATE AND HEROD.

According to all the Evangelists it was in the morning when the Jewish magistrates, after having declared Jesus worthy of death,[1] caused him to be led away to the Roman procurator, Pontius Pilate (Matt. xxvii. 1 ff. parall. ; John xviii. 28). According to Matthew and Mark, Jesus was bound preparatory to his being conducted before Pilate, according to John xviii. 12, immediately on his arrest in the garden ; Luke says nothing of his being bound. To this measure of sending him to Pilate they were compelled, according to John xviii. 31, by the circumstance that the Sanhedrim was deprived of the authority to execute the punishment of death (without the concurrence of the Roman government):[2] but at all events the Jewish rulers must in this instance have been anxious to call in the agency of the Romans, since only their power could afford security against an *uproar among the people* θόρυβος ἐν τῷ λαῷ, which the former feared as a result of the execution of Jesus during the feast time (Matt. xxvi. 5 parall.).

Arrived at the Prætorium, the Jews, according to the representation of the fourth gospel, remained without, from fear of Levitical defilement, but Jesus was led into the interior of the building : so that Pilate must alternately have come out when he would speak to the Jews, and have gone in again when he proceeded to question Jesus (xviii. 28 ff.). The synoptists in the sequel re-present Jesus as in the same locality with Pilate and the Jews, for in them Jesus immediately hears the accusations of the Jews, and answers them in the presence of Pilate. Since they, as well as John, make the condemnation take place in the open air (after the condemnation they represent Jesus as being led into the Prætorium, Matt. xxvii. 27, and Matthew, like John, xix. 13, de-scribes Pilate ascending the *judgment seat* βῆμα, which according to Josephus[3] stood in the open air), without mentioning any change of place in connexion with the trial : they apparently conceived the whole transaction to have passed on the outer place, and supposed, in divergency from John, that Jesus himself was there.

The first question of Pilate to Jesus is according to all the gospels : *Art thou the king of the Jews ?* σὺ εἶ ὁ βασιλεὺς τῶν Ἰουδαίων, i.e. the Messiah ? In the two first Evangelists this question is not introduced by any accusation on the part of the Jews (Matt. v. 11 ; Mark v. 2) ; in John, Pilate, stepping out

---

[1] According to Babl. Sanhedrin, ap. Lightfoot, p. 486, this mode of procedure would have been illegal. It is there said : *Judicia de capitalibus finiunt eodem die si sint ad absolutionem ; si vero sint ad damnationem, finiuntur die sequente.*

[2] Besides this passage of John : ἡμῖν οὐκ ἔξεστιν ἀποκτεῖναι οὐδένα, *It is not lawful for us to put any man to death,* there is no other authority for the existence of this state of things than an obscure and variously interpreted tradition, Avoda Zara f. viii. 2 (Lightfoot, p. 1123 f.) : *Rabh Cahna dicit, cum ægrotaret R. Jsmaël bar Jose, miserunt ad eum, dicentes : dic nobi, ô Domine, duo aut tria, quæ aliquando dixisti nobis nomine patris tui. Dicit iis ——— quadraginta annis ante excidium templi migravit Synedrium et sedit in tabernis. Quid sibi vult hæc traditio ? Rabh Isaac, bar Abdimi dicit: non judicârunt judicia mulctativa. Dixit R. Nachman bar Isaac : ne dicat, quod non judicârunt judicia mulctativa, sed quod non judicârunt judicia capitalia.* With this may be compared moreover the information given by Josephus, Antiq. xx. ix. 1, that it *was not lawful for Ananus* (the high priest) *to assemble the Sanhedrim without the consent of the procurator.* On the other hand the execution of Stephen (Acts vii.) without the sanction of the Romans might seem to speak to the contrary ; but this was a tumultuary act, undertaken perhaps in the confidence that Pilate was absent. Compare on this point Lücke, 2, s. 631 ff.

[3] De bell. Jud. II. ix. 3.

of the Prætorium, asks the Jews what accusation they have to bring against Jesus (xviii. 29), on which they insolently reply : *If he were not a malefactor, we would not have delivered him up unto thee* : an answer by which they could not expect to facilitate their obtaining from the Roman a ratification of their sentence,[4] but only to embitter him.   After Pilate, with surprising mildness, has rejoined that they may take him and judge him according to their law— apparently not supposing a crime involving death—and the Jews have opposed to this permission their inability to administer the punishment of death : the procurator re-enters and addresses to Jesus the definite question : *Art thou the king of the Jews ?* which thus here likewise has no suitable introduction. This is the case only in Luke, who first adduces the accusations of the San-hedrists against Jesus, that he stirred up the people and encouraged them to refuse tribute to Cæsar, giving himself out to be *Christ a king*, Χριστὸν βασιλέα (xxiii. 2).

If in this manner the narrative of Luke enables us to understand how Pilate could at once put to Jesus the question whether he were the king of the Jews ; it leaves us in all the greater darkness as to how Pilate, immedi-ately on the affirmative answer of Jesus, could without any further inquiries declare to the accusers that he found no fault in the accused.   He must first have ascertained the grounds or the want of grounds for the charge of exciting the populace, and also have imformed himself as to the sense in which Jesus claimed the title of *king of the Jews*, before he could pronounce the words : *I find no fault in this man.*   In Matthew and Mark, it is true, to the affirmation of Jesus that he is the king of the Jews is added his silence, in opposition to the manifold accusations of the Sanhedrists—a silence which surprises Pilate : and this is not followed by a precise declaration that no fault is to be found in Jesus, but merely by the procurator's attempt to set Jesus at liberty by coupling him with Barabbas ; still what should move him even to this attempt does not appear from the above gospels.   On the other hand, this point is sufficiently clear in the fourth gospel.   It is certainly surprising that when Pilate asks whether he be really the King of the Jews, Jesus should reply by the counter-question, whether he say this of himself or at the suggestion of another.   In an accused person, however conscious of innocence, such a question cannot be held warrantable, and hence it has been sought in every possible way to give the words of Jesus a sense more consonant with pro-priety : but the question of Jesus is too definite to be a mere repulse of the accusation as absurd,[5] and too indefinite to be regarded as an inquiry, whether the Procurator intended the title βασιλεὺς τῶν Ἰουδαίων in the Roman sense (ἀφ' ἑαυτοῦ) or in the Jewish (ἄλλοι σοι εἶπον).[6]   And Pilate does not so un-derstand it, but as an unwarrantable question to which it is a mark of his in-dulgence that he replies ;—in the first instance, it is true, with some impatience, by the second counter-question, whether he be a Jew, and thus able of him-self to have information concerning a crime so specifically Jewish ; but here-upon he good-naturedly adds that it is the Jews and their rulers by whom Jesus has been delivered to him, and that he is therefore at liberty to speak more particularly of the crime which these lay to his charge.   Now on his Jesus gives Pilate an answer which, added to the impression of his whole appearance, might certainly induce in the Procurator a conviction of his in-nocence.   He replies, namely, that his *kingdom* βασιλεία is not *of this world* ἐκ τοῦ κόσμου τούτου, and adduces as a proof of this, the peaceful, passive con-duct of his adherents on his arrest (v. 36).   On the further question of Pilate,

---

[4] As Lücke supposes, s. 631.
[5] Calvin, in loc.
[6] Lücke and Tholuck, in loc.

whether, since Jesus has thus ascribed to himself a kingdom, although no earthly one, he then claims to be a king? he replies that certainly he is so, but only in so far as he is born to be a witness to the truth: whereupon follows the famous question of Pilate : *What is truth ?* τί ἐστιν ἀλήθεια; Although in this latter reply of Jesus we cannot but be struck by its presenting the peculiar hue of thought which characterizes the author of the fourth gospel, in the use of the idea of *truth* ἀλήθεια, as we were before surprised at the unwarrantable nature of the counter-question of Jesus ; still this account in John renders it conceivable how Pilate could immediately step forth and declare to the Jews that he found no fault in Jesus.   But another point might easily create suspicion against this narrative of John.   According to him the trial of Jesus went forward in the interior of the Prætorium, which no Jew would venture to enter ; who then are we to suppose heard the conversation of the Procurator with Jesus, and was the informant who communicated it to the author of the fourth gospel ?   The opinion of the older commentators that Jesus himself narrated these conversations to his disciples after the resurrection is renounced as extravagant ; the more modern idea that perhaps Pilate himself was the source of the information concerning the trial, is scarcely less improbable, and rather than take refuge, with Lücke, in the supposition that Jesus remained at the entrance of the Prætorium, so that those standing immediately without might with some attention and stillness (?) have heard the conversation, I should prefer appealing to the attendants of the Procurator, who would scarcely be alone with Jesus.   Meanwhile it is easily conceivable that we have here a conversation, which owes its origin solely to the Evangelist's own combination, and in this case we need not bestow so much labour in ascertaining the precise sense of Pilate's question : *what is truth ?* since this would only be an example of the fourth Evangelist's favourite form of dialogue, the contrast of profound communications on the part of Jesus, with questions either of misapprehension or of total unintelligence on the part of the hearers, as xii. 34, the Jews ask   *who is this Son of man ?* τίς ἐστιν οὗτος ὁ υἱὸς τ. α. ; so here Pilate : *what is truth ?* τί ἐστιν ἀλήθεια ;[7]

Before the introduction of Barabbas, which in all the other Evangelists comes next in order, Luke has an episode peculiar to himself.   On the declaration of Pilate that he finds no guilt in the accused, the chief priests and their adherents among the multitude persist in asserting that Jesus stirred up the people by his agency as a teacher from Galilee to Jerusalem : Pilate notices the word Galilee, asks whether the accused be a Galilean, and when this is confirmed, he seizes it as a welcome pretext for ridding himself of the ungrateful business, and sends Jesus to the Tetrarch of Galilee, Herod Antipas, at that time in Jerusalem in observance of the feast ; perhaps also designing as a secondary object, what at least was the result, to conciliate the petty prince by this show of respect for his jurisdiction.   This measure, it is said, gave great satisfaction to Herod, because having heard much of Jesus, he had long been desirous to see him, in the hope that he would perhaps perform a miracle.   The Tetrarch addressed various questions to him, the Sanhedrists urged vehement accusations against him, but Jesus gave no answer ; whereupon Herod with his soldiers betook themselves to mockery, and at length, after arraying him in a gorgeous robe, sent him back to Pilate (xxiii. 4 ff.). This narrative of Luke's, whether we consider it in itself or in its relation to the other gospels, has much to astonish us.   If Jesus as a Galilean really belonged to the jurisdiction of Herod, as Pilate, by delivering the accused to him, appears to acknowledge : how came Jesus (and the question is equally

[7] Comp. Kaiser, bibl. Theol. I, s. 252.

difficult whether we regard him as the sinless Jesus of the orthodox system, or
as the one who in the history of the tribute-penny manifested his subjection
to the existing authorities) to withhold from him the answer which was his
due ? and how was it that Herod, without any further procedures, sent him
away again from his tribunal ? To say, with Olshausen, that the interrogation
before Herod had elicited the fact that Jesus was not born in Nazareth and
Galilee, but in Bethlehem, and consequently in Judæa, is on the one hand an
inadmissible appeal to the history of the birth of Jesus, of the statements in
which there is no further trace in the whole subsequent course of Luke's gospel ; and on the other hand, a totally accidental birth in Judæa, such as that
represented by Luke, the parents of Jesus, and even Jesus himself, being both
before and after resident in Galilee, would not have constituted Jesus a
Judæan ; but above all we must ask, through whom was the Judæan origin of
Jesus brought to light, since it is said of Jesus that he gave no answer, while
according to all the information we possess, that origin was totally unknown
to the Jews ?   It would be preferable to explain the silence of Jesus by the
unbecoming manner of Herod's interrogation, which manifested, not the
seriousness of the judge, but mere curiosity ; and to account for his being
sent back to Pilate by the fact, that not only the arrest, but also a part of the
ministry of Jesus had occurred within the jurisdiction of Pilate.   But why do
the rest of the Evangelists say nothing of the entire episode ? Especially
when the author of the fourth gospel is regarded as the Apostle John, it is not
easy to see how this omission can be explained.   The common plea, that he
supposed the fact sufficiently known from the synoptists, will not serve here,
since Luke is the sole Evangelist who narrates the incident, and thus it does
not appear to have been very widely spread ; the conjecture, that it may probably have appeared to him too unimportant,[8] loses all foundation when it is
considered that John does not scorn to mention the leading away to Annas,
which nevertheless was equally indecisive ; and in general, the narrative of
these events in John is, as Schleiermacher himself confesses, so consecutive
that it nowhere presents a break in which such an episode could be inserted.
Hence even Schleiermacher at last takes refuge in the conjecture that possibly the sending to Herod may have escaped the notice of John, because it
happened on an opposite side to that on which the disciple stood, through a
back door ; and that it came to the knowledge of Luke because his informant
had an acquaintance in the household of Herod, as John had in that of
Annas : the former conjecture, however, is figuratively as well as literally
nothing more than a back door ; the latter, a fiction which is but the effort of
despair.   Certainly if we renounce the presupposition that the author of the
fourth gospel was an apostle, we lose the ground of attack against the narrative of Luke, which in any case, since Justin knows of the consignment to
Herod,[9] is of very early origin.   Nevertheless, first, the silence of the other
Evangelists in a portion of their common history, in which, with this exception, there prevails an agreement as to the principal stages in the development
of the fate of Jesus ; and secondly, the internal difficulties of the narrative,
remain so suspicious, that it must still be open to us to conjecture, that the
anecdote arose out of the effort to place Jesus before all the tribunals that
could possibly be gathered together in Jerusalem ; to make every authority
not hierarchical, though treating him with ignominy, still either explicitly or
tacitly acknowledge his innocence ; and to represent him as maintaining his
equable demeanour and dignity before all.   If this be probable with respect

---

[8] Schleiermacher, über den Lukas, s. 291.
[9] Dial. cum Tryph. 103.

to the present narrative, in which the third Evangelist stands alone, a similar conjecture concerning the leading away to Annas, in which we have seen that the fourth Evangelist stands alone, would only be warded off by the circumstance that this scene is not described in detail, and hence presents no internal difficulties.

After Jesus, being sent back by Herod, was returned upon his hands, Pilate, according to Luke, once more called together the Sanhedrists and the people, and declared, alleging in his support the judgment of Herod as accordant with his own, his wish to dismiss Jesus with chastisement; for which purpose he might avail himself of the custom of releasing a prisoner at the feast of the passover.[10] This circumstance, which is somewhat abridged in Luke, is more fully exhibited in the other Evangelists, especially in Matthew. As the privilege to entreat the release of a prisoner belonged to the people, Pilate, well knowing that Jesus was persecuted by the rulers out of jealousy, sought to turn to his advantage the better disposition of the people towards him; and in order virtually to oblige them to free Jesus, whom, partly out of mockery of the Jews, partly to deter them from his execution as degrading to themselves, he named the Messiah or King of the Jews, he reminded them that their choice lay between him and a *notable prisoner*, δέσμιος ἐπίσημος, Barabbas,[11] whom John designates as a *robber*, λῃστής, but Mark and Luke as one who was imprisoned for insurrection and murder. This plan however failed, for the people, suborned, as the two first Evangelists observe, by their rulers, with one voice desired the release of Barabbas and the crucifixion of Jesus.

As a circumstance which had especial weight with Pilate in favour of Jesus, and moved him to make the proposal relative to Barabbas as urgently as possible, it is stated by Matthew that while the procurator sat on his tribunal, his wife,[12] in consequence of a disturbing dream, sent to him a warning to incur no responsibility in relation to that just man (xxvii. 19). Not only Paulus, but even Olshausen, explains this dream as a natural result of what Pilate's wife might have heard of Jesus and of his capture on the preceding evening; to which may be added as an explanatory conjecture, the notice of the *Evangelium Nicodemi*, that she was *pious*, θεοσεβής, and *judaizing*, ἰουδαΐζουσα.[13] Nevertheless, as constantly in the New Testament, and particularly in the Gospel of Matthew, dreams are regarded as a special dispensation from heaven, so this assuredly in the opinion of the narrator happened *non sine numine*; and hence it should be possible to conceive a motive and an object for the dispensation. If the dream were really intended to prevent the death of Jesus, taking the orthodox point of view, in which this death was necessary for the salvation of man, we must be led to the opinion of some of the ancients, that it may have been the devil who suggested that dream to the wife of the procurator, in order to hinder the propitiatory death;[14] if on the

---

[10] It is doubted whether this custom, of which we should have known nothing but for the N. T., was of Roman or Jewish origin; comp. Fritzsche and Paulus, in loc., and Baur, über die ursprungliche Bedeutung des Passahfestes, u. s. f., Tüb. Zeitschr. f. Theol. 1832, 1, s. 94.

[11] According to one reading, the full name of this man was *Jesus Barabbas*, which we mention here merely because Olshausen finds it " remarkable." *Bar Abba* meaning *Son of the father*, Olshausen exclaims : All that was essential to the Saviour appears in the murderer as caricature! and he quotes as applicable to this case the verse : *ludit in humanis divina potentia rebus*. For our own part, we can only see in this idea of Olshausen's a *lusus humanæ impotentiæ*.

[12] In the *Evang. Nicodemi* and in later ecclesiastical historians she is called *Procula* Πρόκλη. Comp. Thilo. Cod. Apocr. N. T., p. 522, Paulus, exeg. Handb., 2, b, s. 640 f.

[13] Cap. II. s. 520, ap. Thilo.

[14] Ignat. ad Philippens. iv. : φοβεῖ δὲ τὸ γύναιον, ἐν ὀνείροις αὐτὸ καταταράττων καὶ παύειν πειρᾶται τὰ κατὰ τὸν σταυρόν. (*The devil) terrifies the woman, troubling her in her dreams, and endeavours to put a stop to the things of the cross.* The Jews in the Evang. Nicodemi, c.

contrary, the dream were not intended to prevent the death of Jesus, its object must have been limited to Pilate or his wife. But as far as Pilate was concerned, so late a warning could only aggravate his guilt, without sufficing to deter him from the step already half taken ; while that his wife was converted by means of this dream, as many have supposed,[15] is totally unattested by history or tradition, and such an object is not intimated in the narrative. But, as the part which Pilate himself plays in the evangelical narrative is such as to exhibit the blind hatred of the fellow-countrymen of Jesus in contrast with the impartial judgment of a Gentile ; so his wife is made to render a testimony to Jesus, in order that, not only out of the mouth of *babes and sucklings* (Matt. xxi. 16), but also out of the mouth of a weak woman, praise might be prepared for him ; and to increase its importance it is traced to a significant dream. To give this an appearance of probability, similar instances are adduced from profane history of dreams which have acted as presentiments and warnings before a sanguinary catastrophe : [16] but the more numerous are these analogous cases, the more is the suspicion excited that as the majority of these, so also the dream in our evangelical passage, may have been fabricated after the event, for the sake of heightening its tragical effect.

When the Jews, in reply to the repeated questions of Pilate, vehemently and obstinately demand the release of Barabbas and the crucifixion of Jesus, the two intermediate Evangelists represent him as at once yielding to their desire ; but Matthew first interposes a ceremony and a colloquy (xxvii. 24 ff.). According to him Pilate calls for water, washes his hands before the people, and declares himself innocent of the blood of this just man. The washing of the hands, as a protestation of purity from the guilt of shedding blood, was a custom specifically Jewish, according to Deut. xxi. 6 f.[17] It has been thought improbable that the Roman should have here intentionally imitated this Jewish custom, and hence it has been contended, that to any one who wished so solemnly to declare his innocence nothing would more readily suggest itself than the act of washing the hands.[18] But that an individual, apart from any allusion to a known usage, should invent extemporaneously a symbolical act, or even that he should merely fall in with the custom of a foreign nation, would require him to be deeply interested in the fact which he intends to symbolize. That Pilate, however, should be deeply interested in attesting his innocence of the execution of Jesus, is not so probable as that the Christians should have been deeply interested in thus gaining a testimony to the innocence of their Messiah : whence there arises a suspicion that perhaps Pilate's act of washing his hands owes its origin to them alone. This conjecture is confirmed, when we consider the declaration with which Pilate accompanies his symbolical act: *I am innocent of the blood of this just man,* ἀθῶός εἰμι ἀπὸ τοῦ αἵματος τοῦ δικαίου τούτου. For that the judge should publicly and emphatically designate as a *just man,* δίκαιος, one whom he was nevertheless delivering over to the severest infliction of the law,—this even Paulus finds so contradictory that he here, contrary to his usual mode of exposition, supposes that the narrator himself expresses in these words his own interpretation of Pilate's symbolical act. It is surprising that he is not also struck by the equal improbability of the answer which is attributed to the Jews on this occasion. After Pilate has declared himself guiltless

II. p. 524, explain the dream as a result of the magic arts of Jesus : γόης ἐστι—ἰδοὺ ὀνειρόπεμπτα ἔπεμψε πρὸς τὴν γυναῖκά σου, *He is a magician—see, he has sent messages in a dream to thy wife.*
[15] E.g. Theophylact, vid. Thilo, p. 523.
[16] Vid. Paulus and Kuinöl, in loc. They especially adduce the dream of Cæsar's wife the night before his assassination.
[17] Comp. Sota, viii. 6.
[18] Fritzsche, in Matth., p. 808.

of the blood of Jesus, and by the addition : *see ye to it*, has laid the responsibility on the Jews, it is said in Matthew that *all the people* πᾶς ὁ λαὸς, cried : *His blood be on us and on our children*, τὸ αἷμα αὐτοῦ ἐφ᾽ ἡμᾶς καὶ τὰ τέκνα ἡμῶν. But this is obviously spoken from the point of view of the Christians, who in the miseries which shortly after the death of Jesus fell with continually increasing weight on the Jewish nation, saw nothing else than the payment of the debt of blood which they had incurred by the crucifixion of Jesus: so that this whole episode, which is peculiar to the first gospel, is in the highest degree suspicious.

According to Matthew and Mark, Pilate now caused Jesus to be scourged, preparatory to his being led away to crucifixion.   Here the scourging appears to correspond to the *virgis cædere*, which according to Roman usage preceded the *securi percutere*, and to the scourging of slaves prior to crucifixion.[19]   In Luke it has a totally different character.   While in the two former Evangelists it is said : *When he had scourged Jesus, he delivered him to be crucified*, τὸν δὲ 'Ι. φραγελλώσας παρέδωκεν ἵνα σταυρωθῇ : in Luke, Pilate repeatedly (v. 16 and 22) makes the proposal : *having chastised him I will let him go*, παιδεύσας αὐτὸν ἀπολύσω : i. e. while there the scourging has the appearance of a mere accessory of the crucifixion, here it appears to be intended as a substitute for the crucifixion : Pilate wishes by this chastisement to appease the hatred of the enemies of Jesus, and induce them to desist from demanding his execution.   Again, while in Luke the scourging does not actually take place,—because the Jews will in nowise accede to the repeated proposal of Pilate : in John the latter causes Jesus to be scourged, exhibits him to the people with the purple robe and the crown of thorns and tries whether his pitiable aspect, together with the repeated declaration of his innocence, will not mollify their embittered minds : this, however, proving also in vain (xix. 1 ff.).   Thus there exists a contradiction between the Evangelists in relation to the scourging of Jesus, which is not to be conciliated after the method of Paulus, namely by paraphrasing the words τὸν 'Ι. φραγελλώσας παρέδοκεν ἵνα σταυρωθῇ in Matthew and Mark thus : Jesus, whom he had already before scourged in order to save him, suffered this in vain, since he was still delivered over to crucifixion. But, acknowledging the difference in the accounts, we must only ask, which of the two has the advantage as regards historical probability ?   Although it is certainly not to be proved that scourging before crucifixion was a Roman custom admitting no exception: still, on the other hand, it is a purely harmonistic effort to allege, that scourging was only made to precede crucifixion in cases where the punishment was intended to be particularly severe,[20] and that consequently Pilate, who had no wish to be cruel to Jesus, can only have caused him to be scourged with the special design which Luke and John mention, and which is also to be understood in the narratives of their predecessors.   It is far more probable that in reality the scourging only took place as it is described by the two first Evangelists, namely, as an introduction to the crucifixion, and that the Christian legend (to which that side of Pilate's character, in virtue of which he endeavoured in various ways to save Jesus, was particularly welcome as a testimony against the Jews) gave such a turn even to the fact of the scourging as to obtain from it a new attempt at release on the part of Pilate.   This use of the fact is only incipient in the third gospel, for here the scourging is a mere proposal of Pilate : whereas in the fourth, the scourging actually takes place, and becomes an additional act in the drama.

---

[19] Comp. in particular the passages cited by Wetstein, on Matth. xxvii. 26.
[20] Paulus, ut sup. s. 647.

With the scourging is connected in the two first gospels and the fourth, the maltreatment and mockery of Jesus by the soldiers, who attired him in a purple robe, placed a crown of thorns on his head,[21] put, according to Matthew, a reed in his hand, and in this disguise first greeted him as King of the Jews, and then smote and maltreated him.[22] Luke does not mention any derision on the part of the soldiers here, but he has something similar in his narrative of the interrogation of Jesus before Herod, for he represents this prince *with his men of war*, σύν τοῖς στρατεύμασιν αὐτοῦ, as mocking Jesus, and sending him back to Pilate in a *gorgeous robe*, ἐσθὴς λαμπρά. Many suppose that this was the same purple robe which was afterwards put on Jesus by the soldiers of Pilate ; but it must rather have been thrice that Jesus had to wear this disguise, if we take the narrative of John into the account and at the same time refuse to attribute error to any of the synoptists : first in the presence of Herod (Luke); secondly, before Pilate brought Jesus forth to the Jews, that he might excite their compassion with the words : *Behold the man*, ἴδε ὁ ἄνθρωπος (John) ; thirdly, after he was delivered to the soldiers for crucifixion (Matthew and Mark). This repetition is as improbable as it is probable that the one disguising of Jesus, which had come to the knowledge of the Evangelists, was assigned by them to different places and times, and ascribed to different persons.

While in the two first gospels the process of trial is already concluded before the scourging, and in the third, on the rejection of his proposal to scourge and release Jesus by the Jews, Pilate forthwith delivers him to be crucified : in the fourth Evangelist the scene of the trial is further developed in the following manner. When even the exhibition of Jesus scourged and disguised avails nothing, but his crucifixion is obstinately demanded, the procurator is incensed, and cries to the Jews, that they may take him and crucify him themselves, for he finds no fault in him. The Jews reply that according to their law he must die, since he had made himself the *Son of God* υἱὸς θεοῦ ; a remark which affects Pilate with a superstitious fear, whence he once more leads Jesus into the Prætorium, and inquires concerning his origin (whether it be really heavenly), on which Jesus gives him no answer, and when the procurator seeks to alarm him by reminding him of the power which he possesses over his life, refers to the higher source from whence he had this power. Pilate, after this reply, seeks (yet more earnestly than before) to release Jesus ; but at last the Jews hit upon the right means of making him accede to their will, by throwing out the intimation that, if he release Jesus who has opposed himself to Cæsar as an usurper, he cannot be *Cæsar's friend*. Thus, intimidated by the possibility of his being calumniated to Tiberius, he mounts the tribunal, and, since he cannot prosecute his will, betakes himself to derision of the Jews in the question, whether they then wish that he should crucify their king ? Whereupon they, keeping to the position which they had last taken with such evident effect, protest that they will have no king but Cæsar. The procurator now consents to deliver Jesus to be crucified, for which purpose, as the two first Evangelists remark, the purple mantle was removed, and he was again attired in his own clothes.

---

[21] From the explanation of Paulus, s. 649 f., it appears highly probable that the στέφανος ἐξ ἀκανθῶν was not a crown of sharp thorns, but one taken from the nearest hedge, in order to deride Jesus by the *vilissima corona, spineola* (Plin. H. N. xxi. 10).

[22] A similar disguising of a man, in derision of a third party, is adduced by Wetstein, (p. 533 f.) from Philo, in Flaccum.

§ 132.

THE CRUCIFIXION.

Even concerning the progress of Jesus to the place of crucifixion there is a divergency between the synoptists and John, for according to the latter Jesus himself carried his cross thither (xix. 17), while the former state that one Simon a Cyrenian bore it in his stead (Matt. xxvii. 32 parall.). The commentators indeed, as if a real agreement were assumed as a matter of course, reconcile these statements thus : at first Jesus himself endeavoured to bear the cross, but as the attempt made it obvious that he was too much exhausted, it was laid on Simon.[1] But when John says : *And he bearing his cross went forth into — Golgotha, where they crucified him,* καὶ βαστάζων τὸν σταυρὸν αὐτοῦ ἐξῆλθεν εἰς—Γολγοθᾶ· ὅπου αὐτὸν ἐσταύρωσαν : he plainly presupposes that the cross was borne by Jesus on the way thither.[2] But the statement so unanimously given by the synoptists respecting the substitution of Simon appears the less capable of being rejected, the more difficult it is to discover a motive which might lead to its fabrication. On the contrary, this individual trait might very probably have remained unknown in the circle in which the fourth gospel had its origin, and the author might have thought that, according to the general custom, Jesus must have carried his cross. All the synoptists designate this Simon as a *Cyrenian,* i.e. probably one who had come to Jerusalem to the feast, from the Libyan city of Cyrene, where many Jews resided.[3] According to all, the carrying of the cross was forced upon him, a circumstance which can as little be urged for as against the opinion that he was favourable to Jesus.[4] According to Luke and Mark, the man came directly *out of the country,* ἀπ᾽ ἀγροῦ, and as he attempted to pass by the crowd advancing to the place of crucifixion, he was made use of to relieve Jesus. Mark designates him yet more particularly as *the father of Alexander and Rufus,* who appear to have been noted persons in the primitive church (comp. Rom. xvi. 13 ; Acts xix. 33 (?) ; 1 Tim. i. 20 (?) ; 2 Tim. iv. 14 (?)).[5]

On the way to the place of execution, according to Luke, there followed Jesus, lamenting him, a great company, consisting especially of women, whom he however admonished to weep rather for themselves and their children, in prospect of the terrible time, which would soon come upon them (xxiii. 27 ff.). The details are taken partly from the discourse on the second advent, Luke xxi. 23 ; for as there it is said, Οὐαὶ δὲ ταῖς ἐν γαστρὶ ἐχούσαις, καὶ ταῖς θηλαζούσαις, ἐν ἐκείναις ταῖς ἡμέραις, so here Jesus says, that the days are coming in which αἱ στεῖραι, καὶ κοιλίαι αἳ οὐκ ἐγέννησαν, καὶ μαστοὶ οἳ οὐκ ἐθήλασαν, will be pronounced blessed ; partly from Hosea x. 8, for the words τότε ἄρξονται λέγειν τοῖς ὄρεσι κ.τ. λ. (*then shall they begin to say to the mountains,* etc.) are almost exactly the Alexandrian translation of that passage.

The place of execution is named by all the Evangelists *Golgotha,* the Chaldaic אַגֻּלְגָּלְתָּא, and they all interpret this designation by κρανίου τόπος *the place of a skull,* or κρανίον *a skull* (Matt. v. 33 parall.). From the latter name it might appear that the place was so called because it resembled a skull in form ; whereas the former interpretation, and indeed the nature of the case,

---

[1] Thus Paulus, Kuinöl, Tholuck and Olshausen in their Commentaries ; Neander, L. J. Chr., s. 634.
[2] Fritzsche, in Marc. 684 : *Significat Joannes, Jesum suam crucem portavisse, donec ad Calvariæ locum pervenisset.*
[3] Joseph., Antiq. xiv. vii. 2.
[4] It is used in the former way by Grotius ; in the latter, by Olshausen, 2. s. 481,
[5] Comp. Paulus, Fritzsche, and De Wette, in loc.

renders it probable that it owed its name to its destination as a place of execution, and to the bones and skulls of the executed which were heaped up
there.   Where this place was situated is not known, but doubtless it was out
of the city ; even that it was a hill, is a mere conjecture.[6]

The course of events after the arrival at the place of execution is narrated
by Matthew (v. 34 ff.) in a somewhat singular order.   First, he mentions the
beverage offered to Jesus; next, he says that after they had nailed him to
the cross, the soldiers shared his clothes among them ; then, that they sat
down and watched him ; after this he notices the superscription on the cross,
and at length, and not as if supplying a previous omission, but with a particle
expressive of succession in time (τότε), the fact that two thieves were crucified
with him.   Mark follows Matthew, except that instead of the statement about
the watching of the cross, he has a determination of the time at which Jesus
was crucified : while Luke more correctly relates first the crucifixion of the
two malefactors with Jesus, and then the casting of lots for the clothes ; and
the same order is observed by John.   But it is inadmissible on this account
to transpose the verses in Matthew (34, 37, 38, 35, 36), as has been proposed ;[7] and we must rather abandon the author of the first gospel to the
charge, that in his anxiety not to omit any of the chief events at the crucifixion of Jesus, he has neglected the natural order of time.[8]

As regards the mode of the crucifixion there is now scarcely any debated
point, if we except the question, whether the feet as well as the hands were
nailed to the cross.   As it lay in the interest of the orthodox view to prove
the affirmative : so it was equally important to the rationalistic system to
maintain the negative.   From Justin Martyr [9] down to Hengstenberg [10] and
Olshausen, the orthodox find in the nailing of the feet of Jesus to the cross
a fulfilment of the prophecy Ps. xxii. 17, which the LXX. translates : ὤρυξαν
χεῖράς μου καὶ πόδας, but it is doubtful whether the original text really speaks
of piercing, and in no case does it allude to crucifixion : moreover the
passage is nowhere applied to Christ in the New Testament.   To the rationalists, on the contrary, it is at once more easy to explain the death of Jesus
as a merely apparent death, and only possible to conceive how he could
walk immediately after the resurrection, when it is supposed that his feet
were left unwounded ; but the case should rather be stated thus : if the
historical evidence go to prove that the feet also of Jesus were nailed, it
must be concluded that the resuscitation and the power of walking shortly
after, either happened supernaturally or not at all.   Of late there have stood
opposed to each other two learned and profound investigations of this point,
the one by Paulus against, the other by Bähr, in favour of—the nailing of
the feet.[11]   From the evangelical narrative, the former opinion can principally allege in its support, that neither is the above passage in the Psalms
anywhere used by the Evangelists, though on the presupposition of a nailing
of the feet it was so entirely suited to their mode of accounting for facts, nor
in the history of the resurrection is there any mention of wounds in the feet,
together with the wounds in the hands and side (John xx. 20, 25, 27).   The

---

[6] Vid. Paulus and Fritzsche, in loc. Winer, bibl. Realw. art. Golgotha.
[7] Wassenbergh, Diss. de trajectionibus N. T. in Balcknaer's scholæ in ll. quosdam N. T.
2, p. 31.
[8] Comp. Schleiermacher, über den Lukas, s. 295 ; Winer, N. T. Gramm., s. 226, and
Fritzsche, in Matt., p. 814.
[9] Apol. i. 35.   Dial. c. Tryph. xcvii.
[10] Christologie des A. T. 1, a, s. 182 ff.
[11] Paulus, exeg. Handbuch 3, b, s. 669-754 ; Bähr, in Tholuck's liter. Anzeiger für christl.
Theol. 1835, No. 1-6. Comp. also Neander, L. J. Chr., s. 636, Anm.

other opinion appeals not without reason to Luke xxiv. 39, where Jesus invites the disciples to behold his hands and his feet (ἴδετε τὰς χεῖράς μου καὶ τοὺς πόδας μου): it is certainly not here said that the feet were pierced, but it is difficult to understand how Jesus should have pointed out his feet merely to produce a conviction of the reality of his body. The fact that among the fathers of the church, those who, living before Constantine, might be acquainted with the mode of crucifixion from personal observation, as Justin and Tertullian, suppose the feet of Jesus to have been nailed, is of weight. It might indeed be concluded from the remark of the latter : *Qui (Christus) solus a populo tam insigniter crucifixus est*,[12] that for the sake of the passage in the Psalms these fathers supposed that in the crucifixion of Christ his feet also were pierced by way of exception ; but, as Tertullian had before called the piercing of the hands and feet the *propria atrocia crucis*, it is plain that the above words imply, not a special manner of crucifixion, but the special manner of death by crucifixion, which does not occur in the Old Testament, and by which therefore Jesus was distinguished from all the characters therein celebrated. Among the passages in profane writers, the most important is that of Plautus, in which, to mark a crucifixion as extraordinarily severe, it is said : *offigantur bis pedes, bis brachia*.[13] Here the question is : does the extraordinary feature lie in the *bis*, so that the nailing of the feet as well as of the hands only once is presupposed as the ordinary usage ; or was the *bis offigere* of the hands, i.e. the nailing of both the hands, the usual practice, and the nailing of the feet an extraordinary aggravation of the punishment? Every one will pronounce the former alternative to be the most accordant with the words. Hence it appears to me at present, that the balance of historical evidence is on the side of those who maintain that the feet as well as the hands of Jesus were nailed to the cross.

It was before the crucifixion, according to the two first Evangelists, that there was offered to Jesus a beverage, which Matthew (v. 34) describes as *vinegar mingled with gall*, ὄξος μετὰ χολῆς μεμιγμένον, Mark (v. 23) as *wine mingled with myrrh*, ἐσμυρνισμένον οἶνον, but which, according to both, Jesus (Matthew says, after having tasted it) refused to accept. As it is not understood with what object gall could be mixed with the vinegar, the χολὴ of Matthew is usually explained, by the aid of the ἐσμυρνισμένον of Mark, as implying bitter vegetable ingredients, especially myrrh ; and then either οἶνον *wine* is actually substituted for ὄξος *vinegar*, or the latter is understood as sour wine ;[14] in order that the beverage offered to Jesus may thus appear to have been the stupefying draught consisting of wine and strong spices, which, according to Jewish usage, was presented to those about to be executed, for the purpose of blunting their susceptibility to pain.[15] But even if the text admitted of this reading, and the words of this interpretation, Matthew would assuredly protest strongly against the real gall and the vinegar being thus explained away from his narrative, because by this means he would lose the fulfilment of the passage in the psalm of lamentation elsewhere used messianically : (LXX.) καὶ ἔδωκαν εἰς τὸ βρῶμά μου χολήν, καὶ εἰς τὴν δίψαν μου ἐπότισάν με ὄξος, *they gave me also gall for my meat, and in my thirst they gave me vinegar to drink* (Ps. lxix. 21). Matthew incontestably means, in accordance with this prophecy, real gall with vinegar, and the comparison

---

[12] Adv. Marcion, iii. 19.

[13] Mostellaria, ii. 1.

[14] Vid. Kuinöl, Paulus, in loc.

[15] Sanhedrim, f. xliii. 1, ap. Wetstein, p. 635 : *Dixit R. Chaja, f. R. Ascher, dixisse R. Chasdam : exeunti, ut capite plectatur, dant bibendum granum turis in poculo vini, ut alienetur mens ejus, sec. d. Prov.* xxxi. 6 : *date siceram pereunti et vinum amaris anima.*

with Mark is only calculated to suggest the question, whether it be more probable that Mark presents the incident in its original form, which Matthew has remodelled into a closer accordance with the prophecy; or that Matthew originally drew the particular from the passage in the Psalm, and that Mark so modified it as to give it an appearance of greater historical probability?

In order to come to a decision on this question we must take the two other Evangelists into consideration. The presentation to Jesus of a drink mingled with vinegar is mentioned by all four, and even the two who have the vinegar mingled with gall, or the myrrhed wine, as the first drink offered to Jesus, mention afterwards the offering of simple vinegar. According to Luke, this *offering of vinegar*, ὄξος προσφέρειν, was an act of derision committed by the soldiers not very long after the crucifixion, and before the commencement of the darkness (v. 36 f.); according to Mark, shortly before the end, three hours after the darkness came on, one of the bystanders, on hearing the cry of Jesus : my God, my God, etc., presented vinegar to him, likewise in derision, by means of a sponge fixed on a reed (v. 36) ; according to Matthew, one of the bystanders, on the same cry, and in the same manner, presented vinegar to him, but with a benevolent intention, as we gather from the circumstance that the scoffers wished to deter him from the act (v. 48 f.);[16] whereas in John it is on the exclamation : *I thirst*, that some fill a sponge with vinegar from a vessel standing near, and raise it on a stem of hyssop to the mouth of Jesus (v. 29). Hence it has been supposed that there were three separate attempts to give a beverage to Jesus : the first before the crucifixion, with the stupefying drink (Matthew and Mark); the second after the crucifixion, when the soldiers in mockery ⸢offered him some of their ordinary beverage, a mixture of vinegar and water called *posca*[17] (Luke) ; and the third, on the complaining cry of Jesus (Matt., Mark and John).[18] But if the principle of considering every divergent narrative as a separate event be once admitted, it must be consistently carried out : if the beverage mentioned by Luke must be distinguished from that of Matthew and Mark on account of a difference in the time, then must that of Matthew be distinguished from that of Mark on account of the difference in the design ; and, again, the beverage mentioned by John must not be regarded as the same with that of the two first synoptists, since it follows a totally different exclamation. Thus we should obtain in all five instances in which a drink was offered to Jesus, and we should at least be at a loss to understand why Jesus after vinegar had already been thrice presented to his lips, should yet a fourth time have desired to drink. If then we must resort to simplification, it is by no means only the beverage in the two first gospels, and that in the fourth, which, on account of the agreement in the time and manner of presentation, are to be understood as one ; but also that of Mark (and through this the others) must be pronounced identical with that of Luke, on account of their being alike offered in derision. Thus there remain two instances of a drink being offered to Jesus, the one before the crucifixion, the other after ; and both have a presumptive support from history, the former in the Jewish custom of giving a stupefying draught to persons about to be executed, the other in the Roman custom, according to which the soldiers on their expeditions,—and the completing an execution was considered as such,—were in the habit of taking with them their *posca*. But together with this possible historical root, there is a possible prophetic one in Ps. lxix., and the two have an opposite

[16] Vid. Fritzsche, in loc.
[17] Comp. Paulus, in loc.
[18] Thus Kuinöl, in Luc., p. 710 f. ; Tholuck, s. 316.

influence : the latter excites a suspicion that the narrative may not have anything historical at its foundation ; the former throws doubt on the explanation that the whole story has been spun out of the prophecies.

On once more glancing over the various narratives, we shall at least find that their divergencies are precisely of a nature to have arisen from a various application of the passage in the Psalms. The eating of gall and the drinking of vinegar being there spoken of, it appears as if in the first instance the former particular had been set aside as inconceivable, and the fulfilment of the prophecy found in the circumstance (very possibly historical, since it is mentioned by all the four Evangelists), that Jesus had vinegar presented to him when on the cross. This might either be regarded as an act of compassion, as by Matthew and John, or of mockery, with Mark and Luke. In this manner the words : *they gave me vinegar to drink*, ἐπότισάν με ὄξος, were indeed literally fulfilled, but not the preceding phrase : *in my thirst*, εἰς τὴν δίψαν μου ; hence the author of the fourth gospel might think it probable that Jesus actually complained of thirst, i.e. cried, *I thirst*, διψῶ, an exclamation, which he expressly designates as a fulfilment of the *scripture*, γραφὴ, by which we are doubtless to understand the above passage in the Psalms (comp. Ps. xxii. 16) ; nay, since he introduces the ἵνα τελειωθῇ ἡ γραφὴ, *that the scripture might be fulfilled*, by εἰδὼς ὁ Ἰησοῦς, ὅτι πάντα ἤδη τετέλεσται, *Jesus, knowing that all things were now accomplished*, he almost appears to mean that the fulfilment of the prophecy was the sole object of Jesus in uttering that exclamation : but a man suspended on the cross in the agonies of death is not the one to occupy himself with such typological trifling—this is only the part of his biographer who finds himself in perfect ease. Even this addition, however, only showed the fulfilment of one half of the messianic verse, that relating to the vinegar : there still remained what was said of the gall, which, as the concentration of all bitterness, was peculiarly adapted to be placed in relation to the suffering Messiah. It is true that the presentation of the *gall*, χολὴ, as *meat*, βρῶμα, which the prophecy strictly taken required, was still suppressed as inconceivable : but it appeared to the first Evangelist, or to the authority which he here follows, quite practicable to introduce the gall as an ingredient in the vinegar, a mixture which Jesus might certainly be unable to drink, from its unpalatableness. More concerned about historical probability than prophetic connexion, the second Evangelist, with reference to a Jewish custom, and perhaps in accordance with historical fact, converted the vinegar mingled with gall, into wine mingled with myrrh, and made Jesus reject this, doubtless from a wish to avoid stupefaction. As however the narrative of the vinegar mingled with gall reached these two Evangelists in company with the original one of the presentation of simple vinegar to Jesus ; they were unwilling that this should be excluded by the former, and hence placed the two side by side. But in making these observations, as has been before remarked, it is not intended to deny that such a beverage may have been offered to Jesus before the crucifixion, and afterwards vinegar also, since the former was apparently customary, and the latter, from the thirst which tormented the crucified, natural : it is merely intended to show, that the Evangelists do not narrate this circumstance, and under such various forms, because they knew historically that it occurred in this or that manner, but because they were convinced dogmatically that it must have occurred according to the above prophecy, which however they applied in different ways.[19]

During or immediately after the crucifixion Luke represents Jesus as

[19] Comp. also Bleek, Comm. zum Hebräerbrief, 2, s. 312, Anm. ; De Wette, exeg. Handb. 1, 3, s. 198.

saying : *Father, forgive them, for they know not what they do* (v. 34); an intercession which is by some limited to the soldiers who crucified him,[20] by others, extended to the real authors of his death, the Sanhedrists and Pilate.[21] However accordant such a prayer may be with the principles concerning love to enemies elsewhere inculcated by Jesus (Matt. v. 44), and however great the internal probability of Luke's statement viewed in this light : still it is to be observed, especially as he stands alone in giving this particular, that it may possibly have been taken from the reputed messianic chapter, Isa. liii., where in the last verse, the same from which the words : *he was numbered with the transgressors*, μετὰ ἀνόμων ἐλογίσθη are borrowed, it is said : יַפְגִּיעַ לַפֹּשְׁעִים (*he made intercession for the transgressors*), which the LXX. erroneously translate διὰ τὰς ἀνομίας αὐτῶν παρεδόθη, *he was delivered for their transgressions*, but which already the *Targum Jonathan* renders by *pro peccatis* (it should be *peccatoribus*) *deprecatus est*.

All the Evangelists agree in stating that two malefactors δύο κακοῦργοι (Matthew and Mark call them λῃστὰς *thieves*) were crucified, one on each side of Jesus ; and Mark, if his 28th verse be genuine, sees in this a literal fulfilment of the words : *he was numbered with the transgressors*, which, according to Luke xxii. 37, Jesus had the evening before quoted as a prophecy about to be accomplished in him. Of the further demeanour of these fellow-sufferers, John says nothing ; the two first Evangelists represent them as reviling Jesus (Matt. xxvii. 44 ; Mark xv. 32) : whereas Luke narrates that only one of them was guilty of this offence, and that he was rebuked by the other (xxiii. 39 ff.). In order to reconcile this difference, commentators have advanced the supposition, that at first both criminals reviled Jesus, but that subsequently one of them was converted by the marvellous darkness ;[22] more modern ones have resorted to the supposition of an *enallage numeri* :[23] but without doubt those only are right who admit a real difference between Luke and his predecessors.[24] It is plain that the two first Evangelists knew nothing of the more precise details which Luke presents concerning the relation of the two malefactors to Jesus. He narrates, namely, that when one of them derided Jesus by calling upon him, if he were the Messiah, to deliver himself and them, the other earnestly rebuked such mockery of one with whom he was sharing a like fate, and moreover as a guilty one with the guiltless, entreating for his own part that Jesus would remember him when he should come into his *kingdom* βασιλεία : whereupon Jesus gave him the promise that he should that very day be with him *in Paradise* ἐν τῷ παραδείσῳ. In this scene there is nothing to create difficulty, until we come to the words which the second malefactor addresses to Jesus. For to expect from one suspended on the cross a future coming to establish the messianic kingdom, would presuppose the conception of the whole system of a dying Messiah, which before the resurrection the apostles themselves could not comprehend, and which therefore, according to the above representation of Luke, a *thief* must have been beforehand with them in embracing. This is so improbable, that it cannot excite surprise to find many regarding the conversion of the thief on the cross as a miracle,[25] and the supposition which commentators call in to their aid,

[20] Kuinöl, in Luc. p. 710.
[21] Olshausen, p. 484 ; Neander, s. 637.
[22] Thus Chrysostom and others.
[23] Beza and Grotius.
[24] Paulus, s. 763 ; Winer, N. T. Gramm., s. 143 ; Fritzsche, in Matth., p. 817.
[25] Vid. Thilo, Cod. apocr. 1, s. 143. Further apocryphal information concerning the two malefactors crucified with Jesus is to be found in the evang. infant. arab. c. xxiii. ap. Thilo, p. 92 f. ; comp. the note p. 143 ; in the evang. Nicod. c. ix. 10, Thilo, p. 581 ff. ; c. xxvi. p. 766 ff.

namely, that the man was no common criminal, but a political one, perhaps concerned in the insurrection of Barabbas,[26] only serves to render the incident still more inconceivable. For if he was an Israelite inclined to rebellion, and bent on liberating his nation from the Roman yoke, his idea of the Messiah was assuredly the most incompatible with the acknowledgment as such, of one so completely annihilated in a political view, as Jesus then was. Hence we are led to the question, whether we have here a real history and not rather a creation of the legend? Two malefactors were crucified with Jesus : thus much was indubitably presented by history (or did even this owe its origin to the prophecy, Isa. liii. 12 ?). At first they were suspended by the side of Jesus as mute figures, and thus we find them in the narrative of the fourth Evangelist, into whose region of tradition only the simple statement, that they were crucified with Jesus, had penetrated. But it was not possible for the legend long to rest contented with so slight a use of them : it opened their mouths, and as only insults were reported to have proceeded from the bystanders, the two malefactors were at first made to join in the general derision of Jesus, without any more particular account being given of their words (Matt. and Mark). But the malefactors admitted of a still better use. If Pilate had borne witness in favour of Jesus ; if shortly after, a Roman centurion—nay, all nature by its miraculous convulsions—had attested his exalted character : so his two fellow-sufferers, although criminals, could not remain entirely impervious to the impression of his greatness, but, though one of them did indeed revile Jesus agreeably to the original form of the legend, the other must have expressed an opposite state of feeling, and have shown faith in Jesus as the Messiah (Luke). The address of the latter to Jesus and his answer are besides conceived entirely in the spirit of Jewish thought and expression ; for according to the idea then prevalent, paradise was that part of the nether world which was to harbour the souls of the pious in the interval between their death and the resurrection : a place in paradise and a favourable remembrance in the future age were the object of the Israelite's petition to God, as here to the Messiah ;[27] and it was believed concerning a man distinguished for piety that he could conduct those who were present at the hour of his death into paradise.[28]

To the cross of Jesus was affixed, according to the Roman custom,[29] a *superscription* ἐπιγραφὴ (Mark and Luke), or a *title* τίτλος (John) which contained *his accusation* τὴν αἰτίαν αὐτοῦ (Matthew and Mark), consisting according to all the Evangelists in the words : ὁ βασιλεὺς τῶν Ἰουδαίων, *the King of the Jews*. Luke and John state that this superscription was couched in three different tongues, and the latter informs us that the Jewish rulers were fully alive to the derision which this form of superscription reflected on their nation, and on this account entreated Pilate, but in vain, for an alteration of the terms (v. 21 f.).

Of the soldiers, according to John four in number, who crucified Jesus, the Evangelists unanimously relate that they parted the clothes of Jesus among themselves by lot. According to the Roman law *de bonis damnatorum* [30] the vestments of the executed fell as *spolia* to the executioners, and in so far that

[26] Paulus and Kuinöl, in loc.
[27] Confessio Judæi ægroti, ap. Wetstein, p. 820 :—*da portionem meam in horto Edenis, et memento mei in seculo futuro, quod absconditum est justis.* Other passages are given, ib., p. 819.
[28] Cetuboth, f. ciii. ap. Wetstein, p. 819 : *Quo die Rabbi moriturus erat, venit vox de cœlo, dixitque : qui præsens aderit morienti Rabbi, ille intrabit in paradisum.*
[29] Vid. Wetstein, in loc. Matth.
[30] Quoted in Wetstein, p. 536 ; compare, however, the correction of the text in Paulus, ex. handb. 3, b, s. 751.

statement of the Evangelists has a point of contact with history. But, like most of the features in this last scene of the life of Jesus, it has also a point of contact with prophecy. It is true that in Matthew the quotation of the passage Ps. xxii. 18 is doubtless an interpolation; but on the other hand the same quotation is undoubtedly genuine in John (xix. 24) : ἵνα ἡ γραφὴ πληρωθῇ ἡ λέγουσα· (verbally after the LXX.) διεμερίσαντο τὰ ἱμάτιά μου ἑαυτοῖς, καὶ ἐπὶ τὸν ἱματισμόν μου ἔβαλον κλῆρον, *that the scripture might be fulfilled which saith, They parted my raiment among them, and for my vesture they did cast lots.* Here also, according to the assertion of orthodox expositors, David the author of the psalm, under divine guidance, in the moments of inspiration chose such figurative expressions as had a literal fulfilment in Christ.[31]   Rather we must say, David, or whoever else may have been the author of the psalm, as a man of poetical imagination used those expressions as mere metaphors to denote a total defeat; but the petty, prosaic spirit of Jewish interpretation, which the Evangelists shared without any fault of theirs, and from which orthodox theologians, by their own fault however, have not perfectly liberated themselves after the lapse of eighteen centuries, led to the belief that those words must be understood literally, and in this sense must be shown to be fulfilled in the Messiah.   Whether the Evangelists drew the circumstance of the casting of lots for the clothes more from historical information which stood at their command, or from the prophetic passage which they variously interpreted, must be decided by a comparison of their narratives.   These present the divergency, that while according to the synoptists all the clothes were parted by lot, as is evident from the words : διεμερίσαντο τὰ ἱμάτια αὐτοῦ, βάλλοντες κλῆρον, *they parted his garments, casting lots,* in Matthew (v. 35), and the similar turn of expression in Luke (v. 34), but still more decidedly from the addition of Mark : τίς τί ἄρῃ, *what every man should take* (v. 24) : in John it is the *coat* or *tunic,* χιτὼν, alone for which lots are cast, the other garments being parted equally (v. 23 f.).   This divergency is commonly thought of much too lightly, and is tacitly treated as if the synoptical representation were related to that of John as the indefinite to the definite.   Kuinöl in consideration of John translates the words διεμερίζαντο βάλλοντες of Matthew thus : *partim dividebant, partim in sortem conjiciebant* : but the meaning is not to be thus distributed, for the διεμερίζαντο, *they parted,* states *what* they did, the βάλλοντες κλῆρον, *casting lots, how* they did it : besides Kuinöl passes in total silence over the words τίς τί ἄρῃ, because they undeniably imply that lots were cast for several articles : while according to John the lots had reference only to one garment.   If it be now asked, which of the two contradictory narratives is the correct one, the answer given from the point of view to which the comparative criticism of the gospels has at present attained is, that the eye-witness John gives the correct particulars, but the synoptists had merely received the indefinite information, that in parting the clothes of Jesus the soldiers made use of the lot, and this, from unacquaintance with the more minute particulars, they understood as if lots had been cast for all the garments of Jesus.[32]   But not only does the circumstance that it is John alone who expressly cites the passage in the Psalms prove that he had an especial view to that passage : but, in general, this divergency of the Evangelists is precisely what might be expected from a difference in the interpretation of that supposed prophecy.   When the psalm speaks of the parting of the garments and a casting of lots for the vesture : the second particular is, according to the genius of the Hebrew language which abounds in parallel-

---

[31] Tholuck, in loc.
[32] E. G. Theile, zur Biographie Jesu, § 36, Anm. 13.

ism, only a more precise definition of the first, and the synoptists, correctly understanding this, make one of the two verbs a participle. One however who did not bear in mind this peculiarity of the Hebrew style, or had an interest in exhibiting the second feature of the prophecy as specially fulfilled, might understand the *and*, which in reality was indicative only of more precise definition, as denoting addition, and thus regard the casting of lots and the distribution as separate acts. Then the ἱματισμὸς (לְבוּשׁ?) which was originally a synonyme of ἱμάτια (בְּגָדִים) must become a distinct garment, the closer particularization of which, since it was not in any way conveyed in the word itself, was left to choice. The fourth Evangelist determined it to be the χιτών, *tunic*, and because he believed it due to his readers to show some cause for a mode of procedure with respect to this garment, so different from the equal distribution of the others, he intimated that the reason why it was chosen to cast lots for the tunic rather than to divide it, probably was that it had no seam (ἄρραφος) which might render separation easy, but was woven in one piece (ὑφαντὸς δι' ὅλου).[33] Thus we should have in the fourth Evangelist exactly the same procedure as we have found on the side of the first, in the history of the entrance into Jerusalem : in both cases the doubling of a trait originally single, owing to a false interpretation of the ו in the Hebrew parallelism ; the only difference being that the first Evangelist in the passage referred to is less arbitrary than the fourth is here, for he at least spares us the tracing out of the reason why two asses must then have been required for one rider. The more evident it thus becomes that the representation of the point in question in the different Evangelists is dependent on the manner in which each interpreted that supposed prophecy in the Psalms : the less does a sure historical knowledge appear to have had any share in their representation, and hence we remain ignorant whether lots were cast on the distribution of the clothes of Jesus, nay whether in general a distribution of clothes took place under the cross of Jesus ; confidently as Justin appeals in support of this very particular to the Acts of Pilate, which he had never seen.[34]

Of the conduct of the Jews who were present at the crucifixion of Jesus, John tells us nothing ; Luke represents the people as standing to look on, and only the *rulers* ἄρχοντες and the soldiers as deriding Jesus by the summons to save himself if he were the Messiah, to which the latter adds the offer of the vinegar (v. 35 ff.) ; Matthew and Mark have nothing here of mockery on the part of the soldiers, but in compensation they make not only the *chief priests*, *scribes*, and *elders*, but also the *passers by*, παραπορευόμενοι, vent insults against Jesus (v. 39 ff., 29 ff.). The expressions of these people partly refer to former discourses and actions of Jesus ; thus, the sarcasm : *Thou that destroyest the temple and buildest it again in three days, save thyself* (Matt. and Mark), is an allusion to the words of that tenor ascribed to Jesus ; while the reproach : *he saved others, himself he cannot save*, or *save thyself* (in all three), refers to his cures. Partly however the conduct of the Jews towards Jesus on the cross, is depicted after the same psalm of which Tertullian justly says that it contains *totam Christi passionem*.[35] When it is said in Matthew and Mark : *And they that passed by reviled him, wagging their heads and saying :* οἱ δὲ παραπορευόμενοι ἐβλασφήμουν αὐτὸν, κινοῦντες τὰς κεφαλὰς αὐτῶν καὶ λέγοντες· (Luke says of the *rulers* ἄρχοντες *they derided him* ἐξεμυκτήριζον), this is certainly nothing else than a mere reproduction of what

---

[33] Expositors observe in connexion with this particular, that the coat of the Jewish high priest was also of this kind. Jos. Antiq. iii. vii. 4—The same view of the above difference has been already presented in the Probabilia, p. 80 f.
[34] Apol. i. 35.
[35] Adv. Marcion, ut sup.

stands in Ps. xxii. 8 (LXX.) : *All they that see me laugh me to scorn, they shoot out the lip and shake the head :* πάντες οἱ θεωροῦντές με ἐξεμυκτήρισάν με, ἐλάλησαν ἐν χείλεσιν, ἐκίνησαν κεφαλὴν ; and the words which are hereupon lent to the Sanhedrists in Matthew : *He trusted in God ; let him deliver him now if he will have him,* πέποιθεν ἐπὶ τὸν θεὸν, ῥυσάσθω νῦν αὐτὸν, εἰ θέλει αὐτὸν, are the same with those of the following verse in that Psalm : *He trusted in the Lord that he would deliver him : let him deliver him, seeing he delighted in him,* ἤλπισεν ἐπὶ Κύριον, ῥυσάσθω αὐτόν· σωσάτω αὐτὸν, ὅτι θέλει αὐτόν.   Now though the taunts and shaking of the head on the part of the enemies of Jesus may, notwithstanding that the description of them is drawn according to the above Old Testament passage, still very probably have really happened : it is quite otherwise with the words which are attributed to these mockers.   Words which, like those above quoted, are in the Old Testameut put into the mouth of the enemies of the godly, could not be adopted by the Sanhedrists without their voluntarily assuming the character of the ungodly : which they would surely have taken care to avoid.   Only the Christian legend, if it once applied the Psalm to the sufferings of Jesus, and especially to his last hours, could attribute these words to the Jewish rulers, and find therein the fulfilment of a prophecy.

The two first Evangelists do not tell us that any one of the twelve was present at the crucifixion of Jesus : they mention merely several Galilean women, three of whom they particularize : namely, Mary Magdalene ; Mary the mother of James the Less and of Joses ; and, as the third, according to Matthew, the mother of the sons of Zebedee, according to Mark, Salome, both which designations are commonly understood to relate to the same person (Matt. v. 55 f. ; Mark v. 40 f.) : according to these Evangelists the twelve appear not yet to have reassembled after their flight on the arrest of Jesus.[36]   In Luke, on the contrary, among *all his acquaintance,* πάντες οἱ γνωστοὶ αὐτοῦ, whom he represents as beholding the crucifixion (v. 49) the twelve would seem to be included : but the fourth gospel expressly singles out from among the disciples the one *whom Jesus loved,* i.e. John, as present, and among the women, together with Mary Magdalene and the wife of Cleopas, names instead of the mother of James and John, and the mother of Jesus himself.   Moreover, while according to all the other accounts the acquaintances of Jesus stood *afar off,* μακρόθεν, according to the fourth gospel John and the mother of Jesus must have been in the closest proximity to the cross, since it represents Jesus as addressing them from the cross, and appointing John to be his substitute in the filial relation to his mother (v. 25 ff.).   Olshausen believes that he can remove the contradiction which exists between the synoptical statement and the presupposition of the fourth gospel as to the position of the friends of Jesus, by the conjecture that at first they did indeed stand at a distance, but that subsequently some approached near to the cross : it is to be observed, however, in opposition to this, that the synoptists mention that position of the adherents of Jesus just at the close of the scene of crucifixion and death, immediately before the taking down from the cross, and thus presuppose that they had retained this position until the end of the scene ; a state of the case which cannot but be held entirely consistent with the alarm which filled the minds of the disciples during those days, and still more with feminine timidity.   If the heroism of a nearer approach might perhaps be expected from maternal tenderness : still, the total silence of the synoptists, as the interpreters of the common evangelical tradition, renders the

---

[36] Justin, Apol. i. 50, and elsewhere, even speaks of apostacy and denial on the part of all the disciples after the crucifixion.

historical reality of that particular doubtful. The synoptists cannot have known anything of the presence of the mother of Jesus at the cross, otherwise they would have mentioned her as the chief person, before all the other women ; nor does anything appear to have been known of a more intimate relation between her and John : at least in the Acts (i. 12 f.) the mother of Jesus is supposed to be with the twelve in general, his brothers, and the women of the society. It is at least not so easy to understand how the memory of that affecting presence and remarkable relation could be lost, as to conceive how the idea of them might originate in the circle from which the fourth gospel proceeded. If this circle be imagined as one in which the Apostle John enjoyed peculiar veneration, on which account our gospel drew him out of the trio of the more confidential associates of Jesus, and isolated him as the beloved disciple : it will appear that nothing could be more strikingly adapted to confirm this relation than the statement that Jesus bequeathed, as it were, the dearest legacy, his mother (in reference to whom, as well as to the alleged beloved disciple, it must have been a natural question, whether she had left the side of Jesus in this last trial), to John, and thus placed this disciple in his stead,—made him *vicarius Christi.*

As the address of Jesus to his mother and the favourite disciple is peculiar to the fourth gospel : so, on the other hand, the exclamation, *My God, my God, why hast thou forsaken me ?* ἠλὶ, ἠλὶ, λαμὰ σαβαχθανί ; is only found in the two first gospels (Matt. v. 46 ; Mark v. 34). This exclamation, with the mental state from which it proceeded, like the agony in Gethsemane, constitutes in the opinion of the church a part of the vicarious suffering of Christ. As however in this instance also it was impossible to be blind to the difficulties of the supposition, that the mere corporeal suffering, united with the external depression of his cause, overwhelmed Jesus to such a degree that he felt himself forsaken by God, while there have been both before and after him persons who, under sufferings equally severe, have yet preserved composure and fortitude : the opinion of the church has here also, in addition to the natural corporeal and spiritual affliction, supposed as the true cause of that state of mind in Jesus, a withdrawal of God from his soul, a consciousness of the divine wrath, which it was decreed that he should bear in the stead of mankind, by whom it was deserved as a punishment.[37] How, presupposing the dogma of the church concerning the person of Christ, a withdrawal of God from his soul is conceivable, it is the part of the defenders of this opinion themselves, to decide. Was it the human nature in him which felt so forsaken ? Then would its unity with the divine have been interrupted, and thus the very basis of the personality of Christ, according to the above system, removed. Or the divine ? In that case the second person in the Godhead would have been separated from the first. As little can it have been the God-man, consisting of both natures, that felt forsaken by God, since the very essence of this is the unity and inseparableness of the divine and the human. Thus urged by the self-contradiction of this supranaturalistic explanation, to fall back on the natural mode of accounting for the above exclamation by the sense of external suffering, and yet repelled from the idea that Jesus should have been so completely subdued by this, commentators have attempted to mollify the sense of the exclamation. It consists of the opening words of Ps. xxii., a passage which is classical for this last scene in the life of Jesus. Now this psalm begins with a complaining description of the deepest suffering, but in the course of its progress soars into joyful hope of deliverance ; hence it has been supposed that the words which Jesus immediately utters do not give his entire

---

[37] Vid. Calvin, Comm. in harm. evv. in Matth. xxvii. 46 ; Olshausen, in loc.

experience, and that in thus reciting the first verse he at the same time quotes the whole psalm and especially its exulting close, just as if he meant to say : It is true that I, like the author of this psalm, appear now forsaken of God, but in me, as in him, the divine succour will only be so much the more glorified.[38] But if Jesus uttered this exclamation with a view to the bystanders, and in order to assure them that his affliction would soon be merged in triumph, he would have chosen the means the least adapted to his purpose, if he had uttered precisely those words of the Psalm which express the deepest misery ; and instead of the first verse he would rather have chosen one from the 10th to the 12th, or from the 20th to the end.   If however in that exclamation he meant merely to give vent to his own feeling, he would not have chosen this verse if his actual experience in these moments had been, not what is there expressed, but what is described in the succeeding verses.   Now if this experience was his own, and if, all supernatural grounds of explanation being dismissed, it proceeded from his external calamities ; we must observe that one who, as the gospels narrate of Jesus, had long included suffering and death in his idea of the Messiah, and hence had regarded them as a part of the divine arrangements, could scarcely complain of them when they actually arrived as an abandonment by God ; rather, on the above supposition, we should be led to think that Jesus had found himself deceived in the expectations which he had previously cherished, and thus believed himself forsaken by God in the prosecution of his plan.[39]   But we could only resort to such conjectures if the above exclamation of Jesus were shown to have an historical foundation.   In this respect the silence of Luke and John would not, it is true, be so serious a difficulty in our eyes, that we should take refuge in explanations like the following :   John suppressed the exclamation, lest it should serve to countenance the Gnostic opinion, by admitting the inference that the Æon which was insusceptible of suffering, departed from Jesus in that moment.[40]   But the relation of the words of Jesus to the 22nd Psalm does certainly render this particular suspicious.   If the Messiah was once conceived of as suffering, and if that psalm was used as a sort of programme of his suffering — for which it was by no means necessary as an inducement that Jesus should have really quoted one of its verses on the cross :—the opening words of the psalm which are expressive of the deepest suffering must appear singularly adapted to be put into the mouth of the crucified Messiah.   In this case the derisive speech[41] of the bystanders, *he calleth for Elias*, etc., can have had no other origin than this—that the wish for a variety of taunts to complete this scene after the model of the psalm, was met by the similarity of sound between the ἠλὶ in the exclamation lent to Jesus, and the name of Elias which was associated with the Messiah.*

Concerning the last words which the expiring Jesus was heard to utter, the Evangelists differ.   According to Matthew and Mark, it was merely a *loud*

---

[38] Thus Paulus, Gratz, in loc.   Schleiermacher, Glaubenslehre, 2, s. 154, Anm.

[39] Such is the inference drawn by the author of the Wolfenbüttel Fragments, von Zweck Jesu und seiner Jünger, s. 153.

[40] Schneckenburger, Beiträge, s. 66 f.

[41] According to Olshausen, s. 495, there is no syllable in this speech by which such a meaning is intimated ; on the contrary, a secret horror had already diffused itself over the minds of the scoffers, and they trembled at the thought that Elias might appear in the storm. But when one who attempts to give a beverage to Jesus is dissuaded under the pretext of waiting to see *if Elias would come to save him*, εἰ ἔρχεται Ἡλίας, σώσων αὐτὸν, this pretext is plainly enough shown to be meant in derision, and hence the horror and trembling belong only to the unscientific animus of the biblical commentator, which makes him contemplate the history of the passion above all else, as a *mysterium tremendum*, and causes him to discover even in Pilate a depth of feeling which is nowhere attributed to this Roman in the gospels.

voice, φωνὴ μεγάλη, with which he departed (v. 50, 37) ; according to Luke it was the petition : *Father, into thy hands I commend my spirit, πάτερ, εἰς χεῖράς σου παραθήσομαι τὸ πνεῦμά μου* (v. 46) ; while according to John it was on the brief expression : *it is finished, τετέλεσται,* that he bowed his head and expired (v. 30).

Here it is possible to reconcile the two first Evangelists with one or other of the succeeding ones by the supposition, that what the former describe indefinitely as a loud cry, and what according to their representation might be taken for an inarticulate expression of anguish, the others, with more particularity, give in its precise verbal form. It is more difficult to reconcile the two last gospels. For whether we suppose that Jesus first commended his soul to God, and hereupon cried : *it is finished ;* or vice versâ ; both collocations are alike opposed to the intention of the Evangelists, for the expression of Luke *καὶ ταῦτα εἰπὼν ἐξέπνευσεν* cannot be rendered, as Paulus would have it, by : *soon* after he had said this, he expired ; and the very words of the exclamation in John define it as the last utterance of Jesus ; the two writers forming different conceptions of the closing words. In the account of Luke, the common form of expression for the death of Jesus : *παρέδωκε τὸ πνεῦμα (he delivered up his spirit)* appears to have been interpreted as an actual commending of his soul to God on the part of Jesus, and to have been further developed with reference to the passage Ps. xxxi. 5 : *(Lord) into thy hands I commend my spirit, (κύριε) εἰς χεῖράς σου παραθήσομαι τὸ πνεῦμά μου* (LXX.),—a passage which from the strong resemblance of this Psalm to the 22nd would be apt to suggest itself.[12] Whereas the author of the fourth gospel appears to have lent to Jesus an expression more immediately proceeding from his position in relation to his messianic office, making him express in the word *τετέλεσται it is finished* the completion of his work, or the fulfilment of all the prophecies (with the exception, of course, of what could only be completed and fulfilled in the resurrection).

Not only these last words, however, but also the earlier expressions of Jesus on the cross, will not admit of being ranged in the succession in which they are generally supposed. The speeches of Jesus on the cross are commonly reckoned to be seven ; but so many are not mentioned by any single Evangelist, for the two first have only one : the exclamation *my God, my God,* etc. *ἠλὶ, ἠλὶ, κ. τ. λ.* Luke has three ; the prayer of Jesus for his enemies, the promise to the thief, and the commending of his spirit into the hands of the Father ; John has likewise three, but all different : the address to his mother and the disciple, with the exclamations, *I thirst διψῶ* and *It is finished τετέλεσται.* Now the intercessory prayer, the promise and the recommendation of Mary to the care of the disciple, might certainly be conceived as following each other : but the *διψῶ* and the *ἠλὶ* come into collision, since both exclamations are followed by the same incident, the offering of vinegar by means of a sponge on a reed. When to this we add the entanglement of the *τετέλεσται* with the *πάτερ κ. τ. λ.,* it should surely be seen and admitted, that no one of the Evangelists, in attributing words to Jesus when on the cross, knew or took into consideration those lent to him by the others ; that on the contrary each depicted this scene in his own manner, according as he, or the legend which stood at his command, had developed the conception of it to suit this or that prophecy or design.

A special difficulty is here caused by the computation of the hours. According to all the synoptists the darkness prevailed *from the sixth hour until the ninth hour, ἀπὸ ἕκτης ὥρας ἕως ὥρας ἐννάτης* (in our reckoning, from twelve at midday to three in the afternoon); according to Matthew and Mark, it was

---

about the ninth hour that Jesus complained of being forsaken by God, and shortly after yielded up the ghost; according to Mark it was *the third hour* ὥρα τρίτη (nine in the morning) when Jesus was crucified (v. 25). On the other hand, John says (xix. 14) that it was about the sixth hour (when according to Mark Jesus had already hung three hours on the cross) that Pilate first sat in judgment over him. Unless we are to suppose that the sun-dial went backward, as in the time of Hezekiah, this is a contradiction which is not to be removed by a violent alteration of the reading, nor by appealing to the ὡσεὶ (*about*) in John, or to the inability of the disciples to take note of the hours under such afflictive circumstances ; at the utmost it might perhaps be cancelled if it were possible to prove that the fourth gospel throughout proceeds upon another mode of reckoning time than that used by the synoptists.[43]

---

[43] Thus Rettig. exegetische Analekten, in Ullmann's und Umbreit's Studien, 1830, 1, s. 106 ff.; Tholuck. Glaubwürdigkeit, s. 307 ff.; comp. on the various attempts at reconciliation Lücke and De Wette, in loc. Joh.

CHAPTER IV.

DEATH AND RESURRECTION OF JESUS.

§ 133.

PRODIGIES ATTENDANT ON THE DEATH OF JESUS.

ACCORDING to the evangelical accounts, the death of Jesus was accompanied by extraordinary phenomena. Three hours before, we are told, a darkness diffused itself, and lasted until Jesus expired (Matt. xxvii. 45 parall.); in the moment of his death the veil of the temple was torn asunder from the top to the bottom, the earth quaked, the rocks were rent, the graves were opened, and many bodies of departed saints arose, entered into the city, and appeared to many (Matt. v. 51 ff. parall.). These details are very unequally distributed among the Evangelists : the first alone has them all ; the second and third merely the darkness and the rending of the veil : while the fourth knows nothing of all these marvels.

We will examine them singly according to their order. The *darkness* σκότος which is said to have arisen while Jesus hung on the cross, cannot have been an ordinary eclipse of the sun, caused by the interposition of the moon between his disc and the earth,[1] since it happened during the Passover, and consequently about the time of the full moon. The gospels however do not directly use the terms ἔκλειψις τοῦ ἡλίου (*eclipse of the sun*), the two first speaking only of *darkness* σκότος in general ; and though the third adds with somewhat more particularity: καὶ ἐσκοτίσθη ὁ ἥλιος, *and the sun was darkened*, still this might be said of any species of widely extended obscuration. Hence it was an explanation which lay near at hand to refer this darkness to an atmospheric, instead of an astronomical cause, and to suppose that it proceeded from obscuring vapours in the air, such as are especially wont to precede earthquakes.[2] That such obscurations of the atmosphere may be diffused over whole countries, is true ; but not only is the statement that the one in question extended ἐπὶ πᾶσαν or ὅλην τήν γῆν, i.e., according to the most natural explanation, over the entire globe, to be subtracted as an exaggeration of the narrator :[3] but also the presupposition, evident in the whole tenor of their representation, that the darkness had a supernatural cause, appears destitute of foundation from the want of any adequate object for such a miracle. Since then, with these accessory features the event does not in itself at once carry the conviction of its credibility, it is natural to inquire if it have any extrinsic confirmation. The fathers

---

[1] The Evang. Nicodemi makes the Jews very absurdly maintain : *there happened an eclipse of the sun in the ordinary course* ἔκλειψις ἡλίου γέγονε κατὰ τὸ εἰωθός, c. xi. p. 592, ap. Thilo.

[2] Thus Paulus and Kuinöl, in loc.; Hase, L. J. § 143 ; Neander, L. J. Chr. s. 639 f.

[3] Comp. Fritzsche and De Wette, in loc. Matth.

of the church appeal in its support to the testimony of heathen writers, among whom Phlegon especially in his χρονικοῖς is alleged to have noticed the above darkness :[4] but on comparing the passage preserved by Eusebius, which is apparently the one of Phlegon alluded to, we find that it determines merely the Olympiad, scarcely the year, and in no case the season and day of this darkness.[5] More modern apologists appeal to similar cases in ancient history, of which Wetstein in particular has made a copious collection. He adduces from Greek and Roman writers the notices of the eclipses of the sun which occurred at the disappearance of Romulus, the death of Cæsar,[6] and similar events ; he cites declarations which contain the idea that eclipses of the sun betoken the fall of kingdoms and the death of kings ; lastly he points to Old Testament passages (Isa. l. 3 ; Joel iii. 20 ; Amos viii. 9 ; comp. Jer. xv. 9) and rabbinical dicta, in which either the obscuring of the light of day is described as the mourning garb of God,[7] or the death of great teachers compared with the sinking of the sun at ʼmid-day,[8] or the opinion advanced that at the death of exalted hierarchical personages, if the last honours are not paid to them, the sun is wont to be darkened.[9] But these parallels, instead of being supports to the credibility of the evangelical narrative, are so many premises to the conclusion, that we have here also nothing more than the mythical offspring of universally prevalent ideas,—a Christian legend, which would make all nature put on the weeds of mourning to solemnize the tragic death of the Messiah.[10]

The second prodigy is the rending of the veil of the temple, doubtless the inner veil before the Holy of Holies, since the word פָּרֹכֶת, used to designate this, is generally rendered in the LXX. by καταπέτασμα. It was thought possible to interpret this rending of the veil also as a natural event, by regarding it as an effect of the earthquake. But, as Lightfoot has already justly observed, it is more conceivable that an earthquake should rend stationary fixed bodies such as the rocks subsequently mentioned, than that it should tear a pliant, loosely hung curtain. Hence Paulus supposes that the veil of the temple was stretched and fastened not only above but also below and at the sides. But first. this is a mere conjecture : and secondly, if the earthquake shook the walls of the temple so violently, as to tear a veil which even though stretched, was still pliant : such a convulsion would rather have caused a part of the building to fall, as is said to have been the case in the Gospel of the Hebrews : [11] unless it be chosen to add, with Kuinöl, the conjecture that the veil was tender from age, and might therefore be torn by a slight concussion. That our narrators had no such causes in their minds is proved by the fact that the second and third Evangelists are silent concerning the earthquake, and that the first does not mention it until after the rending of the veil. Thus if this event really happened we must regard it as a miracle. Now the object of the divine Providence in effecting such a miracle could

---

[4] Tertull. Apologet. c. xxi. ; Orig. c. Cels. ii. 33, 59.
[5] Euseb. can. chron. ad. Ol. 202, Anm. 4 ; comp. Paulus, s. 765 ff.
[6] Serv. ad Virgil. Georg. i. 465 ff. : *Constat, occiso Cæsare in Senatu pridie Idus Martias, solis fuisse defectum ab hora sexta usque ad noctem.*
[7] Echa R. iii. 28.
[8] R. Bechai Cod. Hakkema : *Cum insignis Rabbinus fato concederet, dixit quidam : iste dies gravis est Israëli, ut cum sol occidit ipso meridie.*
[9] Succa, f. xxix. 1 : *Dixerunt doctores : quatuor de causis sol deficit : prima, ob patrem domus judicii mortuum, cui exequiæ non fiunt ut decet*, etc.
[10] Vid. Fritzsche, in loc. ; comp. also De Wette, exeg. Handb. 1, 1, s. 238 ; Theile, zur Biogr. Jesu, § 36.
[11] Hieron. ad Hedib. ep. cxlix. 8 (comp. his Comm. in loc.) : *In evangelio autem, quod hebraicis literis scriptum est, legimus, non velum templi scissum, sed superliminare templi miræ magnitudinis corruisse.*

only have been this : to produce in the Jewish cotemporaries of Jesus a deep impression of the importance of his death, and to furnish the first promulgators of the gospel with a fact to which they might appeal in support of their cause. But, as Schleiermacher has shown, nowhere else in the New Testament, either in the apostolic epistles or in the Acts, or even in the Epistle to the Hebrews, in connexion with the subject of which it could scarcely fail to be suggested, is this event mentioned : on the contrary, with the exception of this bare synoptical notice, every trace of it is lost ; which could scarcely have been the case if it had really formed a ground of apostolical argument. Thus the divine purpose in ordaining this miracle must have totally failed ; or, since this is inconceivable, it cannot have been ordained for this object— in other words, since neither any other object of the miracle, nor yet a mode in which the event might happen naturally can be discovered, it cannot have happened at all. In another way, certainly, a peculiar relation of Jesus to the veil of the temple is treated of in the Epistle to the Hebrews. While before Christ, only the priests had access into the holy place, and into the Holy of Holies only the high priest might enter once in the year with the blood of atonement ; Christ, as the eternal high priest, entered by his own blood *into the holy place within the veil*, into the Holy of Holies in heaven, whereby he became the *forerunner*, πρόδρομος, of Christians, and opened access to them also, founding an *eternal redemption*, αἰώνιον λύτρωσιν (vi. 19 f., ix. 6, 12, x. 19 f.). Even Paulus finds in these metaphors so close an affinity to our narrative, that he thinks it possible to number the latter among those fables which according to Henke's definitions are to be derived *e figurato genere dicendi ;* [12] at least the event, even if it really happened, must have been especially important to the Christians on account of its symbolical significance, as interpreted by the images in the Epistle to the Hebrews : namely, that by Christ's death the veil of the Jewish worship was rent asunder, and access to God opened to all by means of *worship in the Spirit*. But if, as has been shown, the historical probability of the event in question is extremely weak, and on the other hand, the causes which might lead to the formation of such a narrative without historical foundation very powerful ; it is more consistent, with Schleiermacher, entirely to renounce the incident as historical, on the ground that so soon as it began to be the practice to represent the office of Christ under the images which reign throughout the Epistle to the Hebrews, nay, in the very earliest dawn of this kind of doctrine, on the first reception of the Gentiles, who were left free from the burthen of Jewish observances, and who thus remained without participation in the Jewish sacrifices, such representations must have entered into the Christian hymns (and the evangelical narratives).[13]

On the succeeding particulars of the earthquake and the rending of the rocks, we can only pronounce a judgment in connexion with those already examined. An earthquake by which rocks are disparted, is not unprecedented as a natural phenomenon : but it also not seldom occurs as a poetical or mythical embellishment of the death of a distinguished man ; as, for example, on the death of Cæsar, Virgil is not content with eclipsing the sun, but also makes the Alps tremble with unwonted commotion.[14] Now as we have only been able to view the prodigies previously mentioned in the latter light, and as, besides, the historical validity of the one before us is weakened by the fact that it rests solely on the testimony of Matthew ; we must pronounce upon

---

[12] The possibility of this is admitted by Neander also, but with the presupposition of some fact as a groundwork (s. 640 f.).

[13] Ueber den Lukas, s. 293. Comp. De Wette, exeg. Handb., 1, 1, s. 240.

[14] Georg. i. 463 ff.

this also in the words of Fritzsche : *Messiæ obitum atrocibus ostentis, quibus, quantus vir quummaxime exspirâsset, orbi terrarum indicaretur, illustrem esse oportebat.*[15] The last miraculous sign at the death of Jesus, likewise peculiar to the first Evangelist, is the opening of the graves, the resurrection of many dead persons, and their appearance in Jerusalem. To render this incident conceivable is a matter of unusual difficulty. It is neither in itself clear how it is supposed to have fared with these ancient Hebrew 'saints, ἁγίοις,[16] after their resurrection ; [17] nor is anything satisfactory to be discovered concerning a possible object for so extraordinary a dispensation.[18] Purely in the resuscitated themselves the object cannot apparently have lain, for had it been so, there is no conceivable ground why they should be all awaked precisely in the moment of the death of Jesus, and not each at the period prescribed by the course of his own development. But if the conviction of others was the object, this was still less attained than in the miracle of the rending of the veil, for not only is any appeal to the apparition of the saints totally wanting in the apostolic epistles and discourses, but also among the Evangelists, Matthew is the only one by whom it is recorded. A special difficulty arises from the position which the determination of time : *after his [resurrection,* μετὰ τὴν ἔγερσιν αὐτοῦ, occupies between the apparently consecutive stages of the event. For if we connect these words with what precedes, and thus suppose that at the moment of the death of Jesus, the deceased saints were only re-animated, and did not come out of their graves until after his resurrection,—this would have been a torment for the damned rather than a guerdon for the holy ; if, on the contrary, we unite that determination of time to what follows, and thus interpret the Evangelist's meaning to be, that the resuscitated saints did indeed come out of their graves immediately on their being reanimated at the moment that Jesus died, but did not go into the city until after his resurrection,—any reason for the latter particular is sought in vain. It is but an inartificial way of avoiding these difficulties to pronounce the whole passage an interpolation, without any critical grounds for such a decision.[19] A more dexterous course is pursued by the rationalistic expositors, when they endeavour to subtract the miraculous from the event, and by this means indirectly to remove the other difficulties. Here, as in relation to the rending of the veil, the earthquake is regarded as the chief agent : this, it is said, laid open several tombs, particularly those of some prophets, which were found empty, because the bodies had either been removed by the shock, or become decomposed, or fallen a prey to wild beasts. After the resurrection of Jesus, those who were friendly to him in Jerusalem being filled with thoughts of resurrection from the dead, these thoughts, together with the circumstance of

---

[15] When Hase, § 143, writes : "The earth trembled, mourning for her greatest Son," we see how the historian in speaking of this feature, which he maintains to be historical, involuntarily becomes a poet ; and when in the second edition the author qualifies the phrase by the addition of an "as it were : " it is further evident that his historical conscience had not failed to reproach him for the license.

[16] Only such must be here thought of, and not *sectatores Christi,* as Kuinöl maintains. In the Evang. Nicodemi, c. xvii., there are indeed adherents of Jesus, namely, Simeon (Luke ii.) and his two sons, among those who come to life on this occasion ; but the majority in this apocryphal book also, and as well in the ἀναφορὰ Πιλάτου (Thilo, p. 810), according to Epiphanius, orat. in sepulchrum Chr. 275, Ignat. ad Magnes. IX. and others (comp. Thilo, p. 780 ff.), are Old Testament persons, as Adam and Eve, the patriarchs and prophets.

[17] Comp. the various opinions in Thilo, p. 783 f.

[18] Comp. especially Eichhorn, Einl. in d. N. T. 1, s. 446 ff.

[19] Stroth, von Interpolationen im Evang. Matth. In Eichhorn's Repertorium, 9, s. 139. It is hardly a preferable expedient to regard the passage as an addition of the Greek translator. See Kern, Ueber den Urspr. des Evang. Matth. s. 25 and 100.

the graves being found empty, excited in them dreams and visions in which they believed that they beheld the pious ancestors who had been interred in those graves.[20] But the fact of the graves being found empty would scarcely, even united with the news of the resurrection of Jesus, have sufficed to produce such visions, unless there had previously prevailed among the Jews the expectation that the Messiah would recall to life the departed saints of Israel. If however this expectation existed, it would more probably give birth to the legend of a resurrection of the saints coincident with the death of Jesus than to dreams; whence Hase wisely discards the supposition of dreams, and attempts to find a sufficient explanation of the narrative in the emptiness of the graves on the one hand, and the above Jewish expectation on the other.[21] But on a nearer view it appears that if once this Jewish idea existed there needed no real opening of the graves in order to give rise to such a mythus: accordingly Schneckenburger has left the emptiness of the graves out of his calculation.[22] When, however, he yet speaks of visionary appearances which were seen by the adherents of Jesus in Jerusalem, under the excitement produced by his resurrection, he is not less inconsequent than Hase, when he omits the dreams and yet retains the laying open of the graves; for these two particulars being connected as cause and effect, if one of them be renounced as unhistorical so also must the other.

In opposition to this view it is remarked, not without an appearance of reason, that the above Jewish expectation does not suffice to explain the origin of such a mythus.[23] The actual expectation may be more correctly stated thus. From the epistles of Paul (1 Thess. iv. 16; comp. 1 Cor. xv. 22 f.) and more decidedly from the Apocalypse (xx. 4 f.), we gather that the first Christians anticipated, as a concomitant of the return of Christ, a resurrection of the saints, who would thenceforth reign with Christ a thousand years; only at the end of this period, it was thought, would the rest of the dead arise, and from this second resurrection the former was distinguished as *the first resurrection* ἡ ἀνάστασις ἡ πρώτη, or *the resurrection of the just* τῶν δικαίων (Luke xiv. 14?), in place of which Justin has *the holy resurrection* ἡ ἁγία ἀνάστασις.[24] But this is the Christianized form of the Jewish idea; for the latter referred, not to the return, but to the first advent of the Messiah, and to a resurrection of Israelites only.[25] Now in the statement of Matthew likewise, that resurrection is assigned to the first appearance of the Messiah; for what reason, however, it is there connected with his death, there is certainly no indication in the Jewish expectation taken in and by itself, while in the modification introduced by the adherents of Jesus there would appear rather to have lain an inducement to unite the resurrection of the saints with his own; especially as the connecting of it with his death seems to be in contradiction with the primitive Christian idea elsewhere expressed, that Jesus was the *first-begotten from the dead*, πρωτότοκος ἐκ τῶν νεκρῶν (Col. i. 18; Rev. i. 5), *the first fruits of them that sleep*, ἀπαρχὴ τῶν κεκοιμημένων (1 Cor. xv. 20). But we do not know whether this idea was universal, and if some thought it due to the messianic dignity of Jesus to regard him as the first who rose from the dead, there are obvious motives which might in other cases lead to the representation that already at the death of Jesus there was a resurrection of

[20] Thus Paulus and Kuinöl, in loc. The latter calls this explanation a mythical one.
[21] Leben Jesu, § 148.
[22] Ueber den Urspr. s. 67.
[23] Paulus, exeg. Handb., 3, b. s. 798.
[24] Dial. c. Tryph. cxiii.
[25] See the collection of passages relative to this subject in Schöttgen, 2, p. 570 ff.; and in Bertholdt's Christologia, § 35.

saints.   First there was an external motive : among the prodigies at the death
of Jesus an earthquake is mentioned, and in describing its violence it was
natural to add to the rending of the rocks another feature which appears elsewhere in accounts of violent earthquakes,[26] namely, the opening of the graves :
here then was an inviting hinge for the resurrection of the saints.   But there
was also an internal motive : according to the ideas early developed in the
Christian community, the death of Jesus was the specially efficacious point in
the work of redemption, and in particular the descent into Hades connected
with it (1 Pet. iii. 19 f.) was the means of delivering the previously deceased
from this abode ; [27] hence from these ideas there might result an inducement
to represent the bonds of the grave as having been burst asunder for the
ancient saints precisely in the moment of the death of Jesus.   Besides, by
this position, yet more decidedly than by a connexion with the resurrection
of Jesus, the resuscitation of the righteous was assigned to the first appearance of the Messiah, in accordance with the Jewish idea, which might very
naturally be echoed in such a narrative, in the Judaizing circles of primitive
Christendom ; while at the same time Paul and also the author of the
Apocalypse already assigned the *first resurrection* to the second and still
future advent of the Messiah.   It was then apparently with reference to this
more developed idea, that the words *after his resurrection* were added as a
restriction, probably by the author of the first gospel himself.

The synoptists conclude their description of the events at the death of
Jesus, with an account of the impression which they made more immediately
on the Roman centurion whose office it was to watch the crucifixion.   According to Luke (v. 47) this impression was produced by τὸ γενόμενον (*what was
done*), i.e., since he had beforehand mentioned the darkness, by the departure
of Jesus with an audible prayer, that being the particular which he had last
noticed ; indeed Mark, as if expounding Luke, represents the exclamation :
truly this man was the Son of God as being called forth from the centurion
by the circumstance that Jesus *so cried out, and gave up the ghost*, οὕτω κράξας
ἐξέπνευσεν (v. 39).   Now in Luke, who gives a prayer as the last utterance of
Jesus, it is possible to conceive that this edifying end might impress the
centurion with a favourable opinion of Jesus : but how the fact of his expiring
with a loud cry could lead to the inference that he was the Son of God, will
in no way appear.   Matthew however gives the most suitable relation to the
words of the centurion, when he represents them as being called forth by the
earthquake and the other prodigies which accompanied the death of Jesus :
were it not that the historical reality of this speech of the centurion must
stand or fall with its alleged causes.   In Matthew and Mark this officer
expresses the conviction that Jesus is in truth the *Son of God*, in Luke, that
he is a *righteous man*.   The Evangelists in citing the former expression
evidently intend to convey the idea that a Gentile bore witness to the
Messiahship of Jesus ; but in this specifically Jewish sense the words cannot
well have been understood by the Roman soldier : we might rather suppose
that he regarded Jesus as a son of God in the heathen sense, or as an innocent man unjustly put to death, were it not that the credibility of the whole
synoptical account of the events which signalized the death of Jesus being
shaken, this, which forms the top stone as it were, must also be of doubtful
security ; especially when we look at the narrative of Luke, who besides the
impression on the centurion adds that on the rest of the spectators, and makes
them return to the city with repentance and mourning—a trait which appears

---

[26] See the passages collected by Wetstein.
[27] See this idea further developed in the Evang. Nicod. c xviii. ff.

to represent, not so probably what the Jews actually felt and did, as what in the opinion of the Christians they *ought* to have felt and done.

§ 134.

THE WOUND BY A SPEAR IN THE SIDE OF JESUS.

While the synoptists represent Jesus as hanging on the cross from the ὥρα ἐννάτη, i.e. three in the afternoon, when he expired, until the ὀψία, i.e. probably about six in the evening, without anything further happening to him : the fourth Evangelist interposes a remarkable episode. According to him, the Jews, in order to prevent the desecration of the coming sabbath, which was a peculiarly hallowed one, by the continued exposure of the bodies on the cross, besought the Procurator that their legs might be broken and that they might forthwith be carried away. The soldiers, to whom this task was committed, executed it on the two criminals crucified with Jesus ; but when they perceived in the latter the signs of life having already become extinct, they held such a measure superfluous in his case, and contented themselves with thrusting a spear into his side, whereupon there came forth blood and water (xix. 31–37).

This event is ordinarily regarded as the chief voucher for the reality of the death of Jesus, and in relation to it the proof to be drawn from the synoptists is held inadequate. According to the reckoning which gives the longest space of time, that of Mark, Jesus hung on the cross from the third to the ninth hour, that is, six hours, before he died ; if, as to many it has appeared probable, in the two other synoptists the commencement of the darkness at the sixth hour marks also the commencement of the crucifixion, Jesus, according to them, hung only three hours living on the cross ; and if we presuppose in John the ordinary Jewish mode of reckoning the hours, and attribute to him the same opinion as to the period of the death of Jesus, it follows, since he makes Pilate pronounce judgment on him only about the sixth hour, that Jesus must have died after hanging on the cross not much more than two hours. But crucifixion does not in other cases kill thus speedily. This may be inferred from the nature of the punishment, which does not consist in the infliction of severe wounds so as to cause a rapid loss of blood, but rather in the stretching of the limbs, so as to produce a gradual rigidity ; moreover it is evident from the statements of the Evangelists themselves, for according to them Jesus, immediately before the moment which they regard as the last, had yet strength to utter a loud cry, and the two thieves crucified with him were still alive after that time ; lastly, this opinion is supported by examples of individuals whose life has lasted for several days on the cross, and who have only at length expired from hunger and similar causes.[1] Hence fathers of the church and older theologians advanced the opinion, that the death of Jesus, which would not have ensued so quickly in a natural way, was accelerated supernaturally, either by himself or by God ;[2] physicians and more modern theologians have appealed to the accumulated corporeal and spiritual sufferings of Jesus on the evening of the night prior to his crucifixion ;[3] but they also for the most part leave open the possibility that what appeared to the Evangelists the supervention of death itself, was

---

[1] The instances are collected in Paulus, exeg. Handb., 3, b. s. 781 ff. ; Winer, bibl. Realwörterb. 1, s. 672 ff. ; and Hase, § 144.

[2] According to Tertullian by the former, according to Grotius by the latter ; see Paulus, s. 784, Anm.

[3] Thus Gruner and others ap. Paulus, s. 782 ff. ; Hase, ut sup. ; Neander, L. J. Chr. s. 647.

only a swoon produced by the stoppage of the circulation, and that the wound with the spear in the side first consummated the death of Jesus.

But concerning this wound itself, the place, the instrument, and the manner of ¦its infliction—concerning its object and effects, there has always been a great diversity of opinion. The instrument is called by the Evangelist a λόγχη, which may equally signify either the light javelin or the heavy lance ; so that we are left in uncertainty as to the extent of the wound. The manner in which the wound was inflicted he describes by the verb νύσσειν, which sometimes denotes a mortal wound, sometimes a slight scratch, nay, even a thrust which does not so much as draw blood ; hence we are ignorant of the depth of the wound : though since Jesus, after the resurrection, makes Thomas lay only his fingers in the print of the nails, but, in or even merely on the wound in the side, his hand (John xx. 27), the stroke of the spear seems to have made a considerable wound. But the question turns mainly on the place in which the wound was made. This John describes as the πλευρὰ side, and certainly if the spear entered the left side between the ribs and penetrated into the heart, death must inevitably have ensued : but the above expression may just as properly imply the right side as the left, and in either side any spot from the shoulder to the hip. Most of these points indeed would be at once decided, if the object of the soldier had been to kill Jesus, supposing he should not be already dead ; in this case he would doubtless have pierced Jesus in the most fatal place, and as deeply as possible, or rather, have broken his legs, as was done to the two thieves : but since he treated Jesus otherwise than his fellow sufferers, it is evident that in relation to him he had a different object, namely, in the first place to ascertain by this stroke of the spear, whether death had really taken place—a conclusion which he believed might securely be drawn from the flowing of blood and water out of the wound.

But this result of the wound is in fact the subject on which there is the least unanimity. The fathers of the Church, on the ground that blood no longer flows from corpses, regarded the *blood and water*, αἷμα καὶ ὕδωρ, which flowed from the corpse of Jesus as a miracle, a sign of his superhuman nature.[4] More modern theologians, founding on the same experience, have interpreted the expression as a hendiadys, implying that the blood still flowed, and that this was a sign that death had not yet, or not until now taken place.[5] As, however, blood is itself a fluid, the *water* ὕδωρ added to the *blood* αἷμα cannot signify merely the fluid state of the latter, but must denote a peculiar admixture which the blood flowing from the side of Jesus contained. To explain this to themselves, and at the same time obtain the most infallible proof of death, others have fallen on the idea that the water mixed with the blood came out of the pericardium, which had been pierced by the spear, and in which, especially in such as die under severe anguish, a quantity of fluid is said to be accumulated.[6] But—besides that the piercing of the pericardium is a mere supposition—on the one hand, the quantity of such fluid, where no dropsy exists, is so trifling, that its emission would not be perceptible ; and on the other hand, it is only a single small spot in front of the breast where the pericardium can be so struck that an emission outward is possible : in all other cases, whatever was emitted would be poured into the cavity of the thorax.[7]

---

[4] Orig. c. Cels. ii. 36 : τῶν μὲν οὖν ἄλλων νεκρῶν σωμάτων τὸ αἷμα πήγνυται, καὶ ὕδωρ καθαρὸν οὐκ ἀποῤῥεῖ· τοῦ δὲ κατὰ τὸν Ἰησοῦν νεκροῦ σώματος τὸ παράδοξον, καὶ περὶ τὸ νεκρὸν σῶμα ἦν αἷμα καὶ ὕδωρ ἀπὸ τῶν πλευρῶν προχυθέν. Comp. Euthymius in loc. ἐκ νεκροῦ γὰρ ἀνθρώπου, κἂν μυριάκις νύξῃ τις, οὐκ ἐξελεύσεται αἷμα. ὑπερφυὲς τοῦτο τὸ πρᾶγμα, καὶ τρανῶς διδάσκον, ὅτι ὑπὲρ ἄνθρωπον ὁ νυγείς.

[5] Schuster, in Eichhorn's Bibl. 9, s. 1036 ff.

[6] Gruner, Comm. de morte J. Chr. vera, p. 47 ; Tholuck, Comm. z. Joh. s. 318.

[7] Comp. Hase, ut sup.

Without doubt the idea which was present in the Evangelist's mind was rather the fact, which may be observed in every instance of blood-letting, that the blood, so soon as it has ceased to take part in the vital process, begins to divide itself into *placenta* and *serum ;* and he intended by representing this separation as having already taken place in the blood of Jesus, to adduce a proof of his real death.[8] But whether this outflow of blood and water in perceptible separation be a possible proof of death,—whether Hase and Winer be right when they maintain that on deep incisions in corpses the blood sometimes flows in this decomposed state ; or the fathers, when they deem this so unprecedented that it must be regarded as a miracle in Jesus,—this is another question. A distinguished anatomist has explained the state of the fact to me in the following manner :[9] Ordinarily, within an hour after death the blood begins to coagulate in the vessels, and consequently no longer to flow on incisions ; only by way of exception in certain species of death, as nervous fevers, or suffocation, does the blood retain its fluidity in the corpse. Now if it be chosen to place the death on the cross under the category of suffocation—which, however, from the length of time that crucified persons have often remained alive, and in relation to Jesus especially, from his being said to have spoken to the last, appears impracticable ; or if it be supposed that the wound in the side followed so quickly on the instant of death that it found the blood still fluid,—a supposition which is discordant with the narratives, for they state Jesus to have been already dead at three in the afternoon, while the bodies must have been taken away only at six in the evening : then, if the spear struck one of the larger blood vessels, blood would have flowed, but without water ; if, however, Jesus had already been dead about an hour, and his corpse was in the ordinary state : nothing at all would have flowed. Thus either blood or nothing : in no case blood and water, because the *serum* and *placenta* are not separated in the vessels of the corpse as in the basin after blood-letting. Hardly then had the author of this trait in the fourth gospel himself seen the αἷμα καὶ ὕδωρ flowing out of the side of Jesus, as a sign that his death had taken place ; rather, because after blood-letting he had seen the above separation take place in the blood as it lost its vitality, and because he was desirous to show a certain proof of the death of Jesus, he represented those separate ingredients as flowing out of his wounded corpse.

The Evangelist assures us, with the most solicitous earnestness, that this really happened to Jesus, and that his account is trustworthy, as being founded on personal observation (v. 35). According to some, he gives this testimony in opposition to docetic Gnostics, who denied the true corporeality of Jesus:[10] but wherefore then the mention of the *water ?* According to others, on account of the noteworthy fulfilment of two prophecies by that procedure with respect to the body of Jesus.[11] But, as Lücke himself says, though John does certainly elsewhere, even in subordinate points, seek a fulfilment of prophecy, he nowhere attaches to it so extraordinary a weight as he would here have done according to this supposition. Hence it appears the most natural supposition that the Evangelist intended by those assurances to confirm the truth of the death of Jesus,[12] and that he merely appended the refer-

[8] Winer, ut sup.
[9] Comp. the similar statement of an anatomist in De Wette, in loc. and Tholuck ut sup.
[10] Wetstein and Olshausen, in loc. ; comp. Hase, ut sup.
[11] Lücke, in loc.
[12] Thus Less, Auferstehungsgeschichte, s. 95 f. ; Tholuck, in loc. According to Weisse (die evang. Gesch. 1, s. 102, 2, s. 237 ff.) the Evangelist referred to a passage of the apostolic epistle, under a misapprehension of its meaning, namely, to 1 John v. 6 : οὗτός ἐστιν ὁ ἐλθὼν δί ὕδατος καὶ αἵματος, Ἰ. ὁ Χρ. · οὐκ ἐν τῷ ὕδατι μόνον, ἀλλ' ἐν τῷ ὕδατι καὶ τῷ αἵματι.

ence to the fulfilment of Scripture as a secondary illustrative addition. The absence of an historical indication, that so early as the period of the composition of the fourth gospel, there existed a suspicion that the death of Jesus was only apparent, does not suffice, in the paucity of information at our command concerning that period, to prove that a suspicion so easy of suggestion had not actually to be combated in the circle in which the above gospel arose, and that it may not have given occasion to the adduction of proofs not only of the resurrection of Jesus, but also of his death.[13] Even in the Gospel of Mark a similar effort is visible. When this Evangelist, in narrating Joseph's entreaty for the body of Jesus, says : *And Pilate marvelled if he were already dead* (v. 44) : this suggests the idea that he lent to Pilate an astonishment which he must have heard expressed by many of his cotemporaries concerning the rapidity with which the death of Jesus had ensued; and when he proceeds to state that the procurator obtained from the centurion certain information that Jesus *had been some time dead*, πάλαι ἀπέθανε : it appears as if he wished, in silencing the doubt of Pilate, to silence that of his cotemporaries also ; but in that case he can have known nothing of a wound with a spear, and its consequences, otherwise he would not have left unnoticed this securest warrant of death having really taken place : so that the representation in John has the appearance of being a fuller development of a tendency of the legend already visible in Mark.

This view of John's narrative is further confirmed by his citation of Old Testament passages, as fulfilled in this event. In the stroke of the spear he sees the fulfilment of Zech. xii. 10 (better translated by John than by the LXX.), where Jehovah says to the Israelites וְהִבִּיטוּ אֵלַי אֵת אֲשֶׁר דָּקָרוּ *they shall look on him whom they have pierced*, in the sense, that they will one day return to him whom they had so grievously offended.[14] The word דָּקַר, *to pierce*, understood literally, expresses an act which appears more capable of being directed against a man than against Jehovah : this interpretation is supported by the variation in the reading אֵלָיו ; and it must have been confirmed by the succeeding context, which proceeds in the third person thus : *and they shall mourn for him, as one mourneth for his only son, and shall be in bitterness for him, as one that is in bitterness for his first-born.* Hence the Rabbins interpreted this passage of the Messiah *ben Joseph*, who would be pierced by the sword in battle,[15] and the Christians might refer it, as they did so many passages in Psalms of lamentation, to their Messiah, at first understanding the piercing either figuratively or as implying the nailing of the hands (and feet) in crucifixion (comp. Rev. i. 7) ; until at last some one, who desired a more decisive proof of death than crucifixion in itself afforded, interpreted it as a special piercing with the spear.

If then this trait of the piercing with the spear proceeded from the combined interests of obtaining a proof of death, and a literal fulfilment of a prophecy : the rest must be regarded as merely its preparatory groundwork. The piercing was only needful as a test of death, if Jesus had to be early taken down from the cross, which according to Jewish law (Deut. xxi. 22 ; Josh. viii 29, x. 26, f.—an exception occurs in 2 Sam. xxi. 6 ff.[16]) must in any case be before night ; but in particular in the present instance (a special circumstance which John alone notes), before the commencement of the passover. If Jesus died unusually soon, and if the two who were crucified

[13] Comp. Kaiser, bibl. Theol. 1, s. 253.
[14] Rosenmüller, Schol. in V. T. 7, 4, p. 340.
[15] Vid. ap. Rosenmüller, in loc. ; Schöttgen, 2, p. 221 ; Bertholdt, § 17, not. 12.
[16] Comp. Joseph. b. j. iv. v. 2. Sanhedrin, vi. 5, ap. Lightfoot, p. 499.

with him were yet to be taken down at the same time, the death of the latter must be hastened by violent means. This might be done likewise by means of a stroke of the spear : but then the piercing, which in Zech. xii. 10 was predicted specially of the Messiah, would equally happen to others. Thus in their case it would be better to choose the breaking of the legs, which would not, indeed, instantaneously superinduce death, but which yet made it ultimately certain as a consequence of the mortification produced by the fracture. It is true that the *crurifragium* appears nowhere else in connexion with crucifixion among the Romans, but only as a separate punishment for slaves, prisoners of war, and the like.[17] But it was not the less suitable in a prophetic point of view ; for was it not said of the Paschal lamb with which Jesus was elsewhere also compared (1 Cor. v. 7) : *not a bone of him shall be broken* (Exod. xii. 46) ? so that both the prophecies were fulfilled, the one determining what should happen exclusively to Jesus, the other what should happen to his fellow-sufferers, but not to him.

§ 135.

BURIAL OF JESUS.

According to Roman custom the body of Jesus must have remained suspended until consumed by the weather, birds of prey, and corruption ;[1] according to the Jewish, it must have been interred in the dishonourable burying place assigned to the executed :[2] but the evangelical accounts inform us that a distinguished adherent of the deceased begged his body of the procurator, which, agreeably to the Roman law,[3] was not refused, but was immediately delivered to him (Matt. xxvii. 57 parall.). This man, who in all the gospels is named Joseph, and said to be derived from Arimathea, was according to Matthew a rich man and a disciple of Jesus, but the latter, as John adds, only in secret ; the two intermediate Evangelists describe him as an honourable member of the high council, in which character, Luke remarks, he had not given his voice for the condemnation of Jesus, and they both represent him as cherishing messianic expectations. That we have here a personal description gradually developed into more and more preciseness is evident. In the first gospel Joseph is a disciple of Jesus—and such must have been the man who under circumstances so unfavourable did not hesitate to take charge of his body ; that, according to the same gospel, he was a *rich man* ἄνθρωπος πλούσιος already reminds us of Isa. liii. 9, where it is said וַיִּתֵּן אֶת־רְשָׁעִים קִבְרוֹ וְאֶת־עָשִׁיר בְּמֹתָיו which might possibly be understood of a burial with the rich, and thus become the source at least of this predicate of Joseph of Arimathea. That he entertained messianic ideas, as Luke and Mark add, followed of course from his relation to Jesus ; that he was a *counsellor*, βουλευτής, as the same Evangelists declare, is certainly a new piece of information : but that as such he could not have concurred in the condemnation of Jesus was again a matter of course ; lastly, that he had hitherto kept his adherence to Jesus a secret, as John observes, accords with the peculiar position in relation to Jesus which this Evangelist gives to certain exalted adherents, especially to Nicodemus, who is subsequently associated with Joseph. Hence it must not be at once supposed that the additional particu-

---

[17] Vid. Lipsius, de cruce, L. II. cap. 14.
[1] Comp. Winer, 1, s. 802.
[2] Sanhedrin, ap. Lightfoot, p. 499.
[3] Ulpian, xlviii. 24, 1 ff.

lars which each succeeding Evangelist gives, rest on historical information which he possessed over and above that of his predecessors.

While the synoptists represent the interment of Jesus as being performed by Joseph alone, with no other beholders than the women, John, as we have observed, introduces Nicodemus as an assistant ; a particular, the authenticity of which has been already considered in connexion with the first appearance of Nicodemus.[4]   This individual brings spices for the purpose of embalming Jesus ; a mixture of myrrh and aloes, in the quantity of about a hundred pounds.   In vain have commentators laboured to withdraw from the word λίτρα, which John here uses, the signification of the Latin *libra*, and to substitute a smaller weight : [5] the above surprising quantity is, however, satisfactorily accounted for by the remark of Olshausen, that the superfluity was a natural expression of the veneration of those men for Jesus.   In the fourth gospel the two men perform the office of embalming immediately after the taking down of the body from the cross, winding it in linen clothes after the Jewish practice ; in Luke the women, on their return home from the grave of Jesus, provide spices and ointments, in order to commence the embalming after the sabbath (xxiii. 56, xxiv. 1) ; in Mark they do not buy the *sweet spices* ἀρώματα until the sabbath is past (xvi. 1) ; while in Matthew there is no mention of an embalming of the body of Jesus, but only of its being wrapped in a *clean linen cloth* (xxvii. 59).

Here it has been thought possible to reconcile the difference between Mark and Luke in relation to the time of the purchase of the spices, by drawing over one of the two narrators to the side of the other.   It appeared the most easy to accommodate Mark to Luke by the supposition of an *enallage-temporum ;* his verb ἠγόρασαν, *they bought*, used in connexion with the day after the sabbath, being taken as the pluperfect, and understood to imply, in accordance with the statement of Luke, that the women had the spices in readiness from the evening of the burial.[6]   But against this reconciliation it has already been remarked with triumphant indignation by the Fragmentist, that the aorist, standing between a determination of time and the statement of an object, cannot possibly signify anything else than what happened at that time in relation to that object, and thus the words ἠγόρασαν ἀρώματα, *they bought sweet spices*, placed between διαγενομένου τοῦ σαββάτου, *The sabbath being past*, and ἵνα ἐλθοῦσαι ἀλείψωσιν αὐτὸν, *that they might come and anoint him*, can only signify a purchase made after the sabbath had elapsed.[7]   Hence Michaelis, who undertook to vindicate the histories of the burial and resurrection from the charge of contradiction urged by the Fragmentist, betook himself to the opposite measure, and sought to conform Luke to Mark.   When Luke writes : ὑποστρέψασαι δὲ ἡτοίμασαν ἀρώματα καὶ μύρα, *and they returned, and bought sweet spices and ointments*, he does not, we are told, mean that they had made this purchase immediately after their return, and consequently on the evening of the burial : on the contrary, by the addition καὶ τὸ μὲν σάββατον ἡσύχασαν κατὰ τὴν ἐντολὴν, *and rested the sabbath day, according to the commandment*, he himself gives us to understand that it did not happen until the sabbath was past, since between their return from the grave and the commencement of the sabbath at six in the evening, there was no time left for the purchase.[8]   But when Luke places his ἡτοίμασαν (*they prepared*) between

---

[4] Vol. II. § 80.
[5] Michaelis, Begräbniss- und Auferstehungsgeschichte, s. 68 ff.
[6] Thus Grotius ; Less, Auferstehungsgeschichte, s. 165.
[7] See the fifth Fragment, in Lessing's viertem Beitrag zur Geschichte und Literatur, s. 467 f.   Comp. concerning these differences also Lessing's Duplik.
[8] Michaelis, ut sup. s. 102 ff.

ὑποστρέψασαι (*being returned*) and ἡσύχασαν (*they rested*), this can as little signify something occurring after the rest of the sabbath, as in Mark the similarly placed word ἠγόρασαν can signify something which had happened before the sabbath. Hence more recent theologians have perceived that each of these two Evangelists must be allowed to retain the direct sense of his words ; nevertheless they have believed it possible to free both the one and the other from the appearance of error by the supposition that the spices prepared before the sabbath were not sufficient, and that the women, agreeably to Mark's statement, really bought an additional stock after the sabbath.[9] But there must have been an enormous requirement of spices if first the hundred pounds weight contributed by Nicodemus had not sufficed, and on this account the women on the evening before the sabbath had laid ready more spices, and then these too were found insufficient, so that they had to buy yet more on the morning after the sabbath.

Thus however, in consistency, it is necessary to solve the second contradiction which exists between the two intermediate Evangelists unitedly and the fourth, namely, that according to the latter Jesus was embalmed with a hundred weight of ointment before being laid in the grave, while according to the former the embalming was deferred until after the sabbath. But as far as the quantity was concerned, the hundred pounds of myrrh and aloes were more than enough : that which was wanting, and had to be supplied after the sabbath, could only relate to the manner, *i.e.* that the spices had not yet been applied to the body in the right way—because the process had been interrupted by the arrival of the sabbath.[10] But, if we listen to John, the interment of Jesus on the evening of his death was performed καθὼς ἔθος ἐστὶ τοῖς Ἰουδαίοις ἐνταφιάζειν, *as the manner of the Jews is to bury*, i.e. *ritè*, in due form, the corpse being wound in the *linen clothes* ὀθόνια *with the spices* μετὰ τῶν ἀρωμάτων (v. 40), which constituted the whole of Jewish embalming, so that according to John nothing was wanting in relation to the manner ;[11] not to mention that if the women, as Mark and Luke state, bought fresh spices and placed them in readiness, the embalming of Nicodemus must have been defective as to quantity also. Thus in the burial of Jesus as narrated by John nothing objective was wanting : nevertheless, it has been maintained that subjectively, as regarded the women, it had not been performed, i.e. they were ignorant that Jesus had already been embalmed by Nicodemus and Joseph.[12] One is astonished that such a position can be advanced, since the synoptists expressly state that the women were present at the interment of Jesus, and beheld, not merely the place (ποῦ τίθεται, Mark), but also the manner in which he was interred (ὡς ἐτέθη, Luke).

There is a third divergency relative to this point between Matthew and the rest of the Evangelists, in so far as the former mentions no embalming either before or after the sabbath. This divergency, as it consists merely in the silence of one narrator, has been hitherto little regarded, and even the Fragmentist admits that the wrapping of the body in a clean linen cloth, mentioned by Matthew, involves also the Jewish method of embalming. But in this instance there might easily be drawn an argument *ex silentio*. When we read in the narrative of the anointing at Bethany the declaration of Jesus, that the woman by this deed had anointed his body for burial (Matt. xxvi. 12 parall.) : this has indeed its significance in all the narratives, but a peculiarly striking

---

[9] Kuinöl, in Luc. p. 721.
[10] Thus Tholuck, in loc.
[11] See the Fragments, ut sup. s. 469 ff.
[12] Michaelis, ut sup. s. 99 f. ; Kuinöl and Lücke leave open the choice between this expedient and the former.

one in Matthew, according to whose subsequent narrative no anointing took place at the burial of Jesus,[13] and this fact appears to be the only sufficient explanation of the special importance which the Evangelical tradition attached to the action of the woman. If he who was revered as the Messiah did not, under the pressure of unfavourable circumstances, receive at his burial the due honour of embalmment : then must the thoughts of his adherents revert with peculiar complacency to an event in the latter part of his life, in which a humble-minded female votary, as if foreboding that this honour would be denied to him when dead, rendered it to him while yet living. Viewed in this light the different representation of the anointing in the other Evangelists would have the appearance of a gradual development of the legend. In Mark and Luke it still remains, as in Matthew, that the corpse of Jesus is not really embalmed : but, said the legend, already outstepping the narrative of the first gospel, the embalming was designed for him,—this intention was the motive for the resort of the women to his grave on the morning after the sabbath, and its execution was only prevented by the resurrection. In the fourth gospel, on the other hand, this anointing, from being first performed on him by anticipation while he was yet living, and then intended for him when dead, resolved itself into an actual embalming of his body after death : in conjunction with which, however, after the manner of legendary formations, the reference of the earlier anointing to the burial of Jesus was left standing.

The body of Jesus, according to all the narrators, was forthwith deposited in a tomb hewn out of a rock, and closed with a great stone. Matthew describes this tomb as καινὸν, *new ;* an epithet which Luke and John more closely determine by stating that no man had yet been laid therein. We may observe in passing, that there is as much reason for suspicion with respect to this newness of the grave, as with respect to the unridden ass in the history of the entrance of Jesus, since here in the same way as there, the temptation lay irresistibly near, even without historical grounds, to represent the sacred receptacle of the body of Jesus as never having been polluted by any corpse. But even in relation to this tomb the Evangelists exhibit a divergency. According to Matthew it was the property of Joseph, who had himself caused it to be hewn in the rock ; and the two other synoptists also, since they make Joseph unhesitatingly dispose of the grave, appear to proceed on the same presupposition. According to John, on the contrary, Joseph's right of property in the grave was not the reason that Jesus was laid there; but because time pressed, he was deposited in the new sepulchre, which happened to be in a neighbouring garden. Here again the harmonists have tried their art on both sides. Matthew was to be brought into agreement with John by the observation, that a manuscript of his gospel omits the αὐτοῦ (*his own*) after μνημείῳ ; while an ancient translation read, instead of ὃ ἐλατόμησεν (*which he had hewn*),—ὃ ἦν λελατομημένον (*which was hewn*) : [14] as if these alterations were not obviously owing already to harmonizing efforts. Hence the opposite side has been taken, and it has been remarked that the words of John by no means exclude the possibility that Joseph may have been the owner of the tomb, since both reasons—the vicinity, and the fact that the grave belonged to Joseph—may have co-operated.[15] But the contrary is rather the truth : namely, that the vicinity of the grave when alleged as a motive, excludes the fact of possession : a house in which I should take shelter from a shower, because it is near, would not be my own ; unless indeed I were the owner of

[13] Comp. De Wette, in loc. Matth.
[14] Michaelis, ut sup. s. 45 ff.
[15] Kuinöl, in Matth. p. 786 ; Hase, § 145 ; Tholuck, Comm. s. 320.

two houses, one near and one more distant, of which the latter was my proper dwelling : and in like manner a grave, in which a person lays a relative or friend who does not himself possess one, because it is near, cannot be his own, unless he possess more than one, and intend at greater leisure to convey the deceased into the other ; which however in our case, since the near grave was from its newness adapted above all others for the interment of Jesus, is not easily conceivable. If according to this the contradiction subsists, there does not appear in the narratives themselves any ground for decision in favour of the one or of the other.[16]

§ 136.

THE WATCH AT THE GRAVE OF JESUS.

On the following day, the Sabbath,[1] the chief priests and Pharisees, according to Matthew (xxvii. 62 ff.) came to Pilate, and with reference to the prediction of Jesus, that he should rise again after three days, requested him to place a watch by his grave, lest his disciples should take occasion from the expectation which that prediction had awakened, to steal his body and then spread a report that he was risen again. Pilate granted their request, and accordingly they went away, sealed the stone, and placed the watch before the grave. The subsequent resurrection of Jesus (we must here anticipate so far), and the angelic appearances which accompanied it, so terrified the guards, that they became *as dead men*, ὡσεὶ νεκροὶ,—forthwith, however, hastened to the city and gave an account of the event to the chief priests. The latter, after having deliberated on the subject in an assembly with the elders, bribed the soldiers to pretend that the disciples had stolen the body by night ; whence, the narrator adds, this report was disseminated, and was persisted in up to his time (xxviii. 4, 11 ff.).

In this narrative, peculiar to the first gospel, critics have found all kinds of difficulties, which have been exposed with the most acumen by the author of the Wolfenbüttel Fragments, and after him by Paulus.[2] The difficulties lie first of all in this : that neither the requisite conditions of the event, nor its necessary consequences, are presented in the rest of the New Testament history. As regards the former, it is not to be conceived how the Sanhedrists could obtain the information, that Jesus was to return to life three days after his death : since there is no trace of such an idea having existed even among his disciples. They say : *We remember that that deceiver said, while he was yet alive*, etc. If we are to understand from this that they remembered to have heard him speak to that effect ; Jesus, according to the evangelical accounts, never spoke plainly of his resurrection in the presence of his enemies ; and the figurative discourses which remained unintelligible to his confidential disciples, could still less be understood by the Jewish hierarchs,

---

[16] A confusion of the κῆπος *garden* near to the place of execution, where according to John Jesus was buried, with the garden of Gethsemane, where he was taken prisoner, appears to have given rise to the statement of the Evang. Nicodemi, that Jesus was crucified ἐν τῷ κήπῳ, ὅπου ἐπιάσθη *in the garden where he was apprehended.* C. ix. p. 580, ap. Thilo.

[1] Τῇ ἐπαύριον, ἥτις ἐστὶ μετὰ τὴν παρασκευὴν (*the next day, that followed the day of the preparation*), is certainly a singular periphrasis for the sabbath, for it is a strangely inappropriate mode of expression to designate a solemn day, as the day after the previous day : nevertheless we must abide by this meaning so long as we are unable to evade it in a more natural manner than Schneckenburger in his chronology of the Passion week, Beiträge, s. 3 ff.

[2] The former, ut sup. s. 437 ff. ; the latter in the exeg. Handb. 3, b, s. 837 ff. Comp. Kaiser, bibl. Theol. 1, s. 253.

who were less accustomed to his mode of thought and expression.   If, however, the Sanhedrists merely intend to say, that they had heard from others
of his having given such a promise : this intelligence could only have
proceeded from the disciples ; but as these had not, either before or after the
death of Jesus, the slightest anticipation of his resurrection, they could not
have excited such an anticipation in others ;—not to mention that we have
been obliged to reject as unhistorical the whole of the predictions of the
resurrection lent to Jesus in the gospels.   Equally incomprehensible with this
knowledge on the part of the enemies of Jesus, is the silence of his friends,
the Apostles and the other Evangelists besides Matthew, concerning a circumstance so favourable to their cause.   It is certainly applying too modern
a standard to the conduct of the disciples to say with the Wolfenbüttel Fragmentist, that they must have entreated from Pilate a letter under his seal in
attestation of the fact that a watch had been set over the grave : but it must
be held surprising that in none of the apostolic speeches is there anywhere an
appeal to so striking a fact, and that even in the gospels, with the exception
of the first, it has left no discoverable trace.   An attempt has been made to
explain this silence from the consideration, that the bribing of the guards by
the Sanhedrim had rendered an appeal to them fruitless : [3] but truth is not so
readily surrendered to such obvious falsehoods, and at all events, when the
adherents of Jesus had to defend themselves before the Sanhedrim, the mention of such a fact must have been a powerful weapon.   The cause is already
half given up when its advocates retreat to the position, that the disciples probably did not become acquainted with the true cause of the event immediately, but only later, when the soldiers began to betray the secret.[4]   For
even if the guards in the first instance merely set afloat the tale of the theft,
and thus admitted that they had been placed by the grave, the adherents of
Jesus could already construe for themselves the real state of the case, and
might boldly appeal to the guards, who must have been witnesses of something quite different from the theft of a corpse.   But lest we be told of the
invalidity of an argument drawn from the merely negative fact of silence, there
is something positive narrated concerning a part of the adherents of Jesus,
namely, the women, which is not reconcilable with the fact of a watch being
placed at the grave.   Not only do the women who resort to the grave on the
morning after the Sabbath, intend to complete the embalming which they
could not hope to be permitted to do, if they knew that a watch was placed
before the grave, and that this was besides sealed : [5] but according to Mark
their whole perplexity on their way to the grave turns upon the question, who
will roll away the stone for them from the grave ; a clear proof that they knew
nothing of the guards, since these either would not have allowed them to
remove the stone, however light, or if they would have allowed this, would
also have helped them to roll away a heavier one ; so that in any case the
difficulty as to the weight of the stone would have been superfluous.   But
that the placing of the watch should have remained unknown to the women is,
from the attention which everything relative to the end of Jesus excited in
Jerusalem (Luke xxiv. 18), highly improbable.

But within the narrative also, every feature is full of difficulties, for, according to the expression of Paulus, no one of the persons who appear in it, acts
in accordance with his character.   That Pilate should have granted the re-

---

[3] Michaelis, Begräbniss- und Auferstehungsgeschichte, s. 206 ; Olshausen 2, s. 506.
[4] Michaelis, ut sup.
[5] Olshausen overlooks the latter point when he (ut sup.) says the watch had not received
the command to prevent the completion of the interment.

quest of the Jewish magistrates for a watch, I will not say without hesitation, but so entirely without ridicule, must be held surprising after his previous conduct;[6] such minor particulars might however be merely passed over by Matthew in his summary mode of recounting the incidents. It is more astonishing that the guards should have been so easily induced to tell a falsehood which the severity of Roman discipline made so dangerous, as that they had failed in their duty by sleeping on their post; especially as, from the bad understanding which existed between the Sanhedrim and the procurator, they could not know how far the mediation promised by the former would avail. But the most inconceivable feature is the alleged conduct of the Sanhedrim. The difficulty which lies in their going to the heathen procurator on the Sabbath, defiling themselves by approaching the grave, and placing a watch, has certainly been overstrained by the Fragmentist; but their conduct, when the guards, returning from the grave, apprised them of the resurrection of Jesus, is truly impossible. They believe the assertion of the soldiers that Jesus had arisen out of his grave in a miraculous manner. How could the council, many of whose members were Sadducees, receive this as credible? Even the Pharisees in the Sanhedrim, though they held in theory the possibility of a resurrection, would not, with the mean opinion which they entertained of Jesus, be inclined to believe in his resurrection; especially as the assertion in the mouth of the guards sounded just like a falsehood invented to screen a failure in duty. The real Sanhedrists, on hearing such an assertion from the soldiers, would have replied with exasperation: You lie! you have slept and allowed him to be stolen; but you will have to pay dearly for this, when it comes to be investigated by the procurator. But instead of this, the Sanhedrists in our gospel speak them fair, and entreat them thus: Tell a lie, say that you have slept and allowed him to be stolen: moreover, they pay them richly for the falsehood, and promise to exculpate them to the procurator. This is evidently spoken entirely on the Christian presupposition of the reality of the resurrection of Jesus; a presupposition however which is quite incorrectly attributed to the members of the Sanhedrim. It is also a difficulty, not merely searched out by the Fragmentist, but even acknowledged by orthodox expositors,[7] that the Sanhedrim, in a regular assembly, and after a formal consultation, should have resolved to corrupt the soldiers and put a lie into their mouths. That in this manner a college of seventy men should have officially decided on suggesting and rewarding the utterance of a falsehood, is, as Olshausen justly observes, too widely at variance with the decorum, the sense of propriety, inseparable from such an assembly. The expedient of supposing that it was merely a private meeting, since only the *chief priests* and *elders*, not the *scribes*, are said to have embraced the resolution of bribing the soldiers,[8] would involve the singularity, that in this assembly the *scribes* were absent, while in the shortly previous interview with the procurator, where the *scribes* are represented by the Pharisees who formed their majority, the *elders* were wanting: whence it is evident rather that, it being inconvenient invariably to designate the Sanhedrim by a full enumeration of its constituent parts, it was not seldom indicated by the mention of only some or one of these. If it therefore remains that according to Matthew the high council must in a formal session have resolved on bribing the guards: such an act of baseness could only be attributed to the council as

---

[6] Olshausen indeed is here still so smitten with awe, that he supposes Pilate to have been penetrated with an indescribable feeling of dread on hearing this communication from the Sanhedrists, s. 505.

[7] Olshausen, s 506.

[8] Michaelis, ut sup. s. 198 f.

such, by the rancour of the primitive Christians, among whom our anecdote
arose.

These difficulties in the present narrative of the first gospel have been felt
to be so pressing, that it has been attempted to remove them by the suppo-
position of interpolation ; [9] which has lately been moderated into the opinion,
that while the anecdote did not indeed proceed from the Apostle Matthew
himself, it was not however added by a hand otherwise alien to our gospel,
but was inserted by the Greek translator of the Hebrew Matthew.[10]   Against
the former supposition the absence of all critical authority is decisive ; the
appeal of those who advance the other opinion to the unapostolic character of
the anecdote, would not warrant its separation from the context of the main
narrative, unless that narrative itself were already proved to be of apostolic
origin ; while the anecdote is so far from presenting any want of connexion
with the rest, that, on the contrary, Paulus is right in his remark that an interpolator (or inserting translator) would scarcely have given himself the trouble
to distribute his interpolation in three different places (xxvii. 62–66 ; xxviii.
4, 11–15), but would have compressed it into one passage, or at most two.
Neither can the question be settled so cheaply as Olshausen imagines, when he
concludes that the entire narrative is apostolic and correct, save that the Evangelist erred in representing the corruption of the guards as being resolved on
in full council, whereas the affair was probably managed in secret by Caiaphas
alone : as if this assembly of the council were the sole difficulty of the narrative, and as if, when errors had insinuated themselves in relation to this particular, they might not extend to others also.[11]

Paulus correctly points out how Matthew himself, by the statement : *and
this saying is commonly reported among the Jews to this day,*—indicates a cal-
umnious Jewish report as the source of his narrative.   But when this theologian expresses the opinion that the Jews themselves propagated the story, that
they had placed a watch at the grave of Jesus, but that the guards had permitted his body to be stolen : this is as perverted a view as that of Hase, when
he conjectures that the report in question proceeded first of all from the
friends of Jesus, and was afterwards modified by his enemies.   For as regards
the former supposition, Kuinöl has already correctly remarked, that Matthew
merely designates the assertion respecting the theft of the corpse as a Jewish
report, not the entire narrative of the placing of a watch ; neither is there any
reason to be conceived why the Jews should have fabricated such a report as
that a watch was set at the grave of Jesus : Paulus says, it was hoped thereby
to render the assertion that the body of Jesus was stolen by his disciples more
easy of acceptation with the credulous : but those must indeed have been
very credulous who did not observe, that the placing of the watch was the very
thing to render a furtive removal of the body of Jesus improbable.   Paulus
appears to represent the matter to himself thus : the Jews wished to obtain
witnesses as it were to the accusation of a theft, and for this purpose fabricated
the story of the guard being placed by the grave.   But that the guards with
open eyes quietly beheld the disciples of Jesus carry away his body, no one
could credit : while, if they saw nothing of this, because they slept, they gave
no testimony, since they could then only by inference arrive at the conclusion,
that the body might have been stolen : a conclusion which could be drawn
just as well without them.   Thus in no way can the watch have belonged to
the Jewish basis of the present narrative ; but the report disseminated among

---

[9] Stroth, in Eichhorn's Repertorium, 9, s. 141.
[10] Kern, über den Ursprung des Ev. Matth. Tüb. Zeitschrift, 1834, 2, s. 100 f. ; comp.
123.   Compare my Review, Jahrbücher f. wiss. Kritik, Nov. 1834 ; now in the Charakteristiken u. Kritiken, s. 280.   [11] Hase, L. J., § 145.

the Jews consisted, as the text also says, merely in the assertion that the disciples had stolen the body. As the Christians wished to oppose this calumny, there was formed among them the legend of a watch placed at the grave of Jesus, and now they could boldly confront their slanderers with the question : how can the body have been carried away, since you placed a watch at the grave and sealed the stone? And because, as we have ourselves proved in the course of our inquiry, a legend is not fully convicted of groundlessness until it has been shown how it could arise even without historical grounds : it was attempted on the side of the Christians, in showing what was supposed to be the true state of the case, to expose also the origin of the false legend, by deriving the falsehood propagated among the Jews from the contrivance of the Sanhedrim, and their corruption of the guards. Thus the truth is precisely the reverse of what Hase says, namely, that the legend probably arose among the friends of Jesus and was modified by his enemies :—the friends first had an inducement to the fiction of the watch, when the enemies had already spoken of a theft.[12]

§ 137.

FIRST TIDINGS OF THE RESURRECTION.

That the first news of the grave of Jesus being opened and empty on the second morning after his burial, came to the disciples by the mouth of women, is unanimously stated by the four Evangelists : but in all the more particular circumstances they diverge from each other, in a way which has presented the richest material for the polemic of the Wolfenbüttel Fragmentist, and on the other hand has given abundant work to the harmonists and apologists, without there having been hitherto any successful attempt at a satisfactory mediation between the two parties.[1]

Leaving behind the difference which is connected with the divergencies in the history of the burial, as to the object of the women in resorting to the grave,—namely, that according to the two intermediate Evangelists they intended to embalm the body of Jesus, according to the two others merely to pay a visit to the grave,—we find, first, a very complicated divergency relative to the number of the women who made this visit. Luke merely speaks indefinitely of many women ; not alone those whom he describes xxiii. 55, as having come with Jesus from Galilee, and of whom he mentions by name, Mary Magdalene, Joanna, and Mary the mother of James, but also *certain others with them*, τινὲς σὺν αὐταῖς (xxiv. 1). Mark has merely three women ; two of those whom Luke also names, but as the third, Salome instead of Joanna (xvi. 1). Matthew has not this third woman, respecting whom the two intermediate Evangelists differ, but merely the two Maries concerning whom they agree (xxviii. 1). Lastly, John has only one of these, Mary Magdalene (xx. 1). The time at which the women go to the grave is likewise not determined with uniformity ; for even if the words of Matthew, *In the end of the sabbath, as it began to dawn toward the first day of the week*, ὀψὲ σαββάτων, τῇ ἐπιφωσκούσῃ εἰς μίαν σαββάτων, make no difference,[2] still the addition of Mark : *at the rising of the sun*, ἀνατείλαντος τοῦ ἡλίου, are in contradiction with the expressions *when it was yet dark*, σκοτίας ἔτι οὔσης, in John, and *very early in the morning*, ὄρθρου βαθέος, in Luke.—In relation to the circumstances in which the women first saw the grave there may appear to be a difference, at

---

[12] Comp. Theile, zur Biogr. Jesu, § 37 ; Weisse, die Evang. Gesch. 2, s. 343 f.
[1] Comp. Theile, ut sup.
[2] Comp. Fritzsche, in loc., and Kern, Tüb. Zeitschr. 1834, 2, s. 102 f.

least between Matthew and the three other Evangelists. According to the latter, as they approach and look towards the grave, they see that the stone has already been rolled away by an unknown hand: whereas the narrative of the first Evangelist has appeared to many to imply that the women themselves beheld the stone rolled away by an angel.—Manifold are the divergencies as to what the women further saw and learned at the grave, According to Luke they enter into the grave, find that the body of Jesus is not there, and are hence in perplexity, until they see standing by them two men in shining garments, who announce to them his resurrection. In Mark, who also makes them enter into the grave, they see only one young man in a long white garment, not standing, but sitting on the right side, who gives them the same intelligence. In Matthew they receive this information before they enter into the grave, from the angel, who after rolling away the stone had sat upon it. Lastly, according to John, Mary Magdalene, as soon as she sees the stone taken away, and without witnessing any angelic appearance, runs back into the city.—Moreover the relation in which the disciples of Jesus are placed with respect to the first news of his resurrection is a different one in the different gospels. According to Mark, the women, out of fear, tell no one of the angelic appearance which they have beheld; according to John, Mary Magdalene has nothing more to say to John and Peter, to whom she hastens from the grave, than that Jesus is taken away; according to Luke, the women report the appearance to the disciples in general, and not merely to two of them; while according to Matthew, as they were in the act of hastening to the disciples, Jesus himself met them, and they were able to communicate this also to the disciples. In the two first gospels nothing is said of one of the disciples himself going to the grave on hearing the report of the women; according to Luke, Peter went thither, found it empty and returned wondering, and from Luke xxiv. 24 it appears that other disciples besides him went thither in a similar manner; according to the fourth gospel Peter was accompanied by John, who on this occasion was convinced of the resurrction of Jesus. Luke says that Peter made his visit to the sepulchre after he had already been informed by the women of the angelic appearance; but in the fourth gospel the two disciples go to the grave before Mary Magdalene can have told them of such an appearance; it was only when she had proceeded a second time to the grave with the two disciples, and when they had returned home again, that, stooping into the sepulchre, she saw, according to this gospel, *two angels in white, sitting, the one at the head and the other at the feet, where the body of Jesus had lain,* by whom she was asked, why she wept? and on turning round she beheld Jesus himself; a particular of which there is a fragmentary notice in Mark v. 9, with the additional remark, that she communicated this news to his former companions.

It has been thought possible to reconcile the greater part of these divergencies by supposing, instead of one scene variously described, a multiplicity of different scenes; for which purpose the ordinary grammatical and other artifices of the harmonists were pressed into the service. That Mark might not contradict the σκοτίας ἔτι οὔσης *while it was yet dark* of John, the apologists did not scruple to translate the words ἀνατείλαντος τοῦ ἡλίου by *orituro sole*; the contradiction between Matthew and the rest, when the former appears to say that the women saw the stone rolled away by the angel, seemed to be more easy of solution, not indeed by supposing, with Michaelis,[4] that καὶ ἰδοὺ (*and behold!*) denotes a recurrence to a previous event, and that

---

[3] Kuinöl, in Marc. p. 194 f.
[4] Michaelis, ut sup. s. 112.

ἀπεκύλισε has the signification of a pluperfect (an expedient which has been justly combated by modern criticism in opposition to Lessing, who was inclined to admit it);[5] but by understanding the ἦλθε v. 1 to express a yet unfinished progress of the women towards the grave, in which case the καὶ ἰδοὺ and what follows may, in accordance with its proper meaning, relate something that happened after the departure of the women from their home, but before their arrival at the grave.[6] In relation to the number and the visit of the women, it was in the first place urged that even according to John, although he mentions only Mary Magdalene by name,—several women must have accompanied her to the grave, since he makes her say after her return to the two disciples: *we know not where they have laid him*;[7] a plural, which certainly intimates the presence of other but unspecified persons, with whom Mary Magdalene, whether at the grave itself or on her return, had conversed on the subject before she came to the Apostles. Thus, it is said, Mary Magdalene went to the grave with the other women, more or fewer of whom are mentioned by the other Evangelists. As however she returned without having, like the other women, seen an angel, it is supposed that she ran back alone as soon as she saw the stone rolled away : which is accounted for by her impetuous temperament, she having been formerly a demoniac.[8] While she hastened back to the city, the other women saw the appearances of which the synoptists speak.—To all it is maintained, the angels appeared within the grave ; for the statement in Matthew that one sat outside on the stone, is only a pluperfect : when the women came he had already withdrawn into the sepulchre, and accordingly, after their conversation with him, the women are described as *departing from the sepulchre*, ἐξελθοῦσαι ἐκ τοῦ μνημείου (v. 8):[9] in which observation it is only overlooked that between the first address of the angel and the above expression, there stands his invitation to the women to come with him into the grave and see the place where Jesus had lain. In relation to the difference that according to the two first Evangelists the women see only one angel, according to the third, two, even Calvin resorts to the miserable expedient of supposing a synecdoche, namely that all the Evangelists certainly knew of two angels, but Matthew and Mark mention only the one who acted as speaker. Others make different women see different appearances : some, of whom Matthew and Mark speak, seeing only one angel ; the others, to whom Luke refers, and who came earlier or perhaps later than the above, seeing two ;[10] but Luke makes the same two Maries who, according to his predecessors, had seen only one angel, narrate to the Apostles an appearance of two angels. It is also said that the women returned in separate groups, so that Jesus might meet those of whom Matthew speaks without being seen by those of Luke ; and though those of Mark at first tell no one from fear, the rest, and they themselves afterwards, might communicate what they had seen to the disciples.[11]—On hearing the report brought by several women, Peter, according to Luke, straightway goes to the grave,

[5] Schneckenburger, über den Urspr. des ersten kanon. Evang., s. 62 f. Comp. the Wolfenbüttel Fragmentist in Lessing's viertem Beitrag, s. 472 ff. On the other hand, Lessing's Duplik, Werke, Donauösch. Ausg. 6. Thl. s. 394 f.

[6] De Wette, in loc.

[7] Michaelis, s. 150 ff.

[8] Paulus, exeg. Handb. 3, b, s. 825.

[9] Michaelis, s. 117.

[10] Michaelis, s. 146.—Celsus stumbled at this difference respecting the number of the angels, and Origen replied that the Evangelists mean different angels : Matthew and Mark the one who had rolled away the stone, Luke and John those who were commissioned to give information to the women, c. Cels. v. 56.

[11] Paulus, in loc. Matth.

finds it empty and turns away wondering. But according to the hypothesis which we are now detailing, Mary Magdalene had run back a considerable time before the other women, and had brought with her to the grave Peter and John. Thus Peter, first on hearing the imperfect intelligence of Mary Magdalene that the grave was empty, must have gone thither with John ; and subsequently, on the account of the angelic appearance brought by the other women, he must have gone a second time alone : in which case it would be particularly surprising that while his companion arrived at a belief in the resurrection of Jesus on the very first visit, he himself had not attained further than wonder even on the second. Besides, as the Fragmentist has already ably shown, the narrative in the third gospel of the visit of Peter alone, and that in the fourth of the visit of Peter and John, are so strikingly similar even in words,[12] that the majority of commentators regard them as referring to a single visit, Luke having only omitted to notice the companion of Peter : in support of which opinion they can appeal to Luke xxiv. 24. But if the visit of the two Apostles, occasioned by the return of Mary Magdalene, be one and the same with that occasioned by the return of the other women, then the return of the women is also not a double one ; if however they returned in company with each other, we have a contradiction. After the two Apostles are returned without having seen an angel, Mary, who remains behind, as she looks into the grave, all at once sees two. What a strange playing at hide and seek must there have been on the part of the angels, according to the harmonistic combination of these narratives ! First only one shows himself to one group of women, to another group two show themselves ; both forthwith conceal themselves from the disciples ; but after their departure both again become visible. To remove these intermissions Paulus has placed the appearance presented to Mary Magdalene before the arrival of the two disciples : but by this violent transposition of the order chosen by the narrator, he has only confessed the impossibility of thus incorporating the various Evangelists with each other. Hereupon, as Mary Magdalene raises herself from looking into the grave and turns round, she sees Jesus standing behind her. According to Matthew, Jesus appeared to Mary Magdalene and the other Mary, when they had already set out on their way to the city, consequently when they were at some distance from the grave. Thus Jesus would have first appeared to Mary Magdalene alone, close to the grave, and a second time when she was on her way from thence, in the company of another woman. In order to avoid the want of purpose attaching to the repetition of an appearance of Jesus after so short an interval, commentators have here called in the above supposition, that Mary Magdalene had previously separated herself from the women of whom Matthew speaks :[13] but in that case, since Matthew has besides Mary Magdalene only the other Mary, it would have been only one woman to whom Jesus appeared on the way from the grave : whereas Matthew throughout speaks of several (ἀπήντησεν αὐταῖς).

---

[12] I subjoin the table sketched by the Fragmentist (ut sup. s. 477 f.) :
" 1. Luke xxiv. 12 : Peter ran to the grave, ἔδραμεν.
   John xx. 4 : Peter and John ran, ἔτρεχον.
2. Luke v. 12 : Peter looked in, παρακύψας.
   John v. 5 : John looked in, παρακύψας.
3. Luke v. 12 : Peter saw the clothes lying alone, βλέπει τὰ ὀθόνια κείμενα μόνα.
   John v. 6, 7 : Peter saw the clothes lie, and the napkin not lying with the clothes : θεωρεῖ τὰ ὀθόνια κείμενα, καὶ τὸ σουδάριον οὐ μετὰ τῶν ὀθονίων κείμενον.
4. Luke v. 12 : Peter went home, ἀπῆλθε πρὸς ἑαυτὸν.
   John v. 10 : Peter and John went home again, ἀπῆλθον πάλιν πρὸς ἑαυτούς."
[13] Kuinöl, in Matth., p. 800 f.

To escape from this restless running to and fro of the disciples and the women, this phantasmagoric appearance, disappearance, and reappearance of the angels, and the useless repetition of the appearances of Jesus before the same person, which result from this harmonistic method, we must consider each Evangelist by himself: we then obtain from each a quiet picture with simple dignified features; one visit of the women to the grave, or according to John, two; one angelic appearance; one appearance of Jesus, according to John and Matthew; and one visit to the grave by one or two of the disciples, according to Luke and John.

But with the above difficulties of the harmonistic method of incorporation as to the substance, there is associated a difficulty as to form, in the question, how comes it, under the presuppositions of this mode of viewing the gospels, that from the entire series of occurrences, each narrator has selected a separate portion for himself,—that of the many visits and appearances not one Evangelist relates all, and scarcely one the same as his neighbour, but for the most part each has chosen only one for representation, and each again a different one? The most plausible answer to this question has been given by Griesbach in a special treatise on this subject.[14] He supposes that each Evangelist recounts the resurrection of Jesus in the manner in which it first, became known to him: John received the first information from Mary Magdalene, and hence he narrates only what he learned from her; to Matthew (for without doubt the disciples, as strangers visiting the feast, resided in different quarters of the city), the first news was communicated by those women to whom Jesus himself appeared on their way from the grave, and hence he relates only what these had experienced. But here this explanation already founders on the facts, that in Matthew, of the women who see Jesus on their way homeward, Mary Magdalene is one; and that in John, Mary Magdalene, after her second visit to the grave, in which Jesus appeared to her, no longer went to John and Peter alone, but to the disciples in general, and communicated to them the appearance she had seen and the commission she had received: so that Matthew in any case must also have known of the appearance of Jesus to Mary Magdalene.[15] Further, when, according to this hypothesis, Mark narrates the history of the resurrection as he had learned it in the house of his mother who lived in Jerusalem (Acts xii. 12); Luke, as he had received it from Joanna, whom he alone mentions: we cannot but wonder at the tenacity with which, according to this, each must have clung to the narrative which he had happened first to receive, since the resurrection of Jesus must have been the subject of all others on which there was the most lively interchange of narratives among his adherents, so that the ideas concerning the first tidings of the event must have found their level. To remove these difficulties, Griesbach has further supposed, that the disciples had it in their intention to compare the discordant accounts of the women and reduce them to order; when, however, the resuscitated Jesus himself appeared in the midst of them, they neglected this, because they now no longer founded their faith on the assertions of the women, but on the appearances which they had themselves witnessed: but the more the information of the women fell into the background, the less conceivable is it, how in the sequel each could so obstinately cling to what this or that woman had chanced first to communicate to him.

If then the plan of incorporation will not lead to the desired end,[16] we

[14] Progr. de fontibus, unde Evangelistæ suas de resurrectione Domini narrationes hauserint. Opusc. acad. ed. Gabler, Vol. 2, p. 241 ff.
[15] Comp. Schneckenburger, ut sup. s. 64 f., Anm.
[16] On this subject comp. De Wette, exeg. Handb. I, I, s. 245; Ammon, Fortbildung des Christenthums zur Weltreligion, 2, I, s. 6; Theile, zur Biogr. Jesu, § 37.

must try that of selection, and inquire whether we must not adhere to one of the four accounts, as pre-eminently apostolic, and by this rectify the others ; in which inquiry here as elsewhere, from the essential equality of the external evidence, only the internal character of the separate narratives can decide.

From the number of those accounts concerning the first intelligence of the resurrection of Jesus which have any claim to the rank of autoptical testimonies, modern criticism has excluded that of the first gospel ; [17] and we cannot, as in other instances, complain of this disfavour as an injustice.   For in many respects the narrative of the first gospel here betrays itself to have been carried a step farther in traditional development than that of the other gospels.   First, that the miraculous opening of the grave is seen by the women—if indeed Matthew intends to say this—could scarcely, had it really been the case, have been so entirely lost from remembrance as it is in the other Evangelists, but might very well be formed gradually in tradition ; further, that the rolling away of the stone was effected by the angel, evidently rests only on the combination of one who did not know any better means of answering the question, how the great stone was removed from the grave, and the guards taken out of the way, than to use for both purposes the angel presented to him in the current narratives of the appearance witnessed by the women ; to which he added the earthquake as a further embellishment of the scene.   But besides this, there is in the narrative of Matthew yet another trait, which has anything but an historical aspect. After the angel has already announced the resurrection of Jesus to the women, and charged them to deliver to the disciples the message that they should go into Galilee, where they would see the risen one : Jesus himself meets them and repeats the message which they are to deliver to the disciples.   This is a singular superfluity.   Jesus had nothing to add to the purport of the message which the angel had given to the women ; hence he could only wish to confirm it and render it more authentic.   But to the women it needed no further confirmation, for they were already filled with *great joy* by the tidings of the angel, and thus were believing ; while for the disciples even that confirmation did not suffice, for they remained incredulous even to the account of those who assured them that they had seen Jesus, until they had seen him themselves.   Thus it appears that two different narrations, as to the first news of the resurrection, have here become entangled with each other ; the one representing angels, the other Jesus himself, as the medium by which the women were informed of the event and sent with a message to the disciples :—the latter evidently the later tradition.

The pre-eminence in originality denied to the narrative of Matthew, is here as elsewhere awarded to that of John.   Traits so characteristic, says Lücke, as that on the visit to the grave the *other disciple* went faster than Peter and came to the spot before him, attest the authenticity of the gospel even to the most sceptical.   But the matter has yet another aspect.   It has been already remarked, at an earlier point of our inquiry, that this particular belongs to the effort, which the fourth gospel exhibits in a peculiar manner, to place John above Peter.[18]   We may now discuss the point with more particularity, by comparing the account in Luke already mentioned of the visit of Peter to the grave, with the account in the fourth gospel of the visit of the two disciples.   According to Luke (xxiv. 12), Peter runs to the grave : according to John (xx. 3 ff.), Peter and the favourite disciple go together, but so that

---

[17] Schulz, über das Abendmahl, s. 321 f. ; Schneckenburger, ut sup. s. 61 ff.
[18] Vol. II. § 74.

the latter runs faster, and comes first to the grave. In the third gospel, Peter stoops down, looks into the sepulchre, and sees the linen clothes : in the fourth, John does this, and sees the same. In the third gospel, nothing is said of an entering into the grave : but the fourth makes Peter enter first, and look more closely at the linen clothes, then John also, and the latter with the result that he begins to believe in the resurrection of Jesus.[19] That in these two narratives we have one and the same incident, has been above shown probable from their similarity even in the expressions. Thus the only question is : which is the original narrative, the one nearest to the fact? If that of John : then must his name have been gradually lost out of the narrative in the course of tradition, and the visit to the grave ascribed to Peter only ; which, since the importance of Peter threw all others into the shade, is easily conceivable. We might rest contented with this conclusion, regarding these two parallel narratives by themselves : but in connexion with the whole suspicious position which the fourth gospel assigns to John in relation to Peter, the contrary relation of the two narratives must here again be held the more probable. As in the entrance into the high priest's palace, so in the visit to the grave of Jesus, only in the fourth gospel is John given as a companion to Peter ; as in the former case it is he who gains an entrance for Peter, so in the latter he runs before him and casts the first glance into the grave, a circumstance which is repeatedly mentioned. That afterwards Peter is the first to enter into the grave, is only an apparent advantage, which is allowed him out of deference to the common idea of his position : for after him John also enters, and with a result of which Peter could not boast, namely, that he believed in the resurrection of Jesus, and thus was the first who attained to that degree of faith. From this effort to make John the first-born among the believers in the resurrection of Jesus may also be explained the divergency, that according to the narrative of the fourth gospel alone, Mary Magdalene hastens back to the two disciples before she has yet seen an angel. For had she beforehand witnessed an angelic appearance, which she would not any more than the women in Matthew have mistrusted, she would have been the first believer, and would have won the precedence of John in this respect ; but this is avoided by representing her as coming to the two disciples immediately after perceiving the emptiness of the grave, and under the disquietude excited in her by this circumstance. This presupposition serves also to explain why the fourth gospel makes the woman returning from the grave go, not to the disciples in general, but only to Peter and John. As, namely, the intelligence which, according to the original narrative, was brought to all the disciples, occasioned, according to Luke, only Peter to go to the grave, and as moreover, according to Mark (v. 7), the message of the women was destined more especially for Peter : the idea might easily be formed, that the news came to this disciple alone, with whom the object of the fourth Evangelist would then require that he should associate John. Only after the two disciples had come to the grave, and his John had attained faith, could the author of the fourth gospel introduce the appearances of the angel and of Jesus himself, which were said to have been granted to the women. That instead of these collectively he names only Mary Magdalene—although as has been earlier remarked, he xx. 2 presupposes at least a subsequent meeting between her and other women—this might certainly, under other circumstances, be regarded as the original representation, whence the synoptical one arose by a process of generalization : but it might just as

---

[19] Concerning this sense of ἐπίστευσεν, and its not being contradicted by οὔπω γὰρ ᾔδεισαν τὴν γραφὴν κ. τ. λ. (v. 9), see the correct view in Lücke, in loc.

well be the case that the other women, being less known, were eclipsed by Mary Magdalene. The description of the scene between her and Jesus, with the non-recognition of him at the first moment, etc., certainly does honour to the ingenuity and pathos of the author; [20] but here also there is an unhistorical superfluity similar to that in Matthew. For here the angels have not, as in the other Evangelists, to announce the resurrection to Mary Magdalene, and to make a disclosure to her; but they merely ask her, *Why weepest thou*? whereupon she complains to them of the disappearance of the body of Jesus, but, without waiting for any further explanation, turns round and sees Jesus standing. Thus as in Matthew the appearance of Jesus, since it is not represented as the principal and effective one, is a superfluous addition to that of the angel: so here the angelic appearance is an idle, ostentatious introduction to the appearance of Jesus.

If we turn to the third account, that of Mark, to ascertain whether he may not perhaps be the nearest to the fact: we find it so incoherent, and composed of materials so little capable of being fitted together, that such a relation is not to be thought of. After it has been already narrated that early in the morning of the day succeeding the Sabbath the women came to the grave of Jesus, and were informed by an angel of his resurrection, but out of fear said nothing to any one of the appearance which they had seen (xvi. 1–8): at v. 9, as if nothing had previously been said either of the resurrection or of the time at which it happened, the narrator proceeds : *Now when Jesus was risen early the first day of the week, he appeared first to Mary Magdalene, out of whom he had cast seven devils*, ἀναστὰς δὲ πρωὶ πρώτῃ σαββάτων ἐφάνη πρῶτον Μαρίᾳ τῇ Μαγδαληνῇ. This statement also does not suit the foregoing narrative, because this is not formed on the supposition of an appearance specially intended for Mary Magdalene : on the contrary, as she is said to be informed by an angel of the resurrection of Jesus, together with two other women, Jesus could not have appeared to her beforehand ; while afterwards, on her way to the city, she was in company with the other women, when, according to Matthew, they were all actually met by Jesus. Whether on this account we are to regard the end of the gospel of Mark, from v. 9, as a later addition,[21] is indeed doubtful, from the want of decisive critical grounds, and still more from the abruptness of the conclusion ἐφοβοῦντο γὰρ, *for they were afraid*, which the gospel would then present : but in any case we have here a narrative which the author, without any clear idea of the state of the fact and the succession of the events, hastily compiled out of the heterogeneous elements of the current legend, which he knew not how to manage.

In the narrative of Luke there would be no special difficulty : but it has a suspicious element in common with the others, namely, the angelic appearance, and moreover, in a twofold form. What had the angels to do in this scene? Matthew tells us : to roll away the stone from the grave ; on which it has already been remarked by Celsus, that according to the orthodox presupposition, the Son of God could find no such aid necessary for this purpose : [22] he might indeed find it suitable and becoming. In Mark and Luke the angels appear more as having to impart information and commissions to the women : but as, according to Matthew and John, Jesus himself appeared immediately after, and repeated those commissions, the delivery of them by angels was superfluous. Hence, nothing remains but to say : the angels belonged to the

---

[20] Weisse is of a different opinion, ut sup. s. 355, Anm.
[21] As Paulus, Fritzsche, Credner, Einleitung, 1, § 49. Comp. De Wette, exeg. Handb. 1, 2, s. 199 f. A middle view in Hug, Einl. in d. N. T. 2, § 69.
[22] Orig. c. Cels. v. 52 : ὁ γὰρ τοῦ θεοῦ παῖς, ὡς ἔοικεν. οὐκ ἐδύνατο ἀνοῖξαι τὸν τάφον, ἀλλ' ἐδεήθη ἄλλου ἀποκινήσοντος τὴν πέτραν.

embellishment of the great scene, as celestial attendants who had to open to the Messiah the door by which he meant to issue forth ; as a guard of honour on the spot from which the once dead had just departed with recovered life. But here occurs the question : does this species of pomp exist in the real court of God, or only in the childish conception formed of it by antiquity?

Hence commentators have laboured in various ways to transform the angels in the history of the resurrection into natural appearances. Setting out from the account of the first gospel in which the angel is said to have *a form* or *countenance like lightning*, ἰδέα ὡς ἀστραπὴ, and to effect the rolling away of the stone and the prostration of the guards, while an earthquake is connected with his appearance : it no longer lay far out of the way to think of a flash of lightning, which struck the stone with force sufficient to shatter it, and cast the guards to the earth ; or of an earthquake which, accompanied by flames bursting out of the ground, produced the same effect ; in which case the flames and the overwhelming force of the phenomenon were taken by the watching soldiers for an angel.[23] But partly the circumstance that the angel seated himself on the stone after it had been rolled away, partly, and still more decidedly, the statement that he spoke to the women, renders this hypothesis insufficient. Hence an effort has been made to complete it by the supposition that the sublime thought, Jesus is risen! which on the discovery that the grave was empty began to arise in the women and gradually to subdue their first doubts, was ascribed by them, after the oriental mode of thought and language, to an angel.[24] But how comes it that in all the gospels the angels are represented as clothed in white, shining garments? Is that too an oriental figure of speech? The oriental may indeed describe a good thought which occurs to him as being whispered to him by an angel : but to depict the clothing and aspect of this angel, passes the bounds of the merely figurative even among orientals. In the description of the first gospel the supposed lightning might be called to aid, in the conjecture that the effect thereby produced on the senses of the women was ascribed by them to an angel, which, with reference to that lightning, they depicted as one clothed in shining garments. But, according to the other Evangelists, the rolling away of the stone, *ex hypothesi* by the lightning, was not seen by the women ; on the contrary, when they went or looked into the grave, the white forms appeared to them in a perfectly tranquil position. According to this, it must have been something within the grave which suggested to them the idea of white-robed angels. Now in the grave, according to Luke and John, there lay the white linen clothes in which the body of Jesus had been wrapt : these, which were recognized simply as such by the more composed and courageous men, might, it is said, by timid and excited women, in the dark grave and by the deceptive morning twilight, be easily mistaken for angels.[25] But how should the women, who must have expected to find in the grave a corpse enveloped in white, be prompted by the sight of these clothes to a thought so strange, and which then lay so remote from their anticipations, as that they might be an angel who would announce to them the resurrection of their deceased master? It has been thought in another quarter quite superfluous here to advance so many ingenious conjectures as to what the angels may have been, since, among the four narratives, two expressly tell us what they were : namely, natural men, Mark calling his angel

[23] Schuster, in Eichhorn's allg. Biblioth. 9, s. 1034 ff. : Kuinöl, in Matth., p. 779.
[24] Friedrich, über die Engel in der Auferstehungsgeschichte. In Eichhorn's allg. Bibl. 6, s. 700 ff. Kuinöl, ut sup.
[25] Thus a treatise in Eichhorn's allg. Bibl. 8, s. 629 ff., and in Schmidt's Bibl. 2, s. 545 f. ; also Bauer, hebr. Myth. 5, s. 259.

a *young man*, νεανίσκον, Luke his two angels, *two men*, ἄνδρας δύο.[26] Whom then are we to suppose these men to have been? Here again the door is opened for the supposition of secret colleagues of Jesus, who must have been unknown even to the two disciples :—these men seen at the grave may have been the same who met him in the so-called Transfiguration, perhaps Essenes, white being worn by this sect,—or whatever else of the like conjectures the antiquated pragmatism of a Bahrdt or Venturini has to offer. Or will it rather be chosen to suppose a purely accidental meeting? or, lastly, with Paulus, to leave the matter in an obscurity, from the midst of which, so soon as it is endeavoured to clear it up by definite thoughts, the two forms of the secret colleagues invariably present themselves? A correct discernment will here also rather recognize the forms of the Jewish popular conception, by which the primitive Christian tradition held it necessary to glorify the resurrection of its Messiah : a recognition, which at once solves in the most simple manner the differences in the number and modes of appearance of those celestial beings.[27]

Herewith, however, it is at the same time acknowledged that we can succeed no better with the plan of selection than with that of incorporation ; but must rather confess, that in all the evangelical accounts of these first tidings of the resurrection, we have before us nothing more than traditional reports.[28]

§ 138.

APPEARANCES OF THE RISEN JESUS IN GALILEE AND IN JUDEA, INCLUDING THOSE MENTIONED BY PAUL AND BY APOCRYPHAL WRITINGS.

The most important of all the differences in the history of the resurrection turns upon the question, what locality did Jesus design to be the chief theatre of his appearances after the resurrection? The two first gospels make Jesus, before his death, when retiring to the Mount of Olives, utter this promise to his disciples : *After I am risen again I will go before you into Galilee* (Matt. xxvi. 32 ; Mark xiv. 28) ; the same assurance is given to the women by the angels on the morning of the resurrection, with the addition : *there shall ye see him* (Matt. xxviii. 7 ; Mark xvi. 7); and in Matthew, besides all this, Jesus in his own person commissions the women to say to the disciples : *that they go into Galilee, and there shall they see me* (xxviii. 10). In Matthew the journey of the disciples into Galilee, with the appearance of Jesus which they there witnessed (the only one to the disciples recorded by this Evangelist), is actually narrated in the sequel. Mark, after describing the amazement into which the women were thrown by the angelic appearance, breaks off in the enigmatical manner already mentioned, and appends some appearances of Jesus, which,—as the first happens immediately after the resurrection, and therefore necessarily in Jerusalem, and no change of place is mentioned before the succeeding ones, while the earlier direction to go into Galilee is lost sight of,—must all be regarded as appearances in and around Jerusalem. John knows nothing of a direction to the disciples to go into Galilee, and makes Jesus show himself to

---

[26] Paulus, exeg. Handb. 3, b, s. 829, 55, 60, 62.

[27] Fritzsche, in Marc. in loc., *Nemo—quispiam primi temporis Christianis tam dignus videri poterat, qui de Messia in vitam reverso nuntium ad homines perferret, quam angelus, Dei minister, divinorumque consiliorum interpres et adjutor.* Then on the differences in relation to the number of the angels, etc. : *Nimirum insperato Jesu Messiæ in vitam reditui miracula adjecere alii alia, quæ Evangelistæ religiose, quemadmodum ab suis auctoribus acceperant, literis mandârunt.*

[28] Kaiser, bibl. Theol. 1, s. 254 ff.

the disciples on the evening of the day of resurrection, and again eight days after, in Jerusalem; the concluding chapter, however, which forms an appendix to his gospel, describes an appearance by the Sea of Galilee. In Luke, on the other hand, not only is there no trace of an appearance in Galilee, Jerusalem with its environs being made the sole theatre of the appearances of Christ which this gospel relates; but there is also put into the mouth of Jesus when, on the evening after the resurrection, he appears to the assembled disciples in Jerusalem, the injunction : *tarry ye in the city of Jerusalem* (in the Acts i. 4, more definitely expressed by the negative, *that they should not depart from Jerusalem*), *until ye be endued with power from on high* (xxiv. 49). Here two questions inevitably arise : 1st, how can Jesus have directed the disciples to journey into Galilee, and yet at the same time have commanded them to remain in Jerusalem until Pentecost? and 2ndly, how could he refer them to a promised appearance in Galilee, when he had the intention of showing himself to them that very day in and near Jerusalem?

The first contradiction which presents itself more immediately between Matthew and Luke, has by no one been more pointedly exhibited than by the Wolfenbüttel Fragmentist. If, he writes, it be true, as Luke says, that Jesus appeared to his disciples in Jerusalem on the day of his resurrection, and commanded them to remain there, and not to depart thence until Pentecost : then is it false that he commanded them within the same period to journey into Galilee, that he might appear to them there, and vice versâ.[1] The harmonists indeed affected to regard this objection as unimportant, and only remarked briefly, that the injunction to remain in a city was not equivalent to an arrest, and did not exclude walks and excursions in the neighbourhood; and that Jesus merely forbade the removal of residence from Jerusalem, and the going out into all the world to preach the gospel, before the given term should arrive.[2] But the journey from Jerusalem to Galilee is not a mere walk, but the longest expedition which the Jew could make within the limits of his own country ; as little was it an excursion for the apostles, but rather a return to their home : while what Jesus intended to prohibit to the disciples in that injunction cannot have been the going out into all the world to preach the gospel, since they would have no impulse to do this before the outpouring of the Spirit ; nor can it have been the removal of residence from Jerusalem, since they were there only as strangers visiting at the feast : rather Jesus must have meant to deter them from that very journey which it was the most natural for them to take, i.e. from the return to their native province Galilee, after the expiration of the feast days. Besides this—and even Michaelis confesses himself obliged to wonder here—if Luke does not mean by that prohibition of Jesus to exclude the journey into Galilee, why is it that he alludes to this by no single word? and in like manner, if Matthew knew that his direction to go into Galilee was consistent with the command to remain in the metropolis, why has he omitted the latter, together with the appearances in Jerusalem? This is certainly a plain proof that the accounts of the two Evangelists are based on a different idea as to the theatre on which the risen Jesus appeared.

In this exigency of having to reconcile two contradictory commands given on the same day, the comparison with the Acts presented a welcome help by indicating a distinction of the times. Here, namely, the command of Jesus that the disciples should not leave Jerusalem is placed in his last appearance, forty days after the resurrection, and immediately before the ascension : at

[1] In Lessing's Beiträgen, ut sup. s. 485.
[2] Michaelis, s. 259 f. ; Kuinöl, in Luc., p. 743.

the close of the gospel of Luke it is likewise in the last interview, terminating in the ascension, that the above command is given.   Now though from the summary representation of the gospel taken by itself, it must be believed that all occurred on the very day of the resurrection : we nevertheless see, it is said, from the history of the Acts by the same author, that between v. 43 and 44 in the last chapter of his gospel we must interpose the forty days from the resurrection to the ascension.   Herewith, then, the apparent contradiction between these two commands vanishes : for one who in the first instance indeed enjoins a journey into Galilee, may very well forty days later, after this journey has been made, and the parties are once more in the metropolis, now forbid any further removal from thence.[3]   But as the dread of admitting a contradiction between different New Testament authors is no ground for departing from the natural interpretation of their expressions : so neither can this be justified by the apprehension that the same author may in different writings contradict himself ; since if the one were written somewhat later than the other, the author may in the interim have been on many points otherwise informed, than when he composed his first work.   That this was actually the case with Luke in relation to that part of the life of Jesus which followed his resurrection, we shall have reason to be convinced when we come to the history of the ascension : and this conclusion removes all ground for interposing nearly five weeks between the ἔφαγεν, v. 43, and εἶπε δὲ, v. 44, in defiance of their obviously immediate connexion ; at the same time, however, it does away with the possibility of reconciling the opposite commands of Jesus in Matthew and Luke by a distinction of times.

Meanwhile, even admitting that this contradiction might be in some way or other removed, still, even without that express command which Luke mentions, the mere facts as narrated by him and his predecessor and successor, remain irreconcilable with the injunction which Jesus gives to the disciples in Matthew.   For, asks the Fragmentist, if the disciples collectively twice saw him, spoke with him, touched him, and ate with him, in Jerusalem ; how can it be that they must have had to take the long journey into Galilee in order to see him?[4]   The harmonists, it is true, boldly reply : when Jesus causes his disciples to be told that they will see him in Galilee, it is by no means said that they will see him nowhere else, still less that they will not see him in Jerusalem.[5]   But, the Fragmentist might rejoin, after his manner : as little as one who says to me, go to Rome, there you shall see the Pope, can mean that the Pope will indeed first come through my present place of residence, so as to be seen by me here, but afterwards I must yet go to Rome, in order to see him again there : so little would the angel in Matthew and Mark, if he had had any anticipation of the appearance in Jerusalem on the very same day, have said to the disciples : go into Galilee, there will Jesus show himself to you ; but rather : be comforted, you shall yet see him here in Jerusalem before evening.   Wherefore the reference to the more remote event, when there was one of the same kind close at hand? wherefore an appointment by means of the women, for the disciples to meet Jesus in Galilee, if the latter foresaw that he should on the same day personally speak with the disciples?   With reason does the latest criticism insist on what Lessing had previously urged ;[6] namely, that no rational person would make an appointment with his friends through a third party for a joyful reunion at a distant place, if he were certain of seeing

---

[3] Schleiermacher, über den Lukas, s. 299 f. ; Paulus, s. 910.
[4] Ut sup. s. 486.
[5] Griesbach, Vorlesungen über Hermeneutik des N. T., mit Anwendung auf die Leidens und Auferstehungsgeschichte Christi, herausgegeben von Steiner, s. 314.
[6] Duplik, Werke, 6 Bd. s. 352.

them repeatedly on the same day in their present locality.[7] If thus the angel and Jesus himself, when they in the morning by means of the women directed the disciples to go into Galilee, cannot yet have known that he would show himself to them on the evening of the same day in and near Jerusalem: he must in the morning have still held the intention of going immediately into Galilee, but in the course of the day have embraced another purpose. According to Paulus,[8] an indication of such an original intention is found in Luke, in the travelling of Jesus towards Emmaus, which lay in the direction of Galilee; while the reason for the alteration of plan is supposed by the same expositor, with whom in this instance Olshausen agrees,[9] to have been the belief of the disciples, as more particularly manifested to Jesus on occasion of the journey to Emmaus. How so erroneous a calculation on the part of Jesus can consist with the orthodox view of his person, is Olshausen's care; but even regarding him in a purely human character, there appears no sufficient reason for such a change of mind. Especially after Jesus had been recognised by the two disciples going to Emmaus, he might be certain that the testimony of the men would so accredit the assertion of the women, as to lead the disciples with at least a glimmering ray of faith and hope into Galilee. But in general, if a change of mind and a diversity of plan in Jesus before and after that change, really existed: why does no one Evangelist take any notice of such a retractation? Why does Luke speak as if he knew nothing of the original plan; Matthew, as if he knew nothing of a subsequent alteration; John, as if the principal theatre of the appearances of the risen Jesus had been Jerusalem, and he had only by way of supplement at length showed himself in Galilee? Lastly, why does Mark speak so as to make it evident that, having gathered the original direction to go into Galilee from Matthew, and the succeeding appearances in Jerusalem and its environs from Luke or elsewhere, he was unable, nor did he even make the attempt, in any way to reconcile them; but placed them together as he found them, rough hewn and contradictory.

According to this we must agree with the latest criticism of the gospel of Matthew, in acknowledging the contradiction between it and the rest in relation to the locality of the appearances of Jesus after the resurrection: but, it must be asked, can we also approve the verdict of this criticism when it at once renounces the representation of the first gospel in favour of that of the other Evangelists.[10] If, setting aside all presuppositions as to the apostolic origin of this or that gospel, we put the question: which of the two divergent accounts is the best adapted to be regarded as a traditional modification and development of the other? we can here refer, not merely to the general nature of the accounts, but also to a single point at which the two touch each other in a characteristic manner. This is the address of the angel to the women, in which according to all the synoptists Galilee is mentioned, but in a different way. In Matthew the angel, as has been already noticed, says of Jesus: *he goeth before you into Galilee,—lo, I have told you* (xxviii. 7), προάγει ὑμᾶς εἰς τὴν Γαλιλαίαν—ἰδοὺ εἶπον ὑμῖν. In Mark he says the same, except that instead of the latter addition, by which in Matthew the angel seeks to impress his own words on the women, he has the expression: *as he said unto you*, καθὼς εἶπεν ὑμῖν, with which he refers to the earlier prediction of Jesus concerning this circumstance. If we first compare these two representations: the confirmatory *I have told you*, εἶπον ὑμῖν, might easily appear superfluous

[7] Schneckenburger, über den Urspr. des ersten kanon. Evang., s. 17 f.
[8] Exeg. Handb. 3, b. s. 835.
[9] Bibl. Comm. 2, s. 524.
[10] This is done by Schulz, über das Abendm. s. 321; Schneckenburger, ut sup.

and nugatory; while on the other hand the reference to the earlier prediction of Jesus by *he said*, εἶπεν, might seem more appropriate, and on this
the conjecture might be founded that perhaps Mark has here the correct and
original phrase, Matthew a variation not unaccompanied by a misunderstanding.[11] But if we include the account of Luke in the comparison, we find here,
as in Mark, the words : *remember how he spake unto you when he was yet in
Galilee*, μνήσθητε, ὡς ἐλάλησεν ὑμῖν ἔτι ὢν ἐν τῇ Γαλιλαίᾳ, a reference to an
earlier prediction of Jesus, not however referring to Galilee, but delivered in
Galilee. Here the question occurs : is it more probable that Galilee, from
being the designation of the locality in which the prophecy of the resurrection
was uttered, should at a later period be erroneously converted into a designation of the locality where the risen one would appear; or the contrary ? In
order to decide this, we must ascertain in which of the two positions the mention of Galilee is the more intrinsically suited to the context. Now that on
the announcement of the resurrection it was an important point whether and
where the risen Jesus was to be seen, is self-evident; it was of less moment,
in referring to an earlier prediction, to specify where this prediction was
uttered. Hence from this comparison of the passages it might already be
held more probable that it was originally said, the angels directed the disciples to go into Galilee, there to see the risen one (Matt.) ; but afterwards,
when the narratives of the appearances of Jesus in Judea had gradually supplanted those in Galilee, a different turn was given to the mention of Galilee
in the address of the angel, so as to make it imply that already in Galilee
Jesus had predicted his resurrection (Luke) ; whereupon Mark appears to
have taken a middle course, since he with Luke refers the εἶπον (changed into
εἶπεν) to Jesus, but with Matthew retains Galilee as the theatre, not of the
earlier prediction of Jesus, but of the coming appearance.

If we next take into consideration the general character of the two narratives and the nature of the case, there exist the same objections to the
supposition that Jesus after his resurrection appeared several times to his
disciples in and near Jerusalem, but that the remembrance of this fact was
lost, and the same arguments in favour of the opposite supposition, as we
have respectively applied to the analogous alternatives in relation to the
various journeys to the feasts and Judæan residences of Jesus.[12] That the
appearances of the risen Jesus in Jerusalem should undesignedly, that is, by
a total obliteration of them from the minds of individuals, have sunk into
oblivion in Galilee, where according to this presupposition the tradition of
Matthew was formed, is difficult to conceive, both from the pre-eminent importance of these appearances, which, as for example those before the assembled eleven and before Thomas, involved the surest attestations of the reality
of his resurrection, and also from the organizing influence of the community
in Jerusalem ; while that the Judæan appearances of Jesus were indeed known
in Galilee, but intentionally suppressed by the author of the first gospel, in
order to preserve the honour for his province alone, would presuppose an
exclusivism, an opposition of the Galilean Christians to the church at Jerusalem, of which we have not the slightest historical trace. The other contrary
possibility, that perhaps originally only Galilean appearances of the risen
Jesus were known, but that tradition gradually added appearances in Judea
and Jerusalem, and that at length these completely supplanted the former,
may on many grounds be heightened into a probability. First, as respects

---

[11] On which account Michaelis, s. 118 f., is of opinion that εἶπεν was the original reading
in Matthew also. Comp. Weisse, die Evang. Gesch. 2, s. 347 f.
[12] Vol. I. § 57.

the time, the tidings of the resurrection of Jesus were the more striking, the more immediately his appearances followed on his burial and resurrection : if however he first appeared in Galilee, such an immediate sequence of the events could not exist ; further, it was a natural idea that the resurrection of Jesus must have been attested by appearances in the place where he died ; lastly, the objection that Jesus after his pretended resurrection only appeared to his own friends, and in a corner of Galilee, was in some degree repelled when it could be alleged that on the contrary, he walked as one arisen from the dead in the metropolis, in the midst of his furious enemies, though indeed he was neither to be taken nor seen by them. But when once several appearances of Jesus were laid in Judea and Jerusalem, the appearances in Galilee lost their importance, and might thenceforth either be appended in a subordinate position, as in the fourth gospel, or even be entirely overlooked, as in the third. This result, drawn from the possible mode of legendary formation, not being opposed, as in the inquiry concerning the theatre of the ministry of the living Jesus, by a contrary one drawn from the circumstances and designs of Jesus : we may, in contradiction to the criticism of the day. decide in favour of the first gospel, whose account of the appearance of the risen Jesus recommends itself as the more simple and free from difficulty.[13]

As regards the appearances of the risen Jesus taken singly, the first gospel has two : one on the morning of the resurrection to the women (xxviii. 9 f.), and one, the time of which is undetermined, before the disciples in Galilee (xxviii. 16 f.). Mark, in what is indeed a merely summary statement, enumerates three : the first, to Mary Magdalene on the morning of the resurrection (xvi. 9 f.); a second, to two disciples going into the country (xvi. 12) ; and a third, to the eleven as they sat at meat, doubtless in Jerusalem (xvi. 14). Luke narrates only two appearances : that before the disciples going to Emmaus on the day of the resurrection (xxiv. 13 ff.), and the last, before the eleven and other disciples in Jerusalem, according to xxiv. 36 ff., on the evening of the same day, according to the Acts i. 4 ff. forty days later ; but when the travellers to Emmaus, on rejoining the apostles, are greeted by them, before Jesus has appeared in the midst of them, with the information : *the Lord is risen indeed, and hath appeared to Simon* (xxiv. 34) : here a third appearance is presupposed, which was granted to Peter alone. John has four such appearances : the first, to Mary Magdelene at the grave (xx. 14 ff.) ; the second to the disciples when the doors were shut (xx. 19 ff.) ; the third, likewise in Jerusalem, eight days later, when Thomas was convinced (xx. 26 ff.) ; the fourth, of which the time is unspecified, at the Galilean sea (xxi.). But here we have also to take into consideration a statement of the Apostle Paul, who 1 Cor. xv. 5 ff., if we deduct the appearance of Christ granted to himself, enumerates five appearances after the resurrection, without however giving any precise description of them : one to Cephas ; one to the twelve ; one before more than five hundred brethren at once ; one to James ; and lastly, one before all the apostles.

Now how shall we make an orderly arrangement of these various appearances ? The right of priority is, in John, and still more expressly in Mark, claimed for that to Mary Magdalene. The second must have been the meeting of Jesus with the women returning from the grave, in Matthew ; but as Mary Magdalene was likewise among these, and there is no indication that she had previously seen Jesus, these two appearances cannot be regarded as

---

[13] The opinion that the true locality of the appearances of the risen Jesus before the disciples was Galilee, is concurred in by Weisse, 2, s. 358 ff. ; but in accordance with his fundamental supposition concerning the synoptical gospels, he gives the preference to the narrative of Mark before that of Matthew.

distinct, but rather as one under two different garbs. Paul, who in the above named passage speaks as if he meant to enumerate all the appearances of the resuscitated Christ, of which he knew, omits the one in question ; but it may perhaps be said in explanation of this, that he did not choose to adduce the testimony of women. As the order in which he enumerates his Christophanies, to judge from the succession of εἶτα and ἔπειτα and the conclusion with ἔσχατον, appears to be the order of time : [14] according to him the appear ance before Cephas was the first that happened before a man. This would agree well with the representation of Luke, in which the journeyers to Emmaus, on rejoining the disciples in Jerusalem, are met by them with the information that Jesus is really arisen and has appeared to Simon, which might possibly be the case before his interview with those two disciples. As the next appearance, however, according to Luke, we must number that last named, which Paul would not mention, perhaps because he chose to adduce ¢ nly those which were seen by apostles, and from among the rest only those which happened before great masses of witnesses, or more probably, because it was unknown to him. Mark xvi. 12 f. evidently refers to the same appearance ; the contradiction, that while in Luke the assembled disciples meet those coming from Emmaus with the believing exclamation : *the Lord is risen*, etc., in Mark the disciples are said to have remained incredulous even to the account of those two witnesses, probably proceeds from nothing more than an exaggeration of Mark, who will not lose his hold of the contrast between the most convincing appearances of Jesus and the obstinate unbelief of the disciples. The appearance on the way to Emmaus is in Luke immediately followed by that in the assembly of the *eleven* and others. This is generally held to be identical with the appearance before the *twelve* mentioned by Paul, and with that which John narrates when Jesus on the evening after the resurrection entered while the doors were closed among the disciples, out of whose number, however, Thomas was wanting. It is not fair to urge in opposition to this identification the *eleven* of Luke, as at variance with the statement of John that only ten apostles were present, any more than the *twelve* of Paul, from which number Judas at least must be deducted ; moreover the similar manner in which the two Evangelists describe the entrance of Jesus by ἔστη ἐν μέσῳ αὐτῶν and ἔστη εἰς τὸ μέσον, and the greeting cited in both instances : εἰρήνη ὑμῖν, appear to indicate the identity of the two appearances ; nevertheless, if we consider that the handling of the body of Jesus, which in John first happens eight days later, and the eating of the broiled fish, which John assigns to the still later appearance in Galilee, are connected by Luke with that scene in Jerusalem on the day of the resurrection : it is evident that either the third Evangelist has here compressed several incidents into one, or the fourth has divided one into several—whichever alternative may be chosen. This appearance before the apostles in Jerusalem however, as has been above remarked, according to Matthew could not have happened, since this Evangelist makes the *eleven* journey to Galilee in order to see Jesus. Mark, and Luke in his gospel, annex the ascension to this appearance, and thus exclude all subsequent ones. As the next appearance, the apostle Paul has that before five hundred brethren, which is generally regarded as the same with the one which Matthew places on a mountain in Galilee : [15] but at this only the eleven are stated to have been present, and moreover the discourse of Jesus on the occasion, consisting principally of official instructions, appears more suited to this narrow circle. Paul next adduces an appearance to James, of which there is also an

---

[14] Vid Billroth's Commentar, in loc.
[15] Paulus, exeg. Handb. 3, b. s. 897 ; Olshausen, 2, s. 541.

apocryphal account, in the Hebrew gospel of Jerome, according to which however it must have been the first of all.[16] Here there would be space for that appearance in which, according to the fourth gospel eight days after the resurrection of Jesus, Thomas was convinced; wherewith Paul would closely agree, if his expression, *to all the apostles*, τοῖς ἀποστόλοις πᾶσιν (v. 7), which he uses in relation to this appearance, were really to be understood of a full assembly of the eleven in distinction from the earlier one, when Thomas was not present: which however, as Paul, according to the above presupposition, had described this also as an appearance before *the twelve*, is impossible; on the contrary, the apostle intends as well by the δώδεκα, *twelve*, as by οἱ ἀπόστολοι πάντες, *all the apostles*, the collective body of apostles (whose proper number was then indeed incomplete by one man), in opposition to the individuals (Cephas and James) of whom in each case he had just before spoken, as having witnessed a Christophany. If however we were nevertheless to regard the fifth appearance of Jesus according to Paul as identical with the third in John: it would only be the more clearly evident that the fourth of Paul, before the five hundred brethren, cannot have been the one in Galilee recorded by Matthew. For as, in John, the third took place in Jerusalem, the fourth in Galilee: Jesus and the apostles must in that case have gone into Galilee after the first appearances in Jerusalem, and have met on the mountain; then have returned to Jerusalem where Jesus showed himself to Thomas; then again have proceeded into Galilee where the appearance by the sea occurred; and lastly, have once more returned to Jerusalem for the ascension. In order to avoid this useless journeying backwards and forwards, and yet to be able to combine those two appearances, Olshausen lays the appearance before Thomas in Galilee: an inadmissible violence, since not only is there no mention of a change of place between this and the foregoing, which is by implication represented as happening in Jerusalem, but the place of assembly is in both instances described in the same manner; nay the addition, *the doors being shut*, will not allow the supposition of any other locality than Jerusalem, because in Galilee, where there was less excitement against Jesus from the enmity of the priesthood, there cannot be supposed to have been the same reason for that precaution, in *the fear of the Jews*. Thus, first where the Judean appearances close with that happening eight days after the resurrection, we should obtain room to insert the Galilean appearances of Matthew and John. But these have the peculiar position, that each claims to be the first, and that of Matthew at the same time the last.[17] By the tenor of his whole narrative, and expressly by adding, after the statement that the disciples went to a mountain in Galilee, the words: *where Jesus had appointed them*, οὗ ἐτάξατο αὐτοῖς ὁ Ἰ., Matthew marks this appearance as the one to which Jesus had referred on the morning of the resurrection, first by the angel, and then in his own person; but no one concerts a second meeting in a particular place, leaving the first undetermined: consequently, as an unforeseen earlier meeting is incompatible with the evan-

---

[16] Hieron. de viris illustr. ii. : *Evangelium quoque, quod appellatur secundum Hebræos,—post resurrectionem Salvatoris refert: Dominus autem, postquam dedisset sindonem servo sacerdotis* (apparently in relation to the watch at the grave, which is here represented as a sacerdotal instead of a Roman guard; vid. Credner, Beiträge zur Einl. in das N. T. s. 406 f.), *ivit ad Jacobum et apparuit ei. Juraverat enim Jacobus, se non comesturum panem ab illa hora, qua biberat calicem Domini, donec videret eum resurgentem a dormientibus* (on the inconceivableness of such a vow, despairing as the disciples were, comp. Michaelis, s. 122): *Rursusque post paululum: Afferte, ait Dominus, mensam et panem. Statimque additur: Tulit panem et benedixit ac fregit, et dedit Jacobo justo et dixit ei: frater mi, comede panem tuum, quia resurrexit filius hominis a dormientibus.*
[17] Lessing, Duplik, s. 449 ff.

gelical idea of Jesus,[18] that meeting, since it was the concerted one, was also the first in Galilee. If thus the appearance at the sea of Tiberias in John, cannot possibly be placed before that on the mountain in Matthew : so the latter will just as little suffer the other to follow it, since it is a formal leave-taking of Jesus from his disciples. Moreover, it would be more than ever difficult to understand how the appearance in John could be made out, in accordance with the Evangelist's own statement, to be the third φανέρωσις of the risen Christ before his disciples (xxi. 14), if that of the first gospel must also be supposed to precede it. Meanwhile, even allowing the priority to the former, this numerical notice of John remains sufficiently perplexing. We might, it is true, deduct the appearances before the women, because, though John himself narrates that to Mary Magdalene, he does not take it into his account ; but if we number that to Cephas as the first, and that on the way to Emmaus as the second : then this Galilean appearance, as the third, would fall between the above and that before the eleven on the evening of the resurrection, which would presuppose a rapidity of locomotion totally impossible ; nay, if that appearance before the assembled eleven is the same with the one at which, according to John, Thomas was absent, the third appearance of John would fall before his first. Perhaps, however, when we consider the expression : *showed himself to his disciples,* ἐφανερώθη τοῖς μαθηταῖς αὐτοῦ, we ought to understand that John only numbers such appearances as happened before several disciples at once, so that those before Peter and James should be deducted. In that case, we must number as the first, the appearance to the two disciples going to Emmaus ; as the second, that before the assembled eleven on the evening of the resurrection : and thus in the eight days between this and the one before Thomas, the journey into Galilee would fall somewhat more conveniently,—but also the third appearance of John would fall before his second. Perhaps, then, the author of the fourth gospel held the two disciples whom Jesus met on the way to Emmaus too small a number, to entitle this Christophany to rank as a φανεροῦσθαι τοῖς μαθηταῖς. On this supposition the entrance of Jesus among the assembled disciples in the evening would be the first appearance ; hereupon the five hundred brethren to whom Jesus showed himself at once would surely be numerous enough to be taken into the reckoning : so that the Galilean appearance of John, that is, his third, must be inserted after this, but then it would still fall before that to Thomas and *all the apostles,* which John enumerates as the second. Perhaps, however, the appearance of Jesus before the five hundred is to be placed later, so that after that entrance of Jesus among the assembled disciples would first follow the scene with Thomas, after this the appearance at the sea of Galilee, and only then the sight of Jesus granted to the five hundred. But if the appearance before Thomas is to be reckoned the same with the fifth in Paul's enumeration, this apostle must have reversed the order of his two last appearances, a transposition for which there was no reason : on the contrary, it would have been more natural to place last the appearance before the five hundred brethren, as the most important. Thus nothing remains but to say : John understood under the word μαθηταῖς merely a greater or a smaller assembly of the apostles ; but among the five hundred there was no apostle ; hence he omitted these also, and thus correctly numbered the appearance at the sea of Tiberias as the third : if indeed this could have happened before the one on the mountain in Galilee, which, we have seen, to be inconceivable. The above expedients resorted to by way of accommodation are in part ridiculous enough : but Kern has lately surpassed them all by a suggestion which he advances with great

[18] As Kern admits, Hauptthats. Tüb. Zeitschr. 1836, 3, s. 57.

confidence, namely, that John here intends to number, not the appearances, but the days on which appearances took place, so that τοῦτο ἤδη τρίτον ἐφανερώθη ὁ Ἰ. τοῖς μαθηταῖς, *this is now the third time that Jesus showed himself to the disciples*, means : now had Jesus already appeared to his disciples on three separate days : namely, four times on the day of the resurrection ; then once eight days after ; and now again some days later.[19] Renouncing such expedients, nothing remains but to acknowledge that the fourth Evangelist numbers only those appearances of Jesus to his disciples, which he had himself narrated ; and the reason of this can scarcely have been that the rest, from some cause or other, appeared to him less important, but rather that he knew nothing of them.[20] And again, Matthew with his last Galilean appearance, can have known nothing of the two in Jerusalem recorded by John ; for if in the first of these ten apostles had been convinced of the reality of the resurrection of Jesus, and in the second Thomas also : it could not have been that at that later appearance on the mountain in Galilee some of the eleven (for only these are represented by Matthew as going thither) still doubted (οἱ δὲ ἐδίστασαν, v. 17). Lastly, if Jesus here delivered to his disciples the final command to go into all the world teaching and baptizing, and gave them the promise to be with them until the end of the existing age, which is manifestly the tone of one who is taking leave : he cannot subsequently, as is narrated in the introduction to the Acts, have communicated to them his last commands and taken leave of them at Jerusalem. According to the conclusion of the gospel of Luke, this farewell departure on the contrary occurs much earlier than can be supposed in accordance with Matthew ; and in the close of the gospel of Mark, where Jesus is represented as parting from his disciples in Jerusalem on the very day of his resurrection, partly the same words are put into his mouth as, according to Matthew, are spoken in Galilee, and in any case later than on the day of the resurrection. The fact, that the two books of the same author, Luke, diverge so widely from each other in relation to the time during which Jesus appeared to his disciples after his resurrection, that one determines this time to have been a single day, the other, forty days, cannot be taken into more particular consideration until we have reached a farther point of our inquiry.

Thus the various evangelical writers only agree as to a few of the appearances of Jesus after his resurrection ; the designation of the locality in one excludes the appearances narrated by the rest ; the determination of time in another leaves no space for the narratives of his fellow Evangelists ; the enumeration of a third is given without any regard to the events reported by his predecessors ; lastly, among several appearances recounted by various narrators, each claims to be the last, and yet has nothing in common with the others. Hence nothing but wilful blindness can prevent the perception that no one of the narrators knew and presupposed what another records ; that each again had heard a different account of the matter ; and that consequently at an early period, there were current only uncertain and very varied reports concerning the appearances of the risen Jesus.[21]

This conclusion, however, does not shake the passage in the first Epistle to the Corinthians which, (it being undoubtedly genuine,) was written about the year 59 after Christ, consequently not 30 years after his resurrection. On this authority we must believe that many members of the primitive church

---

[19] Hauptthatsachen, ut sup. s. 47.

[20] Comp. De Wette, exeg. Handb. 1, 3, s. 205, 210 ; Weisse, die evang. Gesch. 2, s. 409.

[21] Comp. Kaiser, bidl. Theol. 1, s. 254 ff. ; De Wette ut sup. ; Ammon, Fortbildung, 2, 1, Kap. 1 ; Weisse, die Evang. Gesch., 2, 7 tes Buch.

who were yet living at the time when this epistle was written, especially the apostles, were convinced that they had witnessed appearances of the risen Christ. Whether this involves the admission that some objective reality lay at the foundation of these appearances, will hereafter become the subject of inquiry ; concerning the present point, the divergencies of the Evangelists, especially in relation to the locality, the passage of Paul offers nothing decisive, since he has given no particular description of any of those appearances.

§ 139.

QUALITY OF THE BODY AND LIFE OF JESUS AFTER THE RESURRECTION.

But how are we to represent to ourselves this continuation of the life of Jesus after the resurrection, and especially the nature of his body in this period ? In order to answer this question we must once more cast a glance over the separate narratives of his appearances when risen.

According to Matthew, Jesus on the morning of the resurrection meets (ἀπήντησεν) the women as they are hastening back from the grave ; they recognize him, embrace his feet in sign of veneration, and he speaks to them. At the second interview on the Galilean mountain the disciples see him (ἰδόντες), but some still doubt, and here also Jesus speaks to them. Of the manner in which he came and went, we have here no precise information.

In Luke, Jesus joins the two disciples who are on their way from Jerusalem to the neighbouring village of Emmaus (ἐγγίσας συνεπορεύετο αὐτοῖς) ; they do not recognize him on the way, a circumstance which Luke attributes to a subjective hindrance produced in them by a higher influence (οἱ ὀφθαλμοὶ αὐτῶν ἐκρατοῦντο, τοῦ μὴ ἐπιγνῶναι αὐτὸν), and only Mark, who compresses this event into few words, to an objective alteration of his form (ἐν ἑτέρᾳ μορφῇ). On the way Jesus converses with the two disciples, after their arrival in the village complies with their invitation to accompany them to their lodging, sits down to table with them, and proceeds according to his wont to break and distribute bread. In this moment the miraculous spell is withdrawn from the eyes of the disciples, and they know him : [1] but in the same moment he becomes invisible to them (ἄφαντος ἐγένετο ἀπ' αὐτῶν). Just as suddenly as he here vanished, he appears to have shown himself immediately after in the assembly of the disciples, when it is said that he all at once stood in the midst of them (ἔστη ἐν μέσῳ αὐτῶν), and they, terrified at the sight, supposed that they saw a spirit. To dispel this alarming idea, Jesus showed them his hands and feet, and invited them to touch him, that by feeling his *flesh and bones* then might convince themselves that he was no spectre ; he also caused a piece of broiled fish and of honeycomb to be brought to him, and ate it in their presence. The appearance to Simon is in Luke described by the expression ὤφθη ; Paul in the first Epistle to the Corinthians uses the same verb for all the Christophanies there enumerated, and Luke in the Acts comprises all the appearances of the risen Jesus during the forty days under the expressions ὀπτανόμενος (i. 3) and ἐμφανῆ γενέσθαι (x. 40). In the same manner Mark describes the appearance to Mary Magdalene by ἐφάνη, and those to the disciples on the way to Emmaus and to the eleven by ἐφανερώθη. John describes the appearance at the sea of Tiberias by ἐφανέρωσεν ἑαυτὸν, and to all the Christophanies narrated by him he applies the word ἐφανερώθη. Mark and Luke add, as the close of the earthly life of the risen Jesus, that he was

---

[1] That it was the marks of the nails in the hand, which became visible in the act of breaking bread, by which Jesus was recognized (Paulus, exeg. Handb. 3, b. s. 882 ; Kuinol, in Luc. p. 734.) is without any intimation in the text.

taken away from before the eyes of the disciples, and (by a cloud, according to Acts i. 9) carried up to heaven.

In the fourth gospel Jesus first stands behind Mary Magdalene as she is turning away from the grave; she however, does not recognize him even when he speaks to her, but takes him for the gardener, until he (in the tone so familiar to her) calls her by her name. When on this she attempts to manifest her veneration, Jesus prevents her by the words: *Touch me not, μή μου ἄπτου*, and sends her with a message to the disciples. The second appearance of Jesus in John occurred under peculiarly remarkable circumstances. The disciples were assembled, from fear of the hostile Jews, with closed doors: when all at once Jesus came and stood in the midst of them, greeted them, and presented—apparently to their sight only—his hands and feet, that they might recognize him as their crucified master. When Thomas, who was not present, refused to be convinced by the account of his fellow disciples of the reality of this appearance, and required for his satisfaction himself to see and touch the wounds of Jesus: the latter, in an appearance eight days after, granted him this proof, making him touch the marks of the nails in his hands and the wound in his side. Lastly, at the appearance by the sea of Galilee, Jesus stood on the shore in the morning twilight, without being known by the disciples in the ship, asked them for fish, and was at length recognized by John, through the rich draught of fishes which he procured them; still, however, the disciples, when come to land, did not venture to ask him whether it were really he. Hereupon he distributed among them bread and fish, of which he doubtless himself partook, and finally held a conversation with John and Peter.[2]

Now the general ideas which may be formed of the life of Jesus after his resurrection are two: either it was a natural and perfectly human life, and accordingly his body continued to be subject to the physical and organic laws; or his life was already of a higher, superhuman character, and his body supernatural and transfigured: and the accounts, taken unitedly, present certain traits to which, on the first view, each of these two ideas may respectively appeal. The human form with its natural members, the possibility of being known by means of them, the continuance of the marks of the wounds, the human speech, the acts of walking and breaking bread,—all these appear to speak in favour of a perfectly natural life on the part of Jesus even after the

[2] The part of this conversation which relates to John, has already (§ 116) been considered. In that relating to Peter, the thrice repeated question of Jesus: *Lovest thou me?* has reference, according to the ordinary opinion, to his as often repeated denial; but to the words: *When thou wast young, thou girdedst thyself, and walkedst whither thou wouldest, but when thou shalt be old, thou shalt stretch forth thy hands, and another shalt gird thee, and carry thee whither thou wouldest not, ὅτε ἦς νεώτερος, ἐζώννυες σεαυτὸν καὶ περιεπάτεις ὅπου ἤθελες· ὅταν δὲ γηράσῃς, ἐκτενεῖς τὰς χεῖράς σου καὶ ἄλλος σε ζώσει καὶ οἴσει ὅπου οὐ θέλεις* (v. 18 f.), the Evangelist himself gives the interpretation, that Jesus spoke them to Peter, *signifying by what death he should glorify God.* He must here have alluded to the crucifixion, which, according to the ecclesiastical legend (Tertull. de præscr. hær. xxxvi. Euseb. H. E. ii. 25) was the death suffered by this apostle, and to which in the intention of the Evangelist the words *Follow me,* v. 20 and 22 (i.e. follow me in the same mode of death) also appear to point. But precisely the main feature in this interpretation, the stretching forth of the hands, is here so placed as to render a reference to crucifixion impossible, namely, before the leading away against the will; on the other hand, the girding, which can only signify binding for the purpose of leading away, should stand before the stretching forth of the hands on the cross. If we set aside the interpretation which, as even Lücke (s. 703) admits, is given to the words of Jesus *ex eventu* by the narrator: they appear to contain nothing more than the commonplace of the helplessness of age contrasted with the activity of youth, for even the phrase, *shall carry thee whither thou wouldest not,* does not outstep this comparison. But the author of John xxi., whether the words were known to him as a declaration of Jesus or otherwise, thought them capable of being applied in the manner of the fourth gospel, as a latent prophecy of the crucifixion of Peter.

resurrection. If it were possible still to demur to this, and to conjecture, that even a higher, heavenly corporeality might give itself such an aspect and perform such functions : all doubts must be quelled by the further statement, that Jesus after the resurrection consumed earthly food, and allowed himself to be touched. Such things are indeed ascribed even to higher beings in old myths, as for example, eating to the heavenly forms from whom Abraham received a visit (Gen. xviii. 8), and palpability to the God that wrestled with Jacob (Gen. xxxii. 24 ff.) : but it must nevertheless be insisted that in reality both these conditions can only belong to material, organized bodies. Hence not only the rationalists, but even orthodox expositors, consider these particulars as an irrefragable proof that the body and life of Jesus after the resurrection must be regarded as remaining still natural and human.[3] This opinion is further supported by the remark, that in the state of the risen Jesus there is observable precisely the same progress as might be expected in the gradual, natural cure of a person severely wounded. In the first hours after the resurrection he is obliged to remain in the vicinity of the grave ; in the afternoon his strength suffices for a walk to the neighbouring village of Emmaus ; and only later is he able to undertake the more distant journey into Galilee. Then also in the permission to touch his body there exists the remarkable gradation, that on the morning of the resurrection Jesus forbids Mary Magdalene to touch him, because his wounded body was as yet too suffering and sensitive ; but eight days later, he himself invites Thomas to touch his wounds. Even the circumstance that Jesus after his resurrection was so seldom with his disciples and for so short a time, is, according to this ex-planation, a proof that he had brought from the grave his natural, human body, for such an one would necessarily feel so weak from the wounds and torture of the cross, as always after short periods of exertion to require longer inter-vals of quiet retirement.

But the New Testament narratives, as we have seen, also contain particulars which favour the opposite idea of the corporeality of Jesus after the resurrec-tion : hence the advocates of the opinion hitherto detailed must undertake so to interpret these apparently antagonistic features that they may no longer present a contradiction. Here it may seem that the very expressions by which the appearances of Jesus are ordinarily introduced, as ὤφθη, used of the appearance in the burning bush (Exod. iii. 2, LXX.) ; ὀπτανόμενος, of the appearance of the angel in Tobit xii. 19 ; ἐφάνη, of the angelic appearances in Matt. i. and ii., may seem already to point to something supernatural. As still more decided indications, the idea of a natural going and coming which may be presupposed in some scenes, is contradicted in others by a sudden appearance and disappearance ; the supposition of an ordinary human body is opposed by the frequent non-recognition on the part of friends, nay, by the express mention of *another form*, ἑτέρα μορφῇ ; above all, the palpability of the body of Jesus appears to be opposed by the capability which, according to the first impression from the text, is lent to him in John, namely, that of entering through closed doors. But, that Mary Magdalene mistook Jesus at first for the gardener, is thought even by commentators who ordinarily are not diffident of the miraculous, to be most probably accounted for by the supposition that Jesus had borrowed clothes from the gardener, who very likely dwelt near to the grave ; moreover, say these writers, both in this instance and in the journey to Emmaus, the disfiguration of the countenance of Jesus by the sufferings of crucifixion may have contributed to prevent his

---

[3] Paulus, exeg. Handb. 3, b. s. 834 ff. ; L. J. 1, b. s. 265 ff. ; Ammon, ut sup. ; Hase, L. J. § 149; Michaelis, ut sup., s. 251 f. Comp. also Neander, L. J. Chr. s. 650.

being recognized, and these two circumstances are alone to be understood from the expression ἑτέρα μορφῇ, *another form*, in Mark.[4] As to the disciples going to Emmaus, in the joyful astonishment caused by the sudden recognition of him whom they had believed dead, Jesus, it is said, may easily have withdrawn from them unobserved in the most natural manner; which, however, they, to whom the whole fact of the resuscitation of Jesus was a miracle, might regard as a supernatural disappearance.[5] Nor, we are told, do the expressions : ἔστη ἐν μέσῳ αὐτῶν or εἰς τὸ μέσον *he stood in the midst of them,* especially in John, where they are accompanied by the ordinary words ἦλθεν *he came,* and ἔρχεται *he comes,* imply anything supernatural, but merely the startling arrival of one who had just been spoken of, without his being expected ; and the assembled disciples took him for a spirit, not because he entered in a miraculous manner, but because they could not believe in the real resuscitation of their deceased master.[6] Lastly, even the trait which is supposed to be decisive against the opinion that the body of the risen Jesus was a natural and human one,— the coming when the doors were shut ἔρχεσθαι θυρῶν κεκλεισμένων in John,—has long been interpreted even by orthodox theologians so as no longer to present any obstacle to that opinion. We will not discuss explanations such as that of Heumann, according to which the *doors* were not those of the house in which the disciples were assembled, but the doors of Jerusalem in general, and the statement that they were shut is an intimation of its having been that hour of the night in which it was customary to close the doors, while the *fear of the Jews* represents the motive, not for the closing of the doors, but for the assembling of the disciples. Apart from these expedients, Calvin himself pronounces the opinion that the body of the risen Jesus passed *per medium ferrum et asseres,* to be *pueriles argutiæ,* for which the text gives no occasion, since it does not say that Jesus entered *per januas clausas,* but only that he suddenly appeared among his disciples, *cum clausæ essent januæ.*[7] Still Calvin upholds the entrance of Jesus of which John here speaks as a miracle, which must consequently be supposed to consist in this, that Jesus entered *cum fores clausæ fuissent, sed quæ Domino veniente subito patuerunt ad nutum divinæ majestatis ejus.*[8] While more modern orthodox divines only contend for the less definite position, that in the entrance of Jesus some miracle took place, its precise character being unascertained :[9] Rationalism has found means entirely to banish the miraculous from the event. The closed doors, we are told, were opened to Jesus by human hands ; which John omits to notice, only because it is understood as a matter of course, nay, it would have been absurd of him to say : they opened the doors for him, and he went in.[10]

But in thus interpreting the words ἔρχεται τῶν θυρῶν κεκλεισμένων, theologians have been by no means unprejudiced. Least of all Calvin ; for when he says, the papists maintain a real penetration of the body of Jesus through closed doors in order to gain support for their tenet that the body of Christ is immense, and contained in no place, *ut corpus Christi immensum esse, nulloque loco contineri obtineant :* it is plain that he combats that interpretation of the words of John merely to avoid giving any countenance to the offensive

---

[4] Tholuck, in loc., comp. Paulus, exeg. Handb, 3, b. s. 866, 881. A similar natural explanation has lately been adopted by Lücke, from Hug.

[5] Paulus, ut sup. s. 882.

[6] Paulus, ut sup. 883, 93 ; Lücke, 2, s. 684 f.

[7] Calvin, Comm. in Joh. in loc., p. 363 f. ed. Tholuck.

[8] Thus Suicer, Thes. s. v. θύρα.; comp. Michaelis, s. 265.

[9] Tholuck and Olshausen, in loc.

[10] Griesbach, Vorlesungen über Hermeneutik, s. 305 ; Paulus, s. 835. Comp. Lücke, 2, s. 683 ff.

doctrine of the ubiquity of Christ's body. The more modern expositors, on the other hand, were interested in avoiding the contradiction which to our perceptions is contained in the statement, that a body can consist of solid matter, and yet pass without hindrance through other solid matter : but as we know not whether this was also a contradiction in the view of the New Testament writers, the apprehension of it gives us no authority to discard that interpretation, providing it be shown to be in accordance with the text. We might certainly, on a partial consideration, understand the expression *the doors being shut*, τῶν θυρῶν κεκλεισμένων, as an intimation of the anxious state into which the disciples were thrown by the death of Jesus. But already the circumstance that this particular is repeated on the appearance of Jesus before Thomas excites doubts, since if the above was the only meaning, it was scarcely worth while to repeat the observation.[11] But as in fact in this second instance the above cause for the closing of the doors no longer exists, while the words τῶν θυρῶν κεκλεισμένων are immediately united with ἔρχεται, *he comes :* what was before the most apparent meaning, namely, that they are intended to determine the manner of the coming of Jesus, is here heightened into a probability.[12] Further, the repeated statement that Jesus came when the doors were closed is again followed by the words ἔστη εἰς τὸ μέσον, which even in connexion with ἦλθεν, to which they are related as a more precise determination, imply that Jesus suddenly presented himself, without his approach having been seen : whence it is undeniably evident that the writer here speaks of a coming without the ordinary means, consequently, of a miraculous coming. But did this miracle consist in passing through the boards of the doors? This is combated even by those who espouse the cause of miracles in general, and they confidently appeal to the fact, that it is nowhere said, he entered *through* the closed doors διὰ τῶν θυρῶν κεκλεισμένον.[13] But the Evangelist does not mean to convey the precise notion that Jesus, as Michaelis expresses himself, passed straight through the pores of the wood of which the doors were made ; he merely means that the doors were shut and remained so, and nevertheless Jesus suddenly stood in the chamber,—walls, doors, in short all material barriers, forming no obstacle to his entrance. Thus in reply to their unjust demand of us, to show them in the text of John a precise determination which is quite away from the intention of this writer, we must ask them to explain why he has not noticed the (miraculous) opening of the doors, if he presupposed such a circumstance? In relation to this point Calvin very infelicitously refers to Acts xii. 6 ff., where it is narrated of Peter, that he came out of the closed prison ; no one, he says, here supposes that the doors remained closed, and that Peter penetrated through wood and iron. Assuredly not ; because here it is expressly said of the iron gate of the prison which led into the city, that it *opened to him of its own accord* (v. 10). This observation serves to give so lively and graphic an idea of the miracle, that our Evangelist would certainly not, in two instances, have omitted a similar one, if he had thought of a miraculous opening of the doors.

Thus in this narrative of John the supernatural will not admit of being removed or diminished : nor is the natural explanation more satisfactory in relation to the expressions by which Luke describes the coming and going of Jesus. For if, according to this Evangelist, his coming was *a standing in the midst of the disciples*, στῆναι ἐν μέσῳ τῶν μαθητῶν, his going *a becoming invisible to them*, ἄφαντος γίνεσθαι ἀπ᾽ αὐτῶν : the concurrence of these two representa-

---

[11] Vid. Tholuck and De Wette, in loc.
[12] Comp. Olshausen, 2, s. 531, Anm.
[13] Thus, besides Calvin, Lücke, ut sup. ; Olshausen, 530 .

tions, taken in connexion with the terror of the disciples and their mistaking him for a spirit, will hardly allow the supposition of anything else than a miraculous appearance. Besides, if we might perhaps form some idea how Jesus could enter in a natural manner without being observed into a room filled with men : we should still be at a loss to imagine how it could be possible for him, when he sat at table at Emmaus, apparently with the two disciples alone, to withdraw himself from them unobserved, and so that they were not able to follow him.[14]

That Mark, under the words ἑτέρα μορφῇ understands a form miraculously altered, ought never to have been denied ; [15] but this is a point of minor importance, because it involves only the narrator's own interpretation of the circumstance which had been already stated, but with a different explanation, by Luke : namely, that the two disciples did not know Jesus. That ·Mary Magdalene took Jesus for the gardener, was hardly, in the view of the Evangelist, the consequence of his having borrowed the gardener's clothes : rather, the spirit of the narrative would require us to explain her not knowing him by supposing that her eyes were *held* (κρατεῖσθαι, Luke xxiv. 16), or that Jesus had assumed *another form ;* while her taking him for the gardener might then be simply accounted for by the fact that she met the unknown man in the garden. Nor are we authorized by the evangelical narratives to suppose a disfiguration of Jesus by the sufferings of the cross, and a gradual healing of his wounds. The words *Touch me not* in John, if they were to be regarded as a prohibition of a touch as painful, would be in contradiction, not merely with Matthew, according to whom Jesus on the same morning—that of the resurrection—allowed the women to embrace his feet, but also with Luke, according to whom he on the same day invited the disciples to handle him ; and we must then ask, which representation is correct ? But there is nothing at all in the context to intimate that Jesus forbade Mary to touch him for fear of pain ; he may have done so from various motives : concerning which, however, the obscurity of the passage has hitherto precluded any decision.[16]

But the most singularly perverted inference is this : that the infrequent and brief interviews of Jesus with his disciples after the resurrection are a proof that he was as yet too weak for long and multiplied efforts, and consequently was undergoing a natural cure. On this very supposition of his needing bodily tendance, he should have been not seldom, but constantly, with his disciples, who were those from whom he could the most immediately expect such tendance. For where are we to suppose that he dwelt in the long intervals between his appearances ? in solitude ? in the open air ? in the wilderness and on mountains ? That was no suitable abode for an invalid, and nothing remains but to suppose that he must have been concealed among secret colleagues of whom even his disciples knew nothing. But thus to conceal his real abode even from his own disciples, to show himself to them only seldom, and designedly to present and withdraw himself suddenly, would be a kind of double dealing, an affectation of the supernatural, which would exhibit Jesus and his cause in a light foreign to the object itself so far as it lies before us in our original sources of information, and only thrown upon it by the dark lantern of modern, yet already obsolete, conceptions. The

---

[14] Olshausen, ut sup. s. 530.
[15] Comp. Fritzsche, in Marc. p. 725.
[16] See the various explanations in Tholuck and Lücke, of whom the latter finds an alteration of the reading necessary. Even Weisse's interpretation of the words (2, s. 395 ff.), although I agree with the general tenor of the explanation of which it forms a part, I must regard as a failure.

opinion of the Evangelists is no other than that the risen Jesus, after those short appearances among his followers, withdrew like a higher being into invisibility, from which, on fitting occasions, he again stept forth.[17]

Lastly, on the presupposition that Jesus by his resurrection returned to a purely natural existence, what conception must be formed of his end? In consistency he must be supposed, whether at the end of a longer [18] or a shorter time after his resuscitation, to have died a natural death; and accordingly Paulus intimates that the too intensely affected body of Jesus, notwithstanding it had recovered from the death-like rigidity produced by crucifixion, was yet completely worn out by natural maladies and consuming fever.[19] That this is at least not the view of the Evangelists concerning the end of Jesus is evident, since two of them represent him as taking leave of his disciples like an immortal, the others as being visibly carried up to heaven. Thus before the ascension, at the latest, if until then Jesus had retained a natural human body, it must have undergone a change which qualified him to dwell in the heavenly regions; the sediment of gross corporeality must have fallen to the earth, and only its finest essence have ascended. But of any natural remains of the ascended Jesus the Evangelists say nothing; and as the disciples who were spectators of his ascension must have observed them had there been such, nothing is left for the upholders of this opinion but the expedient of certain theologians of the Tübingen school, who regard as the residuum of the corporeality of Jesus, the cloud which enveloped him in his ascension, and in which what was material in him is supposed to have been dissolved and as it were evaporated.[20] As thus the Evangelists neither represent to themselves the end of the earthly life of Jesus after the resurrection as a natural death, nor mention any change undergone by his body at the ascension, and moreover narrate of Jesus in the interval between the resurrection and ascension things which are inconceivable of a natural body: they cannot have represented to themselves his life after the resurrection as natural, but only as supernatural, nor his body as material and organic, but only as transfigured.

In the point of view held by the Evangelists, this conception is not contradicted even by those particulars which the friends of the purely natural opinion respecting the life of the risen Jesus are accustomed to urge in their support. That Jesus ate and drank was, in the circle of ideas within which the gospels originated, as far from presupposing a real necessity, as the meal of which Jehovah partook with two angels in the tent of Abraham: the power of eating is here no proof of a necessity for eating.[21] That he caused himself to be touched, was the only possible mode of refuting the conjecture that an incorporeal spectre had appeared to the disciples; moreover, divine existences, not merely in Grecian, but also (according to the passage above quoted, Gen. xxxii. 24) in Hebrew antiquity, sometimes appeared palpable, in distinction from unsubstantial shades, though they otherwise showed themselves as little bound by the laws of materiality as the palpable Jesus, when

---

[17] Comp. on this subject especially Weisse, ut sup. s. 339 ff.

[18] Brennecke, biblischer Beweis, dass Jesus nach seiner Auferstehung noch 27 Jahre leibhaftig auf Erden gelebt, und zum Wohle der Menschheit in der Stille fortgewirkt habe. 1819.

[19] Ut sup. s. 793, 925.   Comp. Briefe über den Rationalismus, s. 240.

[20] Noch etwas über die Frage : warum haben die Apostel Matthäus und Johannes nicht ebenso wie die zwei Evangelisten Markus und Lukas die Himmelfahrt ausdrücklich erzählt? In Süskind's Magazin, 17, s. 165 ff.

[21] Joann. Damasc. de f. orth. 4, 1 : εἰ καὶ ἐγεύσατο βρώσεως μετὰ τὴν ἀνάστασιν, ἀλλ' οὐ νόμῳ φύσεως· οὐ γὰρ ἐπείνασεν· οἰκονομίας δὲ τρόπῳ, τὸ ἀληθὲς πιστούμενος τῆς ἀναστάσεως, ὡς αὐτή ἐστιν ἡ σάρξ ἡ παθοῦσα καὶ ἀναστᾶσα.

he suddenly vanished, and was able to penetrate without hindrance into a room of which the door was closed.[22]

It is quite another question, whether on our more advanced position, and with our more correct knowledge of nature, those two different classes of particulars can be held compatible with each other. Here we must certainly say : a body which consumes visible food, must itself be visible ; the consumption of food presupposes an organism, but an organism is organized matter, and this has not the property of alternately vanishing and becoming visible again at will.[23] More especially, if the body of Jesus was capable of being felt, and presented perceptible flesh and bones, it thus exhibited the impenetrability of matter, proper to it as solid : if on the other hand he was able to pass into closed houses and rooms, unhindered by the interposition of walls and doors, he thus proved that the impenetrability of solid matter did not belong to him. Since then according to the evangelical accounts he must at the same time have had and not have had the same property : the evangelical representation of the corporeality of Jesus after the resurrection is manifested to be contradictory. And this contradiction is not of such a kind that it is divided among the different narrators ; but the account of one and the same Evangelist includes those contradictory features within itself. The brief account of Matthew, it is true, implies in the embracing of the feet of Jesus by the women (v. 9) only the attribute of palpability, without at the same time presenting an opposite one ; with Mark the case is reversed, his statement that Jesus appeared *in another form* (v. 12) implying something supernatural, while on the other hand he does not decidedly presuppose the opposite ; in Luke, on the other hand, the permission to touch his body and the act of eating speak as decidedly in favour of organic materiality, as the sudden appearance and disappearance speak against it ; but the members of this contradiction come the most directly into collision in John, where Jesus, immediately after he has entered into the closed room unimpeded by walls and doors,[24] causes the doubting Thomas to touch him.

§ 140.

DEBATES CONCERNING THE REALITY OF THE DEATH AND RESURRECTION OF JESUS.*

The proposition : a dead man has returned to life, is composed of two such contradictory elements, that whenever it is attempted to maintain the

---

[22] The vagueness of the conception which lies at the foundation of the evangelical accounts is well expressed by Origen, when he says of Jesus : καὶ ἦν γε μετὰ τὴν ἀνάστασιν αὐτοῦ ὡσπερεὶ ἐν μεθορίῳ τινὶ τῆς παχύτητος τοῦ πρὸ τοῦ πάθους σώματος, καὶ τοῦ γυμνὴν τοιούτον σώματος φαίνεσθαι ψυχήν. *After the resurrection, he existed in a form which held the mean between the materiality of his body before his passion, and the state of the soul when altogether destitute of such body* (c. Cels. ii. 62).

[23] Hence even Kern admits that he knows not how to reconcile that particular in Luke with the rest, and regards it as of later, traditional origin (Hauptthats., ut sup. s. 50). But what does this admission avail him, since he still has, from the narrative of John, the quality of palpability, which equally with the act of eating belongs to the "conditions of earthly life, the relations of the material world," to which the body of the risen Jesus, according to Kern's own presupposition, "was no longer subjected " ?

[24] Many fathers of the church and orthodox theologians held the capability thus exhibited by Jesus of penetrating through closed doors, not altogether reconcileable with the representation, that for the purpose of the resurrection the stone was rolled away from the grave, and hence maintained : *resurrexit Christus clauso sepulchro, sive nondum ab ostio sepulchri revoluto per angelum lapide.* Quenstedt, theol. didact. polem. 3, p. 542.

one, the other threatens to disappear. If he has really returned to life, it is natural to conclude that he was not wholly dead ; if he was really dead, it is difficult to believe that he has really become living.[1]

When we form a correct opinion of the relation between soul and body, not abstractly separating the two, but conceiving them at once in their identity, the soul as the interior of the body, the body as the exterior of the soul, we know not how to imagine, to say nothing of comprehending, the revivification of a dead person. What we call the soul is the governing centre which holds in combination the powers and operations of the body ; its function, or rather the soul itself, consists in keeping all other processes of which the body is susceptible in uninterrupted subjection to the superior unity of the process of organic life, which in man is the basis of his spiritual nature : so soon as this regulating power ceases to act, the supremacy in the various parts of the body is assumed by these other, inferior principles, whose work in its prosecution is corruption. When once these have acceded to the dominion, they will not be inclined to render it back to their former monarch, the soul ; or rather this is impossible, because, quite apart from the question of the immortality of the human spirit (*Geist*), the soul (*Seele*) as such ceases in the same moment with its dominion and activity, which constitute its existence ; consequently, in a revivification, even if resort be had to a miracle, this must consist in the direct creation of a new soul.

Only in the dualism which has become popular on the subject of the relation between body and soul, is there anything to favour the opinion of the possibility of a revivification properly so called. In this system, the soul in its relation to the body is represented as like a bird, which, though it may for a time have flown out of the cage, can yet be once more caught and replaced in its former abode ; and it is to such figures that an imaginative species of thought cleaves, in order to preserve the notion of revivification. But even in this dualistic view, the inconceivability of such an event is rather concealed than really diminished. For in the most abstract separation, the co-existence of the body and soul cannot be held as indifferent and lifeless as that of a box and its contents ; on the contrary, the presence of the soul in the body produces effects, which again are the conditions whereby that presence is rendered possible. Thus so soon as the soul has forsaken the body, there is a cessation in the latter of those activities which according to the dualistic idea were the immediate expressions of the influence of the soul ; at the same time, the organs of these activities—brain, blood, etc., begin to stagnate ; a change which is coincident with the moment of death. Thus if it could occur to the departed soul, or be imposed on it by another, to re-enter its former dwelling-place : it would find this dwelling, even after the first moments, uninhabitable in its noblest parts, and unfit for use. To restore, in the same way as an infirm member, the most immediate organs of its activity, is an impossibility to the soul, since in order to effect anything in the body it has need of the service of these very organs : thus the soul, although remanded into the body, must suffer it to decay, from inability to exercise any influence over it ; or there must be added to the miracle of its reconveyance into the body, the second miracle of a restoration of the lifeless bodily organs : an immediate interposition of God in the regular course of nature, irreconcileable with enlightened ideas of the relation of God to the world.

Hence the cultivated intellect of the present day has very decidedly stated the following dilemma : either Jesus was not really dead, or he did not really rise again.

---

[1] Comp. Schleiermacher's Weihnachtsfeier, s. 117 f.

Rationalism has principally given its adhesion to the former opinion. The short time that Jesus hung on the cross, together with the otherwise ascertained tardiness of death by crucifixion, and the uncertain nature and effects of the wound from the spear, appeared to render the reality of the death doubtful. That the agents in the crucifixion, as well as the disciples themselves, entertained no such doubt, would be explained not only by the general difficulty of distinguishing deep swoons and the rigidity of syncope from real death, but also from the low state of medical science in that age; while at least one example of the restoration of a crucified person appeared to render conceivable a resuscitation in the case of Jesus also. This example is found in Josephus, who informs us that of three crucified acquaintances whose release he begged from Titus, two died after being taken down from the cross, but one survived.[2] How long these people had hung on the cross Josephus does not mention; but from the manner in which he connects them with his expedition to Thekoah, by stating that he saw them on his return from thence, they must probably have been crucified during this expedition, and as this, from the trifling distance of the above place from Jerusalem, might possibly be achieved in a day, they had in all probability not hung on the cross more than a day, and perhaps a yet shorter time. These three persons, then, can scarcely have hung much longer than Jesus, who, according to Mark, was on the cross from nine in the morning till towards six in the evening, and they were apparently taken down while they still showed signs of life; yet with the most careful medical tendance only one survived. Truly it is difficult to perceive how it can hence be shown probable that Jesus, who when taken from the cross showed all the signs of death, should have come to life entirely of himself, without the application of medical skill.[3]

According to a certain opinion, however, these two conditions—some remains of conscious life, and careful medical treatment—were not wanting in the case of Jesus, although they are not mentioned by the Evangelists. Jesus, we are told, seeing no other way of purifying the prevalent messianic idea from the admixture of material and political hopes, exposed himself to crucifixion, but in doing so relied on the possibility of procuring a speedy removal from the cross by early bowing his head, and of being afterwards restored by the medical skill of some among his secret colleagues; so as to inspirit the people at the same time by the appearance of a resurrection.[4] Others have at least exonerated Jesus from such contrivance, and have admitted that he really sank into a deathlike slumber; but have ascribed to his disciples a preconceived plan of producing apparent death by means of a potion, and thus by occasioning his early removal from the cross, securing

---

[2] Joseph. vita, 75 : πεμφθεὶς δὲ ὑπὸ Τίτου Καίσαρος σὺν Κερεαλίῳ καὶ χιλίοις ἱππεῦσιν εἰς κώμην τινὰ Θεκώαν λεγομένην, πρὸς κατανόησιν, εἰ τόπος ἐπιτήδειός ἐστι χάρακα δέξασθαι, ὡς ἐκεῖθεν ὑποστρέφων εἶδον πολλοὺς αἰχμαλώτους ἀνεσταυρωμένους, καὶ τρεῖς γνωρίσας συνήθεις μοὶ γενομένους, ἤλγησα τὴν ψυχήν, καὶ μετὰ δακρύων προσελθὼν Τίτῳ εἶπον. Ὁ δ᾽ εὐθὺς ἐκέλευσεν καθαιρεθέντας αὐτοὺς θεραπείας ἐπιμελεστάτης τυχεῖν. καὶ οἱ μὲν δύο τελευτῶσιν θεραπευόμενοι, ὁ δὲ τρίτος ἔζησεν. And when I was sent by Titus Cæsar with Cerealius and 1,000 horsemen, to a certain village called Thecoa, in order to know whether it were a place fit for a camp, as I came back, I saw many captives crucified; and remembered three of them as my former acquaintance. I was very sorry at this in my mind, and went with tears in my eyes to Titus, and told him of them ; so he immediately commanded them to be taken down, and to have the greatest care taken of them, in order to their recovery ; yet two of them died under the physician's hands, while the third recovered. For the arguments of Paulus on this passage, see exeg. Handb. 3, b, s. 786 ; and in the Appendix, s. 929 ff.

[3] Bretschneider, über den angeblichen Scheintod Jesu am Kreuze, in Ullmann's und Umbreit's Studien, 1832, 3, s. 625 ff. ; Hug, Beiträge zur Geschichte des Verfahrens bei der Todesstrafe der Kreuzigung, Freiburger Zeitschr. 7, s. 144 ff.

[4] Bahrdt, Ausführung des Plans und Zwecks Jesu. Comp. on the other hand, Paulus, exeg. Handb. 3, b, 793 f.

his restoration to life.[5]   But of all this our evangelical sources give no
intimation, and for conjecturing such details we have no ground.   Judicious
friends of the natural explanation, who repudiate such monstrous productions
of a system which remodels history at will, have hence renounced the supposition of any remains of conscious life in Jesus, and have contented themselves, for the explanation of his revivification, with the vital force which
remained in his still young and vigorous body, even after the cessation of
consciousness ; and have pointed out, instead of premeditated tendance by
the hands of men, the beneficial influence which the partly oleaginous substances applied to his body must have had in promoting the healing of his
wounds, and, united with the air in the cave, impregnated with the perfumes
of the spices, in reawakening feeling and consciousness in Jesus ; [6] to all
which was added as a decisive impulse, the earthquake and the lightning
which on the morning of the resurrection opened the grave of Jesus.[7]   Others
have remarked, in opposition to this, that the cold air in the cave must have
had anything rather than a vivifying tendency ; that strong aromatics in a confined space would rather have had a stupefying and stifling influence ; [8] and
the same effect must have been produced by a flash of lightning bursting
into the grave, if this were not a mere figment of rationalistic expositors.

Notwithstanding all these improbabilities, which are against the opinion
that Jesus came to life after a merely apparent death by the operation of
natural causes, this nevertheless remains so far possible, that if we had secure
evidence of the resuscitation of Jesus, we might, on the strength of such
certainty as to the result, supply the omissions in the narrative, and approve
the opinion above presented,—with the rejection, however, of all precise
conjectures.   Secure evidence of the resurrection of Jesus, would be the
attestation of it in a decided and accordant manner by impartial witnesses.
But the impartiality of the alleged witnesses for the resurrection of Jesus, is
the very point which the opponents of Christianity, from Celsus down to the
Wolfenbüttel Fragmentist, have invariably called in question.   Jesus showed
himself to his adherents only : why not also to his enemies, that they too
might be convinced, and that by their testimony posterity might be precluded
from every conjecture of a designed fraud on the part of his disciples ? [9]   I
cannot certainly attach much weight to the replies by which apologists have
sought to repel this objection, from that of Origen, who says : *Christ avoided
the judge who condemned him, and his enemies, that they might not be smitten
with blindness* ; [10] to the opinions of the modern theologians, who by their
vacillation between the assertion that by such an appearance the enemies
of Jesus would have been compelled to believe, and the opposite one, that
they would not have believed even on such evidence,—mutually confute one
another.[11]   Nevertheless, it can still be urged in reply to that objection, that

---

[5] Xenodoxien, in der Abh. : Joseph und Nikodemus.   Comp. on the other hand Klaiber's
Studien der würtemberg. Geistlichkeit, 2, 2, s. 84 ff.
[6] Paulus, exeg. Handb. 3, b, s. 785 ff. L. J. 1, b, s. 281 ff.
[7] Schuster, in Eichhorn's allg. Biblioth. 9, s. 1053.
[8] Winer, bibl. Realw. 1, s. 674.
[9] Orig. c. Cels. ii. 63 : Μετὰ ταῦτα ὁ Κέλσος οὐκ εὐκαταφρονήτως τὰ γεγραμμένα κακολογῶν,
φησὶν, ὅτι ἐχρῆν, εἴπερ ὄντως θείαν |δύναμιν ἐκφῆναι ἤθελεν ὁ ’Ι., αὐτοῖς τοῖς ἐπηρεάσασι καὶ
τῷ καταδικάσαντι καὶ ὅλως πᾶσιν ὀφθῆναι.—67 : οὐ γὰρ—ἐπὶ τοῦτ’ ἐπέμφθη τὴν ἀρχήν,
ἵνα λάθῃ.   Comp. the Wolfenbüttel Fragmentist, in Lessing, s. 450, 60, 92 ff. ; Woolston,
Disc. 6.   Spinoza, ep. 23, ad Oldenburg, p. 558 f. ed. Gfrörer.
[10] Ut sup. 67 : ἐφείδετο γὰρ καὶ τοῦ καταδικάσαντος καὶ τῶν ἐπηρεασάντων ὁ Χριστὸς, ἵνα
μὴ παταχθῶσιν ἀορασίᾳ.
[11] Comp. Mosheim, in his translation of the work of Origen against Celsus, on the
passage above quoted ; Michaelis, Anm. zum fünften Fragment, s. 407.

the adherents of Jesus, from their hopelessness, which is both unanimously attested by the narratives, and is in perfect accordance with the nature of the case, here rise to the rank of impartial witnesses. If they had expected a resurrection of Jesus and we had then been called upon to believe it on their testimony alone : there would certainly be a possibility and perhaps also a probability, if not of an intentional deception, yet of an involuntary self-delusion on their part ; but this possibility vanishes in proportion as the disciples of Jesus lost all hope after his death. Now even if it be denied that any one of the gospels proceeded immediately from a disciple of Jesus, it is still certain from the epistles of Paul and the Acts that the Apostles themselves had the conviction that they had seen the risen Jesus. We might then rest satisfied with the evangelical testimonies in favour of the resurrection, were but these testimonies in the first place sufficiently precise, and in the second, in agreement with themselves and with each other. But in fact the testimony of Paul, which is intrinsically consistent and is otherwise most important, is so general and vague, that taken by itself, it does not carry us beyond the subjective fact, that the disciples were convinced of the resurrection of Jesus ; while the more fully detailed narratives of the gospels, in which the resurrection of Jesus appears as an objective fact, are, from the contradictions of which they are convicted, incapable of being used as evidence, and in general their account of the life of Jesus after his resurrection is not one which has connexion and unity, presenting a clear historical idea of the subject, but a fragmentary compilation,[12] which presents a series of visions, rather than a continuous history.

If we compare with this account of the resurrection of Jesus, the precise and internally consistent attestation of his death : we must incline to the other side of the dilemma above stated, and be induced to doubt the reality of the resurrection rather than that of the death. Hence Celsus chose this alternative, deriving the alleged appearance of Jesus after the resurrection, from the self-delusion of the disciples, especially the women, either dreaming or waking ; or from what appeared to him still more probable, intentional deception :[13] and more modern writers, as, for example, the Wolfenbüttel Fragmentist, have adopted the accusation of the Jews in Matthew, namely, that the disciples stole the body of Jesus, and afterwards fabricated, with slender agreement, stories of his resurrection and subsequent appearances.[14] This suspicion is repelled by the remark of Origen, that a spontaneous falsehood on the part of the disciples could not possibly have animated them to so unflinching an announcement of the resurrection of Jesus amid the greatest perils ;[15] and it is a just argument of modern apologists that the astonishing revolution from the deep depression and utter hopelessness of the disciples at the death of Jesus, to the strong faith and enthusiasm with which they proclaimed him as the Messiah on the succeeding Pentecost, would be inexplicable unless in the interim something extraordinarily encouraging had taken place—something, in fact, which had convinced them of his resur-

---

[12] Hase, L. J., § 149 ; Diss. : *librorum sacrorum de J. Chr. a mortuis revocato atque in cælum sublato narrationem collatis vulgaribus illa ætate Judæorum de morte opinionibus interpretari conatus est* C. A. Frege, p. 12 f. ; Weisse, die evang. Gesch. 2, s. 362 ff.

[13] Orig. c. Cels. ii. 55 : τίς τοῦτο εἶδε (the pierced hands of Jesus, and, in general, his appearances after the resurrection), γυνὴ πάροιστρος, ὡς φατέ, καὶ εἴ τις ἄλλος τῶν ἐκ τῆς αὐτῆς γοητείας, ἤτοι κατά τινα διάθεσιν ὀνειρώξας, ἢ κατὰ τὴν αὐτοῦ βούλησιν δόξῃ πεπλανημένῃ φαντασιωθείς, ὅπερ δὴ μυρίοις συμβέβηκεν· ἢ, ὅπερ μᾶλλον, ἐκπλῆξαι τοὺς λοιποὺς τῇ τερατείᾳ ταύτῃ θελήσας, καὶ διὰ τοῦ τοιούτου ψεύσματος ἀφορμὴν ἄλλοις ἀγύρταις παρασχεῖν.

[14] The 5th Fragment, in Lessing's 4th Beitrag. Woolston, Disc. 8.

[15] Ut sup. 56.

rection.[16]   But that this cause of conviction was precisely a real appearance
of the risen Jesus—that, indeed it was necessarily an external event at all—
is by no means proved.   If we chose to remain on supranatural ground, we
might with Spinoza suppose that a vision was produced by miraculous means
in the minds of the disciples, the object of which was to make evident to
them, in a manner accordant with their powers of comprehension and the
ideas of their age, that Jesus by his virtuous life had risen from spiritual
death, and that to those who followed his example he would grant a similar
resurrection.[17]   With one foot at least on the same ground stands the supposition of Weisse, that the departed spirit of Jesus really acted on the
disciples whom he had left behind ; in connexion with which he refers to
the apparitions of spirits, the impossibility of which remains unproved.[18]
In order to escape from the magic circle of the supernatural, others have
searched for natural external causes which might induce the belief that Jesus
had risen and had been seen after his resurrection.   The first impetus to
this opinion, it has been conjectured, was given by the circumstance that on
the second morning after the burial his grave was found empty, the linen
clothes which lay in it being taken first for angels and then for an appearance
of the risen Jesus himself : [19] but if the body of Jesus was not reanimated,
how are we to suppose that it came out of the grave ?   Here it would
be necessary to recur to the supposition of a theft : unless the intimation
of John, that Jesus on account of haste was laid in a strange grave, were
thought available for the conjecture that perhaps the owner of the grave
caused the corpse to be removed : which however the disciples must subsequently have learned, and which in any case has too frail a foundation
in the solitary statement of the fourth gospel.

Far more fruitful is the appeal to the passage of Paul (1 Cor. xv. 5 ff.), as
the most appropriate starting point in this inquiry, and the key to the comprehension of all the appearances of Jesus after his resurrection.[20]   When
Paul there places the Christophany which occurred to himself in the same
series with the appearances of Jesus in the days after his resurrection : this
authorizes us, so far as nothing else stands in the way of such an inference,
to conclude that, for aught the Apostle knew, those earlier appearances were
of the same nature with the one experienced by himself.   Now with respect
to the latter as narrated to us in the Acts (ix. 1 ff., xxii. 3 ff., xxvi. 12 ff.),
it is no longer possible, after the analysis of Eichhorn [21] and Ammon,[22]
to retain it as an external, objective appearance of the real Christ ; even

---

[16] Ullmann, Was setz die Stiftung der Christlichen Kirche durch einen Gekreuzigten
voraus?   In his Studien, 1832, 3, s. 589 f. (Röhr) ; Briefe über den Rationalismus, s. 28,
236.   Paulus, exeg. Handb. 3, b, s. 826 f. ; Hase, § 146.

[17] Spinoza, ut sup.: *Apostolos omnes omnino credidisse, quod Christus a morte resurrexerit,
et ad cælum revera ascenderit—ego non nego.   Nam ipse etiam Abrahamus credidit, quod
Deus apud ipsum pransus fuerit—cum tamen hæc et plura alia hujusmodi apparitiones
seu revelationes fuerint, captui et opinionibus eorum hominum accommodatæ, quibus Deus
mentem suam iisdem revelare voluit.   Concludo itaque Christi a mortuis resurrectionem revera
spiritualem, et solis fidelibus ad eorum captum revelata fuisse, nempe quod Christus æternitate
donatus fuit, et a mortuis (mortuos hic intelligo eo sensu, quo Christus dixit : sinite mortuos
sepelire mortuos suos) surrexit, simul atque vita et morte singularis sanctitatis exemplum dedit,
et eatenus discipulos suos a mortuis suscitat, quatenus ipsi hoc vitæ ejus et mortis exemplum
sequuntur.*

[18] Die evang. Gesch. 2, s. 426 ff.

[19] Versuch über die Auferstehung Jesu, in Schmidt's Bibliothek, 2, 4, s. 545 ff.

[20] Ibid., s. 537 ; Kaiser, bibl. Theol. 1, s. 258 f. ; Frege, ut sup. p. 13.

[21] In his allg. Bibliothek, 6, 1, s. 1 ff.

[22] Comm. exeg. de repentina Sauli—conversione.   In his opusc. theol. ; Fortbildung des
Christenth. 2, 1, Kap. 3.   Comp. also my Streitschriften, 2tes Heft, s. 52 ff.

Neander [23] does not positively dare to maintain more than an internal influence of Christ on the mind of Paul, only appending in a very beseeching manner the supposition of an external appearance ; and even that internal influence he himself renders superfluous by detailing the causes which might in a natural manner produce such a revolution in the disposition of the man thus : the favourable impression of Christianity, of the doctrine, life and conduct of its adherents, which he had here and there received, especially on the occasion of the martyrdom of Stephen, threw his mind into a state of excitement and conflict, which he might indeed for a time forcibly repress, perhaps even by redoubled zeal against the new sect, but which must at last find vent in a decisive spiritual crisis, concerning which it need not surprise us that in an oriental it took the form of a Christophany. If according to this we have in the Apostle Paul an example, that strong impressions from the infant Christian community might carry an ardent mind that had long striven against it, to a pitch of exaltation which issued in a Christophany, and a total change of sentiment : surely the impression of the sublime personality of Jesus would suffice to inspire into his immediate disciples, struggling with the doubts concerning his messiahship which his death had excited in them, the experience of similar visions. They who think it necessary and desirable in relation to the Christophany of Paul to call in the aid of external natural phenomena, as thunder and lightning, may also seek to facilitate the explanation of the appearances of the risen Jesus which his immediate disciples believed themselves to have previously had, by the supposition of similar incidents.[24] Only it must be observed that, as Eichhorn's explanation of the event in the life of Paul proved a failure from his maintaining as historical every single detail in the New Testament narrative, as the blindness of Paul and his cure, the vision of Ananias, and so on, which he could only transform into natural occurrences by a very strained interpretation : so it would inevitably render impossible the psychological explanation of the appearances of Jesus, to acknowledge as historical all the evangelical narratives concerning them, especially those of the tests which Thomas applied by touching the wounds of Jesus, and which Jesus himself afforded by taking material nourishment ; and indeed these narratives, from the contradiction which they are shown to present, have not the slightest claim to such a character. The two first gospels, and our chief informant in this matter, the Apostle Paul, tell us nothing of such tests, and it is quite natural that the Christophanies which, in the actual experience of the women and Apostles, may have floated before them as visions of much the same character as that which Paul had on the way to Damascus, when once received into tradition, should by reason of the apologetic effort to cut off all doubts as to their reality, be continually more and more consolidated so that the mute appearances became speaking ones, the ghostlike form was exchanged for one that ate, and the merely visible body was made palpable also.

Here however there presents itself a distinction, which seems at once to render the event in the history of Paul unavailable for the explanation of those earlier appearances. To the Apostle Paul, namely, the idea that Jesus had risen and appeared to many persons was delivered as the belief of the sect which he persecuted ; he had only to receive it into his conviction and to vivify it in his imagination until it became a part of his own experience : the earlier disciples, on the contrary, had before them as a fact merely the death of their Messiah,—the notion of a resurrection on his part they could nowhere

---

[23] Gesch. der Pflanzung und Leitung der Christl. Kirche durch die Apostel, 1, s. 75 ff.
[24] This is done in the treatise in Schmidt's Bibliothek, and by Kaiser, ut sup.

gather, but must, according to our conception of the matter, have first produced it ; a problem which appears to be beyond all comparison more difficult than that subsequently presented to the Apostle Paul. In order to form a correct judgment on this subject, we must transport ourselves yet more completely into the situation and frame of mind into which the disciples of Jesus were thrown by his death. During several years' intercourse with them he had constantly impressed them more and more decidedly with the belief that he was the Messiah ; but his death, which they were unable to reconcile with their messianic ideas, had for the moment annihilated this belief. Now when, after the first shock was past, the earlier impression began to revive : there spontaneously arose in them the psychological necessity of solving the contradiction between the ultimate fate of Jesus and their earlier opinion of him — of adopting into their idea of, the Messiah the characteristics of suffering and death. As, however, with the Jews of that age to comprehend meant nothing else than to derive from the sacred scriptures : they turned to these, to ascertain whether they might not perhaps find in them intimations of a suffering and dying Messiah. Foreign as the idea of such a Messiah is to the Old Testament, the disciples, who wished to find it there, must nevertheless have regarded as intimations of this kind, all those [poetical and prophetic passages which, like Isa. liii., Ps. xxii., represented the man of God as afflicted and bowed down even to death. Thus Luke states as the chief occupation of the risen Jesus in his interview with the disciples, that *beginning at Moses and all the prophets, he expounded unto them in all the scriptures the things concerning himself*, i. e. that *Christ ought to have suffered such things* (xxiv. 26 f., 44 ff.). When they had in this manner received into their messianic idea ignominy, suffering and death, the ignominiously executed Jesus was not lost, but still remained to them : by his death he had only entered into his messianic glory (Luke xxiv. 26) in which he was invisibly *with them always, even unto the end of the world* (Matt. xxviii. 20). But how could he fail, out of this glory, in which he lived, to give tidings of himself to his followers ? and how could they, when their mind was opened to the hitherto hidden doctrine of a dying Messiah contained in the scriptures, and when in moments of unwonted inspiration their *hearts burned within them* (Luke xxiv. 32),—how could they avoid conceiving this to be an influence shed on them by their glorified Christ, an opening of their understanding by him (v. 45), nay, an actual conversing with him ? [25] Lastly, how conceivable is it that in individuals, especially women, these impressions were heightened, in a purely subjective manner, into actual vision ; that on others, even on [whole assemblies, something or other of an objective nature, visible or audible, sometimes perhaps the sight of an unknown person, created the impression of a revelation or appearance of Jesus : a height of pious enthusiasm which is wont to appear elsewhere in religious societies peculiarly oppressed and persecuted. But if the crucified Messiah had truly entered into the *highest* form of blessed existence, he ought not to have left his body in the grave : and if in precisely such Old Testament passages as admitted of a typical relation to the sufferings of the Messiah, there was at the same time expressed the hope : *thou wilt not leave my soul in hell, neither wilt thou suffer thy holy one to see corruption* (Ps. xvi. 10 ; Acts ii. 27) ; while in Isa. liii. 10, he who had been represented as led to the slaughter and buried, was yet promised a prolongation of his days : what was more natural to the disciples than to reinstate their earlier Jewish ideas, which the death of Jesus had disturbed, namely, *that the Christ remaineth for ever* (John xii. 34), through the medium of an actual revivification of their dead

[25] Comp. Weisse, ut sup. p. 398 ff.

master, and, as it was a messianic attribute one day to call the dead bodily
from the grave, to imagine also as returning to life in the manner of a resurrection?

Meanwhile, if the body of Jesus was interred in a known place, and could
there (so far as we are not at liberty to suppose a theft, or an accidental removal) be sought for and exhibited : it is difficult to conceive how the disciples in Jerusalem itself, and not quite two days after the interment, could
believe and declare that Jesus was risen, without refuting themselves, or
meeting with refutation from their adversaries, (to whom however they appear
to have made the first disclosure as to the resurrection of their Messiah at
Pentecost,) by ocular demonstration at the grave.[26] Now it is here that the
narrative of the first gospel, which has been unjustly placed below the others,
presents an explanatory and satisfactory indication. According to this gospel
also the risen Jesus does indeed appear in Jerusalem, but only to the women,
and so entirely as a mere preparation for a succeeding interview, nay, so
superfluously, that we have already questioned the truth of this appearance,
and pronounced it to be a later modification of the legend of the angelic
appearance, which Matthew nevertheless also included in his narrative.[27] The
sole important appearance of Jesus after the resurrection occurs, according
to Matthew, in Galilee, whither an angel, and Jesus himself on the last evening
of his life and on the morning of the resurrection, most urgently directed his
disciples, and where the fourth gospel also, in its appendix, places an appearance of the resuscitated Jesus. That the disciples, dispersed by their alarm,
at the execution of their Messiah, should return to their home in Galilee,
where they had no need, as in the metropolis of Judea, the seat of the enemies
of their crucified Christ, to shut the doors *for fear of the Jews*, was natural.
Here was the place where they gradually began to breathe freely, and where
their faith in Jesus, which had been temporarily depressed, might once more
expand with its former vigour. But here also, where no body lay in the grave
to contradict bold suppositions, might gradually be formed the idea of the
resurrection of Jesus ; and when this conviction had so elevated the courage
and enthusiasm of his adherents that they ventured to proclaim it in the metropolis, it was no longer possible by the sight of the body of Jesus either to
convict themselves, or to be convicted by others.

According to the Acts, it is true, the disciples so early as on the next
Pentecost, seven weeks after the death of Jesus, appeared in Jerusalem with
the announcement of his resurrection, and were themselves already convinced
of it on the second morning after his burial, by appearances whch they witnessed. But how long will it yet be, until the manner in which the author of
the Acts places the first appearance of the disciples of Jesus with the announcement of the new doctrine, precisely on the festival of the announcement of
the old law, be recognized as one which rests purely on dogmatical grounds ;
which is therefore historically worthless, and in no way binds us to assign so
short a duration to that time of quiet preparation in Galilee ? As regards the
other statement—it might certainly require some time for the mental state of
the disciples to become exalted in the degree necessary, before this or that
individual amongst them could, purely as an operation of his own mind, make
present to himself the risen Christ in a visionary manner ; or before whole
assemblies, in moments of highly wrought enthusiasm, could believe that they
heard him in every impressive sound, or saw him in every striking appearance :
but it would nevertheless be conceived, that, as it was not possible that he

[26] Comp. Friedrich, in Eichhorn's Biblioth. 7, s. 223.
[27] Comp. also Schmidt's Biblioth. 2, s. 548.

should be held by the bonds of death (Acts ii. 24), he had passed only a short time in the grave.　As to the more precise determination of this interval, if it be held an insufficient explanation, that the sacred number three would be the first to suggest itself ; there is a further idea which might occur,—whether or not it be historical that Jesus was buried on the evening before a sabbath,— namely, that he only remained in the grave during the rest of the sabbath, and thus rose *on the morning after the sabbath* πρωὶ πρώτῃ σαββάτῳ which by the known mode of reckoning might be reconciled with the round number of three days.[28]

When once the idea of a resurrection of Jesus had been formed in this manner, the great event could not be allowed to have happened so simply, but must be surrounded and embellished with all the pomp which the Jewish imagination furnished.　The chief ornaments which stood at command for this purpose, were angels : hence these must open the grave of Jesus, must, after he had come forth from it, keep watch in the empty place, and deliver to the women, who (because without doubt women had had the first visions) must be the first to go to the grave, the tidings of what had happened.　As it was Galilee where Jesus subsequently appeared to them, the journey of the disciples thither, which was nothing else than their return home, somewhat hastened by fear, was derived from the direction of an angel ; nay, Jesus himself must already before his death, and, as Matthew too zealously adds, once more after the resurrection also, have enjoined this journey on the disciples. But the further these narratives were propagated by tradition, the more must the difference between the locality of the resurrection itself and the appearances of the risen one, be allowed to fall out of sight as inconvenient ; and since the locality of the death and resurrection was not transferable, the appearances were gradually placed in the same locality as the resurrection,—in Jerusalem, which as the more brilliant theatre and the seat of the first Christian Church, was especially appropriate for them.[29] *

---

[28] May the three days' abode of Jonah in the whale have had any influence on this determination of time ? or the passage in Hosea quoted above, § 111, note 3 ? † The former is indeed only placed in this connexion in one gospel, and the latter is nowhere used in the N. T.

[29] Compare with this explanation the one given by Weisse, in the 7th chapter of his work above quoted.　He agrees with the above representation in regarding the death of Jesus as real, and the narratives of the grave being found empty as later fabrications ; the point in which he diverges is that above mentioned—that in his view the appearances of the risen Jesus are not merely psychological and subjective, but objective magical facts.

CHAPTER V.

THE ASCENSION.

---

§ 141.

THE LAST COMMANDS AND PROMISES OF JESUS.

In the last interview of Jesus with his disciples, which according to Mark and Luke closed with the ascension, the three first Evangelists (the fourth has something similar on the very first interview) represent Jesus as delivering testamentary commands and promises, which referred to the establishment and propagation of the messianic kingdom of earth.

With regard to the commands, Jesus in Luke (xxiv. 47 f. ; Acts i. 8) in parting from his disciples appoints them to be witnesses of his messiahship, and charges them to preach *repentance and remission of sins* in his name from Jerusalem to the uttermost parts of the earth. In Mark (xvi. 15 f.) he enjoins them to go into all the world and bring to every creature the glad tidings of the messianic kingdom founded by him ; he who believes and is baptized will be saved, he who believeth not, will (in the future messianic judgment) be condemned. In Matthew (xxviii. 19 f.) the disciples are also commissioned to make disciples of *all nations* πάντα τὰ ἔθνη, and here baptism is not mentioned incidentally merely, as in Mark, but is made the subject of an express command by Jesus, and is besides more precisely described as a baptism *in the name of the Father, of the Son, and of the Holy Ghost,* εἰς τὸ ὄνομα τοῦ πατρὸς καὶ τοῦ υἱοῦ καὶ τοῦ ἁγίου πνεύματος.

The impediments to the supposition that Jesus delivered to his disciples the express command to carry the announcement of the gospel to the Gentiles, have been already pointed out in an earlier connexion.[1] But that this more definite form of baptism proceeded from Jesus, is also opposed by the fact, that such an allocation of Father, Son, and Spirit does not elsewhere appear, except as a form of salutation in apostolic epistles (2 Cor. xiii. 14 : *the grace of our Lord Jesus Christ,* etc.) ; while as a more definite form of baptism it is not to be met with throughout the whole New Testament save in the above passage of the first gospel : for in the apostolic epistles and even in the Acts, baptism is designated as a βαπτίζειν εἰς Χριστὸν Ἰησοῦν, or εἰς τὸ ὄνομα τοῦ Κυρίου Ἰησοῦ *baptising in Christ Jesus,* or *in the name of the Lord Jesus,* or their equivalent (Rom. vi. 3 ; Gal. iii. 27 ; Acts ii. 38, viii. 16, x. 48, xix. 5), and the same threefold reference to God, Jesus, and the Holy Spirit is only found in ecclesiastical writers, as, for example, Justin.[2] Indeed the formula in Matthew sounds so exactly as if it had been borrowed from the ecclesiastical

---

[1] Vol. II. § 68.
[2] Apol. i. 61.

ritual, that there is no slight probability in the supposition that it was transferred from thence into the mouth of Jesus. But this does not authorize us
to throw the passage out of the text as an interpolation,[3] since, if everything in
the gospels which cannot have happened to Jesus, or which cannot have been
done or spoken by him in the manner there described, were to be pronounced foreign to the original text, the interpolations would soon become
too numerous. So far it is with justice that others have defended the
genuineness of the baptismal formula ;[4] but their grounds for the assertion
that it was delivered in this manner by Jesus himself are insufficient : the
two opinions then resolve themselves into a third, namely, that this more
definite form of baptism does indeed belong to the original context of the
first gospel, but without having been so delivered by Jesus.[5] Jesus had,
during his life, predicted in divers ways the propagation of his kingdom
beyond the limits of the Jewish nation, perhaps also had intimated the introduction of baptism to be his will ; and—whether it be the fact that, as we
learn in the fourth gospel, the disciples already practised baptism in the lifetime of Jesus, or that they first made this rite a sign of reception into the new
messianic society after his death,—in any case it was entirely in the manner
of the legend to place the injunction to baptize, as well as to go out into all
the world, in the mouth of the departing Christ as a last declaration of his
will.

The promises which Jesus gives to his adherents in parting from them, are
in Matthew, where they are directed exclusively to the eleven, limited simply
to the assurance that he, to whom as the exalted Messiah all power was delivered both in heaven and on earth, would be invisibly with them during the
present *age*, αἰών, until at the *consummation* συντέλεια of this term, he should
enter into permanent visible communion with them : precisely the expression of
the belief which was formed in the first Christian community, when the equilibrium was recovered after the oscillations caused by the death of Jesus.—In
Mark, the last promises of Jesus seem to be gathered from the popular opinion
concerning the gifts of the Christians, which was current at the period of the
composition of this gospel. Of the *signs*, σημεῖα, which are here promised to
believers in general, the *speaking with (new) tongues*, λαλεῖν γλώσσαις (καιναῖς)
in the sense intended 1 Cor. xiv., not in the manner described in Acts ii.
which is a mythical modification,[6] actually appeared in the primitive church ;
as also the *casting out of devils* δαιμόνια ἐκβάλλειν ; and it may even be conceived that sick persons were cured in a natural manner by faith in the *laying
on of hands*, ἐπίθεσις χειρῶν by a Christian : on the contrary the *taking up of
serpents* ὄφεις αἴρειν (comp. Luke x. 19) and the power of drinking poisons
with impunity, have never had any existence except in the superstitious belief
of the vulgar, and such signs of discipleship would have been the last to
which Jesus would have attached any value.—In Luke, the object of the last
promise of Jesus is the *power from on high* δύναμις ἐξ ὕψους, which according
to the *promise of the Father*, ἐπαγγελία τοῦ πατρὸς, he would send on the
apostles, and the impartation of which they were to await in Jerusalem (xxiv.
49) ; and in Acts i. 5 ff. Jesus more precisely designates this impartation of
power as a baptism with the *Holy Spirit*, πνεῦμα ἅγιον, which in a few days
would be granted to the disciples in order to qualify them for the announcement of the gospel. These passages of Luke, which place the impartation of

---

[3] As is done by Teller, im excurs. 2, ad Burneti I. de fide et offic. Christ. p. 262.
[4] The work of Beckhaus, über die Aechtheit der sog. Taufformel, 1794, met with
general approval.
[5] Comp. De Wette, exeg. Handb. 1, 1, s. 246.
[6] Comp. Baur, in der Tübinger Zeitschrift für Theologie, Jahrgang 1830, 2, s. 75 ff.

the Holy Spirit in the days after the ascension, seem to be in contradiction with the statement of the fourth gospel, that Jesus communicated the Holy Spirit to his disciples in the days of his resurrection, nay, on his very first appearance in the circle of the eleven. In John xx. 22 f. we read, that Jesus, appearing among the disciples when the doors were closed, breathed on them and said : *Receive ye the Holy Ghost,* λάβετε πνεῦμα ἅγιον, wherewith he connected the authority to remit and retain sins.

If this were the only passage relating to the impartation of the Spirit, every one would believe that the disciples had it commuicated to them by Jesus when he was personally present among them, and not first after his exaltation to heaven. But in accordance with the harmonizing interest, it has been concluded, first by Theodore of Mopsuestia, and recently by Tholuck,[7] that the word λάβετε, *receive, in John,* must be taken in the sense of λήψεσθε, *ye shall receive,* because ·*according to Luke* the Holy Spirit was not imparted to the disciples until later, at Pentecost. But as if he wished to preclude such a wresting of his words, the Jesus of John adds to them the symbolical action of breathing on the disciples, which unmistakably represents the *receiving* of the Holy Spirit as a present fact,[8] It is true that expositors have found out a way of eluding even this act of breathing, by attributing to it the following signification : as certainly as Jesus now breathes upon them, so certainly will they at a future time receive the Holy Ghost.[9] But the act of breathing upon a person is as decided a symbol of a present impartation as the laying on of hands, and as those on whom the apostles laid their hands were immediately filled with the Spirit (Acts viii. 17, xix. 6), so, according to the above narrative, the author of the fourth gospel must have thought that the Apostles on that occasion received the Spirit from Jesus. In order to avoid the necessity of denying, in opposition to the clear meaning of John, that an impartation of the Spirit actually took place immediately after the resurrection, or of coming into contradiction with Luke, who assigns the outpouring of the Spirit to a later period, expositors now ordinarily suppose that the Spirit was granted to the Apostles both at the earlier and the later period, the impartation at Pentecost being only an increasing and perfecting of the former.[10] Or more correctly, since Matthew x. 20 speaks of the *Spirit of the Father* as already sustaining the disciples in their first mission : it is supposed that they were first endowed with some extraordinary power before that mission, in the lifetime of Jesus ; that on the occasion in question, shortly after his resurrection, he heightened this power ; but that all the fulness of the Spirit was not poured out upon them until Pentecost.[11] What constitutes the distinction between these steps, and especially in what the increase of the gifts of the Spirit consisted in the present instance, is, however, as Michaelis has already remarked, not easy to discern. If in the first instance the apostles were endowed with the power of working miracles (Matt. x. 1, 8) together with the gift of speaking freely (παρρησία) before tribunals (v. 20), it could only be a more correct insight into the spirituality of his kingdom that Jesus communicated to them by breathing on them ; but of this they were still destitute immediately before the ascension, when, according to Acts i. 6, they asked whether, with the impartation of the Spirit, within the next few days, would be associated the restoration of the kingdom to Israel. If however it be supposed that each

[7] Comm. z. Joh., s. 332.
[8] Lücke, Comm. z. Joh. 2, s. 686 ; De Wette, s. 204.
[9] Less, Auferstehungsgeschichte, s. 281 ; Kuinöl, in loc.
[10] Lücke, s. 687.
[11] Vid. ap. Michaelis, Begräbniss- und Auferstehungsgeschichte, s. 268 ; Olshausen, 2, s.

successive impartation of the Spirit conferred no new powers on the disciples, but was merely an addition in measure to that which was already present in all its diversified powers : [12] it must still be held surprising that no Evangelist mentions, together with an earlier impartation, a later amplification ; but instead of this, besides an incidental mention of the Spirit as enabling the disciples to defend themselves before tribunals, in Luke (xii. 12),—which, since it is not here, as in Matthew, connected with a mission, may be regarded merely as a reference to the time after the later outpouring of the Spirit,—each of the Evangelists mentions only one impartation, and represents this as the first and last.   This is, indeed, a clear proof that, to place in juxtaposition three impartations and to regard them as so many different degrees, is only an effort to harmonize the gospels by introducing into them what is foreign to the text.

Thus there are in the New Testament three distinct opinions concerning the impartation of the Spirit to the disciples of Jesus ; and in two respects they form a climax.   As regards the time, Matthew places the impartation the earliest—within the period of the natural life of Jesus ; Luke, the latest— in the time after his complete departure from the earth ; John in an intermediate position—in the days of the resurrection.   As regards the conception of the fact, it is the simplest in Matthew, the least perceptible to the senses, for he has no special and external act of impartation ; John already has such a feature, in the act of breathing on the disciples ; while with Luke, in the Acts, the gentle breathing has become a violent storm, which shakes the house, and with which other miraculous appearances are united.   These two series of gradations stand in opposite relations to historical probability.   That the *Spirit* $\pi\nu\epsilon\hat{\upsilon}\mu\alpha$, which, whether it be regarded as natural or as supernatural, is in either case the animating power of the messianic idea in its Christian modification, was communicated to the adherents of Jesus so early as Matthew narrates, is contradicted by his own representation, for according to him, that Christian modification—the introduction of the characteristics of suffering and death into the idea of the Messiah,—was not comprehended by the disciples long after the mission described in Matt. x. ; and as the discourse of instructions there given contains other particulars also, which will only suit later times and circumstances : it is easy to imagine that the promise in question may have been erroneously referred to that earlier period.   Only after the death and resurrection of Jesus can we conceive what the New Testament calls the $\pi\nu\epsilon\hat{\upsilon}\mu\alpha$ $\mathring{\alpha}\gamma\iota o\nu$ to have been developed in the disciples, and in so far the representation of John stands nearer to reality than that of Matthew ; but, as certainly the revolution in the sentiments of the disciples described in the foregoing section, had not taken place so early as two days after the crucifixion : the account of John does not approach so near to the truth as that of Luke, who allows an interval of at least fifty days for the formation of the new opinions in the disciples.   The position of the narratives with respect to historical truth is reversed by the other climax.   For in proportion as a narrative represents the impartation of a spiritual power as perceptible to the senses, the formation of a sentiment which might spring from natural causes as miraculous, the origin of a faculty which can only have been developed gradually, as instantaneous : in the same proportion does such a narrative diverge from the truth ; and in this respect, Matthew would stand at the least distance from the truth, Luke at the greatest.   If we therefore recognise in the representation of the latter the most mature product of tradition, it may be wondered how tradition can have wrought in two opposite ways: receding

---

[12] This is Tholuck's opinion, ut sup.

from the truth in relation to the determination of the manner and form of the impartation, approaching the truth in relation to the determination of the time. But this is explained as soon as it is considered, that in the changes in the determination of the time, tradition was not guided by critical inquiry after truth—this might well have caused surprise,—but by the same tendency that led to the other alteration, namely, to present the impartation of the Spirit as a single miraculous act. If Jesus was said to have shed the Spirit on his disciples by a special act : it must seem appropriate to assign this act to his state of glorification, and thus either with John to place it after the resurrection, or with Luke after the ascension ; indeed the fourth Evangelist expressly remarks that in the lifetime of Jesus, the Spirit was not yet given, *because Jesus was not yet glorified* (vii. 39).

This interpretation of the opinion of the fourth Evangelist concerning the impartation of the Spirit to the disciples, is attested as the correct one by the fact, that it throws unexpected light on an obscurity in his gospel with respect to which we were previously unable to come to a decision. In relation to the farewell discourses of Jesus, it was not possible to settle the dispute, whether what Jesus there says of his return is to be referred to the days of his resurrection, or to the outpouring of the Spirit, because the description of that return as a *seeing again* seemed to speak as decidedly for the former, as the observation that in that time they would no longer ask him anything, and would understand him fully, for the latter : a dispute which is decided in the most welcome manner, if it can be shown to be the opinion of the narrator that the impartation of the Spirit fell in the days of the resurrection.[13] At first indeed it might be thought, that this impartation, especially as in John it is connected with the formal appointment of his disciples as his envoys, and the communication of the authority to remit and retain sins (comp. Matt. xviii. 18), would have been more appropriate at the close than the commencement of the appearances of the risen Jesus, and in a full assembly of the Apostles than in one from which Thomas was absent ; but on this account to suppose with Olshausen that the Evangelist for the sake of brevity merely appends the impartation of the Spirit to the first appearance, though it really belonged to a later interview, is an inadmissible violence ; and we must rather allow, that the author of the fourth gospel regarded this first appearance of Jesus as the principal one, and the one eight days later as merely supernumerary in favour of Thomas. The appearance chap. xxi. is also a supplement, which the author, when he wrote his gospel, either had not known, or at least did not recollect.

§ 142.

THE SO-CALLED ASCENSION CONSIDERED AS A SUPERNATURAL AND AS A NATURAL EVENT.

The ascension of Jesus is reported to us in the New Testament in three different narratives, which in point of fulness of detail and picturesqueness of description form a progressive series. Mark, who in the last portion of his gospel is in general very brief and abrupt, only says, that after Jesus had spoken to the disciples for the last time, he was received up (ἀνελήφθη) into heaven and sat on the right hand of God (xvi. 19). With scarcely more definiteness it is said in the gospel of Luke that Jesus led his disciples *out as far as Bethany*, ἔξω ἕως εἰς Βηθανίαν, and while he here with uplifted hands

---

[13] Comp. Weisse, die evang. Geschichte, 2, s. 418.

gave them his blessing, he was parted from them (διέστη), and carried up into heaven (ἀνεφέρετο) ; whereupon the disciples fell down and worshipped him, and forthwith returned to Jerusalem with great joy (xxiv. 50 ff.).   In the introduction to the Acts, Luke gives more ample details concerning this scene.   On the mount of Olives, where Jesus delivered to his disciples his last commands and promises; he was taken up before their eyes (ἐπήρθη), and a cloud received him out of their sight.   While the disciples were watching him, as he went up into heaven on the clond, there suddenly stood by them two men in white apparel, who induced them to desist from thus gazing after him by the assurance, that the Jesus now taken from them would come again from heaven in the same manner as he had just ascended into heaven ; on which they were satisfied, and returned to Jerusalem (i. 1–12).

The first impression from this narrative is clearly this : that it is intended as a description of a miraculous event, an actual exaltation of Jesus into heaven, as the dwelling-place of God, and an attestation of this by angels ; as orthodox theologians, both ancient and modern, correctly maintain.   The only question is, whether they can also help us to surmount the difficulties which stand in our way when we attempt to form a conception of such an event ?   One main difficulty is this : how can a palpable body, which has still *flesh and bones*, and eats material food, be qualified for a celestial abode ? how can it so far liberate itself from the laws of gravity, as to be capable of an ascent through the air ? and how can it be conceived that God gave so preternatural a capability to Jesus by a miracle?[1]   The only possible reply to these questions is, that the grosser elements which the body of Jesus still retained after the resurrection, were removed before the ascension, and only the finest essence of his corporeality, as the integument of the soul, was taken by him into heaven.[2]   But as the disciples who were present at the ascension observed no residuum of his body which he had left behind, this leads either to the above mentioned absurdity of an evaporation of the body of Jesus, or to Olshausen's process of subtilization which, still incomplete even after the resurrection, was not perfected until the moment of the ascension ; a process which must have been conducted with singularly rapid retrograde transitions in these last days, if the body of Jesus, when penetrating into the closed room where the disciples were assembled, is to be supposed immaterial ; immediately after when Thomas touched him, material ; and lastly, in the ascension, again immaterial.   The other difficulty lies in the consideration, that according to a just idea of the world, the seat of God and of the blessed, to which Jesus is supposed to have been exalted, is not to be sought for in the upper regions of the air, nor, in general, in any determinate place ;—such a locality could only be assigned to it in the childish, limited conceptions of antiquity. We are well aware that he who would attain to God and the circle of the blessed would make a superfluous circuit, if he thought it necessary for this purpose to soar aloft into the higher regions of the firmament ; and the more intimately Jesus was acquainted with God and divine things, the farther certainly would he be from making such a circuit, or from being caused to make it by God.[3]   Thus there would be no other resource than to suppose a divine accommodation to the idea of the world in that age, and to say : God in order to convince the disciples of the return of Jesus into the higher world, although this world is in reality by no means to be sought for in the

---

[1] Gabler, in the neuesten theol. Journal 3, s. 417, and in the Vorrede zu Griesbach's opusc. acad. p. xcvi. comp. Kuinöl, in Marc., p. 222.

[2] Seiler, ap. Kuinöl, ut. sup. s. 223.

[3] Comp. Paulus, exeg. Handb. 3, b, s. 921 ; De Wette, Religion und Theologie, s. 161.

upper air, nevertheless prepared the spectacle of such an exaltation.[4] But
this is to represent God as theatrically arranging an illusion.

As an attempt to set us free from such difficulties and absurdities, the
natural explanation of this narrative must needs be welcome.[5] This distinguishes in the evangelical accounts of the ascension, what was actually beheld,
and what was inferred by reasoning. Certainly, when it is said in the Acts :
while they beheld, he was taken up, βλεπόντων αὐτῶν ἐπήρθη : the exaltation to
heaven seems here to be represented as a fact actually witnessed. But the
Rationalists tell us that we are not to understand ἐπήρθη, as signifying an
elevation above the earth, but only that Jesus, in order to bless the disciples,
drew up his form and thus appeared more elevated to them. They then
bring forward the word διέστη, *he was parted from them*, in the conclusion of
Luke's gospel, and interpret it to mean that Jesus in taking leave of his disciples removed himself farther from them. Hereupon, they continue, in the
same way as on the mount of Transfiguration, a cloud was interposed between
Jesus and the disciples, and together with the numerous olive-trees on the
mount, concealed him from their sight ; a result which, on the assurance ot
two unknown men, they regarded as a reception of Jesus into heaven. But,
when Luke in the Acts immediately connects ἐπήρθη with the statement, *and
a cloud received him*, καὶ νεφέλη ὑπέλαβεν αὐτὸν : he implies that the *taking up*
was an introduction to the being received by the cloud ; which it would not
be if it were a mere drawing up of the body, but only if it were an exaltation
of Jesus above the earth, since only in this case could a cloud float under,
carry, and envelop him, which is the idea expressed by ὑπέλαβεν. Again, in
the Gospel of Luke, the fact that *he was parted from them* is represented as
something which took place *while he blessed them*, ἐν τῷ εὐλογεῖν αὐτον αὐτοὺς ;
now no one when pronouncing a benediction on another, will remove from
him : whereas it appears very suitable, that Jesus while communicating his
blessing to the disciples should be carried upward, and thus, while rising, have
continued to extend over them his outstretched hand as a symbol of his
blessing. Thus the natural explanation of the disappearance in the cloud
falls to the ground of itself ; while in the supposition that the two individuals
clothed in white apparel were natural men, Paulus only disguises a final and
strongly marked essay of the opinion espoused by Bahrdt and Venturini, that
several epochs in the life of Jesus, especially after his crucifixion, were brought
about by the agency of secret colleagues. And Jesus himself—what, according to this opinion, must we suppose to have become of him after this last
separation from his disciples ? Shall we, with Bahrdt, dream of an Essene
lodge, into which he retired after the completion of his work ? and with
Brennecke appeal, in proof that Jesus long continued silently to work for the
welfare of mankind, to his appearance for the purpose of the conversion ot
Paul ? But, taking the narrative of the Acts as historical, this was connected
with circumstances and effects which could be produced by no natural man,
even though a member of a secret order. Or shall we with Paulus suppose,
that shortly after the last interview the body of Jesus sank beneath the
injuries it had received? This could not have happened in the very
next moments after he had appeared still active among his disciples, so that
the two men who joined them might have been witnesses of his decease,—
who, even admitting this, would not have spoken in accordance with the
truth ; but if he continued to live for any length of time he must have had

[4] Kern, Hauptthatsachen, Tüb. Zeitschrift, 1836, 3, s. 58, Comp. Steudel (Glaubenslehre, s. 323), who supposes the ascension to have been a vision which God produced in the
disciples. Against this comp. my Streitschriften, I, s. 152 ff.
[5] See especially Paulus, ut sup. s. 910 ff. ; L. J. I, b, s. 318 ff.

the intention to remain for that period in the concealment of a secret society; and to this must then be supposed to belong the two men clothed in white, who, doubtless with his previous sanction, persuaded the disciples that he had ascended into heaven.[6] But this is a mode of representation, from which in this instance as in every other, a sound judgment must turn away with aversion.

§ 143.

INSUFFICIENCY OF THE NARRATIVES OF THE ASCENSION.   MYTHICAL CON-
CEPTION OF THOSE NARRATIVES.

Among all the New Testament histories of miracles, the ascension least demanded such an expenditure of perverted acumen, since the attestations to its historical validity are peculiarly weak,—not only to us who, having no risen Jesus, can consequently have no ascended one, but apart from all prior conclusions and in every point of view.   Matthew and John, who according to the common idea were the two eyewitnesses among the Evangelists, do not mention it; it is narrated by Mark and Luke alone, while in the rest of the New Testament writings decided allusions to it are wanting.   But this absence of allusions to the ascension in the rest of the New Testament is denied by orthodox expositors.   When, say they, Jesus in Matthew (xxvi. 64), declares before the high priest, that hereafter the Son of Man will be seen sitting at the right hand of God : this presupposes an exaltation thither, consequently an ascension; when in John (iii. 13), he says, no one hath ascended into heaven but the Son of Man who came from heaven, and at another time (vi. 62) tells the disciples that they will hereafter see him ascend where he was before; further, when on the morning of the resurrection he declares that he is not yet ascended to his Father, implying that he is about to do so (xx. 17): there could hardly be more explicit allusions to the ascension; again, when the apostles in the Acts so often speak of an exaltation of Jesus to the right hand of God (ii. 33, v. 31, comp. vii. 56), and Paul represents him as *ascended up far above all heavens* ἀναβὰς ὑπεράνω πάντων τῶν οὐρανῶν (Ephes. iv. 10), Peter, as *gone into heaven* πορευθεὶς εἰς οὐρανὸν (1 Pet. iii. 22) : there can be no doubt that they all knew of his ascension.[1] All these passages, however, with the exception perhaps of John vi. 62, where a *SEEING the Son of Man ascend*, θεωρεῖν ἀναβαίνοντα τὸν υἱὸν τοῦ ἀνθρώπου, is spoken of, contain only in general his exaltation to heaven, without intimating that it was an external, visible fact, that took place in the presence of the disciples.   Rather, when we find Paul in 1 Cor. xv. 5 ff. ranking the appearance of Jesus to himself, which occurred long after the alleged ascension, with the Christophanies before this epoch, so entirely without any pause or indication of a distinction : we must doubt, not merely that all the appearances which he enumerates besides his own can have occurred before the ascension,[2] but whether the Apostle can have had any knowledge at all of an ascension as an external fact which closed the earthly life of Jesus.   As to the author of the fourth gospel,—in his metaphorical language, we are not compelled by the word θεωρῆτε, any more than by the ὄψεσθε in relation to the angels ascending and descending upon Jesus, i. 52, to ascribe to him a knowledge of

---

[6] Briefe über den Rationalismus, s. 146, Anm. 28.
[1] Seiler, ap. Kuinöl, ut sup. s. 221; Olshausen, s. 591 f.   Comp. Griesbach, locorum N. T. ad ascensionem Christi in cœlum spectantium sylloge. In his opusc. acad. ed. Gabler, vol. 2, s. 484 ff.
[2] Schneckenburger, über den Urspr. u. s. f., s. 19.

the visible ascension of Jesus, of which he gives no intimation at the conclusion of his gospel.

Commentators have, it is true, taken all possible pains to explain the want of a narrative of the ascension in the first and fourth gospels, in a way which may not prove inimical either to the authority of the writings, or to the historical value of the fact. They maintain that the Evangelists who are silent on the subject, held it either unnecessary, or impossible, to narrate the ascension. They held it unnecessary, say these expositors, either intrinsically, from the minor importance of the event;[3] or extrinsically, on the consideration that it was generally known as a part of the evangelical tradition;[4] John in particular supposed it to be known from Mark and Luke;[5] or lastly, both Matthew and John omitted it as not belonging to the earthly life of Jesus, to the description of which their writings were exclusively devoted.[6] But we must contend, on the contrary, that the life of Jesus, especially that enigmatical life which he led after his return from the grave, absolutely required such a close as the ascension. Whether it were generally known or not, whether it were important or unimportant,—the simple æsthetic interest which dictates even to an uncultivated author, that a narrative should be wound up with a conclusion, must have led every evangelical writer who knew of the ascension to mention it, though it were but summarily at the end of his history, in order to avoid the strange impression left by the first gospel and still more by the fourth, as narratives losing themselves in vague obscurity. Hence our apologists resort to the supposition that the first and fourth Evangelists held it impossible to give an account of the ascension of Jesus, because the eyewitnesses, however long they might gaze after him, could still only see him hovering in the air and encircled by the cloud, not entering heaven and taking his place on the right hand of God.[7] But in the ideas of the ancient world, to which heaven was nearer than to us, an entrance into the clouds was in itself a real ascent into heaven, as we see from the stories of Romulus and Elijah.

Thus it is undeniable that the above Evangelists were ignorant of the ascension: but the conclusion of the most recent criticism, that this ignorance is a reproach to the first Evangelist as a sign of his unapostolic character,[8] is the less in place here, because the event in question is rendered suspicious not merely by the silence of two Evangelists, but also by the want of agreement between those who narrate it. Mark is at variance with Luke, nay, Luke is at variance with himself. In the account of the former, it appears as if Jesus had ascended into heaven immediately from the meal in which he appeared to the eleven, consequently from out of a house in Jerusalem; for the phrases: *he appeared with the eleven as they sat at meat, and upbraided them—and he said—So then after the Lord had spoken unto them he was received up into heaven,* etc., ἀνακειμένοις—ἐφανερώθη καὶ ὠνείδισε —καὶ εἶπεν—Ὁ μὲν οὖν κύριος, μετὰ τὸ λαλῆσαι αὐτοῖς, ἀνελήφθη κ. τ. λ. have an immediate dependence on each other, and it is only by violence that a change of place or a distinction of time can be introduced.[9] Now an ascent into

[3] Olshausen, s. 593 f.
[4] Even Fritzsche, weary at the conclusion of his labour, writes in Matth., p. 835: *Matthæus Jesu in cœlum abitum non commemoravit, quippe nemini ignotum.*
[5] Michaelis, ut sup. 352.
[6] The treatise: Warum haben nicht alle Evangelisten die Himmelfahrt Jesu ausdrücklich miterzählt? in Flatt's Magazin, 8, s. 67.
[7] The above-named Treatise in Flatt's Magazin.
[8] Schneckenburger, ut sup. s. 19 f.
[9] As by Kuinöl, p. 208 f. 217.

heaven directly out of a room is certainly not easy to imagine; hence Luke represents it as taking place in the open air.   In his gospel he makes Jesus immediately before his ascension, lead out his disciples *as far as Bethany* ἕως εἰς Βηθανίαν, but in the Acts he places the scene on the *mount called Olivet* ὄρος τὸ καλούμενον ἐλαιῶνα ; this, however, cannot be imputed to him as a contradiction, since Bethany lay in the neighbourhood of the mount of Olives.[10] But there is a more important divergency in his statement of time ; for in his gospel, as in Mark, we are left to infer that the ascension took place on the same day with the resurrection : whereas in the Acts it is expressly remarked, that the two events were separated by an interval of forty days.   It has already been remarked that the latter determination of time must have come to the knowledge of Luke in the interim between the composition of the gospel and that of the Acts.   The more numerous the narratives of appearances of the risen Jesus, and the more various the places to which they were assigned : the less would the short space of a day suffice for his life on earth after the resurrection ; while the determination of the lengthened period which had become necessary to forty days precisely, had its foundation in the part which this number is known to have played in the Jewish, and already in the Christian legend.   The people of Israel were forty years in the wilderness ; Moses was forty days on mount Sinai ; he and Elias fasted forty days ; and Jesus himself previous to the temptation remained the same length of time without nourishment in the wilderness.   As, then, all these mysterious intermediate states and periods of transition were determined by the number forty : this number presented itself as especially appropriate for the determination of the mysterious interval between the resurrection and ascension of Jesus.[11]

As regards the description of the event itself, it might be thought admissible to ascribe the silence of Mark, and of Luke in his gospel, concerning the cloud and the angels, purely to the brevity of their narratives ; but since Luke at the close of his gospel narrates circumstantially enough the conduct of the disciples—how they fell down and worshipped the ascended Jesus, and returned to the city with great joy : so he would doubtless have pointed out the information communicated to them by angels as the immediate source of their joy, had he known anything of such a particular at the time when he composed his first writing.   Hence this feature seems rather to have been gradually formed in tradition, in order to render due honour to this last point also in the life of Jesus, and to present a confirmation of the insufficient testimony of men as to his exaltation into heaven by the mouth of two heavenly witnesses.

As, according to this, those who knew of an ascension of Jesus, had by no means the same idea of its particular circumstances : there must have been in general two different modes of conceiving the close of the life of Jesus ; some regarding it as a visible ascension, others not so.[12]   When Matthew makes Jesus before the tribunal of the high priest predict his exaltation to the right hand of the divine power (xxvi. 64), and after his resurrection declare that now all power is given to him in heaven and earth (xxviii. 18) ; and nevertheless has nothing of a visible ascension, but on the contrary puts into the mouth

---

[10] Nevertheless comp. De Wette on the Acts, i. 12.
[11] Vid. Vol. i., § 56, and the authors there cited.   The reference to a reckoning in Daniel, in Paulus, exeg. Handb. 3, b. s. 923, appears to me too artificial.
[12] On this subject comp. especially Ammon, Ascensus J. C., in cœlum historia biblica.   In his opusc. nov. p. 43 ff. Fortbildung des Christenth. 2, 1, s. 13 ff. ; also Kaiser, bibl. Theol. 1, s. 83 ff. ; de Wette, exeg. Handb. 1, 1, s. 247 ; Weisse, die evang. Gesch. 2, p. 375 ff.

of Jesus the assurance : *I am with you alway, even unto the end of the world,*
ἐγὼ μεθ᾽ ὑμῶν εἰμι πάσας τὰς ἡμέρας ἕως τῆς συντελείας τοῦ αἰῶνος (v. 20) : it is
evident that the latent idea, on which his representation is founded, is that
Jesus, doubtless immediately on his resurrection, ascended invisibly to the
Father, though at the same time remaining invisibly with his followers ; and
that out of this concealment he, as often as he found it expedient, revealed
himself in Christophanies. The same view is to be discerned in the Apostle
Paul, when in 1 Cor. xv. he undistinguishingly places the appearance to himself of the Christ already ascended into heaven, in one series with the earlier
Christophanies ; and also the author of the fourth gospel and the rest of the
New Testament writers only presuppose what must necessarily be presupposed
according to the messianic passage : *Sit thou at my right hand,* Ps. cx. 1 : that
Jesus was exalted to the right hand of God ; without deciding anything as to
the manner of the exaltation, or representing to themselves the ascension as
a visible one. The imagination of the primitive Christians must however have
felt a strong temptation to depict this exaltation as a brilliant spectacle.
When it was once concluded that the Messiah Jesus had arrived at so exalted
a position, it would appear desirable to gaze after him, as it were, on his way
thither. If it was expected, in accordance with the prophecy of Daniel, that
his future return from heaven would be a visible descent in the clouds : this
would naturally suggest that his departure to heaven should be represented
as a visible ascent on a cloud ; and when Luke makes the two white-apparelled
angels, who joined the disciples after the removal of Jesus, say : *this same
Jesus, who is taken up from you into heaven, shall so come in like manner as ye
have seen him go into heaven* (Acts i. 11) : we need only take the converse of
this declaration in order to have before us the genesis of the conception of the
ascension of Jesus ; for the mode of conclusion was this : as Jesus will at some
future time return from heaven in the clouds, so he must surely have departed
thither [13] in the same manner.

Compared with these primary incentives, the Old Testament precedents
which the ascension of Jesus has in the translation of Enoch (Gen. v. 24 ;
comp. Wis. xliv. 16, xlix. 16 ; Heb. xi. 5), and especially in the ascension of
Elijah (2 Kings ii. 11 ; comp. Wis. xlviii. 9 ; 1 Macc. ii. 58), together with
the Grecian and Roman apotheoses of Hercules and Romulus, recede into
the background. Apart from the question whether the latter were known to
the second and third Evangelists ; the statement relative to Enoch is too
vague ; while the chariot and horses of fire that transported Elijah were not
adapted to the milder spirit of Christ. Instead of this the enveloping cloud
and the removal while holding a farewell conversation, may appear to have
been borrowed from the later representation of the removal of Moses, which
however in other particulars has considerable divergencies from that of Jesus.[14]
Perhaps also one trait in the narrative of the Acts may be explained out of
the history of Elijah. When this prophet, before his translation, is entreated
by his servant Elisha that he will bequeath him a double measure of his spirit :
Elijah attaches to the concession of this boon the condition : *if thou see me
when I am taken from thee, it shall be so unto thee ; but if not, it shall not be
so ;* whence we might perhaps gather the reason why Luke (Acts i. 9) lays

---

[13] This is also Hase's opinion, L. J. § 150.

[14] Joseph. Antiq. iv., viii. 48, it is said of Moses : *And as he was going to embrace Eleazar
and Joshua, and was still discoursing with them, a cloud stood over him on a sudden, and he
disappeared in a certain valley, although he wrote in the holy books that he died, which was
done out of fear, lest they should venture to say that because of his extraordinary virtue, he
went to God.* Philo, however, vita Mosis, opp. ed. Mangey, vol. ii. p. 179, makes the soul
only of Moses ascend into heaven.

stress on the fact that the disciples beheld Jesus as he went up ($\beta\lambda\epsilon\pi\acute{o}\nu\tau\omega\nu$ $a\mathring{v}\tau\mathring{\omega}\nu$ $\mathring{\epsilon}\pi\acute{\eta}\rho\theta\eta$) : namely, because, according to the narrative concerning Elijah, this was necessary, if the disciples were to receive the spirit of their master.

CONCLUDING DISSERTATION.

THE DOGMATIC IMPORT OF THE LIFE OF JESUS.

---

§ 144.

NECESSARY TRANSITION FROM CRITICISM TO DOGMA. *

THE results of the inquiry which we have now brought to a close, have apparently annihilated the greatest and most valuable part of that which the Christian has been wont to believe concerning his Saviour Jesus, have uprooted all the animating motives which he has gathered from his faith, and withered all his consolations. The boundless store of truth and life which for eighteen centuries has been the aliment of humanity, seems irretrievably dissipated; the most sublime levelled with the dust, God divested of his grace, man of his dignity, and the tie between heaven and earth broken. Piety turns away with horror from so fearful an act of desecration, and strong in the impregnable self-evidence of its faith, pronounces that, let an audacious criticism attempt what it will, all which the Scriptures declare, and the Church believes of Christ, will still subsist as eternal truth, nor needs one iota of it to be renounced. Thus at the conclusion of the criticism of the history of Jesus, there presents itself this problem: to re-establish dogmatically that which has been destroyed critically.

At the first glance, this problem appears to exist merely as a challenge addressed by the believer to the critic, not as a result of the moral requirements of either. The believer would appear to need no re-establishment of the faith, since for him it cannot be subverted by criticism. The critic seems to require no such re-establishment, since he is able to endure the annihilation resulting from his own labours. Hence it might be supposed that the critic, when he seeks to rescue the dogma from the flames which his criticism has kindled, acts falsely in relation to his own point of view, since, to satisfy the believer, he treats what is valueless for himself as if he esteemed it to be a jewel; while in relation to the believer, he is undertaking a superfluous task, in labouring to defend that which the latter considers in no way endangered.

But on a nearer view the case appears otherwise. To all belief, not built on demonstration,†doubt is inherent, though it may not be developed; the most firmly believing Christian has within him the elements of criticism as a latent deposit of unbelief, or rather as a negative germ of knowledge, and only by its constant repression can he maintain the predominance of his faith, which is thus essentially a re-established faith. And just as the believer is intrinsically a sceptic or critic, so, on the other hand, the critic is intrinsically a believer. In proportion as he is distinguished from the naturalistic theologian, and the free-thinker,—in proportion as his criticism is conceived in the spirit of the nineteenth century,—he is filled with veneration for every religion,

₇₅₇

and especially for the substance of the sublimest of all religions, the Christian, which he perceives to be identical with the deepest philosophical truth ; and hence, after having in the course of his criticism exhibited only the differences between his conviction and the historical belief of the Christian, he will feel urged to place that identity in a just light.

Further, our criticism, though in its progress it treats of details, yet on be-coming part of our internal conviction, resolves itself into the simple element of doubt, which the believer neutralizes by an equally simple *veto*, and then spreads anew in undiminished luxuriance all the fulness of his creed.   But hereby the decisions of criticism are only dismissed, not vanquished, and that which is believed is supported by no intermediate proof, but rests absolutely on its own evidence.   Criticism cannot but direct itself against this absence of intermediate proof, and thus the controversy which seemed ended is re-newed, and we are thrown back to the beginning of our inquiry ; yet with a difference which constitutes a step forward in the discussion.   Hitherto our criticism had for its object the data of Christianity, as historically presented in the evangelical records ; now, these data having been called in question in their historical form, assume that of a mental product, and find a refuge in the soul of the believer ; where they exist, not as a simple history, but as a re-flected history, that is, a confession of faith, a received dogma.   Against this dogma, presenting itself totally unsupported by evidence, criticism must in-deed awake, as it does against all deficiency of proof, in the character of a negativing power, and a contender for intermediate proof : it will, however, no longer be occupied with history, but with doctrines.   Thus our historical criticism is followed up by dogmatical criticism, and it is only after the faith has passed through both these trials, that it is thoroughly tested and consti-tuted science.

This second process through which the faith has to pass, ought, like the first, to be made the subject of a distinct work : I shall here merely give a sketch of its most important features, that I may not terminate an historical criticism without pointing out its ultimate object, which can only be arrived at by dogmatical criticism as a sequel.*

§ 145.

THE CHRISTOLOGY OF THE ORTHODOX SYSTEM.

The dogmatic import of the life of Jesus implicitly received, and developed on this basis, constitutes the orthodox doctrine of the Christ. †

Its fundamental principles are found in the New Testament.   The root of faith in Jesus was the conviction of his resurrection.   He who had been put to death, however great during his life, could not, it was thought, be the Messiah : his miraculous restoration to life proved so much the more strongly that he *was* the Messiah.   Freed by his resurrection from the kingdom of shades, and at the same time elevated above the sphere of earthly humanity, he was now translated to the heavenly regions, and had taken his place at the right hand of God (Acts ii. 32 ff., iii. 15 ff., v. 30 ff. ; and elsewhere).   Now, his death appeared to be the chief article in his messianic destination ; accord-ing to Isa. liii., he had suffered for the sins of his people and of mankind (Acts viii. 32 ff. ; comp. Matt. xx. 28 ; John i. 29, 36 ; 1 John ii. 2) ; his blood poured out on the cross, operated like that which on the great day of atone-ment the high priest sprinkled on the mercy-seat (Rom. iii. 25) ; he was the pure lamb by whose blood the believing are redeemed (1 Pet. i. 18 f.) ; the eternal, sinless high priest, who by the offering of his own body, at once effected that, which the Jewish high priests were unable to effect, by their perpetually repeated sacrifices of animals (Heb. x. 10 ff., etc.). But, thenceforth, the Messiah who was exalted to the right hand of God, could not have been a common man : not only was he anointed with the divine spirit in a greater measure than any prophet (Acts iv. 27, x. 38); not only did he prove himself to be a divine messenger by miracles and signs (Acts ii. 22) ; but also, according as the one idea or the other was most readily formed, either he was supernaturally engendered by the Holy Spirit (Matt. and Luke i.), or he had descended as the Word and Wisdom of God into an earthly body (John i.). As, before his appearance on the earth, he was in the bosom of the Father, in divine majesty (John xvii. 5) : so his descent into the world of mortals, and still more his submission to an ignominious death, was a voluntary humiliation, to which he was moved by his love to mankind (Phil. ii. 5 ff.). The risen and ascended Jesus will one day return to wake the dead and judge the world (Acts i. 11, xvii. 31) ; he even now takes charge of his church (Rom. viii. 34 ; 1 John ii. 1), participating in the government of the world, as he originally did in its creation (Matt. xxviii. 18 ; John i. 3, 10 ; Col. i. 16 f.). In addition to all this, every trait in the image of the Messiah as sketched by the popular expectation, was attributed with necessary or gratuitous modifications to Jesus ; nay, the imagination, once stimulated, invented new characteristics.

How richly fraught with blessing and elevation, with encouragement and consolation, were the thoughts which the early Church derived from this view of the Christ ! By the mission of the Son of God into the world, by his delivery of himself to death for the sake of the world, heaven and earth are reconciled (2 Cor. v. 18 ff. ; Eph. i. 10 ; Col. i. 20) ; by this most stupendous sacrifice, the love of God is securely guaranteed to man (Rom. v. 8 ff., viii. 31 ff. ; 1 John iv. 9), and the brightest hopes are revealed to him. Did the Son of God become man ? Then are men his brethren, and as such the children of God, and heirs with Christ to the treasure of divine bliss (Rom. viii. 16 f., 29). The servile relation of man to God, as it existed under the law, has ceased ; love has taken the place of the fear of the punishment threatened by the law (Rom. viii. 15 ; Gal. iv. 1 ff.). Believers are redeemed from the curse of the law by Christ's sacrifice of himself, inasmuch as he suffered a death on which the law had laid a curse (Gal. iii. 13). Now, there is no longer imposed on us the impossible task of satisfying all the demands of the law (Gal. iii. 10 f.)—a task which, as experience shows, no man fulfils (Rom. i. 18–iii. 20), which, by reason of his sinful nature, no man can fulfil (Rom. v. 12 ff.), and which only involves him who strives to fulfil it, more and more deeply in the most miserable conflict with himself (Rom. vii. 7 ff.) : whereas he who believes in Christ, and confides in the atoning efficacy of his death, possesses the favour of God ; not by works and qualifications of his own, but by the free mercy of God, is the man who throws himself on that mercy just before God, by which all self-exaltation is excluded (Rom. iii. 31 ff.). As the Mosaic law is no longer binding on the believer, he being dead to it with Christ (Rom. vii. 1 ff.) ; as, moreover, by the eternal and all-sufficient sacrifice of Christ, the Jewish sacrificial and priestly service is abolished (Heb.) ; therefore the partition wall which separated the Jews and Gentiles is broken down : the latter, who before were aliens and strangers to the theocracy, without God and without hope in the world, are now invited to participate in the new covenant, and free access is opened to them to the paternal God ; so that the two portions of mankind, formerly separated by hostile opinions, are now at peace with each other, members in common of the body of Christ—stones in the spiritual building of his Church (Eph. ii. 11 ff.). But to have justifying faith in the death of Christ, is, virtually, to die with him spiritually—that is, to die to sin ; and as Christ arose from the dead to a new and immortal life, so must the believer in him arise from the death of sin to a new life of righteousness and holiness, put off the old man and put on the new (Rom. vi. 1 ff.). In this, Christ himself aids him by his Spirit, who fills those whom he inspires with spiritual strivings, and makes them ever more and more free from the slavery of sin (Rom. viii. 1 ff.). Nor alone spiritually, will the Spirit of Christ animate those in whom he dwells, but corporeally also, for at the end of their earthly course, God, through Christ, will resuscitate their bodies, as he did the body of Christ (Rom. viii. 11). Christ, whom the bonds of death and the nether world could not hold, has vanquished both for us, and has delivered the believer from the fear of these dread powers which rule over mortality (Rom. viii. 38 f. ; 1 Cor. xv. 55 ff. ; Heb. ii. 14 f.). His resurrection not only confers atoning efficacy on his death (Rom. iv. 25), but at the same time is the pledge of our own future resurrection, of our share in Christ in a future life, in his messianic kingdom, to the blessedness of which he will, at his second advent, lead all his people.   Meanwhile, we may console ourselves that we have in him an Intercessor, who from his own experience of the weakness and frailty of our nature, which he himself assumed, and in which he was in all points tempted as we are, but without sin, knows how much indulgence and aid we need (Heb. ii. 17 f., iv. 15 f.).

The expediency of describing in compendious forms the riches of their faith in Christ, was early felt by his followers.   They celebrated him as *Christ that died, yea rather, that is risen again, who is even at the right hand of God, who also maketh intercession for us*, Χριστὸς ὁ ἀποθανων, μᾶλλον δὲ καὶ ἐγερθεὶς, ὃς καὶ ἔστιν ἐν δεξιᾷ τοῦ θεοῦ, ὃς καὶ ἐντυγχάνει ὑπὲρ ἡμῶν (Rom. viii. 34) ; or with more particularity as *Jesus Christ our Lord, who was made of the seed of David according to the flesh, and declared to be the Son of God with power, according to the Spirit of holinesss, by the resurrection from the dead*, Ἰ. Χ. ὁ Κύριος, γενόμενος ἐκ σπέρματος Δαβὶδ κατὰ σάρκα, ὁρισθεὶς υἱὸς θεοῦ ἐν δυνάμει κατὰ πνεῦμα ἁγιωσύνης, ἐξ ἀναστάσεως νεκρῶν (Rom. i. 3 f.) ; and as *confessedly the great mystery of godliness*, ὁμολογουμένως μέγα τῆς εὐσεβείας μυστήριον, the following propositions were presented : *God was manifest in the flesh, justified in the Spirit, seen of angels, preached unto the Gentiles, believed on in the world, received up into glory*, θεὸς ἐφανερώθη ἐν σαρκὶ, ἐδικαιώθη ἐν πνεύματι, ὤφθη ἀγγέλοις, ἐκηρύχθη ἐν ἔθνεσιν, ἐπιστεύθη ἐν κόσμῳ, ἀνελήφθη ἐν δόξῃ (1 Tim. iii. 16).

The baptismal formula (Matt. xxviii. 19), by its allocation of Father, Son, and Holy Ghost, presented a sort of framework in which to arrange the materials of the new faith.   On this basis was constructed in the first centuries what was called the rule of faith, *regula fidei*, which in divers forms, some more concise, others more diffuse, some more popular, others more subtle, is found in the different fathers.[1]   The more popular form at length settled into what is called the creed of the apostles.   This symbol, in that edition of it which is received in the evangelical church, has in its second and most elaborate article on the Son, the following points of belief : *et (credo) in Jesum Christum, filium ejus (Dei patris) unicum, Dominum nostrum ; qui conceptus est de Spiritu Sancto, natus ex Maria virgine ; passus sub Pontio Pilato, crucifixus, mortuus et sepultus, descendit ad inferna ; tertia die resurrexit a mortuis, ascendit ad cœlos, sedet ad dextram Dei patris omnipotentis ; inde venturus est, judicare vivos et mortuos.*

---

[1] Iren adv. hær. i. 10.   Tertull. de præscr. hær. xiii. adv. Prax. ii. de veland. virg. i. Orig. de principp. prooem. iv

Together with this popular form of the confession of faith in relation to Christ, there was also framed a more rigorous and minute theological digest, occasioned by the differences and controversies which early arose on certain points. The fundamental thesis of the Christian faith, that *the Word was made flesh*, ὁ λόγος σὰρξ ἐγένετο, or, *God was manifested in the flesh*, θεὸς ἐφανερώθη ἐν σαρκὶ, was endangered on all sides, one questioning the Godhead, another the manhood, and a third the veritable union of the two natures.

It is true that those who, like the Ebionites, denied the Godhead, or like that sect of the Gnostics called Docetæ, the manhood of Christ, separated themselves too decidedly from the Christian community, which on her part maintained that *it was necessary that the mediator of God and man should unite both in friendship and harmony by means of a proper relationship to each, and that while he represented man to God, he should reveal God to man*, ἔδει τὸν μεσίτην θεοῦ τε καὶ ἀνθρώπων διὰ ἰδίας πρὸς ἑκατέρους οἰκειότητος εἰς φιλίαν καὶ ὁμόνοιαν τοὺς ἀμφοτέρους συναγαγεῖν, καὶ θεῷ μὲν παραστῆσαι τὸν ἄνθρωπον, ἀνθρώποις δὲ γνωρίσαι τὸν θεόν.[2] But when it was merely the plenitude of the one nature or the other, which was contested,—as when Arius maintained that the being who became man in Christ was indeed divine, but created, and subordinate to the supreme God; when, while ascribing to Christ a human body, he held that the place of the soul was occupied by that superior being; when Apollinaris maintained that not only the body of Jesus was truly human, but his soul also, and that the divine being only served in the stead of the third principle in man, the νοῦς *(understanding)*;—these were opinions to which it was easier to give a Christian guise. Nevertheless the Church rejected the Arian idea of a subordinate God become man in Jesus, for this reason among others less essential, that on this theory the image of the Godhead would not have been manifested in Christ;[3] and she condemned the idea of Arius and Apollinaris, that the human nature of Christ had not the human ψυχὴ *(soul)*, or the human νοῦς *(understanding)*, for this reason chiefly, that only by the union of the divine, with an entire human nature, could the human race be redeemed.[4]

Not only might the one or the other aspect of the nature of Christ be defaced or put out of sight, but in relation also to the union of the two, there might be error, and again in two opposite directions. The devout enthusiasm of many led them to believe, that they could not draw too closely the newly-entwined bond between heaven and earth; hence they no longer wished to distinguish between the Godhead and manhood in Christ, and since he had appeared in one person, they acknowledged in him only one nature, that of the Son of God made flesh. Others, more scrupulous, could not reconcile themselves to such a confusion of the divine and the human: it seemed to them blasphemous to say that a human mother had given birth to God: hence they maintained that she had only borne the man whom the Son of God selected as his temple; and that in Christ there were two natures, united indeed so far as the adoration of his followers was concerned, but distinct as regarded their essence. To the Church, both these views appeared to encroach on the mystery of the incarnation: if the two natures were held to be permanently distinct, then was the union of the divine and human, the vital point of Christianity, destroyed; if a mixture of the two were admitted, then neither nature in its individual quality was capable of a union with the other, and thus again no true unity would be attained. Hence both these opinions

---

[2] Iren. adv. hær. iii. xviii. 7.

[3] Athanas. contra Arianos, orat. 2, 33.

[4] Gregor. Naz. Or. 51, p. 740, B.: τὸ γὰρ ἀπρόσληπτον ἀθεράπευμον. ὃ δὲ ἥνωται τῷ θεῷ, τοῦτο καὶ σώζεται.

were condemned, the latter in the person of Eutyches, the former, not with equal justice, in that of Nestorius ; and as the Nicene creed established the true Godhead of Christ, so that of Chalcedon established his true and perfect manhood, and the union of the two natures in one undivided person.[5] When subsequently there arose a controversy concerning the will of Christ, analogous to that concerning his nature, the Church, in accordance with its previous decisions, pronounced that in Christ, as the God-man, there were two wills, distinct but not discordant, the human will being subordinate to the divine.[6]

In comparison with the controversies on the being and essence of Christ, the other branch of the faith, the doctrine of his work, was developed in tranquillity. The most comprehensive view of it was this : the Son of God, by assuming the human nature, gave it a holy and divine character [7]—above all he endowed it with immortality ; [8] while in a moral view, the mission of the Son of God into the world being the highest proof of the love of God, was the most efficacious means of awakening a return of love in the human breast.[9] To this one great effect of the appearance of Christ, were annexed collateral benefits : his salutary teaching, his sublime example, were held up to view,[10] but especial importance was attached to the violent death which he suffered. The idea of substitution, already given in the New Testament, was more fully developed : the death of Jesus was regarded, now as a ransom paid by him to the devil for the liberation of mankind, who had fallen into the power of the evil one through sin ; now as a means devised by God for removing guilt, and enabling him to remit the punishment threatened to the sins of man, without detriment to his truthfulness, Christ having taken that punishment on himself.[11] The latter idea was worked up Anselm, in his book entitled *Cur Deus homo*, into the well known theory of satisfaction, by which the doctrine of Christ's work of redemption is placed in the closest connexion with that of his person. Man owes to God perfect obedience ; but the sinner—and such are all men—withholds from God the service and honour which are His due. Now God, by reason of his justice, cannot suffer an offence against his honour : therefore, either man must voluntarily restore to God that which is

---

[5] — ἕνα καὶ τὸν αὐτὸν ὁμολογεῖν υἱὸν τὸν κύριον ἡμῶν Ἰ. Χ. συμφώνως ἅπαντες ἐκδιδάσκομεν, τέλειον τὸν αὐτὸν ἐν θεότητι, καὶ τέλειον τὸν αὐτὸν ἐν ἀνθρωπότητι, θεὸν ἀληθῶς καὶ ἄνθρωπον ἀληθῶς τὸν αὐτὸν ἐκ ψυχῆς λογικῆς καὶ σώματος, ὁμοούσιον τῷ πατρὶ κατὰ τὴν θεότητα, καὶ ὁμοούσιον τὸν αὐτὸν ἡμῖν κατὰ τὴν ἀνθρωπότητα, κατὰ πάντα ὅμοιον ἡμῖν χωρὶς ἁμαρτίας· πρὸ αἰώνων μὲν ἐκ τοῦ πατρὸς γεννηθέντα κατὰ τὴν θεότητα, ἐπ' ἐσχάτων δὲ τῶν ἡμερῶν τὸν αὐτὸν δι' ἡμᾶς καὶ διὰ τὴν ἡμετέραν σωτηρίαν ἐκ Μαρίας τῆς παρθένου τῆς θεοτόκου κατὰ τὴν ἀνθρωπότητα, ἕνα καὶ τὸν αὐτὸν Χριστὸν, υἱὸν, κύριον, μονογενῆ, ἐκ δύο φύσεων ἀσυγχύτως, ἀτρέπτως, ἀδιαιρέτως, ἀχωρίστως γνωριζόμενον· οὐδαμοῦ τῆς τῶν φύσεων διαφορᾶς ἀνῃρημένης διὰ τὴν ἕνωσιν, σωζομένης δὲ μᾶλλον τῆς ἰδιότητος ἑκατέρας φύσεως, καὶ εἰς ἓν πρόσωπον καὶ μίαν ὑπόστασιν συντρεχούσης· οὐκ εἰς δύο πρόσωπα μεριζόμενον ἢ διαιρούμενον, ἀλλ' ἕνα καὶ τὸν αὐτὸν υἱὸν καὶ μονογενῆ, θεὸν λόγον, κύριον Ἰ. Χ.

[6] The 6th Œcumenical Synod of Constantinople declared : δύο φυσικὰ θελήματα οὐχ ὑπεναντία,—ἀλλ' ἑπόμενον τὸ ἀνθρώπινον αὐτοῦ θέλημα —καὶ ὑποτασσόμενον τῷ θείῳ αὐτοῦ καὶ πανσθενεῖ θελήματι

[7] Athanas. de incarn. 54 : αὐτὸς ἐνηνθρώπησεν, ἵνα ἡμεῖς θεοποιηθῶμεν. Greg. Nyt. Orat. cass. 35 : τότε τε κατεμίχθη πρὸς τὸ θεῖον, ἵνα τὸ ἡμέτερον τῇ πρὸς τὸ θεῖον ἐπιμιξίᾳ γένηται θεῖον. Joann. Damasc. de f. orth. iii. 20 : πάντα ἀνέλαβεν (τὰ ἀδιάβλη τὰ πάθη τοῦ ἀνθρώπου ὁ Χ.) ἵνα πάντα ἁγιάσῃ. Greg. Naz. or. ii. 23 f. Hilar. Pictav. de trin. ii. 24 : *humani generis causa Dei filius natus ex virgine est—ut homo factus ex virgine naturam in se carnis acciperet perque hujus admixtionis societatem sanctificatum in eo universi generis humani corpus existeret.* For other expressions of the kind, see Münscher, Dogmengesch., herausg. von Cölln, I, § 97, Anm. 10.

[8] Münscher, § 96, Anm. 5, s. 423 f.

[9] Augustin, de Catechiz. rudib. 7.

[10] Vid. Münscher, § 96.

[11] Ibid. § 97.

God's, nay, must, for complete satisfaction, render to him more than he has hitherto withheld ; or, God must as a punishment take from man that which is man's, namely, the happiness for which he was originally created. Man is not able to do the former ; for as he owes to God all the duties that he can perform, in order not to fall into sin, he can have no overplus of merit, wherewith to cover past sins. On the other hand, that God should obtain satisfaction by the infliction of eternal punishment, is opposed to his unchangeable goodness, which moves him actually to lead man to that bliss for which he was originally destined. This, however, cannot happen consistently with divine justice, unless satisfaction be made for man, and according to the measure of that which has been taken from God, something be rendered to him, greater than all else except God. But this can be none other than God himself ; and as, on the other hand, man alone can satisfy for man : it must therefore be a God-man who gives satisfaction. Moreover this cannot consist in active obedience, in a sinless life, because every reasonable being owes this to God on his own behalf ; but to suffer death, the wages of sin, a sinless being is not bound, and thus the satisfaction for the sins of man consists in the death of the God-man, whose reward, since he himself, as one with God, cannot be rewarded, is put to the account of man.

This doctrinal system of the ancient church concerning the person and work of Christ, passed also into the confessions of the Lutheran churches, and was still more elaborately developed by their theologians.[12] With regard to the person of Christ, they adhered to the union of the divine and human natures in one person : according to them, in the act of this union, *unitio personalis*, which was simultaneous with the conception, it was the divine nature of the Son of God which adopted the human into the unity of its personality ; the state of union, the *unio personalis*, was neither essential, nor yet merely accidental, neither mystical nor moral, still less merely verbal, but a real and supernatural union, and eternal in its duration. From this union with the divine nature, there result to the human nature in Christ certain preeminent advantages : namely, what at first appears a deficiency, that of being in itself impersonal, and of having personality only by its union with the divine nature ; further, impeccability, and the possibility of not dying. Besides these special advantages, the human nature of Christ obtains others also from its union with the divine. The relation of the two natures is not a dead, external one, but a reciprocal penetration, a περιχώρησις ; an union not like that of two boards glued together, but like that of fire and metal in glowing iron, or of the body and soul in man. This communion of natures, *communio naturarum*, is manifested by a communication of properties, *communicatio idiomatum*, in virtue of which the human nature participates in the advantages of the divine, and the divine in the redeeming work of the human. This relation is expressed in the propositions concerning the person, *propositionibus personalibus*, and those concerning the properties, *idiomaticis* ; the former are propositions in which the concrete of the one nature, i.e. the one nature as conceived in the person of Christ, is predicated of the other, as in 1 Cor. xv. 47 : *the second man is the Lord from heaven ;* the latter are propositions in which determinations of one or the other nature, are referred to the entire person (*genus idiomaticum*), or in which acts of the entire person are referred to one or the other nature (*genus apotelesmaticum*), or lastly, in which attributes of the one nature are transferred to the other, which however is only

---

[12] Comp. Form. Concord., Epit. und Sol. decl. VIII. p. 605 ff. and 761 ff. ed. Hase. Chemniz, de duabus naturis in Christo libellus, and loci theol., loc. 2, de filio ; Gerhard. II. th. 1, p. 640 ff. (ed. 1615) ; Quenstedt, theol. didact. polem. P. 3, c. 3. Comp. De Wette, bibl. Dogm. § 64 ff.

possible from the divine to the human, not from the human to the divine (*genus auchematicum*).

In passing through the successive stages of the work of redemption, Christ with his person endowed with two natures, experienced, according to the expression of the dogmatical theologians, founded on Phil. ii. 6 ff., two states, *statum exinanitionis*, and *statum exaltationis*.   His human nature in its union with the divine, participated from the moment of conception in divine properties : but as during his earthly life Jesus made no continuous use of them, that life to the time of his death and burial, is regarded as a state of humiliation : whereas, with the resurrection, or even with the descent into hell, commenced the state of exaltation which was consummated by the *sessio ad dextram patris*.

As to the work of Christ, the doctrine of our Church attributes to him a triple office.   As prophet, he has revealed to man the highest truth, the divine decree of redemption, confirming his testimony by miracles ; and he still unceasingly controls the announcement of this truth.   As high priest, he has, on the one hand, by his irreproachable life, fulfilled the law in our stead (*obedientia activa*) ; on the other, he has borne, in his sufferings and death, the punishment which impended over us (*obedientia passiva*), and now perpetually intercedes for us with the Father.   Lastly, as king, he governs the world, and more particularly the Church, which he will lead from the conflicts of earth to the glory of heaven, completing its destiny by the general resurrection and the last judgment.

§ 146.

OBJECTIONS TO THE CHRISTOLOGY OF THE CHURCH.

The Reformed Church did not go thus far with the Lutherans in their doctrine of the person of Christ, for they did not admit the last and boldest consequence drawn by the latter from the union of the manhood and Godhead—the *communicatio idiomatum*, or communication of properties.   The Lutherans themselves did not hold that the properties of the human nature were communicated to the divine, nor that all the properties of the divine nature, eternity for example, could be communicated to the human ;[1] and this gave occasion on the part of the Reformed Church, to the following objection : the communication of properties must be reciprocal and complete, or it is none at all ; moreover, by the communication of the properties of an infinite nature to a finite one, the latter is not less annihilated as to its essence than an infinite nature would be, were it to receive the properties of a finite one.[2]   When the Lutherans sought shelter in the position, that the properties of the one nature were only so far shared by the other, as according to its character is possible, *uti per suam indolem potest*,[3] they in fact did away altogether with the *communicatio idiomatum ;* and indeed this doctrine has been explicitly given up even by orthodox theologians since Reinhard.

But the simple root of this complicated exchange of properties, the union of the divine and human natures in one person, has also met with contradiction.

The Socinians denied it on the ground that two natures, each of which alone constitutes a person, cannot be united to form a single person, especially when they possess properties so opposite, as where the one is immortal,

---

[1] See the Oratio appended to the locus de pers. et offic. Chr. Gerhard, ut sup. p. 719 ff.
[2] Vid. Gerhard, II. th.1, p. 685 ff. ; Marheineke, Instit. symb. § 71 f.
[3] Reinhard, Vorles. über die Dogm. s. 354, conformably to the proposition urged by the Reformed against the Lutherans : *Nulla natura in se ipsam recipit contradictoria*, Planck, Gesch. des protest. Lehrbegriffs, Bd. 6, s. 782.

the other mortal, the one uncreated, the other created ; [4] and the Rationalists agree with them, insisting more particularly that the formulæ of the Church, in which the above union is defined, are almost entirely negative, thus presenting no conception to the mind, and that in a Christ, who by the aid of a divine nature dwelling within him, withstood evil and kept himself from sin, the man who is destitute of such aid can have no true example.[5]

The essential and tenable points of the rationalistic objections to this doctrine, have been the most acutely perceived and arranged by Schleiermacher, who, on this subject as on many others, has brought the negative criticism of the dogmas of the Church to completeness.[6] Before all else he finds it a difficulty, that by the expression, *divine nature* and *human nature*, divinity and humanity are placed under one category, and what is more, under the category of nature, which essentially denotes only a limited being, conceived by means of its opposite. Further, while ordinarily one nature is common to many individuals or persons, here one person is supposed to partake of two different natures. Now if by person be meant the permanent conscious unity of a living being, and by nature, the sum of the laws which govern the conditions of life in that being : it is not to be conceived, how two opposite systems of conditions can have but one centre. The absurdity of this doctrine becomes, according to Schleiermacher, especially evident in the supposition of two wills in Christ, since, for consistency, two wills must be associated with two understandings, and as the understanding and will constitute the personality, Christ would on this supposition be inevitably divided into two persons. It is true that the two wills are supposed always to will in unison : but, on the one hand, there results from this only a moral, not a personal unity ; on the other hand, this unison of wills is not possible in relation to the divine and the human will, since the latter, which from its very essence can only exercise itself on particulars as they present themselves in succession, can as little will the same with the former, whose object is the whole in its development, as the human understanding, which acts by reasoning, can think the same with the divine understanding, which acts intuitively. Hence it evidently follows also that a communication of properties between the two natures is not to be admitted.

The doctrine of the work of Christ did not escape a similar criticism. Passing over what has been objected in point of form to the division of this work into three offices, the ideas of revelation and miracles, under the head of the prophetic office, were chiefly called in question. It was argued that these ideas agreed neither objectively with just conceptions of God and the world in their reciprocal relation, nor subjectively with the laws of the human intellect ; that the perfect God could not have created a world which from time to time needed the extraordinary interposition of the Creator, nor more particularly a human nature which was incapable of attaining its destination by the development of its innate faculties ; that the immutable Being could not operate on the world first in this manner, then in that, at one time mediately, at another immediately, but that he must always have operated on it in the same manner, namely, in himself and on the whole immediately, but

---

[4] Fausti Socini de Christi natura disputatio. Opp. Bibl. Fr. Pol. 1, p. 784 ; Catech. Racov. Q. 96 ff. Comp. Marheineke, Instit. symb. § 96. Spinoza, also, ep. 21, ad Oldenburg, Opp. ed. Gfrörer, p. 556, says : *Quod quædam ecclesiæ his adduut, quod Deus naturam humanam assumpserit, monui expresse, me, quid dicant, nescire ; imo, ut verum fatear, non minus absurde mihi loqui videntur, quam si quis mihi diceret, quod circulus naturam quadrati induerit.*

[5] (Röhr) Briefe über den Rationalismus, s. 378 ff. ; Wegscheider Inst. theol. § 128 ; Bretschneider, Handb. der Dogm. 2, § 137 ff. ; also Kant, Relig. innerhalb der Gränzen der blossen Vernunft. 2tes St. 2ter Absch. b.

[6] Glaubenslehre, 2, §§ 96–98.

for us and on individuals mediately; that to admit an interruption of the order of nature, and of the development of humanity, would be to renounce all rational thought, while, in the particular case in question, a revelation or miracle is not confidently to be recognized as such, since, in order to be sure that certain results have not proceeded from the powers of nature and the faculties of the human mind, a perfect knowledge of the resources of both would be requisite, and of such a knowledge man is not possessed.[7]

But the main difficulty lay in the office of high priest, attributed to Jesus—in the doctrine of the atonement. That which especially drew forth objections was the human aspect which in Anselm's system was given to the relation of God to the Son of man. As it well becomes man to forgive offences without exacting vengeance, so, thought Socinus, might God forgive the offences committed against him by men, without satisfaction.[8] To meet this objection Hugo Grotius argued, that not as in consequence of personal injuries, but to maintain the order of the moral world inviolable, or in virtue of his *justitia rectoria*, God cannot forgive sins without satisfaction.[9] Nevertheless, granting the necessity for satisfaction, it did not appear to be met by the death of Jesus. While Anselm, and still more decidedly Thomas Aquinas,[10] spoke of a *satisfactio superabundans*, Socinus denied that Christ had even borne as much punishment as men have deserved; for every individual man having deserved eternal death, consequently, as many substitutes as sinners ought to have suffered eternal death; whereas in this case, the single Christ has suffered merely temporal death, and that as an introduction to the highest glory; nor did this death attach to his divine nature, so that it might be said to have infinite value, but only to his human nature. On the other hand, Duns Scotus,[11] in opposition to Thomas, and subsequently Grotius and the Arminians (equi-distant from orthodoxy and Socinianism), adopted the expedient of maintaining, that the merit of Christ was indeed in itself finite like its subject, his human nature, and hence was inadequate as a satisfaction for the sins of the world; but that God accepted it as adequate out of his free grace. But from the admission that God can content himself with an inadequate satisfaction, and thus can forgive a part of the guilt without satisfaction, it follows necessarily, that he must also be able thus to forgive the whole. Besides these more precise definitions, however, the fundamental idea of the whole fabric, namely, that one individual can take upon himself the punishment due to the sins of another, has been attacked as an ignorant transference of the conditions of a lower order of relation to a higher. Moral transgressions, it has been said, are not transmissible obligations; it is not with them as with debts of money, which it is immaterial to the creditor who pays, provided they are paid; rather it is essential to the punishment of sin, that it should fall on the guilty only.[12] If, according to this, the so-called passive obedience of Christ cannot have been vicarious, still less can his active obedience have been so, since as man he was bound to render this on his own behalf.[13]

In relation to the kingly office of Christ, the hope of his second advent to

---

[7] Spinoza, tract. theol. polit. c. vi. p. 133. ed. Gfrörer, and ep. 23, ad Oldenburg, p. 558 f. Briefe über den Rat., 4ter, 5ter, 6ter, 12ter. Wegscheider, §§ 11, 12. Schleiermacher, §§ 14, 47.

[8] Prælect. theol. c. xv.

[9] In the work : defensio fidei cath. de satisfactione Chr. adv. F. Socinum.

[10] Summa, P. 3, Q. 48, A. 2.

[11] Comm. in Sentt. L. 3, Dist. 19.

[12] See, besides Socinus, Kant, Relig. innerhalb der Grenzen der blossen Vernunft, 2tes Stück, 1ter Abschn., c.

[13] Töllner, Der thätige Gehorsam Christi untersucht. 1768.

judge the world lost ground in the sentiment of the Church, in proportion as the opinion obtained, that every individual enters on a state of complete retribution immediately after death, for this opinion made the general judgment appear superfluous.[14]

§ 147.

THE CHRISTOLOGY OF RATIONALISM.

The Rationalists, rejecting the doctrine of the Church concerning Christ, his person, and his work, as self-contradictory, useless, nay, even hurtful to the true morality of the religious sentiment, propounded in its stead a system which, while it avoided all contradictions, yet in a certain sense retained for Jesus the character of a divine manifestation, which even, rightly considered, placed him far higher, and moreover embodied the strongest motives to practical piety.[1]

According to them, Jesus was still a divine messenger, a special favourite and charge of the Deity, inasmuch as, furnished by the disposition of Providence with an extraordinary measure of spiritual endowment, he was born in an age and nation, and guided in a career, the most favourable to his development into that for which he was destined ; and, especially, inasmuch as he was subjected to a species of death that rendered possible his apparent resurrection, on which depended the success of his entire work, and was encompassed by a series of circumstances which actually brought that resurrection to pass. The Rationalists hold that their idea of the Christ is not essentially below the orthodox one, as regards his natural endowments and his external destiny, for in their view also he is the greatest man that ever trod the earth—a hero, in whose fate Providence is in the highest degree glorified : while, as regards the internal development and free agency of Jesus, they believe their doctrine essentially to surpass that of the Church. The Christ of the Church, they contend, is a mere automaton, whose manhood lies under the control of his Godhead like a lifeless instrument, which acts with moral perfection because it has no power to sin, and for this reason can neither have moral merit, nor be the object of affection and reverence : according to the rationalistic view, on the contrary, Jesus had implanted in him by God the natural conditions only of that which he was ultimately to become, and his realization of this destiny was the result of his own spontaneity. His admirable wisdom he acquired by the judicious application of his intellectual powers, and the conscientious use of all the aids within his reach ; his moral greatness, by the zealous culture of his moral dispositions, the restraint of his sensual inclinations and passions, and a scrupulous obedience to the voice of his conscience : and on these alone rested all that was exalted in his personality, all that was encouraging in his example.

As regards the work of Jesus, the rationalistic view is, that he has endeared himself to mankind by this above all else, that he has taught them a religion to which for its purity and excellence is justly ascribed a certain divine power and dignity ; and that he has illustrated and enforced this religion by the brilliant example of his own life. This prophetic office of Christ is with Socinians and Rationalists the essence of his work, and to this they refer all the rest, especially what the doctrine of the Church comprehends under the office of high priest. With them the so-called active obedience has value

---

[14] Wegscheider, § 199.
[1] Compare with what follows especially the Briefe über den Rationalismus, s. 372 ff. ; Wegscheider, §§ 128, 133, 140.

solely as an example ; and the death of Jesus conduces to the forgiveness of
sins, solely by furthering the reformation of the sinner in one of these two
ways : either, as a confirmation of his doctrine, and a type of the devoted
fulfilment of duty, it serves to kindle a zeal for virtue ; or, as a proof of the
love of God to man, of his inclination to pardon the converted sinner, it
invigorates moral courage.[2]

If Christ was no more, and did no more, than this rationalistic doctrine
supposes, it is not easy to see how piety has come to make him her special
object, or dogmatism to lay down special propositions concerning him.
Consistent Rationalists have in fact admitted, that what the orthodox dogma
calls Christology, forms no integral part of the rationalistic system, since this
system consists indeed of a religion which Christ taught, but not of a religion
of which he is the object ; that, viewing Christology as the doctrine of the
Messiah, it is merely an accommodation to the Jewish mind,—that even
taken in a more noble sense, as the doctrine of the life, the actions, and the
fate of Jesus as a divine messenger, it does not belong to a system of faith,
for the universal truths of religion are as little connected with our ideas concerning the person of him who first enunciated them, as are the philosophical
propositions in the systems of Leibnitz and Wolf, of Kant, Fichte, and
Schelling, with the opinions we may happen to form of the persons of their
authors ; that what relates to the person and work of Jesus belongs, not to
religion itself, but to the history of religion, and must either be prefixed to a
system of religious doctrine as an historical introduction, or appended to it
as an elucidatory sequel.[3]   Accordingly Henke, in his *Lineaments*, has removed Christology from its wonted position as an integral part of systematic
theology, and has placed it as a subdivision under the head of anthropology.

Thus, however, Rationalism enters into open war with the Christian faith,
for it seeks to thrust into the background, nay, to banish from the province
of theology, that which is its essential point, and corner-stone.   But this very
opposition is decisive of the insufficiency of the rationalistic system, proving
that it does not perform what is demanded from every system of religious
doctrine :*namely, first, to give adequate expression to the faith which is the
object of the doctrine ; and secondly, to place this expression in a relation,
whether positive or negative, to science.   Now the Rationalists, in the effort
to bring the faith into harmony with science, restrict its expression ; for a
Christ who is only a distinguished man, creates indeed no difficulty to the
understanding, but is not the Christ in whom the Church believes.

§ 148.

THE ECLECTIC CHRISTOLOGY OF SCHLEIERMACHER.

It is the effort of this theologian to avoid both these ungrateful results, and
without prejudice to the faith, to form such a conception of the doctrine of the
Christ as may be proof against the attacks of science.[1]   On the one hand, he
has adopted in its fullest extent the negative criticism directed by Rationalism
against the doctrine of the Church, nay, he has rendered it even more searching ; on the other hand, he has sought to retain what Rationalism had lost,

---

[2] For the different views, see Bretschneider, Dogm. 2, s. 353, systematische Entwicklung,
§ 107.
[3] Röhr, Briefe, s. 36, 405 ff.
[1] Schleiermacher, on his Glaubenslehre, to Dr. Lücke, 2tes Sendschreiben, Studien, 2, 3,
s. 481 ff.

the essential part of positive Christianity : and thus he has saved many in these days from the narrowness of Supranaturalism, and the emptiness of Rationalism. This simplification of the faith Schleiermacher effects in the following manner : he does not set out, with the Protestant, from the doctrine of Scripture, nor with the Catholic from the decision of the church, for in both these ways he would have to deal with a precise, developed system, which, having originated in remote centuries, must come into collision with the science of the present day; but he sets out from the consciousness of the Christian, from that internal experience resulting to the individual from his connexion with the Christian community, and he thus obtains a material which, as its basis is feeling, is more flexible, and to which it is easier to give dialectically a form that satisfies science.

As a member of the Christian church—this is the point of departure in the Christology of Schleiermacher [2]—I am conscious of the removal of my sinfulness, and the impartation of absolute perfection : in other words, in communion with the church, I feel operating upon me the influence of a sinless and perfect principle. This influence cannot proceed from the Christian community as an effect of the reciprocal action of its members on each other ; for to every one of these sin and imperfection are inherent, and the co-operation of impure beings can never produce anything pure as its result. It must be the influence of one who possessed that sinlessness and perfection as personal qualities, and who moreover stands in such a relation to the Christian community, that he can impart these qualities to its members : that is, since the Christian church could not exist prior to this impartation, it must be the influence of its founder. As Christians, we find something operated within us ; hence, as from every effect we argue to its cause, we infer the influence of Christ, and from this again, the nature of his person, which must have had the powers necessary to the exertion of this influence.

To speak more closely, that which we experience as members of the Christian church, is a strengthening of our consciousness of God, in its relation to our sensuous existence ; that is, it is rendered easier to us to deprive the senses of their ascendancy within us, to make all our impressions the servants of the religious sentiment, and all our actions its offspring. According to what has been stated above, this is the effect wrought in us by Christ, who imparts to us the strength of his consciousness of God, frees us from the bondage of sensuality and sin, and is thus the Redeemer. In the feeling of the strengthened consciousness of God which the Christian possesses by his communion with the Redeemer, the obstructions of his natural and social life are not felt as obstructions to his consciousness of God ; they do not interrupt the blessedness which he enjoys in his inmost religious life ; what has been called evil, and divine chastisement, is not such for him : and as it is Christ who by receiving him into the communion of his blessedness, frees him therefrom, the office of expiation is united to that of redemption.

In this sense alone is the doctrine of the church concerning the threefold office of Christ to be interpreted. He is a prophet, in that by the word—by the setting forth of himself, and not otherwise,—he could draw mankind towards himself, and therefore the chief object of his doctrine was his own person ; he is at once a high priest and a sacrifice, in that he, the sinless one, from whose existence, therefore, no evil could be evolved, entered into communion with the life of sinful humanity, and endured the evils which adhere to it, that he might take us into communion with his sinless and blessed life : in other words, deliver us from the power and consequences of sin and evil,

[2] Glaubenslehre, 2, §§ 92-105.

and present us pure before God ; lastly, he is a king, in that he brings these blessings to mankind in the form of an organized society, of which he is the head.

From this which Christ effects, we gather what he is. If we owe to him the continual strengthening of the consciousness of God within us, this consciousness must have existed in him in absolute strength, so that it, or God in the form of the consciousness, was the only operative force within him, and this is the sense of the expression of the church—God became man in Christ. If, further, Christ works in us a more and more complete conquest over sensuality, in himself there must have been an absolute conquest over it ; in no moment of his life can the sensual consciousness have disputed the victory with his consciousness of God ; never can a vacillation or struggle have had place within him : in other words, the human nature in him was sinless, and in the stricter sense, that, in virtue of the essential predominance within him of the higher powers over the lower, it was impossible for him to sin. By this peculiarity of his nature he is the Archetype, the actualization of the ideal of humanity, which his church can only approach, never surpass ; yet must he,—for otherwise there could be no true fellowship between him and us,—have been developed under the ordinary conditions of human life : the ideal must in him have been perfectly historical, each phasis of his actual life must have borne the impress of the ideal ; and this is the proper sense of the church formula, that the divine and human nature were in him united into one person.

Only thus far can the doctrine of the Christ be deduced from the experience of the Christian, and thus far, according to Schleiermacher, it is not opposed to science : whatever in the dogma of the church goes beyond this,— as, for example, the supernatural conception of Jesus, and his miracles, also the facts of the resurrection and ascension, and the prophecies of his second coming to judge the world,—ought not to be brought forward as integral parts of the doctrine of the Christ. For he from whose influence upon us comes all the strengthening of our consciousness of God, may have been the Christ, though he should not have risen bodily from the dead, and ascended into heaven, etc. : so that we believe these facts, not because they are involved in our internal ¡experience, but only because they are stated in Scripture ; not so much, therefore, in a religious and dogmatical, as in an historical manner.

This Christology is undeniably a beautiful effort of thought, and as we shall presently see, does the utmost towards rendering the union of the divine and the human in Christ conceivable ; but if its author supposed that he kept the faith unmutilated and science unoffended, we are compelled to pronounce that he was in both points deceived.[3]

Science opens its attack on the proposition, that the ideal man was historically manifested in the person of Christ. It did not escape Schleiermacher himself that this was a dangerous point. No sooner has he put forth the above proposition, than he reflects on the difficulty of supposing that the ideal should be realized in one historical individual ; since, in other cases, we never find the ideal realized in a single appearance, but only in an entire cycle of appearances, which reciprocally complete each other.[*] It is true that this theologian does not hold the character of Christ, as the ideal man, to extend to the manifold relations of human life, so as to be the archetype for all the

---

[3] This opinion has been already put forth in the most noted reviews of Schleiermacher's system ; comp. Braniss, über Schleiermacher's Glaubenslehre ; H. Schmid, über Schl. Glaubensl. s. 263 ff. ; Baur, die christl. Gnosis, s. 626 ff., and the Review of Rosenkranz, Jahrb. für wiss. Kritik, 1831.

science, art, and policy, that are developed in human society ; he confines it to the domain of the consciousness of God. But, as Schmid has justly observed, this does not alter the case, for the consciousness of God also, being, in its development and manifestation, subject to the conditions of finiteness and imperfection ; the supposition that even in this department exclusively, the ideal was manifested in a single historical individual, involves a violation of the laws of nature by a miracle. This, however, is far from alarming Schleiermacher ; on the contrary, he maintains that this is the place, and the only place, in which the Christian doctrine must necessarily admit a miracle, since the originating of the person of Christ can only be conceived as the result of a special divine act of creation. It is true, he limits the miraculous to the first introduction of Christ into the series of existences, and allows the whole of his further development to have been subject to all the conditions of finite existence : but this concession cannot repair the breach, which the supposition only of one miracle makes in the scientific theory of the world. Still less can any help be derived from vague analogies like the following : as it is still possible that matter should begin to agglomerate and thence to revolve in infinite space ; so science must admit, that there may be in the domain of spiritual life an appearance, which in like manner we can only explain as the commencement, the first point, in a higher process of development.[4]

This comparison suggests the observation made by Braniss, namely, that it would be contrary to the laws of all development to regard the initial member of a series as the greatest—to suppose that in Christ, the founder of that community, the object of which is the strengthening of the consciousness of God, the strength of this consciousness was absolute, a perfection which is rather the infinitely distant goal of the progressive development of the community founded by him. Schleiermacher does indeed attribute to Christianity perfectibility in a certain sense : not as a capability of surpassing Christ in his nature, but solely in the conditions of its manifestation. His view is this : the limitation, the imperfection of the relations of Christ, the language in which he expressed himself, the nationality within which he was placed, modified his thoughts and actions, but in their form alone ; their essence remained nevertheless the perfect ideal. Now if Christianity in its progressive advancement in doctrine and practice, rejects more and more of those temporal and national limitations by which the actions and teaching of Jesus were circumscribed ; this is not to surpass Christ, it is rather to give a more perfect expression of his inner life. But, as Schmid has satisfactorily shown, an historical individual is that which appears of him, and no more ; his internal nature is known by his words and actions, the condition of his age and nation are a part of his individuality, and what lies beneath this phenomenal existence as the essence, is not the nature of this individual, but the human nature in general, which in particular beings operates only under the limitations of their individuality, of time, and of circumstances. Thus to surpass the historical appearance of Christ, is to rise nearer, not to his nature, but to the idea of humanity in general ; and if we are to suppose that it is still Christ whose nature is more truly expressed, when with the rejection of the temporal and national, the essential elements of his doctrine and life are further developed : it would not be difficult, by a similar abstraction, to represent Socrates, as the one who in this manner cannot be surpassed.

As neither an individual in general, nor, in particular, the commencing point in an historical series, can present the perfect ideal : so, if Christ be regarded decidedly as man, the archetypal nature and development which Schleiermacher ascribes to him, cannot be brought to accord with the laws of human existence. Impeccability, in the sense of the impossibility of sinning, as it is supposed to exist in Christ, is a quality totally incompatible with the human nature ; for to man, in consequence of his agency being liable to guidance by the motives of the senses as well as of the reason, the possibility of sinning is essential. And if Christ was entirely free from in- ward conflict, from all vacillation of the spiritual life between good and evil, he could not be a man of like nature with us ; for the action and re-action between the spiritual nature in general and the external world, and, in par- ticular, between the superior religious and moral powers, and the operations of the mind in subordination to the senses, necessarily manifests itself as a conflict.[5]

If, on the one side, the Christology in question is far from satisfying science, it is equally far, on the other side, from satisfying the faith. We will not enter into those points in which, instead of the decisions of the church, it at leasts offers acceptable substitutes (concerning which, however, it may be doubted whether they are a full compensation).[6] Its disagreement with the faith is the most conspicuous in the position, that the facts of the resur- rection and ascension do not form essential parts of the Christian faith. For the belief in the resurrection of Christ is the foundation stone, without which the Christian church could not have been built ; nor could the cycle of Christian festivals, which are the external representation of the Christian faith, now suffer a more fatal mutilation than by the removal of the festival of Easter : the Christ who died could not be what he is in the belief of the church, if he were not also the Christ who rose again.

Thus the doctrine of Schleiermacher concerning the person and conditions of Christ, betrays a twofold inadequacy, not meeting the requirements either of the faith of the church, or of science. It is clear, however, from his doctrine of the work of Christ, that in order to satisfy the former so far as is here done, such a contradiction of the latter was quite unnecessary, and an easier course might have been pursued. For resting merely on a backward inference from the inward experience of the Christian as the effect, to the person of Christ as the cause, the Christology of Schleiermacher has but a frail support, since it cannot be proved that that inward experience is not to be explained without the actual existence of such a Christ. Schleiermacher himself did not overlook the probable objection that the church, induced merely by the relative excellence of Jesus, conceived an ideal of absolute perfection, and transferred this to the historical Christ, from which combina- tion she continually strengthens and vivifies her consciousness of God : but he held this objection to be precluded by the observation, that sinful humanity, by reason of the mutual dependence of the will and the under- standing, is incapable of conceiving an immaculate ideal. But, as it has been aptly remarked, if Schleiermacher claims a miracle for the origination of his real Christ, we have an equal right to claim one for the origination of the ideal of a Christ in the human soul.[7] Meanwhile, it is not true that sinful human nature is incapable of conceiving a sinless ideal. If by this ideal be understood merely a general conception, then the conception of the perfect and the sinless is as necessarily co-existent with the consciousness of imperfection and sinfulness as the conception of infinity with that of finiteness ; since the two

[5] Schmid, ut sup.
[6] Comp. Rosenkranz, ut sup. s. 935 ff.
[7] Baur, ut sup. s. 653.

ideas conditionate one another, and the one is not possible without the other. If, on the other hand, by this ideal be meant a concrete image, the conception of a character in which all the individual features are portrayed, it may be admitted that a sinful individual or age cannot depict such an image without blemish ; but of this inability the age or individual itself is not conscious, not having any superior standard, and if the image be but slightly drawn, if it leave room for the modifications of increased enlightenment, it may continue to be regarded as immaculate even by a later and more clear-sighted age, so long as this age is inclined to view it under the most favourable light.

We may now estimate the truth of the reproach, which made Schleiermacher so indignant, namely, that his was not an historical, but an ideal Christ. It is unjust in relation to the opinion of Schleiermacher, for he firmly believed that the Christ, as construed by him, really lived ; but it is just in relation to the historical state of the facts, because such a Christ never existed but in idea ; and in this sense, indeed, the reproach has even a stronger bearing on the system of the church, because the Christ therein presented can still less have existed. Lastly, it is just in relation to the consequence of Schleiermacher's system, since to effect what Schleiermacher makes him effect, no other Christ is necessary, and, according to the principles of Schleiermacher respecting the relation of God to the world, of the supernatural to the natural, no other Christ is possible, than an ideal one :—and in this sense the reproach attaches specifically to Schleiermacher's doctrine, for according to the premises of the orthodox doctrine, an historical Christ is both possible and necessary.

§ 149.

CHRISTOLOGY INTERPRETED SYMBOLICALLY.   KANT.   DE WETTE.

The attempt to retain in combination the ideal in Christ with the historical, having failed, these two elements separate themselves : the latter falls as a natural residuum to the ground, and the former rises as a pure sublimate into the ethereal world of ideas. Historically, Jesus can have been nothing more than a person, highly distinguished indeed, but subject to the limitations inevitable to all that is mortal : by means of his exalted character, however, he exerted so powerful an influence over the religious sentiment, that it constituted him the ideal of piety ; in accordance with the general rule, that an historical fact or person cannot become the basis of a positive religion until it is elevated into the sphere of the ideal.[1]

Spinoza made this distinction when maintaining, that to know the historical Christ is not necessary to felicity, but only to know the ideal Christ, namely the eternal wisdom of God, which is manifested in all things, in the human mind particularly, and in a pre-eminent degree in Jesus Christ—that wisdom which alone teaches man what is true and false, good and bad.[2]

According to Kant, also, it ought not to be made a condition of salvation to believe, that there was once a man who by his holiness and merit gave satisfaction for himself and for all others; for of this the reason tells us

[1] Thus Schmid, ut sup. s. 267.
[2] Ep. 21, ad Oldenburg.   Opp. ed. Gfrörer, p. 556 :—*dico, ad salutem non esse omnino necesse, Christum secundum carnem noscere ; sed ed æterno illo filio Dei, h. e. Dei æterna sapientia, quæ sese in omnibus rebus, et maxime in mente humana, et omnium maxime in Christo Jesu manifestavit, longe aliter sentiendum. Nam nemo absque hac ad statum beatitudinis potest pervenire, utpote quæ sola docet, quid verum et falsum, bonum et malum sit.*

nothing ; but it *is* the duty of men universally to elevate themselves to the ideal of moral perfection deposited in the reason, and to obtain moral strength by the contemplation of this ideal.   Such moral faith alone man is bound to exercise, and not historical faith.[3]

Taking his stand on this principle, Kant proceeds to interpret the doctrines of the Bible and the church as symbols of the ideal.   It is humanity, or the rational part of this system of things, in its entire moral perfection, that could alone make a world the object of divine Providence, and the end of creation. This idea of a humanity well-pleasing to God, has existed in God from all eternity ; it proceeds from his essence, and is therefore no created thing, but his eternal Son, the Word, through whom, that is, for whose sake, all things were created, and in whom God loved the world.   As this idea of moral perfection has not man for its author, as it has been introduced into him even without his being able to conceive how his nature can have been susceptible of such an idea, it may be said to have come down to us from heaven, and to have assumed the human nature, and this union with us may be regarded as an abasement of the Son of God.   This ideal of moral perfection, so far as it is compatible with the condition of a being dependent on necessities and inclinations, can only be conceived by us under the form of a man.   Now just as we can obtain no idea of the amount of a force, but by calculating the degree of resistance which it can overcome, so we can form no estimate of the strength of the moral disposition, but by imagining hard conflicts in which it can triumph : hence the man who embodies the perfect ideal must be one who would voluntarily undertake, not only to perform every duty of man on his own behalf, and by precept and example to disseminate the good and the true around him as extensively as possible ; but also, though tempted by the strongest allurements, to submit to all sufferings, even to the most ignominious death, for the welfare of mankind.

In a practical relation this idea has its reality completely within itself, and it needed no exemplification in experience in order to become a model binding on us, since it is enshrined as such in our reason.   Nay, this ideal remains essentially confined to the reason, because it cannot be adequately represented by any example in outward experience, since such an example would not fully disclose the inward disposition, but would only admit of our forming dubious inferences thereon.   Nevertheless, as all men ought to be conformed to this ideal, and consequently must be capable of such conformity, it is always possible in experience that a man may appear, who in his teaching, course of life, and sufferings, may present an example of a man well-pleasing to God : but even in this manifestation of the God-man, it would not properly be that which is obvious to the senses, or can be known by experience, which would be the object of saving faith ; but the ideal lying in the reason, which we should attribute to this manifestation of the God-man, because he appeared to us to be conformed to it—that is, indeed, so far only as this can be concluded from outward experience.   Inasmuch as all of us, though naturally generated men, feel bound, and consequently able, ourselves to present such an example, we have no reason to regard that exemplification of the ideal man as supernaturally generated, nor does he need the attestation of miracles; for besides the moral faith in the idea, nothing further is requisite than the historical conviction that his life was conformed to that idea, in order to accredit him as its personification.

He who is conscious of such a moral disposition, as to have a well-founded confidence, that under temptations and sufferings similar to those which are

---

[3] Religion innerhalb der Gränzen der blossen Vernunft. drittes Stück, 1te Abthl. vii.

attributed to the ideal man, as a touchstone of his moral disposition, he would adhere unalterably to this exemplar, and faithfully follow his steps, such a man alone is entitled to consider himself an object of the divine complacency. To elevate himself to such a state of mind, man must depart from evil, cast off the old man, crucify the flesh; a change which is essentially connected with a series of sorrows and sufferings. These the former man has deserved as a punishment, but they fall on the new: for the regenerated man, who takes them on himself, though physically and in his empirical character, as a being determined by the senses, he remains the former man; is morally, as an intellectual being, with his changed disposition, become a new man. Having by this change taken upon him the disposition of the Son of God, that which is strictly a substitution of the new man for the old, may be represented, by a personification of the idea, as a substitution of the Son of God, and it may be said, that the latter himself, as a substitute, bears for man, for all who practically believe in him, the guilt of sin; as a redeemer, satisfies supreme justice by suffering and death; and as an intercessor, imparts the hope of appearing justified before the judge: the suffering which the new man, in dying to the old, must perpetually incur through life, being conceived in the representative of mankind, as a death suffered once for all.[4]

Kant, like Schleiermacher (whose Christology in many respects recalls that of Kant),[5] carries his appropriation of the Christology of the church no further than the death of Christ: of his resurrection and ascension, he says, that they cannot be available to religion within the limits of pure reason, because they would involve the materiality of all existences. Still, in another light, he employs these facts as symbols of the ideas of the reason; as images of the entrance into the abode of blessedness, that is, into communion with all the good: while Tieftrunk has yet more decidedly given it as his opinion, that without the resurrection, the history of Jesus would terminate in a revolting catastrophe; that the eye would turn away with melancholy and dissatisfaction from an event, in which the pattern of humanity fell a victim to impious rage, and in which the scene closed with a death as unmerited as sorrowful; that the history requires to be crowned with the fulfilment of the expectation towards which the moral contemplations of every one are irresistibly drawn—with the passage into a compensating immortality.[6]

In the same manner, De Wette ascribed to the evangelical history, as to every history, and particularly to the history of religion, a symbolical, ideal character, in virtue of which it is the expression and image of the human mind and its various operations. The history of the miraculous conception of Jesus represents the divine origin of religion; the narratives of his miracles, the independent force of the human mind, and the sublime doctrine of spiritual self-reliance; his resurrection is the image of the victory of truth, a fore-shadowing of the future triumph of good over evil; his ascension, the symbol of the eternal majesty of religion. The fundamental religious ideas which Jesus enunciated in his teaching, are expressed with equal clearness in his history. This history is an expression of devoted enthusiasm, in the courageous ministry of Jesus, and in the victorious power of his appearance; of resignation, in his contest with the wickedness of men, in the melancholy of his premonitory discourses, and above all in his death. Christ on the cross is the image of humanity purified by self-sacrifice; we ought all to crucify ourselves with him, that we may rise with him to new life. Lastly,

---

[4] Ut sup. 2tes Stück, 1ter Abschn. 3tes Stück, 1te Abthlg.
[5] This is shown by Baur, christl. Gnosis, s. 660 ff.
[6] Censur des christl. protestantischen Lehrbegriffs, 3, s. 180.

the idea of devotion was the key-note in the history of Jesus, every moment of his life being dedicated to the thought of his heavenly Father.[7]

At an earlier period, Horst presented this symbolical view of the history of Jesus with singular clearness. Whether, he says, all that is narrated of Christ happened precisely so, historically, is a question indifferent to us, nor can it now be settled. Nay, if we would be candid with ourselves, that which was once sacred history for the Christian believer, is, for the enlightened portion of our cotemporaries, only fable : the narratives of the supernatural birth of Christ, of his miracles, of his resurrection and ascension, must be rejected by us as at variance with the inductions of our intellect. Let them however only be no longer interpreted merely by the understanding as history, but by the feelings and imagination, as poetry ; and it will be found that in these narratives nothing is invented arbitrarily, but all springs from the depths and divine impulses of the human mind. Considered from this point of view, we may annex to the history of Christ all that is important to religious trust, animating to the pure dispositions, attractive to the tender feelings. That history is a beautiful, sacred poem of the human race—a poem in which are embodied all the wants of our religious instinct ; and this is the highest honour of Christianity, and the strongest proof of its universal applicability. The history of the gospel is in fact the history of human nature conceived ideally, and exhibits to us in the life of an individual, what man ought to be, and, united with him by following his doctrine and example, can actually become. It is not denied that what to us can appear only sacred poetry, was to Paul, John, Matthew and Luke, fact and certain history. But it was the very same internal cause which made the narratives of the gospel sacred fact and history to them, which makes those narratives to us a sacred mythus and poetry. The points of view only are different : human nature, and in it the religious impulse, remains ever the same. Those first Christians needed in their world, for the animating of the religious and moral dispositions in the men of their time, history and fact, of which, however, the inmost kernel consisted of ideas : to us, the facts are become superannuated and doubtful, and only for the sake of the fundamental ideas, are the narratives of those facts an object of reverence.[8]

This view was met immediately on the part of the church by the reproach, that instead of the riches of divine reality which faith discovers in the history of Christ, it palmed upon us a collection of empty ideas and ideals ; instead of a consolatory work effected, an overwhelming obligation. For the certainty, that God once actually united himself with human nature, the admonition that man ought to obtain divine dispositions, offers a poor compensation: for the peace which the redemption completed by Christ brings to the believer, it is no equivalent to put before him the duty of freeing himself from sin. By this system, man is thrust out of the reconciled world in which Christianity places him, into an unreconciled world, out of a world of happiness into a world of misery ; for where reconciliation has yet to be effected, where happiness has yet to be attained, there is at present enmity and unhappiness. And, in truth, the hope of entire deliverance from these conditions, is, according to the principles of this system, which only admits an infinite approximation towards the idea, a deceptive one ; for that which is only to be reached in an endless progression, is in fact unattainable.

But not the faith alone, science also in its newest development, has found

---

[7] Religion und Theologie, 2ter Abschnitt, Kap. 3; comp. bibl. Dogmatik, § 255 ; kirchliche, § 64 ff.

[8] Ideen über Mythologie u. s. w. in Henke's neuer Magazin, b. s. 454 ff. Comp. Henke's Museum, 3, s. 455.

this system unsatisfactory. Science has perceived that to convert ideas simply into an obligatory possibility, to which no reality corresponds, is in fact to annihilate them ; just as it would be to render the infinite finite, to represent it as that which lies beyond the finite.* Science has conceived that the infinite has its existence in the alternate production and extinction of the finite ; that the idea is realised only in the entire series of its manifestations ; that nothing can come into existence which does not already essentially exist ; and, therefore, that it is not to be required of man, that he should reconcile himself with God, and assimilate his sentiments to the divine, unless this reconciliation and this assimilation are already virtually effected.

§ 150.

THE SPECULATIVE CHRISTOLOGY.

Kant had already said that the good principle did not descend from heaven merely at a particular time, but had descended on mankind invisibly from the commencement of the human race ; and Schelling laid down the proposition : the incarnation of God is an incarnation from eternity.[1] But while the former understood under that expression only the moral instinct, which, with its ideal of good, and its sense of duty, has been from the beginning implanted in man ; the latter understood under the incarnate Son of God the finite itself, in the form of the human consciousness, which in its contradistinction to the infinite, wherewith it is nevertheless one, appears as a suffering God, subjected to the conditions of time.

In the most recent philosophy this idea has been further developed in the following manner.[2] When it is said of God that he is a Spirit, and of man that he also is a Spirit, it follows that the two are not essentially distinct. To speak more particularly, it is the essential property of a spirit, in the distribution of itself into distinct personalities, to remain identical with itself, to possess itself in another than itself. Hence the recognition of God as a spirit implies, that God does not remain as a fixed and immutable Infinite encompassing the Finite, but enters into it, produces the Finite, Nature, and the human mind, merely as a limited manifestation of himself, from which he eternally returns into unity. As man, considered as a finite spirit, limited to his finite nature, has not truth ; so God, considered exclusively as an infinite spirit, shut up in his infinitude, has not reality. The infinite spirit is real only when it discloses itself in finite spirits ; as the finite spirit is true only when it merges itself in the infinite. The true and real existence of spirit, therefore, is neither in God by himself, nor in man by himself, but in the God-man ; neither in the infinite alone, nor in the finite alone, but in the interchange of impartation and withdrawal between the two, which on the part of God is revelation, on the part of man religion.

If God and man are in themselves *one*, and if religion is the human side of this unity : then must this unity be made evident to man in religion, and become in him consciousness and reality. Certainly, so long as man knows not that he is a spirit, he cannot know that God is man : while he is under the guidance of nature only, he will deify nature ; when he has learned to submit

---

[1] Vorlesungen über die Methode des akademischen Studiums, s. 192.
[2] Hegel's Phänomenologie des Geistes, s. 561 ff. ; Vorlesungen über die Philos. der Relig. 2, s. 234 ff. Marheineke, Grundlehren der christl. Dogmatik. s. 174 ff. Rosenkranz, Encyklopädie der theol. Wissenschaften, s. 38ff., 148 ff. ; comp. my Streitschriften, 3tes Heft, s. 76 ff.

himself to law, and thus to regulate his natural tendencies by external means, he will set God before him as a lawgiver.   But when, in the vicissitudes of the world's history, the natural state discloses its corruptions, the legal its misery; the former will experience the need of a God who elevates it above itself, the latter, of a God who descends to its level.   Man being once mature enough to receive as his religion the truth that God is man, and man of a divine race; it necessarily follows, since religion is the form in which the truth presents itself to the popular mind, that this truth must appear, in a guise intelligible to all, as a fact obvious to the senses: in other words, there must appear a human individual who is recognised as the visible God.   This God-man uniting in a single being the divine essence and the human personality, it may be said of him that he had the Divine Spirit for a father and a woman for his mother.   His personality reflecting itself not in himself, but in the absolute substance, having the will to exist only for God, and not at all for itself, he is sinless and perfect.   As a man of Divine essence, he is the power that subdues nature, a worker of miracles; but as God in a human manifestation, he is dependent on nature, subject to its necessities and sufferings— is in a state of abasement.   Must he even pay the last tribute to nature? does not the fact that the human nature is subject to death preclude the idea that that nature is one with the divine?   No: the God-man dies, and thus proves that the incarnation of God is real, that the infinite spirit does not scorn to descend into the lowest depths of the finite, because he knows how to find a way of return into himself, because in the most entire alienation of himself, he can retain his identity.   Further, the God-man, in so far as he is a spirit reflected in his infinity, stands contrasted with men, in so far as they are limited to their finiteness: hence opposition and contest result, and the death of the God-Man becomes a violent one, inflicted by the hands of sinners; so that to physical degradation is added the moral degradation of ignominy and accusation of crime.   If God then finds a passage from heaven to the grave, so must a way be discoverable for man from the grave to heaven: the death of the prince of life is the life of mortals.   By his entrance into the world as God-man, God showed himself reconciled to man; by his dying, in which act he cast off the limitations of mortality, he showed moreover the way in which he perpetually effects that reconciliation: namely, by remaining, throughout his manifestation of himself under the limitations of a natural existence, and his suppression of that existence, identical with himself.   Inasmuch as the death of the God-man is merely the cessation of his state of alienation from the infinite, it is in fact an exaltation and return to God, and thus the death is necessarily followed by the resurrection and ascension.

The God-man, who during his life stood before his cotemporaries as an individual distinct from themselves, and perceptible by the senses, is by death taken out of their sight; he enters into their imagination and memory: the unity of the divine and human in him, becomes a part of the general consciousness; and the church must repeat spiritually, in the souls of its members, those events of his life which he experienced externally.   The believer, finding himself environed with the conditions of nature, must, like Christ, die to nature—but only inwardly, as Christ did outwardly,—must spiritually crucify himself and be buried with Christ, that by the virtual suppression of his own sensible existence, he may become, in so far as he is a spirit, identical with himself, and participate in the bliss and glory of Christ.

§ 151.

LAST DILEMMA.

Thus by a higher mode of argumentation, from the idea of God and man in their reciprocal relation, the truth of the conception which the church forms of Christ appears to be confirmed, and we seem to be reconducted to the orthodox point of view, though by an inverted path : for while there, the truth of the conceptions of the church concerning Christ is deduced from the correctness of the evangelical history ; here, the veracity of the history is deduced from the truth of those conceptions. That which is rational is also real; the idea is not merely the moral imperative of Kant, but also an actuality. Proved to be an idea of the reason, the unity of the divine and human nature must also have an historical existence. The unity of God with man, says Marheineke,[1] was really and visibly manifested in the person of Jesus Christ; in him, according to Rosenkranz,[2] the divine power over nature was concentrated, he could not act otherwise than miraculously, and the working of miracles, which surprises us, was to him natural. His resurrection, says Conradi,[3] is the necessary sequel of the completion of his personality, and so little ought it to surprise us, that, on the contrary, we must rather have been surprised if it had not happened.

But do these deductions remove the contradictions which have exhibited themselves in the doctrine of the church, concerning the person and work of Christ? We need only to compare the structures, which Rosenkranz in his Review has passed on Schleiermacher's criticism of the Christology of the church, with what the same author proposes as a substitute in his Encyclopædia, in order to perceive, that the general propositions on the unity of the divine and human natures, do not in the least serve to explain the appearance of a person, in whom this unity existed individually, in an exclusive manner. Through I may conceive that the divine spirit in a state of renunciation and abasement becomes the human, and that the human nature in its return into and above itself becomes the divine ; this does not help me to conceive more easily, how the divine and human natures can have constituted the distinct and yet united portions of an historical person. Though I may see the human mind in its unity with the divine, in the course of the world's history, more and more completely establish itself as the power which subdues nature ; this is quite another thing, than to conceive a single man endowed with such power, for individual, voluntary acts. Lastly, from the truth, that the suppression of the natural existence is the resurrection of the spirit, can never be deduced the bodily resurrection of an individual.

We should thus have fallen back again to Kant's point of view, which we have ourselves found unsatisfactory : for if the idea have no corresponding reality, it is an empty obligation and ideal. But do we then deprive the idea of all reality? By no means : we reject only that which does not follow from the premises.[4] If reality is ascribed to the idea of the unity of the divine and human natures, is this equivalent to the admission that this unity must actually have been once manifested, as it never had been, and never more will be, in one individual? This is indeed not the mode in which Idea realizes itself; it is not wont to lavish all its fulness on one exemplar, and

---

[1] Dogmatik, § 326.
[2] Encyklopädie, s. 160.
[3] Selbstbewusstsein und Offenbarung, s. 295 f. Comp. Bauer, Recens. des L. J., Jahrbücher f. wiss. Kritik, 1836, Mai, s. 699 ff.
[4] Compare with this my Streitschriften, 3 Heft, s. 68 ff. 125,

be niggardly towards all others[5]—to express itself perfectly in that one individual, and imperfectly in all the rest: it rather loves to distribute its riches among a multiplicity of exemplars which reciprocally complete each other—in the alternate appearance and suppression of a series of individuals. And is this no true realization of the idea? is not the idea of the unity of the divine and human natures a real one in a far higher sense, when I regard the whole race of mankind as its realization, than when I single out one man as such a realization? is not an incarnation of God from eternity, a truer one than an incarnation limited to a particular point of time.

This is the key to the whole of Christology, that, as subject of the predicate which the church assigns to Christ, we place, instead of an individual, an idea ; but an idea which has an existence in reality, not in the mind only, like that of Kant. In an individual, a God-man, the properties and functions which the church ascribes to Christ contradict themselves ; in the idea of the race, they perfectly agree. Humanity is the union of the two natures—God become man, the infinite manifesting itself in the finite, and the finite spirit remembering its infinitude ; it is the child of the visible Mother and the invisible Father, Nature and Spirit ; it is the worker of miracles, in so far as in the course of human history the spirit more and more completely subjugates nature, both within and around man, until it lies before him as the inert matter on which he exercises his active power;[6] it is the sinless existence, for the course of its development is a blameless one, pollution cleaves to the individual only, and does not touch the race or its history. It is Humanity that dies, rises, and ascends to heaven, for from the negation of its phenomenal life there ever proceeds a higher spiritual life ; from the suppression of its mortality as a personal, national, and terrestrial spirit, arises its union with the infinite spirit of the heavens. By faith in this Christ, especially in his death and resurrection, man is justified before God ; that is, by the kindling within him of the idea of Humanity, the individual man participates in the divinely human life of the species. Now the main element of that idea is, that the negation of the merely natural and sensual life, which is itself the negation of the spirit (the negation of negation, therefore), is the sole way to true spiritual life.[7]

This alone is the absolute sense of Christology : that it is annexed to the person and history of one individual, is a necessary result of the historical form which Christology has taken.* Schleiermacher was quite right when he foreboded, that the speculative view would not leave much more of the historical person of the Saviour than was retained by the Ebionites. The phenomenal history of the individual, says Hegel, is only a starting point for the mind. Faith, in her early stages, is governed by the senses, and therefore contemplates a temporal history ; what she holds to be true is the external, ordinary event, the evidence for which is of the historical, forensic kind—a fact to be proved by the testimony of the senses, and the moral confidence inspired by the witnesses. But mind having once taken occasion by this external fact, to bring under its consciousness the idea of humanity as one with God, sees in the history only the presentation of that idea ; the object of faith is completely changed ; instead of a sensible, empirical fact, it has

---

[5] With this should be compared the explanation in the Streitschriften, ut sup. s. 119.

[6] Of this also there is an explanation in the Streitschriften, 3, s. 166 f.

[7] Herein lies the answer to the objection which Schaller (der historische Christus und die Philosophie, s. 64 ff.) has made to the above view; namely, that it teaches only a substantial, not a personal unity of man with God. That unity which exists in the determination of the race has already been present in individuals separately, according to the different measure of their religious development, and thus the substantial unity has become, in different degrees, a personal unity.

become a spiritual and divine idea, which has its confirmation no longer in history but in philosophy. When the mind has thus gone beyond the sensible history, and entered into the domain of the absolute, the former ceases to be essential ; it takes a subordinate place, above which the spiritual truths suggested by the history stand self-supported ; it becomes as the faint image of a dream which belongs only to the past, and does not, like the idea, share the permanence of the spirit which is absolutely present to itself.[8] Even Luther subordinated the physical miracles to the spiritual, as the truly great miracles. And shall we interest ourselves more in the cure of some sick people in Galilee, than in the miracles of intellectual and moral life belonging to the history of the world—in the increasing, the almost incredible dominion of man over nature—in the irresistible force of ideas, to which no unintelligent matter, whatever its magnitude, can oppose any enduring resistance ? Shall isolated incidents, in themselves trivial, be more to us than the universal order of events, simply because in the latter we presuppose, if we do not perceive, a natural cause, in the former the contrary ?   This would be a direct contravention of the more enlightened sentiments of our own day, justly and conclusively expressed by Schleiermacher. The interests of pity, says this theologian, can no longer require us so to conceive a fact, that by its dependence on God it is divested of the conditions which would belong to it as a link in the chain of nature ; for we have outgrown the notion, that the divine omnipotence is more completely manifested in the interruption of the order of nature, than in its preservation.[9] Thus if we know the incarnation, death and resurrection, the *duplex negatio affirmat*, as the eternal circulation, the infinitely repeated pulsation of the divine life ; what special importance can attach to a single fact, which is but a mere sensible image of this unending process ?   Our age demands to be led in Christology to the idea in the fact, to the race in the individual : a theology which, in its doctrines on the Christ, stops short at him as an individual, is not properly a theology, but a homily.

In what relation, then, must the pulpit stand to theology,—nay, how is the continuance of a ministry in the church possible when theology has reached this stage?   This is the difficult question which presents itself to us in conclusion.*

§ 152.†

RELATION OF THE CRITICAL AND SPECULATIVE THEOLOGY TO THE CHURCH.

Schleiermacher has said, that when he reflected on the approaching crisis in theology, and imagined himself obliged to choose one of two alternatives, either to surrender the Christian history, like every common history, as a spoil to criticism, or to hold his faith in fee to the speculative system ; his decision was, that for himself, considered singly, he would embrace the latter, but that, regarding himself as a member of the church, and especially as one of its teachers, he should be induced rather to take the opposite course. For the idea of God and of man on which, according to the speculative system, the truth of the Christian faith rests, is indeed a precious jewel, but it can be possessed only by a few, and he would not wish to be that privileged individual in the church, who alone among thousands held the faith on its true grounds.   As a member of the church, he could have no satisfaction but in

[8] Vorlesungen über die Philosophie der Religion, 2, s. 263 ff.   Compare the collection of the several propositions of Hegel on the person of Christ and the evangelical history, in my Streitschriften, 3 Heft, s. 76.
[9] Glaubenslehre, 1, s. 47.

perfect equality, in the consciousness that all receive alike, both in kind and manner, from the same source. And as a teacher and spokesman to the church, he could not possibly attempt the task of elevating old and young, without distinction, to the idea of God and of man : he must rather attack their faith as a groundless one, or else endeavour to strengthen and confirm it while knowing it to be groundless. As thus in the matter of religion an impassable gulf would be fixed between two parties in the church, the speculative theology threatens us with the distinction of an esoteric and exoteric doctrine, which ill accords with the declaration of Christ, that all shall be taught of God. The scientific alone have the foundation of the faith : the unscientific have only the faith, and receive it only by means of tradition. If the Ebionitish view, on the contrary, leave but little of Christ, yet this little is equally attainable by all, and we are thereby secured from the hierarchy of speculation, which ever tends to merge itself in the hierarchy of Rome.[1]

Here we see presented, under the form of thought belonging to a cultivated mind, the same opinion which is now expressed by many in a less cultivated fashion : namely, that the theologian who is at once critical and speculative, must in relation to the church be a hypocrite. The real state of the case is this. The church refers her Christology to an individual who existed historically at a certain period : the speculative theologian to an idea which only attains existence in the totality of individuals ; by the church the evangelical narratives are received as history : by the critical theologian, they are regarded for the most part as mere mythi. If he would continue to impart instruction to the church, four ways are open to him : *

First, the attempt already excluded by the above observations of Schleiermacher, namely, to elevate the church to his own point of view, and for it, also, to resolve the historical into the ideal :—an attempt which must necessarily fail, because to the Church all those premises are wanting on which the theologian rests his speculative conclusions ; and upon which, therefore, only an enthusiast for interpretation would venture.

The second and opposite measure would be, to transport himself to the point of view of the church, and for the sake of imparting edification ecclesiastically, to descend from the sphere of the ideal into the region of the popular conception. This expedient is commonly understood and judged too narrowly. The difference between the theologian and the church is regarded as a total one ; it is thought, that in answer to the question, whether he believes in the history of Christ, he ought to say exactly, no ; whereas he says, yes : and this is a falsehood. It is true, that if in the discourses and instructions of the spiritual teacher, the main interest were an historical one, this would be a correct representation of the case : but, in fact, the interest is a religious one,—it is essential religion which is here communicated under the form of a history ; hence he who does not believe in the history as such, may yet appreciate the religious truths therein contained, equally with one who does also receive the history as such : the distinction is one of form merely, and does not affect the substance. Hence it is an evidence of an uncultivated mind, to denounce as a hypocrite a theologian who preaches, for example, on the resurrection of Christ, since, though he may not believe in the reality of that event as a single sensible fact, he may, nevertheless, hold to be true the representation of the process of spiritual life, which the resurrection of Christ affords. Strictly considered, however, this identity of the substantial truth,

---

[1] In the 2ten Sendschreiben on his Glaubenslehre.

exists only in the apprehension of him who knows how to distinguish the substance from the form of religion, *i.e.*, of the theologian, not of the church, to whom he speaks. The latter can conceive no faith in the dogmatical truth of the resurrection of Christ, for example, apart from a conviction of its historical reality : and if it come to discover that the theologian has not this conviction, and yet preaches on the resurrection, he must appear in the eyes of the church a hypocrite, and thus the entire relation between the theologian and the church would be virtually cancelled.

In this case, the theologian, though in himself no hypocrite, would appear such to the church, and would be conscious of this misconstruction. If not-withstanding this, he should continue to instruct the church under the form of its own conceptions, he would ultimately appear a hypocrite to himself also, and would be driven to the third, desperate course, of forsaking the ministerial office. It avails nothing to say, he has only to descend from the pulpit, and mount the professor's chair, where he will not be under the necessity of withholding his scientific opinions from such as are destined to science; for if he, whom the course of his own intellectual culture has obliged to renounce the ministerial office, should by his instructions lead many to the same point, and thus render them also incapable of that office, the original evil would only be multiplied. On the other hand, it could not be held good for the church, that all those who pursue criticism and speculation to the results above presented, should depart from their position as teachers. For no clergyman would any longer meddle with such inquiries, if he thus ran the risk of being led to results which would oblige him to abandon the ministerial office ; criticism and philosophy would fall into the hands of those who are not professed theologians, and to the theologian nothing would remain but the faith, which then could not possibly long resist the attacks of the critical and speculative laity. But where truth is concerned, the possible consequences have no weight; hence the above remark ought not to be made. Thus much, however, may be maintained in relation to the real question : he whom his theological studies have led to an intellectual position, respecting which he must believe, that he has attained the truth, that he has penetrated into the deepest mysteries of theology, cannot feel either inclined or bound just at this point in his career to abandon theology : on the contrary, such a step would be unnatural, nay, impossible.*

He will therefore seek another expedient ; and as such there presents itself a fourth, which is not, like the two first, one-sided, nor like the third, merely negative, but which offers a positive mode of reconciling the two extremes— the consciousness of the theologian, and that of the church. In his discourses to the church, he will indeed adhere to the forms of the popular conception, but on every opportunity he will exhibit their spiritual significance, which to him constitutes their sole truth, and thus prepare—though such a result is only to be thought of as an unending progress—the resolution of those forms into their original ideas in the consciousness of the church also. Thus, to abide by the example already chosen, at the festival of Easter, he will indeed set out from the sensible fact of the resurrection of Christ, but he will dwell chiefly on the being buried and rising again with Christ, which the Apostle himself has strenuously inculcated. This very course every preacher, even the most orthodox, strictly takes, as often as he draws a moral from the evangelical text on which he preaches : for this is nothing else than the transition from the externally historical to the inward and spiritual. It is true, we must not overlook the distinction, that the orthodox preacher builds his moral on the text in such a way, that the latter remains as an historical foundation ; whereas, with the speculative preacher, the transition from the biblical history or the church doctrine, to the truth which he thence derives, has the negative effect of annihilating the former. Viewed more closely, however, the transition of the orthodox preacher from the evangelical text to the moral application, is not free from this negative tendency ; in proceeding from the history to the doctrine he implies at least thus much : the history is not enough, it is not the whole truth, it must be transmuted from a past fact into a present one, from an event external to you, it must become your own intimate experience : so that with this transition, the case is the same as with the proof of the existence of God, in which the cosmical existence, which is the point of departure, apparently remains as a foundation, but is in fact negatived as a true existence, and merged in the absolute. Nevertheless, there remains a marked distinction between these two propositions : since, and in so far as, this has happens, so and so is your duty and your consolation—and : this is indeed related as having happened once, but the truth is, that it always so happened, and both in and by you ought to happen. At least, the community will not receive both as identical ; and thus, here again, in every excess or diminution which the more or less spontaneous relation of the teacher to critical theology, together with the variety in the degrees of culture of the community, introduces,—the danger is incurred that the community may discover this difference, and the preacher appear to it, and consequently to himself, a hypocrite.

In this difficulty, the theologian may find himself driven either directly to state his opinions, and attempt to elevate the people to his ideas : or, since this attempt must necessarily fail, carefully to adapt himself to the conception of the community ; or, lastly, since, even on this plan, he may easily betray himself, in the end to leave the ministerial profession.

We have thus admitted the difficulty with which the critical and speculative views are burthened, with reference to the relation of the clergyman to the church ; we have exhibited the collision into which the theologian falls, when it is asked, what course remains for him in so far as he has adopted such views ? and we have shown that our age has not arrived at a certain decision on this subject. But this collision is not the effect of the curiosity of an individual ; it is necessarily introduced by the progress of time and the development of Christian theology ; it surprises and masters the individual, without his being able to guard himself from it. Or rather he can do this with slight labour, if he abstain from study and thought, or, if not from these, from freedom of speech and writing. Of such there are already enough in our day, and there was no need to make continual additions to their number through the calumniation of those who have expressed themselves in the spirit of advanced science. But there are also a few, who, notwithstanding such attacks, freely declare what can no longer be concealed—and time will show whether by the one party or the other, the Church, Mankind, and Truth are best served.

ANNOTATIONS TO THE TEXT

EDITOR'S NOTES

THESE notes are keyed to the pagination of the text printed in this volume. The points on the pages to which the notes refer are designated by asterisks and daggers. The notes are restricted to the most important substantive variations between the German editions, major interpretive issues, and questions of text and translation. Often a substantive revision signals a significant interpretive question, making it possible to consider these two matters in the same note. But because of space restrictions, it has been possible to consider only a small portion of the total number of variations between the editions. To locate some passages it has been necessary to give page and line count. Running heads and footnotes are not included in line counts. When the count is from the top of the page it is abbreviated "t"; from the bottom, "b." For example, "136/10t–2b" means "page 136, line 10 from top through line 2 from bottom."

§ 1.

39 * There is no indication of the source of this "amplification." Perhaps it represents an effort by Dr. Brabant to interpret Strauss on the basis of conversations and correspondence with him.

§ 10.

61 * The last two sentences of this paragraph replace, in the second, third, and fourth editions, a separate concluding paragraph of § 10 in the first edition. The paragraphs that follow were added in the third edition and retained in the fourth.

§ 11.

65 * Following this point the several German editions and the English translation vary considerably.

The second edition adds about three-quarters of a page in which Strauss explains further how he applies the concept of myth to the entire history of the life of Jesus. This additional material is dropped in the third and fourth editions.

Following the paragraph beginning, "The most extended application ...," the third and fourth editions add an additional section of nearly three pages, which is not contained in the Eliot translation. Strauss explains, in discussing August Tholuck's *Die Glaubwürdigkeit der evangelischen Geschichte* (Hamburg, 1837), how, in view of external considerations, the possibility of mythical treatment was greater for the Evangelists in regard to the childhood stories of Jesus than to his later life. But once myth is allowed into the childhood stories, it is impossible to mark it off from any other period of Jesus' life—all the more so if it is employed in the exposition of the baptism narrative at the beginning of Jesus' public ministry. Strauss concludes this section, however, by stating: "It is by no means to be asserted that [myth] is equally extensive throughout. To the contrary, it is obvious that in those parts of the life of Jesus where he is brought into public light more historical ground is to be found than in those segments which had elapsed in the darkness of private life." This additional section adds an important qualification not found in the earlier editions, namely, that myth is not equally extensive throughout the Gospels and that authentic historical materials are to be found in the parts dealing with the public ministry of Jesus.

The paragraph beginning, "The most extended application . . . ," is the only material following this point that is common to all four German editions, and is also the only paragraph included in the translation. This fact seems to indicate that the Brabants were acquainted with all the German editions and at certain points compared them critically, exercising an editorial judgment.

§ 12.

68   * The second and subsequent editions conclude § 12 with the last two paragraphs. The first edition does not contain them, but continues for approximately twenty pages of German text with arguments defending the mythical view of the Gospel history. Much of this material was reworked and included in §§ 13–14 of the second edition. The reasons for the addition of §§ 13–16 in the second and third editions are discussed in the Editor's Introduction, pp. xxv–xxix.

§ 13.

73   * The last two sentences of this paragraph were added in the third and fourth editions. They do little to resolve the question of Johannine authorship, since it could be argued on the basis of what is said here that the Gospel of John derived either from the Apostle or from the Presbyter, or from neither. For Strauss's vagueness on this question, see the Editor's Introduction, pp. xxxix–xl.

74   * In this paragraph Strauss is tantalizingly close to the position of modern form criticism. He denies the existence of a hypothetical Proto-Gospel, an eyewitness source from which the canonical Gospels were supposed to have drawn their materials. Rather he allows for a period of oral tradition (*die mündliche Überlieferung*, translated "orally circulated Gospel"), which only gradually came to be written down, and which went through many literary revisions. One of the first of these written documents was the Gospel of the Hebrews (believed by some nineteenth century critics to be a written source behind the present Gospel of Matthew). These oral traditions *might* have originated with particular apostles or disciples who were eyewitnesses, but there is no way of testing this. Indeed, Strauss's great problem is that he did not possess the tools of form criticism by which to analyze the formative process of *oral* traditions. He has no way of tracing these traditions back to their more primitive forms and of reaching historical bedrock. Thus he is led to the conclusion, stated in the next paragraphs, that "unhistorical legends" or "a mass of myths" began to form in Palestine shortly after Jesus' death. Strauss has proven to be correct about the oral transmission of the Gospel traditions; but given the critical tools of his day, there was no way to bridge the gulf from the events themselves to the earliest written documents. He did not shy away from the radical character of this conclusion because it harmonized with his theological and philosophical perspective.

§ 14.

80   * This footnote, added in the second and subsequent editions, is intended as a further elaboration of the author's claim to an "absence of presupposition" in the Preface to the first edition. Strauss had been challenged on this claim by Wilhelm Hoffmann and other critics.

§ 15.

86   * § 15 was added in the third and fourth editions. For a discussion of the contents of this section, see the Editor's Introduction, pp. xxvi–xxvii.

§ 16.

87   * This section was added in the second and subsequent editions and comprises wholly new material. The reasons for its addition, together with an analysis of its contents, are discussed in the Editor's Introduction, pp. xxviii–xxix.

§ 34.

166   * This is the approximate point where George Eliot took over the translation from Rufa Brabant (Hennell) in January 1844. According to Sara Hennell, Rufa Brabant completed 257 pages in the first volume of the fourth German edition,

which corresponds to this point in the English text. (Gordon S. Haight, ed., *The George Eliot Letters* [New Haven: Yale University Press, 1954], I:171n.) Eliot also confirms that her "first page is 257," but she is not certain whether starting there will leave a page or so untranslated. Accordingly, she asks Sara Hennell, "Will you be so kind as to ascertain exactly how far Mrs. H's translation has proceeded, and send me the intermediate pages? Perhaps, however, I had better translate the whole §. It is the 34th about the magi—may they be anathema!" (*Letters*, I:174–75).

§ 40.

193   * The third edition omits the remainder of this paragraph, concluding it with the following sentence: "Now whether or not we agree with Tholuck that the Jewish doctors requested that the remarkable child be seated near them, we seem to have at most an exaggerated expression of the narrator, which, however, does not invalidate the essential truth of his report."

194   * From this point to the end of § 40 the third edition differs substantially from the others. It is conceivable, Strauss now suggests, that already in his twelfth year Jesus had some intimation of his future Messiahship. "The consciousness of God as his Father, with whom he stood in an especially internal spiritual and intellectual communion, is the most natural germ from which Jesus' consciousness of his messianic position must have later developed."

§ 41.

196   * The third edition omits this section entirely, which is identical in the other editions.

§ 43.

201   * The Eliot translation follows the third edition rather than the fourth for lines 11–19t. This peculiar and rare lapse of Eliot might be explained by the fact that she was working with loose sheets of the German text, which were passed back and forth between herself, Sara Hennell, and the publisher. This sheet might have been lost and a sheet from the third edition substituted for it. It so happens that the text on the page of the fourth edition ends at the point where it rejoins the reading of the third ("amid the concourse . . .").

§ 44.

213   * At this point the third edition introduces a paragraph not contained in any of the other editions, which argues that, while unlikely, it is not impossible that the duration of John's ministry was limited to six months.

§ 46.

230   * From p. 221/2b to the end of § 46 the third edition differs considerably from the others. Strauss is no longer willing to argue so forcefully or directly from the historical inauthenticity of the Fourth Gospel to conclusions which, to be sure, do not really differ in substance from those in the other editions.

§ 47.

234   * In the third edition Strauss argues differently, freeing Jesus from any direct, substantive dependence on the Baptist as far as his messianic idea is concerned, and advancing the first of the legendary additions to the tradition (John's delayed and qualified testimony concerning Jesus) into historical fact. These revisions constitute a crucial concession on the part of Strauss, for they mark the beginning of his attempt to rescue Jesus from the opprobrium of being a messianic fanatic, who shared with John the apocalyptic notion of the inbreaking of the messianic kingdom. The question as to whether Jesus himself was decisively stamped by the apocalyptic preaching of the Baptist continues to be hotly debated among New Testament scholars today. See the articles on "Apocalypticism" in *Journal for Theology and the Church* 6 (New York: Herder and Herder, 1969), especially the comments by Ernst Käsemann on the relations between Jesus and John the Baptist, pp. 39–40, 102–5, 115–18. After Strauss, Johannes Weiss was the first to develop a thoroughly apocalyptic interpretation of Jesus' preaching. See his book, *Jesus' Proclamation of the Kingdom of God*, ed. Richard H. Hiers and D. Larrimore Holland (Philadelphia: Fortress Press, 1971).

§ 49.

237 * In the third edition, this section is completely reworked, with different conclusions. As to whether Jesus was not yet aware of his messianic destiny at the time
of baptism, the third edition argues that it is unlikely that Jesus could have come
to a decisive clarity about his messianic role shortly thereafter, without its having
already developed as a part of his self-consciousness by the time he reached intellectual maturity, at the age of thirty. Regarding the sinlessness of Jesus, Strauss
now contends that it is unthinkable that he who later was empowered to forgive
sins and baptize by the Spirit should have required forgiveness and purification
by another.

§ 51.

246 * The third edition ends the section at this point, after the addition of one more
sentence, contending that an invention of the baptism scene is unlikely because it
would be perceived to subordinate Jesus to John, and that it is not improbable
that "Jesus, who knew himself to be the Messiah, should have submitted himself
to baptism in order to inaugurate the messianic kingdom."

§ 57.

271 * In the third edition, Strauss decides decisively in favor of the Fourth Evangelist who has Jesus make several trips to Jerusalem during his public ministry.

§ 61.

283 * The last three paragraphs of this section differ in the third edition, where
Strauss argues that the title, Son of Man, while understood by the Jews to refer
to the Messiah (cf. John 12:34), nevertheless was not the *customary* designation
for the Messiah (cf. Matt. 16:13 ff.). Jesus preferred this title as a self-designa-
tion to that of Messiah or Son of David, because it avoided the political connotations of the latter, and its unusualness permitted a new conception of
the Messiah.

Strauss's conclusions in this section (especially as formulated in the first,
second, and fourth editions) are of great significance for his analysis of Jesus'
messianic consciousness (§§ 62–69) and the discourses on the second advent (§§
115–16). From the point of view of modern form criticism and redaction criticism, his work on the Son of Man materials is not satisfactory. He assumes, after
a hurried and poorly documented argument, that the Jews identified the Danielic
Son of Man with the Messiah, that Jesus understood the title fundamentally in
the Danielic, apocalyptic sense, and that he came to regard himself as this Son of
Man. He notices that many of the sayings seem to refer to a third person, but
attributes these to an earlier period in Jesus' career when he was not yet fully
conscious of his identity. He does not distinguish between different literary and
theological *types* of Son of Man sayings—apocalyptic, suffering, and earthly.
Modern investigations have made such a distinction and argue that (at best) one
of these types of Son of Man sayings can be attributed to Jesus, but that the
others have been added by the primitive tradition. Either Jesus referred to the
apocalyptic Son of Man as a figure other than himself, and the tradition added
other sayings in which *Jesus* is identified as the Son of Man; or Jesus referred to
himself as the Son of Man in a *nonapocalyptic*, earthly sense, in which case the
primitive Jewish-Christian community added the apocalyptic sayings and assumed
Jesus' identity with the Danielic figure; or possibly none of these types of sayings can be traced to Jesus. For a discussion of the issues, see Norman Perrin,
Rediscovering the Teaching of Jesus (New York: Harper & Row, 1967), pp.
164–99, 259–60.

§ 62.

284 * In the third edition, this section follows § 64, and it differs significantly. The
third edition does not seriously consider the possibility that Jesus was initially
uncertain of his messianic identity. Rather he concealed it from public disclosure
to avoid awakening the political idea of the messianic kingdom in the popular
mind because it was his life's work to prepare for this kingdom in a spiritual
sense. Indeed, Jesus' injunction to his disciples not to disclose the messianic secret

is coupled with the prediction of his forthcoming suffering and death, which means that his death was to be the sole means by which he hoped to free the messianic idea of his contemporaries from its earthly ingredients.

284 † This "indisputable fact" is now regarded as highly questionable by New Testament scholarship. Here Strauss is curiously brief and uncritical in assessing the evidence. The probable reasons for his failure to apply the mythical interpretation in this instance are discussed in the Editor's Introduction, p. xxxii.

288 * In the last paragraph of this section, the first and second editions vary, and the fourth edition follows the reading of the first, not the second (the entire section is changed in the third edition). The second edition presents as a hypothesis the conclusion reached in the first, that Jesus originally took the same position as the Baptist in relation to the messianic kingdom, and only gradually came to think of himself as the Messiah. To this is opposed another, more plausible hypothesis, that a figure of epochal significance like Jesus could not have remained uncertain of his mission once he had entered upon it, and that therefore it must be assumed that Jesus understood himself to be the Messiah from the time of his baptism, but that he did not express this publicly for pedagogical reasons: he did not wish to obtrude himself upon his followers by peculiar or alien explanations, but rather to allow his identity to become self-evident from his activity and impact as a whole.

§ 63.

288 † This section is completely rewritten in the third edition. Strauss now contends that "in his sayings Jesus elevated the title 'Son of God' from its Jewish-theocratic sense to a religious-metaphysical significance."

§ 66.

295 * In the third edition the word "balance" is removed from the title, and the entire section is rewritten. Strauss no longer attempts to "balance" the data supporting political and spiritual elements in the messianic plan of Jesus; that plan is now construed as purely spiritual. The data supporting the "appearance" of a political element (as adduced by Reimarus and presented in the preceding section) are reconsidered and found unconvincing. (1) In view of the Sermon on the Mount, the parables, and other teachings of Jesus, it cannot be seriously maintained that he did not clarify his concept of the messianic kingdom to show that it entails a purely moral-religious spiritual community. (2) The task of Jesus' disciples was merely to announce the nearness of the kingdom, not to define it. (3) Jesus' promise of the twelve thrones (Matt. 19:28) is merely a figurative way of saying that one's present activity on behalf of the kingdom will be the measure of one's future share in its glory and blessedness. (4) For his entry into Jerusalem, Jesus chose the animal of the king of peace (the ass rather than the white horse); the philippic against the scribes and Pharisees and the cleansing of the temple are to be viewed as actions of a religious and moral reformer rather than of a ruler. (5) His lamentation over Jerusalem indicates that he had intended to bring about a rebirth of his people but not to engage in direct political activity on their behalf.

These changes are among the most significant of the third edition. Gone is the entire discussion on p. 296 of the apocalyptic character of Jesus' messianic expectation, which did not set its hopes upon a political revolution but upon direct divine intervention at the coming of the Son of Man upon the clouds of heaven —an apocalyptic expectation which in Strauss's view marks Jesus as an enthusiast with whom we can have little sympathy today. Albert Schweitzer regarded this as one of the most important passages in Strauss's work, and rightly considered it to anticipate the eschatological interpretation defended by Johannes Weiss and himself. (Albert Schweitzer, *The Quest of the Historical Jesus*, 3rd ed. [London: Adam & Charles Black, 1954], pp. 92–93.)

§ 68.

300 * In the third edition this section is completely revised. Strauss now concludes that the weight of evidence favors the view that Jesus broadened the messianic kingdom to include Gentiles.

§ 78.

345   * Strauss's discussion of the parables is curious in several respects. His chief interest is in comparing parallel versions of parables and their external connections, to determine which of the Evangelists has preserved the more primitive versions, and to examine the workings of synoptic tradition. Nowhere does he direct attention to the phenomenon of the parable as such or attempt a definition of its literary form and function. He says merely that the parable "is a kind of problem, to be solved by the reflection of the hearer" (p. 345). He appears to reject the traditional allegorical interpretation and to anticipate the work of Adolf Jülicher by suggesting that the parables convey a single point (or "moral," p. 349) of broad applicability. He interprets only two parables in any detail— the unjust steward (Luke 16:1–13), and the rich man and Lazarus (Luke 16:19–31)—both of which cast Jesus into a rather unfavorable light on Strauss's accounting. According to the latter parable, for example, "the measure of future recompense is not the amount of good done, or wickedness perpetrated, but of evil endured, and fortune enjoyed" (p. 351)—a point of view Strauss obviously finds distasteful, both for its high estimation of poverty (see also p. 337) and for the notion of a future recompense. This selection of parables for special attention appears highly arbitrary. Note too that Strauss ends his discussion with a group of parables which he claims are related to the second advent of Christ (pp. 352–55). This would imply that the parables of Jesus are self-referential, and that he spelled out the details of his messianic coming in parabolic detail, both of which are quite unlikely although congruent with Strauss's general portrayal of Jesus.

§ 83.

382   * The number for n. 8 should appear here.

386   * In the third edition frequent alterations occur in §§ 80–83, suggesting that the *content*, but not the *form*, of many of the Johannine discourses may be considered authentic. These changes are culminated by an altered conclusion to the last paragraph of this section. Following the remark that the discourses of Jesus in the Fourth Gospel, by contrast with those in the Synoptics, are joined together by "transitions in which one thought develops itself out of another, and a succeeding proposition is frequently but an explanatory amplification of the preceding" (p. 386/17t), the third edition reads as follows: "Either we have here a truer account than that found in the Synoptics, namely, one which, aside from isolated elements, restores the original connection and transitions—one which, however, is no longer ascribed to the Johannine Gospel by even its most ardent friends; or we have what has fallen asunder in memory in the [Synoptic] discourses here restored to unity by the Evangelist's own intellectual efforts, indeed in such a fashion that he has dissolved the brittle, solid units (for the most part in his own mind) into a pliable mass, from which he has constructed the discourses lying before us in forms for which he must assume the major responsibility. Thus all that can be ventured by a critical examination of the New Testament agrees essentially with what [C. G.] Bretschneider says in his most recent, revised estimate of the Johannine discourses: John allowed Jesus to speak less often in the way that he really spoke in detail, than in a way that was conformable with the impression John had of the entire appearance and teaching of Jesus. The question still at stake concerns two matters: first, how much in these discourses still belongs to Jesus himself; second, whether on this view the composition of the Fourth Gospel can be attributed to the Apostle John. The first question I have already sought to answer in what precedes; in regard to the second, I do not venture to assert that the Johannine discourses contain anything that represents a formidable obstacle to their being interpreted in part from the individual character of John and in part from the composition of the Gospel in his old age." See the Editor's Introduction, pp. xxxix-xl.

§ 84.

387   * This section provides an important supplement to the discussion in § 13 of external grounds for determining the historical credibility of the canonical Gos-

pels. Here, in effect, Strauss sums up the *internal* grounds of credibility based on his analysis of individual Gospel narratives up to this point. See the Editor's Introduction, p. xxx.

§ 88.

402   * The third edition completely alters the conclusion of this section, beginning at p. 400/10b. The question of the chronological difference between the Synoptists and the Fourth Evangelist is left open. More importantly, the cleansing of the temple is more thoroughly spiritualized than in the other editions where Strauss goes to lengths to assure that this incident had no revolutionary political significance, and appears to represent the cleansing of the temple as a product of Jesus' messianic enthusiasm, by which he expected, perhaps, to propel events to their denouement and thus initiate by supernatural means the messianic age. Also lacking in the third edition is a discussion of the possible nonhistoricity of the incident.

§ 89.

409   * The last two paragraphs of the section are altered in the third edition, where it is argued that the Johannine account (12:1 ff.) is the most historically reliable. It is puzzling, Strauss continues, that the name of Mary has been dropped from Matthew and Mark; but the Lukan version (7:36 ff.) can be explained by its association with another tradition, which lies at the base of the story of the woman taken in adultery in John 8:1 ff., a story whose authenticity can be contested.

§ 90.

409   † This section is omitted entirely by the third edition, thus avoiding a discussion damaging to the apostolic authorship of John. Instead, Strauss merely briefly questions the authenticity of John 8:1–11 at the end of the preceding section.

§ 91.

415   * Beginning with the last three paragraphs of this section, the text of the third edition differs completely and continues for six pages.

In this expanded material, Strauss introduces a third category of miracles: *unusual powers of nature*, analogous to animal magnetism (hypnotism); these cures are *natural* but *uncommon* or *extraordinary*, as distinguished from *supernatural* or *absolute* miracles on the one hand, and cures based on the *ordinary powers of nature* on the other. Included in this category are cures involving touch, cures based on the hypnotic power of will or on clairvoyance, and cures at a distance ("far seeing" or mental telepathy). Jesus healed by making use of the ordinary and extraordinary powers of nature, but not in a supernatural or absolute fashion. Having introduced this third category, Strauss now attempts to de-emphasize its significance, manifesting an ambivalence characteristic of the third edition. Such curative powers stand in only an accidental relation to the moral worth and piety of the healer. The hypnotic clairvoyance and telepathy of the somnambulist often are accompanied by a state of mental depression. Hence these "miraculous" incidents of themselves can by no means prove that Jesus was the founder of the true religion. Yet, in agreement with Schleiermacher (*The Christian Faith*, § 14), Strauss writes, "It is natural to expect that, corresponding to new points of development in spiritual life, new phenomena of a bodily character should also occur, brought about by the new spiritual power. Accordingly it may be presupposed of Christ that he, who exercised such a remarkable influence on the rest of human nature, should also . . . have given evidence of a remarkable power to effect the bodily side of human nature."

In this chapter Strauss categorizes the miracles by type and treats them in an order of descending historical probability, moving from the cures (§§ 92–99), to resuscitations of the dead (§ 100), to miracles in the strict sense, involving Jesus' power over inanimate nature (§§ 101–4). The fact that precedence is given to the expulsion of demons (§§ 92–93) reflects Strauss's judgment that these narratives can be traced back to historical roots more frequently than other types of cures (although he offers no methodologically precise way of doing so). In the third edition, Strauss attempts to upgrade the authenticity of some of the cures, earlier dismissed as legendary, by assigning them to the third category of miracles, analogous to animal magnetism. Accordingly, important alterations occur in §§ 93 (expulsion of demons), 96 (cures of paralytics), and 97 (involuntary cures). The shift of § 96 forward by two sections in the third edition means that Strauss upgrades the cures of paralytics to the point where they surpass in credibility the cures of lepers and of the blind. The cures of lepers, cures of the blind, cures at a distance, and cures on the Sabbath are not materially assisted by the animal magnetism hypothesis. Nor does Strauss alter his judgment of any of the miracles in the first category, miracles in the strict sense.

§ 96.

452 * In the third edition this section precedes §§ 94 and 95 (see ed.n. 415*) and is heavily revised. Examples from the field of animal magnetism allow us to conjecture that Jesus possessed a hypnoticlike healing power, and the paralytics a faith highly stimulated by the words of Jesus, in which case the cures of paralytics belong to a type of phenomenon for which there is observable historical evidence.

§ 101.

496 * In the first edition, this section has the title, *Sturm-, See- und Fischgeschichten,* "Storm, Sea, and Fish Stories." It was changed to *Seeanekdoten* in the second and subsequent editions; similar changes are made in the text wherever the offensive phrase occurs. Emanuel Hirsch states that Strauss's critics often "complained of the heartless coldness of the investigation, but were able to object formally only to a single chapter title, 'Storm, Sea and Fish Stories'." (*Geschichte der neuern evangelischen Theologie* 5 [Gütersloh: C. Bertelsmann Verlag, 1954], p. 497.) Cf. the *Kaltblütigkeit* mentioned in the Preface to the first edition.

496 † This sentence, inserted first in the third edition, specifies more clearly the distinction implied all along between miracle in the broad or loose sense and miracle in the strict or absolute sense. Following C. H. Weisse, Strauss makes this distinction by using the terms *Wunder* and *Mirakel.*

501 * It is just this tendency that has led William R. Farmer (*The Synoptic Problem* [New York: Macmillan, 1964]) and others to regard Mark as the latest, not the earliest, of the Gospels. Assuming the lateness of Mark, Strauss elsewhere notes its apparent tendency to exaggerate and expand miracle stories by comparison with Matthew and Luke (pp. 389–90), but he makes no attempt to utilize this insight critically because he is not interested in the synoptic problem as such. If on the other hand Mark is the earliest Gospel, then Matthew and Luke can be viewed as abbreviating and in other ways modifying the Markan miracle traditions. For this argument, see H. J. Held, "Matthew as Interpreter of the Miracle Stories," in G. Bornkamm, G. Barth, and H. J. Held, *Tradition and Interpretation in Matthew* (Philadelphia: Westminster Press, 1963), pp. 165–299.

§ 112.

573 * This paragraph is modified in the third edition: it is not merely *possible* that Jesus himself came to view suffering and death as a part of the office and destination of the Messiah; it is *necessarily the case* in view of his messianic plan and conduct. "If he . . . unambiguously understood himself to be the Messiah, and indeed in such a way as to have completely overcome and spiritualized the sensual political messianic idea of his people, then the reserve with which he explained his Messiahship and his sparse hints aimed at correcting the earthly messianic hopes of his disciples can only be explained on the assumption that he expected his violent death to serve as a factual and most potent corrective of these errors."

Following this variation, the third edition rejoins the reading of the others to the end of the section. It is remarkable how generally conservative Strauss's conclusion is (in all editions). He attributes to Jesus a prediction of his passion and death and an interpretation of its efficacy in "moral" and "psychological," if not soteriological, terms. Thus Jesus himself, not the primitive kerygma, is the source of the idea of the suffering and dying Messiah. This helps to explain why Strauss is able to accept as authentic all of the Son of Man sayings, including those in which the suffering and death of the Son of Man are predicted (ed.n. 283*). In effect, Jesus is credited by Strauss with combining the apocalyptic Son of Man of Daniel with the Suffering Servant of Isaiah 53 (without, however, the propitiatory element).

§ 115.

584   * Here we may observe an interesting contrast between Strauss and Reimarus (the "Fragmentist"). For the latter, Jesus remained purely political in his intention: his plan failed, and the apostles introduced the apocalyptic predictions. Strauss on the other hand credits Jesus, not the primitive church, with the apocalypses (§ 116), which rescues him from being a political Messiah, but at the cost of making him an enthusiast.

585   * Strauss's meaning at this point is not entirely clear. Does he have in mind the inference that Jesus was in error, or the inference (by Reimarus) that the apostles engaged in premeditated deception, or both? If the former, then Christianity does appear to have been "fatally wounded," for the subsequent analysis shows, to Strauss's satisfaction, that there is no way of avoiding the fact that Jesus intimately associated his own second coming with the destruction of Jerusalem. (See the next note.)

590   † This paragraph is added in the third edition and retained in the fourth. It is an important addition, for it contains an acknowledgment by Strauss that a philosophical interpretation of the second coming more congenial with his own immanental views—"instead of a merely future, to make it a perpetual coming" —does not accord with the meaning of the New Testament apocalypses. The only remaining possibility is that these texts represent a *vaticinium post eventum* and hence cannot be attributed to Jesus, but Strauss rejects that possibility in the next section. Thus he is left with the conclusion that the futuristic eschatology and illusory apocalypticism of Jesus render him unintelligible to our age, although he can be understood as a product of his own. Or as he himself expresses it earlier in this section, "Such inferences from the discourse before us would inflict a fatal wound on Christianity" (pp. 584–85). It is curious that this paragraph, which renders the problem so painfully obvious, should be added in the third edition, where attempts are made elsewhere (e.g., § 66) to moderate Jesus' eschatology.

§ 116.

591   * For "history" read "visions." The list of errata in the fourth German edition corrects *Geschichte* to *Gesichte*.

596   * The preceding two paragraphs were heavily revised in the second and subsequent editions. The first edition is more radical, for it ascribes to Jesus an anticipation of his glorification as the heavenly Son of Man in his own lifetime and a postponement of this rather fanatic dream when the inevitability of his death became apparent. It is also more critical, because it recognizes the prediction of the destruction of the temple and the devastation of Jerusalem to be a *vaticinium post eventum*. On the other hand, Strauss may have come to sense an inconsistency in attributing the sayings about Jerusalem to the Evangelists, and the sayings about the heavenly Son of Man to Jesus. In other words, if some apocalyptic elements in the discourses of Jesus can be attributed to the primitive church, why should not all of them, including the apocalyptic Son of Man sayings? Indirectly, the existence of a primitive Christian apocalyptic is admitted in the first edition, but is removed in the second and subsequent editions, which trace all apocalyptic elements to Jesus. In this respect the first edition is closer to modern scholarship on the matter. But Strauss never doubts that Jesus regarded himself as the apocalyptic Son of Man in the Danielic sense. It is curious that in the third edition Strauss does not argue from a *vaticinium post eventum*, in view of the fact that he removes the suggestion from § 66 that Jesus was an apocalyptic enthusiast (see ed.n. 295*); this is one of several inconsistencies in the third edition. Perhaps Strauss wanted to avoid an association with the more radical position of the first edition. Perhaps,

too, the accuracy of the predictions of the destruction of Jerusalem could be taken as proof of Jesus' superior religious consciousness.

§ 117.

602   * For § 62 read § 63.

§ 124.

634   * Beginning at p. 633/12t the editions vary. The first edition is the most radical. The words "do this in remembrance of me" are attributed to the primitive community rather than to Jesus. That Jesus might have had a last-minute foreboding of his near and violent death is rejected. The section ends with an analysis of Jesus' assurance that he would no more drink of the fruit of the vine until he drank it new in the kingdom of the Father (Matt. 26:29 par.). Thus the first edition ends on a negative note: there is no evidence that Jesus had a presentiment of his near end, and the cultic aspects of the Last Supper must be traced to Christian legend.

The second and fourth editions (which are identical) ameliorate the severity of this conclusion by allowing for the possible authenticity of "do this in remembrance of me" through the suggestion that Jesus may have had some significant intention in distributing bread and wine among his disciples; and, by the addition of a new concluding paragraph and other changes, they leave open the possibility that Jesus contemplated his death as a near event, thus making bread and wine the symbols of his body and blood, even perhaps uttering the words preserved by Paul and Luke. In the third edition Strauss removes the suggestion that Jesus might even yet expect the messianic kingdom to commence during his life.

§ 128.

656   * This paragraph is important for Strauss's understanding of Jesus' attitude toward his death. He accepts as historical Jesus' admission to the claim of Messiahship when questioned by the Sanhedrin (Matt. 26:63–64 par.), and adds that Jesus probably became convinced that he would enter into his messianic glorification as the Son of Man only upon his speedy return after death, which he here predicts. This conclusion harmonizes with Strauss's contention that "Jesus held and expressed the conviction that he was the Messiah" (p. 284), and with his interpretation of the discourses on the second advent (§§ 115–16). But the suggestion made here (in all the editions) that Jesus may at first have expected to enter into his messianic glorification without the intervention of death, and that the necessity of suffering dawned upon him only in the extremity of the moment, is found elsewhere only in the first edition (ed.n. 596*).

Strauss never argues for the historical authenticity of the scene before the Sanhedrin; he simply assumes it. As with the whole question of Jesus' claim to Messiahship, he is curiously uncritical, while other parts of the passion story are readily dismissed as legendary.

§ 132.

688   * Strauss's argument that the opening words of Psalm 22 "must appear singularly adapted to be put into the mouth of the crucified Messiah" by the Evangelists is hardly convincing in light of the persistent difficulty experienced by the church from the beginning in interpreting them. Strauss himself notes some of the strained exegesis of this passage at the beginning of the paragraph.

§ 140.

735   * Some comments on Strauss's interpretation of the resurrection may be appropriate at this point:

In this and the preceding three sections Strauss demonstrates with devastating effectiveness that it is no longer possible to regard the empty tomb and appearance traditions as factual historical reports. He shows it is impossible to harmonize divergencies in the accounts of the empty tomb (§ 137); he discloses contradictions in the place and time of the alleged appearances of Jesus (§ 138); and he shows that the Evangelists can only have intended to represent the post-resurrection body of Jesus as supernatural and transfigured, yet they predicate impossibly contradictory attributes of this body (§ 139). The unavoidable conclusion is that the resurrection stories cannot be regarded as historical reports but as theological interpretations of some sort of definitive experience on the part of the primitive Christian community (§ 140).

Strauss is the author of the so-called subjective vision hypothesis. The experience that gave rise to the idea of a "resurrection" was a visionary experience on the part of the first disciples, enthusiastically engendered by the psychological need to resolve the contradiction between the death of Jesus and belief in his Messiahship. For Strauss this is both a *subjective* and a *visionary* experience: he wants to show how an individual disciple "could, *purely as an operation of his own mind*, make present to himself the risen Christ in a *visionary* manner" (p. 743).

The subjectivity of the experience is accounted for by a psychological interpretation. As already noted, psychology permitted Strauss a more refined rationalism, which marks him as a distinctly modern man. The psychological interpretation means for Strauss that the resurrection experience of the disciples has no extrasubjective source and reality: it is purely a product of their own minds, reinforced by a growing communal enthusiasm. He rejects as magical and supernatural any attempts to attribute the Easter experience to the agency of the risen Jesus (e.g., by Spinoza and Weisse, pp. 740, 744, n. 29). Thus, as he puts it, he is "induced to doubt the reality of the resurrection" (p. 739), at least as something which happened to Jesus.

The experience is clearly a visionary one for Strauss: note his preference for the term "Christophany." This is not, to be sure, an external physical vision or epiphany, as Strauss thinks is intended by the Evangelists and Paul in their use of the term ὀphthē ("appeared") ; rather it is a subjective vision or hallucination, induced by a state of excitement, anticipation, or "pious enthusiasm." Once the visionary character of the experience is granted, it is possible to avoid Strauss's subjective-psychological explanation only on miraculous grounds or by a dubious appeal to extrasensory perception (e.g., Wolfhart Pannenberg). Thus Strauss's constant stressing of the visionary aspect helps to support his psychological interpretation (as the only alternative to supernaturalism), and it has the incidental effect of making the early Christians, like their leader, enthusiasts.

Strauss assumes, without argument or analysis, that the word "resurrection" (*anastasis*) means the "revivification of a dead person" (p. 736), the return to life of a dead man (p. 735). Such a concept is blatantly supernatural, violating the known laws of nature and history. Therefore a rational person must conclude either that Jesus was not really dead, or that he did not again become living (p. 736). Strauss opts for the latter. In the *Glaubenslehre* (II:736), he criticizes Schleiermacher's interpretation of the resurrection as "the living action of Christ" in "the corporate life he founded," for it is impossible, claims Strauss, to imagine "the duration of an individual dissolved from his historical conditions and absolutely uprooted." In other words, Strauss allows the concept of "resurrection" to be defined by supernaturalism, and clearly he has no interest, as Schleiermacher did, in finding a way to conceive of the personal presence of the risen Jesus, now active in the redemption of humanity.

744   * Footnote 29 is added in the third and fourth editions. The first edition has no footnote at all. The second edition has a different, longer footnote, in which Strauss argues that the story of the resurrection is a good instance of the fact that the mythical interpretation does not intend to destroy history as such but rather to establish a firm historical basis for the Gospel stories whenever possible. In this instance, however, the factual historical basis of the resurrection accounts is not the revivification of Jesus itself but the *belief* in his revivification. But, Strauss adds, to demonstrate that the early Christian community really did believe that Jesus was raised from the dead and appeared to his disciples by no means entails a reversion from the mythical standpoint to the natural interpretation.

744   † The cross-reference should be to § 113, note 3 (the error is in the German of the fourth edition), and the text is Hosea 6:2: "After two days he will revive us; on the third day he will raise us up, that we may live before him."

§ 144.

757   * The translation of the section head should read: "Necessary Transition *of*
Criticism to Dogma" (*Nothwendiger Übergang der Kritik in das Dogma*). George
Eliot misconstrued the meaning of the heading, and indeed of the section as a
whole. She was aware of the obscurity in meaning as she interpreted it, and consequently tried to read *Dogma* as *Dogmatik*. (Haight, *Letters*, I:208–9.) But
Strauss's intention in the Concluding Dissertation is not to make a transition
from criticism to dogmatics, but rather to transfer the *critical operation* to
dogma. The transition is from the criticism of *history* to the criticism of *dogma*.
"Dogma" here means Christian faith as it has been formulated in doctrines,
creeds, dogmatic systems, "theology." Criticism must be brought to bear upon the
doctrinal as well as historical forms of Christian faith (i.e., upon the history of
doctrine as well as upon the Gospels)—both of which remain at the level of *Vorstellung*—in order to raise faith to the level of knowledge (*Wissen*) or *Begriff*. In
this process, the identity in *content* of Christian faith and philosophical truth
will be disclosed. Strauss takes up the second phase of this critical task in his next
book, *The Christian Faith, Its Doctrinal Development and Conflict with Modern
Science* (1840–41). In this work he subjects the history of Christian doctrine to
the same destructive criticism as that brought to bear upon the Gospel stories in
The Life of Jesus, thus completing the project he had envisioned since 1831,
although the promised speculative reconstruction of the truth of Christian faith is
lacking, and the work ends on a thoroughly negative note. Strauss gives a brief
sketch of dogmatic criticism as it applies to the doctrine *of Christ* in §§ 145–50 of
the Concluding Dissertation of the present work, treating first the orthodox doctrine of Christ and its criticism by Socinianism and rationalism, then the Christol-
ogies of rationalism, Schleiermacher, Kant, de Wette, Hegel, and the Hegelians—
each of which discloses the weaknesses of its predecessors.

The Eliot translation of § 144 is faulty or imprecise at several points. Dr. Brabant had prepared an English rendering of the Concluding Dissertation, but when
Eliot tried to utilize it she found it consisted only of unfinished notes. (Haight,
Letters, I:194.) Possibly she adopted some of Dr. Brabant's readings or para-
phrasings in this section. The translation gives evidence of an attempt at interpretation, which only renders matters more obscure.

757   † A better translation: "To all belief that is not yet knowledge" (*in jedem
Glauben, der noch nicht Wissen ist*).

758   * The last two paragraphs of the translation are flawed by efforts at interpretation that only render the meaning more obscure. Circumlocutions are sought for
vermitteln ("mediate"), *Unmittelbarkeit* ("immediacy"), *Wissen* ("knowledge"),
and other terms. The passage is very difficult, but a careful reading of it will provide hints at what Strauss *intended*, but did not precisely execute, in his dogmatic
criticism. A revised translation is provided here:

> Furthermore, our [historical] criticism, though in its progress it
> treats of details, yet on becoming part of consciousness resolves itself
> once again into the simplicity of undeveloped doubt, which the
> believing consciousness neutralizes by an equally simple veto; and
> after the rejection of such doubt what is believed again spreads out
> in undiminished fulness. But hereby criticism is only set aside, not
> overcome, and therefore what is believed is not truly mediated, but
> remains in its immediacy. Criticism cannot but direct itself against
> this immediacy, and thus the apparently completed process is re-
> peated, and we are thrown back to the beginning of the investigation; yet
> with a difference which constitutes a step forward in the matter. Hitherto
> the object of criticism was the Christian content as it lies before us in
> the Gospel reports as the history of Jesus. Now this content, called into
> question by doubt, reflects upon itself and seeks a refuge in the interiority
> of the believer, where however it exists not as mere history but as self-

reflected history, i.e., as confession and dogma. Against this dogma appearing in its immediacy, as against every form of immediacy, criticism must indeed awaken in the form of negativity and a striving for mediation. So this is no longer, as before, historical criticism but dogmatic criticism, and it is only after faith has passed through both these tests that it is truly mediated or has becoming knowledge. This second process through which faith has to pass ought, like the first, to be made the subject of a distinct work. I shall here merely give a sketch of its most important features, that I may not terminate the historical criticism without pointing to its ultimate goal, which only lies beyond dogmatic criticism.

"Mediation" refers to the process by which the content of faith is subjected to the critical categories of consciousness, and the distinction between objective religious belief (*Vorstellung*) and subjective truth (*Begriff*) is dialectically transscended.

§ 145.

758 † A more precise translation of this sentence: "The dogmatic import of the life of Jesus, adhered to in its immediacy [*in seiner Unmittelbarkeit festgehalten*] and developed on this basis, constitutes the orthodox doctrine of Christ."

§ 147.

768 * The term is *Glaubenslehre* and should be translated "doctrine of faith" instead of "system of religious doctrine." The distinction is important because in the preceding paragraph Strauss uses the other term, *Religionslehre*, and the point is that, whereas what the rationalists do is appropriate in a *Religionslehre*, it is not adequate for a *Glaubenslehre*, which is supposed to provide an exposition of Christian faith.

§ 148.

770 * The translation omits *vollständig* ("completely") before "realized" in the first part of the sentence. The qualification is important for Schleiermacher.

§ 149.

777 * A more literal translation of this sentence: "Science has perceived that to convert ideas into a mere ought [*Sollen*], to which no being [*Sein*] corresponds, is in fact to annihilate them, just as it would be to finitize the infinite to represent it as permanently beyond the finite [*als bleibendes Jenseits des Endlichen*]." The point is that if the infinite is conceived undialectically, as *permanently* beyond the finite, not engaged in the alternate positing and annulment (*Setzen und Wiederaufheben*) of the finite, it is in effect finitized, for finitude *alone* is devoid of dialectical process. These concluding sentences represent, of course, the Hegelian critique of Kant.

§ 151.

780 * In place of this sentence the first and second editions have a full paragraph in which it is argued that the annexing of the content of Christology to the person and history of one individual is purely fortuitous: Jesus was at best an accidental occasion for the emergence of the idea of humanity, given the subjective needs of the time and the pathos of his suffering and death. The relation to Jesus as an individual is no longer necessary for a scientifically reconstructed Christology. This paragraph was omitted in the third and fourth editions.

Its omission in the *third* edition is easy to understand. Prior to this paragraph, Strauss had argued only that the idea cannot be exclusively identified with a single individual but with the human race as a whole. But this in itself would not deny Jesus a peculiar and essential role in the coming to consciousness of this idea, even if he was not in an archetypal sense the God-man. The omitted paragraph makes just this denial—a denial contradicted by the new concluding section of the third edition (ed.n. 781†).

By omitting this paragraph and adding a mediating Christology at the end of the work, the *context* of the concluding paragraph of this section (beginning at p. 780/12b, "Schleiermacher was quite right ..."), found in all four editions, is altered in the third edition. The paragraph now represents a position that Strauss intends to *refute* or *qualify* in the third edition. It is not the case, after all, that "when the mind ... has gone beyond the sensible history, and entered into the domain of the absolute, the former ceases to be essential"; rather, Jesus continues to have permanent significance as the founder and chief exemplar of Christian religious consciousness (see the concluding section of the third edition). In the first, second, and fourth editions, the concluding paragraph of this section represents Strauss's *own* view. It is a puzzle, therefore, why he did not restore the omitted paragraph in the fourth edition.

In the two versions of his argument, Strauss represents the two possibilities inherent in Hegel's Christology: that Jesus had only a fortuitous relation to the idea of the Christ, which first arose in the faith of the community and would later free itself of him completely (the first, second, and fourth editions); or that Jesus, while not the God-man in the orthodox sense, nevertheless by the force of his personality, God-consciousness, teaching, and death is the essential agent by whom the idea of God-manhood was and continues to be mediated to humanity as a whole (the third edition). Strauss was the first, in the *Streitschriften*, No. 3, pp. 55–126, to call attention to the systematic ambiguities in Hegel's Christology.

781   * This paragraph is omitted in the third edition.

§ 152.

781   † Instead of this section, the third edition has its own concluding section, "Attempts at Mediation. Conclusion," which is completely different. It is translated in full on pp. 798–802. In connection with this change, see ed.n. 780*.

782   * These four ways are envisioned as early as 1830 in a letter to Christian Märklin. They are enumerated in somewhat different form: first, to force oneself back to faith, which is impossible; second, to prune the faith rationalistically in its mediation to the people, which would be shameful and contrary to duty; third, to leave the ministry, which is the way of the student radicals; finally, to find every opportunity to transfigure the forms of religious imagery (*Vorstellungen*) into those of speculative-theological concepts (*Begriffe*), while continuing to use the religious images when necessary. Strauss to Märklin, 26 December 1830 (*Ausgewählte Briefe*, pp. 4–6).

783   * In this last sentence, Strauss undoubtedly expresses his own personal dilemma. He believed himself to be a theologian and could not bring himself to abandon the career of theology. Yet, since both the ministerial office and the professor's chair were denied him, this third alternative was forced upon him.

CONCLUDING SECTION OF THE THIRD EDITION OF
*THE LIFE OF JESUS**

§ 150†
ATTEMPTS AT MEDIATION. CONCLUSION

INDEED, only when scientific Christology has passed beyond Jesus as a person will it be forced to turn back to a consideration of him again and again. "All actions, including world-historical actions, culminate with individuals as subjects giving actuality to the substantial."[1] Generally speaking, the various directions in which the wealth of the divine life is set forth in humanity

[1] Hegel, *Rechtsphilosophie*, § 348.
* Translated by John C. Shelley.
† The section numbers in the third edition vary; this section replaces § 152 of the fourth edition.

(e.g., in art and science) are represented by great individuals.[2] Especially in the field of religion, at least within the domain of monotheism, all new epochs and characteristic formations are attached to a prominent personality. Should Christianity alone be made an exception to this rule? Should the most forceful spiritual creation be without a demonstrable founder, simply the result of the collision of scattered powers and causes?

Criticism welcomes the urging it has received from various voices[3] to turn expressly to this side of the matter, which was never denied by it. As a result of this sort of reflection, Jesus belongs to the category of highly gifted individuals who in the various spheres of life are called to raise the development of Spirit in humanity to higher levels. These are individuals whom in fields outside of religion, namely those of art and science, we are accustomed to call geniuses. To be sure, Christ is not hereby once again introduced into the properly Christian sanctuary, but first only into the Chapel of Alexander Severus,* where he stands next to Orpheus and Homer, not only next to Moses but also Muhammad—indeed, where he dare not scorn the company of Alexander and Caesar, of Raphael and Mozart. To be sure, this unsettling association will be partially annulled by the consideration that within the various spheres in which the divinely inspired creative power of genius can unfold, that of religion is not merely the most preeminent, but is more precisely related to others as the midpoint of a circle, because in religion alone the divine Spirit touches man in immediate self-consciousness, but in all the other spheres through some sort of agency—of ideas, images, colors, sounds, etc. Thus it can be said of the religious founder in an entirely different sense than of the poet, philosopher, etc., that God reveals himself in him. A second consideration is that even within the religious domain, Christ, as the founder of the highest religion, transcends the other religious founders.

In the highest sphere of spiritual life, that of the most intimate union of divine and human natures, Christ stands as the greatest among all who have been ingeniously creative. But this only applies to the course of affairs up to the present time; for the future, it seems, we have no guarantee that another will not come who would be related to Christ as an equal or indeed as a superior, even if Christians do not expect another. Just as Socrates and Plato followed Thales and Parmenides, and within the religious domain itself Christ followed Moses; just as the possibility is presupposed in all other fields that the future may place beside or in front of the geniuses who have emerged thus far, equal or even superior geniuses—so it seems that even in the field of religion this possibility may not be denied. To be sure, just as every people generally has its fixed periods of advance, flowering, and decay, so there is a moment after which, even in the various spheres of its spiritual life, no higher revelations are to be expected but rather the golden age is followed by the silver, the bronze, etc. But the life-process of a single nation cannot be held forth when it is a question of a religion that is common to many peoples. It is certainly true that, neither within the confines of a single people nor outside it, are later geniuses in a field necessarily superior to earlier ones. The distinction is often only qualitative, and not always quanti-

[2] Cf. my *Streitschriften*, No. 3, p. 70.

[3] Ullmann, in his review of the *Leben Jesu* in *Theologische Studien und Kritiken* (1836), pp. 813 ff., and in the *Antwortschreiben*, pp. 26 ff.; Schweizer, "Das Leben Jesu von Strauss, im Verhältniss zur Schleiermacher'schen Dignität des Religionsstifters," *Theologische Studien und Kritiken* (1837), p. 465; Schaller, *Der historische Christus und die Philosophie*, pp. 96 ff. Cf. my *Streitschriften*, No. 3, pp. 70, 149 ff.

* Roman Emperor, 222–235. A syncretist who wanted to unite many religions, he placed a bust of Christ in his private chapel along with images of leaders of other faiths.

tative. Hardly anyone will say that Sophocles was a greater poet than Homer, that Caesar and Napoleon were greater generals than Alexander. The more precise situation is that these later figures stand over the earlier ones not by virtue of the quantity of their talent or personal achievement, but insofar as not only the legacy of the earlier heroes in their subject area, but generally the intellectual achievement of the periods between them and their earlier counterparts, stand at their disposal for use and assimilation. So Napoleon is certainly not to be called a greater military genius than Caesar, but he solved more complex problems of strategy, which in Caesar's time were not yet posed or could not be solved because of a lack of means. Just as little will one want to say of Shakespeare, either that he was a greater poet than Homer or Sophocles, or that his work stands as a greater artistic accomplishment than that of the Greeks. Still, insofar as he poetically assimilated a more highly developed consciousness of humanity, or had to solve deeper or more complex problems, he stands higher— as indeed in this respect Goethe stands over Shakespeare. In any case such a later genius would be closer to later generations than the earlier one, would be more closely akin to their intellectual level of development, and would therefore be a more suitable model and point of contact. Consequently, even one hypothetically coming still later, although in himself not a higher, more talented religious genius than Christ, would be nearer and more closely related to believers living at a later time.

Surely there are areas in which we unhesitatingly deny for all time the future appearance of one who is superior to or even equal with what has already been accomplished, not merely within a certain nation but in humanity generally. One such area in the field of art is that of sculpture. Here even the most gifted artist cannot from a rational point of view hope to surpass or even equal the artists of antiquity. Surely the reason for this is not so much talent as external circumstances, which in Greece favored the perception of the beautiful human body in such a way that repetition is inconceivable. Should we now suppose that the present and future circumstances of humanity, and the retreat of the life of feeling and imagination—that incontestable birthplace of religion—behind the reflective intellect, make a further development in the field of religion inconceivable? This would be doubtful because with the example of sculpture, at least, the extinction of productivity is accompanied by a loss of interest in an art form that is unable to compete in wealth of intellectual content with poetry, for example, and therefore can no longer afford to progressive humanity the same high satisfaction as it did for the Greeks.

In order, therefore, to eradicate the disquieting possibility of which we speak, we would have to prove that nothing higher can be imagined than the peculiar excellence of the religious personality and work of Jesus himself, and by the nature of the case the inconceivability of a future equal would also be demonstrated.

In the first place, the antithesis of the human and divine, which is posited in every human consciousness but existed most sharply in the consciousness of the Israelite people, was dissolved in the self-consciousness of Jesus. According to the first three Gospels, he knew God as his Father and God's affairs as his own; he was conscious of acknowledging God perfectly and allowed his will to be merged into the divine. According to John, he articulated positively his unity with the Father and presented himself as the visible revelation of him. In any case according to both representations this was neither a mere feigning nor a transient surge of Jesus' feeling in single heightened moments; rather his entire life and all his sayings and actions were permeated with this consciousness as from the soul. If religion is the awakening in the human spirit of the relationship between God and man, then the stages of the religious life mount up from the dull lack of consciousness of this distinction, through an ever more highly developing estrangement and imperfect efforts at compensation in the religions of nature and of law, to the complete conquest of this schism in self-conscious spiritual unity, which accordingly is the goal of religious development, the insuperable highest stage. If this unity existed in Christ, then in the religious aspect he is unsurpassable for all time; however much in the other domains of the spiritual life—e.g., in philosophical thought and in the investigation and mastery of nature—the standpoint of his time, whose limits he shared in these matters, has already been surpassed and may yet in the future be surpassed.

But are feeling and immediate self-consciousness, which surely constitute the nearest seat and center of religion, really so completely independent of the other spiritual activities and their respective levels of development, especially the development of reflective thought and the world view conditioned by it? Hardly anyone will want to maintain that the highest achievement of religion, the unity of the divine and the human in immediate self-consciousness, could have been attained within polytheism; and the progress of the latter to monotheism was not induced by an elevation of feeling, but by a sharpening of thought and an enlargement of world views. Even within the sphere of monotheism the imagery of intervening angels, of a devil opposing the divine plans, of an extraordinary activity of God that is not congruent with his ordinary, natural work, indeed often conflicts with it, of a temporal beginning and future end of the world process—such imagery belonging to objective thinking cannot possibly exist without having a disturbing effect on feeling, within which the religious unity of the divine and the human takes place. A purer form of that unity must be expected of ages and levels of culture which reject that dross. Because, however, this unity is the fundamental basis achieved by Christ, above which piety by nature cannot possibly lift itself to a higher level, and because all further developments in religion must be only formal in nature, religious progress in the future, as in the recent past, will proceed more in degrees than in epochs, such as the giant stride by which Jesus brought mankind forward on the course of its religious development. The unity of God and man has not appeared in human self-consciousness with any greater creative power than in Jesus, having penetrated and transfigured his entire life uniformly and without perceptible darkness. In this respect the thesis is correct that the starting point of a sequence in the realm of the spiritual life is also to be considered the greatest—to be sure, not the absolutely greatest, whose achievement would in no respect allow of an improvement, but in the sense that an idea in its first appearance is usually the most powerful and frequently permeates its first bearers so thoroughly that they become what has recently been called plastic figures.

But why, even if none higher than Christ is to be expected, should it not be conceivable that at least one person, or even many, after him and through him would succeed in attaining the same absolute stage of religious life? There would be no objection if they attained this stage through him, for in this respect they would already stand beneath him. In the realm of the religious as well as the moral, no one can accomplish something for another but rather the second, third, or tenth person who brings a frame of mind or a deed to reality has to accomplish the same spiritual task as the first. More superficial and in fact not worth refuting is the assurance that only one God-man is necessary for the founding of the kingdom of God on earth, indeed that a plurality of God-men would be inexpedient because the one would necessarily weaken the impact of the other, reducing him from an absolute and incomparable status to a merely relative one, and obscuring, moreover, the unity of revelation and the destination of mankind for a single kingdom of God.[4] According to another argument, the fall and the subsequent incongruity between humanity and its ideal account for the fact that the human race could attain its archetype, the complete representation of the personality of the divine λόγος in the form of creaturely personality, only once, in a single individual.[5] But the further implementation of this notion leaves the matter as obscure as the beginning, and the whole thing is suspended in midair by its connection to a sinful fall as a deed brought about by the fault of the human race, which accordingly might have been avoided. Obviously, then, this sort of proof has its peculiar difficulties. But in fact one worries here about dreams and grapples with shadows, insofar as it is a question not of a concretely given experience but only of abstract possibilities. Religion has no need to engage in such broodings of the intellect any more than a rational man lets himself be alarmed by calculating the possibility of a collision of the earth with a passing comet. Eager reflection of this sort will simply disturb the peace as long as it is not in the position to point out in reality a single person who might have the courage and the right to stand next to Jesus in religious matters.

Therefore, by putting aside the concepts of sinlessness and absolute perfection as unattainable, we conceive Christ as the one in whose self-consciousness the unity of the divine and the human first appeared with sufficient energy to reduce to a disappearing minimum all hindrances of this unity in the whole range of his soul and life. He is the one who to this extent remains unique and unequaled in world history, without, however, having to deprive the religious consciousness first achieved and expressed by him of purification and further development in details through the progressive formation of the human spirit.[6]

[4] Kern, "Hauptthatsachen," *Tübinger Zeitschrift für Theologie*, (1836), No. 2, pp. 33 f.

[5] Weisse, *Die evangelische Geschichte*, II, 536.

[6] For these concluding paragraphs see my essay, "Vergängliches und Bleibendes im Christenthum," *Freihafen* (1838), No. 3, pp. 1–48.

BIBLIOGRAPHIES

MODERN AUTHORS CITED BY STRAUSS

INCLUDED here are most of the post-Reformation works cited by Strauss in the footnotes, up to and including his own contemporaries and critics. We have been unable to trace approximately thirty titles. Journal articles are not listed. Some important books mentioned only in the third edition are included, in order to supplement the Editor's Introduction and the Annotations. Works are cited in the edition used by Strauss, or in the edition closest to the period 1835–1840 if no indication of the edition is provided by the footnote.

anon. *Ueber Offenbarung und Mythologie, als Nachtrag zur Religion innerhalb der Grenzen der reinen Vernunft.* Berlin, 1799.

Ammon, Christoph Friedrich von. *Ascensus Jesu Christi in coelum historia biblica,* in *Opuscula Theologica.* Erlangen, 1797.

——. *Die Fortbildung des Christenthums zur Weltreligion. Eine Ansicht der höheren Dogmatik.* 2nd ed. 4 vols. Leipzig, 1836–40.

——. *Die Geschichte des Leben Jesu mit steter Rücksicht auf die vorhandenen Quellen.* 3 vols. 1842–47.

Bahrdt, Carl Friedrich. *Ausführung des Plans und Zwecks Jesu.* In *Briefen an Wahrheit suchende Leser.* 12 vols. 1784–98.

——. *Uebersetzung des Neuen Testaments. Die neuesten Offenbarung Gottes in Briefen und Erzählungen verdeutscht.* 2 parts. Riga, 1773.

Bauer, Georg Lorenz. *Handbuch der Geschichte der hebräischen Nation.* 2 parts. Nuremberg, 1800–1804.

——. *Hebräische Mythologie des Alten und Neuen Testaments, mit Parallelen aus der Mythologie anderer Völker, vornehmlich der Griechen und Römer.* 2 vols. Leipzig, 1835.

Baumgarten-Crucius, Ludwig Friedrich Otto. *Grundzüge der biblischen Theologie.* Jena, 1828.

Baur, Ferdinand Christian. *Apollonius von Tyana und Christus, oder das Verhältniss des Pythagoreismus zum Christenthum. Ein Beitrag zur Religionsgeschichte der ersten Jahrhunderte nach Christus.* Tübingen, 1832.

——. *Die christliche Gnosis, oder die christliche Religions-Philosophie in ihrer geschichtlichen Entwicklung.* Tübingen, 1835.

——. *Programma de Ebionitarum origene et doctrina, ab Essenis repetenda.* Tübingen, 1831.

——. *Symbolik und Mythologie, oder die Naturreligion des Alterthums.* 2 parts. Stuttgart, 1824–25.

Bengel, Johann Albert. *Gnomon Novi Testamenti.* 3rd ed. 2 vols. Tübingen, 1773.

———. *Ordo temporum a principio per periodos oeconomiae divinae*. Edited by Eberhard Friedrich Hellwag. Stuttgart, 1770.

Bertholdt, Leonhard. *Christologia Judaeorum Jesu apostolorumque aetate in compendium redacta observationibusque illustrata*. Erlangen, 1811.

———. *Daniel*. 1806.

———. *Historisch-kritische Einleitung in sämmtliche kanonische und apokryphische Schriften des alten und neuen Testaments*. 6 parts. Erlangen, 1812–19.

———. *Verosimilia de origine evangelii Joannis*, in *Opuscula academica exegetici potissimum argumenti colleg*. Edited by G. B. Winer. Leipzig, 1824.

Billroth, Johann Gustav Friedrich. *Commentar zu den Briefen des Paulus an die Corinther*. Leipzig, 1833.

Bleek, Friedrich. *Der Brief an die Hebräer*. Berlin, 1828.

Bohlen, Peter von. *Die Genesis, historisch-kritisch erläutert*. Königsberg, 1835.

Bolten, Johann Adrian. *Der Bericht des Matthäus von Jesu dem Messia*. Altona, 1792.

Braniss, Christlieb Julius. *Ueber Schleiermachers Glaubenslehre; ein kritischer Versuch*. Berlin, 1824.

Brennecke, Jacob Andreas. *Biblischer Beweis, dass Jesus nach seiner Auferstehung noch 27 Jahre leibhaftig auf Erden gelebt, und zum Wohle der Menschheit in der Stille fortgewirkt habe*. 2nd ed. 1819.

Bretschneider, Carl Gottlieb. *Handbuch der Dogmatik der evangelisch-lutherischen Kirche*. 3rd ed. Leipzig, 1828.

———. *Probabilia de Evangelii et Epistolarum Joannis, Apostoli, indole et origine*. Leipzig, 1820.

Chemniz, Martin. *De duabus naturis in Christo*. Jena, 1591.

———. *Loci theologici*. 6 parts. Frankfurt & Wittenberg, 1653.

Conradi, Kasim. *Selbstbewusstseyn und Offenbarung, oder Entwickelung des religiösen Bewusstseyns*. Mainz, 1831.

Credner, Karl August. *Einleitung in das Neue Testament*. Part I, sections 1 & 2. Halle, 1836.

Creuzer, Georg Friedrich. *Symbolik und Mythologie der alten Völker*. 2nd ed. 6 parts. Leipzig & Darmstadt, 1819–23.

Dähne, August Ferdinand. *Geschichtliche Darstellung der jüdisch-alexandrinischen Religions-Philosophie*. Halle, 1834.

Daub, Carl. *Judas Ischariot, oder das Böse in Verhältnis zum Guten*. 2 parts. Heidelberg, 1816–18.

de Wette, Wilhelm Martin Leberecht. *Commentar über die Psalmen*. Heidelberg, 1811.

———. *Kritik der Israelischen Geschichte*. Part I: *Kritik der Mosaischen Geschichte*. Halle, 1807.

———. *Kurzgefasstes exegetisches Handbuch zum Neuen Testament*. 3 vols. Leipzig, 1836–48.

———. *Lehrbuch der christlichen Dogmatik, in ihrer historischen Entwickelung dargestellt*. Part I: *Biblische Dogmatik Alten und Neuen Testaments; oder kritische Darstellung der Religionslehre des Hebräismus, des Judenthums und Urchristenthums*. 3rd ed. Berlin, 1831.

———. *Lehrbuch der Hebräisch-Judischen Archäologie*. 2nd ed. Leipzig, 1830.

———. *Lehrbuch der historisch kritischen Einleitung in die Bibel Alten und Neuen Testaments*. 4th ed. 2 parts. Berlin, 1833–34.

———. *De Morte Christi expiatoria*, in *Opuscula Theologica*. Berlin, 1830.

———. *Ueber Religion und Theologie. Erläuterung zu seinem Lehrbuche der Dogmatik*. 2nd. ed. Berlin, 1821.

Döpke, J. Chr. C. *Die Hermeneutik der neutestamentlichen Schriftseller.* Part I. Leipzig, 1829.

Eck, Johann Christian Friedrich. *Versuch die Wundergeschichten des Neuen Testaments aus natürlichen Ursachen zu erklären, oder der Beweis von den Wundern in seiner wahren Gestalt.* Berlin, 1795.

Eckermann, Jacob Christoph Rudolph. *Handbuch für das systematische Studium der christlichen Glaubenslehre.* 4 vols. Altona, 1801–3.

———. *Theologische Beyträge.* 6 vols. Altona, 1794–99.

Eichhorn, Johann Gottfried. *Einleitung in das Alte Testament.* 4th ed. 5 vols. Göttingen, 1823–24.

———. *Einleitung in das Neue Testament.* 2nd ed. 3 vols. Leipzig, 1820, 1810, 1812.

———. *Urgeschichte.* Edited by J. P. Gabler. 2 parts in 3 vols. Altdorf & Nuremberg, 1790–93.

Eisenmenger, Johann Andreas. *Entdecktes Judenthum.* 2 vols. Königsberg, 1711.

Ersch, Johann Samuel, and Gruber, Johann Gottfried. *Allgemeine Encyclopädie der Wissenschaften und Künste.* 3 sections. Leipzig, 1818–89.

Eschenmayer, Christoph Adolph Adam von. *Der Ischariothismus unserer Tage. Eine Zugabe zu dem jüngst erscheinenen Werke: Das Leben Jesu von Strauss, I. Theil.* Tübingen, 1835.

Fleck, Ferdinand Florens. *De Regno Divino liber exegeticus historicus quatuor Evangelistarum doctrinam complectens.* Leipzig, 1829.

Fritzsche, Chr. Friedrich. *Prüfung der Gründe, mit welchen neuerlich die Aechtheit der Bücher Mosis bestritten worden ist.* Leipzig, 1814.

George, J. F. Leopold. *Mythus und Sage. Versuch einer wissenschaftlichen Entwicklung dieser Begriffe und ihres Verhältnisses zum christlichen Glauben.* Berlin, 1837.

Gesenius, Friedrich Heinrich Wilhelm. *Hebräisches und aramäisches Handwörterbuch über das Alte Testament.* 2nd ed. Leipzig, 1823.

———. *Der Prophet Jesaia.* 3 parts. Leipzig, 1820–21.

Gfrörer, August Friedrich. *Kritische Geschichte des Urchristenthums.* Vol. I; part 2: *Philo und die alexandrinische Theosophie.* Stuttgart, 1831.

Gieseler, Johann Carl Ludwig. *Historisch-kritischer Versuch über die Entstehung und die frühesten Schicksale der schriftlichen Evangelien.* Leipzig, 1818.

———. *Lehrbuch der Kirchengeschichte.* 3rd ed. 6 vols. Bonn, 1829–57.

Glass, Solomon. *Philologiae Sacrae.* 2nd ed. Jena, 1645.

Gramberg, Carl Peter Wilhelm. *De Angelologia Veteris Testamenti.* Züllichau, 1827.

Gratz, Peter Aloys. *Kritisch-historischer Kommentar über das Evangelium des Matthäus.* 2 parts. Tübingen, 1821–23.

Greiling, Johann Christoph. *Das Leben Jesu von Nazareth.* Halle, 1813.

Griesbach, Johann Jacob. *Commentarius criticus in textum Graecum Novi Testamenti.* 2 parts. Jena, 1793–1811.

———. *Commentatio, qua Marci Evangelium totum e Matthaei et Lucae commentariis decerptum esse monstratur.* Commentationes Theologicae, edited by J. C. Velthusen, C. J. Kuinoel and G. A. Ruperti. Leipzig, 1794.

———. *Progr. de fontibus, unde Evangelistae suas de resurrectiones Domini narrationes hauserint.* In *Opuscula Academica,* edited by Johann Philip Gabler. Jena, 1824–25.

———. *Vorlesungen über Hermeneutik des Neuen Testaments, mit Anwendung auf die Leidens und Auferstehungsgeschichte Christi.* Edited by J. C. S. Steiner. Nuremberg, 1815.

Grotius, Hugo. *Defensio fidei catholicae de satisfactione Christi adversüs Faustum Socinum.* 2nd ed. Leiden, 1617.

Gruner, C. F. F. *De Iesu Christi morte vera n. syncoptica.* Heidelberg, 1800.

———. *De Iesu Christi morte vera non simulata.* Halle, 1805.

Guerike, Heinrich Ernst Ferdinand. *Beiträge zur historisch-kritischen Einleitung ins Neue Testament.* 2 vols. Halle, 1828–31.

Hävernick, Heinrich Andreas Christian. *Commentar über das Buch Daniel.* Hamburg & Berlin, 1832.

Hase, Carl August von. *Das Leben Jesu.* 2nd ed. Leipzig, 1835.

Hegel, Georg Wilhelm Friedrich. *Grundlinien der Philosophie des Rechts.* Berlin, 1821.

———. *Die Phänomenologie des Geistes.* Bamberg & Würzberg, 1807.

———. *Vorlesungen über der Philosophie der Religion.* Edited by Philipp Marheinecke. 2 vols. Berlin, 1832.

Hengstenberg, Ernst Wilhelm. *Christologie des Alten Testaments.* 3 parts. Berlin, 1829–35.

Henke, Heinrich Philipp Conrad. *Johannes Apostolus nonnullorum Jesu apophthegmatum.* Sylloge Commentationum theologicarum, edited by D. J. Pott and G. A. Ruperti. Helmstadt, 1800–1807.

———. *Lineamenta institutionum Fidei Christianae historico-criticarum.* Helmstadt, 1795.

Henneberg, J. V. *Philologischer, historischer und kritischer Kommentar über die Geschichte des Leidens und Todes Jesu, nach den Evangelien des Matthäus, Markus, und Lukas.* Leipzig, 1822.

Herder, Johann Gottfried von. *Christliche Schriften.* Vol. II: *Vom Erlöser der Menschen.* Vol. III: *Von Gottes Sohn der Welt Heiland nach Johannes Evangelium.* Leipzig, 1794–98.

Hess, Johann Jacob. *Bibliothek der heiligen Geschichte.* 2 parts. Zürich, 1791–92.

———. *Geschichte der drey letzten Lebensjahre Jesu.* 2 vols. Tübingen, 1779.

———. *Lebensgeschichte Jesu.* 2 vols. Zürich, 1781.

Heydenreich, August Ludwig Christian. *Ueber die Unzulässigkeit des mythischen Auffassung des Historischen im Neuen Testament und im Christenthum.* 2 parts. Frankfurt, 1831–33.

Hitzig, Ferdinand. *Der Prophet Jesaja.* Heidelberg, 1833.

Hoffmann, Wilhelm. *Das Leben Jesu kritisch bearbeitet von Dr. D. F. Strauss, geprüft für Theologen und Nichttheologen.* Stuttgart, 1836.

Hug, Johann Leonhard von. *Einleitung in die Schriften des Neuen Testaments.* 3rd ed. 2 parts. Stuttgart, 1821.

Ideler, Carl Wilhelm. *Handbuch der mathematischen und technischen Chronologie.* 2 vols. Berlin, 1825–26.

Iken, Conrad. *Dissertationes Philologico-Theologicae.* 2 vols. The Netherlands, 1749–70.

Kaiser, Gottlieb Philipp Christian. *Die biblische Theologie.* 2 parts. Erlangen, 1813–21.

Kant, Imanuel. *Die Religion innerhalb der Grenzen der blossen Vernunft.* Königsberg, 1794.

Kelle, K. G. *Vorurtheilsfreie Würdigung der mosaischen Schriften.* 3 parts. Freiberg, 1812.

Klopstock, Friedrich Gottlieb. *Der Messias. Ein Heldengedicht.* Halle, 1749.

Köster, Friedrich Burchard. *Immanuel, oder Characteristik der neutestamentlichen Wundererzählung.* Leipzig, 1821.

Kuinöl, C. Th. *Commentarius in Libros Nov. Test. historicos.* Vol. I: *Evangelium*

Matthaei. 3rd ed. Leipzig, 1823. Vol. II: *Evangelia Marci et Lucae.* 3rd ed. Leipzig, 1824.

Lange, Johann Peter. *Ueber den geschichtlichen Charakter der kanonischen Evangelien, insbesondere der Kindheitsgeschichte Jesu, mit Beziehung auf 'das Leben Jesu von D. F. Strauss'.* Duisburg, 1836.

Lavater, Johann Caspar. *Jésus Messías. Oder, die Evangelien und Apostelgeschichte, in Gesangen.* Zürich, 1783–84.

Leland, John. *A View of the Principal Deistical Writers That Have Appeared in England in the Last and Present Century.* 3rd ed. 3 vols. London, 1754–56.

Less, Gottfried. *Auferstehungsgeschichte Jesu nach allen vier Evangelisten.* Göttingen, 1779.

Lessing, Gotthold. *Eine Duplik.* Braunschweig, 1778.

———. *Fragmente des Wolfenbüttelschen Ungenannten.* 4th ed. Berlin, 1835. (Author: Hermann Samuel Reimarus.)

———. *Werke.* Donaueschingen Ausgabe. 8 vols. Berlin, 1840.

Lightfoot, John. *Horae Hebraicae et Talmudicae.* Cambridge, 1658.

Lipsius, Justus. *De Cruce libri tres.* Antwerp, 1593.

Lücke, Gottfried Christian Friedrich. *Commentar über die Schriften des Evangelisten Johannes.* 2nd ed. 3 parts. Bonn, 1833–34.

Marheinecke, Philipp Conrad. *Die Grundlehren der christlichen Dogmatik als Wissenschaft.* 2nd ed. Berlin, 1827.

———. *Institutiones Symbolicae, Doctrinarum Catholicorum, Protestantium.* Berlin, 1830.

Matthäi, Georg Christian Rudolf. *Der Religionsglaube der Apostel Jesu, nach seinem Inhalte, Ursprunge und Werthe.* 2 vols. Göttingen, 1826–29.

———. *Synopse der vier Evangelien, nebst Kritik ihrer Wundererzählungen.* Göttingen, 1826.

Meyer, Heinrich August Wilhelm. *Kritisches exegetisches Handbuch über das Evangelium des Johannes.* Göttingen, 1834.

Michaelis, Johann David. *Anhang, oder das 5e Fragment der Lessingschen Beyträge selbst.* Halle, 1775.

———. *Anmerkungen für Ungelehrte zu seiner Uebersetzung des Neuen Testaments.* 4 parts. Göttingen, 1790–92.

———. *Einleitung in die göttlichen Schriften des Neuen Bundes.* 2 vols. Göttingen, 1788.

———. *Erklärung der Begräbniss- und Auferstehungsgeschichte Christi.* Halle, 1783.

———. *Gründliche Erklärung des mosaischen Rechts.* 6 parts. Frankfurt, 1779.

Mosheim, Johann Lorenz von. *Diss. de vera notione coenae Domini,* annexed to Ralph Cudworth, *Syst. intellectuale huj. universi.* Jena, 1733.

Müller, Carl Ottfried. *Prolegomena zu einer wissenschaftlichen Mythologie.* Göttingen, 1825.

Münscher, Wilhelm. *Handbuch der christlichen Dogmengeschichte.* 3rd ed. 4 vols. Marburg, 1817–18.

Münter, F. *Der Stern der Weisen. Untersuchung über das Geburtsjahr Christi.* Copenhagen, 1827.

Neander, Johann August Wilhelm. *Allgemeine Geschichte der christlichen Religion und Kirche.* 6 vols. in 11 parts. Hamburg, 1825–52.

———. *Geschichte der Pflanzung und Leitung der christlichen Kirche durch die Apostel.* 2 vols. Hamburg, 1832–33.

———. *Das Leben Jesu Christi in seinem geschichtlichen Zusammenhange und seiner geschichtlichen Entwicklung.* Berlin & Hamburg, 1837.

————. *Dr. Neanders auf höhere Verlassung abgefasstes Gutachten über das Buch des Dr. Strauss' "Leben Jesu" und das in Beziehung auf die Verbreitung desselben zu beachtende Verfahren.* 1836.

Olshausen, Hermann. *Biblischer Commentar über sämmtliche Schriften der Neuen Testaments.* 3rd ed. 7 vols. in 9 parts. Königsberg, 1837–66.

Osiander, Johann Ernst. *Apologie des Lebens Jesu gegen den neuesten Versuch, es in Mythen aufzulösen.* Tübingen, 1837.

Paulus, Heinrich Eberhard Gottlob. *Exegetisches Handbuch über die drei ersten Evangelien.* Wohlfeile Ausgabe. 3 parts. Heidelberg, 1830–33.

————. *Das Leben Jesu, als Grundlage einer reinen Geschichte des Urchristenthums.* 2 vols. Heidelberg, 1828.

————. *Philologisch-kritischer Commentar über das Neue Testament.* 4 parts. Leipzig, 1804–5.

Planck, Gottlieb Jacob. *Geschichte des Christenthums in der Periode seiner Einführung in die Welt durch Jesum und die Apostel.* 2 vols. Göttingen, 1818.

————. *Geschichte der Entstehung der Veränderungen und der Bildung unsers protestantischen Lehrbegriffs vom Anfang der Reformation bis zu der Einführung der Concordienformel.* 6 vols. Leipzig, 1791–1800.

Pott, David Justus and Ruperti, Georg Alexander. *Sylloge commentationum theologicarum.* 8 vols. Helmstadt, 1800–1807.

Quenstedt, Johannes Andreas. *Theologia didactico-polemica, sive systema theologicum.* 3rd ed. Wittenberg, 1696.

Reinhard, Franz Volkmar. *Versuch über den Plan, welchen der Stifter der christlichen Religion . . . entwarf.* 5th ed. Wittenberg, 1830.

————. *Vorlesungen über die Dogmatik.* Sulzbach, 1811.

Röhr, Johann Friedrich. *Briefe über den Rationalismus. Zur Berichtigung der schwankenden und zweideutigen Urtheile, die in neuesten dogmatischen Consequenz-Streitigkeiten über denselben gefällt worden sind.* Aachen, 1813. (Published anonymously.)

Rosenkranz, Johann Karl Friedrich. *Encyclopädie der theologischen Wissenschaften.* Halle, 1831.

Rosenmüller, Johann Georg. *Scholia in Novum Testamentum.* 6th ed. 5 vols. Nuremberg, 1815–31.

Saunier, H. *Ueber die Quellen des Evangeliums des Marcus. Ein Beitrag zu den Untersuchungen über die Entstehung unsrer kanonischen Evangelien.* Berlin, 1825.

Schaller, Julius. *Der historische Christus und die Philosophie. Kritik der Grundidee des Werks das Leben Jesu von D. F. Strauss.* Leipzig, 1838.

Schelling, Friedrich Wilhelm Joseph. *Vorlesungen über die Methode des akademischen Studiums.* Tübingen, 1803.

Schiller, Friedrich. *Sämmtliche Werke.* New ed. 18 vols. Stuttgart, 1826–27.

Schleiermacher, Friedrich Daniel Ernst. *Der christliche Glaube nach den Grundsätzen der evangelischen Kirche.* 2 vols. Berlin, 1821–22. 2nd ed., 1830.

————. *Ueber die Schriften des Lukas. Ein kritischer Versuch.* 1st Part. Berlin, 1817.

————. *Sammlung zerstreuter, theologischer Aufsätze des Friedrich Schleiermacher.* Reutlingen, 1830. (Includes the two *Sendschreiben* to Lücke published in *Theologische Studien und Kritiken,* 1829.)

————. *Die Weihnachtsfeier. Ein Gespräch.* 2nd ed. Berlin, 1827.

Schmid, Heinrich. *Ueber Schleiermacher's Glaubenslehre mit Beziehung auf die Reden über die Religion.* Leipzig, 1835.

Schneckenburger, Matthias. *Beiträge zur Einleitung ins Neue Testament und zur Erklärung seiner schwierigen Stellen.* Stuttgart, 1832.

―――. *Ueber das Evangelium der Aegypter. Ein historisch-kritischer Versuch.* Bern, 1834.

―――. *Ueber den Ursprung des ersten kanonischen Evangeliums. Ein kritischer Versuch.* Stuttgart, 1834.

Schöttgen, Christian. *Horae Hebraicae et Talmudicae in universum Novum Testamentum.* 2 vols. Dresden & Leipzig, 1733–42.

Schott, Heinrich August. *Commentarius exeg. dogm. in eos Jesu Christi sermones qui de redita ejus ad judicium agunt.* Jena, 1819.

Schulz, David. *Die christliche Lehre vom heiligen Abendmahl nach dem Grundtexte des neuen Testaments.* 2nd ed. Leipzig, 1831.

Schulze, Johann David. *Der schriftstellerische Charakter und Werth des Johannes, zum Behuf der Specialhermeneutik seiner Schriften untersucht und bestimmt.* Leipzig, 1811.

Semler, Johann Salomo. *Abhandlung von freier Untersuchung des Canons; nebst Antwort auf die Tübingische Vertheidigung der Apocalypsis.* 4 parts. Halle, 1771-75.

―――. *Beantwortung der Fragmente eines Ungenannten, insbesondere vom Zweck Jesu und seiner Jünger.* 2 parts. Halle, 1780.

Sieffert, Friedrich Ludwig. *Ueber den Ursprung des ersten kanonischen Evangeliums. Eine kritische Abhandlung.* Königsberg, 1832.

Socinus, Faustus Paulus. *De Jesu Christi filii Dei natura sive essentia, nec non de peccatorum per ipsum expiationne disputatio adversus A. Volanum.* 2nd ed. Raków, 1627.

―――. *Praelectiones Theologicae.* Edited by V. Schmalz. Raków, 1609.

Spanheim, Friedrich. *Dubia Evangelica.* 3 parts. Geneva, 1651–55.

Spinoza, Benedict. *Corpus philosophorum optimae notae, qui ab restauratione litterarum ad Kantium usque floruerunt.* Edited by August Friedrich Gfrörer. Stuttgart, 1830.

―――. *Tractatus Theologica-Politicus.* Amsterdam, 1670.

Stäudlin, Carl Friedrich. *Geschichte der Sittenlehre Jesu.* 4 vols. Göttingen, 1799–1832.

Starke, Christoph. *Synopsis bibliothecae exegeticae Novi Testament oder Auszug der grundlichen Auslegung der Heiligen Schrift des Neuen Testaments.* 3 parts. Leipzig, 1763–67.

Steudel, Johann Christian Friedrich. *Die Glaubenslehre der evangelisch-protestanischen Kirche, nach ihrer guten Begründung, mit Rücksicht auf das Bedürfniss der Zeit.* Tübingen, 1834.

―――. *Vorläufig zu Beherzigendes bey Würdigung der Frage über die historische oder mythische Grundlage des Lebens Jesu.* Tübingen, 1835.

Storr, Gottlob Christian. *Doctrina christianae pars theoretica e sacris litteris repetita.* Stuttgart, 1807.

―――. *Opuscula academica ad interpretationem librorum sacrorum pertinentia.* 3 vols. Tübingen, 1796–1803.

―――. *Ueber den Zwek der evangelischen Geschichte und der Briefe Johannis.* 2nd ed. Tübingen, 1810.

Süskind, Friedrich Gottlieb von. *Vermischte Aufsätze, meist theologischen Inhalts.* Edited by K. Fr. Süskind. Stuttgart, 1831.

Suicer, Joannes Casper. *Thesaurus Ecclesiasticus e patribus Graecis.* Amsterdam, 1682.

Theile, Carl Gottfried Wilhelm. *Zur Biographie Jesu.* Leipzig, 1837.
Thiess, Johann Otto. *Neuer kritischer Kommentar über das Neue Testament.* 2 vols. Halle, 1804–6.
Thilo, Johann Carl. *Codex Apocryphus Novi Testamenti.* Vol. I. Leipzig, 1832.
Tholuck, Friedrich August Gottgetreu. *Commentar zum Evangelio Johannis.* 4th ed. Hamburg, 1833.
———. *Die Glaubwürdigkeit der evangelischen Geschichte, zugleich eine Kritik des Lebens Jesu von Strauss.* Hamburg, 1837.
———. *Philologisch-theologische Auslegung der Bergpredigt Christi nach Matthäus.* 2nd ed. Hamburg, 1835.
Tieftrunk, Johann Heinrich. *Censur des christlichen protestantischen Lehrbegriffs nach den Principien der Religionskritik.* 2nd ed. 3 parts. Berlin, 1794–96.
Töllner, Johann Gottlieb. *Untersuchung der thätige Gehorsams Jesu Christi.* Breslau, 1768.
Ullmann, Carl. *Historisch oder mythisch! Beiträge zur Beantwortung den gegenwärtigen Lebensfrage der Theologie.* Hamburg, 1838.
Usteri, Leonhard. *Commentatio critica, in qua Evangelium Johannis genuinum esse—ostenditur.* Zürich, 1823.
Vater, Johann Severin. *Commentar über den Pentateuch.* 3 parts. Halle, 1802–5.
Vatke, Wilhelm. *Die biblische Theologie, wissenschaftlich dargestellt.* Vol. I: *Die Religion des Alten Testaments nach den kanonischen Büchern entwickelt.* Part 1. Berlin, 1835.
Venturini, Karl Heinrich Georg. *Natürliche Geschichte des grossen Propheten von Nazareth.* 4 parts. Copenhagen, 1800.
Wegscheider, Julius August Ludwig. *Institutiones theologiae Christianae dogmaticae.* 7th ed. Halle, 1833.
———. *Versuch einer vollständigen Einleitung in das Evangelium des Johannes.* Göttingen, 1806.
Weisse, Christian Hermann. *Die evangelische Geschichte kritisch und philosophisch bearbeitet.* 2 vols. Leipzig, 1838.
Wettstein, Johann Jacob. Ἡ καιγη διαθηκη. *Novum testamentum Graecum . . . cum lectionibus variantibus . . . nec non commentario pleniore.* Amsterdam, 1751.
Wilke, Christian Gottlob. *Tradition und Mythe. Ein Beitrag zur historischen Kritik der kanonischen Evangelien überhaupt, wie besondere zur Würdigung des mythischen Idealismus im Leben Jesu von Strauss.* Leipzig, 1837.
Winer, Georg Benedict. *Biblisches Realwörterbuch zum Handgebrauch für Studierende, Kandidaten, Gymnasiallehre und Prediger.* 2nd ed. 2 vols. Leipzig, 1833–35.
———. *Grammatik des neutestamentlichen Sprachidioms als sichere Grundlage der neutestamentlichen Exegese bearbeitet.* 3rd ed. Leipzig, 1830.
———. *De onkeloso ejusque paraphrasi Chaldaica.* Leipzig, 1820.
Woolston, Thomas. *A Discourse on the Miracles of Our Savior.* 6 parts. London, 1727–29.
Wurm, Johann Friedrich. *De Ponderum, nummorum, mensurarum ac de anni ordinandi rationibus, apud Romanos et Graecos.* Stuttgart, 1821.

WORKS BY AND ABOUT STRAUSS

1. MAJOR WRITINGS BY DAVID FRIEDRICH STRAUSS
Der alte und der neue Glaube. Ein Bekenntniss. Leipzig, 1872.
August Wilhelm von Schlegel. Leipzig, 1849.

Ausgewählte Briefe von David Friedrich Strauss. Edited by Eduard Zeller. Bonn, 1895.

Briefe von David Friedrich Strauss an L. Georgii. Edited by Heinrich Maier. Tübingen, 1912.

"Der Briefwechsel zwischen Strauss und Baur." Edited by Ernst Barnikol. *Zeitschrift für Kirchengeschichte* 73 (1962): 74–125.

Briefwechsel zwischen Strauss und Vischer. Edited by Adolf Rapp. 2 vols. Stuttgart, 1952–53.

Charakteristiken und Kritiken. Leipzig, 1839.

Christian Märklin. Ein Lebens- und Charakterbild aus der Gegenwart. Mannheim, 1851.

Die christliche Glaubenslehre in ihrer geschichtlichen Entwicklung und im Kampfe mit der modernen Wissenschaft dargestellt. 2 vols. Tübingen & Stuttgart, 1840–41.

Der Christus des Glaubens und der Jesus der Geschichte. Eine Kritik des Schleiermacher'schen Lebens Jesu. Berlin, 1865.

Gesammelte Schriften von David Friedrich Strauss. Edited by Eduard Zeller. 12 vols. Bonn, 1876–78.

Die Halben und die Ganzen. Eine Streitschrift gegen Schenkel und Hengstenberg. Berlin, 1865.

Hermann Samuel Reimarus und seine Schutzschrift für die vernünftigen Verehrer Gottes. Leipzig, 1862.

Justinus Kerner. Zwei Lebensbilder aus den Jahren 1839 und 1862. Marbach, 1953.

Kleine Schriften biographischen, literar- und kunstgeschichtlichen Inhalts. Leipzig, 1862.

Kleine Schriften. Berlin, 1866.

Das Leben Jesu, für das deutsche Volk bearbeitet. 2 vols. Leipzig, 1864. Many subsequent editions.

Das Leben Jesu, kritisch bearbeitet. 2 vols.
   1st ed. Tübingen, 1835–36. Reprint: Darmstadt: Wissenschaftliche Buchgesellschaft, 1969.
   2nd ed. Tübingen, 1837.
   3rd ed. Tübingen, 1838–39.
   4th ed. Tübingen, 1840.

Lessings Nathan der Weise. Berlin, 1864.

Poetisches Gedenkbuch. Gedichte aus dem Nachlasse. Edited by Eduard Zeller. Bonn, 1878.

Der politische und der theologische Liberalismus. Halle, 1848.

Der Romantiker auf dem Throne der Cäsaren, oder Julian der Abtrünnige. Mannheim, 1847.

Sechs theologisch-politische Volksreden. Stuttgart & Tübingen, 1848.

Streitschriften zur Vertheidigung meiner Schrift über das Leben Jesu und zur Charakteristik der gegenwärtigen Theologie. 3 numbers. Tübingen, 1837.

Ulrich von Hutten. 3 parts in 2 vols. Leipzig, 1858, 1860.

"Vergängliches und Bleibendes im Christenthum." *Freihafen* I:3 (1838): 1–48.

Voltaire: Sechs Vorträge. Leipzig, 1870.

Zwei friedliche Blätter. Über Justinus Kerner, und Über Vergängliches und Bleibendes im Christenthum. Altona, 1839.

2. ENGLISH TRANSLATIONS OF WRITINGS BY STRAUSS

The Life of Jesus Critically Examined. Translated from the 4th German edition by George Eliot (Mary Ann Evans).
   1st ed. 3 vols. London: Chapman Brothers, 1846.

2nd ed. 1 vol. London: Swan Sonnenschein, and New York: Macmillan, 1892. Reissued, 1898. With an Introduction by Otto Pfleiderer.

American edition. New York: Calvin Blanchard, 1855 (1 vol. ed.). 1860 (2 vol. ed.). Reprint of 1860 edition: St. Clair Shores, Michigan: Scholarly Press, 1970. No introduction or annotations.

The Life of Jesus, or, A Critical Examination of His History. [Translated from the 2nd and 3rd German editions.] 4 vols. London: Henry Hetherington, and Birmingham: Joseph Taylor, 1841(?)–1844. An American edition of the first volume, with "Christ" instead of "Jesus" in the title, was published in New York by G. Vale, 1845 (2nd ed., date of 1st ed. not ascertainable). Translator(s) unknown. A vastly inferior work.

A New Life of Jesus. 2 vols. London & Edinburgh, 1865.

The Old Faith and the New. Translated from the 6th German edition by Mathilde Blind. London & New York, 1874.

Soliloquies on the Christian Religion. London, 1845.

Ulrich von Hutten: His Life and Times. Translated from the 2nd German edition by Mrs. G. Sturge. London, 1874.

3. SELECTED SECONDARY BIBLIOGRAPHY

Works published prior to 1840 and cited by Strauss in *The Life of Jesus* are listed in the Bibliography of Modern Authors.

Backhaus, Günther. *Kerygma und Mythos bei David Friedrich Strauss und Rudolf Bultmann.* Hamburg-Bergstedt, 1956.

Barth, Karl. *David Friedrich Strauss als Theologe, 1839–1939.* Zürich, 1939.

──────. *Protestant Thought: From Rousseau to Ritschl.* Translated by Brian Cozens. New York, 1959. Pp. 362–89.

Baur, Ferdinand Christian. *Kritische Untersuchungen über die kanonischen Evangelien.* Tübingen, 1847. Pp. 40–76.

Brazill, William J. *The Young Hegelians.* New Haven, 1970. Pp. 95–132.

Brown, Jerry Wayne. *The Rise of Biblical Criticism in America, 1800–1870: The New England Scholars.* Middletown, Conn., 1969. Chap. IX.

Hartlich, Christian, and Sachs, Walter. *Der Ursprung des Mythosbegriffes in der modernen Bibelwissenschaft.* Tübingen, 1952. Chap. 5.

Harvey, Van A. "D. F. Strauss' *Life of Jesus* Revisited." *Church History* 30 (1961): 191–211.

Hausrath, Adolf. *David Friedrich Strauss und die Theologie seiner Zeit.* 2 vols. Heidelberg, 1876, 1878. The most important critical study of Strauss.

Hirsch, Emanuel. *Geschichte der neuern evangelischen Theologie* 5. Gütersloh: C. Bertelsmann Verlag, 1954. Pp. 492–518.

Kohut, A. *David Friedrich Strauss als Denker und Erzieher.* Leipzig, 1908.

Maier, Heinrich. *An der Grenze der Philosophie. Melanchthon-Lavater-David Friedrich Strauss.* Tübingen, 1909.

Müller, Gotthold. *Identität und Immanenz: Zur Genese der Theologie von David Friedrich Strauss.* Zürich, 1968. The most important study of Strauss's early development.

Parker, Theodore. "D. F. Strauss's *Das Leben Jesu.*" *Christian Examiner* 28 (1840): 273–316.

Schweitzer, Albert. *The Quest of the Historical Jesus.* Translated by W. Montgomery, 3rd ed. London, 1954. Chaps. VII, VIII, IX.

Zeller, Eduard. *David Friedrich Strauss in seinem Leben und seinen Schriften.* 2nd ed. Bonn, 1874. Eng. trans.: London, 1874.

Ziegler, Theobald. *David Friedrich Strauss.* 2 vols. Strassburg, 1908.